P9-DGH-639

WEBSTER'S

TWO IN ONE

DICTIONARY AND THESAURUS

Copyright © 1997 V. Nichols
Distributed by Nichols Industries, LTD.

All rights reserved. No part of this publication may be reproduced or transmitted in any form, by electronic or mechanical means, to include photocoping, or by any storage or retrieval system, without written permission from the copyright owner.

Printed in the United States of America.

A, a The first letter of the English alphabet; the highest grade, meaning excellent or best.
aah *v.* to exclaim in joy
aard-vark *n.* a burrowing African animal which resembles the anteater and feeds on ants and termites
aard-wolf *n.* hyena-like mammal feeding chiefly on carrion and insects
ab-a-ca *n.* a plant from the Philippines whose leafstalks are the source of Manila hemp
a-back *adv.* unexpectedly; by surprise; startled; confused
abac-te-ri-al *adj.* not being caused by bacteria
ab-a-cus *n.* a frame holding parallel rods with beads used for manual computation **abacuses n., abaci n.**
a-baft *adv.* toward the stern of a ship
ab-a-lo-ne *n.* a member of the genus of gastropod mollusks that will cling to rocks and have a shell which is flat and lined with mother of pearl.
a-ban-don *v.* to yield utterly; to desert; to forsake; to withdraw protection, support, or help **abandonment n., abandoner n.**
a-ban-don-ed *adj.* to be deserted; to be foresaken
a-base *v.* to lower in rank, position, prestige, or estimation; to cast down, to humble **abasement** *n*
a-bash *v.* embarrass **abashment n.**
a-bate *v.* reduce in quantity, or value, to deduct; to make less **abatement n., abater n.**
ab-ba-cy *n.* a jurisdiction or an office of an abbot
ab-ba-tial *adj.* to be pertaining or related to an abbey or abbot.
ab-be *n.* a French title given to a priest.
ab-bess *n.* the femal superior of an abbey of nuns and possessing the same authority as an abbot
ab-bey *n.* monastery **abbeys pl.**
ab-bot *n.* the superior of the monastery
ab-bre-vi-ate *v.* make briefer; to shorten to reduce to a briefer form, as a word or phrase **abbreviated, abbreviating** *v.*
ab-bre-vi-a-tion *n.* shortened form of a word or phrase
ABC soil *n.* a type of soil where there are three well-defined layers.
ab-di-cate *v.* to relinquish power or responsibility formally
ab-do-men *n.* the part of the human body that lies between the thorax and the pelvis and contains the stomach, spleen, liver, kidneys, bladder, pancreas, and intestines **abdominal adj.**
ab-duct *v.* carry away wrongfully by force or fraud; to kidnap; to draw aside, or away; to move apart **abductor n.**
a-beam *adv. or adj.* right angles to the keel of a ship
a-bed *adv.* in bed; on a bed; to bed
ab-er-rant *adj.* straying from the right course; wandering; varying from **aberrance n., aberrantly adv.**
a-bet *v.* incite **abetment n., abettor n.**
ab-hor *v.* dislike intensely **abhorrer n.**
a-bide *v.* to tolerate; to remain; to last; to conform to **abider n., abided v.**
a-bil-i-ty *n.* state of being able; competence; **-ties** *n., pl.*
ab-ject *adj.* sunk to a low condition **abjection** *n.*, **abjectly adv., -ness n.**
ab-jure *v.* renounce solemnly **abjured v.**
a-blaze *adv.* on fire, glowing
a-ble *adj.* having sufficient ability
a-ble--bodied *adj.* having a strong body **ablebodies adj.**
ab-lu-tion *n.* washing of the body as a part of religious rites **ablutionary adj.**
ab-ne-gate *v.* deny; to refuse or renounce **abnegator n., abnegation n.**
ab-nor-mal *adj.* not normal **-ity** *n.*
a-board *adv.* on board a ship, onto
a-bode *n.* temporary dwelling place
a-bol-ish *v.* put an end to, destroy
a-bom-i-na-ble *adj.* detestable; loathsome **abominably adv.**
a-bort *v.* to terminate or cause to terminate an operation or procedure before completion **aborter n.**
a-bor-tion *n.* induced termination of pregnancy before the fetus can survive **abortionist n.**
a-bound *v.* to have plenty
a-bout *adv.* approximately, all sides
a-bove *adv.* higher or greater than
ab-ra-ca-dab-ra *n.* a word believed to have magical powers, used in casting spells; nonsense, foolish talk
a-brade *v.* to wear or rub off **abrading** *v.*
a-breast *adv.* or *adj.* side by side
a-bridge *v.* to make smaller, fewer or shorter while maintaining essential contents **abridger** *n*
a-broad *adv.* widely, beyond
ab-ro-gate *v.* put an end to **-ed v.**
ab-rupt *adj.* happening suddenly
ab-scess *n.* infected sore containing pus **abscessed adj.**
ab-scind *v.* to sever; to separate
ab-scond *v.* to flee from justice
ab-sence *n.* being absent, not present inattention
ab-sent *adj.* not present **absently adv.**
ab-sent--mind-ed *adj.* always forgetting things; not paying attention
ab-so-lute *adj.* unconditional
ab-solve *v.* to set free from guilt
ab-sorb *v.* to take in **absorbable adj.**
ab-sorp-tion *n.* the act of giving full attention or having great interest.
ab-stain *v.* refrain from doing something **abstainer n.**
ab-ste-mi-ous *adj.* showing moderation **abstemiously adv.**
ab-sten-tion *n.* the act of holding off from using or doing something
ab-stract *v.* summarize **abstractable adj.**
ab-struse *adj.* difficult to understand **abstruseness n., abstrusely adv.**
ab-surd *adj.* clearly unreasonable **absurdness** *n.*, **absurdly adv.**
a-bun-dance *n.* ample supply; plenty
a-buse *v.* use in an improper or wrong way **abusable adj., abuser n.**
a-but *v.* to border **abutted, abutting** *v.*
a-but-ment *n.* bridge support

a-bys-mal *adj.* extension downward, inward, or inward **abysmally** *adv.*
a-byss *n.* deep crack or gap in the earth, great space, bottomless
a-ca-cia *n.* thorny tree or shrub
a-cad-e-my *n.* private school
a-can-thus *n.* a prickly plant, native to the Mediterranean region
acap-pel-la *adj.* singing without instrumental accompaniment
a-cat-a-lec-tic *adj.* not stopping short; having the complete number or syllables, in a line of verse
ac-cede *v.* to consent **-ed v., -ing v.**
ac-cel-er-ate *v.* work faster; to increase, gain **acceleratingly adv.**
ac-cent *n.* emphasize **accentless** *adj.*
ac-cept *v.* take what is given
ac-cept-able *adj.* satisfactory; proper, capable of being accepted
ac-cep-tance *n.* approval, being accepted or acceptable
ac-cess *n.* admission, entrance
ac-ces-si-ble *adj.* easy access or approach **accessibleness n., accessibly adv.**
ac-ces-sion *n.* in Computer Science, the act of obtaining data from storage; the ability to store data
ac-ces-sory *n.* **-ies** contributing
ac-ci-dent *n.* unexpected happening **accidental** *adj.*, **accidentally adv.**
ac-claim *v.* greet with strong approval, praise **acclaimer n.**
ac-cli-mate *v.* become accustomed
ac-co-lade *n.* award; praise
ac-com-mo-date *v.* to give room or lodging; to adjust **accommodating adj.**
ac-com-mo-da-tion *n.* adjustment; change to fit new conditions.
ac-com-pa-ni-ment *n.* something that goes well with another, unit
ac-com-pa-nist *n.* someone who plays a musical accompaniment
ac-com-pa-ny *v.* go along with
ac-com-plice *n.* companion in crime
ac-com-plish *v.* to do **accomplishment** *n.*
ac-cord *n.* harmony **accordance** *n.*
ac-cord-ing-ly *adv.* in a proper way
ac-cor-di-on *n.* musical instrument
ac-cost *v.* approach in an unfriendly manner, speak in a challenging or aggressive manner
ac-count *n.* description; record **accountable** *adj.*
ac-count-able *adj.* liable to be held responsible; able to be explained
ac-coun-tan-cy *n.* the profession of an accountant.
ac-count-ing *n.* system of keeping business records or accounts
ac-cred-it *v.* give official power
ac-crete *v.* grow together
ac-crue *v.* to increase at certain times **accruable adj., accrued v.**
ac-cu-mu-late *v.* collect or gather
ac-cu-ra-cy *n.* exactness; precision; the fact of being accurate or without mistakes
ac-cu-rate *adj.* without mistakes; careful and exact **accurately adv.**
ac-curs-ed *adj.* unpleasant **-ness n.**
ac-cu-sa-tion *n.* charge of guilty
ac-cu-sa-tive *adj.* relating to the direct object of a preposition or of a verb
ac-cuse *v.* find fault with; charge someone with breaking the law
ac-custom *v.* familiarize by habit **accustomed** *adj.*, **accustomation n.**
ace *n.* playing card marked with one spot; score in tennis
ac-e-tate *n.* salt, acetic acid
a-ce-tic acid *n.* main ingredient for production of vinegar
a-cet-y-lene *n.* inflammable gas
ache *v.* have a dull, steady pain
a-chieve *v.* to succeed **achievement** *n.*
achro-ma-tism *n.* a quality of giving of images practically free from extraneous colors.
ac-id *n.* a chemical compound **acidity** *n.*, **acidness n., acidly adv.**
acid rock *n.* song lyrics suggesting drug related experiences
a-cid-u-late *v.* to become or make acid **acidulated v., acidulating v.**
ack-ack *n.* anti-aircraft fire or gun
ac-know-ledge *v.* to admit the truth **acknowledgement** *n.*, **-able adj.**
ac-me *n.* the highest point
ac-ne *n.* skin disease; pimples
ac-o-lyte *n.* altar boy, assistant
ac-o-nite *n.* a poisonous plant
a-corn *n.* nut of the oak tree
a-cous-tic *adj.* having to do with sound **acoustical adj., acoustically adv.**
a-cous-tics *n.* study of sound
ac-quaint *v.* to make familiar **acquaintance** *n.*, **acquaintanceship**
ac-qui-esce *v.* agree without arguing **acquiesced v., acquiescing v.**
ac-quire *v.* become the owner **acquirement** *n.*, **acquired, v.**
acquired immunity *n.* immunity against disease
ac-qui-si-tion *n.* something acquired
ac-quit *v.* rule not guilty **acquital** *n.*
a-cre *n.* a measurement of land, great quantity **acreage** *n.*
ac-rid *adj.* a sharp, bitter taste **acridity** *n.*, **acridness n., -ly adv.**
ac-ri-mo-ni-ous *adj.* bitter in speech or manner **acrimoniousness n.**
ac-ro-bat *n.* one skilled in gymnastic feats **acrobatic** *adj.*, **-lly adv.**
ac-ro-pho-bi-a *n.* unusual fear of being at great heights
a-cross *prep.* side to side, opposites
acrylic fiber *n.* synthetic textile fiber
act *n.* a thing done; a deed **-ing** *adj.*
ac-tion *n.* process of doing or acting, act of will, bringing about
ac-ti-vate *v.* put into action **activation n., activated v., -ing v.**
ac-tive *adj.* full of action; busy, quick **actively** *adv.*, **activeness n.**
ac-tiv-ism *n.* action to affect changes in government **activistic adj.**
act of God *n.* uncontrollable happening caused by nature
ac-tor *n.* performer **actorish adj.**
ac-tress *n.* female actor **-es n.**
ac-tu-al *adj.* existing in fact; real
ac-tu-ate *v.* put into mechanical motion or action **actuation** *n.*

a-cute *adj.* sharp and quick
acutely *adv.*, **acuteness n., -er adj.**
ad-age *n.* proverb, metaphorical
ad-a-mant *adj.* standing firm
a-dapt *v.* to adjust to new conditions
adaption, adaptness *n.*
add *v.* join together **addable adj.**
ad-der *n.* poisonous snake
ad-dict *n.* a person with a strong habit with a drug **addiction** *n.*
ad-di-tion *n.* adding of numbers to find the total **additional** *adj.*
ad-dle *v.* become or make confused
ad-dress *v.* to speak to; place where mail or goods can be delivered
ad-duce *v.* offer as proof or give as a reason **adducer n., -ed v., -ing v.**
ad-e-noids *n.* lymphoid tissue growths which obstructs breathing, relating to the adenoids
a-dept *adj.* highly skilled **adeptly** *adv.*, **adeptness** *n.*
ad-e-quate *adj.* sufficient **-ly adv.**
ad-here *v.* to stick and not come loose **adhered v., adhering v.**
ad-her-ent *n.* one who follows a leader **adherently adv.**
ad-he-sive *adj.* having a sticky surface **adhesively adv., adhesiveness n.**
a-dieu *n.* good-by **adieus, adieux pl.**
ad-in-ter-im *adj.* in the meantime
ad-ja-cent *adj.* close to or nearby
ad-jec-tive *n.* word used to describe a noun or pronoun **adjectively adv.**
ad-join *v.* be next to, attach or add
ad-journ *v.* close a meeting or session, to relocate **adjournment** *n.*
ad-judge *v.* decide by judicial procedure **adjudged v., adjudging v.**
ad-jure *v.* ask urgently **adjuration** *n.*
adjust *v.* to arrange or change **adjustability** *n.*, **adjustable adj.**
ad-just-er *n.* person who estimates damages for settlement **adjustor n.**
ad-lib *v.* to improvise **adlibbed v.**
ad-man *n.* person working in the business of advertising
ad-min-is-ter *v.* direct or manage
ad-min-is-tra-tion *n.* people who manage a school, or company **administrator** *n.*, **-al adj., -ist n.**
ad-mi-ra-ble *adj.* worthy of being admired **admirableness adv.**
ad-mi-ral *n.* highest ranking naval officer, is above a vice-admiral
ad-mire *v.* regard with wonder
ad-mis-si-ble *adj.* capable of being admitted **admissibility n.**
ad-mit *v.* to confess; give the right to enter or access **admittance** *n.*
ad-mix-ture *n.* blend; mingling
ad-mon-ish *v.* to give a person advice **admonishtion** *n.* **admonishingly adv.**
a-do *n.* fuss, excitement
a-do-be *n.* building material made from clay and straw
ad-o-les-cence *n.* between childhood and adulthood, growing up
a-dopt *v.* legally take into one's family **adoption** *n.*, **-ability n.**
a-dor-a-ble *adj.* very likable **-ness n.**
a-dore *v.* to love greatly; to worship
a-dorn *v.* to add splendor or beauty, to decorate **adornment** *n.*
a-drift *adv.* floating freely; having no purpose, without guidance
a-droit *adj.* skillful and clever, with the hands **adroitly** *adv.*
ad-ulate *v.* give greater praise **adulation** *n.*, **adulator n., -ed v.**
a-dult *n.* person who is fully grown **adulthood** *n.*, **adultness n., -ly adv.**
a-dul-ter-ate *v.* to make impure
a-dul-tery *n.* voluntary sexual intercourse with someone other than a spouse
ad-vance *v.* to move ahead **-ment** *n.*
ad-vanced *adj.* ahead in time
ad-van-tage *n.* better chance **advantageous** *adj.*
ad-vent *n.* the four Sundays before Christmas as a season of prayer
ad-ven-ture *n.* an exciting experience **adventured v., adventuring v.**
ad-verb *n.* word used to describe a verb or adjective **adverbial** *adj.*
ad-verse *adj.* opposed; against someone or something, opposite
ad-ver-si-ty *n.* bad luck or misfortune, a condition of suffering
ad-ver-tise *v.* draw public attention to a product **advertiser** *n.*
ad-vice *n.* opinion on a course of action, recommendation
ad-vis-ed-ly *adv.* deliberately
ad-vise-ment *n.* careful thought
ad-viser *n.* person who gives an opinion, one who gives advice
advocate *v.* write or speak in favor of **advocated v., advocating n.**
aer-ate *v.* to purify, to supply
aer-i-al *adj.* antenna for television or radio **aerially adv.**
aer-i-al-ist *n.* aerial acrobat
aer-o-bics *n.* strenuous exercise for the heart **aerobically adv.**
aer-o-nau-tics *pl., n.* science of designing aircraft **aeronautical adj.**
aer-o-sol *n.* liquid substance under pressurized conditions
aes-thet-ic *adj.* having a love for or judgements concerning beauty
a-far *adv.* far away, great distance
af-fa-ble *adj.* good natured; friendly
af-fair *n.* an event or happening
af-fect *v.* to move emotionally **affecting** *adj.*, **affectability n.**
af-fec-tion *n.* fond feeling for another **affectionless adj.**
af-fec-tion-ate *adj.* loving and gentle **affectionately** *adv.*
af-fi-da-vit *n.* sworn written statement, has made an oath
af-fil-i-ate *v.* join or associate with common ownership **affiliation** *n.*
af-fin-i-ty *n.* natural attraction or liking, relationship by marriage
af-firm *v.* to declare positively **affirmative** *n.*, **affirmable adj.**
af-fix *n.* to attach; to add at the end
af-flict *v.* a persistent cause of suffering or pain **affliction** *n.*
af-flu-ence *n.* wealth; abundance
af-ford *v.* be able to provide
af-fray *n.* noisy fight

af-front *v.* to confront
af-ghan *n.* a knitted or crocheted blanket of colored wool
a-fire *adv.* burning, on fire
a-float *adv.* floating on water
a-flut-ter *adj.* nervously excited
a-foot *adj.* walking, on foot
a-fore-men-tioned *adj.* mentioned before, previously
a-foul *adv.* tangled, in conflict with
a-fraid *adj.* filled with fear; reluctant, unwanting of a situation
a-fresh *adj.* to something again
aft *adv.* toward the rear of a ship
af-ter *adv. prep.* following
af-ter-math *n.* consequence
af-ter-thought *n.* idea occurring later, not thought of originally
a-gain *adv.* once more
a-gainst *prep.* in exchange for
a-gape *adv.* open-mouthed, wide
ag-ate *n.* type of quartz
age *n.* length of time a person has lived **aged v., aging v.**
aged *adj.* grown or become old
age-less *adj.* existing forever
a-gen-cy *n.* business that acts for others **agencies n.**
a-gen-da *n.* list of things to be done
a-gent *n.* one who acts as the representative of another
ag-glom-er-ate *v.* to collect
ag-gran-dize *n.* to extend, to make greater **aggrandizement** *n.*
ag-gra-vate *v.* to annoy, bothersome
ag-gre-gate *adj.* to gather together
ag-gres-sion *n.* hostile action
ag-gres-sive *adj.* pushy; offensive
a-ghast *adj.* appalled, amazement
ag-ile *adj.* ability to move easily
ag-i-tate *v.* to stir or move with violence **agitation, agitator** *n.*
a-gleam *adj.* gleaming, reflecting
ag-nos-tic *n.* disbeliever in God
a-go *adj. & adv.* in the past
a-gog *adj.* excited, interest
ag-o-nize *v.* afflict with great anguish **agonized, agonizing** *adj.*
ag-o-ny *n., pl.* **-nies** mental distress
a-gree *v.* to give consent **agreed n. agreeable** *adj.*, **agreeness** *n.*
a-gree-ment *n.* harmony
ag-ri-cul-ture *n.* raising of livestock and crops, cultivation of soil
a-ground *adv. & adj.* stranded; beached, on or onto a shore
a-head *adv.* in advance
a-hoy *interj.* nautical greeting
aid *v.* to give help
AIDS *n.* Acquired Immune Deficiency Syndrome
ail *v.* to feel sick, pain
aim *v.* to direct a weapon; to direct purpose **aimless adj., aimlessness n.**
air *n.* nitrogen and oxygen mixture; a breeze **airlessness n.**
air conditioner *n.* equipment to control temperature indoors
air-craft *n.* a machine that flies
air-field *n.* paved runways at an airport **airfields n.**
air-mail & air mail *n.* mail sent via air
air-port *n.* airplane terminal
air raid *n.* bombing attack
air-ship *n.* dirigible; lighter-than-air aircraft having propulsion
aisle *n.* passageway between rows of seats
a-jar *adv. & adj.* partially opened
a-kin *adj.* related, as in a family
al-a-bas-ter *n.* white, fine-grained gypsum **alabastrine adj.**
a-lac-ri-ty *n.* readiness; eagerness
a la mode *n.* pie served with ice cream, fashionable
a-larm *n.* a warning of danger; bell or buzzer of a clock **alarming** *adv.*
a-las *interj.* expressive of anxiety
a-late *or* **alated** *adj.* having wings
alb *n.* white robe worn by the clergy
al-ba-core *n.* large marine fish
al-ba-tross *n.* large sea bird
al-bi-no *n.* person with abnormal whiteness of the skin and hair
al-bum *n.* a book for photographs, etc, for making a collection
al-bu-men *n.* white of an egg
al-caz-ar *n.* a spanish fortress or palace
al-co-hol *n.* intoxicating liquor
al-co-hol-ism *n.* a habit or addiction, continuous use of a drug
al-cove *n.* partly enclosed extension of a room, an arched opening
ale *n.* beverage similar to beer
a-lert *adj.* vigilant; watchful **alertly** *adv.*, **alertness** *n.*
al-fal-fa *n.* plant grown for forage
al-fres-co *adv. & adj.* outside
al-ge-bra *n.* form of math
a-li-as *n., pl.* aliases assumed name
al-i-bi *n.* form of defense
a-li-en *adj.* owing allegiance to a country, differing in nature
a-light *v.* to dismount; to come down **alightment n., alighting v.**
a-lign *v.* to arrange in a line
a-like *adj.* similar; having close resemblance **alikeness n.**
al-i-mo-ny *n.* court ordered allowance for support
a-live *adj.* having life
al-ka-loid *n.* nitrogen containing organic bases obtained from plants
all *adj.* being a whole amount
al-lay *v.* to calm; to pacify **-er** *n.*
al-lege *v.* to assert; to be true
al-le-giance *n.* loyalty to one's nation, obligation, devotion
al-le-lu-ia *interj.* expressing praise to God
al-ler-gist *n.* doctor specializing in allergies
al-ler-gy *n.* **-gies** abnormal reaction to environmental substances
al-le-vi-ate *v.* make more bearable **allevition** *n.*, **alleviator n.**
al-ley *n.* passageway behind buildings, narrow street **alley's n.**
al-li-ga-tor *n.* large amphibious reptiles having broad heads
al-lo-cate *v.* to assign **allocation n.**
allot *v.* to distribute or set aside. **alloted v., allotting v., allotter n.**
al-low *v.* to make a provision for; to per-

mit **allowable** *adj.*
al-low-ance *n.* a regular amount of money, food, etc **allowanced v.**
all right *adj.* meets satisfaction; dependable, agreeable, dependable
all-round *adj.* versatile
all-star *adj.* composed entirely of star performers or participants
al-lude *n.* refer to something indirectly, to play with
al-lure *v.* to entice; to tempt **allurement** *n.*, **allured v.**, **alluring v.**
al-lu-sion *n.* a hint **allusive adj.**
al-ly *v.* unite in a close relationship or bond **allied v.**, **allying v.**
al-ma ma-ter *n.* the school or university attended by a person
al-ma-nac *n.* an annual calender publication containing data
al-might-y *adj.* having absolute power, having control
al-mond *n.* oval nut
al-most *adv.* not quite
alms *pl., n.* money given to the poor
a-loft *adv.* toward the upper rigging of a ship, a great height, in air
a-lo-ha *interj.* hawaiian greeting
a-lone *adj.* away from other people
a-long *adv.* following the length or path through woods, grass, etc.
a-loof *adj.* distant; indifferent, at a distance **aloofness** *n.*
a-loud *adv.* audibly, loud mannered
alp *n.* high mountain, large
al-pac-a *n.* a mammal related to the llama, having fine woolly hair
al-pen-stock *n.* long staff used by mountain climbers for support
al-pha *n.* first letter of the Greek alphabet, something that is first
al-pha-bet *n.* letters arranged in order, used in writing
al-pha-bet-ize *v.* to arrange in alphabetical order
al-read-y *adv.* by this or a specified time in the past
al-so *adv.* likewise; in addition
al-tar *n.* elevated holy table
al-ter *v.* to change or make different
al-ter-ca-tion *n.* noisy quarrel
al-ter-na-tive *n.* choice between two or more possibilities
al-ter-na-tor *n.* electric generator producing alternating current
al-though *conj.* even though
al-tim-e-ter *n.* instrument for measuring altitude
al-ti-tude *n.* height above sea level
al-to *n.* low female singing voice
al-to-geth-er *adv.* entirely
al-tru-ism *n.* selfless concern for others, unconcerned
a-lu-mi-num *n.* silvery metallic element, used in science
a-lum-na *n.* a female graduate of a school or university
a-lum-nus *n.* a male graduate of a school or university
al-ways *adv.* forever; at all times
am *n.* first person, singular
a-mal-ga-mate *v.* to mix; to blend **amalgation**, *n.*
a-man-dine *adj.* garnished with almonds, to decorate with almonds
am-a-teur *n.* one who lacks expertise **amateurish** *adj.*
a-maze *v.* to astound **amazement** *n.*
am-bass-a-dor *n.* official representative of a country
am-ber *n.* brownish-yellow resin
am-bi-ance *n.* environment
am-bi-dex-trous *adj.* using both hands with equal facility
am-bi-ent *adj.* surrounding, circling
am-big-u-ous *adj.* uncertain; doubtful **ambiguousness n.**
am-bi-tion *n.* strong desire to succeed **ambitionless adj.**
am-bi-tious *adj.* challenging
am-ble *v.* move at a leisurely pace, to make comfortable **ambler** *n.*
am-bu-lance *n.* vehicle to transport the injured or sick to a hospital
am-bush *n.* surprise attack
a-me-lio-rate *v.* to make better
a-men *interj.* ending of a prayer
a-me-na-ble *adj.* responsible **-ility** *n.*
a-mend *v.* to correct; to improve, make better **amendment** *n.*
a-mends *pl., n.* compensation for injury or sickness
a-men-i-ty *n.* agreeableness
a-merce *v.* to punish, correct
America *n.* United States of America, a free country
A-mer-ica-n *n.* a native U.S. citizen
am-e-thyst *n.* purple gemstone
a-mi-a-ble *adj.* friendly and pleasant
am-i-ca-ble *adj.* harmonious **amicability** *n.*
a-mid *prep.* to be in the middle of something, to be occupied
a-mi-go *n.* friend
a-miss *adj.* out of order or place
am-mo-nia *n.* colorless, pungent gas
am-mu-ni-tion *n.* projectiles fired from guns or other weapons
am-ne-sia *n.* the loss of memory
am-nes-ty *n.* pardon for political offenders
a-mor-al *adj.* neither moral nor immoral
a-mor-phous *adj.* something which is lacking definite form
am-or-tize *v.* liquidate a loan
a-mount *n.* sum or total quantity
am-per-age *n.* strength of an electric current, hot wires
am-pere *n.* unit of electric current
am-per-sand *n.* sign that represents and (&), used as an abbreviation
am-phet-a-mine *n.* a drug
am-phib-i-an *n.* an animal able to live on land and in water
am-ple *adj.* sufficient; abundant
am-pul *n.* small, sealed vial
am-pu-tate *v.* to remove a limb from the body, get rid of **amputation** *n.*
a-muck *adv.* in an uncontrolled manner, uncontrollable
am-u-let *n.* charm worn to protect against evil, protection
a-muse *v.* entertain **amusement** *n.*
an *adj.* one sort of, others
a-nad-ro-mous *adj.* migrating up river to

breed in fresh water
an-a-gram *n.* formation of a new word from another
a-nal *adj.* relating to the anus
an-al-ge-sia *n.* inability to feel pain **analgesic** *adj.*
a-nal-o-gous *adj.* similar, alikeness
a-nal-y-sis *v.* examining parts
an-a-lyze *v.* to make an analysis of
an-ar-chy *n.* state of policial disorder, absence of government
a-nat-o-mize *v.* examine in great detail, to look over carefully
a-nat-o-my *n.* structure of an organ **anatomical** *adj.*
an-ces-tor *n.* forefather
an-ces-try *n.* line of descent
an-chor *n.* device to keep a ship from drifting, to keep in place
an-chor-age *n.* place for anchoring a ship
an-cho-vy *n.* small fish
an-cient *adj.* very old **ancientness** *n.*
and *conj.* along with; as well as; added to, to put with
an-dan-te *adv.* slow in tempo
and-i-ron *n.* heavy metal support for logs in a fireplace
an-dro-gen *n.* hormone that maintains masculine characteristics
an-ec-dote *n.* short account of a story, a long story short
a-ne-mi-a *n.* condition in which blood does not have enough red corpuscles, in hemoglobin
a-nent *prep.* regarding; concerning
an-es-thet-ic *n.* drug used during an operation to take away pain
a-new *adv.* again, to do over
an-gel *n.* an immortal being **angelic** *adj.*
an-ger *n.* feeling of extreme hostility
an-gi-na *n.* disease marked by painful choking spasms
an-gle *v.* shape that makes a corner
An-glo *n.* root word meaning "English", Anglo-American
an-go-ra *n.* silky hair of the Angora rabbit; used in sweater making
an-gry *adj.* feeling of anger, hostility toward someone **angrily** *adv.*
an-guish *n.* great suffering or grief
an-gu-lar *adj.* gaunt; bony; lean
an-hy-drous *adj.* does not contain any water, without
an-i-mal *n.* any four-footed creature; beast; having four feet
an-i-mate *v.* give life or spirit to something that is still **animation**
an-i-mos-i-ty *n.* hostility
an-ise *n.* licorice-flavored herb
an-kle *n.* joint that connects the foot with the leg, support
an-klet *n.* short sock
an-nals *n.* descriptive record
an-neal *v.* treatment to make glass less brittle, not fragile
an-nex *v.* join a smaller thing to a larger one **annexation** *n.*
an-ni-hi-late *v.* destroy completely
an-ni-ver-sa-ry *n., pl.* -ries date on which something happened at an earlier time in history
an-nounce *v.* to give notice, to make public **announcement** *n.*
an-nounc-er *n.* performer on radio or television who entertains
an-noy *v.* to bother **annoyance** *n.*
an-nu-al *adj.* recurring the same time each year; again
an-nu-i-ty *n.* annual payment of an income; once a year
an-nul *v.* to cancel a marriage or a law **annulment** *n.*
an-nun-ci-ate *v.* to proclaim
a-noint *v.* apply oil in a religious ceremony; to bless someone
a-non *adv.* in a short period of time
a-non-y-mous *adj.* an unknown or withheld name, agency
an-oth-er *adj.* additional
an-swer *n.* written or spoken reply
ant *n.* small insect
an-tag-o-nize *v.* arouse hostility
ant-eat-er *n.* animal with a long snout which feeds on ants
an-te-ce-dent *adj.* event that precedes another; afterwards
an-te-lope *n.* swift-running mammal; quick-running
an-te me-rid-i-em *n.* time before noon; before 12 o'clock
an-ten-na *n.* feelers of an insect; aerial; helps in movement
an-te-ri-or *adj.* toward or at the front; a head of
an-te-room *n.* waiting room
an-them *n.* hymn of praise
an-ther *n.* part of the flower
an-thol-o-gy *n.* collection of stories
an-thra-cite *n.* hard coal
an-thrax *n.* infectious disease found in cattle and sheep
an-thro-poid *n.* gorillas
an-thro-pol-o-gy *n.* study on the origin, and development of man
an-ti *n.* one who opposes policy or proposal; against; not for
an-ti-bi-ot-ic *n.* substance used as a germ killer; a medicine
an-ti-bod-y *n.* proteins that counteract diseases; help heal
an-tic *n.* mischievous caper or act
an-tic-i-pate *v.* to look forward; excitement **anticipation** *n.*
an-ti-cli-max *n.* letdown or decline
an-ti-dote *n.* substance to counteract poison **-al** *adj.*
an-ti-freeze *n.* substance, mixed with water to lower the freezing point
an-ti-his-ta-mine *n.* a drug to relieve symptoms of allergies
an-ti-knock *n.* substance to reduce engine knock in a vehicle
an-ti-mo-ny *n.* silver-white metallic element used in medicines
an-ti-pasto *n.* appetizer
an-ti-per-spi-rant *n.* sustance to reduce perspiration and odor
an-ti-pode *n.* a direct opposite
an-tique *n.* an object that is over 100 years old
an-tiquity *n., pl.* **antiquities** quality of being old
an-ti-Sem-ite *n.* person hostile toward Jews; against

an-tith-e-sis *n.* direct opposition
ant-ler *n.* horns of a deer
an-to-nym *n.* word opposite in meaning **antonymous adj., antonymy n.**
a-nus *n.* lower opening of the alimentary canal; anal
an-vil *n.* block for forming metal
anx-i-e-ty *n.* state of uncertainty
anx-ious *adj.* worried; upset
any *adj.* no matter which
any-body *pron.* anyone; any person
any-how *adv.* in any way; whatever
any-thing *pron.* any occurrence
any-time *adv.* at any time
any-way *adv.* in any manner
any-where *adv.* to any place
a-or-ta *n.* main artery from the heart; branching out from heart
a-pace *adv.* rapid in pace; faster
a-part *adv.* separate or at a distance
a-part-heid *n.* non-white racial discrimination in South Africa
a-part-ment *n.* suite in a building
ap-a-thy *n.* lack of emotions or feelings; lack of concern
ape *n.* large mammal
ap-er-ture *n.* an opening
a-pex *n.* the highest point
a-pha-sia *n.* loss of the ability to express ideas; loss of expression
aphid *n.* small insects which move
aph-o-rism *n.* brief statement of truth; giving the truth
aph-ro-dis-i-ac *adj.* arousing the sexual desire
a-pi-ary *n.* place where bees are kept; collection of hives
a-piece *adv.* for or to each one
a-plomb *n.* poise; confident
ap-o-gee *n.* point most distant from earth; toward the outer layer
a-pol-o-get-ic *adj.* expression of apology; giving sympathy
ap-o-plex-y *n.* loss of muscular control; non-movement
a-pos-tle *n.* person sent on a mission; to accomplish something
a-pos-tro-phe *n.* mark (') of punctuation used in writing
ap-pall *v.* overcome by shock or dismay **appalled v., appalling v.**
ap-pa-ra-tus *n.* instrument for a specific operation or useage
ap-par-el *v.* to adorn; clothes
ap-par-ent *adj.* open to the mind; visible; open minded
ap-pa-ri-tion *n.* unusual appearance
ap-peal *n.* an earnest plea **appealable adj. appealingly** *adv.*
ap-pear *v.* to come into public view, in sight **appearance** *n.*
ap-pease *v.* to pacify; to quiet
ap-pel-late *adj.* review the decisions of the lower courts
ap-pend *v.* add an appendix
ap-pen-dec-to-my *n.* a surgical removal of the appendix
ap-petite *n.* craving or desire for food **appetitive adj.**
ap-pe-tiz-er *n.* food served before a meal for enjoyment
ap-plaud *v.* express approval by clapping; agreeable
ap-ple *n.* edible fruit having sweatness; with seeds
ap-ple-jack *n.* brandy
ap-pli-ance *n.* equipment designed for a particular use
ap-pli-ca-ble *adj.* appropriate; suitable **applicability n.**
ap-pli-cant *n.* person applying for a job with an organization
ap-pli-ca-tion *n.* request or petition
ap-ply *v.* to put into use; useage
ap-point *v.* to fix or set officially **appointment** *n.*
ap-por-tion *v.* divide and share; divided into portions **apportment** *n.*
ap-po-site *adj.* pertinent
ap-prais-al *n.* evaluation of property
ap-praise *v.* estimate the value of; to set a value **appraiser** *n.*
ap-pre-ci-ate *v.* recognize the worth
ap-pre-hend *v.* anticipate with anxiety; arrest; seize; take away
ap-pre-hen-sive *adj.* view the future with anxiety or alarm
ap-pren-tice *n.* person learning a trade through on-hands training
ap-prise *v.* to inform; make aware
ap-proach *v.* to come near; in contact **approachable** *adj.*
ap-prove *v.* express a favorable opinion; to agree with
ap-prox-i-mate *adj.* almost exact **approximately** *adv.*
apri-cot *n.* oval, orange-colored fruit having sweatness
apron *n.* garment used to protect clothing; protection against
ap-ro-pos *adv.* by the way
apse *n.* polygonal projection of a church, semicircular
apt *adj.* appropriate **aptly** *adv.*
ap-ti-tude *n.* natural talent or ability
aqua *n.* water, greenish-blue color
aqua-naut *n.* scuba diver
aquar-i-um *n.* an artificial pond
aq-ue-ous *adj.* resembling water
ar-a-ble *adj.* land suitable for plowing; fit for cultivation
ar-bi-tra-tor *n.* a person chosen to decide a dispute; settlement
ar-bor *n.* garden shelter
ar-bor-vi-tae *n.* ever-green tree
arc *n.* Something that is curved or arched.
arch *n.* the structure that spans over an open area; usually curved
ar-chae-ol-o-gy *n.* scientific study of ancient times **archaeologist** *n.*
arch-bishop *n.* a bishop of the highest rank; the highest
arch-di-o-cese *n.* district of an archbishop **archdiocesan adj.**
ar-cher-y *n.* art of shooting with a bow and arrow **archer** *n.*
ar-chi-tect *n.* person who designs and supervises construction
arch-way *n.* an arch over a passage
arc-tic *adj.* extremely cold or frigid
ar-dor *n.* extreme warmth or passion; to have feelings for
ar-e-a *n.* flat piece of ground

a-re-na *n.* area for public entertainment; usually a spherical shape
ar-go-sy *n.* fleet of ships
ar-gue *v.* to dispute, quarrel; to disagree on something **argument** *n.*
ar-gyle *n.* knitted diamond-shaped designs in solid or outline
ar-id *adj.* dry; insufficient rain
a-right *adv.* correctly
a-rith-me-tic *adj.* branch of math
ark *n.* ship Noah built
arm *n.* upper limb of the human body extended outward **armer** *n.*
ar-ma-da *n.* fleet of warships
ar-ma-dil-lo *n.* burrowing nocturnal animal
ar-ma-ment *n.* military supplies and weapons needed for strength
ar-ma-ture *n.* main moving part of an electric device
arm-chair *n.* chair with armrests
arm-ful *n.* as much as the arm can hold; what can be carried
arm-hole *n.* an opening in a garment for the arm to go through
ar-mi-stice *n.* mutual agreement; truce; trusting agreement; bond
arm-let *n.* band worn on the upper arm made of cloth or metal
ar-moire *n.* large wardrobe
ar-mor *n.* covering to protect the body made of metal
ar-mory *n.* place where military equipment is stored
arm-pit *n.* hollow area under connection of the arm and shoulder
arm-rest *n.* support for the arm on a chair
arm-twist-ing *n.* direct pressure to achieve a desired effect
ar-my *n.* the land forces of a country; to defend a country
a-ro-ma *n.* distinctive fragrance or odor, long lasting **aromatic** *adj.*
a-round *adv.* to or on all sides
around-the-clock *adj.* lasting for a period of 24 hours; one day
arouse *v.* wake up from a sleep
ar-peg-gi-o *n.* chord produced in succession
ar-rack *n.* alcoholic beverage
ar-raign *v.* called before a court **arraignment** *n.*
ar-range *v.* put in correct order or sequence **arrangement** *n.*
ar-rant *adj.* extreme; without moderation; noforiously
ar-ras *n.* wall hanging of tapestry
ar-ray *v.* place or set in order; arrange **arrayer** *n.*
ar-rears *n., pl.* state of being behind, as an obligation, etc.
ar-rest *n.* to capture; to seize
arrest-ee *n.* person under arrest
ar-rest-ing *adj.* very impressive or striking; catching the attention of
ar-rhyth-mia *n.* alteration in rhythm of the heartbeat; irregular
ar-rhyth-mic *adj.* lacking regularity or rhythm; irregularity
ar-ri-ve *v.* reach or get to a destination; to make an appearance
ar-ro-gance *n.* overbearing manner **arrogant adj., arrogantly** *adv.*
ar-row *n.* weapon shot from a bow; sign to show direction
ar-row-head *n.* striking end of an arrow; part which does damage
ar-row-root *n.* starch-yielding plant
ar-rowy *adj.* to move swiftly
ar-se-nal *n.* collection of weapons; place where military equipment is stored; manufacturing of weapon
ar-se-nic *n.* element used to make insecticide or weed killer
ar-son *n.* fraudulent burning of property; destroying **arsonist** *n.*
art *n.* human expression of objects by painting, etc.
ar-ter-y *n.* blood vessel that carries blood from the heart to the body
ar-te-sian well *n.* well that produces water without a pump; natural
art form *n.* form of an artistic expression
art glass *n.* glass designed for decorative purposes
ar-thral-gia *n.* pain in one or more joints **arthralgic adj.**
ar-thritic *n.* person who has arthritis; pain in joints
ar-thri-tis *n.* inflammation of joints
ar-thro-pod *n.* animal with jointed limbs and segmented body, as a spider and other insects
ar-ti-choke *n.* plant with an edible thistle-like head; produces fruit
ar-ti-cle *n.* term or clause in a contract; a paragraph or section
ar-tic-u-late *adj.* able to express oneself clearly; feelings
ar-ti-fact *n.* something made by man showing human modification **artifactual adj.**
ar-ti-fice *n.* artful or clever skill
ar-ti-fi-cial *adj.* not genuine; made by man **artificialy** *adv.*
ar-til-lery *n.* weapons, especially cannons used in wars
ar-ti-san *n.* a craftsman
art-ist *n.* a person who practices the fine arts of painting, etc.
ar-tiste *n.* an expert in the theatrical profession; actor or actress
ar-tis-tic *adj.* characteristic of an artist; unique in design
art-ist-ry *n.* ability, or quality of workmanship; artistic ability
art-less *adj.* crude; simple; lacking art and skill **artlessly** *adv.*
art-mobile *n.* trailer that carries an art collection for exhibition on road tours; transportation of art
art-work *n.* the artistic work of an artist; expression of an artist
as *adv.* in the manner like; similar to; the same as
as-bes-tos *n.* mineral form of magnesium silicate used in fire-proofing; for putting out fires
as-cend *v.* to rise up from a lower level; to climb; to mount
as-cen-dant *adj.* rising; moving up
as-cent *n.* a way up; a slope

as-cer-tain *v.* to find out for certain; to make sure; to be correct
as-cet-icism *n.* practice of strict self-denial; measure of discipline
as-cot *n.* scarf or broad tie
as-cribe *v.* assign or attribute to something **ascribable,** *v.*
a-sex-u-al *adj.* lacking sexual reproductive organs **asexuality** *n.*
ash *n.* tree with a hard, elastic wood
a-shamed *adj.* feeling guilt, or shame; feeling unworthy; embarrassed
ashamedly *adv.*
a-shore *adv.* on or to the shore
ash-tray *n.* container or receptacle for discarding tobacco ashes
aside *adv.* out of the way; to one side; off to the side
ask *v.* to request; to seek information; to find out about
askance *adv.* with suspicion or distrust
askew *adv. or adj.* out of line, not straight; in a different direction
a-slant *adv.* in a slanting direction
a-sleep *adv.* in a state of sleep
a-slope *adv.* in a slanting or sloping position or direction
a-so-cial *adj.* selfish, not social
as-par-a-gus *n.* a vegetable with tender shoots; edible
as-pect *n.* the situation, position, view, or appearance of something
as-pen *n.* a tree known as the trembling poplar, having leaves that flutter in the lightest wind
as-peri-ty *n., pl.* **-ties** roughness in manner or sound
as-per-sion *v.* false charges or slander; defamation; maligning
as-phalt *n.* a sticky, thick, blackish-brown mixture of petroleum tar
as-phyx-i-ate *v.* to suffocate, to prevent from breathing
asphyxiation *n.*, **asphyxiator n.**
as-pic *n.* a savory jelly made from fish, meat; used to garnish meat
as-pi-rate *v.* to give pronunciation with a full breathing sound
as-pire *v.* to desire with ambition; to strive towards something that is higher
aspiringly *adv.*
as-pi-rin *n.* medication used for the relief of pain and fever
ass *n.* a hoofed animal; a donkey
as-sail *v.* to attack violently with words or blows **assailant** *n.*
as-sas-sin *n.* murderer especially one that murders a politically important person either for fanatical motives or for hire
as-sas-si-nate *v.* to murder a prominent person by secret or sudden attack
-tion, -or *n.*
as-sault *n.* a very violent physical or verbal attack on a person
assaulter *n.*, **assaultive adj.**
as-say *n.* to evaluate or to assess; to try; to attempt **assayer** *n.*
as-sem-blage *n.* a collection of things or people; a gathering
as-sem-ble *v.* to put together the parts of something; to come together as a group **assembly** *n.*
as-sem-bly-man *n.* a member of an assembly line; a part of
as-sent *v.* to agree on something
as-sert *v.* to declare or state positively, to maintain; to defend
as-sess *v.* to fix or assign a value to something **assessor** *n.*
as-sess-ment *n.* the official determination of value for tax purposes; the amount assessed
as-set *n.* a value placed on goods owned by a person
as-sev-er-ate *v.* to state positively, firmly, and seriously
as-sign *v.* to designate as to duty; to give or allot; to attribute
assignable *adj.*, **assignor n.**
as-sign-ee *n.* the person appointed to act for another
as-sign-ment *n.* a given amount of work or task to undertake; a post, position, or office to which one is assigned; to be completed
as-sim-i-late *v.* to take in, to understand; to make similar **assimilation** *n.*
as-sist *v.* to give support, to aid, to give help **assistance, assistant** *n.*
as-size *n.* a fixed or customary standard;
as-so-ci-ate *v.* to connect or join together *n.* a partner, colleague, or companion
as-so-ci-a-tion *n.* an organized body of people having a common interest; a society; as one
as-so-nance *n.* the repetition of sound in words or syllables
as-sort *v.* to distribute into groups of a classification; divide
as-sort-ed *adj.* made up of different or various kinds
as-sort-ment *n.* the act or state of being assorted; a collection of different things or persons
as-suage *v.* to quiet, pacify; to put an end to by satisfying to soothe; to lessen intensity **assuagement** *n.*
as-sua-sive *adj.* having a smooth, pleasant effect or quality
as-sume *v.* to take upon oneself to complete a job or duty; to take responsibility for; complete
assumeable *adj.*, **assumeably** *adv.*
as-sump-tion *n.* an idea or statement believed to be true without proof; taken for granted
as-sur-ance *n.* a statement made to inspire confidence of mind or manner; to give word
as-sure *v.* to give the feeling of confidence; to make sure
as-sured *adj.* satisfied as to the truth or certainty **assuredly** *adv.*
as-sur-er *n.* a person who gives assurance to someone or something
as-ter *n.* a plant having white, bluish, purple, or pink daisy-like flowers
as-ter-isk *n.* the character (*) used to indicate letters omitted or as a reference to a footnote
a-stern *adv. & adj.* toward the rear or back of an aircraft or ship
as-ter-oid *n.* one of thousands of small

moving planets between Jupiter and Mars

asth-ma *n.* a respiratory disease marked by labored breathing, accompanied by wheezing **asthmatic** *adj.*, **cally** *adv.*

as though *conj.* as if

astig-ma-tism *n.* a defect of the lens of an eye resulting in blurred or imperfect images

a-stir *adj.* to be out of bed, awake; in motion; to be up and around

as to *prep.* with reference to or regard to; concerning

as-ton-ish *v.* to strike with sudden fear, wonder, or surprise

as-ton-ish-ing *adj.* causing surprise or astonishment **astonishingly** *adv.*

as-ton-ish-ment *n.* the state of being amazed or astonished

as-tound *v.* to fill with wonder and bewilderment **astoundingly** *adv.*

as-tra-khan *n.* the curly fur from a young lamb of the southeast U.S.S.R.

as-tral *adj.* resembling, or related to the stars; in resemblence

a-stray *adv.* away from a desirable or proper path; different path

a-stride *prep.* one leg on either side of something; placed or lying on both sides of; extending across or over

astride *adv.*

as-trin-gent *adj.* able to draw together or to constricting tissue

astringency *n.*, **astringently adv.**

as-tro-dome *n.* a large stadium covered by a dome for protection

as-tro-labe *n.* instrument formerly used to determine the altitude of a celestial body

as-trol-o-gy *n.* the study of the supposed influences of the planets and stars and their movements and positions on human affairs **-ical** *adj.*, astrologer *n.*

as-tro-naut *n.* person who travels in a spacecraft beyond the earth's atmosphere; explores space

as-tro-nau-tics *n.* the technology and science of the construction and operation of a spacecraft **-cal** *adj.*

as-tro-nom-i-cal *adj.* relating to astronomy; something enormously large **astronomically** *adv.*

as-tron-o-my *n.* the science of the celestial bodies and their motion, magnitudes, and constitution

astronomer *n.*

as-tro-phys-ics *n.* branch of astronomy dealing with the chemical and physical constitution of the celestial bodies

astrophysicist *n.*, **astrophysical adj.**

as-tute *adj.* sharp in discernment; very shrewd **astutely** *adv.*, **astuteness** *n.*

a-sun-der *adv.* separate into parts or positions apart from each other

asy-lum *n.* a refuge or institution for the care of the needy or sick

at *prep.* to indicate presence, occurrence, or condition

at-a-vism *n.* a hereditary characteristic that skips several generations

atavistic *adj.*

at-el-ier *n.* an artist's workshop

a-the-ism *n.* the disbelief that God exists;

athe-ist *n.* a person who does not believe in the existence of God

a-thirst *adj.* having a strong, eager desire for something

ath-lete *n.* person who participates in the playing of sports

ath-lete's foot *n.* a contagious skin infection of the feet (a fungus)

ath-let-ic *adj.* relating to athletes

a-thwart *adv.* opposition to the expected or right

a-tilt *adj. & adv.* inclined upward or tilted in some way

Atlantic Ocean *n.* the second largest ocean in the world

at-las *n.* a collection or book of maps for states and countries

at-mos-phere *n.* a gaseous mass that surrounds a celestial body

at-oll *n.* an island of coral that encircles a lagoon

at-om *n.* the smallest unit of an element

atom bomb *or* **atomic bomb** *n.* a bomb that explodes violently

a-ton-al *adj.* marked by the deliberate avoidance of a traditional key or tonal center **atonally** *adv.*

a-tone *v.* to make amends

a-tone-ment *n.* amends for a wrongdoing; reconciliation

atop *adj.* on the top of something

atri-um *n.* one of the four chambers of the heart

a-tro-cious *adj.* cruel or evil

a-troc-i-ty *n.*, *pl.* **-ties** the condition of being atrocious

a-tro-phy *v.* decrease in size or wasting away; progressive decline

at-tach *v.* to fasten or become fastened

attachable *adj.*

at-ta-che *n.* an expert on the diplomatic staff of an embassy

attache case *n.* a briefcase or a small suitcase used for carrying important materials

at-tach-ment *n.* the state of being attached; a tie of affection or loyalty; together

at-tack *v.* to threaten with force or violence, to assault

at-tain *v.* to arrive at or reach a goal

attainability *n.*, **attainable adj.**

at-tain-der *n.* the loss of civil rights that occurs following a criminal conviction or sentencing

at-tain-ment *n.* accomplishment; achievement; reached a goal

at-taint *v.* to disgrace or stain; to achieve or obtain by effort

at-tar *n.* the fragrant oil from flowers; fragrance

at-tempt *v.* to make an effort to do something

at-tend *v.* to be present; to take charge of or to look after

at-ten-dance *n.* the number of times a person attends something

at-ten-dant *n.* one who provides a service for another; caregiver

at-ten-tion *n.* observation, or mental concentration **attentiveness** *n.*

at-ten-u-ate *v.* to lessen the force, amount or value; to become thin
attenuation *n.*, **attenuated v.**
at-test *v.* ive testimony or sign one's name as a witness **attestation** *n.*
at-tic *n.* the space directly below the roof of a building; for storage
at-tire *n.* a person's dress or clothing worn on a daily basis
at-ti-tude *n.* a mental position; the feeling one has for oneself
at-tor-ney *n.*, *pl.* **attorneys** person with legal training who is appointed by another to transact business for him
attorney general *n.* the chief law officer of a state or nation
at-tract *v.* to draw by appeal
at-trib-ute *v.* explain by showing a cause
attributable *adj.*
at-tune *v.* bring something into harmony
attunement n.
atwit-ter *adj.* excited; nervously concerned about something
au-burn *adj.* a reddish brown color; moderately brown
au cou-rant *adj.* fully familiar or informed; aware of surroundings
auc-tion *n.* a public sale of merchandise to the highest bidder
auctioneer *n.*,**auctioned v., -ing v.**
auc-to-ri-al *adj.* having to do with an author; writer
au-da-cious *adj.* bold, daring, or fearless; insolent **audaciously** *adv.*
au-di-ble *adj.* capable of being heard and understandable
au-di-ence *n.* a group of spectators or listeners
au-di-o *adj.* relating to sound or its high-fidelity reproduction
au-dit *n.* verification or examination of financial accounts
au-di-tion *n.* trial performance given by an entertainer as to demonstrate ability
au-di-tor *n.* a person who listens or hears; one who audits accounts
au-di-to-ri-um *n.* a large room in a public building or a school that holds many people
au-di-to-ry *adj.* related to the organs or sense of hearing
aught *n.* zero (0)
aug-ment *v.* to add to or increase; to enlarge **augmentable adj., augmentor n.**
au jus *adj.* served in the juices obtained from roasting
auk *n.* sea bird living in the arctic regions and cold regions
aunt *n.* sister of a person's father or mother
au-ra *n.*, *pl.* **auras, aurae** an emanation said to come from a person's or an animal's body
au-ral *adj.* relating to the ear or the sense of hearing
au-re-ate *adj.* of a brilliant golden color or radiance
au re-voir *interj.* used in expressing farewell to someone
au-ri-cle *n.* the two of the four upper chambers of the heart
au-ro-ra *n.* the brilliant display of moving and flashing lights in the night sky **auroral** *adj.*
aus-tere *adj.* stern in manner and appearance **austereness n.**
aus-tral *adj.* southern
au-then-tic *adj.* real; genuine; worthy of acceptance; original
au-then-ti-cate *v.* to prove that something is true or genuine
authenticity *n.*, **authentication n.**
author *n.* a person who writes an original literary work **author** *v.*
au-thor-i-tar-i-an *adj.* blind submission and absolute, unquestioned obedience to authority
au-thor-i-ty *n.*, *pl.* **-ties** group or person with power; an expert
au-thor-ize *v.* give authority; to approve; to justify **authorzation** *n.*
au-tism *n.* absorption in a self-centered mental state, such as fantasies, daydreams or hallucinations
autistic *adj.*
au-to-bahn *n.* highway in Germany
au-to-bi-og-ra-phy *n.*, *pl.* **-phies** the life story of a person, written by that person **autobiographer** *n.*
au-toch-tho-nous *adj.* native to an area or region of land
au-toc-ra-cy *n.* government by one person who has unlimited power
au-to-di-dact *n.* a person who has taught himself to do something
au-to-graph *n.* a handwritten signature
autography n.
au-to-mate *v.* to operate by automation
automatable adj
au-to-mat-ic *adj.* operating with very little control **automatically** *adv.*
automatic pilot *n.* the device for automatically steering aircraft and ships in one direction
au-to-ma-tion *n.* the equipment used to acquire automation
au-to-mo-bile *n.* a four-wheeled passenger vehicle commonly propelled by an internalcombustion engine
automobilist n.
au-to-mo-tive *adj.* relating to self-propelled vehicles
au-top-sy *n.*, *pl.* **-sies** the examination of a body after death to determine the cause of death
au-to-stra-da *n.* an expressway in Italy
au-tumn *n.* the season between summer and winter **-al n.**
aux-il-ia-ry *adj.* providing help or assistance to someone
auxin *n.* hormone in a plant that stimulates growth
a-vail *v.* to be of advantage or use; to use; to result in
a-vail-able *adj.* present and ready for immediate use; attainable
av-a-lanche *n.* a large mass of rock or snow that slides or falls down a mountainside or hill
a-vant--garde *n.* people who invent new ideas and styles in a certain field of study
a-venge *v.* to take revenge for something

avenger *n.*
av-e-nue *n.* a street lined with trees
a-ver *v.* to state positively
av-er-age *n.* typical or usual, not being exceptional; regularly
a-verse *adj.* having a feeling of repugnance
a-ver-sion *n.* a feeling of strong dislike; the act of turning away
a-vert *v.* prevent or keep from happening; to ward off
a-vi-ary *n.* a place where birds are kept and confined
a-vi-a-tion *n.* the operation of planes and other aircraft
a-vi-a-tor *n.* pilot of an aircraft
av-id *adj.* greedy avidly *adv.*
av-o-ca-do *n.* pear-shaped edible fruit from the avocado tree
av-o-ca-tion *n.* activity in addition to the regular work; a hobby
a-void *v.* to stay away from; to shun
a-void-ance *n.* the act of making something void
a-vouch *v.* to guarantee
a-vow *v.* state openly on a subject
a-wait *v.* to wait for something
a-wake *v.* to be alert or watchful
a-ward *v.* confer as being deserved or merited
a-ware *adj.* being conscious of something; knowing of all things
a-wash *adj.* flooded; to be washed by water; to ruin by water
a-way *adv.* at a distance; apart from
awe *n.* a feeling of wonder awe *v.*
a-wea-ry *adj.* tired
a-weigh *adj.* hang just clear of a ship's anchor
awe-some *adj.* expressive of awe
aw-ful *adj.* very unpleasant; disagreeable awfully *adv.*
a-while *adv.* for a short time
a-whirl *adj.* to spin around
awk-ward *adj.* not graceful; clumsy awkwardly *adv.*
awl *n.* tool used to make holes in leather or in wood
awn *n.* the part of a piece of grass which resembles a bristle
awn-ing *n.* structure that serves as a shelter over a window
a-wry *adv.* in a twisted or turned position; other than upright
ax *or* **axe** *n.* tool used to split wood
ax-i-om *n.* something assumed to be true without proof
ax-is *n.* the line around an object or body that rotates
ax-le *n.* shaft around which a wheel or pair of wheels revolve
a-yah *n.* nursemaid or maid in India
a-zal-ea *n.* a shrub grown for their many colored flowers
AZT *abbr.* azidothymidine; a drug that improves the symptoms of Acquired Imune Difficiency Syndrome
Az-tec *n.* Indian people of Mexico
az-ure *n.* blue color of the sky; the unclouded sky
azurite *n.* a mineral consisting of blue basic carbonate of copper

B, b The second letter of the English alphabet.
baa *n.* the bleating of a sheep
babble *v.* to chatter senselessly
babe *n.* a very young child or infant
ba-bel *n.* babbling noise of many people talking at the same time
ba-boon *n.* a species of the monkey family baboonish *adj.*
ba-bush-ka *n.* a headpiece that is made by folding a kerchief into a triangle
ba-by *n., pl. babies* infant, very young child babish *adj.*
baby grand *n.* a type of piano
ba-by--sit *v.* to take care of small children in the absence of their parents
bac-ca-lau-re-ate *n.* a college degree
bach-e-lor *n.* an unmarried male
ba-cil-lus *n., pl.* **bacilli** rod-like microscopic organism
back *n.* the rear part of the human body back-less *adj.*
back-ache *n.* a pain in the back
back-bite *v.* gossip or speak in a nasty way back-biter *n.*
back-board *n.* a board that gives support
back-bone *n.* spinal column
back-drop *n.* a curtain or scene behind the back of a stage set
back-er *n.* someone who gives support
back-field *n.* football players behind the line of scrimmage
back-fire *n.* explosion of ignited fuel in an engine backfire *v.*
back-gam-mon *n.* a board game
back-ground *n.* area behind which objects are represented
back-hand *n.* a stroke in the game of tennis
back-ing *n.* support; endorsment
back-lash *n.* violent backward movement back-lash-er *n.*
back-log *n.* accumulation of unfinished work
back-pack *n.* equipment to carry items on the back
back-pedal *v.* to move backward or retreat
back-rest *n.* a support given to the back
back room *n.* a room in the rear of a building
back-saw *n.* saw with metal ribson its backside
back-seat *n.* the seat in the back of an automobile, ets.; an inferior position
back-side *n.* the buttocks
back-slide *v.* to lapse back into a less desirable condition
back-spin *n.* a spin which rotates in the reverse direction.
back-stage *n.* area behind the performing area in a theatre
back-stop *n.* screen to stop a ball
back-stretch *n.* side opposite the homestretch on a racecourse
back-stroke *n.* a swimming stroke
back-swept *adj.* slanting or swept backward
back-talk *n.* a smart or insolent reply
back-track *v.* to retrace one's previous steps or course

back-up *n.* alternative or substitute
back-ward *adv.* in a reverse order **backwardness** *n.*
back-wash *n.* a backward flow of water
back-wa-ter *n.* a body of water turned back by an obstruction
back-woods *n., pl.* heavily wooded area **back-woods-man** *n.*
ba-con *n.* salted and smoked pork
bac-te-ri-cide *n.* substance that kills bacteria
bad *adj.* naughty or disobedient; inferior in quality or performance
badger *n.* burrowing mammal *v.* harass
bad-min-ton *n.* a court game
baf-fle *v.* to perplex
bag *n.* flexible container for storing, or carrying something
ba-gel *n.* round roll with a chewy texture
bag-gage *n.* personal belongings of a traveler
bag-gy *adj.* loose **baggily** *adv.*
bag-pipe *n.* a wind instrument **bagpiper** *n.*
ba-guette *n.* a long, narrow rectangle gem
bag-worm *n.* type of moth larva
bail *n.* money given to guarantee appearance of prisoners
bail-iff *n.* officer who guards prisoners
bail-i-wick *n.* office of a bailiff
bails-man *n.* person who puts up bail for another
bait *v.* to lure
bake *v.* to cook in an oven **baker** *n.*
baker's dozen *n.* thirteen pieces
baking powder *n.* leavening agent
baking soda *n.* sodium bicarbonate
bal-a-lai-ka *n.* musical instrument
bal-ance *n.* scale for weighing of something
bal-co-ny *n.* platform projecting from the wall of a building
bald *adj.* lacking hair on the head
bal-der-dash *n.* nonsense
bale *n.* large, bound package or bundle
ba-lee *n.* a whalebone
balk *v.* to refuse to go on **balky** *adj.*
ball *n.* round object
bal-lad *n.* folk song
bal-last *n.* heavy material for stability
ball bearing *n.* bearing to reduce friction
bal-le-ri-na *n.* a female ballet dancer
bal-let *n.* artistic expression of dance **bal-let-ic** *adj.*
bal-loon *n.* a bag inflated with gas
bal-lot *n.* slip of paper used in voting
ball-point *n.* self-inking writing pen
bal-ly-hoo *n.* exaggerated advertising
balm *n.* a fragrant soothing ointment
ba-lo-ney *n., Slang* nonsense
bal-sa *n.* wood very light in weight
bal-us-ter *n.* upright post supporting a handrail
bam-boo *n.* tall grass with hollow stems
bam-boo-zle *v.* to trick
ban *v.* to prohibit
ba-nal *adj.* trite
ba-nan-a *n.* crescent-shaped yellow fruit
band *n.* a group of musicians
band-age *n.* strip of cloth to protect an injury **bandage** *v.*
ban-dan-na *n.* brightly colored handkerchief
ban-deau *n.* narrow band worn in the hair
ban-dit *n.* a gangster or robber **banditry** *n.*
ban-do-leer *n.* a belt
ban-dy *adv.* crooked
bane *n.* cause of destruction or ruin
ban-gle *n.* a bracelet
ban-ish *v.* to drive away **banishment** *n.*
ban-jo *n.* a stringed instrument
bank *n.* land at rivers edge; establishment for saving and lending money
bank-rupt *n.* person legally insolvent
ban-ner *n.* flag
ban-nock *n.* unleavened or flat cake
ban-quet *n.* elaborate dinner or feast
ban-yan *n.* a tree
bap-tism *n.* Christian sacrament
bap-tize *v.* sprinkle with water during baptism
barb *n.* fishhook point
bar-bar-i-an *n.* uncivilized culture
bar-be-cue *n.* outdoor pit for roasting meat
bar-bell *n.* exercise bar with weights
bar-ber *n.* person who cuts and dresses hair
bard *n.* a poet
bare *adj.* exposed to view **bareness** *n.*
bare-back *adv. & adj.* ride without a saddle
bare-ly *adv.* sparsely
barf *v. Slang* to vomit
bar-gain *n.* agreement on the sale of an item
barge *n.* a flat-bottomed boat
bar-i-tone *n.* male voice between tenor and bass
bark *n.* outer covering of a tree
bar-ley *n.* type of grain for making whiskey and beer
barn *n.* a farm building
bar-na-cle *n.* fish attached to an underwater surface
ba-rom-et-er *n.* device recording atmospheric changes
ba-roque *adj.* ornate artistic style
bar-rack *n.* building for housing soldiers
bar-ra-cu-da *n.* fish with a narrow body
bar-rage *n.* discharge of missiles
bar-rel *n.* round wooden container
bar-ren *adj.* sterile
bar-rette *n.* bar used to hold hair in place
bar-ri-cade *n.* barrier
bar-ri-er *n.* structure to restrict entrance
bar-room *n.* place to purchase alcoholic beverages
bar-tend-er *n.* one who serves drinks at a bar
bar-ter *v.* to trade
ba-salt *n.* volcanic rock
base *n.* fundamental part; headquarters
base-ball *n.* game using a ball and bat
base-ment *n.* foundation of a home
bash *v.* hit with a heavy blow
bash-ful *adj.* shy
ba-sic *adj.* forming the basis
BASIC *n.* computer programming language

bas-il *n.* an herb
bas-o-lisk *n.* tropical American lizard
ba-sin *n.* a washbowl
ba-sis *n., pl.* **bases** the main part
bask *v.* relax in the warmth of the sun
bas-ket *n.* woven straw, container **basketry** *n.*
bas-ket-ball *n.* game played on a court
bass *n.* fresh water fish
bas-si-net *n.* infant's crib
bas-soon *n.* a woodwind instrument
bas-tard *n.* an illegitimate child
baste *v.* loose stitch; moisten meat
bat *n.* wooden stick; nocturnal flying mammal
bath *n.* the act of washing the body
bat-tal-ion *n.* a military unit
bat-ten *v.* to secure
bat-ter *v.* beat or strike continuously
bat-tery *n.* device for storing electricity
bat-tle *n.* combat between opposing forces
bawd *n.* a prostitute
bawl *v.* cry loudly
bay *n.* inlet of a body of water
bay-o-net *n.* spear-like weapon
ba-zaar *n.* a fair
be *v.* to exist; a verb to show action
beach *n.* sandy shore of a lake or river
bea-con *n.* signaling device
bead *n.* ball with a hole for threading
beak *n.* bill of a bird
beak-er *n.* widemouthed cup for drinking
beam *n.* wood or metal used in construction
bean *n.* edible seed pod
bear *n.* **bears** large mammal *v.* to endure
beard *n.* hair growing on the chin **beardless** *adj.*
beast *n.* four-legged animal **beastly** *adj.*
beat *v.* to strike repeatedly
be-a-tif-ic *adj.* showing extreme bliss
beau *n.* sweetheart
beau-ty *n.* quality pleasing to the eye **beautifully,** *adv.*
be-cause *conj.* for a reason; since
beck *n.* a summons
be-come *v.* come to be
bed *n.* furniture for sleeping
be-dazzle *v.* confuse with bright lights
bed-bug *n.* wingless insect
bed-lam *n.* state of confusion
be-drag-gled *adj.* limp and wet; soiled
bee *n.* a stinging insect
beef *n.* cow, steer, or bull meat **beefy** *adj.*
beer *n.* an alcoholic beverage
beet *n.* red root vegetable
bee-tle *n.* an insect
be-fit *v.* be suitable
be-fore *adv.* earlier
be-friend *v.* be a friend to someone
beg *v.* ask for charity **beggar** *n.*
be-gan *v.* past tense of begin
be-get *v.* to produce
be-gin *v.* to start
be-go-nia *n.* a tropical plant
be-grudge *v.* envy someone's possessions
be-guile *v.* to delight
be-half *n.* support or interest of another
be-have *v.* function in a certain manner
be-head *v.* remove the head from the body
be-hind *adv.* at the back; slow in arriving
be-hold *v.* to look at
beige *n. or adj.* light brownish, grey color
being *n.* existence
be-lat-ed *adj.* tardy **belatedly** *adv.*
belch *v.* to expel stomach gas
bel-fry *n.* bell tower
be-lief *n.* something trusted or believed
be-lieve *v.* to accept as true or real
be-lit-tle *v.* speak in a slighting manner
bell *n.* hollow instrument that sounds when struck
bell--bot-toms *pl., n.* pants with flared legs
bel-lig-er-ent *adj.* hostile **belligerence** *n.*
bel-low *v.* make a deep, powerful roar
bel-lows *n.* instrument that produces air
bel-ly *n.* the abdomen
be-long *n.* to be a part of
be-loved *adj.* to be dearly loved
be-low *adv.* at a lower level or place
belt *n.* band worn around the waist
belt-way *n.* a highway
be-muse *v.* to bewilder
bench *n.* long seat
bend *v.* arch; curve
beneath *adv.* below; underneath
ben-e-dict *n.* newly married bachelor
ben-e-dic-tion *n.* a blessing
ben-e-fac-tion *n.* a gift
ben-e-fice *n.* fixed capital assets
be-nef-i-cence *n.* quality of being kind
ben-e-fi-cial *adj.* helpful **beneficially** *adv.*
ben-e-fit *n.* aid; help
be-nev-o-lence *n.* act of kindness **benevolent** *adj.*
be-nign *adj.* having a kind disposition
ben-i-son *n.* blessing
bent *adj.* curved
be-numb *v.* to dull
be-queath *v.* leave by a will; to hand down
be-rate *v.* scold severely
be-reave *v.* to suffer the loss of a loved one **bereavement** *n.*
be-ret *n.* a round, woolen cap
berg *n.* a large mass of ice; iceberg
ber-i-ber-i *n.* nervous disorder
berry *n., pl.* **berries** an edible fruit
ber-serk *adj.* destructively violent
berth *n.* space for a ship or boat to dock
be-seech *v.* to ask
be-side *prep.* at the side of; next to
be-siege *v.* to harass with requests
be-smear *v.* to soil
be-som *n.* broom made of twigs
be-spat-ter *v.* to soil
be-speak *v.* to indicate; foretell
best *adj.* exceeding all others in quality
bes-tial *adj.* animal-like **bestially** *adv.*
be-stir *v.* to rouse into action
best man *n.* attendant at a wedding
be-stow *v.* to give honor
be-stride *v.* to straddle
bet *n.* amount risked on a stake or wager

be-take *v.* move or to go
be-tide *v.* to happen to; to take place
be-to-ken *v.* show by a visible sign
be-tray *v.* to be disloyal or unfaithful
be-troth *v.* promise to take or give in marriage **betrothal** *n.*
be-trothed *n.* person engaged to be married
bet-ter *adj.* more suitable, useful
be-tween *prep.* in the middle; shared by two
be-twixt *prep.* between
bev-el *n.* angle at which one surface meets another
bev-er-age *n.* refreshing liquid to drink
bev-y *n.* a flock of birds
be-wail *v.* express regret or sorrow
be-ware *v.* cautious
be-wilder *v.* to perplex or puzzle **bewilderment** *n.*
be-witch *v.* fascinate completely
be-yond *prep.* outside the reach or scope of
bez-el *n.* flange or groove
be-zique *n.* card game
bi-a-ly *n.* baked roll with onions on top
bi-an-nu-al *adj.* twice a year; semiannual
bi-as *n.* diagonal line; prejudice
bib *n.* protective cloth for small children
Bi-ble *n.* book of Old and New Testaments
bib-u-lous *adj.* inclined to drink
bi-cen-ten-ni-al *adj.* every 200 years
bi-ceps *n.* large muscle of the upper arm
bick-er *v.* to argue
bi-con-cave *adj.* bowing in on two sides
bi-cus-pid *n.* tooth with two roots
bi-cy-cle *n.* two-wheeled vehicle
bid *v.* to offer to pay a certain price
bid-dy *n.* hen
bide *v.* to wait
bi-det *n.* a basin for bathing genital and anal areas
bi-en-ni-al *adj.* every two years **biennially** *adv.*
bier *n.* stand on which a coffin is placed
bi-fo-cal *adj.* having two focal lengths
bi-fur-cate *v.* divide into two parts
big *adj.* very large in intensity; grownup
big-a-my *n.* married to two people at the same time **bigamist** *n.*
big head *adj.* conceited person
big--hearted *adj.* generous and kind
big-ot *n.* person devoted to one group
big-wig *n.* person of authority
bi-ki-ni *n.* scanty, two-piece bathing suit
bi-lat-er-al *adj.* having two sides
bile *n.* liquid that is secreted by the liver
bilge *n.* inside hull of a ship
bi-lin-gual *adj.* fluent in two languages
bil-ious *adj.* gastric distress
bilk *v.* to swindle
bill *n.* itemized fees for services rendered
bill-board *n.* sign for advertisements
bill-fold *n.* wallet
bil-liards *n.* game played on a table
bil-lion *n.* one thousand million
bil-lion-aire *n.* wealthy person
bill of lading *n.* list of merchandise shipped
bil-low *n.* large swell of water; wave **billowy** *adj.*
bil-ly club *n.* wooden club for protection
billy goat *n.* male goat
bi-month-ly *adj., pl.* **bimonthlies** every two months
bin *n.* storage place
bi-na-ry *adj.* having two different parts
bind *v.* to bandage
bind-er *n.* a notebook
bind-er-y *n.* place where books are bound
binge *n.* a spree
bin-go *n.* a game of chance
bin-oc-u-lar *n.* device to bring objects far away into focus
bi-o-chem-is-try *n.* chemistry of biological processes
bi-o-de-grad-a-ble *adj.* decomposable by natural processes
bi-ol-o-gy *n.* science of living organisms **biological** *adj.*
bi-o-phys-ics *n.* the physics of living organisms
bi-op-sy *n.* examination for the detection of a disease
bi-par-ti-san *adj.* support by two parties **bipartisanship** *n.*
bi-plane *n.* glider or airplane
birch *n.* tree with close-grained wood **birch-en adj.**
bird *n.* warm-blooded, egg-laying animal **bird-like adj.**
bird-brain *n., Slang* a person who acts silly
bird-ie *n.* stroke under par; a shuttlecock
bi-ret-ta *n.* priests cap
birth *n.* beginning of existence
birth control *n.* a technique to control or prevent the number of children born; lessening
birth-day *n.* the day a person is born; day of origin
birth-mark *n.* an unusual mark on the skin at birth
birth-rate *n.* ratio of births to a population
bis *adv.* again; encore
bis-cuit *n.* type of bread or cracker
bi-sect *v.* to divide
bi-sex-u-al *adj.* relating to or having characteristics of both sexes
bish-op *n.* Christian clergyman
bi-son *n.* large buffalo
bisque *n.* creamy soup made from fish or of the flesh of birds
bis-sex-tile *adj.* the extra day occurring in a leap year
bis-tro *n.* bar or small nightclub
bit *n.* tiny piece
bitch *n.* a female dog; spiteful woman
bite *v.* crush with the teeth **bitingly** *adv.*
bit-ter *adj.* a sharp, unpleasant taste; disagreeable taste
bit-ter-sweet *n.* root, with a bitter, then a sweet taste
bi-valve *n.* a mollusk
biv-ou-ac *n.* temporary military camp

under little shelter
bi-week-ly *n.* every two weeks
bi-year-ly *n.* every two years
bi-zarre *adj.* extremely strange and odd; out of the ordinary
blab *v.* reveal a secret indiscreetly
black *adj.* very dark in color; depressing
black--and--blue *adj.* discolored skin caused by bruising
black-ball *n.* vote to prevent admission; vote against
black belt *n.* expert in karate
black-berry *n.* plant with black berries; edible fruit
black-board *n.* slate-like board written on with chalk
black box *n.* container that protects the tape recordings of airline
black eye *n.* bruise around the eye
black-head *n.* dirt that clogs the pores and creates blemishes
black-jack *n.* card game
blacklight *n.* invisible infrared light
black-mail *n.* threat of exposing a past discreditable act
black market *n.* selling illegal merchandise
black-out *n.* temporary loss of electrical power
black-smith *n.* person who shapes iron
blacksmithing n.
black-top *n.* asphalt
black widow *n.* a poisonous spider
blad-der *n.* sac that holds urine
blade *n.* cutting part of a knife
blame *v.* to find fault **blameless** *n.*
blanch *v.* remove color; scald vegetables
bland *adj.* tasteless
blan-dish *v.* coax; flatter
blank *adj.* empty; confused
blankly *adv.*
blan-ket *n.* covering used on a bed
blare *v.* loud sound
blar-ney *n.* talk that is deceptive
blast *n.* strong gust of air; sound of a horn
blast-off *n.* launching of a space ship
bla-tant *adj.* offensively loud; shameless; obvious, conspicuous
blaze *n.* a sudden burst of fire
bla-zon *v.* to make known; to announce; armorial bearings
bleach *v.* remove the color from a fabric; to make white or lighter
bleach-ers *pl., n.* tiered planks used for seating of spectators
bleak *adj.* depressing; barren; cold; harsh
bleat *n.* the cry of a sheep or goat
bleed *v.* to lose blood, as from an injury; to feel anguish or pain
bleep *n.* a signal with a quick, loud sound
blem-ish *n.* a flaw or defect
blend *v.* to mix together smoothly
bless *v.* to confer prosperity or well-being
bless-ed *adj.* Holy; enjoying happiness; bringing pleasure
bless-ing *n.* a short prayer before a meal; the act of one that blesses
blight *n.* disease of plants
blimp *n.* a large aircraft
blind *adj.* not having eyesight; unable to see; unable to discern
blind-ers *pl., n.* flaps restricting side vision
blind-fold *v.* cover the eyes with a cloth; unable to see
blink *v.* open and close the eyes quickly
blink-er *n.* a light to indicate turns
blintz *n.* hin pancake stuffed with fillings
blip *v.* erase sounds from a recording; a short crisp sound
bliss *n.* great happiness or joy
blissful *adj.*
blis-ter *n.* swelling of skin containing a watery liquid
blithe *adj.* carefree or casual
blitheness *n.*
blitz *n.* a sudden attack
bliz-zard *n.* a severe winter storm
bloat *v.* to swell or puff out
blob *n.* a small shapeless mass
bloc *n.* group formed for a common purpose
block *n.* solid piece of matter
blockage *n.*
block-ade *n.* the closure of an area
blond *adj.* a golden or flaxen color
blondish *adj.*
blonde *adj.* a person with blond hair; having light hair
blood *n.* the red fluid circulated by the heart, arteries, and capilaries
blood count *n.* the number of white and red corpuscles in a specific amount of blood
blood-hound *n.* breed of hunting dogs remarkable for senses
blood-shot *adj.* red irritation of the eyes; inflammation
blood vessel *n.* canal in which blood flows and circulates
bloom *v.* bear flowers; to flourish
blooming *adj.*
bloom-ers *n., pl.* loose pants gathered at the knee or just below the knee
bloop-er *n.* embarrassing mistake made in public
blot *n.* a spot
blotch *n.* area of skin that is discolored; difference in shade
blouse *n.* loosely fitting shirt or top
blow *v.* move or be in motion because of a current of air
blow--by--blow *adj.* very descriptive
blow dry *v.* dry one's hair with a hair dryer; to dry completely
blow-out *n.* the sudden deflation of a tire; a bursting by pressure
blow-torch *n.* handheld tool to melt soft metals
blow-up *n.* photo enlargement
blubber *n.* fat removed from whales
blue *n.* the color of a clear sky
blue baby *n.* infant with inadequate oxygen in the blood
blue-berry *n., pl.* **blueberries** small, seedless berry
blue-collar *adj.* wage earners who do manual labor

blue-fish *n.* game fish of the tropical waters; various dark fishes
blue-grass *n.* folk music
blue jay *n.* a bird
blue-nose *n.* a snob
blue-print *n.* reproduction of technical drawings or plans
blue ribbon *n.* award for first place in a contest or competition
blues *pl., n.* style of jazz music
blue spruce *n.* an evergreen tree
bluff *v.* mislead
blun-der *n.* an error or mistake
blun-der-buss *n.* gun with a flared muzzle; a blundering person
blunt *adj.* abrupt; dull
blur *v.* to smudge or smear; to become hazy
blush *v.* to turn red in the face; to feel ashamed **blushingly** *adv.*
blus-ter *n.* violent noisy wind in a storm
bo-a *n.* large nonvenomous snake
boar *n.* wild pig
board *n.* piece of sawed lumber; area where games are played
board-walk *n.* wooden walkway along a beach
boast *v.* to brag
boat *n.* a small open craft or ship
boat-swain *n.* petty officer in charge of the rigging
bob *v.* move up and down in a quick, jerky movement
bob-bin *n.* spool that holds thread
bobby socks *pl., n.* ankle sock
bob-cat *n.* wildcat
bob-sled *n.* sled with steering controls **bobsledder n.**
bod-ice *n.* upper piece of a dress
bod-y *n.* main part; physical part of a person **bodily** *adv.*
body-guard *n.* person hired to protect another from harm
body-surf *v.* surf on without a surfboard **bodysurfer n.**
bog-gle *v.* pull away from with astonishment
bo-gus *adj.* counterfeit; worthless
bo-he-mi-an *n.* unconventional lifestyle
boil *v.* heat liquid till it bubbles
boil-er *n.* vessel used to heat water for power
bois-ter-ous *adj.* violent; undisciplined **boisterously** *adv.*
bold *adj.* courageous **boldly** *adv.*
bold-face *n.* style of printing type
bo-le-ro *n.* a short jacket
bo-lo-gna *n.* smoked sausage
bol-ster *n.* round pillow
bolt *n.* threaded metal pin
bomb *n.* weapon detonated upon impact; to attack with bombs
bom-bard *v.* attack with missiles or bombs **bombardment** *n.*
bom-bast *n.* very ornate speech
bomber *n.* military aircraft
bo-na fide *adj.* genuine; authentic
bo-nan-za *n.* great prosperity
bon-bon *n.* candy
bond *n.* something that fastens or binds; together
bond-age *n.* slavery
bone *n.* calcified tissue of the skeleton
bone--dry *adj.* without water
bon-er *n., Slang* mistake or blunder
bon-fire *n.* an open outdoor fire
bo-ni-to *n.* game fish related to the tuna; medium sized
bon-kers *adj., Slang* acting crazy
bon-net *n.* a woman's hat
bon-sai *n.* a small ornamental shrub
bo-nus *n.* over and above what is expected; extra
bon voyage *n.* a farewell wish
boo *n.* expression of disapproval
boog-ie *v., Slang* dance to rock and roll music
book *n.* bound, printed literary work
book-case *n.* shelving for storing books
book-end *n.* support for holding books
book-ie *n., Slang* a bookmaker
book-ing *n.* engagement
book-keep-ing *n.* recording transactions of a business **bookeeper** *n.*
book-worm *n.* one who reads a lot
boo-mer-ang *n.* curved, missile that returns to the thrower
boon *n.* something beneficial
boon-docks *pl., n. Slang* an out-of-the-way place; country with brush
boor *n.* person with little refinement; peasant
boost *v.* lift by pushing up from below; an increase in amount
boost-er *n.* promoter
boot *n.* a protective covering for the foot usually with high tops
boot camp *n.* a military camp used for basic training
booth *n.* small compartment or area **booths pl.**
boot-leg *v., Slang.* sell, or transport liquor illegally
bo-rax *n.* cleaning compound
bor-der *n.* margin or edge
bore *v.* make a hole using a drill
born *adj.* brought into life or being
bor-ough *n.* self-governing town
bor-row *v.* receive money with the intentions of returning it
bos-om *n.* the female's breasts
boss *n.* supervisor **bossiness** *n.*
bot-a-ny *n.* science of plants **otanical** *adj.,* **botanist** *n.*
botch *v.* ruin something by clumsiness; accidental
both *adj.* two in conjunction with one; together as one
both-er *v.* to pester **bothersome** *adj.*
bot-tle *n.* receptacle made of glass
bot-tle-neck *n.* narrow passage
bot-tom *n.* lowest or deepest part **bottomless** *adj.*
bot-u-lism *n.* food poisoning
bough *n.* large branch of a tree
bouil-lon *n.* a clear seasoned broth made from lean meat
boul-der *n.* large round rock
boul-e-vard *n.* broad city street
bounce *v.* rebound or cause to rebound **bounced v., bouncing v.**
bounc-er *n.* person who removes disorderly people
bounc-ing *adj.* lively and spirited

bound-a-ry *n.* a limit or border
bound-en *adj.* under an obligation
bound-less *adj.* without limits
boundlessly *adv.*
boun-te-ous *adj.* plentiful or generous; excess
boun-ti-ful *adj.* abundant; plentiful
bounty *n.* reward for the return of something
bou-quet *n.* cut flowers
bour-bon *n.* whiskey
bour-geois *pl., n.* member of the middle class society
bout *n.* a contest
bou-tique *n.* small retail shop
bou-ton-niere *n.* flower worn in the buttonhole of a man's jacket
bo-vine *adj.* relating to an ox or cow
bow *n.* front section of a boat
bow-el *n.* digestive tract
bow-ie knife *n.* thick-bladed hunting knife which is curved cconcavely
bowl *n.* container for food or liquids
bow-leg *n.* outward curvature of the leg
bowlegged adj.
bowling alley *n.* building used for bowling
bowl over *v.* astound
box *n.* small container or chest
box-car *n.* enclosed railway car
box-er *n.* person who boxes professionally
box office *n.* where tickets are purchased for an upcoming event
boy *n.* male youth or child
boyhood *n.*
boy-cott *v.* a means of protest
bra *n.* brassiere
brace *n.* device that supports something; something with connects
brace-let *n.* ornamental band for the wrist; for show
brack-en *n.* large species of fern
brack-et *n.* support to hold a shelf
brack-ish *adj.* distasteful
brad *n.* small nail
brag *v.* assert or talk boastfully
brag-ga-do-ci-o *n., pl.* cockiness or arrogant manner
brag-gart *n.* person who brags
braid *v.* interweave three or more strands;; to make by braiding
braille *n.* system of printing for the blind; reading with fingers
brain *n.* large mass of nerve tissue enclosed in the cranium brainless *adj.*
brain-storm *n.* sudden idea or inspiration; a harebrained idea
brain-wash-ing *n.* intensive indoctrination
brain wave *n.* rhythmic fluctuation between parts of the brain
braise *v.* brown meat, then simmer
brake *n.* device to stop or slow a vehicle; to decrease in speed
brake fluid *n.* liquid contained in hydraulic brake cylinders
bran *n.* husk of cereal grains
branch *n.* extension from the trunk of a tree; extension outward
brand *n.* trademark or label; mark of shame brander n.
bran-dish *v.* to wave or flourish a weapon; an aggressive manner
brand name *n.* a company's trademark
brand-new *adj.* unused
bran-dy *n.* an alcoholic liquor
brandied *adj.*
brash *adj.* unthinking; insolent; impudent
brass *n.* alloy of zinc, copper and other metals
bras-siere *n.* woman's undergarment with bust support
brat *n.* an ill-mannered child
brat-wurst *n.* fresh pork sausage
brave *adj.* having courage
bra-vo *Interj.* expressing approval
brawl *n.* noisy fight
brawn *n.* well-developed muscles
bray *v.* make a loud cry like a donkey; loudness
braze *v.* to solder
bra-zen *adj.* shameless or impudent
bra-zier *n.* person who works with brass; a utensil for holding coals
breach *n.* a break in friendly relations; ruptered or torn condition
bread *n.* leavened food made from flour and yeast *Slang* Money
breadth *n.* distance from side to side; a comprehensive quality
breadwinner *n.* one who supports a household; a means of livelihood
break *v.* to collapse or give way
breakdown *n.* failure to function
breaker *n.* a wave
breakfast *n.* the first meal of the day
breakthrough *n.* sudden advance in technique; breaking through an obstruction
breast *n.* milk-producing glandular organs; used in breast-feeding
breast-bone *n.* the sternum
breast-stroke *n.* a swimming stroke
breathe *v.* draw air into and expel from the lungs breathless *adj.*
breath-tak-ing *adj.* awesome
breathtakingly *adv.*
breech *n., pl.* breeches the buttocks
breed *v.* genetic strain of domestic animals; to produce
breeze *n.* slight gentle wind
breeze-way *n.* roofed area between two buildings
bre-vi-ar-y *n.* book of prayers and psalms for the canonical hours
brev-i-ty *n., pl.* -ties brief duration
brew *v.* to make beer
brew-er-y *n.* plant where beer is brewed and produced
bribe *v.* induce by giving a token of value
bric--a--brac *n.* collection of objects usually having a value
brick *n.* molded block of baked clay used in building
brick-lay-er *n.* person who lays bricks side by side
bride *n.* women just married
bride-groom *n.* man just married
brides-maid *n.* woman who attends a bride
bridge *n.* structure over water

bri-dle *n.* harness to guide a horse
brief *n.* concise, formal statement of a case **briefly** *adv.*
brief-case *n.* a small bag for carrying papers and books
bri-er *n.* prickly plant
brig *n.* prison on a ship; sailing ship
bri-gade *n.* military unit
bright *adj.* brilliant in color; vivid **brightness** *n.*
bril-liant *adj.* radiant; intelligent
brim *n.* edge or rim of a cup
brim-stone *n.* sulfur
brin-dle *adj.* having dark streaks or flecks; a brindled animal
brine *n.* water contained in the oceans
bring *v.* to carry to a certain place
brink *n.* upper edge of a very steep slope
bri-quette *n.* brick-shaped piece of charcoal
brisk *adj.* moving or acting quickly
bris-ket *n.* meat from the breast of an animal
bris-tle *n.* short, stiff, coarse hair
britch-es *pl., n.* trousers
brit-tle *adj.* fragile
broach *n.* tapered tool for enlarging a hole
broad *adj.* covering a wide area **-ly** *adv.*
broad-cast *v.* to make widely known
broad-cloth *n.* cloth with a lustrous finish
broad-mind-ed *adj.* fair
broad-side *n.* side of a ship above the water; used on one side
bro-cade *n.* silk fabric
broc-co-li *n.* green vegetable
bro-chure *n.* pamphlet
brogue *n.* strong regional accent
broil *v.* cook by direct radiant heat **broiler** *n.*
broke *adj.* completely without money; without something
bro-ken *adj.* separated violently into parts; damaged or altered
bro-ken-hearted *adj.* overcome by grief or despair
bro-mide *n.* a sedative
bron-chi-al *adj.* pertaining to the bronchi **bronchially adv.**
bron-co *n.* wild horse
bron-to-saur *n.* very large dinosaur
bronze *n.* alloy of tin, copper, and zinc **bronzed v., bronzing v.**
brooch *n.* decorative pin
brood *n.* the young of an animal
brood-er *n.* enclosed heated area for raising young chickens
brook *n.* small fresh-water stream
broom *n.* long-handled implement for sweeping
broth *n.* liquid from cooking meats
broth-er *n.* male who shares the same parents as another
brow *n.* ridge above the eye
brow-beat *v.* bully
brown *n.* color between yellow and red in hue; medium lightness
brown bag-ging *n.* practice of bringing one's lunch to work
brown-ie *n.* chewy chocolate cake
browse *v.* look over something casually; glance at
bruise *n.* discoloration of the skin
brunch *n.* late breakfast and an early lunch combined together
bru-net *adj.* person with dark brown hair
brush *n.* device for painting or grooming the hair
bru-tal *adj.* very harsh or cruel **brutally** *adv.*
bub-ble *n.* round hollow object
bu-bon-ic plague *n.* contagious fatal disease
buck *n.* male deer
buck-et *n.* vessel used to carry liquids; pail
buckle *v.* to warp
bud *n.* something not developed completely; not yet mature
bud-dy *n.* companion
budge *v.* move slightly
bud-get *n.* money for a certain purpose; financial position
buff *v.* shine
buf-fa-lo *n.* wild ox
buff-er *n.* a special tool used to polish or shine something
buf-fet *n.* a side table for serving food; counter for refreshments
buf-foon *n.* clown
bug *n.* small insect; listening device
bu-gle *n.* brass instrument without keys
build *v.* erect by uniting materials
build-ing *n.* roofed and walled structure built for permanent use
bulb *n.* light for electric lamps
bulge *n.* swelling of the surface
bulk *n.* large mass
bulk-head *n.* retaining wall on the waterfront; an upright partition
bull *n.* adult male in cattle
bull-doze *v.* dig up land
bull-dozer *n.* machine for moving earth; one that buldozes
bul-let *n.* projectile fired from a gun **bulletproof adj.**
bul-le-tin *n.* a public notice
bull-head-ed *adj.* stubborn
bul-lion *n.* refined gold or silver
bull-pen *n.* area where pitchers warm up; a cell where prisoners are held until brought to court
bull's eye *n.* center of a target
bul-ly *n.* mean or cruel person
bul-rush *n.* tall grass
bul-wark *n.* strong support
bum *n.* one who begs from others
bum-ble-bee *n.* large bee
bump *v.* collide with
bump-er *n.* device that absorbs shock and prevents damage
bumper--to--bumper *adj.* long line of vehicles moving very slowly
bump-kin *n.* awkward country person **bumpkinly adj., -ish adj.**
bump-tious *adj.* forward; pushy
bun *n.* plain or sweet small breads; tightly rolled hair
bunch *n.* group of items
bun-co *n.* swindling scheme
bun-dle *n.* anything wrapped or held together

bundle up *v.* dress warmly
bun-ga-low *n.* one-story cottage
bun-gle *v.* act awkwardly **bungling adj., bungler** *n.*,**bunglingly adv.**
bun-ion *n.* painful swelling of the big toe
bunk *n.* narrow bed
bunk-er *n.* tank for storing fuel on a ship **bunkered v., bunkering v.**
bun-ny *n.* small rabbit
bunt *v.* tap a pitched ball with a half swing; middle part of square sail
bunt-ing *n.* hooded blanket for a baby; various stout-billed birds
buoy *n.* floating channel marker
buoy-an-cy *n.* tendency to remain afloat; ability to recover quickly
bur-den *n.* something hard to bear; a duty; something that is carried
bu-reau *n.* low chest; body of non-elected officials in government
bur-geon *v.* put forth new life
bur-glar *n.* person who steals **-ize** *v.*
bur-i-al *n.* act of burying
burl *n.* growth on a tree
bur-lap *n.* coarse cloth woven from hemp; lightweight material
bur-lesque *n.* theatrical entertainment **burlesqued v., burlesquely adv.**
burn *v.* be destroyed by fire; consume fuel and give off heat
bur-nish *v.* to polish; make shiny
burp *n.* a belch
bur-ro *n.* a small donkey
bur-row *n.* tunnel dug in the ground by an animal for burrying
bur-si-tis *n.* inflammation of the joints
burst *adj.* explode and experience a sudden outbreak
bus *n.* large passenger vehicle
bus boy *n.* waiter's assistant; person who cleans the tables
bus-by *n.* a fur hat
bush *n.* a low plant with branches near the ground; a dense tuft or growth; land that is covered intensely with undergrowth
bushed *adj., Slang* extremely exhausted; tired
bush-el *n.* a unit of dry measurement which equals four pecks; a container that holds a bushel
bush-ing *n.* metal lining that reduces friction; electrical
bush-mas-ter *n.* the largest New World venomous snake
bush-whack *v.* to travel through thick woods by cutting bushes and small trees; to ambush **bushwhacker** *n.*
busi-ness *n.* person's professional dealings or occupation; an industrial or commercial establishment; role; function
bust *n.* a sculpture that resembles the upper part of a human body; the breasts of a women *v.* to break or burst; to become short of money *Slang* to place a person under arrest
bus-tle *n.* a padding that gives extra bulk to the back of a woman's skirt **bustled v., bustling v.**
bus-y *adj.* full of activity; engaged in some form of work **busily** *adv.*, **business** *n.*
busy-body *n.* an inquisitive person who interferes with someone else's business
but *conj.* on the contrary to; other than; if not; except for the fact
bu-tane *n.* a gas produced from petroleum, used as a fuel refrigerant and aerosol propellant
butch-er *n.* one who slaughters animals and dresses them for food **butchered v., butchering v.**
butt *n.* the object of ridicule; the thick large or blunt end of something. *v.* To hit with horns or the head; to place end to end
but-ter *n.* a yellow substance churned from milk
but-ter-cup *n.* a colorful plant with glossy yellow flowers
but-ter-fat *n.* the natural fat from milk that floats to the top of unpasteurized milk
but-ter-fin-gers *n.* an awkward or clumsy person
but-ter-fly *n.* a narrow-bodied insect with four broad, colorful wings; resembles a butterfly
but-ter-milk *n.* the liquid that remains after butter has been churned from milk
but-ter-scotch *n.* a candy made from brown sugar and melted butter
but-tocks *pl., n.* the two round fleshy parts of the rump
but-ton *n.* a small disk that interlocks with a buttonhole
but-ton-hole *n.* the slit through which a button is inserted
but-tress *n.* a support made of either brick or stone
bux-om *adj.* lively; full of life; happy; pleasantly plump
buy *v.* to purchase in exchange for money. *n.* Anything that is bought
buy-er *v.* a person who buys from a store or an individual
buzz *v.* to make a low vibrating sound, as a bee; to signal
buz-zard *n.* a broad-winged vulture from the same family as the hawk
buzz-er *n.* an electrical signaling device that makes a buzzing sound; the sound of a buzzer
by *prep.* up to and beyond; to go past; not later than
bye *n.* a position in which a contestant has no opponent after pairs are drawn for a tournament, and, therefore, advances to the next round
bye-bye *Slang* farewell
by-gone *adj.* gone by; past
by-law *n.* a rule or law governing internal affairs of a group or organization
by--product *n.* material that is left over when something is manufactured but also has a market value of its own
byte *n.* in computer science, a sequence of adjacent binary digits operated on as a unit
by-word *n.* well-known proverb; an object of contempt or derision

C, c The third letter of the English alphabet.
cab *n.* a taxicab; the compartment where a person sits to drive a large truck or machinery
ca-bal *n.* a group that conspires against a government or other public institution
ca-ban-a *n.* a small shelter on the beach with living facilities
cab-a-ret *n.* a restaurant that provides dancing and live entertainment
cab-bage *n.* a plant with large, edible green leaves, eaten as a vegetable
cab-in *n.* a small house; a private room on a ship
cab-in boy *n.* a male employee, on a ship, that waits on passengers and officers
cab-i-net *n.* a storage unit
cab-i-net-maker *n.* a person who specialized in the construction of furniture
ca-ble *n.* a very heavy rope having great strength
ca-ble car *n.* a means of transportation on a cable, either by rail or air
cable--gram *n.* a message or telegram sent by underwater cable
cable stitch *n.* a knitting stitch that produces the look of a cable
cable television *n.* a private television system which picks up signals from television stations and transmits them by cable
ca-boo-dle *n. Slang* the entire unit, amount, or colletion
ca-boose *n.* the last car of a train
ca-ca-o *n.* any tree of the chocolate family; the dried seed of the cacao tree from which chocolate and cocoa are made
cach-a-los *n.* a sperm whale
cache *n.* a safe place
ca-chet *n.* a mark of distinctionor authenticity
cack-le *v.* to laugh with the characteristic shrill noise a hen makes after laying an egg
ca-coph-o-ny *n.* a harsh and disagreeable sound
cac-tuws *n.* a leafless plant with a thick, prickly surface, which grows primarily in hot and dry regions
cad *n.* an ungentlemanly man
ca-dav-er *n.* a dead body
ca-dev-er-ous *adj.* pale and gaunt
cad-die *n.* a person employed by a golfer to assist him by carrying his clubs during the game of golf
ca-dence *n.* a rhythmic movement
ca-den-za *n.* an elaborate ornamental section for a soloist near the end of a conceto
ca-det *n.* a military student
cadge *v.* to beg or to receive by begging; to mooch
cad-mi-um *n.* a metallic element, bluish-white in color, used in storage batteries and solders
cad-re *n.* the group of trained personnel that forms the heart of an organization
ca-du-ce-us *n.* the symbol of the medical profession, a winged staff entwined with two serpents entwined around it.
cae-su-ra *n.* a pause or break in a line of verse or poetry
caf-e-te-ri-a *n.* a restaurant with self-service
caf-feine *n.* a stimulant **caffeinic** *adj.*
caf-tan *n.* a loose-fitting, full-length garment worn in the Near East
cage *n.* a box-like structure enclosed with bars or grating for the confinement of animals.
ca-gey *adj.* shrewd, wary, or cautious
ca-hoot *n.* a questionable relationship withan associate
ca-jole *v.* to wheedle or coax someone into doing something
cake *n.* a sweet dessert
cal-a-mine *n.* a lotion for skin irritations
ca-lam-i-ty *n.* a misfortune **calamitously** *adv.*
cal-ci-fy *v.* to become stony **calcification** *n.*
cal-ci-um *n.* an element found in teeth and bones
cal-cu-late *v.* to estimate something **calculable, calculated** *adj.*
cal-dron *n.* a cooking kettle
calf *n.* the offspring of a domestic cow
cal-i-co *n.* a cotton fabric used in clothing
call *v.* to call out; to telephone
cal-lus *n.* thickening of the skin
calm *adj.* an absence of motion
cal-o-rie *n.* a measurement of food energy
cam-el *n.* a desert animal living in Africa and Asia
cam-e-o *n.* a precious gem
cam-er-a *n.* an apparatus for taking pictures
cam-i-sole *n.* a short sleeveless undergarment for women
cam-ou-flage *v.* to disguise or conseal something from view
camp *n.* a temporary lodging
cam-pus *n.* the grounds of a college
can *v.* to be physically or mentally able
ca-nal *n.* a man-made water channel
ca-nar-y *n.* a small, colorful songbird
ca-nas-ta *n.* a card game
can-cel *v.* to invalidate or annul **cancelation** *n.*
can-cer *n.* a malignant tumor **-ous** *adj.*
can-di-date *n., pl.* a person seeking an office **candidacy** *n.*
can-dle *n.* a wax tallow burned to produce light
cane *n.* a walking stick
ca-nine *adj.* of the dog family
can-is-ter *n.* a container to store food in
can-ker *n.* an erosive sore in the mouth which causes great discomfort
can-ni-bal *n.* a person who eats human flesh
can-non *n.* a heavy war weapon
can-ny *adj.* cautious
ca-noe *n.* a light-weight, slender boat **canoeist** *n.*
can-on *n.* the laws of a church
can-o-py *n.* a cloth covering over a bed

can-tan-ker-ous *adj.* bad-tempered; ill-natured **cantankerously** *adv.*
can-teen *n.* a container for carrying water
can-ter *n.* movement that is slower than a gallop
can-vas *n.* a fabric used in making tents
can-vass *v.* to solicit opinions or votes; to examine very carefully
can-yon *n.* a deep, narrow gorge
cap *n.* a covering for the head
ca-pa-ble *adj.* having the ability to perform
ca-pac-i-ty *n.* the volume of something; the ability to hold
cape *n.* a covering for the shoulders
cap-il-lary *n.* small vessels that connect
cap-i-tal *n.* the seat of government
ca-pit-u-late *v.* to surrender **-tor** *n.*
ca-pon *n.* a young rooster
cap-size *v.* to overturn in a boat
cap-sule *n.* a gelatinous case for oral medicine
cap-tain *n.* the chief leader of a group
cap-tion *n.* a subtitle
cap-ti-vate *v.* to hold the attention of someone or thing
cap-tive *n.* a prisoner
cap-ture *v.* to take by force **captuer** *n.*
ca-rafe *n.* a wine bottle
car-a-mel *n.* a chewy candy
car-at *n.* a unit of weight for gems
car-a-van *n.* a group of people traveling together
car-bo-hy-drate *n.* organic compounds
car-bon *n.* a nonmetallic element **carbonize** *v.*, **carbonic** *adj*
carbon monoxide *n.* a poisonous gas
car-bun-cle *n.* an infection of the skin
car-bu-re-tor *n.* a device to mix vapor, fuel, and air
car-ci-no-ma *n.* a malignant tumor
car-di-ac *adj.* of the heart
car-di-gan *n.* a sweater with buttons down the front
car-di-ol-o-gy *n.* the study of the heart **cardiologist** *n.*, **cardiological** *adj*
card-sharp *n.* a person who cheates when playing cards
care *n.* a feeling of concern
ca-reer *n.* an occupation
care-free *adj.* free from all worries
care-ful *adj.* exercising care
ca-ress *v.* to touch gently
car-go *n.* freight
car-il-lon *n.* a set of tuned bells in a tower
car-nage *n.* a massacre
car-ni-val *n.* an amusement show
car-ol *n.* a song
car-pen-ter *n.* one who works with lumber
car-pet *n.* a floor covering
car-rot *n.* an orange root vegetable
car-ry *v.* to transport from one place to another
car-tel *n.* a group of companies organized to control prices, etc.
car-ti-lage *n.* connective tissue
car-toon *n.* a funny caricature **-ist** *n.*
cart-wheel *n.* a sideways handspring
cas-cade *n.* a waterfall
case *n.* a particular occurrence
cash *n.* money
cash-ew *n.* an edible nut
cash-ier *n.* an employee who handles cash
ca-si-no *n.* a public place for gambling
cask *n.* a barrel
cas-ket *n.* a coffin
cas-se-role *n.* a dish used for baking
cas-sette *n.* tape used in tape recorders
cast *v.* hurl or throw with force **castway** *adj.*
cast-er *n.* a small set of swiveling rollers
cas-ti-gate *v.* to punish or criticize severely
cas-tle *n.* a fort
cast-off *adj.* to discarded or throw away
cas-trate *v.* to spay
ca-su-al *adj.* informal
ca-su-al-ty *n.* one injured or killed
cat-a-combs *n.* underground passage
cat-a-log *n.* publication listing of names and addresses
cat-a-ma-ran *n.* a pleasure boat
ca-tas-tro-phe *n.* a terrible disaster
catch *v.* to capture or seize
cat-e-go-ry *n.* a grouping of something
ca-ter *v.* to provide food
cat-er-pil-lar *n.* the larva of a moth or butterfly
cat-fish *n.* a freshwater fish
ca-the-dral *n.* a large church
cat-nap *n.* a short nap
CAT scan *n.* x-ray; using computerized axial tomography
cat-tle *n.*, *pl.* farm animals
cau-cus *n.* the meeting of a political party
cau-li-flow-er *n.* a vegetable
caulk *v.* to seal seams against leakage
cause *v.* to produce a result
cause-way *n.* a highway through a marsh tract
cau-ter-ize *v.* to burn with a hot instrument
cau-tion *n.* a warning
cav-al-cade *n.* horse-drawn carriages
cav-al-ry *n.* army troops on horseback
cave *n.* an underground tomb or chamber
cav-i-ar *or* **cav-i-are** *n.* eggs of a large fish
cav-i-ty *n.* a decayed place in a tooth
cease *v.* to stop
cease-fire *v.* to stop fighting
cease-less *adj.* endless **ceasely** *adv.*
ce-dar *n.* an evergreen tree
ceil-ing *n.* an overhead covering of a room
cel-e-brate *v.* to observe with ceremonies **celebration** *n.*
cel-leb-ri-ty *n.*, *pl.* **-ies** a famous person
cel-er-y *n.* a vegetable with an edible stalk
ce-les-tial *adj.* heavenly
cell *n.* a small room in a prison
cel-lar *n.* an underground area of a house
cel-lu-lite *n.* a fatty deposit
cel-lu-lose *n.* a carbohydrate
ce-ment *n.* a hard construction material
cem-e-ter-y *n.* a place for burying the

dead
cen-sor *n.* a person who examines films **censorship** *n.*
cen-sure *n.* an expression of criticism
cen-sus *n.* the count of the population
cen-ter *n.* the equal distance from all sides
cen-tral *adj.* the center or main part **centralize** *v.*
cen-tu-ry *n.* a period of 100 years
ce-ram-ic *adj.* material made by firing clay
ce-re-al *n.* an edible grain; breakfast food
cer-a-bel-lum *n.* the lower part of the brain
cer-e-brum *n.* the upper part of the brain
cer-e-mo-ny *n.* a ritual
cer-tain *adj.* to be very sure **-ly** *adv.*
cer-tif-i-cate *n.* a document stating the truth
cer-ti-fy *v.* to declare in writing to be true
ces-sa-tion *n.* the act of stopping or ceasing
ces-sion *n.* the act of giving up rights
chafe *v.* to become sore by rubbing
chafing dish *n.* a dish for cooking food
cha-grin *n.* the feeling of disappointment
chain *n.* connecting links
chair *n.* a seat with four legs and a back
chair-man *n.* a person presiding at a meeting
cha-let *n.* a cottage
chal-ice *n.* a drinking goblet
chalk *n.* a soft mineral used for writing
chal-lah *n.* a loaf of braided bread
chal-lis *n.* a lightweight printed cloth
cham-ber *n.* a judge's office
chamber-maid *n.* maid at a hotel
champ *n.* a champion
cham-pagne *n.* a white sparkling wine
chance *n.* accidental
chan-cel *n.* an area of a church
chan-cel-lor *n.* a chief director **-ship** *n.*
chan-croid *n.* a lesion in the genital area
chan-de-lier *n.* a large light fixture
change *v.* to become or make different; alter
chan-nel *n.* the deepest part of a harbor, lake or river
chant *n.* a melody sung on the same note
cha-os *n.* total disorder
chap *n., Slang* a fellow
chap-el *n.* a place to worship
chap-er-on *n.* a woman who supervises younger women
chap-lain *n.* clergyman
chaps *pl., n.* leather overpants
chap-ter *n.* one division or part of a book
char-ac-ter *n.* a persons quality or trait
char-coal *n.* a material used for fuel
chard *n.* an edible white beet
charge *v.* to give full responsibility to; price
charg-er *n.* an apparatus to recharge a battery
char-i-ot *n.* a horse-drawn vehicle
char-i-ty *n.* money given to the needy
cha-ri-va-ri *n.* a playful serenade to newlyweds
charm *n.* an ability to please; ornament
chart *n.* a map
char-ter *n.* an official document
chase *v.* to run after
chasm *n.* a deep crack in the earth's surface
chas-sis *n.* the framework for automobiles
chaste *adj.* pure
chas-tise *v.* to reprimand
chat *v.* to converse in a friendly manner
chat-tel *n.* movable personal property
chauf-feur *n.* a person who drives someone
cheap *adj.* inexpensive; low in cost
cheapen *v.* to lessen the value
cheap-skate *n.* one who tries to avoid spending money
cheat *v.* to break the rules **cheater** *n.*
check *v.* to restrain; examine for correctness
check-book *n.* a book with blank checks
check-ers *n.* a board game
check-mate *n.* a winning chess move
ched-dar *n.* a firm, smooth cheese
cheek *n.* the fleshy part of the face
cheek-bone *n.* the facial bone below the eyes
cheerful *adj.* having good spirits
cheer-leader *n.* person who cheers at a sporting event
cheese *n.* food made from the curd of milk
cheese burg-er *n.* a hamburger with cheese
cheese-cake *n.* dessert cake
chee-tah *n.* a swift-running wildcat
chef *n.* a male cook
che-mise *n.* woman's loose undergarment
chem-ist *n.* a person versed in chemistry
che-mo-ther-a-py *n.* a treatment for cancer
che-nille *n.* a soft cord used to make rugs, etc.
cher-ish *v.* to hold dear
cher-ry *n.* fruit tree bearing red fruit
cher-ub *n.* an angel resembling a child
chess *n.* game for two played on a chessboard **chessman** *n.*
chest *n.* the part of the upper body
chest-nut *n.* a tree with edible nuts
chev-ron *n.* an insignia or emblem
chew *v.* to crush or grind with the teeth
chic *adj.* fashionable
chick *n.* a young chicken
chick-a-dee *n.* a bird
chick-en *n.* a domestic fowl
chicken pox *n.* a contagious childhood disease
chick-pea *n.* a plant with edible pea-like seeds
chic-le *n.* the juice of a tropical tree
chic-o-ry *n.* a herb used in salads
chide *v.* to scold or find fault
chief *n.* a person of highest rank; a boss
chief-tain *n.* a head of a group, or tribe
chif-fon *n.* a sheer fabric
chif-fo-nier *n.* a tall chest of drawers
chig-ger *n.* an insect

chi-gnon *n.* hair worn on the back of the neck
child *n.* a young person of either sex **childish** *adj.*
child abuse *n.* the sexual or physical maltreatment of a child
child-birth *n.* the act of giving birth
chil-i *n.* a hot pepper
chill *v.* to reduce to a lower temperature
chill-y *adj.* very cold condition
chime *n.* a set of bells tuned to a scale
chi-me-ra *n.* an absurd fantasy
chim-ney *n.* a flue for smoke to escape
chim-pan-zee *n.* an ape
chin *n.* the lower part of the face
chi-na *n.* fine porcelain from China
chin-chil-la *n.* a rodent from South America
chintz *n.* printed, glazed cotton fabric
chintz-y *adj.* cheap
chip *n.* a small broken off piece; disk used in the game of poker
chip-munk *n.* striped rodent
chi-ro-prac-tic *n.* a method of therapy **chiropractor** *n.*
chirp *n.* the high-pitched sound of a bird
chis-el *n.* tool with a sharp edge to shape
chit *n.* voucher for food or drink
chit-chat *n.* casual conversation
chiv-al-ry *n.* brave qualities of a knight
chive *n.* herb used as flavoring in cooking
chlo-rine *n.* compound used to purify water
chock *n.* wedge placed under a wheel
choc-o-late *n.* ground cacao nuts **chocolaty** *adj.*
choice *n.* select or choose
choir *n.* an organized group of singers
chok-er *n.* short necklace
cho-les-ter-ol *n.* fatty substance present in blood cells
choose *v.* select or pick out
chop *v.* cut by making downward stroke
choppy *adj.* rough
chop-sticks *pl., n.* sticks of wood for eating
cho-ral *adj.* sung by a choir or chorus
cho-rale *n.* hymn with a simple melody
chore *n.* a daily task
cho-re-a *n.* acute nervous disease
cho-re-og-ra-phy *n.* creation of a dance routine in ballets
chor-is-ter *n.* a member of a choir
cho-rus *n.* a group of people singing together
cho-sen *adj.* preferred above all others
chow *n., Slang* food
chow-der *n.* soup made with fish or clams
Christ *n.* Jesus; The Messiah
chris-ten *v.* to baptize; give a Christian name
Christ-mas *n.* December 25th; believed to be the birthday of Jesus Christ by Christians
chrome *n.* anything plated with chromium
chron-ic *adj.* frequently recurring
chron-i-cle *n.* record of events in order
chry-san-the-mum *n.* cultivated plants
chub-by *adj.* plumb
chuck-hole *n.* hole in the street
chuck-le *v.* laugh quietly **-er** *n.*
chum *n.* a close friend or pal
chunk *n.* a thick piece; a lump
churl *n.* a rude person
churn *n.* container for making butter
chut-ney *n.* condiment made with fruit
ci-der *n.* juice from apples
ci-gar *n.* rolled tobacco leaves
cig-a-rette *n.* amount of tobacco rolled in thin paper
cinch *n.* strap for holding a saddle
cin-der *n.* piece of burned wood
cin-e-ma *n.* a motion picture
cin-e-mat-o-garaph *n.* movie pro-jector
cin-e-ma-tog-ra-phy *n.* art of photographing a motion picture
cin-na-mon *n.* bark of a tree used for spice
ci-pher *n.* zero
cir-ca *prep.* approximate
cir-cle *n.* process that ends at its starting point
cir-cuit *n.* path where electric current flows
cir-cu-lar *adj.* moving in a circle
cir-cu-late *v.* pass from place to place
cir-cum-cise *v.* remove skin on the male penis
cir-cum-fer-ence *n.* perimeter of a circle
cir-cum-scribe *v.* confine within boundaries
cir-cum-stance *n.* fact to consider when making a decision
cir-cum-stan-tial *adj.* not essential
cir-cum-stan-ti-ate *adj.* provide circumstantial evidence
cir-cum-vent *v.* gain advantage
cir-cus *n.* show featuring clowns, and trained animals
cir-rho-sis *n.* liver disease
cir-rus *n.* white, wispy cloud
cis-tern *n.* man-made tank for holding rain water
cit-a-del *n.* fortress
ci-ta-tion *n.* official summons from a court
cit-i-zen *n.* native or naturalized person
cit-ron *n.* fruit
cit-y *n.* place larger than a town
civ-et *n.* cat-like mammal
civ-ic *adj.* relating to or of a city
ci-vil-ian *n.* person not in active duty in the military or police force
civ-i-li-za-tion *n.* high level development
civ-i-lize *v.* tame
claim *v.* to hold something to be true **claimable** *adj.*
clair-voy-ance *n.* visualize objects hidden from the senses
clam *n.* freshwater bivalve mollusks
clam-ber *v.* climb using both hands and feet **clamberer** *n.*
clam-my *adj.* damp, cold, and sticky
clam-or *n.* loud noise or outcry
clamp *n.* device for holding things
clan *n.* group of people who are related
clan-des-tine *adj.* done in secrecy
clang *v.* make a loud, ringing sound

clap *v.* applaud
clap-board *n.* board covering for a house
clap-per *n.* part of a bell
clar-i-fy *v.* become or make clearer
clar-i-net *n.* woodwind instrument
clash *v.* to collide; conflict
clasp *n.* hook to hold objects together
class *n.* group with common interest
clas-sic *adj.* belonging in a certain category
clas-si-fy *v.* arrange into the same category
clause *n.* group of words part of a complex sentence
claus-tro-pho-bia *n.* fear of enclosed places
clav-i-chord *n.* key-board instrument
clav-i-cle *n.* bone that connecting breastbone and shoulder blade
claw *n.* sharp, curved nail on the foot of an animal
clay *n.* pliable earth that hardens when fired
clean *adj.* free from impurities
cleanse *v.* make pure or clean **-er** *n.*
clear *adj.* not cloudy; able to see easily
clearance *n.* distance between two objects
cleat *n.* metal projection to prevent slipping
cleav-er *n.* knife used by butchers
clef *n.* musical staff symbol
cler-gy *n.* women and men religious leaders
cler-gy-man *n.* member of the clergy
cler-i-cal *adj.* trained for office duties
clerk *n.* clerical worker in an office
clev-er *adj.* mentally quick **cleverness** *n.*
cli-ent *n.* a patron; a customer
cli-en-tele *n.* collection of customers
cliff *n.* steep edge or face of a rock
cli-mate *n.* weather conditions **-tic** *adj.*
cli-max *n.* point of greatest intensity
climb *v.* move to a higher location
clinch *v.* to settle definitively
cling *v.* hold fast to; to grasp or stick
clin-ic *n.* medical establishment
clink *v.* cause a light ringing sound
clip *v.* cut off
clip-per *n.* fast sailing vessel
clique *n.* exclusive group of people
clob-ber *v., Slang* hit repeatedly
cloche *n.* woman's close-fitting hat
clock *n.* instrument that measures time
clog *v.* to choke up
clone *n.* identical reproduction
close *adj.* near, as in time; nearly even
clos-et *n.* compartment or room for storage
clot *n.* thick or solid mass, as of blood
cloth *n.* fabric, used to cover a table
clothe *v.* provide clothes
cloud *n.* something that obscures
clout *n.* a heavy blow with the hand; influence
clove *n.* a spice
clo-ver *n.* herb with trifoliolate leaves
clover-leaf *n.* junction of highway
clown *n.* professional comedian **-ish** *adj.*
cloy *v.* make sick with too much sweetness
club *n.* heavy wooden stick
clump *n.* thick cluster
clum-sy *adj.* lacking coordination
clus-ter *n.* a group of something
clutch *v.* to seize and hold tightly
clut-ter *n.* confused mass of disorder
coach *n.* director of athletics, drama, etc.
co-ad-ju-tor *n.* assistant
coal *n.* mineral widely used for fuel; ember
co-a-lesce *v.* come together
co-ali-tion *n.* temporary alliance
coarse *adj.* lacking refinement **-ness** *v.*
coast *n.* land bordering the sea
coat *n.* outer garment
coax *v.* persuade by gentleness **coaxingly** *adv.*
cob *n.* male swan; a corncob
co-balt *n.* metallic element resembling iron and nickel
cob-ble *v.* make or repair shoes
co-bra *n.* venomous snake
cob-web *n.* fine thread spun into a web
co-caine *n.* narcotic used as a local anesthetic
coch-le-a *n.* spiral tube of the inner ear
cock *n.* adult male in the domestic fowl; the rooster
cock-a-too *n.* crested parrot
cock-le *n.* edible bivalve mollusk
cock-ney *n.* dialect of East End Londoners
cock-pit *n.* compartment where the pilot and the crew sit
cock-roach *n.* fast running nocturnal insect
co-co *n.* fruit of the coconut palm
co-coa *n.* powder from kernels of the cacao
co-coon *n.* silky, protective case spun by insect larvae
cod *n.* large fish of the North Atlantic
cod-dle *v.* to cook just below boiling point
code *n.* set of rules; set of secret words
co-ed-u-ca-tion *n.* educational system for both men and women
co-erce *v.* dominate with force
co-ex-ist *v.* exist together
cof-fee *n.* beverage prepared from ground beans
cof-fin *n.* box for burying a corpse
cog *n.* series of a teeth on the rim of a wheel
co-gent *adj.* forceful **cogently** *adv.*
cog-i-tate *v.* think carefully about
co-gnac *n.* fine brandy made in France
co-hab-it *v.* live as husband and wife
co-here *v.* stick or hold together
co-hort *n.* group of people united in one effort
coif *n.* hat worn under a nun's veil
coil *n.* series of connecting rings
coin *n.* piece of metal used as money
co-in-cide *v.* happen at the same time
co-in-ci-dence *n.* two events happening at the same time
coke *n.* arbonaceous fuel; cocaine
cold *adj.* having a low temperature **coldness** *n.*
cold--blooded *adj.* without feeling

col-ic *n.* sharp pain in the abdomen caused by muscular cramps
col-i-se-um *n.* large amphitheater
col-lab-o-rate *v.* work with another person
col-lapse *v.* fall; to give way
col-lar *n.* part of a garment around the neck
col-lar-bone *n., Anat.* the clavicle
col-late *v.* assemble in correct sequence
col-lat-er-al *adj.* security for a loan
col-league *n.* one who works in the same profession
col-lect *v.* gather or assemble
col-lege *n.* institution of higher education
col-lide *v.* come together with impact
col-lo-quy *n.* formal conference
col-lusion *n.* secret agreement
co-lon *n.* punctuation mark (:); section of the large intestine
colo-nel *n.* an officer in the armed forces **colonelcy** *n.*
col-o-ny *n.* group of emigrants living in a new land
col-or *n.* a hue or tint **colorful** *adj.*
col-or-a-tion *n.* arrangement of different colors or shades
col-or--blind *adj.* not able to distinguish colors
col-or-fast *adj.* color that will not fade
col-os-sal *adj.* large or gigantic in size
colt *n.* very young male horse **-ish** *adj.*
col-umn *n.* decorative, supporting pillar
col-um-nist *n.* person who writes a newspaper column
co-ma *n.* deep unciousness sleep
comb *n.* instrument for aranging the hair
com-bat *v.* oppose; to struggle
com-bi-na-tion *n.* series of numbers or letters to open locks
com-bine *v.* unite; to merge
com-bus-ti-ble *adj.* capability of burning
come *v.* arrive; to approach
com-e-dy *n.* humorous, entertaining performance
com-et *n.* celestial body orbiting the sun **cometic** *adj.*
com-fort *v.* console in time of grief or fear
com-fort-er *n.* heavy quilt; one who comforts
com-ic *adj.* characteristic of comedy
com-i-cal *adj.* funny
com-ma *n.* punctuation mark (,) indicating a break or series
com-mand *v.* to give orders; to dominate
com-mem-o-rate *v.* honor the memory of **commemorative** *adj.*
com-mence *v.* begin; start
com-mence-ment *n.* graduation ceremony
com-mend *v.* give praise **-able** *adj.*
com-men-su-rate *adj.* equal in duration **commensurately** *adv.*
com-ment *n.* statement of observation
com-merce *n.* exchanging of products
com-mer-cial *adj.* relating to a product
com-mis-er-ate *v.* feel sympathy for someone
com-mis-sary *n.* store on a military base
com-mis-sion *n.* moneys paid sales
com-mit-tee *n.* people appointed perform a task or function
com-mode *n.* movable wash-stand
com-mo-dore *n.* naval officer
com-mon *adj.* general, ordinary
common denominatior *n.* number that can be evenly divided
com-mu-ni-ca-ble *adj.* capable of being transmitted, as with a disease **communicably** *adv.*
com-mu-ni-cate *v.* make known
com-mu-ni-ca-tion *n.* act of transmitting ideas
com-mun-ion *n.* mutual sharing of feelings and thoughts
com-mu-nism *n.* system of government
com-mu-ni-ty *n.* group of people living in the same area
com-mute *v.* travel to one's job each day
com-pact *adj.* packed together
com-pan-ion *n.* an associate
com-pan-ion-a-ble *adj.* friendly **companionably** *adv.*
com-pa-ny *n.* gathering of persons for a social purpose
com-pa-ra-ble *adj.* capable of comparison
com-pare *v.* note the likenesses of
com-part-ment *n.* enclosed area
com-pass *n.* instrument to determine geographic direction
com-pas-sion *n.* sympathy for someone
com-pat-i-ble *adj.* live together harmoniously
com-pa-tri-ot *n.* person of the same country **compatriotic** *adj.*
com-pel *v.* urge or force action
com-pen-dium *n.* short summary
com-pen-sate *v.* make up for; to pay
com-pete *v.* to engage in a contest
com-pe-tent *adj.* having sufficient ability
com-pe-ti-tion *n.* a trial of skill or ability **competitive** *adj.*
com-pet-i-tor *n.* one who competes against another
com-pile *v.* to put together information from other documents
com-plain-ant *n.* person filing a formal charge
com-plaint *n.* expression of dissatisfaction, or resentment
com-plai-sance *n.* willingness to please
com-ple-ment *n.* something that adds to
com-plete *adj.* having all the necessary parts; whole
com-plex *adj.* consisting of intricate parts
com-plex-ion *n.* natural color and texture of the skin
com-pli-ance *n.* agreement
com-pli-cate *v.* make or become complex
com-pli-ment *n.* expression of praise
com-pli-men-ta-ry *adj.* giving a compliment
com-ply *v.* to consent
com-po-nent *n.* a constituent part
com-port *v.* conduct oneself in a certain way
com-pose *v.* make up from elements or parts **composer** *n.*
com-pos-ite *adj.* made from separate elements

com-po-si-tion *n.* artistic literary work
com-post *n.* fertilizing mixture of vegetable matter
com-po-sure *n.* tranquillity
com-pote *n.* fruit preserved or stewed in syrup
com-pound *n.* combination of two or more parts **compounable** *adj.*
com-pre-hend *v.* to perceive **-sion** *n.*
com-pre-hen-sive *adj.* large in scope
com-pres-sor *n.* a machine that for compressing air
com-prise *v.* to be made up of
com-pro-mise *n.* settling of differences
comp-trol-ler *n.* person who examines accounts
com-pute *v.* determine by the use of math; to make calculations
com-puter *n.* electronic machine which performs logical calculations
computerize *v.* process or store information on a computer
com-rade *n.* associate who shares one's interest or occupation
con *v. Slang* to swindle or trick
con-cat-e-nate *v.* join, or link together
con-cave *adj.* hollowed and curved inward **concavly** *adv.*
con-ceal *v.* keep from sight; to hide **concealment** *n.*
con-cede *v.* yield to a privilege; acknowledge as true **conceded** *adj.*
con-ceive *v.* become pregnant; to create a mental image
con-cen-trate *v.* give intense thought to something
con-cen-tra-tion *n.* state of being concentrated
con-cept *n.* generalized idea **conceptual** *adj.*
con-cep-tion *n.* union of sperm and egg
con-cern *n.* sincere interest **-ed** *adj.*
con-cert *n.* musical performance
con-cer-to *n.* one or more solo instruments in a composition
con-ces-sion *n.* act of conceding
con-ces-sion-aire *n.* operator or holder of a concession
conch *n.* a tropical marine mollusk
con-cil-i-ate *v.* win over or to gain a friendship **conciliation** *n.*
con-cise *adj.* short and to the point
con-clave *n.* private or secret meeting to elect a new pope
con-clude *v.* bring to an end **conclusion** *n.*
con-com-i-tant *adj.* accompanying
con-cord *n.* accord; harmony
con-course *n.* open space for passage of crowds
con-crete *n.* construction material
con-cu-pis-cence *n.* a strong sexual desire
con-cur *v.* to agree or express approval
con-cur-rent *adj.* acting together
con-cus-sion *n.* sudden and violent jolt
con-demn *v.* to find to be wrong **condemnable** *adj.*
con-dense *v.* to make more compact **condenser** *n.*
con-di-ment *n.* relish, or sauce used to season food
con-di-tion *n.* state or existence of something
con-di-tion-al *adj.* tentative **conditionally** *adv.*
con-di-tioned *adj.* prepared for a certain process or action
con-di-tion-er *n.* application that improves a substance
con-dom *n.* thin rubber sheath to cover the penis during sexual intercourse
con-do-min-i-um *n.* building in which all units are owned separately
con-done *n.* to forgive
con-duct *v.* lead and direct a band; lead the way
con-duc-tor *n.* person who conducts a musical ensemble
con-duit *n.* pipe to pass electric wires through
cone *n.* solid body tapered evenly to a point
con-fab-u-late *v.* chat informally
con-fec-tion-er-y *n.* candy and sweets
con-fed-er-a-cy *n.* union of southern states
con-fed-er-ate *n.* ally or friend
con-fer *v.* consult with another **conferment** *n.*
con-fer-ence *n.* meeting for discussion
con-fess *v.* to make known or tell something
con-fet-ti *pl., n.* small pieces of paper thrown during a happy occasion
con-fide *v.* entrust a secret to another **confiding** *adj.*
con-fi-dence *n.* a feeling of self-assurance
con-fi-den-tial *adj.* hold as a secret **confidentiality** *n.*
con-fig-u-ra-tion *n.* arrangement of parts or things
con-fine *v.* keep within a certain boundary or limit **confinement** *n.*
con-firm *v.* establish or support the truth of something
con-fir-ma-tion *n.* act of confirming to show proof
con-fis-cate *v.* seize for public use; to officially seize **confiscation** *n.*
con-flict *n.* a battle; a clash **-tive** *adj.*
con-form *v.* similar in form or character **conformably** *adv.*
con-for-ma-tion *n.* the manner in which something is shaped
con-found *v.* to amaze, to confuse
con-front *v.* stand face to face with defiance **confrontation** *n.*
con-fuse *v.* mislead or bewilder
con-fu-sion *n.* state of being confused; disorder
con-fute *v.* prove to be invalid or false **confutable** *adj.*
con-geal *v.* jell; to solidify
con-gen-ial *adj.* having agreeable characteristics
con-gen-i-tal *adj.* existing from the time of birth, but not from heredity
con-gest *v.* enlarge with an excessive accumulation of blood; to clog, as with traffic **congestion** *n.*
con-glom-er-ate *n.* business consisting of many different companies

con-grat-u-late *v.* acknowledge an achievement with praise
con-grat-u-la-tions *pl., n.* expression of or the act of congratulating
con-gre-gate *v.* assemble together in a crowd **congregator** *n.*
con-gre-ga-tion *n.* group of people meeting for worship
Con-gress *n.* united States legislative body **congressional** *adj.*
con-gru-ent *adj.* agreeing to conform
con-jec-ture *n.* guess or conclusion based on incomplete evidence **conjectural** *adj.*
con-join *v.* to unite
con-ju-gate *adj.* change the form of a verb; to join in pairs **-ly** *adv.*
con-junct *adj.* combined
con-junc-tion *n.* act of joining; the state of being joined
con-junc-ti-va *n.* the membrane lining of the eyelids
con-junc-tive *adj.* connective
con-junc-ti-vi-tis *n. Pathol.* inflammation of the membrane that lines the eyelids
con-jure *v.* bring into the mind; to appeal or call on solemnly
con-nect *v.* join; to unite
con-nec-tion *n.* association of one person or thing to another
con-nec-tive *adj.* capable of connecting; tending to connect **connectivity** *n.*
con-nive *v.* ignore a known wrong, therefore implying sanction **connivance** *n.*
con-nois-seur *n.* a person whose expertise in an area of art or taste allows him to be a judge; an expert
con-no-ta-tion *n.* the associative meaning of a word in addition to the literal meaning
con-note *v.* imply along with the literal meaning
con-nu-bi-al *adj.* having to do with marriage or the state of marriage
con-quer *v.* subdue; to win
con-science *n.* ability to recognize right and wrong
con-sci-en-tious *adj.* honest
con-scious *adj.* aware of one's own existence and environment
con-script *n.* one who is drafted for a service or a job
con-se-crate *v.* declare something to be holy **consecration** *n.*
con-sec-u-tive *adj.* following in uninterrupted succession **consecutively** *adv.*
con-sen-sus *n.* a collective opinion
con-sent *v.* to agree; give permission
con-se-quent *adj.* following as a natural result or effect **consequentially** *adv.*
con-serv-a-tive *adj.* opposed to change **consequentively** *adv.*
con-ser-va-to-ry *n.* a school of dramatic art or music
con-serve *v.* save something from decay, loss, or depletion **conservable** *adj.*
con-sider *v.* seriously think about; to examine mentally
con-sid-er-a-ble *adj.* large in amount or extent; important considerably *adv.*
con-sid-er-a-tion *n.* taking into account of circumstance before forming an opinion
con-sign *v.* commit to the care of another; to deliver merchandise **consignable** *adj.* **consignment** *n.*
con-sist *v.* be made up of
con-sis-ten-cy *n.* degree of texture, viscosity, or density **consistent** *adj.*
con-sole *v.* give comfort to someone **consolable** *adj.*
con-sol-i-date *v.* combine in one or to form a union of; to form a compact mass **consolidation** *n.*
con-so-nant *n.* sound in speech other than a vowel **consonantly** *adv.*
con-sort *n.* spouse; companion or partner; agreement
con-spic-u-ous *adj.* noticeable **-ly** *adv.*
con-spir-a-cy *n.* plan or act of two or more persons to do an evil act
con-spire *v.* plan a wrongful act in secret **conspirator** *n.*
con-sta-ble *n.* peace officer
con-stant *adj.* unchanging; steady in action, purpose, and affection **constancy** *n.*, **constantly** *adv.*
con-ster-na-tion *n.* sudden confusion or amazement
con-sti-pa-tion *n.* condition of the bowels characterized by inability to empty the bowels
con-stit-u-ent *adj.* having the power to elect a representative
con-sti-tu-tion *n.* fundamental laws that govern a nation; structure or composition
con-strain *v.* restrain by physical or moral means **constrained** *adj.*
con-straint *n.* the threat or use of force; confinement
con-struct *v.* to create, make, or build **constructor** *n.*
con-struc-tion *n.* the act of constructing or building something **-al** *adj.*
con-struc-tive *adj.* useful; helpful; advancing, or improving **constructively** *adv.*, **-ness** *n.*
con-strue *v.* interpret; to translate
con-sul *n.* an official that resides in a foreign country
con-sult *v.* seek advice or information from; to compare views **consulter** *n.*
con-sume *v.* to ingest; to eat or drink; to absorb **consumable** *adj.*
consumer *n.* person who buys services or goods
con-sump-tion *n.* fulfillment; the act of consuming
con-sump-tive *adj.* tending to destroy or waste away
con-tact *n.* place, or junction where two or more surfaces or objects touch
con-ta-gion *n.* transmitting of a disease by contact
con-tain *v.* include or enclose
con-tain-er *n.* something that holds or carries
con-tam-i-nate *v.* pollute or make inferior
con-temn *v.* scorn or despise
con-tem-plate *v.* to ponder **-ation** *n.*
con-tempt *n.* viewing something as mean,

vile, or worthless
con-temp-tu-ous *adj.* feeling or showing contempt
con-tend *v.* dispute; to fight; to debate; to argue
con-tent *n.* something contained within; subject matter of a book **-ment** *n.*
con-ten-tion *n.* competition
con-test *n.* a competition; strife; conflict **contestant** *n.*
con-text *n.* a sentence, or phrase
con-ti-nent *n.* one of the seven large masses of the earth
con-tin-ue *v.* maintain without interruption; to resume **continuance** *n.*
con-ti-nu-i-ty *n.* quality of being continuous
con-tin-u-ous *adj.* uninterrupted or unbroken
con-tort *v.* severely twist out of shape **contortive** *adj.*
con-tor-tion-ist *n.* an acrobat who exhibits unnatural body positions
con-tour *n.* the outline of a body, figure, or mass
con-tra-band *n.* illegal or prohibited traffic; smuggled goods
con-tra-cep-tion *n.* voluntary prevention of impregnation **-tive** *adj. or n.*
con-tract *n.* formal agreement between two or more parties
con-trac-tion *n.* a shortening of a word by using an apostrophe (')
con-trac-tile *adj.* having the power to contract
con-tra-dict *v.* express the opposite side or idea **contradiction** *n.*
con-tral-to *n., pl.* **-tos** lowest female singing voice
con-tra-puntal *adj.* relating to counterpoint
con-trast *v.* note the differences between two or more people, things, etc.
con-tra-vene *v.* be contrary; to violate
con-trib-ute *v.* give something to someone **contribution** *n.*
con-trol *v.* have the authority to regulate, direct, or dominate a situation **controlable** *adj.*
con-trol-ler *n.* the chief accounting officer of a business
con-tro-ver-sy *n.* a dispute; a debate; a quarrel **controversial** *adj.*
co-nun-drum *n.* a riddle with an answer that involves a pun
con-va-lesce *v.* grow strong after a long illness **convalescent** *adj.*
con-vene *v.* meet or assemble formally
con-ven-ience *n.* quality of being suitable
con-vent *n.* local house of a religious order, especially for nuns
con-ven-tion *n.* formal meeting; a regulatory meeting between people, or nations
con-ven-tion-al *adj.* commonplace
con-verge *v.* come to a common point
con-ver-sa-tion *n.* an informal talk
converse *v.* involve oneself in conversation with another
con-ver-sion *n.* state of changing to adopt new opinions or beliefs **conversional** *adj.*
con-vex *adj.* curved outward
con-vey *v.* transport; pass information on to someone else
con-vict *v.* prove someone guilty
con-vince *v.* persuade to believe without doubt
con-voy *n.* group of vehicles traveling together
con-vulse *v.* move or shake violently
con-vul-sion *n.* an involuntary muscular contraction
cook *v.* apply heat to food; to prepare food
cook-ie *n.* sweet, flat cake
cool *adj.* without warmth
coop *n.* enclosed area to contain chickens
co-op-er-ate *v.* work together **-tion** *n.*
co-op-er-a-tive *adj.* willing to cooperate with others
coot *n.* bird
cop *n., Informal* police officer
cope *v.* to struggle or contend with something
cop-ier *n.* machine that makes copies
co-pi-lot *n.* assistant pilot on an aircraft
co-pi-ous *n.* large in quantity; abundant
cop-per *n.* metallic element; conductor of electricity
cop-per-head *n.* venomous snake
cop-ra *n.* dried coconut meat
cop-u-late *v.* have sexual intercourse
copy *v.* reproduce an original
copy-right *n.* satutory right to distribute literary work
copy writer *n.* person who writes copy
co-quette *n.* woman who flirts
cor-al *n.* small sea creature
coral snake *n.* venomous snake
cord *n.* string or twine; an insulated wire
cor-dial *adj.* warm-hearted and sincere
cor-don *n.* circle of ships to guard an area
cor-du-roy *n.* durable ribbed cotton fabric
core *n.* innermost part of something
cork *n.* elastic bark of the oak tree
cork-screw *n.* device for removing corks from bottles
corn *n.* vegetable
corn bread *n.* bread made from crushed cornmeal
corn cob *n.* cone where kernels grow
corncrib *n.* building for storing corn
cor-ne-a *n.* membrane of the eyeball
cor-ner *n.* angle where surfaces meet
corner back *n.* the defensive halfback
corner-stone *n.* stone that forms part of a building
cor-net *n.* brass musical instrument
corn-row *v.* braid the hair in rows
corn-starch *n.* starch made from corn used to thicken food
corn syrup *n.* sweet syrup
cor-nu-co-pi-a *n.* a curved goat's horn
co-rol-la *n.* petals of a flower
cor-ol-lary *n.* something that naturally follows or accompanies
cor-o-nar-y *adj.* relating to the arteries of the heart muscles
coronary thrombosis *n.* blockage of the coronary artery

cor-po-ral *n.* noncommissioned officer
cor-po-rate *adj.* combined into one joint body
cor-po-ra-tion *n.* group of merchants
corps *n.* branch of the armed forces
corpse *n.* dead body
cor-pu-lence *n.* excessive body fat; obesity
cor-pus-cle *n.* living cell in the blood
cor-pus delicti *n.* evidence pertaining to a crime
cor-ral *n.* enclosure for containing animals
cor-rect *v.* make free from fault or mistakes **correctable** *adj.*
cor-rel-a-tive *adj.* having a mutual relation
cor-re-spond *v.* communicate by written words **correspondence** *n.*
cor-ri-dor *n.* long hall
cor-ri-gen-dum *n.* an error accompanied by its correction
cor-ri-gi-ble *adj.* able to correct
cor-rob-o-rate *v.* support with evidence **corroboration** *n.*
cor-rode *v.* eat away **corrosion** *n.*
cor-rupt *adj.* dishonest; evil
cor-sage *n.* small bouquet of flowers
cor-sair *n.* pirate; a fast moving vessel
cor-set *n.* woman's undergarment for support
cor-tège *n.* a funeral procession
cor-tex *n.* external layer of an organ
cor-ti-sone *n.* hormone from the adrenal cortex
cor-us-cate *v.* to sparkle
cor-vette *n.* armed warship
co-ry-za *n.* acute inflammation of the respiratory system
co-sign *v.* sign a document jointly
co-sig-na-to-ry *n.* one who cosigns a document
cos-met-ic *n.* preparation to beautify the face
cos-me-tol-o-gy *n.* study of cosmetics **cosmetologist** *n.*
cos-mog-o-ny *n.* creation of the universe
cos-mo-naut *n.* a Soviet astronaut
cos-mo-pol-i-tan *adj.* being at home anywhere in the world
cos-mos *n.* orderly systematic universe
cos-set *v.* to pamper; pet
cost *n.* amount paid or charged for a purchase
cos-tive *adj.* causing constipation
cos-tume *n.* clothes worn for playing a part or dressing up in a disguise
cot *n.* small, often collapsible bed
cot-tage *n.* small house
cotter pin *n.* metal pin with flared ends
cot-ton *n.* fabric created by the weaving cotton fibers
cotton candy *n.* spun sugar
cot-ton-mouth *n.* water moccasin snake
couch *n.* piece of furniture
cou-gar *n.* mountain lion, panther, and puma
cough *v.* suddenly expel air from the lungs
could *v.* past tense of can
could-n't *contr.* could not
cou-lomb *n.* unit to measure electricity
coun-cil *n.* group of people assembled for consultation; advisory body **councilman** *n.*
coun-sel *n.* advice through consultation
coun-sel-or *n.* a lawyer
count *v.* find the total number of units; to name numbers in order
count-down *n.* counting in descending order
coun-te-nance *n.* expression of the face
coun-ter-act *v.* oppose; make ineffective
coun-ter-at-tack *n.* attack made in response to an enemy attack
coun-ter-bal-ance *n.* a weight that balances another; counterpoise
coun-ter-claim *n.* contrary claim made to offset another
coun-ter-clock-wise *adj. & adv.* opposite direction
coun-ter-es-pi-o-nage *n.* espionage aimed at thwarting enemy espionage
coun-ter-feit *v.* closely imitate or copy
coun-ter-foil *n.* stub of a check or ticket
coun-ter-man *n.* one who works at a counter
coun-ter-mand *v.* reverse a command by issuing a contrary order
coun-ter-of-fen-sive *n.* a military offensive
coun-ter-pane *n.* a covering
coun-ter-part *n.* one who complements another
coun-ter-plea *n.* plea in answer to a previous plea
coun-ter-point *n., Mus.* combined melodies
coun-ter-pro-duct-ive *adj.* hinder rather than aid
coun-ter-vail *v.* counteract
coun-ter-weight *n.* an equivalent weight
count-ess *n.* wife of an earl or count
count-ing house *n.* room used for keeping books
count-less *adj.* too numerous to be counted
coun-tri-fied *adj.* rural; unsophisticated
coun-try *n.* the land of one's birth
coun-try-man *n.* a compatriot
coun-try-side *n.* rural area
coun-ty *n.* territorial division
cou-pe *n.* car with two doors
cou-ple *n.* a pair; a few
cou-plet *n.* rhyming lines of poetry
cou-pon *n.* form to obtain a discount
cour-age *n.* strength to face danger without fear **courageous** *adj.*
cou-ri-er *n.* a messenger
course *n.* a series or sequence; a series of studies
court *n.* a place where trials are conducted; area marked off for game playing
cour-te-ous *adj.* respect for others
cour-te-san *n.* prostitute
cour-te-sy *n.* courteous behavior
court-house *n.* building holding courts of law
court-yard *n.* open space enclosed by walls
cous-in *n.* child of one's uncle or aunt
cove *n.* small inlet or bay
cov-e-nant *n.* formal, binding agreement

cov-er *v.* place something on or over
cov-et *v.* to crave possessions of someone else
cov-ey *n.* small drain that runs under a road
cum-ber-some *adj.* unwieldy
cum-mer-bund *n.* group of birds
cow *n.* mature female of cattle
cow-ard *n.* one showing great fear or timidity **cowardice** *n.*
cowl *n.* hood or long hooded cloak
cox-comb *n.* conceited foolish person
cox-swain *n.* one who steers a boat
coy *adj.* quieting or shy
coy-o-te *n.* small wolf-life animal
coz-en *v.* swindle, cheat, or deceive; win over by coaxing
co-zy *adj.* comfortable and warm; snug
crab *n.* one of numerous crustaceans
crab-by *adj.* ill-tempered and cross
crack *v.* to break without completely separating *n.* addictive form of cocaine
cra-dle *n.* small bed for infants
craft *n.* special skill or ability
crag *n.* steep, jagged rock or cliff
cram *v.* pack tightly; prepare hastily for an exam
cramp *n.* painful contraction of a muscle; abdominal pain
cran-ber-ry *n.* tree with tart red berries
crane *n.* large bird; machine for lifting heavy objects
cra-ni-um *n.* the skull
crank *n.* device to turn a shaft
crank-y *adj.* grouchy **crankiness** *n.*
cran-ny *n.* small crevice
craps *v.* gambling game with two dice
crash *v.* break noisily; collapse
crate *n.* container for shipping or storage
cra-ter *n.* depression in a volcano
cra-vat *n.* a necktie
crave *v.* desire intensely
cra-ven *adj.* lacking courage
crav-ing *n.* intense longing or desire
craw *n.* the stomach of a lower animal
crawl *v.* move on hands and knees; progress slowly
cray-on *n.* stick of wax used for coloring
craze *v.* to become insane
cra-zy *adj.* insane **craziness** *n.*
creak *v.* squeaking or grating noise
cream *n.* fatty part of milk; pale yellow-white color
crease *n.* line made by folding and pressing
cre-ate *v.* bring something into existence
cre-a-tion *n.* something created
cre-a-tive *adj.* inventive; imaginative **creativeness** *n.*
cre-a-tor *n.* God
crea-ture *n.* a living being
cre-den-za *n.* a buffet or sideboard
cred-i-ble *adj.* reasonable grounds for belief
cred-it *n.* money available in a bank; acknowledgment; college unit
cred-u-lous *adj.* gullible
creed *n.* religious belief
creek *n.* narrow stream
creel *n.* wicker basket for holding fish
creep *v.* advance at a slow pace
cre-mate *v.* reduce to ashes by burning
cre-o-sote *n.* oily liquid mixture
cre-pus-cu-lar *adj.* relating to twilight
cre-scen-do *adv.* gradually increasing in loudness
cres-cent *n.* quarter shape of the moon
cress *n.* plant with edible leaves
crest *n.* top line of a mountain or hill; ridge of a wave or roof
cre-tin-ism *n.* condition of physical stunting and mental deficiency
cre-tonne *n.* cotton or linen cloth
cre-vasse *n.* deep crack in a glacier
crev-ice *n.* narrow crack
crew *n.* group of people that work together
crew-el *n.* yarn used in embroidery
crib *n.* small baby's bed with high sides
crick-et *n.* leaping insect; a game
crime *n.* an act forbidden by law
crimp *v.* to pinch in or together
crimson *n.* deep purplish color
cringe *v.* shrink or recoil in fear
crin-kle *v.* wrinkle
crin-o-line *n.* fabric used for stiffening garments
crip-ple *n.* one who is partially disabled
cri-sis *n.* an uncertain time; turning point of a disease
crisp *adj.* brittle; brisk or cold
crisp-er *n.* compartment to keep fruits and vegetables fresh
criss-cross *v.* mark with intersecting lines
cri-te-ri-on *n., pl.* **criteria** rule by which something can be judged
crit-ic *n.* one who expresses an opinion
crit-i-cal *adj.* tending to criticize harshly **critically** *adv.*
crit-i-cize *v.* to find fault with
croak *n.* hoarse, raspy cry of a frog
cro-chet *n.* needlework with a hooked needle
crock *n.* earthenware pot or jar
croc-o-dile *n.* large, tropical reptiles
cro-cus *n.* first spring plant.
crone *n.* old woman
cro-ny *n.* close friend
crook *n.* bend or curve; dishonest person
croon *v.* sing in a gentle, low voice
crop *n.* plants harvested for use or for sale
cro-quet *n.* outdoor game
cro-quette *n.* small patty of minced food
cross *n.* an upright post with a crossbar
cross-breed *v.* breeding different species
crotch *n.* angle formed by the junction of two parts
crouch *v.* bend at the knees
croup *n.* spasmodic loud, harsh cough
crou-pi-er *n.* one who collects and pays bets at a gambling table
crou-ton *n.* piece of toasted bread
crow *n.* large, black bird
crowd *n.* large group of people together
crown *n.* head covering made of precious metal and jewels
CRT *abbr.* Cathode Ray Tube
cru-cial *adj.* extremely important
cru-ci-fy *v.* put to death on a cross
crude *adj.* lacking refinement
cruel *adj.* inflicting suffering **cruelty** *n.*

cru-et *n.* container for oil or vinegar
cruise *v.* drive or sail about for pleasure
crumb *n.* fragment of bread
crum-ble *v.* break into small pieces
crunch *v.* chew with a crackling noise
cru-sade *n.* religious journey
crush *v.* squeeze or force to damage
crust *n.* hardened exterior of bread; shell of a pie
crus-ta-cean *n.* crabs, lobsters, etc.
crutch *n.* support to or an aid for walking
crux *n.* a main or central feature
cry *v.* shed tears
crypt *n.* underground chamber or vault
cryp-tic *adj.* intended to be obscure
cryp-tog-ra-phy *n.* deciphering of messages in secret code
crys-tal *n.* glassware
crystal ball *n.* globe for seeing the future
crys-tal-lize *v.* to form crystals; coat with crystals
cub *n.* young of the lion, wolf, or bear
cub-by-hole *n.* small enclosed area
cube *n.* solid with six equal squares
cubic *adj.* having three dimensions
cu-bi-cle *n.* small partitioned area
cu-bit *n.* ancient unit of measurement
cu-cum-ber *n.* fruit with a green rind of the gourd family
cud *n.* food rechewed by cattle
cud-dle *v.* caress fondly and hold close
cue *n.* signal to an actor
cuff *n.* lower part of a sleeve or pants
cui-sine *n.* style of preparing food
cull *v.* select the best
cul-mi-nate *v.* reach the highest point
cul-prit *n.* person guilty of a crime
cult *n.* system of religious worship
cul-ti-vate *v.* improve land by fertilizing and plowing
cul-ture *n.* form of civilization, beliefs, arts, and customs
cul-vert *n.* drain that runs under a road
cum-ber-some *adj.* unwieldy.
cum-mer-bund *n.* wide sash worn by men
cu-mu-lus *n.* white, fluffy cloud
cun-ning *adj.* crafty
cup *n.* container with handle for drinking
cu-po-la *n.* rounded roof
cu-ra-tor *n.* person in charge of a museum
curb *n.* control; edge of a street
curd *n.* portion of milk for making cheese
cure *n.* recovery from a sickness
cur-few *n.* an order to be home at a certain hour
cu-ri-o *n.* unusual or rare object
cu-ri-ous *adj.* inquisitive **curiousity** *n.*
curl *v.* twist into curves
cur-rant *n.* small seedless raisin
cur-ren-cy *n.* money in circulation
cur-rent *adj.* occur in the present time
cur-ric-u-lum *n.* courses offered in a school
cur-ry *n.* spice
cur-ry-comb *n.* special comb to curry a horse
curse *n.* a wish for harm to come to someone or something
cursor *n.* computer screen indicator
cur-sive *n.* flowing writing
curt *adj.* abrupt; rude
cur-tail *v.* shorten
cur-tain *n.* material that covers a window
curt-sy *n.* a bow
cush-ion *n.* pillow with a soft filling
cus-pid *n.* pointed tooth
cus-pi-dor *n.* spittoon
cuss *v.* use profane language
cus-tard *n.* baked dessert milk, eggs, sugar, and flavoring
cus-to-di-an *n.* one who has the custody or care of something
cus-to-dy *n.* the act of guarding; the care and protection of a minor
cus-tom *n.* accepted practice of a community or people; the usual manner of doing something
customary *adj.*
customs *n.* tax one must pay on imported goods
custom--built *adj.* built to one's special order
cus-tomer *n.* person with whom a merchant or business person must deal
cus-tom house *n.* office of business where customs are paid
cut *v.* penetrate with a sharp edge, as with a knife
cut-and-dried *adj.* without changes
cut back *v.* to reduce
cute *adj.* attractive in a delightful way
cut glass *n.* glass shaped and decorated by using a cutting instrument
cut-lass *n.* thick, short, curved sword formerly was used by sailors aboard warships
cut-lery *n.* cutting instruments used to prepare food for cooking
cut-let *n.* a thin piece of meat **cut-off** *n.* a short cut; the act of cutting something off
cut-out *n.* something intended to be cut or already cut out
cut--rate *adj.* offering merchandise at a lower than normal price
cut-ter *n., Naut.* a fast-sailing vessel with a single mast
cut-throat *n.* a murderer
cut up *v.* act foolishly
cy-a-nide *n., Chem.* a poison
cyc-la-men *n.* a plant with red, white, or pink flowers
cy-cle *n.* time in which an event occurs repeatedly; a bicycle or motorcycle
cy-clist *n.* a person who rides a cycle
cyn-ic *n.* one who believes that all people have selfish motives
cy-no-sure *n.* person or object that attracts admiration
cy-press *n.* evergreen tree
cys-tic fi-bro-sis *n.* disease of the lungs and pancreas
cys-ti-tis *n.* inflammation of the bladder
cy-tol-ogy *n.* scientific study of cell formation
cza-ri-na *n.* the woman married to the czar of Russia

D, d The fourth letter of the English alphabet.
dab *v.* touch with light, short strokes
dab-ble *v.* play in a liquid with the hands
da ca-po *adv.* from the beginning
dachs-hund *n.* small long bodied dog with long drooping ears
dac-tyl *n.* the fact that the three syllables have the fist one longest like the joints of the finger
dac-ty-lol-o-gy *n.* the art of communicating ideas by signs made with the fingers; sigh language
dac-ty-lous *adj.* having fingers or toes
dad *n., Informal* father
dad-dy--long-legs *n.* an insect with very long legs
daf-fo-dil *n.* a bulbous plant with yellow flowers
daf-fy *adj.* weak-minded or silly
daft *adj.* crazy; foolish; insane **daftly** *adv.* **daftness** *n.*
dag-ger *n.* pointed, short-edged weapon
da-querre-o-type *n.* a very early photogrqphic process which used silver-coated metallic plates that were sensitive to light.
dahl-ia *n.* perennial plant having tuberous roots
dai-ly *adj.* to occur or happen every day of the week
dai-ly dou-ble *n.* a bet that is won by picking the winners of two specified races occurring on the same day
dain-ty *adj.* delicately beautiful; having or showing refined taste **daintiness** *n.*
dai-qui-ri *n.* cocktail made with rum and lime juice
dair-y *n.* business that processes milk for resale **dairymaid** *n.* **dairyman** *n.*
dai-sy *n.* plant with yellow and white flowers
dale *n.* a small valley
dal-ly *v.* waste time; to dawdle; to flirt **dallier** *n.*, **dalliance** *n.*
dam *n.* barrier to control water level
dam-age *n.* injury to person or property **damageable** *adj.*, **damagingly** *adv.*
dam-a-scene *v.* to ornament wavy designs on metal, by laying with a precious metal
dam-ask *n.* reversible fabric
dame *n.* mature woman
damn *v.* to swear or curse at; to pronounce as bad, worthless, or a failure **damnation** *n.*, **damnableness** *n.*
damp *adj.* between dry and wet
dam-sel *n.* a maiden; a young unmarried woman
dam-son *n.* tree with an oval purple plum of the same name
dance *v.* move rhythmically to music
dan-de-lion *n.* a weed of North America; an herb; having yellow flowers
dan-dle *v.* to move a child or infant up and down on the knees or in the arms with a gentle movement
dan-druff *n.* scaly material which forms on the scalp and is shed
dan-dy *n.* elegantly dressed man; fine appearance **dandyish** *adj.*
dan-ger *n.* exposure to injury, evil, or loss, a case of danger
dan-ger-ous *adj.* unsafe **dangerously** *adv.* **dangerousness** *n.*
dan-gle *v.* hang loosely and swing to and fro **danglingly adv., dangler n.**
dank *adj.* damp; wet and cold **dankness** *n.*, **dankly** *adv.*
dan-seuse *n.* female ballet dancer
dap-per *adj.* stylishly dressed
dap-ple *v.* to make variegated in color
dare *v.* have courage to take a risk or undertan an adventure; to challenge a person as to show proof of courage; **dare-devil** *n.* reckless or bold person **daredevilry n, daredeviltry n.**
dark *adj.* dim; to have little or no light
dark-en *v.* make dark or become dark **darkish** *adj.*, **darkly** *adv.*
dar-ling *n.* someone who is very dear; favorite person; a person tenderly loved **darlingly** *adv.*
darn *v.* mend a hole **darner** *n.*
dart *n.* pointed missile
dash *v.* to move quickly; to rush; to finish or perform a duty in haste; with sudden speed **dasher** *n.*
da-ta *pl., n.* facts or figures from which conclusions may be drawn
data bank *n.* location in a computer where information is stored
date *n.* a particular point in time; the exact time at which something happens; an edible fruit **date** *v.*
date-line *n.* the date of newspaper publication; imaginary line
da-tum *n.* single piece of information **datums pl., data** *n.*
daub *v.* coat or smear with grease, plaster or an adhesive substance
daugh-ter *n.* female offspring of a man or woman; realtion to parent
daughter--in--law *n.* one's son's wife **daughters-in-law pl.**
daunt *v.* intimidate or discourage
dav-it *n.* small crane on the side of a ship used for boats or anchors
daw-dle *v.* waste time **dawdler n.**
dawn *n.* the beginning of a new day; to begin to understand, perceive or develop; first light appearance
day *n.* period of fime between dawn and night-fall; one rotation of the earth
day-care *n.* supervision and training for children of working parents
daze *v.* stun or bewilder with a heavy blow or shock **dazedly** *adv.*
D--Day *n., Milit.* June 6, 1944
dea-con *n.* clergyman who ranks immediately below a priest
dead *adj.* without life; dormant
dead-end *n.* cannot progress
deadline *n.* time when something must be finished; the final day
dead-ly *adj.* very dangerous; likely to cause death
deaf *adj.* totally or partially unable to hear; refusing or unwilling to listen
deal *v.* pass out playing cards; to be concerned with a certain matter
deal-er-ship *n.* franchise to sell a certain item in a specified area, as a car dealer
deal-ing *n., Slang* involved in the buying

and selling of illegal drugs
dean *n.* head administrator of a college, or university **deanship** *n.*
dear *adj.* greatly cherished; loved **dearly** *adv.*, **dearness n.**
death *n.* termination; permanent cessation of all vital functions
deathly *adj.* fatal; causing death
death-trap *n.* unsafe structure
death-watch *n.* vigil kept on a person who is dying
deb *n.* debutante
de-ba-cle *n.* sudden downfall or failure
de-base *v.* lower in character or value **debasement** *n.*, **debaser** *n.*
de-bate *v.* discuss or argue opposing points **debatable** *adj.*
de-bauch *v.* to corrupt **debauchment** *n.*
de-ben-ture *n.* voucher given as an acknowledgment of debt
de-bil-i-tate *v.* make feeble or weak
deb-it *n.* item recorded in an account; a sum of items entered
de-brief *v.* question or interrogate to obtain information
de-bris *n.* discarded or scattered remains or waste
debt *n.* that which someone owes as money or goods or services
debt-or *n.* person owing a debt to another, usually money, etc.
de-bug *v.* find and remove a concealed listening device; to remove errors
de-bunk *v.* expose false pretensions
de-but *n.* first public appearance; beginning of a new career; introduction
deb-u-tante *n.* young woman making her debut in society
dec-ade *n.* period of ten years; a set of ten; division of the rosary
de-ca-dence *n.* process of deterioration or decay; a period of decline
de-caf-fein-at-ed *adj.* having the caffeine removed; without
dec-a-gon *n., Geom.* a polygon with ten sides and ten angles
dec-a-gram *n.* in the metric system, weight equal to 10 grams
de-cal *n.* design or picture that is transferred by decalsomania
de-cal-co-ma-ni-a *n.* process of transferring pictures or designs to somehting
dec-a-li-ter *n.* in the metric system, measure equal to 10 liters
dec-a-logue *n.* the Ten Commandments; a basic set of rules
dec-a-me-ter *n.* in the metric system, measure equal to 10 feet
de-camp *v.* break camp; to leave or depart suddenly **decampment n.**
de-cant-er *n.* decorative stoppered bottle for serving wine or other liquids
de-cap-i-tate *v.* cut off the head; to behead **decapitation n.**
de-cath-lon *n.* an athletic event with ten different track and field events
de-cay *v.* decline; to rot
de-cease *v.* die **decedent** *n.*
de-ceit *n.* falseness; deception
de-ceive *v.* mislead by falsehood; to lead into error; to delude
de-cel-er-ate *v.* decrease in velocity
de-cen-ni-al *adj.* happening once every 10 years; for a period of ten
de-cent *adj.* satisfactory; generous; adequate **decently adv.**
de-cen-tral-ize *v.* divide the administrative functions among local authorities
de-cep-tion *n.* act of deceiving
de-cep-tive *adj.* having the power to deceive **deceptively adv.**
de-ci-bel *n.* measurement of sound
de-cide *v.* to make up one's mind; to settle **decided v., deciding v.**
de-cid-ed *adj.* definite or unquestionable; determination **decidedly adv.**
de-cid-u-ous *adj.* shedding or falling off at maturity
dec-i-gram *n.* in the metric system, the tenth part of a gram
dec-i-li-ter *n.* in the metric system, the tenth part of a liter
dec-i-mal *n.* proper fraction based on the number 10
decimal point *n.* period to the left of a decimal fraction
dec-i-mate *v.* destroy or kill a large proportion of something
dec-i-meter *n.* in the metric system, the tenth part of a meter
de-ci-pher *v.* to decode; to translate from code to text **decipherable** *adj.*
de-ci-sion *n.* a judgment or conclusion; act of deciding
de-ci-sive *adj.* ending uncertainty
deck *n.* set of playing cards; platform; resembling a ship's deck
deck hand *n.* member of a ship's crew who performs manual duties
de-claim *v.* speak loudly and rhetorically; to give speech **declamation n.**
de-clare *v.* to state formally or officially **declaration** *n.*, **declarative** *adj.*
de-clas-si-fy *v.* make public
de-clen-sion *n.* sloping downward; a decline; falling off or away
de-cline *v.* reject or refuse something **declinable adj., declinational** *adj.*
de-cliv-i-ty *n.* steep down-ward slope or surface **declivitous, declivous** *adj.*
de-coct *v.* extract by boiling; condense; to make concentrate **decoction** *n.*
de-code *v.* convert from coded message into plain language **decoder n.**
de-com-pose *v.* decay **decomposition** *n.*
de-com-press *v.* relieve of pressure
de-con-ges-tant *n.* agent that relieves congestion
de-con-tam-i-nate *v.* make free of contamination **decontamination n.**
de-con-trol *v.* remove all controls
de-cor *n.* style of decorating
dec-o-rate *v.* adorn with fashionable or beautiful things; dress up
dec-o-ra-tion *n.* art, process, or act of decorating; a thing or group of things which decorate; an emblem
dec-o-ra-tive *adj.* ornamental; suitable for decoration **decoratively** *adv.*
de-co-rum *n.* proper behavior
de-coy *n.* artificial animal to lure game
de-crease *v.* grow less or smaller
de-cree *n.* formal order
de-crep-it *adj.* worn out by old age

de-cry *v.* denounce
ded-i-cate *v.* commit oneself to a certain cause **dedicated v.**
de-duce *v.* derive a conclusion by reasoning
de-duct *v.* subtract or take away from
deed *n.* notable achievement or feat
deem *v.* judge or consider
deep *adj.* extending far below a surface **deepness** *n.*
deep-en *v.* become or make deep or deeper **deepened v., deepening v.**
deep-freeze *v.* quick-freeze food
deep--root-ed *adj.* firmly implanted
deep-six *v., Slang* to throw overboard; toss out
deer *n., pl.* **deer** hoofed ruminant mammal
deer fly *n.* bloodsucking flies
deer-skin *n.* deer's hide or leather made from it
de-es-ca-late *v.* decreased gradually
de-face *v.* spoil or mar the surface of something
de fac-to *adj.* actually exercising authority
de-fal-cate *v.* to misuse funds; to embezzle
de-fame *v.* to slander
de-fault *v.* neglect to fulfill an obligation
de-feat *v.* to win a victory
de-feat-ism *n.* accepting defeat as inevitable
def-e-cate *v.* discharge feces from the bowels
de-fect *n.* lack of perfection; a fault
de-fec-tive *adj.* imperfect; less than normal intelligence
de-fend *v.* protect
de-fend-ant *n.* person charged in a lawsuit; being on the devensive
de-fense *n.* action of defending
de-fer *v.* delay or postpone
de-fi-ance *n.* strong opposition
de-fi-cient *adj.* lacking a necessary element **deficiently adv.**
def-i-cit *n.* deficiency in amount
de-flate *v.* remove air; collapse
de-flect *v.* turn aside; swerve from a course **deflector n.**
de-flower *v.* rob one's virginity; to violate **deflowerer n.**
de-fog *v.* remove fog from
de-for-est *v.* to clear of trees
de-form *v.* distort the form of; to spoil the natural form of
de-fraud *v.* cheat; to swindle
de-fray *v.* make payment on something **defrayable** *adj.*
de-frost *v.* cause to thaw out; to remove the ice or frost from
deft *adj.* skillful and neat in one's actions **deftness** *n.*
de-funct *adj.* deceased
de-fuse *v.* remove the detonator or fuse from; to make less dangerous or harmful
de-fy *v.* confront or resist boldly; to dare **defier** *n.*, **defying** *n.*
de-gauss *v.* neutralize a magnetic field **degausser n.**
de-gen-er-ate *v.* decline in quality or value; to become worse
de-grade *v.* reduce in rank; demote
de-gree *n.* succession of stages or steps; academic title; amount
de-horn *v.* remove the horns from an animal **dehorner n.**
de-hu-man-ize *v.* deprive of human qualities or personality
de-hu-mid-i-fy *v.* remove moisture from **dehumidifier** *n.*, **dehumidification** *n.*
de-hy-drate *v.* lose moisture or water; to deprive **dehydrator n.**
de-ice *v.* keep free of ice **deicer** *n.*
de-i-fy *v.* glorify or idealize; raise in high regard **deified** *n.*, **deifying** *n.*
deign *v.* to grant
de-ism *n.* belief in the existence of God; but not that he has control
de-ject *v.* lower the spirits; to dishearten; to make gloomy
de-ject-ed *adj.* sad; low in spirit
de ju-re *adv., L.* legally or rightfully
de-lay *v.* put off until a later time; to defer **delayer n., delaying adj.**
de-le *n., Print* mark in typesetting to delete **deled v., deleing v.**
de-lec-ta-ble *adj.* giving great pleasure **delectability n., delectableness** *n.*
de-lec-ta-tion *n.* enjoyment or pleasure; delight
del-e-gate *n.* representative for another; a deputy or agent
del-e-ga-tion *n.* state of being delegated **deleted v., deleting v.**
de-lete *v.* cancel; to take out by cutting or erasing **deletion** *n.*, **deleting** *n.*
del-e-te-ri-ous *adj.* causing physical injury; harmful **deleteriously** *adv.*
delft *n.* glazed earthenware
del-i *n., Slang* delicatessen
de-lib-er-ate *v.* say or do something intentionally **deliberateness** *n.*
del-i-ca-cy *n.* select or choice food
del-i-cate *adj.* exquisite and fine in quality **delicately adv.**
del-i-ca-tes-sen *n.* specialty store
de-li-cious *adj.* enjoyable and pleasant to the taste **deliciously** *adv.*
de-li-cious *n.* variety of red, sweet apples **deliciously adv.**
de-light *n.* a giving of great joy or pleasure **delighted** *adj.*
de-light-ful *adj.* extremely pleasing
de-lim-it *v.* set or prescribe the limits
de-lir-i-um *n.* temporary mental disturbance characterized by confusion, disorder speech, and hallucinations
delirium tremens *n.* acute delirium resulting from use of alcohol
de-liv-er *v.* to hand over; assist at a birth of an offspring **delivered** *v.*, **-ing** *v.*
de-liv-er-y *n.* act of conveying; process or act of giving birth **deliveries** *pl.*
del-phin-ium *n.* perennial plant
delta ray *n.* electron ejected from ionizing radiation
de-lude *v.* mislead the mind; to deceive
del-uge *v.* flood with water; to overwhelm **deluging** *v.*, **deluged** *v.*
de-lu-sion *n.* false belief in spite of contrary evidence **delusionary** *adj.*
de luxe *adj.* elegance or luxury

delve *v.* search carefully for information
de-mag-net-ize *v.* remove the magnetic properties **demagnetiation** *n.*
dem-a-gogue *n.* person who appeals to the emotions to gain power or fame
de-mand *v.* ask for in a firm tone; claim as due **demander** *n.*, **demandable** *adj.*
de-mar-cate *v.* set boundaries or limits
de-mean *v.* behave or conduct oneself in a particular manner
de-mean-or *n.* person's conduct to others
de-men-tia *n.* irreversible deterioration of the mind **demential** *adj.*
de-mer-it *n.* a defect
de-mesne *n.* manor house; a domain
dem-i-god *n.* mythological, semidivine being **demigoddess** *n.*
dem-i-john *n.* narrow-necked bottle
de-mil-i-ta-rize *v.* remove the military characteristics from
dem-i-monde *n.* class of women supported by wealthy lovers
de-mise *n.* death; a transfer of an estate by lease or will **demised** *v.*, **-ing** *v.*
dem-i-tasse *n.* small cup of very strong black coffee; the cup used to serve
dem-o *n.* demonstration to show product
de-mo-bi-lize *v.* disband; release from the military service **-ation** *n.*
de-moc-ra-cy *n., pl.* **democracies** form of government by and for the people
dem-o-crat *n.* one who believes in social and political equality
de-mog-ra-phy *n.* study of the characteristics of human population
de-mol-ish *v.* tear down; to raze
dem-o-li-tion *n.* a process of demolishing something **demolitionist** *n.*
de-mon *n.* evil spirit; a devil
de-mon-e-tize *v.* deprive the currency of its standard value **demonization** *n.*
de-mo-ni-ac *adj.* like or befitting a demon **demonically** *adv.*
de-mon-ol-o-gy *n.* belief or study in demons
de-mon-stra-ble *adj.* obvious or apparent
dem-on-strate *v.* show or prove by evidence **demonstration** *n.*
de-mon-stra-tive *adj.* able to prove beyond any doubt; conclusive
de-mor-al-ize *v.* undermine the morales
de-mote *v.* reduce in rank, or grade **demotion** *n.*
de-mul-cent *n.* a soothing substance
de-mur *v.* take issue; to object
de-mure *adj.* reserved and modest
de-murrer *n.* plea to dismiss a lawsuit
den *n.* shelter for animals; small room
de-na-ture *v.* change the nature of
den-drol-ogy *n.* botanical study of trees
den-gue *n., Pathol.* infectious tropical disease transmitted by mosquitoes
de-ni-al *n.* refusal to comply with a request or truth
den-i-grate *v.* to slander
den-im *n.* strong cotton used for jeans
de-nom-i-nate *v.* give a name to
de-nom-i-na-tion *n.* name of a group or classification
de-nom-i-na-tor *n.* the bottom half of a fraction
de-no-ta-tion *n.* meaning of or object designated by a word
de-note *v.* make known
de-noue-ment *n.* final solution of a novel
de-nounce *v.* condemn openly; accuse formally
dense *adj.* thick; slow to understand; stupid
den-si-ty *n.* state or quality of being dense
dent *n.* small surface depression
den-tal *adj.* pertaining to the teeth
dental floss *n.* a strong thread to clean between the teeth
dental hygienist *n.* dental professional who provides preventive dental care
den-ti-frice *n.* preparation for cleaning the teeth
den-tine *n.* calcified part of the tooth
den-tist *n.* licensed dental doctor
den-ti-tion *n.* number, and arrangement of teeth
den-ture *n.* set of artificial teeth
de-nude *v.* remove all covering; cause to be naked
de-nun-ci-a-tion *n.* disapproval of a person or action; an accusation
de-ny *v.* declare untrue; refuse to acknowledge
de-o-dor-ant *n.* product to prevent unpleasant odors
de-o-dor-ize *v.* destroy the odor of
de-ox-i-dize *v.* remove oxygen from
de-part *v.* leave; to go away; to deviate
de-part-ment *n.* the distinct division of something
de-part-men-tal-ize *v.* divide into organized departments
department store *n.* large retail store usually in many places
de-par-ture *n.* act of taking leave; deviation
de-pend *v.* rely on
de-pend-a-ble *adj.* trust-worthy **dependability** *n.*
de-pend-ence *n.* trust or reliance
de-pend-ent *adj.* needing the help of another for support
de-pict *v.* represent in a picture
de-pil-a-to-ry *n.* chemical which removes hair
de-plane *v.* disembark or leave an aircraft
de-plete *v.* exhaust, empty, or use up
de-plor-a-ble *adj.* very bad; grievous; wretched **deplorably** *adv.*
de-plore *v.* show great disapproval of something
de-ploy *v.* spread out; place or position according to plans **deployment** *n.*
de-po-lit-i-cize *v.* remove the political status or aspect from
de-po-nent *n.* a person testifing under an oath
de-pop-u-late *v.* lower the population by massacre or disease
de-port *v.* banish from a country
de-port-ment *n.* one's conduct
de-pose *v.* remove position or office
de-pos-it *v.* set something down; put money in a bank
dep-o-si-tion *n.* in law, written testimony given under oath

de-pos-i-to-ry *n.* place for safekeeping
de-pot *n.* railroad station
de-prave *v.* render bad or worse
depravity *n.*
dep-re-cate *v.* express regret or disapproval; belittle
de-pre-ci-ate *v.* lessen in value or price
de-pre-ci-a-tion *n.* loss in value from usage
de-press *v.* make gloomy; lower the spirits
de-pres-sant *adj.* act to lower the nervous activities
de-press-ed *adj.* sad; low in spirits
de-press-ed area *n.* area with severe unemployment
de-pres-sion *n.* severe decline in business; condition of deep dejection
de-pres-sive *adj.* related to psychological depression
de-prive *v.* take something away from; to keep from using
depth *n.* distance downward; intensity of of sound; comprehension
depth charge *n.* underwater bomb
dep-u-ta-tion *n.* person acting for another or others
de-pute *v.* appoint as a deputy, an agent; delegate; to transfer
dep-u-tize *v.* to appoint as a deputy
dep-u-ty *n.* person designated act for or assist a sheriff
de-rail *v.* cause a train to run off the rails **derailment** *n.*
de-range *v.* to disturb the normal order of
der-by *n.* horse race for 3-year-olds; stiff hat with narrow brim
de-reg-u-late *v.* remove from regulation or control
der-e-lict *adj.* neglectful; remiss
der-e-lic-tion *n.* voluntary neglect
de-ride *v.* ridicule
de ri-gueur *adj.* required by manners, custom, or fashion
der-i-va-tion *n.* process of deriving
de-riv-a-tive *adj.* made from derived elements
de-rive *v.* receive or obtain from a source
der-mal *adj.* relating to or of the skin
der-ma-ti-tis *n., Pathol.* inflammation of the skin
der-ma-tol-o-gy *n.* the medical study of the skin and the diseases
dermatologist *n.*
der-o-gate *v.* to take away from; to distract
de-rog-a-tory *adj.* effect of belittling; lessening
der-rick *n.* machine to lift heavy loads; framework of an oil well
der-ri-ere *n.* the buttocks
der-ring--do *n.* daring action or spirit
de-salt *v.* remove the salt from sea water
des-cant *v.* play or sing a varied melody
de-scend *v.* move from a higher to a lower level
de-scen-dent *n.* offspring from another individual
de-scen-dant *adj.* proceeding downward
de-scent *n.* a slope; lowering in level or status
de-scribe *v.* explain in written or spoken words **describable** *adj.*
de-scrip-tion *n.* discourse to give a mental image of something
de-scry *v.* catch sight of
des-e-crate *v.* violate something sacred
desecration *n.*
de-seg-re-gate *v.* eliminate racial segregation in
de-sen-si-tize *v.* make less sensitive
des-ert *v.* abandon or forsake
des-ert *n.* dry, barren region
de-ser-tion *n.* act of deserting or leaving
de-serve *v.* be worthy of or entitled to
de-served *adj.* merited; earned
deservingly *adv.*
des-ic-cant *n.* silica gel to absorb moisture
des-ic-cate *v.* preserve food by drying; dehydrate
de-sid-er-a-tum *n.* desired and necessary thing
de-sign *v.* sketch preliminary outlines; create in the mind
des-ig-nate *v.* assign a name or title to; specify
de-sign-ing *adj.* relating to the art making designs
de-sir-a-ble *adj.* attractive, or valuable
desirableness *n.*
de-sire *v.* long for; to wish
de-sir-ous *adj.* have a craving or strong desire
de-sist *v.* stop doing something
desk *n.* school and office furniture for writing
des-o-late *adj.* forlorn; forsaken
desolately *adv.*
des-o-la-tion *n.* wasteland; de-serted; loneliness
de-spair *v.* lose or give up hope
des-per-a-do *n.* a dangerous, or violent criminal
des-per-ate *adj.* rash, without care; intense
des-per-a-tion *n.* state of being desperate
des-pi-ca-ble *adj.* hateful; contemptable
de-spise *v.* regard with contempt
de-spite *prep.* notwithstanding.
de-spoil *v.* rob; strip of possessions by force
de-spond *v.* lose hope, courage, or spirit
de-spon-den-cy *n.* dejection of spirits from loss hope
des-pot *n.* an absolute ruler; a tyrant
des-sert *n.* sweet food, as pastry, etc.
des-ti-na-tion *n.* goal; end of journey
des-tine *v.* determined in advance
des-ti-ny *n.* fate; predetermined course of events
des-ti-tute *adj.* impoverished; poor
destitution *n.*
de-stroy *v.* ruin; to to demolish; to kill
de-stroy-er *n.* one that destroys; small maneuverable warship
de-struct *n., Aeros.* deliberate destruction of a defective missile
de-struc-ti-ble *adj.* capable of being destroyed
des-ue-tude *n.* condition or state of disuse
de-sul-fur-ize *v.* remove sulfur from

des-ul-to-ry *adj.* something occuring by chance
de-tach *v.* unfasten, or separate
de-tached *adj.* apart; separate
de-tach-ment *n.* process of separating
de-tail *n.* part considered sep-arately; task
de-tain *v.* keep from proceeding
de-tect *v.* find out; to expose or uncover, as a crime **detectable** *adj.*
de-tec-tive *n.* person that investigates crimes
de-tent *n.* a pawl
de-ten-tion *n.* hold in custody
de-ter *v.* prevent someone from acting by intimidation **determent** *n.*
de-ter-gent *n.* cleansing agent
de-te-ri-o-rate *v.* to worsen; to depreciate **deterioration** *n.*
de-ter-mi-nate *adj.* definitely fixed or limited; conclusive
de-ter-mine *v.* settle or decide conclusively **determination** *n.*
de-ter-mined *adj.* having a fixed purpose
de-ter-rent *n.* something which deters **deterrently** *adv.*
de-test *v.* dislike strongly **detestable** *adj.*
de-throne *v.* remove from the throne
det-o-nate *v.* explode suddenly violently **detonation** *n.*
det-o-na-tor *n.* fuse used to detonate an explosive
de-tour *n.* deviation from a direct route
de-tox-i-fy *v.* free oneself from dependence on drugs or alcohol **detoxification** *n.*
de-tract *v.* take away from; to divert **detraction** *n.*
de-train *v.* leave a railroad train **detrainment** *n.*
det-ri-ment *n.* damage; injury; loss **detrimental** *adj.*
de-tri-tus *n.* loose fragments from disintegration
deuce *n.* two
deut-sche mark *n.* standard monetary unit of Germany
de-val-u-ate *v.* reduce or lessen the value of **devaluation** *n.*
dev-as-tate *v.* destroy; to ruin **devastation** *n.*
de-vel-op *v.* expand the potentialities; to enlarge; process film
de-vel-op-er *n.* person who builds and sells homes; chemical to process film
de-vel-op-ment *n.* group of homes; improvement
de-vi-ant *adj.* stray from the norm **deviantance** *n.*
de-vi-ate *v.* turn away from prescribed behavior or course
de-vice *n.* something built and used for a specific purpose
dev-il *n.* spirit of evil, the ruler of Hell; Satan; wicked person
dev-il-ish *adj.* resemble or have the characteristics of a devil
dev-il--may--care *adj.* reckless
dev-il-ment *n.* reckless mischief
devil's advocate *n.* one who argues for the sake of arguing
dev-il-try *n.* malicious mischief; cruelty or wickedness
de-vi-ous *adj.* leading away from the direct course **deviously** *adv.*
de-vise *v.* form in the mind; contrive; give real estate by will
de-vi-see *n.* person to whom a devise is made
de-vi-sor *n.* person who devises property
de-vi-tal-ize *v.* make weak
de-void *adj.* empty; lacking
de-voir *n.* act or expression of courtesy or respect
de-volve *v.* pass duty or authority on to a successor
de-vote *v.* apply oneself completely to some activity
de-vot-ed *adj.* feeling or showing loyalty **devotedly** *adv.*
dev-o-tee *n.* enthusiastic supporter
de-vo-tion *n.* strong attachment or affection **devotionly** *adv.*
de-vout *adj.* extreemely and earnestly religions; showing sincerity **devoutly** *adv.*
dew *n.* moisture condensed from the atmosphere in small drops onto cool surfaces
dew-claw *n.* rudimentary toe in some dogs and other mammals
dew-lap *n.* the loosee skin under the throat and neck of cattle and certain dogs
dex-ter-i-ty *n.* proficiency or skill in using the hands or body; cleverness; skillful
deex-ter-ous *adj.* skillful or adroit in the use of the hands
di-a-gram *n.* a sketch, plan or outline designed to demonstrate the similarity among partsof a whole
di-al *n.* graduated circular plate or face where a measurement is indicated by means of a pointer
di-a-logue *n.* conversation involving two or more persons
di-am-e-ter *n.* a straight line which passes through the center of a circle
di-a-met-ri-cal *adj.* along or relating to a diameter
dia-mond *n.* a very hard highly refractive colorless or white crystalline of carbon used as a gem
di-a-pa-son *n.* full range of a voice or an instrument
di-a-per *n.* baby's pants of absorbent material
di-aph-a-nous *adj.* transparent or translucent
di-a-phragm *n., Anat.* muscular wall between chest and abdomen; contraceptive device
di-ar-rhe-a *n.,Pathol.* disorder of the intestines
di-a-ry *n.* a daily record
di-as-tro-phism *n., Geol.* processes through which the earth's crust are formed
di-a-ther-my *n., pl.* **diathermies** *Med.* generation of heat in the body tissues
di-as-to-le *n.* rhythmnical expansion of the heart
di-a-tom *n.* various tiny planktonic algae
di-a-tom-ic *adj.* having two atoms in a

m·lecule
di-a-·on-ic *adj., Mus.* relating to a musical scale having eight tones to an octave
di-a-tribe *n.* malicious criticism
dib-ble *n.* gardener's pointed tool for planting bulbs
dice *pl., n.* small cubes used in a game of chance
di-chot-o-my *n., pl.* **dichotomies** division into two mutually exclusive subclasses
dick-er *v.* haggle or work towards a deal or bargain
dick-ey *n.* a woman's blouse front worn under a jacket
di-cot-y-le-don *n.* plant having two seed leaves
dic-tate *v.* speak aloud for another to record or transcribe **dictation** *n.*
dic-ta-ting ma-chine *n.* phonographic machine which records speech
dic-ta-tor *n.* person having absolute authority and supreme governmental powers **dictatorship** *n.*
dic-ta-to-ri-al *adj.* tending to dictate
dic-tion *n.* arrangement of words in speaking and writing
dic-tion-ar-y *n.* book containing words, definitions and usages
dic-tum *n.* authoritative utterance
did *v.* past tense of do
di-dac-tic *adj.* inclined to teach excessively
did-dle *v.* cheat; to swindle
did-n't *contr.* did not
die *v.* expire; to stop living
die casting *n.* process of giving an alloy or metal a desired shape
die-hard *n.* stubborn person
diel-drin *n.* highly toxic chemical used as an insecticide
di-e-lec-tric *n., Elect.* nonconductor of electricity
die-sel *n.* vehicle driven by a diesel engine
diesel engine *n.* internalcombustion engine run by an air-fuel mixture
die-sink-er *n.* person who engraves metal dies
di-et *n.* regulated selection of food and drink
di-e-tet-ics *pl., n.* study of diet and regulations of a diet
di-eth-yl-bes-trol *n.* a synthetic estrogen to treat menstrual disorders
di-e-ti-tian *n.* diet planner
dif-fer *v.* have different opinions
dif-fer-ence *n.* state, or degree of being different or unlike
dif-fer-ent *adj.* not the same
dif-fer-en-tia *n.* a specific difference
dif-fer-en-tial *adj.* showing a difference or differences
dif-fer-en-ti-ate *v.* show, or distinguish the difference
dif-fi-cult *adj.* hard to do, or accomplish; hard to please
dif-fi-cul-ty *n., pl.* **difficulties** quality or state of being difficult
dif-fi-dent *adj.* lacking confidence in oneself; timid **diffidently** *adv.*
dif-frac-tion *n., Phys.* modification of light rays
dif-fuse *v.* spread freely in all directions; to scatter
dig *v.* break up the earth
di-gest *v.* summarize; change ingested food into usable form
di-gest-ion *n.* dissolving food in the stomach
dig-it *n.* toe or finger
dig-i-tal *adj.* expressed in digits, as for computer use
digital computer *n.* computer using data resented as digits to perform operations
dig-i-tal-is *n.* drug prepared from dried leaves of foxglove
dig-ni-fied *adj.* stately; poised
dig-ni-fy *v.* to give distinction to something
dig-ni-tary *n., pl.* **dignitaries** person of high rank
dig-ni-ty *n., pl.* **dignities** quality being excellent
di-graph *n.* pair of letters that represents a single sound
di-gress *v.* to wander
dik-dik *n.* small African antelope
dike *n.* embankment made of earth, control flood waters
di-lap-i-dat-ed *adj.* state of decay or disrepair
di-late *v.* become larger **dilateable** *adj.*
dil-a-to-ry *adj.* delaying; slow; tardy
di-lem-ma *n.* perplexing situation
dil-et-tante *n.* superficial interest in something
dil-i-gent *adj.* industrious
dill *n.* aromatic herb
di-lute *v.* reduce concentration
dim *adj.* dull
dime *n.* U. S. coin worth ten cents
di-men-sion *n.* measurable extent
di-min-ish *v.* make smaller
di-min-u-en-do *adv.* gradually lessening in volume
di-min-u-tive *adj.* very small
dim-ple *n.* depression in the skin
din *n.* loud noise
dine *v.* to eat dinner
di-nette *n.* small dining room
din-ghy *n., pl.* **dinghies** a small rowboat
din-ky *adj., Informal* insignificant or small; tiny **dinkier adv.**
din-ner *n.* last meal of the day
di-no-saur *n., Paleon.* extinct reptiles **dinosauric adj.**
dip *v.* put into a liquid momentarily
diph-the-ri-a *n., Pathol.* acute infectious disease
di-plo-ma *n.* document from school
dip-lo-mat *n.* government representative
dip-per *n.* long-handled cup
dip-so-ma-ni-a *n.* insatiable craving for alcohol
dire *adj.* dreadful or terrible
di-rect *v.* give orders
di-rec-tion *n.* act of directing; instruction
di-rect-ly *adv.* immediately; at once
di-rec-tor *n.* person who manages
di-rec-to-ry *n., pl.* **directories** book listing data

dirge *n.* slow mournful song
dir-i-gi-ble *n.* lighter-than-air plane
dirn-dl *n.* dress with a full skirt
dirt *n.* soil or earth
dirt-y *adj.* not clean **dirtiness** *n.*
dis-a-ble *v.* to incapacitate
dis-ad-van-tage *n.* unfavorable inferior condition
dis-a-gree *v.* vary in opinion **disagreeable** *adj.*
dis-al-low *v.* refuse to allow
dis-ap-pear *v.* vanish **disappearance** *n.*
dis-ap-point *v.* fail to satisfy
dis-ap-pro-ba-tion *n.* disapproval
dis-ap-prove *v.* refuse to approve
dis-arm *v.* make harmless
dis-ar-range *v.* disturb the order **disarramgement** *n.*
dis-ar-ray *n.* state of confusion or disorder
dis-as-sem-ble *v.* to take apart
dis-as-so-ci-ate *v.* break away or detach from an association
dis-as-ter *n.* event that causes distress; a suden misfortune
dis-a-vow *v.* disclaim or deny
dis-band *v.* disperse
dis-bar *v.* expelled from the legal profession **disbarment** *n.*
dis-be-lieve *v.* refuse to believe
dis-burse *v.* pay out money
disc *or* **disk** *n., Informal* phonograph record that holds information
dis-card *v.* to throw out
dis-cern *v.* understand
dis-charge *v.* to release
dis-ci-ple *n.* follower
dis-ci-pline *n.* train; punishment to correct poor behavior
dis-claim *v.* to deny interest in or assocation with
dis-close *v.* make known **discloseure** *n.*
dis-co *n., pl.* **discos** discotheque
dis-color *v.* alter or change the color of
dis-com-fit *v.* defeat in battle
dis-com-fort *n.* uneasiness; pain
dis-com-mode *v.* inconvenience
dis-com-pose *v.* disrupt composure of something
dis-con-cert *v.* upset
dis-con-nect *v.* break the connection of something
dis-con-so-late *adj.* unhappy
dis-con-tent *n.* dissatisfaction
dis-con-tin-ue *v.* bring to an end
dis-cord *n.* lacking harmony
dis-co-theque *n.* nightclub with
dis-count *v.* sell for lower price than usual or regular price
dis-coun-te-nance *v.* look upon with disfavor; weary
dis-cour-age *v.* deprived of enthusiasm or courage
dis-course *n.* conversation; lengthy discussion
dis-cour-te-ous *adj.* lacking courteous manners
dis-cov-er *v.* make known or visible **discoverable** *adj.*
dis-cred-it *v.* cast disbelief on
dis-creet *adj.* tactful; careful of appearances; modest
dis-crep-an-cy *n., pl.* **discrepancies** difference in facts
dis-crete *adj.* separate; made up of distinct parts
dis-cre-tion *n.* act of being discreet
dis-crim-i-nate *v.* distinguish between
dis-cur-sive *adj.* covering a wide field of subjects in a quick manner
dis-cuss *v.* to talk
dis-dain *v.* ignore; scorn
dis-ease *n.* sickness; illness **diseased** *adj.*
dis-em-bark *v.* unload
dis-em-body *v.* to free from the body
dis-en-chant *v.* free from false beliefs; disbeliefs
dis-en-gage *v.* to set free
dis-en-tan-gle *v.* free from involvement; know nothing of
dis-fig-ure *v.* deform appearance
dis-fran-chise *v.* deprive the legal right
dis-gorge *v.* to regurgitate; to pour out
dis-grace *n.* loss of honor
dis-guise *v.* alter appearance
dis-gust *v.* version
dish *n.* eating utensil
dis-har-mo-ny *n.* discord
dis-heart-en *v.* lose spirit
di-shev-el *v.* disarrange
dis-hon-est *adj.* lacking honesty
dis-hon-or *n.* disgrace
dis-il-lu-sion *v.* to disenchant
dis-in-fect *v.* free from infection
dis-in-gen-u-ous *adj.* lacking frankness
dis-in-her-it *v.* deprive of inheritance
dis-in-te-grate *v.* break into small particles; decompose
dis-in-ter-est-ed *adj.* unselfish, or not interested
dis-join *v.* to become detached
dis-like *v.* regard with disapproval
dis-lo-cate *v.* put out of place
dis-lodge *v.* remove from
dis-loy-al *adj.* untrue to obligations or duty **disloyalty adj.**
dis-mal *adj.* depressing
dis-man-tle *v.* to take apart
dis-may *v.* disheartened
dis-mem-ber *v.* cut into pieces
dis-miss *v.* to discharge
dis-mount *v.* get down from
dis-o-bey *v.* refuse or fail to obey
dis-o-blige *v.* act contrary to wishes
dis-or-der *n.* confussion
dis-or-gan-ize *v.* destroy or break up the unity; unorganizational
dis-own *v.* refuse to claim as one's own **disownment n.**
dis-patch *v.* send off on a particular destination
dis-pel *v.* drive or away
dis-pense *v.* give out
dis-perse *v.* scatter in various directions; to give out or distribute
dis-place *v.* change the position of
dis-play *v.* put in view
dis-please *v.* cause disapproval or annoyance of; to be offensive to
dis-pose *v.* put in place; arrange
dis-prove *v.* prove to be false
dis-pute *v.* to debate or argue
dis-qual-i-fy *v.* deprive of the required conditions

dis-qui-si-tion *n.* formal inquiry
dis-re-gard *v.* to neglect
dis-re-pute *n.* state of low esteem
dis-re-spect *n.* lack of respect
dis-robe *v.* undress
dis-rupt *v.* throw into disorder
dis-sat-is-fy *v.* fail to satisfy
dis-sect *v.* cut into pieces
dis-sem-ble *v.* conceal; disguise
dis-sem-i-nate *v.* spread; distribute
dis-sen-sion *n.* difference of opinion
dis-sent *v.* differ in opinion
dis-ser-ta-tion *n.* written essay
dis-serv-ice *n.* ill turn
dis-sim-i-lar *adj.* different
dis-sim-u-late *v.* dissemble
dis-si-pate *v.* disperse or drive
dis-so-ci-ate *v.* break association
dis-solve *v.* cause to fade away
dis-so-nance *n., Mus.* lack of agreement; unagreeable
dis-suade *v.* alter the course of action; to change direction
dis-tance *n.* separation in time or space **distanced v., distancing v.**
dis-tant *adj.* separate by a specified amount of time or space
dis-taste *v.* feeling aversion to
dis-tem-per *n.* contagious viral disease of dogs
dis-tend *v.* expand
dis-till *v.* extract by distillation
dis-til-late *n.* the condensed substance sep-arated by distillation
dis-tinct *adj.* clearly seen
dis-tinc-tion *n.* act of distinguishing
dis-tinc-tive *adj.* serving to give style or distinction to
dis-tin-guish *v.* to recognize as beeing different
dis-tort *v.* to twist or bend out of shape **distortion** *n.*
dis-tract *v.* to draw or divert one's atten-tion **distractingly adv.**
dis-trait *adj.* absentminded
dis-traught *adj.* deeply agitated with doubt or anxiety
dis-trict *n.* an administrative or political section of a territory; a division of space **district v.**
dis-turb *v.* to destroy the tranquillity of; to unsettle mentally **disturber**
ditch *n.* trench in the earth
dive *v.* to plunge into water headfirst; to submerge
di-verge *v.* to move or extend in different directions from a common point **diverged v., diverging v.**
di-veerse *adj.* unlike in characteristics; different; not similar
di-ver-si-fy *v.* to give variety to some-thing; to engage in varied operations
di-ver-sion *n.* the act of diverting from a course or activity
di-vert *v.* to undress or strip, especially of clothing or dispossess of property
di-vide *v.* to separate into parts; to cause to be apart
di-vi-sion *n.* separation; something which divides or marks off
div-ot *n.* a square of turf or sod
diz-zy *adj.* having a whirling sensation in the head
do-cent *n.* a teacher at a college or university; conducts groups
doc-ile *adj.* easily led, taught, or managed **docility** *n.*
dock *n.* a landing slip or pier for ships or boats; a loading area for trucks or trains
dock-et *n.* a brief written summary of a document
doc-tor *n.* a person trained and licensed to practive medicine
doc-tor-ate *n.* the degreee, status, or title of a doctor
doc-trine *n.* something taught as a body of principles
doc-u-ment *n.* official paper **documentation n.**
doc-u-men-ta-ry *adj.* relating to or based on documents
dodge *v.* avoid by moving suddenly
doe *n.* mature female deer
does-n't *contr.* does not
dog *n.* domesticated carnivorous mam-mal
dog-ged *adj.* stubbornly determined
dog-ma *n.* rigidly held doctrine
dog-mat-ic *adj.* marked by an authorita-tive assertion
dol-drums *pl., n.* a period of listlessness
dole *n.* distribution of food or money to the needy
dole-ful *adj.* filled with sadness
doll *n.* child's toy
dol-lar *n.* standard monetary unit of the U.S.
dol-men *n.* prehistoric monument
do-lor-ous *adj.* marked by grief; mourn-ful
dol-phin *n.* aquatic mammal
dolt *n.* stupid person
do-main *n.* territory under one gov-ernment
dome *n.* round shaped roof
do-mes-tic *adj.* relating to house-hold
dom-i-cile *n.* dwelling place
dom-i-nant *adj.* prevailing
dom-i-nate *v.* rule or control
dom-i-no *n.* a small rectangular block with dots on the face
don *v.* to put on
don-key *n., pl.* **donkeys** domesticated ass
do-nor *n.* one who donates or con-tributes
don't *contr.* do not
doo-dle *v.* to scribble or draw aimlessly
doom *n.* an unhappy destiny
door *n.* means of entrance or exit
dope *n.* drug or narcotic
dor-mant *adj.* asleep; state of rest
dor-sal *adj., Anat.* of or relating to back
do-ry *n., pl.* **dories** small flatbottomed boat
dose *n.* measured amount of medicine take at one time
dos-si-er *n.* complete data on a person
dot *n.* small round mark
dote *v.* show excessive affection
dou-ble *adj.* twice as much
double--cross *v., Slang* to betray
double--deck-er *n.* vehicle with two decks for passengers

doubt *v.* **doubter** *n.* uncertain of something
dough *n.* soft pastry mixture of flour and other ingredients
dough-nut *or* **donut** *n.* small cake made of rich, light dough
douse *v.* plunge into liquid or throw water on
dove *n.* any of numerous pigeons
dow-dy *adj.* not neat or tidy; old-fashioned **dowdiest** *adj.*
dow-el *n.* round wooden object that fastens two joined pieces
down *adv.* from higher to lower
down-er *n., Slang* depressant drug; a barbiturate
doz-en *n.* twelve of a kind
drab *adj.* unexciting; yellow-brown **drabness** *n.*
draft *n.* current of air; sketch or plan *Milit.* mandatory selection for service **draftee** *n.*
drag *v.* pull along by force
drag-on *n.* mythical, serpent-like monster
drain *v.* to draw off liquid gradually
drake *n.* male duck
dram *n.* small drink; a small portion
dra-ma *n.* a play recounting a serious story
drape *v.* to cover or adorn with something
dras-tic *adj.* extreme or severe
draw *v.* cause to move toward a position to sketch
draw-back *n.* undesirable feature
draw-bridge *n.* bridge that is raised or lowered
drawer *n.* one that draws pictures; a sliding receptacle in furniture
draw-ing *n.* picture; process of choosing lots
drawl *v.* to speak slowly
dray *n.* heavy cart used for hauling
dread *v.* fear greatly
dread-ful *adj.* inspiring dread; awful
dream *n.* series of thoughts or images which occur during sleep or the REM state of sleep
drea-ry *adj.* bleak and gloomy; dull **dreariness** *n.*
dredge *v.* remove sand or mud from under water **dredger** *n.*
dregs *pl., n.* sediment of a liquid
drench *v.* wet thoroughly
dress *n.* an outer garment for women and girls to put clothes on
drib-ble *v.* to slobber or drool; to bounce a ball repeatedly
drift *v.* to be carried along by a current to move about aimlessly
drill *n.* tool used in boring holes; the act of training soldiers by repeated exercise
drink *v.* to take liquid into the mouth and swallow
drip *v.* to fall in drops *n.* the sound made by falling drops
drive *v.* to propel, push, or press onward
driv-el *v.* to slobber
driz-zle *n.* fine, quiet, gentle rain
droll *adj.* whimsically comical
drom-e-dar-y *n.* one-humped camel
drone *n.* a male bee; unmanned boat or aircraft
drool *v.* to let saliva dribble from the mouth
droop *v.* to hang or bend downward
drop *n.* tiny, rounded mass of liquid; smallest unit of liquid measure
drop *v.* fall in drops; let fall
drop-sy *n., Med.* diseased condition with excessive water in the body
dross *n.* impurity forming molten metal
drought *n.* prolonged period of dryness; being without water
drove *n.* herd of cattle
drown *v.* die by suffocating in a liquid of any kind
drowse *v.* to doze
drub *v.* hit with a stick
drudge *n.* person who does menial tasks **drudgery** *n.*
drug *n.* substance for treatment of disease or illness
drum *n.* musical percussion instrument
drunk *adj.* intoxicated with alcohol
drunk-ard *adj.* person habitually drunk
drupe *n.* one seeded fruit, as the peach
dry *adj.* free from moisture; having no rain; thirsty
dry--clean *v.* clean fabrics with chemical solvents
dry goods *n.* textile fabrics
du-al *adj.* made up or composed of two parts
dub *v.* confer knighthood upon; nickname
du-bi-ous *adj.* causing doubt; unsettled in judgment
duch-ess *n.* wife or widow of a duke
duck *n.* swimming birds with short necks and legs
duct *n.* bodily tube or canal
duc-tile *adj.* capable of being shaped
dud *n., Informal* bomb or explosive round which fails to detonate; a failure
dude *n., Informal* a city person vacationing on a ranch
dudg-eon *n.* displeased, or indignant mood
due *adj.* owed; payable
dues *n., pl.* fee or charge for membership
du-el *n.* premeditated combat between two people
du-et *n.* musical composition for two performers **duetted** *v.*
duf-fel bag *n.* large cloth bag for personal belongings
duke *n.* noble ranking below a prince; a nobleman of the highest hereditary rank **dukedom** *n.*
dul-cet *adj.* melodious
dul-ci-mer *n.* musical stringed instrument of trapezoidal shape played with light hammers held in hands **dulcimore** *n.*
dull *adj.* stupid; with a blunt edge or point; not exciting **dullness** *n.*
du-ly *adv.* in a proper or due manner
dumb *adj.* unable to speak; uneducated **dumbness** *n.*
dumb-bell *n.* short bar with weights

dumb-waiter *n.* small elevator used to convey food or dishes, from one floor to another
dum-dum bullet *n.* small-arms bullet designed to expand on contact
dum-found *v.* to confound with amazement
dum-my *n.* one who is stupid; hand in bridge
dump *v.* throw down or discard; dispose of garbage
dump-ling *n.* mass of dough cooked in soup or stew
dun *v.* press a debtor for payment
dun *adj.*
dunce *n.* slow-witted person
dune *n.* hill of sand drifted by the wind
dung *n.* excrement of animals; manure
dun-ga-ree *n.* sturdy, cotton fabric, especially blue denim; pants or overalls made from this material
dun-geon *n.* dark, underground prison chamber
dunk *v.* dip a piece of food into liquid before eating
du-o-de-num *n., pl.* **-denums** first portion of the small intestine
dupe *n.* person who is easily deceived
du-pli-cate *n.* identical; exact copy of an original **duplication** *n.*
du-ra-ble *adj.* able to continue for a long period of time without deterioration **durability** *n.*
du-ra-tion *n.* period of time during which something lasts or exists
du-ress *n.* constraint by fear or force; forced restraint
dur-ing *prep.* throughout the time of; within the time of
dusk *n.* earliest part of the evening, just before darkness
dust *n.* fine, dry particles of dirt
duty *n.* something a person must do; a moral obligation
dwarf *n.* a human being, or animal of a much smaller than normal size **dwarfish** *adj.*
dwell *v.* to live, as an inhabitant **-er** *n.*
dwell-ing *n.* house or building in which one lives
dwin-dle *v.* to waste away
dye *v.* fix a color in or stain materials; color with a dye
dying *adj.* coming to the end of life; about to die
dy-nam-ic *adj.* forceful; energic; productive activity or change; of or relating to energy, motion, or force **-al adj.**
dy-nam-ics *n., Phys.* part of physics dealing with force, energy, and motion and the relationship between them
dy-na-mo *n.* machine producing electric current
dys-en-ter-y *n.* infection of the lower intestinal tract
dys-lex-i-a *n.* an impairment in one's ability to read **dyslexic** *adj.*
dys-pep-sia *n.* indigestion
dys-pro-si-um *n.* metallic element
dys-tro-phy *n.* various neuromuscular disorders, especially muscular dystrophy

E, e The fifth letter of the English alphabet.
each *adj.* everyone
each other *pron.* each of two or more in reciprocal action or relation
ea-ger *adj.* marked by enthusiastic interest **eagerness** *n.*
eager beaver *n.* one who is extremely zealous in performing his assigned duties and in volunteering for more
ea-gle *n.* large, powerful bird
eagle eye *n.* the ability to see or observe with exceptional keeness; one that observes
eagle ray *n.* any of several widely distributed large active stingrays with broad pectoral fins like wings
ea-glet *n.* young eagle
eal-dor-man *n.* a chief officer in Anglo-Saxon England who is in a district
ear *n., Anat.* hearing organ in vertebrates
ear-ache *n.* a type of pain which is located in the ear
ear-drum *n.* the tympanic membrane of the ear
earl *n.* British nobleman **earldom** *n.*
ear-ly *adj.* occurring before the usual time
early bird *n.* an early riser; a person who arrives early
earn *v.* payment for work done or services rendered **earner** *n.*
ear-nest *n.* serious intent **earnestly, earnestness** *n.*
earn-ings *pl., n.* something earned, such as a salary
earth *n.* the outer layer of the world; ground; soil; dirt
ease *n.* state of being comfortable
ea-sel *n.* frame used to support a canvas or picture
east *n.* the direction in which the sun rises **eastly** *adj. & adv.*, **eastward** *adj. & adv.*
Easter *n.* Christian festival that celebrates the resurrection of Christ
easy *adj.* little difficulty **easily** *adv.*, **easiness** *n.*
easy going *adj.* to be taking life easy; without worry, concern, or hastle
eat *v.* chew and swallow food; to erode **eater** *n.*
eaves *n.* the overhangingedge of a roof
ebb *n.* recede of a tide towards the sea; leassening; to weaken
ebb tide *n.* the tide while at ebb; a period of decline
eb-o-ny *n., pl.* **ebonies** dark, hard, colored wood; black or very deep brown
e-bul-lient *adj.* filled with enthusiasm
eb-ul-li-tion *n.* the process of boiling or bubbling; a sudden release of emotion
ec-cen-tric *adj.* different or peculiar
ec-cle-si-as-ti-cal *n.* a clergyman; a person officially serving a church
ech-e-lon *n.* formation of military troops
e-chi-no-derm *n.* the phylum of marine animals which have spiny shells and radial bodies

ech-o *n., pl.* **echoes** repetition of a sound
ec-lec-tic *adj.* having components from diverse sources **eclectic** *n.*
e-clipse *n.* total or partial blocking of one celestial body by another
e-clip-tic *n., Astron.* the suns apparent path
ec-logue *n.* short pastoral poem in dialogue form
e-col-o-gy *n.* scientific study of the environment **ecologist** *n.*
ec-o-nom-ic *adj.* science relating to the necessities of life
ec-o-nom-i-cal *adj.* not wasteful **economically** *adv.*
ec-o-nom-ics *pl., n.* science which studies wealth
e-con-o-mize *v.* to manage thriftily **economizer** *n.*
e-con-o-my *n., pl.* **economies** system for the management of resources and production of goods
ec-ru *n.* light yellowish brown
ec-sta-sy *n., pl.* **ecstasies** state of intense joy or delight
ec-u-men-i-cal *adj.* worldwide; un-iversal
ec-ze-ma *n.* noncontagious skin disease marked by itching and scaly patches
ed-dy *n., pl.* **eddies** wind or water running against the main current
edge *n.* cutting side of a blade; sharpness
ed-i-ble *adj.* safe or fit for consumption
e-dict *n.* public decree
ed-i-fy *v.* improve or educate
ed-it *v.* correct for publication; to compile for an edition **editor** *n.*
e-di-tion *n.* form in which a book is published
ed-i-to-ri-al *n.* article in a newspaper or magazine **editorially** *adv.*
ed-u-cate *v.* supply with training or schooling **educator** *n.*
e-duce *v.* to call forth or bring out
eel *n., pl.* **eel** *or* **eels** snake-like fish
ee-rie *or* **ee-ry** *adj.* weird; scary; spooky **eerily** *adv.*, **eeriness** *n.*
ef-face *v.* remove or rub out
ef-fect *n.* power to produce a desired result
ef-fec-tive *adj.* producing an expected effect or result **effectiveness** *n.*
ef-fem-i-nate *adj.* having a more woman-like quality or trait
ef-fer-ent *adj., Physiol.* carrying away or outward from an organ or part **efferently** *adv.*
ef-fete *adj.* exhausted of effectiveness or force
ef-fi-ca-cious *adj.* producing an intended effect **efficaciously** *adv.*
ef-fi-cient *adj.* adequate in performance with minimum effort
ef-fi-gy *n., pl.* **effigies** image of a hated person
ef-flo-res-cence *n.* slow process of development
ef-flu-vi-um *n., pl.* **effluvivia** *or* **effluviums** unpleasant vapor of something
ef-fort *n.* earnest attempt or achievement **effortless** *adj.*
ef-fron-ter-y *n., pl.* **effronteries** shameless; boldness; impudence
ef-ful-gent *adj.* shining brilliantly
ef-fu-sion *n.* unrestrained outpouring of feeling
egg *n.* reproductive cell of female animals
egg-beat-er *n.* tool with rotating blades used to mix food
egg-nog *n.* drink of beaten eggs, sugar, and milk or cream
egg-plant *n.* a purple, egg-shaped, edible fruit
e-go *n.* self thinking
e-go-cen-tric *adj.* thinking of oneself as the object of all experiences
e-go-ma-ni-a *n.* self obsession
e-gre-gious *adj.* remarkably bad
e-gress *n.* act of coming out; means of departing
e-gret *n.* white wading birds
ei-der *n.* large sea duck found in northern regions
eight *n.* cardinal number which follows seven
ei-ther *pron.* one or the other; *adv.* likewise; also
e-jac-u-late *v.* eject abruptly; to exclaim
e-ject *v.* to throw out; to expel **ejection, ejector** *n.*
eke out *v.* obtain with great effort
e-lab-o-rate *adj.* planned or carried out with great detail
e-lapse *v.* slip or glide away
e-las-tic *adj.* capable of easy adjustment
e-late *v.* make proud of **elation** *n.*
el-bow *n., Anat.* outer joint of the arm between the upper arm and forearm
elbow-room *n.* ample room to move about
eld-er *adj.* older; senior
e-lect *v.* choose or select by vote
e-lec-tric *or* **e-lec-tri-cal** *adj.* relating or pertaining to electricity
e-lec-tric-i-ty *n., Phys., Chem.* force that causes bodies to attract or repel each other; form of energy
e-lec-tro-cute *v.* kill by the use of electric current **electrocution** *n.*
e-lec-trode *n.* a conductor of electricity into or out of a battery
e-lec-tro-mag-net *n.* magnet that operates through an electric source
e-lec-tron *n., Elect.* subatomic particle with a negative electric charge
e-lec-tro-type *n.* duplicate metal plate used in printing
el-e-gance *n.* refinement in appearance
el-e-gy *n., pl.* **elegies** poem expressing sorrow for one who is dead **elegist** *n.*
el-e-ment *n.* constituent part
el-e-men-ta-ry *adj.* fundamental; essential
el-e-phant *n.* large mammal having a long, flexible trunk
el-e-vate *v.* lift up or raise
e-lev-en *n.* cardinal number equal to ten plus one **eleventh** *n.*
elf *n., pl.* **elves** imaginary being with magical powers
e-lic-it *v.* bring or draw out
e-lide *v.* to omit; to slur over in pronun-

ciation
e-lim-i-nate *v.* get rid of or remove
e-lite *n.* most skilled members of a group
e-lix-ir *n., Phar.* sweetened aromatic liquid of alcohol and water
elk *n.* large deer
el-lipse *n., Geom.* closed curve oval in shape
elm *n.* various valuable timber and shade trees
el-o-cu-tion *n.* art of effective public speaking
e-lope *v.* run away, especially in order to marry
el-o-quent *adj.* having the power to speak fluently
else *adj.* different; other; more
else-where *adv.* to or in another place
e-lu-ci-date *v.* make clear, clarify; to explain
e-lude *v.* to evade or avoid
e-ma-ci-ate *v.* to become extremely thin **emaciation** *n.*
em-a-nate *v.* to come or give forth
e-man-ci-pate *v.* liberate; to set free **emancipation** *n.*
e-mas-cu-late *v.* to castrate
em-balm *v.* treat a corpse with preservatives to protect from decay
em-bank *v.* support, protect or defend **enbankment** *n.*
em-bar-go *n., pl.* **embargoes** a restraint on trade
em-bark *v.* to set out on a venture
em-bar-rass *v.* feel selfconscious; to confuse **embarrassment** *n.*
em-bas-sy *n., pl.* **embassies** headquarters of an ambassador
em-bat-tle *v.* to prepare for battle
em-bed *v.* to enclose tightly in a surrounding mass
em-bel-lish *v.* to adorn; to decorate **embellishment** *n.*
em-ber *n.* small piece of glowing coal
em-bez-zle *v.* take money or other items fraudulently
em-bit-ter *v.* to create feelings of hostility **embitterment** *n.*
em-bla-zon *v.* decorate in bright colors
em-blem *n.* symbol of something; a distinctive design
em-bod-y *v.* give a bodily form to
em-bold-en *v.* to encourage; to make bold
em-bo-lism *n., Med.* blockage of a blood vessel
em-bon-point *n.* plumpness; stoutness
em-boss *v.* shape or decorate with raised designs
em-brace *v.* to clasp or hold in the arms
em-bro-cate *v.* moisten and rub liquid medicine
em-broi-der *v.* to decorate with ornamental needlework
em-broil *v.* to throw into confusion **embroilment** *n.*
em-bry-o *n., pl.* **embryos** organism in the early development stage **embryonic** *adj.*
em-cee *n., Informal* master of ceremonies emcee *v.*
e-mend *v.* correct or remove faults **emendation** *n.*
em-er-ald *n.* bright-green gemstone
e-merge *v.* to rise into view
e-mer-gen-cy *n., pl.* **emergencies** sudden and unexpected situation
e-mer-i-tus *adj.* retired from active duty with honor
e-met-ic *adj.* medicine used to induce vomiting
em-i-grate *v.* to move from one country or region **emigration** *n.*
e-mi-gre *n.* refugee
em-i-nent *adj.* high in esteem or rank **eminently** *adv.*
em-is-sar-y *n., pl.* **emissaries** person sent out on a mission
e-mit *v.* to send forth; to throw or give out
e-mol-lient *n.* substance for softening of the skin **emollient** *adj.*
e-mol-u-ment *n.* profit; compensation
e-mote *v.* to show emotion
e-mo-tion *n.* strong feeling of sorrow, hate and love
em-pa-thy *n., Physiol.* understanding the feelings of another person
em-pen-nage *n.* rear section of an aircraft
em-per-or *n.* ruler of an empire
em-pha-sis *n., pl.* **emphases** importance attached to anything
em-pire *n.* nations governed by a single supreme authority
em-pir-i-cal *or* **em-pir-ic** *adj.* gained from observation or experience **empirically** *adv.*
em-place-ment *n.* platform for guns or military equipment
em-ploy *v.* engage the service or use of **-able** *adj.*, **emoloyer, employment** *n.*
em-ploy-ee *or* **em-ploy-e** *n.* person who works for another in return for pay
em-po-ri-um *n., pl.* **emporiums** *or* **emporia** large store which carries general merchandise
em-pow-er *v.* to authorize; to delegate
em-press *n.* woman who rules an empire
emp-ty *adj.* containing nothing; lacking substance
em-u-late *v.* strive to equal, by imitating
e-mul-sion *n., Chem.* mixture of small droplets, one within the other
en-a-ble *v.* to make able
en-act *v.* to make into law; to decree **enactment** *n.*
e-nam-el *n.* protective coating
en-am-or *v.* to inflame with love; to charm
en-camp *v.* to form or stay in a camp **encampment** *n.*
en-cap-su-late *v.* enclose or encase in a capsule
en-ceph-a-li-tis *n., Pathol.* inflammation of the brain
en-chain *v.* put in chains
en-chant *v.* to put under a spell **enchantment** *n.*
en-cir-cle *v.* to form a circle around **encirclement** *n.*
en-close *v.* to surround on all sides
en-co-mi-um *n., pl.* **encomiums** *or* **encomia** high praise

en-com-pass *v.* to surround
en-core *n.* audience's demand for a repeat performance
en-coun-ter *n.* unexpected meeting or conflict
en-cour-age *v.* inspire with courage or hope **encouragement** *n.*
en-croach *v.* intrude upon the rights of another **encroacher, encroachment** *n.*
en-crust *v.* cover with a crust; to crust
en-cum-ber *v.* hinder or burden with difficulties
en-cy-clo-pe-di-a *n.* a book of references covering a broad range of subjects
en-cyst *v.* to become enclosed in a sac **encystment** *n.*
end *n.* terminal point where something is concluded
en-dan-ger *v.* to expose to danger **endangerment** *n.*
en-dear *v.* to make beloved or dear **endearingly** *adv.*
endearment *n.* state of being endeared
en-deav-or *n.* attempt to attain or do something
en-dem-ic *adj.* peculiar to a particular area
en-dog-e-nous *adj., Biol.* originating or growing from within
en-dor-phin *n.* painkilling hormones secreted by the brain
en-dorse *v.* to write one's signature on the back of a check **endorsement** *n.*
en-dow *v.* to bestow upon **endowment** *n.*
en-dure *v.* to undergo
end-wise *adv.* on end; lengthwise
en-e-ma *n.* injection of a liquid into the rectum for cleansing
en-e-my *n.* a hostile force
en-er-gy *n., pl.* **energies** vigor; growth *Phys.* electric power
en-er-vate *v.* to weaken
en-fee-ble *v.* to weaken **enfeeblement** *n.*
en-fold *v.* enclose; wrap in layers
en-force *v.* impose by force or firmness **enforceable** *adj.*, **enforcement** *n.*
en-fran-chise *v.* to grant to give a franchise to
en-gage *v.* to secure or bind; pledge to marry
en-gen-der *v.* to exist
en-gine *n.* mechanical machine
en-gorge *v.* to swallow greedily **engorgement** *n.*
en-graft *v., Bot.* join or fasten
en-grave *v.* to etch into a surface
en-gross *v.* occupy attention
en-gulf *v.* enclose completely
en-hance *v.* make greater **-ment** *n.*
e-nig-ma *n.* anything puzzling
en-join *v.* to prohibit
en-joy *v.* feel joy or find pleasure
en-large *v.* make larger in size
en-list *v.* enroll or sign up for
en-mesh *v.* to entangle
en-mi-ty *n., pl.* **enmities** deep hatred; hostility
en-no-ble *v.* to confer the rank of nobility
en-nui *n.* boredom; weariness
e-nor-mity *n., pl.* **enormities** wickedness
e-nor-mous *adj.* very great in size **enormously** *adv.*
e-nough *adj.* adequate to satisfy demands
en-rage *v.* put into a rage
en-rap-ture *v.* to delight
en-rich *v.* make rich or richer
en-roll *or* **en-rol** *v.* to enter one's name on a register or record
en-sconce *v.* to settle securely
en-sem-ble *n.* group of complementary parts that are in harmony
en-shrine *v.* to hold saced
en-shroud *v.* cover with a shroud
en-sign *n.* identifying flag; commissioned Navy officer
en-slave *v.* to put in bondage **enslavement** *n.*
en-snare *v.* to catch; to trap
en-sue *v.* to follow as a consequence
en-sure *v.* to make certain of
en-tail *v.* necessary accompaniment or result **entailment** *n.*
en-tan-gle *v.* to complicate; to confuse **entanglement** *n.*
en-ter *v.* go into; to penetrate; to begin
en-ter-prise *n.* large or risky undertaking; project with risks
en-ter-tain *v.* to amuse; consider **entertainment** *n.*
en-thrall *v.* to fascinate; captivate **enthrallment** *n.*
en-thu-si-asm *n.* intense feeling
en-tice *v.* to attract by arousing desire
en-tire *adj.* whole; complete
en-ti-tle *v.* furnish with a right
en-ti-ty *n., pl.* **entities** something that exists alone
en-tomb *v.* to place in a tomb **entombment** *n.*
en-to-mol-o-gy *n.* study of insects
en-trails *pl., n.* internal organs of man
en-trance *n.* the means or place of entry
en-trance *v.* to fascinate
en-trap *v.* catch in a trap **entrapment** *n.*
en-treat *v.* to make an earnest request of
en-trench *v.* to fix or sit firmly **entrenchment** *n.*
en-tre-pre-neur *n., Fr.* person who undertakes business ventures
en-trust *v.* transfer to another for care
en-try *n., pl.* **entries** opening or place for entering
en-twine *v.* twine about or together
e-nu-mer-ate *v.* count off one by one
e-nun-ci-ate *v.* to pronounce with clarity; to announce
en-ve-lope *n.* paper covering for a letter
en-ven-om *v.* to make poisonous; to embitter
en-vi-a-ble *adj.* highly desirable
en-vi-ron-ment *n.* surroundings
en-vi-ron-men-tal-ist *n.* person who tries to preserve the natural environment
en-vi-rons *pl., n.* surrounding region; a place
en-vis-age *v.* form a mental image of; to visualize
en-voy *n.* messenger or agent; a diplomatic representative
en-vy *n., pl.* **envies** resentment for someone else's possessions
e-o-li-an *adj., Geol.* caused by or transmitted by the wind

e-on *n.* indefinite period of time
ep-au-let *or* **ep-au-lette** *n.* shoulder ornament on a military uniform
e-pergne *n.* centerpiece for holding flowers
e-phed-rine *n., Chem.* alkaloid used to relieve nasal congestion
e-phem-er-al *adj.* lasting a very short time
ep-ic *n.* long narrative poem
ep-i-cure *n.* a person having refined tastes
ep-i-dem-ic *adj.* something that effects many individuals
ep-i-der-mis *n., Anat.* outer nonvascular layer of the skin
ep-i-gram *n.* clever, witty observation
ep-i-lep-sy *n., Pathol.* nervous disorder with attacks of unconsciousness
ep-i-logue *or* **ep-i-log** *n.* short speech given by an actor to the audience at the end of a play; an appended chapter placed at the end of a novel or book, etc.
ep-i-neph-rine *or* **ep-i-neph-rin** *n., Biochem.* a hormone secreted by the adrenal medulla of the adrenal glands
e-piph-a-ny *n.* Christian festival held on January 6th
e-pis-co-pa-cy *n., pl.* **episcopacies** government of a church by bishops
e-pis-co-pal *adj.* pertaining to or governed by bishops
e-pis-co-pate *n.* term, rank, or position of a bishop
ep-i-sode *n.* a section of a poem, novel, etc., that is complete in itself **episodic** *adj.*
e-pis-tle *n.* a formal letter **Epistle** one of the letters in the New Testament
ep-i-taph *n.* inscription, as on a tomb or gravestone
ep-i-the-li-um *n.* thin membranous tissue covering the outer bodily surface
ep-i-thet *n.* word used to characterize something
e-pit-o-me *n.* concise summary; typical example
e-pit-o-mize *v.* be a perfect example
ep-och *n.* point in time marking a new era
ep-ox-y *n., pl.* **epoxies** *Chem.* corrosion-resistant resin used glues and coatings
eq-ua-ble *adj.* not changing; evenly proportioned
e-qual *adj.* same quantity, or value; having the same privileges or rights
e-qual-ize *v.* become or make equal **equalization** *n.*
e-qua-nim-i-ty *n.* composure
e-quate *v.* consider or make equal
e-qua-tion *n.* act of being equal; mathematical statement of equality, usually shown as (=)
e-qua-tor *n.* imaginary circle around the earth
eq-uer-ry *n.* the officer in charge of the horses of royalty
e-ques-tri-an *n.* person who rides or performs on a horse
e-qui-an-gu-lar *adj., Geom.* having all angles equal
e-qui-dis-tant *adj.* having equal distances
e-qui-lat-er-al *adj.* having all sides equal
e-qui-lib-ri-um *n.* balance between two opposing forces; state of adjustment, or balance
e-quine *adj.* pertaining to or like a horse
e-qui-nox *n.* twice a year the sun crosses the equator and days and nights are equal in time
e-quip *v.* furnish with what is needed for any undertaking
eq-ui-page *n.* carriage that is equipped with horses and attendants
e-quip-ment *n.* material provided for a special purpose
e-qui-poise *n.* a state of balance
eq-ui-ta-ble *adj.* being impartial in treatment or judgment **equitableness** *n.*
eq-ui-ta-tion *n.* art or act of horse riding
eq-ui-ty *n.* fairness or impartiality; value of property beyond a mortgage or liability
e-quiv-a-lent *adj.* being equal **equivalence** *n.*
e-quiv-o-cal *adj.* ambiguous; questionable **equivocally** *adv.*
e-quiv-o-cate *v.* use intentionally evasive or vague language **equivocation** *n.*
-er *n., suff.* person concerned with a trade; one from a certain area, as a northerner
e-ra *n.* historical period in history
e-rad-i-cate *v.* to destroy utterl
e-rase *v.* remove something written **erasable** *adj.*
er-bi-um *n., Chem.* metallic, silvery, rare-earth element
ere *prep., Poet.* prior to; before
e-rect *adj.* in a vertical position; standing up straight; upright
ere-long *adv., Archaic* before long
er-e-mite *n.* a hermit
er-go *conj. & adv.* consequently; therefore
er-got *n.* disease of cereal plants; drug used to contract involuntary muscles
er-mine *n.* weasel with white fur
e-rode *v.* wear away gradually; to corrode
e-rog-e-nous *adj.* responsive to sexual stimulation
e-ro-sion *n.* state of being eroded
e-ro-sive *adj.* tending to erode **erosiveness** *n.*
e-rot-ic *adj.* pertaining to or promoting sexual desire
err *v.* make a mistake; to sin
er-rand *n.* trip to carry a message or perform a task
er-rant *adj.* wandering in search of adventure; straying from what is proper
er-rat-ic *adj.* lacking a fixed course; inconsistent **erratically** *adv.*
er-ra-tum *n., pl.* **errata** an error in writing or printing
er-ro-ne-ous *adj.* having or contain an error **erroneously** *adv.*
er-ror *n.* something done incorrectly; a mistake
er-satz *adj.* substitute usually inferior; artificial
erst-while *adj., Archaic* former

e-ruct *v.* to belch **eructation** *n.*
er-u-dite *adj.* scholarly
er-u-di-tion *n.* informed; great learning
e-rupt *v.* burst forth violently; explode with steam, lava, etc
er-y-sip-e-las *n.* an acute, inflammatory, skin disease resulting from streptococcus
es-ca-late *v.* intensify, increase, or enlarge
es-ca-la-tor *n.* a moving stairway
es-cal-lop *n. & v.* variation of scallop
es-ca-pade *n.* reckless behavior; a prankish trick
es-cape *v.* break free from confinement, restraint, etc.
es-cape-ment *n., Mech.* device in timepieces to control the movement of the wheel
es-cap-ism *n.* escape from unpleasant realities through day-dreams
escapist *n. & adj.*
es-ca-role *n.* endive leaves used for salads
es-carp-ment *n.* a steep slope or drop
-escense *n., suff.* give off light in a certain way, as florescence
es-chew *v.* shun or avoid
es-cort *n.* person accompanying another to give protection
es-cri-toire *n.* a writing desk
es-crow *n.* money placed in the custody of a third party until specified conditions are met
es-cutch-eon *n.* surface with an emblem bearing a coat of arms
-ese *n. & adj., suff.* anative of; in the language or style of
e-soph-a-gus *n., pl.* **esophagi** *Anat.* membranous tube through which food passes to the stomach
es-o-ter-ic *adj.* confidential; kept secret
es-pa-drille *n.* canvas shoe
es-pal-ier *n.* framework used to train shrubs to grow a particular way
es-pe-cial *adj.* having a very special place; exceptional **especially** *adv.*
es-pi-o-nage *n.* act of spying to obtain secret intelligence
es-pla-nade *n.* flat, open stretch of land along a shoreline
es-pou-sal *n.* support or adoption of a cause
es-pouse *v.* to make something one's own; to take as a spouse
es-pres-so *n.* strong coffee brewed by steam pressure
es-prit *n.* spirit; wit; mental liveliness
es-prit de corps *n., Fr.* a group's spirit of enthusiasm to the common goals of the group
es-py *v.* catch a quick view
-esque *adj., suff.* resembling
es-quire *n.* title of courtesy or respect
-ess *n., suff.* female
es-say *n.* short composition dealing with a single topic
es-sence *n.* the most important element; being
es-sen-tial *adj.* indispensable necessary **essentially** *adv.*
-est *adj. & adv., suff.* used to form the superlative degree of adverbs and adjectives
es-tab-lish *v.* make permanent, or secure; to create or find
es-tab-lish-ment *n.* a place of residence; those of influence and status in a society
es-tate *n.* large piece of land containing a large house
es-teem *v.* regard with respect
es-ter *n., Chem.* organic compounds formed by the reaction of an acid with an alcohol
es-ti-ma-ble *adj.* worthy of respect or admiration
es-ti-mate *v.* give an approximate opinion or calculation **estimation** *n.*
es-ti-val *adj.* pertaining to or of summer
es-ti-vate *v.* pass the summer in a state of dormancy
es-trange *v.* arouse hated; disassociate or remove oneself
es-tro-gen *n., Biochem.* steroid hormones that regulate female reproductive functions
es-tu-ar-y *n., pl.* **-ies** wide mouth of a river where the current meets the sea
etch *v.* engrave or cut into the surface by the action of acid **etcher** *n.*
etch-ing *n.* process of engraving using a sharp instrument and acid
e-ter-nal *adj.* existing without beginning or end; unending
e-ter-ni-ty *n., pl.* **externities** forever; the immeasurable extent of time
eth-ane *n., Chem.* gasous hydrocarbon contained in crude petroleum
eth-a-nol *n., Chem.* the intoxicant in liquors, wines, and beers; alcohol
e-ther *n., Chem.* an anesthetic
e-the-re-al *adj.* highly refined; delicate
eth-ic *n.* the system of moral values
eth-i-cal *adj.* conforming to right principles of conduct
eth-nic *adj.* relating to or of a cultural, or racial group
eth-nog-ra-phy *n., pl.* **ethnographies** branch of anthropology dealing with primitive human cultures
eth-nol-o-gy *n., pl.* **-gies** the study of racial groups, their cultures, and origins
eth-yl-ene *n., Chem.* flammable gas used as a fuel
e-ti-ol-o-gy *n.* science and study of causes or origins
et-i-quette *n.* prescribed rules of behavior in society
-ette *n., suff.* small; female
et-y-mol-o-gy *n., pl.* **-gies** branch of linguistics that deals with etymologies
eu-ca-lyp-tus *n.* large, native Australian tree with aromatic leaves
Eu-cha-rist *n.* the Christian sacrament of Communion
eu-chre *n.* card game for two to four players
eu-gen-ics *n.* science of improving the physical and mental qualities of human beings
eu-lo-gize *v.* deliver a eulogy for **eulogist** *n.*
eu-lo-gy *n., pl.* **eulogies** a speech that

honors a person or thing
eu-nuch *n.* a castrated man
eu-phe-mism *n.* substitution for a word thought to be too strong
eu-pho-ny *n., pl.* **-nies** agreeable sound of spoken words
eu-pho-ri-a *n.* very strong feeling of elation or well-being **euphoric** *adj.*
eu-re-ka *interj.* an expression of triumph
eu-sta-chian tube *n., Anat.* passage between the middle ear and the pharynx
eu-tha-na-sia *n.* act of putting to death painlessly a person suffering from an incurable disease
eu-then-ics *n.* study of improving the physical and mental qualities of human beings
e-vac-u-ate *v.* to leave a threatened area **evacuation** *n.*
e-vac-u-ee *n.* a person evacuated from a hazardous place
e-vade *v.* to elude; to get away from by using tricks
e-val-u-ate *v.* to determine the value of; to appraise **evaluation** *n.*
ev-a-nesce *v.* to fade away
ev-a-nes-cent *adj.* vanishing or passing quickly; fleeting
e-van-gel-i-cal *adj.* relating to the Christian gospel
e-van-gel-ism *n.* preaching and spreading of the gospel
e-van-gel-ist *n.* Protestant preacher or missionary
e-van-gel-ize *v.* to preach the gospel
e-vap-o-rate *v.* convert into vapor; remove the liquid or moisture from milk
e-va-sive *adj.* being intentionally vague **evasively** *adv.*
eve *n.* the evening before a special holiday; evening
e-ven *adj.* having a level surface; equally matched
e-ven-hand-ed *adj.* fair; impartial **evenhandedly** *adv.*
eve-ning *n.* the time between sunset and bedtime
e-ven-song *n.* an evening prayer
e-vent *n.* a significant occurrence; something that takes place **eventful** *adj.*
e-ven-tide *n.* evening
e-ven-tu-al *adj.* expected to happen in due course of time **eventually** *adv.*
e-ven-tu-al-i-ty *n.* the conceivable outcome
e-ven-tu-ate *v.* to come out eventually
ev-er *adv.* at any time; throughout the entire course of time
ev-er-glade *n.* tract of low, swampy land
ev-er-green *adj.* tree with green foliage throughout the year
ev-er-last-ing *adj.* existing or lasting forever **everlastingly** *adv.*
ev-er-more *adv., Poet.* for and at all time to come; always
e-vert *v.* to turn inside out or outward
eve-ry *adj.* without exceptions
eve-ry-body *pron.* every person
eve-ry-day *adj.* happening every day; daily
eve-ry-one *pron.* every person
eve-ry-place *adv.* everywhere
eve-ry-thing *pron.* all things; the essential thing
eve-ry-where *adv.* in, at, or to everyplace
e-vict *v.* to put out a tenant by legal process **eviction** *n.*
ev-i-dence *n.* facts on which a conclusion can be based
ev-i-dent *adj.* easily seen; obvious **evidently** *adv.*
e-vil *adj.* morally bad or wrong; low in public esteem
e-vil-do-er *n.* person who does evil to another
e-vil--mind-ed *adj.* obsessed with evil thoughts or intentions
e-vince *v.* demonstrate or indicate clearly
e-vis-cer-ate *v.* remove the vital part of something
e-voke *v.* call or summon forth to produce a reaction
ev-o-lu-tion *n.* gradual process of development or change **-ary** *adj.*
e-volve *v.* develop or change gradually; developed by evolutionary processes
ewe *n.* female sheep
ew-er *n.* wide-mouthed pitcher or jug
ex- *pref.* former
ex-ac-er-bate *v.* make more severe or worse
ex-act *adj.* accurate in every detail
ex-acting *adj.* making severe demands; rigorous **exactingly** *adv.*
ex-act-i-tude *n.* the quality of being exact
ex-ag-ger-ate *v.* represent something as being greater than it really is **exaggeration** *n.*
ex-alt *v.* raise in honor, rank, etc.; to praise or glorify **exalted** *adj.*
ex-am *n., Slang* an examination
ex-am-i-na-tion *n.* a test of skill or knowledge
ex-am-ine *v.* observe or inspect; to test by questions
ex-ample *n.* representative as a sample; one worthy of imitation
ex-as-per-ate *v.* make frustrated or angry
ex-ca-vate *v.* dig a hole or cavity **excavation** *n.*
ex-ceed *v.* surpass in quantity; to go beyond the limit
ex-ceed-ing-ly *adv.* greater than
ex-cel *v.* surpass or to do better than others
ex-cel-lence *n.* quality of being superior; superior quality
ex-cel-lent *adj.* the best quality
ex-cel-si-or *n.* wood shavings to protect delicate materials
ex-cept *prep.* with the omission or exclusion of; aside from
ex-cep-tion *n.* something that is excluded or does not conform
ex-cep-tion-a-ble *adj.* open to objection **exceptionably** *adv.*
ex-cep-tion-al *adj.* unusual; well above average **exceptionally** *adv.*
ex-cerpt *n.* passage from a book, etc.
ex-cess *n.* amount beyond what is necessary
ex-ces-sive *adj.* exceeding what is necessary; extreme

ex-change *v.* return for something else; trade
ex-cheq-uer *n.* treasury of a nation
ex-cise *n.* internal tax on the sale of a commodity
ex-cise *v.* remove surgically
ex-cit-a-ble *adj.* be easily excited **excitableness** *n.*
ex-cite *v.* stir up strong emotion; simulate the emotions of **excitant** *n.*
ex-claim *v.* cry out abruptly
ex-cla-ma-tion *n.* a sudden forceful utterance
ex-clude *v.* keep out; to omit from consideration
ex-clu-sive *adj.* intended for a single source; having no duplicate **-ly** *adv.*
ex-com-mu-ni-cate *v.* deprive the right of church membership **-ation** *n.*
ex-co-ri-ate *v.* to censure harshly
ex-cre-ment *n.* bodily waste
ex-cre-ta *pl., n.* excretions from the body such as sweat
ex-crete *v.* eliminate waste matter from the body
ex-cru-ci-at-ing *adj.* intensely painful **excruciatingly** *adv.*
ex-cul-pate *v.* free from wrong doing **exculpation** *n.*
ex-cur-sion *n.* short trip for pleasure
ex-cur-sive *adj.* go in one direction and then another; digressive
ex-cuse *v.* ask forgiveness or pardon for oneself; apologize for **excuseable** *adj.*
ex-e-cra-ble *adj.* extremely bad **-ness** *n.*
ex-e-crate *v.* to detest; abhor
ex-e-cute *v.* to carry out; put to death by the legal authority
ex-e-cu-tion *n.* act of executing a task; the death penalty
ex-e-cu-tion-er *n.* a person who carries out a legal execution
ex-ec-u-tive *n.* administrator in an organization; branch of government responsible for activating the laws of a country
ex-ec-u-tor *n.* person appointed to carry out the execution of a will
ex-em-plar *n.* something serving as a worthy model; a typical example
ex-em-pla-ry *adj.* worthy of imitation; commendable
ex-em-pli-fy *v.* show by giving examples
ex-empt *v.* free or excuse from an obligation or duty **exemption** *n.*
ex-er-cise *n.* the act of training or developing oneself
ex-ert *v.* put oneself through a strenuous effort **exertion** *n.*
ex-hale *v.* breathe out
ex-haust *v.* make extremely tired; drain oneself of strength
ex-haust *n.* discharge of waste gases; device through which waste gases are released
ex-hib-it *v.* display for public view
ex-hi-bi-tion-ism *n.* practice of drawing undue attention to oneself
ex-hil-a-rate *v.* to elate or refresh
ex-hort *v.* to urge by earnest appeal
ex-hume *v.* ig up and remove from a grave **exhumation** *n.*
ex-i-gen-cy *n.* urgency
ex-ig-u-ous *adj.* extremely small; scanty
ex-ile *n.* banishment; one who has been driven from his or her country
ex-ist *v.* have actual being or reality
ex-is-tence *n.* state of existing, or occurring
ex-is-ten-tial *adj.* based on experience **existentially** *adv.*
ex-is-ten-tial-ism *n.* a philosophy that stresses the active role of the will rather than of reason
ex-it *n.* a way or passage out
ex-o-bi-ol-o-gy *n.* the study of extraterrestrial life
ex-o-dus *n.* a departure of large numbers of people
ex-on-er-ate *v.* free one from accusation or blame; free from responsibility
ex-or-bi-tant *adj.* beyond usual and proper limits
ex-or-cise *v.* cast out or expel an evil spirit by prayers **exorcism** *n.*
ex-o-ther-mic *adj.* releasing rather than absorbing heat
ex-ot-ic *adj.* strangely different and fascinating
ex-pand *v.* increase the scope, or size; develop more fully **expandable** *adj.*
ex-panse *n.* a wide, open stretch
ex-pan-sion *n.* amount of increase in volume
ex-pan-sive *adj.* broad and extensive
ex-pa-ti-ate *v.* to talk or write at length
ex-pa-tri-ate *v.* to leave one's country and reside in another
ex-pect *v.* look forward to something as probable or certain
ex-pec-tan-cy *n.* state of expecting; expectation
ex-pec-tant *adj.* pregnant
ex-pec-ta-tion *n.* something that is expected and looked forward to
ex-pec-to-rant *n.* medicine used to promote expectoration
ex-pec-to-rate *v.* to spit
ex-pe-di-en-cy *n.* quality of being expedient
ex-pe-di-ent *adj.* determined by selfish interests only
ex-pe-dite *v.* speed up the progress of something
ex-pe-di-tion *n.* a journey for a definite purpose
ex-pe-di-tion-ar-y *adj.* sent on military service abroad
ex-pe-di-tious *adj.* quick; speedy
ex-pel *v.* drive or force out
ex-pend *v.* to pay out or use up
ex-pend-a-ble *adj.* available for spending **expendability** *n.*
ex-pen-di-ture *n.* an amount spent
ex-pense *n.* outlay or consumption of money; funds allotted to cover incidental costs
ex-pen-sive *adj.* high-priced
ex-pe-ri-ence *n.* the knowledge or skill acquired from actual participation or training in an activity
ex-pe-ri-enced *adj.* be knowledgeable through actual practices, etc
ex-per-i-ment *n.* test performed to dem-

onstrate a truth **experimental** *adj.*
ex-pert *n.* a person having great knowledge, or skill
ex-per-tise *n.* specialized skill in a particular area
ex-pi-ate *v.* to make amends for
ex-pire *v.* to come to an end; to exhale
ex-plain *v.* make understandable; to account for
ex-ple-tive *n.* an exclamation, often profane
ex-pli-cate *v.* to clear up the meaning of
ex-plic-it *adj.* plainly expressed; straightforward
ex-plode *v.* burst or blow up violently with a loud noise
ex-ploit *n.* a deed or act that is notable
ex-plore *v.* examine in a systematic way
ex-plo-sion *n.* sudden, violent release of energy
ex-plo-sive *n.* a chemical preparation that explodes
ex-po-nent *n.* person who speaks for a cause or group
ex-port *v.* send merchandise to other countries for resale
ex-pose *v.* lay open, as to ridicule; to lay bare; to reveal the identity of someone
ex-po-si-tion *n.* a statement of intent; a public exhibition
ex post facto *adj., L.* after the fact
ex-pos-tu-late *v.* try to dissuade against an action
ex-po-sure *n.* an indication of which way something faces
ex-pound *v.* give a detailed statement of something
ex-press *v.* to formulate in words; to comunicate
ex-pres-sion *n.* communication of feeling; a facial ok that conveys a feeling
ex-pres-sive *adj.* serving to indicate or express; full of expression
ex-press-way *n.* a multilane highway
ex-pro-pri-ate *v.* take property from the owner for public use
ex-pul-sion *n.* act of expelling
ex-punge *v.* to delete or remove; to erase
ex-pur-gate *v.* remove objectionable material from a play, etc.
ex-qui-site *adj.* intricately beautiful in craftsmanship
ex-tant *adj.* still in existence; not destroyed; surviving
ex-tem-po-ra-ne-ous *adj.* performing with little or no advance preparation; not memorized **-ously** *adv.*
ex-tem-po-rize *v.* do, with little or no advance preparation
ex-tend *v.* open to full length; to prolong; offer the hand
ex-ten-sion *n.* additional time to pay a debt
ex-ten-sive *adj.* wide-spread; far-reaching
ex-tent *n.* degree to which anything is extended; the size
ex-ten-u-ate *v.* minimize the seriousness of something
ex-te-ri-or *adj.* the outside; the external layer
ex-ter-mi-nate *v.* to destroy completely **exterminator** *n.*
ex-ter-nal *adj.* outside; exterior
ex-tinct *adj.* no longer existing
ex-tin-guish *v.* put an end to; to make extinct **extinguishable** *adj.*
ex-tir-pate *v.* pull up by the roots
ex-tol *v.* to praise highly
ex-tort *v.* obtain money by threat, or abuse of authority **extortist** *n.*
ex-tra *adj.* over and above what is normal
ex-tract *v.* pull or draw out by force
ex-trac-tion *n.* act of extracting; one's origin or ancestry
ex-tra-cur-ric-u-lar *adj.* outside the usual duties
ex-tra-dite *v.* surrender by extradition
ex-tra-di-tion *n.* legal surrender of a criminal for trial
ex-tra-dos *n.* the upper curve of an arch
ex-tra-ga-lac-tic *adj.* coming from beyond the galaxy
ex-tra-mar-i-tal *adj.* adulterous
ex-tra-mu-ral *adj.* involving teams from different schools
ex-tra-ne-ous *adj.* coming from without **extraneously** *adv.*
ex-tra-or-di-nar-y *adj.* beyond what is usual; remarkable
ex-tra-sen-so-ry *adj.* beyond the range of normal perception
ex-tra-ter-res-tri-al *adj.* orginating outside the earth
ex-trav-a-gant *adj.* overly lavish; wasteful; unrestrained **extravagantly** *adv.*
ex-trav-a-gan-za *n.* a lavish, showy entertainment
ex-treme *adj.* going far beyond the bounds of moderation; of the highest or utmost degree **extremely** *adv.*
ex-trem-ist *n.* person who resorts to extreme measures
ex-trem-i-ty *n.* utmost or farthest point; appendage or limb of the body
ex-tri-cate *v.* free from entanglement; to disengage
ex-trin-sic *adj.* outside the nature of something; external
ex-tro-vert *n.* out going person
ex-trude *v.* push or thrust out; to protrude
ex-u-ber-ant *adj.* full of high spirits **exuberance** *n.*
ex-ude *v.* to ooze or trickle forth, as sweat
ex-ult *v.* jubilant; to rejoice greatly **exultation** *n.*
ex-ur-bi-a *n.* well-to-do residential area
eye *n.* an organ of sight; central area of a hurricane
eye-ful *n.* a satisfying or complete view
eye opener *n.* a startling revelation
eye-sight *n.* power of sight; the range of vision
eye-sore *n.* something ugly that offends the sight
eye-strain *n.* fatigue or discomfort of the eyes, caused by excessive or improper use and marked by symptoms such as pain and headache
eye-wit-ness *n.* a person who has seen something and can testify to it firsthand

F, f The sixth letter of the English alphabet.
fa-ba-ceous *adj.* or or relating to the legume family
Fa-bi-an *adj.* of, relating to, or in the manner of the Roman general Quintus Fabius Maximus known for his defeat of Hannibal in the Secon Punic War by the avoidance of decisive contests
fa-ble *n.* a fictitious story having a moral
fabler *n.*
fa-bled *adj.* to tell something in the form of a fable
fab-li-au *n.* a type of tale that is usually cynical and comic and was popular in the 12th and 13th centuries
fab-ric *n.* cloth produced by knitting or spinning fibers
fab-ri-cant *n.* manufacturer
fab-ri-cate *v.* make or manufacture; build **fabrication** *n.*
fab-u-lar *adj.* of, relating to, or having the form of a fable
fab-u-list *adj.* a creator or writer of fables; liar
fab-u-lous *adj.* incredible
fa-cade *n., Arch.* face or front of a building
face *n.* front surface of the head
face angle *n.* an angle formed by two edges of polyhedral angle
face card *n.* a king, queen, or jack in a deck of cards
face--cloth *n.* washcloth
face--down *adv.* with the face down
face fly *n.* European fly that is similar to the house fly, is widely established in North America, and causes great distress in livestock by clustering about the face
face--harden *v.* to harden the suface of
face--lift-ing *n.* plastic surgery for improving the facial appearance
face--off *n.* putting a puck into play by dropping it between two players
face--plate *n.* the type of glass which is located on the front of a kinescope where the image of an object can be seen
fac-er *n.* a stunning check or defeat
face--saver *n.* something that saves space
face--saving *n.* the act of preserving one's dignity
fac-et *n.* polished surface on a gemstone; aspect of a person
fa-ce-tious *adj.* humorous **-ly** *adv.*
fact--to--face *adj.* being within each other's sight or presence
face-up *v.* to meet without shrinking
face value *n.* apparent value of something
fa-cial *adj.* near, of, or for the face
facial index *n.* the ratio of the breadth of the face to its length times 100
facial nerve *n.* cranial nerves that supply mnnotor fibers to the muyscles of the face and jaw
fac-ile *adj.* requiring little effort
fa-cil-i-tate *v.* make easier
fa-cil-i-ty *n.* ease in performance, or doing something
fac-ing *n.* lining sewn to a garment
fac-sim-i-le *n.* an exact copy
fact *n.* something that actually occurred; piece of information
fact finder *n.* one that tries to determine the realities of a case
fac-tion *n.* self-seeking group in a government
fac-tious *adj.* creating friction; divisive
fac-ti-tious *adj.* produced by man rather than nature
fac-ti-tive *adj.* relating to a transitive verb that in some constructions requires an objective complement as well as an object
fac-tor *n.* one transacting business for another for commission
fac-tor-age *n.* the charges made by a factor for certain services
factor analysis *n.* the transformation of statistical data into linear combinations of variables that are not correlated
fac-to-ry *n.* plant where goods are manufactured
fac-to-tum *n.* employee having many duties and responsibilites
fac-tu-al *adj.* consisting of or based on facts
fac-ul-ty *n.* natural ability or power; branch of learnig or teaching
fad *n.* temporary fashion **-ish** *adj.*
fade *v.* lose brightness gradually
fa-er-ie *n. variation of* fairy
fag *v.* exhaust by hard work
fag end *n.* frayed end of a rope or cloth
fag-ot *n.* bundle of sticks, etc. used for fuel
fag-got-ing *n.* a method of ornamenting cloth by pulling out horizontal threads and typing the remaining vertical threads into hourglass shaped bunches
Fahr-en-heit *adj.* temperature scale in which the freezing point of water is 32 degrees and the boiling point is 212 degrees
fa-ience *n.* earthenware decorated with a colorful opaque glaze
fail *v.* be totally ineffective; receive a grade below standard
fail-ing *n.* a minor fault; a defect
faille *n.* ribbed material
fail--safe *adj.* a system designed to prevent equipment failure
fail-ure *n.* a breaking down in strength, or efficiency
faint *adj.* having little vigor; lacking brightness; dizzy
faint-hearted *adj.* lacking courage
fair *adj.* visually light in coloring; not stormy; exhibit of livestock, etc.
fair ball *n.* batted ball with in the foul lines
fair--haired *adj.* having blonde or light colored hair; favored, favorite
fair--mind-ed *adj.* just and impartial
fair-way *n.* part of a golf course between the tee and the green
fair-y *n.* a tiny imaginary being
fair-y-land *n.* delightful, enchanting place
fair-y tale *n.* fictitious tale of fanciful

creatures
fait ac-com-pli *n.* irreversible accomplished fact or deed
faith *n.* belief in the value, or trustworthiness of someone or something
faith-ful *adj.* true and trustworthy in obligations, etc. **faithfully** *adv.*
fake *adj.* having a misleading appearance; not genuine
fal-con *n.* bird of prey
fall *v.* drop down from a higher place; collapse
fal-la-cious *adj.* deceptive; misleading
fal-li-ble *adj.* capable of making an mistake **fallibility** *n.*
fall-ing--out *n.* fight, or quarrel
fall-ing star *n.* a meteor
fall--off *n.* a decrease in something
fal-lo-pi-an tube *n.* ducts serving as a passage for the ovum
fall-out *n.* descent of minute particles of radioactive material
fal-low *n.* unplanted plowed ground; light brown color
false *adj.* incorrect; deliberately untrue **falsely** *adv.*
false face *n.* mask used as a disguise on Halloween
false-hood *n.* act of lying; untrue statement
fal-set-to *n.* high male singing voice
fal-si-fy *v.* give an untruthful account; misrepresent
fal-ter *v.* be uncertain in action or voice **faleringly** *adv.*
fame *n.* public esteem
fa-mil-iar *adj.* being well-acquainted with
fa-mil-i-ar-i-ty *n.* the knowledge of something
fa-mil-iar-ize *v.* make oneself familiar with something **familarization** *n.*
fam-i-ly *n.* a group of people connected by blood or marriage
fam-ine *n.* widespread scarcity of food
fam-ish *v.* to starve
fa-mous *adj.* well-known; renowned
fan *n.* device for putting air into motion
fa-nat-ic *n.* one moved by enthusiasm
fan-ci-er *n.* person having a special interest in something
fan-cy *n.* imagination whimsical nature
fan-cy--free *adj.* unattached
fan-fare *n.* short, loud trumpet flourish
fang *n.* long, pointed tooth
fan-jet *n.* aircraft with turbojet engines
fan-ny *n.* *Slang* the buttocks
fan-ta-sia *n.* composition according to the composer's fancy
fan-ta-size *v.* create mental pictures
fan-tas-tic *adj.* unreal; wildly exaggerated **fantastically** *adv.*
fan-ta-sy *n.* creative imagination
far *adv.* at a considerable distance
farce *n.* theatre comedy with ludicrous situations
fare *n.* fee paid for hired transportation
fare-well *n.* goodby
far--fetched *adj.* highly improbable
far--flung *adj.* widely distributed
far-i-na-ceous *adj.* rich in, or composed of starch
farm *n.* land used for agriculture raising animals
far--off *adj.* remote
far--out *adj.* very unconventional
far-ra-go *n.* a confused mixture
far-row *n.* litter of pigs
far--sighted *adj.* seeing distance objects more clearly than nearby things
far-ther *adv.* at a more distant point
far-ther-most *adj.* most distant
far-thest *adj.* at the greatest distance
far-thing *n.* something of little worth
fas-ci-nate *v.* attract irresistibly; captivate **-nation** *n.*
fas-cism *n.* one-party system of government
fashion *n.* mode or manner of dress
fast *adj.* swift; rapid
fast *v.* abstain from food
fast-back *n.* car with a downward slope roof
fast-en *v.* connect; securely fix something **fastener** *n.*
fast--food *n.* restaurant specializes in foods prepared and served quickly
fas-tid-i-ous *adj.* delicate or refined
fat *adj.* obese; plump
fat-al *adj.* causing death; inevitable **fatally** *adv.*
fa-tal-ism *n.* belief that things are predetermined by fate
fa-tal-i-ty *n.* death caused by a disaster or accident
fat cat *n.*, *Slang* powerful and wealthy person
fate *n.* predetermine events
fate-ful *adj.* governed by fate
fa-ther *n.* male parent **Father** a priest
fath-om *n.* length equal to six feet
fath-om-less *adj.* too deep to measure
fa-tigue *n.* condition of extreme tiredness
fatigues military clothes
fat-ty *adj.* greasy
fat-u-ous *adj.* silly and foolish
fau-cet *n.* valve to draw liquids from a pipe
faugh *interj.* exclamation of contempt
fault *n.* impairment or defect
fault-find-er *n.* a petty critic
fau-vism *n.* art movement noted for flamboyant colors
faux pas *n.* a false step; a social blunder
fa-vor *n.* a helpful or considerate act
fa-vor-a-ble *adj.* expressing approval **favorableness** *n.*
fa-vor-ite *n.* preferred above all others **favoritism** *n.*
fawn *n.* a young deer; yellowish brown color
fay *n.* fairy or elf
faze *v.* to disconcert
fe-al-ty *n.* loyalty owed to a feudal lord
fear *n.* anticipation of danger
fear-less *adj.* without fear; brave
fea-si-ble *adj.* capable of be[illegible] complished
feast *n.* a delicious meal
feat *n.* notable achievemen[illegible]
feath-er *n.* protective cov[illegible] **feathery** *adj.*
feather bed *n.* feather[illegible]

feather-stitch *n.* an embroidery stitch
feather-weight *n.* light weight boxer
fea-ture *n.* appearance or shape of the face
feb-ri-fuge *n.* medicine used to reduce fever
feb-rile *adj.* relating to a fever
fe-ces *pl. n.* bodily waste; excrement
feck-less *adj.* weak; worthless
fe-cund *adj.* fruitful; productive
fe-cun-date *v.* make fertile
fed-er-al *adj.* agreement between two or more states
fed-er-ate *v.* unite in a federal union
fed-er-a-tion *n.* two or more states joining a confederacy
fe-do-ra *n.* soft hat
fed up *adj.* extremely annoyed
fee *n.* fixed charge; charge for a professional service
fee-ble *adj.* very weak
feeble minded *adj.* mentally deficient
feed *v.* supply with food
feel *v.* perceive through the sense of touch
feel-ing *n.* sensation by touch
feign *v.* make a false show of; to fabricate **feigned** *adj.*
feint *n.* deceptive or misleading movement
fe-lic-i-tate *v.* to wish happiness **felicitation** *n.*
fe-lic-i-tous *adj.* most appropriate
fe-lic-i-ty *n.* great hapiness; bliss
fe-line *adj.* relating to cats
fel-low *n.* boy or man
fel-low-ship *n.* group with common interests
fel-ly *n.* rim of a wooden wheel
fel-on *n.* one who has committed a felony
fel-o-ny *n.* serious crime
felt *n.* unwoven fabric
fe-male *n.* sex that produces ova
fem-i-nine *adj.* pertaining to the female sex **femininity** *n.*
femme fa-tale *n.* seductive, charming woman
fe-mur *n.* leg bone
fen *n.* low marshy land
fence *n.* boundary or barrier
fenc-ing *n.* sport of using a foil or saber
fend *v.* ward off
fend-er *n.* covering for the wheel of a car
fen-nel *n.* herb of the carrot family
fe-ral *adj.* not tame or domesticated
fer--de--lance *n.* snake
fer-men-ta-tion *n.* decomposition of complex organic compounds
fern *n.* flowerless, seedless plants
fe-ro-cious *adj.* extremely savage
fer-ret *n.* small, red-eyed polecat
fer-rous *adj.* containing iron
fer-rule *n.* cap at the end of a cane
fer-ry *n.* boat to transport people and vehicles
fer-tile *adj., Biol.* ability to reproduce
fer-til-ize *v.* make fertile
fer-til-iz-er *n.* manure which enriches
[illegible]ick to punish children

fer-vent *adj.* passionate; very hot
fer-vor *n.* great intensity
fes-cue *n.* tough perennial grass
fes-ter *v.* develop pus
fes-ti-val *n.* holiday or celebration
fes-toon *n.* garland of flowers, etc.
fet-a *n.* Greek cheese white in color
fetch *v.* go after and return with
fetch-ing *adj.* very attractive or pleasing
fete *n.* large elaborate party
fet-id *adj.* having a foul odor; stinking **fetidly** *adv.*
fet-ish *n.* object having magical powers
fet-lock *n.* tuft of hair on the back of the leg of a horse
fet-ter *n.* chain to prevent escape
fe-tuc-ci-ne *n.* pasta
fe-tus *n.* unborn organism carried within the womb
feud *n.* bitter family quarrel
fe-ver *n.* abnormally high body temperature
fever blister *n.* cold sore
few *adj.* small in number
fey *adj.* acting as if under a spell
fez *n.* red felt, black-tasseled hat
fi-an-ce *n.* man engaged to be married
fi-an-cee *n.* woman engaged to be married
fi-as-co *n.* complete or total failure
fi-at *n.* positive order or decree
fib *n.* trivial lie
fi-ber *n.* piece of synthetic material
fiber-board *n.* tough building material
fiber-glass *n.* non-flammable material of spun glass
fiber optics *pl., n.* light transmitted through flexible glass rods
fib-ril-la-tion *n., Pathol.* uncoordinated contraction of the muscle of the heart
-fic *adj., suffix* causing; rendering
-fication *n., suffix* production
fi-chu *n.* scarf
fick-le *adj.* inconstant; changeable
fic-tion *n.* something created or imaginary **fictional** *adj.*
fic-ti-tious *adj.* nonexistent; imaginary **fictitiously** *adv.*
fid-dle *v.* play a violin; spend time on a fruitless activity
fiddler crab *n.* small burrowing crab
fid-dle-sticks *interj.* to express mild disgust
fi-del-i-ty *n.* faithfulness or loyalty
fidg-et *v.* move nervously or restlessly
fidgets *pl, n.* condition of being nervous **fidgetity** *adj.*
fief *n.* feudal estate
field *n.* piece of cultivated land
field marshal *n.* army official in Europe
fiend *n.* evil spirit or demon
fierce *adj.* savage and violent
fier-y *adj.* composed of fire
fi-es-ta *n.* religious holiday or festival
fife *n.* small, shrilltoned instrument
fig *n.* tree bearing an edible fruit
fight *v.* argue or quarrel **fighting** *n.*
fight-er *n.* person who fights; airplane
fig-ment *n.* invention or fabrication
fig-u-ra-tive *adj.* containing a figure of speech **figuratively** *adv.*
fig-ure *n.* symbol that represents a num-

ber; human form or body
figure eight *n.* ice skating maneuver
figure-head *n.* person with nominal leadership
fig-u-rine *n.* molded figure; a statuette
fil-a-ment *n.* finely spun thread, or wire
fil-bert *n.* edible nut; **filch** *v.* to steal
file *n.* device for storing papers; grinding tool
fi-let *n.* filet of meat or fish
filet mi-gnon *n.* small, tender cut of beef
fil-i-al *adj.* relating to a son or daughter
fil-i-buster *n.* attempt to hinder legislative action
fil-i-gree *n.* lace-like ornamental work
fill *v.* supply fully; satisfy a need; put into **filling** *n.*
fill-er *n.* something added to increase weight or bulk
fil-lip *n.* snap of the finger
fil-ly *n.* female horse
film *n.* photosensitive paper used in photography
film-strip *n.* strip of film for projection on a screen
fil-ter *n.* device used to purify
filth *n.* dirty or foul
filth-y *adj.* covered with filth; dirty **filthiness** *n.*
fin *n.* extension of the body for swimming
fi-na-gle *v., Slang* get something by trickery
fi-nal *adj.* pertaining to the end; last **finally** *adv.*
fi-na-le *n.* last part; final scene in a play
fi-nal-ist *n.* person in the final round of a contest
fi-nal-ize *v.* put into final form **finalization** *n.*
fi-nance *n.* science of monetary affairs **financial** *adj.*
fin-an-cier *n.* expert in large-scale financial affairs
finch *n.* small bird
find *v.* come upon unexpectedly
find-ing *n.* something discovered
fine *adj.* superior in skill or quality; healthy **finely** *adv.*
fin-er-y *n.* elaborate jewels and clothes
fin-esse *n.* highly refined skill
fin-ger *n.* digits of the hand
finger-board *n.* wood on the neck of a stringed instrument
finger bowl *n.* bowl of water for cleansing the fingers
finger-nail *n.* transparent covering of the dorsal surface of each finger
fin-i-al *n.* ornamental projection on a lamp shade
fin-ick-y *adj.* hard to please; choosy
fi-nis *n.* the end
fin-ish *v.* bring to an end; to conclude **finished** *adj.*
fi-nite *adj.* having bounds or limits
fink *n.* person who breaks a strike; unsavory person
fir *n.* evergreen tree
fire *n.* chemical reaction of burning
fire alarm *n.* device to alert an outbreak of fire
fire-arm *n.* small weapon
fire-ball *n.* very bright meteor
fire-break *n.* strip of land cleared to prevent a fire from spreading
fire-bug *n.* one who enjoys setting fire
fire-cracker *n.* small explosive set off to make noise
fire engine *n.* vehicle to carry firemen and their equipment
fire escape *n.* emergency exit from a building
fire extinguisher *n.* apparatus containing fire-extinguishing chemicals
fire fighter *n.* person who fights fires as an occupation
fire-fly *n.* insect that glows at night
fire-proof *adj.* resistant to fires
fire-trap *n.* unsafe building
fire-works *pl. n.* explosives for entertainment
firm *adj.* solid or unyielding to pressure
fir-ma-ment *n.* the sky
first *adj.* preceding all others
first aid *n.* temporary medical care
first-born *n.* child who is born first
first class *n.* highest group in a classification
first-hand *adj.* directly from the original source
firth *n.* narrow inlet or arm of the sea
fis-cal *adj.* relating to the finances or treasury of a nation
fish *n., pl.* cold-blooded, aquatic animal **fishing** *n.*
fish-y *adj.* creating doubt of suspicion
fis-sile *adv.* capable of being separated
fis-sion *n.* process of splitting into parts
fis-sure *n.* narrow crack in a rock
fist *n.* the hand closed tightly
fit *v.* be the proper size and shape; be in good physical condition
fitch *n.* hide of a polecat
fit-ful *adj.* capricious; restless
fit-ing *adj.* suitable or proper
five *n.* number equal to 4 + 1
fix *v.* make firm; mend; repair
fix-a-tion *n.* state of being fixed
fix-ture *n.* part or appendage of a house
fizz *n.* hissing or bubbling sound
flab *n.* excessive, loose body tissue
flabbergast *v.* overwhelm with shock; astound
flac-cid *adj.* lacking resilience or firmness
flac-on *n.* small, decorative bottle
flag *n.* banner of a country or nation
flag-el-lant *n.* whipping for sexual excitement
fla-grant *adj.* disgraceful; notorious
flair *n.* aptitude or talent for something
flak *n.* antiaircraft fire
flake *n.* thin piece peeled off a surface
flam-boy-ant *adj.* ornate; showy; florid
flame *n.* mass of burning vapor from a fire
fla-men-co *n.* a fiery percussive dance
flame-out *n.* failure of a jet aircraft engine while in flight
fla-min-go *n.* large, tropical wading bird
flam-ma-ble *adj.* capable of catching fire
flange *n.* collar used to strengthen or guide a wheel
flank *n.* fleshy part of the hip

flan-nel *n.* woven wool fabric
flap-per *n.* woman of the 1920's
flare *v.* blaze up with a bright light
flash *v.* burst into a brilliant fire or light
flash-back *n.* interruption of a story, for something that happened earlier
flash card *n.* card with numbers, letters, etc. used as a learning tool
flash-y *adj.* tastelessly showy; gaudy
flask *n.* glass container used in laboratories
flat *adj.* extending horizontally; prostrate or prone
flat-bed *n.* truck without sides
flat-car *n.* railroad car with no roof or sides
flat-ten *v.* to knock down; make flat
flat-ter *v.* praise extravagantly
flat-ter-y *n.* insincere compliments
flat-top *n.* aircraft carrier; short haircut
flat-u-lent *adj.* having gas in the intestine
flat-ware *n.* eating utensils
flaunt *v.* display showily
flau-tist *n.* a flutist
fla-vor *n.* distinctive taste of something **flavorful** *adj.*
fla-vor-ing *n.* substance used to increase the flavor
flaw *n.* defect or blemish
flaw-less *adj.* without defects; perfect
flax *n.* plant that yields linseed oil
flay *v.* remove the skin of; to scold harshly
flea *n.* blood-sucking, parasitic
flea market *n.* place to sell secondhand items
fleck *n.* tiny spot
fledg-ling *n.* a young bird; immature or inexperienced person
flee *v.* run away; to move swiftly away
fleece *n.* soft wool covering a sheep
fleet *n.* number of warships
flesh *n.* soft tissue of the human body
flesh-ly *adj.* pertaining to the body; sensual; worldly
fleur-de-lis *n., pl.* **fleurs-de-lis** heraldic emblem
flex *v.* to contract a muscle
flex-i-ble *adj.* capable of being bent; capable of adjusting to new situations; pliable
flex time *n.* system allowing employees to set their own work schedules
flick *n.* light, quick snapping movement
flick-er *v.* burn or shine unsteadily
fli-er *n.* aviator; printed advertisement of handbill
flight *n.* a scheduled airline trip
flight-y *adj.* inclined to act in a fickle fashion **flightiness** *n.*
flim-flam *n. Slang* swindle; trick; hoax
flim-sy *adj.* lacking substance; of inferior workmanship
flinch *v.* wince or pull back in pain
fling *v.* throw or toss violently; period devoted to self-indulgence
flip *v.* throw suddenly with a jerk
flip--flop *n.* sound of something flapping loosely; sudden reverse of direction
flip-pant *adj.* showing disrespect
flip-per *n.* flat limb of a seal for swimming
flip side *n.* reverse or opposite side
flirt *v.* make teasing romantic overtures **flirtation** *n.*
flit *v.* move rapidly or abruptly
flit-ter *v.* to flutter
float *n.* suspend on water; cork on a fishing line
flock *n.* group of animals
floe *n.* large, flat mass of floating ice
flog *v.* beat hard with a whip or stick **flogger** *n.*
flood *n.* an overflow of water onto land
flood-gate *n.* valve to control flow or depth of water
flood-light *n.* intensely bright beam of light
floor *n.* level base of a room
floor exercise *n.* competitive gymnastics event with tumbling maneuvers
floor show *n.* entertainment at a night club
flop *v.* fall down clumsily
flop house *n.* cheap, rundown hotel
floppy disk *n.* flexible plastic disk used to record and store computer data
flo-ra *n.* plants grown in a specific region
flo-ral *adj.* pertaining to flowers
flor-id *adj.* rosy color or redness; ornate; covered with flowers
flo-rist *n.* one who grows or sells flowers **floristry** *n.*
floss *n.* embroidery thread; dental floss
flo-til-la *n.* fleet of small vessels
flot-sam *n.* debris from sunken ships
floun-der *v.* struggle clumsily for footing; flat fish
flour *n.* ground meal of wheat
flour-ish *v.* thrive; prosper and succeed
flout *v.* show open contempt for **floutingly** *adv.*
flow *v.* move freely, as a fluid
flow-er *n.* cluster of colored petals
flub *v.* botch; to make a mess of
fluc-tu-ate *v.* shift irregularly; to change **fluctuation** *n.*
flue *n.* pipe for escaping smoke
flu-ent *adj.* capable of flowing; facile in speech **fluently** *adv.*
flu-id *n.* substance, as water cap-able of flowing
fluke *n.* flat fish; stroke of good luck
flunk *v., Slang* fail an examination or course
flun-ky *n.* person who does menial work; servant
flu-o-res-cence *n., Chem., Phys.* electromagnetic radiation
fluorescent lamp *n.* tubular electric lamp
fluor-i-date *v.* sodium compound to prevent tooth decay
flu-o-rine *n.* pale yellow, gasous element
flu-o-ro-scope *n.* instrument used for observing the human body by means of x-rays
flur-ry *n.* sudden gust of wind; brief, light fall of snow
flush *v.* flow or rush out suddenly; become red in the face
flus-ter *v.* make nervous or confused
flute *n.* highpitched, woodwind instrument
flut-ist *n.* a flute player

flut-ter *v.* flap or wave irregularly
flux *n.* a constant flow or movement
flux-ion *n.* constant change
fly *v.* move through the air on wings or wing-like parts; travel by air
flyable *adj.*
flying saucer *n.* unidentified moving objects in the sky described as being saucershaped
fly-wheel *n.* rotating wheel to regulate the speed of a machine shaft
foal *n.* young horse, especially one under a year old
foam *n.* mass of bubbles on liquid; roth **foamy** *adj.*
fob *n.* chain attached to a pocket watch
fo-cus *v.* produce a sharp clear image of; adjust a lens
fod-der *n.* coarse feed for livestock
foe *n.* enemy in war; adversary
fog *n.* vapor mass of condensed water lying close to the ground
fog-horn *n.* horn sounded to give warning in a fog
fo-gy *n.* a person with old-fashioned attitudes and ideas
foi-ble *n.* minor flaw; weakness
foil *v.* prevent from being successful; to thwart
foist *v.* pass off as valuable or genuine; force to accept by deceit
fold *v.* double or lay one part over another
fol-de-rol *n.* pretty but useless ornament
fo-li-age *n.* leaves on plants and trees
fo-li-o *n.* folder for loose papers
folk *n., pl.* **folk** *or* **folks** ethnic group of people forming a nation or tribe; a person's parents
fol-li-cle *n.* small anatomical cavity
fol-low *v.* proceed or come after; to pursue
fol-ly *n., pl.* **fillies** an instance of foolishness; costly or unprofitable undertaking
fo-ment *v.* to rouse; to incite; treat with moist heat
fond *adj.* affectionate; cherished with great affection **fondness** *n.*
fon-dant *n.* sweet soft preparation of sugar used in candies
fon-dle *v.* stroke or caress tenderly
fond-ly *adv.* in a willingly credulous manner
fon-due *n.* preparation of melted cheese and wine for dipping food into
font *n.* receptacle that holds baptismal or holy water; assortment of printing type
food *n.* substance consisting of carbohydrates and protein to sustain life
fool *n.* one lacking good sense or judgment
foot *n., pl.* **feet** lower extremity of the leg upon which one stands; unit of measurement equal to 12 inches
foot-ball *n.* game played with an inflated ball
foot-bridge *n.* bridge for pedestrians
foot-hill *n.* hill at the foot of a mountain
foot-hold *n.* place to support the foot
foot-ing *n.* stable position for placement of the feet; a foundation
foot-locker *n.* trunk for personal belongings
foot-loose *adj.* having no ties; free to move about
foot-note *n.* note of reference below the text; a commentary
foot-path *n.* narrow path for people on foot
foot-print *n.* outline of the foot on a surface
foot-stool *n.* low stool for resting the feet
foot-work *n.* use of the feet, as in boxing
fop *n.* man concerned with his appearance **foppish** *adj.*
for *prep.* used to indicate the extent of something; behalf of someone; to be in favor of
for-age *n.* food for domestic animals; search for supplies or food **forager** *n.*
for-ay *n.* a raid to plunder
for-bear *v.* refrain from; to cease from **forbearance** *n.*
for-bid *v.* command not to do something; to prohibit by law
forbidding *adj.* very difficult; disagreeable
force *n.* energy or power; strength; intellectual influence **forceful** *adj.*
force-meat *n.* ground meat, fish, etc., used in stuffing
for-ceps *n.* **forceps** *pl.* instrument resembling a pair of tongs used in surgery
forc-i-ble *adj.* achieved or accomplished by force
ford *n.* shallow place in a body of water for crossing
fore *adj. & adv.* situated in, at, or toward the front; golfer's warning
fore--and--aft *adj.* from stem to stern
fore-arm *n.* part of the arm between the elbow and the wrist
fore-bear *or* **for-bear** *n.* an ancestor
fore-bode *v.* give a warning in advance; have a premonition of something evil
fore-cast *v.* estimate in advance; predict the weather
fore-cas-tle *n.* living quarters for the crew of a merchant ship
fore-close *v.* recall a mortgage in default; to exclude; to shut out
fore-fa-ther *n.* ancestor
fore-fin-ger *n.* finger next to the thumb
fore-foot *n.* front foot of an animal
fore-front *n.* very front of something; the vanguard
fore-go *v.* to precede in time, place, etc.
for-eign *adj.* outside one's native country
for-eign-er *n.* person from a different place or country; an alien
fore-knowl-edge *n.* prior knowledge of something
fore-lock *n.* lock of hair growing over the forehead
fore-man *n.* person who oversees a group of people; spokesperson for a jury
fore-most *adj. & adv.* first in rank or order
fo-ren-sic *adj.* relating to a formal debate
fore-or-dain *v.* appoint advance; predestine

fore-see *v.* know or see beforehand **foreseeable** *adj.*
fore-sight *n.* capacity of foreseeing; concern for the future **forsighted** *adj.*
for-est *n.* tract of land covered with trees
forest ranger *n.* man in charge of protecting a public forest
fore-tell *v.* tell in advance; to predict
for-ev-er *adv.* for eternity; without end
fore-warn *v.* warn in advance
for-feit *n.* something taken away as punishment; a penalty **forfeitable** *adj.*
for-gath-er *v.* come together; to assemble
forge *n.* furnace to heat metals; a smithy *v.* give shape to; defraud
for-get *v.* lose the memory of **-ful** *adj.*
for-give *v.* pardon; to cease to feel resentment against
for-go *or* **fore-go** *v.* to give up or refrain from **forgoer** *n.*
fork *n.* eating utensil with prongs; division in a river or road
for-lorn *adj.* left in distress; hopeless; forsaken **forlornly** *adv.*
form *n.* contour of something; human body; manner determined by etiquette; fitness training; document
form *suff.* having the form or shape of; cuneiform
for-mal *adj.* adhering to convention; explicit; correct manners
for-mal-de-hyde *n.* colorless, gaseous chemical used as a disinfectant
for-mat *n.* style of a publication; basic design
for-ma-tion *n.* a given arrangement
for-ma-tive *adj.* having the power to form; pertaining to growth, or development
for-mer *adj.* previous; being the first of two persons mentioned or referred to
for-mer-ly *adv.* previously
for-mi-da-ble *adj.* extremely difficult; causing fear by size or strength **formidably** *adv.*
for-mu-la *n.* prescribed rules to be used; milk substitute for infants
for-mu-late *v.* state or express as a formula **formulation** *n.*
for-ni-ca-tion *n.* illicit sexual intercourse
for-sake *v.* abandon or renounce; to give up
for-sooth *adv.* in truth; certainly
for-swear *v.* renounce emphatically or upon oath; swear falsely; to perjure oneself
for-syth-i-a *n.* shrub with earlyblooming, bright, yellow flowers
fort *n.* fortified enclosure for defense against an enemy
forte *n.* activity one does with excellence; person's strong point
forth *adv.* out from seclusion; forward in order, place, or time
forth-with *adv.* at once; promptly
for-ti-fy *v.* provide physical strength; give courage to; enrich food with vitamins, etc.
for-ti-tude *n.* strength of mind; courage
fort-night *n.* period of two weeks **fortnightly** *adj. & adv.*
for-tress *n.* a fort
for-tu-i-tous *adj.* occurring by chance; lucky; fortunate
for-tu-nate *adj.* having good fortune
for-tune *n.* force that determines events; large amount of money
for-tune--tell-er *n.* person who predicts the future
for-ty *n.* number equal to four times ten
forty winks *n., Slang* short nap
fo-rum *n.* public market-place in ancient Rome where business is transacted; a judicial assembly
for-ward *adj.* toward a place or time in advance **forwardy** *adv.*
fos-sil *n.* remains of a past geologic age
fos-ter *v.* give parental care to; nurture
foul *adj.* spoiled or rotten; vulgar or obscene; dirty
found *v.* establish; to set up; melt metal and pour into a mold
foun-da-tion *n.* base of a building; make-up base
foun-dry *n.* place where metal is cast
fount *n.* a fountain; abundant source
foun-tain *n.* natural spring of water from the earth; artifically created spray of water
four-score *adj.* four times twenty; eighty
fourth *n.* gear in a motor vehicle
Fourth of July *n.* American Independence Day
fowl *n.* bird used as food or hunted as game
fox *n.* wild mammal; sly or crafty person
fox-hole *n.* shallow pit dug by a soldier to protect him from enemy fire
fox--trot *n.* ballroom dance
fox-y *adj.* sly or crafty; sharp
foy-er *n.* lobby of a hotel, theatre, etc.; entrance hall
fra-cas *n.* noisy quarrel or disturbance
frac-tion *n.* small part of; quantity less than a whole number **fractional** *adj.*
frac-ture *n.* act of breaking; broken bone
frag-ile *adj.* easily broken; frail
frag-ment *n.* broken or detached part
fra-grant *adj.* having an agreeable sweet odor **frangrance** *n.*
frail *adj.* physically weak; fragile
frame *v.* enclosed border for a picture
frame-up *Slang* make someone appear guilty
fran-chise *n.* license to market a company's goods **franchiser** *n.*
fran-gi-ble *adj.* breakable; delicate **frangibility** *n.*
frank-furt-er *n.* smoked sausage made of beef or beef and pork
frank-in-cense *n.* aromatic gum resin used as incense
fran-tic *adj.* emotionally out of control with worry or fear **frantically** *adv.*
fra-ter-nal *adj.* pertaining to brothers **fraternalism** *n.*
frat-er-nize *v.* associate with others in a friendly way; mingle
frat-ri-cide *n.* killer of one's brother or sister **fratricidal** *adj.*
fraud *n.* deception for unlawful gain; imposter
fraud-u-lent *adj.* practicing fraud **fraudulently** *adv.*

fraught *adj.* accompanied by something specified
fray *n.* heated argument or dispute
fraz-zle *v., Slang* wear out; completely fatigue
freak *n.* seemingly capricious event; person with abnormalities; **freak out** experience hallucinations from drug use **freakish** *adj.*
freck-le *n.* brownish, suninduced spots on the skin
free *adj.* not imprisoned; costing nothing; under no obligation
free-bie *n.* something given or received with out charge
free-dom *n.* state of being free; independence
freeze *v.* become ice through loss of heat; set prices at a certain level
freight *n.* mode of shipping cargo; charge for shipping freight
freight-er *n.* ship for transporting cargo
fren-zy *n.* state of excitement or violent agitation
fre-quent *adj.* happening often or time after time
fres-co *n.* art of painting on moist plaster
fresh *adj.* newlymade, or obtained; not stale **freshness** *n.*
fresh-man *n.* first year student in college
fret *v.* anxious or irritated; ripple water **fretfully** *adv.*
fri-a-ble *adj.* easily crumbled; brittle **friableness** *n.*
fri-ar *n.* member of a Roman Catholic order
fric-as-see *n.* dish of meat or poultry in gravy
fric-tion *n.* rubbing one surface against another; a conflict or clash **-al** *adj.*
friend *n.* close personal companion **friendship** *n.*
frieze *n.* decorative band along a wall
frig-ate *n.* square-rigged warship
fright *n.* sudden alarm or fear
fright-en *v.* fill with fear; arousing fear **frighteningly** *adv.*
frig-id *adj.* very cold; sexually unresponsive **frigidity** *n.*
frill *n.* decorative ruffle; gathered border
fringe *n.* edging that consists of hanging threads, or loops
frisk *v.* skip or leap about playfully; to search someone for a concealed weapon by running the hands over the clothing quickly
frit-ter *v.* squander or waste little by little
friv-o-lous *adj.* trivial; insignificant; not serious; silly
frizz *v.* form into small, tight curls **frizziness** *n.*
fro *adv.* away from; back, as running to and fro
frock *n.* loosefitting robe; a robe worn by monks
frol-ic *n.* merriness; a playful, carefree occasion; playful
from *prep.* starting at a particular time or place; used to indicate a source; used to indicate differentiation, as knowing right from left
frond *n.* large leaf of a tropical fern, usually divided into smaller leaflets
front *n.* forward surface of an object or body; area or position located ahead
fron-tier *n.* part of an international border or the area adjacent to it; an unexplored area of knowledge or thought **frontiersman** *n.*
fron-tis-piece *n.* an illustration that usually precedes the title page of a book
frost *n.* feathery covering of minute ice crystals on a cold surface; icing on a cake **frostiness** *n.*
froth *n.* mass of bubbles on or in a liquid, resulting from agitation or fermentation; a salivary foam, as of an animal, resulting from disease **frothiness** *n.*
frou-frou *n.* rustling sound, as of silk; a frilly dress or decoration
frown *v.* contract the brow as in displeasure or concentration; to look on with distaste or disapproval
frow-zy *adj.* appearing unkempt
fro-zen *adj.* changed into, or made into ice; extremely cold, as a climate; immobilized or made rigid, as by fear; kept at a fixed level
fruc-tose *n.* sugar
fru-gal *adj.* economical; thrifty
fruit *n., pl.* **fruit** *or* **fruits** ripened, mature, seed-bearing part of a flowering plant, as a pod or berry; edible, fleshy plant part an apple or plum **-ful** *adj.*
fru-i-tion *n.* accomplishment of something worked for or desired; the state of bearing fruit
frump-y *adj.* unfashionable; dowdy **frumpiness** *n.*
frus-trate *v.* keep from attaining a goal or fulfilling a desire; to thwart
fry *v.* cook in hot fat or oil, especially over direct heat; *n.* dish of any fried food
fud-dy--dud-dy *n., pl.* **fuddy-duddies** an old-fashioned person
fuel *n.* combustible matter consumed to generate energy, such as wood, coal, or oil burned to generate heat; *v.* take in or supply with fuel; to stimulate, as an argument **fueler** *n.*
fu-gi-tive *adj.* fleeing or having fled, as from arrest, pursuit, etc. *n.* One who flees or tries to escape
ful-crum *n., pl.* **fulcrums** *or* **fulcra** point on which a lever turns
ful-fill *v.* convert into actuality; to effect; to carry out; to satisfy **fulfillment** *n.*
ful-minate *v.* condemn severely; to explode
ful-some *adj.* offensively insincere **fulsomeness** *n.*
fum-ble *v.* to blunder; to mishandle a baseball or football; *n.* a fumbled ball
fume *n., often* **fumes** irritating smoke, gas, or vapor; *v.* to show or feel anger or distress
fu-mi-gate *v.* subject to fumes in order to exterminate vermin or insects **-gator** *n.*
fun *n.* enjoyment; amusement
func-tion *n.* characteristics or proper ac-

tivity of a person or thing; specific occupation, duty, or role; an official ceremony

fund *n.* a sum of money reserved for a specific purpose; *v.* to furnish or accumulate a fund for

fun-da-men-tal *adj.* basic or essential; of major significance

fu-ner-al *n.* service performed in conjunction with the burial or cremation of a dead person

fun-gus *n.* **funguses** numerous sporebearing plants including mushrooms **fungal** *adj.*

fu-nic-u-lar *n.* a cable railway along which cable cars are drawn up a mountain counterbalancing one another

funk *n.* cowardly fright or panic; fear; a state of depression

funk-y *adj., Slang* an earthy quality that is characteristic of the blues **-iness** *n.*

fun-nel *n.* coneshaped utensil for pouring liquid

fur-be-low *n.* decorative ruffle on clothing

fur-bish *v.* make bright by rubbing; renovate

fu-ri-ous *adj.* extremely angry; fit of rage **furiously** *adv.*

furl *v.* roll up and secure something

fur-lough *n.* permission to be absent from duty

fur-nace *n.* device to produce intense heat

fur-nish *v.* outfit or equip with furniture **furnisher** *n.*

fur-ni-ture *n.* beds, lamps, chairs and tables, etc.

fu-ror *n.* violent anger; an uproar

fur-rier *n.* dealer in furs

fur-row *n.* long, narrow trench; deep wrinkle in the skin

fur-tive *adj.* done in secret; obtained underhandedly

fu-ry *n.* uncontrolled anger; turbulence

fuse *n.* electrical safety device; device to detonate explosives

fu-see *n.* friction match; signal flare

fus-si-lage *n.* central section of an airplane

fu-sil-lade *n.* discharge of a number of firearms

fu-sion *n.* the act or procedure of melting together by heat; a blend produced by fusion; a nuclear reactio in which nuclei of a light element combine to form mor massive nuclei, with the release of huge amounts of energy

fuss *v.* argue; bother

fussy *adj.* giving close attention to details

fu-tile *adj.* ineffectual; serving no useful purpose; hopeless

fu-til-i-ty *n.* the state or quality of being futile

fu-ture *n.* time yet to come **future** *adj.*

fu-tur-is-tic *adj.* relating to the future

fuzz *n.* small particles of fibers that may sometime collect as a ball **fuzzy** *adj.*

fyke *n.* a long net bag that is kept open with hoops

G, g The seventh letter of the English alphabet.

gab *v., Slang* talk or chat idly

gab-ar-dine *n.* a firm cotton, wool, or rayon material, having a diagonal raised weave, used for suits or coats

gab-ble *v.* to speak rapidly or incoherently gabble *n.*

Gabriel *n.* a special messenger of God mentioned in the Bible

gad *v.* to wander about restlessly

gad-a-bout *n., Slang* person who seeks excitement

gad--fly *n.* a fly that bites or annoys cattle and horses; an irritating, critical, but often constructively provocative person.

gadg-et *n., Slang* small or tool for various jobs

gad-o-lin-i-um *n.* a metallic element, silvery-white in color, of the lanthanide series, symbolized by Gd

Gae-a *n.* in Greek mythology, the mother and wife of Uranus, the goddess of earth.

Geal *n.* one of the Celts of Scotland, Ireland, or the Isle of Man

gaff *n.* sharp iron hook used for landing fish

gaffe *n.* a mistake which is made and it is a blunder or stupid

gaf-fer *n.* an old man

gag *n.* wadded cloth, forced into the mouth to prevent speach *Slang* practical joke

ga-ga *adj. Slang* crazy; silly

gage *n.* something, as a wadded cloth, forced into or over the mouth to prevent someone from speaking or crying out; an obstacle to or any restraint of free speech, such as by censorship; *Slang* a practical joke

gag-gle *n.* flock of geese

gai-e-ty *n., pl.* **gaieties** state of being happy; cheerfulness

gai-ly *adv.* doing something in a cheerfully or gay manner

gain *v.* to earn or acquire possession

gain-er *n.* the person who gains something

gain-ful *adj.* producing profits

gain-say *v.* to deny; to contradict

gait *n.* a way or manner of moving on foot; one of the foot movements in which a horse steps or runs

gai-ter *n.* a covering, as of leather or canvas, that covers the leg and extends from the knee to the instep; an old-fashioned shoe with a high top and elastic sides

gal *n., Slang* a girl

ga-la *n.* festive celebration

ga-lac-tic *adj.* referring to or pertaining to the Mifkey Way or the galaxies

ga-lac-tose *n.* the sugar typically occurring in lactose

gal-ax-y *n., pl.* **galaxies** *Astron.* very large cluster of stars

gale *n., Meteor.* very powerful wind

ga-le-na *n.* a metallic, dull gray mineral that is the principal or of lead

gall *n., Physiol.* bitter fluid secreted by

the liver; bile
gal-lant *adj.* polite and attentive to women
gal-lant-ry *n.* nobility and bravery
gall-blad-der *or* **gall bladder** *n.* small sac under the right liver that stores bile
gal-le-on *n.* large sailing ship
gal-ler-y *n., pl.* **-ries** group of spectators; building that displays works of art
gal-ley *n., pl.* **galleys** a long medieval ship ;that was propelled by sails and oars; the long tray used bvy printers to hold set type; a printer's proof made from composed type, used to detect and correct errors
gal-ley proof *n.* the proof which is taken from a galley to enable corrections before a page is printed
gal-ley slave *n.* the person who is condemned to work in a galley; a person who is overworked
gal-li-cism *n.* the French idiom which can be used in another language
gal-li-mau-fry *n.* a mixture or a medley of something
gall-ing *adj.* to be annoying or bothersome to another
gal-li-nule *n.* a wading bird with dark iridescent plumage
gal-li-um *n.* a slivery metallic element used in semiconductor technology and as a component or various low-melting alloys, symbolized by Ga
gal-li-vant *v.* roam about in search of pleasure
gal-lon *n.* liquid measurement equal to 4 quarts
gal-lop *n.* horse's gait
gal-lows *n.* framework used for execution by hanging
gall-stone *n., Pathol.* small, stony mass that forms in the gall bladder
ga-loot *n.* a person who is clumsy or uncouth
ga-lore *adj.* in great numbers
ga-losh *n.* waterproof overshoes which are worn in bad weather
ga-lumph *v.* to bump along
gal-van-ic *adj.* producing with shocking, or by galvanism
gal-va-nism *n.* electricity produced by chemical action
gal-va-nize *v.* to protect iron or steel with rust resistant zinc
gal-va-nom-e-ter *n., Electr.* apparatus that detects electric and its strength and direction
gam-bit *n.* an opening in chess where a piece is sacrificed
gam-ble *v.* to take a chance
gam-bol *v.* frolic, skip, or leap about in play
gam-brel roof *Archit.* a ridged roof with the slop broken on each side, the lower slope steeper than the upper
game *n.* contest having rules; animals or birds hunted for sport or food
game-cock *n.* a rooster which is bred and trained for to sport of cockfighting
game-keep-er *n.* n a person in charge of protecting and maintaining wildlife on a private preserve
gam-ete *n., Biol.* mature reproductive cells
gam-in *n.* homeless child
gam-mer *n.* eiderly woman
gam-ut *n.* whole range or extent of anything
gan-der *n.* male goose *Slang* quick glance
gang *n.* group of persons who work together or socialize regularly
gan-gling *adj.* tall and thin
gan-grene *n., Pathol.* the death and decay of tissue in the body
gang-ster *n.* member of a criminal gang
gap *n.* opening or wide crack
gape *v.* open the mouth wide
gar *n.* fish having a spearlike snout and elongated body
garb *n.* clothing
gar-bage *n.* food wastes; trash
gar-ble *v.* mix up or confuse
gar-den *n.* place for growing plants
gar-de-nia *n.* tropical shrub with fragrant white flowers
gar-gan-tu-an *adj.* of enormous size
gar-gle *v.* to cleanse or medicate the back of the mouth and throat
gar-ish *adj.* too showy and bright; gaudy
gar-land *n.* wreath of flowers or leaves
gar-lic *n.* plant having a strong odor, resembling an onion
gar-ment *n.* article of clothing
gar-ner *v.* gather and store
gar-net *n.* dark-red gemstone
gar-nish *v.* to add decoration
gar-ret *n.* room in an attic
gar-ri-son *n.* military post
gar-ter *n.* band worn to hold a stocking in place
gas *n., pl.* **gases** combustible mixture used as fuel; gasoline
gash *n.* long, deep cut
gas-ket *n., Mech.* seal to prevent the escape of fluid or gas
gas-o-hol *n.* fuel blended from unleaded gasoline and ethanol
gasp *v.* labored attempts to breathe
gas-tric *adj.* pertaining to the stomach
gas-tri-tis *n., Pathol.* inflammation of the stomach lining
gas-tron-o-my *n.* art of good eating
gate *n.* movable opening in a wall or fence
gath-er *v.* bring or come together into one place
gaud-y *adj.* too highly decorated for good taste
gauge *or* **gage** *n.* standard measurement
gaunt *adj.* thin in appearance
gaunt-let *or* **gant-let** *n.* challenge to fight
gauze *n.* loosely-woven material used for bandages
gav-el *n.* mallet used to call for order
ga-vi-al *n.* large crocodile
gawk *v.* to gape; to stare stupidly
gawk-y *adj.* Clumsy or awkward
gay *adj.* merry; happy
gaze *v.* to look steadily at something to stare
ga-zette *n.* newspaper

gear *n., Mech.* toothed wheel
gee-zer *n., Slang* an old man
geld *v.* to castrate
gem-ol-o-gy *or* **gem-mol-o-gy** *n.* study of gems
gen-der *n.* quality of being either male or female
gene *n., Biol.* means by which hereditary characteristics are given
ge-ne-al-o-gy *n., pl.* **-ies** record or study of ones ancestory
gen-er-al-ize *v.* draw a general conclusion from facts or observations
gen-er-al-i-za-tion *n.* something arrived at by generalizing
gen-er-ate *v.* cause to be; to produce
gen-er-a-tion *n.* group of individuals born about the same time
ge-ner-ic *adj.* relating to an entire class or group; general
gen-er-ous *adj.* sharing freely; abundant
gen-e-sis *n., pl.* **-ses** act or state of originating
ge-net-ic *adj.* pertaining to the development of something
gen-ial *adj.* cheerful, pleasant and good-humored
gen-i-tal *adj.* pertaining to the reproductive organs
genitals *pl.,n.* the external sexual organs
gen-i-tive *adj., Gram.* indicating origin, source, or possession
gen-ius *n., pl.* **-ses** exceptional intellectual ability a strong, natural talent
gen-o-cide *n.* systematic extermination of a race or cultural group
gen-teel *adj.* refined or well-bred
gen-tian *n.* annual or perennial plant
Gen-tile *n.* a Christian; non-Jew
gen-tle *adj.* not harsh, mild in manner
gen-tle-man *n.* man of noble birth and social position
gen-tle-wom-an *n.* woman of noble birth and social position
gen-try *n.* people of high social standing
gen-u-flect *v.* to bend down on one knee
gen-u-ine *adj.* real; not counterfeit
ge-o-cen-tric *adj.* relating to the earth's center
ge-og-ra-phy *n., pl.* **-hies** the scientific study of the earth's features and population
ge-om-e-try *n., pl.* **ies** mathematics dealing with lines, planes, and solids
ge-o-ther-mal *adj.* relating to the internal heat of the earth
ger-i-at-rics *pl., n.* medical study that deals with diseases and hygiene of old age
germ *n.* small cell from which a new organism may develop
ger-mane *adj.* relevant to what is being considered or discussed
germ cell *n.* egg or sperm cell
ger-mi-cide *n.* agent used to destroy or disease germs
ger-mi-nate *v.* to grow, develop, or sprout
gest *n.* notable deed or feat
ges-tic-u-late *v.* make expressive gestures
ges-ture *n.* bodily motion, especially with the hands in speaking
get *v.* to receive or come into the possession of
get-up *n.* an outfit; a costume
gey-ser *n.* natural spring that ejects hot water and steam
ghast-ly *adj.* horrible; terrifying
gher-kin *n.* very small pickle
ghet-to *n.* section of a city in which members of an ethnic group lives
ghost *n.* the spirit of a dead person which is believed to appear to or haunt living persons; a spirit
gib-ber *v.* to talk or chatter incoherently or unintelligibly
gib-ber-ish *n.* meaningless speech
gib-bet *n.* a gallows *v.* To execute by hanging on a gibbet
gib-bon *n.* a slender, long-armed Asian ape
gibe *v.* to ridicule or make taunting remarks **giber** *n.*
gib-let *n., or* **giblets** the heart, liver, and gizzard of a fowl
gid-dy *adj.* affected by a reeling or whirling sensation; dizzy
giddily *adv.*, **giddiness** *n.*
gift *n.* something that is given from one person to another
gifted *adj.* having a special ability; talented
gig *n.* a light, two-wheeled carriage drawn by one horse. *Naut.* A speedy, light rowboat
gi-gan-tic *adj.* of tremendous size; huge
gigantically *adv.*
gig-gle *v.* to laugh in highpitched, repeated, short sounds
giggler *n.*, **giggly** *adj.*
gig-o-lo *n.*, a man who is supported by a woman not his wife
gild *v.* to coat with a thin layer of gold; to brighten or adorn
gilded *adj.*, **gilding, gilder** *n.*
gill *n., Zool.* the organ, as of fishes and various other aquatic invertebrates, used for taking oxygen from water
gilt *adj.* covered with or of the color of gold
gim-crack *n.* a cheap and useless object of little or no value
gim-let *n.* a small, sharp tool with a bar handle and a pointed, spiral tip used for boring holes
gimp *n., Slang* a person who walks with a limp; a cripple
gin *n.* an aromatic, clear, alcoholic liquor distilled from grain and flavored with juniper berries
gin-ger *n.* a tropical Asian plant with a pungent aromatic root, used in medicine and cooking
ginger ale *n.* an effervescent soft drink flavored with ginger
gin-ger-ly *adv.* doing something very cautiously
ging-ham *n.* a cotton fabric woven in solid colors and checks
gin-gi-vi-tis *n., Pathol.* inflammation of the gums
gin rummy *n.* a variety of the card game rummy

gird *v.* to surround, encircle, or attach with or as if with a belt
gird-er *n.* a strong, horizontal beam, as of steel or wood
gir-dle *n.* a cord or belt worn around the waist; a supporting undergarment worn by women
girl *n.* a female child or infant; a young, unmarried woman
girth *n.* the circumference or distance around something
gis-mo *n., Slang* a part or device whose name is unknown or forgotten
gist *n.* the central or main substance
give *v.* to make a present of; to bestow; donate or contribute; to apply
giv-en *adj.* bestowed; presented
giz-zard *n.* the second stomach in birds
gla-brous *adj., Biol.* having no hair or down **glabrousness** *n.*
glacial epoch *Geol.* a portion of geological time when ice sheets covered much of the earth's surface
glad *adj.* displaying, experiencing, or affording joy and pleasure; being happy
glad-den *v.* to make glad
glade *n.* a clearing in a forest
glad-some *adj.* giving cheer
glam-or-ize *or* **glam-our-ize** *v.* to make glamorous
glam-our *or* **glam-or** *n.* alluring fascination or charm
glance *v.* to take a brief or quick look at something
gland *n., Anat.* any of various body organs which excrete or secrete substances
glare *v.* to stare fiercely or angrily
glau-co-ma *n., Pathol.* a disease of the eye
glau-cous *adj.* yellowish green
gleam *n.* a momentary ray or beam of light
glean *v.* to collect or gather facts by patient effort **-er** *n.,* **-ings** *pl., n.*
glee *n.* joy; merriment
glen *n.* a small, secluded valley
glib *adj.* spoken easily and fluently; superficial **glibly** *adv.,* **glibness** *n.*
glide *v.* to pass or move smoothly with little or no effort **glidingly** *adv.*
glid-er *n.* one that glides; *Aeron.* an aircraft without an engine
glim-mer *n.* a faint suggestion; an indication; a dim unsteady light
glimpse *n.* a momentary look
glis-san-do *n., pl.* **-di** a rapid passing from one tone to another by a continuous change of pitch
glis-ten *v.* to shine softly as reflected by light
glitch *n.* a minor mishap or malfunction
glit-ter *n.* a brilliant sparkle
gloam-ing *n.* twilight
gloat *v.* to express, feel, or observe with great malicious pleasure or selfsatisfaction **gloater** *n.*
glob *n.* a drop of something
glob-al *adj.* spherical; involving the whole world **globalize** *v.*
globe *n.* a spherical object; anything that is perfectly rounded
glob-u-lin *n., Biochem.* any of a class of simple proteins found widely in blood, milk, tissue, muscle and plant seeds
gloom *n.* partial or total darkness **gloomily** *adv.,* **gloominess** *n.*
glop *n., Slang* a messy mixture of food; something that is considered worthless
glo-ri-fy *v.* to worship and give glory to **glorification** *n.*
glo-ri-ous *adj.* magnificent **-ly** *adv.*
glory *n., pl.* **-ies** distinguished praise or honor
gloss *n.* the sheen or luster of a polished surface
glos-sa-ry *n., pl.* **-ries** a list of words and their meanings
glot-tis *n., pl.* **-ises** *or* **-ides** *Anat.* the opening or cleft between the vocal cords
glow *v.* to have a bright, warm, ruddy color
glow-er *v.* to look sullenly or angrily at; to glare
glox-in-i-a *n.* a tropical South American plant
glu-cose *n., Chem.* a substance less sweet than cane sugar, found as dextrose in plants and animals and obtained by hydrolysis
glut *v.* to feed or supply beyond capacity. *n.* An overabundance
glu-ten *n.* a mixture of plant proteins that is used as an adhesive **glutenous** *adj.*
glut-ton *n.* someone who eats immoderately
glyc-er-ol *n., Chem.* a sweet, oily, syrupy liquid derived from fats and oils
gly-co-side *n., Chem.* any of a group of carbohydrates which, when decomposed, produce glucose or other sugar
gnarl *n.* a hard, protruding knot on a tree **gnarled** *adj.*
gnash *v.* to grind or strike the teeth together
gnat *n.* a small, winged insect, specially one that bites or stings
gnaw *v.* to bite or eat away with persistence **gnawer** *n.*
gnome *n.* in folklore, a dwarf-like creature
go *v.* to proceed or pass along; to leave; pass, as of time *n.* an attempt; a try
go--ahead *n.* permission; a signal to move ahead or proceed
goal *n.* a purpose
goat-ee *n.* a short, pointed beard on a man's chin
goat-skin *n.* the skin of a goat
gob *n.* a piece or lump of something
gob-ble *v.* to eat and swallow food greedily
gob-bler *n.* a male turkey
go--be-tween *n.* a person who acts as an agent between two parties
gob-let *n.* a drinking glass
gob-lin *n.* in folklore, an ugly, grotesque creature said to be mischievous and evil
god *n.* someone considered to be extremely important or valuable
God *n.* the Supreme Being

god-less *adj.* not recognizing a god **godlessness** *n.*
god-ly *adj.* filled with love for God.
god-send *n.* something received unexpectedly that is needed or wanted
go--get-ter *n.* an enterprising, aggressive person
gog-gle *n., pl.* **-gles** spectacles or eyeglasses to protect the eyes
go-ing *n.* the act of moving, leaving, or departing
goi-ter *n., Pathol.* any abnormal enlargement of the thyroid gland **goitrous** *adj.*
gold *n.* a soft, yellow, metallic element that is highly ductile and resistant to oxidation
gold-en *adj.* made of or containing gold; bright yellow in color
gold-fish *n.* a reddish or brass-colored freshwater fish
Gol-go-tha *n.* the place near Jerusalem where Jesus was crucified; also known as Calvary
Go-li-ath *n.* in the Bible, a giant Philistine killed by David with a stone from a sling shot
gon-ad *n., Anat.* the male or female sex gland where the reproductive cells develop; an ovary or testis
gon-do-la *n.* a long, narrow, flat-bottomed boat
gong *n.* a heavy metal disk with a deep resonant tone
gon-o-coc-cus *n., pl.* **-cocci** the bacterium which causes gonorrhea **gonococcic** *adj.*
gon-or-rhe-a *n., Pathol.* a contagious venereal infection transmitted chiefly by sexual intercourse
goo *n.* any sticky substance
goo-ber *n., Regional* a peanut
good *adj.* having desirable or favorable qualities or characteristics; morally excellent **better, best** *adj.*
Good Book *n.* the Bible
good--by *or* **good--bye** *interj.* used to express farewell *n.* a farewell; a parting word
good--look-ing *adj.* handsome
good--na-tured *adj.* having an easygoing and pleasant disposition
good-ness *n.* the state or quality of being good
good-y *n., pl.* **-ies** something that is good to eat; a prissy person
goof *n., Slang* a mistake *v.* to blunder; to make a mistake
goof--off *n.* a person who shuns responsibility or work
goof-y *adj.* ridiculous; silly
gook *n., Slang* a slimy, sludgy, or dirty substance
goon *n., Slang* a thug or hoodlum hired to intimidate or injure someone
goose *n., pl.* **geese** a large water bird related to swans and ducks
go-pher *n.* a burrowing rodent with large cheek pouches
gore *v.* to stab or pierce *n.* blood that has been shed
gorge *n.* a deep, narrow ravine; deep or violent disgust **gorger** *n.*
gor-geous *adj.* beautiful; dazzling
go-ril-la *n.* a large African jungle ape
gorse *n.* a spiny plant bearing fragrant yellow flowers
go-ry *adj.* covered or stained with blood; resembling gore
gos-hawk *n.* a large, shortwinged hawk formerly used in falconry
gos-ling *n.* a young goose
gos-pel *or* **Gos-pel** *n.* the teachings of Christ and the apostles
gos-sa-mer *n.* the fine film or strands of a spider's web floating in the air **gossamer** *adj.*
gos-sip *n.* idle, often malicious talk *v.* to spread or engage in gossip
got *v.* past tense of get
gour-mand *n.* a person who takes excessive pleasure in eating
gour-met *n.* someone who appreciates and understands fine food and drink
gout *n., Pathol.* a disease caused by a defect in metabolism and characterized by painful inflammation of the joints **gouty** *adj.*
gov-ern *v.* to guide, rule, or control by right or authority **governable** *adj.*
gov-ern-ment *n.* the authoritative administration of public policy and affairs of a nation, state or city **-al** *adj.*
gov-er-nor *n.* one who governs, as the elected chief executive of any state in the United States **governorship** *n.*
grab *v.* to snatch or take suddenly **grabber** *n.*, **grabby** *adj.*
gra-ben *n., Geol.* an elongated depression in the earth, caused by the downward faulting of a portion of the earth's crust
grace *n.* seemingly effortless beauty, ease, and charm of movement or form
gra-da-tion *n.* a gradual and orderly arrangement or progression according to quality, size, rank, or other value **gradational** *adj.*
grade *n.* a step or degree
gra-di-ent *n.* a slope or degree of inclination *Phys.* a rate of change in variable factors, as temperature or pressure
grad-u-al *adj.* moving or changing slowly by degrees **-ly** *adv.*, **-ness** *n.*
grad-u-ate *v.* to receive or be granted an academic diploma or degree upon completion of a course of study
grad-u-a-tion *n.* the state of graduating; a commencement ceremony
graf-fi-to *n., pl.* **graffiti** an inscription or drawing made on a public wall
gra-ham *n.* whole wheat flour
grail *n.* the legendary cup used by Christ at the Last Supper
grain *n.* a small, hard seed or kernel of cereal, wheat, or oats; the seeds or fruits of such plants as a group; texture; basic nature
grain alcohol *n.* ethanol
grain-y *adj.* having a granular texture **graininess** *n.*
gram *n.* a metric unit of mass and weight equal to 1/1000 kilogram and

nearly equal to one cubic centimeter of water at its maximum density
gram-mar *n.* the study and description of the classes of words, their relations to each other, and their arrangement into sentences
gram molecule *n., Chem.* the quantity of a compound, expressed in grams, that is equal to the molecular weight of that compound
gran-a-ry *n., pl.* **-ries** a building for storing threshed grain
grand *adj.* large in size, extent, or scope; magnificent
gran-deur *n.* the quality or condition of being grand
gran-dil-o-quent *adj.* speaking in or characterized by a pompous or bombastic style **grandiloquence** *n.*
gran-di-ose *adj.* impressive and grand; pretentiously pompous **-ly** *adv.*,
grand mal *n., Pathol.* a form of epilepsy characterized by severe convulsions and loss of consciousness
gran-ite *n.* a hard, coarsegrained igneous rock composed chiefly of quartz, mica, and orthoclase
gran-ite-ware *n.* ironware utensils coated with hard enamel
gran-ny *or* **gran-nie** *n.* a grandmother; an old woman
gra-no-la *n.* rolled oats mixed with dried fruit and seeds
grant *v.* to allow; to consent to
granter, grantor *n.*
gran-u-lar *adj.* composed or seeming to be composed or containing grains or granules **granularity** *n.*
gran-u-late *v.* to make or form into granules or crystals **-tion** *n.*
gran-ule *n.* a very small grain or particle
graph *n.* a diagram representing the relationship between sets of things
graph-ic *or* **graph-i-cal** *adj.* describing in full detail
graph-ite *n.* a soft black form of carbon having a metallic luster and slippery texture, used in lead pencils, lubricants, paints, and coatings
graphitic *adj.*
graph-ol-o-gy *n.* the study of handwriting for the purpose of analyzing
graphologist *n.*
grap-nel *n.* a small anchor with several flukes at the end
grap-ple *n.* an instrument with iron claws used to fasten an enemy ship alongside for boarding **-er** *n.*
grasp *v.* to seize and grip firmly *n.* the power to seize and hold
grasp-ing *adj.* urgently desiring material possessions; greedy
graspingly *adv.*, **graspingness** *n.*
grass *n.* any of numerous plants having narrow leaves and jointed stems *Slang* Marijuana **-iness** *n.*, **-y** *adj.*
grate *v.* to reduce, shred or pulverize by rubbing against a rough or sharp surface *n* a rasping noise **-er** *n.*, **-ing** *adj.*
grate *n.* a framework or bars placed over a window or other opening
grate-ful *adj.* thankful or appreciative for benefits or kindnesses
gratefully *adv.*
grat-i-fy *v.* to give pleasure or satisfaction to **gratification** *n.*
grat-ing *n.* a grate
grat-is *adv. & adj.* free
grat-i-tude *n.* the state of appreciation and gratefulness
gra-tu-i-tous *adj.* given or obtained without payment; unjustified
gratuitously *adv.*,
gra-tu-i-ty *n., pl.* **-ies** a gift given in return for a service rendered
gra-va-men *n., pl.* **-mens** *or* **-mina** in law, the part of an accusation or charge weighing most heavily against the accused
grave *n.* a burial place for a dead body *adj.* very serious or important in nature
grav-el *n.* loose rock fragments often with sand *Pathol.* the deposit of sand-like crystals that form in the kidneys
gra-vim-e-ter *n.* an implement for determining specific gravity **gravimetry** *n.*
grav-i-tate *v.* to be drawn as if by an irresistible force
grav-i-ta-tion *n., Physics* the force or attraction any two bodies exert towards each other **-ive** *adj.*, **-ally** *adv.*
grav-i-ty *n., pl.* **-ies** the gravitational force mani-fested by the tendency of material bodies to fall toward the center of the earth
gray-ling *n., pl.* **-ling** *or* **-lings** any of several freshwater food and game fish with a small mouth and a large dorsal fin
gray matter *n.* the grayish-brown nerve tissue of the spinal cord and brain
graze *v.* to feed upon growing grasses or herbage
grease *n.* melted or soft animal fat *v.* to lubricate or coat with grease
great *adj.* very large in size or volume; very good or firstrate **greatly** *adv.*,
great-heart-ed *adj.* noble in spirit
greed *n.* selfish desire to acquire more than one needs or deserves
greed-y *adj.* excessively eager to acquire or gain something
green-er-y *n., pl.* **-ies** green foliage or plants
green--eyed *adj.* jealous
green thumb *n.* a special skill for making plants thrive
greet *v.* to address someone in a friendly way; to welcome **greeter** *n.*
greet-ing *n.* a word of salutation.
gre-gar-i-ous *adj.* habitually associating with others as in groups, flocks, or herds; sociable
grem-lin *n.* a mischievous elf
gre-nade *n.* a small explosive device detonated by a fuse and thrown by hand or projected from a rifle
grew *v.* past tense of grow
grid *n.* an arrangement of regularly spaced bars
grid-dle *n.* a flat pan used for cooking
grid-i-ron *n.* a metal framework used for broiling meat, fish, and other foods; a

football field

grief *n.* deep sadness or mental distress caused by a loss

griev-ance *n.* a real or imagined wrong which is regarded as cause for complaint or resentment

grieve *v.* to cause, or feel sorrow

grille *or* **grill** *n.* a grating with open metalwork

grim *adj.* stern or forbidding in appearance or character; gloomy; dismal **grimly** *adv.*, **grimness** *n.*

grim-ace *n.* a facial expression of pain, disgust

grime *n.* dirt, especially soot clinging to or coating a surface **griminess** *n.*, **grimy** *adj.*

grin *v.* to smile broadly

grind *v.* to reduce to fine particles; to sharpen; *n.* a person who works hard

grip *n.* a firm hold; a grasp; the ability to seize or maintain a hold

gripe *v.* to cause sharp pain or cramps in the bowels; to anger

grippe *n.* influenza **grippy** *adj.*

gris-ly *adj.* ghastly; gruesome

gris-tle *n.* cartilage of meat

grit *n.* small, rough granules; having great courage and fortitude **gritty** *adj.*

grits *pl., n.* coarsely ground hominy; coarse meal

griz-zle *v.* to become gray

gro-cer *n.* a storekeeper who deals in various household supplies

grog-gy *adj.* dazed, weak, or not fully conscious, as from a blow **groggily** *adv.*

groom *n.* a person hired to tend horses; a stableman; a bridegroom

gro-tesque *adj.* incongruous or ludicrous in appearance; bizarre; outlandish

grot-to *n., pl.* **-toes** *or* **-tos** a cave or cave-like structure

grouch *n.* an habitually irritable or complaining person **grouchily** *adv.*,

ground *n.* the surface of the earth

ground *v.* past tense of grind

ground hog *n.* a woodchuck

ground-less *adj.* without foundation or basis

group *n.* a collection or assemblage of people, or things

grov-el *v.* to lie or crawl face downward, as in fear; to act with abject humility

grow *v.* to increase in size, develop, and reach maturity; to expand; to increase **grower** *n.*

grub *v.* to dig up by the roots; to lead a dreary existence

grub-by *adj.* sloppy, unkempt

grudge *n.* a feeling of ill will, rancor, or deep resentment

gru-el *n.* a thin liquid made by boiling meal in water or milk

gru-el-ing *or* **gru-el-ling** *adj.* extremely tiring **gruelingly** *adv.*

grue-some *adj.* causing horror or fright **gruesomely** *adv.*,

gruff *adj.* brusque and rough in manner; harsh in sound; hoarse **gruffly** *adv.*, **gruffness** *n.*

grum-ble *v.* to complain in low, throaty sounds; to growl **grumbler** *n.*

grump-y *adj.* irritable and moody; ill tempered

grun-gy *adj., Slang* dirty, run-down, or inferior in condition

grunt *n.* the deep, guttural sound of a hog

guar-an-tee *n.* the promise or assurance of the durability or quality of a product; something held or given as a pledge or security

guar-an-ty *n., pl.* **-ies** a pledge or promise to be responsible for the debt, duty, or contract of another person

guard *v.* to watch over or shield from danger or harm; to keep watch

guard-i-an *n.* one who is legally assigned responsibility for the care of the person unable to be do for himself **guardianship** *n.*

gub-ba *v., Slang* to tickle the neck area

guess *v.* to make a judgment or form an opinion on uncertain or incomplete knowledge

guest *n.* one who is the recipient of hospitality from another

guf-faw *n.* a loud burst of laughter **guffaw** *v.*

guid-ance *n.* the act, process, or result of guiding

guide *n.* one who leads or directs another **guider** *n.*

guilt *n.* the condition of having committed a crime or wrongdoing; the feeling of responsibility for having done something wrong

gul-let *n., Pathol.* the passage from the mouth to the stomach; esophagus; the throat

gul-li-ble *adj.* easily cheated

gul-ly *n., pl.* **-ies** a ditch cut in the earth by running water

gump-tion *n., Slang* boldness; initiative; enterprise

gust *n.* a sudden, violent rush of wind or air; a sudden outburst **gustily** *adv.*, **gusty** *adj.*

gus-ta-to-ry *adj.* of or pertaining to the sense of taste

gus-to *n.* hearty enjoyment

gut *n.* the alimentary canal or part of it *v.* to disembowel guts bowels; entrails

guts-y *n., Slang* courageous

guy *n., Slang* a man; a fellow

gym-na-si-um *n., pl.* **-ums** *or* **-sia** a building equipped for indoor sports

gy-ne-col-o-gy *n.* the branch of medicine dealing with the female reproductive organs **gynecological**,

gyp *v., Informal* to swindle, cheat, or defraud *n.* a fraud **gypper** *n.*

gy-rate *v.* to rotate or revolve around a fixed point or axis *adj.* coiled or winding about **gyratory** *adj.*

gy-ro *n.* a gyroscope or gyrocompass

gy-ro-scope *n.* a spinning wheel or disk whose spin axis maintains its angular orientation when not subjected to external torques

gy-ro-sta-bi-liz-er *n.* a gyroscopic instrument designed to reduce the rolling motion of ships

H, h The eighth letter of the English alphabet.
ha-be-as cor-pus *n.* in law, a writ commanding a person to appear before a judge or court for the purpose of releasing that person from unlawful detention or restraint
hab-er-dash-er *n.* a person who deals in men's clothing and men's furnishings
ha-bil-i-ment *n.* clothing characteristic of an office, rank, or occasion
hab-it *n.* involuntary pattern of behavior acquired by frequent repetition
hab-it-a-ble *adj.* suitable for habitation **habitably** *adv.*
hab-i-tat *n.* the region in which an animal or plant lives or grows
hab-i-ta-tion *n.* a place of residence
hab-it--form-ing *adj.* producing physiological addiction
ha-bit-u-al *adj.* practicing by or acting according to havit; resorted to on a regular basis; regular
hab-i-tude *n.* habitual mode of behavior
ha-ci-en-da *n.* a large estate or ranch in Spanish speaking countries
hack *v.* to cut with repeated irregular blows; to manage ;successfully; *n.* a tool used for hacking; taxi driver
hack-le *n.* one of the long, slender, often narrow glossy feathers on the neck of a rooster; the hair on the back of the neck, especially of a dog, that rise in anger or fear
hack-ney *n.* a horse of medium size for ordinary driving or riding
hackney coach *n.* a four-wheeled carriage for hire having six seats
hack-neyed *adj.* trite
hack-saw *n.* a saw in a narrow frame for cutting metal
had-dock *n.* a food fish
hade *n.* the angle maade by a rock fauult or vein
had-n't *cont.* had not
haft *n.* a handle of a weapon or tool
hag *n.* a malicious, ugly old woman; a witch **haggish** *adj.*
hag-gard wornout, exhausted, and gaunt look, as from hunger or fatigue
hag-gle *v.* to argue or bargain on price or terms **haggler** *n.*
hag-i-og-ra-phy *n., pl.* **hagiographies** biography of the lives of saints or revered persons
hai-ku *n.* an unrhymed Japanese verse form with three short lines
hail *n.* precipitation of small, hard lumps of ice and snow; a hailstone; an exclamation, greeting, acclamation
hail-stone *n.* a type of hard pellet made of frozen snow and ice
hair *n.* one of the pigmented filaments that grow from the skin of most mammals; a covering of such structures, as on the human head and on the skin; a slim margin
hair-breadth *adj.* extremely close or narrow; an extremely small space or margin
hair-brush *n.* an instrument used for grooming the hair
hair-cloth *n.* a wiry, stiff fabric of horsehair.
hair-line *n.* a fine line or crack
hair-rasing *adj.* causing fear or horror
hake *n.* a marine food fish related to the cod
hal-berd *n.* a medieval weapon used in the 15th and 16th centuries
hal-cy-on *adj.* calm and tranquil; peaceful; prosperous
hale *adj.* healthy and robust; free from defect *v.* to compel to go **haleness** *n.*
half *n., pl.* **halves** one of two equal parts into which a thing is divisible
half--wit *n.* a mentally disturbed person
hal-ite *n.* large crystal or masses of salt; salt rock
hal-i-to-sis *n.* a condition of having bad breath
hal-le-lu-jah *interj.* used to express joy, praise, or jubilation **hallelujah** *n.*
hal-low *v.* to sanctify; to make holy; to honor
hal-lu-ci-na-tion *n.* an illusion of seeing something that is nonexistent **hallucinate** *v.*
hal-lu-ci-no-gen *n.* a drug or other agent which causes hallucination **hallucinogenic** *adj.*
ha-lo *n.* a ring of colored light surrounding the head; an aura of glory
hal-o-gen *n.* any of the group of nonmentallic elements including flourine, chlorine, bromine, iodine, and astatine **halogenous** *adj.*
hal-ter *n.* a rope or strap for leading or tying an animal
halve *v.* to divide into two equal parts
hal-yard *n.* a rope for hoisting or lowering a sail, flag, or yard
ham *n.* the meat of a hog's thigh
ham-let *n.* a small rural village or town
ham-mer *n.* a hand tool with a heavy head used to drive or strike forcefully
ham-mock *n.* a hanging bed or couch of fabric or heavy netting
ham-per *v.* to interfere with movement or progress of
ham-ster *n.* any of various rodents with large cheek pouches and a short tail
ham-string *n.* either of two tendons located at the back of the human knee
hand *n.* the part of the arm below the wrist, consisting of the palm, four fingers and a thumb
hand-gun *n.* a gun that can be held and fired with one hand
hand-i-craft *or* **hand-craft** *n.* skill and expertise in working with the hands
han-dle *v.* to touch, pick up, or hold with the hands
hand-made *adj.* made by hand or by a hand process
hand-maid *or* **hand-maid-en** *n.* a female maid or personal servant
hand-y *adj.* easy to use or reach; helpful or useful
hang *v.* to be attached to from above and unsupported from below
han-gar *n.* a building for housing aircraft
han-ger *n.* a device from which some-

thing may be hung or on which something hangs
hang-up *n.*, *Slang* a psychological or emotional problem; an obstacle
hank *n.* a loop, coil, or piece of hair, thread, or yarn
han-ker *v.* to have a yearning or craving for something
Ha-nuk-kah *or* **Ha-nu-kah** *n.* an eight-day Jewish holiday remembering the rededication of the Temple in Jerusalem
hao-le *n.* a person who is not of the Hawaiian race, especially a Caucasian
hap-haz-ard *adj.* occurring by accident; happening by chance or at random
hap-less *adj.* unfortunate; unlucky **haplessly** *adv.*
hap-pen *v.* to occur or come to pass; to take place; to discover by chance
hap-pen-ing *n.* a spontaneous event or performance
happen-stance *n.* an event occurring by chance
hap-py *adj.* enjoying contentment and well-being; glad, joyous, satisfied or pleased **happiness** *n.*
ha-rass *v.* to disturb or annoy constantly; to torment persistently **harassment** *n.*
har-bin-ger *n.* a person that initiates or pioneers a major change
har-bor *n.* a place of refuge or shelter; a bay or cove; an anchorage for ships
hard *adj.* difficult to perform, endure, or comprehend; solid in texture or substance **hardness** *n.*
hard copy *n.* in computer science, the printed information or data from a computer
hard disk *n.* in computer science, magnetic storage consisting of a rigid disk of aluminum coated with a magnetic recording substance; contained within a removable cartridge or mounted in the hard disk of a microcomputer
hard-en *v.* to make or become hard or harder
har-di-hood *n.* resolute courage; audacious boldness; vitality; vigor
hard-ly *adj.*, *Slang* very little; almost certainly not. *adv.* forcefully; painfully
hard-ship *n.* a painful, difficult condition
hard-tack *n.* a hard, crackerlike biscuit made with flour and water
hard-ware *n.* manufactured machine parts, such as tools and utensils; the mechanical components of a computer installation
har-dy *adj.* bold and robust
hark *v.* to listen closely
har-le-quin *n.* a jester; a clown
har-lot *n.* a prostitute
harm *n.* emotional or physical damage or injury. *v.* to cause harm to **harmful** *adj.*
harm-less *adj.* without harm
har-mon-ic *adj.* relating to musical harmony
har-mo-ni-ous *adj.* pleasing to the ear **harmoniously** *adv.*
har-mo-ny *n.*, *pl.* **-ies** complete agreement, as of feeling or opinion; pleasing sounds
har-ness *n.* the working gear, other than a yoke, of a horse or other draft animal **harnesser** *n.*
harp *n.* a musical instrument having a triangular upright frame with strings plucked with the fingers
har-poon *n.* a barbed spear used in hunting whales and large fish **harpoon** *v.*
harp-si-chord *n.* a piano-like instrument whose strings are plucked by using quills or leather points **harpsichordist** *n.*
har-py *n.*, *pl.* **harpies** a vicious woman; a predatory person
har-ri-dan *n.* a mean, hateful old woman
har-ri-er *n.* a slender, narrow-winged hawk that preys on small animals
har-row *n.* a tool with sharp teeth for breaking up and smoothing soil
har-ry *v.* to harass
harsh *adj.* disagreeable; extremely severe **harshly** *adv.*
hart *n.* a fully grown male deer after it has passed its fifth year
har-um-scar-um *adj.* reckless
har-vest *n.* the process or act of gathering a crop
hash-ish *n.* the leaves and flowering tops of the hemp plant
has-sle *n.*, *Slang* a quarrel or argument
has-sock *n.* a firm upholstered cushion used as a footstool
haste *n.* speed; swiftness of motion or action **hasten** *v.*
hasty *adj.* rapid; swift; made or done with excessive speed **hastily** *adv.*
hat *n.* a covering for the head with a crown and brim
hatch *n.* a small opening or door, as in a ship's deck
hatch-et *n.* a small ax with a short handle
hate *v.* to feel hostility or animosity toward; to dislike intensely
haugh-ty *adj.* arrogantly proud; disdainful
haul *v.* to pull or draw with force; to move or transport
haunch *n.* the hip; the buttock and upper thigh of a human or animal
haunt *v.* to appear to or visit as a ghost or spirit; to linger in the mind **haunting** *adj.*
haut-bois *or* **haut-boy** *n.* an oboe
hau-teur *n.* a disdainful arrogance
have *v.* to hold or own, as a possession or as property **have to** need to; must **have had it** suffered or endured all that one can tolerate
hav-oc *n.* mass confusion; wide-spread destruction
haw *n.* a hesitating sound made by a speaker who is groping for words
haw-ser *n.* a heavy cable or rope for towing or securing a ship
hay *n.* alfalfa or grass that has been cut and dried for animal food
hay-wire *adj.*, *Slang* broken; emotionally out of control
haz-ard *n.* a risk; chance; an accident or source of danger **hazardous** *adj.*
ha-zel-nut *n.* the edible nut of the hazel

haz-y *adj.* lacking clarity; vague
hazily *adv.*, **haziness** *n.*
head *n.* the upper part of a human or animal body, containing the brain
head-ing *n.* a title or caption that acts as a front, beginning, or upper part of anything
head-set *n.* a pair of headphones
head-strong *adj.* not easily restrained; obstinate
heal *v.* to restore to good health; to mend **healable** *adj.*, **healer** *n.*
health *n.* the overall sound condition or function of a living organism at a particular time **healthful** *adj.*
heap *n.* a haphazard assortment of things
hear *v.* to perceive by the ear; to listen with careful attention
hear-ing *n.* one of the five senses; the range by which sound can be heard
heark-en *v.* to listen carefully
hear-say *n.* information heard from another; common talk; rumor
heart *n.* the hollow, primary muscular organ of vertebrates which circulates blood throughout the body; the emotional center, such as in love, hate, consideration, or compassion
heart-ache *n.* emotional grief; sorrow; mental anguish
heart attack *n.* an acute malfunction or interrupted heart function
hearth *n.* the floor of a fireplace, furnace
heart-y *adj.* marked by exuberant warmth; full of vigor; nourishing
heat *n.* a quality of being hot or warm; a degree of warmth; depth of feeling
hea-then *n.* a person or nation that does not recognize the God of Christianity, Judaism, or Islam; in the Old Testament
heave *v.* to raise or lift, especially forcibly
heav-en *n.* the sky; the region above and around the earth; the abode of God, the angels, and the blessed souls of the dead **heavenly** *adj.*
heav-y *adj.* of great weight; very thick or dense
heck-le *v.* to badger or annoy, as with questions, comments, or gibes
heckler *n.*
hec-tic *adj.* intensely active, rushed, or excited
he'd *conj.* he had; he would
he-don-ism *n.* the doctrine devoted to the pursuit of pleasure
heed *v.* to pay attention; to take notice of something
heft *n.*, *Slang* weight; bulk. *v.* to gauge or estimate the weight of by lifting
heft-y *adj.* bulky; heavy; sizable
he-gem-o-ny *n.* dominance or leadership, as of one country over another
he-gi-ra *n.* a journey or departure to flee an undesirable situation
heif-er *n.* a young cow, particularly one that has not produced a calf
height *n.* the quality of being high; the highest or most advanced point
Heim-lich maneuver *n.* an emergency maneuver used to dislodge food from a choking person's throat; the closed fist is placed below the rib cage and pressed inward to force air from the lungs upward
hei-nous *adj.* extremely wicked; hateful or shockingly wicked
heir *n.* a person who inherits another's property or title
heist *v.*, *Slang* to take from; to steal *n.* a robbery
hel-i-cal *adj.* of or pertaining to the shape of a helix
hel-i-con *n.* a large, circular tuba that encircles the player's shoulder
hel-i-cop-ter *n.* an aircraft propelled by rotors which can take off vertically
he-li-um *n.* an extremely light, nonflammable, odorless, gaseous element, symbolized by He
hell *or* **Hell** *n.* the abode of the dead souls condemned to eternal punishment
he'll *contr.* he will
helm *n.* a wheel or steering apparatus for a ship
hel-met *n.* a protective covering for the head made of metal, leather, or plastic
helms-man *n.* one who guides a ship
help *v.* to assist or aid. *n.* Assistance; relief; one hired to help
helper *n.*, **helpful** *adj.*
hel-ter--skel-ter *adv.* in a confused or hurried manner; in an aimless way *adj.* rushed and confused
helve *n.* a handle on a tool such as an axe or hatchet
he--man *n.* *Slang* a man marked by strength; a muscular man
he-ma-tol-o-gy *n.* the branch of biological science that deals with blood and blood-generating organs
hematologist *n.*
hem-i-sphere *n.* a half sphere that is divided by a plane passing through its center
he-mo-glo-bin *n.* the respiratory pigment in the red blood cells of vertebrates containing iron and carrying oxygen to body tissues
he-mo-phil-i-a *n.*, *Pathol.* an inherited blood disease characterized by severe, protracted, sometimes spontaneous bleeding
hem-or-rhage *n.* bleeding, especially excessive bleeding **hemorrhage** *v.*
hem-or-rhoid *n.*, *Pathol.* a painful mass of dilated veins in swollen anal tissue
he-mo-stat *n.* an agent that stops bleeding; a clamp-like instrument for preventing or reducing bleeding
hen *n.* a mature female bird
hence-forth, hence-for-ward *adv.* from this time on
hep-a-rin *n.*, *Biochem* a substance found especially in liver tissue having the power to slow or prevent blood clotting
her-ald *n.* a person who announces important news
her-ald-ry *n.*, *pl.* **-ries** the art or science of tracing genealogies
herb-age *n.* grass or vegetation used especially for grazing

her-bar-i-um *n., pl.* **herbariums** *or* **herbaria** a collection of dried plant specimens that are scientifically arranged for study
her-bi-cide *n.* a chemical agent used to kill weeds
her-bi-vore *n.* a herbivorous animal
her-biv-o-rous *adj.* feeding chiefly on plant life or vegetables **-ly** *adv.*
her-cu-le-an *adj.* of unusual size, force, or difficulty
here-af-ter *adv.* from now on; at some future time
here-by *adv.* by means or by virtue of this
he-red-i-tar-y *adj.* passing or transmitted from an ancestor to a legal heir
he-red-i-ty *n.* the genetic transmission of physical traits from parents to offspring
here-in *adv.* in or into this place
here-of *adv.* relating to or in regard to this
her-e-sy *n., pl.* **heresies** a belief in conflict with orthodox religious beliefs
here-to *adv.* to this matter, proposition, or thing
here-with *adv.* together or along with this; hereby
her-maph-ro-dite *n.* a person having both male and female reproductive organs
her-met-ic *or* **her-met-i-cal** *adj.* tightly sealed against air and liquids **hermetically** *adv.*
her-mit *n.* a person who lives in seclusion, often for religious reasons
her-ni-a *n.* the protrusion of a bodily organ, as the intestine, through an abnormally weakened wall that usually surrounds it; a rupture **hernial** *adj.*
he-ro *n., pl.* **heroes** a figure in mythology and legend renowned for exceptional courage and fortitude
heroic couplet *n.* a verse consisting of two rhyming lines of iambic pentameter
her-o-in *n.* a highly addictive narcotic derivative of morphine
her-o-ine *n.* a woman of heroic character
her-o-ism *n.* heroic behavior
her-pes *n., Pathol.* a viral infection, characterized by small blisters on the skin or mucous membranes
her-pe-tol-o-gy *n.* the scientific study and treatment of reptiles and amphibians
her-ring *n.* a valuable food fish of the North Atlantic
hertz *n.* a unit of frequency equalling one cycle per second
he's *contr.* he has; he is
hes-i-tant *adj.* given to hesitating **hesitancy** *n.*
hes-i-tate *v.* to pause or to be slow before acting, speaking, or deciding **hesitation** *n.*
het-er-o-sex-u-al *adj.* of or having sexual desire to the opposite sex **heterosexuality** *n.*
hew *v.* to make or shape with or as if with an axe
hex *n.* one held to bring bad luck; a jinx *v.* to put under an evil spell; to bewitch
hex-a-gon *n.* a polygon having six sides and six angles
hex-am-e-ter *n.* a line of verse containing six metrical feet
hi-a-tus *n.* a slight gap, break, or lapse in time from which something is missing
hi-ba-chi *n., pl.* **hibachis** a deep, portable charcoal grill used for cooking food
hi-ber-nate *v.* to pass the winter in an inactive, dormant, sleep-like state
hi-bis-cus *n.* a chiefly tropical shrub or tree
hick *n., Slang* a clumsy, unsophisticated country person
hide *v.* to put, or keep out of sight; to keep secret; to obscure from sight; *n.* the skin of an animal
hid-e-ous *adj.* physically repulsive; extremely ugly
hi-er-ar-chy *n., pl.* **hierarchies** an authoritative body or group of things or persons arranged in successive order
hi-er-o-glyph-ic *n.* a pictorial symbol representing an idea, object, or sound **hieroglyphically** *adv.*
high *adj.* extending upward; located at a distance above the ground
high-fa-lu-tin *adj.* pretentious or extravagant in manner or speech
high-ness *n.* the state of being high
high--pres-sure *adj., Informal* using insistent persuasive methods or tactics
high--spirited *adj.* unbroken in spirit; proud
high--strung *adj.* very nervous and excitable
hi-lar-i-ous *adj.* boisterously happy or cheerful
hill *n.* a rounded, elevation of the earth's surface, smaller than a mountain **hilly** *adj.*
hilt *n.* the handle of a dagger or sword **to the hilt** fully; completely; thoroughly
him *pron.* the objective case of the pronoun he
him-self *pron.* that identical male one; a form of the third person, singular masculine pronoun
hind *adj.* located at or toward the rear part; posterior
hin-der *v.* to interfere with the progress or action of
hind-most *adj.* farthest to the rear or back
hin-drance *n.* the act of hindering or state of being hindered
hind-sight *n.* comprehension or understanding of an event after it has happened
hip *n.* the part of the human body that projects outward below the waist and thigh; the hip joint
hip *n.* the bright, red seed case of a rose
hip *adj., Slang* said to be aware of or informed about current goings on
hip-pie *or* **hip-py** *n., pl.* **hippies** a young person who adopts unconventional dress and behavior
hip-po-pot-a-mus *n.* a large, aquatic

mammal, native to Africa
hire *v.* to obtain the service of another for pay
his *adj.* the possessive case of the pronoun he
hir-sute *adj.* covered with hair
hiss *n.* a sound resembling a prolonged, sibilant sound, as that of
his-tol-o-gy *n., pl.* **-ies** the study of the minute structures of animal and plant tissues as seen through a microscope **histological** *adj.*
his-to-ri-an *n.* a person who specializes in the writing or study of history
his-tor-ic *adj.* significant or famous in history
his-to-ry *n., pl.* **-ries** past events, especially those involving human affairs
his-tri-on-ics *pl., n.* theatrical arts; feigned emotional display
hitch *v.* to fasten or tie temporarily, with a hook or knot *Slang* to unite in marriage
hith-er *adv.* to this place *adj.* situated toward this side
hith-er-to *adv.* up to now
hive *n.* a natural or man-made structure serving as a habitation for honeybees
hives *pl., n.* any of various allergic conditions marked by itching welts
hoarse *adj.* having a husky, gruff, or croaking voice
hoars-en *v.* to become or make hoarse
hoar-y *adj.* ancient; aged; gray or white with age
hoax *n.* a trick or deception
hob-by *n., pl.* **hobbies** an activity or interest undertaken for pleasure during one's leisure time
hob-gob-lin *n.* an imaginary cause of terror or dread
hob-nob *n.* to associate in a friendly manner
ho-bo *n., pl.* **hoboes** *or* **hobos** a vagrant who travels aimlessly about; a tramp
hod *n.* a V-shaped trough held over the shoulder to carry loads, as bricks or mortar
hodge-podge *n.* a jumbled mixture or collection
Hodg-kin's disease *n., Pathol.* a disease characterized by progressive enlargement of the lymph nodes, lymphoid tissue, and spleen, generally fatal
hoe *n.* a tool with a long handle and flat blade used for weeding
hoist *v.* to haul or raise up *n.* a machine used for raising large objects
hold *v.* to take and keep as in one's hand; to grasp
hold-ing *n.* property, as land, money, or stocks
hole *n.* a cavity or opening in a solid mass or body
ho-li-ness *n.* the state of being holy
hol-ler *v.* to shout loudly; to yell **holler** *n.*
hol-low *adj.* having a cavity or space within; concaved or sunken
hol-mi-um *n.* a metallic element of the rare-earth group, symbolized by Ho
hol-o-grah *n.* a handwritten document, as a letholstered
ho-ly *adj.* regarded with or characterized by divine power
Holy Communion *n.* the Eucharist
Holy Ghost *n.* the third person of the Trinity
Holy Land *n.* palestine
Holy Spirit *n.* the Holy Ghost
hom-age *n.* great respect or honor
home *n.* the place where one resides; a place of origin
ho-me-op-a-thy *n.* a system of treating a disease with minute doses of medicines that produce the symptoms of the disease being treated
ho-me-o-sta-sis *n., Biol.* a state of equilibrium that occurs between different but related functions or elements **homeostatic** *adj.*
home-spun *adj.* something made, woven, or spun at home; anything that is simple and plain
home-y *or* **hom-y** *adj.* suggesting the coziness, intimacy, and comforts of home
hom-i-cide *n.* the killing of one person by another
hom-i-let-ic *n.* pertaining to the nature of a sermon
hom-i-ly *n., pl.* **homilies** a sermon, particularly one based on a Biblical text
ho-mo-ge-ne-ous *adj.* of the same or similar nature or kind
hom-o-graph *n.* a word that is identical to another in spelling, but different from it in origin and meaning
hom-o-nym *n.* a word that has the same sound and often the same spelling as another but a different meaning and origin
hom-o-phone *n.* one of two or more words that have the same sound but different spelling, origin, and meaning
Ho-mo sa-pi-ens *n.* the scientific name for the human race
ho-mo-sex-u-al *adj.* having sexual attraction or desire for persons of the same sex **homosexuality** *n.*
hon-cho *n., pl.* **honchos** the main person in charge; the boss; the manager
hon-est *adj.* not lying, cheating, or stealing; having or giving full worth or value
honey-suck-le *n.* a shrub or vine bearing a tubular, highly fragrant flower
hon-ky--tonk *n., Slang* a cheap bar or nightclub
hon-or *n.* high regard or respect; personal integrity; reputation; privilege
hon-or-ar-y *adj.* relating to an office or title bestowed as an honor, without the customary powers, duties, or salaries
hood *n.* a covering for the head and neck; cover of an automobile engine **hooded** *adj.*
hood *suff.* the quality or state of; sharing a given quality or state
hood-lum *n.* a young, tough, wild, or destructive fellow
hoo-doo *n.* voodoo *Slang* one who is thought to bring bad luck

hoo-ey *n., & interj., Slang* nonsense
hoof *n., pl.* **hooves** the horny covering of the foot in various mammals; *Slang* to dance; to walk; **on the hoof** alive; not butchered
hook *n.* a curved or bent piece of metal used to catch, drag, suspend, or fasten something
hook-er *n., Slang* a prostitute
hook-worm *n.* a parasitic intestinal worm with hooked mouth parts
hook-y *n., Slang* truant **to play hooky** to be out of school without permission
hoop-la *n., Slang* noise and excitement
hoose-gow *n., Slang* a jail
hoot *n.* the loud sound or cry of an owl **hooter** *n.,* **hoot** *v.*
hoot *n., Slang* a very insignificant amount **not give a hoot** not caring
hope *v.* to want or wish for something with a feeling of confident expectation **to hope against hope** to continue hoping for something even when it may be in vain **hopeful** *adj. & n.*
hop-per *n.* one that hops; a jumping insect; a receptacle in which coal, sand, grain, or other materials are held ready for discharge
horde *adj.* a large crowd
ho-ri-zon *n.* the line along which the earth and sky seem to meet
hor-mone *n., Physiol.* an internal secretion carried by the bloodstream to other parts of the body where it has a specific effect
hor-net *n.* any of various wasps which are capable inflicting a severe sting
horn-swog-gle *v.* to deceive
hor-o-scope *n.* a chart or diagram of the relative positions of the planets and signs of the zodiac at a certain time, as that of a person's birth; used to predict the future
hor-ri-ble *adj.* shocking; inducing or producing horror *Informal* excessive; inordinate **horribly** *adv.*
hor-rid *adj.* horrible
hor-ri-fy *v.* to cause a feeling of horror; to dismay or shock
hor-ror *n.* the painful, strong emotion caused by extreme dread, fear, or repugnance
horse sense *n., Slang* common sense
hor-ti-cul-ture *n.* the art or science of raising and tending fruits, vegetables, flowers, or ornamental plants **horticultural** *adj.*
ho-san-na *interj.* used to praise or glorify God
ho-sier-y *n.* stockings and socks
hos-pice *n.* a lodging for travelers or the needy
hos-pi-ta-ble *adj.* treating guests with warmth and generosity; receptive
hos-pi-tal *n.* an institution where the injured or sick receive medical, surgical, and emergency care
hos-pi-tal-i-ty *n.* hospitable treatment, disposition, or reception
host *n.* one who receives or entertains guests
hos-tage *n.* a person held as security that promises will be kept or terms met by a third party
host-ess *n.* a woman who entertains socially; a woman who greets patrons at a restaurant and escorts them to their tables
hos-tile *adj.* of or relating to an enemy; antagonistic
hos-til-i-ty *n., pl.* **-ies** a very deepseated opposition or hatred; war
hot *adj.* having heat that exceeds normal body temperature; electrically charged, as a hot wire *Slang* recently and or illegally obtained
hot air *n., Slang* idle talk
hot-el *n.* a business that provides lodging, meals, entertainment, and other services for the public
hot-foot *v.* to hasten
house *n.* a building that serves as living quarters for one or more families; home
how *adv.* in what manner or way; to what effect; in what condition or state; for what reason; with what meaning
how-dy *interj.* a word used to express a greeting
how-ev-er *adv.* in whatever manner or way *conj.* never-the-less
howl *v.* to utter a loud, sustained, plaintive sound, as the wolf **howl-er** *n.*
how-so-ev-er *adv.* to whatever degree or extent
hub *n.* the center of a wheel; the center of activity
hud-dle *n.* a crowd together
huff *n.* a fit of resentment or of ill temper
hug *v.* to embrace; to hold fast; to keep, cling, or stay close to
huge *adj.* of great quantity, size, or extent
hulk *n.* a heavy, bulky ship; the body of an old ship no longer fit for service
hulk-ing *adj.* unwieldy or awkward
hull *n.* the outer cover of a fruit or seed; the framework of a boat
hul-la-ba-loo *n.* a confused noise; a great uproar
hum *v.* to make a continuous low-pitched sound; to be busily active; to sing with the lips closed **hummer** *n.*
hu-man *adj.* of, relating to, or typical of man
hu-mane *adj.* to be marked by compassion, sympathy, or consideration for others
hum-ble *adj.* marked by meekness or modesty; unpretentious; lowly
hum-drum *n., Slang* boring; dull
hu-mid *adj.* containing or characterized by a large amount of moisture; damp
hu-mid-i-ty *n.* a moderate amount of wetness in the air; dampness
hu-mil-i-ate *v.* to reduce one's dignity or pride to a lower position **-tion** *n.*
hu-mor *n.* something that is or has the ability to be comical or amusing
hunch *n.* a strong, intuitive feeling about a future event or result
hun-ger *n.* a strong need or desire for food

hurl *v.* to throw something with great force
hur-rah *interj.* used to express approval, pleasure, or exultation
hur-ri-cane *n.* a tropical cyclone with winds exceeding 74 miles per hour
hur-ry *v.* to move or cause to move with haste *n.* the act of hurrying
hurriedly *adv.*
hurt *v.* to experience or inflict with physical pain; to cause physical or emotional harm to; to damage **-ful** *adj.*
hus-band *n.* a man who is married
hush *v.* to make or become quiet; to calm; to keep secret *n.* a silence
hus-sy *n., pl* **-ies** a saucy or mischievous girl; a woman with doubtful morals
hus-tle *v.* to urge or move hurriedly along; to work busily and quickly *Slang* to make energetic efforts to solicit business or make money
hustle, hustler *n.*
hy-brid *n.* an offspring of two dissimilar plants or of two animals of different races, breeds, varieties, or species
hy-dro-gen *n.* a colorless, normally odorless, highly flammable gas that is the simplest and lightest of he elements, symbolized by H
hy-dro-pho-bi-a *n.* a fear of water
hydrophobic *adj.*
hy-giene *n.* the science of the establishment and maintenance of good health and the prevention of disease
hy-men *n.* the thin membrane that partly closes the external vaginal orifice
hymn *n.* a song of praise giving thanks to God; a song of joy **hymn** *v.*
hype *v., Slang* to put on; to stimulate; to promote or publicize extravagantly
hy-per-ac-tive *adj.* abnormally active
hyperactivity *n.*
hy-per-ten-sion *n.* the condition of abnormally high blood pressure
hy-phen *n.* a punctuation mark (-) used to show connection between two or more words **hyphen** *v.*
hyp-no-sis *n., pl.* **hypnoses** a state that resembles sleep but is brought on or induced by another person whose suggestions are accepted by the subject
hyp-not-ic *adj.* inducing sleep; an agent,such as a drug, which induces sleep
hyp-no-tism *n.* the study or act of inducing hypnosis
hyp-no-tize *v.* to induce hypnosis; to be dazzled by; to be overcome by suggestion
hy-po-chon-dri-a *n.* a mental depression accompanied by imaginary physical ailments
hys-ter-ec-to-my *n., pl.* **-ies** surgery on a female which partially or completely removes the uterus
hys-ter-ia *n.* a psychological condition characterized by emotional excess and or unreasonable fear
hys-ter-ic *n.* a person suffering from hysteria; a fit of uncontrollable laughter
hys-ter-i-cal *adj.* emotionally out of control **hysterically** *adv.*

I, i the ninth letter of the English alphabet; the Roman numeral for one.
I *pron.* the person speaking or writing *n.* the self; the ego
I *or* **i** *abbr.* island; isle
IAAF *abbr.* International Amateur Athletic Federation
i-amb *or* **i-am-bus** *n.* a metrical foot consisting of a short or unstressed syllable followed by an accented syllable
i-at-ro-gen-ic *adj.* induced inadvertently by a physician or his treatment
iatrogenically *adv.*
ib *or* **ibid** *abbr., L.* ibidem, in the same place
I band *n.* a type of isotropic band that is of the striated muscle fiber
Ibe-ri-an *n.* a person who is a member of the group of people who inhabited the Caucasus in Asia
i-bex *n.* an Old World mountain goat with long curved horns
i-bis *n.* a long-billed wading bird related to the heron and stork
ice *n.* solidly frozen water; a dessert of crushed ice which is flavored and sweetened *Informal* extreme coldness of manner *v.* to change into ice; to cool or chill; to cover with icing
icily *adv.*, **iciness** *n.*, **icy** *adj.*
ice age *n., Geol.* a time of widespread glaciation
ice bag *n.* a small, flexible, waterproof bag designed to hold ice, used on parts of the body
ice-berg *n.* a thick mass of floating ice separated from a glacier
ice-boat *n.* a vehicle with runners and usually a sail, used for sailing over ice; an icebreaker
ice-bound *adj.* obstructed or covered by ice
ice-box *n.* a structure designed for holding ice in which food and other perishables are stored
ice-break-er *n.* a sturdy vessel for breaking a path through icebound waters; a pier or dock apron for deflecting floating ice from the base of a pier or bridge
ice cap *n.* an extensive perennial covering of ice and snow that covers a large area of land
ice cream *n.* a smooth mixture of milk, cream, flavoring, sweeteners, and other ingredients, beaten and frozen
ice hock-ey *n.* a version of hockey played on ice
ice-house *n.* a building where ice is stored
Ice-land *n.* an island country in the North Atlantic near the Arctic Circle
Icelander *n.*, **Icelandic** *adj.*
ice milk *n.* a food similar to ice cream but made with skim milk
ice pack *n.* a large mass of floating, compacted ice; a folded bag filled with ice and applied to sore parts of the body
ice pick *n.* a pointed tool used for breaking ice into small pieces

ice skate *n.* shoe or boot with a runner fixed to it for skating on ice
ice-skate *v.*
ich-thy-ol-o-gy *n.* the zoological study of fishes **ichthyologic, ichthyological** *adj.*, **ichthyologist** *n.*
i-ci-cle *n.* hanging spike of ice formed by dripping water that freezes
ic-ing *n.* sweet preparation for coating cakes and cookies
i-con *or* **i-kon** *n.* a sacred Christian pictorial representation of Jesus Christ, the Virgin Mary, or other sacred figures
i-con-o-clast *n.* one who opposes the use of sacred images; one who attacks traditional or cherished beliefs
iconoclasm *n.*, **iconoclastic** *adj.*
id *n., Psychol.*. the unconscious part of the psyche associated with instinctual needs and drives
I'd *contr.* I had; I should; I would
i-de-a *n.* something existing in the mind; conception or thought; an opinion; a plan of action
i-de-al *n.* concept or imagined state of perfection; highly desirable; perfect; an ultimate objective; an honorable principle or motive *adj.* conforming to absolute excellence **ideally** *adv.*
i-de-al-ism *n.* the practice or tendency of seeing things in ideal form; pursuit of an ideal; a philosophical system believing that reality consists of ideas or perceptions
idealist *n.*, **idealistic** *adj.*
i-de-al-ize *v.* to regard or represent as ideal **idealization** *n.*
i-dem *pron. & adj., L.* the same; used to indicate a previously mentioned reference
i-den-ti-cal *adj.* being the same; exactly equal or much alike; designating a twin or twins developed from the same ovum **identically** *adv.*
i-den-ti-fi-ca-tion *n.* the act of identifying; the state of being identified; a means of identity
i-den-ti-fy *v.* to recognize the identity of; to establish as the same or similar; to equate; to associate oneself closely with an individual or group
identifiable *adj.*
i-den-ti-ty *n., pl.* **identities** the condition or state of being a specific person or thing and recognizable as such; the condition or fact of being the same as something else
id-e-o-gram *or* **id-e-o-graph** *n.* pictorial symbol used in a writing system to represent an idea or thing, as Chinese characters; a graphic symbol, as $ or %
i-de-ol-o-gy *n., pl.* **ideologies** body of ideas that influence a person, group, culture, or political party
ideological *adj.*
ides *pl., n.* in the ancient Roman calendar, the fifteenth day of March, May, July, and October or the thirteenth day of the other months
id-i-o-cy *n., pl.* **-cies** a condition of an idiot
id-i-om *n.* form of expression having a meaning that is not readily understood from the meaning of its component words; the dialect of people or a region; a kind of language or vocabulary
idiomatic *adj.*, **idiomatically** *adv.*
id-i-o-syn-cra-sy *n., pl.* **-sies** peculiarity, as of behavior **idiosyncratic** *adj.*, **idiosyncratically** *adv.*
id-i-ot *n.* a mentally deficient person; an extremely foolish or stupid person
idiotic *adj.*, **idiotically** *adv.*
i-dle *adj.* doing nothing; inactive; moving lazily; slowly; running at a slow speed or out of gear; unemployed or inactive
idleness, idler *n.*, **idly** *adv.*
i-dol *n.* a symbol or representation of a god or deity that is worshiped; a person or thing adored
i-dol-a-try *n.* the worship of idols; blind adoration; devotion; to admire
idolater *n.*, **idolatrous** *adj.*
i-dol-ize *v.* to admire with excessive admiration or devotion; to worship as an idol **idolization, idolizer** *n.*
i-dyll *or* **i-dyl** *n.* a poem or prose piece about country life; a scene, event, or condition of rural simplicity; a romantic interlude
idyllic *adj.*, **idyllically** *adv.*
-ie *suff.* little; dear
if-fy *adj., Slang* marked by unknown qualifies or conditions
ig-loo *n.* dome-shaped Eskimo dwelling often made of blocks of snow
ig-ne-ous *adj., Geol.* relating to fire; formed by solidification from a molten magma
ig-nite *v.* to start or set a fire; to render luminous by heat
ig-ni-tion *n.* an act or action of igniting; a process or means for igniting the fuel mixture in an engine
ig-no-ble *adj.* dishonorable in character or purpose; not of noble rank
ignobly *adv.*
ig-no-min-i-ous *adj.* marked by or characterized by shame or disgrace; dishonorable **ignominy** *n.*
ig-no-ra-mus *n.* totally ignorant person
ig-no-rant *adj.* lacking education or knowledge; not aware; lacking comprehension **ignorance** *n.*
ig-nore *v.* to pay no attention to; to reject
ignorable *adj.*
i-gua-na *n.* large, dark-colored tropical American lizard
il-e-i-tis *n.* inflammation of the ileum
il-e-um *n., pl.* **ilea** the lower part of the small intestine between the jejunum and the large intestine
ilk *n.* sort; kind
ill *adj.* not healthy; sick; destructive in effect; harmful; hostile; unfriendly; not favorable; not up to standards *adv.* in an ill manner; with difficulty; scarcely *n.* evil; injury or harm; something causing suffering
I'll *contr.* I will; I shall
ill--ad-vised *adj.* done without careful

thought or sufficient advice
ill--bred *adj.* ill-mannered; impolite; rude
il-le-gal *adj.* contrary to law or official rules **illegality** *n.*, **illegally** *adv.*
il-leg-i-ble *adj.* not readable; not legible **illegibly** *adv.*, **illegibility** *n.*
il-le-git-i-mate *adj.* against the law; unlawful; born out of wedlock **illegitimacy** *n.*, **illegitimately** *adv.*
ill--fat-ed *adj.* destined for misfortune; doomed; unlucky
ill--fa-vored *adj.* unattractive; objectionable; offensive; unpleasant
ill--got-ten *adj.* obtained in an illegal or dishonest way
ill--hu-mored *adj.* irritable; cross **ill-humoredly** *adv.*
il-lic-it *adj.* not permitted by custom or law; unlawful **illicitly** *adv.*
il-lit-er-ate *adj.* unable to read and write; uneducated **illiteracy, illiterate** *n.*
ill--man-nered *adj.* lacking or showing a lack of good manners; rude
ill--na-tured *adj.* disagreeable or unpleasant disposition
ill-ness *n.* sickness; a state of being in poor health
il-log-i-cal *adj.* contrary to the principles of logic; not logical **illogicality** *n.*, **illogically** *adv.*
ill--tem-pered *adj.* having or showing a cross temper or disposition
il-lu-mi-nate *v.* to give light; to make clear; to provide with understanding; to decorate with pictures or designs **illumination, illuminator** *n.*
ill--use *v.* to treat cruelly or unjustly *n.* unjust treatment
il-lu-sion *n.* a misleading perception of reality; an overly optimistic idea or belief; misconception **illusive, illusory** *adj.*
il-lus-trate *v.* to explain or clarify, especially by the use of examples; to clarify by serving as an example; to provide a publication with explanatory features **illustrator** *n.*
il-lus-tra-tion *n.* the act of illustrating; an example or comparison used to illustrate
il-lus-tra-tive *adj.* serving to illustrate
il-lus-tri-ous *adj.* greatly celebrated; renowned **illustriousness** *n.*
ill will *n.* unfriendly or hostile feelings; malice
I'm *contr.* I am
im-age *n.* a representation of the form and features of someone or something; an optically formed representation of an object made by a mirror or lens; a mental picture of something imaginary *v.* to make a likeness of; to reflect; to depict vividly
im-age-ry *n.*, *pl.* **-ies** mental pictures; existing only in the imagination
im-ag-in-a-ble *adj.* capable of being imagined **imaginably** *adv.*
im-ag-i-nar-y *adj.* existing only in the imagination
im-ag-i-na-tion *n.* the power of forming mental images of unreal or absent objects; such power used creatively; resourcefulness **imaginative** *adj.*, **imaginatively** *adv.*
im-ag-ine *v.* to form a mental picture or idea of; to suppose; to guess
i-ma-go *n.*, *pl.* **-goes** *or* **-gines** an insect in its sexually mature adult stage
i-mam *n.* a prayer leader of Islam; rulers that claim descent from Muhammad
im-bal-ance *n.* a lack of functional balance; defective coordination
im-be-cile *n.* a mentally deficient person **imbecile, imbecilic** *adj.*, **imbecility** *n.*
im-bibe *v.* to drink; to take in **imbiber** *n.*
im-bri-cate *adj.* with edges over-lapping in a regular arrangement, as roof tiles or fish scales
im-bro-glio *n.*, *pl.* **-glios** a complicated situation or disagreement; a confused heap; a tangle
im-bue *v.* to saturate, as with a stain or dye
im-i-ta-ble *adj.* capable or worthy of imitation
im-i-tate *v.* to copy the actions or appearance of another; to adopt the style of; to duplicate; to appear like **imitator** *n.*
im-i-ta-tion *n.* an act of imitating; something copied from an original
im-mac-u-late *adj.* free from sin, stain, or fault; impeccably clean **immaculately** *adv.*
im-ma-nent *adj.* existing within; restricted to the mind; subjective **immanence, immanency** *n.*, **-ly** *adv.*
im-ma-te-ri-al *adj.* lacking material body or form; of no importance or relevance **immaterially** *adv.*, **immaterialness** *n.*
im-ma-ture *adj.* not fully grown; undeveloped; suggesting a lack of maturity **immaturely** *adv.*, **-ity** *n.*
im-meas-ur-a-ble *adj.* not capable of being measured **immeasurably** *adv.*
im-me-di-a-cy *n.*, *pl.* **-ies** the quality of being immediate; directness; something of urgent importance
im-me-di-ate *adj.* acting or happening without an intervening object, agent, or cause; directly perceived; occurring at once; close in time, location, or relation **immediately** *adv.*
im-me-mo-ri-al *adj.* beyond the limits of memory, tradition, or records
im-mense *adj.* exceptionally large **immensely** *adv.*, **immensity** *n.*
im-merse *v.* to put into a liquid; to baptize by submerging in water; to engross; to absorb **immersible** *adj.*, **immersion** *n.*
im-mi-grant *n.* one who leaves his country to settle in another
im-mi-grate *v.* to leave one country and settle in another **immigration** *n.*
im-mi-nent *adj.* about to happen **imminence** *n.*
im-mo-bile *adj.* not moving or incapable of motion **immobility** *n.*
im-mo-bi-lize *v.* to render motionless **immobilization** *n.*

impatience *n.*, **impatiently** *adv.*
im-pawn *v.* to put or place something in pawn
im-peach *v.* to charge with misconduct in public office before a proper court of justice; to make an accusation against
impeachable *adj.*, **impeachment** *n.*
im-pearl *v.* to form something into pearls
im-pec-ca-ble *adj.* having no flaws; perfect; not capable of sin
impeccably *adv.*
im-pe-cu-ni-ous *adj.* having no money
impecuniousness *n.*
im-ped-ance *n.* a measure of the total opposition to the flow of an electric current, especially in an alternating current circuit
im-pede *v.* to obstruct or slow down the progress of
im-ped-i-ment *n.* one that stands in the way; something that impedes, especially an organic speech defect
im-ped-i-men-ta *pl., n.* things that impede or encumber, such as baggage
im-pel *v.* to spur to action; to provoke; to drive forward; to propel
impeller *n.*
im-pend *v.* to hover threateningly; to be about to happen
im-pen-dent *adj.* to be near at hand
im-pen-e-tra-bil-i-ty *n.* the inability of two parts of anything to occupy the same space at exactly the same time
im-pen-e-tra-ble *adj.* not capable of being penetrated; not capable of being seen through or understood; unfathomable
impenetrability *n.*, **-bly** *adv.*
im-pen-i-tence *n.* the quality of being impenitent
im-pen-i-tent *adj.* not sorry; unrepentant
impenitence *n.*
im-per-a-tive *adj.* expressing a command or request; empowered to command or control; compulsory
imperative *n.*, **imperatively** *adv.*
im-pe-ra-tor *n.* the commander in chief of the ancient Romans
im-per-cep-ti-ble *adj.* not perceptible by the mind or senses; extremely small or slight
imperceptibly *adv.*
im-per-cep-tive *adj.* not being perceptive
im-per-cip-i-ent *adj.* bbeing not percipient
imperf *abbr.* imperforate
im-per-fect *adj.* not perfect; of or being a verb tense which shows an uncompleted or continuous action or condition *n.* the imperfect tense
imperfectly *adv.*
im-per-fect- fun-gus *n.* a type of fungus of which only the conidial stage is known
im-per-fec-tion *n.* the quality or condition of being imperfect; a defect
im-per-fec-tive *adj.* to be expressing action as being imcomplete
im-per-fo-rate *adj.* to have no opening; lacking a normal opening
im-pe-ri-al *adj.* of or relating to an empire or emperor; designating a nation or government having dependent
im-mod-er-ate *adj.* exceeding normal bounds
immoderately *adv.*
im-mod-est *adj.* lacking modesty; indecent; boastful
immodestly *adv.*, **immodesty** *n.*
im-mo-late *v.* to kill, as a sacrifice; to destroy completely
immolator *n.*
im-mor-al *adj.* not moral
immorally *adv.*
im-mo-ral-i-ty *n., pl.* **-ies** lack of morality; an immoral act or practice
im-mor-tal *adj.* exempt from death; lasting forever, as in fame *n.* a person of lasting fame
immortality *n.*, **immortally** *adv.*
im-mov-a-ble *adj.* not capable of moving or being moved
immovably *adv.*
im-mune *adj.* not affected or responsive; resistant, as to a disease
immunity *n.*
im-mu-nize *v.* to make immune
immunization *n.*
im-mu-nol-o-gy *n.* the study of immunity to diseases
immunologic, immunological *adj.*, **-ally** *adv.*
im-mu-no-sup-pres-sive *adj.* acting to suppress a natural immune response to an antigen
im-mure *v.* to confine by or as if by walls; to build into a wall
im-mu-ta-ble *adj.* unchanging or unchangeable
immutability *n.*, **-bly** *adv.*
imp *n.* a mischievous child
im-pact *n.* a collision; the impetus or force produced by a collision; an initial, usually strong effect *v.* to pack firmly together; to strike or affect forcefully
im-pac-ted *adj.* wedged together at the broken ends, as an impacted bone; wedged inside the gum in such a way that normal eruption is prevented, as an impacted tooth
im-pac-tion *n.* something wedged in a part of the body
im-pair *v.* to diminish in strength, value, quantity, or quality
impairment *n.*
im-pa-la *n.* large African antelope, the male of which has slender curved horns
im-pale *v.* to pierce with a sharp stake or point; to kill by piercing in this fashion
impalement *n.*
im-pal-pa-ble *adj.* not perceptible to touch; not easily distinguished
impalpability *n.*, **impalpably** *adv.*
im-part *v.* to grant; to bestow; to make known; to communicate
im-par-tial *adj.* not partial; unbiased
impartiality *n.*, **impartially** *adv.*
im-pass-a-ble *adj.* impossible to travel over or across
im-passe *n.* a road or passage having no exit; a difficult situation with no apparent way out; a deadlock
im-pas-sioned *adj.* filled with passion
im-pas-sive *adj.* unemotional; showing no emotion; expressionless
impassively *adv.*
im-pa-tient *adj.* unwilling to wait or tolerate delay; expressing or caused by irritation at having to wait; restlessly eager; intolerant

colonies; majestic; regal *n.* a pointed beard on the lower lip or chin **imperially** *adv.*

im-pe-ri-al-ism *n.* the national policy or practice of acquiring foreign territories or establishing dominance over other nations **imperialist** *n.*, **imperialistic** *adj.*

imperial moth *n.* a large New World moth with yellow wings and brownish or purplish markings

im-per-il *v.* to put in peril; endanger

im-pe-ri-ous *adj.* commanding; domineering; urgent **imperiousness** *n.*, **imperiously** *adv.*

im-per-ish-a-ble *adj.* not perishable **imperishably** *adv.*

im-pe-ri-um *n.* an absolute dominion; the right to employ the force of the state

im-per-ma-nence *n.* the state of being impermanent

im-per-ma-nent *adj.* not permanent; temporary **impermanence** *n.*, **-ly** *adv.*

im-per-me-a-ble *adj.* not permeable **impermeability** *n.*, **impermeably** *adv.*

im-per-mis-si-ble *adj.* not permissible; not allowed

im-per-son-al *adj.* having no personal reference or connection; showing no emotion or personality **-ly** *adv.*

im-per-son-al-ize *v.* to make something impersonal

im-per-son-ate *v.* to assume the character or manner of **impersonation, impersonator** *n.*

im-per-ti-nence *n.* the instance of impertinence

im-per-ti-nent *adj.* overly bold or disrespectful; not pertinent; irrelevant **impertinence** *n.*, **impertinently** *adv.*

im-per-turb-a-ble *adj.* unshakably calm **imperturbability** *n.*, **imperturbably** *adv.*

im-per-vi-ous *adj.* incapable of being penetrated or affected **imperviously** *adv.*, **imperviousness** *n.*

im-pe-ti-go *n.* a contagious skin disease marked by pustules

im-pet-u-ous *adj.* marked by sudden action or emotion; impulsive **impetuosity** *n.*, **impetuously** *adv.*

im-pe-tus *n.* a driving force; an incitement; a stimulus; momentum

im-pi-e-ty *n., pl.* **-ies** the quality of being impious; irreverence

im-pinge *v.* to strike or collide; to impact; to encroach **impingement** *n.*

im-pi-ous *adj.* not pious; irreverent; disrespectful **impiously** *adv.*

imp-ish *adj.* mischievous **impishly** *adv.*, **impishness** *n.*

im-pla-ca-ble *adj.* not capable of being placated or appeased **implacability** *n.*, **implacably** *adv.*

im-plant *v.* to set in firmly; to fix in the mind; to insert surgically **implant, implantation** *n.*

im-plau-si-ble *adj.* difficult to believe; unlikely **-bility** *n.*, **implausibly** *adv.*

im-ple-ment *n.* a utensil or tool *v.* to put into effect; to carry out; to furnish with implements **implementation** *n.*

im-pli-cate *v.* to involve, especially in illegal activity; to imply

im-pli-ca-tion *n.* the act of implicating or state of being implicated; the act of implying; an indirect expression; something implied

im-plic-it *adj.* contained in the nature of someone or something but not readily apparent; understood but not directly expressed; complete; absolute

im-plode *v.* to collapse or burst violently inward **implosion** *n.*

im-plore *v.* to appeal urgently to **implorer** *n.*, **imploringly** *adv.*

im-ply *v.* to involve by logical necessity; to express indirectly; to suggest

im-po-lite *adj.* rude

im-pol-i-tic *adj.* not expedient; tactless

im-pon-der-a-ble *adj.* incapable of being weighed or evaluated precisely **imponderable** *n.*

im-port *v.* to bring in goods from a foreign country for trade or sale; to mean; to signify; to be significant *n.* something imported; meaning; significance; importance **importer** *n.*

im-por-tance *n.* the quality of being important; significance

im-por-tant *adj.* likely to determine or influence events; significant; having fame or authority **importantly** *adv.*

im-por-ta-tion *n.* the act or business of importing goods; something imported

im-por-tu-nate *adj.* persistent in pressing demands or requests **-ly** *adv.*

im-por-tune *v.* to press with repeated requests **importunity, importuner** *n.*

im-pose *v.* to enact or apply as compulsory; to obtrude or force oneself or a burden on another; to take unfair advantage; to palm off **imposition** *n.*

im-pos-ing *adj.* awesome; impressive **imposingly** *adv.*

im-pos-si-ble *adj.* not capable of existing or happening; unlikely to take place or be done; unacceptable; difficult to tolerate or deal with **impossibility** *n.*, **impossibly** *adv.*

im-post *n.* a tax or duty

im-pos-tor *or* **im-pos-ter** *n.* one who assumes a false identity or title for the purpose of deception

im-pos-ture *n.* deception by the assumption of a false identity

im-po-tent *adj.* without strength or vigor; having no power; ineffectual; incapable of sexual intercourse **impotence, impotency** *n.*, **impotently** *adv.*

im-pound *v.* to confine in or as if in a pound; to seize and keep in legal custody; to hold water, as in a reservoir **impoundment** *n.*

im-pov-er-ish *v.* to make poor; to deprive or be deprived of natural richness or fertility **impoverishment** *n.*

im-prac-ti-ca-ble *adj.* incapable of being done or put into practice **impracticableness, impracticability** *n.*, **impracticably** *adv.*

im-prac-ti-cal *adj.* unwise to put into effect; unable to deal with practical or financial matters efficiently

impracticality *n.*
im-pre-cise *adj.* not precise
im-preg-nate *v.* to make pregnant; to fertilize, as an ovum; to fill throughout; to saturate **impregnation, -tor** *n.*
im-pre-sa-ri-o *n., pl.* **-os** a theatrical manager or producer, especially the director of an opera company
im-press *v.* to apply or produce with pressure; to stamp or mark with or as if with pressure; to fix firmly in the mind; to affect strongly and usually favorably *n.* the act of impressing; a mark made by impressing; a stamp or seal for impressing **impressible** *adj.*, **impresser** *n.*
im-pres-sion *n.* a mark or design made on a surface by pressure; an effect or feeling retained in the mind as a result of experience; an indistinct notion or recollection; a satiric or humorous imitation; the copies of a publication printed at one time
im-pres-sion-a-ble *adj.* easily influenced
im-pres-sion-ism *n.* a style of late nineteenth century painting in which the immediate appearance of scenes is depicted with unmixed primary colors applied in small strokes to simulate reflected light
impressionist *n.*, **impressionistic** *adj.*
im-pres-sive *adj.* making a strong impression; striking
impressively *adv.*, **impressiveness** *n.*
im-pri-ma-tur *n.* official permission to print or publish; authorization
im-print *v.* to make or impress a mark or design on a surface; to make or stamp a mark on; to fix firmly in the mind *n.* a mark or design made by imprinting; a lasting influence or effect; a publisher's name, often with the date and place of publication, printed at the bottom of a title page
im-pris-on *v.* to put in prison
imprisonment *n.*
im-prob-a-ble *adj.* not likely to occur or be true **improbability** *n.*, **-bly** *adv.*
im-promp-tu *adj.* devised or performed without prior planning or preparation
impromptu *adv.*
im-prop-er *adj.* unsuitable; indecorous; incorrect **improperly** *adv.*
improper fraction *n.* a fraction having a numerator larger than or the same as the denominator
im-pro-pri-e-ty *n., pl.* **-ies** the quality or state of being improper; an improper act or remark
im-prove *v.* to make or become better; to increase something's productivity or value **improvable** *adj.*
im-prove-ment *n.* the act or process of improving or the condition of being improved; a change that improves
im-prov-i-dent *adj.* not providing for the future **improvidence** *n.*, **improvidently** *adv.*
im-pro-vise *v.* to make up, compose, or perform without preparation; to make from available materials
improvisation, improviser, improvisator *n.*, **improvisatory, improvisatorial** *adj.*, **-torially** *adv.*
im-pru-dent *adj.* not prudent; unwise
imprudence *n.*, **imprudently** *adv.*
im-pu-dent *adj.* marked by rude boldness or disrespect
impudence *n.*, **impudently** *adv.*
im-pugn *v.* to attack as false; to cast doubt on
im-pulse *n.* a driving force or the motion produced by it; a sudden spontaneous urge; a motivating force; a general tendency *Physiol.* a transfer of energy from one neuron to another
im-pul-sive *adj.* acting on impulse rather than thought; resulting from impulse; uncalculated **impulsively** *adv.*, **impulsiveness** *n.*
im-pu-ni-ty *n.* exemption from punishment
im-pure *adj.* not pure; unclean; unchaste or obscene; mixed with another substance; adulterated; deriving from more than one source or style
impurely *adv.*, **impurity** *n.*
im-pute *v.* to attribute something as a mistake, to another; to charge
imputation *n.*
in *abbr.* inch
in ab-sen-tia *adv.* in the absence of
in-ac-ces-si-ble *adj.* not accessible
inaccessibility *n.*, **inaccessibly** *adv.*
in-ac-tive *adj.* not active or inclined to be active; out of current use or service
inactively *adv.*, **inactivity, -ness** *n.*
in-ad-e-quate *adj.* not adequate
inadequacy *n.*, **inadequately** *adv.*
in-ad-ver-tent *adj.* unintentional; accidental; inattentive
inadvertently *adv.*
in-al-ien-a-ble *adj.* not capable of being given up or transferred
inalienably *adv.*, **inalienability** *n.*
in-ane *adj.* without sense or substance
inanely *adv.*, **inanity** *n.*
in-an-i-mate *adj.* not having the qualities of life; not animated
inanimately *adv.*, **inanimateness** *n.*
in-a-ni-tion *n.* exhaustion, especially from malnourishment
in-ap-pre-cia-ble *adj.* too slight to be significant **inappreciably** *adv.*
in-ar-tic-u-late *adj.* not uttering or forming intelligible words or syllables; unable to speak; speechless; unable to speak clearly or effectively; unexpressed **inarticulately** *adv.*, **inarticulateness** *n.*
in-as-much as *conj.* because of the fact that; since
in-au-gu-ral *adj.* of or for an inauguration
in-au-gu-rate *v.* to put into office with a formal ceremony; to begin officially
inauguration, inaugurator *n.*
in-be-tween *adj.* intermediate *n.* an intermediate or intermediary
in between *adv. & prep.* between
in-board *adj.* within a ship's hull; close to or near the fuselage of an aircraft
inboard *adv.*
in-born *adj.* possessed at birth; natural;

hereditary
in-bound *adj.* incoming
in-breed *v.* to produce by repeatedly breeding closely related individuals
inc *or* **Inc** *abbr.* income; increase; incorporated
In-ca *n., pl.* **-ca** *or* **-cas** an Indian people who ruled Peru before the Spanish conquest in the sixteenth century
Incan *adj.*
in-cal-cu-la-ble *adj.* not calculable; indeterminate; unpredictable; very large
incalculably *adv.*
in-can-des-cent *adj.* giving off visible light when heated; shining brightly; ardently emotional or intense
incandescence *n.*
incandescent lamp *n.* a lamp in which a filament is heated to incandescence by an electric current
in-can-ta-tion *n.* a recitation of magic charms or spells; a magic formula for chanting or reciting
in-ca-pac-i-tate *v.* to render incapable; to disable; in law, to disqualify
incapacitation *n.*
in-ca-pac-i-ty *n., pl.* **-ies** inadequate ability or strength; a defect; in law, a disqualification
in-car-cer-ate *v.* to place in jail
incarceration *n.*
in-car-na-tion *n.* the act of incarnating or state of being incarnated; the embodiment of God in the human form of Jesus; one regarded as personifying a given abstract quality or idea
in-cen-di-ary *adj.* causing or capable of causing fires; of or relating to arson; tending to inflame; inflammatory
incendiary *n.*
in-cense *v.* to make angry *n.* a substance, as a gum or wood, burned to produce a pleasant smell; the smoke or odor produced
in-cen-tive *n.* something inciting one to action or effort; a stimulus
in-cep-tion *n.* a beginning; an origin
inceptive *adj.*
in-cer-ti-tude *n.* uncertainty; lack of confidence; instability
in-ces-sant *adj.* occurring without interruption; continuous
incessantly *adv.*
in-cest *n.* sexual intercourse between persons so closely related that they are forbidden by law to marry
incestuous *adj.*, **incestuously** *adv.*
inch *n.* a unit of measurement equal to 1/12th of a foot *v.* to move slowly
in-cho-ate *adj.* in an early stage; incipient
-ly *adv.*, **inchoateness** *n.*
in-ci-dence *n.* the extent or rate of occurrence
in-ci-dent *n.* an event; an event that disrupts normal procedure or causes a crisis
in-ci-den-tal *adj.* occurring or likely to occur at the same time or as a result; minor; subordinate *n.* a minor attendant occurrence or condition
incidentally *adv.*
in-cin-er-ate *v.* to burn up
incineration *n.*
in-cin-er-a-tor *n.* one that incinerates; a furnace for burning waste
in-cip-i-ent *adj.* just beginning to appear or occur
incipience *n.*, **incipiently** *adv.*
in-cise *v.* to make or cut into with a sharp tool; to carve into a surface; to engrave
in-ci-sion *n.* the act of incising; a cut or notch, especially a surgical cut
in-ci-sive *adj.* having or suggesting sharp intellect; penetrating; cogent and effective; telling
incisively *adv.*, **incisiveness** *n.*
in-ci-sor *n.* a cutting tooth at the front of the mouth
in-cite *v.* to provoke to action
incitement, inciter *n.*
in-clem-ent *adj.* stormy or rainy; unmerciful
inclemency *n.*
in-cli-na-tion *n.* an attitude; a disposition; a tendency to act or think in a certain way; a preference; a bow or tilt; a slope
in-cline *v.* to deviate or cause to deviate from the horizontal or vertical; to slant; to dispose or be disposed; to bow or nod *n.* an inclined surface
in-clude *v.* to have as a part or member; to contain; to put into a group or total
inclusion *n.*, **inclusive** *adj.*, **-ly** *adv.*
in-cog-ni-to *adv. & adj.* with one's identity hidden
in-co-her-ent *adj.* lacking order, connection, or harmony; unable to think or speak clearly or consecutively
incoherence *n.*, **incoherently** *adv.*
in-com-bus-ti-ble *adj.* incapable of burning
incombustible *n.*
in-come *n.* money or its equivalent received in return for work or as profit from investments
income tax *n.* a tax on income earned by an individual or business
in-com-ing *adj.* coming in or soon to come in
in-com-men-su-rate *adj.* not commensurate; disproportionate; inadequate
incommensurately *adv.*
in-com-mode *v.* to inconvenience; to disturb
in-com-mu-ni-ca-do *adv. & adj.* without being able to communicate with others
in-com-pa-ra-ble *adj.* incapable of being compared; without rival
incomparably *adv.*
in-com-pat-i-ble *adj.* not suited for combination or association; inconsistent
incompatibility *n.*, **incompatibly** *adv.*
in-com-pe-tent *adj.* not competent
incompetence, incompetency, *n.*
in-com-plete *adj.* not complete
incompletely *adv.*, **incompleteness** *n.*
in-con-gru-ous *adj.* not corresponding; disagreeing; made up of diverse or discordant elements; unsuited to the surrounding or setting
incongruity *n.*, **incongruously** *adv.*
in-con-se-quen-tial *adj.* without importance; petty
inconsequentially *adv.*
in-con-sid-er-a-ble *adj.* unimportant; trivial
inconsiderably *adv.*

in-con-sid-er-ate *adj.* not considerate; thoughtless **inconsiderately** *adv.*, **inconsiderateness** *n.*
in-con-sol-a-ble *adj.* not capable of being consoled **inconsolably** *adv.*
in-con-spic-u-ous *adj.* not readily seen or noticed **inconspicuously** *adv.*, **inconspicuousness** *n.*
in-con-stant *adj.* likely to change; unpredictable; faithless; fickle **inconstancy** *n.*, **inconstantly** *adv.*
in-con-ti-nent *adj.* not restrained; uncontrolled; unable to contain or restrain something specified; incapable of controlling the excretory functions **incontinence** *n.*, **incontinently** *adv.*
in-con-tro-vert-i-ble *adj.* unquestionable; indisputable **incontrovertibly** *adv.*
in-con-ven-ience *n.* the quality or state of being inconvenient; something inconvenient *v.* to cause inconvenience to; to bother
in-con-ven-ient *adj.* not convenient **inconveniently** *adv.*
in-cor-po-rate *v.* to combine into a unified whole; to unite; to form or cause to form a legal corporation; to give a physical form to; to embody **incorporation, incorporator** *n.*
in-cor-po-re-al *adj.* without material form or substance **incorporeally** *adv.*
in-cor-ri-gi-ble *adj.* incapable of being reformed or corrected **incorrigibility, incorrigible** *n.*, **incorrigibly** *adv.*
in-cor-rupt-i-ble *adj.* not capable of being corrupted morally; not subject to decay **incorruptibility** *n.*, **incorruptibly** *adv.*
in-crease *v.* to make or become greater or larger; to have offspring; to reproduce *n.* the act of increasing; the amount or rate of increasing **increasingly** *adv.*
in-cred-i-ble *adj.* too unlikely to be believed; unbelievable; extraordinary; astonishing **incredibility** *n.*, **incredibly** *adv.*
in-cred-u-lous *adj.* skeptical; disbelieving; expressive of disbelief **incredulity** *n.*, **incredulously** *adv.*
in-cre-ment *n.* an increase; something gained or added, especially one of a series of regular additions **incremental** *adj.*
in-crim-i-nate *v.* to involve in or charge with a wrongful act, as a crime **incrimination** *n.*, **incriminatory** *adj.*
in-cu-bate *v.* to warm and hatch eggs, as by bodily heat or artificial means; to maintain a bacterial culture in favorable conditions for growth **incubation** *n.*
in-cu-ba-tor *n.* a cabinet in which a desired temperature can be maintained, used for bacterial culture; an enclosure for maintaining a premature infant in a controlled environment; a temperature controlled enclosure for hatching eggs
in-cu-bus *n., pl.* **-buses** *or* **-bi** an evil spirit believed to seize or harm sleeping persons; a nightmare; a nightmarish burden
in-cul-cate *v.* to impress on the mind by frequent repetition or instruction **inculcation, inculcator** *n.*
in-cul-pate *v.* to incriminate
in-cum-bent *adj.* lying or resting on something else; imposed as an obligation; obligatory; currently in office *n.* a person who is currently in office **incumbency** *n.*, **incumbently** *adv.*
in-cu-nab-u-lum *n., pl.* **-la** a book printed before 1501
in-cur *v.* to become liable or subject to, especially because of one's own actions **incurrence** *n.*
in-cu-ri-ous *adj.* lacking interest; detached
in-cur-sion *n.* a sudden hostile intrusion into another's territory
in-cus *n., pl.* **incudes** an anvil-shaped bone in the middle ear of mammals
in-debt-ed *adj.* obligated to another, as for money or a favor; beholden **indebtedness** *n.*
in-de-cent *adj.* morally offensive or contrary to good taste **indecency** *n.*, **indecently** *adv.*
in-de-ci-pher-a-ble *adj.* not capable of being deciphered or interpreted
in-de-ci-sion *n.* inability to make up one's mind; irresolution
in-de-ci-sive *adj.* without a clear-cut result; marked by indecision **indecisively** *adv.*, **indecisiveness** *n.*
in-dec-o-rous *adj.* lacking good taste or propriety **indecorously** *adv.*, **indecorousness** *n.*
in-deed *adv.* most certainly; without doubt; in reality; in fact *interj.* used to express surprise, irony, or disbelief
in-de-fat-i-ga-ble *adj.* tireless **indefatigably** *adv.*
in-de-fin-a-ble *adj.* not capable of being defined **indefinableness** *n.*, **indefinably** *adv.*
in-def-i-nite *adj.* not decided or specified; vague; unclear; lacking fixed limits **indefinitely** *adv.*, **-ness** *n.*
in-del-i-ble *adj.* not able to be erased or washed away;permanent **indelibly** *adv.*
in-del-i-cate *adj.* lacking sensitivity; tactless **indelicacy** *n.*, **indelicately** *adv.*
in-dem-ni-fy *v.* to secure against hurt, loss, or damage; to make compensation for hurt, loss, or damage **indemnification, indemnifier** *n.*
in-dem-ni-ty *n., pl.* **-ties** security against hurt, loss, or damage; a legal exemption from liability for damages; compensation for hurt, loss, or damage
in-dent *v.* to set in from the margin, as the first line of a paragraph; to notch the edge of; to serrate; to make a dent or depression in; to impress; to stamp *n.* an indentation
in-den-ta-tion *n.* the act of indenting or the state of being indented; an angular cut in an edge; a recess in a surface
in-den-ture *n.* a legal deed or contract; a contract obligating one party to work for another for a specified period of time *v.* to bind into the service of

another

in-de-pend-ence *n.* the quality or state of being independent

In-de-pend-ence Day *n.* July 4, a legal holiday in the United States, commemorating the adoption of the Declaration of Independence in 1776

in-de-pend-ent *adj.* politically self-governing; free from the control of others; not committed to a political party or faction; not relying on others, especially for financial support; providing or having enough income to enable one to live without working *n.* one who is independent, especially a candidate or voter not committed to a political party **independently** *adv.*

in--depth *adj.* thorough; detailed

in-de-scrib-a-ble *adj.* surpassing description; incapable of being described **indescribably** *adv.*

in-de-ter-mi-nate *adj.* not determined; not able to be determined; unclear or vague **indeterminacy** *n.*, **indeterminately** *adv.*

in-dex *n., pl.* **-dexes** *or* **-dices** a list for aiding reference, especially an alphabetized listing in a printed work which gives the pages on which various names, places, and subjects are mentioned; something serving to guide or point out, especially a printed character calling attention to a paragraph or section; something that measures or indicates; a pointer, as in an instrument; in mathematics, a small number just above and to the left of a radical sign indicating what root is to be extracted; any number or symbol indicating an operation to be performed on a expression; a number or scale indicating change in magnitude, as of prices, relative to the magnitude at some specified point usually taken as one hundred (100) *v.* to provide with or enter in an index; to indicate; to adjust through

in-dex-a-tion *n.* the linkage of economic factors, as wages or prices, to a cost-of-living index so they rise and fall within the rate of inflation

in-dex fin-ger *n.* the finger next to the thumb

in-dex of re-frac-tion *n.* the quotient of the speed of light in a vacuum divided by the speed of light in a medium under consideration

In-di-an *n.* a native or inhabitant of India; a member of any of various aboriginal peoples of the Americas

Indian Ocean *n.* an ocean that extends from southern Asia to Antarctica and from eastern Africa to southeastern Australia

In-di-an sum-mer *n.* a period of mild weather in late autumn

in-di-cate *v.* to point out; to show; to serve as a sign or symptom; to signify; to suggest the advisability of; to call for **indication, indicator** *n.*

in-dic-a-tive *adj.* serving to indicate; of or being a verb mood used to express actions and conditions that are objective facts *n.* the indicative mood; a verb in the indicative mood

in-dict *v.* to accuse of an offense; to charge; to make a formal accusation against by the findings of a grand jury **indictable** *adj.*, **indictor, indictment** *n.*

in-dif-fer-ent *adj.* having no marked feeling or preference; impartial; neither good nor bad **indifference** *n.*, **indifferently** *adv.*

in-dig-e-nous *adj.* living or occurring naturally in an area; native

in-di-gent *adj.* impoverished; needy **indigence** *n.*

in-di-ges-tion *n.* difficulty or discomfort in digesting food

in-dig-nant *adj.* marked by or filled with indignation **indignantly** *adv.*

in-dig-na-tion *n.* anger aroused by injustice, unworthiness, or unfairness

in-dig-ni-ty *n., pl.* **-ies** humiliating treatment; something that offends one's pride

in-di-go *n., pl.* **-gos** *or* **-goes** a blue dye obtained from a plant or produced synthetically; a dark blue

in-di-go bunt-ing *n.* a small North American bird, the male of which has deep-blue plumage

in-di-go snake *n.* a non-venomous bluish-black snake found in the southern United States and northern Mexico

in-di-rect *adj.* not taking a direct course; not straight to the point **indirection** *n.*, **indirectly** *adv.*

in-dis-creet *adj.* lacking discretion **indiscreetly** *adv.*, **indiscretion** *n.*

in-dis-pen-sa-ble *adj* necessary; essential **indispensability, indispensable** *n.*, **indispensably** *adv.*

in-dite *v.* to write; to compose; to put down in writing **inditer** *n.*

in-di-um *n.* a soft, silver-white, metallic element used for mirrors and transistor compounds, symbolized by In.

in-di-vid-u-al *adj.* of, for, or relating to a single human being **individually** *adv.*

in-di-vis-i-ble *adj.* not able to be divided

in-doc-tri-nate *v.* to instruct in a doctrine or belief; to train to accept a system of thought uncritically **indoctrination** *n.*

In-do--Eu-ro-pe-an *n.* a family of languages comprising most of the languages of Europe and parts of southern Asia **Indo-European** *adj.*

in-do-lent *adj.* disinclined to exert oneself; lazy **indolence** *n.*

in-dom-i-ta-ble *adj.* incapable of being subdued or defeated **-ably** *adv.*

in-du-bi-ta-ble *adj.* too evident to be doubted **indubitably** *adv.*

in-duce *v.* to move by persuasion or influence; to cause to occur; to infer by inductive reasoning **inducer** *n.*

in-duce-ment *n.* the act of inducing; something that induces

in-duct *v.* to place formally in office; to admit as a new member; to summon into military service **inductee** *n.*

in-duc-tance *n.* a circuit element, usually

a conducting coil, in which electromagnetic induction generates electromotive force

in-duc-tion *n.* the act of inducting or of being inducted; reasoning in which conclusions are drawn from particular instances or facts; the generation of electromotive force in a closed circuit by a magnetic field that changes with time; the production of an electric charge in an uncharged body by bringing a charged body close to it

in-dulge *v.* to give in to the desires of, especially to excess; to yield to; to allow oneself a special pleasure **-ger** *n.*

in-dus-tri-al *adj.* of, relating to, or used in industry **industrially** *adv.*

in-dus-tri-ous *adj.* working steadily and hard; diligent
industriously *adv.*, **industriousness** *n.*

in-dus-try *n., pl.* **-tries** the commercial production and sale of goods and services; a branch of manufacture and trade; industrial management as distinguished from labor; diligence

in-e-bri-ate *v.* to make drunk; to intoxicate **inebriated,**
inebriant *adj. & n.*, **inebriation** *n.*

in-ef-fa-ble *adj.* beyond expression; indescribable **ineffably** *adv.*

in-ef-fi-cient *adj.* wasteful of time, energy, or materials
inefficiency *n.*, **inefficiently** *adv.*

in-e-luc-ta-ble *adj.* not capable of being avoided or overcome **ineluctably** *adv.*

in-ept *adj.* awkward or incompetent; not suitable **ineptitude, ineptness** *n.*,
ineptly *adv.*

in-e-qual-i-ty *n., pl.* **-ies** the condition or an instance of being unequal; social or economic disparity; lack of regularity; in mathematics, an algebraic statement that a quantity is greater than or less than another quantity

in-eq-ui-ty *n., pl.* **-ies** injustice; unfairness

in-ert *adj.* not able to move or act; slow to move or act; sluggish; displaying no chemical activity
inertly *adv.*, **inertness** *n.*

in-er-tia *n.* the tendency of a body to remain at rest or to stay in motion unless acted upon by an external force; resistance to motion or change
inertial *adj.*, **inertially** *adv.*

in-ev-i-ta-ble *adj.* not able to be avoided or prevented **inevitability** *n.*,
inevitably *adv.*

in-ex-o-ra-ble *adj.* not capable of being moved by entreaty; unyielding
inexorably *adv.*

in-ex-pe-ri-ence *n.* lack of experience

in-ex-pli-ca-ble *adj.* not capable of being explained **inexplicably** *adv.*

in ex-tre-mis *adv.* at the point of death

in-ex-tri-ca-ble *adj.* not capable of being untied or untangled; too complex to resolve **inextricably** *adv.*

in-fal-li-ble *adj.* not capable of making mistakes; not capable of failing; never wrong **infallibility** *n.*, **infallibly** *adv.*

in-fa-mous *adj.* having a very bad reputation; shocking or disgraceful
infamously *adv.*

in-fa-my *n., pl.* **-ies** evil notoriety or reputation; the state of being infamous; a disgraceful, publicly known act

in-fan-cy *n., pl.* **-ies** the condition or time of being an infant; an early stage of existence; in law, minority

in-fant *n.* a child in the first period of life; a very young child; in law, a minor

in-fan-ti-cide *n.* the killing of an infant

in-fan-tile *adj.* of or relating to infants or infancy; immature; childish

in-fan-tile pa-ra-ly-sis *n.* poliomyelitis

in-fan-try *n., pl.* **-ries** the branch of an army made up of soldiers who are trained to fight on foot **infantryman** *n.*

in-farct *n.* an area of dead tissue caused by an insufficient supply of blood
infarcted *adj.*, **infarction** *n.*

in-fat-u-ate *v.* to arouse an extravagant or foolish love in
infatuated *adj.*, **infatuation** *n.*

in-fect *v.* to contaminate with disease-causing microorganisms; to transmit a disease to; to affect as if by contagion
infective *adj.*

in-fec-tion *n.* invasion of a bodily part by disease-causing microorganisms; the condition resulting from such an invasion; an infectious disease

in-fe-lic-i-tous *adj.* not happy; unfortunate; not apt, as in expression
infelicity *n.*, **infelicitously** *adv.*

in-fer *v.* to conclude by reasoning; to deduce; to have as a logical consequence; to lead to as a result or conclusion **inferable** *adj.*

in-fer-ence *n.* a conclusion based on facts and premises

in-fe-ri-or *adj.* located under or below; low or lower in order, rank, or quality
inferior, inferiority *n.*

in-fer-nal *adj.* of, like, or relating to hell; damnable; abominable **infernally** *adv.*

in-fer-no *n.* a place or condition suggestive of hell

in-fest *v.* to spread in or over so as to be harmful or offensive **infestation** *n.*

in-fi-del *n.* one who has no religion; an unbeliever in a religion, especially Christianity

in-field *n.* in baseball, the part of a playing field within the base lines
infielder *n.*

in-fil-trate *v.* to pass or cause to pass into something through pores or small openings; to pass through or enter gradually or stealthily **infiltration** *n.*

in-fi-nite *adj.* without boundaries; limitless; immeasurably great or large; in mathematics, greater in value than any specified number, however large; having measure that is infinite
infinite *n.*, **infinitely** *adv.*

in-fin-i-tes-i-mal *adj.* immeasurably small **infinitesimally** *adv.*

in-fin-i-ty *n., pl.* **-ies** the quality or state of being infinite; unbounded space, time, or amount; an indefinitely large number

in-firm *adj.* physically weak, especially from age; feeble; not sound or valid
in-fir-ma-ry *n., pl.* **-ries** an institution for the care of the sick or disabled
in-flame *v.* to set on fire; to arouse to strong or excessive feeling; to intensify; to produce, affect or be affected by inflammation
in-flam-ma-ble *adj.* tending to catch fire easily; easily excited
in-flam-ma-tion *n.* localized redness, swelling, heat, and pain in response to an injury or infection
in-flate *v.* to fill and expand with a gas; to increase unsoundly; to puff up; to raise prices abnormally **inflatable** *adj.*
in-fla-tion *n.* the act or process of inflating; a period during which there is an increase in the monetary supply, causing a continuous rise in the price of goods
in-flect *v.* to turn; to veer; to vary the tone or pitch of the voice, especially in speaking; to change the form of a word to indicate number, tense, or person **inflective** *adj.*, **inflection** *n.*
in-flex-i-ble *adj.* not flexible; rigid; not subject to change; unalterable **inflexibility** *n.*, **inflexibly** *adv.*
in-flict *v.* to cause to be suffered; to impose **inflicter, inflictor, -tion** *n.*
in-flo-res-cence *n.* a characteristic arrangement of flowers on a stalk **inflorescent** *adj.*
in-flu-ence *n.* the power to produce effects, especially indirectly or through an intermediary; the condition of being affected; one exercising indirect power to sway or affect *v.* to exert influence over; to modify **influential** *adj.*
in-flu-en-za *n.* an acute, infectious viral disease marked by respiratory inflammation, fever, muscular pain, and often intestinal discomfort; the flu
in-flux *n.* a stream of people or things coming in
in-form-ant *n.* one who discloses or furnishes information which should remain secret
in-for-ma-tive *adj.* providing information; instructive
in-frac-tion *n.* a violation of a rule
in-fra-red *adj.* of, being, or using electromagnetic radiation with wave lengths longer than those of visible light and shorter than those of microwaves
in-fra-son-ic *adj.* producing or using waves or vibrations with frequencies below that of audible sound
in-fra-struc-ture *n.* an underlying base or foundation; the basic facilities needed for the functioning of a system
in-fringe *v.* to break a law; to violate; to encroach; to trespass **infringement** *n.*
in-fu-ri-ate *v.* to make very angry or furious; to enrage **infuriatingly** *adv.*, **infuriation** *n.*
in-fuse *v.* to introduce, instill or inculcate, as principles; to obtain a liquid extract by soaking a substance in water **infusion** *n.*
-ing *suff* used in forming the present participle of verbs and adjectives resembling participles; activity or action; the result or a product of an action
in-gen-ious *adj.* showing great ingenuity; to have inventive ability; clever **ingeniously** *adv.*, **ingeniousness** *n.*
in-ge-nu-i-ty *n., pl.* **-ies** cleverness; inventive skill
in-gen-u-ous *adj.* frank and straightforward; lacking sophistication
in-gest *v.* to take or put food into the body by swallowing **ingestion** *n.*, **ingestive** *adj.*
in-gle-nook *n.* a recessed area or corner near or beside a fireplace
in-glo-ri-ous *adj.* not showing courage or honor; dishonorable **ingloriously** *adv.*
in-got *n.* a mass of cast metal shaped in a bar or block
in-grain *v.* to impress firmly on the mind or nature *n.* fiber or yarn that is dyed before being spun or woven
in-grained *adj.* to be worked into the inmost texture; deep-seated
in-grate *n.* a person who is ungrateful
in-gra-ti-ate *v.* to gain favor or confidence of others by deliberate effort or manipulation **ingratiatingly** *adv.*, **ingratiation** *n.*, **ingratiatory** *adj.*
in-grat-i-tude *n.* lack of gratitude
in-gre-di-ent *n.* an element that enters into the composition of a mixture; a part of anything
in-gress *n.* a going in or entering of a building **ingression** *n.*, **ingressive** *adj.*
in-grown *adj.* growing into the flesh; growing abnormally within or into **ingrowing** *adj.*
in-gui-nal *adj., Anat.* of, pertaining to, or located in the groin
in-hab-it *v.* to reside in; to occupy as a home **inhabitability, inhabiter, inhabitation** *n.*, **inhabitable** *adj.*
in-hab-i-tant *n.* a person who resides permanently, as distinguished from a visitor
in-ha-la-tion *n.* the act of inhaling
in-ha-la-tor *n.* a device that enables a person to inhale air, anesthetics, medicated vapors, or other matter
in-hale *v.* to breathe or draw into the lungs, as air or tobacco smoke; the opposite of exhale **inhalation** *n.*
in-hal-er *n.* one that inhales; a respirator
in-here *v.* To be an essential or permanent feature; to belong
in-her-ent *adj.* forming an essential element or quality of something **inherently** *adv.*
in-her-it *v.* to receive something, as property, money, or other valuables, by legal succession or will *Biol.* to receive traits or qualities from one's ancestors or parents **inheritable** *adj.*, **inheritor** *n.*
in-her-i-tance *n.* the act of inheriting; that which is inherited or to be inherited by legal transmission to a heir
in-her-i-tance tax *n.* a tax imposed on an inherited estate
in-hib-it *v.* to restrain or hold back; to

prevent full expression
inhibitable *adj.*, **inhibitor, inhibiter** *n.*, **inhibitive, inhibitory** *adj.*
in-hi-bi-tion *n.* the act of restraining, especially a self-imposed restriction on one's behavior; a mental or psychological restraint
in--house *adj.* of, relating to, or carried on within an organization
in-hu-man *adj.* lacking pity, emotional warmth, or kindness; monstrous; not being of the ordinary human type **inhumanly** *adv.*
in-hu-mane *adj.* lacking compassion or pity; cruel **inhumanely** *adv.*
in-hu-man-i-ty *n., pl.* **-ties** the lack of compassion or pity; an inhumane or cruel act
in-im-i-cal *adj.* harmful opposition; hostile; malign **inimically** *adv.*
in-im-i-ta-ble *adj.* incapable of being matched; unique **inimitably** *adv.*
in-iq-ui-ty *n., pl.* **-ies** the grievous violation of justice; wickedness; sinfulness **iniquitous** *adj.*
in-i-tial *adj.* of or pertaining to the beginning *n.* the first letter of a name or word *v.* to mark or sign with initials **initially** *adv.*
in-i-ti-ate *v.* to begin or start; to admit someone to membership in an organization, fraternity, or group; to instruct in fundamentals *adj.* initiated **initiator** *n.*, **initiatory** *adj.*
in-i-ti-a-tive *n.* the ability to originate or follow through with a plan of action; the action of taking the first or leading step *Govt.* the power or right to propose legislative measures
in-ject *v.* to force a drug or fluid into the body through a blood vessel or the skin with a hypodermic syringe; to throw in or introduce a comment abruptly **injection** *n.*
in-junc-tion *n.* an authoritative command or order; in law, a court order requiring the party to do or to refrain from some specified action **-tive** *adj.*
in-jure *v.* to cause physical harm, damage, or pain
in-ju-ri-ous *adj.* causing injury, damage or hurt; slanderous; abusive **injuriously** *adv.*, **injuriousness** *n.*
in-ju-ry *n., pl.* **-ies** damage or harm inflicted or suffered
in-jus-tice *n.* the violation of another person's rights; an unjust act; a wrong
ink *n.* any of variously colored liquids or paste, used for writing, drawing, and printing **inker** *n.*
ink-horn *n.* a small container to hold ink
ink-ling *n.* a slight suggestion or hint; a vague idea or notion
ink-stand *n.* a stand or device for holding writing tools and ink
ink-well *n.* a small container or reservoir for holding ink
ink-y *adj.* resembling ink in color; dark; black; containing or pertaining to ink
in-laid *adj.* ornamented with wood, ivory, or other materials embedded flush with the surface
in-land *adj.* pertaining to or located in the interior of a country **inlander** *n.*
in--law *n.* a relative by marriage
in-lay *v.* to set or embed something, as gold or ivory, into the surface of a decorative design
in-let *n.* a bay or stream that leads into land; a passage between nearby islands
in-mate *n.* a person who dwells in a building with another; one confined in a prison, asylum, or hospital
inn *n.* a place of lodging where a traveler may obtain meals and/or lodging
in-nards *pl. n., Slang* the internal organs or parts of the body; the inner parts of a machine
in-nate *adj.* inborn and not acquired; having as an essential part; inherent **innately** *adv.*
in-ner *adj.* situated or occurring farther inside; relating to or of the mind or spirit
in-ner ear *n.* the part of the ear which includes the semicircular canals, vestibule, and cochlea
in-ner-most *adj.* most intimate; farthest within
in-ner tube *n.* a flexible, inflatable rubber tube placed inside a tire
in-ning *n.* in baseball, one of nine divisions of a regulation baseball game, in which each team has a turn at bat
innings *pl.* in the game of cricket, the time or period during which one side bats
inn-keep-er *n.* the proprietor or manager of an inn
in-no-cent *adj.* free from sin, evil, or moral wrong; pure; legally free from blame or guilt; not maliciously intended; lacking in experience or knowledge; naive **innocence, innocent** *n.*, **innocently** *adv.*
in-noc-u-ous *adj.* having no harmful qualities or ill effect; harmless
in-nom-i-nate bone *n., Anat.* one of the two large, irregular bones which form the sides of the pelvis
in-no-vate *v.* to introduce or begin something new **innovative** *adj.*, **innovator** *n.*
in-nu-en-do *n., pl.* **-dos** or **-does** an indirect or oblique comment, suggestion or hint
in-nu-mer-a-ble *adj.* too numerous or too much to be counted; countless
in-oc-u-late *v.* to introduce a mild form of a disease or virus to a person or animal in order to produce immunity **inoculation** *n.*
in-op-er-a-ble *adj.* unworkable; incapable of being treated or improved by surgery
in-op-er-a-tive *adj.* not working; not functioning
in-op-por-tune *adj.* inappropriate; untimely; unsuitable **inopportunely** *adv.*, **inopportuneness** *n.*
in-or-di-nate *adj.* exceeding proper or normal limits; not regulated; unrestrained **inordinately** *adv.*
in-or-gan-ic *adj.* not having or involving

living organisms, their remains, or products

in-pa-tient *n.* a patient admitted to a hospital for medical treatment

in-put *n.* the amount of energy delivered to a machine; in computer science, information that is put into a data-processing system *Elect.* the voltage, current, or power that is delivered to a circuit

in-quest *n.* a legal investigation into the cause of death

in-quire *v.* to ask a question; to make an investigation **inquirer** *n.*, **inquiringly** *adv.*

in-quir-y *n., pl.* **-ies** the act of seeking or inquiring; a request or question for information; a very close examination; an investigation or examination of facts or evidence

in-qui-si-tion *n.* a former Roman Catholic tribunal established to seek out and punish heretics; an interrogation that violates individual rights; an investigation **inquisitor** *n.*, **inquisitorial** *adj.*

in-quis-i-tive *adj.* curious; probing; questioning **inquisitively** *adv.*, **inquisitiveness** *n.*

in-sane *adj.* afflicted with a serious mental disorder impairing a person's ability to function; the characteristic of a person who is not sane **insanely** *adv.*, **insanity** *n.*

in-san-i-tar-y *adj.* not sanitary; not hygienic and dangerous to one's health

in-scribe *v.* to write, mark, or engrave on a surface; to enter a name in a register or on a formal list; to write a short note on a card *Geom.* to enclose one figure in another so that the latter encloses the former **inscriber** *n.*

in-scru-ta-ble *adj.* difficult to interpret or understand; incomprehensible **-bility, inscrutableness** *n.*, **inscrutably** *adv.*

in-sect *n., Zool.* any of a numerous cosmopolitan class of small to minute winged invertebrate animals with 3 pairs of legs, a segmented body, and usually 2 pairs of wings

in-sec-ti-cide *n.* a substance for killing insects

in-sec-tiv-o-rous *adj.* feeding on insects

in-se-cure *adj.* troubled by anxiety and apprehension; threatened; not securely guarded; unsafe; liable to break, fail, or collapse **insecurely** *adv.*, **insecurity** *n.*

in-sem-i-nate *v.* to introduce semen into the uterus of; to make pregnant; to sow seed **insemination, inseminator** *n.*

in-sen-sate *adj.* showing a lack of humane feeling; unconscious

in-sen-si-ble *adj.* deprived of consciousness; unconscious; incapable of perceiving or feeling; unmindful; unaware **insensibility** *n.*, **insensibly** *adv.*

in-sen-ti-ent *adj.* without sensation or consciousness **insentience** *n.*

in-sep-a-ra-ble *adj.* incapable of being separated or parted **inseparability** *n.*, **inseparably** *adv.*

in-sert *v.* to put in place; to set *n.* in printing, something inserted or to be inserted **insertion** *n.*

in-set *v.* to set in; to implant; to insert

in-shore *adj.* near or moving toward the shore **inshore** *adv.*

in-side *n.* the part, surface, or space that lies within

insides *n.* The internal parts or organs **inside** *adj.*

in-sid-er *n.* one having special knowledge or access to confidential information

in-sid-i-ous *adj.* cunning or deceitful; treacherous; seductive; attractive but harmful **insidiously** *adv.*, **invidiousness** *n.*

in-sight *n.* perception into the true or hidden nature of things **insightful** *adj.*, **insightfully** *adv.*

in-sig-ni-a *n., pl.* **-nia** *or* **-nias** a badge or emblem used to mark membership, honor, or office

in-sin-cere *adj.* not sincere; hypocritical **insincerely** *adv.*, **insincerity** *n.*

in-sin-u-ate *v.* to suggest something by giving a hint; to introduce by using ingenious and sly means **insinuating** *adv.*, **insinuation** *n.*

in-sip-id *adj.* lacking of flavor; tasteless; flat; dull; lacking interest **insipidly** *adv.*, **insipidness** *n.*

in-sist *v.* to demand or assert in a firm way; to dwell on something repeatedly, as to emphasize **insistence** *n.*, **insistent** *adj.*, **insistently** *adv.*

in-so-far *adv.* to such an extent

in-sole *n.* the fixed inside sole of a shoe or boot; a removable strip of material put inside a shoe for protection or comfort

in-sol-u-ble *adj.* incapable of being dissolved; not soluble; not capable of being solved **insolubility, insolubleness** *n.*, **insolubly** *adv.*

in-sol-vent *adj.* in law, unable to meet debts; bankrupt

in-som-ni-a *n.* the chronic inability to sleep **insomniac** *n.*

in-sou-ci-ant *adj.* lighthearted and cheerful; unconcerned; not bothered **insouciance** *n.*

in-spect *v.* to examine or look at very carefully for flaws; to examine or review officially **-ion, inspector** *n.*

in-spi-ra-tion *n.* the stimulation within the mind of some idea, feeling, or impulse which leads to creative action; a divine or holy presence which inspires; the act of inhaling air **inspirational** *adj.*, **inspirationally** *adv.*

in-spire *v.* to exert or guide by a divine influence; to arouse and create high emotion; to exalt; to inhale; breathe in **inspirer** *n.*, **inspiringly** *adv.*

inst *abbr.* instant; institute; institution

in-sta-bil-i-ty *n., pl.* **-ties** lacking stability

in-stall *or* **in-stal** *v.* to put in position for service; to place into an office or position; to settle **installation, installer** *n.*

in-stall-ment *or* **in-stal-ment** *n.* one of

several payments due in specified amounts at specified intervals

in-stance *n.* an illustrative case or example; a step in proceedings *v.* to illustrate

in-stant *n.* a very short time; a moment; a certain or specific point in time *adj.* instantaneously; immediate; urgent

in-stan-ta-ne-ous *adj.* happening with no delay; instantly; completed in a moment **instantaneously** *adv.*

in-stant-ly *adv.* immediately; at once

in-stead *adv.* in lieu of that just mentioned

in-step *n., Anat.* the arched upper part of the human foot

in-sti-gate *v.* to urge forward; to stir up; to foment; to provoke **instigation, instigator** *n.*

in-still *or* **in-stil** *v.* to introduce by gradual instruction or effort; to pour in slowly by drops **instillation, instiller** *n.*

in-stinct *n.* the complex and normal tendency or response of a given species to act in ways essential to its existence, development, and survival **-tive, instinctual** *adj.*, **instinctively** *adv.*

in-sti-tute *v.* to establish or set up; to find; to initiate; to set in operation; to start *n.* an organization set up to promote or further a cause; an institution for educating

in-sti-tu-tion *n.* the principle custom that forms part of a society or civilization; an organization which performs a particular job or function, such as research, charity, or education; a place of confinement such as a prison or mental hospital **institutionalize** *v.*, **institutional** *adj.*, **institutionally** *adv.*

in-struct *v.* to impart skill or knowledge; to teach; to give orders or direction **instructive** *adj.*

in-struc-tion *n.* The act of teaching or instructing; important knowledge; a lesson; an order or direction

in-struc-tor *n.* one who instructs; a teacher; a low-rank college teacher, not having tenure **instructorship, instructress** *n.*

in-stru-ment *n.* a mechanical tool or implement; a device used to produce music; a person who is controlled by another; a dupe; in law, a formal legal document, deed, or contract

in-stru-men-tal *adj.* acting or serving as a means; pertaining to, composed for, or performed on a musical instrument **instrumentally** *adv.*

in-stru-men-tal-ist *n.* a person who plays or performs with a musical instrument

in-stru-men-tal-i-ty *n., pl.* **-ies** anything that serves to accomplish a purpose; means or agency

in-stru-men-tā-tion *n.* the use of instruments or work performed with instruments *Mus.* the arrangement of music for instruments

in-sub-or-di-nate *adj.* not obedient; not obeying orders **insubordinately** *adv.*, **insubordination** *n.*

in-sub-stan-tial *adj.* unreal; imaginary; not solid or firm; flimsy **insubstantiality** *n.*

in-suf-fi-cient *adj.* inadequate; not enough **insufficiently** *adv.*, **insufficiency** *n.*

in-su-lar *adj.* of or related to an island; typical or suggestive of life on an island; narrow-minded; limited in customs, opinions, and ideas **insularity** *n.*

in-su-late *v.* to isolate; to wrap or surround with nonconducting material in order to prevent the passage of heat, electricity, or sound into or out of; to protect with wrapping or insulation **insulation, insulator** *n.*

in-su-lin *n., Biochem.* the hormone released by the pancreas, essential in regulating the metabolism of sugar; a preparation of this hormone removed from the pancreas of a pig or an ox, used in the treatment of diabetes

in-sult *v.* to speak or to treat with insolence or contempt; to abuse verbally *n.* an act or remark that offends someone **insulter** *n.*, **insulting** *adj.*, **insultingly** *adv.*

in-su-per-a-ble *adj.* insurmountable; not able to be overcome **insuperability** *n.*, **insuperably** *adv.*

in-sur-ance *n.* protection against risk, loss, or ruin; the coverage an insurer guarantees to pay in the event of death, loss, or medical bills; a contract guaranteeing such protection on future specified losses in return for annual payments; any safeguard against risk or harm **insurability** *n.*, **-able** *adj.*

in-sure *v.* to guarantee against loss of life, property, or other types of losses; to make certain; to ensure; to buy or issue insurance **insurability** *n.*, **insurable** *adj.*

in-sured *n.* a person protected by an insurance policy

in-sur-er *n.* the person or company which insures someone against loss or damage

in-sur-mount-a-ble *adj.* incapable of being overcome **insurmountably** *adv.*

in-sur-rec-tion *n.* an open revolt against an established government **insurrectional** *adj.*, **insurrectionist** *n* **insurrectionary** *adj. & n.*,

in-sus-cep-ti-ble *adj.* immune; incapable of being infected **insusceptibility** *n.*

in-tact *adj.* remaining whole and not damaged in any way **intactness** *n.*

in-take *n.* the act of taking in or absorbing; the amount or quantity taken in or absorbed

in-tan-gi-ble *adj.* incapable of being touched; vague or indefinite to the mind **intangibility, intangibleness** *n.*, **intangibly** *adv.*

in-te-ger *n.* any of the numbers 1, 2, 3, etc., including all the positive whole numbers and all the negative numbers and zero; a whole entity

in-te-gral *adj.* being an essential and indispensable part of a whole; made up, from, or formed of parts that constitute a unity

in-te-grate *v.* to make into a whole by joining parts together; to unify; to be open to people of all races or ethnic groups **integration** *n.*, **integrative** *adj.*

in-teg-ri-ty *n.* uprightness of character; honesty; the condition, quality, or state of being complete or undivided

in-tel-lect *n.* the power of the mind to understand and to accept knowledge; the state of having a strong or brilliant mind; a person of notable intellect

in-tel-lec-tu-al *adj.* pertaining to, possessing, or showing intellect; inclined to rational or creative thought *n.* a person who pursues and enjoys matters of the intellect and of refined taste **intellectuality** *n.*, **intellectually** *adv.*

in-tel-lec-tu-al-ize *v.* to examine objectively so as not to become emotionally involved **intellectualization, intellectualizer** *n.*

in-tel-li-gence *n.* the capacity to perceive and comprehend meaning; information; news; the gathering of secret information, as by military or police authorities; information so collected

in-tel-li-gent *adj.* having or showing intelligence **intelligently** *adv.*

in-tel-li-gi-ble *adj.* having the capabilities of being understood; understanding

in-tend *v.* to have a plan or purpose in mind; to design for a particular use **intended** *adj.*

in-tense *adj.* extreme in strength, effect, or degree; expressing strong emotion, concentration, or strain; profound **intensely** *adv.*, **intenseness** *n.*

in-ten-si-fy *v.* to become or make more intense or acute **intensification** *n.*

in-ten-si-ty *n.*, *pl.* **-ies** the quality of being intense or acute; a great effect, concentration, or force

in-ten-sive *adj.* forceful and concentrated; marked by a full and complete application of all resources **intensively** *adv.*

intensive care *n.* the hospital care provided for a gravely ill patient in specially designed rooms with monitoring devices and life-support systems

in-tent *n.* a purpose, goal, aim, or design **intently** *adv.*, **intentness** *n.*

in-ten-tion *n.* a plan of action; purpose, either immediate or ultimate

in-ten-tion-al *adj.* deliberately intended or done **-lity** *n.*, **intentionally** *adv.*

in-ter *v.* to place in a grave; bury **interment** *n.*

inter- *pref.* mutually; with each other; together; among or between

in-ter-act *v.* to act on each other or with each other **interaction** *n.*, **interactive** *adj.*

in-ter-breed *v.* to crossbreed; to breed together two different species

in-ter-cede *v.* to argue or plead on another's behalf **interceder** *n.*

in-ter-cept *v.* to interrupt the path or course of; to seize or stop **intercept, interception** *n.*

in-ter-cep-tor *or* **in-ter-cept-er** *n.* one who or that which intercepts; a fighter plane designed for the pursuit and interception of enemy aircraft

in-ter-ces-sion *n.* an entreaty or prayer on behalf of others **intercessor** *n.*, **intercessional, intercessory** *adj.*

in-ter-change *v.* to put each in the place of another; to give and receive in return *n.* the intersection of a highway which allows traffic to enter or turn off without obstructing other traffic **interchangeable** *adj.*, **interchanger** *n.*

in-ter-col-le-gi-ate *adj.* involving or pertaining to two or more colleges

in-ter-com *n.*, *Informal* a two-way communication system, as used in different areas of a home or business

in-ter-com-mu-ni-cate *v.* to communicate with each other **-tion** *n.*, **intercommunicative** *adj.*

in-ter-con-ti-nen-tal *adj.* pertaining to or involving two or more continents

in-ter-course *n.* mutual exchange between persons or groups; communication; sexual intercourse

in-ter-dict *v.* to forbid or prohibit by official decree **interdiction, interdictor** *n.*, **interdictory** *adj.*

in-ter-est *n.* curiosity or concern about something; that which is to one's benefit; legal or financial right, claim, or share, as in a business; a charge for a loan of money, usually a percent of the amount borrowed

in-ter-est-ed *adj.* having or displaying curiosity; having a right to share in something **interestedly** *adv.*

in-ter-est-ing *adj.* stimulating interest, attention, or curiosity **interesting** *adv.* **interestingness** *n.*

in-ter-face *n.* a surface forming a common boundary between adjacent areas; in computer science, the software or hardware connecting one device or system to another **interface** *v.*, **interfacial** *adj.*

in-ter-fere *v.* to come between; to get in the way; to be an obstacle or obstruction **interference** *n.*

in-ter-ga-lac-tic *adj.* between galaxies

in-ter-im *n.* a time between events or periods *adj.* temporary.

in-te-ri-or *adj.* of, or contained in the inside; inner; away from the coast or border; inland; private; not exposed to view

in-ter-ject *v.* to go between other parts or elements; to add something between other things **interjector** *n.*, **interjectory** *adj.*

in-ter-jec-tion *n.* a word used as an exclamation to express emotion, as *Oh! Heavens! Super!* **interjectional** *adj.*

in-ter-lace *v.* to join by weaving together; to intertwine; to blend

in-ter-lin-e-ar *adj.* situated or inserted between lines of a text

in-ter-lock *v.* to join closely

in-ter-loc-u-tor *n.* one who takes part in a conversation

in-ter-loc-u-to-ry *adj.* having the nature of a dialogue; in law, pronounced

while a suit is pending and temporarily in effect
in-ter-lope *v.* to intrude or interfere in the rights of others
in-ter-lude *n.* a period of time that occurs in and divides some longer process; light entertainment between the acts of a show, play, or other more serious entertainment
in-ter-mar-ry *v.* to marry someone who is not a member of one's own religion, class, race, or ethnic group
intermarriage *n.*
in-ter-me-di-ar-y *n., pl.* **-ies** a mediator *adj.* coming between; intermediate
in-ter-me-di-ate *adj.* situated or occurring in the middle or between
intermediately *adv.*,**intermediateness** *n.*
in-ter-min-gle *v.* to blend or become mixed together
in-ter-mis-sion *n.* a temporary interval of time between events or activities; the pause in the middle of a performance
in-ter-mit-tent *adj.* ceasing from time to time; coming at intervals
in-tern *or* **in-terne** *n.* a medical school graduate undergoing supervised practical training in a hospital *v.* to confine, as in wartime
internment, internship *n.*
in-ter-nal *adj.* of or pertaining to the inside; pertaining to the domestic affairs of a country; intended to be consumed by the body from the inside
in-ter-nal--com-bus-tion en-gine *n.* an engine in which fuel is burned inside the engine
in-ter-nal med-i-cine *n.* the branch of medicine that studies and treats the nonsurgical diseases
in-ter-na-tion-al *adj.* pertaining to or involving two or more nations
internationally *adv.*
in-ter-na-tion-al-ism *n.* the policy of cooperation among nations where politics and economics are concerned
internationalist *n.*
in-ter-nec-ine *adj.* mutually destructive to both sides; involving struggle within a group
in-tern-ee *n.* a person who is confined or interned
in-ter-nist *n.* a physician who is a specialist in internal medicine
in-ter-play *n.* action, movement, or influence between or among people
interplay *v.*
in-ter-po-late *v.* to insert between other things or elements; to change something by introducing additions or insertions **interpolation, interpolator** *n.*
in-ter-pose *v.* to put between parts; to put in or inject a comment into a conversation or speech; to intervene
interposer, interposition *n.*
in-ter-pret *v.* to convey the meaning of something by explaining or restating; to present the meaning of something, as in a picture; to take words spoken or written in one language and put them into another language **-able** *adj.*, **interpretation, interpreter** *n.*
in-ter-pre-ta-tive *or* **in-ter-pre-tive** *adj.* of or based on interpreting; to provide an interpretation **interpretatively** *adv.*
in-ter-ra-cial *adj.* between, among, or affecting different races
in-ter-reg-num *n., pl.* **-nums** *or* **-na** an interval between two successive reigns; a break in continuity
in-ter-re-late *v.* to have or to put into a mutual relationship
interrelation, interrelationship *n.*
in-ter-ro-gate *v.* to question formally
interrogation, interrogator *n.*
in-ter-rog-a-tive *adj.* asking or having the nature of a question *n.* a word used to ask a question **interrogatively** *adv.*
in-ter-rupt *v.* to break the continuity of something; to intervene abruptly while someone else is speaking or performing **interrupter, interruption** *n.*, **interruptive** *adj.*
in-ter-scho-las-tic *adj.* conducted between or among schools
in-ter-sect *v.* to divide by cutting through or across; to form an intersection; to cross
in-ter-sec-tion *n.* a place of crossing; a place where streets or roads cross; in mathematics, the point common to two or more geometric elements
in-ter-sperse *v.* to scatter among other things **interspersion** *n.*
in-ter-state *adj.* between, involving, or among two or more states
in-ter-stel-lar *adj.* among or between the stars
in-ter-stice *n.* the small space between things **interstitial** *adj.*
in-ter-twine *v.* to unite by twisting together **intertwinement** *n.*
in-ter-ur-ban *adj.* between or among connecting urban areas
in-ter-val *n.* the time coming between two points or objects; a period of time between events or moments *Mus.* the difference in pitch between two tones
in-ter-vene *v.* to interfere or take a decisive role so as to modify or settle something; to interfere with force in a conflict **intervention** *n.*
in-ter-view *n.* a conversation conducted by a reporter to elicit information from someone; a conversation led by an employer who is trying to decide whether to hire someone
interview *v.*, **interviewer** *n.*
in-ter-weave *v.* to weave together; to intertwine
in-tes-tate *adj.* having made no valid will; not disposed of by a will
intestacy *n.*
in-tes-tine or in-tes-tines n. *Anat.* the section of the alimentary canal from the stomach to the anus
intestinal *adj.*, **intestinally** *adv.*
in-ti-mate *adj.* characterized by close friendship or association
intimately *adv.*, **intimacy, -ness** *n.*
in-tim-i-date *v.* to make timid or fearful; to frighten; to discourage or suppress by threats or by violence

intimidation, intimidator *n.*
in-to *prep.* to the inside of; to a form or condition of; to a time in the midst of
in-tol-er-a-ble *adj.* not tolerable; unbearable **intolerability, intolerableness** *n.*, **intolerably** *adv.*
in-tol-er-ant *adj.* not able to endure; not tolerant of the rights or beliefs of others **intolerance** *n.*, **intolerantly** *adv.*
in-to-na-tion *n.* the manner of speaking, especially the meaning and melody given to speech by changing levels of pitch
in-tone *v.* to utter or recite in a monotone; to chant **intoner** *n.*
in to-to *adv., L.* totally
in-tox-i-cate *v.* to make drunk; to elate or excite **intoxicant, intoxication** *n.*
intra- *prefix* within
in-tra-cel-lu-lar *adj.* within a cell or cells
in-tra-cra-ni-al *adj.* within the skull
in-trac-ta-ble *adj.* hard to manage; difficult to cure or treat
in-tra-dos *n., pl.* **-dos** *or* **-doses** the interior curve of an arch or vault
in-tra-mu-ral *adj.* taking place within a school, college, or institution; competition limited to a school community
in-tra-mus-cu-lar *adj.* within a muscle
in-tran-si-gent *adj.* refusing to moderate a position; uncompromising **intransigence, intransigency, intransigent** *n.*
in-tra-oc-u-lar *adj.* within the eyeball
in-tra-state *adj.* within a state
in-tra-u-ter-ine *adj.* within the uterus
in-tra-u-ter-ine de-vice *n.* a metal or plastic loop, ring, or spiral inserted into the uterus as a means of contraception
in-tra-ve-nous *adj.* within a vein **intravenously** *adv.*
in-trep-id *adj.* courageous; unshaken by fear; bold **intrepidly** *adv.*, **intrepidness** *n.*
in-tri-cate *adj.* having many perplexingly entangled parts or elements; complex; difficult to solve or understand **intricacy** *n.*, **intricately** *adv.*
in-trigue *v.* to arouse the curiosity or interest; to fascinate; to plot; to conspire; to engage in intrigues *n.* a secret or illicit love affair; a secret plot or plan **intriguer** *n.*
in-trin-sic *adj.* belonging to the true or fundamental nature of a thing; inherent **intrinsically** *adv.*
in-tro-duce *v.* to present a person face to face to another; to make acquainted; to bring into use or practice for the first time; to bring to the attention of **introducer, introduction** *n.*, **introductory** *adj.*
in-tro-it *or* **In-tro-it** *n.* a hymn or psalm sung at the beginning of a Roman Catholic Mass
in-tro-vert *n., Psychol.* a person who directs his interest to himself and not to friends or social activities **introversion** *n.*, **introversive, introverted** *adj.*
in-trude *v.* to thrust or push oneself in; to come in without being asked or wanted
in-tu-it *v.* to understand through intuition
in-tu-i-tion *n.* the direct knowledge or awareness of something without conscious attention or reasoning; knowledge that is acquired in this way **intuitive** *adj.*, **intuitively** *adv.*
in-un-date *v.* to overwhelm with abundance or excess, as with work **inundation** *n.*
in-ure *v.* to become used to accepting something which is undesirable **inurement** *n.*
in-vade *v.* to enter by force with the intent to conquer or pillage; to penetrate and overrun harmfully; to violate; to encroach upon **invader** *n.*
in-va-lid *n.* a chronically sick, bedridden, or disabled person **invalid** *adj. & v.*
in-val-id *adj.* disabled by injury or disease; not valid; unsound **invalidity** *n.*, **invalidly** *adv.*
in-val-i-date *v.* to nullify; to make invalid **invalidation, invalidator** *n.*
in-val-u-able *adj.* priceless; of great value; to be of great help or use **invaluably** *adv.*, **invaluableness** *n.*
in-var-i-a-ble *adj.* constant and not changing **invariably** *adv.*
in-va-sion *n.* the act of invading; an entrance made with the intent of overrunning or occupying **invasive** *adj.*
in-veigh *v.* to angrily protest **inveigher** *n.*
in-vei-gle *v.* to win over by flattery **inveiglement, inveigler** *n.*
in-vent *v.* to devise or create by original effort or design **inventor** *n.*
in-ven-tion *n.* the act or process of inventing; a new process, method, or device conceived from study and testing
in-ven-tive *adj.* skillful at invention or contrivance; ingenious **inventively** *adv.*, **inventiveness** *n.*
in-ven-to-ry *n., pl.* **-ies** a list of items with descriptions and quantities of each; the process of making such a list **inventory** *v.*
in-verse *adj.* reversed in order or sequence; inverted *n.* something opposite **inversely** *adv.*
in-ver-sion *n.* the act of inverting or the state of being inverted; that which is inverted
in-vert *v.* to turn upside down; to reverse the position, condition, or order of something **inverter** *n.*, **invertible** *adj.*
in-ver-te-brate *adj.* lacking a backbone or spinal column **invertebrate** *n.*
in-vest *v.* to use money for the purchase of stocks or property in order to obtain profit or interest; to place in office formally; to install; to make an investment **investor** *n.*
in-ves-ti-gate *v.* to search or inquire into; to examine carefully **-tive** *adj.*, **investigation, investigator** *n.*
in-ves-ti-ture *n.* the ceremony or act of

investing or installing someone in a high office
in-vest-ment *n.* the act of investing money or capital to gain interest or income; property acquired and kept for future benefit
in-vig-o-rate *v.* to give strength or vitality to **invigoratingly** *adv.*, **-tion** *n.*
in-vin-ci-ble *adj.* incapable of being defeated **invincibility** *n.*, **invincibly** *adv.*
in-vi-o-la-ble *adj.* secure from profanation; safe from assault
inviolability *n.*, **inviolably** *adv.*
in-vi-o-late *adj.* not violated
inviolately *adv.*, **inviolateness** *n.*
in-vis-i-ble *adj.* not capable of being seen; not visible; not open to view; hidden **invisibility** *n.*, **invisibly** *adv.*
in-vi-ta-tion *n.* the act of inviting; the means or words that request someone's presence or participation
in-vite *v.* to request the presence or participation of; to make a formal or polite request for; to provoke; to entice; to issue an invitation
in-vit-ing *adj.* tempting; attractive
invitingly *adv.*
in-vo-ca-tion *n.* an appeal to a deity or other agent for inspiration, witness, or help; a prayer used at the opening of a ceremony or service
in-voice *n.* an itemized list of merchandise shipped or services rendered, including prices, shipping instructions, and other costs; a bill **invoice** *v.*
in-voke *v.* to call upon for aid, support, or inspiration; to conjure **invoker** *n.*
in-vol-un-tar-y *adj.* not done by choice or willingly *n. Physiol.* muscles which function without an individual's control **involuntariness** *n.*
in-volve *v.* to include as a part; to make a participant of; to absorb; to engross
involvement *n.*
in-vul-ner-a-ble *adj.* to be immune to attack; impregnable; not able to be physically injured or wounded
invulnerability *n.*, **invulnerably** *adv.*
in-ward *adj.* situated toward the inside, center, or interior; of or existing in the mind or thoughts
inwardness *n.*, **inwardly** *adv.*
i-o-dine *n.* a grayish-black, corrosive, poisonous element, symbolized by I; a solution made up of iodine, alcohol, and sodium iodide or potassium iodide which is used as an antiseptic
i-on *n., Physics.* an atom or group of atoms which carries a positive or negative electric charge as a result of having lost or gained one or more electrons
i-on-ize *v.* to convert completely or partially into ions **ionization** *n.*
IOU *abbr.* I owe you
ip-so fac-to *adv., L.* by that very fact or act
IQ *abbr.* intelligence quotient
i-ras-ci-ble *adj.* easily provoked to anger; quick-tempered **irascibly** *adv.*, **irascibility, irascibleness** *n.*
i-rate *adj.* raging; angry **irately** *adv.*
ir-i-des-cent *adj.* displaying the colors of the rainbow in shifting hues and patterns **iridescence** *n.*
i-ris *n., pl.* **irises** *or* **irides** the pigmented part of the eye which regulates the size of the pupil by contracting and expanding around it *Bot.* a plant with narrow sword-shaped leaves and large, handsome flowers, as the gladiolus and crocus
I-rish *adj.* pertaining to Ireland and its people or their language
irk *v.* to annoy or to weary
Iron Age *n.* the most recent of three early stages of human progress, following the Stone Age and the Bronze Age
i-ron-bound *adj.* bound with iron; unyielding
i-ron-clad *adj.* covered with protective iron plates; strict; unbreakable
iron curtain *n.* an impenetrable political and ideological barrier between the Soviet bloc and the rest of the world
i-ron-ic *adj.* marked by or characterized by irony **ironical** *adj.*, **ironically** *adv.*
iron lung *n.* a tank which encloses the entire body with the exception of the head and regulates the respiration of a patient by alternately increasing and decreasing air pressure
i-ron-stone *n.* a heavy, white, glazed pottery
i-ro-ny *n., pl.* **-ies** a literary device for conveying meaning by saying the direct opposite of what is really meant
ir-ra-di-ate *v.* to subject to ultraviolet light, radiation, or similar rays
irradiation, irradiator *n.*
ir-ra-tion-al *adj.* unable to reason; contrary to reason; absurd; in mathematics, a number which is not expressible as an integer or a quotient of integers **irrationality** *n.*, **irrationally** *adv.*
ir-rec-on-cil-a-ble *adj.* not able or willing to be reconciled
irreconcilability *n.*, **irreconcilably** *adv.*
ir-re-deem-a-ble *adj.* not capable of being recovered, bought back, or paid off; not convertible into coin
ir-re-duc-i-ble *adj.* not having the capabilities of reduction, as to a smaller amount
irreducibility *n.*, **irreducibly** *adv.*
ir-ref-ra-ga-ble *adj.* cannot be refuted or disproved **irrefragably** *adv.*
ir-re-fut-able *adj.* cannot be disproved
irrefutability *n.*, **irrefutably** *adv.*
ir-reg-u-lar *adj.* not according to the general rule or practice; not straight, uniform, or orderly; uneven *n.* one who is irregular **irregularity** *n.*, **irregularly** *adv.*
ir-rel-e-vant *adj.* not pertinent or related to the subject matter **-ly** *adv.*, **irrelevance, irrelevancy** *n.*
ir-re-lig-ious *adj.* lacking in religion; opposed to religion **irreligiously** *adv.*, **irreligiousness, irreligion** *n.*
ir-re-mis-si-ble *adj.* unpardonable, as for sin **irremissibility** *n.*

ir-re-mov-a-ble *adj.* not removable
irremovably *adv.*
ir-rep-a-ra-ble *adj.* unable to be set right or repaired **irreparability** *n.*, **irreparably** *adv.*
ir-re-place-a-ble *adj.* unable to be replaced
ir-re-press-i-ble *adj.* impossible to hold back or restrain
irrepressibility *n.*, **irrepressibly** *adv.*
ir-re-proach-a-ble *adj.* blameless; not meriting reproach **-ness** *n.*, **irreproachably** *adv.*
ir-re-sist-i-ble *adj.* completely fascinating; impossible to resist
irresistibility *n.*, **irresistibly** *adv.*
ir-res-o-lute *adj.* lacking resolution; indecisive; lacking firmness of purpose
irresolutely *adv.*, **irresoluteness** *n.*
ir-re-spec-tive *adj.* regardless of
ir-re-spon-si-ble *adj.* lacking in responsibility; not accountable
irresponsibility *n.*, **irresponsibly** *adv.*
ir-re-triev-a-ble *adj.* unable to be retrieved or recovered
ir-rev-er-ence *n.* a lack of reverence; a disrespectful action
irreverent *adj.*, **irreverently** *adv.*
ir-re-vers-i-ble *adj.* impossible to reverse
irreversibility *n.*, **irreversibly** *adv.*
ir-rev-o-ca-ble *adj.* unable or incapable of being turned in the other direction; incapable of being repealed, annulled or undone **irrevocability** *n.*, **irrevocably** *adv.*
ir-ri-gate *v.* to water the land or crops artificially, as by means of ditches or sprinklers; to refresh with water *Med.* to wash out with a medicated fluid or water **irrigation, irrigator** *n.*, **irrigational** *adj.*
ir-ri-ta-ble *adj.* easily annoyed; ill-tempered *Pathol.* to respond abnormally to stimuli
irritability, irritableness *n.*, **irritably** *adv.*
ir-ri-tate *v.* to annoy or bother; to provoke; to be sore, chafed, or inflamed **irritator, irritation** *n.*, **irritant** *adj. & n.*, **irritatingly** *adv.*
ir-rupt *v.* to burst or rush in; to invade **irruption** *n.*, **-ive** *adj.*, **irruptively** *adv.*
IRS *abbr.* Internal Revenue Service.
is *v.* third person, singular, present tense of the verb to be
-ish *suffix* of or belonging to a nationality or ethnic group; characteristic of; the approximate age of; the approximate time of; somewhat
is-land *n.* a piece of land smaller than a continent, completely surrounded by water **islander** *n.*
isle *n.* a small island
ism *n.*, *Slang* a distinctive cause, doctrine, or theory
-ism *suffix* practice; process; a manner of behavior characteristic of person or thing; a system of principles
is-n't *contr.* is not
i-so-late *v.* to set apart from the others; to put by itself; to place or be placed in quarantine **isolation, isolator** *n.*
i-so-la-tion-ism *n.* a national policy of avoiding political or economic alliances or relations with other countries **isolationist** *n.*
i-so-mer *n.* a compound having the same kinds and numbers of atoms as another compound but differing in chemical or physical properties due to the linkage or arrangement of the atoms **isomeric** *adj.*
i-sos-ce-les tri-an-gle *n.* a triangle which has two equal sides
i-so-therm *n.* a line on a map linking points that have the same temperature **isothermal** *adj.*
i-so-tope *n.* any of two or more species of atoms of a chemical element which contain in their nuclei the same number of protons but different numbers of neutrons **isotopic** *adj.*, **isotopically** *adv.*
i-so-trop-ic *adj.* having the same value in all directions **isotropy** *n.*
Is-rae-li *adj.* of or pertaining to the country of Israel or its inhabitants **Israeli, Israel** *n.*
is-sue *n.* the act of giving out; something that is given out or published; a matter of importance to solve *Med.* a discharge as of pus or blood *v.* to come forth; to flow out; to emerge; to distribute or give out, as supplies **issuable** *adj.*, **issuer** *n.*
isth-mus *n.* a narrow strip of land which connects two larger pieces of land **isthmian** *adj.*
i-tal-i-cize *v.* to print in italics **italicization** *n.*
itch *v.*, **itchiness** *n.*, **itchy** *adj.*
-ite *suffix* a native or inhabitant of; an adherent of; a sympathizer or follower
i-tem *n.* a separately-noted unit or article included in a category or series; a short article, as in a magazine or newspaper
i-tem-ize *v.* to specify by item; to list **itemizer, itemization** *n.*
it-er-ate *v.* to state or do again; to repeat **iteration** *n.*
i-tin-er-ant *adj.* traveling from place to place; wandering
i-tin-er-ar-y *n., pl.* **-ies** a scheduled route of a trip
it'll *contr.* it will; it shall
its *adj.* the possessive case of the pronoun it
it's *contr.* it is; it has
I've *contr.* I have
i-vo-ry *n., pl.* **-ies** a hard, smooth, yellowish-white material which forms the tusks of elephants, walruses, and other animals; any substance similar to ivory **ivory** *adj.*
ivory tower *n.* a condition or attitude of withdrawal from the world and reality
i-vy *n., pl.* **-ies** a climbing plant having glossy evergreen leaves
-ization *n. suffix* the process, action, or result of doing a specified thing
-ize *suffix* to cause to become or resemble
iz-zard *n.* the letter z

J, j The tenth letter of the English alphabet.

Ja *abbr.* joint account; judge advocate

jab *v.* to poke or thrust sharply with short blows; a rapid punch **jabbingly** *adv.*

jab-ber *v.* to speak quickly or without making sense

jab-i-ru *n.* a large white bird resembling the stork

jab-ot *n.* ruffle or decoration on the front of a blouse, dress, or shirt

ja-bot-i-ca-ba *n.* a shrubby tree of the tropics

ja-cal *n.* a small hut

jac-a-mar *n.* a tropical, brilliantly colored, insectivorous bird of tropical America

ja-ca-na *n.* a small aquatic bird having long, straight claws that are adapted for walking on floating objects such as aquatic plants

jac-a-ran-da *n.* a tall tropical tree; or the fragrant wood of such a tree

jack *n.* the playing card that ranks just below a queen and bears a representation of a knave; any of various tools or devices used for raising heavy objects; the male of certain animals; a man or boy; fellow; a small flag on a ship that indicates nationality

jacks *n.* game played with a set of six-pronged metal pieces and a small ball

jack-al *n.* an African or Asian dog-like, carnivorous mammal

jack-a-napes *n.* an impudent person

jack-ass *n.* a male donkey or ass; a stupid person or one who acts in a stupid fashion

jack-boot *n.* a heavy military boot which reaches above the knee

jack-daw *n.* a glossy, black, crow-like bird

jack-et *n.* a short coat worn by men and women; an outer protective cover for a book; the skin of a cooked potato

Jack Frost *n.* a name given to frost or winter weather

jack-hammer *n.* a tool operated by air pressure, used to break pavement and to drill rock

jack--in--the--box *n.* a toy consisting of a small box from which a puppet springs up when the lid is unfastened

jack--in--the--pul-pit *n.* a common herb which grows from a turnip-shaped bulb

jack-knife *n.* a large pocketknife; a dive executed by doubling the body forward with the knees unbent and the hands touching the ankles and then straightening before entering the water; to bend in the manner of a jacknife

jack-leg *adj.* deficient in skill; an amateur

jack-light *n.* a light used for hunting or fishing at night; to fish or hunt with a light

jack--of--all--trades *n.* a person who is able to do many types of work

jack--o--lan-tern *n.* a lantern made from a hollowed out pumpkin which has been carved to resemble a face

jack pine *n.* large pine tree

jack-pot *n.* any post, prize, or pool in which the amount won is cumulative

jack rabbit *n.* a large American hare with long back legs and long ears

jade *n.* hard, translucent, green gemstone

jad-ed *adj.* fatigued; dulled; worn-out

jag *n.* a very sharp projection or point *Slang* a binge or spree

jag-ged *adj.* having jags or sharp notches; serrated **jaggedly** *adv.*, **jaggedness** *n.*

jag-uar *n.* large, spotted, feline mammal of tropical America with a tawny coat and black spots

jai alai *n.* game similar to handball in which players catch and throw a ball with long, curved, wicker baskets strapped to their arms

jail *n.* a place of confinement for incarceration

jail-bird *n., Slang* a prisoner or ex-prisoner

jail-break *n.* prison escape using force

jail de-liv-er-y *n.* the freeing of a prisoner by prisoners

jail-er *n.* the officer in charge of a jail and its prisoners

ja-lop-y *n., pl.* **-ies** *Slang* an old, rundown automobile

ja-lou-sie *n.* a window, blind, or door having adjustable horizontal slats

jam *v.* to force or wedge into a tight position *Mus.* to be a participant in a jazz session *Slang* to be in a **jam** *n.* a preserve of whole fruit boiled with sugar

jamb *n.* the vertical sidepiece of a door

jam-ba-lay-a *n.* a food dish made of rice, vegetables and various kinds of meats

jam-bo-ree *n.* a large, festive gathering

jam session *n.* an informal gathering of a group of jazz musicians

jan-gle *v.* to make a harsh unmusical sound *n.* a discordant sound **jangler** *n.*

jan-i-tor *n.* person who cleans and cares for a building **janitorial** *adj.*

ja-pan *n.* black varnish used for coating objects

jape *v.* to joke; to make fun of or mock by words or actions **japer, japery** *n.*

jar *n.* deep, cylindrical vessel with a wide mouth; a harsh sound *v.* to strike against or bump into; to affect one's feelings unpleasantly

jar-di-niere *n.* decorative pot or stand for flowers or plants

jar-gon *n.* technical or specialized vocabulary used among members of a particular profession **jargonistic** *adj.*

jar-gon-ize *v.* to write or communicate jargon; a means of expressing oneself with jargon

jas-mine *or* **jes-sa-mine** *n.* a shrub with fragrant yellow or white flowers

jas-per *n.* an opaque red, brown, or yellow variety of quartz

ja-to *n.* takeoff of an airplane which is assisted by an auxiliary rocket engine

jaun-dice *n., Pathol.* a diseased condition of the liver due to the presence of bile pigments in the blood

jaunt *n.* short journey for pleasure

jaun-ty *adj.* having a buoyantly carefree and self-confident air or matter about oneself **-ily** *adv.* **-iness** *n.*

jaunt-ing car *n.* a light weight, open air cart that has two seats, set back to back or facing each other, with an area in front for the driver

Ja-va *n., Slang* coffee

jave-lin *n.* a light spear thrown as a weapon

jave-lin throw *v.* to wound or strike with a javelin

jaw *n., Anat.* either of the two bony structures forming the framework of the mouth and holding the teeth

jaw-bone *n.* one of the bones of the jaw, especially the lower jaw

jaw-break-er *n.* very hard piece of candy. *Slang* A word which is hard to pronounce

jay *n.* any of various corvine birds of brilliant coloring

jay-hawk-er *n.* the nickname for a person who is a native of Kansas

jay-walk *v., Slang* to cross a street carelessly, violating traffic regulations and or signals **jaywalker** *n.*

jazz *n.* kind of music which has a strong rhythmic structure with frequent syncopation and often involving ensemble and solo improvisation **-er** *n.*, **-y** *adj.*

jeal-ous *adj.* suspicious or fearful of being replaced by a rival; resentful or bitter **-ly** *adv.*, **-ness**, *n.*

jean *n.* strong, twilled cotton cloth **jeans** Pants made of denim

jeep *n.* small, military, and civilian vehicle with four-wheel drive

jeer *v.* speak or shout derisively **jeer** *n.*, **jeringly** *adv.*

Je-ho-vah *n.* God, in the Christian translations of the Old Testament

je-june *adj.* lacking in substance or nourishment; immature

je-ju-num *n., pl.* **-na** *Anat.* part of the small intestine which extends from the duodenum to the ileum

jel-ly *n. pl.* **-ies** food preparation made with pectin or gelatin and having a somewhat elastic consistency; a food made of boiled and sweetened fruit juice and used as a filler or spread; *v.* to make into jelly; to become or take the form of jelly; to become gelatinous; to assume or cause to assume definite form

jel-lybean *n.* small candy having a hard, colored coating over a gelatinous center

jel-ly-fish *n., pl.* **fishes** any of a number of freeswimming marine animals of jelly-like substance

jeop-ard-ize *v.* to put in jeopardy; to expose to loss or danger

jeop-ard-y *n.* exposure to loss or danger

jer-bo-a *n.* any of a type of small, nocturnal rodent of Asia and Africa with long hind legs

jer-e-mi-ad *n.* lament or prolonged complaint

Jer-emi-ah *n.* Hebrew prophet of the seventh century B.C.

jerk *v.* give a sharp twist or pull to *n.* sudden movement, as a tug or twist *Physiol.* involuntary contraction of a muscle resulting from a reflex action **jerky, jerkily** *adv.*, **jerkiness** *n.*

jer-kin *n.* close-fitting jacket, usually sleeveless

jerk-wa-ter *adj.* of little importance

jer-ry--build *v.* build flimsily and cheaply

jer-sey *n., pl.* **-seys** a soft ribbed fabric of wool, cotton, or other material; a knitted sweater, jacket, or shirt; fawn-colored, small dairy cattle which yield milk rich in butter fat

jest *n.* action or remark intended to provoke laughter; a joke; a playful mood **jester** *n.*

Jes-u-it *n.* member of the Society of Jesus, a religious order founded in 1534

Jesus *n.* founder of Christianity, son of Mary and regarded in the Christian faith as Christ the son of God, the Messiah; also referred to as Jesus Christ or Jesus of Nazareth

jet *n.* sudden spurt or gush of liquid or gas emitted through a narrow opening; a jet airplane **jet** *adj.*

jet lag *n.* mental and physical fatigue resulting from rapid travel through several time zones

jet set *n.* international social group of wealthy individuals who travel from one fashionable place to another for pleasure **jet setter** *n.*

jet stream *n.* high-velocity wind near the troposphere, generally moving from west to east often at speeds exceeding 250 mph.; a high-speed stream of gas or other fluid expelled from a jet engine or rocket

jet-ti-son *v.* throw cargo overboard; to discard a useless or hampering item

jet-ty *n., pl.* **-ies** wall made of piling rocks, or other material which extends into a body of water to protect a harbor or influence the current; a pier

Jew *n.* descendant of the ancient Hebrew people; a person believing in Judaism

jew-el *n.* precious stone used for personal adornment; a person or thing of very rare excellence or value *v.* furnish with jewels **jewelry** *n.*

jew-eler *or* **jew-el-ler** *n.* person who makes or deals in jewelry

Jew's harp *n.* small musical instrument held between the teeth when played, consisting of a U-shaped frame with a flexible metal piece attached which is plucked with the finger to produce twanging sounds

jib *n., Naut.* triangular sail set on a stay extending from the head of the foremast to the bowsprit

jif-fy *or* **jiff** *n.* short time

jig *n.* any of a variety of fast, lively dances; the music for such a dance *Mech.* device used to hold and guide a tool **jig** *v.*

jig-ger *n.* small measure holding 1 1/2

oz. used for measuring liquor *Naut.* small sail in the stern of a sailing craft

jig-gle *v.* move or jerk lightly up and down *n.* jerky, unsteady movement

jig-saw *n.* saw having a slim blade set vertically, used for cutting curved or irregular lines

jigsaw puzzle *n.* puzzle consisting of many irregularly shaped pieces which fit together and form a picture

jilt *v.* discard a lover *n.* woman or girl who discards a lover

jim-my *n., pl.* **-ies** short crowbar, often used by a burglar *v.* to force open or break into with a jimmy

jim-son-weed *n.* tall, coarse, foul-smelling, poisonous annual weed with large, trumpet-shaped purplish or white flowers

jin-gle *v.* make a light clinking or ringing sound *n.* short, catchy song or poem, as one used for advertising

jin-go-ism *n.* extreme nationalism which is marked by a belligerent foreign policy **jingoist** *n.*, **jingoistic** *adj.*

jinn *n., pl.* **jin-ni** in the Moslem legend, a spirit with supernatural powers

jinx *n., Slang* person or thing thought to bring bad luck

jit-ney *n.* vehicle carrying passengers for a small fee

jit-ter *v., Slang* to be intensely nervous **jittery** *adj.*

jit-ter-bug *n., Slang* lively dance or one who performs this dance **jitterbug** *v.*

jit-ters *n.* nervousness

jive *n., Slang* jazz or swing music and musicians

job *n.* anything that is done; work that is done for a set fee; the project worked on; a position of employment **jobless** *adj.*, **joblessness** *n.*

job-ber *n.* one who buys goods in bulk from the manufacturer and sells them to retailers; a person who works by the job; a pieceworker

job-name *n. Computer Science.* code that is assigned to a specific job instruction in a computer program, for the operator's use

jock *n., Slang* male athlete in college; a person who participates in athletics

jock-ey *n.* person who rides a horse as a professional in a race

joc-u-lar *adj.* marked by joking; playful **jocularity** *n.*, **jocularly** *adv.*

joc-und *adj.* cheerful; merry; suggestive of high spirits and lively mirthfulness **jocundity** *n.*, **jocundly** *adv.*

jog *n.* slight movement or a slight shake; the slow steady trot of a horse; to exercise by running at a slow but steady pace **jogger** *n.*

jog-gle *v.* move or shake slightly

john *n., Slang* toilet; a prostitute's client

John *n.* one of the twelve Apostles

John Doe *n., Law* person in a legal proceeding whose true name is unknown

john-ny-cake *n.* thin bread made with cornmeal

John the Baptist *n.* baptizer of Jesus Christ

join *v.* bring or put together so as to form a unit

join-er *n.* person whose occupation is to build articles by joining pieces of wood

joint *n.* place where two or more things or parts are joined; a point where bones are connected **adj.** marked by cooperation, as a joint effort

join-ture *n., Law* settlement of property arranged by a husband which is to be used for the support of his wife after his death

joist *n.* any of a number of small parallel beams set from wall to wall to support a floor

joke *n.* something said or done to cause laughter, such as a brief story with a punch line; something not taken seriously *v.* to tell or play jokes **jokingly** *adv.*

jok-er *n.* person who jokes; a playing card

jol-li-fi-ca-tion *n.* merrymaking.

jol-ly *adj.* full of good humor; merry **jollity** *n.*, **jolly** *v.*

jolt *v.* knock or shake about *n.* sudden bump or jar, as from a blow **jolty** *adj.*

jon-quil *n.* widely grown species of narcissus related to the daffodil

josh *v., Slang* make good-humored fun of someone

joss *n.* Chinese idol or image

jos-tle *v.* make one's way through a crowd by pushing, elbowing, or shoving

jot *v.* make a brief note of something *n.* tiny bit

jounce *v.* bounce; to bump; to shake **jouncey** *adj.*

jour-nal *n.* diary or personal daily record of observations and experiences; in bookkeeping, a book in which daily financial transactions are recorded

jour-nal-ese *n.* vocabulary and style of writing supposedly characteristic of most newspapers

jour-nal-ism *n.* occupation, collection, writing, editing, and publishing of newspapers and other periodicals **-ist** *n.*, **-istic** *adj.*, **journalistically** *adv.*

jour-ney *n.* trip from one place to another over a long distance

jour-ney-man *n., pl.* **-men** worker who has served an apprenticeship in a skilled trade

joust *n.* formal combat between two knights on horseback as a part of a medieval tournament

Jove *Interj.* mild expression of surprise or emphasis

jo-vi-al *adj.* good-natured; good-humored; jolly **joviality** *n.*

jowl *n.* fleshy part of the lower jaw; the cheek **jowly** *adj.*

joy *n.* strong feeling of great happiness; delight **joyfully** *adv.*, **-fulness** *n.*, **-less** *adj.*, **-lessly** *adv.*

joy-ous *adj.* joyful; causing or feeling joy **joyously** *adv.*

joy ride *Slang* ride taken for pleasure only
joy stick *Slang* control stick of an airplane or video game
ju-bi-lant *adj.* exultantly joyful or triumphant; expressing joy
jubilance *n.*, **jubilantly** *adv.*
ju-bi-la-tion *n.* rejoicing; exultation
ju-bi-lee *n.* special anniversary of an event; any time of rejoicing
Ju-da-ism *n.* religious practices or beliefs of the Jews; a religion based on the belief in one God
judge *v., Law* public officer who passes judgment in a court *v.* decide authoritatively after deliberation
judg-ment or **judge-ment** *n.* ability to make a wise decision or to form an opinion; the act of judging *Law* sentence or determination of a court
judgmental *adj.*
ju-di-ca-ture *n.* function or action of administration of justice; law, courts, or judges as a whole
ju-di-cial *adj.* pertaining to the administering of justice, to courts of law, or to judges **judicially** *adv.*
ju-di-ci-ar-y *adj.* of, or pertaining to judges, courts, or judgments *n.* department of the government which administers the law
ju-di-cious *adj.* having, showing, or exercising good sound judgement
judiciously *adv.*, **judiciousness** *n.*
ju-do *n.* system or form of self-defense, developed from jujitsu in Japan
jug *n.* small pitcher or similar vessel for holding liquids
jug-ger-naut *n.* destructive force or object
jug-gle *v.* keep several objects continuously moving from the hand into the air; to practice fraud or deception
juggler *n.*
jug-u-lar *adj., Anat.* of or pertaining to the region of the throat or the jugular vein
jugular vein *n., Anat.* one of the large veins on either side of the neck
juice *n.* liquid part of a vegetable, fruit, or animal *Slang* electric current
juic-er *n.* device for extracting juice from fruit
juic-y *adj.* full of; abounding with juice; full of interest; richly rewarding, especially financially
ju-jit-su *or* **ju-jut-su** *n.* Japanese system of using holds, throws, and stunning blows to subdue an opponent
juke box *n.* large, automatic, coin-operated record player equipped with push buttons for the selection of records
ju-lep *n.* mint julep
ju-li-enne *adj.* cut into thin strips *n.* clear meat soup containing vegetables chopped or cut into thin strips
jum-ble *v.* to mix in a confused mass; to throw together without order
jum-bo *n.* very large person, animal, or thing *adj.* extremely large
jump *v.* spring from the ground, floor, or other surface into the air by using a muscular effort of the legs and feet; to move in astonishment
jump-er *n.* one who or that which jumps; a sleeveless dress, usually worn over a blouse
jump-y *adj.* nervous; jittery **jumpiness n.**
jump suit *n.* one piece clothing worn by parachutes
jun-co *n.* any of various small birds of North America
junc-tion *n.* place where lines or routes meet, as roads or railways; the process of joining or the act of joining
junc-ture *n.* point where two things join; a crisis; an emergency; a point in time
June beetle *or* **June bug** *n.* large, brightly colored beetle which flies in June and has larvae that live in the soil and often destroy crops
jun-gle *n.* densely covered land with tropical vegetation, usually inhabited by wild animals
jun-gle fe-ver *n.* disease of tropical regions where fever accompanies sickness
jun-gle-gym *n.* a structure with bars upon children can climb
jun-gle rot *n.* skin disease, such as a fungus
jun-ior *adj.* younger in years or rank, used to distinguish the son from the father of the same first name; the younger of two *n.* third year of high school or college
junior college *n.* college offering a two year course which is equivalent to the first two years of a four year college
junior high school *n.* school which includes the 7th, 8th, and 9th grades
ju-ni-per *n.* evergreen shrub or tree of Europe and America with dark blue berries, prickly foliage, and fragrant wood
jun-ket *n.* party, banquet, or trip **-teer** *n.*
junk-ie *or* **junk-y** *n., Slang* drug addict that uses heroin
ju-ry *n., pl.* **-ies** group of legally qualified persons summoned to serve on a judicial tribunal
just *adj.* fair and impartial in acting or judging; morally right
justly *adv.*, **justness** *n.*
jus-tice *n.* principle of moral or ideal rightness; conformity to the law
jus-ti-fy *v.* to be just, right, or valid; to declare guiltless; to adjust or space lines to the proper length
jut *v.* extend beyond the main portion; to project
ju-ve-nile *adj.* young; youthful; not yet an adult *n.* a young person; an actor who plays youthful roles; a child's book
ju-ve-nile de-lin-quent *n.* a person who is guilty of violations of the law, but is too young to be punished as an adult criminal; a young person whose behavior is out of control
jux-ta-pose *v.* put side by side; to place together

K, k The eleventh letter of the English alphabet.

kaa-ba *n.* building in the Great Mosque at Mecca that contains the sacred stone said to have been turned black in color, by the tears of the repentant pilgrims or by the sins of people; who have rubbed or touched it

ka-bob *n.* small cubes of meat cooked with vegetables

ka-bu-ki *n.* traditional Japanese drama in which dances and songs are performed in a stylized fashion

Kad-dish *n.* a Jewish prayer recited by mourners after the death of a relative and during other daily prayers in the synagogue

kaf-fee-klatsch *n.* informal conversation over coffee

kaf-ir *n.* a grain sorghum that is cultivated in dry areas, having a tough leafy stalk and is used for fodder

kai-nite *n.* a mineral that is used as a fertilizer and a source of magnesium and potassium

kai-ser *n.* an Austrian ruler from 1804-1918; an emperor; the title given to German rulers between the years of 1871 and 1918

ka-ka *n.* a New Zealand parrot, having an olivebrown color

ka-ka-po *n.* a large parrot

kale *n.* a green cabbage having crinkled leaves which do not form a tight head

ka-lie-do-scope *n.* a tubular instrument rotated to make successive symmetrical designs by using mirrors reflecting the changing patterns made by pieces of loose colored glass ath the end of a tube

kal-yard school *n.* a school of writers form the 19th century who wrote about Scottish life in a very sentimental manner, using heavy dialect

kal-mi-a *n.* an evergreen shrub of North America, having pink, ;white, or purple flowers

kame *n.* short ridge of gravel and sand that remains after glacial ice melts

kam-ik *n.* boot made of sealskin, knee-high in length and worn in the eastern arctic regions

ka-mi-ka-ze *n.* a Japanese pilot in World War II trained to make a suicidal crash; an aircraft loaded with explosives used in a suicide attack

kam-pong *n.* a group of dwellings or a local village in countries that speak Malay

kan-ga-roo *n., pl.* **-roo, roos** various herbivorous marsupials, of Australia, with short forelegs, large hind limbs, capable of jumping, and a large tail

kangaroo court *n.* self-appointed, illegal court, usually marked by incompetence or dishonesty

ka-o-lin *or* **ka-o-line** *n.* fine clay used in ceramics

ka-pok *n.* silky fiber manufactured from the fruit of the silk-cotton tree and used for stuffing cushions and life preservers

ka-put *adj., Slang* destroyed or out of order

kar-a-kul *n.* any of a breed of fat-tailed sheep of central Asia having a narrow body and coarse wiry, brown fur

kar-at *n.* unit of measure for the fineness of gold

ka-ra-te *n.* Japanese art of self-defense

kar-ma *n.* over-all effect of one's behavior, held in Hinduism and Buddhism to determine one's destiny in a future existence **kar-mic** *adj.*

ka-ross *n.* animal skins sewn together into the shape of a square and won by natives; a throw rug made from animal skins

kar-y-o-lymph *n.* the transparent substance surrounding the nucleus of a cell

ka-ty-did *n.* various green insects related to grasshoppers and crickets, having specialized organs on the wings of the male that make a shrill sound when rubbed together

katz-en-jam-mer *n.* a feeling of uneasiness, worry, or nervousness, that follows intoxication

kay-ak *n.* watertight Eskimo boat with a light frame and covered with sealskin **kayaker** *n.*

ka-zoo *n.* toy musical instrument with a paper membrane which vibrates symathelically when a player hums into the tube

kedge *n.* small anchor *v.* pull a ship by the rope of an anchor

keel *n.* central main stem on a ship or aircraft which runs lengthwise along the center line from bow to stern, to which a frame is built upwards *v.* to capsize. *keel over.* fall over suddenly; turn upside down **-ed** *adj.* **-less** *adj.*

keel-haul *v.* drag a person under the keel of a ship as a form of punishment

keel-son *n., Naut.* structural member fastened above and parallel to the keel to give additional strength

keen *adj.* having a sharp edge or point; acutely painful or harsh; intellectually acute; strong; intense *Slang* great *n.* wailing lament especially for the dead **keenly** *adv.*, **keenness** *n.*

keep *v.* to have and hold; to not let go; to maintain, as business records; to know a secret and not divulge it; to protect and defend

keep-sake *n.* memento or souvenir

keg *n.* small barrel

keg-ler *n.* bowler

kelp *n.* any of a large brown seaweeds

kel-pie *n.* sheep dog originally bred in Australia

ken-nel *n.* shelter for or a place where dogs or cats are bred, boarded, or trained **kennel** *v.*

ke-no *n.* game of chance resembling bingo; a lottery game

kep-i *n.* French military cap having a flat, round top and a visor

ker-a-tin *n.* fibrous protein which forms the basic substance of nails, hair, horns, and hoofs **keratinous** *adj.*

ker-a-ti-tis *n.* inflammation of the cornea
ker-chief *n.* piece of cloth usually worn around the neck or on the head; scarf; a handkerchief
ker-nel *n.* grain or seed, as of corn, enclosed in a hard husk; the inner substance of a nut; the central, most important part
ker-o-sene *or* **ker-o-sine** *n.* oil distilled from petroleum or coal and used for illumination
kes-trel *n.* small falcon, with gray and brown plumage
ketch *n.* small sailing vessel with two masts
ketch-up *n.* thick, smooth sauce made from tomatoes
ket-tle *n.* pot used for cooking
ket-tle-drum *n.* musical instrument with a parchment head which can be tuned by adjusting the tension
key *n.* an instrument by which the bolt of a lock is turned *adj.* of general importance
key-board *n.* bank of keys, as on a piano, typewriter, or computer terminal *v.* to set by means of a keyed typesetting machine; to generate letters by means of a word processor **keyboarder** *n.*
key club *n.* private club that offers entertainment amd serves liquor
key-note *n., Mus.* first and harmonically fundamental tone of a scale; main principle or theme
keynote address *n.* opening speech that outlines issues for discussion
key-punch *n.* machine operated from a keyboard that uses punched holes in tapes or cards for data processing systems **keypunch** *n.*, **keypuncher** *v.*
key-stone *n.* wedge-shaped stone at the center of an arch that locks its parts together; an essential part
key-stroke *n.* stroke of a key, as of a typewriter
key-way *n.* groove for a key
kg *abbr.* kilogram
khak-i *n.* yellowish brown or olive-drab color; a sturdy cloth being khaki in color **khakis** uniform of khaki cloth
khan *n.* Asiatic title of respect; a medieval Turkish, Mongolian or Tartar ruler **khanate** *n.*
khe-dive *n.* ruler of Egypt from 1867 to 1914 governing as a viceroy of the sultan of Turkey
kibble *n.*coarsely ground grain
kib-itz *v.* Slang look on and offer meddlesome advice to others **kibitzer** *n.*
kick *n.* sudden forceful thrust with the foot
kick-stand *n.* metal rod for holding up a two-wheeled bike
kick up *n.* provoke; to stir up
kid *n.* young goat; leather made from the skin of a young goat *Slang* child; youngster *v.* mock or tease playfully to deceive for fun; to fool **kidder** *n.*
kid leather *n.* soft pliable leather made from goatskin or lambskin
kid-nap *v.* seize and hold a person; unlawfully, often for ransom **kidnapper** *n.*
kid-ney *n., pl.* **-neys** either of two organs situated in the abdominal cavity of vertebrates whose function is to keep proper water balance in the body and to excrete wastes in the form of urine
kidney bean *n.* bean grown for its edible seeds
kidvid *n., Slang* television programming for children
kiel-ba-sa *n.* smoked Polish sausage
kill *n.* put to death; nullify; cancel; to slaughter for food
kill-deer *n., pl.* **-deer, -deers** bird characterized by a plaintive, penetrating cry
killer whale *n.* black and white carnivorous whale, found in the colder waters of the seas
kil-lick *n.* small anchor usually made from a stone
kill-joy *n.* one who spoils the enjoyment of others
kiln *n.* oven or furnace for hardening or drying a substance, especially one for firing ceramics, pottery, etc.
ki-lo *n.* kilogram
kil-o-bit *n.* in computer science, one thousand binary digits
ki-lo-cy-cle *n.* unit equal to one thousand cycles, one thousand cycles per second
kil-o-gram *n.* measurement of weight in the meteric system equal to slightly more than one third of a pound
kil-o-ton *n.* one thousand tons; an explosive power equal to that of one thousand tons of TNT
kil-o-watt *n.* unit of power equal to one thousand watts
kil-o-watt-hour *n.* unit of electric power consumption of one thousand watts throughout one hour
kilt *n.* knee-length wool skirt with deep pleats, usually of tartan, worn especially by men in the Scottish Highlands
kil-ter *n.* good condition; proper or working order
ki-mo-no *n.* loose, Japanese robe with a wide sash; a loose robe worn chiefly by women
kin *n.* one's relatives by blood
kin-der-gar-ten *n.* school or class for young children from the ages of four to six
kin-der-gart-ner *n.* child who attends kindergarten
kind-heart-ed *adj.* a sympathetic nature **-ly** *adv.* **kindheartedness** *n.*
kin-dle *v.* ignite; to catch fire; to stir up; to arouse; to excite, as the feelings **kindler** *n.*
kin-dling *n.* easily ignited material such as, sticks, wood chips, etc. used to start a fire
kin-dred *n.* a person's relatives by blood *adj.* having a like nature; similar **kindredness** *n.*
kin-e-mat-ics *n.* the branch of dynamics

that deals with motion considered apart from force and mass
kinematical *adj.*, **-ally** *adv.*
kin-e-scope *n.* cathoderay tube in a television set which translates received electrical into a visable picture on a screen; a film of a television on broadcast
ki-net-ic *adj.* of, or pertaining to, or produced by motion
king-bolt *n.* verticle central vehicle to the front axle
king crab *n.* large crablike crustacean common in the coastal waters of Japan, Alaska, and Siberia
king-pin *n.* foremost pin of a set arranged in order for playing bowling or tenpins; the most important or essential person
kink *n.* tight twist or knotlike curl; a sharp painful muscle cramp; a mental quirk *v.* to form or cause to form a kink.
kink-a-jou *n.* tropical American mammal having large eyes, brown fur and a long prehensile tail
kink-y *adj.* tightly curled; sexually uninhibited **kinkily** *adv.*, **kinkiness** *n.*
ki-osk *n.* small building used as a refreshment booth or newsstand
kip *n.* untanned skin of a calf, a lamb and or an adult of any small breed
kip-per *n.* salted and smoked herring or salmon *v.* to cure by salting, smoking, or drying
kir-tle *n.* woman's long skirt
kis-met *n.* fate; appointed lot
kitch-en *n.* room in a house or building used to prepare and cook food
kite *n.* light-weight framework of wood and paper designed to fly in a steady breeze at the end of a string; any of various predatory birds of the hawk family having a long, usually forked tail
kith *or* **kin** *n.* acquaintances or family
kitsch *n.* anything that is pretentious and in poor taste
kit-ten *n.* young cat
kit-ty--cor-nered *adj.* diagonally; catercornered
klep-to-ma-ni-a *n.* obsessive desire to steal or impulse to steal, especially without economic motive
klutz *n.*, *Slang* stupid or clumsy person **klutziness** *n.*, **klutzy** *adj.*
km *abbr.* kilometer
knack *n.* natural talent; aptitude
knap-sack *n.* supply or equipment bag, as of canvas or nylon, worn strapped across the shoulders
knave *n.* tricky; or dishonest person **knavish** *adj.*, **-ishness** *n.*
knead *v.* work dough into a uniform mass; to shape by or as if by kneading
knee *n.* joint in the human body which connects the calf with the thigh
knell *v.* sound a bell, especially when rung for a funeral; to toll *n.* act or instance of knelling; a signal of disaster
knick-ers *pl. n.* short loose-fitting pants gathered at the knee
knick-knack *n.* trinket; trifling article
knight *n.* medieval soldier serving a monarch; a chess piece bearing the shape of a horse's head **knighthood** *n.*, **knightly** *adj.*
knish *n.* baked or fried dough stuffed with meat, cheese, or potatoes
knit *v.* to form by intertwining thread or yarn, by interlocking loops of a single yarn by means of needles; to fasten securely; to draw together **knit** *n.*
knitting needle *n.* long, slender, pointed rod for knitting
knob *n.* rounded protuber-ance; a lump; a rounded mountain; a rounded handle **knobed** *adj.*
knock *v.* hit or strike with a hard blow; to criticize; to collide
knock-down *adj.* designed to be easily assembled for storage or shipment
knockdown--drag--out *adj.* extremely violent or bitter
knock-er *n.* one who or that which knocks; as a metal ring for knocking on a door
knock-knee *n.* condition in which one or both knees turn inward and knock or rub together while walking **knock-kneed** *adj.*
knoll *n.* small round hill; a mound
knot *n.* interwinding as of string or rope; a fastening made by tying together lengths of material, as string; a unifying bond, especially of marriage; a hard node on a tree from which a branch grows *Naut.* unit of speed
knot-hole *n.* hole in lumber left by the falling out of a knot
knout *n.* whip or scourge for flogging criminals **knout** *v.*
know *v.* perceive directly as fact or truth; to believe to be true; to be certain of
ko-a-la *n.* Australian marsupial which has large hairy ears, gray fur, and feeds on eucalyptus leaves
kohl-ra-bi *n.* a variety of cabbage having a thick stem and eaten as a vegetable
kook *n.*, *Slang* crazy or eccentric person
ko-sher *adj.* conformant to eat according to Jewish dietary laws *Slang* appropriate; proper.
kow-tow *v.* show servile deference
kraal *n.* a village of southern African natives; an enclosure for animals in southern Africa.
krem-lin *n.* the citadel of Moscow which houses the major Soviet government offices; the Soviet government
kryp-ton *n.* a white, inert gaseous chemical used mainly in fluorescent lamps, symbolized by Kr
ku-dos *n.* acclaim or prestige resulting from notable achievement or high position
kum-quat *n.* small, round orange fruit having a sour pulp and edible rind
ky-ack *n.* a packsack for either side of a packsaddle
ky-pho-sis *n.* the abnormal backward curve of the spine
ky-rie *n.* a short prayer that consists of the words "Lord, have mercy"

L, l The twelfth letter of the English alphabet; the Roman numeral for fifty.
lab *n.* laboratory
la-bel *n.* something that identifies or describes **label** *v.*
la-bi-al *adj.* pertaining to or of the labia or lips
la-bi-um *n., pl.* **labia** any of the four folds of the vulva
la-bor *n.* physical or manual work done for hire
lab-o-ra-to-ry *n., pl.* **-ies** a place equipped for conducting scientific experiments, research, or testing
labor camp *n.* a group of prisoners who have been forced into labor; a place for migrant farm workers
la-bored *adj.* bearing the marks of constraint and effort; produced with a great amount of labor; heavy
la-bo-ri-ous *adj.* toilsome; not easy; requiring much labor; diligent in service or work; industrious
la-bor-ite *n.* a person who promotes the theories, interests, and practices of a labor organization.
la-bret *n.* a decorative ornament worn by primitive tribes or people, usually made from a piece of wood, bone, ets. and placed through a pierced lip
la-brum *n.* the upper part of the mouth or an crustacean or insect
lab-y-rinth *n.* a system of winding, intricate passages; a maze **-thine** *adj.*
lac-er-ate *v.* to open with a jagged tear **laceration** *n.*
lach-ry-mal or **lac-ri-mal** *adj.* relating to or producing tears
lack *n.* the deficiency or complete absence of something
lack-a-dai-si-cal *adj.* lacking life, interest, or spirit; melancholy
lack-ey *n.* a male servant of very low status
lack-lus-ter *adj.* lacking sheen
lac-tate *v.* to secrete or to milk **lactation** *n.*
lac-te-al *adj.* of, resembling, or like milk
lac-tic acid *n.* a limpid, syrupy acid that is present in sour milk, molasses, some fruits, and wines
lac-tose *n., Biochem.* a white, odorless, crystalline sugar
la-cu-na *n., pl.* **-nas, -nae** a space from which something is missing
lad *n.* a boy or young man
lad-en *adj.* heavily burdened; oppressed; loaded **laden** *v.*
lad-ing *n.* cargo; freight
la-dle *n.* a cup-shaped vessel with a deep bowl and a long handle **ladle** *v.*
la-dy *n., pl.* **ladies** a woman showing refinement, cultivation, and often high social position
lag *v.* to stray or fall behind; to move slowly
la-gniappe *n.* a small gift which is given to a purchaser by a storekeeper
lain *v.* past tense of lie
lais-sez--faire *n.* a policy stating that a government should exercise very little control in trade and industrial affairs

bowl and a long handle **ladle** *v.*
la-dy *n., pl.* **ladies** a woman showing refinement, cultivation, and often high social position
lag *v.* to stray or fall behind; to move slowly
la-gniappe *n.* a small gift which is given to a purchaser by a storekeeper
lain *v.* past tense of lie
lais-sez--faire *n.* a policy stating that a government should exercise very little control in trade and industrial affairs
la-i-ty *n.* laymen, as distinguished from clergy
lake *n.* a large inland body of either salt or fresh water
lamb *n.* a young sheep; the meat of a lamb used as food
lam-baste or **lambast** *v., Slang* to thrash or beat
lam-bent *adj.* lightly and playfully brilliant **lambency** *n.*
lame *adj.* disabled or crippled **lamely** *adv.*, **lameness** *n.*
la-me *n.* a brocaded fabric woven with gold or silver thread
lame duck *n.* an officeholder who has been defeated but continues in office until the inauguration of his or her successor
la-ment *v.* to express sorrow
lam-i-na *n., pl.* **-nae, -nas** a thin scale or layer *Bot.* the blade or flat part of a leaf
lam-i-nate *v.* to form or press into thin sheets **laminated** *adj.*
lamp *n.* a device for generating heat or light
lam-poon *n.* a satirical, but often humorous, attack in verse or prose
lam-prey *n. ,pl.* preys an eel-like fish
lance *n.* a spear-like implement used as a weapon by mounted knights or soldiers
land *n.* the solid, exposed surface of the earth as distinguished from the waters
lan-dau *n.* a four-wheeled vehicle with a closed carriage and a back seat with a collapsible top
land-er *n.* a space vehicle for landing on a celestial body
land--fill *n.* a system of trash and garbage disposal in which the waste is burned in low-lying land so as to build up the ground surface; a section built up by landfill
land grant *n.* a grant of land made by a government, especially for railroads, roads, or agricultural colleges
land-ing *n.* the act of coming, going, or placing ashore from any kind of vessel or craft; the act of descending and settling on the ground in an airpland
land-scape *n.* a view or vista of natural scenery as seen from a single point
lane *n.* a small or narrow path between walls, fences, or hedges
lan-guage *n.* the words, sounds, pronunciation and method of combining words
lan-guid *adj.* lacking in energy **languidly** *adv.*, **languidness** *n.*

lan-guish *v.* to become weak
lank *adj.* slender; lean
lan-o-lin *n.* wool grease obtained from sheep's wool and refined for use in ointments and cosmetics
lan-yard *n.* a piece of rope or line used to secure objects on ships
lap-in *n.* rabbit fur that is sheared and dyed
lap-is laz-u-li *n.* a semiprecious stone that is azure blue in color
lap-pet *n.* a flap or fold on a headdress or on a garment
lapse *n.* a temporary deviation or fall to a less desirable state
lar-ce-ny *n., pl.* **-ies** the unlawful taking of another person's property
lar-der *n.* a place, such as a pantry or room, where food is stored
large *adj.* greater than usual or average in amount or size
lar-gess *or* **lar-gesse** *n.* liberal or excessive giving to an inferior; generosity
lar-go *adv., Mus.* in a very slow, broad, and solemn manner **largo** *adj. & n.*
lar-i-at *n.* a long, light rope with a running noose at one end to catch livestock
lark *n.* a bird having a melodious ability to sing
lar-va *n., pl.* **larvae** the immature, wingless, often worm-like form of a newly hatched insect
lar-ynx *n., pl.* **larynges** *or* **larynxes** the upper portion of the trachea which contains the vocal cords
lash *v.* to strike or move violently or suddenly
lass *n.* a young girl or woman
las-si-tude *n.* a condition of weariness; fatigue
last *adj.* following all the rest; of or relating to the final death
Last Supper *n.* the last meal eaten by Jesus Christ and his disciples, before his crucifixion
latch *n.* a device used to secure a gate or door, consisting of a bar that usually fits into a notch
latch onto to grab onto
latch-et *n.* a narrow leather strap or thong used to fasten a shoe
latch-key *n.* a key for opening an outside door
late *adj.* coming, staying, happening after the proper or usual time; having recently died **-ness** *n.*, **-ly** *adv.*
lat-er-al *adj.* relating to or of the side **laterally** *adv.*
la-tex *n.* the milky, white fluid that is produced by certain plants, such as the rubber tree
lath *n.* a thin, narrow strip of wood nailed to joists, rafters, or studding
lathe *n.* a machine for holding material while it is spun and shaped by a tool
lat-i-tude *n.* the angular distance of the earth's surface north or south of the equator
la-trine *n.* a public toilet
lat-ter *adj.* being the second of two persons or two things
laud *v.* to praise; to extol **laudable** *adj.*, **laudably** *adv.*
laugh *v.* to express amusement, satisfaction **laughable** *adj.*
laun-dry *n., pl.* **-ies** an establishment where laundering is done professionally
lau-re-ate a person honored for his accomplishment
la-va *n.* molten rock which erupts or flows from an active volcano
lav-a-to-ry *n., pl.* **-ies** a room with permanently installed washing and toilet facilities
lav-en-der *n.* an aromatic plant having spikes of pale violet flowers
lav-ish *adj.* generous and extravagant in giving or spending **lavisher** *n.*, **lavishly** *adv.*
law *n.* a rule of conduct or action, recognized by custom or decreed by formal enactment, considered binding on the members of a nation, community, or group
law-ren-ci-um *n.* a short-lived radioactive element
law-suit *n.* a case or proceeding brought before a court of law for settlement
law-yer *n.* a person trained in the legal profession who acts for and advises clients or pleads in court
lax *adj.* lacking disciplinary control **laxity, laxness** *n.*
lax-a-tive *n.* a medicine taken to stimulate evacuation of the bowels
lay *v.* to cause to lie; to place on a surface; past tense of lie
lay-er *n.* a single thickness, coating, or covering that lies over or under another **layered** *adj.*, **layer** *v.*
lay-off *n.* a temporary dismissal of employees
la-zy *adj.* unwilling to work; sluggish **lazily** *adv.*, **laziness** *n.*
la-zy-bones n. *Slang* a lazy person
L--do-pa *n.* a drug used in treating Parkinson's disease
lea *n., Poetic.* a grassy field or meadow
leach *v.* to cause a liquid to pass through a filter
lead *v.* to go ahead so as to show the way; to control the affairs or action of
lead poisoning *n.* poisoning of a person's system by the absorption of lead or any of its salts
leaf *n., pl.* **leaves** a flat out-growth from a plant structure or tree
leak *n.* an opening, as a flaw or small crack, permitting an escape or entrance of light or fluid **leakage, leakiness** *n.*
lean *v.* to rest or incline the weight of the body for support **leanly** *adv.*, **-ness** *n.*
lean-ing *n.* an inclination
learn *n.* the process of acquiring knowledge **learner** *n.*
lease *n.* a contract for the temporary use or occupation of property or premises in exchange for payment of rent
leash *n.* a strong cord or rope for restraining a dog or other animal
least-wise *adv., Slang* at least

leath-er *n.* an animal skin or hide with the hair removed
leave *v.* to go or depart from
leav-en *n.* an agent of fermentation, as yeast, used to cause batters and doughs to rise **leaven** *v.*
lech-er-y *n.* unrestrained indulgence in sexual activity **-er** *n.*, **-ous** *adj.*
lec-i-thin *n.* any of a group of phosphorus containing compounds found in plant and animal tissues
lec-tern *n.* a stand or tall desk, usually with a slanted top
lec-ture n. a speech on a specific subject
led *v., p.t. & p.p.* past tense of lead
ledg-er *n.* a book in which sums of money received and paid out are recorded
lee *n.* the side of a ship sheltered from the wind
leech *n.* any of various carnivorous or bloodsucking worms
leek *n.* a culinary herb of the lily family, related to the onion
leer *n.* a sly look or sideways glance expressing desire
lee-way *n., Naut.* the lateral drift of a plane or ship away from the correct course
left *adj.* pertaining to or being on the side of the body that faces north when the subject is facing east
leg-a-cy *n., pl.* **-ies** personal property, money, and other valuables that are bequeathed by will
le-gal *adj.* of, pertaining to, or concerned with the law or lawyers **-ity, -ization** *n.*, **legalize** *v.*, **legally** *adv.*
le-gal-ism *n.* a strict conformity to the law, especially when stressing the letter and forms of the law rather than the spirit of justice
le-ga-tion *n.* the official diplomatic mission in a foreign country, headed by a minister
le-ga-to *adv., Music* smooth and flowing with successive notes connected **legato** *adj. & n.*
leg-end *n.* an unverifiable story handed down from the past **legendary** *adj.*
leg-horn *n.* a hat made from finely plaited wheat straw
leg-i-ble *adj.* capable of being read **legibility** *n.*, **legibly** *adv.*
le-gion *n.* any various honorary or military organizations
leg-is-late *v.* to pass or make laws
leg-is-la-tion *n.* the act or procedures of passing laws
leg-is-la-ture *n.* a body of persons officially constituted and empowered to make and change laws
leg-ume *n.* a plant of the pea or bean family
lei *n., pl.* **leis** a wreath of flowers worn around the neck; the customary greeting of welcome in the state of Hawaii
lei-sure *n.* the time of freedom from work or duty **leisurely** *adj. & adv.*
lem-on *n.* an oval citrus fruit grown on a tree
lem-on-ade *n.* a drink made from water, lemon juice, and sugar
lend *v.* to allow the temporary use or possession of something **lender** *n.*
length *n.* the linear extent of something from end to end
length-wise *adv. & adj.* of or in the direction or dimension of length
le-ni-ent *adj.* gentle, forgiving, and mild **leniently** *adv.*
len-i-tive *adj.* having the ability to ease pain
lent *v.* past tense of lend
len-til *n.* a leguminous plant, having broad pods and containing edible seeds
leop-ard *n.* a large member of the cat family of Africa and Asia
le-o-tard *n.* a close-fitting garment worn by dancers and acrobats
lep-er *n.* one who suffers from leprosy
lep-re-chaun *n.* a mischief elf of Irish folklore
lep-ro-sy *n., Pathol.* a chronic communicable disease characterized by nodular skin lesions and the progressive destruction of tissue **leprotic** *adj.*
les-bi-an *n.* a homosexual woman
lese maj-es-ty *or n.* an offense against a ruler or supreme power of state
le-sion *n., Pathol.* an injury; a wound
less *adj.* smaller; of smaller or lower importance or degree
-less *suffix.* without; lacking
les-see *n.* one who leases a property
les-son *n.* an instance from which something is to be or has been learned
let *v.* to give permission; to allow
le-thal *adj.* pertaining to or being able to cause death
leth-ar-gy *n., Pathol.* a state of excessive drowsiness or abnormally deep sleep; laziness **lethargic** *adj.*
let's *contr.* let us
let-ter *n.* a standard character or sign used in writing or printing to represent an alphabetical unit or speech
leu-ke-mi-a *n., Pathol.* a generally fatal disease of the blood **leukemic** *adj.*
le-vee *n.* an embankment along the shore of a body of water, built to prevent over-flowing
lev-el *n.* a relative position, rank, or height on a scale. *v.* To make or become flat or level **-er, -ness** *n.*
lever *n.* a handle that projects and is used to operate or adjust a mechanism
lev-i-tate *v.* to rise and float in the air in apparent defiance of gravity **levitation** *n.*
Le-vit-i-cus *n.* the third book of the Old Testament
lev-i-ty *n., pl.* **-ies** lack of seriousness; frivolity; lightness
lev-y *v.* to impose and collect by authority or force, as a fine or tax
lewd *adj.* preoccupied with sex; lustful **lewdness** *n.*
lex-i-cog-ra-phy *n.* the practice or profession of compiling dictionaries
lex-i-con *n.* a dictionary; a vocabulary or list of words that relate to a certain

subject, occupation, or activity
li-a-bil-i-ty *n., pl.* **-ies** the condition or state of being liable
li-a-ble *adj.* legally or rightly responsible
li-ai-son *n.* a communication, as between different parts of an armed force or departments of a government
li-ar *n.* a person who tells falsehoods
li-bel *n., Law* a written statement in published form that damages a person's character or reputation
lib-er-al *adj.* characterized by generosity or lavishness in giving; abundant; ample; inclining toward opinions or policies that favor progress or reform, such as religion or politics
liberal arts *pl. n.* academic courses that include literature, philosophy, history, languages, etc.
lib-er-ate *v.* to set free, as from bondage, oppression
lib-er-ty *n., pl.* **-ies** the state of being free from oppression
li-bi-do *n.* one's sexual desire or impulse; the psychic energy drive that is behind all human activities
li-brar-i-an *n.* a person in charge of a library
li-brar-y *n., pl.* **-ies** a collection of books, pamphlets, magazines, and reference books kept for reading, reference, or borrowing
lice *n.* plural of louse
li-cense *n.* an official document that gives permission to engage in a specified activity or to perform a specified act
li-cen-ti-ate *n.* a person licensed to practice a specified profession
li-cen-tious *adj.* lacking in moral restraint; immoral
li-chen *n.* any of various flowerless plants consisting of fungi, commonly growing in flat patches on trees and rocks
lichened, lichenous *adj.*
lic-it *adj.* lawful **licitly** *adv.*
lick *v.* to pass the tongue over or along the surface of something
lick-e-ty--split *adv.* full speed
lic-o-rice *n.* a perennial herb of Europe, the dried root of which is used to flavor medicines and candy
lid *n.* a hinged or removable cover for a container; an eyelid
lidded, lidless *adj.*
lie *v.* to be in or take a horizontal recumbent position; to recline *n.* a false or untrue statement
liege *n.* a feudal lord or sovereign
lien *n.* the legal right to claim, hold, or sell the property of another to satisfy a debt or obligation
lieu *n.* place; stead **in lieu of** In place of
lieu-ten-ant *n.* a commissioned officer
life *n., pl.* **lives** the form of existence that distinguishes living organisms from dead organisms or inanimate matter in the ability to carry on metabolism, respond to stimuli, reproduce, and grow
lifer *n.* **Slang** a person sentenced to life in prison
life-time *n.* the period between one's birth and death
life zone *n.* a biogeographic zone
lift *v.* to raise from a lower to a higher position; to elevate; to take from; to steal
liftoff *n.* the vertical takeoff or the instant of takeoff of an aircraft or spacecraft
lig-a-ment *n.* a tough band of tissue joining bones or holding a body organ in place **ligamentous** *adj.*
li-gate *v.* to tie with a ligature
lig-a-ture *n.* something, as a cord, that is used to bind
light *n.* electromagnetic radiation that can be seen by the naked eye; a source of fire, such as a match
lightness *n.*
light-ning *n.* the flash of light produced by a high-tension natural electric discharge into the atmosphere
lig-ne-ous *adj.* of or resembling wood; woody
lig-nite *n.* a brownish-black soft coal
lig-ro-in *n.* a volatile, flammable fraction of petroleum used as a solvent
lik-en *v.* to describe as being like; to compare
like-ness *n.* resemblance; a copy
like-wise *adv.* in a similar way
lilt *n.* a light song; a rhythmical way of speaking
lil-y *n., pl.* **-ies** any of various plants bearing trumpet-shaped flowers
limb *n.* a large bough of a tree; an animal's appendage used for movement or grasping; an arm or leg
lim-ber *adj.* bending easily; pliable; moving easily; agile
lime *n.* a tropical citrus edible green fruit; calcium oxide
lime-light *n.* a focus of public attention; the center of attention
lim-er-ick *n.* a humorous verse of five lines
lim-it *n.* a boundary; a maximum or a minimum number or amount
limn *v.* to describe; to depict by drawing
limner *n.*
li-mo-nite *n.* natural iron oxide used as an ore of iron
lim-ou-sine *n.* a luxurious large vehicle; a small bus used to carry passengers to airports and hotels
limp *v.* to walk lamely. *adj.* Lacking or having lost rigidity; not firm or strong
lim-pet *n.* any of numerous marine gastropod mollusks having a conical shell and adhering to tidal rocks
lim-pid *adj.* transparently clear
limpidity *n.*, **limpidly** *adv.*
lin-den *n.* any of various shade trees having heart-shaped leaves
lin-e-age *n.* a direct line of descent from an ancestor
lin-e-a-ment *n.* a contour, shape, or feature of the body and especially of the the face
lin-e-ar *adj.* of, pertaining to, or resembling a line; long and narrow
lin-en *n.* thread, yarn, or fabric made of

flax; household articles, such as sheets and pillow cases
ling *n.* any of various marine food fishes related to the cod
lin-ger *v.* to be slow in parting or reluctant to leave; to be slow in acting; to procrastinate **linger** *n.*, **-ingly** *adv.*
lin-ge-rie *n.* women's undergarment
lingo *n., pl.* **goes** language that is unfamiliar; a specialized vocabulary
lin-guist *n.* one who is fluent in more than one language
lin-i-ment *n.* a liquid or semiliquid medicine applied to the skin
lin-ing *n.* a material which is used to cover an inside surface
lin-net *n.* a small Old World finch
li-no-le-um *n.* a floor covering
lin-seed *n.* the seed of flax, used in paints and varnishes
lin-tel *n.* a horizontal beam across the top of a door which supports the weight of the structure above
li-on *n.* a large carnivorous mammal of the cat family, found in Africa and India
li-on-ize *v.* to treat someone as a celebrity
liq-ue-fy *or* **liq-ui-fy** *v.* to make liquid **liquefaction** *n.*
li-queur *n.* a sweet alcoholic beverage; a cordial
liq-ui-date *v.* to settle a debt by payment or other settlement; to close a business by settling accounts and dividing up assets; to get rid of, to kill **liquidation, liquidator** *n.*
liq-uor *n.* a distilled alcoholic beverage
lisle *n.* a fine, tightly twisted cotton thread
lisp *n.* a speech defect or mannerism marked by lisping
list *n.* a series of numbers or words; a tilt to one side
list-less *adj.* lacking energy or enthusiasm **listlessly** *adv.*
lit-a-ny *n., pl.* **-ies** a prayer in which phrases recited by a leader are alternated with answers from a congregation
li-tchi *or* **li-chee** *n.* a Chinese tree, bearing edible fruit
lit-er-al *adj.* conforming to the exact meaning of a word **literally** *adv.*, **literalistic** *adj.*
lit-er-al-ism *n.* adherence to the explicit sense of a given test; literal portrayal; realism **literalist** *n.*
lit-er-ar-y *adj.* pertaining to literature; appropriate to or used in literature
lit-er-ate *adj.* having the ability to read and write **literacy** *n.*
lithe *adj.* bending easily; supple **lithely** *adv.*, **litheness** *n.*
lith-i-um *n.* a silver-white, soft metallic element symbolized by Li
li-thog-ra-phy *n.* a printing process **lithograph** *n. & v.*
li-thol-o-gy *n.* the microscopic study and classification of rocks **lithologist** *n.*
lit-i-gate *v.* to conduct a legal contest by judicial process **litigant, litigation** *n.*
lit-ter-bug *n.* one who litters a public area
lit-to-ral *adj.* relating to or existing on a shore *n.* a shore
lit-ur-gy *n., pl.* **-ies** a prescribed rite or body of rites for public worship
live-li-hood *n.* a means of support or subsistence
live-ly *adj.* vigorous **liveableness** *n.*
liv-er *n.* the large, very vascular, glandular organ of vertebrates which secretes bile
live-stock *n.* farm animals raised for human use
live wire *n., Slang* an energetic person
liv-id *adj.* discolored from a bruise; very angry
liz-ard *n.* one of various reptiles, usually with an elongated scaly body
load *n.* a mass or weight that is lifted or supported; anything, as cargo
loaf *n., pl.* **loaves** a food, especially bread, that is shaped into a mass *v.* to spend time in idleness
loam *n.* soil that consists chiefly of sand, clay, and decayed plant matter
loan *n.* money lent with interest to be repaid; something borrowed for temporary use *v.* to lend
loath *adj.* averse
loathe *v.* to dislike intensely
loath-ing *n.* intense dislike
loath-some *adj.* arousing disgust **loathsomely** *adv.*, **loathsomeness** *n.*
lob *v.* to hit or throw in a high arc
lob-by *n., pl.* **-ies** a foyer, as in a hotel or theatre; a group of private persons trying to influence legislators
lobe *n.* a curved or rounded projection or division, as the fleshy lower part of the ear **lobar, lobed** *adj.*
lob-lol-ly *n., pl.* **-ies** a mudhole; mire
lo-bo *n.* the gray wolf
lo-bot-o-my *n., pl.* **-mies** surgical severance of nerve fibers by incision into the brain
lob-ster *n.* any of several large, edible marine crustaceans
lob-ule *n.* a small lobe; a subdivision of a lobe
lo-cal *adj.* pertaining to, being in, or serving a particular area or place **locally** *adv.*
lo-cale *n.* a locality where a particular event takes place; the setting or scene, as of a novel
lo-cate *v.* to determine the place, position, or boundaries of; to look for and find **locator** *n.*
loch *n., Scot.* a lake
lock *n.* a device used, as on a door, to secure or fasten
lock-et *n.* a small, ornamental case for a keepsake, often a picture, worn as a pendant on a necklace
lock-jaw *n.* tetanus
lock-smith *n.* a person who makes or repairs locks
lo-co *adj., Slang* insane
lo-co-mo-tion *n.* the act of moving
lo-co-mo-tive *n.* a self-propelled vehicle

that is generally electric or diesel-powered and is used for moving railroad cars
lo-cust *n.* any of numerous grasshoppers which often travel in swarms and damage vegetation
loft *n.* one of the upper, generally unpartitioned floors of an industrial buildings
loge *n.* a small compartment, especially a box in a theatre; a small partitioned area
log-gi-a *n.* a roofed but open arcade along the front of a building; an open balcony
log-ic *n.* the science dealing with the principles of reasoning, especially of the method and validity of deductive reasoning
log-i-cal *adj.* something marked by consistency of reasoning **logically** *adv.*
lo-gis-tics *pl., n.* the methods of procuring, maintaining, and replacing material and personnel **logistic** *adj.*
lo-go-type *n.* identifying symbol for a company or publication
lo-gy *adj.* something marked by sluggishness **-iness** *n.*
loins the thighs and groin; the reproductive organs
loi-ter *v.* to stay for no apparent reason; to dawdle or delay **loiterer** *n.*
loll *v.* to move or act in a lax, lazy or indolent manner
lol-ly-gag *v., Slang* to fool around
lone *adj.* single; isolated; sole
lone-ly *adj.* being without companions **loneliness** *n.*
lon-er *n.* a person who avoids the company of others
long-bow *n.* a wooden bow that is approximately five to six feet in length
lon-gev-i-ty *n.* long life; long duration; seniority
lon-gi-tude *n.* the angular distance that is east and west of the prime meridian at Greenwich, England
lon-gi-tu-di-nal *adj.* of or relating to the length; relating to longitude
look *v.* to examine with the eyes; to see; to glance, gaze, or stare at
look-out *n.* a person positioned to keep watch
loom *v.* to come into view as a image; to seem to be threatening
loo-ny *or* **loo-ney** *adj.* **loony** *n.* crazy
loose *adj.* not fastened; not confined or fitting; free
loot *n.* goods, usually of significant value, taken in time of war; goods that have been stolen *v.* to plunder
lope *v.* to run with a steady gait **lope, lopper** *n.*
lop-sid-ed *adj.* larger or heavier on one side than on the other; tilting to one side **lopsidedly** *adv.*, **-ness** *n.*
lo-qua-cious *adj.* overly talkative **loquaciously** *adv.*, **loquacity** *n.*
Lord *n.* God. a man having dominion and power over other people
lore *n.* traditional fact; knowledge that has been gained through education or experience
lorn *n.* forlorn
lose *v.* to mislay; to fail to keep **loser** *n.*
loss *n.* the suffering or damage used by losing; someone or something that is lost. **losses** *pl. n.* killed, wounded, or captured
lost *adj.* unable to find one's way
lot *n.* fate; fortune; a parcel of land having boundaries
lo-tion *n.* a liquid medicine for external use on the hands and body
lounge *v.* to move or act in a lazy, relaxed manner. *n.* A room, as in a hotel or theatre; a couch **-er** *n.*
louse *n., pl.* **lice** a small, wingless biting or sucking insect which lives as a parasites on various animals and also on human beings.
lous-y *adj.* lice infested *Slang* mean; poor; inferior
lout *n.* an awkward, stupid person **loutish** *adj.*
love *n.* intense affection for another arising out of kinship or personal ties; a strong feeling of attraction resulting from sexual desire
lov-er *n.* a person who loves another; a sexual partner
low *adj.* not high; being below or under normal height, rank, or level; depressed
low-brow *n.* an uncultured person
low-down *n.* the whole truth; all the facts *adj.* despicable; mean; depressed
low frequency *n.* a radiowave frequency between 30 and 300 kilohertz
low-key *or* **low-keyed** *adj.* restrained
low-ly *adj.* low in position or rank **lowliness** *n.*
low profile *n.* a deliberately inconspicuous life style or posture
lox *n.* smoked salmon; liquid oxygen.
loy-al *adj.* faithful in allegiance to one's country and government; faithful to a person, cause, ideal
loy-al-ist *n.* one who is or remains loyal to political cause, party, government, or sovereign
lu-au *n.* a traditional Hawaiian feast
lub-ber *n.* an awkward, clumsy or stupid person; an inexperienced sailor
lu-bri-cant *n.* a material, as grease or oil, applied to moving parts to reduce friction
lu-bri-cous *adj.* smooth, unstable; shifty **lubricity** *n.*
lu-cid *adj.* easily understood; mentally clear; rational; shining **lucidity** *n.*
Lucifer *n.* the devil; Satan
lu-cra-tive *adj.* producing profits or great wealth
lu-cre *n.* money; profit
lu-cu-brate *v.* to study or work laboriously
lu-di-crous *adj.* amusing or laughable through obvious absurdity; ridiculous
luge *n.* a small sled
lu-gu-bri-ous *adj.* mournful; dejected; especially exaggeratedly
lull *v.* to cause to rest or sleep; to cause

to have a false sense of security
lul-la-by *n., pl.* **-bies** A song to lull a child to sleep
lum-ba-go *n.* painful rheumatic pain of the muscles and tendons of the lumbar region
lum-bar *adj.* part of the back and sides between the lowest ribs and the pelvis
lum-ber *n.* timber, sawed or split into boards
lu-mi-nar-y *n., pl.* **-ies** a celestial body, as the sun; a notable person
lu-mi-nes-cence *n.* an emission of light without heat, as in fluorescence
lu-mi-nous *adj.* emitting or reflecting light; bathed in steady light; illuminated
lum-mox *n.* a clumsy oaf
lump *n.* a projection; a protuber-ance; a swelling
lu-na-cy *n., pl.* **-ies** insanity
lu-nar *adj.* of, relating to, caused by the moon
lu-na-tic *n.* a crazy person
lunch-eon *n.* a lunch
lung *n.* one of the two spongy organs that constitute the basic respiratory organ of air-breathing vertebrates
lunge *n.* a sudden forward movement
lu-pus *n.* a bacterial disease of the skin
lure *n.* a decoy; something appealing; *v.* to attract or entice with the prospect of reward or pleasure
lurk *v.* to lie in concealment, as in an ambush
lus-cious *adj.* very pleasant to smell or taste; appealing to the senses
lush *adj.* producing luxuriant growth or vegetation *Slang* An alcoholic **-ly** *adv.*
lust *n.* intense sexual desire; an intense longing; a craving **lustful** *adj.*
lus-ter *or* **lus-tre** *n.* a glow of reflected light; sheen; brilliance or radiance
lust-y *adj.* vigorous; healthy; robust; lively **lustily** *adv.*
lute *n.* a medieval musical stringed instrument
lux-u-ri-ant *adj.* growing or producing abundantly; lush; plentiful **-ly** *adv.*
lux-u-ri-ate *v.* to enjoy luxury or abundance
lymph node *n.* a roundish body of lymphoid tissue; lymph gland
lynch *v.* to execute without author-ity or the due process of law
lynx *n.* a wildcat *adj.* having acute eyesight
lyre *n.* an ancient Greek stringed instrument related to the harp
lyr-ic *adj.* concerned with thoughts and feelings; romantic; appro-priate for singing. *n.* a lyric poem
lyrically *adv.*, **lyricism** *n.*
ly-ser-gic acid di-eth-yl-am-ide *n.* an organic compound which induces psychotic symptoms similar to those of schizophrenia; LSD
ly-so-some *n.* a cellular organelle containing various hydrolytic enzymes
lysosomal *adj.*
ly-so-zyme *n.* a basic bateriolytic protein present in human tears and saliva

M, m The thirteenth letter of the English alphabet.
ma-ca-bre *adj.* suggesting death and decay **macabrly** *adv.*
mac-ad-am *n.* pavement for roads consisting of layers of compacted, broken stone, usually cemented with asphalt and tar *v.* the laving down of layers of small stones, held together with asphalt or tar
mac-a-ro-ni *n.* dried pasta made into short tubes and prepared as food
mac-a-roon *n.* small cookie
ma-caw *n.* the largest type of tropical American parrots
mace *n.* an aromatic spice made by grinding the cover of the nutmeg
mac-e-doine *n.* a jellied salad, or mixture of diced vegetables or fruits
mac-er-ate *v.* to make a solid substance soft **maceration** *n.*
ma-chet-e *n.* a large, heavy type of knife used for cutting sugarcane
mach-i-nate *v.* to plot
ma-chine *n.* device built to use energy to do work **machinery** *n.*, **machinable** *adj.*, **machined v.**
ma-chin-er-y *n.* a collection of machines as a whole; the mechanism or operating parts of a machine; literary devices
machine shop *n.* a work are where materials, especially metals, are cut and desigtned by machine tools
machine tool *n.* a machine that is power-driven and used for chaping or cutting metals, wood, etc.
ma-chin-ist *n.* the person who operates, assembles and repairs machines for others
ma-chis-mo *n.* an exaggerated sense of masculinity; a strong sense of
ma-cho *adj.* exhibiting machismo in character; agressive
mack-er-el *n.* kind of fish that is found in the Atlantic Ocean
mack-in-tosh *n.* raincoat
mac-ra-me *n.* the craft of tying knots in a geometrical pattern
mac-ro-bi-ot-ic *adj.* being an extremely restricted diet to promote longevity; for the well-being of
ma-cron *n.* the (-) placed over a vowel to indicate a long sound
mac-ro-scop-ic *adj.* large enough to be seen by the naked eye
mad *adj.* being angry; insane **madder adj. madness** *n.*, **madly** *adv.*
mad-am *n.* title used to address a married woman; a polite address
made *v.* past tense of make
mad-e-moi-selle *n.* an unmarried French girl; used as a title
made--to--order *adj.* to be custom-made; designed a certain way
made--up *adj.* being fabricated; invented; falsely devised
mad-house *n.* a place of confusion uproar and disorder
mad-ri-gal *n., Music* unaccompanied song **madrigalist** *n.*
mael-strom *n.* any irresistible or dangerous force; whirlpool

maes-tro *n.* a person mastering any art; a composer or conductor
mag-a-zine *n.* publication of reading marterial; explosives storehouse
ma-gen-ta *n.* a purplish red color or hue; known as fuchsine
mag-got *n.* the legless larva insects; an eccentric idea **maggoty** *adj.*
mag-ic *n.* art of illusions
magically *adv.*, **magical** *adj.*
mag-is-trate *n.* civil officer of law
magistratically *adv.*
mag-ma *n.* the molten rock beneath the earth's surface
mag-nan-i-mous *adj.* being forgiving; generous **-ness** *n.*, **-ly** *adv.*
mag-nate *n.* kind of business tycoon
mag-ne-sia *n.* a light, white powder used in medicine as an antacid
mag-ne-si-um *n.* a light, silvery metallic element which burns with a hot flame; the form of light
mag-net *n.* body attracting other magnetic material
magnetically *adv.*, **magnetize** *v.*
mag-net-ic *adj.* pertaining to magnetism or a magnet **magnetically adv.**
mag-net-ite *n.* a black iron oxide in mineral form of the spinel group
mag-net-ize *v.* to have magnetic properties **magnetizable adj.**
mag-ne-to *n.* small alternator that uses magnets to operate
mag-nif-i-cent *adj.* beautiful
magnificence *n.*, **magnificently** *adv.*
mag-ni-fy *v.* increase in size
magnification *n.*, **magnifiable** *adj.*
mag-nil-o-quent *adj.* speaking in a lofty manner **magniloquently adv.**
mag-ni-tude *n.* the greatness in size
mag-no-lia *n.* flowering tree
mag-num *n.* wine bottle holding about two quarts
mag-pie *n.* large, noisy bird
ma-ha-ra-ja *n.* a king or prince who rules an Indian state
ma-ha-ra-ni *n.* the wife of the maharaja; a Hindu princess
ma-hat-ma *n.* a title of respect
ma-hog-a-ny *n.*, *pl.* **mahoganies** trees with hard wood; brownish
maid *n.* a young unmarried woman or girl
maid-en *n.* young girl
maid-en-hair *n.* a delicate fern with dark stems and lightgreen, feathery fronds
maid-en name *n.* woman's family name before marriage
mail *n.* printed matter **mailable adj.**, **mailbox** *n.*, **mailed** *adj.*
mail order *n.* goods which are ordered and sent by mail
maim *v.* to cripple or disfigure another
maimer *n.*
main *adj.* being most important part
mainly *adv.*
main-land *n.* the land part of a country as distinguished from an island
main-line *v.* to inject a drug directly into a vein; main highway
main-stream *n.* a main direction or line of thought or influence
main-tain *v.* keep in existence
maintainer *n.*, **maintainable** *adj.*
maize *n.* type of corn
maj-es-ty *n.* stateliness; one's exualted dignity **majesties pl.**
ma-jor *adj.* being greater in importance, rank, or dignity
ma-jor-ette *n.* a young woman who marches and twirls a baton in her hand usually in a parade
ma-jor-i-ty *n.* the state of having a greater number of something
ma-jor med-i-cal *n.* a type of insurance policy which one has
make *v.* create; cause to happen
maker *n.*, **makable** *adj.*
make--be-lieve *n.* something pretended; imagined; fantasy
make--up *n.* composition
mal-a-chite *n.* a green basic copper carbonate of copper
mal-a-droit *adj.* lacking skill
maladroitness *n.*, **maladroitly** *adv.*
mal-a-dy *n.*, *pl.* **maladies** chronic disease or sickness
mal-aise *n.* the vague discomfort sometimes indicating the beginning of an illness
mal-a-prop-ism *n.* foolish misuse of a word; misapplication of a word
mal-ap-ro-pos *adj.* being not appropriate in style
ma-lar-i-a *n.*, disease caused by the bite of sporozoan parasites in the red blood cells **malarious** *adj.*
ma-lar-key *n.* foolish or insincere talk
mal-con-tent *adj.* unhappy with surroundings; dissatisfied
mal-de-mer *n.* seasickness
male *adj.* being a man
mal-e-dic-tion *n.* a curse; execration; to speak evil of
mal-for-ma-tion *n.* a defective form of something; wrong-doing
mal-func-tion *n.* the failure to work
mal-ice *n.* the desire to harm others
maliciously *adv.*, **maliciousness n.**
ma-lign *v.* to speak evil of
malignly *adv.*, **maligner** *n.*
ma-lig-nant *adj.*, *Pathol.* to be relating to tumors **malignantly** *adv.*, **-cy** *n.*
ma-lin-ger *v.* pretend sickness to avoid work **malingerer** *n.*
mal-lard *n.* wild duck
mal-let *n.* hammer with a short handle; barrel-shaped head
mal-nour-ished *adj.* being underfed; lacking food; without food
mal-oc-clu-sion *n.* improper alignment of the teeth
mal-prac-tice *n.* the mistreatment by a doctor; negligent
malt *n.* grain **malty** *adj.*
mal-treat *v.* to treat another unkindly
maltreatment *n.*
mam-mal *n.* the group of animals who suckle their young **mammalian** *adj.*
mam-mog-ra-phy *n.* x-ray of the breast for detection of cancer
mam-moth *n.* extinct form of an elephant with large, curved tusks
man *n.* the adult male; the human race; a

human being; manhood
man-a-cle *n.* handcuffs
man-age *v.* direct or control
manageable *adj.*, -ability *n.*
man-ag-er *n.* one in charge of a situation
managership *n.*
man-a-tee *n.* type of aquatic mammal with a broad round tail
man-date *n.* an order or command
man-da-to-ry *adj.* required
man-do-lin *n.* a musical instrument
mandolinist *n.*
mane *n.* long and heavy hair growing on animals necks maned *adj.*
mange *n.* the skin disease of the dogs marked by the loss of hair
man-ger *n.* the box for animal feed
man-gle *v.* to disfigure or to mutilate
mangled, mangling v.
man-grove *n.* tropical tree
man-han-dle *v.* to handle roughly
manhandled *adj.*
man-hole *n.* sewer drain
ma-ni-a *n.* the desire for something
man-i-cot-ti *n.* pasta
man-i-cure *n.* the taking care of the fingernails manicurist *n.*
man-i-fest *n.* the list of cargo a vehicle carries manifestation *n.*
man-i-fold *adj.* to be having many parts, or types; having a variety
ma-nip-u-late *v.* to manage shrewdly
manipulation *n.*
man-kind *n.* human race
man--made *adj.* not developed naturally; made by mankind
man-ner *n.* way in which things are done
mannerless *adj.*
man-or *n.* estate manorial *adj.*
man-slaugh-ter *n.*, *Law* the unlawful killing of another without malice
man-tel *n.* shelf over a fireplace
mantelpiece *n.*
man-til-la *n.* light scarf
man-u-al *adj.* operated by the hand
manually *adv.*
man-u-fac-ture *v.* make a product
manufacturer *n.*, -able *adj.*
ma-nure *n.* animal dung used for fertilizer on crops and grass
man-u-script *n.* a typed copy of an article, or book
man-y *adj.* indefinite number
map *n.* plane surface of a region
mapper *n.*, mapped v.,mapping v.
ma-ple syr-up *n.* concentrating the sap of the sugar maple
mar *v.* deface marer *n.*
mar-a-thon *n.* the foot race of 26 miles
mar-ble *n.* the limestone
marblize *v.*, marbling *n.*
march *v.* to walk with measured steps
marching *n.*
mare *n.* female of the horse
mar-ga-rine *n.* kind of butter substitute
mar-gin *n.* edge of printed text
marginal *adj.*, marginally *adv.*
mar-i-jua-na *n.* kind of hallucinogenic drug; a wild tobacco
ma-ri-na *n.* harbor for boats
mar-i-nade *n.* brine for soaking meat, fish, or vegetables
ma-rine *adj.* to be pertaining to the sea
mariner *n.*
mar-i-o-nette *n.* puppet operated by strings
mark *n.* visible impression
mar-ket *n.* public place to purchase or sell goods
mar-riage *n.* the legal union of two people in wedlock
marriageability *n.*, -able *adj.*
mar-row *n.* the tissue in bone cavities
marrowy *adj.*
marsh *n.* low, wet land; swamp
marshy *adj.* marshiness *n.*
mar-shal *n.* military officer
marsh-mal-low *n.* kind of soft confection which is edible
mar-su-pi-al *n.* animals with external pouches such as a kangaroo
mar-tial arts *pl., n.* self-defense, such as karate
mar-ti-ni *n.* cocktail of gin and dry vermouth; vodka may be used
mar-tyr *n.* person who would die for a cause martyrdom *n.*
mar-zi-pan *n.* paste of almonds, sugar and egg whites made into candy shaped into various forms
mar-vel *n.* be in awe
mas-car-a *n.* the cosmetic used for coloring the eyelashes
mas-cot *n.* object to bring good luck
mas-cu-line *adj.* male sex
mash *n.* the mixture to distill alcohol; to gain the affection of
mask *n.* covering to conceal the face
mas-o-chism *n.* the sexual pleasure from pain masochistic *adj.*, masochist *n.*
ma-son *n.* brick layer
mas-quer-ade *n.* a costume party or gathering for entertainment
mass *n.* body of matter with no form; a Eucharistic celebration
mas-sa-cre *n.* savage killing of human beings massacrer *n.*
mas-sage *n.* rub down of one's body to relieve tension massager *n.*
mas-sive *adj.* of great intensity
mast *n.* pole which supports the sails of boats
mas-ter *n.* person with the control
mas-ter-piece *n.* work of art
mas-ti-cate *v.* to chew -able adj.
mas-to-don *n.* kind of extinct mammal which differ from mammoths
mas-tur-ba-tion *n.* ones sexual stimulation without intercourse
mat-a-dor *n.* bullfighter
match *n.* identical; piece of wood that ignites matcher *n.*
ma-te-ri-al-ize *v.* to take form or shape; to make material
ma-te-ri-el *n.* the equipment or the supplies used by an organization
ma-ter-nal *adj.* relating to mother
maternally *adv.*, maternalistic *adj.*
math-e-mat-ics *n.* the study of form, quantity and magnitude of numbers
mathematically *adv.*, -cal *adj.*
mat-i-nee *n.* afternoon movie
mat-ri-cide *n.* one who kills his mother
matricidal adj.

ma-tric-u-late *v.* enroll into a college
matriculation *n.*
mat-ri-mo-ny *n.* ceremony of marriage
matrimonial *adj.*
ma-tron *n.* married woman
mat-ter *n.* the substance of anything
ma-ture *adj.* completely developed
maturity *n.*, **maturer adj.**, **-est adj.**
mat-zo *n.* flat piece of unleavened bread eaten at the Passover
maud-lin *adj.* sentimental
maul *n.* heavy hammer
maun-der *v.* talk incoherent
mau-so-le-um *n.* large tomb
mav-er-ick *n.* an unbranded calf
max-i-mum *n.* greatest possible quantity or value
may *v.* permitted or allowed
may-be *adv.* perhaps
may-on-naise *n.* the dressing used for salads and sandwiches
may-or *n.* chief magistrate of a city or town **mayoralty** *n.*
maze *n.* a complicated network of passages **mazy** *adj.*
mead *n.* alcoholic beverage
mead-ow *n.* a tract of grassland
mea-ger *adj.* thin; lean in quantity
meagerness *n.*, **meagerly** *adv.*
mean *v.* purpose or intent; bad tempered
meanness *n.*
me-an-der *v.* wander about
meanderingly *adv.*, **-drous** *adj.*
mea-sles *n.* kind of contagious disease marked by red circular spots
mea-sly *adj.* very small
meas-ure *n.* the dimension of anything
measurer *n.*
meat *n.* tissue of an animal used as food; the core of something
me-chan-ic *n.* person skilled with tools
mechanical *adj.*
mech-a-nism *n.* the parts of a machine which help it run
med-al *n.* an award **medalist** *n.*
med-dle *v.* to interfere in other's affairs or business **meddlesome** *adj.*, **-er** *n.*
me-di-al *adj.* being situated in the middle; between two
me-di-ate *v.* to help settle or decide a dispute **mediative adj.**
med-ic *n.* intern; corpsman
med-i-cal *adj.* the study of medicine
medically *adv.*
med-i-cine *n.* the treatment of diseases or illness
me-di-o-cre *adj.* being common; plain
mediocrity *n.*
med-i-tate *v.* in contemplative thought
meditator *n.*, **meditative** *adj.*
me-di-um *n.* the middle; intermediary professing to give messages from the dead
med-ley *n.* a jumble; musical composition made up of songs
meek *adj.* to be lacking in spirit
meekness *n.*
meet *v.* to come upon
meg-a-ton *n.* weight equal to one million tons
mel-an-chol-y *adj.* gloomy or sad
-iness *n.* **melancholically** *adv.*
mel-a-no-ma *n.*, *pl.* **melanomas** *or* **melanomata** malignant mole
mel-io-rate *v.* to improve
meliotor *n.*, **meliorateable** *adj.*
mel-lif-er-ous *adj.* to be producing or yielding honey
mel-o-dra-ma *n.* type of dramatic presentation **-tic** *adj.*, **-tics** *n.*
mel-on *n.* the fruit of the gourd family eaten raw as fruits
melt *v.* change from solid to liquid
melter *n.*, **meltable** *adj.*
melt-down *n.* melting of a nuclear-reactor core
mem-ber *n.* a person belonging to a club **membership** *n.*, **-less** *adj.*
mem-brane *n.* thin layer of skin
membranous *adj.*
me-men-to *n.* keepsake
mem-oir *n.* an autobiography of a person; a remembrance
mem-o-ra-ble *adj.* worth remembering
memorably *adv.*
mem-o-rize *v.* to commit to one's memory **-zation** *n.*, **-zable** *adj.*
men-ace *n.* a threatening person
menacly *adv.*
me-nar-che *n.* beginning of the menstruation cycle
me-ni-al *adj.* requiring little skill
menially *adv.*
men-o-pause *n.*, *Physiol.* time of final menstruation **menopausal** *adj.*
men-tal *adj.* of the mind
men-tal re-tar-da-tion *n.* a mental deficiency
men-tion *v.* refer to briefly
mentioner *n.*, **mentionable** *adj.*
men-u *n.* the list of the food at a restaurant
mer-can-tile *adj.* to be relating to commerce
mer-ce-nar-y *n.* a greedy person
mercenarily *adv.*
mer-cer-ize *v.* to treat cotton yarn
mer-chan-dise *n.* goods bought and sold
merchandiser *n.*
mer-chant *n.* person who operates a retail business
mer-cu-ry *n.* the silvery liquid found in thermometers
mer-cy *n.*, *pl.* **mercies** kind treatment
-iless *adj.*, **mercifully** *adv.*
mere *adj.* no more than is stated
merely *adv.*, **merest adj.**
merge *v.* to unite as one **mergence** *n.*
mer-it *n.* act worthy of praise
meritedly *adv.*, **meritless** *adj.*
mer-maid *n.* an imaginary sea creature half woman half fish
mer-ry-go-round *n.* kind of carrousel; seats in animal form
me-sa *n.* flat-topped hill
mesh *n.* open spaces in wire
mess *n.*, *pl.* **messes** disorderly confused heap
mes-sage *n.* the information which is sent from one person to another by word of mouth
mes-sen-ger *n.* one who does errands for another person
mess-y *adj.* untidy; dirty

me-tab-o-lism *n.* chemical changes in living cells
met-a-gal-ax-y *n.* the universe
met-a-mor-pho-sis *n.* change in the structure and formation of living animals **metamorphoses pl.**
me-te-or *n.* moving particle in the solar system resembling light
me-te-or-ol-o-gy *n.* the science of weather forecasting **-al** *adj.*
meth-a-done *n.* man-made narcotic used to treat heroin addiction
meth-od *n.* the process of carrying out something
me-tic-u-lous *adj.* very precise **meticulously** *adv.*
met-ro *n.* subway system
met-ro-nome *n.* instrument designed to mark musical time **-nomic** *adj.*
me-trop-o-lis *n.* the large capital city of a state, country or region
mew *n.* hideaway
mez-za-nine *n.* the lowest balcony
mi-crobe *n.* minute living organism **microbial** *adj.*
mi-cro-com-put-er *n.* type of computer using a microprocessor
mi-cro-film *n.* film used to record reduced size printed material
mi-cro-phone *n.* instrument which amplifies sound
mi-cro-proc-es-sor *n.* semiconductor processing unit
mi-cro-scope *n.* device to magnify small objects
mi-cro-scop-ic *adj.* very small; minute **microscopically** *adv.*
mi-cro-wave *n.* a rather short electromagnetic wave
mi-cro-wave o-ven *n.* the oven using microwaves to heat food quickly
mid-day *n.* noon
mid-dle *adj.* the center
midg-et *n.* very small person
mid-night *n.* 12 o'clock p.m.
mid-point *n.* near the middle
mid-riff *n.* midsection of the human torso; a section of garment
mid-ship-man *n.* person who is in training at the U.S. Naval Academy; a student
mid-term *n.* the middle of academic an term
miff *n.* a displeasure
might *n.* a force **mighty** *adj.*, **-ily** *adv.*
mi-graine *n.* kind of severe headaches **migrainous adj.**
mi-grant *n.* a person constantly moving to find work
mi-grate *v.* move from place to place **-tory** *adj.*, **migration** *n.*
mild *adj.* gentle in manner **mildness** *n.*, **mildly** *adv.*
mile *n.* 5,280 feet
mil-i-ta-rize *v.* train for war
mi-li-tia *n.* armed forces used only in an emergency
Milk-y Way *n.* luminous galaxy in the solar system
mil-li-ner *n.* one who designs, makes, or sells women's hats
mil-lion *n.* number equal to 1,000 x 1,000; a very large number
mim-e-o-graph *n.* kind of duplicating machine which uses stencils
mim-ic *v.* imitate another person **mimical** *adj.*
mince *v.* to chop something into small pieces **mincing** *adj.*, **mincer** *n.*
mind *n.* organ for thought **mindful** *adj.*, **mindfulness** *n.*
mine *n.* underground excavation; personal belongings
min-er-al *n.* an inorganic crystalline
min-e-stro-ne *n.* kind of thick vegetable soup
min-gle *v.* to mix together
min-i-a-ture *n.* copy greatly reduced in size; smaller than usual
mini-disk *n.* 5.25 inch floppy disk used for storing important data
min-i-mum *n.* least amount
min-is-ter *n.* pastor of a church **ministerial** *adj.*
mink *n.* an animal with valuable fur
min-now *n.* small, fresh water fish
mi-nor *adj.* not of legal age
mi-nor-i-ty *n., pl.* **minorities** smaller in number of two groups
min-u-et *n.* kind of slow, stately dance; graceful
mi-nus *prep., Math.* reduced, by subtraction of numbers
min-ute *n.* 60 seconds in time; small in size; short space of time
mir-a-cle *n.* kind of supernatural event; extremely unusual
mi-rage *n.* optical illusion
mir-ror *n.* a glass which reflects images as they are seen
mirth *n.* a merriment or a joyousness **mirthfulness** *n.*, **mirthful** *adj.*
mis-an-thrope *n.* the hatred or distrusts of mankind
mis-ap-pro-pri-ate *v.* to embezzle money **misappropriation** *n.*
mis-car-riage *n.* the premature birth of a fetus before it is viable
mis-cel-la-ne-ous *adj.* mixed variety of parts, etc.; many different
mis-chief *n.* a behavior causing harm or damage something
mis-con-ceive *v.* to misunderstand the meaning of something
mis-de-mean-or *n., Law* a crime less serious than a felony
mis-er *n.* person who hoards money **miserly** *adj.*, **miserliness** *n.*
mis-er-a-ble *adj.* very unhappy
mis-er-ly *n.* the state of great unhappiness; depression
mis-fire *v.* fail to explode
mis-fit *n.* one not adjusted to his environment; a poor fit
mis-for-tune *n.* bad luck
mis-giv-ing *n.* the feeling of doubt
mis-han-dle *v.* to manage inefficiently, wrong, or ignorantly
mis-hap *n.* an unfortunate accident
mish-mash *n.* jumble or hodgepodge
mis-in-ter-pret *v.* understand incorrectly **misinterpreter** *n.*
mis-judge *v.* make a mistake in judgment **misjudgment** *n.*

mis-lay *v.* lose something
mis-lead *v.* to deceive
misleader *n.*, **misleading** *adj.*
mis-no-mer *n.* an inappropriate name
misnomered adj.
mi-sog-a-my *n.* the hatred of the marriage
mis-pro-nounce *v.* to pronounce incorrectly or in an incorrect way
mi-sog-y-ny *n.* the hatred of women
Miss *n.* the title for unmarried girl
mis-sile *n.* object that shot at a target
mis-sion *n.* kind of task to be carried out to obtain a result
mis-take *n.* wrong decision
mis-tle-toe *n.* parasitic plant
mis-tress *n.* a woman in authority
mis-trust *v.* have doubt
mite *n.* very small insect
mit-i-gate *v.* to make less painful
mitigator *n.*, **mitigative** *adj.*
mitt *n.* the women's hand warmer; baseball glove
mix *v.* blend; combine; unite
mixable *adj.*, **mixability** *n.*
mix-up *n.* state of confusion
moan *n.* dull sound of pain
moat *n.* kind of trench around a castle
moatlike adj.
mob *n.* an unruly crowd or group of people **mobbish** *adj.*
mock-up *n.* a model used for demonstration
mode *n.* a method of doing something
mod-el *n.* clothing displayer
mod-er-ate *adj.* not excessive
moderateness *n.*, **moderately** *adv.*
mod-ern *adj.* up-to-date
mod-ern-ize *v.* to improve on something
modernzation *n.*
mod-est *adj.* shy; reserved
modesty *n.*, **modestly** *adv.*
mod-i-fy *v.* make different in form
modifier *n.*, **modifiable** *adj.*
mod-ule *n.* a series of standardized components **modular** *adj.*
mod-us op-er-an-di *n.* the method of operating; procedure
moist *adj.* sightly wet; damp
moisten *v.*, **moistly** *adv.*
mois-ture *n.* dampness
moisturize *v.*, **moisturizer** *n.*
mo-lar *n.* the grinding tooth
mo-las-ses *n.* the light brown syrup produced from sugar
mold *n.* growth produced on damp organic matter; pattern
moldy *adj.*, **moldeer** *n.*
mole *n.* spot on the human skin
mol-e-cule *n.* smaliest part retaining its identity
mo-lest *v.* to accost someone sexually
molestation *n.*
mol-li-fy *v.* make less angry
molifier *n.*, **molifiable** *adj.*
molt *v.* to cast off or shed feathers
molter *n.*
mol-ten *adj.* transform to liquid form by heat **moltenly** *adv.*
mo-men-tous *adj.* being of a great importance
mo-men-tum *n.*, *pl.* **-ta** *or* **-tums** increasing force; body in motion
mon-arch *n.* one who reigns an empire or kingdom; ruler
mon-as-ter-y *n.*, *pl.* **monasteries** the place where monks work and live
mon-e-tar-y *adj.* to be relating to money
monetarily *adv.*
mon-ey *n.* the medium of exchange
mon-grel *n.* the mixed breed animal
mo-ni-tion *n.* the caution or warning about something
monk *n.* a member of a religious order
monkishness *n.*, **monkishly** *adv.*
mon-key *n.*, *pl.* **monkeys** member of the primates, excluding man
mon-o-cle *n.* the eyeglass used for one eye
mo-nog-a-my *n.* sexual relationship with only one person
mon-o-logue *n.* speech by one person
monologuist *n.*
mon-o-ma-ni-a *n.* mental disorder
monomaniacal *adj.*
mon-o-nu-cle-o-sis *n.* kind of infectious disease
mo-nop-o-ly *n.*, *pl.* **monopolies** the exclusive ownership
mon-o-rail *n.* train traveling on a single rail to a specific destination
mon-o-the-ism *n.* the belief there is just one God; the one and only
mon-o-tone *n.* the sounds uttered in a single unvarying tone **-ic** *adj.*
mo-not-o-nous *adj.* lacking variety
monotoness *n.*, **monotonously** *adv.*
mon-ox-ide *n.* oxide containing one oxygen atom per molecule
mon-soon *n.* periodic wind
mon-ster *n.* animal having abnormal form
mon-tage *n.* a composite picture
month-ly *adj.* being payable each month; twelve times a year
mon-u-ment *n.* the object in memory of a person **monumental** *adj.*, **-ally** *adv.*
mooch *v.* *Slang* acquire by begging
moocher *n.*
mood *n.* the temporary state of one's mind
mood-y *adj.* being gloomy
moodiness *n.*, **moodily** *adv.*
moon *n.* earth's only satellite
moony *adj.*, **mooniness** *n.*
moon-lit *adj.* lit by the moon
moor *v.* fasten with anchors
moose *n.* very large deer
moot *v.* debate; argue
mope *v.* to be dejected
mo-ped *n.* motorbike
mor-al *adj.* referring to conduct of right or wrong
mo-rale *n.* an individual's state of mind
mor-a-to-ri-um *n.* temporary pause
mor-bid *adj.* gruesome; gloomy
morbidness *n.*, **morbidly** *adv.*
more *adj.* being of greater number or degree
more-o-ver *adv.* furthermore
mo-res *n.*, *pl.* moral customs of a social group
morgue *n.* place to keep dead bodies until they are claimed

morn-ing *n.* the early part of the day; before noon
mo-roc-co *n.* soft leather made of goatskin tanned with sumac
mo-ron *n.* an adult with a low intelligence level **moronism** *n.*, **moronic** *adj.*, **moronity** *n.*
mor-ose *adj.* marked by gloom **morosity** *n.*, **morosely** *adv.*
mor-phine *n.* a highly addictive narcotic, derived from opium
mor-sel *n.* a small quantity of food
mor-tal *adj.* to having caused death; about to cause death
mort-gage *n.* conveyance as security for the repayment of a debt
mor-ti-cian *n.* undertaker
mo-sa-ic *n.* decorative inlaid design of tile
moss *n.* small green plants
most *adj.* majority of; greatest in quantity
mo-tel *n.* establishment which provides lodging for travelers
moth *n.* nocturnal insect
moth-er *n.* female parent
mo-tif *n.* the main element or theme of something
mo-tile *adj.* being capable of moving alone
mo-tion *n.* the act of changing position; a proposal for action
mo-tive *n.* the need or the desire to act **motivator n.**
mo-tor *n.* the device which develops energy for motion
mot-tle *v.* marked with spots or streaks of colors
mot-to *n.* phrase, or word expressing purpose
mound *n.* small hill of earth
mourn *v.* to express one's grief or sorrow over something
mov-ie *n.* motion picture
mow *v.* to cut down
much *adj.* being of great amount or quantity; many in number
muck *n.* moist, sticky soil
mu-cus *n.* the liquid secreted by glands in the body
mud *n.* the mixture of water and solid material such as earth
muf-fle *v.* to suppress; to deaden sound; to conceal or protect
mug *n.* large drinking cup
mug-gy *adj.* being humid and being sultry **muggily adv., -ness n.**
mul-ber-ry *n.* trees having an edible fruit
mulch *n.* protective covering of compost or wood chips
mull *v.* ponder; think over
multi- *prefix* multiple; two or more
mul-ti-far-i-ous *adj.* having great variety **multifariousness n.**
mul-ti-ple *adj.* to be consisting of more than one individual or part
mul-ti-ply *v.* increase in amount or number
mul-ti-tude *n.* large amount or number of something
mum *adj.* not speaking
mum-ble *v.* to speak in a confused indistinct manner
mum-my *n., pl.* **mummies** body embalmed for burial **mummify** *v.*
munch *v.* chew noisily
mun-dane *adj.* relating to the world **mundanely** *adv.*
mu-nic-i-pal *adj.* relating to local affairs; local self-government
mu-ral *n.* kind of painting created on a wall
mur-der *n.* the crime of killing a person by will
mur-mur *n.* a low sound
mus-cle *n.* bodily tissue which produces strength
mus-cu-lar *adj.* brawny
mu-sic *n.* the organized tones in sequences; melodious
mu-si-cian *n.* a performer of music
mus-lin *n.* a sheer, or coarse fabric
muss *v.* to mess up
mus-sel *n.* a type of freshwater bivalve mollusk
must *v.* to be forced to
mus-tache *n.* hair growing on the human upper lip
mus-tang *n.* wild horse
mus-tard *n.* from the seeds of the mustard plant
mus-ter *v.* to come or bring things together
musn't *contr.* must not
mute *adj.* unable to speak
mu-ti-late *v.* maim or cripple
mu-ti-ny *n., pl.* **mutinies** revolt against lawful authority
mutt *n., Slang* a dog that is of a mixed breed
mut-ter *v.* to speak or utter in a low voice with the lips partialy closed
mut-ton *n.* the flesh of a fully grown sheep used for food
mu-tu-al *adj.* having the same relationship **mutuality** *n.*
my *adj.* of myself *interj.* to express surprise, dismay, or pleasure
my-ce-li-um *n., pl.* **mycelia** the mass of filaments which form the main structure of a fungus
my-col-o-gy *n.* scientific study of fungi
my-e-li-tis *n.* the inflammation of the spinal cord or the bone marrow
my-elo-ma *n.* the tumor of the bone marrow
myo-car-dio-graph *n.* recording tool which traces the action of the heart muscles
myo-car-di-um *n.* muscular layer of the heart; along the heart wall
my-o-pia *n.* a visual defect
myr-i-ad *adj.* having large, indefinite aspects
myr-mi-don *n.* loyal follower
myr-tle *n.* evergreen shrub
my-self *pron.* one identical with me
mys-ter-y *n., pl.* **mysteries** something that is not understood
mys-tic *n.* person practicing or believing in mysticism **mystical** *adj.*, **-cally** *adv.*
mys-ti-fy *v.* to perplex
my word *interj.* an expression of astonishment

N, n. The fourteenth letter of the English alphabet.
nab *v., Slang* to seize
na-cho *n.* a tortilla, often small and triangular in shape, topped with cheese or chili sauce and baked
nag *v.* to bother by scolding or constant complaining *n.* a worthless horse
nagger *n.*
nai-ad *n. Gr. Mythol.* a nymph presiding over and living in springs, brooks, and fountains
nail *n.* a thin pointed piece of metal for hammering into wood and other material to hold pieces together
nail-brush *n.* a small brush with firm bristles used to clean the hands and nails
nail-file *n.* a small instrument with a rough surface, used to shape the fingernails
na-ive *adj.* simple andtrusting; not sophisticated; lacking careful judgment; ingenuous
na-ked *adj.* without clothes on the body; nude; exposed; uncovered
nakedly *adv.*, **nakedness** *n.*
nam-by--pam-by *adj.* weak; indecisive; lacking in substance
name *n.* a title or word by which something or someone is known *v.* to give a name **nameable** *adj.*
name--call-ing *n.* the use of offending names to induce condemnation or rejection
name-less *adj.* having no name; anonymous
name-plate *n.* a plaque or plate bearing ones name, company, or title; the title of a book or other publication that is displayed on the cover of the first page
name-sake *n.* a person named after someone with the same name
na-nism *n.* unusullyt small in size; dwarfism
nan-ny *n.* a child's nurse; one who cares for small cildren
nan-ny goat *n.* a female domestic goat
nap *n.* a short rest or sleep, often during the day; to drowse; the surface of a piece of leather or fabric
na-palm *n.* a mixture of aluminum soaps used in jelling gasonling for use in bombsor by flame throwers
nape *n.* the back of the neck
nap-kin *n.* a cloth or soft paper, used at the dinner table for wiping the lips and fingers
na-po-le-on *n.* a pastry of several flaky layers filed with custard cream
nar-cis-sism *n.* the excessive admiration with oneself; self-love
nar-cis-sus *n.* a widely grown type of bulbous plant
nar-co-sis *n.* a deep drug induced state of stupor or unconsciousness
nar-cot-ic *n.* a drug which dulls the senses, relieves pain, and induces a deep sleep; if abused, it can become habit-forming and cause convulsions or comas
nar-rate *v.* to tell a story or give a description in detail
narration *n.*, **narrator** *v.*
nar-row *adj.* slender or small in width
narrowly *adj.*
narrow--mind-ed *adj.* lacking sympathy or tolerance
nar-whal *n.* an aquatic mammal of the Arctic regions, closely related to the white whale
na-sal *adj.* of or pertaining to the nose
na-stur-tium *n.* a five-petaled garden plant usually having red, yellow, or orange flowers
nas-ty *adj.* dirty, filthy, or indecent
nastily *adv.*, **nastiness** *n.*
na-tal *adj.* pertaining to or associated with birth
na-tion *n.* a group of people made up of one or more nationalities under one government **-al** *adj.*, **nationally** *adv.*
na-tion-al-ism *n.* devotion to or concern for one's nation
na-tion-al-i-ty *n.* the fact or condition of belonging to a nation
na-tion-al-ize *v.* to place a nation's resources and industries under the control of the state
na-tive *n.* a person born in a country or place *adj.* belonging to one by nature or birth
na-tiv-i-ty *n.* birth, circumstances, or con-ditions; the birth of Christ
nat-u-ral *adj.* produced or existing by nature; not artificial *Mus.* a note that is not sharp or flat
naturalness *n.*, **naturally** *adv.*
natural child-birth *n.* childbirth with little stress or pain; childbirth requiring training for the mother and father and medical supervision, but without the use of drugs, anesthesia, or surgery
nat-u-ral-ize *v.* to confer the privileges and rights of full citizenship
naturalization *n.*
na-ture *n.* the universe and its phenomena; kind, sort, or type
natured *adj.*
naught *n.* nothing; the number 0
naugh-ty *adj.* unruly; not proper
naughtily *adv.*, **naughtiness** *n.*
nau-se-a *n.* an upset stomach with a feeling that one needs to vomit **-ous** *adj.*
nau-ti-cal *adj.* pertaining to ships or seamanship **nautically** *adv.*
na-val *adj.* of or relating to ships
na-vel *n.* a small mark or scar on the abdomen where the umbilical cord was attached
nav-i-ga-ble *adj.* sufficiently deep and wide enough to allow ships to pass
nav-i-gate *v.* to plan the course of a ship or aircraft; to steer a course
navigation, navigator *n.*
na-vy *n.* one of a nation's organizations for defense; a nation's fleet of ships; a very dark blue
Ne-an-der-thal *adj.* suggesting a caveman in behavior or appearance; primitive or crude **Neanderthal** *n.*
neap tide *n.* a tide in the minimum range which occurs twice a month
near *adv.* at, to, or within a short time or

distance *adj.* closely or intimately related **nearness** *n.*
near-by *adj. & adv.* adjacent
near-sight-ed *adj.* able to see clearly at short distances only
neat *adj.* tidy and clean; free from disorder and dirt **neatly** *adv.*, **neatness** *n.*
neb-u-lous *adj.* confused or vague
nec-es-sar-y *adj.* unavoidable **necessarily** *adv.*
ne-ces-si-tate *v.* to make necessary; to oblige; to require
ne-ces-si-ty *n., pl.* **-ies** the condition of being necessary
neck *n.* the part of the body which connects the head and trunk; a narrow part or projection, as of land, a stringed instrument, or bottle. *v.* to caress and kiss
neck-tie *n.* a narrow strip of material worn around the neck
nec-tar *n.* a good-tasting beverage; a sweet fluid in various flowers, gathered by bees to help make honey **nectarous** *adj.*
nee *n.* born; the surname a woman was born with
need *n.* the lack of something desirable, useful, or necessary
nee-dle *n.* a slender, pointed steel implement which contains an eye through which thread is passed
needle-point *n.* decorative stitching done on canvas
need-n't *contr.* need not
ne-far-i-ous *adj.* extremely wicked
ne-gate *v.* to nullify; to deny; to rule out **negation** *n.*
neg-a-tive *adj.* expressing denial or disapproval; not positive **negatively** *adj.*, **negativeness** *n.*
neglect *v.* to ignore; to pay no attention to **neglectful** *adj.*
neg-li-gee *n.* a woman's loose-fitting dressing gown
neg-li-gent *adj.* to neglect what needs to be done; neglectful
ne-go-ti-ate *v.* to confer with another person to reach an agreement **negotiation, negotiator** *n.*
Ne-gro *n.* a member of the Black race; a black person
ne-groid *adj.* of or relating to the Black race **negroid** *n.*
neigh-bor *n.* one who lives near another; fellowman
neighbor-hood *n.* a section or small region that possesses a specific quality
nei-ther *adj.* not one or the other *pron.* Not the one or the other *conj.* Not either; also not
neo *prefix* recent; new
neo-dym-i-um *n.* a metallic element of the rare-earth group, symbolized by Nd.
ne-on *n.* an inert gaseous element used in lighting fixtures, symbolized by Ne
ne-o-nate *n.* a newborn child less than a month old
ne-o-na-tol-o-gy *n.* the medical study of the first 60 days of a baby's life
neo-phyte *n.* a novice; a beginner.
ne-o-plasm *n.* a tumor tissue serving no physiologic function **neoplastic** *adj.*
neph-ew *n.* the son of one's sister, brother, sister-in-law, or brother-in-law
ne-phrit-ic *adj.* relating to the kidneys
nep-o-tism *n.* the act of showing favoritism to relatives or friends in the work force **nepotist** *n.*
nep-tu-ni-um *n.* a radioactive metallic element, symbolized by Np
nerve *n.* the bundles of fibers which convey sensation and originate motion through the body
nerv-ous *adj.* affecting the nerves or the nervous system **-ly** *adv.*, **-ness** *n.*
nervous system *n., Physiol.* the body system that coordinates, regulates, and controls the various internal functions and responses to stimuli
nest *n.* a shelter, or home built by a bird to hold its eggs and young
nest egg *n.* a supply of money accumulated or saved for future use
nes-tle *v.* to settle snugly; to lie close to **nestler** *n.*
net *n.* a meshed fabric made of cords, ropes, threads, or other material knotted or woven together; the profit, weight, or price which remains after all additions, subtractions, or adjustments have been made
neth-er *adj.* situated below or beneath
net-tle *n.* a plant having toothed leaves covered with stinging hairs
net-work *n.* a system of interlacing tracks, channels, or lines
neu-ral *adj.* relating to a nerve or the nervous system
neu-ral-gia *n.* pain that occurs along the course of a nerve
neu-ri-tis *n.* an inflammation of a nerve which causes pain, the loss of reflexes, and muscular decline **neurotic** *adj.*
neu-rol-o-gy *n.* the medical and scientific study of the nervous system and its disorders **neurological** *adj.*, **neurologist** *n.*
neu-ron *or* **neu-rone** *n., Anat.* a granular cell nerve which is the main functional unit of the nervous system
neu-ro-sis *n.* any one of various functional disorders of the mind or emotions having no physical cause **neurotic** *adj., n.*, **neurotically** *adv.*
neu-ter *adj.* neither feminine nor masculine *n.* a castrated animal
neu-tral *adj.* not supporting either side of a debate, quarrel, or party; a color which does not contain a decided hue *Chem.* neither alkaline nor acid **neutrality** *n.*, **neutrally** *adv.*
neu-tral-ize *v.* to make or declare neutral
neu-tron *n.* an uncharged particle in the nucleus of an atom
nev-er *adv.* not ever
nev-er-the-less *adv.* nonetheless
new *adj.* not used before; unaccustomed; unfamiliar
news *n., pl.* current information and happenings
news-cast *n.* a television or radio news

broadcast
news-pa-per *n.* a weekly or daily publication which contains recent news and information
news-print *n.* an inexpensive machinefinished paper made from wood pulp and used chiefly for newspapers and some paperback books
New Testament *n.* the second part of the Christian Bible containing the Gospels, Acts, Epistles, and the Book of Revelation
next *adj.* immediately following or proceeding
nib-ble *v.* to bite a little at a time
nibble, nibbler *n.*
nice *adj.* pleasing; enjoyable
nicely *adv.*, **niceness** *n.*
niche *n.* a recess or alcove in a wall, usually used for displays
nick *n.* a small chip or cut on a surface; the final critical moment
nick-el *n.* a hard, silver, metallic element used in alloys and symbolized by Ni; a United States coin worth five cents
nick-el-o-de-on *n.* a movie theatre which charged five cents for admission; a coin-operated juke box
nick-name *n.* the familiar form of a proper name, expressed in a shortened form **nickname** *v.*
nic-o-tine *or* **nicotin** *n.* a poisonous alkaloid found in tobacco and used in insecticides and medicine
niece *n.* a daughter of one's sister or brother or one's sister-in-law or brother-in-law
nigh *adv.* near in relationship, time, or space
night *n.* the time between dusk and dawn or the hours of darkness
nightcap *n.* an alcoholic drink usually taken before retiring for the night
night-in-gale *n.* a songbird with brownish plumage, noted for the sweet, nocturnal song of the male
night-mare *n.* a frightening and horrible dream
nim-ble *adj.* marked by a quick, light movement; quick-witted
nimbleness *n.*, **nimbly** *adv.*
nin-com-poop *n.* a silly or stupid person
nine *n.* the cardinal number that is equal to 8+1 **nine** *adj., pron.*
ni-o-bi-um *n.* a gray, metallic element used in alloys, symbolized by Nb
nip *v.* to pinch, bite, or grab something
nipper *n.*
nip-ple *n.* the small projection of a mammary gland through which milk passes
ni-tro-gen *n.* a nonmetallic gaseous element which is essential to life, symbolized by N
ni-tro-glyc-er-in *n.* a highly flammable, explosive liquid, used to make dynamite and, in medicine, to dilate blood vessels
no *adv.* used to express rejection
no-bel-i-um *n.* a radioactive element, symbolized by No
Nobel prize *n.* an award given to people with achievements in literature, economics, medicine, and other fields, established by the last will and testament of Alfred Nobel
no-bil-i-ty *n., pl.* **-ies** the state or quality of being noble
no-ble *adj.* morally good; superior in character or nature **-ness** *n.*, **-y** *adv.*
no-bod-y *pron.* not anybody
noc-tur-nal *adj.* pertaining to or occurring during the night; active at night and quiet during the daylight hours
nocturnally *adv.*
nod *n.* a quick downward motion of the head as one falls off to sleep; a downward motion of the head indicating acceptance or approval
node *n.* a swollen or thickened enlargement
no-el *n.* a Christmas carol
noise *n.* a sound which is disagreeable or loud; in computer science, unwanted data in an electronic signal
noisy *adj.*, **noisily** *adv.*
no-mad *n.* a member of a group of people who wander from place to place **nomadic** *adj.*, **nomadism** *n.*
no-men-cla-ture *n.* the set of names used to describe the elements of art, science, and other fields
nom-i-nal *adj.* of or relating to something that is in name or form only
nominally *adv.*
nom-i-nate *v.* to select a candidate for an elective office; to appoint or designate to a position **nomination, -tor** *n.*
nom-i-nee *n.* a person nominated for a position or office
non- *prefix* not
non-a-ge-nar-i-an *adj.* a person between the ages of 90 and 100 years
non-cha-lant *adj.* giving an effect of casual unconcern **-ance** *n.*, **-ly** *adv.*
non com-pos men-tis *adj.* mentally unbalanced; not of sound mind
non-con-form-ist *n.* a person who does not feel compelled to follow or accept his community's customs or traditions
none *pron.* not any; not one
non-sec-tar-i-an *adj.* not associated with or restricted to one religion, faction, or sect
non-sense *n.* something that seems senseless or foolish; something which is very unimportant **nonsensical** *adj.*
non seq-ui-tur *n.* an inference that does not follow as the logical result of what has preceded it
non-sex-ist *adj.* not discriminating on the basis of gender
noo-dle *n.* a flat strip of dried dough made with eggs and flour *Slang* the head
nook *n.* a corner, recess, or secluded place
noon *n.* the middle of the day; 12:00 o'clock
noose *n.* a loop of rope secured by a slipknot, allowing it to decrease in size as the rope is pulled
nor *conj.* not either; or not
norm *n.* a rule, model, or pattern typical

nu-bile *adj.* suitable or ready for marriage
nu-cle-ar *adj.* pertaining to and resembling a nucleus
nu-cle-us *n.*, *pl.* **-clei** *or* **-cleuses** a central element around which other elements are grouped
nude *adj.* unclothed; naked **nudity, nudist** *n.*
nudge *v.* to poke or push gently **nudge** *n.*
nug-get *n.* a lump, as of precious metal
nui-sance *n.* a source of annoyance
null *adj.* invalid; having no value or consequence; having no legal value **nullification** *n.*
nul-li-fy *v.* to counteract
numb *adj.* lacking physical sensation; paralyzed or stunned **numbness** *n.*
num-ber *n.* a word or symbol which is used in counting or which indicates how many or which one in a series
number-less *adj.* too many to be counted
nu-meral *n.* a symbol, figure, letter, word, or a group of these which represents a number
nu-mer-a-tor *n.* the term in mathematics indicating how many parts are to be taken; the number in a fraction which appears above the line
nu-mer-ous *adj.* consisting or made up of many units
nun *n.* a woman who has joined a religious group and has taken vows to give up worldly goods and never to marry
nup-tial *adj.* of or pertaining to a wedding **nuptials** *pl.*, *n.* a wedding
nurse *n.* a person who is specially trained to care for disabled or sick persons *v.* To feed a baby from a mother's breast; to provide care to a sick or disabled person
nurs-er-y *n.*, *pl.* **-ies** a room reserved for the special use of infants or small children; a business or place where trees, shrubs, and flowers are raised and sold
nur-ture *n.* the upbringing, care, or training of a child **nurture** *v.*, **nurturer** *n.*
nut *n.* a hard-shelled fruit or seed which contains an inner, often edible kernal *Slang* a person who does crazy or silly things
nu-tri-ent *n.* a substance which nourishes or promotes growth and repairs natural wastage of organic life
nu-tri-tion *n.* the process by which a living being takes in food and uses it to live and grow **nutritive, nutritional** *adj.*, **nutritionally** *adv.*
nu-tri-tious *adj.* nourishing and healthy **nutritiously** *adv.*
nuts *adj.*, *Slang* foolish, crazy
nuz-zle *v.* to gently rub against something with the nose; to cuddle
ny-lon *n.* a strong, elastic material; yarn or fabric made from nylon **nylons** stockings made of nylon
nys-tag-mus *n.* the rapid involuntary movement of the eyeballs
nystagmic *adj.*

for a particular group
nor-mal *adj.* ordinary, average, usual; having average intelligence; standard **normalcy, normality** *n.*, **normally** *adv.*
north *n.* the direction to a person's left while facing east
nose *n.* the facial feature containing the nostrils; the sense of smell
nose-dive *n.* a sudden plunge as made by an aircraft
nos-tal-gia *n.* a yearning to return to the past **nostalgic** *adj.*
nos-tril *n.* the external openings of the nose
nos-y *or* **nos-ey** *adj.* snoopy; inquisitive; prying
not *adv.* in no manner; used to express refusal or denial
no-ta-ble *adj.* remarkable; distinguished *n.* a person or thing which is notable **notably** *adv.*
no-ta-rize *v.* to acknowledge and certify as a notary public
notary public *n.* a person who is legally authorized as a public officer to witness and certify documents
no-ta-tion *n.* a process or system of figures or symbols used in specialized fields to represent quantities, numbers, or values **notational** *adj.*
notch *n.* a v-shaped indentation or cut
note *n.* a record or message in short form *Mus.* a tone or written character
not-ed *adj.* famous; well-known
noth-ing *n.* not any thing; no part or portion *adv.* in no way; not at all
no-tice *n.* an announcement; a notification *v.* to give notice; to become aware of **noticeable** *adj.*, **-ably** *adv.*
no-ti-fy *v.* to give notice of; to announce **notifier, notification** *n.*
no-tion *n.* an opinion; a general concept; an idea **notions** *pl.*, *n.* small useful articles, as thread or buttons
no-to-ri-ous *adj.* having a widely known and usually bad reputation
not-with-stand-ing *prep.* in spite of *adv.* nevertheless; anyway *conj.* although
noun *n.* a word which names a person, place, or thing
nour-ish *v.* to furnish with the nutriment and other substances needed for growth and life **nourishing** *adj.*, **nourishment** *n.*
nou-veau riche *n.* a person who has recently become rich
no-va *n.*, *pl.* **-vae** *or* **-vas** a star which flares up and fades away after a few years or months
nov-el *n.* an inventive narrative dealing with human experiences; a book
nov-el-ty *n.*, *pl.* **-ies** something unusual or new
nov-ice *n.* a person who is new and unfamiliar with an activity or business
now *adv.* at the present time
no-where *adv.* not in or at any place
nox-ious *adj.* harmful; obnoxious
noz-zle *n.* a projecting spout or vent of something
nu-ance *n.* a slight variation
nub *n.* a knob; a small piece or lump

O, o The fifteenth letter of the English alphabet.
O *n.* a word used before a name when talking to that person; an interjection
oaf *n.* a stupid or clumsy person
oafish *adj.*, **oafishly** *adv.*
oak *n.* a large tree of durable wood bearing acorns **oaken** *adj.*
oar *n.* a long pole, flat at one end, used in rowing a boat
oar-lock *n.* a u-shaped device, on a pivot used to hold an oar during rowing.
oars-man *n.* a person who is skilled in the use of oars
oasis *n.*, *pl.* **oases** a fertile section in the desert which contains water
oat *n.* a cultivated cereal grass whose grain or seed is used as food
oat-cake *n.* a thin, brittle cake made of oatmeal
oath *n.* a solemn promise in the name of God or on a Bible
oat-meal *n.* a cooked cereal food made from rolled oats
ob-bli-ga-to *adj.* necessary to; indispensable
ob-du-rate *adj.* stubborn **obduracy** *n.*
o-be-di-ence *n.* the havit of obeying; compliance; submission
o-be-di-ent *adj.* obeying or willing to do what one is fold **obedience** *n.*
ob-e-lisk *n.* a tall, four-sided stone pillar which slopes from a pointed top
o-bese *adj.* very fat **obesity** *n.*
o-bey *v.* to carry out instructions **obeyer** *n.*
ob-fus-cate *v.* to obscure; to confuse, muddle, or bewilder
o-bi *n.* a sash that is tied over a kimono and worn by the Japanese female
o-bit *n. Slang* an obituary
o-bit-u-ar-y *n.*, *pl.* **-ies** a published announcement that a person has died
ob-ject *v.* to voice disapproval *Grammar* a word in a sentence which explains who or what is acted upon
object ball *n.* in billiards the first ball struck by the cue ball.
object glass *n.* the lens or combination of lenses in a microscope or telescope, that first receives the rays from an object and forms the image through the eyepiece
ob-jec-tion *n.* a feeling of opposition or disagreement, etc.; the reason for a disagreement
ob-jec-tion-a-ble *adj.* provoking diapproval or protest; offensive or represhensible
ob-jec-tive *adj.* pertaining to or dealing with material objects rather than mental concepts
ob-la-tion *n.* a religious offering or the act of sacrifice
ob-li-ga-tion *n.* a promise or feeling of duty; something one must do because one's conscience or law demands it
ob-lig-a-to-ry *adj.* binding legally or morally; imperative, compulsory; recording an obligation
o-blige *v.* to constrain; to put in one's debt by a service or favor
obliger *n.*, **obligingly** *adv.*
ob-li-gee *n.* the person to whom another is obligated or bound by a legal agreement
o-bling-ing *adj.* disposed to do favors or perform special services; willing; kind
ob-li-gor *adj.* a person who is legally bound to discharge an obligation
o-blique *adj.* inclined; not level or straight up and down
obliqueness, obliquity *n.*
ob-liq-ui-ty *n.* divergence from ones moral standards, an instance of mental deviation; a confusing statement
o-blit-er-ate *v.* to blot out or eliminate completely; to wipe out
obliteration, obliterator *n.*, **obliterative** *adj.*
o-bliv-i-on *n.* the condition of being utterly forgotten
ob-liv-i-ous *adj.* not aware or conscious of what is happening; unmindful
obliviously *adv.*, **obliviousness** *n.*
ob-long *adj.* rectangular; longer in one direction than the other **oblong** *n.*
ob-lo-quy *n.* abusive languange; a strongly condemnatory utterance
ob-nox-ious *adj.* very unpleasant; repugnant **obnoxiousness** *n.*
o-boe *n.* a double-reed, tube-shaped woodwind instrument
oboist, ob-scene *adj.* indecent
ob-scene *adj.* indecent; disgusting; objectionable; tending to 9incit lust
ob-scure *adj.* remote; not clear; faint *v.* to make dim; to conceal by covering
obscurely *adv.*, **obscurity** *n.*
ob-serve *v.* to pay attention; to watch
observable, observant *adj.*, **observably** *adv.*, **observer** *n.*
ob-ser-vant *adj.* paying strict attention to something
ob-ser-va-tion *n.* the act of observing something; that which is observed; a judgment or opinion
observational *adj.* **-ally** *adv.*
ob-ser-va-to-ry *n.*, *pl.* **-ies** a building or station furnished with instruments for studying the natural phenomenon
ob-sess *v.* to preoccupy the mind with an idea or emotion **obsession** *n.*
ob-so-lete *adj.* no longer in use; out-of-date **obsolescence** *n.*, **obsolescent** *adj.*
ob-sta-cle *n.* an obstruction; anything which opposes or stands in the way of
ob-ste-tri-cian *n.* a physician who specializes in the care of a woman during pregnancy and childbirth
ob-stet-rics *pl.*, *n.* the branch of medicine which deals with pregnancy and childbirth
ob-sti-na-cy *n.* the instance, state, or quality of being obstinate
ob-sti-nate *adj.* stubbornly set to an opinion or course of action
obstinacy *n.*, **obstinately** *adv.*
ob-strep-er-ous *adj.* noisy, unruly, or boisterous in resistance to advice or control
ob-struct *v.* to block, hinder or impede
obstructor, obstruction *n.*, **-tive** *adj.*
ob-struc-tion-ism *n.* the deliberate inter-

ference the progress or business
ob-tain *v.* to acquire or gain possession of **obtainable** *adj.*, **obtainer** *n.*
ob-trude *v.* to thrust forward without request or warrant; to call attention to oneself
ob-tuse *adj.* lacking acuteness of feeling; insensitive; not distinct or clear to the senses, as pain or sound
ob-vert *v.* to turn in order to present a different view or surface
ob-vi-ate *v.* to counter or prevent by effective measures
ob-vi-ous *adj.* easily seen, discovered, or understood
oc-ca-sion *n.* the time an event occurs; the event itself; a celebration *v.* to bring about
oc-ca-sion-al *adj.* appearing or occurring irregularly or now and then
oc-ci-den-tal *adj.* western
oc-cip-i-tal bone *n. Anat.* the bone which forms the back of the skull
oc-cult *adj.* concealed *n.* the action or influence of supernatural agencies or secret knowledge of them
occultist, occultism *n.*
oc-cult-ism *n.* study or belief in the influence or action of supernatural powers
oc-cu-pan-cy *n.* the state or act of being occupied; the act of holding in possession
oc-cu-pant *n.* a person who acquired title by occupancy
oc-cu-pa-tion *n.* a job, profession, or vocation; a foreign military force which controls an area
occupational therapy *n. Med.* the treatment of mental, nervous, or physical disabilities by means of work designed to promote recovery or readjustment
oc-cu-py *v.* to take and retain possession of; to live in **occupier** *n.*
oc-cur *v.* to suggest; to have something come to mind; to happen
occurrence *n.*, **-rent** *adj. and n.*
o-cean *n.* an immense body of salt water which covers 3/4 of the earth's surface
oceanic *adj.*
ocean-ar-i-um *n.* a large contained marine aquarium used for the display of fish
o-ce-an-ic *adj.* pertaining to , occurring in the ocean
ocean-front *n.* an area or building that faces the ocean
ocean-going *adj.* being capable or designed for ocean travel
o-ce-an-og-ra-phy *n.* the science of oceanic phenomena dealing with underwater research
o-cean sunfish *n.* a large tropical fish having short bodies and very long fines
oc-el-lat-ed *adj.* having eyelike markings
o-cel-lus *n.* the simple eye of an insect that is present in both the larval and adult
o-cel-lot *n.* a leopardlike cat, both nocturnal and arboreal
och-loc-ra-cy *n.* rule by the common people
och-lo-pho-bia *n.* the morbid fear of mobs and crowds
o'clock *adv.* of, or according to the clock
o-co-til-lo *n.* a desert shrub, characterized by thorny stems and bright red flowers
oc-ta-chord *n.* a musical instrument with eight strings; a standard scale of eight notes
oc-ta-gon *n.* a polygon with eight angles and eight sides
octagonal *adj.*, **octagonally** *adv.*
oc-ta-he-dron *n.* a solid having eight sides
oc-tam-er-ous *adj.* divided into or consisting of eight parts
oc-tane *n.* any of several hydrocarbon compounds which occur in petroleum
oc-tave *n., Music* a tone on the eighth degree above or below another tone
Oc-to-ber *n.* the 10th month of the calendar year, having 31 days
oc-to-ge-nar-i-an *n.* a person between the ages of 80 and 90
oc-to-pus *n., pl.* **-es** *or* **-pi** a cephalopod with a sac-like body and eight tentacles containing double rows of suckers
oc-u-lar *adj.* of or relating to the eye
OD *n. Slang* an overdose of a drug; one who has taken an overdose *v.* to overdose; to die from an overdose
odd *adj.* unusual; strange; singular; left over; not even **oddly** *adv.*, **oddness** *n.*
odds *pl, n.* an equalizing advantage given to a weaker opponent
ode *n.* a lyric poem usually honoring a person or event
o-dom-e-ter *n.* a device in a vehicle used to measure distance traveled **-try** *n.*
o-dor *n.* a smell; a sensation which occurs when the sense of smell is stimulated
od-ys-sey *n.* a long voyage marked by many changes of fortune; a spiritual quest
of *prep.* proceeding; composed of; relating to
off *adv.* from a position or place; no longer connected or on *adj.* canceled *prep.* away from
of-fend *v.* to make angry; to arouse resentment; to break a law **offender** *n.*
of-fense *n.* a violation of a duty, rule, or a propriety; the act of causing displeasure; the act of assaulting or attacking
of-fen-sive *adj.* disagreeable or unpleasant; causing resentment; insulting
of-fer *v.* to present for acceptance or rejection; to present as an act of worship; to make available
of-fer-ing *n.* the act of one who offers; a contribution, as money, given to the support of a church
off-hand *adv. or adj.* without preparation or premeditation
of-fice *n.* a place where business or professional duties are conducted
of-fi-cer *n.* a person who holds a title, or position of authority

of-fi-cial *adj.* something derived from proper authority *n.* one who holds a position or office; a person who referees a game such as football, basketball, or soccer
officialism *n.*, **officially** *adv.*
of-fi-ci-ate *v.* to carry out the duties and functions of a position or office
of-fi-cious *adj.* offering one's services or advice in an unduly forward manner
officiously *adv.*, **officiousness** *n.*
off-spring *n., pl.* **-springs** the descendants of a person, plant, or animal
of-ten *adv.* frequently
oh *interj.* used to express surprise, fear, or pain
oil *n.* any of various substances, usually thick, which can be burned or easily melted; a lubricant *v.* to lubricate
oil field *n.* an area rich in petroleum; an area which has been made ready for oil production
oint-ment *n.* an oily substance used on the skin as an aid to healing or to soften the skin
o-kra *n.* a tall tropical and semitropical plant with green pods that can be either fried or cooked in soups
old *adj.* having lived or existed for a long time; of a certain age *n.* former times
old-en *adj.* of or relating to times long past; ancient
old--fash-ioned *adj.* pertaining to or characteristic of former times or old customs; not modern or up-to-date
Old Glory *n.* the flag of the United States of America
Old Testament *n.* the first of two parts of the Christian Bible, containing the history of the Hebrews, the laws of Moses, the writings of the prophets, the Holy Scriptures of Judaism, and other material
Old World *n.* the eastern hemisphere, including Asia, Europe, and Africa
ol-fac-tory *adj.* pertaining to the sense of smell
oli-gar-chy *pl., n.* **-ies** a government controlled by a small group for corrupt and selfish purposes; the group exercising such control
ol-ive *n.* a small oval fruit from an evergreen tree with leathery leaves and yellow flowers, valuable as a source of oil
O-lym-pic Games *pl., n.* international athletic competition held every four years, based on an ancient Greek festival
om-buds-man *pl. n.* **-men** a government official appointed to report and receive grievances against the government
om-e-let *or* **om-e-lette** *n.* a dish made from eggs and other items, such as bacon, cheese, and ham, and cooked until set
o-men *n.* a phenomenon which is thought of as a sign of something to come, whether good or bad
om-i-nous *adj.* fore-shadowed by an omen or by a presentiment of evil; threatening
o-mis-sion *n.* the state or act of being omitted; anything neglected or left out
o-mit *v.* to neglect; to leave out
om-ni-bus *n.* a public vehicle designed to carry a large number of people; a bus *adj.* covering a complete collection of objects or cases
om-nip-o-tent *adj.* having unlimited or infinite power or authority
om-nis-cient *adj.* knowing all things; having universal or complete knowledge
om-niv-or-ous *adj.* feeding on both vegetable and animal substances; absorbing everything **omnivorously** *adv.*
on *prep.* positioned upon; indicating proximity; indicating direction toward; with respect to *adv.* in a position of covering; forward
once *adv.* a single time; at any one time *conj.* As soon as
once-over *n., Slang* a swift but comprehensive glance
on-col-o-gy *n.* the study of tumors
oncological, -gic *adj.*, **oncologist** *n.*
one *adj.* single; undivided *n.* a single person; a unit; the first cardinal number (1). **oneself** *pron.* one's own self
one--sid-ed *adj.* partial to one side; unjust **one-sidedness** *n.*
on-ion *n.* an edible bulb plant having a pungent taste and odor
on--line *adj. Computer Science* controlled directly by a computer
on-ly *adj.* sole; for one purpose alone *adv.* without anyone or anything else *conj.* except; but
on-o-mat-o-poe-ia *n.* the use of a word, as buzz or hiss, which vocally imitates the sound it denotes
onomatopoeic, onomatopoetic *adj.*
on-shore *adj.* moving or coming near or onto the shore **onshore** *adv.*
on-slaught *n.* a fierce attack
on-to *prep.* to a position or place; aware of
o-nus *n.* a burden; a responsibility or duty which is difficult or unpleasant; the blame
on-ward *adv.* moving forward in time or space **onwards** *adj.*
on-yx *n.* a gemstone; a chalcedony in layers of different colors
oo-dles *pl., n., Slang* a great or large quantity
ooze *n.* a soft deposit of slimy mud on the bottom of a body of water; muddy or marshy ground; a bog *v.* to flow or leak slowly; to disappear little by little
o-pal *n.* a translucent mineral composed of silicon, often marked with an iridescent play of colors **opaline** *adj.*
o-paque *adj.* not transparent; dull; obscure **opacity, opaqueness** *n.*
OPEC *abbr.* Organization of Petroleum Exporting Countries.
o-pen *adj.* having no barrier; not covered, sealed, locked, or fastened *n.* a contest for both amateurs and professionals *v.* to begin or start
openness *n.*, **openly** *adv.*

open-and-shut *adj.* easily settled; simple to decide
op-era *n.* a drama having music as a dominant factor, an orchestral accompaniment, acting, and scenery
op-er-ate *v.* to function, act, or work effectively; to perform an operation, as surgery **operative** *adj.*
op-er-a-tion *n.* the process of operating; the system or method of operating; a series of acts to effect a certain purpose; a process; a procedure performed on the human body with surgical instruments to restore health; various mathematical or logical processes
op-er-a-tor *n.* a person who operates a machine; the owner or person in charge of a business *Slang* a shrewd person
oph-thal-mol-o-gy- *n.* a branch of medical science dealing with diseases of the eye, its structure, and functions
o-pin-ion *n.* a judgment held with confidence; a conclusion held without positive knowledge
o-pi-um *n.* a bitter, highly addictive drug; a narcotic
o-pos-sum *n., pl.* **-sum** *or* **-sums** a nocturnal animal which hangs by its tail and carries its young in a pouch
op-po-nent *n.* an adversary; one who opposes another
op-por-tune *adj.* occurring at the right or appropriate time
opportunist *n.,* **opportunely** *adv.*
op-por-tu-ni-ty *n., pl.* **-ies** a favorable position; a chance for advancement
op-pose *v.* to be in direct contention with; to resist; to be against
opposable *adj.,* **opposition** *n.*
op-po-site *adj.* situated or placed on opposing sides **oppositeness** *n.*
op-press *v.* to worry or trouble the mind; to weigh down; to burden as if to enslave **oppression, oppressor** *n.*
op-tic *adj.* pertaining or referring to sight or the eye
op-ti-cal *adj.* pertaining to sight; constructed or designed to assist vision **optically** *adv.*
op-ti-cian *n.* a person who makes eyeglasses and other optical articles
op-ti-mism *n.* a doctrine which emphasizes that everything is for the best
op-ti-mum *n., pl.* **-ma** the degree or condition producing the most favorable result *adj.* conducive to the best result
op-tion *n.* the act of choosing or the power of choice; a choice **-ally** *adv.*
op-tion-al *adj.* left to one's decision; elec-tive; not required
op-tom-e-try *n.* the occupation or profession of examining the eyes and prescribing corrective lenses
op-u-lence *n.* wealth in abundance; affluence
or *conj.* a word used to connect the second of two choices or possibilities, indicating uncertainty *suffix* indicating a person or thing which does something
or-a-cle *n.* a seat of worship where ancient Romans and Greeks consulted the gods for answers; a person of unquestioned wisdom **oracular** *adj.*
o-ral *adj.* spoken or uttered through the mouth; taken or administered through the mouth **orally** *adv.*
oral contraceptive *n.* a pill containing hormones, taken monthly to prevent pregnancy
or-ange *n.* a citrus fruit which is round and orange in color *adj.* Yellowish-red
o-rang-u-tan *n., pl.* **-tans** a large, anthropoid ape, having brownish-red hair and very long arms
o-rate *v.* to speak in an elevated manner
orb *n.* a globe or sphere
or-bit *n.* the path of a celestial body or a manmade object *v.* to revolve or move in an orbit; to circle **orbital** *adj.*
or-chard *n.* land that is devoted to the growing of fruit trees
or-ches-tra *n.* a group of musicians performing together on various instruments **orchestral** *adj.*
orchestra pit *n.* in theatres, the space reserved for musicians
or-chid *n.* a plant found the world over having three petals in various colors
or-dain *v.* to appoint as a minister, priest, or rabbi by a special ceremony; to decree
or-deal *n.* a painful or severe test of character or endurance
or-der *n.* a condition where there is a logical arrangement or disposition of things; sequence or suc-cession; method; an instruction for a person to follow; a request for certain objects *v.* to command; to demand
orderly *adj.* neat, tidy.
or-di-nance *n.* a command, rule, or order; a law issued by a municipal body
or-di-nar-y *adj.* normal; having no exceptional quality; common; average; plain
ore *n.* a natural underground substance, as a mineral or rock, from which valuable matter is extracted
o-reg-a-no *n.* a bushy perennial herb of the mint family, used as a seasoning for food
or-gan *n.* a musical instrument of pipes, reeds, and keyboards which produces sound by means of compressed air; a part of an animal, human, or plant that performs a definite function, as the heart, a kidney, or a stamen
or-gan-dy *or* **or-gan-die** *n., pl.* **-ies** a translucent, stiff fabric of cotton or silk
or-gan-ic *adj.* effecting or pertaining to the organs of an animal or plant; of or relating to the process of growing plants with natural fertilizers with no chemical additives **organically** *adv.*
or-gan-i-za-tion *n.* the state of being organized or the act of organizing; a group of people united for a particular purpose **organizational** *adj.*
or-gan-ize *v.* to assemble or arrange with

an orderly manner; to arrange by planning **organization** *n.*

or-gasm *n.* **Physiol.** intensive emotional excitement; the culmination of a sexual act

o-ri-ent *v.* to determine the bearings or right direction with respect to another source

Orient *n.* the countries located east of Europe **Oriental** *adj.*

or-i-fice *n.* an opening through which something may pass; a mouth

or-i-gin *n.* the cause or beginning of something; the source; a beginning place

o-rig-i-nal *adj.* belonging to the first or beginning *n.* a new idea produced by one's own imagination; the first of a kind **originality** *n.*, **originally** *adv.*

or-i-ole *n.* a songbird having brightly colored yellow and black plumage in the males

or-na-ment *n.* a decoration. *v.* To adorn or beautify **ornamental** *adj.*, **ornamentally** *adv.*, **ornamentation** *n.*

or-nate *adj.* excessively ornamental; elaborate; showy, as a style of writing

or-phan *n.* a child whose parents are deceased **orphan** *v.*, **orphanage** *n.*

or-ris *n.* any of several species having a fragrant root and used in medicine, perfumes, and cosmetics

or-tho-don-tics *n.* the branch of dentistry dealing with the correction and prevention of irregularities of the teeth

or-tho-dox *adj.* following established traditions and beliefs, especially in religion

Orthodox Judaism *n.* the branch of Jewish faith which accepts the Mosaic Laws as interpreted in the Talmud

or-tho-pe-dics *n.* the branch of surgery or manipulative treatment concerned with the disorders of the bones, joints, and muscles **orthopedist** *n.*

os-cil-late *v.* to swing back and forth with regular motion, as a pendulum **oscillation, oscillator** *n.*, **-tory** *adj.*

os-mi-um *n.* a hard, but brittle metallic element symbolized as OS

os-mo-sis *n.* the tendency of fluids separated by a semipermeable membrane to pass through it and become mixed and equal in strength **osmotic** *adj.*

os-ten-ta-tion *n.* the act of displaying pretentiously in order to excite

osteo *n. comb. form* bone; pertaining to the bones

os-te-op-a-thy *n.* a medical practice based on the theory that diseases are due chiefly to abnormalities of the body, which can be restored by manipulation of the parts by therapeutic measures

os-teo-po-ro-sis *n.* a disorder causing gradual deterioration of bone tissue, usually occurring in older women

os-tra-cize *v.* to exile or exclude from a group; to shut out

oth-er *adj.* additional; alternate; different from what is implied or specified *pron.* a different person or thing

oth-er-wise *adv.* under different conditions of circumstances

ot-ter *n.*, *pl.* **-ter** *or* **-ters** web-footed aquatic mammals, related to the weasel

ouch *n. interj.* an exclamation to express sudden pain

ought *v.* used to show or express a moral duty or obligation; to be advisable or correct

ounce *n.* a unit of weight which equals 1/16 of a pound

our *adj.* of or relating to us ourselves *pron.* the possessive case of the pronoun we **ourselves** our own selves

oust *v.* to eject; to remove with force

out *adv.* away from the center or inside *adj.* away *n.* a means of escape *prep.* through; forward from

out-age *n.* a loss of electricity

out-break *n.* a sudden outburst; an occurrence

out-cast *n.* a person who is excluded; a homeless person

out-come *n.* a consequence or result

out-dated *adj.* old-fashioned and obsolete

out-do *v.* to excel in achievement

out-fit *n.* the equipment or tools required for a specialized purpose; the clothes a person is dressed in *v.* to supply

out-land-ish *adj.* extremely ridiculous, unusual, or strange

out-last *v.* to exceed; to outlive; to last longer that something else in comparison

out-law *n.* a person who habitually defies or breaks the law; a criminal *v.* to ban; prohibit; to deprive of legal protection

out-let *n.* an exit

out-line *n.* a rough draft showing the main features of something **outline** *v.*

out-look *n.* a person's point of view; an area offering a view of something

out-num-ber *v.* to go over or exceed in number

out-pa-tient *n.* a patient who visits a clinic or hospital for treatment but does not spend the night

out-post *n.* troops stationed at a distance away from the main group as a guard against attack; a frontier or outlying settlement

out-put *n.* production or yield during a given time

out-rage *n.* an extremely violent act of violence or cruelty; the violent emotion such an act engenders **outrageous** *adj.*, **outrage** *v.*

out-right *adj.* free from reservations or complications; complete; entire

out-side *n.* the area beyond the boundary lines or surface; extreme *adv.* outdoors

out-spo-ken *adj.* spoken without reserve; candid **outspokenly** *adv.*

out-stand-ing *adj.* excellent; prominent; unsettled, as a bill owed; projecting

out-ward *adj.* pertaining to the outside or exterior; superficial **outwards** *adv.*
out-wit *v.* to trick, baffle, or outsmart with ingenuity
o-val *adj.* having the shape of an egg; an ellipse
o-va-ry *n., pl.* **-ies** one of the pair of female reproductive glands **-rian** *adj.*
o-va-tion *n.* an enthusiastic display of approval for a person or a performance; applause
ov-en *n.* an enclosed chamber used for baking, drying, or heating
o-ver-act *v.* to act in an exaggerated way
o-ver *prep.* above; across; upon *adv.* covering completely; thoroughly; again; repetition *adj.* higher; upper *prefix* excessive, as overstuffed or overcrowded
over-act *v.* to act in an exaggerated way
over-all *adj.* including or covering everything; from one side or end to another; generally *n.* pants with a bib and shoulder straps
over-arm *adj.* thrown or executed with the arms raised above the shoulders
over-bear *v.* to crush or bear down by superior force or weight **overbearing** *adj.*
over-board *adv.* over the side of a boat or ship into the water
over-cast *adj.* gloomy; obscured *Meteor.* clouds covering more than 9/10 of the sky
over-coat *n.* a coat worn over a suit for extra warmth
over-come *v.* to prevail; to conquer or defeat **overcomer** *n.*
over-con-fi-dence *n.* extreme or excessive confidence
over-do *v.* to do anything excessively; to overcook
over-dose *n.* to take an excessive dose of medication, especially narcotics
over-draw *v.* to withdraw money over the limits of one's credit
over-drive *n.* a gearing device in a vehicle that turns a drive shaft at a greater speed than that of the engine, therefore decreasing power output
over-due *adj.* past the time of return or payment
over-flow *v.* to flow beyond the limits of capacity; to overfill
over-hand *v.* to execute something with the hand above the level of the elbow or shoulder **overhanded** *adv.*
over-haul *v.* to make all needed repairs
over-head *n.* the operating expenses of a company, including utilities, rent, and upkeep *adj.* situated above the level of one's head
over-look *v.* to disregard or fail to notice something purposely; to ignore
over-night *adj.* lasting the whole night; from dusk to dawn **overnight** *adv.*
over-pass *n.* a raised section of highway which crosses other lines of traffic *v.* to cross, pass over, or go through something; to overlook
over-plus *n.* a surplus of something
over-ride *v.* to disregard; to take precedence over; to declare null and void
over-rule *v.* to put aside by virtue of higher authority
over-run *v.* to spread out; to extend or run beyond
over-seas *adv.* abroad, across the seas **overseas** *adj.*
over-see *v.* to supervise; to direct **overseer** *n.*
overseer *n.* one who oversees
over-sexed *adj.* having an overactive interest in sex
over-shoe *n.* a galosh worn over a shoe for protection from snow or water
over-sight *n.* a mistake made inadvertently
over-size or oversized *adj.* larger than the average size of something
over-step *v.* to go beyond a limit or restriction
overt *adj.* open to view
over--the--counter *adj.* not traded on an organized security ex-change; of or relating to drugs or medicine which can be purchased without a prescription
over-throw *v.* to remove from power by force; to bring about destruction
over-time *n.* the time worked beyond or before the specified hours
over-whelm *v.* to overcome completely; to make helpless
o-void *adj.* having the shape of an egg
ovu-late *n.* to discharge or produce eggs from an ovary
o-vum *n., pl.* **ova** the female reproductive cell
owe *v.* to be in debt for a certain amount; to have a moral obligation
owl *n.* a predatory nocturnal bird, having large eyes, a short hooked bill, and long powerful claws **owlish** *adj.*
own *adj.* belonging to oneself *v.* to possess; to confess; to admit **owner** *n.*
ox *n., pl.* **oxen** a bovine animal used domestically in much the same way as a horse; an adult castrated bull
ox-ford *n.* a shoe which is laced and tied over the instep
ox-ide *n.* a compound of oxygen and another element
oxy-ac-id *n.* an acid containing oxygen
ox-y-gen *n.* a colorless, odorless, tasteless gaseous element essential to life, symbolized by O
ox-y-gen-ate *v.* to combine or treat with oxygen
oxygen mask *n.* a device worn over the mouth and nose through which a person can receive oxygen as an aid to breathing
ox-y-gen tent *n.* the protective cover that is placed over the upper body of a patient, and makes it possible for delivering and retaining pure oxygen to aid breathing
oys-ter *n.* an edible marine mollusk
o-zone *n.* a pale-blue gas formed of oxygen with an odor like chlorine, formed by an electrical discharge in the air *Slang* fresh air

P, p The sixteenth letter of the English alphabet.
pab-u-lom *n.* type of food such as in absorable solution
pa-ca *n.* type of large and borwn rodent that is from Central and South America having white spots
pace *n.* a person's step in walking or the length of a person's step; stride
pace *v.*, **pacer** *n.*
pace car *n.* the automobile that leads a field of competitors around the track, in order to warm up the engines then falls out and does not continue in the race
pace lap *n.* the warm up lap before the start of a car race
pace-mak-er *n.* the person who sets the pace for another in a race; a type of surgically implanted electronic instrument used to stabilize or stimulate the heartbeat
pac-er *n.* one that paces
pa-chi-si *n.* another name for the game Parcheesi; ancient board game played with dice
pach-y-derm *n.* a group of animals which contains the elephant, the rhinoceros, and hippo; animals having thisk skins
pach-y-san-dra *n.* a type of species of the evergreen trailing herbs of the box family and is grown for the purpose of ground cover in areas that are shaded
pa-cif-i-ca-tion *n.* the state of something being pacified or calmed
pac-i-fi-er *n.* a person or something that will pacify another; nipple shaped device for babies to such on
pac-i-fism *n.* the policy dealing with the establishment of universal peace between all nations; opposition to violence or war as a means of settling problems or disputes
pac-i-fy *v.* to quiet or soothe anger or distress; to calm **pacification** *n.*
pack *n.* a bundle; a group or number of things tied or wrapped up
pack-age *n.* something tied up, wrapped or bound together
pack-age deal *n.* an agreement or offer that involves a number of related items, the items offered
pack-age store *n.* a retail establishment that sells alcoholic beverages only in sealed containers
pack animal *n.* an animal used to carry heavy packs
pack-board *n.* a metal fram that is usuallyt covered with canvas, used to carry goods and equipment over ones shoulder
pack-er *n.* a person who packs; one who works in an establishment that packs meat; a machine that automatically packs
pack-et *n.* a type of parcelor package that is small in size and can be used to carry or hold small items
pack-ing *n.* the action of a person who packs
pack-ing house *n.* a place where food, such as meats, are made and packed in order to be sent to the market for sale
pack-man *n.* a perosn who carries a pack and tries to sell his wares; a peddler
pack rat *n.* a type of rodent located in North America that has a habit of hiding or hoarding the items that it finds; one who collects uesless items
pack-sack *n.* a flexible baglike case of material or leather designed with straps for carrying items of ones back
pack-sad-dle *n.* a saddle that is used on pack animals for carrying objects
pack-thread *n.* the twine or rope that is used for the purpose of binding packages together to make carrying easier for carrying
pact *n.* an agreement between nations, groups, or people
pad-dy wag-on *n.*, *Slang* a police vehicle
pa-dre *n.* a title used in Spain and Italy for a priest
pa-gan *n.* a person who does not acknowledge God in any religion; a heathen **pagan** *adj.*, **paganism** *n.*
page *n.* a person hired to deliver messages or run errands; one side of the leaf of a book or letter
pag-eant *n.* an elaborate exhibition or spectacular parade for public celebration **pageantry** *n.*
pa-go-da *n.* a sacred Buddhist tower built as a memorial or shrine
paid *v.* past tense of pay
pail *n.* a cylindrical container usually having a handle
pain *n.* the unpleasant feeling resulting from injury or disease **-ful**, **-less** *adj.*
paint *n.* a mixture of colors or pigments which are spread on a surface as protection or as a decorative coating **painter**, **painting** *n.*
pair *n.*, *pl.* **pairs**, pair two things which are similar and used together
pa-ja-mas *pl.*, *n.* a loose fitting garment for sleeping, consisting of a jacket and pants
pal-ace *n.* the royal residence of a sovereign **palatial** *adj.*
pal-at-a-ble *adj.* pleasant to the taste
pale *n.* the pointed stake of a fence; a picket **palely** *adv.*
pal-ette *n.* a thin oval board with a hole for the thumb, on which an artist lays and mixes colors
pal-in-drome *n.* a word, number, or sentence which reads the same backward or forward
pal-i-sade *n.* a fence made of stakes for protection
pall *n.* a heavy cloth used to cover a bier or coffin
pal-la-di-um *n.* a silvery-white metallic element symbolized by Pd.
pall-bear-er *n.* a person who assists in carrying a coffin at a funeral
pal-lid *adj.* deficient in color
pal-lor *n.* lacking color; paleness
palm *n.* the inner area of the hand between the fingers and the wrist
pal-sy *n.*, *pl.* **-ies** paralysis; the loss of

ability to control one's movements
pam-per *v.* to treat with extreme care
pam-phlet *n.* a brief publication which is not permanently bound
pan-a-ce-a *n.* a remedy for all diseases, difficulties, or ills
pan-cake *n.* a thin, flat cake made from batter and fried on a griddle
pan-cre-as *n., Anat.* a large, irregularly shaped gland situated behind the stomach which releases digestive enzymes and produces insulin **-tic** *adj.*
pan-da *n.* a large bear-like animal of China and Tibet
pan-de-mo-ni-um *n.* a place marked with disorder and wild confusion
pan-der or panderer *n.* a go-between in sexual affairs; a pimp
pan-el *n.* a flat, rectangular piece of material, often wood, which for-ms a part of a surface **panelist** *n.*
pan-ic *n.* a sudden unreasonable fear which overpowers **panicky** *adj.*
pan-nier *n.* one of a pair of large baskets which are carried on either side of an animal
pan-o-ply *n., pl.* **-lies** the complete equipment of a warrior
pan-o-ram-a *n.* an unlimited or complete view in all directions
pan-sy *n., pl.* **-ies** a garden plant with flowers bearing blossoms
pant *v.* to breathe in rapid or short gasps; to yearn
pan-the-ism *n.* the belief that the laws and forces of nature are all manifestations of God
pantheist *n.*, **pantheistic** *adj.*
pan-ther *n.* a black leopard in its unspotted form
pan-to-mime *n.* communication done solely by means of facial and body gestures
pan-try *n., pl.* **-ies** a closet or room for storage
pants *pl, n.* trousers; underpants
pap *n.* a soft food for invalids or babies
pa-pa-cy *n., pl.* **-ies** the dignity or jurisdiction of a pope
pa-per *n.* a substance made of pulp from wood and rags
pa-poose *n.* a North American Indian child or baby
pa-pri-ka *n.* a dark red seasoning powder made by grinding red peppers
Pap test *n.* a test in which a smear of bodily secretion from the uterus is examined for the early detection of cancer
par-a-ble *n.* a short, fictitious story which illustrates a moral lesson
par-a-chute *n.* a folding umbrella-shaped apparatus of light fabric used to make a safe landing after a free fall from an airplane
pa-rade *n.* an organized public procession **parader** *n.*
par-a-dise *n.* a state or place of beauty, bliss or delight; heaven
paradisiac, paradisiacal *adj.*
par-a-dox *n.* a statement which seems opposed to common sense or contradicts itself **paradoxical** *adj.*, **paradoxically** *adv.*
par-a-gon *n.* a pattern or model of excellence or perfection
par-a-graph *n.* a section of a composition dealing with a single idea, containing one or more sentences
par-a-keet *n.* a small parrot with a long, wedge-shaped tail
par-al-lel *adj.* moving in the same direction but separated by a distance, as railroad tracks
parallel *v.* **parallelism** *n.*
par-al-lel-o-gram *n.* a four-sided figure having parallel opposite sides which are equal
pa-ral-y-sis *n., pl.* **-ses** complete or partial loss of the ability to feel any sensation or to move **-tic** *adj. & n.*
par-a-lyze *v.* to cause to be inoperative or powerless
par-a-med-ic *n.* a person trained to give emergency medical treatment until a doctor is available
par-a-mount *adj.* superior to all others in rank, importance, and power
par-a-noi-a *n.* mental insanity marked by systematic delusions of persecution or grandeur
par-a-pher-na-lia *n.* personal effects or belongings
par-a-phrase *v.* to put something written or spoken into different words while retaining the same meaning
par-a-site *n., Biol.* an organism which lives, grows, feeds, and takes shelter in or on another organism
par-a-sol *n.* a small umbrella used as protection from the sun
par-boil *v.* to precook something in boiling water
par-cel *n.* a wrapped package; a portion of land **parcel** *v.*
parch *v.* to become very dry from intense heat
parch-ment *n.* goatskin or sheepskin prepared with a pumice stone and used as a material for writing or drawing
par-don *v.* to forgive someone for an offense **pardonable** *adj.*, **pardonably** *adv.*, **pardon** *n.*
pare *v.* to cut away or remove the outer surface gradually
par-e-go-ric *n.* a medication used to relieve stomach pains
par-ent *n.* a mother or father; a forefather; an ancestor
parenthood *n.*, **parental** *adj.*
pa-ren-the-sis *n., pl.* **-ses** one of a pair of curved lines ( ) used to enclose a qualifying or explanatory remark
park *n.* a tract of land used for recreation
par-ka *n.* a cloth jacket with an attached hood
Par-kin-son's disease *n., Pathol.* a progressive disease marked by partial facial paralysis, muscular tremor, weakness, and impaired muscular control
par-lia-ment *n.* the assembly which

constitutes the lawmaking body of various countries

par-lor *n.* a room for entertaining visitors or guests

pa-ro-chi-al *adj.* belonging to a local parish; having to do with a parish

par-o-dy *n., pl.* **-ies** a composition, song, or poem which mimics another in a ridiculous way

pa-role *n.* the conditional release of a prisoner before his sentence expires **parole** *v. & adj.*

par-ox-ysm *n.* a violent attack or outburst; a spasm

par-ri-cide *n.* the crime of murdering one's parents **parricidal** *adj.*

par-rot *n.* a brightly colored, semitropical bird

par-ry *v.* to avoid something; to turn aside **parry** *n.*

parse *v.* to identify the parts of speech in a sentence and to indicate their relationship to each other

par-si-mo-ny *n.* extreme reluctance to use one's resources or to spend money **-ious** *adj.*, **parsimoniously** *adv.*

pars-ley *n.* an herb with curly leaves which is used for seasoning and garnishing

pars-nip *n.* a plant from the carrot family cultivated for its long, edible root

par-son *n.* a pastor or clergyman

parsonage *n.* the home provided by a church for its parson

part *n.* a segment, portion, or division of a whole

par-take *v.* to have a share or part; to take

par-tial *adj.* incomplete; inclined to favor one side more than the other **partiality** *n.*, **partially** *adv.*

par-tic-i-pate *v.* to join in or share; to take part

par-ti-cle *n.* a very small piece of solid matter

par-tic-u-lar *adj.* having to do with a specific person, group, thing, or category **particularly** *adv.*

part-ing *n.* a division; a separation; the place where a division or separation occurs *adj.* done, given, or said on departing

par-ti-tion *n.* a separation or division *v.* to divide

part-ner *n.* one who shares something with another

part-ner-ship *n.* two or more persons who run a business together and share in the profits and losses

par-tridge *n., pl.* **partridges** a plump or stout-bodied game bird

par-ty *n., pl.* **-ies** a group of persons who gather for pleasure or entertainment

pass *v.* to proceed; to move; to transfer; to go away or come to an end

pas-sage *n.* the act of going, proceeding, or passing

pas-sen-ger *n.* one who travels in a vehicle, car, plane, or boat

pas-sion *n.* a powerful feeling; lust; sexual desire; an outburst of strong feeling

pas-sive *adj.* not working, acting, or operating; inactive **passivity** *n.*

pass-port *n.* an official permission issued to a person allowing him to travel out of this country and to return

past *adj.* having to do with or existing at a former time *n.* Before the present time

pas-tel *n.* a crayon made of ground pigments; a drawing made with crayons of this kind

pas-teur-i-za-tion *n.* the process of killing disease-producing microorganisms by heating the liquid to a high temperature

pas-time *n.* spending spare time in a pleasant way; a diversion

pas-tor *n.* a Christian clergyman in charge of a church or congregation

pas-tor-al *adj.* referring to the duties of a pastor

past par-ti-ci-ple *n.* a participle used with reference to actions and conditions in the past

pas-try *n.* food made with dough or having a crust made of dough

pas-ture *n.* an area for grazing of domestic animals

pat *v.* to tap lightly with something flat *n.* a soft, caressing stroke

patch *n.* a piece of fabric used to repair a weakened or torn area in a garment **patchy, patchable** *adj.*

pat-ent *n.* a governmental protection assuring an inventor the exclusive right of manufacturing, using, exploiting, and selling an invention *adj.* evident **patentee, patency** *n.*, **patently** *adv.*

pa-ter-nal *adj.* relating to or characteristic of a father; inherited from a father **paternally** *adv.*, **paternalism** *n.*

path *n.* a track or course; a route; a course of action

pa-thet-ic *adj.* rousing pity, tenderness, or sympathy **pathetically** *adv.*

pa-thol-o-gy *n.* the science that deals with facts about diseases, their nature and causes **-ic, -ical** *adj.*, **-gist** *n.*

pa-thos *n.* a quality in a person that evokes sadness or pity

pa-tience *n.* the quality, state, or fact of being patient; the ability to be patient

pa-tient *adj.* demonstrating uncomplaining endurance under distress

pa-ti-o *n.* an area attached to a house, used for enjoyment and entertainment

pa-tri-arch *n.* the leader of a tribe or family who rules by paternal right; a very old and revered man **patriarchal** *adj.*

pa-tri-ot *n.* a person who loves and defends his country **patriotic** *adj.*, **patriotism** *n.*

pa-trol *n.* walking around an area for the purpose of maintaining or observing security **patrol** *v.*

pa-tron *n.* a person who fosters, protects, or supports some person, enterprise, or thing; a regular customer **patroness** *n.*

pat-sy *n., pl.* **-ies** *Slang* a person who is taken advantage of

pat-tern *n.* anything designed or shaped to serve as a guide in making something else; a sample
pat-ty *n., pl.* **-ies** a small, flat piece of chopped meat
pau-per *n.* a very poor person who depends on charity **pauperism** *n.*, **pauperize** *v.*
pause *v.* to linger, hesitate, or stop for a time **pause** *n.*
pave *v.* to surface with gravel, concrete, asphalt, or other material
pavement *n.* a surface that has been paved
pa-vil-ion *n.* a large, roofed structure used for shelter
paw *n.* the foot of an animal *v.* To handle clumsily or rudely
pay *v.* to give a person what is due for a debt, purchase, or work completed; to compensate
pay-ment *n.* the act of paying
pay-roll *n.* the amount of money to be paid to a list of employees
pea *n.* a round edible seed contained in a pod and grown on a vine
peace *n.* a state of physical or mental tranquillity; calm; serenity; the absence of war **peaceable, -ful** *adj.*
peach *n.* a round, sweet, juicy fruit
pea-cock *n.* a male bird with brilliant blue or green plumage and a long iridescent tail
peak *n.* a projecting edge or point; the top *v.* to bring to the maximum
pea-nut *n.* a nutlike seed which ripens underground; the plant bearing this nut
pear *n.* a juicy, edible fruit which grows on a tree
peas-ant *n.* a farmhand or rustic workman; an uneducated person of the lowest class
peat *n.* the black substance formed when plants begin to decay in wet ground, as bogs **peaty** *adj.*
peb-ble *n.* a small, smooth stone
pe-can *n.* a large tree of the central and southern United States with an edible oval, thin-shelled nut
peck *v.* to strike with the beak; to eat without any appetite, taking only small bites
pec-tin *n.* a complex carbohydrate found in ripe fruits and used in making jelly **pectic** *adj.*
pe-cu-liar *adj.* odd; strange **peculiarity** *n.*, **peculiarly** *adv.*
ped-al *n.* a lever usually operated by the foot
ped-dle *v.* to travel around in an attempt to sell merchandise
ped-es-tal *n.* a support or base for a statue **to put on a pedestal** to hold something in high respect
pe-des-tri-an *n.* a person traveling by foot
pe-di-at-rics *n.* the branch of medicine dealing with the care of children and infants **pediatric** *adj.*, **pediatrician** *n.*
ped-i-cure *n.* the cosmetic care of the toenails and feet
ped-i-gree *n.* a line of ancestors, especially of an animal of pure breed
ped-i-ment *n.* a broad, triangular architectural or decorative part above a door
pe-dom-e-ter *n.* an instrument which indicates the number of miles one has walked
pe-dun-cle *n., Biol.* a stalk-like support in some plants and animals
peek *v.* to look shyly or quickly from a place of hiding; to glance
peel *n.* the natural rind or skin of a fruit *v.* to pull or strip the skin or bark off **peeler** *n.*
peen *n.* the ball-shaped end of a hammer opposite the flat, striking surface
peep *v.* to utter a very small and weak sound, as of a young bird
peer *v.* to look searchingly
pee-vish *adj.* irritable in mood **peevishly** *adv.*, **peevishness** *n.*
peg *n.* a small pin **peg** *v.*
pei-gnoir *n.* a woman's loose fitting dressing gown
pe-koe *n.* a superior black tea made from young or small leaves
pel-i-can *n.* a large, webfooted bird with a large pouch under the lower bill for the temporary storage of fish
pel-let *n.* a small round ball made from paper or wax; a small bullet
pelt *n.* the skin of an animal with the fur
pel-vis *n., pl.* **-vises** *or* **-ves** the structure of the vertebrate skeleton which rests on the lower limbs, supporting the spinal column
pen *n.* an instrument used for writing **pen** *v.*
pe-nal *adj.* of or pertaining to punishment or penalties
pen-al-ty *n., pl.* **-ties.** the legal punishment for an offense or crime
pen-ance *n.* a voluntary act to show sorrow or repentance for sin
pen-cil *n.* a writing or drawing implement made from graphite
pen-dant *or* **pen-dent** *n.* an ornament which hangs from a necklace
pend-ing *adj.* not yet decided; imminent *prep.* during; until
pen-du-lous *adj.* hanging downward so as to swing
pen-du-lum *n.* a suspended object free to swing back and forth
pen-e-trate *v.* to force a way through or into; to pierce **-ing** *adj.*, **penetration** *n.*
pen-guin *n.* a webfooted, flightless, marine bird
pen-i-cil-lin *n.* a powerful antibiotic derived from mold and used to treat certain types of bacterial infections
pen-in-su-la *n.* a piece of land projecting into water from a larger land mass
pe-nis *n., pl.* **-nises** *or* **-nes** the male sex organ
pen-i-tent *adj.* having a feeling of guilt or remorse for one's sins or misdeeds; sorry **penitence** *n.*
pen-ny *n., pl.* **-ies** a U. S. coin worth one cent ($.01)
pen-sion *n.* the amount of money a per-

son receives regularly after retirement
pen-sive *adj.* involved in serious, quiet reflection
pen-ta-gon *n.* any object or building having five sides and five interior angles
pent-house *n.* an apartment built on the roof of a building
pe-on *n.* a servant; a person engaged in menial work
pe-o-ny *n., pl.* **-nies** a plant with a large, fragrant red, white, or pink flower
peo-ple *n., pl.* **people** human beings
pep-per *n.* a strong, aromatic condiment *v.* to pelt or sprinkle
pep-tic *adj.* pertaining to or aiding digestion
per an-num *adv.* for, by, or in each year; annually
per-cale *n.* a closely woven cotton fabric
per--cap-i-ta *adj. & adv., Latin* of each individual
per-ceive *v.* to become aware of by the senses; to understand; to feel or observe **-able** *adj.*, **-ably** *adv.*
per-cent-age *n.* the rate per hundred; a part or proportion in relation to a whole
per-cept *n.* a mental impression of something perceived
perch *n.* a place on which birds rest or alight; any place for standing or sitting
per-cip-i-ent *adj.* having the power of perception **percipience, percipiency** *n.*
per-co-late *v.* to pass or cause to pass through a porous substance; to filter **percolation, percolator** *n.*
per-en-ni-al *adj.* lasting from year to year; perpetual **perennially** *adv.*
per-fect *adj.* having no defect or fault **perfectly** *adv.*, **perfectness** *n.*
per-form *v.* to execute or carry out an action **performance** *n.*
per-fume *n.* a fragrant substance which emits a pleasant scent; one distilled from flowers
per-haps *adv.* possibly; maybe; not sure
per-i-gee *n.* the point of an orbit when a satellite of the earth is closest to the earth
per-il *n.* a source of danger; exposure to the chance of injury **perilous** *adj.*, **perilously** *adv.*
pe-ri-od *n.* an interval of time marked by certain conditions
pe-riph-er-y *n., pl.* **-ies** the outer part, boundary, or surface **peripheral** *adj.*
per-ish *v.* to ruin or spoil; to suffer an untimely or violent death
per-i-win-kle *n.* any of several edible marine snails
per-jure *v.* to give false testimony while under oath
per-ma-nent *adj.* continuing in the same state; lasting indefinitely; enduring
per-me-ate *v.* to spread through; to pervade
per-mis-sion *n.* the act of permitting something; consent
per-mit *v.* to consent to; to allow
per-ni-cious *adj.* very harmful; malicious **perniciously** *adv.*
per-ox-ide *n., Chem.* oxide containing the highest proportion of oxygen for a given series
per-pen-dic-u-lar *adj.* being at right angles to the plane of the horizon **perpendicularity** *n.*
per-pe-trate *v.* to perform; to commit; to be guilty
per-pet-u-al *adj.* lasting or continuing forever or an unlimited time **perpetually** *adv.*
per-plex *v.* to confuse or be confused; to make complicated **perplexing** *adj.*
per-se-cute *v.* to harass or annoy persistently; to oppress because of one's religion, beliefs, or race
per-se-vere *v.* to persist in any purpose or idea; to strive in spite of difficulties
per-sim-mon *n.* a tree having reddish orange, edible fruit
per-sist *v.* to continue firmly despite obstacles; to endure
per-son *n.* a human being; an individual
per-son-al *adj.* belonging to a person or persons
per-son-i-fy *v.* to think of or represent as having human qualities or life; to be a symbol of **personifier, -fication** *n.*
per-son-nel *n.* the body of people working for a business or service
per-spec-tive *n.* a painting or drawing technique in which objects seem to have depth and distance
per-spi-ra-tion *n.* the salty fluid excreted from the body by the sweat glands
per-spire *v.* to give off perspiration
per-suade *v.* to cause to convince or believe by means of reasoning or argument
per-tain *v.* to relate to; to refer to; to belong as a function, adjunct or quality
per-ti-na-cious *adj.* adhering firmly to an opinion, belief, or purpose; stubbornly persistent **pertinacity** *n.*
per-ti-nent *adj.* relating to the matter being discussed
per-turb *v.* to disturb, make anxious, or make uneasy; to cause confusion
per-vade *v.* to spread through every part of something; to permeate **pervasive** *adj.*
per-ver-sion *n.* the act of being led away from the accepted course; a deviant form of sexual behavior **perverted** *adj.*
pes-si-mism *n.* the tendency to take a gloomy view of affairs or situations and to anticipate the worst **pessimist** *n.*, **pessimistic** *adj.*
pest *n.* a person or thing which is a nuisance; an annoying person or thing; a destructive insect, plant, or animal
pes-ter *v.* to harass with persistent annoyance; to bother
pes-ti-cide *n.* a chemical substance used to destroy rodents, insects, and pests
pes-ti-lence *n.* a widespread and often fatal infectious disease
pet *n.* an animal, bird, or fish one keeps for companionship
pet-al *n., Bot.* one of the leaf-like parts of

a flower
pe-tite *adj.* small in size; little
pe-ti-tion *n.* a solemn request or prayer; a formal written request addressed to a group or person in authority **petitioner** *n.*
pet-ri-fy *v.* to convert into a stony mass; to make fixed or immobilize, as in the face of danger
pe-tro-le-um *n.* an oily, thick liquid which develops naturally below the ground surface, used in products such as gasoline, fuel oil, and kerosene
pet-ty *adj.* to have little importance or value; insignificant; trivial
pe-tu-nia *n.* a widely grown tropical plant
pew *n.* a row of bench-like seats for seating people in church
pew-ter *n.* an alloy of tin with copper
pfen-nig *n., pl.* **-nigs** *or* **-nige** a small coin of Germany
phal-lus *n., pl.* **-li** *or* **-luses** a representation of the penis, often as a symbol of generative power **phallic** *adj.*
phan-tasm *n.* the creation of an imaginary image; a fantasy; a phantom
phar-ma-cy *n., pl.* **-cies** a drugstore
phar-ynx *n., pl.* **-ynges** *or* **-ynxes** the part of the throat located between the palate and the esophagus
phase *n.* any decisive stage in development or growth
phe-nom-e-non *n.* something that can be observed or perceived; a rare occurrence
phi-lan-der *v.* to make love without feeling or serious intentions **philanderer** *n.*
phi-lat-e-ly *n.* the collection and study of postage stamps and postmarked material **philatelist** *n.*
phil-har-mon-ic *adj.* pertaining to a symphony orchestra
phi-los-o-phy *n., pl.* **-ies** the logical study of the nature and source of human knowledge or human values; the set of values
pho-bi-a *n.* a compulsive fear of a specified situation or object
phone *n., Slang* a telephone *v.* to call or communicate by telephone
phon-ic *adj.* pertaining to sounds in speech; using the same symbol for each sound **phonically** *adv.*
pho-no-graph *n.* a machine which uses a needle to reproduce sound from a grooved disc or record
pho-ny *adj. Informal* counterfeit; fraudulent; not real or genuine
phos-phate *n., Chem.* a salt or phosphoric acid which contains mostly phosphorus and oxygen
phos-pho-rus *n.* a highly flammable, poisonous, nonmetallic element
pho-to *n. Slang* a photograph
pho-to-cop-y *v.* to reproduce printed material using a photographic process **photocopier, photocopy** *n.*
pho-to-graph *n.* a picture or image recorded by a camera **photography** *n.*
pho-to-syn-the-sis *n., Biochem.* the chemical process by which plants use light to change carbon dioxide and water into carbohydrates, releasing oxygen as a byproduct **photosynthesize** *v.*, **photosynthetic** *adj.*
phrase *n., Gram.* a brief or concise expression which does not contain a predicate
phre-nol-o-gy *n.* the study of or the theory that the conformation of the human skull indicates the degree of intelligence and character
phys-i-cal *adj.* relating to the human body apart from the mind or emotions
phy-si-cian *n.* a person licensed to practice medicine
phys-ics *n.* the scientific study which deals with energy, matter, motion, and related areas of science
phys-i-ol-o-gy *n., pl.* **-ies** the scientific study of living animals, plants, and their activities and functions
phys-i-o-ther-a-py *n.* the treatment of disease or physical defects by the use of heat and massage.
pi-ca *n.* a printer's type size of 12 points, equal to about 1/6 inch
pic-co-lo *n.* a small flute with a brilliant sound pitched an octave above the flute
pick *v.* to select or choose
pick-le *n.* a cucumber preserved in a solution of brine or vinegar
pic-nic *n.* an outdoor social gathering where food is provided **picnicker** *n.*
pic-ture *n.* a visual representation on a surface, which is printed, drawn or photographed
piece *n.* an element, unit, or part of a whole
piece-meal *adv.* gradually
pier *n.* a structure extending into the water, used to secure, protect, and provide access to vessels
pierce *v.* to penetrate or make a hole in something
pi-e-ty *n., pl.* **-ties** devoutness toward God
pig *n.* a cloven footed mammal with short legs, bristly hair, and a snout for rooting
pi-geon *n.* a bird with short legs, a sturdy body, and a small head
pig-gy-back *adv.* carried on the back and shoulders
pig-ment *n.* a material used as coloring matter, suitable for making paint
pike *n.* a long pole with a sharp, pointed steel head
pile *n.* a quantity of anything thrown in a heap
pil-fer *v.* to steal in little quantities **pilferage** *n.*
pil-grim *n.* a person who travels to a sacred place; a wanderer
pill *n.* a small tablet containing medicine which is taken by mouth **the pill** *Slang* an oral contraceptive drug taken by women
pil-lar *n.* a freestanding column which serves as a support
pil-low *n.* a cloth case filled with feathers

or other soft material
pi-lot *n.* a person who is licensed to operate an aircraft
pi-men-to *n.* a sweet pepper used as a stuffing for olives or as a relish
pimp *n.* a person who arranges customers for prostitutes
pim-ple *n.* a small eruption of the skin, having an inflamed base
pimpled, pimply *adj.*
pin *n.* a small, stiff piece of wire with a blunt head and a sharp point
pin-a-fore *n.* a sleeveless apron-like garment
pin-cer *n.* an implement having two handles and a pair of jaws working on a pivot
pinch *v.* to squeeze between a finger and thumb causing pain or discomfort
pine *n., Bot.* any of various cone-bearing evergreen trees
pine-ap-ple *n.* a tropical American plant with spiny, curved leaves bearing a large edible fruit *Slang* a hand grenade
pink-eye *n., Pathol.* an acute, contagious conjunctivitis of the eye
pin-na-cle *n.* the highest peak
pi-noch-le *or* **pi-noc-le** *n.* a card game for two, three, or four people, played with a double deck of 48 cards
pint *n.* a liquid or dry measurement equal to half of a quart or two cups
pin-to *n., pl.* **-tos** *or* **-toes** a horse with spots
pin-worm *n.* a nematode parasite which infests the human intestines and rectum
pi-o-neer *n.* one of the first settlers of a new region or country
pi-ous *adj.* reverently religious; devout
piously *adv.*, **piousness** *n.*
pipe *n.* a hollow cylinder for conveying fluids
pique *n.* a feeling of resentment or irritation
pi-rate *n.* a robber of the high seas
piracy *n.*, **piratical** *adj.*
pis-til *n.* the seed-producing female reproductive organ of a flower
pis-tol *n.* a small hand-held firearm
pis-ton *n., Mech.* a solid cylinder fitted into a larger cylinder, moving back and forth under liquid pressure
pit *n.* an artificial or manmade hole in the ground; a slight indentation in the skin
pitch *n.* a thick, sticky, dark substance which is the residue of the distillation of petroleum or coal tar
pith *n., Bot.* the sponge-like soft tissue at the center of the branch or stem of many plants
pit-i-ful *adj.* evoking or meriting pity
pitifully *adv.*
pit-y *n., pl.* **-ies.** a feeling of compassion or sorrow
piv-ot *n.* a thing or person upon which development, direction, or effect depends *v.* to turn
piz-za *n.* an Italian food consisting of a doughy crust covered with tomato sauce, cheese, and other toppings and then baked
place *n.* a region; an area; a building or location used for a special purpose
place-ment *n.* the act of being placed
pla-cen-ta *n., pl.* **-tas** *or* **-tae** *Anat.* the vascular, membranous structure which supplies a fetus with nourishment before its birth
plague *n.* anything that is troublesome *Pathol.* a highly contagious and often fatal epidemic disease
plaid *n.* a rectangular wool cloth or garment, usually worn by men and women, having a crisscross or checkered design
plain *adj.* level; flat; clear; open, as in view; not rich or luxurious; not highly gifted or cultivated
plainly *adv.*, **plainness** *n.*
plain-tiff *n.* a person who brings suit
plan *n.* a scheme or method for achieving something
plane *n.* a tool for smoothing or leveling a wood surface
plan-et *n., Astron.* a celestial body which is illuminated by light from the star around which it revolves
plank *n.* a broad piece of wood
plant *n.* a living organism belonging to the vegetable kingdom
plaque *n.* a flat piece, made from metal, porcelain, ivory, or other materials, engraved for mounting
plas-ma *n.* the clear fluid part of blood, used for transfusions
plas-tic *n.* a synthetically made material which is molded and then hardened into objects **plasticity** *n.*, **plasticize** *v.*
plastic surgery *n.* surgery dealing with the restoration or repair of deformed or destroyed parts of the body or skin
plate *n.* a shallow, flat vessel made from glass, crockery, plastic, or other material from which food is served or eaten
pla-teau *n.* an extensive level expanse of elevated land
plat-form *n.* any elevated or raised surface used by speakers; a formal declaration of principles or policy of a political party
plat-i-num *n.* a silver-white, metallic element which is corrosiveresistant, used in jewelry
pla-toon *n.* a military unit subdivision commanded by a lieutenant
plat-ter *n.* a large, oblong, shallow dish for serving food
plau-si-ble *adj.* seeming to be probable
play *v.* to amuse or entertain oneself, as in recreation; to take part in a game *n.* a dramatic presentaton
playful *adj.* lightly humorous
plea *n.* an urgent request; in law, an allegation made by either party in a law suit
plead *v.* to ask earnestly
pleas-ant *adj.* giving or promoting the feeling of pleasure **-ly** *adv.*
please *v.* to make happy; to give pleasure
pleas-ur-a-ble *adj.* pleasant
pleas-ure *n.* a feeling of satisfaction or

enjoyment
pleat *n.* a fold in a cloth made by doubling the cloth back and fastening it down
plebe *n.* a freshman or first year student at the United States Naval Academy
pledge *n.* a solemn promise; a deposit of something as security for a loan; a promise to join a fraternity
plen-ti-ful *adj.* having great abundance
plen-ty *n.* an ample amount
pleu-ra *n., pl.* **pleurae** *Anat.* the membranous sac which envelops the lungs and provides a lining for the thoracic cavity
pli-a-ble *adj.* flexible
pli-ers *pl. n.* a pincers-like implement used for holding, bending, or cutting
plight *n.* a distressing circumstance, situation, or condition
plod *n.* to walk in a heavy way
plow *n.* an implement for breaking up or turning over the soil
pluck *v.* to remove by pulling out or off **plucker** *n.*
plug *n.* anything used to stop or close a hole or drain *Electr.* a two-pronged device attached to a cord and used in a jack or socket to make an electrical connection **plugger** *n.*
plum *n.* a small tree bearing an edible fruit with a smooth skin and a single hard seed
plum-age *n.* the feathers of a bird
plumb *n.* a lead weight tied to the end of a string, used to test the exact perpendicular line of something
plumb-er *n.* a person who repairs or installs plumbing in a home or business
plumb-ing *n.* the profession or trade of a plumber
plume *n.* a feather used as an ornament
plun-der *v.* to deprive of goods or property in a violent way **plunderer** *n.*
plunge *v.* to thrust or cast something, as into water
plunk *v.* to put down or place suddenly **plunker** *n.*
plu-ral *adj.* consisting of or containing more than one
plus *prep.* add the symbol (+) which indicates addition
plu-to-ni-um *n.* a radioactive metallic element symbolized by Pu.
ply *v.* to mold, bend, or shape *n.* a layer of thickness; the twisted strands of thread, yarn, or rope
pneu-mo-nia- *n.* an inflammation caused by bacteria, virus of the lungs, or irritation
pock-et *n.* a small pouch within a garment, having an open top and used for carrying items
pod *n., Bot.* aseed vessel, as of a bean or pea *Aeron* a separate and detachable compartment in a spacecraft
po-di-a-try *n.* professional care and treatment of the feet
po-di-um *n.,pl.* **-ia** *or* **-iums** a small raised platform for an orchestra conductor or a speaker
po-em *n.* a composition in verse with language selected for its beauty and sound
po-et *n.* a person who writes poetry
po-et-ry *n.* the art of writing stories, poems, and thoughts into verse
point *n.* the sharp or tapered end of something; a mark of punctuation, as a period (.); a geometric object which does not have property or dimensions other than locaton; a degree, condition, or stage
poise *v.* to bring into or hold one's balance *n.* equilibrium; selfconfidence; the ability to stay calm in all social situations
poi-son *n.* a substance which kills, injures **poisonous** *adj.*
poke *v.* to push or prod at something with a finger or other implement
po-lar *adj.* having to do with the poles of a magnet or sphere
po-lar-ize *v.* to cause something to vibrate in an exact pattern; to break up into opposite groups **-ation** *n.*
pol-i-o-my-e-li-tis *n.* inflammation of the spinal cord causing paralysis; also polio
po-lice *n.* a division or department organized to maintain order. *v.* to patrol; to enforce the law
po-liceman *n.* a member of the police force **policewoman** *n.*
pol-i-cy *n., pl.* **-ies** any plan or principle which guides decision making
pol-ish *v.* to make lustrous and smooth by rubbing; to become refined or elegant
po-lite *adj.* refined, mannerly, and courteous
po-lit-i-cal *adj.* concerned with or pertaining to government; involved in politics
pol-i-ti-cian *n.* a person active in governmental affairs or politics
pol-i-tics *n.* the activities and methods of a political party
poll *n.* the recording of votes in an election; a public survey on a given topic
pol-len *n.* the yellow dust-like powder which contains the male reproductive cells of a flowering plant
pol-lute *v.* to contaminate; to make unclear or impure; to dirty **pollution** *n.*
po-lo-ni-um *n.* a radioactive metallic element symbolized by PO.
pol-ter-geist *n.* a mischievous ghost or spirit which makes much noise
pol-y-es-ter *n.* a strong lightweight synthetic resin used in fibers
pol-y-graph *n.* a machine designed to record different signals given off by the body, as respiration, blood pressure, or heartbeats; may be used to detect a person who may be lying
pol-y-he-dron *n.* a solid bounded by polygons
pom-pa-dour *n.* a hairstyle which is puffed over the forehead
pomp-ous *adj.* a showing or appearance of dignity or importance
pond *n.* a body of still water, smaller in size than a lake

pon-der *v.* to weigh or think about very carefully; to meditate
pon-der-ous *adj.* massive; having great weight
pon-tiff *n.* a pope
po-ny *n., pl.* **-ies** a small horse
pool *n.* a small body of water
poor *adj.* lacking possessions and money; not satisfactory; broke; needy; destitute
pop-lar *n.* a rapid growing tree having a light, soft wood
pop-u-lar *adj.* approved of; widely liked; suited to the means of the people
pop-u-la-tion *n.* the total number of people in a given area, country, or city
por-ce-lain *n.* a hard, translucent ceramic which has been fired and glazed
porch *n.* a covered structure forming the entrance to a house
por-cu-pine *n.* a clumsy rodent covered with long sharp quills
pore *v.* to ponder or meditate on something
pork *n.* the edible flesh of swine
por-no *n., Slang* pornography
por-nog-ra-phy *n.* pictures, films, or writing which deliberately arouse sexual excitement
por-poise *n.* an aquatic mammal with a blunt, rounded snout
port *n.* a city or town with a harbor for loading and unloading cargo from ships; the left side of a ship; a dark-red, sweet, fortified wine
port-a-ble *adj.* capable of being moved easily
por-ter *n.* a person hired to carry baggage
port-fo-li-o *n.* a carrying case for holding papers and other items
por-tion *n.* a section or part of a whole; a share
por-tray *v.* to represent by drawing, writing, or acting
pose *v.* to place or assume a position, as for a picture
po-si-tion *n.* the manner in which something is placed; an attitude; a viewpoint; a job; employment
pos-i-tive *adj.* containing, expressing, or characterized by affirmation; very confident; absolutely certain; not negative
positively *adv.*
pos-se *n.* a deputized group or squad
pos-ses-sion *n.* the fact or act of possessing property; the state of being possessed
pos-ses-sive *adj.* having a strong desire to possess; not wanting to share *n.* the noun or pronoun case which indicates ownership
pos-si-ble *adj.* capable of being true, happening, or being accomplished
possibility *n.*
post *n.* an upright piece of wood or metal support; a position or employment *v.* to put up information in a public place *prefix.* after; in order; or time; behind
post-age *n.* the charge or fee for mailing something
pos-te-ri-or *adj.* located in the back *n.* the buttocks
post-mor-tem *adj.* the examination of a body after death; an autopsy
post-op-er-a-tive *adj.* following surgery
post-pone *v.* to put off; to defer to a later time
post-script *n.* a short message added at the end of a letter
pos-ture *n.* the carriag or position of the body
pot *n.* a rounded, deep container used for cooking and other domestic purposes *Slang* a large sum of money; marijuana
potful *n.*
po-tas-si-um *n.* a silvery-white, highly reactive metallic element
po-ta-to *n., pl.* **-toes** a thick, edible, underground tuber plant native to America
po-tent *adj.* having great strength or physical powers; having a great influence on the mind or morals
po-ten-tial *adj.* possible, but not yet actual
pot-pour-ri *n.* a mixture of sweet-smelling dried flower petals and spices, kept in an airtight jar
pot-ter-y *n., pl.* **-ies** objects molded from clay and fired by intense heat
pouch *n.* a small bag or other container for holding or carrying money, tobacco, and other small articles *Zool.* the sac-like structure in which some animals carry their young
poul-try *n.* domestic fowl as ducks and hens, which are raised for eggs or meat
pound *n., pl.* **pounds** A measure of weight equal to sixteen ounces; a public enclosure where stray animals are fed and housed *v.* to strike repeatedly or with force
pov-er-ty *n.* the condition or state of being poor and needing money
pow-der *n.* a dry substance which has been finely ground or pulverized; dust; an explosive, such as gunpowder *v.* to dust or cover
pow-er-ful *adj.* possessing energy or great force; having authority
prac-ti-cal *adj.* serving an actual use or purpose
pract-ice *n.* a custom or habit of doing something
prai-rie *n.* a wide area of level or rolling land with grass and weeds but no trees
praise *v.* to express approval; to glorify
prank *n.* a mischievous, playful action or trick
pra-seo-dym-i-um *n.* a metallic element of the rare-earth group
prawn *n.* an edible shrimp-like crustacean found in both salt and fresh water
pray *v.* to address prayers to God; to ask or request
prayer *n.* a devout request; the act of praying; a formal or set group of words used in praying
pre- *pref* earlier or prior to something; in front

preach *v.* to advocate; to proclaim; to deliver a sermon **-er, -ment** *n.*, **-y** *adj.*
pre-am-ble *n.* an introduction to something, as a law, which states the purpose and reasons for the matter which follows
pre-cau-tion *n.* a measure of caution or care taken in advance to guard against harm
pre-cede *v.* to be or go before in time, or position
prec-e-dent *n.* an instance which may serve as a rule or example in the future
pre-cept *n.* a rule, order, or commandment meant to guide one's conduct
pre-cinct *n.* an electoral district of a county, township, city, or town; an enclosure with definite boundaries
pre-cious *adj.* having great worth or value; beloved; cherished
pre-cip-i-ta-tion *n.* condensed water vapor which falls as snow, rain, sleet or hail
pre-cip-i-tous *adj.* very steep; marked with very steep cliffs
pre-cise *adj.* exact; definite; strictly following rules
pre-ci-sion *n.* exactness; the quality of being precise
pre-clude *v.* to shut out; to make impossible; to prevent
pre-co-cious *adj.* showing and developing skills and abilities very early in life
pre-con-ceive *v.* to form a notion or conception before knowing all the facts
pre-da-cious *adj.* living by preying on other animals
pred-a-tor *n.* a person who lives or gains by stealing from another person; an animal that survives by killing and eating other animals
pre-des-ti-na-tion *n.* destiny; fate; the act by which God has predestined all events
pred-i-ca-ble *adj.* capable of being predicated: to foretell
pred-i-cate *n. Gram.* the word or words which say something about the subject of a clause or sentence; the part of a sentence which contains the verb *v.* to establish
pre-dict *v.* to tell beforehand; to foretell
pre-dom-i-nant *adj.* superior in strength, authority, or number
pree-mie *n. Slang* a baby born before the expected due date
pre-empt *v.* to take or get hold of before someone else; to take the place of; to do something before someone else has a chance to do it **-ion** *n.*, **-ive** *adj.*
pre-fab-ri-cate *v.* to construct in sections beforehand
pref-ace *n.* the introduction at the beginning of a book or speech
pre-fect *n.* a high administrative official **prefecture** *n.*
pre-fer *v.* to select as being the favorite; to promote
pref-er-ence *n.* a choice; a special liking for anything over another **-ential** *adj.*
pre-fix *v.* to put at the beginning; to put before
preg-nant *adj.* carrying an unborn fetus; significant
pre-his-tor-i-cal *adj.* of or related to the period before recorded history
pre-judge *v.* to judge before one knows all the facts
prej-u-dice *n.* a biased opinion based on emotion rather than reason; bias against a group, race, or creed
pre-lim-i-nar-y *adj.* leading up to the main action
prel-ude *n.* an introductory action *Music* the movement at the beginning of a piece of music
pre-ma-ture *adj.* occurring or born before the natural or proper time **prematurely** *adv.*
pre-med-i-tate *v.* to plan in advance or beforehand
pre-mi-er *adj.* first in rank or importance **premiership** *n.*
pre-na-tal *adj.* existing prior to birth
pre-oc-cu-py *v.* to engage the mind or attention completely
prep *Slang* preparatory school; preparation
prep-a-ra-tion *n.* the process of preparing for something
pre-par-a-to-ry *adj.* serving as preparation
pre-pare *v* to make ready or qualified; to equip
pre-pay *v.* to pay for in advance
pre-pon-der-ate *v.* to have superior importance, weight, force, influence, or other qualities **preponderance** *n.*
prep-o-si-tion *n.*, *Gram.* a word placed in front of a noun or pronoun to show a connection with or to something or someone
pre-pos-ter-ous *adj.* absurd; ridiculous; beyond all reason
prep-pie *n. Slang* a student attending a prep school; a young adult who behaves and dresses very traditionally
pre-rog-a-tive *n.* the unquestionable right belonging to a person
pres-age *n.* an omen or indication of something to come
pre-school *adj.* of or for children usually between the ages of two and five
pre-scribe *v.* to impose as a guide; to recommend
pre-scrip-tion *n.*, *Med.* a physician's written order for medicine
pres-ence *n.* the state of being present; the immediate area surrounding a person or thing
pres-ent *adj.* now going on; not past or future *Gram.* denoting a tense or verb form which expresses a current state or action
pres-en-ta-tion *n.* a formal introduction of one person to another; to present something as an exhibition, show, or product
pre-serv-a-tive *adj.* keeping something from decay or injury **preservation** *n.*
pre-serve *v.* to keep or save from destruction or injury
pre-side *v.* to have a position of authority

or control; to run or control a meeting
pres-i-dent *n.* the chief executive officer of a government, corporation, or association
presidency *n.*, **presidential** *adj.*
press *v.* to act upon or exert steady pressure or force; to squeeze out or extract by pressure; to smooth by heat and pressure **presser** *n.*
pres-sure *n.* the act of or the state of being pressed; a constraining moral force; any burden, force, painful feeling, or influence; the depressing effect of something hard to bear
pres-tige *n.* importance based on past reputation and achievements
pres-to *adv.*, *Music* very fast and quick; at once
pre-sume *v.* to take for granted; to take upon oneself without permission
pre-sump-tion *n.* arrogant conductor speech; something that can be logically assumed true until disproved
pre-tend *v.* to make believe; to act in a false way **pretender** *n.*
pre-tense *n.* a deceptive and false action or appearance
pre-ten-tions *n.* having or making claims to worth, excellence, etc.
pre-text *n.* a motive assumed in order to conceal the true purpose
pret-ty *adj.* pleasant; attractive; characterized by gracefulness; pleasing to look at
pret-zel *v.* a hard, cooked dough usually twisted in a knot and sprinkled with salt
pre-vail *v.* to succeed; to win control over something
pre-vent *v.* to keep something from happening; to keep from doing something
pre-ven-tive *or* **preventative** *adj.* protecting or serving to ward off harm, disease, or other problems
pre-view *or* **prevue** *n.* an advance showing or viewing to invited guests
pre-vi-ous *adj.* existing or occurring earlier **-ly** *adv.*
price *n.* the set amount of money expected or given for the sale of something
prick *n.* a small hole made by a sharp point
pride *n.* a sense of personal dignity; a feeling of pleasure because of something achieved **pride** *v.*
priest *n.* a clergyman in the Catholic church who serves as mediator between God and His worshipers
pri-ma-ry *adj.* first in origin, time, series, or sequence; basic
prime *adj.* first in importance, time, or rank *n.* a period of full vigor, success, or beauty
prim-i-tive *adj.* of or pertaining to the beginning or earliest time; resembling the style or manners of an earlier time
primp *v.* to dress or arrange with superfluous attention to detail
prince *n.* the son of a king; a king
prin-cess *n.* the daughter of a king
prin-ci-pal *adj.* chief; most important; owner *n.* the headmaster or chief official of a school; a sum of money invested or owed which is separate from the interest
prin-ci-ple *n.* the fundamental law or truth upon which others are based; a moral standard
print *n.* an impression or mark made with ink; the design or picture which is transferred from an engraved plate or other impression
printer *n.* a person whose occupation is printing
print-out *n. Computer Science* the output of a computer, printed on paper
pri-or *adj.* previous in order or time
pri-or-i-ty *n.* something which takes precedence; something which must be done or taken care of first
prism *n.* a solid figure with triangular ends and rectangular sides, used to disperse light into a spectrum
pris-on *n.* a place of confinement where people are kept while waiting for a trial or while serving time for breaking the law; jail
pri-vate *adj.* secluded or removed from the public view; secret; intimate; owned or controlled by a group or person rather than by the public
priv-i-lege *n.* a special right or benefit granted to a person
priv-i-leged *adj.* to have or enjoy a given privilege
prize *n.* an award or something given to the winner of a contest
pro *n.* an argument in favor of or supporting something
prob-a-bil-i-ty *n.*, *pl.* **-ies** the state or quality of being probable; a mathematical statement or prediction of the odds of something happening or not happening
prob-a-ble *adj.* likely to become a reality, but not certain or proved
pro-bate *n.* the act of legally proving that a will is genuine
pro-ba-tion *n.* a period used to test the qualifications and character of a new employee; the early release of lawbreakers
probe *n.* an instrument used for investigating an unknown environment; a careful investigation or examination
prob-lem *n.* a perplexing situation or question; a question presented for consideration, solution, or discussion **problematic** *adj.*
pro-ce-dure *n.* a certain pattern or way of doing something; the normal methods or forms to be followed
pro-ceed *v.* to carry on or continue an action or process
pro-ceeds *pl.*, *n.* the profits received from a fundraising venture
proc-ess *n.* the course, steps, or methods toward a desired result *Law* any judicial request or order; in Computer Science, the sequence of operations which gives a desired result *v.* to compile, compute, or assemble; data
pro-ces-sion *n.* a group which moves

along in a formal manner; a parade
pro-ces-sion-al *n.* a hymn sung during a procession *adj.* the opening of a church service
pro-ces-sor *n. Computer Science* the central unit of a computer which processes data
pro-claim *v.* to announce publicly
proc-la-ma-tion *n.* an official public declaration or announcement
pro-cras-ti-nate *v.* to put off, defer, or postpone to a later time
procrastination, procrastinator *n.*
proc-tor *n.* a person in a university or college whose job it is to see that order is maintained during exams
proctorial *adj.*
pro-cure *v.* to acquire; to accomplish
prod *v.* to arouse mentally; to poke with a pointed instrument *n.* a pointed implement used to prod or poke
prod-i-gal *adj.* wasteful expenditure of money, strength, or time; extravagance *n.* one who is a spendthrift or is wasteful
pro-duce *v.* to bear or bring forth by a natural process; to manufacture; to make; to present or bring into view
producer *n.*
prod-uct *n.* something produced, manufactured, or obtained *Math.* the answer obtained by multiplying
pro-duc-tion *n.* the process or act of producing; something produced
pro-fane *adj.* manifesting disrespect toward sacred things; vulgar
pro-fess *v.* to admit or declare openly; to make an open vow
pro-fess-sion-al *adj.* having to do with a job or profession; referring to or engaging in an occupation
pro-fes-sor *n.* a faculty member of the highest rank in a college or university
pro-fi-cient *adj.* highly skilled in a field of knowledge
pro-file *n.* the outline of a person's face or figure as seen from the side; a short biographical sketch indicating the most striking characteristics
prof-it *n.* the financial return after all expenses have been accounted for *v.* to gain an advantage or a financial reward **profitable** *adj.*
pro-found *adj.* deeply held or felt
pro-fuse *adj.* extravagant; giving forth lavishly; over-flowing **profusely** *adv.*
prog-e-ny *n., pl.* **-ies** one's offspring, children, or descendants
prog-no-sis *n., pl.* **-noses** a prediction of the outcome and course a disease may take
pro-gram *n.* any prearranged plan or course; a show or performance, as one given at a scheduled time; in Computer Science, a sequence of commands which tell a computer how to perform a task or sequence of tasks
prog-ress *n.* forward motion or advancement to a higher goal; an advance; steady improvement
pro-hib-it *v.* to forbid legally; to prevent
pro-ject *n.* a plan or course of action; a proposal; a large job
pro-jec-tile *n.* anything hurled forward through the air
pro-jec-tion *n.* the act or state of being projected; the state or part that sticks out
pro-lif-er-ate *v.* to grow or produce with great speed, as cells in tissue formation
pro-logue *n.* an introductory statement at the beginning of a poem, song, or play
pro-long *v.* to extend or lengthen in time
prom-e-nade *n.* an unhurried walk for exercise or amusement; a public place for such a walk
prom-i-nent *adj.* jutting out; widely known; held in high esteem
pro-mis-cu-ous *adj.* lacking selectivity or discrimination
prom-ise *n.* an assurance given that one will or will not do something; a pledge
pro-mote *v.* to raise to a higher rank or position; to work on behalf of
prompt *adj.* arriving on time; punctual; immediate
prone *adj.* lying flat; face down
pronely *adv.*, **proneness** *n.*
prong *n.* a pointed, projecting part, as the end of a sharp instrument or the end of an antler
pro-noun *n., Gram.* a word which can be used in the place of a noun
pro-nounce *v.* to deliver officially; to articulate the sounds **pronunciation** *n.*
proof *n.* the establishment of a fact by evidence
prop *n.* a support to keep something upright
prop-a-gate *v.* to reproduce or multiply by natural causes; to pass on qualities or traits **propagation** *n.*
pro-pel *v.* to thrust or cause to move forward; to motivate
prop-er *adj.* appropriate; especially adapted or suited; conforming to social convention; correct
prop-er-ty *n., pl.* **-ies** any object of value owned or lawfully acquired, as real estate; a piece of land
proph-e-cy *n., pl.* **-ies** a prediction made under divine influence
proph-et *n.* one who delivers divine messages; one who foretells the future
pro-pi-ti-ate *v.* to win the goodwill of; to stop from being angry **propitiation** *n.*
pro-po-nent *n.* one who supports or advocates a cause
pro-por-tion *n.* the relation of one thing to another in size, degree, or amount **proportional, proportionate** *adj.*
pro-pose *v.* to present or put forward for consideration or action; to suggest someone for an office or position; to make an offer; to offer marriage
prop-o-si-tion *n.* a scheme or plan offered for consideration; a subject or idea to be proved or discussed
pro-pri-e-ty *n., pl.* **-ies** the quality or state of being proper in accordance with recognized principles or usage
pro-pul-sion *n.* the act or process of propelling

pro-rate *v.* to distribute or divide proportionately
pro-scribe *v.* to banish; to outlaw
prose *n.* ordinary language, speech, or writing which is not poetry
pros-e-cute *v.* to carry on *Law* to bring suit against a person; to seek enforcement for legal process **prosecution** *n.*
pros-pect *n.* something that has the possibility of future success; a possible customer *v.* to explore
pros-per *v.* to be successful; to achieve success **prosperous** *adj.*
pros-tate *n.* a small gland at the base of the male bladder
pros-ti-tute *n.* one who sells the body for the purpose of sexual intercourse
pros-trate *adj.* lying with the face down to the ground *v.* to overcome
prot-ac-tin-i-um *n.* a radioactive metallic element symbolized by Pa.
pro-tect *v.* to guard or shield from attack of injury; to shield **protective** *adj.*
pro-tein *n., Biochem.* any of a very large group of highly complex nitrogenous compounds occurring in living matter and composed of amino acids which are essential for tissue repair and growth
pro-test *v.* to make a strong formal objection; to object to **protester** *n.*
Prot-es-tant *n.* a member of any of the Christian churches who believes Jesus is the son of God and died for man's sins
pro-to-col *n.* the code and rules of diplomatic and state etiquette
pro-ton *n., Physics* a unit of positive charge equal in magnitude to an electron
pro-tract *v.* to extend in space
pro-trude *v.* to project; to thrust outward
proud *adj.* showing or having a feeling that one is better than the others; having a feeling of satisfaction; having proper self-respect or proper self-esteem
prove *v.* to show with valid evidence that something is true **provable** *adj.*
prov-erb *n.* an old saying which illustrates a truth
pro-vide *v.* to supply or furnish with what is needed
pro-vi-sion *n.* a supply of food or needed equipment
pro-voke *v.* to cause to be angry; to annoy
prox-i-mate *adj.* immediate; direct
prox-y *n., pl.* **proxies** the authority, usually written, to act for another
prude *n.* a person who is very modest, especially in matters related to sex
pru-dent *adj.* cautious; discreet; managing very carefully
psalm *n.* a sacred hymn, taken from the Book of Psalms in the Old Testament
pso-ri-a-sis *n., Pathol.* a noncontagious, chronic, inflammatory skin disease characterized by reddish patches and white scales
psych *v., Slang* to prepare oneself emotionally or mentally; to outwit or outguess
psy-chi-a-try *n.* the branch of medicine which deals with the diagnosis and treatment of mental disorders
psy-chic *adj.* cannot be explained by natural or physical laws *n.* a person who communicates with the spirit world
psy-chol-o-gy *n., pl.* **psychologies** the science of emotions, behavior, and the mind **psychological** *adj.*, **psychologist** *n.*
psy-cho-path *n.* a person suffering from a mental disorder characterized by aggressive antisocial behavior **psychopathic** *adj.*
pu-ber-ty *n.* the stage of development in which sexual reproduction can first occur **pubertal, puberal** *adj.*
pub-lic *adj.* pertaining to or affecting the people or community; for everyone's use
pub-li-ca-tion *n.* the business of publishing; any pamphlet, book, or magazine
pub-lic-i-ty *n.* the state of being known to the public
pub-lish *v.* to print and distribute a book, magazine, or any printed matter to the public **publisher** *n.*
puck *n.* a hard rubber disk used in playing ice hockey
pud-dle *n.* a small pool of water
puff *n.* a brief discharge of air or smoke *v.* to breathe in short heavy breaths
pull *v.* to apply force; to cause motion toward or in the same direction of
pulp *n.* the soft juicy part of a fruit; a soft moist mass
pul-pit *n.* the elevated platform lectern used in a church from which a service is conducted
pul-sate *v.* to beat rhythmically **pulsation**
pulse *n., Physiol.* the rhythmical beating of the arteries caused by the action of the heart **pulse** *v.*
pul-ver-ize *v.* to be reduced to dust or powder by crushing
pump *n.* a mechanical device for moving a gas or liquid *v.* to raise with a pump; to obtain information through persistent questioning
pump-kin *n.* a large, edible yellow-orange fruit having a thick rind and many seeds
punch *n.* a tool used for perforating or piercing; a blow with the fist; a drink made of an alcoholic beverage and a fruit juice or other nonalcoholic beverage
punc-tu-al *adj.* prompt; arriving on time
punc-tu-ate *v.* to mark words or written material with punctuation; to give or show emphasis
punc-ture *v.* to prick or pierce with a pointed instrument *n.* the act or effect of puncturing
pun-gent *adj.* sharp or acrid in smell or taste
pun-ish *v.* to subject a person to confinement or impose a penalty for a crime

pun-ish-ment *n.* a penalty which is imposed for breaking the law or a rule
punk *n.*, *Slang* a young, inexperienced boy *adj.* of or relating to a bizarre style of clothing; relating to punk rock bands
pup *n.* a puppy, young dog, or the young of other animals
pupil *n.* a person who attends school and receives instruction by a teacher
pup-pet *n.* a small figure of an animal or person which is manipulated by hand or by strings **puppeteer**
pur-chase *v.* to receive by paying money as an exchange **purchaser** *n.*
pure *adj.* free from anything that damages, weakens, or contaminates
purge *v.* to make clean; to free from guilt or sin; to rid of anything undesirable
pu-ri-fy *v.* to make clean or pure **purification, purifier** *n.*
pu-ri-ty *n.* the quality of being pure; freedom from guilt or sin
pur-ple *n.* a color between red and violet **purplish** *adj.*
pur-port *v.* to give the appearance of intending; to imply, usually with the intent to deceive
pur-pose *n.* a desired goal; an intention **purposely** *adv.*
purse *n.* a small pouch or bag for money; a handbag; a pocketbook; the sum of money offered as a prize
pur-sue *v.* to seek to achieve; to follow in an attempt to capture **pursuer** *n.*
pur-suit *n.* the act of pursuing an occupation
pur-vey *v.* to supply provisions as a service **purveyor** *n.*
pus *n.* a yellowish secretion formed in infected tissue which contains bacteria
push *v.* to move forward by exerting force; to force oneself through a crowd; to sell illegally *Slang* to sell illegal drugs
put *v.* to cause to be in a location; to bring forward for debate or consideration, as to put up for
pu-ta-tive *adj.* commonly supposed
pu-tre-fy *v.* to cause to decay
putt *n.* in golf, a light stroke made on a putting green to get the ball into the hole
puz-zle *v.* to bewilder; to confuse *n.* a toy, board game, or word game
pyg-my *n.*, *pl.* **pygmies** a very small person or animal; a dwarf
py-lon *n.* a tower serving as a support for electrical power lines
py-or-rhe-a *n.*, *Pathol.* inflammation of the gums and sockets of the teeth
pyr-a-mid *n.* a solid structure with a square base and triangular sides which meet at a point
pyre *n.* a pile of combustible material for burning a dead body
py-ro-ma-ni-a *n.* a compulsion to set fires
py-ro-met-al-lur-gy *n.* chemical metallurgy depending on heat action
py-tho-ness *n.* a woman who practices divination **pythonic adj.**

Q, q The seventeenth letter of the English alphabet.
qat *n.* a small plant found in Africa, the fresh leaf is chewed for a stimulating effect
Qa-tar *n.* country located on the western coast of the Persian Gulf
qi-vi-ut *n.* yarn spun from the fine, soft hair of the musk ox
quack *n.* the harsh, croaking cry of a duck **quack** *v.*, **quackery** *n.*
quad-ran-gle *n.*, *Math* a plane figure with four sides and four angles
quad-rant *n.* a quarter section of a circle, subtending or enclosing a central angle of 90 degrees; an instrument which is used to measure altitudes
qua-draph-o-ny *n.* the recording of sound using four transmission channels
quad-rate *adj.* being square or almost square
qua-drat-ics *n.* a branch of algebra concerned with equations
quad-ra-ture *n.* an arrangement of two celestial bodies with a separation of 90 degrees
qua-dren-ni-um *n.* a period consisting of four years
quad-ri-cen-ten-ni-al *n.* an anniversary celebrating 400 years
quad-ri-ceps *n.* the muscle located in the front of the thigh
qua-dri-ga *n.* a chariot pulled by a team of four horses
qua-drille *n.* a square dance with five or six figures exected by four couples
quad-ril-lion *n.* a thousand trillions; one followed by fifteen zeros
quad-ri-par-tite *adj.* consisting of four persons or parts
quad-ri-ple-gic *n.* a person who is paralyzed in both arms and both legs
qua-dru-ma-na *n.* a group of primates distinguished by hand-shaped feet **quadrumanal** *adj.*
quad-ru-ped *n.* any animal having four feet
quad-ru-ple *adj.* consisting of four parts; multiplied by four
qua-dru-plet *n.* one of four infants born at the same time
qua-dru-pli-cate *n.* consisting of four identical parts
quaff *v.* to drink with abundance
quag-ga *n.* a wild ass of Africa, related to the zebras
quag-mire *n.* an area of soft muddy land that gives way underfoot; a marsh
quail *n.*, *pl.* a small game bird
quaint *adj.* pleasing in an old-fashioned, unusual way
quake *v.* to shake or tremble voilently
Quak-er *n.* the religious sect called the Society of Friends
qual-i-fi-ca-tion *n.* an act of qualifying; the ability, skill, or quality which makes something suitable for a given position
qual-i-fy *v.* to prove something able; restrict; limit; modify
qual-i-ty *n.*, *pl.* , **qualities** a distinguish-

ing character which makes something such as it is

qualm *n.* a sudden feeling of sickness; sensation of uneasiness or boubt

quan-da-ry *n.* a state of perplexity

quan-ti-ty *n.* number; amount; bulk; weight; a portion, as a large amount

quan-tum *n., pl.,* **quanta** an amount or quantity

quar-an-tine *n.* a period of enforced isolation for a specified period of time use to prevent the spread of a contagious disease **quarantine** *v.*

quar-rel *n.* an unfriendly or angry disagreement; a cause for dispute

quar-ri-er *n.* a person who works in a stone quarry

quar-ry *n., pl.* **quarries** an animal hunted for food; an open pit or excavation from which limestone or other material is being extracted

quart *n.* a unit of measurement equaling four cups

quar-ter *n.* one of four equal parts into which anything may be divided; a place of lodging, as a barracks; a U.S. coin equal to 1/4 of a dollar

quar-ter-back *n., Football* the offensive player who directs the plays for his team

quar-ter-deck *n.* the part of a deck, on a ship that is used for ceremonial and offical use only

quarter horse *n.* a horse capable of high speed and great endurance

quar-ter-ly *adj.* a division of time that is divided into three month intervals

quar-ter-mas-ter *n.* the officer in charge of supplies for army troops; a Navy OD officer who steers a ship and handles signaling equipment

quar-tet *n.* a musical composition for four voices or instruments; any group or set of four

quartz *n.* a hard, transparent crystallized mineral

qua-sar *n.* one of the most distant and brightest bodies in the universe; a quasar producing intense visible radiation but not emitting radio signals

quash *v.* to nullify or suppress by judicial action

quay *n.* a landing place beside water for loading ships

quea-sy *adj.* nauseated; sick **queasiness** *n.*

queen *n.* the wife of a king; a woman sovereign or monarch; in chess, the most powerful piece on the board, which can move any number of squares in any direction; the fertile female in a colony of social insects

queer *adj.* strange; unusual; different from the normal *Slang* homosexual

quell *v.* to put down with force

quench *v.* to extinguish or put out; to cool metal by thrusting it into water; to drink to satisfy a thirst

quer-u-lous *adj.* complaining or fretting; expressing complaints

que-ry *n.* an injury; a question *v.* to question **querier** *n.*

quest *n.* a search; pursuit; an expedition to find something

ques-tion *n.* an expression of inquiry which requires an answer;a problem; an unsolved matter; the acat of inquiring or asking

ques-tion-able *adj.* being in doubt; not vertain or sure

question mark *n.* a mark of punctuation, (?), used in writing to indicate a question

ques-tion-naire *n.* a written series of questions to gather statistical information often used for a survey

queue *n., Computer Science* a sequence of stored programs or data on hold for processing

quib-ble *v.* to raise trivial objection

quiche *n.* unsweetened custard baked in a pastry shell

quick *adj.* moving swiftly; occurring in a short time

quick-sand *n.* a bog of very fine, wet sand of considerable depth

quid *n.* a small portion of tobacco; a cow's cud

qui-et *adj.* silent; making very little sound; still; tranquil; calm

quill *n.* a strong bird feather; a spine from a porcupine

quilt *n.* a bed coverlet made of two layers of cloth with a soft substance between and held in place by lines of stitching

qui-nine *n., Chem.* a very bitter, colorless, crystalline powder used in the treatment of malaria

quin-sy *n., Pathol.* a severe inflammation of the tonsils

quin-tes-sence *n.* the most essential and purest form of anything

quin-tet *n.* a musical composition written for five people

quin-tu-ple *adj.* increased five times

quire *n.* twenty-five sheets of paper removed from a complete ream of paper

quirk *n.* a sudden, sharp bend or twist; a personal mannerism

quis-ling *n.* a person who is a traitor, working against his own country from within

quit *v.* to cease; to give up; to depart; to abandon

quite *adv.* to the fullest degree; really; actually

quix-ot-ic *adj.* extravagantly romantic; impractical

quiz *v.* to question, as with an informal oral or written examination

quo-ta *n.* an allotment or proportional share

quo-ta-tion *n.* the exact quoting of words as a passage

quo-ta-tion mark *n.* the marks of punctuation (" ") showing a direct quote

quote *v.* to repeat exactly what someone else has previously stated

quo-tient *n., Math* the amount or number which results when one number is divided by another

R, r The eighteenth letter of the English alphabet.
R *abbr.* radius
ra-ba-to *n.* a wide lace-edged collar of the early 17th century
rab-bet *n.* a recess or groove along the edge of a piece of wood cut to fit another piece to form a joint **-ed** *v.*
rab-bi *n.* an ordained leader of Jews; the leader and teacher of a Jewish congregation **rabbinic** *adj.*
rab-bin-i-cal *adj.* to be referring or pertaining to the rabbis
rab-bit *n.* a burrowing mammal related to but smaller than the hare
rab-bit ears *n.* indoor television antenna, having two extensible rods, connected to a base forming a V shape
rab-bit-eye *n.* a blueberry found in the southeastern part of the United States
rab-bit punch *n.* a hit that is aimed at the back of one's head
rab-bit-ry *n.* the location where rabbits are kept
rab-ble *n.* a disorderly crowd **rabbling, rabbled** *v.*
rab-ble-ment *n.* a rabble; a tumult
rab-ble-rous-er *n.* a person who stirs masses of people to riot
rab-id *adj.* affected with rabies; mad; furious **rabidly** *adv.* **rabidness** *n.*
ra-bies *n.* an acute, infectious viral disease of the central nervous system, often fatal, which is transmitted by the bite of an infected animal
rac-coon *n., pl.* **-coons, -coon** a nocturnal mammal with a black, mask-like face and a black-and-white ringed, bushy tail
race *n.* the zoological division of the human population having common origin and other physical traits, such as hair form and pigmentation; a group of people having such common characteristics or appearances; people united by a common nationality
race *n.* a contest which is judged by speed; any contest, such as a race for an elective office **raced, racer** *n.*
race course *n.* the track on which a rave takes place
race hourse *n.* a type of horse which is bred strictly for the use of racing
ra-ceme *n.* a type of plant bearing flowers along its stalk
rac-er *n.* a person who takes part in a race; one who runs in a race
race-track *n.* the course which is used for the purpose of racing horses
ra-chis *n.* a type of axial structure
ra-cial *adj.* a characteristic of a race of people
rac-ism *n.* a thought or belief that one race is better than another race **racist** *n.*
rack *n.* an open framework or stand for displaying or holding something; an instrument of torture used to stretch the body; a triangular frame used to arrange the balls on a pool table *Mech.* a metal bar with teeth designed to move a cogged bar and produce a rotary or linear motion *v.* to strain, as with great effort in thinking
rack-et or **racquet** *n.* a light-weight bat-like object with netting stretched over an oval frame, used in striking a tennis ball or a shuttlecock
rack-et-eer *n.* a person who engages in acts which are illegal
rac-on-teur *n.* one who is skilled in the act of telling stories
rac-y *adj.* having a spirited or strongly marked quality; slightly improper or immodest **racily** *adv.*, **raciness** *n.*
ra-dar *n.* a system which uses radio signals to detect the presence of an object or the speed the object is traveling
ra-dar as-tron-o-my *n.* astronomy that deals with investigations of the celestial bodies of the solar system by comparing characteristics of reflected radar wave with characteristics of ones transmitted from earth
ra-dar-scope *n.* a screen or oscilloscope that serves as a visual indicator in a radar receiver
rad-dled *adj.* to be in a state of confusion; broken down; worn; lacking composure
ra-di-al *adj.* pertaining to or resembling a ray or radius; developing from a center axis
ra-di-ance *n.* the quality of being shiny; the state of being radiant; relating or emitting to radiant heat
ra-di-ant *adj.* emitting rays of heat or light; beaming with kindness or love; projecting a strong quality **-ly** *adv.*
ra-di-ant heat *n.* heat that is transmitted by radiation
ra-di-ate *v.* to move out in rays, such as heat moving through the air **-ly** *adv.*
ra-di-a-tion *n.* an act of radiating; the process or action of radiating; the process of emitting radiant energy in the form of particles or waves **radiationless** *adj.*, **radiative** *adj.*
ra-di-a-tor *n.* something which radiates
rad-i-cal *adj.* proceeding from a foundation or root; drastic; making extreme changes in views, conditions, or habits; carrying convictions or theories to their fullest application **radically** *adv.*, **radicalness** *n.*
radii *pl. of* radius
ra-di-o *n.* the technique of communicating by radio waves; the business of broadcasting programmed material to the public via radio waves **radioing, radioed** *v.*
ra-dio-ac-tive *adj.* exhibiting radioactivity **radioactively** *adv.*
ra-di-o-ac-tiv-i-ty *n., Physics* a spontaneous emission of electromagnetic radiation, as from a nuclear reaction
ra-di-o-fre-quen-cy *n.* a frequency which is above 15,000 cycles per second that is used in radio transmission
ra-di-o-gram *n.* a type of radiograph
ra-di-ol-o-gy *n.* a science which deals with rays for a radioactive substance

and use for medical diagnosis
radiologist *n.*
rad-ish *n.* the edible root of the radish plant
ra-di-um *n* a radioactive metallic element symbolized by Ra.
ra-di-us *n., pl.* **radii** or **raduses** a line from the center of a circle to its surface or circumference
ra-don *n.* a heavy, colorless, radioactive gaseous element symbolized by Rn
raf-fi-a *n.* a fiber from an African palm tree used for making baskets, hats, and other woven articles
raff-ish *adj.* something that is marked by crudeness or flashy vulgarity
raffishly *adv.*, raffishness *n.*
raf-fle *n.* a game of chance; a lottery in which one buys chances to win something
raft *n.* a floating structure made from logs or planks and used for water trans-portation
raft-er *n.* a timber of a roof which slopes
rag *n.* a cloth which is useless and sometimes used for cleaning purposes
rag-a-muf-fin *n.* a child who is unkempt
rag-bag *n.* a miscellaneous grouping or collection; a bag for holding scrap pieces of material
rag doll *n.* a child's doll that is usually made from scrap material and has a hand painted face
rage *n.* violent anger **raging** *adj.*, raginglу *adv.*
rag-ged *adj.* to be torn or ripped
raggedness *n.*, raggedly *adv.*
rag-weed *n.* a type of plant whose pollen can cause hay fever
raid *n.* a sudden invasion or seizure
raider *n.*
rail *n.* a horizontal bar of metal, wood, or other strong material supported at both ends or at intervals; the steel bars used to support a track on a railroad
rail-bird *n.* a person who sits on or near a race track rail and watches a race or workout
rail-ing *n.* a barrier of wood
rain *n.* the condensed water from atmospheric vapor, which falls to earth in the form of drops
rain-bow *n.* an arc that contains bands of colors of the spectrum and is formed opposite the sun and reflects the sun's rays, usually visible after a light rain shower
rain-coat *n.* a water-resistant or waterproof coat
rain-fall *n.* the amount of measurable precipitation
rain gauge *n.* an instrument used to measure rain fall
rain-making *n.* the act or process of producing or attempting to produce rain by the use of artificial means
raise *v.* to cause to move upward; to build; to make greater in size, price, or amount; to increase the status; to grow; as plants; to rear as children; to stir ones emotions; to obtain or collect as funds or money
rai-sin *n.* a grape dried for eating
rake *n.* a tool with a long handle at the end and a set of teeth at the other end used to gather leaves and other matter; a slope or incline, as the rake of an auditorium rake *v.*
ral-ly *v.* to call together for a purpose *n.* a rapid recovery, as from depression, exhaustion, or any setback; in a meeting whose purpose is to rouse or create support
ram *n.* a male sheep; an implement used to drive or crush by impact; to cram or force into place
RAM *abbr.* random access memory
ram-ble *v.* to stroll or walk without a special destination in mind; to talk without sequence of ideas **ramble** *n.*, ramblingly *adv.*
ram-bunc-tious *adj.* rough or boisterous
rambunctiousness *n.*
ramp *n.* an incline which connects two different levels; movable staircase allows passengers to enter or leave an aircraft
ram-page *n.* a course of destruction or violent behavior *v.* to storm about in a rampage rampageous *adj.*, rampageously *adv.*, rampageousness *n.*
ram-pan-cy *n.* the state or quality of being rampant
ram-pant *adj.* exceeding or growing without control; wild in actions; standing on the hind legs and elevating both forelegs rampantly *adv.*
ram-rod *n.* a metal rod used to drive or plunge the charge into a muzzle-loading gun or pistol; the rod used for cleaning the barrels of a rifle or other firearm
ram-shack-le *adj.* likely to fall apart from poor construction or maintenance
ranch *n.* a large establishment for raising cattle, sheep, or other livestock; a large farm that specializes in a certain crop or animals rancher *n.*
ran-cid *adj.* having a rank taste or smell
ran-dom *adj.* done or made in a way that has no specific pattern or purpose; to select from a group whose members all had an even chance of being chosen
rang *v.* past tense of ring
range *n.* an area over which anything moves; an area of activity; a tract of land over which animals such as cattle and horses graze; an extended line or row especially of mountains; an open area for shooting at a target; large cooking stove with burners and oven. *v.* to arrange in a certain order; to extend or proceed in a particular direction
range finder *n.* instrument that is used in gunnery to determine the distance of a target
rank *n.* a degree of official position or status *v.* to place in order, class, or rank *adj.* a strong and disagreeable odor, smell, or taste
ran-sack *v.* to search or plunder through every part of something

ran-som *n.* the price demanded or paid for the release of a kidnaped person; the payment for the release of a person or property detained **ransom** *v.*
rant *v.* to talk in a wild, loud way
ra-pa-cious *adj.* living on prey seized alive; taking by force; plundering **rapaciously** *adv.*, **rapaciousness,**
rape *n.* the crime of forcible sexual intercourse; abusive treatment **rape** *v.*, **rapist** *n.*
rap-id *adj.* having great speed; completed quickly or in a short time **rapidity, rapidness** *n.*
ra-pi-er *n.* a long, slender, straight sword with two edges
rap-ine *n.* the forcible taking of another's property
rap-port *n.* a harmonious relationship
rapt *adj.* deeply absorbed or carried away with something and not to noticing any-thing else; engrossed **raptness** *n.*, **raptly** *adv.*
rare *adj.* scarce; infrequent; often held in high esteem or admiration because of infrequency **rareness** *n.*
ras-cal *n.* a person full of mischief; a person who is not honest **rascally** *adj.*
rash *adj.* acting without consideration or caution *n.* a skin irritation or eruption caused by an allergic reaction
rasp *n.* a file with course raised and pointed projections *v.* to scrape or rub with a course file; to utter something in a rough, grating voice **rasper** *n.*, **raspy** *adj.*
rasp-berry *n.* a small edible fruit, red or black in color and having many small seeds *Slang* contemptuous sound made by expelling air with the tongue between the lips in order to make a vibration
raspy *adj.* grating; irritable
rat *n.* a rodent similar to the mouse, but having a longer tail *Slang* a despicable person who betrays his friends or associates
rat-a-tat *n.* a sharp tapping, or repeated knocking
ratch-et *n.* a mechanism consisting of a pawl that allows a wheel or bar to move in one direction only
ratch-et wheel *n.* a wheel with teeth that is held place with a engaging handle
rate *n.* the measure of something to a fixed unit; the degree of price or value; a fixed ratio or amount *v.* to appraise
rath-er *adv.* preferably; with more reason or justice; more accurate or precise
rat-i-fy *v.* to approve something in an official way **ratification** *n.*
rat-ing *n.* a relative evaluation or estimate of something
ra-tio *n.*, *pl.* **ratios** the relationship between two things in amount, size, degree, expressed as a proportion
ra-tion *n.* a fixed portion or share *v.* to provide or allot in rations **rationing** *n.*
ra-tion-al *adj.* having the faculty of reasoning; being of sound mind **rationality** *n.*, **-ally** *adv.* **rationalness** *n.*
rat-tan *n.* an Asian palm whose strong stems are used to make wickerworks
rat-tle *v.* to make a series of rapid, sharp noises in quick succession; to talk rapidly; chatter *n.* a baby's toy made to rattle when shaken
rat-tler *n.*, *Slang* a venomous snake which has a series of horny, modified joints which make a rattling sound when moved; a rattlesnake; one that rattle
rat-tle-trap *n.* something that is rickety or rattly
rau-cous *adj.* loud and rowdy; having a rough hoarse sound; disorderly **raucously** *adv.*, **raucousness** *n.*
rav-age *v.* to bring on heavy destruction; devastate
rave *v.* to speak incoherently; to speak with enthusiasm *n.* the act of raving
rav-el *v.* to separate fibers or threads; to unravel **ravelment** *n.*
ra-ven *n.* a large bird, with shiny black feathers *adj.* of or relating to the glossy sheen or color of the raven
ra-vine *n.* a deep gorge with steep sides in the earth's surface, usually created by flowing water
rav-ish *v.* to seize and carry off; to rape **ravishment** *n.*, **ravisher** *n.*
raw *adj.* uncooked; in natural condition; not processed inexperienced; damp, sharp, or chilly **rawly** *adv.*, **rawness** *n.*
ray *n.* a thin line of radiation or light; a small trace or amount; one of several lines coming from a point
ray-on *n.* a synthetic cellulose yarn; any fabric made from such yarn
ra-zor *n.* a sharp cutting instrument used especially for shaving
ra-zor-back *n.* a wild hog of the southeastern United States; the mascot of the University of Arkansas
razz *v.*, *Slang* to heckle; to tease
raz-zle--daz-zel *n.* a state of complete confusion
re- *prefix* again, anew or reverse action
reach *v.* to stretch out; to be able to grasp *n.* the act of stretching out
re-act *v.* to act in response to *Chem.* to undergo a chemical change; to experience a chemical reaction
re-ac-tor *n.* a person, object, device, or substance which reacts to something
read *v.* to visually go over something, as a book, and to understand its meaning; to learn or be informed; to perceive something in a meaning which may or may not actually be there
read-y *adj.* prepared for use or action; quick or prompt; willing
re-a-gent *n* any substance which causes a chemical reaction
re-al *adj.* something which is existing, genuine, true, or authentic *Law* property which is regarded as permanent or immovable
reel-to-reel *adj.* pertaining to magnetic tape which is threaded to a take-up reel, which moves from one reel to another

real estate *n.* land and whatever is attached such as natural resources or buildings

re-al-ism *n.* concern or interest with actual facts and things as they really are **realist** *n.*, **-istic** *adj.*, **-stically** *adv.*

re-al-i-ty *n., pl.* the fact or state of being real or genuine; an actual situation or event

re-al-ize *v.* to understand correctly; to make real **realizable** *adj.*, **realization** *n.*, **realizer** *n.*

re-al-ly *adv.* actually; truly; indeed

realm *n.* a scope or field of any power or influence

ream *n.* a quantity of paper containing 500 sheets

reap *v.* to harvest a crop with a sickle or other implement

rear *n.* the back; *adj.* of or at the rear; *v.* to raise up on the hind legs; to raise as an animal or child

rea-son *n.* a statement given to confirm or justify a belief, promise, or excuse; the ability to decide things, to obtain ideas, to think clearly, and to make logical and rational choices and decisions; *v.* to discuss something logically **reasoning** *n.*

rea-son-a-ble *adj.* moderate; rational **reasonableness** *n.*, **reasonably** *adv.*

re-a-sur-ance *n.* the act of reassuring; reinsurance

re-bate *n.* a deduction allowed on items sold; a discount; money which is returned to the purchaser from the original payment; *v.* to return part of the payment **rebater** *n.*

re-bel *v.* to refuse allegiance; to resist any authority; to react with violence

re-bel-lion *n.* an organized uprising to change or overthrow an existing authority

re-bel-lious *adj.* engaged in rebellion; relating to a rebel or rebellion **rebelliously** *adv.*, **rebelliousness** *n.*

re-birth *n.* a revival or renaissance; reincarnation

re-bound *v.* to spring back; to recover from a setback or frustration; *n.* recoil

re-broad-cast *v.* to repeat or broadcast again **rebroadcast** *n.*

re-buff *v.* to refuse abruptly; to snub **rebuff** *n.*

re-build *v.* to make extensive repairs to something; to reconstruct; remodel

re-buke *v.* to criticize something sharply; to turn back **rebuker** *n.*

re-but *v.* to try and prove someone wrong by argument or evidence **rebuttal** *n.*, **rebutable** *adj.*

re-call *v.* to order or summon to return to ask for something to be returned; so that defects can be fixed or repaired; to remember; to recollect

re-cant *v.* to formally admit that a previously held belief was wrong by making public confession

re-cap *v.* to restore an old tire; to review or summarize something

re-cede *v.* to move back; as floodwater; to withdraw from an agreement

re-ceipt *n.* the written acknowledgment of something received; *pl.*, **receipts** the amount of money received

re-ceive *v.* to take or get something; to greet customers or guests; to accept as true or correct **receiver** *n.*

re-cent *adj.* happening at a time just before the present **recently** *adv.*

re-cep-ta-cle *n.* anything which holds something; an electrical outlet designed to receive a plug

re-cep-tion *n.* the act or manner of receiving something; a formal entertainment of guests, as a wedding reception

re-cep-tion-ist *n.* an employee who greets callers and answers the telephone for a business

re-cep-tive *adj.* able to receive **receptively** *adv.*, **-ness**, **receptivity** *n.*

re-cess *n.* a break in the normal routine of something; a depression or niche in a smooth surface

re-ces-sion *n.* the act of receding; withdrawal; a period or time of reduced economic activity **-ary** *adj.*

rec-i-pe *n.* the directions and a list of ingredients for preparing food

re-cip-ro-cate *v.* to give and return mutually, one gift or favor for another

re-cite *v.* to repeat something from memory; give an account of something in detailt

reck-less *adj.* state of being careless and rash when doing something **-ness** *n.*

reck-on *v.* to calculate; to compute; to estimate; to consider; to assume

reck-on-ing *n.* the act of calculation or counting

re-claim *v.* to redeem; to reform; to recall; to change to a more desirable condition or state

rec-la-ma-tion *n.* the state of being eclaimed

re-cline *v.* to assume a prone position

rec-luse *n.* a person who chooses to live in seclusion

rec-og-ni-tion *n.* an acknowledgment which is formal

re-cog-ni-zance *n.* an amount of money which will be forfeited for a nonperformance of an obligation

rec-og-nize *v.* to experience or identify something or someone as having been known previously; to appreciative **recognizable** *adj.*, **recognizably** *adv.*

re-coil *v.* to fall back or to rebound **recoilless** *adj.*

rec-ol-lect *v.* to remember or recall to the mind **recollection** *n.*

rec-om-mend *v.* to suggest to another as desirable; advise **recommendation** *n.*, **recommedable** *adj.*

rec-om-pense *v.* to reward with something for a service

rec-on-cile *v.* to restore a friendship after an estrangement **reconcilably** *adv.*

rec-on-dite *adj.* being obscure

re-con-di-tion *v.* to return to a good condition

re-con-firm *v.* confirm something again

re-con-nais-sance *n.* an observation of

territory such as that of the enemy
re-con-noi-ter *v.* to survey a region
re-con-sid-er *v.* to think about again with a view to changing a previous action or decision **reconsideration** *n.*
re-con-struct *v.* to build something again
re-con-struc-tion *n.* something which has been reconstructed or rebuilt
re-cord *v.* to write down for future use or permanent reference; to preserve sound on a tape or disk for replay; a phonograph record; *n.* information which is recorded and kept permanently
re-cord-er *n.* a person who records things such as official transactions
re-cord-ing *n.* the act of making a transcription of sounds
rec-ord play-er *n.* the machine which is used to play recordings
re-count *v.* to tell the facts; narrate or describe in detail; to count again; *n.* a second count to check the results of the first count
re-coup *v.* to be reimbursed; to recover
re-course *n.* a turning to or an appeal for help
re-cov-er *v.* to regain something which was lost; to be restored to good health; *Law* to obtain a judgment for damages
re-cov-er-y *n.* the power to regain something
rec-re-ant *adj.* cowardly; unfaithful
re-cre-ate *v.* to create again
rec-re-a-tion *n.* refreshment of body and mind; a pleasurable occupation or exercise **recreational** *adj.*
re-crim-i-nate *v.* the charging of another of the same account **recriminatory, recriminative** *adj.*, **recrimination** *n.*
re-cruit *v.* to enlist someone for military or naval purposes; to look for someone as for a service or employment **recuiter** *n.*
rec-tal *adj.* referring to the rectum of the body
rec-tan-gle *n.* a parallelogram with all right angles **rectangular** *adj.*, **rectangularity** *n.*
rec-ti-fi-er *n.* that which rectifies something
rec-ti-fy *v.* to make correct; *Chem.* to purify by repeated distillations; *Electr.* to make an alternating current a direct current
rec-ti-lin-e-ar *adj.* made up of or indicated by straight lines; bounded by straight lines
rec-ti-tude *n.* rightness in principles and conduct; correctness
rec-to *n.* the right-hand page of a book
rec-tor *n.* a member of the clergy in charge of a parish; a priest in charge of a congregation, church, or parish; the principal or head of a school or of a college
rec-tum *n., pl.* **rectums, recta** *Anat.* the lower terminal portion of the large intestine connecting the colon and anus
re-cum-bent *adj.* lying down or reclining
re-cu-per-ate *v.* to regain strength or to regain one's health; to recover from a financial loss **recuperation** *n.*, **recuperative** *adj.*
re-cur *v.* to happen, to return, or to appear again **recurrence, recurrent** *adj.*
red *n.* having the color which resembles blood, as pigment or dye which colors red; *Slang* a communist; one who is in favor of the overthrow of an existing political of social order; a condition indicating a loss, as in the red
re-deem *v.* to buy back; to pay off; to turn something in, as coupons or rain checks and receive something in exchange
re-demp-tion *n.* the act of redeeming; rescue; ransom; that which redeems; salvation
re-doubt *n.* a small enclosed fortification
re-doubt-a-ble *adj.* to be dreaded **redoubtably** *adv.*
re-dound *v.* to have an effect on something
re-dress *v.* to put something right
red snap-per *n.* a saltwater fish which is red in color and can be found in the Gulf of Mexico and near Florida
red tape *n.* routines which are rigid and may cause a delay in a process
re-duce *v.* to decrease; lessen in number, degree, or amount; to put into order; to lower in rank; to lose weight by dieting
re-duc-tion *n.* the state of being reduced
re-dun-dant *adj.* exceeding what is necessary; repetitive
re-du-pli-cate *v.* to repeat something **reduplication** *n.*
red-wood *n.* a tree found in California which is very tall and wide
re-ech-o *v.* to reverberate again
reed *n.* tall grass with a slender stem, which grows in wet areas; a thin tongue of wood, metal, cane, or plastic; placed in the mouthpiece of an instrument to produce sounds by vibrating **reediness** *n.*, **reedy** *adj.*
reef *n.* a chain of rocks, coral, or sand at or near the surface of the water
reef-er *n.* a jacket which is close-fitting
reek *v.* to emit vapor or smoke; to give off a strong offensive odor
reel *n.* a device which revolves on an axis and is used for winding up or letting out fishing line, rope, or other string-like material; a lively and fast dance
re-e-lect *v.* the act of electing someone again for an office
re-em-pha-size *v.* to stress something or an idea again
re-en-list *v.* to enlist or join a group or an armed force again **reenlistment** *n.*
re-enter *v.* to enter a room or area again
re-ex-am-ine *v.* examine something or someone another time or again **reexamination** *n.*
re-fec-to-ry *n.* the place in colleges where the students dine
re-fer *v.* to direct for treatment, information, or help
ref-e-ree *n.* a person who supervises a game, making sure all the rules are

followed
ref-er-ence *n.* the act of referring some-one to someplace or to some-thing
ref-er-en-dum *n.* a public vote on an item for final approval or for rejection
ref-er-ent *n.* what is referred to such as a person
re-fill *v.* to fill something with an item again
re-fine *v.* to purify by removing unwanted substances or material; to improve refined *adj.* refinement *n.*
re-fin-er-y *n.* a place or location which is used for the purpose of refining, such as sugar
re-fin-ish *v.* the act of putting a new surface onto something, such as wood
re-fit *v.* to repair something
re-flect *v.* to throw back rays of light from a surface; to give an image, as from a mirror; to ponder or think carefully about something
reflection *n.* reflective *adj.*
re-flec-tor *n.* something which is able to reflect things, such as light
re-flex *adj.* turning, casting, or bending backward; *n.* an involuntary reaction of the nervous system to a stimulus
re-for-est *v.* the act of replanting a forest or wooded area with trees -ation *n.*
re-form *v.* to reconstruct, make over, or change something for the better; improve; to abandon or give up evil ways
reformer *n.*, reformed *adj.*
re-for-ma-to-ry *n.* a jail-like institution for young criminals
re-fract *v.* the deflecting something, such as a ray of light refractive *adj.*
re-frac-tion *n.* the state of being refracted or deflected
re-frac-to-ry *adj.* unmanageable; obstinate; difficult to melt; resistant to heat; *n.* something which does not change significantly when exposed to high temperatures
re-frain *v.* to hold back
re-fresh *v.* to freshen something again
re-fresh-ment *n.* something which will refresh someone, such as a cold drink or snack
re-frig-er-ant *n.* an agent which cools something
re-frig-er-ate *v.* to chill or cool; to preserve food by chilling; to place in a refrigerator
re-frig-er-a-tor *n.* a box-like piece of equipment which chills food and other matter
re-fu-el *v.* to put fuel into something again
ref-uge *n.* shelter or protection from harm; any place one may turn for relief or help
ref-u-gee *n.* a person who flees to find safety
re-ful-gent *adj.* state of being radiant or putting off a bright light
re-fund *v.* to return or pay back; to reimburse refundable *adj.* refund *n.*
re-fur-bish *v.* to make clean; to renovate
re-fus-al *n.* the denial of something which is demanded
re-fuse *v.* to decline; to reject; to deny
ref-use *n.* rubbish; trash
re-fute *v.* to overthrow or to disprove with the use of evidence
re-gain *v.* to recover; to reach again
re-gal *adj.* of or appropriate for royalty regally *adv.*
re-gale *v.* to entertain or delight; to give pleasure
re-ga-li-a *n.* something which represents royalty such as a septer
re-gard *v.* to look upon closely; to consider; to have great affection for; *n.* careful attention or thought; esteem or affection; regards greetings of good wishes
re-gard-ful *adj.* state of being mindful
re-gard-less *adj.* state of being careless or showing no regard towards something or someone
re-gat-ta *n.* a boat race
re-gen-cy *n., pl.* regenies the jurisdiction or office of a regent
re-gen-er-ate *v.* to reform spiritually or morally; to make or create anew; to refresh or restore
re-gent *n.* one who rules and acts as a ruler during the absence of a sovereign, or when the ruler is underage
re-gime *n.* an administration
reg-i-men *n.* government control; therapy
reg-i-ment *n.* a military unit of ground troops which is composed of several battalions regimental *adj.*
regimentation *n.*
re-gion *n.* an administrative, political, social, or geographical area
re-gion-al *adj.* typical or pertaining to a geographic region; limited to a particular region
reg-is-ter *n.* something which contains names or occurrences
reg-is-trar *n.* type of person who keeps a register
reg-is-tra-tion *n.* an act of recording things or names
re-gress *v.* to return to a previous state or condition regress, regression *n.*
re-gret *v.* to feel disappointed or distressed about; *n.* a sense of loss or expression of grief; a feeling of sorrow
regretfully, regretably *adv.*, regretful, regretable *adj.*
reg-u-lar *adj.* usual; normal; customary; conforming to set principles, procedures, or discipline; well-ordered; not varying regularity *n.*, regularly *adv.*
reg-u-late *v.* to adjust to a specification or requirement regulative, regulatory *adj.*, regulator *n.*
reg-u-la-tion *n.* a rule that is set down in order to govern an area or people
re-gur-gi-tate *v.* to pour something forth
re-ha-bil-i-tate *v.* to restore; to a former state, by education and therapy
rehabilitation *n.*, rehabilitative *adj.*
re-hash *v.* to rework or go over old material
re-hears-al *n.* the act of practicing for a performance rehearse *v.*

reign *n.* the period in time when the monarch rules over an area
re-im-burse *v.* to repay **reimbursement** *n.*
rein *n.* one of a pair of narrow, leather straps attached to the bit of a bridle and used to control a horse
rein-deer *n.* a large deer found in northern regions, both sexes having antlers
re-in-force *v.* to support; to strengthen with additional people or equipment **reinforcement** *n.*
re-in-state *v.* to restore something to its former position or condition **reinstatement** *n.*
re-it-er-ate *v.* to say or do something over and over again
re-ject *v.* to refuse; to discard as useless **reject, rejection** *n.*
re-joice *v.* to fill with joy; to be filled with joy
re-join *v.* to respond or to answer someone
re-join-der *n.* the answer to a reply made by someone to another
re-ju-ve-nate *v.* to restore to youthful appearance or vigor **rejuvenation** *n.*
re-kin-dle *v.* to inflame something again
re-lapse *v.* to fall back or revert to an earlier condition **relapse** *n.*
re-late *v.* to tell the events of; to narrate; to bring into natural association **relater** *n.*
re-lat-ed *adj.* to be in the same family; connected to each other by blood or by marriage
re-la-tion *n.* the relationship between people by marriage or blood lines **relational** *adj.*
re-la-tion-ship *n.* a connection by blood or family; kinship; friendship; a natural association
rel-a-tive *adj.* relevant; connected; considered in comparison or relation-ship to other; *n.* a member of one's family
rel-a-tiv-i-ty *n.* a condition or state of being relative
re-lax *v.* to make loose or lax; to relieve something from effort or strain; to become less formal or less reserved **relaxation** *n.*, **relaxedly** *adv.*
re-lay *n.* a race in which a fresh team replaces another; *v.* to pass from one group to another
re-lease *v.* to set free from confinement; to unfasten; to free; to relinquish a claim on something **releaser** *n.*
rel-e-gate *v.* to banish someone or something
re-lent *v.* to soften in temper, attitude, or determination; to slacken **relentless** *adj.*
rel-e-vant *adj.* related to matters at hand
re-li-a-ble *adj.* dependable; capable of being relied upon
re-li-ance *n.* confidence and trust; something which is relied upon
re-li-ant *adj.* state of being confident or having reliance
re-lic *n.* something which is very old; a keepsake; an object whose cultural environment has disappeared
re-lief *n.* anything which decreases or lessens anxiety, pain, discomfort, or other unpleasant conditions or feelings
re-lief map *n.* a map which outlines the contours of the land
re-lieve *v.* to lessen or ease pain, anxiety, embarrassment, or other problems; to release or free from a duty by providing a replacement **reliever** *n.*, **relievable** *adj.*
re-lig-ion *n.* an organized system of beliefs, rites, and celebrations centered on a supernatural being power; belief pursued with devotion **religious** *adj.*
re-lin-quish *v.* to release something or someone
re-lish *n.* pleasure; a spicy condiment taken with food to lend it flavor
re-live *v.* to experience something again
re-lo-cate *v.* to move to another area **relocation** *n.*
re-luc-tance *n.* an unwillingness
re-luc-tant *adj.* unwilling; not yielding
re-ly *v.* to trust or depend
re-main *v.* to continue without change; to stay after the departure of others
remainder *n.* something left over; *Math* the difference which remains after division or subtraction
re-mains *pl., n.* what is left after all other parts have been taken away; corpse
re-mand *n.* state of being remanded
re-mark *n.* a brief expression or comment; to take notice; to observe; to comment
re-mark-a-ble *adj.* extraordinary **remarkably** *adv.*
re-me-di-a-ble *adj.* being able to be remedied
rem-e-dy *n., pl.* **remedies** a therapy or medicine which relieves pain; something which corrects an error or fault; *v.* to cure or relieve; to rectify
re-mem-ber *v.* to bring back or recall to the mind; to retain in the mind carefully; to keep a person in one's thought; to recall a person to another as a means of greetings
re-mem-brance *n.* something which is remembered by someone
re-mind *v.* to cause or help to remember
rem-i-nisce *v.* to recall the past things which have happened
rem-i-nis-cence *n.* the practice or process of recalling the past **reminiscent** *adj.*
re-miss *adj.* lax in performing one's duties; negligent **remissness** *n.*
re-mis-sion *n.* a forgiveness; act of remitting
re-mit *v.* to send money as payment for goods; to forgive, as a crime or sin; to slacken, make less violent, or less intense **remittance** *n.*
rem-nant *n.* a small piece or a scrap or something
re-mod-el *v.* to reconstruct something making it like new
re-mon-strance *n.* statement of reasons against an idea or something
re-mon-strate *v.* giving strong reasons against an act or an idea

re-morse *n.* deep moral regret for past misdeeds **remorseful** *adj.*
re-mote *adj.* distant in time; space or relation **remotely** *adv.*, **remoteness** *n.*
re-mount *v.* to mount something again
re-mov-a-ble *adj.* being able to be removed
re-mov-al *n.* the change of a site or place
re-move *v.* to get rid of; to extract; to dismiss from office; to change one's business or residence; *n.* an act of moving **removable** *adj.* **removal** *n.*
re-moved *adj.* state of being separate from others
re-mu-ner-ate *v.* pay an equivalent for a service
ren-ais-sance *n.* a revival or rebirth; the humanistic revival of classical art, literature, and learning in Europe which occurred during the 14th through the 16th centuries
re-nal *adj.* of or relating to the kidneys
re-nas-cence *n.* a revival or a rebirth
rend *v.* to remove from with violence; to split
ren-der *v.* to give or make something available; to submit or give; to represent artistically; to liquefy or melt fat by means of heat **rendering** *n.*
ren-dez-vous *n.* a meeting place that has been prearranged; *v.* to meet at a particular time and place
ren-di-tion *n.* an interpretation or a translation
ren-e-gade *n.* a person who rejects one allegiance for another; an outlaw; a traitor **renegade** *adj.*
re-nege *v.* to fail to keep one's word
re-new *v.* to make new or nearly new by restoring; to resume **renewable** *adj.*, **renewal** *n.*
ren-net *n.* an extract taken from a calf's stomach and used to curdle milk for making cheese
re-nounce *v.* to reject something or someone
ren-o-vate *v.* to return or to restore to a good condition
re-nown *n.* the quality of being widely honored **renowned** *adj.*
rent *n.* the payment made for the use of another's property; *v.* to obtain occupancy in exchange for payment **rental** *n.*
re-nun-ci-a-tion *n.* renouncing
re-or-gan-i-za-tion *n.* the process of reorganizing something
rep. *n., Slang* representative; *v.* represent
re-pair *v.* to restore to good or usable condition; to renew; refresh **repairable** *adj.*
re-pair-man *n.* the person who makes repairs of things that are broken
rep-a-ra-ble *adj.* being able to be corrected
rep-a-ra-tion *n.* the act of repairing something
rep-ar-tee *n.* a quick, witty response or reply
re-pa-tri-ate *v.* to go back to one's own country
re-pay *v.* to pay back money; to do something in return
re-peal *v.* to withdraw officially **repeal** *n.*, **repealer** *n.*
re-peat *v.* to utter something again; to do an action again
re-peat-er *n.* something or person which repeats
re-pel *v.* to discourage; to force away; to create aversion
re-pel-lent *adj.* able to repel
re-pent *v.* to feel regret for something which has occurred; to change one's sinful way **repentance** *n.*, **repentant** *adj.*
re-per-cus-sion *n.* an unforeseen effect produced by an action **repercussive** *adj.*
rep-er-toire *n.* the accomplishments or skills of a person
rep-er-to-ry *n.* a collection of things
rep-e-ti-tion *n.* the act of doing something over and over again; the act of repeating
re-place *v.* to return something to its previous place **replaceable** *adj.*, **replacement** *n.*, **replacer** *n.*
re-plen-ish *v.* to add to something to replace what has gone or been used
re-plete *adj.* having plenty; abounding; full
rep-li-ca *n.* a reproduction or copy of something **replicate** *v.*
re-ply *v.* to give an answer to either verbally or in writing **reply** *n.*
re-port *n.* a detailed account; usually in a formal way; *v.* to tell about; to make oneself available; to give details of **reportable** *adj.*, **reporter** *n.*
re-port card *n.* the report of the students progress
re-port-ed-ly *adv.* to be according to a report
re-pose *n.* the act of being at rest; *v.* to lie at rest **reposeful** *adj.*
re-pos-i-tor-y *n.* the location where things may be placed for preservation
re-pos-sess *v.* to restore ownership of something
rep-re-hend *v.* to show or express disapproval of **reprehension** *n.*, **reprehensible** *adj.*
rep-re-sent *v.* to stand for something; to serve as the official representative for
rep-re-sen-ta-tion *n.* the act of representing
rep-re-sent-a-tive *n.* a person or thing serving as an example or type; *adj.* of or relating to government by representation; typical
re-press *v.* to restrain; hold back; to remove from the conscious mind **repression** *n.*, **repressive** *adj.*
re-prieve *v.* to postpone punishment; to provide temporary relief **reprievable** *adj.*, **reprieve** *n.*, **reprieve**, **reprieving** *v.*
rep-ri-mand *v.* to censure severely; rebuke **reprimand** *n.*
re-print *n.* an additional printing of a book exactly as the previous one **reprint** *v.*, **reprinter** *n.*

re-pri-sal *n.* retaliation with intent to inflect injury in return for injury received
re-proach *v.* to blame; to rebuke
reproachful *adj.*
rep-ro-bate *adj.* the state of being morally depraved
re-pro-duce *v.* to produce an image or copy; *Biol.* to produce an offspring; to recreate or produce; again
reproducer *n.*, **reproducible** *adj.*, **reproduction** *n.*, **reproductive** *adj.*
re-proof *n.* a censure
re-prove *v.* to tell or express a disapproval of something
rep-tile *n.* a cold-blooded, egg-laying vertebrate, as a snake, lizard, or turtle
reptilian *n.*, *adj.*
re-pub-lic *n.* a political unit or state where representatives are elected to exercise the power
re-pub-li-can *adj.* having the character of a republic
re-pub-li-can-ism *n.* the Republican principles
Republican Party *n.* one of the two political parties in the United States
re-pu-di-ate *v.* to cast away; to refuse to pay something
re-pug-nance *n.* the state or condition of being opposed
re-pug-nant *adj.* distasteful; repulsive; offensive
re-pulse *v.* to repel or drive back; to repel or reject rudely; to disgust or be disgusted **repulsion** *n.*
re-pul-sive *adj.* state of causing aversion
rep-u-ta-ble *adj.* to be honorable
reputability *n.*
re-put-a-tion *n.* the commonly held evaluation of a person's character
re-pute *v.* to account or to consider something
re-quest *v.* to ask for something
request *n.*
re-qui-em *n.* the Roman Catholic mass for a deceased person
re-quire *v.* to demand or insist upon
requirement *n.*
req-ui-site *adj.* absolutely needed; necessary
req-ui-si-tion *n.* a demand or a request
re-quit-al *n.* the act of requiting something
re-quite *v.* to reward; to repay someone
re-run *n.* a television show which is shown again
re-sale *n.* the act of selling something again
re-scind *v.* to repeal; to void
rescindable *adj.*, **rescission** *n.*
res-cue *v.* to free from danger; *n.* an act of deliverance **rescuer** *n.*
re-search *n.* a scientific or scholarly investigation; to carefully seek out
researcher *n.*
re-sem-ble *v.* to have similarity to something **resemblance** *n.*
re-sent *v.* to feel angry about
resentful *adj.*, **resentfully** *adv.*, **resentment** *n.*
res-er-va-tion *n.* the act of keeping something back
re-serve *v.* to save for a special reason; to set apart; to retain; to put off; *n.* something that is saved for a future point in time; the portion of a country's fighting force kept inactive until called upon
res-er-voir *n.* a body of water stored for the future; large reserve; a supply
re-side *v.* to dwell permanently; to exist as a quality or attribute **residence** *n.*
res-i-due *n.* matter remaining after treatment or removal of a part; something which remains
re-sign *v.* to give up; to submit to something as being unavoidable; to quit
resignation *n.*
res-in *n.* a plant substance from certain plants and trees used in varnishes and lacquers **resinous** *adj.*
re-sist *v.* to work against or actively oppose; to withstand **resistible** *adj.*
res-o-lute *adj.* coming from or characterized by determination
resolutely *adv.*, **resolution** *n.*
re-solve *v.* to make a firm decision on something; to find a solution
resolvable *adj.*, **resolver** *n.*, **resolution** *n.*
re-sort *v.* to go frequently or customarily *n.* a place, or recreation, for rest, and for a vacation
re-sound *v.* to be filled with echoing sounds; to reverberate; to ring or sound loudly **resounding** *adj.*, **resoundingly** *adv.*
re-source *n.* a source of aid or support which can be drawn upon if needed; **resources** one's available capital or assets **resourceful** *adj.*
re-spect *v.* to show consideration or esteem for; to relate to; *n.* courtesy or considerate treatment
respectfully *adv.* **respectful** *adj.*
res-pi-ra-tion *n.* the process or act of inhaling and exhaling; the act of breathing; the process in which an animal or person takes in oxygen from the air and releases carbon dioxide
respirator *n.*
res-pite *n.* a temporary postponement
re-spond *v.* to answer or reply; to act when prompted by something or someone
re-sponse *n.* a reply; the act of replying
responsive *adj.*
re-spon-si-ble *adj.* trustworthy; in charge; having authority; being answerable for one's actions or the actions of others **responsibility** *n.*
rest *n.* a cessation of all work, activity, or motion; *Mus.* an interval of silence equal in time to a note of same value; *v.* to stop work; to place or lay
restful *adj.*, **restfully** *adv.*
res-tau-rant *n.* a place which serves meals to the public
res-ti-tu-tion *n.* the act of restoring something to its rightful owner; compensation for injury, loss, or damage
res-tive *adj.* nervous or impatient because of a delay **restively** *adv.*,

restiveness *n.*
re-store *v.* to bring back to a former condition; to make restitution of **restoration** *n.*
re-strain *v.* to hold back or be held back; to control, limit, or restrict **restraint** *n.*
re-strict *v.* to confine within limits **restriction** *n.*, **restrictive** *adj.*, **restrictively** *adv.*
re-sult *v.* to happen or exist in a particular way; *n.* the consequence of an action, course, or operation
re-sume *v.* to start again after an interruption **resumption** *n.*
res-u-me *n.* a summary of one's personal history, background, work, and education
re-sus-ci-ate *v.* to return to life; to revive **resuscitation** *n.*, **resuscitator** *n.*
re-tail *v.* the sale of goods or commodities to the public; *v.* to sell to the consumer **retail** *adj.*, **retailer** *n.*
re-tain *v.* to hold in one's possession; to remember; to employ someone, as for his services
re-tain-er *n.* a person or thing that retains; a fee paid for one's services
re-tard *v.* to delay or slow the progress of. **retardant** *n. & adj.*
re-tar-da-tion *n.* a condition in which mental development is slow or delayed; a condition of mental slowness
re-ten-tion *n.* the act or condition of being retained
ret-i-na *n., pl.* **retinas, retinae** the light sensitive membrane lining the inner eyeball connected by the optic nerve to the brain **retinal** *adj.*
re-tire *v.* to depart for rest; to remove oneself from the daily routine of working; *Baseball* to put a batter out **retirement** *n.*, **retired** *adj.*, **retiree** *n.*
re-trace *v.* to go back over
re-tract *v.* to draw back or to take back something that has been said **retractable** *adj.*, **retraction** *n.*
re-tread *v.* to replace the tread of a worn tire **retread** *n.*
re-treat *n.* the act of withdrawing from danger; a time of study; prayer; and meditation in a quiet; isolated location **retreat** *v.*
re-trieve *v.* to regain; to find something and carry it back **retrievable** *adj.*, **retrieval** *n.*
ret-ro-ac-tive *adj.* taking effect on a date prior to enactment
ret-ro-spect *n.* a review of things in the past **retrospectively** *adv.*, **retrospective** *adj.*
re-turn *v.* to come back to an earlier condition; to reciprocate; *n.* the act of sending, bringing, or coming back **returns** *n.* a yield or profit from investments; a report on the results of an election **returnable** *adj.*, **returnee** *n.* **returner** *n.*
re-un-ion *n.* a reuniting; the coming together of a group which has been separated for a period of time
re-veal *v.* to disclose or make known; to expose or bring into view
rev-eil-le *n.* the sounding of a bugle used to awaken soldiers in the morning
rev-el *v.* to take great delight in **reveler** *n.*
rev-e-la-tion *n.* an act of or something revealed; a manifestation of divine truth; **evelation** the last book in the New Testament
re-venge *v.* to impose injury in return for injury received **revengeful** *adj.*, **revenger** *n.*
re-verse *adj.* turned backward in position; *n.* the opposite of something; a change in fortune usually from better to worse; change or turn to the opposite direction; to transpose or exchange the positions of; *Law* to revoke a decision **reverser** *n.*
re-vert *v.* to return to a former practice or belief **reversion** *n.*
re-view *v.* to study or look over something again; to give a report on; *n.* a reexamination; a study which gives a critical estimate of something **reviewer** *n.*
re-vise *v.* to look over something again with the intention of improving or correcting it **reviser** *n.*, **revision** *n.*
re-viv-al *n.* the act or condition or reviving; the return of a film or play which was formerly presented; a meeting whose purpose is religious reawakening
re-vive *v.* to restore, refresh, or recall; to return to consciousness or life
re-voke *v.* to nullify or make void by recalling **revocation** *n.*
re-volt *n.* to try to overthrow authority; to fill with disgust
rev-o-lu-tion *n.* the act or state of orbital motion around a point; the abrupt overthrow of a government; a sudden change in a system
re-volve *v.* to move around a central point; to spin; to rotate **revolvable** *adj.*
re-vue *n.* a musical show consisting of songs, dances, skits, and other similar entertainment
re-ward *n.* something given for a special service; *v.* to give a reward
R.F.D. *abbr.* rural free delivery
rhap-so-dy *n., pl.* rhapsodies an excessive display of enthusiasm
rhe-ni-um *n.* a metallic element symbolized by Re
rhet-o-ric *n.* effective expression in writing or speech; language which is not sincere
Rh fac-tor *n.* a substance found in the red blood cells of 85% of all humans; the presence of this factor is referred to as PH positive; the absence as PH negative
rhi-noc-er-os *n.* a very large mammal with one or two upright horns on the snout
Rhode Is-land *n.* a state located in the northeastern part of the United States
rho-di-um *n.* a metallic element symbol-

ized by Rh
rhu-barb *n.* a garden plant with large leaves and edible stalks used for pies
rhyme *or* **rime** *n.* a word or verse whose terminal sound corresponds with another rhyme *v.* rhymer *n.*
rhy-thm *n.* Music, speech, or movements which are characterized by equal or regularly alternating beats
rhythmical, rhythmic *adj.*
rhythmically *adv.*
RI *abbr.* Rhode Island
rib *n.* one of a series of curved bones enclosed in the chest of man and animals; *Slang* to tease
rib-bon *n.* a narrow band or strip of fabric, such as satin, used for trimming
rice *n.* a cereal grass grown extensively in warm climates
rich *adj.* having great wealth; of great value; satisfying and pleasing in voice, color, tone, or other qualities; extremely productive; as soil or land
rick-rack *n.* a zigzag braid used in trimming
rick-ets *n., Pathol.* a disease occurring in early childhood resulting from a lack of vitamin D and insufficient sunlight, characterized by defective bone growth and deformity
rid *v.* to make free from anything objectionable
rid-dle *v.* to perforate with numerous holes; *n.* a puzzling problem or question which requires a clever solution
ride *v.* to travel in a vehicle or on an animal; to sit on and drive, as a motorcycle
rid-er *n.* one who rides as a passenger; a clause, usually having little relevance, which is added to a document
ridge *n.* a long, narrow crest; a horizontal line formed where two sloping surfaces meet ridge *v.*
ridge-pole *n.* timber located at the top of a roof which is horizontal
rid-i-cule *n.* actions or words intended to make a person or thing the object of mockery ridicule *v.*
ri-dic-u-lous *adj.* to be causing derision or ridicule
rife *adj.* state of being abundant or abounding
rif-fle *n.* ripply water which is caused by a ridge
riff-raff *n.* the rabble; low persons in society
ri-fle *n.* a firearm having a grooved bore designed to be fired from the shoulder
ri-fling *n.* the act of putting or cutting spiral grooves in the barrel of a gun.
rift *n.* a fault; disagreement; a lack of harmony
rig *v.* to outfit with necessary equipment; *n.* the arrangement of sails, masts, and other equipment on a ship; the apparatus used for drilling water or oil wells
right *adj.* in accordance with or conformable to law, justice, or morality; proper and fitting; properly adjusted, disposed, or placed; orderly; sound in body or mind; *n.* the right side, hand, or direction; the direction opposite left; *adv.* immediately; completely; according to justice, morality, or law rightness *n.*
right an-gle *n., Geom.* an angle of 90 degrees; an angle with two sides perpendicular to each other
rig-id *adj.* not bending; inflexible; severe; stern rigidity, rigidness *n.*
rig-or *n.* the condition of being rigid or stiff; stiffness of temper; harshness
rigorous *adj.*, **rigorously** *adv.*
rind *n.* a tough outer layer which may be taken off or pealed off
ring *n.* a circular mark, line, or object; a small circular band worn on a finger; a group of persons acting together; especially in an illegal way; *v.* to make a clear resonant sound, as a bell when struck; *n.* the sound made by a bell
ring-worm *n., Pathol.* a contagious skin disease caused by fungi and marked by discolored, ring-shaped, scaly patches on the skin
rink *n.* a smooth area covered with ice used for hockey or ice-skating; a smooth wooden surface for roller-skating
rinse *v.* to wash lightly with water; *n.* the act of rinsing; a hair coloring or conditioning solution
ri-ot *n.* a wild and turbulent public disturbance; *Slang* an irresistibly amusing person riotous *adj.*
rip *v.* to tear apart violently; to move violently or quickly; *n.* a torn place; **rip-off** *Slang* to steal
rip-cord *n.* a cord which, when pulled, releases a parachute from its pack
ripe *adj.* fully developed or aged; mature ripeness *n.*
rip-ple *v.* to cause to form small waves on the surface of water; to waver gently ripple *n.*
rise *v.* to move from a lower position to a higher one; to extend upward; to meet a challenge or demand; *n.* the act of going up or rising; an elevation in condition or rank
ris-er *n.* a person who rises
ris-i-ble *adj.* being inclined to or causing laughter
risk *n.* a chance of suffering or encountering harm or loss; danger risky *adj.*
rite *n.* a formal religious ceremony; any formal custom or practice
rit-u-al *n.* a prescribed method for performing a religious ceremony; *adj.* pertaining to or practiced as a rite
ritual *adj.*, **ritualism** *n.*
ri-val *n.* one who strives to compete with another; one who equals or almost equals another
riv-er *n.* a relatively large natural stream of water, usually fed by another body of water
ri-vet *n.* a metal bolt used to secure two or more objects
RN *abbr.* Registered Nurse
roach *n.* a European freshwater fish; cockroach; *Slang* the butt of a

marijuana cigarette
road *n.* a public highway used for vehicles, people, and animals; a path or course; a course toward the achievement of something; **road block** *n.* an obstruction in a road, which prevents passage
roam *v.* to travel aimlessly or without a purpose **roamer** *n.*
roar *v.* to utter a deep prolonged sound of excitement; to laugh loudly **roar, roarer** *n.*
roast *v.* to cook meat by using dry heat in an oven; *n.* a cut of meat.
rob *v.* to take property unlawfully from another person **robber** *n.*, **robbery** *n.*
robe *n.* a long loose garment usually worn over night clothes; a long flowing gar-ment worn on ceremonial occasions
rob-in *n.* a large North American bird with a black head and reddish breast
ro-bot *n.* a machine capable of performing human duties
ro-bust *adj.* full of strength and health; rich; vigorous **robustly** *adv.*, **robustness** *n.*
rock *n.* a hard naturally formed material; *Slang* one who is dependable
rock-er *n.* a curved piece, usually of wood, on which a cradle or chair rocks
rock-et *n.* a device propelled with the thrust from a gaseous combustion; *v.* to move rapidly
rode *v.* past tense of ride
ro-dent *n.* a mammal, such as a rat, mouse, or beaver having large incisors used for gnawing
ro-de-o *n.* a public show, contest, or demonstration of ranching skills, as riding and roping
roe *n.* the eggs of a female fish
rogue *n.* a scoundrel or dishonest person; an innocently or playful person
roll *v.* to move in any direction by turning over and over; to sway or rock from side to side, as a ship; to make a deep prolonged sound as thunder; *n.* a list of names; *Slang* a large amount of money
roll-er *n.* a cylinder for crushing, smoothing or rolling something; any of a number of various cylindrical devices
Roman Catholic Church *n.* the Christian church having priests and bishops and recognizing the Pope as its supreme head
ro-mance *n.* a love affair, usually of the young, characterized by ideals of devotion and purity; a fictitious story filled with extravagant adventures **romance** *v.* **romancer** *n.*
Ro-man nu-mer-al *n.* the letter or letters of the Roman system of numbering still used in formal contexts, as: V=5, X=10, L=50, C=100, D=500, M=1000
romp *v.* to run, play, or frolic in a carefree way
rood *n.* a measurement of land which equals 1/4 acre
rook-ie *n.* an untrained person; a novice or inexperienced person
room *n.* a section or area of a building set off by partitions or walls; *v.* to occupy or live in a room
roast *n.* a place or perch on which birds sleep or rest; a piece of meat which has been or is to be roasted
root *n.* the part of a plant which grows in the ground; *Math* a number which, when multiplied by itself, will produce a given quantity; *v.* to search or rummage for something; to turn up the earth with the snout, as a hog **rootless** *adj.*, **rootless** *adj.*
root beer *n.* a type of beverage which is made from herb and root extracts and this if fermented in sugar and yeast
root hair *n.* a type of filament which grows from the tip of a root
root-stock *n.* the source
rope *n.* a heavy cord of twisted fiber; **know the ropes** to be familiar with all of the conditions at hand **roping, roped** *v.*
rop-y *adj.* being stringy; being like a rope
ro-sa-ry *n., pl.* **-ies** a string of beads for counting prayers; a series of prayers
rose *n.* a shrub or climbing vine having sharp prickly stems and variously colored fragrant flowers
ro-se-ate *adj.* being rosy; optimistic; being colored like a rose
rose-bud *n.* a bud of a rose
rose--col-ored *adj.* being pink or rosy; cheerful
rose-mar-y *n.* a type of a green shrub which is located in the Mediterranean region and its leaves are used for seasoning
ro-sette *n.* an ornament gathered to resemble a rose and made of silk or ribbon
rose wa-ter *n.* a fragrant product made from rose petals, steeped in water, and used in cosmetics
rose-wood *n.* a type of tropical South American tree
Rosh Ha-sha-nah *n.* the Jewish New Year
ros-in *n.* a resin which is formed as the oil of turpentine is distilled from crude turpentine
ros-ter *n.* a list of names
ros-trum *n.* the platform that a speaker gives his speach from
ros-y *adj.* being the of roses; cheerful **rosiness** *n.*
rot *v.* to decay
ro-ta-ry *adj.* turning or designed to turn; of or relating to axial rotation
ro-tate *v.* to turn on an axis; to alternate something in sequence **rotatable** *adj.*, **rotation, rotator** *n.*, **rotatory** *adj.*
ROTC *abbr.* Reserve Officer's Training Corps
ro-tis-ser-ie *n.* a rotation device with spits for roasting food
ro-tor *n.* a rotating part of a mechanical device

rot-ten *adj.* decomposed; morally corrupt; very bad
ro-tund *adj.* plump; rounded
rouge *n.* a cosmetic coloring for the cheeks
rough *adj.* having an uneven surface; violent or harsh; *n.* the part of a golf course with tall grass; *v.* to treat roughly; *adv.* in a very rude manner
roughly *adv.*, **roughness** *n.*
rou-lette *n.* a gambling game in which players bet on which slot a small ball will land in
round *adj.* curved; circular; spherical; *v.* to become round; to surround; *adv.* throughout; prescribed duties, places, or actions **roundness** *n.*
rouse *v.* to awaken or stir up
route *n.* a course of travel; *v.* to send in a certain direction
rou-tine *n.* activities done regularly; *adj.* ordinary
rove *v.* to wander over a wide area
rover *n.*, **roving** *adj.*
row *n.* a number of things positioned next to each other; a continuous line; *v.* to propel a boat with oars
roy-al *adj.* relating to a king or queen
roy-al-ty *n.*, *pl.* **royalties** monarchs and or their families; a payment to someone for the use of his invention, copyright, or services
R.S.V.P. *abbr.* respondez s'il vous plait; please reply
rub *v.* to move over a surface with friction and pressure; to cause to become worn or frayed
rub-ber *n.* a resinous elastic material obtained from the coagulated and processed sap of tropical plants or produced synthetically **rubbery** *adj.*
rub-ber ce-ment *n.* a type of adhesive that is liquid and made of rubber
rub-ber-ize *v.* coat or cover something with rubber
rub-ber-neck *v.* to turn the head in order to see something
rub-ber plant *n.* type of plant that is found in East India and yields rubber
rub-ber stamp *n.* a type of rubber plate which is coated with ink and used for the purpose of leaving prints on paper or other objects
rub-bish *n.* worthless trash; nonsense
rubbishy *adj.*
rub-ble *n.* the pieces of broken material or stones
ru-bel-la *n.* the German measles
ru-bi-cund *adj.* state of being of a red color or hue
ru-bid-i-um *n.*, *Symbol* a silvery, highly reactive element symbolized by Rb
ru-bric *n.* a heading, title, or initial letter of a manuscript which appears in red
ru-by *n.*, *pl.* **rubies** a deep-red precious stone
ruck-us *n.*, *Slang* a noisy uproar, or commotion
rud-der *n.*, *Naut.* a broad, flat, hinged device attached to the stern of a boat used for steering
rud-dy *adj.* being red in color or hue
rude *adj.* discourteous; offensively blunt
ru-di-ment *n.* a first step, element, skill, or principle; *Biol.* an undeveloped organ
rue *v.* to repent
rue-ful *adj.* to be causing sorrow or remorse
ruff *n.* a stiff collar which has pleats in it
ruf-fi-an *n.* a lawless, rowdy person
ruf-fle *n.* a pleated strip or frill; a decorative band; *v.* to disturb or destroy the smoothness
rug *n.* a heavy textile fabric used to cover a floor
rug-by *n.* a game similar to football in which the ball is propelled toward the opponents goal by carrying or kicking
rug-ged *adj.* strong; rough; having an uneven or rough surface
ruggedness *n.*, **ruggedly** *adv.*
ru-in *n.* total destruction; *v.* to destroy
ruination *n.*, **ruinous** *adj.*
rule *n.* controlling power; an authoritative direction or statement which regulates the method of doing something; a standard procedure; *v.* to have control over; to make a straight line using a ruler; to be in command
rul-er *n.* a straight edge used for measuring; a person who rules as a sovereign
rul-ing *n.* a type of decision which is handed down by a judge in a trial
rum *n.* a type of liquor made from molasses and is distilled
rum-ba *n.* a type of dance which has a complex rhythm
rum-ble *v.* to make a heavy, continuous sound; *n.* a long deep rolling sound
ru-mi-nant *n.* a cud-chewing animal; as a cow, deer, sheep, or giraffe; an animal which chews something which was swallowed
ru-mi-nate *v.* to chew a cud; to ponder at length **rumination** *n.*, **ruminative** *adj.*, **ruminator** *n.*
rum-mage *v.* to look or search thoroughly by digging or turning things over; to ransack
rum-mage sale *n.* a sale of second-hand objects, conducted to make money
rum-my *n.* a card game in which each player tries to get rid of his hand in sequences of three cards or more of the same suit
ru-mor *n.* an uncertain truth which is circulated from one person to another; gossip; *v.* to speed by rumor
ru-mor-mon-ger *n.* one who aids in the spreading of rumors
rump. the fleshy hind quarter of an animal; the human buttocks
rum-ple *v.* to form into creases or folds; to wrinkle
rum-pus room *n.* a type of room which is used for parties
run *v.* to hurry busily from place to place; to move quickly in such a way that both feet leave the ground for a portion of each step; to make a rapid journey; to be a candidate seeking an office; to drain or discharge; *Law* to

be effective, concurrent with; *n.* a speed faster than a walk; a streak, as of luck; the continuous extent or length of something; an outdoor area used to exercise animals; in baseball, the method of scoring a point by running the bases and returning to home plate

run-a-bout *n.* a type of boat which is open

rund-let *n.* a type of barrel which is small in size

run-down *adj.* the state of being worn down

rung *n.* a bar or board which forms a step of a ladder

run-ner *n.* the person who runs in a race

run-ner--up *n.* a contestant who finishes second in a competition

run-ning *adj.* state of moving fast or rapidly

run-off *n.* that which runs off of something

run of the mill *adj.* ordinary; not special; average

runt *n.* the smallest animal in a litter

run-through *n.* the rehearsal of a play

run-way *n.* a path over which something runs; a platform which extends from a stage into the middle of an auditorium; a strip of paved ground for the landing and takeoff of airplanes

rup-ture *n.* a state of being broken; the act of bursting

ru-ral *adj.* pertaining to the country or country life

ru-ral-ize *v.* the act of moving to or living in the country or the rural area **ruralization** *n.*

ru-ral route *n.* a mail route which runs through the country

ruse *n.* a type of trick

rush *v.* to move quickly; to hurry; to be in a hurry

rus-set *n.* a reddish or yellowish brown color **russet** *adj.*

rust *n.* ferric oxide which forms a coating on iron material exposed to moisture and oxygen; deterioration through neglect; *v.* to form rust

rus-tic *adj.* characteristic of country life; *n.* a simple person **rustically** *adv.*

rus-ti-cate *v.* living and staying in the country or rural area **-tor, -icity** *n.*

rus-tle *v.* to move making soft sounds, such as those made by leaves of a tree

rus-tler *n.* a person who steals cattle

rust-proof *adj.* being unable to rust

rust-y *adj.* to be covered by rust **rustiness** *n.*, **rustily** *adv.*

rut *n.* an indented track made by the wheels of vehicles

ru-ta-ba-ga *n.* type of vegetable which belongs to the mustard family that produces a tuber

ru-the-ni-um *n.* a metallic element symbolized by Ru

rut-ty *adj.* a state of having many ruts

rye *n.* a cultivated cereal grass whose seeds are used to make flour and whiskey

S, s The nineteenth letter of the English alphabet.

sab-a-dil-la *n.* a type of mexican plant such as of the lily family whose seeds can be used for insecticides

sab-bat *n.* the midnight assembly of the diabolists

Sab-ba-tar-i-an *n.* a person who observes the Sabbath on Saturday

Sab-bath *n.* seventh day of the week; set apart as the day of worship for Jews and some Christians; Sunday, the first day of the week, a day set apart as the day of worship by most Christians

sab-bat-i-cal *adj.* to be relating to the sabbath

Sa-bel-li-an *n.* the member of the early Italian people which includes the Sabines and Samnited

sa-ber *n.* lightweight sword

sa-ber saw *n.* a type of light and protable electric saw

sa-ber--toothed tiger *n.* a type of extinct cant which was charaterized by the great development of the upper canines

sa-bine *n.* the member of the people of the Appennines of the ancient times

sa-ble *n.* carnivorous mammal having soft, black or dark fur

sa-ble-fish *n.* a type of large spiny-finned fish which is grey or black and of the Pacific coast

sa-bot *n.* the kind of wooden shoe which is worn by the people in various European countries

sab-o-tage *n.* act of malicious destruction

sab-o-teur *n.* a person who commits sabotage

sac *n.*, *Biol.* membranous pouch in an animal or plant, containing a liquid

sa-ca-huis-te *n.* a kind of bear grass that has long linear leaves and is used for forage

sac-cade *n.* a type of small rapid jerky movement of the eye

sac-cate *adj.* to have the form of a pouch

sac-cha-rate *n.* a tyhpe of a compound of sugar usually with a bivalent metal

sac-char-i-fy *v.* to break some compound into a simple sugar

sac-cha-rim-e-ter *n.* a kind of device which is used for the purpose of measuring the amount of sugar in a solution

sac-cha-rin *n.* white, crystalline powder used as a noncaloric sugar substitute

sac-cha-rine *adj.* pertaining to or like sugar

sac-cha-roi-dal *adj.* being of fine granular texture

sac-cha-rom-e-ter *n.* a type of hydrometer that has a special scale

sac-cu-lar *adj.* to be resembling a sac

sac-cu-late *adj.* to be formed of a series of saccular expansions

sac-cule *n.* a chamber which is the smaller of the membranous labyrinth of the ear

sac-er-do-tal *adj.* pertaining to the priesthood or to priests

sa-chem *n.* a kind of North American

Indian chief
sa-chet *n.* small bag of a sweet-smelling powder used to scent clothes
sack *n.* strong bag for holding articles *Slang* dismissal from a position or job
sack-ing *n.* the material that sacks are constructed from
sack out *v.* to go or to get into bed
sack race *n.* type of race where the contestants jump inside a sack to the finish line
sacque *n.* a type of infant jacket that is short and fastens at the neck
sa-cral *adj.* pertaining to the sacrum
sac-ra-ment *n.* a formal christian rite performed in a chruch, as a baptism
sac-ra-men-tal *adj.* pertaining to the character of the sacrament
sac-ra-men-tal-ism *n.* the use of the sacramental acts or rites
sa-crar-i-um *n.* a kind of ancient Roman shrine ;which holds sacred articles
sa-cred *adj.* dedicated to worship; holy **sacredly** *adv.*
sa-cred mush-room *n.* a type of New World hallucinogenic fungi
sac-ri-fice *n.* practice of offering something *v.* to give up something of value for something else **sacrificial** *adj.*
sad *adj.* marked by sorrow; unhappy; causing sorrow **sadly** *adv.*, **sadness** *n.*
sa-dism *n.*, *Psychol.* condition in which sexual gratification comes from inflicting pain on others; cruelty **sadist** *n.*, **sadistic** *adj.*, **-tically** *adv.*
sa-fa-ri *n.*, *pl.* **safaris** trip or journey; a hunting expedition in Africa
safe *adj.* secure from danger, harm, or evil; unharmed **safely** *adv.*, **safeness** *n.*
sag *v.* droop; to sink from pressure or weight **sag** *n.*
sa-ga *n.* long heroic story
sage *n.* person recognized for judgment and wisdom
said *v.* past tense of say
sake *n.* motive or reason for doing something
sa-la-ry *n.*, *pl.* **salaries** set compensation paid on a regular basis for services rendered **salaried** *adj.*
sale *n.* exchange of goods for a price; disposal of items at reduced prices **salable** *adj.*
sa-li-ent *adj.* projecting beyond a line; conspicuous
sa-li-va *n.* tasteless fluid secreted in the mouth which aids in digestion
sal-i-vate *v.* to secrete saliva
sal-i-va-tion *n.* action or process of salivating
Salk vaccine *n.* vaccine used to immunize against polio
sal-low *n.* a European willow with broad leaves
sal-ly *n.*, *pl.* **sallies.** sudden rush to launch an assault on something or someone
salm-on *n.*, *pl.* **salmons** a large game fish with pinkish flesh
sal-mo-nel-la *n.* bacteria associated with food poison
sa-lon *n.* large drawing room; a business establishment pertaining to fashion
sa-loon *n.* place where alcoholic drinks are sold
salt *n.* white crystalline solid, mainly sodium chloride
sal-ta-tion *n.* sudden movement; dancing
salt-cel-lar *n.* a small personal dish used to hold salt
salt-ed *adj.* seasoned with salt; preserved
sal-tine *n.* a thin, salted cracker
salt mine *n.* a mine from which salt is dug
salt-y *adj.* tasting or containing salt **saltiness** *n.*
sal-u-tar-y *adj.* wholesome; healthful; beneficial
sal-u-ta-tion *n.* an expression; a greeting of good will **salutational** *adj.*
sa-lu-ta-to-ry *n.* message of welcome delivered at com-mencements
sa-lute *v.* to show honor *n.* act of respect or greeting by saluting **saluter** *n.*
sal-u-tif-er-ous *adj.* referring to something healthful or beneficial
salv-a-ble *adj.* something that may be salvaged **salvability** *n.*
salve *n.* medicated ointment used to soothe the pain of a burn or wound
sal-va-tion *n.* preservation from destruction or danger **-al** *adj.*, **-ism** *n.*
salve *v.* to salvage, as a ship
sa-mar-i-um *n.* a metallic element
same *adj.* identical; exactly alike; similar; not changing
sam-ple *n.* portion which represents the whole *v.* to try a little; to examine
san-a-to-ri-um *n.*, *pl.* **sanatoriums** an institution for treating chronic diseases
sanc-ti-fy *v.* to make holy **sanctification** *n.*
sanc-tion *n.* permission from a person of authority; a penalty to ensure compliance
sanc-tu-ar-y *n.*, *pl.* **-ies.** sacred, holy place, as the part of a church, where services are held; a safe place; a refuge
sane *adj.* having a healthy, sound mind; showing good judgment **sanely** *adv.*, **sanity** *n.*
san-i-tar-y *adj.* free from bacteria or filth which endanger health
san-i-tize *v.* to make sanitary; to make clean or free of germs
sank *v.* past tense of sink
sa-pi-ent *adj.* wise
sap-phire *n.* a clear, deep-blue gem, used in jewelry
sar-casm *n.* insulting or mocking statement or remark **sarcastic** *adj.*, **sarcastically** *adj.*
sar-dine *n.* small edible fish of the herring family, often canned in oil
sar-don-ic *adj.* scornful; mockingly cynical
sass *n.*, *Slang* rudeness; a disrespectful manner of speech
sas-sa-fras *n.* dried root of a North American tree, used as flavoring
sat-el-lite *n.* natural or man-made object which orbits a celestial body
sat-in *n.* smooth, shiny fabric made of

silk, nylon, or rayon, having a glossy face and dull back

sat-ire *n.* use of mockery, sarcasm, or humor in a literary work to ridicule or attack human vice

sat-is-fac-tion *n.* anything which brings about a happy feeling; the fulfillment of a need, appetite, or desire

sat-is-fy *v.* fulfill; to give assurance to

sat-u-rate *v.* to make completely wet; to soak or load to capacity **saturation** *n.*

sau-cer *n.* small shallow dish for holding a cup

sav-age *adj.* wild; uncivilized; brutal *n.* vicious or crude person **-ly** *adv.*, **-ry** *n.*

save *v.* rescue from danger, loss, or harm; to prevent loss or waste; to keep for another time in the future

sav-ior *n.* one who saves Christ Savior

sa-voir--faire *n.* social skill

sa-vor *n.* the taste or smell of something to truly enjoy **savory** *adj.*

say *v.* speak aloud; to express oneself in words; to indicate; to show *n.* chance to speak

scab *n.* stiff, crusty covering which forms over a healing wound *Slang* person who continues to work while others are on strike

sca-bies *n.* contagious skin disease characterized by severe itching, caused by a mite under the skin

scald *v.* burn with steam or a hot liquid

scal-lop *n.* marine shellfish

scalp *n.* skin which covers the top of the human head

scal-pel *n.* small, straight knife with a narrow, pointed blade, used in surgery

scamp *n.* scheming or tricky person

scan *v.* examine all parts closely; to look at quickly **scan, scanner** *n.*

scan-dal *n.* something which brings disgrace when exposed to the public; gossip

scan-di-um *n.* metallic element symbolized by Sc.

scant *adj.* not plentiful or abundant; inadequate

scant-ling *n.* dimensions of material used in building

scap-u-la *n., pl.* **scapulae** one pair of large, flat, triangular bones which form the back of the shoulder **-ar** *adj.*

scar *n.* permanent mark which remains on the skin after a sore or injury has healed

scarce *adj.* not common or plentiful; rare **scarceness** *n.*

scar-la-ti-na *n.* mild form of scarlet fever

scar-let *n.* bright or vivid red

scat-ter *v.* spread around

scav-en-ger *n.* an animal, as a vulture, which feeds on decaying or dead animals or plant matter

sce-nar-i-o *n.* synopsis of a dramatic plot

scene *n.* view; the time and place where an event occurs; a public display of temper

scent *n.* smell; an odor *v.* to smell

sched-ule *n.* list or written chart which shows the times at which events will happen

scheme *n.* plan of action; an orderly combination of related parts; a secret plot

schol-ar *n.* student with a strong interest in learning

school *n.* place for teaching and learning

schoon-er *n.* sailing vessel with two or more masts

sci-ence *n.* study and theoretical explanation of natural phenomena in an orderly way; knowledge acquired through experience **scientific** *adj.*

scis-sors *pl., n.* a cutting tool

scle-ro-sis *n., pl.* **scleroses** a hardening of a part of the body, as an artery

scold *v.* accuse or reprimand harshly

sconce *n.* wall bracket for holding candles

scoop *n.* mall, shovel-like tool *v.* lift up or out

scoot *v.* go suddenly and quickly

scope *n.* range or extent of one's actions

scope *suff.* device for seeing or discovering

scorch *v.* burn slightly, changing the color and taste of something; to parch with heat

scorn *n.* contempt; disdain *v.* treat with scorn **scornful** *adj.*

scour *v.* clean by rubbing with an abrasive agent

scout *v.* observe activities in order to obtain information *n.* person whose job is to obtain information

scow *n.* a large barge with a flat bottom and square ends, used to transport freight, gravel, or other cargo

scowl *v.* make an angry look; to frown

scrab-ble *v.* scratch about frantically, as if searching for something **scrabbler** *n.*

scrag-gly *adj.* messy; irregular

scrap *n.* small section or piece

scrape *v.* rub a surface with a sharp object in order to clean *Slang* embarrassing situation

scratch *v.* mark or make a slight cut on; to mark with the fingernails

scrawl *n.* write or draw quickly and often illegibly

scraw-ny *adj.* very thin; skinny

scream *v.* utter a long, sharp cry, as of fear or pain *n.* long piercing cry

screech *v.* make a shrill, harsh noise **screech** *n.*

scrim-shaw *n.* art of carving designs on whale ivory or whalebone

scrip-ture *n.* sacred writing **Scriptures** the Bible

scroll *n.* roll of parchment or similar material used in place of paper

scro-tum *n., pl.* **scrota** external sac of skin which encloses the testes **scrotal** *adj.*

scrub *v.* clean something by rubbing; *Slang* cancel

scrump-tious *adj., Slang* delightful

scru-ple *n.* principle which governs one's actions **scrupulous** *adj.*

scu-ba *n.* apparatus used by divers for underwater breathing

scuff *v.* drag or scrape the feet while walking

sculp-tor *n.* person who creates statues from clay, marble, or other material
scum *n.* thin layer of waste matter floating on top of a liquid
scurf *n.* flaky dry skin; dandruff
scur-ry *v.* move quickly
scut-tle *n.* small opening with a movable lid in the hull of a ship
scythe *n.* tool with a long handle and curved, single-edged blade, used for cutting hay, grain and grass
sea *n.* body of salt water which covers most of the earth
seam *n.* line formed at the joint of two pieces of material
sear *v.* wither or dry up; to shrivel; to burn or scorch
search *v.* look over carefully
search, searcher *n.*
sea-son *n.* one of the four parts of the year **seasonal** *adj.*,
seat *n.* place or spot, as a chair, stool, or bench, on which to sit
se-cede *v.* withdraw from an organization or group **secessionist** *n.*
se-clude *v.* isolate
sec-ond *n.* unit of time equal to 1/60 of a minute; a very short period of time; an object which does not meet first class standards
sec-on-dar-y *adj.* not being first in importance; inferior
se-cret *n.* knowledge kept from others; a mystery
sec-re-tary *n., pl.* **secretaries** person hired to write and keep records for an executive or an organization
secretarial *adj.*
se-crete *v.* produce and give off; to release or discharge
sec-tion *n.* part or division of something; a separate part
sec-u-lar *adj.* relating to something worldly
se-cure *adj.* safe and free from doubt or fear; sturdy or strong; not likely to fail *v.* tie down, fasten, lock, or otherwise protect from risk or harm **-ly** *adv.*
se-cu-ri-ty *n., pl.* **securities** state of being safe and free from danger or risk; protection
se-date *adj.* serene and composed *v.* to keep or be kept calm through the use of drugs **sedative** *n.*
sed-i-ment *n.* material which floats in or settles to the bottom of a liquid
sedimentary *adj.*, **sedimentation** *n.*
se-duce *v.* tempt and draw away from proper conduct **seducer, seduction** *n.*, **sedative** *adj.*
see *v.* have the power of sight; to understand
seed *n.* fertilized plant ovule with an embryo, capable of producing an offspring
seek *v.* search for; to try to reach; to attempt **seeker** *n.*
seem *v.* appear to be; to have the look of **seeming** *adj.*
seep *v.* leak or pass through slowly
seepage *n.*
seer *n.* person who predicts the future
seg-ment *n.* any of the parts into which a thing is divided *v.* divide **-al** *adj.*
seg-re-gate *v.* separate or isolate from others
seg-re-ga-tion *n.* act of separating people based on the color of their skin
seine *n.* fishing net with weights on one edge and floats on the other
seize *v.* grasp or take possession forcibly
sel-dom *adv.* not often
se-lect *v.* to choose from a large group; to make a choice **selection** *adj.*, **-or**
se-le-ni-um *n.* element symbolized by Se.
self *n., pl.* **selves** complete and essential being of a person
self--de-fense *n.* act of defending oneself or one's belongings
sell *v.* exchange a product or service for money **seller** *n.*
se-man-tics *n.* study of word meanings and the relationships between symbols and signs
sem-a-phore *n.* system for signaling by using flags, lights or arms in various positions **semaphore** *v.*
se-men *n.* secretion of the male reproductive system, thick and whitish in color and containing sperm
se-mes-ter *n.* one of two periods of time in which a school year is divided
sem-i-an-nu-al *adj.* occurring twice a year
sem-i-co-lon *n.* punctuation mark (;) having a degree of separation stronger than a comma but less than a period
sem-i-nar *n.* course of study for students engaged in advanced study of a particular subject
sem-i-nar-y *n., pl.* **seminaries** school that prepares ministers, rabbis, or priests for their religious careers **-ian** *n.*
send *v.* cause something to be conveyed from one place to another; to dispatch
se-nile *adj.* having a mental deterioration often associated with old age
senility *n.*
sen-ior *adj.* being the older of two; of higher office or rank; referring to the last year of high school or college
seniority *n.*
sense *n.* sensation; feeling; the physical ability which allows a person to be aware of things around him; the five senses: taste, smell, touch, sight, and hearing
sen-si-bil-i-ty *n., pl.* **sensibilities** ability to receive sensations
sen-si-ble *adj.* capable of being perceived through the senses; sensitive; having good judgment **sensibly** *adv.*
sen-si-tive *adj.* capable of intense feelings **sensitivity** *n.*
sen-sor *n.* device which responds to a signal
sen-su-al *adj.* preoccupied with the gratification of the senses
sensuality *n.*, **sensualous** *adj.*
sent *v.* past tense of send
sen-tence *n.* series of words arranged to express a single complete thought; a prison term for a convicted person
sen-ti-ment *n.* feelings of affection; an

idea, opinion, thought, or attitude based on emotion rather than reason
sentimental *adj.*
sen-ti-nel *n.* who guards
se-pal *n.* one of the leaves which forms a calyx in a flower
sep-a-rate *v.* divide or keep apart by placing a barrier between; to go in different directions; to set apart from others; *adj.* single; individual
separation *n.*
se-quence *n.* set arrangement; a number of connected events; the regular order
ser-e-nade *n.* music performed as a romantic expression of love
se-rene *adj.* calm; peaceful **serenity** *n.*
serf *n.* slave owned by a lord during the Middle Ages
serge *n.* twilled, durable woolen cloth
se-ri-al *adj.* arranged in a series with one part presented at a time
se-ries *pl. n.* number of related items which follow one another
se-ri-ous *adj.* sober; grave; not trivial; important **seriously** *adv.*,
ser-mon *n.* message or speech delivered by a clergyman during a religious service
ser-pent *n.* snake
ser-rate *adj.* having sharp teeth; having a notched edge **serration** *n.*
se-rum *n., pl.* **serums** *or* **sera** yellowish fluid part of the blood which remains after clotting
ser-vant *n.* one employed to care for someone or his property
serve *v.* to take care of; to wait on; to prepare and supply; to complete a term of duty
serv-ice *n.* help given to others; a religious gathering; the military
ses-a-me *n.* tropical plant and its edible seeds
ses-sion *n.* meeting or series of meetings; a meeting set for a specific purpose
set *v.* to put or place; to cause to do; to regulate; to adjust; to arrange; to place in a frame or mounting
set-tee *n.* small couch or bench with arms and a back
set-tle *v.* arrange or put in order; to restore calm
sev-er *v.* cut off or separate **severance** *n.*
sev-er-al *adj.* being more than one or two, but not many; being separate
severally *adv.*
se-vere *adj.* strict; stern; hard; not fancy; extremely painful
severely *adv.*, **severity** *n.*
sew *v.* fasten or fix; to make stitches with thread and needle
sew-age *n.* solid waste material carried away by a sewer
sew-er *n.* conduit or drain pipe used to carry away waste
sex *n.* one of two divisions, male and female, into which most living things are grouped; sexual intercourse
sex-tet *n.* group of six people or things
shab-by *adj.* worn-out; ragged
shack *n.* small, poorly built building
shad *n., pl.* **shad** *or* **shads** edible fish which swims upstream to spawn
shad-ow *n.* area from which light is blocked; a shaded area **shadowy** *adj.*
shaft *n.* long, narrow part of something; a beam or ray of light; a long, narrow underground passage
shal-low *adj.* not deep; lacking intellectual depth
sham *n.* person who is not genuine but pretends to be; a cover for pillows
sham-ble *v.* walk while dragging one's feet
shame *n.* painful feeling of embarrassment or disgrace brought on by doing something wrong; dishonor; disgrace
shank *n.* portion of the leg between the ankle and the knee; a cut of meat from the leg of an animal, such as a lamb
shape *n.* outline or configuration of something; the form of a human body
share *n.* part or portion given to or by one person; one of equal parts, as the capital stock in a corporation *v.* divide or distribute portions **sharer** *n.*
shark *n.* large marine fish which eats other fish and is dangerous to man
sharp *adj.* having a thin edge or a fine point; capable of piercing or cutting; clever; quick-witted; painful
shat-ter *v.* burst suddenly into pieces
shave *v.* remove a thin layer; to cut body hair, as the beard, by using a razor; to come close to
she *pron.* female previously indicated by name
shear *v.* trim, cut, or remove the fleece or hair with a sharp instrument **-er** *n.*
sheath *n.* cover or case for a blade, as a sword
shed *v.* pour out or cause to pour; to throw off without penetrating; to cast off or leave behind, especially by a natural process
sheen *n.* luster
sheep *n., pl.* **sheep** cud-chewing thick-fleeced mammal, widely domesticated for meat and wool
sheer *adj.* very thin; almost transparent; complete; absolute; very steep, almost perpendicular
sheet *n.* large piece of cloth for covering a bed; a single piece of paper
shelf *n., pl.* **shelves** flat piece of wood, metal, plastic, or other rigid material attached to a wall or within another structure, used to hold or store things
shell *n.* hard outer covering of certain organisms
shel-ter *n.* something which gives protection or cover
shelve *v.* put aside; to place on a shelf
shep-herd *n.* person who takes care of a flock of sheep
sher-bet *n.* sweet frozen dessert made with fruit juices, milk or water, egg white, and gelatin
sher-iff *n.* high ranking lawenforcement officer
shield *n.* piece of protective metal or wood held in front of the body; anything which serves to conceal or

protect; a badge or emblem
shield *v.*, **shielder** *n.*
shift *n.* group of people who work together; a woman's loose-fitting dress; *v.* change direction or place
shim-mer *v.* shine with a faint sparkle **shimmerer** *n.*, **shimmery** *adj.*
shin *n.* front part of the leg from the knee to the ankle
shine *v.* give off light; to direct light; to polish shoes
shiner *n.* black eye
shin-gle *n.* thin piece of material, as asbestos, used to cover a roof or side of a house **shingler** *n.*
shin-gles *pl.*, *n.*, *Pathol.* acute, inflammatory viral infection, characterized by skin eruptions along a nerve path
ship *n.* large vessel for deep-water travel or transport; *v.* send or transport
ship-yard *n.* place where ships are built or repaired
shirt *n.* garment worn on the upper part of the body
shiv-er *v.* tremble or shake with excitement or chill **shiver** *n.*, **shivery** *adj.*
shoe *n.* outer cover for a foot
shone *v.* past tense of shine
shoot *v.* kill or wound with a missile, as a bullet, fired from a weapon; to discharge or throw rapidly
shore *n.* land bordering a body of water
short *adj.* having little height or length; less than normal in distance, time, or other qualities; less than the needed amount; **shorts** underpants or outerpants which end at the knee or above; **shortage** a lack in the amount needed; **short-change** give less than the correct amount, as change for money; **short circuit** an electrical malfunction
short-en-ing *n* a fat, such as butter, used to make pastry rich and light
shot *n.* discharging of a gun, rocket, or other device; an attempt; a try; an injection
should *v.* past tense of shall, used to express obligation, duty, or expectation
shoul-der *n.* part of the body located between the neck and upper arm
should-n't *contr.* should not
shout *v.* to yell; *n.* a loud cry
shov-el *n.* tool with a long handle and a scoop, used for picking up material or for digging
show *v.* put within sight; to point out; to explain; to put on display
shrank *v.* past tense of shrink
shrap-nel *n.*, *pl.* **shrapnel** large shell containing metal fragments
shred *n.* a narrow strip or torn fragment; a small amount
shrew *n.* a small mouse-like mammal, having a narrow, pointed snout
shriek *n.* loud, sharp scream or noise
shrill *adj.* high-pitched, sharp sound
shrimp *n.*, *pl.* **shrimp** or **shrimps** small, edible shellfish
shrine *n.* place for sacred relics; a place considered sacred because of an event or person associated with it
shrink *v.* make or become less or smaller; to pull back from; to flinch; *Slang* psychiatrist
shroud *n.* a cloth in which a body is wrapped for burial; *v.* to cover
shrug *v.* to raise the shoulders briefly to indicate doubt or indifference **shrug** *n.*
shrunk *v.* past tense of shrink
shuck *n.* outer husk that covers an ear of corn
shud-der *v.* tremble uncontrollably, as from fear
shuf-fle *v.* drag or slide the feet; to mix together in a haphazard fashion; to rearrange or change
shun *v.* avoid deliberately
shut *v.* move a door, drawer, or other object to close an opening; to lock up; to cease or halt operations
shy *adj.* bashful; timid; easily frightened
sib-ling *n.* one of two or more children from the same parents
sick *adj.* in poor health; ill; nauseated; morbid **sickness** *n.*
sick-le *n.* tool with a curved blade attached to a handle, used for cutting grass or grain
side *n.* surface between the front and back or top and bottom of an object
SIDS *abbr.*, *n.* Sudden Infant Death Syndrome; an unexpected death of a seemingly healthy baby
siege *n.* the action of surrounding a town or port in order to capture it; a prolonged sickness
si-er-ra *n.* rugged chain of mountains or hills
si-es-ta *n.* rest or short nap
sieve *n.* meshed or perforated device which allows small particles to pass through but which holds back larger particles; a device for separating liquids from solids **sieve** *v.*
sigh *v.* to exhale a long, deep breath, usually when tired, sad, or relieved **sigh** *n.*
sight *n.* the ability to see with the eyes; the range or distance one can see
sign *n.* a piece of paper, wood, metal, etc., with information written on it; a gesture that tells or means something
sig-nal *n.* a sign which gives a warning; the image or sound sent by television or radio
sig-na-ture *n.* the name of a person, written by that person; a distinctive mark which indicates identity
sig-nif-i-cance *n.* quality of being important
sig-ni-fy *v.* express or make known by a sign; to indicate **signification** *n.*, **significant** *adj.*
si-lence *n.* state or quality of being silent; quiet
silent *adj.* making no sound; not speaking; mute
sil-i-con *n.* second most common chemical element, found only in combination with another substance
silk *n.* soft, thread-like fiber spun by silkworms; thread or fabric made from silk
sil-ly *adj.* foolish; lacking good sense,

seriousness, or substance **silliness** *n.*
sil-ver *n.* soft, white metallic element used in tableware, jewelry, and coins
sim-i-lar *adj.* almost the same, but not identical
sim-mer *v.* to cook just below boiling; to be near the point of breaking, as with emotion
sim-ple *adj.* easy to do or understand; not complicated; ordinary
sim-plic-i-fy *n.* state of being easy to understand
sim-pli-fy *v.* to make easy or simple **simplification** *n.*
sim-u-late *v.* to have the appearance, effect, or form of **simulation, simulator** *n.*
si-mul-ta-ne-ous *adj.* occurring at exactly the same time **simultaneously** *adj.*
sin *n.* breaking of a religious law or a law of God
since *adv.* at a time before the present; *prep.* during the time later than
sin-cere *adj.* honest; not deceitful; genuine; true **sincerely** *adv.*, **-ity** *n.*
sing *v.* to use the voice to make musical tones; to make a humming or whistling sound **singer** *n.*
singe *v.* to slightly burn the surface of something
sin-gle *adj.* of or referring to only one, separate; individual; unmarried
sin-gu-lar *adj.* separate; one; extraordinary; denoting a single unit, thing or person
sink *v.* to submerge beneath a surface; to go down slowly
si-nus *n.*, *pl.* **sinuses** *Anat.* body cavity; one of eight air spaces in the bones of the face which drain into the nasal cavity
sip *v.* drink in small amounts
si-phon *also* **syphon** *n.* tube through which liquid from one container can be drawn into another by forced air pressure **siphon** *v.*
sir *n.* respectful term used when addressing a man
si-ren *n.* whistle which makes a loud wailing noise, as a warning or signal
sit *v.* rest the body with the weight on the buttocks; to cover eggs for hatching
siz-a-ble *adj.* large in size or dimensions
size *n.* measurement or dimensions of something
siz-zle *v.* make a hissing sound, as of fat frying
skate *n.* device with rollers or a blade which attaches to the shoe and allows one to glide over ice or roll over a wooden or cement surface
skate-board *n.* narrow piece of wood with wheels attached
skel-e-ton *n.* framework of bones that protects and supports the soft tissues and organs
skep-tic *n.* person who doubts or questions **skepticism** *n.*, **skeptical** *adj.*, **skeptically** *adv.*
sketch *n.* rough drawing or outline; a brief literary composition **sketchy** *adj.*
skew *v.* turn or slant; *n.* slant
skid *v.* slide to the side of the road; to slide along without rotating
skill *n.* ability gained through practice; expertise **skilled** *adj.*
skim *v.* remove the top layer; to remove floating matter
skimp *v.* economize; to hold back **-y** *adj.*
skin *n.* tough, outside covering of man and some animals; the outside layer of a vegetable or fruit
skirt *n.* piece of clothing that extends down from the waist
skull *n.* bony part of the skeleton which protects the brain
sky *n.*, *pl.* **skies** upper atmosphere above the earth; the celestial regions
slab *n.* thick piece or slice
slack *adj.* not taut or tense; sluggish; lacking in strength
slain *v.* past tense of slay
slam *v.* shut with force; to strike with a loud impact
slam-mer *n.*, *Slang* jail or prison
slan-der *n.* false statement that deliberately does harm to another's reputation **slanderous** *adj.*
slang *n.* informal language that contains made-up words or common words used in a different or uncommon way
slant *v.* lie in an oblique position; to slope; to report on something giving only one side or viewpoint
slap *n.* sharp blow with an open hand
slash *v.* cut with a fast sweeping stroke; to reduce or limit greatly *n.* long cut
slate *n.* fine grained rock that splits into thin layers, often used as a writing surface or roofing material **slate** *v.*
slaugh-ter *v.* kill livestock for food; to kill in great numbers; *Slang* to soundly defeat **slaughterer** *n.*
slave *n.* person held against his will and made to work for another
sled *n.* vehicle with runners, used to travel on snow or ice
sleek *adj.* smooth and shiny; neat and trim **sleekly** *adv.*
sleep *n.* natural state of rest for the mind and body; *v.* to rest in sleep
sleet *n.* rain that is partially frozen; a combination of snow and rain
sleeve *n.* part of a garment which covers the arm; a case for something
sleigh *n.* vehicle mounted on runners, usually pulled over ice and snow by horses
slen-der *adj.* slim; inadequate in amount **slenderly** *adv.*
slept *v.* past tense of sleep
slice *n.* thin cut; a portion or share
slick *adj.* smooth and slippery; quick; smart; clever
slick-er *n.* raincoat made of yellow oilcloth
slight *adj.* minor in degree; unimportant **slightly** *adv.*
slim *adj.* slender; meager; not much **slimness** *n.*
slime *n.* wet, slippery substance **-y** *adj.*
sling *n.* piece of material, as leather, or a strap which secures something; a piece

of fabric worn around the neck used to support an injured hand or arm
slip *v.* move in a smooth, quiet way; to fall or lose one's balance; *Slang* to become less active, alert, or strong
slith-er *v.* slide or slip in an indirect manner; to move like a snake **slithery** *adj.*
sliv-er *n.* thin, narrow piece of something that has been broken off **sliver** *v.*
slob-ber *v.* dribble from the mouth **slobber** *n.*
slo-gan *n.* phrase used to express the aims of a cause
slope *v.* slant upward or downward
slosh *v.* to splash in a liquid, as water **sloshy** *adj.*
slot *n.* narrow, thin groove or opening; *Slang* place or scheduled time for an event
sloth *n.* laziness; a slow mammal found in South America
slouch *n.* drooping or sagging posture; a lazy person
slow *adj.* moving at a low rate of speed; requiring more time than usual; not lively; sluggish; not interestin; *adv.* at less speed; in a slow manner **slowly** *adv.*, **slowness** *n.*
slug *n.* slow animal related to the snail; a bullet or a lump of metal
sluice *n.* man-made ditch used to move water
slum *n.* crowded urban neighborhood marked by poverty
slum-ber *v.* to sleep; to doze; *n.* **sleep slumberer** *n.*
slump *v.* fall or sink suddenly
slur *v.* to slide over without careful consideration; to pronounce unclearly; *n.* an insult
slush *n.* melting snow **slushy** *adj.*
slut *n.* woman of bad character; a prostitute
sly *adj.* cunning; clever; sneaky **slyly** *adv.*, **slyness** *n.*
smack *v.* slap; press and open the lips with a sharp noise **small** *adj.* little in size, quantity, or extent; unimportant **smallness** *n.*
small-pox *n.* acute, contagious disease marked by high fever and sores on the skin
smart *adj.* intelligent; clever
smash *v.* break into small pieces; to ruin
smear *v.* spread or cover with a sticky, oily, or moist substance; *Slang* discredit one's reputation
smell *v.* notice an odor by means of the olfactory sense organs; *n.* odor
smelt *v.* heat metals or their ores to a high temperature in order to obtain pure metallic constituents
smile *n.* grin
smirk *v.* smile in a conceited way **smirk, smirker** *n.*
smite *v.* hit with great force using the hand
smock *n.* loose-fitting garment worn as a protection for one's clothes while working
smog *n.* mixture of smoke and fog **smoggy** *adj.*
smoke *n.* cloud of vapor released into the air when something is burning
smolder *v.* burn slowly without a flame and with little smoke **smolder** *n.*
smooth *adj.* not irregular; flat; without lumps; *adv.* evenly; *v.* to make less difficult
smor-gas-bord *n.* buffet meal with a variety of foods to choose from
smother *n.* failure to receive enough oxygen to survive; *v.* conceal **smothery** *adj.*
smudge *v.* soil by smearing with dirt; *n.* dirty mark or smear
smug *adj.* complacent with oneself; self-satisfied
smug-gle *v.* import or export goods illegally without paying duty fees **smuggler** *n.*
snack *n.* small amount of food taken between meals
snag *n.* stump or part of a tree; a pull in a piece of fabric
snake *n.* any of a large variety of scaly reptiles, having a long tapering body; *Slang* an untrustworthy person
snap *v.* break suddenly with a sharp, quick sound; to fly off under tension
snare *n.* anything that entangles or entraps; a trap with a noose, used to catch small animals
snarl *v.* speak in an angry way; to cause confusion; to tangle or be tangled
snatch *v.* seize or grasp something suddenly
sneak *v.* act or move in a quiet, sly way; *n.* person who acts in a secret, underhanded way
sneer *v.* express scorn by the look on one's face
sneeze *v.* expel air from the nose suddenly and without control
sniff *v.* inhale through the nose in short breaths with a noise
snip *v.* cut off in small pieces and with quick strokes
snipe *n., pl.* **snipe or snipes** bird with a long bill which lives in marshy places; *v.* to shoot at people from a hidden position **sniper** *n.*
snob *n.* a person who considers himself better than anyone else
snoop *v., Slang* prowl or spy; *n.* one who snoops
snore *v.* to breath with a harsh noise while sleeping **snorer** *n.*
snor-kel *n.* tube that extends above the water, used for breathing while swimming face down
snort *n.* force air through the nostrils with a loud, harsh nois; *Slang* inhale a narcotic through the nose
snow *n.* vapor that forms crystals in cold air and falls to the ground in white flakes **snow** *v.*
snub *v.* treat with contempt or in an unfriendly way
snuff *v.* draw air in through the nostrils **snuff** *n.*
snug *adj.* warm, pleasant, comfortable and safe

so *adv.* to a degree or extent as a result; likewise; also; indeed; *conj.* in order that; therefore
soap *n.* cleansing agent made of an alkali and a fat, and used for washing
soar *v.* glide or fly high without any noticeable movement; to rise higher than usual
sob *v.* weep with short, quick gasps
so-ber *adj.* not drunk or intoxicated; serious; solemn **soberly** *adv.*, **soberness** *n.*
soc-cer *n.* game in which two teams of eleven men each try to kick a ball into the opposing team's goal
so-cia-ble *adj.* capable of friendly social relations; enjoying the company of others **sociableness** *n.*, **sociably** *adv.*
socialism *n.* system in which people as a whole, and not individuals, control and own all property
so-ci-e-ty *n.*, *pl.* **societies** people working together for a common purpose; companionship
so-ci-ol-o-gy *n.* study of society and the development of human society **sociologist** *n.*
sock *n.* short covering for the foot, ankle, and lower part of the leg; a hard blow
sock-et *n.* hollow opening into which something is fitted
so-da *n.* sodium carbonate; a flavored, carbonated drink
sod-den *adj.* completely saturate; very wet; lacking in expression
so-di-um *n.* metallic element symbolized by Na.
sod-om-y *n.* anal sexual intercourse
so-fa *n.* upholstered couch with arms and a back
soft *adj.* not stiff or hard; not glaring or harsh; mild or pleasant; gentle in sound
soft-ware *n.* in computer science, data, as routines, programs and languages, which is essential to the operation of computers
sog-gy *adj.* saturated with a liquid or moisture
sol-ace *n.* comfort in a time of trouble, grief, or misfortune **solacer** *n.*
so-lar *adj.* relating to or connected with the sun; utilizing the sun for power or light; measured by the earth's movement around the sun
so-lar-i-um *n.*, *pl.* **-ia** *or* **-ums** a glassed-in room exposed to the sun's rays
solar system *n.* the sun and the planets, asteroids, and comets that orbit it
sol-der *n.* alloy, as lead or tin, which is melted and used to mend or join other pieces of metal
soldier *n.* enlisted person who serves in the military
sole *n.* bottom of a foot or shoe; single, the only one
sol-emn *adj.* very serious; characterized by dignity; sacred **-ity**, **-ness** *n.*
so-lic-it *v.* try to obtain; to ask earnestly; to beg or entice a person persistently **solicition** *n.*
sol-id *adj.* having a definite firm shape and volume; having no crevices; not hollow; having height, weight and length; with-out interruption **-ify** *v.*
sol-i-taire *n.* single gemstone set by itself; a card game played by one person
sol-i-tude *n.* act of being alone or secluded; isolation
so-lo *n.* musical composition written for and performed by one person or played by one instrument
sol-u-ble *adj.* capable of being dissolved **solubility** *n.*
solve *v.* find the answer to **solvable** *adj.*
som-ber *adj.* dark; gloomy; melancholy
some *adj.* being an indefinite number or quantity; unspecified; *pron.* undetermined or indefinite quantity
some-day *adv.* an unspecified future time
somehow *adv.* in a way
som-nam-bu-lism *n.* act of walking during sleep
son *n.* male offspring
song *n.* piece of poetry put to music; the act or sound of singing
son-ic *adj.* pertaining to sound or the speed of sound
son-net *n.* poem made up of fourteen lines
soon *adv.* in a short time; in the near future; quickly
soot *n.* black powder generated by incomplete combustion of a fuel, such as coal or wood
soothe *v.* make comfortable; to calm
sop *v.* soak up a liquid; to absorb
so-pran-o *n.*, *pl.* **sopranos** *or* **soprani** highest female singing voice
sor-did *adj.* filthy, very dirty; morally corrupt
sore *adj.* tender or painful to the touch, as an injured part of the body; severe or extreme
so-ror-i-ty *n.*, *pl.* **sororities** social organization for women
sor-rel *n.* any of several herbs with sour-tasting leaves, used in salads
sor-row *n.* anguish; mental suffering; an expression of grief **-ful** *adj.*, **-fully** *adv.*
sor-ry *adj.* feeling or showing sympathy or regret; worthless
sort *n.* collection of things having common attributes or similar qualities
sought *v.* past tense of seek
soul *n.* spirit in man that is believed to be separate from the body and is the source of a person's emotional, spiritual, and moral nature
sound *n.* sensation received by the ears from air, water, noise, and other sources; *v.* make a sound; *adj.* free from flaw, disease, or damage **soundless** *adj.*, **soundly** *adv.*
soup *n.* liquid food made by boiling meat and/or vegetables, in water
sour *adj.* sharp to the taste; acid; unpleasant **sourly** *adv.*
source *n.* any point of origin or beginning
south *n.* direction opposite of north; *adv.* to or towards the south; *adj.* from the south **southerly** *adj.*, **southerner** *n.*
south-paw *n.* left-handed person

sou-ve-nir *n.* item kept as a remembrance of something or someplace
sov-er-eign *n.* ruler with supreme power; a monarch
soviet *adj.* having to do with the Soviet Union
sow *v.* scatter or throw seeds on the ground for growth; *n.* a female pig
space *n.* unlimited area in all directions in which events occur and have relative direction; an interval of time; the area beyond the earth's atmosphere
spade *n.* tool with a flat blade used for digging, heavier than a shovel **spade** *v.*
spa-ghet-ti *n.* pasta made in long, thin pieces
span *n.* the section between two limits or supports; *v.* to extend across
spank *v.* strike or slap the buttocks with an open hand as a means of punishment
spare *v.* to refrain from injuring, harming or destroying; to refrain from using
spark *n.* glowing or incandescent particle, as one released from a piece of burning wood or one produced by means of friction; *v.* to give off sparks
spar-kle *v.* emit or reflect light
spar-row *n.* small bird with grayish or brown plumage
sparse *adj.* scant; thinly distributed **sparsely** *adv.*
spasm *n.* involuntary muscle contraction
spat-ter *v.* scatter or splash a liquid
spat-u-la *n.* kitchen utensil with a flexible blade for mixing soft substances
spawn *n.* eggs of fish or other water animals, as oysters or frogs; *v.* to lay eggs
speak *v.* utter words; to express a thought in words
speak-er *n.* person who speaks, usually before an audience
spear *n.* weapon with a long shaft and a sharply pointed head; *v.* strike, pierce
spear-mint *n.* mint plant yielding an aromatic oil used as a flavoring
spe-cial-ist *n.* person, such as a doctor, who devotes his practice to one particular field
spe-cial-ize *v.* focus one's efforts or interests in one field of activity or study
spec-i-men *n.* sample; a representative of a particular thing
speck *n.* small particle, mark, or spot
spec-ta-cle *n.* public display of something unusual **spectacled** *adj.*
spec-trum *n.*, *Physics* band of colors produced when light is passed through a prism or other means, separating the light into different wave lengths
spec-u-late *v.* reflect and think deeply; to take a chance on a business venture in hopes of making a large profit
speech *n.* ability, manner, or act of speaking; a talk before the public
speed *n.* rate of action or movement; quickness; rapid motion; *Slang* a drug used strictly as a stimulant
spell *v.* say out loud or write in proper order the letters which make up a word; to relieve
spellbind *v.* fascinate or hold as if by magic
spend *v.* give out; to use up; to pay; to exhaust
sperm *n.* male cell of reproduction; semen
sphere *n.*, *Math* round object with all points the same distance from a given point; globe, ball, or other rounded object **spherical** *adj.*
sphinx *n.*, *pl.* **sphinxes** *or* **sphinges** ancient Egyptian figure having the head of a man, male sheep, or hawk and the body of a lion; a very mysterious person
spice *n.* pungently aromatic plant used as flavoring in food, as nutmeg, cinnamon, pepper, or curry **spicy** *adj.*
spi-der *n.* eight-legged arachnid
spike *n.* large, thick nail
spill *v.* allow or cause something to flow or run out of something
spin *v.* draw out fibers and twist into thread; to run something around and around **spinner** *n.*
spin-ach *n.* widely cultivated plant with green leaves which are used in salads
spine *n.* spinal column; the backbone; the back of a bound book
spin-ster *n.* unmarried woman; an old maid
spir-it *n.* vital essence of man, considered divine in origin the mind; the Holy Ghost
spir-i-tual *adj.* of, like, or pertaining to the nature of spirit; relating to religion; sacred **-ity** *n.*, **-lze** *v.*
spite *n.* hatred or malicious bitterness; a grudge; ill will **-ful** *adj.*, **-fully** *adv.*
spit-toon *n.* a cuspidor or receptacle for spit
spitz *n.* small dog with a tail which curls over its back
splash *v.* spatter a liquid; to wet or soil with liquid; to make a splash **splashy** *adj.*
splash-down *n.* landing of a missile or spacecraft in the ocean
spleen *n.*, *Anat.* highly vascular, flattened organ which filters and stores blood, located below the diaphragm
splen-did *adj.* illustrious; magnificent
splice *v.* join together by wearing, overlapping, and binding the ends **splice** *n.*
splint *n.* device used to hold a fractured or injured limb in the proper position for healing **splint** *v.*
splotch *n.* discolored and irregularly shaped spot
splutter *v.* make a slight, short spitting sound **splutter** *n.*
spoil *v.* destroy the value, quality, or usefulness
spoke *n.* one of the rods that serve to connect and support the rim of a wheel; *v.* past tense of speak
sponge *n.* any of a number of marine creatures with a soft, porous skeleton which soaks up liquid **spongy** *adj.*

spon-ta-ne-ous *adj.* done from one's own impulse without apparent external cause **spontaneousity** *n.*, **spontaneously** *adv.*
spoof *n.* deception; nonsense
spook *n.*, *Slang* a ghost; *v.* scare or frighten **spooky** *adj.*
spool *n.* small cylinder for holding thread, tape or wire
spoon *n.* eating or cooking utensil; a shiny metallic fishing lure *Slang* make love, as by kissing or caressing **-ful** *n.*
spo-rad-ic *adj.* occurring occasionally or at irregular intervals **sporadically** *adv.*
spore *n.*, *Bot.* reproductive singlecelled structure produced by nonflowering plants; any cell capable of developing into a new organism, seed, or germ
sport *n.* interesting diversion; a particular game or physical activity with set rules
sport-ing *adj.* of or relating to risk taking or gambling; displaying sportsmanship
sports-man-ship *n.* fair play; the ability to win or lose graciously
spot *n.* a small area that differs in size, portion, or color; *Slang* a dangerous or difficult situation
spot-light *n.* powerful light thrown directly at one area
spouse *n.* one's husband or wife; a marriage partner
spout *v.* pour out forcibly, as under pressure; to cause to shoot forth **spouter** *n.*
sprain *n.* wrenching or twisting of a muscle or joint
sprawl *v.* sit or lie in an ungraceful manner; to develop haphazardly **sprawler** *n.*
spray *n.* liquid dispersed in a fine mist or droplets; *v.* disperse or send forth in a spray **sprayer** *n.*
spread *v.* unfold or open fully; to apply or distribute over an area; to force apart; to extend or expand **spread** *v.*
spree *n.* excessive indulgence in an activity; a binge
spright-ly *adj.* Vivacious, lively **sprightliness** *n.*
sprin-kle *v.* scatter in small particles or drops; to rain in small drops **sprinkle** *n.*
sprint *n.* short, fast race **sprinter** *n.*
sprock-et *n.*, *Mech.* tooth-like projection from the rim of a wheel
sprung *v.* past tense of spring
spry *adj.* quick; brisk; energetic
spud *n.*, *Slang* potato
spur *n.* sharp, projecting device worn on a rider's boot, used to nudge a horse
sput-nik *n.* unmanned Soviet earth satellite
sput-ter *v.* throw off small particles in short bursts; to speak in a confused or agitated manner
spu-tum *n.*, *pl.* **sputa** saliva or mucus that is expectorated
spy *n.*, *pl.* **spies** secret agent who obtains information; one who watches other people secretly
squab-ble *v.* engage in a petty argument
squad *n.* small group organized to perform a specific job
squan-der *v.* spend extravagantly or wastefully
square *n.* parallelogram with four equal sides; an implement having a T or L shape used to measure right angles; *Math.* to square root *n.* number which when multiplied by itself gives the given number
squash *n.* edible fruit of the gourd family; a sport played in a walled court with a hard rubber ball and racket
squat *v.* sit on the heels; to crouch; to settle on a piece of land in order to obtain legal title
squaw *n.* American Indian woman
squeak *v.* utter a sharp, penetrating sound
squea-mish *adj.* easily shocked or nauseated **squeamishly** *adv.*
squeeze *v.* press together; to extract by using pressure
squint *v.* view something through partly closed eyes
squirm *n.* twist the body in a wiggling motion **squirm** *v.*
squir-rel *n.* rodent with gray or brown fur, having a long bushy tail and dark eyes
squirt *v.* eject in a thin stream or jet; to wet with a squirt
sta-bi-lize *v.* make firm; to keep from changing **stabilizeation, stabilizer** *n.*
sta-ble *n.* building for lodging and feeding horses or other farm animals
stac-ca-to *adj.*, *Music* Marked by sharp emphasis **staccato** *n. & adv.*
stack *n.* large pile of straw or hay; any systematic heap or pile; a chimney
sta-di-um *n.*, *pl.* **-dia** large structure for holding athletic events or other large gatherings
staff *n.*, *pl.* **staffs** *or* **staves** pole or rod used for a specific purpose; the people employed to assist in the day-to-day affairs of running a business.
stag *n.* adult male of various animals; a man who attends a social gathering without a woman companion
stag-ger *v.* walk unsteadily; to totter
stag-nant *adj.* not flowing; standing still; foul from not moving; inactive **stagnate** *v.*
stair *n.* step or a series of steps
staircase *n.* series or a flight of steps that connect one level to another
stake *n.* bet placed on a game of chance; a sharpened piece of wood for driving into the ground
stale *adj.* having lost freshness; deteriorated; lacking in interest; dull
stalk *n.* main axis of a plant *v.* approach in a stealthy manner
stall *n.* enclosure in a barn, used as a place to feed and confine animals; a sudden loss of power in an engine; a booth used to display and sell *v.* to delay
stal-lion *n.* uncastrated, fully grown male horse
sta-men *n.*, *pl.* **stamens** *Bot.* pollen-

producing organs of a flower
stam-i-na *n.* physical or moral endurance
stam-mer *v.* make involuntary halts or repetitions of a sound or syllable while speaking
stamp *v.* put the foot down with force; to imprint or impress with a die, mark, or design *n.* a postage stamp
stam-pede *n.* sudden rush of panic, as of a herd of horses or cattle
stance *n.* posture or position of a standing person or animal
stand *v.* to be placed in or maintain an erect or upright position; to take an upright position; to remain unchanged; to maintain a conviction; to resist *n.* a device on which something rests; a small booth for selling or displaying items
stand-ard *n.* model which stands for or is accepted as a basis for comparison
stand-ing *n.* status, reputation, or achievement; a measure of esteem *adj.* unchanging
sta-ple *n.* principle commodity grown in an area; a major element; a metal fastener designed to hold materials such as cloth or paper **staple** *v.*, **stapler** *n.*
star *n.*, *Astron.* self-luminous body that is a source of light; any of the celestial bodies that can be seen in the night sky; a symbol having five or six points and resembling a star
star-board *n.* right side of a ship or boat
starch *n.* nutrient carbohydrates that are found in foods such as rice and potatoes *v.* to stiffen clothing by using starch **starchiness** *n.*, **starchy** *adj.*
stare *v.* look with an intent, direct gaze **stare, starer** *n.*
stark *adj.* bare; total; complete; forbidding in appearance **starkness** *n.*, **starkly** *adv.*
star-ling *n.* common black or brown bird
star-tle *v.* cause a sudden surprise; to shock **startle** *n.*
starve *v.* suffer or die from not having food; to suffer from the need of food, love, or other necessities **starvation** *n.*
state *n.* situation, mode, or condition of something; a nation; the governing power or authority of; one of the subdivisions or areas of a federal government, as the United States *v.* make known verbally
stat-ic *adj.* not moving *n.* random noise heard on a radio **-ally** *adv.*
sta-tion *n.* place where someone or something is directed to stand; a scheduled stopping place; the place from which radio and television programs are broadcast
sta-tion-ar-y *adj.* not movable; unchanging
sta-tion-er-y *n.* writing paper and envelopes
sta-tis-tic *n.* estimate using an average or mean on the basis of a sample taken; numerical data
stat-ue *n.* form sculpted from wood, clay, metal, or stone
stave *n* narrow piece of wood used in forming part of a container, as a barrel
stay *v.* remain; to pause; to maintain a position; to halt or stop; to postpone or delay an execution *n.* short visit
stead *n.* position, place, or job of another
stead-y *adj.* firmly placed, fixed or set; not changing
steal *v.* take another person's property; to move in a sly way; to move secretly *Slang* real bargain
steam *n.* water in the form of vapor; the visible mist into which vapor is condensed by cooling **steam** *v.*, **steamy** *adj.*
steel *n.* various mixture of iron, carbon, and other elements; a strong material that can be shaped when heated **steely** *adj.*
stem *n.* main stalk of a plant; the main part of a word to which prefixes and suffixes may be added *v.* stop or retard the progress or flow of something
sten-cil *n.* form cut into a sheet of material, as cardboard or plastic, so that when ink or paint is applied, the pattern will reproduce on paper or another material
ste-nog-ra-phy *n.* skill of writing in shorthand **stenographer** *n.*
step *n.* single completed movement in walking, dancing, or running; the distance of such a step; the part of a ladder that one places the feet on in ascending or descending *Music* musical scale; a degree
ste-re-o *n.* record player with stereophonic sound
ster-e-o-type *n.* conventional opinion or belief; a metal printing plate
ster-ile *adj.* free from microorganisms; sanitary; unable to reproduce
ster-ling *n.* alloy of 92.5% silver and another metal, as copper
stern *adj.* inflexible; harsh *n.* rear of a boat or ship **sternly** *adv.*, **sternness** *n.*
ster-num *n.*, *pl.* **-nums** *or* **-na** long, flat bone located in the chest wall, connecting the collarbones and the cartilage of the first seven pairs of ribs **sternumal** *adj.*
steth-o-scope *n.* instrument used to listen to the internal sounds of the body
stew *v.* cook slowly; to simmer; to boil *n.* dish of stewed meat and potatoes *Slang* to worry
stew-ard *n.* manager of another's financial affairs; a person responsible for maintaining household affairs; a male attendant on an airplane or ship
stick *n.* slender piece of wood; a club, rod, or walking stick *v.* put a hole in something; to pierce; to cling; to become jammed
stiff *adj.* not flexible; not easily bent; awkward *n.*, *Slang* dead body **-ness** *n.*
sti-fle *v.* suffocate; to cut off; to suppress; to keep back
stig-ma *n.*, *pl.* **-mata** *or* **-mas** mark of disgrace **stigmata** part of a flower where pollen is deposited at pollina-

tion **stigmatic** *adj.*
still *adj.* silent; calm; peaceful; until now or another time *adv.* nevertheless **stillness** *n.*
stillbirth *n.* birth of a dead fetus
stilt *n.* one of a pair of long poles with foot supports, used for walking
stim-u-lant *n.* agent which arouses or accelerates physiological activity
stim-u-late *v.* excite to a heightened activity; to quicken **stimulation** *n.*
stim-u-lus *n., pl.* **-li** something that excites to action
sting *v.* prick with something sharp; to feel or cause to feel a smarting pain; to cause or feel sharp pain, either physical or mental *n.* act of stinging; the injury or pain caused by the stinger of a bee or wasp **stinger** *n.*
stin-gy *adj.* not giving freely; cheap
stink *v.* give off a foul odor that is highly offensive
stip-u-late *v.* settle something by agreement; to establish conditions of agreement **stipulation** *n.*
stir *v.* mix a substance by moving round and round; to agitate or provoke
stir-rup *n.* loop extending from a horse's saddle, used to support the rider's foot
stitch *n.* in sewing, a single loop formed by a needle and thread; the section of loop of thread
stock *n.* supply of goods kept on hand; animals living on a farm; a share in ownership, as in a company or corporation; the raw material or the base used to make something *v.* provide with stock *adj.* regular, common, or typical
stock-ade *n.* barrier placed around a fort for protection
stock-ing *n.* knitted covering for the foot
stock-y *adj.* sturdy and compact; built sturdily
stole *n.* long, narrow scarf that is usually worn around a woman's shoulders, as a mink stole *v.* past tense of steal
stom-ach *n., Anat.* organ into which food passes from the esophagus; one of the primary organs of digestion *v.* tolerate or stand; to put up with
stone *n.* rock; compacted earth or mineral matter; a gem or jewel; the seed or pit of certain fruits *Med.* hard rock that forms inside a body organ, as the kidney **stoned** to be overcome by an excessive amount of alcohol or drugs
stood *v.* past tense of stand
stool *n.* seat without a backrest and arms; a small version of this on which to rest the feet; a bowel movement
stoop *v.* bend the body forward and downward from the waist *n.* porch attached to a house
stop *v.* cease; to halt; to refrain from moving, operating, or acting; to block or obstruct
stor-age *n.* act of storing or keeping; in Computer Science, the part of a computer in which all information is held; the memory
store *n.* business offering merchandise for sale; a supply to be used in the future *v.* supply; to accumulate
stork *n.* large, wading bird
storm *n.* atmospheric condition marked by strong winds with rain, sleet, hail, or snow *v.* charge or attack with a powerful force
sto-ry *n., pl.* **-ies.** narration of a fictional tale or account; a lie; a level in a building or house
stout *adj.* strong; sturdy; substantial; courageous
stove *n.* apparatus in which oil, electricity, gas, or other fuels are consumed to provide the heat for cooking
stow *v.* pack or put away
strad-dle *v.* sit or stand with the legs on either side of something; to favor both sides of an issue **-er** *n.*
straight *adj.* being without bends, angles, or curves; upright; erect; honest; undiluted; unmodified; heterosexual **straightly** *adv.*
strain *v.* stretch beyond a proper limit; to injure by putting forth too much effort; to pass through a sieve to separate small particles from larger ones
strait *n.* narrow passageway which connects two bodies of water
strand *n.* land that borders a body of water; one of the threads that are twisted together to form a rope *v.* leave in a difficult situation
strange *adj.* not previously known or experienced;odd; peculiar; inexperienced; alien **-ly** *adv.*
stran-ger *n.* person unknown; a newcomer; an alien
stran-gle *v.* kill by choking **strangler** *n.*
strap *n.* long, narrow strip of leather or other material used to secure objects
strat-e-gy *n., pl.* **-ies** skillful planning and managing of an activity **-gic** *adj.*
stra-tum *n., pl.* **-ta** *or* **-tums** horizontal layer, as of the earth's crust
straw *n.* stalk of dried, threshed grain; a slender, plastic or paper straw used to suck up a liquid
straw-ber-ry *n.* low plant with white flowers and red fruit; the fruit of this plant
stray *v.* roam or wander *n.* lost or wandering animal or person *adj.* lost **strayer** *n.*
streak *n.* narrow line or stripe that is different from the surrounding area; a run of good or bad luck *v.* rush or move rapidly; to make a streak **streaky** *adj.*
stream *n.* small body of flowing water; a steady or continuous succession or procession. *v.* flow in or like a stream
street *n.* public thoroughfare in a town or city with buildings on either or both sides
strength *n.* quality of being strong; power in general; degree of concentration or potency
strengthen *v.* grow strong or stronger
stren-u-ous *adj.* necessitating or charac-

terized by vigorous effort or exertion **strenuously** *adv.*

stress *n.* special significance; an emphasis given to a specific syllable, word, action, or plan; strain or pressure **stressful** *adj.*

stretch *v.* extend fully; to extend forcibly beyond proper limits; to prolong *n.* state or act of stretching **stretchable, stretchy** *adj.*

strew *v.* scatter about

strick-en *adj.* suffering, as from an emotion, illness, or trouble

strict *adj.* holding to or observing rules exactly; imposing absolute standards **strictly** *adv.*, **-ness** *n.*

stride *v.* walk with a long, sweeping step

strike *v.* hit with the hand; to ignite, as with a match; to afflict suddenly with a disease; to discover; to conclude or make; to stop working as a protest against something or in favor of rules or demands presented to an employer

string *n.* strip of thin twine, wire, or catgut used on stringed musical instruments; a series of related acts, items, or events; in Computer Science, data arranged in an ascending or descending sequence according to a command within the data

strin-gent *adj.* of or relating to strict requirements; marked by obstructions or scarcity **stringently** *adv.*

strip *v.* take off the outer covering; to divest or pull rank; to remove one's clothes; to rob

stripe *n.* streak, band, or strip of a different color or texture; a piece of material or cloth worn on the sleeve of a uniform to indicate rank, award, or service

stroke *n.* movement of striking; a sudden action with a powerful effect; a single movement made by the hand or as if by a brush or pen *Path.* sudden interruption of the blood supply to the brain *v.* pass the hand over gently

stroll *v.* walk in a slow, leisurely way

strong *adj.* exerting or possessing physical power; durable; difficult to break **strongly** *adv.*

struc-ture *n.* construction made up of a combination of related parts **structure** *v.*, **structural** *adj.*

strug-gle *v.* put forth effort against opposition

strych-nine *n.* extremely poisonous alkaloid derived from certain plants, used to kill rodents and as a neural stimulant

stub *n.* short, projecting part; the short end of something after the main part has been removed or used

stub-born *adj.* inflexible; difficult to control, handle, or manage

stuc-co *n., pl.* **-coes** *or* **-cos** fine plaster used to coat exterior walls and to decorate interior walls

stud *n.* upright post, as in a building frame, to which sheets of wallboard or paneling are fastened; a small removable button used as an ornament; a male horse used for breeding **stud** *v.*

stu-dent *n.* person who studies at a school or college

stu-di-o *n.* place of work for an artist, photographer, or other creative person; a place for filming movies

stud-y *n., pl.* **-ies** process of applying the mind to acquire knowledge

stum-ble *v.* trip and nearly fall over something; to come upon unexpectedly

stump *n.* part of a tree which remains after the top is cut down *v.* puzzle or be puzzled; to walk heavily; to campaign

stun *v.* render senseless by or as if by a blow

stu-pen-dous *adj.* astonishing or highly impressive **-ness** *n.*, **stupendously** *adv.*

stu-pid *adj.* slow in apprehension or understanding **stupidity** *n.*

stur-dy *adj.* possessing robust strength and health **-ily** *adv.*, **sturdiness** *n.*

stur-geon *n.* large freshwater fish highly valued as a source of caviar

stut-ter *v.* speak with involuntary repetitions of sound **stutter** *n.*

sty *n., pl.* **sties** inflammation of the edge of an eyelid

style *n.* method, manner, or way of performing, speaking, or clothing; elegance, grace, or excellence in performance or appearance **style** *v.*, **stylish** *adj.*

suave *adj.* ingratiating; smoothly pleasant in manner

sub- *prefix* beneath, under, or below

sub-con-scious *adj.* below the level of consciousness

sub-due *v.* bring under control by influence, training, persuasion or force

sub-ject *n.* word in a sentence that defines a person or thing; a person who is under the control of another's governing power **subjection** *n.*

sub-jec-tive *adj.* taking place within, relating to or preceding from an individual's emotions or mind **subjectively** *adv.*, **subjectivity** *n.*

sub-ma-rine *adj.* operating or existing beneath the surface of the sea *n.* ship that travels underwater **submariner** *n.*

sub-merge *v.* plunge under the surface of the water

sub-mit *v.* give into or surrender to another's authority **submission, -tal** *n.*, **submissive** *adj.*

sub-or-di-nate *adj.* being of lower class or rank; minor; inferior **-ation** *n.*, **subordinative** *adj.*

sub-poe-na *n.* legal document requiring a person to appear in court for testimony

sub-se-quent *adj.* following in time, place, or order **subsequently** *adv.*, **subsequentness** *n.*

sub-side *v.* move to a lower level or sink; to become less intense

sub-sid-i-ar-y *adj., pl., n.* **-ies.** providing assistance in a lesser capacity **subsidiaries** *pl., n.*

sub-si-dy *n., pl.* **-dies.** financial aid granted directly to a private commercial enterprise from the government
sub-sist *v.* have continued existence
sub-soil *n.* layer of earth that comes after the surface soil
sub-stance *n.* matter or material of which anything consists
sub-sti-tute *n.* something or someone that takes the place of another
sub-ten-ant *n.* a person who rents property from a tenant
sub-ter-ra-ne-an *adj.* located, situated, or operating underground
sub-ti-tle *n.* explanatory title, as in a document, book, etc.; a written translation that appears at the bottom of a foreign motion picture screen
sub-tract *v.* deduct or take away from
sub-trop-i-cal *adj.* pertaining to regions adjacent to the tropics
sub-urb *n.* residential community near a large city **suburban** *adj.*
sub-way *n.* underground electrical-hypowered train, usually used as a means of transportation
suc-ceed *v.* accomplish what is attempted; to come next or to follow
suc-cess *n.* achievement of something intended or desired; attaining wealth, fame, or prosperity
suc-ces-sion *n.* act or process of following in order; sequence; series; the order, sequence or act by which something changes hands
suc-ces-sive *adj.* following in order or sequence **-ly** *adv.*, **-ness** *n.*
suc-cu-lent *adj.* juicy; full of juice or sap **-ence** *n.*, **succulently** *adv.*
such *adj.* of this or that kind or thing; a great degree or extent in quality *pron.* of a particular degree or kind; a person or thing of such
suck *v.* pull liquid in the mouth by means of a vacuum created by the lips and tongue *n.* action of sucking
su-crose *n.* sugar obtained from the sugar beet or sugar cane
suc-tion *n.* process or act of sucking
sud-den *adj.* happening very quickly without warning or notice; sharp; abrupt; marked by haste **-ly** *adv.*
suds *pl., n.* bubbles or soapy water **sudsy** *adv.*
suede *n.* leather with a soft, napped finish
su-et *n.* hard fat around the kidney and loins of sheep
suf-fer *v.* feel pain or distress; to sustain injury, loss, or damage **sufferer** *n.*
suf-fi-cient *adj.* as much that is needed or desired
suf-fix *n.* form affixed to the end of a word
suf-fo-cate *v.* kill by depriving something or someone of oxygen **suffocation** *n.*
sugar *n.* sweet, watersoluble, crystal-like carbohydrate *Slang* nickname for someone
sug-gest *v.* give an idea for action or consideration; to imply; hint or intimate
sug-ges-tion *n.* act of suggesting; a slight insinuation; hint
su-i-cide *n.* act of taking one's own life **suicidal** *adj.*
suit *n.* set of articles, as clothing, to be used or worn together; in cards, one of the four sets: spades, hearts, clubs, and diamonds that make up a deck *v.* meet the requirements of; to satisfy
sul-fur *also* **sulphur** *n.* light, yellow, nonmetallic element occurring naturally in both combined and free form, used in making matches, gunpowder and medicines
sulk *v.* to be sullenly silent
sul-len *adj.* ill-humored, melancholy; gloomy; depressing
sul-try *adj.* hot and humid; muggy
sum *n.* result obtained by adding; the whole amount, quantity, or number; summary
sum-ma-ry *n., pl.* **-ries.** giving the sum or substance *adj.* a statement covering the main points **summarily** *adv.*
sum-mer *n.* warmest of the four seasons, following spring and coming before autumn
sum-mit *n.* top and highest point, degree, or level
sum-mons *n., pl.* **-monses** order or command to perform a duty; a notice to appear at a certain place
sun *n.* star around which other planets of the solar system orbit; the energy, visible light, and heat, that is emitted by the sun; sunshine **sunny** *adj.*
Sun-day *n.* Christian holy day; the first day of the week
sun-down *n.* time of day the sun sets
sunk-en *adj.* submerged or deeply depressed in
su-per *adj.* exceeding a norm; in excessive intensity or degree; surpassing most others; superior in rank, status or position; excellent *n. Slang* superintendent of a building
su-perb *adj.* of firstrate quality **superbly** *adv.*
su-per-fi-cial *adj.* pertaining to a surface; concerned only with what is not necessarily real
su-pe-ri-or *adj.* of higher rank, grade, or dignity *n.* person who surpasses another in rank or excellence **-ity** *n.*, **superiorly** *adv.*
su-per-la-tive *adj.* of the highest degree of excellence; pertaining to the degree of comparison of an adverb or adjective that shows extreme extent or level **superlatively** *adv.*
su-per-nat-u-ral *adj.* order of existence beyond the natural world; pertaining to a divine power **supernaturaly** *adv.*
su-per-sede *v.* take the place of; to set aside
su-per-son-ic *adj., Aero.* characterized by a speed greater than that of sound
su-per-sti-tion *n.* belief founded, despite evidence that it is irrational; a belief, resulting from faith in magic or chance
su-per-vise *v.* have charge in directing the work of other people **supervision,**

supervisor *n.*, **supervisory** *adj.*
sup-ple-ment *n.* part that compensates for what is lacking **-ary, -tal** *adj.*
sup-ply *v., pl., n.* **-plies.** provide with what is needed; to make available **supplier** *n.*
sup-port *v.* bear or hold the weight of; to tolerate; to give assistance or approval *n.* act of supporting **supportable, -ive** *adj.*, **-er** *n.*
sup-pose *v.* think or assume as true; to consider probable **supposed** *adj.*, **supposedly** *adv.*
su-preme *adj.* of the highest authority, rank, or power
sur-charge *n.* extra fee added to the cost of something; to overcharge
sur-face *n.* exterior or outside boundary of something
surge *v.* increase suddenly *n.* large swell of water
sur-geon *n.* physician who practices surgery
sur-ger-y *n., pl.* **-ies.** branch of medicine in which physical deformity or disease is treated by an operative procedure
sur-mise *v.* guess; conjecture
sur-mount *v.* overcome; be at the top
sur-name *n.* person's family last name
sur-pass *v.* go beyond the limits of; to be greater than
sur-plus *n.* amount beyond what is needed
sur-prise *v.* come upon unexpectedly or suddenly; to cause to feel amazed or astonished **-er** *n.*, **surprisingly** *adv.*
sur-ren-der *v.* give up or yield possession or power *n.* act of surrendering
sur-ro-gate *n.* person who puts himself in the place of another **surrogate** *v.*
sur-round *v.* extend around all edges of something; to enclose or shut in
sur-veil-lance *n.* close observation kept over one, especially as a suspect
sur-vive *v.* continue to exist; to outlast; to outlive
su-shi *n.* Japanese dish of thin slices of fresh, raw fish
sus-pect *v.* have doubt or distrust; to have a suspicion or inkling of someone or something **suspect** *n.*
sus-pense *n.* feeling of being insecure or undecided, resulting from uncertainty
sus-pi-cion *n.* instance of suspecting something wrong without proof
sus-tain *v.* hold up and keep from falling; to suffer or undergo an injury
su-ture *n.* stitching together or joining the edges of an incision or cut
swad-dle *v.* wrap closely, using a long strip of flannel or linen
swag-ger *v.* walk with a proud or conceited air
swarm *n.* large number of insects, as bees; a large group of persons or things **swarm** *v.*, **swarmer** *n.*
swat *v.* hit something with a sharp blow
sway *v.* move or swing from right to left or side by side; to exert influence or control *n.* dominating power
swear *v.* make an affirmation under oath
sweet *adj.* having a sugary, agreeable flavor; arousing pleasant emotions; a beloved or dear person
swerve *v.* turn aside from the regular course
swift *adj.* moving with great speed; accomplished or occurring quickly **swiftly** *adv.*, **swiftness** *n.*
swin-dle *v.* cheat out of property or money; to practice fraud **swindler** *n.*
swirl *v.* move with a whirling, rotating motion **swirl** *n.*
swiv-el *n.* coupling device, ring, or pivot that allows attached parts to rotate or move freely **swivel** *v.*
syl-la-ble *n., Phonet.* word or part of one that consists of a single vocal impulse, usually consisting of one or more vowels or consonants
sym-bol *n.* something that stands for or represents something else
sym-me-try *n., pl.* **-tries.** balance in form, size, and position of parts that are on two sides of an axis
sym-pa-thet-ic *adj.* having or showing kindness or sympathy for others
sym-pa-thy *n., pl.* **-thies.** mutual understanding or affection during a time of sadness or loss
syn-a-gogue *n.* place for Jewish worship and prayer
syn-chro-nize *v.* operate or take place at the same time
syn-di-cate *n.* organization set up to carry out business transactions
syn-o-nym *n.* word that means the same or nearly the same as another
syn-op-sis *n., pl.* **-ses.** shortened statement or narrative
syn-tax *n.* way in which words are put together or arranged to form sentences and phrases
syn-the-sis *n.* the combination of elements or parts to form a whole
syn-the-size *v.* to produce or combine by synthesis
syn-the-siz-er *n.* electronic equipment used to produce and control sound
syn-ton-ic *adj.* adaptive and normally responsive to the interpersonal or social environment **syntonically** *adv.*
syph-i-lis *n.* infectious venereal disease transmissible by direct contact and usually progressing in severity
syph-i-lol-o-gy *n.* a branch medicine dealing with syphilis
sy-ringe *n.* medical instrument used to inject or draw fluids
syr-up *n.* sticky, thick, sweet liquid, used as a topping for food
sys-tal-ic *adj.* to be marked by regular dilatation and contraction
sys-tem *n.* method or way of doing something **systemless** *adj.*
sys-to-le *n., Physiol.* regular rhythmic contraction of the heart that pumps blood through the aorta and pulmonary artery **systolic** *adj.*
sy-zy-gial *adj.* to be pertaining to syzygy
syz-y-gy *n.* a configuration of three celestial bodies in one gravitational system such as the moon, the sun, and earth when an eclipse is taking place

T, t The twentieth letter of the English alphabet.

tab *n.* strip, flap, or small loop that projects from something *slang* bill or total, as for a meal

tab-a-nid *n.* member of large bloodsucking insects such as the horse fly

tab-ard *n.* a type of domestic cat that has a coat which is mottled and striped

tab-er-na-cle *n.* portable shelter or structure used by the Jews during their journey out of Egypt

ta-bes *n/* the wasting that comes with or is accompanying a chronic disease

ta-bes for-sa-lis *n.* disease of the spinal cord

ta-bla *n.* a type of drum which is usually used in pairs of different sizes in the Hindu music

tab-la-ture *n.* a tabular surface or structure

ta-ble *n.* article of furniture

table-cloth *n.* a type of covering that is placed on the top of tables for protection or for decoration

ta-ble-ful *n.* the amount that a table is able to accomodate

ta-ble--hop *v.* to go from one table to another in order to talk with one's friends such as in a restaurant

ta-ble-land *n.* braod flat land; a plateau

table salt *n.* the salt that is suitable for use in cooking and at the table for the food

table-spoon *n.* a unit of measure; a large spoon for serving food

table sugar *n.* a type of white sugar which is granulated and used in foods

tab-let *n.* pad used for writing

ta-ble talk *n.* the conversation which is informal and takes place at the dinner table

ta-ble ten-nis *n.* a type of game that is like lawn tennis and is played on a table top with a plastic ball and wooden paddles

ta-ble-top *n.* a top of a table

ta-ble-ware *n.* the utensils such as forks, knives, and plates that are used on the table to eat with

ta-ble wine *n.* a type of wine that is wserved with the food and does not have more than 14 percent alcohol

tab-loid *n.* small newspaper

ta-boo *n.* custom or rule against doing, using, or mentioning something

tab-u-lar *adj.* pertaining to or arranged in a table or list

ta-chis-to-scope *n.* instrument for testing visual perception

ta-chom-e-ter *n.* instrument for measuring velocity and speed

tach-y-car-di-a *adj.* rapid heart movement or action

ta-chyg-ra-phy *n.* the art of shorthand; stenography

tac-it *adj.* understood; expressed or implied nonverbally; implicit

tac-i-turn *adj.* speaking infrequently **taciturnity** *n.*

tack-le *n.* equipment used for fishing or other sports or occupations **tackled** *v.*

tacky *adj.* slightly sticky; shabby; lacking style or good taste

ta-co *n., pl.* **-cos** type of Mexican or Spanish food made of a tortilla

tact *n.* having the ability to avoid what would disturb or offend someone

tac-tic *n.* way or method of working toward a goal

tad *n.* small boy; an insignificant degree or amount

tae-ni-a-sis *n.* a sickness due to the presence of tapeworms

taf-fe-ta *n.* stiff, smooth fabric of rayon, nylon, or silk **taffetized** *adj.*

taff-rail *n.* rail around the stern of a boat or ship

taf-fy *n.* candy made from sugar, butter and flavoring

taf-fy pull *n.* an informal party where guest make and pull taffy

tag *n.* piece of plastic, metal, paper, or other material that is attached to something in order to identify it; children's game **tagger** *n.*

tag-board *n.* very sturdy cardboard used to make posters, and signs

tail *n.* posterior extremity, extending from the end or back of an animal **Tails** opposite side of a coin from heads

tai-lor *n.* one whose profession is making, mending, and altering clothing *v.* adapt for a specific purpose

taint *v.* spoil, contaminate, or pollute *n.* blemish or stain

take *v.* seize or capture; to get possession of; to move to a different place; to choose

talc *n.* soft, fine-grained, smooth mineral used in making talcum powder

tale *n.* story or recital of relating events that may or may not be true

tal-ent *n.* aptitude, or ability of a person **talented** *adj.*

talk *v.* communicate by words or speech; to engage in chatter or gossip

tall *adj.* greater than average height; of a designated or specified height; imaginary, as a tall tale **tallness** *n.*

tal-low *n.* hard fat rendered from sheep or cattle, used to make candles, lubricants, and soap **tallow** *adj.*

tal-ly *n., pl.* **-ies** record or counting of money, amounts, or scores

tal-on *n.* long, curved claw found on birds or animals

tam-bou-rine *n.* percussion instrument made of a small drum with jingling metal disks around the rim

tame *adj.* not wild or ferocious; domesticated or manageable *v.* make docile or calm **tamely** *adv.*, **tamer**, **tameness** *n.*

tam-per *v.* change, meddle, or alter something; to use corrupt measures; to scheme **tamperproof** *adj.*, **tamperer** *n.*

tan-dem *n.* any arrangement that involves two or more things, animals, or persons arranged one behind the other

tang *n.* sharp, distinct taste, smell, or quality

tan-gent *n.* line that touches a curved line but does not intersect or cross it; a sudden change from one course to another **tangency** *n.*, **tangential** *adj.*
tan-ger-ine *n.* small citrus fruit
tan-gi-ble *adj.* capable of being appreciated or felt by the sense of touch **tangibly** *adv.*
tan-gle *v.* mix, twist, or unite in a confused manner making separation difficult **tangle, tanglement** *n.*
tank *n.* large container for holding or storing a gas or liquid **tankful** *n.*
tan-ta-lize *v.* tease or tempt by holding or keeping something just out of one's reach **tantalizer** *n.*
tan-ta-lum *n.* metallic element symbolized by Ta
tan-trum *n.* fit; an outburst or a rage of bad temper
tap *v.* strike repeatedly, usually while making a small noise; to strike or touch gently
tape *n.* narrow strip of woven fabric
ta-per *n.* very slender candle *v.* become gradually smaller or thinner at one end
tap-es-try *n., pl.* **-ies** thick fabric woven with designs and figures
tap-i-o-ca *n.* bead-like substance used for thickening and for puddings
taps *n. pl. Mil.* bugle call that signals lights out, also sounded at memorial and funeral services
tar-dy *adj.* late; not on time **tardily** *adv.*, **tardiness** *n.*
tar-get *n.* object marked to shoot at; an aim or goal
tar-iff *n.* duty or tax on merchandise coming into or going out of a country
tar-nish *v.* become discolored or dull; to lose luster; to spoil **tarnishable** *adj.*
tar-ot *n.* set of 22 cards used for fortune-telling, each card showing a virtue, an elemental force, or a vice
tar-pau-lin *n.* sheet of waterproof canvas used as a protective covering
tar-ry *v.* linger, or delay
tart *adj.* sharp; sour; cutting, biting in tone or meaning **tartly** *adv.*, **tartness** *n.*
task *n.* bit of work, usually assigned by another; a job
tas-sel *n.* ornamental decoration made from a bunch of string or thread
taste *n.* ability to sense or determine flavor in the mouth; a personal liking or dislike **tasteful, tasteless** *adj.*, **taster** *n.*
tat-tle *v.* reveal the secrets of another by gossiping
tattle-tale *n.* one who betrays secrets concerning others; a person, usually a child, who informs on others
tat-too *n.* permanent design or mark made on the skin by pricking and inserting an indelible dye **tattooer** *n.*
taught *v.* past tense of teach
taut *adj.* tight; emotionally strained **tautly** *adv.*, **tautness** *n.*
tau-tol-o-gy *n., pl.* **-ies** redundancy; a statement which is an unnecessary repetition of the same idea
tav-ern *n.* inn; an establishment or business licensed to sell alcoholic beverages **taverner** *n.*
tax *n.* payment imposed and collected from individuals or businesses by the government *v.* strain
tax-ex-empt *adj.* exempted from tax
tax-i *v.* move along the ground or water surface on its own power before taking off
taxi-cab *n.* vehicle for carrying passengers for money
tax-i-der-my *n.* art or profession of preparing, stuffing, and mounting animal skins **taxidermist** *n.*
tea *n.* small tree or bush which grows where the climate is very hot and damp; a drink made by steeping the dried leaves of this shrub in boiling water
teach *v.* communicate skill or knowledge; to give instruction **teaching** *n.*, **teachable** *adj.*
teach-er *n.* person who teaches; one who instructs
team *n.* two or more players on one side in a game; a group of people trained to work together; two or more animals harnessed to the same implement
tear *v.* become divided into pieces; to separate; to rip into parts or pieces
tear *n.* fluid secreted by the eye to moisten and cleanse *v.* to cry **teary** *adj.*
tease *v.* make fun of; to bother; to annoy
tech-ne-tium *n.* metallic element symbolized by Tc.
tech-ni-cal *adj.* expert; derived or relating to technique; related to industry or mechanics **technically** *adv.*
tech-nique *n.* technical procedure or method of doing something
tech-nol-o-gy *n., pl.* **-ies** application of scientific knowledge to serve man in industry, commerce, medicine and other fields
te-di-ous *adj.* boring; taking a long time **tediously** *adv.*
teem *v.* swarm or crowd; to abound; to be full of
teens *pl., n.* ages between 13 and 19; the years of one's life between 13 and 19
teeth *pl., n.* plural of tooth
tel-e-cast *n.* television broadcast **telecast** *v.*
tel-e-gram *n.* message sent or received by telegraph
tel-e-graph *n.* system for communicating; a transmission sent by wire or radio
te-lep-a-thy *n.* communication by means of mental processes rather than ordinary means **telepathic** *adj.*, **telepathist** *n.*
tel-e-phone *n.* system or device for transmitting conversations by wire
tel-e-pho-to *adj.* relating to a camera lens which produces a large image of a distant object **telephotograph** *n.*
tel-e-scope *n.* instrument which contains a lens system which makes distant objects appear larger and nearer **telescopic** *adj.*

tel-e-thon *n.* long telecast used to raise money for a worthy cause
tel-ex *n.* teletype communications by means of automatic exchanges
tell *v.* relate or describe; to command or order
tem-per *n.* state of one's feelings **temperable** *adj.*
tem-per-a-ment *n.* personality; a characteristic way of thinking, reacting **temperamental** *adj.*
tem-per-ance *n.* moderation; restraint from drinking alcoholic beverages
tem-per-ate *adj.* avoiding extremes; moderate **temperately** *adv.*
tem-per-a-ture *n.* measure of heat or cold in relation to the body or environment; an elevation in body temperature above the normal 98.6
tem-pest *n.* severe storm, with snow, hail, rain, or sleet
tem-ple *n.* place of worship
tem-po *n., pl.* **-pos** *or* **-pi** *Mus.* rate of speed at which a musical composition is to be played
tem-po-rar-y *adj.* lasting for a limited amount of time
tempt *n.* encourage or draw into a foolish or wrong course of action
te-na-cious *adj.* persistent; stubborn **tenaciously** *adv.*, **tenaciousness** *n.*
ten-ant *n.* person who pays rent to occupy another's property **-able** *adj.*
Ten Commandments *n.* ten rules of moral behavior which were given to Moses by God
tend *v.* to be inclined or disposed; to look after
ten-den-cy *n., pl.* **-ies** disposition to act or behave in a particular way
ten-der *adj.* fragile; soft; not hard or tough; painful or sore when touched
ten-don *n.* band of tough, fibrous tissues that connect a muscle and bone
ten-nis *n.* sport played with a ball and racket by 2 or 4 people
ten-or *n.* adult male singing voice, above a baritone
tense *adj.* taut or stretched tightly; nervous **tense** *v.*
ten-sion *n.* condition of stretching or the state of being stretched **tensionless** *adj.*
tent *n.* portable shelter made by stretchin material over a supporting framework
ten-ta-cle *n.* long, unjointed, flexible body part that projects from certain invertebrates, as the octopus
ten-ta-tive *adj.* experimental; not definite **tentatively** *adv.*
ten-ure *n.* the right, state, or period of holding something, as an office or property **-ed, -ial** *adj.*
tep-id *adj.* lukewarm
ter-cen-ten-a-ry *n., pl.* **-ries.** time span of 300 years
term *n.* phrase or word; a limited time or duration
ter-mi-nal *adj.* of, forming, or located at the end; final
ter-mi-nate *v.* bring to a conclusion or end **termination** *n.*
ter-mite *n.* winged or wingless insect which lives in large colonies feeding on wood
ter-race *n.* open balcony or porch
ter-ra cot-ta *n.* hard, baked clay used in ceramic pottery
ter-rain *n.* surface of an area, as land
ter-ra-pin *n.* edible turtle of North America
ter-res-tri-al *adj.* something earthly; not heavenly
ter-ri-ble *adj.* causing fear or terror; intense; extreme; horrid **terribly** *adv.*, **terriblness** *n.*
ter-rif-ic *adj.* terrifying *Informal* excellent; causing amazement **terrifically** *adv.*
ter-ri-fy *v.* fill with fear or terror; to frighten; to menace **terrified, terrifying** *adj.*
ter-ri-to-ry *n., pl.* **-ies** area, usually of great size, which is controlled by a particular government **territorial** *adj.*
ter-ror *n.* extreme fear
ter-ror-ism *n.* the use of intimidation to attain one's goals or to advance one's cause
terse *adj.* brief; using as few words as possible without loss of force or clearness **tersely** *adj.*, **terseness** *n.*
test *n.* examination to determine one's knowledge, skill, intelligence or other qualities **tester** *n.*
tes-ta-ment *n.* legal document which states how one's personal property is to be distributed upon his death
Testament *n.* one of the two sections of the Bible **Testamentary** *adj.*
tes-tate *adj.* having left a valid will
tes-ti-fy *v.* give evidence while under oath **testifier** *n.*
tes-ti-mo-ni-al *n.* formal statement; a gift, dinner, reception, or other sign of appreciation given to a person as a token of esteem
tes-ti-mo-ny *n., pl.* **-ies** a solemn affirmation made under oath
tes-tis *n., pl.* **testes** sperm producing gland of the male
teth-er *n.* rope or chain which fastens an animal to something
text *n.* actual wording of an author's work; the main part of a book **textual** *adj.*
text-book *n.* book used by students to prepare their lessons
tex-tile *n.* cloth made by weaving; yarn or fiber for making cloth **textile** *adj.*
tex-ture *n.* look, surface, or feel of something
thal-li-um *n.* metallic element resembling lead, symbolized by Tl.
than *conj.* in comparison with or to something
thank *v.* express one's gratitude; to credit
thank-ful *adj.* feeling or showing gratitude
thanks *pl., n.* expression of one's gratitude
that *adj., pl.* **those** person or thing present or being mentioned
thaw *v.* change from a frozen state to a

liquid or soft state; to melt **thaw** *n.*
the-a-tre or the-a-ter *n.* building adapted to present dramas, motion pictures, plays, or other performances
the-at-ri-cal *adj.* extravagant; designed for show, display, or effect
theatricals *n.*
theft *n.* act or crime of stealing; larceny
their *adj. & pron.* possessive case of they
the-ism *n.* belief in the existence of God
theist *n.*, **theistic** *adj.*
them *pron.* objective case of they
theme *n.* topic or subject of something
thematic *adj.*
them-selves *pron.* them or they; a form of the third person plural pronoun
then *adv.* at that time; soon or immediately *adj.* being or acting in or belonging to or at that time
thence *adv.* from that place
thenceforth, thence-for-ward *adv.* from that time on
the-oc-ra-cy *n., pl.* **-ies** government by God or by clergymen who think of themselves as representatives of God
-tic *adj.*, **-tically** *adv.*
the-ol-o-gy *n., pl.* **-ies** religious study of the nature of God, beliefs
theologian *n.*
the-o-rize *v.* analyze theories
the-o-ry *n., pl.* **-ies** general principle or explanation which covers the known facts
ther-a-peu-tics *n.* medical treatment of disease **therapeutist** *n.*
ther-a-py *n., pl.* **-ies** treatment of certain diseases **therapist** *n.*
there *adv.* in, at, or about that place; toward, into, or to
thereabouts, thereafter, thereby, therefore, therefrom, *adv.*
ther-mal *adj.* having to do with or producing heat
ther-mo-plas-tic *ad.* pliable and soft when heated or warm but hard when cooled **thermoplastic** *n.*
ther-mo-stat *n.* device that automatically responds to temperature changes and activates equipment to adjust the temperature to correspond with the setting on the device **-ic** *adj.*
the-sau-rus *n., pl.* **-ruses** *or* **-ri** book which contains synonyms and antonyms
these *pron.* plural of this
the-sis *n., pl.* **-ses** formal argument or idea; a paper written by a student that develops an idea
they *pron.* two or more beings just mentioned
they'd *contr.* they had
they'll *contr.* they will
they're *contr.* they are
they've *contr.* they have
thick *adj.* having a heavy or dense consistency
thief *n., pl.* **thieves** person who steals
thieve *v.* take by theft **thievery** *n.*
thigh *n.* part of the leg between the hip and the knee of man
thin *adj.* having very little depth or extent from one side or surface to the other; not fat; slender **thinly** *adv.*
thing *n.* something not recognized or named; an idea, or conception
things one's belongings
think *v.* exercise thought; to use the mind **thinkable** *adj.*
third *n.* next to the second in time or place; the last in a series of three
thirst *n.* uncomfortably dry feeling in the throat and mouth; a desire for liquids
this *pron., pl.* **these** person or thing that is near, present, or just mentioned
this-tle *n.* prickly plant usually producing a purplish or yellowish flower
thith-er *adv.* to that place; there
thong *n.* narrow strip of leather used for binding
tho-rax *n., pl.* **-raxes** *or* **-races** section or part of the human body between the neck and abdomen
tho-ri-um *n.* radioactive metallic element symbolized by Th.
thorn *n.* sharp, pointed, woody projection on a plant stem **thorny** *adj.*
thor-ough *adj.* complete; intensive
thoroughly *adv.*
thor-ough-bred *adj.* being of a pure breed of stock
thor-ough-fare *n.* public highway, road or street
those *adj. & pron.* plural of that
though *adv.* nevertheless; in spite of
thought *n.* process, act, or power of thinking; an idea
thoughtful, thoughtless *adj.*
thrash *v.* to beat or strike with a whip; to move violently about; to defeat
thrasher *n.*
threat *n.* expression or warning of intent to do harm
thresh *v.* to separate seed from a harvested plant mechanically
thresh-old *n.* horizontal piece of wood or other material which forms a doorsill
threw *v.* past tense of throw
thrice *adv.* three times
thrift *n.* careful use of money and other resources
thrill *n.* feeling of sudden intense excitement, fear, or joy
thrilling *adj.*, **thrillingly** *adv.*
thrive *v.* to prosper; to be healthy; to do well in a position
throat *n.* front section or part of the neck containing passages for food and air
throb *v.* to beat, move, or vibrate in a pulsating way
throm-bo-sis *n., pl.* **-ses** development of a blood clot in a blood vessel or in the heart cavity
throng *n.* large group or crowd *v.* to crowd around or into
throt-tle *n.* valve which controls the flow of fuel to an engine
through *prep.* from the beginning to the end
through-out *prep., adv.* in every place; everywhere; at all times
throw *v.* to toss or fling through the air

with a motion of the arm
thru *prep., adv. & adj.* through
thrush *n.* small songbird having a brownish upper body and spotted breast
thrust *v.* to push; to shove with sudden or vigorous force
thru-way *or* **throughway** *n.* major highway; an expressway
thud *n.* dull thumping sound
thug *n.* tough or violent gangster
thuggish *adj.*
thumb *n.* short first digit of the hand
thump *n.* blow with something blunt or heavy
thun-der *n.* loud explosive sound made as air is suddenly expanded by heat and then quickly contracted again
thus *adv.* in this or that way
thwack *v.* strike hard, using something flat
thwart *v.* prevent from happening
thy *adj.* pertaining to oneself
thyme *n.* an aromatic mint herb whose leaves are used in cooking
thy-roid *adj. Anat.* pertaining to the thyroid gland
thy-rox-ine *n.* hormone secreted by the thyroid gland
ti-ar-a *n.* bejeweled crown
tick *n.* one of a series of rhythmical tapping sounds made by a clock; a small bloodsucking parasite
tick-et *n.* printed slip of paper or cardboard allowing its holder to enter a specified event or to enjoy a privilege
tick-le *v.* to stroke lightly so as to cause laughter; to amuse or delight **-ler** *n.*
tid-bit *n.* choice bit of food, news, or gossip
tide *n.* rise and fall of the surface level of the ocean
tid-ings *pl., n.* news; information about events
ti-dy *adj.* well arranged; neat; orderly
tidiness *n.*
tie *v.* to secure or bind with a rope or other similar material; to make a bow or knot in; to match an opponent's score
tier *n.* layer or row placed one above the other **tiered** *adj.*
ti-ger *n.* large carnivorous cat having tawny fur with black stripes
tiger-eye *n.* yellow-brown gemstone
tight *adj.* set closely together; bound or securely firm; not loose *adv.* firmly
tight-en *v.* to become or make tighter
tightener *n.*
tights *pl., n.* skintight stretchable garment
till *prep. & conj.* until; unless or before *v.* to cultivate; to plow.
till-er *n.* machine or person that tills land
tilt *v.* to tip, as by raising one end
tim-ber *n.* wood prepared for building
timber line *n.* height on a mountain beyond which trees cannot grow
time *n.* continuous period measured by clocks, watches, and calendars *adj.* of or pertaining to time
tim-id *adj.* shy
tin *n.* white, soft, malleable metallic element, symbolized by Sn.
tinc-ture *n.* tinge of color; an alcohol solution of some medicinal substance
tin-der *n.* readily combustible substance or material
tine *n.* narrow pointed spike or prong, as of a fork or antler
tinge *v.* to impart a faint trace of color *n.* trace of color
tin-gle *v.* to feel a stinging or prickling sensation
tin-kle *v.* to produce a slight, sharp series of metallic ringing sounds
tin-ny *adj.* pertaining to or composed of tin
tin-sel *n.* thin strips of glittering material used for decorations
tint *n.* slight amount or trace of color *v.* to color
ti-ny *adj.* minute; very small
tip-ple *v.* drink an alcoholic beverage to excess
tip-sy *adj.* partially intoxicated
ti-rade *n.* long, violent speech
tire *v.* become or make weary *n.* outer covering for a wheel, usually made of rubber, serving to absorb shock and to provide traction
tis-sue *n., Biol.* similar cells and their products developed by plants and animals
ti-ta-ni-um *n.* metallic element symbolized by Ti.
tithe *n.* income given voluntarily for the support of a church
tithe *v.*, **tither** *n.*
tit-il-late *v.* excite or stimulate in a pleasurable way
ti-tle *n.* identifying name of a book, poem, play, or other creative work; a name or mark of distinction indicating a rank or an office
to *prep.* toward, opposite or near; in contact with; as far as; used as a function word indicating an action, movement, or condition suggestive of movement; indicating correspondence, dissimilarity, similarity, or proportion
toad *n.* tailless amphibian
toaster *n.* device for toasting bread
to-bac-co *n.* plant widely cultivated for its leaves
to-bog-gan *n.* long sled-like vehicle without runners
to-day *adv.* on or during the present day
tod-dle *v.* walk unsteadily
toddler *n.* small child
tod-dy *n., pl.* **-ies** drink made with hot water, sugar, spices, and liquor
toe *n.* one of the extensions from the front part of a foot; the part of a stocking, boot or shoe
tof-fee *n.* chewy candy made of butter and brown sugar
to-geth-er *adv.* in or into one group, mass, or body; regarded jointly
toil *v.* to labor very hard and continuously **toilsome** *adj.*
toi-let *n.* porcelain apparatus with a

flushing device, used as a means of disposing body wastes
toi-lette *n.* act of washing, dressing, or grooming oneself
tol-er-ate *v.* to put up with; to endure; to suffer
toll *n.* fixed charge for travel across a bridge or along a road *v.* to sound a bell in repeated single, slow tones
tom *n.* male turkey or cat
tom-a-hawk *n.* ax used as a weapon or tool by North American Indians
to-ma-to *n., pl.* **-toes** garden plant cultivated for its edible fruit; the fruit of such a plant
tomb *n.* vault for burying the dead; a grave
tomb-stone *n.* stone used to mark a grave
to-mor-row *n.* day after the present day
ton *n.* measurement of weight equal to 2,000 pounds
tone *n.* vocal or musical sound that has a distinct pitch *v.* to change or soften the color
tongs *pl., n.* implement with two long arms joined at one end
tongue *n.* muscular organ attached to the floor of the mouth, used in tasting, chewing, and speaking
ton-ic *n.* medicine or other agent used to restore health
to-night *n.* this night; the night that is coming
ton-sil *n.* one of a pair of tissue similar to lymph nodes, found on either side of the throat
ton-sil-lec-to-my *n.* surgical removal of tonsils
too *adv.* also; as well; more than is needed
tool *n.* implement used to perform a task **tooling** *n.*
tooth *n., pl.* **teeth** one of the hard, white structures rooted in the jaw and used for chewing and biting; the small, notched, projecting part of any object, such as a gear, comb or saw
toothed, toothless *adj.*
top *n.* highest part or surface of anything; a covering or lid; the highest degree
to-paz *n.* gemstone
top-coat *n.* outer coat
top-ic *n.* subject discussed in an essay, thesis, speech or other discourse; the theme
top-most *adj.* uppermost
to-pog-ra-phy *n., pl.* **-ies** detailed description of a region or place
top-ple *v.* to fall; to overturn
To-rah *n.* body of law and wisdom contained in Jewish Scripture and oral tradition; a parchment scroll that contains the first five books of the Old Testament
torch *n.* stick of resinous wood which is burned to give light *Slang* to set fire to
tor-ment *n.* extreme mental anguish or physical pain *v.* to cause terrible pain; to pester, harass, or annoy
-ingly *adv.*, **tormentor** *n.*
tor-na-do *n., pl.* **-does** *or* **-dos** whirling, violent windstorm accompanied by a funnel-shaped cloud that travels a narrow path over land
tor-pe-do *n., pl.* **-oes** large, self-propelled, underwater missile launched from a ship, containing an explosive charge
tor-pid *adj.* having lost the power of motion or feeling; dormant
torpidity *n.*, **torpidly** *adv.*
tor-rent *n.* swift, violent stream
torrential *adj.*
tor-rid *adj.* parched and dried by the heat **torridly** *adv.*
tor-sion *n.* act or result of twisting
torsional *adj.*
tor-so *n., pl.* **-sos** *or* **-si** trunk of the human body
tort *n., Law* wrongful act requiring compensation for damages
tor-toise *n.* turtle that lives on the land
tor-tu-ous *adj.* marked by repeated bends, turns, or twists; devious
tortuousness *n.*
tor-ture *n.* infliction of intense pain as punishment
toss *v.* fling or throw about continuously; to throw up in the air *n.* a throw
tot *n.* young child; a toddler
to-tal *n.* whole amount or sum; the entire quantity
adj. absolute; complete
to-tal-i-tar-i-an *adj.* characteristic of a government controlled completely by one party
tote *v.* carry something on one's arm or back
to-tem *n.* animal or plant regarded as having a close relationship to some family clan or group
tot-ter *v.* walk unsteadily
tou-can *n.* brightly colored tropical bird having a very large thin bill
touch *v.* allow a part of the body, as the hands, to feel or come into contact with; join; to come next to; to have an effect on; to move emotionally
touchable *adj.*
tough *adj.* resilient and strong enough to withstand great strain without breaking or tearing; difficult to cut or chew *n.* unruly person; a thug **toughness** *n.*
tou-pee *n.* wig worn to cover a bald spot on one's head
tour *n.* trip with visits to points of interest; a journey **tourism, tourist** *n.*
tour-na-ment *n.* contest involving a number of competitors for a title or championship
tour-ni-quet *n.* device used to temporarily stop the flow of blood through an artery
tou-sle *v.* to mess up
tout *v.* to solicit customers
tow *v.* drag or pull, as by a chain or rope
to-ward or towards *prep.* in the direction of; just before; somewhat before; regarding
tow-el *n.* absorbent piece of cloth used for drying or wiping

tow-er *n.* very tall building or structure; a skyscraper towering *adj.*
town *n.* collection of houses and other buildings larger than a village and smaller than a city
tox-e-mi-a *n.*, *Pathol.* blood poisoning; a condition in which the blood contains toxins
tox-ic *adj.* relating to a toxin; destructive, deadly, or harmful
tox-in *n.* poisonous substance produced by chemical changes in plant and animal tissue
toy *n.* object designed for the enjoyment of children; a small trinket; a bauble
trace *n.* visible mark or sign of a thing, person, or event; something left by some past agent or event
track *n.* mark, as a footprint, left by the passage of anything; a regular course; a set of rails on which a train runs; a circular or oval course for racing
tract *n.* extended area, as a stretch of land
trac-tor *n.* diesel or gasoline-powered vehicle used in farming
tractor trailer *n.* large truck having a cab and no body
trade *n.* business or occupation; skilled labor; a craft; an instance of selling or buying; a swap trader *n.*
trade-mark *n.* brand name which is legally the possession of one company and cannot be used by another
tra-di-tion *n.* customs passed down from one generation to another -al *adj.*
tra-duce *v.* to betray
traf-fic *n.* passage or movement of vehicles; trade, buying and selling
trag-e-dy *n.*, *pl.* -ies extremely sad or fatal event or course of events
trail *v.* to draw, drag, or stream along behind; to follow in the tracks of
trail-er *n.* one who trails; a large vehicle that transports objects and is pulled by another vehicle
trait *n.* quality or distinguishing feature, such as one's character
trai-tor *n.* person who betrays his country
tra-jec-to-ry *n.*, *pl.* -ies curved line or path of a moving object
tram-mel *n.* long, large net used to catch birds or fish
tramp *v.* to plod or walk with a heavy step
tram-ple *v.* to tread heavily; to stomp; to inflict injury, pain trampler *n.*
tram-po-line *n.* canvas device on which an athlete or acrobat may perform
trance *n.* stupor, daze, mental state, or condition, such as produced by drugs or hypnosis
tran-quil *adj.* very calm, quiet
trans-act *v.* to perform, carry out, conduct, or manage business in some way transaction, transactor *n.*
tran-scend *v.* to pass beyond; to exceed; to surpass
tran-scribe *v.* to make copies of something; to adopt or arrange
tran-script *n.* written copy
trans-cription *n.* process or act of transcribing
trans-fer *v.* remove, shift, or carry from one position to another transferable *adj.*
trans-fig-ure *v.* change the outward appearance or form -ation *n.*
trans-fix *v.* to pierce; to hold motionless, as with terror, awe or amazement transfixion *n.*
trans-form *v.* change or alter completely in nature, form or function transformation
trans-fuse *v.* transfer liquid by pouring from one place to another transfusion
trans-gress *v.* to go beyond the limit or boundaries
tran-sient *adj.* not staying or lasting very long; moving from one location to another transiently *adv.*
tran-sit *n.* passage or travel from one point to another
trans-late *v.* change from one language to another while retaining the original meaning translation, translator *n.*
trans-lu-cent *adj.* diffusing and admitting light but not allowing a clear view of the object
trans-mis-sion *n.* act or state of transmitting *Mech.* gears and associated parts of an engine which transmit power to the driving wheels of an automobile or other vehicle
trans-mit *v.* dispatch or convey from one thing, person, or place to another
trans-mute *v.* change in nature, kind, or substance
tran-som *n.* small, hinged window over a doorway
trans-par-ent *adj.* admitting light so that images and objects can be clearly viewed; obvious transparency *n.*
tran-spire *v.* to happen; to take place transpiration *n.*
trans-plant *v.* remove a living plant from where it is growing and plant it in another place; to remove a body organ from one person and implant it in the body of another, as a kidney transplant
trans-port *v.* carry or move from one place to another
trans-pose *v.* reverse the place or order of
trans-sex-u-al *n.* person whose sex has been changed surgically
trap *n.* device for holding or catching animals; anything which deliberately catches or stops people or things *v.* catch in a trap
tra-peze *n.* short horizontal bar suspended by two ropes, used for acrobatic exercise or stunts
trau-ma *n.*, *pl.* -mas *or* -mata severe wound caused by a sudden physical injury; an emotional shock causing lasting and substantial damage to a person's psychological development
tra-vail *n.* strenuous mental or physical exertion
trav-el *v.* journey or move from one

place to another
tra-verse *v.* pass over, across, or through
trawl *n.* strong fishing net which is dragged through water
tray *n.* flat container having a low rim, used for carrying, holding, or displaying something
treach-er-ous *adj.* disloyal; deceptive **treachery** *n.*
tread *v.* to walk along, on, or over; to trample
trea-son *n.* violation of one's allegiance to a sovereign or country, as giving or selling state secrets to another country or attempting to overthrow the government
treas-ure *n.* hidden riches; something regarded as valuable
treas-ur-y *n., pl.* **-ies** place where public or private funds are kept
treat *v.* behave or act toward; regard in a given manner; provide entertainment or food for another at one's own expense or cost
treat-ment *n.* manner or act of treating; medical care
tre-foil *n.* any of various plants having three leaflets with red, purple, yellow, or pink flowers
trek *v.* make a slow and arduous journey **trekker** *n.*
trel-lis *n.* latticework frame used for supporting vines
trem-ble *v.* shake involuntarily, as with fear or from cold **trembler** *n.*, **trembly** *adj.*
tre-men-dous *adj.* extremely huge, large, or vast *Slang* wonderful
trem-or *n.* quick, shaking movement; any continued and involuntary trembling or quavering of the body
trench *n.* ditch; long, narrow excavation in the ground
trend *n.* general inclination, direction, or course; a fad
tres-pass *v.* infringe upon another's property
tres-tle *n.* bar or beam supported by four legs
tri-al *n.* in law, the examination and hearing of a case before a court of law
tri-an-gle *n., Geom.* plane figure bounded by three sides and having three angles **triangular** *adj.*
tribe *n.* group of people composed of several villages, districts, or other groups which share a common language, culture, and name
trib-u-la-tion *n.* great distress or suffering
trib-un-al *n.* decision making body
trib-ute *n.* action of respect or gratitude to someone
tri-ceps *n., Anat.* large muscle at the back of the upper arm
trick *n.* action meant to fool, as a scheme; a prank; a feat of magic **tricky** *adj.*
trick-er-y *n.* deception
trick-le *v.* flow in droplets or a small stream **trickle** *n.*
tri-col-or *n.* French color in the flag **tricolored** *adj.*
tri-cy-cle *n.* small vehicle having three wheels, propelled by pedals
tri-dent *n.* long spear with three prongs, used as a weapon
tried *adj.* tested and proven reliable or useful
tri-en-ni-al *adj.* happening every third year; lasting for a time period of three years
tri-fle *n.* something of little value or importance; a dessert made with cake, jelly, wine, and custard
trig-ger *n.* lever pulled to fire a gun; a device used to release or start an action *v.* to start
trim *v.* clip or cut off small amounts in order to make neater; to decorate *adj.* neat **trim** *n.*
tri-ni-tro-tol-u-ene *n.* very powerful explosive, abbreviated as TNT
trin-ket *n.* small piece of jewelry
tri-o *n.* set or group of three
trip *n.* travel from one place to another; a journey; a loss of balance
tripe *n.* stomach lining of oxen or similar animals, used as food
trip-le *adj.* having three parts
trip-let *n.* one of three born at the same time
tri-pod *n.* three-legged stand
trite *adj.* used too often; common
tri-umph *v.* be victorious *n.* victory **triumphantly** *adv.*
triv-i-al *adj.* insignificant; of little value or importance
trol-ley *n.* streetcar powered by electricity from overhead lines
tro-phy *n., pl.* **-ies** prize or object, such as a plaque, awarded to someone for his success, victory, or achievement
tro-po-sphere *n.* lowest atmosphere between the earth's surface and the stratosphere
troth *n.* good faith; the act of pledging one's fidelity
trou-ble *n.* danger; affliction; need; distress; an effort *v.* bother; to worry; to be bothered **troubler** *n.*
trough *n.* long, narrow, shallow container, especially one that holds food or water for animals
trounce *v.* whip or beat
troupe *n.* group, especially of the performing arts
trou-sers *pl., n.* outer garment that covers the body from the waist down
trous-seau *n.* wardrobe, linens, and other similar articles of a bride
tru-ant *n.* person who is absent from school without permission **truancy** *n.*
truce *n.* agreement to stop fighting; a cease fire
truck *n.* automotive vehicle used to carry heavy loads; any of various devices with wheels designed to move heavy loads **trucker** *n.*
trudge *v.* walk heavily and wearily; plod
true *adj.* in accordance with reality or fact; not false; real; loyal; faithful
trunk *n.* main part of a tree; the human body, excluding the head, arms and

legs; a sturdy box for packing
truss *v.* fasten or tie securely *Med.* support or device worn to keep a hernia in place
trust *n.* confidence or faith in a person or thing
trust-y *adj.* reliable
truth *n., pl.* **truths** facts corresponding with actual events or happenings; sincerity or honesty
truthful *adj.*, **truthfully** *adv.*
try *v.* make an attempt; to make an effort; to strain; to hear or conduct a trial; to place on trial trying *adj.*
tryst *n.* meeting between lovers; a prearranged meeting
tsu-na-mi *n.* extensive and destructive ocean wave caused by an underwater earthquake
tub *n.* round, low, flat-bottomed, vessel with handles on the side
tu-ba *n.* large, brass wind instrument having a low range
tu-ber-cu-lo-sis *n.* contagious lung disease of humans and animals caused by microorganisms
tuck *n.* flattened fold of material, usually stitched in place
tuft *n.* small cluster of feathers, threads, hair, or other material fastened or growing closely together
tug *v.* strain and pull vigorously *n.* hard pull
tu-i-tion *n.* payment for instruction, as at a private school or college
tu-lip *n.* bulb-bearing plant, having upright cup-like blossoms.
tum-ble *v.* fall or cause to fall; to perform acrobatic rolls, somersaults, and similar maneuvers
tum-ble-down *adj.* ramshackle; in need of repair
tum-brel *n.* cart which can discharge its load by tilting
tu-mor *n., Pathol.* swelling on or in any part of the body; an abnormal growth which may be malignant or benign
tu-mult *n.* confusion and noise of a crowd; a riot
tu-na *n., pl.* **-na** *or* **-nas** any of several large marine food fish
tun-dra *n.* treeless area in the arctic regions having a subsoil which is permanently frozen
tune *n.* melody which is simple and easy to remember; agreement
tung-sten *n.* element also known as wolfram, symbolized by W.
tu-nic *n.* loose garment extending to the knees, worn by ancient Romans and Greeks
tun-nel *n.* underground or underwater passageway
tur-ban *n.* Moslem headdress that consists of a long scarf wound around the head
tur-bine *n.* motor having one or more rotary units mounted on a shaft, which are turned by the force of gas or a liquid
tur-bu-lent *adj.* marked by a violent disturbance
tu-reen *n.* large dish used to serve soup or stew
turf *n.* layer of earth with its dense growth of grass and matted roots
tur-moil *n.* state of confusion or commotion
turn-key *n.* person in charge of the keys at a prison
turn-over *n.* process or act of turning over; an upset; a change or reversal
tusk *n.* long, curved tooth, as of an elephant or walrus
tus-sle *n.* hard fight or struggle with a problem or person **tussle** *v.*
tu-tor *n.* person who teaches another person privately
tu-tu *n.* very short ballet skirt
tux-e-do *n.* semiformal dress suit worn by men
tweak *v.* pinch and twist sharply
twice *adv.* double; two times
twid-dle *v.* to turn or twirl in an aimless way
twig *n.* small branch which grows from a larger branch on a tree
twi-light *n.* soft light of the sky between sunset and darkness
twilight sleep *n.* a state of feeling in which pain is dulled
twill *n.* weave that produces the parallel rib on the surface of a fabric
twin *n.* one of two persons born at the same time to the same mother; one of two similar persons or things
twine *v.* weave or twist together
twinge *n.* sudden, sharp pain
twin-kle *v.* gleam or shine with quick flashes; to sparkle
twirl *v.* to rotate or cause to turn around and around
twist-er *n., Slang* tornado; a cyclone; one that twists
twit *v.* tease about a mistake
twitch *v.* move or cause to move with a jerky movement
twit-ter *v.* utter a series of chirping sounds; to chatter nervously
two-bits twenty-five cents
two-faced double-dealing
ty-coon *n., Slang* business person of wealth and power
tyke *n.* small child
type *n.* class or group of persons or things
ty-phoon *n.* tropical hurricane
typ-i-cal *adj.* exhibiting the characteristics of a certain class or group **typically** *adv.*
typ-i-fy *v.* be characteristic or typical of **typification** *n.*
typ-ist *n.* operator of a typewriter
ty-po *n., Slang* error in typewriting or in setting type; any printed error which was not the fault of the author
ty-ran-no-sau-rus *n.* large, flesh-eating dinosaur which walked on its hind legs
tyr-an-ny *n.* harsh, absolute, and unfair rule by a king or other ruler
tyr-an-nize *v.* rule or control completely
ty-rant *n.* absolute, unjust, or cruel ruler control unfairly
ty-ro *n.* a novice; a beginner

U, u The twenty-first letter of the English alphabet.
UAW *abbr.* United Auto Workers
Uban-gi *n.* a woman of Africa that has lips which are distended with wooden disks
ubi-qui-none *n.* the quinone which is able to function as an electron transfer agent in the Kreb's cycle
ubiq-ul-tous *adj.* to be everywhere at the same time
ubiq-ui-ty *n.* a presence in many places or locations at the same time
U-boat *n.* a type of submarine which is used by the Germans
UDC *abbr.* Universal Decimal Classification
ud-der *n.* milk-producing organ pouch of some female animals, having two or more teats
UFO *n.* an unidentified flying object such as a space ship from another planet in the science fiction films
UFT *abbr.* United Federation of Teachers
UG *abbr.* Underground
ugh *interj.* used to express disgust or horror
ug-li-fy *v.* to make something or someone ugly
ug-ly *adj.* offensive; repulsive; unpleasant to look at **ugliest, uglier** *adj.*
uh *interj.* to express hesitation
uh-huh *interj.* used for the purpose of showing or indicating agreement
UK *abbr.* United Kingdom
uki-yo-e *n.* a kind of Japanese art movement which flourished during the 17th to the 19th century
u-ku-le-le *n.* small, four-stringed musical instrument, orginally from Hawaii
ul-cer *n.* festering, inflamed sore on a mucous membrane or on the skin that results in the destruction of the tissue
ul-cero-gen-ic *adj.* to be tending to develop into an ulcer
ulex-ite *n.* a kind of mineral that occurs in loose fibers that is able to transmit light lengthwise with very little diminished intensity
ul-na *n., Anat.* one of the two bones of the forearm
ulot-ri-chous *adj.* to have crisp or woolly hair
ul-ster *n.* a type of long loose overcoat that is of Irish origin and is made of heavy material
ul-ti-ma ra-tio *n.* a final argument or the last resort to a problem
ul-ti-mate *adj.* final; ending; most extreme **ultimately** *adv.*
ul-ti-ma-tum *n., pl* **-tums, -ta** final demand, proposal, or choice
ultra- *prefix.* beyond the scope, range, or limit of something
ul-tra-mod-ern *adj.* extremely advanced or modern in style
ul-tra-son-ic *adj.* relating to sound frequencies inaudible to humans
ul-tra-vi-o-let *adj.* producing radiation having wave-lengths just shorter than those of visible light and longer than those of X rays
um-bil-i-cal cord *n.* structure by which a fetus is attached to its mother, serving to supply food and dispose of waste
um-brel-la *n.* collapsible frame covered with plastic or cloth, held above the head as protection from sun or rain
um-pire *n.* in sports, the person who rules on plays in a game *v.* act as an umpire
ump-teen *adj., Slang* indefinitely large number
un- *prefix* reverse or opposite of an act; removal or release from
un-able *adj.* not having the mental capabilities
un-ac-com-pa-nied *adj.* alone; without a companion *Mus.* Solo
un-ac-count-a-ble *adj.* without an explanation; mysterious; not responsible
un-ac-cus-tomed *adj.* not used to or in the habit of; not ordinary
u-nan-i-mous *adj.* agreed to completely; based on the agreement of all
un-armed *adj.* lacking means for protection
un-as-sum-ing *adj.* modest and not showy
un-at-tach-ed *adj.* not engaged, going steady, or married
un-a-void-able *adj.* inevitable; unstoppable **-ly** *adv.*
un-a-ware *adj.* not realizing
un-bear-a-ble *adj.* not possible to endure; intolerable
un-be-coming *adj.* unattractive; not pleasing; not proper, polite or suitable for the situation
un-be-known *or* **unbeknownst** *adj.* not known; without one's knowledge
un-be-liev-able *adj.* incredible; hard to accept; not to be believed
un-called for *adj.* not necessary or needed; not requested
un-can-ny *adj.* strange, odd, or mysterious; exceptional
un-cer-tain *adj.* doubtful; not sure; not known; hard to predict
un-chang-ed *adj.* having nothing new or different
un-civ-i-lized *adj.* without culture or refinement; without an established cultural
un-cle *n.* brother of one's mother or father
un-clean *adj.* immoral; dirty; not decent
un-clothe *v.* uncover or undress
un-com-fort-a-ble *adj.* disturbed; not at ease physically or mentally
un-com-mon *adj.* rare; odd; unusual; extraordinary
un-com-pro-mis-ing *adj.* firm; unwilling to give in or to compromise
un-con-cern *n.* lack of interest; disinterest; indifference
un-con-di-tion-al *adj.* without conditions **unconditionally** *adv.*
un-con-scious *adj.* not mentally aware; done without thought; not on purpose
un-con-sti-tu-tion-al *adj.* contrary to the constitution or the basic laws of a state

or country
un-couth *adj.* acting or speaking crudely, unrefined; clumsy or awkward
un-cov-er *v.* remove the cover from something; to disclose
un-de-cid-ed *adj.* unsettled; having made no firm decision; open to change
un-de-ni-able *adj.* not open to doubt or denial; not possible to contradict
un-der *prep.* below, in place or position; in a place lower than another; less in degree, number, or other quality; inferior in rank, quality, or character; during the reign or period; in accordance with; less than the required amount; insufficient
under *prefix.* location beneath or below; lower in importance or rank
un-der-brush *n.* small bushes, vines, and plants that grow under tall trees
un-der-clothes *pl., n.* clothes worn next to the skin; underwear
un-der-de-vel-oped *adj.* not fully mature or grown; lacking modern communications and industry
un-der-foot *adj.* underneath or below the feet; being so close to one's feet as to be in the way
un-der-go *v.* to have the experience of; to be subjected to
un-der-grad-u-ate *n.* college or university student studying for a bachelor's degree
un-der-hand *adj.* done deceitfully and secretly **underhandedly** *adv.*
un-der-line *v.* to draw a fine directly under something
un-der-mine *v.* to weaken; to make less strong
un-der-neath *adv.* beneath or below; on the under side; lower
un-der-pass *n.* road or walk that goes under another
un-der-priv-i-leged *adj.* deprived of economic and social advantages
un-der-rate *v.* rate or value below the true worth
un-der-score *v.* emphasize
un-der-sell *v.* sell for less than a competitor
un-der-side *n.* side or part on the bottom
un-der-stand *v.* comprehend; to realize
un-der-stand-a-ble *adj.* able to comprehend **-ly** *adv.*
un-der-state *v.* make too little of the actual situation **-ment** *n.*
un-der-stood *adj.* agreed upon by all
un-der-stud-y *v.* to learn another person's part or role in order to be able to replace him if necessary
un-der-take *v.* set about to do a task; to pledge oneself to a certain job; to attempt
un-der-tak-er *n.* person who prepares the dead for burial
un-der-tone *n.* low, quiet voice; a pale or subdued color visible through other colors
un-der-tow *n.* underwater current which runs in the opposite direction of the surface current
un-der-wa-ter *adj.* occurring, happening or used beneath the surface of the water
un-der-write *v.* sign or write at the end of something; to finance; to assume a risk by means of insurance assume responsibility for; to undertake to pay a written pledge of money **underwriter** *n.*
un-de-sir-a-ble *adj.* offensive; not wanted **undesirably** *adv.*
un-do *v.* cancel; to reverse; to loosen or unfasten
un-done *adj.* not finished; unfastened; ruined
un-du-late *v.* to move from side to side with a flowing motion; to have a wavy shape **undulation** *n.*
un-dy-ing *adj.* without end
un-earth *v.* dig up from the earth; to find or discover
unearthly *adj.* strange; not from this world
un-eas-y *adj.* feeling or causing distress or discomfort; embarrassed
un-em-ployed *adj.* without a job; without work **unemployment** *n.*
un-e-qual *adj.* not even; not fair; not of the same size or time
un-e-ven *adj.* not equal; varying in consistency or form; not balanced
un-e-vent-ful *adj.* lacking in significance; calm
un-expect-ed *adj.* surprising; happening without warning **-ly** *adv.*
un-fail-ing *adj.* constant, unchanging
un-fair *adj.* not honest; marked by a lack of justice
un-faith-ful *adj.* breaking a promise or agreement; without loyalty
un-fa-mil-iar *adj.* not knowing; strange; foreign
unfavorable *adj.*, not desired; harmful; unpleasant
un-feel-ing *adj.* without sympathy; hardhearted; without sensation
un-fit *adj.* not suitable; not qualified; in poor body or mental health
un-fold *v.* open up the folds of and lay flat; to reveal gradually
un-fore-seen *adj.* not anticipated or expected
un-for-get-ta-ble *adj.* impossible or hard to forget; memorable
un-for-tu-nate *adj.* causing or having bad luck, damage, or harm
un-found-ed *adj.* not founded or based on fact; groundless; lacking a factual basis
un-friend-ly *adj.* showing a lack of kindness; not friendly
un-furl *v.* unroll or unfold; to open up or out
un-fur-nished *adj.* without furniture
un-god-ly *adj.* wicked; evil; lacking reverence for God **ungodliness** *n.*
un-grate-ful *adj.* not thankful; no appreciation
un-guent *n.* healing or soothing salve; ointment
un-happy *adj.* sad; without laughter or joy; not satisfied or pleased

un-heard *adj.* not heard; not listened to
un-heard--of *adj.* not known or done before; without precedent
un-hook *v.* release or undo from a hook
u-ni-corn *n.* mythical animal resembling a horse, with a horn in the center of its forehead
u-ni-cy-cle *n.* one wheeled vehicle with pedals
un-i-den-ti-fied flying object *n.* flying object that cannot be explained or identified
u-ni-form *n.* identical clothing worn by the members of a group to distinguish them from the general population
uniformly *adv.*
u-ni-fy *v.* come together as one; to unite
un-in-hab-it-ed *adj.* not lived in; empty
un-in-ter-est-ed *adj.* having no interest or concern in; not interested
un-ion *n.* act of joining together of two or more groups or things; a group of countries or states joined under one government; a mar-riage; an organized body of employees who work together to upgrade their working conditions and wages **Union** The United States
u-nique *adj.* unlike any other; sole
u-ni-sex *adj.* adaptable and appropriate for both sexes
u-ni-son *n.* in music, the exact sameness of pitch, as of a tone
u-nit *n.* any one of several parts regarded as a whole; an exact quantity that is used as a standard of measurement; a special section
u-nite *v.* join or come together for a common purpose
United Nations *n.* international organization formed in 1945; comprised of nearly all the countries of the world whose purpose is to promote security, economic development, and peace
United States of America *n.* country bordering the Atlantic and Pacific Oceans, Mexico, and Canada
u-ni-ty *n., pl.* **-ies** fact or state of being one; accord; agreement; harmony
u-ni-valve *n.* mollusk having a one-piece shell, such as a snail
u-ni-ver-sal *adj.* having to do with the world or the universe in its entirety
u-ni-verse *n.* the world, stars, planets, space, and all that is contained
u-ni-ver-si-ty *n., pl.* **-ies** educational institution offering undergraduate and graduate degrees in a variety of academic areas
un-just *adj.* not fair; lacking justice or fairness
un-kempt *adj.* poorly groomed; messy
un-kind *adj.* harsh; lacking in sympathy, concern, or understanding
un-known *adj.* strange; unidentified; not known; not familiar
un-lead-ed *adj.* containing no lead
un-like *prep.* dissimilar; not alike; not equal in strength or quantity
un-lim-it-ed *adj.* having no boundaries or limitations
un-load *v.* take or remove the load; to unburden; to dispose or get rid of by selling in volume
un-lock *v.* open, release, or unfasten a lock; open with a key
un-loose *v.* loosen or undo; to release
un-luck-y *adj.* unfortunate; having bad luck; disappointing or unsuitable
unluckily *adv.*
un-manned *adj.* designed to operate or be operated without a crew of people
un-men-tion-a-ble *adj.* improper or unsuitable
un-mis-tak-a-ble *adj.* very clear and evident; understood; obvious
un-mor-al *adj.* having no moral knowledge
un-nat-u-ral *adj.* abnormal or unusual; strange; artificial
un-nec-es-sar-y *adj.* not needed; not appropriate **unnecessarily** *adv.*
un-nerve *v.* frighten; to upset
un-num-bered *adj.* countless; not identified by number
un-oc-cu-pied *adj.* empty; not occupied
un-pack *v.* remove articles out of trunks, suitcases, or boxes
un-pleas-ant *adj.* not agreeable; not pleasant
un-pop-u-lar *adj.* not approved or liked
un-pre-dict-a-ble *adj.* not capable or being foretold; not reliable
un-pre-pared *adj.* not equipped or ready
un-pro-fes-sion-al *adj.* contrary to the standards of a profession; having no professional status
un-prof-it-a-ble *adj.* showing or giving no profit; serving no purpose
un-qual-i-fied *adj.* lacking the proper qualifications; unreserved
un-rav-el *v.* to separate threads; to solve; to clarify; to come apart
un-re-al *adj.* having no substance or reality
un-rea-son-a-ble *adj.* not according to reason; exceeding all reasonable limits
un-re-li-a-ble *adj.* unable to be trusted; not dependable
un-re-served *adj.* done or given without reserve; unlimited
un-re-strained *adj.* not held back, forced, or affected
un-ru-ly *adj.* disorderly; difficult to subdue or control
un-sat-is-fac-to-ry *adj.* unacceptable; not pleasing
un-screw *v.* to loosen or unfasten by removing screws from
un-scru-pu-lous *adj.* without morals, guiding principles, or rules
un-seat *v.* cause to lose one's seat; to force out of office
un-sel-fish *adj.* willing to share; thinking of another's well-being before one's own
un-set-tle *v.* cause to be upset or excited; to disturb
un-sheathe *v.* draw a sword from a sheath or other case
un-sight-ly *adj.* not pleasant to look at; ugly
un-skilled *adj.* having no skills or training in a given kind of work

ing in a given kind of work
un-sound *adj.* having defects; not solidly made
un-speak-a-ble *adj.* of or relating to something which can not be expressed
un-sta-ble *adj.* not steady or firmly fixed; having the tendency to fluctuate or change
un-stead-y *adj.* not secure; unstable; variable
un-sub-stan-tial *adj.* lacking strength, weight, or solidity
un-suit-a-ble *adj.* unfitting; not suitable; not appropriate for a specific circumstance
un-tan-gle *v.* free from snarls or entanglements
un-thank-ful *adj.* ungrateful
un-think-a-ble *adj.* unimaginable
un-ti-dy *adj.* messy; showing a lack of tidiness
un-tie *v.* unfasten or loosen; to free from a restraint or bond
un-til *prep.* up to the time of *conj.* to the time when; to the degree or place
un-time-ly *adj.* premature; before the expected time
un-told *adj.* not revealed; not told; inexpressible; cannot be described
un-touch-a-ble *adj.* cannot be touched; incapable of being obtained or reached
un-true *adj.* not true; contrary to the truth; not faithful; disloyal
un-truth *n.* something which is not true **untruthful** *adj.*
un-used *adj.* not put to use; never having been used
un-u-su-al *adj.* not usual; uncommon **unusually** *adv.*
un-ut-ter-a-ble *adj.* incapable of being described or expressed; unpronounceable
un-veil *v.* remove a veil from; to uncover; to reveal
un-war-y *adj.* not cautious or careful; careless
un-whole-some *adj.* unhealthy; morally corrupt or harmful
un-will-ing *adj.* reluctant; not willing
un-wind *v.* undo or reverse the winding of; to untangle
un-wise *adj.* lacking good judgment or common sense
un-wor-thy *adj.* not deserving; not becoming or befitting; lacking merit or worth; shameful **-iness** *n.*
up *adv.* from a lower position to a higher one; on, in, or to a higher level, position, or place; to a greater degree or amount; in or into a specific action or an excited state, as they stirred up trouble; under consideration, as up for discussion; in a safe, protected place; totally, completely, as the building was burned up
up-beat *n., Mus.* relatively unaccented beat preceding the down beat *adj.* optimistic; happy
up-bring-ing *n.* process of teaching and rearing a child
up-draft *n.* upward current of air
up-grade *v.* increase the grade, rank, or standard of
up-hill *adv.* up an incline *adj.* hard to accomplish; going up a hill or incline
up-hol-ster *v.* cover furniture with fabric covering
up-keep *n.* cost and work needed to keep something in good condition
up-on *prep.* on
up-per *adj.* higher in status, position or location *n.* the part of a shoe to which the sole is attached
up-per--class *adj.* economically or socially superior
up-right *adj.* having a vertical direction or position; honest *n.* something standing vertically
up-ris-ing *n.* revolt; a rebellion; an insurrection
up-roar *n.* confused, loud noise; a commotion
up-root *v.* detach completely by pulling up the roots
up-set *v.* capsize; to turn over; to throw into confusion or disorder; to overcome; to beat unexpectedly *adj.* capsized; overturned; distressed; troubled
up-stage *adj. & adv.* toward or at the back part of a stage
up-start *n.* one who has risen quickly to power or wealth
up-tight *adv.* nervous, or tense
up-ward *or* **upwards** *adv.* from a lower position to or toward a higher one
u-ra-ni-um *n.* hard, heavy, shiny metallic element that is radioactive
urge *v.* encourage, push, or drive; to recommend persistently and strongly
ur-gent *adj.* requiring immediate attention
urine *n.* in man and other mammals, the yellowish fluid waste produced by the kidneys
Us *pl., pron.* objective case of we; used as an indirect object, direct object
us-a-ble *or* **useable** *adj.* fit or capable of being used **usability** *n.*, **usably** *adv.*
us-age *n.* way or act of using something; the way words are used
use *v.* put into action; to emply for a special purpose; to employ on a regular basis; to exploit for one's own advantage
u-su-al *adj.* ordinary or common; regular; customary **usually** *adv.*, **usualness** *n.*
u-surp *v.* take over by force without authority **usurpation, -er** *n.*
u-ten-sil *n.* tool, implement, or container
u-ter-us *n.* organ of female mammals within which young develop and grow before birth **uterine** *adj.*
u-til-i-ty *n., pl.* **-ies** state or quality of being useful; a company which offers a public service
u-til-ize *v.* make or put to use
ut-most *adj.* of the greatest amount or degree; most distant **utmost** *n.*
u-to-pi-a *n.* condition or place of perfection or complete harmony
u-vu-la *n.* fleshy projection which hangs above the back of the tongue

V, v The twenty-second letter of the English alphabet.
v. *abbr.* verb; version; vowel
va-cant *adj.* empty; not occupied
va-cate *v.* to leave; to cease to occupy
va-ca-tion *n.* period of time away from work for pleasure, or relaxation
vac-ci-nate *v.* inject with a vaccine so as to produce immunity to an infectious disease, as measles or smallpox
vac-ci-na-tion *n.* inoculation with a vaccine
vac-cine *n.* solution of weakened or killed microorganisms, as bacteria or viruses, injected into the body to produce immunity to a disease
vac-u-um *n., pl.* **vacuums, -ua** space which is absolutely empty; a void; a vacuum cleaner
vag-a-bond *n.* homeless person who wanders from place to place
va-gar-y *n., pl.* **vagaries** eccentric or capricious action or idea
va-gi-na *n., pl.* **vaginas, -nae** *Anat.* canal or passage extending from the uterus to the external opening of the female reproductive system
va-gi-ni-tis *n.* inflammation of the vagina
va-grant *n.* roaming from one area to another without a job **vagrancy** *n.*
vague *adj.* not clearly expressed; not sharp or definite **vaguely** *adv.*
vain *adj.* conceited; lacking worth or substance; having to much pride in oneself **vainly** *adv.*
val-ance *n.* decorative drapery across the top of a window
vale *n.* a valley
val-e-dic-to-ri-an *n.* student ranking highest in a graduating class, who delivers a speech at the commencement
val-en-tine *n.* card or gift sent to one's sweetheart on Valentine's Day, February 14th
val-et *n.* man who takes care of another man's clothes and other personal needs; a hotel employee who attends to personal services for guests
val-iant *adj.* brave; exhibiting valor **valiance, valor** *n.*
val-id *adj.* founded on facts or truth *Law* binding; having legal force **validity** *n.*
val-ley *n., pl.* **valleys** low land between ranges of hills or mountains
val-or *n.* bravery **valorous** *adj.*
val-u-a-ble *adj.* of great value or importance; having a high monetary value **valuableless** *adj.*
val-ue *n.* quality or worth of something that makes it valuable; material worth
valve *n.* movable mechanism which opens and closes to control the flow of a substance through a pipe or other passageway
va-moose *v. Slang* leave in a hurry
vam-pire *n.* in folklore, a dead person believed to rise from the grave at night to suck the blood of sleeping persons; a person who preys on others
vam-pire bat *n.* a tropical bat that feeds on the blood of living mammals.
van *n.* large closed wagon or truck
va-na-di-um *n.* metallic element symbolized by V.
van-dal-ism *n.* malicious defacement or destruction of private or public property
vane *n.* metal device that turns in the direction the wind is blowing; a thin rigid blade of an electric fan, propeller, or windmill
va-nil-la *n.* flavoring extract used in cooking and baking
van-ish *v.* disappear suddenly; to drop out of sight; to go out of existence
van-i-ty *n., pl.,* **vanities** conceit; extreme pride in one's ability, possessions, or appearance
van-tage *n.* superior position; an advantage
va-por *n.* moisture or smoke suspended in air, as mist or fog
vaporish, vaporous *adj.*
var-i-able *adj.* changeable; tending to vary; inconstant
variableness *n.,* **variably** *adv.*
var-i-ance *n.* state or act of varying; difference; conflict
var-i-a-tion *n.* result or process of varying; the degree or extent of varying
Mus. a different form or version of a given theme, with modifications in rhythm, melody, or key
var-i-e-gat-ed *adj.* having marks of different colors **variegate** *v.*
va-ri-e-ty *n., pl.,* **varieties** state or character of being varied or various; a number of different kinds; an assortment
var-i-ous *adj.* of different kinds
var-mint *n., Slang* a troublesome animal; an obnoxious person
var-nish *n.* solution paint used to coat or cover a surface with a hard, transparent, shiny film
var-si-ty *n., pl.,* **varsities** best team representing a college, university, or school
var-y *v.* change; to make or become different; to be different
vas-cu-lar *adj., Biol.* having to do with vessels circulating fluids, as blood
va-sec-to-my *n., pl.* **vasectomies** method of male sterilization
vast *adj.* very large or great in size **vastly** *adv.,* **vastness** *n.*
vault *n.* room for storage and safekeeping, as in a bank, usually made of steel; a burial chamber
veg-e-ta-ble *n.* plant, as the tomato, green beans, lettuce, raised for the edible part
veg-e-tar-i-an *n.* person whose diet is limited to vegetables
veg-e-ta-tion *n.* plants or plant life which grow from the soil
ve-hi-cle *n.* a motorized device for transporting goods, equipment, or passengers
veil *n.* a piece of transparent cloth worn on the head or face for concealment or protection
vein *n., Anat.* vessel which transports blood back to the heart after passing

through the body **vein** *v.*
ve-lour *n.* soft velvet-like woven cloth
vel-vet *n.* fabric made of rayon, cotton, or silk
vend-er *or* **vendor** *n.* person who sells, as a peddler
ven-det-ta *n.* fight or feud between blood-related persons
ven-er-a-ble *adj.* meriting or worthy of respect by reason of dignity, position, or age
venereal disease *n.* contagious disease, as syphilis, or gonorrhea, which is typically acquired through sexual intercourse
ve-ne-tian blind *n.* window blind having thin, horizontal slats
ven-i-son *n.* edible flesh of a deer
ven-om *n.* poisonous substance secreted by some animals, as scorpions or snakes **venomous** *adj.*
ve-nous *adj.* of or relating to veins
vent *n.* means of escape or passage from a restricted area; an opening which allows the escape of vapor, heat, or gas
ven-ti-late *v.* expose to a flow of fresh air for refreshing, curing, or purifying purposes
ventilation, ventilator *n.*
ven-ture *n.* course of action involving risk, chance, or danger, especially a business investment
ven-ue *n.* place where a crime or other cause of legal action occurs; the locale of a gathering
verb *n.* part of speech which expresses action, existence, or occurrence
ver-bal *adj.* expressed in speech; expressed orally; not written; relating to or derived from a verb *n.* an adjective, noun or other word which is based on a verb and retains some characteristics of a verb **verbally** *adv.*, **verbalize** *v.*
ver-ba-tim *adv.* word for word
ver-be-na *n.* American garden plant
verge *n.* extreme edge or rim; margin; the point beyond which something begins
ver-min *n.* a destructive, annoying animal which is harmful to one's health
ver-sa-tile *adj.* having the capabilities of doing many different things; having many functions or uses
verse *n.* writing that has a rhyme; poetry; a subdivision of a chapter of the Bible
ver-sion *n.* an account or description told from a particular point of view; a translation from another language, especially a translation of the Bible
ver-so *n., pl.* versos left-hand page
ver-sus *prep.* against; in contrast to; as an alternative of
ver-te-bra *n., pl.* **vertebrae, vertebras** one of the bony or cartilaginous segments making up the spinal column
ver-tex *n., pl.* **vertexes, vertices** highest or topmost point; the pointed top of a triangle
ver-ti-cal *adj.* in a straight up-and-down direction
ver-y *adv.* to a high or great degree; truly; absolutely; exactly
ves-per *n.* evening prayer service; a bell to call people to such a service
ves-sel *n.* hollow or concave utensil, as a bottle, kettle, container, or jar; a hollow craft designed for navigation on water
vest *n.* a sleeveless garment open or fastening in front, worn over a shirt
ves-tige *n.* trace or visible sign of something that no longer exists **vestigial** *adj.*, **vestigially** *adj.*
ves-try *n., pl.* **vestries** room in a church used for meetings
vet *n., Slang* veterinarian; a veteran
vet-er-an *n.* person with a long record or experience in a certain field; one who has served in the military
vet-er-i-nar-i-an *n.* one who is trained and authorized to give medical treatment to animals
vet-er-i-nar-y *adj.* pertaining to the science and art of prevention and treatment of animals
ve-to- *n., pl.* **vetoes** power of a government executive, as the President or a governor, to reject a bill passed by the legislature
vex *v.* to bother or annoy
vi-a *prep.* by way of; by means of
vi-a-duct *n.* bridge, resting on a series of arches
vi-al *n.* small, closed container used especially for liquids
vi-brate *v.* move or make move back and forth or up and down
vi-car-i-ous *adj.* undergoind or serving in the place of someone or something else; experienced through sympathetic or imaginative participation in the experience of another
vice *n.* immoral habit or practice; evil conduct
vi-ce ver-sa *adv.* with the order or meaning of something reversed
vi-chy-ssoise *n.* a soup made from potatoes, chicken stock, and cream, flavored with leeks or onions and usually served cold
vi-cin-i-ty *n., pl.* **-ies** surrounding area or district; the state of being near in relationship or space
vi-cious *adj.* dangerously aggressive; having the quality of immorality
vic-tim *n.* person who is harmed or killed by another **victimize** *v.*
vic-tor *n.* person who conquers; the winner
vic-to-ri-ous *adj.* being the winner in a contest **victoriously** *adv.*
vic-to-ry *n., pl.* **victories** defeat of those on the opposite side
vid-e-o *adj.* being, related to, or used in the reception or transmission of television
vid-e-o disc *n.* disc containing recorded images and sounds
vid-e-o game *n.* computerized game displaying on a display screen
vid-e-o term-in-al *n. Computer Science* computer device having a cathoderay tube for displaying data on a screen

vie *v.* strive for superiority
view *n.* act of examining or seeing; a judgment or opinion
vig-il *n.* a watch with prayers kept on the night before a religious feast; a period of surveillance
vig-or *n.* energy or physical strength; intensity of effect or action
vile *adj.* morally disgusting, miserable, and unpleasant
vil-la *n.* a luxurious home in the country; a country estate
vil-lage *n.* incorporated settlement, usually smaller than a town
vil-lain *n.* evil or wicked person
vin-ai-grette *n.* a small ornamental bottle with a periorated top, used for holding an aromatic preparation such as smelling salts
vin-di-cate *v.* to clear of suspicion; to set free **vindication** *n.*
vin-dic-tive *adj.* showing or possessing a desire for revenge; spiteful
vine *n.* plant whose stem needs support as it climbs or clings to a surface
vin-e-gar *n.* a tart, sour liquid derived from cider or wine
vin-tage *n.* the grapes or wine produced from a particular district in one season
vi-nyl *n.* variety of shiny plastics, similar to leather, often used for clothing and for covering furniture
vi-o-la *n.* stringed instrument, slightly larger and deeper in tone than a violin
vi-o-late *v.* break the law or a rule; to disrupt or disturb a person's privacy **violation** *n.*
vi-o-lence *n.* physical force or activity used to cause harm, damage, or abuse
vi-o-let *n.* small, low-growing plant with blue, purple, or white flowers; a purplish-blue color
vi-o-lin *n.* a small stringed instrument, played with a bow
vi-per *n.* a poisonous snake; an evil or treacherous person
vir-gin *n.* person who has never had sexual intercourse *adj.* in an unchanged or natural state
Vir-go *n.* the sixth sign of the zodiac; a person born betweeb August 23rd and September 22nd
vir-ile *adj.* having the qualities and nature of a man; capable of sexual performance in the male
vir-tu *n.* the love or knowledge of fine objects of art
vir-tue *n.* morality, goodness or uprightness; a special type of goodness **virtuous** *adj.*
vi-rus *n.* any of a variety of microscopic organisms which cause diseases
vi-sa *n.* an offical authorization giving permission on a passport to enter a specific country
vis-cid *adj.* sticky; having an adhesive quality
vise or vice *n.* a tool in carpentry and metalwork having two jaws to hold things in position
vis-i-bil-i-ty *n., pl.* **-ies** degree or state of being visible; the distance that one is able to see clearly
vis-i-ble *adj.* apparent; exposed to view
vi-sion *n.* power of sight; the ability to see; an image created in the imagination; a supernatural appearance
vis-it *v.* journey to or come to see a person or place *n.* a professional or social call *Slang* to chat
vi-su-al *adj.* visible; relating to seeing or sight
vi-tal *adj.* essential to life; very important **vitally** *adv.*
vi-ta-min *n.* any of various substances which are found in foods and are essential to good health
vit-re-ous *adj.* related to or similar to glass
vi-va-cious *adj.* filled with vitality or animation; lively
viv-id *adj.* bright; brilliant; intense; having clear, lively, bright colors
viv-i-fy *v.* give life to
vo-cab-u-lar-y *n., pl.* **vocabularies** list or group of words and phrases, usually in alphabetical order; all the words that a person uses or understands
vo-cal *adj.* of or related to the voice; uttered by the voice; to speak freely and loudly *n.* vocal sound
vogue *n.* leading style or fashion; popularity
voice *n.* sounds produced by speaking; the ability or power to produce musical tones *v.* to express; to utter
void *adj.* containing nothing; empty; not inhabited
voile *n.* a fine, soft, sheer fabric used for making light clothing and curtains
volt-age *n.* amount of electrical power, given in terms of the number of volts
vol-ume *n.* capacity or amount of space or room; a book; a quantity; the loudness of a sound
vol-un-tar-y *adj.* done cooperatively or willingly; from one's own choice
vol-un-teer *n.* one who offers himself for a service of his own free will *adj.* consisting of volunteers
vo-lup-tuous *adj.* full of pleasure; delighting the senses; sensuous; luxury
vom-it *v.* eject contents of the stomach through the mouth
vo-ra-cious *adj.* having a large appetite; insatiable
vote *n.* expression of one's choice by voice, by raising one's hand, or by secret ballot **voter** *n.*
vouch *v.* verify or support as true; to guarantee
vow *n.* solemn pledge or promise, especially one made to God; a marriage vow
vow-el *n.* sound of speech made by voicing the flow of breath within the mouth; a letter representing a vowel
vul-gar *adj.* showing poor manners; crude; improper; immoral or indecent
vul-ner-a-ble *adj.* open to physical injury or attack
vul-ture *n.* large bird of the hawk family, living on dead animals; a greedy person

W, w The twenty-third letter of the English alphabet.
wacky *adj.* amusingly or absurdly irrational
wad *n.* small crumpled mass or bundle
wad-dle *v.* walk with short steps and swing from side to side
waddle, waddler *n.*
wade *v.* walk through a substance as mud or water which hampers one's steps
wad-able *adj.* having the capability of being wadded
wad-ding *n.* materials for wadding or wads; a sheet of loose fibers that is used for stuffing
wad-dle *v.* to walk with short steps and swing from side to side
wa-fer *n.* small, thin, crisp cracker, cookie, or candy
waf-fle *n.* pancake batter cooked in a waffle iron
waft *v.* drift or move gently, as by the motion of water or air **waft** *n.*
wag *v.* move quickly from side to side or up and down *n.* playful, witty person
waggish *adj.*
wage *n.* payment of money for labor or services *v.* to conduct
wa-ger *v.* make a bet
wag-on *n.* four-wheeled vehicle used to transport goods; a station wagon; a child's four-wheeled cart with a long handle
waif *n.* abandoned, homeless, or lost child
wail *n.* loud, mournful cry or weep
waist *n.* narrow part of the body between the thorax and hips **waisted** *adj.*
wait *v.* stay in one place in expectation of; to await; to put off until a later time or date
wait-er *n.* man who serves food at a restaurant
wait-ress *n.* woman who serves food at a restaurant
waive *v.* forfeit of one's own free will; to postpone or dispense with
wake *v.* come to consciousness, as from sleep *n.* vigil for a dead body.
walk *v.* move on foot over a surface; to pass over, go on
walk-out *n.* labor strike against a company
wall *n.* vertical structure to separate or enclose an area *v.* to provide or close up, as with a wall
wal-la-by *n.* small or medium-sized kangaroo
wal-let *n.* flat folding case for carrying paper money
wal-lop *n.* powerful blow; an impact *v.* to move with disorganized haste
walloper *n.*
wall-pa-per *n.* decorative paper for walls, usually having a colorful pattern
wal-nut *n.* edible nut with a hard, light-brown shell; the tree on which this nut grows
wal-rus *n.* large marine mammal of the seal family, having flippers, tusks, and a tough hide
waltz *n.* ballroom dance
wam-pum *n.* polished shells, once used as currency by North American Indians *Slang* Money
wand *n.* slender rod used by a magician
wan-der *v.* travel about aimlessly; to roam; to stray **wanderer** *n.*
wane *v.* decrease in size or extent; to decrease gradually *n.* gradual deterioration
wan-gle *v.* resort to devious methods in order to obtain something wanted
wangler *n.*
want *v.* wish for or desire; to need; to lack; to fail to possess a required amount
war *n.* armed conflict among states or nations
ward *n.* section in a hospital.
v. to keep watch over someone or something
ware *n.* manufactured items of the same general kind; items or goods for sale
ware-house *n.* large building used to store merchandise
warm *adj.* moderate heat; neither hot or cold
warn *v.* give notice or inform beforehand; to call to one's attention; to alert
warp *v.* become bent out of shape; to deviate from a proper course
war-rant *n.* written authorization giving the holder legal power to search, seize, or arrest
warrantable *adj.*
war-ri-or *n.* one who fights in a war or battle
war-y *adj.* marked by caution; alert to danger
wash *v.* cleanse by the use of water; to remove dirt
wash--and--wear *adj.* requiring little or no ironing after washing
wash-board *n.* corrugated board on which clothes are rubbed in the process of washing
washed--out *adj., Slang* tired
wash-er *n.* small disk usually made of rubber or metal having a hole in the center, used with nuts and bolts; a washing machine
wash-ing *n.* clothes and other articles that are washed or to be washed; cleaning
was-n't *contr.* was not
wasp *n.* any of various insects, having a slim body with a constricted abdomen, the female capable of inflicting a painful sting
waste *v.* to be thrown away; to be available but not used completely **-ful** *adj.*
watch *v.* view carefully; to guard; to keep informed
watch-dog *n.* dog trained to guard someone or his property
watch-ful *adj.* carefully observant or attentive **watchfully** *adv.*
watch-man *n.* person hired to keep watch; a guard
wa-ter *n.* clear liquid making up oceans, lakes, and streams; the body fluids as

tears or urine
water moccasin *n.* venomous snake
water polo *n.* water game between two teams
water power *n.* power or energy produced by swift-moving water
wa-ter-proof *adj.* capable of preventing water from penetrating
wa-ter-shed *n.* The raised area between two regions that divides two sections drained by different river sources
wa-ter--ski *v.* travel over water on a pair of short, broad skis while being pulled by a motorboat
wa-ter-spout *n.* tube or pipe through which water is discharged
water table *n.* upper limit of the portion of the ground completely saturated with water
wa-ter-tight *adj.* closed or sealed so tightly that no water can enter
wa-ter-way *n.* navigable body of water; a channel for water
wa-ter-y *adj.* containing water; diluted; lacking effectiveness **wateriness** *n.*
watt *n.* unit of electrical power represented by current of one ampere, produced by the electromotive force of one volt
wave *v.* move back and forth or up and down; to motion with the hand
wa-ver *v.* sway unsteadily; to move back and forth; to weaken in force
waver *n.*, **waveringly** *adv.*
wax *n.* natural yellowish substance made by bees, solid when cold and easily melted or softened when heated
way *n.* manner of doing something; a tendency or characteristic
way-far-er *n.* person who travels on foot
way-lay *v.* attack by ambush
way-ward *adj.* unruly; unpredictable
we *pl., pron.* used to refer to the person speaking and one or more other people
weak *adj.* having little energy or strength; easily broken; having inadequate skills
weakness *n.*, **weakly** *adv.*
wealth *n.* abundance of valuable possessions or property
wean *v.* accustom an infant or small child to food other than a mother's milk or bottle
weap-on *n.* device which can be used to harm another person
wear *v.* to have on or put something on the body; to display **wearable** *adj.*
wea-ri-some *adj.* tedious, boring or tiresome
wea-ry *adj.* exhausted; tired; feeling fatigued **wearily** *adv.*, **-iness** *n.*
wea-sel *n.* mammal with a long tail and short legs; a sly, sneaky person
weath-er *n.* condition of the air or atmosphere in terms of humidity, temperature, and similar features
weath-er-man *n.* man who reports or forecasts the weather
weather vane *n.* device that turns, indicating the direction of the wind
weave *v.* make a basket, cloth, or other item by interlacing threads or other strands of material **weaver** *n.*
web *n.* cobweb; piece of interlacing material which forms a woven structure
wed *v.* take as a spouse; to marry
we'd *contr.* we had; we should
wed-ding *n.* marriage ceremony; an act of joining together in close association
wedge *n.* tapered, triangular piece of wood or metal used to split logs, to add leverage, and to hold something open or ajar
weed *n.* unwanted plant which interferes with the growth of grass, vegetables, or flowers
week *n.* period of seven days, beginning with Sunday and ending with Saturday
week-day *n.* any day of the week except Saturday or Sunday
week-end *n.* end of the week from the period of Friday evening through Sunday evening
weep *v.* to shed tears; to express sorrow, joy, or emotion
wee-vil *n.* small beetle having a downward-curving snout
weigh *v.* determine the heaviness of an object by using a scale; to consider carefully in one's mind
weight *n.* amount that something weighs; heaviness; a heavy object used to hold or pull something down
weight-less *adj.* lacking the pull of gravity; having little weight
weight-y *adj.* burdensome; important
weird *adj.* having an extraordinary or strange character **weirdly** *adv.*
weird-o *n., Slang* person who is very strange
wel-come *v.* extend warm hospitality; to accept gladly
weld *v.* unite metallic parts by applying heat and sometimes pressure, allowing the metals to bond together
wel-fare *n.* state of doing well; governmental aid to help the disabled or disadvantaged
well *n.* hole in the ground which contains a supply of water; a shaft in the ground through which gas and oil are obtained
we'll *contr.* we will; we shall
well--be-ing *n.* state of being healthy, happy, or prosperous
well--done *adj.* completely cooked; done properly
well--groomed *adj.* clean, neat, and properly cared for
well--known *adj.* widely known
well--man-nered *adj.* polite; having good manners
well--mean-ing *adj.* having good intentions
well--to--do *adj.* having more than enough wealth
welsh *v., Slang* cheat by avoiding a payment to someone; to neglect an obligation
welt *n.* strip between the sole and upper part of a shoe; a slight swelling on the body
wel-ter-weight *n.* boxer weighing be-

tween 136 and 147 pounds
went *v.* past tense of go
wept *v.* past tense of weep
were *v.* second person singular past plural of be
we're *contr.* we are
were-n't *contr.* were not
west *n.* direction of the setting sun
western *adj.*
whack *v.* strike with a hard blow, to slap
n. an attempt
whale *n.* very large mammal resembling a fish which lives in salt water
wharf *n.* pier or platform built at the edge of water so that ships can load and unload
what *pron.* which one; which things; which type or kind
what-ev-er *pron.* everything or anything
adj. no matter what
what's *contr.* what is
wheat *n.* grain ground into flour, used to make breads and similar foods
wheel *n.* a circular disk which turns on an axle
wheel-bar-row *n.* vehicle having one wheel, used to transport small loads
wheel-chair *n.* a mobile chair for disabled persons
wheel-er *n.* anything that has wheels
wheeze *v.* breathe with a hoarse whistling sound
n. high whistling sound
whelk *v.* any of various large water snails, sometimes edible
when *adv.* at what time; at which time
pron. what or which time
conj. while; at the time that
whence *adv.* from what source or place; from which
when-ev-er *adv.* at any time; when
conj. at whatever time
where *adv.* at or in what direction or place; in what direction or place
where-a-bouts *adv.* near, at, or in a particular location
n. approximate location
where-as *conj.* it being true or the fact; on the contrary
where-by *conj.* through or by which
wher-ev-er *adv.* in any situation or place
whet *v.* to make sharp; to stimulate
wheth-er *conj.* indicating a choice; alternative possibilities; either
whet-stone *n.* stone used to sharpen scissors, knives, and other implements
whew *n., interj.* used to express relief; or tiredness
whey *n.* clear, water-like part of milk that separates from the curd
which *pron.* what one or ones; the one previously; whatever one or ones; whichever
which-ev-er *pron.* any; no matter which or what
whiff *n.* slight puff; a light current of air; a slight breath or odor
while *n.* length or period of time
conj. during the time that; even though; at the same time
whim *n.* sudden desire or impulse
whim-per *v.* make a weak, soft crying sound
whim-si-cal *adj.* impulsive; erratic; light and spontaneous **whimsically** *adv.*
whine *v.* make a squealing, plaintive sound; to complain in an irritating, childish fashion
whin-ny *v.* neigh in a soft gentle way
whip *v.* spank repeatedly with a rod or stick; to punish by whipping
n. flexible stick or rod used to herd or beat animals **whipper** *n.*
whip-lash *n.* injury to the spine or neck caused by a sudden jerking motion of the head
whip-poor-will *n.* brownish nocturnal bird of North America
whir *v.* move with a low purring sound
whirl *v.* rotate or move in circles; to twirl; to move
whirl-pool *n.* circular current of water
whirl-wind *n.* violently whirling mass of air; a tornado
whirl-y-bird *n., Slang* helicopter
whisk *v.* move with a sweeping motion; move quickly or lightly
whisk-er *n.* hair that grows on a man's face; the long hair near the mouth of dogs, cats, and other animals
whiskers man's beard
whis-key *n.* alcoholic beverage distilled from rye, barley, or corn
whis-per *v.* speak in a very low tone; to tell in secret
whis-tle *v.* make a clear shrill sound by blowing air through the teeth, through puckered lips, or through a special instrument
white *n.* color opposite of black; the part of something that is white or light in color, as an egg or the eyeball; a member of the Caucasian group of people
white-cap *n.* wave having a top of white foam
white--col-lar *adj.* relating to an employee whose job does not require manual labor
white-wash *n.* mixture made of lime and other ingredients and used for whitening fences and exterior walls
whith-er *adv.* what state, place, or circumstance; wherever
whit-tle *v.* cut or carve off small shavings from wood with a knife; to remove or reduce gradually
whittler *n.*
who *pron.* which or what certain individual, person, or group
who'd *contr.* who would; who had
who-ev-er *pron.* whatever person; all or any persons
whole *adj.* complete; having nothing missing; not divided or in pieces
whole-heart-ed *adj.* sincere; totally committed
whole-sale *n.* sale of goods in large amounts to a retailer
whole-some *adj.* contributing to good mental or physical health
wholesomely *adv.*, **-ness** *n.*
whole wheat *adj.* made from the wheat kernel with nothing removed
who'll *contr.* who shall; who will

whol-ly *adv.* totally; exclusively
whom *pron.* form of who used as the direct object of a verb or the object of the preposition
whom-ev-er *pron.* form of whoever used as the object of a preposition or the direct object of a verb
whooping cough *n.* infectious disease of the throat and breathing passages
whooping crane *n.* large bird of North America, nearly extinct
whoosh *v.* make a rushing or gushing sound, as a rush of air
whop-per *n.* something of extraordinary size *Slang* a lie
whore *n.* prostitute
who's *contr.* who is; who has
whose *pron.* belonging to or having to do with one's belongings
why *adj.* for what reason or purpose *conj.* cause, purpose, or reason for which *interj.* expressing surprise or disagreement
wick *n.* soft strand of fibers which extends from a candle or lamp
wick-er *n.* thin, pliable twig used to make furniture and baskets
wick-et *n.* wire hoop in the game of croquet
wide *adj.* broad; covering a large area; completely extended or open *adv.* over a large area; full extent
wide-spread *adj.* fully spread out; over a broad area
wid-ow *n.* woman whose husband is no longer living
wid-ow-er *n.* man whose wife is no longer living
width *n.* distance or extent of something from side to side
wield *v.* use or handle something skillfully; to employ power effectively
wie-ner *n.* frankfurter; a hot dog
wife *n.* married female
wig *n.* artificial or human hair woven together to cover baldness or a bald spot on the head
wig-gle *v.* squirm; to move with rapid side-to-side motions **-er** *n.*
wig-wam *n.* Indian dwelling place
wild *adj.* living in a natural, untamed state; not occupied by man; not civilized; strange and unusual *adv.* out of control *n.* wilderness region not cultivated or settled by man
wild-cat *n.* medium-sized wild, feline animal; one with a quick temper
wil-der-ness *n.* unsettled area; a region left in its uncultivated or natural state
wild-life *n.* animals and plants living in their natural environments
will *n.* mental ability to decide or choose for oneself; strong desire or determination; a legal document stating how one's property is to be distributed after death
wil-low *n.* large tree, usually having narrow leaves and slender flexible twigs
wilt *v.* cause or to become limp; to lose force; to deprive of courage or energy
win *v.* defeat others; to gain victory in a contest; to receive *n.* victory; the act of winning **winner** *n.*
winch *n.* apparatus with one or more drums on which a cable or rope is wound, used to lift heavy loads
wind *n.* natural movement of air **windy** *adj.*
wind *v.* wrap around and around something; to turn, to crank *n.* turning or twisting
wind-bag *n., Slang* person who talks excessively without saying anything of importance
wind-fall *n.* sudden or unexpected stroke of good luck
wind instrument *n.* musical instrument which produces sound when a person forces his breath into it
wind-mill *n.* machine operated or powered by the wind
win-dow *n.* opening built into a wall for light and air; a pane of glass
win-dow-shop *v.* look at merchandise in store windows without going inside to buy
wind-pipe *n.* passage in the neck used for breathing; the trachea
wine *n.* drink containing 10-15% alcohol by volume, made by fermenting grapes
wing *n.* one of the movable appendages that allow a bird or insect to fly; one of the airfoils on either side of an aircraft
wing-spread *n.* extreme measurement from the tips or outer edges of the wings of an aircraft, bird, or other insect
wink *v.* shut one eye as a signal or message
win-ning *adj.* defeating others; captivating *n.* victory
win-some *adj.* very pleasant; charming
win-ter *n.* coldest season, coming between autumn and spring *adj.* relating to or typically of winter
win-ter-green *n.* small plant having aromatic evergreen leaves
wipe *v.* clean by rubbing; to take off by rubbing *n.* act or instance of wiping
wire *n.* small metal rod used to conduct electricity; thin strands of metal twisted together to form a cable; the telephone or telegraph system
wis-dom *n.* ability to understand what is right, true, or enduring; good judgment; knowledge
wise *adj.* having superior intelligence; having great learning; having a capacity for sound judgment marked by deep understanding **wisely** *adv.*
wise-crack *n., Slang* witty remark or joke usually showing a lack of respect
wish *v.* desire or long for something; to command or request *n.* longing or desire
wish-bone *n.* bone of a bird, which, according to the superstition, when broken brings good luck to the person who has the longer end
wish-ful *adj.* having or expressing a wish; hopeful **wishfully** *adv.*
wish-y-wash-y *adj., Slang* not purposeful; indecisive

wisp *n.* tuft or small bundle of hay, straw, or hair; a thin piece
wispy *adj.*
wit *n.* ability to use words in a clever way; a sense of humor
witch *n.* person believed to have magical powers; a mean, ugly, old woman
with *prep.* in the company of; near or alongside; having, wearing or bearing
with-draw *v.* take away; to take back; to retreat
with-draw-al *n.* process of with-drawing; a retreat; the act of removing money from an account
whither *v.* dry up or wilt from a lack of moisture; to lose freshness or vigor
with-hold *n.* hold back or keep
withholding tax *n.* tax on income held back by an employer in payment of one's income tax
with-in *adv.* inside the inner part; inside the limits; inside the limits of time, distance, or degree
with-out *adv.* on the outside; not in possession of
prep. something or someone lacking
with-stand *v.* endure
wit-ness *n.* person who has seen, experienced, or heard something; something serving as proof or evidence
wit-ty *adj.* amusing or cleverly humorous
wiz-ard *n.* very clever person; a person thought to have magical powers *Slang* one with amazing skill
wob-ble *v.* move unsteadily from side to side, as a rocking motion
woe *n.* great sorrow or grief; misfortune
wok *n.* convex metal cooker for stir-frying food
woke *v.* past tense of wake
wolf *n.* carnivorous animal found in northern areas; a fierce person *v.* eat quickly and with greed
wolfish *adj.*, **wolfishly** *adv.*
woman *n.* mature adult human female; a person who has feminine qualities
womanhood *n.* state of being a woman
womb *n.* uterus; place where development occurs
won *v.* past tense of win
won-der *n.* feeling of amazement or admiration *v.* feel admiration; feel uncertainty
won-der-ment *n.* feeling or state of amazement
won-drous *adj.* wonderful; marvelous
won't *contr.* will not
won-ton *n.* noodle dumpling filled with minced pork and served in soup
wood *n.* hard substance which makes up the main part of trees
wood-chuck *n.* rodent having short legs and a heavyset body, which lives in a burrow
wood-en *adj.* made of wood; resembling wood; stiff; lifeless; lacking flexibility
wood-peck-er *n.* bird which uses its bill for drilling holes in trees looking for insects to eat
wood-wind *n.* group of musical instruments which produce sounds when air is blown through the mouthpiece, as the clarinet
wool *n.* soft, thick hair of sheep and other such mammals; a fabric made from such hair
word *n.* meaningful sound which stands for an idea; a comment
word processing *n.* system which produces typewritten documents with automated type and editing equipment
work-er *n.* person who works for wages; an employee; a bee or other insect which performs special work in the colony in which it lives
work-ing *adj.* adequate to permit work to be done; assumed to permit further work
work-man-ship *n.* skill or art of a craftsman; quality given to something in the process of making it
world *n.* planet Earth; the universe; the human race
worn *adj.* made weak or thin from use; exhausted
wor-ry *v.* oncerned or troubled; to tug at repeatedly; to annoy; to irritate
wor-ship *n.* reverence for a sacred object; high esteem or devotion for a person *v.* revere; attend a religious service **worshiper** *n.*
worst *adj.* bad; most inferior; most disagreeable
worth *n.* quality or value of something; personal merit
wor-thy *adj.* valuable or useful; deserving admiration or honor
would-n't *contr.* would not
wound *n.* laceration of the skin *v.* injure by tearing, cutting, or piercing the skin
wow *interj.* expression of amazement, surprise, or excitement
wran-gle *v.* quarrel noisily
wrap *v.* fold in order to protect something; encase or enclose
wrath *n.* violent anger or fury
wreak *v.* inflict punishment upon another person
wreath *n.* decorative ring-like form of intertwined flowers, bows, and other articles
wreck *v.* ruin or damage by accident or deliberately
wrest *v.* twist or pull away in a violent way
wretch *n.* extremely unhappy person; a miserable person
wrig-gle *v.* squirm; move by turning and twisting
wring *v.* squeeze and twist by hand or machine; press together
wrin-kle *n.* small crease on the skin or on fabric
writ *n.*, *Law* written court document directed to a public official or individual ordering a specific action
writhe *v.* twist, as in pain; suffer greatly with pain
wrong *adj.* incorrect; against moral standards; not suitable **wrongly** *adv.*
wrote *v.* past tense of write
wrought *adj.* fashioned; formed; beatened or hammered into shape
wrung *v.* past tense of wring

X, x The twenty-fourth letter of the English alphabet.
Xan-a-du *n.* a place having idyllic beauty
xan-thate *n.* ester or slat of a xanthic acid
xan-thic *adj.* the color yellow or all colors that tend toward the color yellow when relating to flowers
xan-thin *n.* a carotenoid pigment that is soluble in alcohol
xan-thine *n.* a crystalline nitrogen compound, closely related to uric acid, found in blood, urine and certain plant and animal tissues
xan-tho-chroid *adj.* pertaining to the light-complexioned caucasoid race
xan-tho-ma *n.* a skin condition of the eyelids marked by small, yellow, raised nodules or plates
X chro-mo-some *n.* the sex female chromosome, associated with female characteristics; occurs paired in the female and single in the male chromosome pair
xe-bec *n.* a small vessel with three-masts having both lateen and square sails
xe-nic *adj.* relating to, or employing a culture medium that contains one or more unidentified organisms
xe-non *n.* the colorless, odorless gaseous element found in small quantities in the air, symbolized by Xe
xe-no-phile *n.* one attracted to foreign people, styles, manners, etc.
xen-o-phobe *n.* a person who dislikes, fears, and mistrusts foreigners or anything strange **xenophobia** *n.*
xe-rarch *adj.* originating or developing in a dry place
xe-ric *adj.* relating to or requiring only a small amount of moisture
xe-ri-cal-ly *adv.*
xe-roph-i-lous *adj.* tolerant or characteristic of xeric environments
xerophily *n.*
xe-roph-thal-mi-a *n.* a itching soreness of the eyes that is caused by an insufficient amount of vitamin A
xerophthalmic *adj.*
xe-ro-phyte *n.* a plant that can live in a surrounding of extreme heat and drought **xerophytic** *adj.*, **xerophytically** *adv.*, **xerophytism** *n.*
XL *abbr.* extra large
X-mas *abbr., n.* Christmas
X--ra-di-a-tion *n.* treatment with X-rays
X ray *n.* energy that is radiated with a short wavelength and high penetrating power; a black and white negative image or picture of the interior of the body
x--sec-tion *n.* cross section of something **x-sectional** *adj.*
xy-lo-phone *n.* a musical instrument consisting of mounted wooden bars which produce a ringing musical sound when struck with two small wooden hammers **xylophonist** *n.*
xy-lose *n.* a crystalline aldose sugar
xy-lot-o-mous *adj.* capable of cutting or boring wood **xylotomic** *adj.*

Y, y The twenty-fifth letter of the English alphabet.
yacht *n.* a small sailing vessel powdered by wind or motor, used for pleasure cruises **yacht** *v.*
yacht-ing *n.* the sport of sailing in a yacht
yachts-man *n.* a person who sails a yacht **yachtsmanship, -ship** *n.*
yak *n.* a long-haired ox of Tibet and the mountains of central Asia
yam *n.* an edible root; a variety of the sweet potato
Yan-kee *n.* a native of the northern United States **Yankee** *adj.*
yap *v.* to bark in a high pitched, sharp way. *Slang* To talk in a relentess, loud, or stupid manner
yard *n.* a unit of measure that equals 36 inches or 3 feet; the ground around or near a house or building
yard goods *n.* fabric that is sold by the yard
yard-man *n.* a person employed as a worker in a railroad yard
yard-mas-ter *n.* a person in charge of a railroad yard
yard-stick *n.* a graduated measuring stick that equals 1 yard or 36 inches; standard of measurement
yarn *n.* twisted fibers, as of wool, used in knitting or weaving *Slang* An involved tale or story
yawn *v.* to inhale a deep breath with the mouth open wide **yawn, yawner** *n.*
yawn-ing *adj.* expressing tiredness by a yawn
Y-Chro-mo-some *n.* the sex chromosome associated with male characteristics.
ye *pron.* you, used especially in religious contexts, as hymns
yea *adv.* yes; indeed; truly
yeah *adv., Slang* yes
year *n.* a period of time starting on January 1st and continuing through December 31st, consisting of 365 days or 366 days in a leap year
year-book *n.* a book printed each year giving facts about the year; a book printed each year for a high school, college, etc.
year-ling *n.* an animal that is one year old
year-ly *adj.* pertaining to something that happens, appears, or comes once a year, every year
yearn *v.* to feel a strong craving; deep desire; a wistful feeling **yearner, yearning** *n.*
year--round *adj.* lasting or continuing for an entire year
yeast *n.* fungi or plant cells used to make baked goods rise or fruit juices ferment
yell *v.* to cry out loudly. *n.* A loud cry; a cheer to show support for an athletic team
yel-low *n.* the bright color of a lemon; the yolk of an egg *v.* to make or become yellow *adj.* of the color yellow *Slang* cowardly
yel-low fev-er *n.* an acute infectious disease of the tropics, spread by the

bite of a mosquito
yel-low-fin tuna *n.* small tuna with yellow-tipped fins and light flesh
yel-low-jack-et *n.* a small wasp, having bright yellow markings, and usually makes its nest below ground level
yelp *n.* a quick, sharp, shrill cry, as from pain
yen *n.* an intense craving or longing
yeo-man *n.* the owner of a small farm; a petty officer who acts as a clerk
yes *adv.* to express agreement
yes-ter-day *n.* the day before today; a former or recent time *adv.* on the day before the present day
yet *adv.* up to now; at this time; even now; more so *conj.* nevertheless; but
yield *v.* to bear or bring forward; to give up the possession of something; to give way to *n.* an amount that is produced
yield-ing *adj.* ready to yield, comply, or submit; unresisting **yieldingly** *adv.*
yo-del *v.* to sing in a way so that the voice changes from normal to a high shrill sound and then back again
yo-ga *n.* a system of exercises which helps the mind and the body in order to achieve tranquillity and spiritual insight
yo-del *n.* a very unsophisticated country person; a bumpkin
yolk *n.* the yellow nutritive part of an egg
Yom Kip-pur *n.* the Jewish holiday observed with fasting and prayer for the forgiveness of sins
you *pron.* the person or persons addressed
you all *pron., Slang* **y'all** a southern variation used for two or more people in direct address
you'd *contr.* you had; you would
you'll *contr.* you will; you shall
young *adj.* of or relating to the early stage of life; not old *n.* the offspring of an animal **youngster** *n.*
your *adj.* belonging to you or yourself or the person spoken to
you're *contr.* you are
your-self *pron.* a form of you for emphasis when the object of a verb and the subject is the same
youth *n.* the appearance or state of being young; the time of life when one is not considered an adult; a young person
youth-ful *adj.* being of a young age or early stage in life **youthfully** *adv.*, **youthfulness** *n.*
you've *contr.* you have
yowl *v.* to make a loud, long cry or howl **yowl** *n.*
yo-yo *n.* A grooved spool toy with a string wrapped around the spool so it can be spun or moved up and down.
yt-ter-bi-um *n.* a metallic element of the rare-earth group symbolized by Yb
yt-tri-um *n.* a metallic element symbolized by Y
yuc-ca *n.* a tropical plant having large, white flowers and long, pointed leaves
yule *n.* Christmas
yule-tide *n.* the Christmas season

Z, z The twenty-sixth letter of the English alphabet.
za-ny *n., pl* **-nies** a clown; a person who acts silly or foolish *adj.* typical of being clownish **zaniness** *n.*, **zanily** *adv.*
zap *v., Slang* to destroy; to do away with
zeal *n.* great interest or eagerness
zeal-ot *n.* a fanatical person; a fanatic
zeal-ous *adj.* full of interest; eager; passionate **zealously** *adv.*, **zealousness** *n.*
ze-bra *n.* an African mammal of the horse family having black or brown stripes on a white body
zeph-yr *n.* a gentle breeze
ze-ro *n., pl.* **-ros, -roes** the number or symbol "0"; nothing; the point from which degrees or measurements on a scale begin; the lowest point *v.* to aim, point at, or close in on *adj.* pertaining to zero; nonexisting
zest *n.* enthusiasm; a keen quality **zestful** *adj.*, **zestfully**, *adv.*, **zesty** *adj.*
zig-zag *n.* a pattern with sharp turns in alternating directions *adv.* to move in a zigzag course or path **zigzag** *v.*
zilch *n., Slang* nothing; zero
zinc *n.* a bluish-white crystalline metallic element, used as a protective coating for steel and iron, symbolized by Zn
zip *n.* to act or move with vigor or speed *v.* to move with energy, speed, or facility; to open or close with a zipper *Slang* energy; zero; nothing
zip code *n.* the system to speed the delivery of mail by assigning a five digit number, plus four to each postal delivery location in the United States
zip-per *n.* a fastener consisting of two rows of plastic or metal teeth that are interlocked by means of sliding a tab
zir-co-ni-um *n.* a metallic element symbolized by Zr
zit *n., Slang* a pimple
zom-bie *n.* a person who resembles the walking dead; a person who has a strange appearance or behavior
zone *n.* an area or region set apart from its surroundings by some characteristic
zonk *v., Slang* to stun; to render senseless with alcohol or drugs
zoo *n., pl.* **zoos** a public display or collection of living animals
zo-ol-o-gy *n.* the science that deals with animals, animal life, and the animal kingdom **zoologist** *n.*
zoom *v.* to move with a continuous, loud, buzzing sound; to move upward sharply; to move toward a subject with great speed
zuc-chi-ni *n., pl.* **-ni** a summer squash that is long and narrow and has a dark-green, smooth rind
zwie-back *n.* a sweetened bread which is baked, sliced, and toasted to make it crisp
zy-mol-o-gy *n.* the branch of science dealing with ferments and fermentation **zymologic** *adj.*
zy-mo-scope *n.* an instrument that measures yeast's fermenting power

WEBSTER'S

THESAURUS

DICTIONARY FORMAT
OF
SYNONYMS AND ANTONYNMS

DEFINITION OF THESAURUS

SYNONYMS: Words having the same meaning.

Example:
Give *(syn.)* offer, present, supply

ANTONYMS: Words having the opposite meaning.

Example:
Cold *(ant.)* hot, warm, heated

a *(SYN.)* any, one.
abandon *(SYN.)* relinquish, resign, surrender, leave, give up, cease, forsake.
(ANT.) support, keep, fulfill, uphold, depend, stay, maintain, embrace.
abandoned *(SYN.)* depraved, wicked, deserted, desolate, forsaken, rejected.
(ANT.) befriended, cherished, chaste, moral, respectable, virtuous, righteous.
abate *(SYN.)* lessen, curtail, reduce, decrease, restrain, decline, stop.
(ANT.) grow, prolong, increase, extend.
abbey *(SYN.)* nunnery, convent, cloisters, monastery.
abbot *(SYN.)* friar, monk.
abbreviate *(SYN.)* shorten, lessen, abridge, condense, curtail, reduce, cut.
(ANT.) lengthen, increase, expand.
abbreviation *(SYN.)* abridgment, reduction, shortening, condensation.
(ANT.) expansion, extension, amplification, lengthening, dilation.
abdicate *(SYN.)* relinquish, renounce, vacate, waive, desert, forsake, abolish.
(ANT.) maintain, defend, retain, uphold.
abdomen *(SYN.)* paunch, belly, stomach.
abduct *(SYN.)* carry off, take, kidnap.
abettor *(SYN.)* accomplice, ally, confederate, associate, accessory.
(ANT.) opponent, rival, enemy.
abhor *(SYN.)* dislike, hate, loathe, execrate, avoid, scorn, detest, despise.
abhorrent *(SYN.)* loathsome, horrible, detestable, nauseating, hateful.
abide *(SYN.)* obey, accept, tolerate, endure, dwell, stay, reside.
ability *(SYN.)* aptness, capability, skill, dexterity, faculty, power, talent.
(ANT.) incapacity, weakness, inability.
abject *(SYN.)* sordid, infamous, miserable, wretched, mean, contempt.
able *(SYN.)* qualified, competent, fit, capable, skilled, having power.
(ANT.) inadequate, trained, efficient, incapable, weak, incompetent, unable.
abnormal *(SYN.)* uncommon, unnatural, odd, irregular, monstrous, eccentric, unusual, weird, strange.
(ANT.) standard, natural, usual, normal, average.
aboard *(SYN.)* on board.
abolish *(SYN.)* end, eradicate, annul, cancel, revoke, destroy, invalidate.
(ANT.) promote, restore, continue, establish, sustain.
abominable *(SYN.)* foul, dreadful, hateful, revolting, vile, odious, loathsome.
(ANT.) delightful, pleasant, agreeable.
abominate *(SYN.)* despise, detest, hate, dislike, abhor, loathe.
(ANT.) love, cherish, approve, admire.
abomination *(SYN.)* detestation, hatred, disgust, revulsion, antipathy, horror.
abort *(SYN.)* flop, fizzle, miscarry, abandon, cancel.
abortion *(SYN.)* disaster, failure, defeat.
abound *(SYN.)* swarm, plentiful, filled.
(ANT.) scarce, lack.
about *(SYN.)* relating to, involving, concerning, near, around, upon, almost.
above *(SYN.)* higher than, overhead, on, upon, over, superior to.
(ANT.) under, beneath, below.
abrasion *(SYN.)* rubbing, roughness, scratching, scraping, friction, chap.
abrasive *(SYN.)* hurtful, sharp, galling, annoying, grating, irritating, caustic.
(ANT.) pleasant, soothing, comforting.
abreast *(SYN.)* side by side, alongside.
abridge *(SYN.)* condense, cut, abbreviate, make shorter, contract.
(ANT.) increase, lengthen, extend.
abroad *(SYN.)* away, overseas, widely.
(ANT.) at home, privately, secretly.
abrogate *(SYN.)* rescind, withdraw, revoke, annul, cancel, abolish, repeal.
abrupt *(SYN.)* sudden, unexpected, blunt, curt, craggy, precipitous, sharp.
(ANT.) foreseen, smooth, warm, courteous, gradual, smooth, expected.
abscess *(SYN.)* pustule, sore, wound, inflammation.
absence *(SYN.)* nonexistence, deficiency, lack, need, shortcoming.
(ANT.) attendance, completeness, existence, presence.
absent *(SYN.)* away, truant, abroad, departed, inattentive, lacking out, off.
(ANT.) attending, watchful, present.
absolute *(SYN.)* unconditional, entire, actual, complete, thorough, total.
(ANT.) partial, conditional, dependent accountable, restricted, qualified.
absolutely *(SYN.)* positively, really, doubtlessly.
(ANT.) doubtfully, uncertainly.
absolution *(SYN.)* pardon, forgiveness, acquittal, mercy, dispensation.
absolve *(SYN.)* exonerate, discharge, acquit, pardon, forgive, clear, excuse.
(ANT.) blame, convict, charge, accuse.
absorb *(SYN.)* consume, swallow up, engulf, assimilate, imbibe, engage.
(ANT.) discharge, dispense, emit, exude, leak, eliminate, bore, tire, weary, drain.
absorbent *(SYN.)* permeable, spongy, pervious, porous.
(ANT.) moisture-proof, impervious.
abstemious *(SYN.)* abstinent, sparing, cautious, temperate, ascetic.
(ANT.) uncontrolled, indulgent.
abstinence *(SYN.)* fasting, self-denial, continence, do without, sobriety.
(ANT.) greed, excess, self-indulgence.
abstract *(SYN.)* part, appropriate, steal, remove, draw from, separate, abridge.
(ANT.) return, unite, add, replace.
abstracted *(SYN.)* parted, removed, stolen, abridged, taken away.
(ANT.) replaced, returned, added.
abstraction *(SYN.)* idea, image, generalization, thought, opinion.
(ANT.) matter, object, thing, substance.
absurd *(SYN.)* ridiculous, silly, foolish, irrational, nonsensical, impossible.
(ANT.) rational, sensible, sound, meaningful, consistent, reasonable.
abundance *(SYN.)* ampleness, profusion, copiousness, plenty.
(ANT.) insufficiency, want, absence, dearth, scarcity.
abundant *(SYN.)* ample, overflowing, plentiful, rich, teeming, large amount, profuse, abounding.
(ANT.) insufficient, scant, not enough,

scarce, deficient, uncommon, absent.

abuse *(SYN.)* maltreatment, misuse, reproach, defamation, dishonor, mistreat, damage, ill-use, reviling, aspersion, desecration, invective, insult, outrage, profanation, perversion, upbraiding, disparagement, misemploy, misapply, hurt, harm, injure, berate.
(ANT.) plaudit, respect, appreciate, commendation. protect, praise, cherish.

abusive *(SYN.)* harmful, insulting, libelous, hurtful, slanderous, nasty, defamatory, injurious, scathing, derogatory.
(ANT.) supportive, helpful, laudatory, complimentary.

abut *(SYN.)* touch, border, meet, join, verge on, connect with.

abutment *(SYN.)* pier, buttress, bulwark, brace, support.

abysmal *(SYN.)* immeasurable, boundless, endless, stupendous, profound, unbelievable, infinite, overwhelming, consummate.

abyss *(SYN.)* depth, chasm, void, infinitude, limbo, unknowable.

academic *(SYN.)* learned, scholarly, theoretical, erudite, bookish, formal, pedantic.
(ANT.) ignorant, practical, simple, uneducated.

academy *(SYN.)* college, school.

accede *(SYN.)* grant, agree, comply, consent, yield, endorse, accept, admit.
(ANT.) dissent, disagree, differ, oppose.

accelerate *(SYN.)* quicken, dispatch, facilitate, hurry, rush, speed up, forward, hasten, push, expedite.
(ANT.) hinder, retard, slow, delay, quicken.

accent *(SYN.)* tone, emphasis, inflection, stress, consent.

accept *(SYN.)* take, approve, receive, allow, consent to, believe, adopt, admit.
(ANT.) ignore, reject, refuse.

acceptable *(SYN.)* passable, satisfactory, fair, adequate, standard, par, tolerable, unobjectionable.
(ANT.) poor, substandard, inadmissible.

access *(SYN.)* entrance, approach, course, gateway, door, avenue.

accessible *(SYN.)* nearby, attainable, achievable, affable, democratic, accommodating.
(ANT.) remote, unobtainable, unachievable, standoffish, forbidding, unfriendly.

accessory *(SYN.)* extra, addition, assistant, supplement, contributory, accomplice.

accident *(SYN.)* casualty, disaster, misfortune, mishap, chance, calamity, contingency, fortuity, misadventure, mischance, injury, event, catastrophe.
(ANT.) purpose, intention, calculation.

accidental *(SYN.)* unintended, chance, casual, fortuitous, contingent, unplanned, unexpected, unforeseen.
(ANT.) calculated, planned, willed, intended, intentional, on purpose, deliberate.

acclaim *(SYN.)* eminence, fame, glory, honor, reputation, credit, applaud, distinction, approve, notoriety.
(ANT.) infamy, obscurity, disapprove, reject, disrepute.

acclimated *(SYN.)* adapted, habituated, acclimatized, accommodated, seasoned, inured, used to, weathered, reconciled.

accolade *(SYN.)* praise, honor, acclaim, recognition, applause, kudos, bouquet, crown, testimonial, acclamation, salute.

accommodate *(SYN.)* help, assist, aid, provide for, serve, oblige, hold, house.
(ANT.) inconvenience.

accommodating *(SYN.)* obliging, helpful, willing, kind, cooperative, gracious, cordial, sympathetic, unselfish.
(ANT.) unfriendly, selfish, hostile, uncooperative.

accommodation *(SYN.)* change, alteration, adaptation, convenience, adjustment, acclimatization, aid, help, boon, kindness, service, courtesy.
(ANT.) inflexibility, rigidity, disservice, stubbornness, disadvantage.

accommodations *(SYN.)* housing, lodgings, room, place, quarters, board.

accompany *(SYN.)* chaperon, consort with, escort, go with, associate with, attend, join.
(ANT.) abandon, quit, leave, desert, avoid, forsake.

accomplice *(SYN.* accessory, ally, associate, partner in crime, assistant, sidekick, confederate.
(ANT.) opponent, rival, enemy, adversary.

accomplish *(SYN.)* attain, consummate, achieve, do, execute, carry out, fulfill, complete, effect, perform, finish.
(ANT.) fail, frustrate, spoil, neglect, defeat.

accomplished *(SYN.)* proficient, skilled, finished, well-trained, gifted, masterly, polished, able.
(ANT.) unskilled, amateurish, crude.

accomplishment *(SYN.)* deed, feat, statute, operation, performance, action, achievement, transaction.
(ANT.) cessation, inhibition, intention, deliberation.

accord *(SYN.)* concur, agree, award, harmony, conformity, agreement, give, tale, sum, statement, record, grant.
(ANT.) difference, quarrel, disagreement.

accordingly *(SYN.)* consequently, therefore, whereupon, hence, so, thus.

accost *(SYN.)* approach, greet, speak to, address.
(ANT.) avoid, shun.

account *(SYN.)* description, chronicle, history, narration, reckoning, rate, computation, detail, narrative, relation, recital, consider, believe, deem, record, explanation, report, tale, story, anecdote, reason, statement, tale, ledger.
(ANT.) confusion, misrepresentation, distortion.

accountable *(SYN.)* chargeable, answerable, beholden, responsible, obliged, liable.

account for *(SYN.)* justify, explain, substantiate, illuminate, clarify, elucidate.
accredited *(SYN.)* qualified, licensed, deputized, certified, commissioned, vouched for, empowered.
(ANT.) illicit, unofficial, unauthorized.
accrue *(SYN.)* amass, collect, heap, increase, accumulate, gather, hoard.
(ANT.) disperse, dissipate, waste, diminish.
accrued *(SYN.)* accumulated, totaled, increased, added, enlarged, amassed, expanded.
accumulate *(SYN.)* gather, collect, heap, increase, accrue, assemble, compile, hoard, amass.
(ANT.) spend, give away, diminish, dissipate.
accumulation *(SYN.)* heap, collection, pile, store, hoard, stack, aggregation.
accurate *(SYN.)* perfect, just, truthful, unerring, meticulous, correct, all right.
(ANT.) incorrect, mistaken, false, wrong.
accursed *(SYN.)* ill-fated, cursed, condemned, doomed, bedeviled, ruined.
(ANT.) fortunate, hopeful.
accusation *(SYN.)* charge, incrimination, indictment, arraignment.
(ANT.) pardon, exoneration, absolve.
accuse *(SYN.)* incriminate, indict, censure, tattle, denounce, charge, arraign, impeach, blame.
(ANT.) release, vindicate, exonerate, acquit, absolve, clear.
accustom *(SYN.)* addict, familiarize, condition.
accustomed *(SYN.)* familiar with, used to, comfortable with.
(ANT.) strange, unusual, rare, unfamiliar.
ace *(SYN.)* champion, star, king, queen, winner, head.
acerbity *(SYN.)* bitterness, harshness, unkindness, sourness, acidity, unfriendliness, acrimony, coldness, sharpness.
(ANT.) sweetness, gentleness, kindness, tenderness.
ache *(SYN.)* hurt, pain, throb.
achieve *(SYN.)* do, execute, gain, obtain, acquire, accomplish, realize, perform, complete, accomplish, finish, fulfill, reach, attain, secure, procure.
(ANT.) fail, lose, fall short.
achievement *(SYN.)* feat, accomplishment, attainment, exploit, realization, performance, completion, deed.
(ANT.) botch, dud, mess, omission, defeat, failure.
acid *(SYN.)* tart, sour, bitter, mordant, biting, biting.
(ANT.) pleasant, friendly, bland, mild, sweet.
acknowledge *(SYN.)* allow, admit, agree to, concede, recognize, answer, grant, accept, receive.
(ANT.) reject, refuse, disavow, refute, deny.
acme *(SYN.)* summit, top, zenith, peak, crown.
(ANT.) bottom.
acquaint *(SYN.)* inform, teach, enlighten, notify, tell.
acquaintance *(SYN.)* fellowship, friendship, cognizance, knowledge, intimacy, familiarity, companionship, associate, colleague, companion.
(ANT.) inexperience, unfamiliarity, ignorance.
acquiesce *(SYN.)* submit, agree, concur, assent, comply, consent, succumb.
(ANT.) refuse, disagree, rebel, argue.
acquire *(SYN.)* attain, earn, get, procure, assimilate, obtain, secure, gain, appropriate.
(ANT.) miss, surrender, lose, forego, forfeit.
acquirement *(SYN.)* training, skill, learning, achievement, attainment, education, information.
acquisition *(SYN.)* procurement, gain, gift, purchase, proceeds, possession, grant.
acquisitive *(SYN.)* greedy, avid, hoarding, covetous.
acquit *(SYN.)* forgive, exonerate, absolve, cleanse, pardon, excuse, excuse, discharge, found not guilty.
(ANT.) doom, saddle, sentence, condemn.
acrid *(SYN.)* bitter, sharp, nasty, stinging, harsh.
(ANT.) pleasant, sweet.
acrimonious *(SYN.)* sharp, sarcastic, acerb, waspish, cutting, stinging, testy.
(ANT.) soft, kind, sweet, pleasant, soothing.
acrobat *(SYN.)* athlete, gymnast.
act *(SYN.)* deed, doing, feat, execution, accomplishment, performance, action, operation, transaction, law, decree, statute, edict, achievement, exploit, statute, judgment, routine, pretense.
(ANT.) inactivity, deliberation, intention, cessation.
acting *(SYN.)* officiating, substituting, surrogate, temporary, delegated.
action *(SYN.)* deed, achievement, feat, activity, exploit, movement, motion, play, behavior, battle, performance, exercise.
(ANT.) idleness, inertia, repose, inactivity, rest.
activate *(SYN.)* mobilize,energize, start, propel, nudge, push.
(ANT.) paralyze, immobilize, stop, deaden.
active *(SYN.)* working, operative, alert, agile, nimble, supple, sprightly, busy, brisk, lively, quick, industrious, energetic, vigorous, industrious, occupied, vivacious, dynamic, engaged.
(ANT.) passive, inactive, idle, dormant, lazy, lethargic.
activism *(SYN.)* engagement, confrontation, agitation, commitment, aggression, fervor, zeal.
(ANT.) detachment, lethargy, disengagement.
activist *(SYN.)* militant, doer, enthusiast.
activity *(SYN.)* action, liveliness, motion, vigor, agility, exercise, energy, quickness, enterprise, movement, briskness.
(ANT.) idleness, inactivity, dullness,

sloth.

actor *(SYN.)* performer, trouper, entertainer.

actual *(SYN.)* true, genuine, certain, factual, authentic, concrete, real.
(ANT.) unreal, fake, bogus, nonexistent, false.

actuality *(SYN.)* reality, truth, deed, occurrence, fact, certainty.
(ANT.) theory, fiction, falsehood, supposition.

acute *(SYN.)* piercing, severe, sudden, keen,sharp, perceptive, discerning, shrewd, astute, smart, intelligent.
(ANT.) bland, mild, dull, obtuse, insensitive.

adamant *(SYN.)* unyielding, firm, obstinate.
(ANT.) yielding.

adapt *(SYN.)* adjust, conform, accommodate, change, fit, alter, vary, modify.
(ANT.) misapply, disturb.

add *(SYN.)* attach, increase, total, append, sum, affix, augment, adjoin, put together, unite, supplement.
(ANT.) remove, reduce, deduct, subtract, detach, withdraw.

address *(SYN.)* greet, hail, accost, speak to, location, residence, home, abode, dwelling, speech, lecture, greeting, oration, presentation.
(ANT.) avoid, pass by.

adept *(SYN.)* expert, skillful, proficient.
(ANT.) unskillful.

adequate *(SYN.)* capable, commensurate, fitting, satisfactory, sufficient, enough, ample, suitable, plenty, fit.
(ANT.) lacking, scant, insufficient, inadequate.

adhere *(SYN.)* stick fast, grasp, hold, keep, retain, cling, stick to, keep, cleave.
(ANT.) surrender, abandon, release, separate, loosen.

adherent *(SYN.)* follower, supporter.
(ANT.) renegade, dropout, defector.

adjacent *(SYN.)* next to, near, bordering, adjoining, touching, neighboring.
(ANT.) separate, distant, apart.

adjoin *(SYN.)* connect, be close to, affix, attach.
(ANT.) detach, remove,

adjoining *(SYN.)* near to, next, next to, close to, touching, bordering.
(ANT.) distant, remote, separate.

adjourn *(SYN.)* postpone, defer, delay, suspend, discontinue, put off.
(ANT.) begin, convene, assemble.

adjust *(SYN.)* repair, fix, change, set, regulate, settle, arrange, adapt, suit, accommodate, modify, very, alter, fit.

administer *(SYN.)* supervise, oversee, direct, manage, rule, govern, control, conduct, provide, give, execute, preside, apply, contribute, help.

administration *(SYN.)* conduct, direction, management, supervision.

admirable *(SYN.)* worthy, fine, praise-deserving, commendable, excellent.

admiration *(SYN.)* pleasure, wonder, esteem, approval.
(ANT.) disdain, disrespect, contempt.

admire *(SYN.)* approve, venerate, appreciate, respect, revere, esteem, like.
(ANT.) abhor, dislike, despise, loathe, detest, hate.

admissible *(SYN.)* fair, justifiable, tolerable, allowable, permissible.
(ANT.) unsuitable, unfair, inadmissible.

admission *(SYN.)* access, admittance, entrance, pass, ticket.

admit *(SYN.)* allow, assent, permit, acknowledge, welcome, concede, agree, confess, accept, grant, own up to.
(ANT.) deny, reject, dismiss, shun, obstruct.

admittance *(SYN.)* access, entry, entrance.

admonish *(SYN.)* caution, advise against, warn, rebuke, reprove, censure.
(ANT.) glorify, praise.

admonition *(SYN.)* advice, warning, caution, reminder, tip.

ado *(SYN.)* trouble, bother, fuss, bustle, activity, excitement, commotion, action, hubbub, upset, confusion, turmoil.
(ANT.) tranquillity, quietude.

adolescent *(SYN.)* young, youthful, immature, teenage.
(ANT.) grown, mature, adult.

adoration *(SYN.)* veneration, reverence, glorification, worship homage.

adore *(SYN.)* revere, venerate, idolize, respect, love, cherish, esteem, honor.
(ANT.) loathe, hate, despise.

adorn *(SYN.)* trim, bedeck, decorate, ornament, beautify, embellish, glamorize, enhance, garnish, embellish.
(ANT.) mar, spoil, deform, deface, strip, bare.

adrift *(SYN.)* floating, afloat, drifting, aimless, purposeless, unsettled.
(ANT.) purposeful, stable, secure, well-organized.

adroit *(SYN.)* adept, apt, dexterous, skillful, clever, ingenious, expert.
(ANT.) awkward, clumsy, graceless, unskillful, oafish.

adult *(SYN.)* full-grown, mature.
(ANT.) infantile, immature.

advance *(SYN.)* further, promote, bring forward, propound, proceed, aggrandize, elevate, improve, adduce, allege, propose, progress, move, advancement, improvement, promotion, upgrade.
(ANT.) retard, retreat, oppose, hinder, revert, withdraw, flee, retardation.

advantage *(SYN.)* edge, profit, superiority, benefit, mastery, leverage, favor, vantage, gain.
(ANT.) handicap, impediment, obstruction, disadvantage, detriment, hindrance, loss.

adventure *(SYN.)* undertaking, occurrence, enterprise, happening, event, project, occurrence, incident, exploit.

adventurous *(SYN.)* daring, enterprising, rash, bold, chivalrous.
(ANT.) cautious, timid, hesitating.

adversary *(SYN.)* foe, enemy, contestant, opponent, antagonist.

(ANT.) ally, friend.
adverse *(SYN.)* hostile, counteractive, unfavorable, opposed, disastrous, contrary, antagonistic, opposite, unlucky, unfriendly, unfortunate.
(ANT.) favorable, propitious, fortunate, friendly, beneficial.
adversity *(SYN.)* misfortune, trouble, calamity, distress, hardship, disaster.
(ANT.) benefit, happiness.
advertise *(SYN.)* promote, publicize, make known, announce, promulgate.
advertisement *(SYN.)* commercial, billboard, want ad, handbill, flyer, poster, brochure, blurb.
advice *(SYN.)* counsel, instruction, suggestion, warning, information, caution, exhortation, admonition, recommendation, plan, tip, guidance, opinion.
advisable *(SYN.)* wise, sensible, prudent, suitable, fit, proper, fitting.
(ANT.) ill-considered, imprudent, inadvisable.
advise *(SYN.)* recommend, suggest, counsel, caution, warn, admonish.
adviser *(SYN.)* coach, guide, mentor, counselor.
advocate *(SYN.)* defend, recommend, support.
(ANT.) opponent, adversary, oppose, opponent.
aesthetic *(SYN.)* literary, artistic, sensitive, tasteful, well-composed.
(ANT.) tasteless.
affable *(SYN.)* pleasant, courteous, sociable, friendly, amiable, gracious, approachable, communicative.
(ANT.) unfriendly, unsociable.
affair *(SYN.)* event, occasion, happening, party, occurrence, matter, festivity, business, concern.
affect *(SYN.)* alter, modify, concern, regard, move, touch, feign, pretend, influence, sway, transform, change, impress.
affected *(SYN.)* pretended, fake, sham, false.
affection *(SYN.)* fondness, kindness, emotion, love, feeling, tenderness, attachment, disposition, endearment, liking, friendly, friendliness, warmth.
(ANT.) aversion, indifference, repulsion, hatred, repugnance, dislike, antipathy.
affectionate *(SYN.)* warm, loving, tender, fond, attached.
(ANT.) distant, unfeeling, cold.
affirm *(SYN.)* aver, declare, swear, maintain, endorse, certify, state, assert, ratify, pronounce, say, confirm, establish.
(ANT.) deny, dispute, oppose, contradict, demur, disclaim.
afflict *(SYN.)* trouble, disturb, bother, agitate, perturb.
(ANT.) soothe.
affliction *(SYN.)* distress, grief, misfortune, trouble.
(ANT.) relief, benefit, easement.
affluent *(SYN.)* wealthy, prosperous, rich, abundant, ample, plentiful, well-off, bountiful, well-to-do.
(ANT.) poor.
afford *(SYN.)* supply, yield, furnish.
affront *(SYN.)* offense, slur, slight, provocation, insult.
afraid *(SYN.)* faint-hearted, frightened, scared, timid, fearful, apprehensive, cowardly, terrified.
(ANT.) assured, composed, courageous, bold, confident.
after *(SYN.)* following, subsequently, behind, despite, next.
(ANT.) before.
again *(SYN.)* anew, repeatedly, afresh.
against *(SYN.)* versus, hostile to, opposed to, in disagreement.
(ANT.) pro, with, for, in favor of.
age *(SYN.)* antiquity, date, period, generation, time, senility, grow old, senescence, mature, dotage, ripen, mature, era, epoch.
(ANT.) youth, childhood.
aged *(SYN.)* ancient, elderly, old.
(ANT.) youthful, young.
agency *(SYN.)* office, operation.
agent *(SYN.)* performer, doer, worker, actor, operator.
aggravate *(SYN.)* intensify, magnify, annoy, irritate, increase, heighten, nettle, make worse, irk, vex, provoke, embitter, worsen.
(ANT.) soften, soothe, appease, pacify, mitigate, ease, relieve.
aggregate *(SYN.)* collection, entirety, sum, accumulate, total, amount to, compile, conglomeration.
(ANT.) part, unit, ingredient, element.
aggression *(SYN.)* assault, attack, invasion, offense.
(ANT.) defense.
aggressive *(SYN.)* offensive, belligerent, hostile, attacking, militant, pugnacious.
(ANT.) timid, withdrawn, passive, peaceful, shy.
aghast *(SYN.)* surprised, astonished, astounded, awed, thunderstruck, flabbergasted, bewildered.
agile *(SYN.)* nimble, graceful, lively, active, alert, fast, quick, athletic, spry.
(ANT.) inept, awkward, clumsy.
agility *(ANT.)* quickness, vigor, liveliness, energy, activity, motion.
(ANT.) dullness, inertia, idleness, inactivity.
agitate *(SYN.)* disturb, excite, perturb, rouse, shake, arouse, disconcert, instigate, inflame, provoke, jar, incite, stir up, toss.
(ANT.) calm, placate, quiet, ease, soothe.
agitated *(SYN.)* jumpy, jittery, nervous, restless, restive, upset, disturbed, ruffled.
agony *(SYN.)* anguish, misery, pain, suffering, torture, ache, distress, throe, woe, torment, grief.
(ANT.) relief, ease, comfort.
agree *(SYN.)* comply, coincide, conform, assent, accede, tally, settle, harmonize, unite, yield, consent.
(ANT.) differ, disagree, protest, contradict, argue, refuse.
agreeable *(SYN.)* amiable, charming, gratifying, pleasant, suitable, pleasur-

able, welcome, pleasing, acceptable, friendly, cooperative.
(ANT.) obnoxious, offensive, unpleasant, disagreeable, quarrelsome, contentious, touchy.

agreement *(SYN.)* harmony, understanding, unison, contract, pact, stipulation, alliance, deal, bargain, treaty, contract, arrangement, settlement, accord, concord.
(ANT.) variance, dissension, discord, disagreement, difference, misunderstanding.

agriculture *(SYN.)* farming, gardening, tillage, husbandry, cultivation, agronomy.

ahead *(SYN.)* before, leading, forward, winning, inadvance.
(ANT.) behind.

aid *(SYN.)* remedy, assist, helper, service, support, assistant, relief, help.
(ANT.) obstruct, hinder, obstacle, impede, hindrance.

ail *(SYN.)* bother, trouble, perturb, disturb, suffer, feel sick.

ailing *(SYN.)* sick, ill.
(ANT.) hearty, hale, well.

ailment *(SYN.)* illness, disease, affliction, sickness.

aim *(SYN.)* direction, point, goal, object, target, direct, try, intend, intention, end, objective.

aimless *(SYN.)* directionless, adrift, purposeless.

air *(SYN.)* atmosphere, display, reveal, expose, publicize.
(ANT.) conceal, hide.

airy *(SYN.)* breezy, light, gay, lighthearted, graceful, fanciful.

aisle *(SYN.)* corridor, passageway, lane, alley, opening, artery.

ajar *(SYN.)* gaping, open.

akin *(SYN.)* alike, related, connected, similar, affiliated, allied.

alarm *(SYN.)* dismay, fright, signal, warning, terror, apprehension, affright, consternation, fear, siren, arouse, startle, bell.
(ANT.) tranquillity, composure, security, quiet, calm, soothe, comfort.

alarming *(SYN.)* appalling, daunting, shocking.
(ANT.) comforting, calming, soothing.

alcoholic *(SYN.)* sot, drunkard, tippler, inebriate.

alert *(SYN.)* attentive, keen, clear-witted, ready, nimble, vigilant, watchful, observant.
(ANT.) logy, sluggish, dulled, listless.

alias *(SYN.)* anonym, assumed name.

alibi *(SYN.)* story, excuse.

alien *(SYN.)* adverse, foreigner, strange, remote, stranger, different, extraneous.
(ANT.) germane, kindred, relevant, akin, familiar, accustomed.

alight *(SYN.)* debark, deplane, detrain, disembark.
(ANT.) embark, board.

alive *(SYN.)* existing, breathing, living, live, lively, vivacious, animated.
(ANT.) inactive, dead, moribund.

allay *(SYN.)* soothe, check, lessen, calm, lighten, relieve, soften, moderate, quite.
(ANT.) excite, intensify, worsen, arouse.

allege *(SYN.)* affirm, cite, claim, declare, maintain, state, assert.
(ANT.) deny, disprove, refute, contradict, gainsay.

allegiance *(SYN.)* faithfulness, duty, devotion, loyalty, fidelity, obligation.
(ANT.) treachery, disloyalty.

allegory *(SYN.)* fable, fiction, myth, saga, parable, legend.
(ANT.) history, fact.

alleviate *(SYN.)* diminish, soothe, solace, abate, assuage, allay, soften, mitigate, extenuate, relieve, let up, ease, slacken, relax, weaken.
(ANT.) increase, aggravate, augment, irritate.

alley *(SYN.)* footway, byway, path, passageway, aisle, corridor, opening, lane.

alliance *(SYN.)* combination, partnership, union, treaty, coalition, association, confederacy, marriage, pact, agreement, relation, interrelation, understanding, relationship.
(ANT.) separation, divorce, schism.

allot *(SYN.)* divide, mete, assign, give, measure, distribute, allocate, share, grant, dispense, deal, apportion.
(ANT.) withhold, retain, keep, confiscate, refuse.

allow *(SYN.)* authorize, grant, acknowledge, admit, let, permit, sanction, consent, concede, mete, allocate.
(ANT.) protest, resist, refuse, forbid, object, prohibit.

allowance *(SYN.)* grant, fee, portion, ration, allotment.

allude *(SYN.)* intimate, refer, insinuate, hint, advert, suggest, imply, mention.
(ANT.) demonstrate, specify, state, declare.

allure *(SYN.)* attract, fascinate, tempt, charm, infatuate, captivate.

ally *(SYN.)* accomplice, associate, confederate, abettor, assistant, friend, partner.
(ANT.) rival, enemy, opponent, foe, adversary.

almighty *(SYN.)* omnipotent, powerful.

almost *(SYN.)* somewhat, nearly.
(ANT.) completely, absolutely.

alms *(SYN.)* dole, charity, donation, contribution.

aloft *(SYN.)* overhead.

alone *(SYN.)* desolate, unaided, only, isolated, unaided, lone, secluded, lonely, deserted, solitary, single, apart, solo, separate.
(ANT.) surrounded, attended, accompanied, together.

aloof *(SYN.)* uninterested, uninvolved, apart, away, remote, unsociable, standoffish, separate, disdainful, distant.
(ANT.) warm, outgoing, friendly, cordial.

also *(SYN.)* in addition, likewise, too, besides, furthermore, moreover, further.

alter *(SYN.)* adjust, vary, deviate, modify, reserved, change.
(ANT.) maintain, preserve, keep.

alteration *(SYN.)* difference, adjust-

ment, change, modification.
(ANT.) maintenance, preservation.
altercation *(SYN.)* controversy, dispute, argument, quarrel.
alternate *(SYN.)* rotate, switch, spell, interchange.
(ANT.) fix.
alternative *(SYN.)* substitute, selection, option, choice, replacement, possibility.
although *(SYN.)* though, even if, even though, despite, notwithstanding.
altitude *(SYN.)* elevation, height.
(ANT.) depth.
altogether *(SYN.)* totally, wholly, quite, entirely, thoroughly, completely.
(ANT.) partly.
altruism *(SYN.)* kindness, tenderness, generosity, charity, benevolence, liberality.
(ANT.) selfishness, unkindness, cruelty, inhumanity.
always *(SYN.)* evermore, forever, perpetually, ever, unceasingly, continually, constantly, eternally, everlastingly.
(ANT.) never, rarely, sometimes, occasionally.
amalgamate *(SYN.)* fuse, unify, unite, commingle, merge, blend, combine, consolidate.
(ANT.) decompose, disintegrate, separate.
amass *(SYN.)* collect, accumulate, heap up, gather, increase, compile, assemble, store up.
(ANT.) disperse, dissipate, spend.
amateur *(SYN.)* beginner, dilettante, learner, dabbler, neophyte, apprentice, novice, nonprofessional, tyro.
(ANT.) expert, master, adept, professional, authority.
amaze *(SYN.)* surprise, flabbergast, stun, dumbfound, astound, bewilder, aghast, thunderstruck, astonish.
(ANT.) bore, disinterest, tire.
ambiguous *(SYN.)* uncertain, vague, obscure, dubious, equivocal, unclear, deceptive.
(ANT.) plain, clear, explicit, obvious, unequivocal, unmistakable, certain.
ambition *(SYN.)* eagerness, goal, incentive, aspiration, yearning, longing, desire.
(ANT.) indifference, satisfaction, indolence, resignation.
ambitious *(SYN.)* aspiring, intent upon.
(ANT.) indifferent.
amble *(SYN.)* saunter, stroll.
ambush *(SYN.)* trap, hiding place.
amend *(SYN.)* change, mend, better, correct, improve.
(ANT.) worsen.
amends *(SYN.)* compensation, restitution, payment, reparation, remedy, redress.
amiable *(SYN.)* friendly, good-natured, gracious, pleasing, agreeable, outgoing, kindhearted, kind, pleasant.
(ANT.) surly, hateful, churlish, disagreeable, ill-natured, ill-tempered, cross, captious, touchy.
amid *(SYN.)* among, amidst, surrounded by.
amiss *(SYN.)* wrongly, improperly, astray, awry.
(ANT.) properly, rightly, right, correctly, correct.
ammunition *(SYN.)* shot, powder, shells, bullets.
among *(SYN.)* between, mingled, mixed amidst, amid, betwixt, surrounded by.
(ANT.) separate, apart.
amorous *(SYN.)* amatory, affectionate, loving.
amount *(SYN.)* sum, total, quantity, number, price, value, measure.
ample *(SYN.)* broad, large, profuse, spacious, copious, liberal, plentiful, full, bountiful, abundant, great, extensive, generous, wide, enough, sufficient, roomy.
(ANT.) limited, insufficient, meager, small, lacking, cramped, confined, inadequate.
amplification *(SYN.)* magnification, growth, waxing, accrual, enhancement, enlargement, heightening, increase.
(ANT.) decrease, diminishing, reduction, contraction.
amplify *(SYN.)* broaden, develop, expand, enlarge, extend.
(ANT.) confine, restrict, abridge, narrow.
amuse *(SYN.)* divert, please, delight, entertain, charm.
(ANT.) tire, bore.
amusement *(SYN.)* diversion, pastime, entertainment, pleasure, enjoyment, recreation.
(ANT.) tedium, boredom.
amusing *(SYN.)* pleasant, funny, pleasing, entertaining, comical.
(ANT.) tiring, tedious, boring.
analogous *(SYN.)* comparable, corresponding, like, similar, correspondent, alike, correlative, parallel, allied, akin.
(ANT.) different, opposed, incongruous, divergent.
analysis *(SYN.)* separation, investigation, examination.
analyze *(SYN.)* explain, investigate, examine, separate.
ancestral *(SYN.)* hereditary, inherited.
ancestry *(SYN.)* family, line, descent, lineage.
(ANT.) posterity.
anchor *(SYN.)* fix, attach, secure, fasten.
(ANT.) detach, free, loosen.
ancient *(SYN.)* aged, old-fashioned, archaic, elderly, antique, old, primitive.
(ANT.) new, recent, current, fresh.
anecdote *(SYN.)* account, narrative, story, tale.
anesthetic *(SYN.)* opiate, narcotic, sedative, painkiller, analgesic.
angel *(SYN.)* cherub, archangel, seraph.
(ANT.) demon, devil.
angelic *(SYN.)* pure, lovely, heavenly, good, virtuous, innocent, godly, saintly.
(ANT.) devilish.
anger *(SYN.)* exasperation, fury, ire, passion, rage, resentment, temper, indignation, animosity, irritation, wrath,

displeasure, infuriate, arouse, nettle, annoyance, exasperate.
(ANT.) forbearance, patience, peace, self-control.

angry *(SYN.)* provoked, wrathful, furious, enraged, incensed, exasperated, maddened, indignant, irate, mad, inflamed.
(ANT.) happy, pleased, calm, satisfied, content, tranquil.

anguish *(SYN.)* suffering, torment, torture, distress, pain, heartache, grief, agony, misery.
(ANT.) solace, relief, joy, comfort, peace, ecstasy, pleasure.

animal *(SYN.)* beast, creature.

animate *(SYN.)* vitalize, invigorate, stimulate, enliven, alive, vital, vigorous.
(ANT.) dead, inanimate.

animated *(SYN.)* gay, lively, spry, vivacious, active, vigorous, chipper, snappy.
(ANT.) inactive.

animosity *(SYN.)* grudge, hatred, rancor, spite, bitterness, enmity, opposition, dislike, hostility, antipathy.
(ANT.) good will, love, friendliness, kindliness.

annex *(SYN.)* join, attach, add, addition, wing, append.

annihilate *(SYN.)* destroy, demolish, end, wreck, abolish.

announce *(SYN.)* proclaim, give out, make known, notify, publish, report, herald, promulgate, advertise, broadcast, state, tell, declare, publicize.
(ANT.) conceal, withhold, suppress, bury, stifle.

announcement *(SYN.)* notification, report, declaration, bulletin, advertisement, broadcast, promulgation, notice, message.
(ANT.) silence, hush, muteness, speechlessness.

annoy *(SYN.)* bother, irk, pester, tease, trouble, vex, disturb, inconvenience, molest, irritate, harry, harass.
(ANT.) console, gratify, soothe, accommodate, please, calm, comfort.

annually *(SYN.)* once a year.

anoint *(SYN.)* grease, oil.

answer *(SYN.)* reply, rejoinder, response, retort, rebuttal, respond.
(ANT.) summoning, argument, questioning, inquiry, query, ask, inquire.

antagonism *(SYN.)* opposition, conflict, enmity, hostility, animosity.
(ANT.) geniality, cordiality, friendliness.

antagonist *(SYN.)* adversary, rival, enemy, foe, opponent.
(ANT.) ally, friend.

antagonize *(SYN.)* against, provoke, counter, oppose, embitter.
(ANT.) soothe.

anthology *(SYN.)* garland, treasury, collection.

anticipate *(SYN.)* await, foresee, forecast, hope for, expect.

anticipated *(SYN.)* expected, foresight, hoped, preconceived.
(ANT.) dreaded, reared, worried, doubted.

antics *(SYN.)* horseplay, fun, merrymaking, pranks, capers, tricks, clowning.

antipathy *(SYN.)* hatred.

antiquated *(SYN.)* old, out-of-date, outdated, old-fashion.

antique *(SYN.)* rarity, curio, old, ancient, old-fashioned, archaic, out-of-date.
(ANT.) new, recent, fresh.

anxiety *(SYN.)* care, disquiet, fear, concern, solicitude, trouble, worry, apprehension, uneasiness, distress, foreboding.
(ANT.) nonchalance, assurance, confidence, contentment, peacefulness, placidity, tranquillity.

anxious *(SYN.)* troubled, uneasy, perturbed, apprehensive, worried, concerned, desirous, bothered, agitated, eager, fearful.
(ANT.) tranquil, calm, peaceful.

anyway *(SYN.)* nevertheless, anyhow.

apartment *(SYN.)* suite, flat, dormitory.

apathy *(SYN.)* unconcern, indifference, lethargy.
(ANT.) interest, feeling.

aperture *(SYN.)* gap, pore, opening, cavity, chasm, abyss, hole, void.
(ANT.) connection, bridge, link.

apex *(SYN.)* acme, tip, summit, crown, top.

apologize *(SYN.)* ask forgiveness.

apology *(SYN.)* defense, excuse, confession, justification, alibi, explanation, plea.
(ANT.) denial, complaint, dissimulation, accusation.

apostate *(SYN.)* nonconformist, unbeliever, dissenter, heretic, schismatic.
(ANT.) saint, conformist, believer.

appall *(SYN.)* shock, stun, dismay, frighten, terrify, horrify.
(ANT.) edify, please.

appalling *(SYN.)* fearful, frightful, ghastly, horrid, repulsive, terrible, dire, awful.
(ANT.) fascinating, beautiful, enchanting, enjoyable.

apparatus *(SYN.)* rig, equipment, furnishings, gear, tackle.

apparel *(SYN.)* clothes, attire, garb, clothing, garments, dress, robes.

apparent *(SYN.)* obvious, plain, self-evident, clear, manifest, transparent, unmistakable, palpable, unambiguous, ostensible, illusory, visible, seeming, evident, understandable.
(ANT.) uncertain, indistinct, dubious, hidden, mysterious.

apparition *(SYN.)* illusion, ghost, phantom, vision, fantasy, dream.

appeal *(SYN.)* plea, petition, request, entreaty, request, plead, petition, beseech, beg, entreat, attract.
(ANT.) repulse, repel.

appear *(SYN.)* look, arrive, emanate, emerge, arise, seem, turn up.
(ANT.) vanish, withdraw, exist, disappear, evaporate.

appearance *(SYN.)* advent, arrival, aspect, demeanor, fashion, guise, apparition, manner, mien, look, presence.

(ANT.) disappearance, reality, departure, vanishing.

appease *(SYN.)* calm, compose, lull, quiet, relieve, assuage, pacify, satisfy, restraint, lesson, soothe, check, ease, alleviate, still, allay, tranquilize.
(ANT.) excite, arouse, incense, irritate, inflame.

append *(SYN.)* supplement, attach, add.

appendage *(SYN.)* addition, tail, supplement.

appetite *(SYN.)* zest, craving, desire, liking, longing, stomach, inclination, hunger, thirst, relish, passion.
(ANT.) satiety, disgust, distaste, repugnance.

appetizer *(SYN.)* hors d'oeuvre.

applaud *(SYN.)* cheer, clap, hail, approve, praise, acclaim.
(ANT.) disapprove, denounce, reject, criticize, condemn.

appliance *(SYN.)* machine, tool, instrument, device, utensil, implement.

applicable *(SYN.)* fitting, suitable, proper, fit, usable, appropriate, suited.
(ANT.) inappropriate, inapplicable.

apply *(SYN.)* affix, allot, appropriate, use, employ, petition, request, devote, avail, pertain, attach, ask, administer, petition, assign, relate, utilize.
(ANT.) give away, demand, detach, neglect, ignore.

appoint *(SYN.)* name, choose, nominate, designate, elect, establish, assign, place.
(ANT.) discharge, fire, dismiss.

appointment *(SYN.)* rendezvous, meeting, designation, position, engagement, assignment.
(ANT.) discharge, dismissal.

appraise *(SYN.)* value, evaluate, place a value on.

appreciate *(SYN.)* enjoy, regard, value, prize, cherish, admire, go up, improve, rise, respect, think highly of, esteem, appraise.
(ANT.) belittle, misunderstand, apprehend, degrade, scorn, depreciate, undervalue.

apprehend *(SYN.)* seize, capture, arrest, understand, dread, fear, grasp, perceive.
(ANT.) release, lose.

apprehension *(SYN.)* fear, misgiving, dread, uneasiness, worry, fearfulness, anticipation, capture, seizure.
(ANT.) confidence, composure, self-assuredness.

apprehensive *(SYN.)* worried, afraid, uneasy, bothered, anxious, concerned, perturbed, troubled, fearful.
(ANT.) relaxed.

apprentice *(SYN.)* amateur, recruit, novice, learner, beginner.
(ANT.) experienced, professional, master.

approach *(SYN.)* greet, inlet, come near, advance, access, passageway.
(ANT.) avoid, pass by, retreat.

appropriate *(SYN.)* apt, particular, proper, fitting, suitable, applicable, loot, pillage, purloin, rob, steal, embezzle, assign, becoming, apportion, authorize.
(ANT.) improper, contrary, inappropriate, buy, repay, restore, return, unfit, inapt.

approval *(SYN.)* commendation, consent, praise, approbation, sanction, assent, endorsement, support.
(ANT.) reproach, censure, reprimand, disapprove.

approve *(SYN.)* like, praise, authorize, confirm, endorse, appreciate, think well of, ratify, commend, sanction.
(ANT.) criticize, nullify, disparage, frown on, disapprove, deny.

approximate *(SYN.)* near, approach, roughly, close.
(ANT.) correct.

apt *(SYN.)* suitable, proper, appropriate, fit, suited, disposed, liable, inclined, prone, clever, bright, alert, intelligent, receptive.
(ANT.) ill-becoming, unsuitable, unlikely, slow, retarded, dense.

aptness *(SYN.)* capability, dexterity, power, qualification, skill, ability, aptitude.
(ANT.) incompetency, unreadiness, incapacity.

aptitude *(SYN.)* knack, talent, gift, ability.

aqueduct *(SYN.)* gully, pipe, canal, waterway, channel.

arbitrary *(SYN.)* unrestricted, absolute, despotic, willful, unreasonable, unconditional, authoritative.
(ANT.) contingent, qualified, fair, reasonable, dependent, accountable.

arbitrate *(SYN.)* referee, settle, mediate, umpire, negotiate.

architecture *(SYN.)* structure, building, construction.

ardent *(SYN.)* fervent, fiery, glowing, intense, keen, impassioned, fervid, hot, passionate, earnest, eager, zealous, enthusiastic.
(ANT.) cool, indifferent, nonchalant, apathetic.

ardor *(SYN.)* enthusiasm, rapture, spirit, zeal, fervent, eager, glowing, eagerness.
(ANT.) unconcern, apathy, disinterest, indifference.

arduous *(SYN.)* laborious, hard, difficult, burdensome, strenuous, strained.
(ANT.) easy.

area *(SYN.)* space, extent, region, zone, section, expanse, district, neighborhood, size.

argue *(SYN.)* plead, reason, wrangle, indicate, prove, show, dispute, denote.
(ANT.) reject, spurn, ignore, overlook.

argument *(SYN.)* debate, dispute, discussion, controversy.
(ANT.) harmony, accord, agreement.

arid *(SYN.)* waterless, dry, flat, dull, unimaginative, stuffy.
(ANT.) fertile, wet, colorful.

arise *(SYN.)* enter, institute, originate, start, open, commence, emerge.
(ANT.) terminate, end, finish, complete, close.

aristocrat *(SYN.)* noble, gentleman, peer, lord, nobleman.
(ANT.) peasant, commoner.
arm *(SYN.)* weapon, defend, equip, empower, fortify.
armistice *(SYN.)* truce, pact, deal, understanding, peace, treaty, contract.
army *(SYN.)* troops, legion, military, forces, militia.
aroma *(SYN.)* smell, odor, fragrance, perfume, scent.
arouse *(SYN.)* stir, animate, move, pique, provoke, kindle, disturb, excite.
(ANT.) settle, soothe, calm.
arraign *(SYN.)* charge, censure, incriminate, indict, accuse.
(ANT.) acquit, release, vindicate, exonerate, absolve.
arraignment *(SYN.)* imputation, charge, accusation, incrimination.
(ANT.) pardon, exoneration, exculpation.
arrange *(SYN.)* classify, assort, organize, place, plan, prepare, devise, adjust, dispose, regulate, group, prepare.
(ANT.) jumble, scatter, disorder, confuse, disturb, disarrange.
arrangement *(SYN.)* display, grouping, order, array.
array *(SYN.)* dress, adorn, attire, clothe, arrange, order, distribute, exhibit.
(ANT.) disorder, disorganization, disarray.
arrest *(SYN.)* detain, hinder, restrain, seize, withhold, stop, check, obstruct, apprehend, interrupt, catch, capture.
(ANT.) free, release, discharge, liberate.
arrival *(SYN.)* advent, coming.
(ANT.) leaving, departure.
arrive *(SYN.)* come, emerge, reach, visit, land, appear.
(ANT.) exit, leave, depart, go.
arrogance *(SYN.)* pride, insolence.
(ANT.) humbleness, modesty, humility.
arrogant *(SYN.)* insolent, prideful, scornful, haughty, cavalier, proud.
(ANT.) modest, humble.
art *(SYN.)* cunning, tact, artifice, skill, aptitude, adroitness, painting, drawing.
(ANT.) clumsiness, innocence, unskillfulness, honesty.
artful *(SYN.)* clever, sly, skillful, knowing, deceitful, tricky, crafty, cunning.
(ANT.) artless.
article *(SYN.)* story, composition, treatise, essay, thing, report, object.
artificial *(SYN.)* bogus, fake, affected, feigned, phony, sham, unreal.
(ANT.) genuine, true, real, authentic.
artist *(SYN.)* actor, actress, painter, sculptor, singer, designer.
artless *(SYN.)* innocent, open, frank, simple, honest, candid, natural, unskilled, ignorant, truthful, sincere.
(ANT.) artful.
ascend *(SYN.)* rise, scale, tower, mount, go up, climb.
(ANT.) fall, sink, descend, go down.
ascertain *(SYN.)* solve, learn, clear up, answer.
ascribe *(SYN.)* attribute, assign.
ashamed *(SYN.)* shamefaced, humiliated, abashed, mortified, embarrassed.
(ANT.) proud.
ask *(SYN.)* invite, request, inquire, query, question, beg, solicit, demand.
(ANT.) order, reply, insist, answer.
askance *(SYN.)* sideways.
askew *(SYN.)* disorderly, crooked, awry, twisted.
(ANT.) straight.
asleep *(SYN.)* inactive, sleeping.
(ANT.) alert, awake.
aspect *(SYN.)* appearance, look, view, outlook, attitude, viewpoint, phase, part, feature, side.
asphyxiate *(SYN.)* suffocate, stifle, smother, choke, strangle, throttle.
aspiration *(SYN.)* craving, desire, hope, longing, objective, passion, ambition.
aspire *(SYN.)* seek, aim, wish for, strive, desire, yearn for.
ass *(SYN.)* mule, donkey, burro, silly, dunce, stubborn, stupid, fool.
assail *(SYN.)* assault, attack.
assassinate *(SYN.)* purge, kill, murder.
assault *(SYN.)* invade, strike, attack, assail, charge, bombard, onslaught.
(ANT.) protect, defend.
assemble *(SYN.)* collect, gather, meet, congregate, connect, manufacture.
(ANT.) disperse, disassemble, scatter.
assembly *(SYN.)* legislature, congress, council, parliament.
assent *(SYN.)* consent to, concede, agree, approval, accept, comply.
(ANT.) deny, dissent, refusal, denial, refuse.
assert *(SYN.)* declare, maintain, state, claim, express, defend, press, support.
(ANT.) deny, refute, contradict, decline.
assess *(SYN.)* calculate, compute, estimate, levy, reckon, tax, appraise.
asset *(SYN.)* property, wealth, capitol, resources, goods.
assign *(SYN.)* apportion, ascribe, attribute, cast, allot, choose, appropriate, name, elect, appoint, distribute.
(ANT.) release, relieve, unburden, discharge.
assignment *(SYN.)* task, job, responsibility, duty.
assist *(SYN.)* help, promote, serve, support, sustain, abet, aid, back.
(ANT.) prevent, impede, hinder, hamper.
assistance *(SYN.)* backing, help, patronage, relief, succor, support.
(ANT.) hostility, resistance, antagonism, counteraction.
assistant *(SYN.)* accomplice, ally, associate, confederate, abettor.
(ANT.) rival, enemy, adversary.
associate *(SYN.)* affiliate, ally, join, connect, unite, combine, link, mingle, partner, mix.
(ANT.) separate, disconnect, divide, disrupt, estrange.
association *(SYN.)* organization, club, union, society, fraternity, sorority, companionship, fellowship.
assorted *(SYN.)* varied, miscellaneous, classified, different, several, grouped.
(ANT.) alike, same.
assortment *(SYN.)* collection, variety, mixture, conglomeration.

assume *(SYN.)* arrogate, affect, suspect, believe, appropriate, take, pretend.
(ANT.) doff, demonstrate, prove, grant, concede.
assumption *(SYN.)* presumption, guess, theory, supposition, conjecture.
assurance *(SYN.)* confidence, conviction, self-reliance, surety, firmness, courage, promise, pledge, certainty, assertion.
(ANT.) humility, shyness, suspicion, modesty.
assure *(SYN.)* promise, convince, warrant, guarantee, pledge.
(ANT.) equivocate, deny.
astonish *(SYN.)* astound, amaze, surprise, shock.
(ANT.) tire, bore.
astound *(SYN.)* shock, amaze, astonish, stun, surprise, floor.
asylum *(SYN.)* shelter, refuge, home, madhouse, institution.
athletic *(SYN.)* strong, active, able-bodied, gymnastic, muscular.
atone *(SYN.)* repay, make up.
attach *(SYN.)* connect, adjoin, annex, join, append, stick, unite, adjoin, affix.
(ANT.) unfasten, untie, detach, separate, disengage.
attachment *(SYN.)* friendship, liking, regard, adherence, affection, devotion.
(ANT.) estrangement, opposition, alienation, aversion.
attack *(SYN.)* raid, assault, besiege, abuse, censure, offense, seige, invade.
(ANT.) surrender, defense, opposition, aid, defend, protect, repel.
attain *(SYN.)* achieve, acquire, accomplish, gain, get, reach, win.
(ANT.) relinquish, discard, abandon, desert.
attempt *(SYN.)* essay, experiment, trial, try, undertaking, endeavor, effort.
(ANT.) laziness, neglect, inaction.
attend *(SYN.)* accompany, escort, watch, be serve, care for, follow, lackey.
(ANT.) desert, abandon, avoid.
attendant *(SYN.)* waiter, servant, valet.
attention *(SYN.)* consideration, heed, circumspection, notice, watchfulness.
(ANT.) negligence, omission, oversight.
attentive *(SYN.)* careful, awake, alive, considerate, heedful, mindful, wary.
(ANT.) indifferent, unaware, oblivious.
attest *(SYN.)* testify, swear, certify.
attire *(SYN.)* apparel, dress, clothe.
attitude *(SYN.)* standpoint, viewpoint, stand, pose, aspect, position, posture.
attorney *(SYN.)* lawyer.
attract *(SYN.)* enchant, interest, pull, fascinate, draw, tempt, infatuate.
(ANT.) deter, repel, repulse, alienate.
attractive *(SYN.)* enchanting, winning, engaging, pleasant, pleasing, seductive.
(ANT.) unattractive, obnoxious, repellent, repulsive, forbidding.
attribute *(SYN.)* give, apply, place, trait, characteristic, feature, nature, credit.
audible *(SYN.)* distinct, bearable, plain, clear.
(ANT.) inaudible.
augment *(SYN.)* enlarge, increase, raise, expand, broaden, extend.
auspicious *(SYN.)* lucky, timely, favorable, promising, fortunate.
(ANT.) untimely, unfortunate.
authentic *(SYN.)* real, true, genuine, pure, accurate, reliable, legitimate.
(ANT.) false, spurious, artificial.
authenticate *(SYN.)* validate, warrant, guarantee, verify, certify.
author *(SYN.)* father, inventor, maker, originator, writer, composer.
authority *(SYN.)* dominion, justification, power, permission, authorization.
(ANT.) incapacity, denial, prohibition.
authorize *(SYN.)* permit, sanction, legalize, assign, enable, approve, empower.
(ANT.) forbid, prohibit.
autocrat *(SYN.)* monarch, ruler, tyrant.
autograph *(SYN.)* endorse, sign, approve.
automatic *(SYN.)* self-acting, mechanical, involuntary, self-working.
(ANT.) hand-operated, intentional, deliberate, manual.
automobile *(SYN.)* auto, car.
auxiliary *(SYN.)* assisting, helping, aiding.
avail *(SYN.)* help, profit, use, value, benefit, serve, advantage.
available *(SYN.)* obtainable, convenient, ready, handy, accessible, prepared.
(ANT.) unavailable, out of reach, inaccessible, unobtainable.
average *(SYN.* moderate, ordinary, usual, passable, fair, intermediate.
(ANT.) outstanding, exceptional, extraordinary, unusual.
averse *(SYN.)* unwilling, opposed, forced, against, involuntary.
(ANT.) willing.
aversion *(SYN.)* disgust, dislike, distaste, loathing, abhorrence, antipathy.
(ANT.) devotion, enthusiasm, affection, love.
avert *(SYN.)* avoid, prevent, prohibit.
(ANT.) invite.
avid *(SYN.)* greedy, eager.
avocation *(SYN.)* sideline, hobby, minor occupation.
avoid *(SYN.)* elude, forestall, evade, escape, avert, eschew, free, shun.
(ANT.) oppose, meet, confront, encounter, seek.
award *(SYN.)* reward, prize, medal, gift.
aware *(SYN.)* mindful, perceptive, informed, apprised, realizing.
(ANT.) unaware, insensible, ignorant.
away *(SYN.)* absent, departed, distracted, gone, not at home.
(ANT.) present, attentive, attending.
awe *(SYN.)* surprise, respect, dread, astonishment, alarm, fear and wonder.
awful *(SYN.)* frightful, horrible, awe-inspiring, dire, terrible, unpleasant, imposing, solemn, appalling, cruel.
(ANT.) humble, lowly, pleasant, nice, commonplace.
awkward *(SYN.)* unpolished, clumsy, ungraceful, ungainly, cumbersome.
(ANT.) adroit, graceful, skillful.
awry *(SYN.)* askew, wrong, twisted, crooked, disorderly.
(ANT.) straight, right.
axiom *(SYN.)* fundamental, maxim, principle, theorem, adage, apothegm.

babble *(SYN.)* twaddle, nonsense, gibberish, prattle, balderdash, rubbish, chatter, baby talk, poppycock, jabber, maunder, piffle.
baby *(SYN.)* newborn, infant, neonate, babe, teeny, small, wee, little, undersized, midget, papoose, protect, cosset, pamper.
babyish *(SYN.)* infantile, childish, baby, whiny, unreasonable, immature, puerile, foolish, dependent.
(ANT.) mature, adult, sensible, reasonable, grownup.
back *(SYN.)* help, assist, endorse, support, second, ratify, approve, stand by, approve, posterior, rear.
(ANT.) anterior, front, face, undercut, veto, undermine, progress, flow, leading, close, accessible, near.
backbiting *(SYN.)* gossip, slander, abuse, malice, cattiness, aspersion, derogation, belittling, badmouthing.
(ANT.) compliments, praise, loyalty, friendliness, approval.
backbone *(SYN.)* vertebrae, spine, pillar, support, staff, mainstay, basis, courage, determination, toughness, character.
(ANT.) timidity, weakness, cowardice, spinelessness.
backbreaking *(SYN.)* exhausting, fatiguing, tough, tiring, demanding, wearying, wearing, difficult.
(ANT.) light, relaxing, undemanding, slight.
back down *(SYN.)* accede, concede, acquiesce, yield, withdraw, renege.
(ANT.) persevere, insist.
backer *(SYN.)* underwriter, benefactor, investor, patron, sponsor, supporter.
backfire *(SYN.)* flop, boomerang, fail, founder, disappoint.
(ANT.) succeed.
background *(SYN.)* training, training, practice, knowledge, experience.
backing *(SYN.)* help, support, funds, money, assistance, grant, advocacy, subsidy, sympathy, endorsement.
(ANT.) criticism, detraction, faultfinding.
backlog *(SYN.)* inventory, reserve, hoard, amassment, accumulation.
backslide *(SYN.)* relapse, revert, return, weaken, regress, renege.
backward *(SYN.)* dull, sluggish, stupid, loath, regressive, rearward, underdeveloped, slow, retarded.
(ANT.) progressive, precocious, civilized, advanced, forward.
bad *(SYN.)* unfavorable, wrong, evil, immoral, sinful, faulty, improper, unwholesome, wicked, corrupt, tainted, harmful, injurious, defective, poor, imperfect, inferior, substandard, contaminated, inappropriate, unsuited, rotten, unsuitable, sorry, upset, sick, suffering, unpleasant, disagreeable.
(ANT.) good, honorable, reputable, moral, excellent.
badger *(SYN.)* tease, question, annoy, pester, bother, taunt, bait, provoke, torment, harass, hector.
baffle *(SYN.)* confound bewilder, perplex, puzzle, mystify, confuse, frustrate, bewilder.
(ANT.) inform, enlighten.
bag *(SYN.)* catch, snare, poke, sack.
bait *(SYN.)* enticement, captivate, ensnare, tease, torment, pester, worry, entrap, question, entice, lure, trap, harass, tempt, badger.
balance *(SYN.)* poise, stability, composure, remains, residue, equilibrium, compare, weigh, equalize.
(ANT.) unsteadiness, instability.
bald *(SYN.)* bare, hairless, nude, open, uncovered, simple.
(ANT.) covered, hairy.
baleful *(SYN.)* evil immoral sinful, destructive, detrimental, noxious, wicked, bad, villainous, injurious.
(ANT.) good, moral, reputable, excellent, harmless.
balk *(SYN.)* unwilling, obstinate, stubborn, hesitate, check, stop.
(ANT.) willing.
ball *(SYN.)* cotillion, dance, globe, sphere, spheroid.
ballad *(SYN.)* poem, song, ditty.
balloon *(SYN.)* puff up, enlarge, swell.
(ANT.) shrivel, shrink.
ballot *(SYN.)* choice, vote, poll.
balmy *(SYN.)* soft, gentle, soothing, fragrant, mild.
(ANT.) tempestuous, stormy.
ban *(SYN.)* prohibit, outlaw, disallow, block, bar, exclude, obstruct, prohibition, taboo, forbid.
(ANT.) allow, permit.
banal *(SYN.)* hackneyed, corny, vapid, trite, overused, humdrum.
(ANT.) striking, original, fresh, stimulating, novel.
band *(SYN.)* company, association, crew, group, society, belt, strip, unite, gang.
bandit *(SYN.)* thief, robber, highwayman, outlaw, marauder.
bang *(SYN.)* hit, strike, slam.
banish *(SYN.)* drive away, eject, exile, oust, deport, dismiss, expel.
(ANT.) receive, accept, shelter, admit, harbor, embrace, welcome.
bank *(SYN.)* barrier, slope, storage, treasury, row, series, string, shore.
banner *(SYN.)* colors, standard, pennant, flag.
banquet *(SYN.)* feast, celebration, festival, dinner, affair.
banter *(SYN.)* joke, tease, jest.
bar *(SYN.)* counter, impediment, saloon, exclude, obstacle, barricade, obstruct, shut out, hindrance, forbid, block, barrier, obstruction.
(ANT.) allow, permit, aid, encouragement.
barbarian *(SYN.)* brute, savage, boor, ruffian, rude, uncivilized, primitive, uncultured, coarse, cruel, barbaric, crude.
(ANT.) permit, allow, encouragement.
barbarous *(SYN.)* savage, remorseless, cruel, uncivilized, rude, unrelenting, merciless, crude, ruthless, inhuman.
(ANT.) kind, civilized, polite, humane, refined, tasteful, cultivated.

barber *(SYN.)* coiffeur, hairdresser.
bare *(SYN.)* naked, nude, uncovered, undressed, unclothed, unfurnished, plain, barren, empty, disclose, reveal, publicize, bald, expose, scarce, mere.
(ANT.) dressed, garbed, conceal, covered, hide, disguise, clothed.
barefaced *(SYN.)* impudent, bold, insolent, brazen, shameless, audacious, impertinent, rude.
barely *(SYN.)* hardly, scarcely, just.
bargain *(SYN.)* agreement, arrangement, deal, contract, arrange, sale.
baroque *(SYN.)* ornamented, elaborate, embellished, ornate.
barren *(SYN.)* unproductive, bare, unfruitful, infertile, sterile, childless.
(ANT.) productive, fruitful, fertile.
barricade *(SYN.)* fence, obstruction, shut in, fortification, barrier.
(ANT.) free, open, release.
barrier *(SYN.)* fence, wall, bar, railing, obstacle, hindrance, fortification, restraint, impediment, limit, barricade.
(ANT.) assistance, aid, encouragement.
barter *(SYN.)* exchange, deal, trade.
base *(SYN.)* bottom, rest, foundation, establish, found, immoral, evil, bad, wicked, depraved, selfish, worthless, cheap, debased, poor, support, stand, low, abject, menial.
(ANT.) exalted, righteous, lofty, esteemed, noble, honored, refined, valuable.
bashful *(SYN.)* timorous, abashed, shy, coy, timid, diffident, modest, sheepish, embarrassed, humble, recoiling, uneasy, awkward, ashamed.
(ANT.) fearless, outgoing, adventurous, gregarious, aggressive, daring.
basic *(SYN.)* underlying, chief, essential, main, fundamental.
(ANT.) subsidiary, subordinate.
basis *(SYN.)* presumption, support, base, principle, groundwork, presupposition,foundation, postulate, ground, assumption, premise, essential.
(ANT.) implication, trimming, derivative, superstructure.
basket *(SYN.)* hamper, creel, dossier, bassinet.
bastion *(SYN.)* mainstay, support, staff, tower, stronghold.
bat *(SYN.)* strike, hit, clout, stick, club, knock, crack.
batch *(SYN.)* group, set, collection, lot, cluster, bunch, mass, combination.
bath *(SYN.)* washing, shower, tub, wash, dip, soaping.
bathe *(SYN.)* launder, drench, swim, cover, medicate, immerse, wet, dip, soak, suffuse, rinse, saturate.
bathing suit *(SYN.)* maillot, swimsuit, trunks.
bathos *(SYN.)* mawkishness, soppiness, slush, sentimentality.
bathroom *(SYN.)* powder room, toilet, bath, lavatory.
baton *(SYN.)* mace, rod, staff, billy, crook, stick, fasces.
battalion *(SYN.)* mass, army, swarm, mob, drove, horde, gang, legion, regiment.
batten *(SYN.)* thrive, flourish, fatten, wax, expand, bloom, boom, grow.
(ANT.) decrease, weaken, fail.
batter *(SYN.)* pound, beat, hit, pommel, wallop, bash, smash, mixture, strike.
battery *(SYN.)* series, troop, force, rally, muster, set.
battle *(SYN.)* strife, fray, combat, struggle, contest, skirmish, conflict, fight, war, flight, warfare, action, campaign, strive against.
(ANT.) truce, concord, agreement, settlement, harmony, accept, concur, peace.
battlement *(SYN.)* parapet, rampart, fort, bastion, stronghold, escarpment.
bauble *(SYN.)* plaything, toy, trinket.
bawd *(SYN.)* procuress, prostitute.
bawdy *(SYN.)* vulgar, smutty, filthy, dirty, obscene, pornographic.
bawl *(SYN.)* sob, shout, wail, cry loudly, bellow, weep, cry.
bawl out *(SYN.)* scold, upbraid, censure, berate, reprove, reprimand.
bay *(SYN.)* inlet, bayou, harbor, lagoon, cove, sound, gulf.
bazaar *(SYN.)* fair, market, marketplace.
beach *(SYN.)* sands, seashore, waterfront, seaside, strand, coast, shore.
beacon *(SYN.)* light, signal, watchtower, guide, flare, warning, alarm.
bead *(SYN.)* globule, drop, pill, blob.
beak *(SYN.)* nose, bill, proboscis.
beam *(SYN.)* gleam, ray, girder, crossmember, pencil, shine, glisten, smile, glitter, gleam.
beaming *(SYN.)* joyful, bright, happy, radiant, grinning.
(ANT.) sullen, gloomy, threatening, scowling.
bear *(SYN.)* carry, support, take, uphold, suffer, convey, allow, stand, yield, endure, tolerate, produce, sustain, brook, transport, undergo, permit, suffer, abide, tolerate.
(ANT.) evade, shun, avoid, refuse, dodge.
bearable *(SYN.)* sufferable, supportable, manageable, tolerable.
(ANT.) terrible, painful, unbearable, awful, intolerable.
bearing *(SYN.)* course, direction, position, posture, behavior, manner, carriage, relation, reference, connection, application, deportment, air, way, conduct.
bearings *(SYN.)* orientation, whereabouts, location, direction, position, reading, course.
bear on *(SYN.)* affect, relate to.
bear out *(SYN.)* confirm, substantiate, justify, verify, prove.
bear up *(SYN.)* carry on, endure.
bear with *(SYN.)* tolerate, forbear.
beast *(SYN.)* monster, savage, brute, creature, animal.
beastly *(SYN.)* detestable, mean, low, hateful, loathsome, nasty, unpleasant, despicable, obnoxious, brutal, brutish, offensive.

(ANT.) considerate, sympathetic, refined, humane, fine, pleasant.

beat *(SYN.)* pulse, buffet, pound, defeat, palpitate, hit, thump, belabor, knock, overthrow, thrash, pummel, rout, smite, throb, punch, subdue, pulsate, dash, strike, overpower, vanquish, conquer, batter, conquer, overcome, blow.
(ANT.) stroke, fail, defend, surrender, shield.

beaten *(SYN.)* disheartened, dejected, licked, discouraged, hopeless, downcast, down, depressed.
(ANT.) eager, hopeful, cheerful.

beatific *(SYN.)* uplifted, blissful, elated, happy, wonderful, joyful, divine.
(ANT.) awful, hellish, ill-fated, accursed.

beating *(SYN.)* whipping, drubbing, flogging, lashing, scourging, walloping.

beau *(SYN.)* lover, suitor, swain, admirer.

beautiful *(SYN.)* pretty, fair, lovely, charming, comely, handsome, elegant, attractive.
(ANT.) repulsive, hideous, unsightly, foul, homely, plainness, unattractive, ugly, ugliness.

beauty *(SYN.)* handsomeness, fairness, charm, pulchritude, attractiveness, loveliness, comeliness, grace, allegiance.
(ANT.) ugliness, disfigurement, homeliness, plainness, deformity, eyesore.

becalm *(SYN.)* calm, quiet, smooth, still, hush, repose, settle.

because *(SYN.)* inasmuch as, as, since, for.

because of *(SYN.)* as a result of, as a consequence of.

beckon *(SYN.)* call, signal, summon, motion, gesture, wave.

becloud *(SYN.)* obfuscate, confuse, befog, confound, obscure, muddle.
(ANT.) illuminate, clarify, solve.

become *(SYN.)* change, grow, suit, be appropriate, befit.

becoming *(SYN.)* suitable, meet, befitting, appropriate, fitting, seemly, enhancing, attractive, pleasing, flattering, tasteful, smart, adorning, ornamental.
(ANT.) unsuitable, inappropriate, incongruent, ugly, unattractive, improper.

bed *(SYN.)* layer, cot, vein, berth, stratum, couch, accumulation, bunk, deposit, cradle.

bedazzle *(SYN.)* glare, blind, dumbfound, flabbergast, bewilder, furbish, festoon.

bedeck *(SYN.)* deck, adorn, beautify, smarten, festoon, garnish.

bedevil *(SYN.)* worry, fret, irk, torment, harass, pester, nettle, tease, vex, plague.
(ANT.) soothe, calm, delight, please.

bedlam *(SYN.)* tumult, uproar, madhouse, commotion, confusion, racket, rumpus, pandemonium.
(ANT.) calm, peace.

bedraggled *(SYN.)* shabby, muddy, sodden, messy, sloppy.
(ANT.) dry, neat, clean, well-groomed.

bedrock *(SYN.)* basis, foundation, roots, basics, essentials, fundamentals, bottom, bed, substratum, core.
(ANT.) top, dome, apex, nonessentials.

bedroom *(SYN.)* chamber, bedchamber.

beef *(SYN.)* brawn, strength, heft, gripe, sinew, fitness, huskiness, might.

beef up *(SYN.)* reinforce, vitalize, nerve, buttress, strengthen.
(ANT.) sap, weaken, enervate, drain.

beefy *(SYN.)* solid, strong, muscular, heavy, stocky.

befall *(SYN.)* occur, come about, happen.

before *(SYN.)* prior, earlier, in advance, formerly.
(ANT.) behind, following, afterward, latterly, after.

befriend *(SYN.)* welcome, encourage, aid, stand by.
(ANT.) dislike, shun, desert, avoid.

befuddle *(SYN.)* stupefy, addle, confuse, rattle, disorient.

beg *(SYN.)* solicit, ask, implore, supplicate, entreat, adjure, petition, beseech, request, importune, entreat, implore.
(ANT.) grant, cede, give, bestow, favor.

beget *(SYN.)* sire, engender, produce, create, propagate, originate, breed, generate, procreate, father.
(ANT.) murder, destroy, kill, abort, prevent, extinguish.

beggar *(SYN.)* scrub, tatterdemalion, pauper, wretch, ragamuffin, vagabond, starveling.

begin *(SYN.)* open, enter, arise, initiate, commence, start, inaugurate, originate, institute, create.
(ANT.) terminate, complete, finish, close, end, stop.

beginner *(SYN.)* nonprofessional, amateur, apprentice.
(ANT.) veteran, professional.

beginning *(SYN.)* outset, inception, origin, source, commencement, start, opening, initiation, inauguration.
(ANT.) termination, completion, end, close, consummation, closing, ending, finish.

begrime *(SYN.)* soil, dirty, smear, muddy, splotch, tarnish.
(ANT.) wash, clean, freshen, launder.

begrudge *(SYN.)* resent, envy, stint, withhold, grudge.

begrudging *(SYN.)* hesitant, reluctant, resentful, unwilling, forced.
(ANT.) willing, eager, quick, spontaneous.

beguiling *(SYN.)* enchanting, interesting, delightful, intriguing, engaging, bewitching, attractive, enthralling, captivating.
(ANT.) boring, dull, unattractive, tedious.

behalf *(SYN.)* benefit, welfare, support, aid, part, interest.

behave *(SYN.)* deport, comport, manage, act, demean, bear, interact, carry, operate, conduct.
(ANT.) rebel, misbehave.

behavior *(SYN.)* manners, carriage, disposition, action, deed, bearing,

deportment, conduct, demeanor.
(ANT.) rebelliousness, misbehavior.
behead *(SYN.)* decapitate, guillotine, decollate.
behest *(SYN.)* order, command, decree, mandate, bidding.
behind *(SYN.)* after, backward, at the back, in back of.
(ANT.) frontward, ahead, before.
behold *(SYN.)* look, see, view, notice, observe, perceive, sight.
(ANT.) overlook, ignore.
being *(SYN.)* life, existing, existence, living, actuality, organism, individual.
(ANT.) death, nonexistence, expiration.
belabor *(SYN.)* repeat, reiterate, pound, explain, expatiate, din.
belated *(SYN.)* late, delayed, overdue, tardy.
(ANT.) well-timed, early.
belch *(SYN.)* emit, erupt, gush, disgorge, bubble, eructation, burp.
beleaguered *(SYN.)* bothered, beset, annoyed, beset, harassed, badgered, vexed, plagued, victimized.
belie *(SYN.)* distort, misrepresent, twist, disappoint.
belief *(SYN.)* trust, feeling, certitude, opinion, conviction, persuasion, credence, confidence, reliance, faith, view, creed, assurance.
(ANT.) heresy, denial, incredulity, distrust, skepticism, doubt.
believe *(SYN.)* hold, apprehend, fancy, support, accept, conceive, suppose, imagine, trust, credit.
(ANT.) doubt, reject, distrust, disbelieve, question.
believer *(SYN.)* adherent, follower, devotee, convert, zealot.
(ANT.) doubter, critic, scoffer, skeptic.
belittle *(SYN.)* underrate, depreciate, minimize, decry, disparage, diminish, demean, slight, discredit, militant, depreciate, humiliate.
(ANT.) esteem, admire, flatter, overrate, commend.
bell *(SYN.)* pealing, ringing, signal, tolling, buzzer, chime.
belligerent *(SYN.)* aggressive, warlike, hostile, offensive, combative, militant.
(ANT.) easygoing, compromising, peaceful.
bellow *(SYN.)* thunder, roar, scream, shout, yell, howl.
bellwether *(SYN.)* leader, pilot, guide, ringleader, boss, shepherd.
belly *(SYN.)* stomach, abdomen, paunch.
belonging *(SYN.)* loyalty, relationship, kinship, acceptance, rapport.
belongings *(SYN.)* property, effects, possessions.
beloved *(SYN.)* adored, sweet, loved, cherished, prized, esteemed, valued, darling.
below *(SYN.)* under, less, beneath, underneath, lower.
(ANT.) aloft, overhead, above, over.
belt *(SYN.)* girdle, sash, strap, cummerbund, band, waistband, whack, hit, wallop, punch.
bemoan *(SYN.)* mourn, lament, grieve, sorrow, regret, deplore.
bend *(SYN.)* turn, curve, incline, submit, bow, lean, crook, twist, yield, stoop, crouch, agree, suppress, oppress, mold, kneel, deflect, subdue, influence.
(ANT.) resist, straighten, break, stiffen.
beneath *(SYN.)* under, below.
(ANT.) above, over.
benediction *(SYN.)* thanks, blessing, prayer.
beneficial *(SYN.)* salutary, good, wholesome, advantageous, useful, helpful, serviceable, profitable.
(ANT.) harmful, destructive, injurious, disadvantageous, unwholesome, deleterious, detrimental.
benefit *(SYN.)* support, help, gain, avail, profit, account, favor, aid, good, advantage, serve, interest, behalf, service.
(ANT.) handicap, calamity, trouble, disadvantage, distress.
benevolence *(SYN.)* magnanimity, charity, tenderness, altruism, humanity, philanthropy, generosity, liberality, beneficence, good will.
(ANT.) malevolence, unkindness, cruelty, selfishness, inhumanity.
benevolent *(SYN.)* kindhearted, tender, merciful, generous, altruistic, obliging, kind, good, well-wishing, philanthropy, liberal, unselfish, kindly, disposed, openhearted, humane, benign, friendly.
(ANT.) malevolent, greedy, wicked, harsh.
bent *(SYN.)* curved, crooked, resolved, determined, set, inclined, firm, decided.
(ANT.) straight.
berate *(SYN.)* scold.
beseech *(SYN.)* appeal, entreat, plead, ask, beg, implore.
beset *(SYN.)* surround, attack.
besides *(SYN.)* moreover, further, except for, also, as well, furthermore.
besiege *(SYN.)* assault, attack, siege, bombard, raid, charge.
bespeak *(SYN.)* engage, reserve, indicate, show, signify, express.
best *(SYN.)* choice, prime, select.
(ANT.) worst.
bestial *(SYN.)* brutal, beastly, savage, cruel.
bestow *(SYN.)* confer, place, put, award, give, present.
(ANT.) withdraw, withhold.
bet *(SYN.)* gamble, give, stake, wager, pledge, ante.
betray *(SYN.)* reveal, deliver, expose, mislead, trick, deceive, exhibit, show.
(ANT.) shelter, protect, safeguard.
betrothal *(SYN.)* marriage, engagement, contract.
better *(SYN.)* superior, preferable, improve.
(ANT.) worsen.
between *(SYN.)* among, betwixt.
beware *(SYN.)* take care, watch out, look sharp, be careful.
bewilder *(SYN.)* perplex, confuse, mystify, baffle, puzzle, overwhelm.
(ANT.) clarify, enlighten.

bewitch *(SYN.)* captivate, charm, delight, enchant.
beyond *(SYN.)* past, farther, exceeding.
bias *(SYN.)* slant, inclination, proneness, turn, bent, penchant, tendency, disposition, propensity, partiality, predisposition, leaning, proclivity, prejudice, influence, warp, slanting, predilection.
(ANT.) fairness, justice, even-handedness, equity, detachment, impartiality.
bible *(SYN.)* guide, handbook, gospel, manual, sourcebook, guidebook.
bibulous *(SYN.)* guzzling, intemperate, sottish, alcoholic.
(ANT.) sober, moderate.
bicker *(SYN.)* dispute, argue, wrangle, quarrel.
(ANT.) go along with, agree.
bid *(SYN.)* order, command, direct, wish, greet, say, offer, instruct, invite, purpose, tender, proposal.
bidding *(SYN.)* behest, request, decree, call, charge, beck, summons, solicitation, invitation, instruction, mandate.
bide *(SYN.)* stay, tarry, delay, wait, remain.
big *(SYN.)* large, huge, bulky, immense, colossal, majestic, august, monstrous, hulking, gigantic, massive, great, enormous, tremendous, outgoing, imporant, kind, bighearted, considerable, generous, grand.
(ANT.) small, little, tiny, immature, petite.
big-hearted *(SYN.)* good-natured, liberal, generous, unselfish, open-handed, unstinting, charitable, magnanimous.
(ANT.) cold, selfish, mean, uncharitable.
bigoted *(SYN.)* intolerant, partial, prejudiced, biased, unfair, chauvinist.
bigotry *(SYN.)* bias, blindness, intolerance, unfairness, prejudice, ignorance, passion, sectarianism.
(ANT.) acceptance, open-mindedness.
big-shot *(SYN.)* somebody, brass hat, big gun.
(ANT.) underling, nobody, nebbish, cipher.
bijou *(SYN.)* gem, bauble, jewel, ornament.
bile *(SYN.)* spleen, rancor, anger, bitterness, peevishness, ill-humor, nastiness, resentment, discontent, irascibility.
(ANT.) cheerfulness, affability, pleasantness.
bilge *(SYN.)* hogwash, drivel, gibberish, rubbish, bosh, foolishness, twaddle.
bilious *(SYN.)* petulant, crabby, ill-natured, cross, peevish, crotchety, cranky.
(ANT.) happy, agreeable, pleasant, good-natured.
bilk *(SYN.)* defraud, trick, cheat, hoodwink, deceive, fleece, rook, bamboozle.
bill *(SYN.)* charge, invoice, account, statement.
billet *(SYN.)* housing, quarters, berth, shelter, barrack, installation.
billingsgate *(SYN.)* swearing, scurrility, cursing, abuse, vulgarity, gutter, profanity.
billow *(SYN.)* surge, swell, rise, rush, peaking, magnification, amplification, augmentation, increase, intensification.
(ANT.) lowering, decrease.
bin *(SYN.)* cubbyhole, box, container, chest, cubicle, crib, receptacle, can.
bind *(SYN.)* connect, restrain, band, fasten, oblige, obligate, engage, wrap, connect, weld, attach, tie, require, restrict.
(ANT.) unlace, loose, unfasten, untie, free.
binding *(SYN.)* compulsory, obligatory, mandatory, compelling, unalterable, imperative, indissoluble, unconditional, unchangeable.
(ANT.) adjustable, flexible, elastic, changeable.
binge *(SYN.)* fling, spree, carousal, toot.
birth *(SYN.)* origin, beginning, infancy, inception.
(ANT.) finish, decline, death, disappearance, end.
biscuit *(SYN.)* bun, roll, cake, muffin, bread, rusk.
bit *(SYN.)* fraction, portion, scrap, fragment, particle, drop, speck, harness, small amount, restraint, morsel, sum.
bite *(SYN.)* gnaw, chew, nip, sting, pierce, mouthful, snack, morsel.
biting *(SYN.)* cutting, sharp, acid, sneering, sarcastic.
(ANT.) soothing, kind, gentle, agreeable.
bitter *(SYN.)* distasteful, sour, acrid, pungent, piercing, vicious, severe, biting, distressful, stinging, distressing, ruthless, hated, hostile, grievous, harsh, painful, tart.
(ANT.) sweet, mellow, pleasant, delicious.
bizarre *(SYN.)* peculiar, strange, odd, uncommon, queer, unusual.
(ANT.) usual, everyday, ordinary, inconspicuous.
black *(SYN.)* sooty, dark, ebony, inky, swarthy, soiled, filthy, dirty, stained, somber, depressing, sad, dismal, gloomy.
(ANT.) white, clean, pristine, glowing, pure, cheerful, sunny, bright.
blackball *(SYN.)* turn down, ban, blacklist, exclude, snub, reject, debar.
(ANT.) accept, include, invite, ask, bid.
blacken *(SYN.)* tar, ink, black, darken, besoot, smudge, begrime, discredit, defile, dull, dim, tarnish, ebonize, denounce, sully, libel, blemish, defame.
(ANT.) exalt, honor, whiten, brighten, shine, bleach.
blackmail *(SYN.)* bribe, payment, bribery, extortion, shakedown, coercion.
blackout *(SYN.)* faint, coma, unconsciousness, oblivion, amnesia, stupor, swoon.
bladder *(SYN.)* saccule, sac, vesicle, pouch, pod, cell, blister, container,

cyst.

blade *(SYN.)* cutter, lancet, knife, sword.

blah *(SYN.)* lifeless, flat, jejune, lukewarm, stale, insipid, tasteless, pedestrian, tedious, dreary, uninteresting.
(ANT.) spirited, fascinating, vibrant, vigorous.

blame *(SYN.)* upbraid, criticize, fault, guilt, accuse, rebuke, charge, implicate, impeach, tattle, condemn, indict, responsibility, censure, denounce, reproach.
(ANT.) exonerate, credit, honor, absolve.

blameless *(SYN.)* moral, innocent, worthy, faultless.
(ANT.) blameworthy, culpable, guilty.

blanch *(SYN.)* whiten, bleach, decolorize, peroxide, fade, wash out, dim, dull.

bland *(SYN.)* soft, smooth, gentle, agreeable, vapid, insipid, mild, polite.
(ANT.) harsh, outspoken, disagreeable.

blandish *(SYN.)* praise, compliment, overpraise, cajole, puff, adulate, salve, fawn, court, toady, butter up, please, jolly.
(ANT.) insult, deride, criticize, belittle.

blandisher *(SYN.)* adulator, booster, sycophant, eulogist, apple polisher, flunkey.
(ANT.) knocker, faultfinder, belittler.

blandishment *(SYN.)* applause, cajolery, honey, adulation, plaudits, acclaim, fawning, compliments.
(ANT.) carping, belittling, criticism, deprecation.

blank *(SYN.)* unmarked, expressionless, uninterested, form, area, void, vacant, empty.
(ANT.) marked, filled, alert, animated.

blanket *(SYN.)* quilt, coverlet, cover, comforter, robe, padding, carpet, wrapper, mantle, envelope, housing, coat, comprehensive, universal, across-the-board, panoramic, omnibus.
(ANT.) limited, detailed, restricted, precise.

blare *(SYN.)* roar, blast, resound, jar, scream, swell, clang, peal, trumpet, toot, hoot.

blasphemous *(SYN.)* profane, irreverent, impious, godless, ungodly, sacrilegious, irreligious.
(ANT.) reverent, reverential, religious, pious.

blasphemy *(SYN.)* profanation, impiousness, cursing, irreverence, sacrilege, abuse, ecration, swearing, contempt.
(ANT.) respect, piety, reverence, devotion.

blast *(SYN.)* burst, explosion, discharge, blowout.

blasted *(SYN.)* blighted, withered, ravaged, decomposed, spoiled, destroyed.

blastoff *(SYN.)* launching, expulsion, launch, shot, projection.

blatant *(SYN.)* shameless, notorious, brazen, flagrant, glaring, bold, obvious.
(ANT.) deft, subtle, insidious, devious.

blaze *(SYN.)* inferno, shine, flare, marking, fire, outburst, holocaust, notch, flame.
(ANT.) die, dwindle.

bleach *(SYN.)* pale, whiten, blanch, whitener.
(ANT.) darken, blacken.

bleak *(SYN.)* dreary, barren, cheerless, depressing, gloomy, windswept, bare, cold, dismal, desolate, raw, chilly.
(ANT.) lush, hopeful, promising, cheerful.

bleary *(SYN.)* hazy, groggy, blurry, fuzzy, misty, clouded, overcast, dim, blear.
(ANT.) clear, vivid, precise, clear-cut.

bleed *(syn.)* pity, lose blood, grieve, sorrow.

blemish *(SYN.)* injury, speck, flaw, scar, disgrace, imperfection, stain, fault, blot.
(ANT.) purity, embellishment, adornment, perfection.

blend *(SYN.)* beat, intermingle, combine, fuse, unify, consolidate, unite, amalgamate, conjoin, mix, coalesce, intermix, join, merge, compound, combination, stir, mixture, commingle, mingle.
(ANT.) separate, decompose, analyze, disintegrate.

bless *(SYN.)* thank, celebrate, extol, glorify, adore, delight, praise, gladden, exalt.
(ANT.) denounce, blaspheme, slander, curse.

blessed *(SYN.)* sacred, holy, consecrated, dedicated, hallowed, sacrosanct, beatified, joyful, delighted, joyous, sainted, canonized, blissful.
(ANT.) miserable, sad, dispirited, cheerless.

blessing *(SYN.)* benison, sanction, favor, grace, benediction, invocation, approbation, approval, compliment, bounty, windfall, gift, benefit, advantage, kindness, felicitation, invocation.
(ANT.) disapproval, execration, curse, denunciation, malediction, rebuke, displeasure, condemnation, adversity, misfortune, mishap, calamity.

blight *(SYN.)* decay, disease, spoil, sickness, wither, ruin, damage, harm, decaying, epidemic, affliction, destroy.

blind *(SYN.)* sightless, unmindful, rash, visionless, ignorant, unsighted, unconscious, discerning, heedless, oblivious, purblind, unknowing, screen, unaware, thoughtless, shade, unthinking, cover, curtain, without thought, headlong.
(ANT.) discerning, sensible, calculated, perceiving, perceptive, aware.

blink *(SYN.)* bat, glance, flicker, wink, twinkle.

bliss *(SYN.)* ecstasy, rapture, glee, elation, joy, blessedness, gladness, happiness, delight, felicity, blissfulness.
(ANT.) woe, sadness, sorrow, grief,

unhappiness, torment, wretchedness, misery.

blissful *(SYN.)* happy, elated, rapturous, ecstatic, paradisiacal, joyous, enraptured.

blister *(SYN.)* bleb, swelling, welt, sore, blob, bubble, inflammation, boil, canker.

blithe *(SYN.)* breezy, merry, airy, lighthearted, light, gay, fanciful, graceful.
(ANT.) morose, grouchy, low-spirited, gloomy.

blitz *(SYN.)* strike, onslaught, thrust, raid, lunge, drive, incursion, assault, sally.

blizzard *(SYN.)* storm, snowstorm, snowfall, gale, tempest, blast, blow, swirl.

bloat *(SYN.)* distend, puff up, inflate, swell.
(ANT.) deflate.

blob *(SYN.)* bubble, blister, pellet, globule.

block *(SYN.)* clog, hinder, bar, impede, close, obstruct, barricade, blockade, obstruction, hindrance, obstacle, impediment, retard, check, stop.
(ANT.) forward, promote, aid, clear, advance, advantage, assist, further, open.

blockade *(SYN.)* barrier, fortification, obstruction, barricade.

blockhead *(SYN.)* dunce, dolt, fool, sap, idiot, simpleton, chump, booby, bonehead, woodenhead.

blood *(SYN.)* murder, gore, slaughter, bloodshed, ancestry, lineage, heritage.

bloodcurdling *(SYN.)* hair-raising, terrifying, alarming, chilling, stunning, scary.

bloodless *(SYN.)* dead, torpid, dull, drab, cold, colorless, passionless, lackluster.
(ANT.) passionate, vital, ebullient, animated, vivacious.

bloodshed *(SYN.)* murder, killing, slaying, blood bath, massacre, carnage.

bloodthirsty *(SYN.)* murderous, cruel.

bloody *(SYN.)* cruel, pitiless, bloodthirsty, inhuman, ruthless, ferocious, murderous.
(ANT.) kind, gentle.

bloom *(SYN.)* thrive, glow, flourish, blossom, flower.
(ANT.) wane, decay, dwindle, shrivel, wither.

blooming *(SYN.)* flush, green, vigorous, thriving, vital, abloom, healthy, fresh, booming.
(ANT.) flagging, declining, whithering.

blooper *(SYN.)* muff, fluff, error, bungle, botch, blunder, fumble, howler, indiscretion.

blossom *(SYN.)* bloom, flower, flourish.
(ANT.) shrink, wither, dwindle, fade.

blot *(SYN.)* stain, inkblot, spot, inkstain, blemish, dishonor, disgrace, spatter, obliterate, soil, dry.

blot out *(SYN.)* wipe out, destroy, obliterate, abolish, annihilate, cancel, expunge, strike out, shade, darken, shadow, overshadow, obfuscate, cloud, eclipse.

blow *(SYN.)* hit, thump, slap, cuff, box, shock, move, drive, spread, breeze, puff, whistle, inflate, enlarge.

blowout *(SYN.)* blast, explosion, burst.

blue *(SYN.)* sapphire, azure, gloomy, sad, unhappy, depressed, dejected, melancholy.
(ANT.) cheerful, optimistic, happy.

blueprint *(SYN.)* design, plan, scheme, chart, draft, prospectus, outline, proposal, conception, project, layout.

blues *(SYN.)* dumps, melancholy, depression, doldrums, moodiness, dejection, despondency, gloominess, moroseness.

bluff *(SYN.)* steep, perpendicular, vertical, abrupt, precipitous, rough, open, frank, hearty, blunt, fool, mislead, pretend, deceive, fraud, lie, fake, deceit.

blunder *(SYN.)* error, flounder, mistake, stumble.

blunt *(SYN.)* solid, abrupt, rough, dull, pointless, plain, bluff, edgeless, unceremonious, obtuse, rude, outspoken, unsharpened, rounded, worn, crude, direct, impolite, short, curt, gruff.
(ANT.) tactful, polite, subtle, polished, suave, sharp, keen, pointed, diplomatic.

blur *(SYN.)* sully, dim, obscure, stain, dull, confuse, cloud, smear, stain, smudge.
(ANT.) clear, clarify.

blush *(SYN.)* redden.

board *(SYN.)* embark, committee, wood, mount, cabinet, food, get on, lumber.

boast *(SYN.)* vaunt, flaunt, brag, glory, crow, exaggerate, bragging.
(ANT.) humble, apologize, minimize, deprecate.

body *(SYN.)* remains, bulk, mass, carcass, form, company, corpus, society, firmness, group, torso, substance, collection, cadaver, trunk, group, throng, company, crowd, band.
(ANT.) spirit, intellect, soul.

bogus *(SYN.)* counterfeit, false, pretend, fake, phony.
(ANT.) genuine.

boil *(SYN.)* seethe, bubble, pimple, fume, pimple, cook, swelling, rage, foam, simmer, stew.

boisterous *(SYN.)* rough, violent, rowdy, noisy, tumultuous.
(ANT.) serene.

bold *(SYN.)* daring, forward, pushy, striking, brave, dauntless, rude, prominent, adventurous, fearless, insolent, conspicuous, defiant, arrogant, cavalier, brazen, unafraid, intrepid, courageous, valiant, heroic, gallant, disrespectful, impudent, shameless.
(ANT.) modest, bashful, cowardly, timid, retiring, flinching, fearful, timorous, polite, courteous, deferential.

bolt *(SYN.)* break away, fastener, flee, take flight, lock.

bombard *(SYN.)* shell, open fire, bomb, rake, assail, attack.

bond *(SYN.)* fastener, rope, tie, cord, connection, attachment, link, tie, promise.
(ANT.) sever, separate, untie, disconnect.
bondage *(SYN.)* slavery, thralldom, captivity, imprisonment, servitude, confinement, vassalage, enslavement.
(ANT.) liberation, emancipation, free, independence, freedom.
bonds *(SYN.)* chains, cuffs, fetters, shackles, irons, bracelets.
bone up *(SYN.)* learn, master, study, relearn.
bonus *(SYN.)* more, extra, premium, gift, reward, bounty.
bony *(SYN.)* lean, lank, thin, lanky, rawboned, fleshless, skinny, gangling, weight.
(ANT.) plump, fleshy, stout.
book *(SYN.)* manual, textbook, work, booklet, monograph, brochure, tract, volume, pamphlet, treatise, publication, hardcover, paperback, novel, workbook, text.
bookish *(SYN.)* formal, scholarly, theoretical, academic, learned, scholastic, erudite.
(ANT.) simple, ignorant.
boom *(SYN.)* advance, grow, flourish, progress, gain, increase, roar, beam, rumble, reverberate, thunder, prosper, swell, thrive, pole, rush.
(ANT.) decline, fail, recession.
booming *(SYN.)* flourishing, blooming, thriving, vigorous, prospering, exuberant.
(ANT.) waning, dying, failing, declining.
boon *(SYN.)* gift, jolly, blessing, pleasant, godsend, windfall.
boondocks *(SYN.)* sticks, backwoods.
boor *(SYN.)* lout, clown, oaf, yokel, rustic, vulgarian, ruffian.
boorish *(SYN.)* coarse, churlish, uncivil, ill-mannered, ill-bred, uncivilized, crude, uncouth.
(ANT.) polite, cultivated, cultivated, well-mannered.
boost *(SYN.)* push, lift, help, hoist, shove.
(ANT.) depress, lower, belittle, submerge, disparage, decrease, decline, reduction, downturn.
booster *(SYN.)* supporter, fan, rooter, plugger, follower.
boot *(SYN.)* shoe, kick.
booth *(SYN.)* enclosure, cubicle, stand, compartment, box.
bootless *(SYN.)* purposeless, ineffective, profitless, useless.
(ANT.) favorable, successful, useful.
bootlicker *(SYN.)* flunky, fawner, toady, sycophant.
booty *(SYN.)* prize, plunder, loot.
booze *(SYN.)* spirits, drink, liquor, alcohol.
border *(SYN.)* fringe, rim, verge, boundary, edge, termination, brink, limit, brim, outskirts, frontier, margin.
(ANT.) interior, center, mainland, core, middle.
borderline *(SYN.)* indeterminate, halfway, obscure, inexact, indefinite, unclear.
(ANT.) precise, absolute, definite.
border on *(SYN.)* approximate, approach, resemble, echo, parallel, connect.
bore *(SYN.)* tire, weary, hole, perforate, pierce, drill.
(ANT.) arouse, captivate, excite, interest.
boredom *(SYN.)* ennui, doldrums, weariness, dullness, tedium.
(ANT.) stimulation, motive, activity, stimulus, excitement.
boring *(SYN.)* monotonous, dull, dead, flat, tedious, wearisome, trite, prosaic, humdrum, long-winded.
born *(SYN.)* hatched, produced.
borrow *(SYN.)* copy, adopt, simulate, mirror, assume, usurp, plagiarize, take.
(ANT.) allow, advance, invent, originate, credit, lend.
bosom *(SYN.)* chest, breast, feelings, thoughts, mind, interior, marrow, heart.
boss *(SYN.)* director, employer, oversee, direct, foreman, supervisor, manager.
(ANT.) worker, employee, underling.
bossy *(SYN.)* overbearing, arrogant, domineering, lordly, tyrannical, highhanded, arbitrary, oppress.
(ANT.) flexible, easygoing, cooperative.
botch *(SYN.)* blunder, bungle, fumble, goof, muff, mishandle, mismanage.
(ANT.) perform, realize.
bother *(SYN.)* haunt, molest, trouble, annoy, upset, fleeting, transient, harass, inconvenience, momentary, disturb, passing, pester, tease, irritate, worry, vex.
(ANT.) prolonged, extended, long, protracted, lengthy, comfort, solace.
bothersome *(SYN.)* irritating, vexatious, worrisome, annoying, distressing, troublesome, disturbing.
bottle *(SYN.)* container, flask, vessel, decanter, vial, ewer, jar.
bottleneck *(SYN.)* obstacle, obstruction, barrier, block, blockage, detour.
bottom *(SYN.)* basis, fundament, base, groundwork, foot, depths, lowest part, underside, foundation, seat, buttocks, rear, behind.
(ANT.) top, peak, apex, summit, topside.
bough *(SYN.)* branch, arm, limb.
bounce *(SYN.)* recoil, ricochet, rebound.
bound *(SYN.)* spring, vault, hop, leap, start, surrounded, jump, limit, jerk, boundary, bounce, skip, tied, shackled, trussed, fettered, certain, sure, destined, compelled, required.
(ANT.) unfettered, free.
boundary *(SYN.)* bound, limit, border, margin, outline, circumference, perimeter, division, frontier, edge.
boundless *(SYN.)* limitless, endless, inexhaustible, unlimited, eternal, infinite.
(ANT.) restricted, narrow, limited.
bounteous *(SYN.)* plentiful, generous, liberal, abundant.
(ANT.) scarce.
bountiful *(SYN.)* bounteous, fertile,

plentiful, generous, abundant.
(ANT.) sparing, infertile, scarce.
bounty *(SYN.)* generosity, gift, award, bonus, reward, prize, premium.
bourgeois *(SYN.)* common, ordinary, commonplace, middle-class, conventional.
(ANT.) upper-class, unconventional, loose, aristocratic.
bout *(SYN.)* round, contest, conflict, test, struggle, match, spell, fight.
bow *(SYN.)* bend, yield, kneel, submit, stoop.
bowels *(SYN.)* entrails, intestines, innards, guts, stomach.
bowl *(SYN.)* container, dish, pot, pottery, crock, jug, vase.
bowl over *(SYN.)* fell, floor, overturn, astound, nonplus, stagger, jar.
bow out *(SYN.)* give up, withdraw, retire, resign, abandon.
box *(SYN.)* hit, fight, crate, case, container.
boxer *(SYN.)* prizefighter, fighter.
boy *(SYN.)* male, youngster, lad, kid, fellow, buddy, youth.
(ANT.) girl, man.
boycott *(SYN.)* picket, strike, ban, revolt, blackball.
boy friend *(SYN.)* date, young man, sweetheart, courtier, beau.
brace *(SYN.)* strengthen, tie, prop, support, tighten, stay, strut, bind, truss, crutch.
bracelet *(SYN.)* armband, bangle, circlet.
bracing *(SYN.)* stimulating, refreshing, restorative, fortifying, invigorating.
bracket *(SYN.)* join, couple, enclose, relate, brace, support.
brag *(SYN.)* boast, flaunt, vaunt, bluster, swagger.
(ANT.) demean, debase, denigrate, degrade, depreciate, deprecate.
braid *(SYN.)* weave, twine, wreath, plait.
brain *(SYN.)* sense, intelligence, intellect, common sense, understanding, reason.
(ANT.) stupid, stupidity.
brake *(SYN.)* decelerate, stop, curb.
(ANT.) accelerate.
branch *(SYN.)* shoot, limb, bough, tributary, offshoot, part, division, expand, department, divide, spread, subdivision.
brand *(SYN.)* make, trademark, label, kind, burn, trade name, mark, stamp, blaze.
brave *(SYN.)* bold, daring, gallant, valorous, adventurous, heroic, magnanimous, chivalrous, audacious, valiant, courageous, fearless, intrepid, unafraid.
(ANT.) weak, cringing, timid, cowardly, fearful, craven.
brawl *(SYN.)* racket, quarrel, fracas, riot, fight, melee, fray, disturbance, dispute, disagreement.
brawn *(SYN.)* strength, muscle.
(ANT.) weakness.
brazen *(SYN.)* immodest, forward, shameless, bold, brassy, impudent, insolent, rude.
(ANT.) retiring, self-effacing, modest, shy.
breach *(SYN.)* rupture, fracture, rift, break, crack, gap, opening, breaking, quarrel, violation.
(ANT.) observation.
break *(SYN.)* demolish, pound, rack, smash, burst, rupture, disobey, violate, crack, infringe, crush, squeeze, transgress, fracture, shatter, wreck, crash, atomize, disintegrate, collapse, splinter, crack, gap, breach, opening, rupture.
(ANT.) restore, heal, join, renovate, mend, repair.
breed *(SYN.)* engender, bear, propagate, father, beget, rear, conceive, train, generate, raise, procreate, nurture, create, mother, produce, originate, generate, raise, train, nurture.
(ANT.) murder, abort, kill.
breeze *(SYN.)* air, wind, zephyr, breath.
(ANT.) calm.
breezy *(SYN.)* jolly, spry, active, brisk, energetic, lively, carefree, spirited.
brevity *(SYN.)* briefness, conciseness.
(ANT.) length.
brew *(SYN.)* plot, plan, cook, ferment, prepare, scheme.
bribe *(SYN.)* buy off.
bridle *(SYN.)* control, hold, restrain, check, harness, curb, restraint, halter.
(ANT.) release, free, loose.
brief *(SYN.)* curt, short, fleeting, passing, compendious, terse, laconic, succinct, momentary, transient, temporary, concise, compact, condensed.
(ANT.) long, extended, prolonged, lengthy, protracted, comprehensive, extensive, exhaustive.
brigand *(SYN.)* bandit, robber, thief.
bright *(SYN.)* luminous, gleaming, clever, witty, brilliant, lucid, vivid, clear, smart, intelligent, lustrous, clever, shining, shiny, sparkling, shimmering, radiant, cheerful, lively, gay, happy, lighthearted, keen, promising, favorable, encouraging.
(ANT.) sullen, dull, murky, dark, gloomy, dim, lusterless, boring, colorless, stupid, backward, slow.
brilliant *(SYN.)* bright, clear, smart, intelligent, sparkling, shining, alert, vivid, splendid, radiant, glittering, talented, ingenious, gifted.
(ANT.) mediocre, dull, lusterless, second-rate.
brim *(SYN.)* border, margin, lip, rim, edge.
(ANT.) middle, center.
bring *(SYN.)* fetch, take, carry, raise, introduce, propose.
(ANT.) remove, withdraw.
brink *(SYN.)* limit, verge, rim, margin, edge.
brisk *(SYN.)* fresh, breezy, cool, lively, spry, refreshing, spirited, jolly, energetic, quick, active, animated, nimble, spry, agile, sharp, keen, stimulating, invigorating.
(ANT.) musty, faded, stagnant, decayed, hackneyed, slow, lethargic, sluggish, still, dull, oppressive.

briskness *(SYN.)* energy, exercise, motion, rapidity, agility, action, quickness, activity, vigor, liveliness, movement.
(ANT.) inertia, idleness, sloth, dullness, inactivity.
bristle *(SYN.)* flare up, anger, rage, seethe, get mad.
brittle *(SYN.)* crumbling, frail, breakable, delicate, splintery, crisp, fragile, weak.
(ANT.) tough, enduring, unbreakable, thick, strong, sturdy, flexible, elastic, supple.
broach *(SYN.)* set afoot, introduce, inaugurate, start, mention, launch, advance.
broad *(SYN.)* large, wide, tolerant, expanded, vast, liberal, sweeping, roomy, expansive, extended, general, extensive, full.
(ANT.) restricted, confined, narrow, constricted, slim, tight, limited, negligible.
broadcast *(SYN.)* distribute, announce, publish, scatter, circulate, spread, send, transmit, relay.
broaden *(SYN.)* spread, widen, amplify, enlarge, extend, increase, add to, expand, stretch, deepen, magnify.
(ANT.) tighted, narrow, constrict, straiten.
broad-minded *(SYN.)* unprejudiced, tolerant, liberal, unbigoted.
(ANT.) prejudiced, petty, narrow-minded.
brochure *(SYN.)* booklet, pamphlet, leaflet, mailing, circular, tract, flier.
broil *(SYN.)* cook, burn, heat, roast, bake, scorch, fire, grill, singe, sear, toast.
broken *(SYN.)* flattened, rent, shattered, wrecked, destroyed, reduced, smashed, crushed, fractured, ruptured, interrupted, burst, separated.
(ANT.) whole, integral, united, repaired.
brokenhearted *(SYN.)* disconsolate, forlorn, heartbroken, sad, grieving.
bromide *(SYN.)* banality, platitude, stereotype, commonplace, slogan, proverb.
brooch *(SYN.)* clasp, pin, breastpin, broach.
brood *(SYN.)* study, consider, ponder, reflect, contemplate, meditate, young, litter, offspring, think, muse, deliberate.
brook *(SYN.)* rivulet, run, branch, stream, creek.
brother *(SYN.)* comrade, man, kinsman, sibling.
(ANT.) sister.
brotherhood *(SYN.)* kinship, kindness, fraternity, fellowship, clan, society, brotherliness, bond, association, relationship, solidarity.
(ANT.) strife, discord, acrimony, opposition.
brotherly *(SYN.)* affectionate, fraternal, cordial, sympathetic, benevolent, philanthropic, humane, kindred, communal, altruistic.
brow *(SYN.)* forehead, eyebrow.
browbeat *(SYN.)* bully, domineer, bulldoze, intimidate, henpeck, oppress, grind.
brown study *(SYN.)* contemplation, reflection, reverie, musing, thoughtfulness, deliberation, rumination, self-communion.
browse *(SYN.)* scan, graze, read, feed.
bruise *(SYN.)* hurt, injure, wound, damage, abrasion, injury, contusion, mark, damage, harm, wound.
brunt *(SYN.)* force, impact, shock, strain, oppression, severity.
brush *(SYN.)* rub, wipe, clean, bushes, remove, shrubs, broom, whisk, paintbrush, hairbrush, underbrush, thicket.
brush-off *(SYN.)* dismissal, snub, slight, rebuff, turndown.
brusque *(SYN.)* sudden, curt, hasty, blunt, rough, steep, precipitate, rugged, craggy, gruff, surly, abrupt, short, bluff.
(ANT.) smooth, anticipated, courteous, expected, gradual, personable.
brutal *(SYN.)* brute, cruel, inhuman, rude, barbarous, gross, sensual, ferocious, brutish, coarse, bestial, carnal, remorseless, ruthless, savage, mean, savage, pitiless, barbaric.
(ANT.) kind, courteous, humane, civilized, gentle, kindhearted, mild.
brute *(SYN.)* monster, barbarian, beast, animal, wild, savage.
bubble *(SYN.)* boil, foam, seethe, froth.
buccaneer *(SYN.)* sea robber, privateer, pirate.
buck *(SYN.)* spring, jump, vault, leap.
bucket *(SYN.)* pot, pail, canister, can.
buckle *(SYN.)* hook, fastening, fastener, bend, wrinkle, clip, clasp, distort, catch, strap, fasten, collapse, yield, warp.
bud *(SYN.)* develop, sprout.
buddy *(SYN.)* companion, friend, partner, pal.
budge *(SYN.)* stir, move.
budget *(SYN.)* schedule, ration.
buff *(SYN.)* shine, polish, burnish, rub.
buffet *(SYN.)* bat, strike, clout, blow, knock, beat, crack, hit, slap, cabinet, counter, server.
buffoon *(SYN.)* jester, fool, clown, jokester, zany, comedian, chump, boor, dolt.
bug *(SYN.)* fault, hitch, defect, catch, snag, failing, rub, flaw, snarl, weakness, annoy, pester, hector, vex, nag.
bugbear *(SYN.)* bogy, specter, demon, devil, fiend.
build *(SYN.)* found, rear, establish, constructed, raise, set up, erect, assemble.
(ANT.) raze, destroy, overthrow, demolish, undermine.
building *(SYN.)* residence, structure, house, edifice.
build-up *(SYN.)* gain, enlargement, increase, praise, commendation, promotion, jump, expansion, uptrend, testimonial, plug, puff, blurb, endorsement, compliment.
(ANT.) reduction, decrease, decline.
bulge *(SYN.)* lump, protuberance, bump, swelling, extend, protrude.

(ANT.) hollow, shrink, contract.
bulk *(SYN.)* lump, magnitude, volume, size, mass, most, majority.
bulky *(SYN.)* great, big, huge, large, enormous, massive, immense, monstrous, clumsy, cumbersome.
(ANT.) tiny, little, small, petite, handy.
bull *(SYN.)* push, force, press, drive, thrust, bump.
bulldoze *(SYN.)* cow, bully, coerce, thrust, push.
bulletin *(SYN.)* news, flash, message, statement, newsletter, circular.
bullheaded *(SYN.)* dogged, stiff-necked, stubborn, mulish, rigid, pigheaded, willful, tenacious, unyielding.
(ANT.) flexible, submissive, compliant.
bully *(SYN.)* pester, tease, intimidate, harass, domineer.
bulwark *(SYN.)* wall, bastion, abutment, bank, dam, rampart, shoulder, parapet, backing, maintainer, embankment, safeguard, reinforcement.
bum *(SYN.)* idler, loafer, drifter, hobo, wretch, dwadler, beggar, vagrant.
bumbling *(SYN.)* bungling, inept, blundering, clumsy, incompetent, awkward, maladroit, lumbering, ungainly.
(ANT.) facile, handy, dexterous.
bump *(SYN.)* shake, push, hit, shove, prod, collide, knock, bang, strike.
bumpkin *(SYN.)* hick, yokel, rustic.
bumptious *(SYN.)* arrogant, self-assertive, conceited, forward, overbearing, pushy, boastful, obtrusive.
(ANT.) sheepish, self-effacing, retiring, shrinking, unobtrusive, diffident.
bumpy *(SYN.)* uneven, jolting, rough, jarring, rocky, coarse, craggy, irregular.
(ANT.) flat, smooth, flush, polished.
bunch *(SYN.)* batch, bundle, cluster, company, collection, flock, group.
bundle *(SYN.)* package, mass, collection, batch, parcel, packet, box, carton.
bungalow *(SYN.)* ranch house, cabana, cabin, cottage, lodge, summer house.
bungle *(SYN.)* tumble, botch, foul up, boggle, mess up, louse up, blunder.
bunk *(SYN.)* berth, rubbish, nonsense, couch, bed, cot.
buoyant *(SYN.)* light, jolly, spirited, effervescent, blithe, sprightly, lively, resilient, vivacious, afloat, floating, cheery, cheerful.
(ANT.) hopeless, dejected, sullen, depressed, heavy, despondent, sinking, low, pessimistic, downcast, glum.
burden *(SYN.)* oppress, afflict, trouble, encumber, tax, weight, load, worry, contents, trial, lade, overload.
(ANT.) lighten, alleviate, ease, mitigate, console, disburden.
burdensome *(SYN.)* arduous, cumbersome, bothersome, oppressive, irksome, trying, hard, difficult.
bureau *(SYN.)* office, division, department, unit, commission, board, chest.
bureaucrat *(SYN.)* clerk, official, functionary, servant, politician.
burglar *(SYN.)* thief, robber.
burial *(SYN.)* interment, funeral.
burly *(SYN.)* husky, beefy, heavyset, brawny, strapping.
(ANT.) skinny, scrawny.
burn *(SYN.)* scorch, blaze, scald, sear, char, incinerate, fire, flare, combust, flame, consume.
(ANT.) quench, extinguish.
burnish *(SYN.)* polish, shine, buff, wax.
burrow *(SYN.)* tunnel, search, seek, dig, excavate, hunt, den, hole.
burst *(SYN.)* exploded, broken, erupt.
bury *(SYN.)* hide, inhume, conceal, immure, cover, inter, entomb, secrete.
(ANT.) reveal, display, open, raise.
business *(SYN.)* employment, profession, trade, work, art, engagement, vocation, occupation, company, concern, firm, partnership, corporation.
(ANT.) hobby, avocation, pastime.
bustle *(SYN.)* noise, flurry, action, trouble, fuss, ado, stir, excitement, commotion.
(ANT.) calmness, composure, serenity, peacefulness.
bustling *(SYN.)* humming, busy, stirring, vibrant, bubbling, alive, active, moving, jumping, astir, zealous.
busy *(SYN.)* careful, industrious, active, patient, assiduous, diligent, perseverant, hardworking, employed.
(ANT.) unconcerned, indifferent, apathetic, lethargic, careless, inactive, unemployed, lazy, indolent.
busybody *(SYN.)* gossip, tattletale, pry, meddler, snoop.
but *(SYN.)* nevertheless, yet, however, though, although, still.
butcher *(SYN.)* kill, murder, slaughter, assassinate, slay, massacre.
(ANT.) save, protect, vivify, animate, resuscitate.
butt *(SYN.)* bump, ram, bunt, shove, jam, drive, punch, blow, push, thrust, propulsion.
buttocks *(SYN.)* hind end, rump, posterior, backside, behind, bottom, rear.
button *(SYN.)* clasp, close, fasten, hook.
buttress *(SYN.)* support, brace, stay, frame, prop, reinforcement, bulwark, backing, encourage, sustain, reassure, boost, bolster, steel.
buxom *(SYN.)* well-developed, chesty, ample, fleshy, full figured, zaftig.
buy *(SYN.)* procure, get, purchase, acquire, obtain.
(ANT.) vend, sell.
buzz *(SYN.)* whir, hum, thrum, drone.
by *(SYN.)* near, through, beside, with, from, at, close to.
bygone *(SYN.)* bypast, former, earlier, past, older, onetime, forgotten.
(ANT.) immediate, present, current, modern.
bypass *(SYN.)* deviate from, go around, detour around.
by-product *(SYN.)* offshoot, spin-off, effect, extra, outgrowth, bonus, appendage, side effect, supplement, extension, side issue, rider.
bystander *(SYN.)* onlooker, watcher, viewer, observer, witness, kibitzer.
byway *(SYN.)* passage, detour, path.
byword *(SYN.)* adage, proverb, axiom, shibboleth, apothegm, motto, slogan.

cab *(SYN.)* coach, taxi, car, hack, taxicab, carriage.
cabin *(SYN.)* cottage, shack, shanty, hut.
cabinet *(SYN.)* ministry, council, committee, case, cupboard.
cable *(SYN.)* wire, cord, rope, telegraph.
cafeteria *(SYN.)* cafe, diner, restaurant.
calculate *(SYN.)* count, compute, figure, estimate, consider, tally, determine.
(ANT.) guess, miscalculate, assume.
calculating *(SYN.)* crafty, shrewd, scheming, cunning.
(ANT.) simple, guileless, direct, ingenuous.
calculation *(SYN.)* figuring, reckoning, computation, estimation.
calendar *(SYN.)* timetable, schedule, diary.
call *(SYN.)* designate, name, yell, cry, ask, shout, speak, cry out, exclaim.
calling *(SYN.)* occupation, profession, trade.
callous *(SYN.)* insensitive, impenitent, obdurate, unfeeling, hard, heartless.
(ANT.) soft, compassionate, tender.
calm *(SYN.)* appease, lull, quiet, soothe, composed, tranquilize, tranquil.
(ANT.) disturbed, emotional, turmoil.
campaign *(SYN.)* cause, crusade, movement.
canal *(SYN.)* gully, tube, waterway.
cancel *(SYN.)* eliminate, erase, delete, repeal, revoke, void.
(ANT.) perpetuate, confirm, ratify.
candid *(SYN.)* free, blunt, frank, plain, open, sincere, honest, straightforward.
(ANT.) sly, contrived, wily, scheming.
candidate *(SYN.)* applicant, aspirant, nominee.
canine *(SYN.)* pooch, dog, puppy.
canny *(SYN.)* artful, skillful, shrewd, cautious, careful, cunning.
canopy *(SYN.)* awning, screen, shelter.
canyon *(SYN.)* gully, arroyo, ravine.
cap *(SYN.)* top, cover, crown, lid.
capability *(SYN.)* ability, capacity, dexterity, qualification.
(ANT.) incapacity, disability.
capable *(SYN.)* clever, qualified, able.
(ANT.) unfitted, incapable, inept.
capacity *(SYN.)* capability, power, ability, talent, content, skill, volume.
(ANT.) inability, stupidity, incapacity.
capital *(SYN.)* important, property, wealth, money, city, cash, assets.
(ANT.) unimportant, trivial, secondary.
captain *(SYN.)* commander, authority, supervisor, leader, commander.
captivate *(SYN.)* fascinate, charm, delight.
captivity *(SYN.)* detention, imprisonment, custody, confinement, bondage.
(ANT.) liberty, freedom.
capture *(SYN.)* catch, grip, apprehend, clutch, arrest, snare, seize, nab.
(ANT.) set free, lose, liberate, throw.
cardinal *(SYN.)* chief, primary, important, prime, leading, major, essential.
(ANT.) secondary, auxiliary.
care *(SYN.)* concern, anxiety, worry, caution, solicitude, attention, regard, charge, ward, attention, regard.
(ANT.) neglect, disregard, indifference.
career *(SYN.)* occupation, profession, job, calling, vocation, trade.
carefree *(SYN.)* lighthearted, happy, unconcerned, breezy, jolly, lively.
careful *(SYN.)* prudent, thoughtful, attentive, cautious, painstaking, scrupulous, discreet, watchful.
(ANT.) nice, careful, heedless, messy.
careless *(SYN.)* imprudent, heedless, unconcerned, inattentive, lax.
(ANT.) careful, cautious, painstaking.
cargo *(SYN.)* freight, load, freightload, shipment.
carriage *(SYN.)* bearing, conduct, action, deed, behavior, demeanor, disposition, deportment.
carry *(SYN.)* convey, transport, support, bring, sustain, bear, hold, move, transfer, take.
(ANT.) drop, abandon.
carve *(SYN.)* hew, shape, cut, whittle, chisel, sculpt.
case *(SYN.)* state, covering, receptacle, condition, instance, example, occurrence, illustration, sample.
cast *(SYN.)* fling, toss, throw, pitch, form, company, shape, mold, hurl.
castle *(SYN.)* mansion, palace, chateau.
casual *(SYN.)* chance, unexpected, informal, accidental, incidental, offhand, unplanned, spontaneous.
(ANT.) planned, expected, calculated, formal, deliberate, dressy.
casualty *(SYN.)* calamity, fortuity, mishap, loss, injured, dead, wounded, accident, misfortune.
(ANT.) purpose, intention, calculation.
catalog *(SYN.)* classify, roll, group, list, inventory, directory, index, record.
catastrophe *(SYN.)* mishap, calamity, disaster, adversity, accident, ruin.
(ANT.) fortune, boon, triumph, blessing, advantage, welfare.
catch *(SYN.)* hook, snare, entrap, ensnare, capture, grip, apprehend.
(ANT.) lose, free, liberate, throw, release.
category *(SYN.)* class, caste, kind, order, genre, rank, classification.
cause *(SYN.)* effect, incite, create, induce, inducement, occasion, incentive, prompt, reason, motive.
caution *(SYN.)* heed, vigilance, care, prudence, counsel, warning, wariness.
(ANT.) carelessness, abandon, recklessness.
cautious *(SYN.)* heedful, scrupulous, attentive, prudent, thoughtful, discreet.
(ANT.) improvident, headstrong, heedless, foolish, forgetful, indifferent.
cave *(SYN.)* grotto, hole, shelter, lair, den, cavern.
cave in *(SYN.)* fall in, collapse.
cavity *(SYN.)* pit, hole, crater.
cavort *(SYN.)* caper, leap, frolic, hop, prance.
cease *(SYN.)* desist, stop, abandon, discontinue, relinquish, end, terminate, leave, surrender, resign.
(ANT.) occupy, continue, persist, begin, endure, stay.
cede *(SYN.)* surrender, relinquish, yield.
celebrate *(SYN.)* honor, glorify, com-

memorate, keep, solemnize, extol, observe, commend, praise.
(ANT.) decry, overlook, profane, disregard, disgrace.
celebrated *(SYN.)* eminent, glorious, distinguished, noted, illustrious, famed, well-known, popular, renowned, famous.
(ANT.) obscure, hidden, anonymous, infamous, unknown.
celebrity *(SYN.)* somebody, personage, heroine, hero, dignitary, notable.
celestial *(SYN.)* godlike, holy, supernatural, divine, paradisiacal, utopian, transcendent, superhuman.
(ANT.) diabolical, profane, mundane, wicked.
cement *(SYN.)* solidify, weld, fasten, secure.
cemetery *(SYN.)* graveyard.
censure *(SYN.)* denounce, reproach, upbraid, blame, disapproval, reprehend, condemn, criticism, disapprove, criticize, reprove.
(ANT.) commend, approval, forgive, approve, praise, applaud, condone.
center *(SYN.)* heart, core, midpoint, middle, nucleus, inside, hub, focus.
(ANT.) rim, boundary, edge, border, periphery, outskirts.
central *(SYN.)* chief, necessary, main, halfway, dominant, mid, middle, inner, focal, leading, fundamental, principal.
(ANT.) side, secondary, incidental, auxiliary.
ceremonious *(SYN.)* correct, exact, precise, stiff, outward, external, solemn, formal.
(ANT.) material, unconventional, easy, heartfelt.
ceremony *(SYN.)* observance, rite, parade, formality, pomp, ritual, protocol, solemnity.
(ANT.) informality, casualness.
certain *(SYN.)* definite, assured, fixed, inevitable, sure, undeniable, positive, confident, particular, special, indubitable, secure, unquestionable.
(ANT.) probable, uncertain, doubtful, questionable.
certainly *(SYN.)* absolutely, surely, definitely.
(ANT.) dubiously, doubtfully, questionably.
certainty *(SYN.)* confidence, courage, security, assuredness, firmness, assertion, statement.
(ANT.) humility, bashfulness, modest, shyness.
certificate *(SYN.)* affidavit, document.
certify *(SYN.)* validate, affirm, verify, confirm, authenticate, substantiate.
certitude *(SYN.)* confidence, belief, conviction, feeling, faith, persuasion, trust.
(ANT.) doubt, incredulity, denial, heresy.
cessation *(SYN.)* ending, finish, stoppage, termination, conclusion, end.
chafe *(SYN.)* heat, rub, warm, annoy, disturb.
chagrin *(SYN.)* irritation, mortification, embarrassment, annoyance, vexation, worry, bother, shame, annoy, irk, humiliation, irritate, vex, frustrate, humiliate, embarrass, mortify, exasperate, disappoint, disappointment.
chain *(SYN.)* fasten, bind, shackle, restrain.
chairman *(SYN.)* speaker.
challenge *(SYN.)* question, dare, call, summon, threat, invite, threaten, demand.
chamber *(SYN.)* cell, salon, room.
champion *(SYN.)* victor, winner, choice, best, conqueror, hero, support, select.
chance *(SYN.)* befall, accident, betide, disaster, opportunity, calamity, occur, possibility, prospect, happen, luck, fate, take place.
(ANT.) design, purpose, inevitability, calculation, certainty, intention.
change *(SYN.)* modification, alternation, alteration, mutation, variety, exchange, shift, alter, transfigure, veer, vary, variation, substitution, substitute, vicissitude.
(ANT.) uniformity, monotony, settle, remain, endure, retain, preserve, steadfastness, endurance, immutability, stability.
changeable *(SYN.)* fitful, fickle, inconstant, unstable, shifting, wavering.
(ANT.) stable, uniform, constant, unchanging.
channel *(SYN.)* strait, corridor, waterway, artery, duct, canal, way, trough, groove, passageway.
chant *(SYN.)* singing, incantation, hymn, intone, sing, carol, psalm, song, ballad.
chaos *(SYN.)* confusion, jumble, turmoil, anarchy, disorder, muddle.
(ANT.) organization, order, tranquillity, tidiness, system.
chaotic *(SYN.)* confused, disorganized, disordered, messy.
(ANT.) neat, ordered, systematic, organized.
chap *(SYN.)* break, fellow, person, crack, split, man, rough, individual, boy.
chaperon *(SYN.)* associate with, escort, convoy, accompany, consort with.
(ANT.) avoid, desert, leave, abandon, quit.
chapter *(SYN.)* part, section, division.
char *(SYN.)* scorch, singe, burn, sear.
character *(SYN.)* description, class, kind, repute, mark, individuality, disposition, traits, personality, reputation, symbol, features, quality, eccentric, nature.
characteristic *(SYN.)* exclusive, distinctive, special, mark, feature, property, typical, unique, attribute, distinguishing, trait, quality.
charge *(SYN.)* arraignment, indictment, accusation, sell for, attack, assail, assault, indict, blame, allegation, care, custody, imputation.
(ANT.) pardon, flee, exculpation, excuse, absolve, retreat, exoneration.
charitable *(SYN.)* benevolent, generous, liberal, altruistic, kind, obliging, considerate, unselfish.
(ANT.) petty, mean, harsh, wicked,

greedy, narrow-minded, stingy, malevolent.

charity *(SYN.)* benevolence, kindness, magnanimity, altruism, generosity.
(ANT.) malevolence, cruelty, selfishness.

charm *(SYN.)* allure, spell, enchantment, attractiveness, magic, witchery, amulet, talisman, lure, enchant, bewitch, fascinate, captivate.

charmer *(SYN.)* siren, temptress, enchantress, vamp, seductress, seducer, enchanter.

charming *(SYN.)* attractive, enchanting, fascinating, alluring, appealing, winsome, agreeable, bewitching, winning.
(ANT.) revolting, repugnant, repulsive.

chart *(SYN.)* design, plan, cabal, plot, sketch, stratagem, map, diagram, conspiracy, graph, intrigue.

charter *(SYN.)* lease, hire, rent, alliance.

chase *(SYN.)* hunt, run after, pursue, trail, follow, persist, scheme.
(ANT.) escape, flee, abandon, elude, evade.

chasm *(SYN.)* ravine, abyss, canyon, gorge.

chaste *(SYN.)* clear, immaculate, innocent, sincere, bare, clean, modest, pure, decent, virtuous, virginal, sheer, absolute, spotless.
(ANT.) polluted, tainted, foul, impure, sinful, worldly, sullied, defiled.

chasten *(SYN.)* chastise, restrain, punish, discipline.

chastise *(SYN.)* punish, castigate, correct.
(ANT.) release, acquit, free, exonerate.

chat *(SYN.)* argue, jabber, blab, plead, consult, converse, lecture, discuss, talk, conversation, tattle.

chatter *(SYN.)* dialogue, lecture, speech, conference, talk, discourse.
(ANT.) silence, correspondence, writing.

cheap *(SYN.)* poor, common, inexpensive, shabby, low-priced, beggary, low-cost, shoddy, mean, inferior.
(ANT.) honorable, dear, noble, expensive, costly, well-made, elegant, dignified.

cheat *(SYN.)* deceive, fool, bilk, outwit, victimize, dupe, gull, hoodwink, circumvent, swindler, cheater, trickster, phony, fraud, defraud, charlatan, crook, chiseler, con artist, hoax, swindle.

check *(SYN.)* dissect, interrogate, analyze, contemplate, inquire, question, scrutinize, arrest, stop, halt, block, curb, control, investigate, review, examine, test, counterfoil, stub, barrier, watch.
(ANT.) overlook, disregard, advance, foster, continue, promote, omit, neglect.

checkup *(SYN.)* medical examination, physical.

cheek *(SYN.)* nerve, effrontery, impudence, gall, impertinence.

cheer *(SYN.)* console, gladden, comfort, encourage, applause, encouragement, joy, glee, gaiety, mirth, soothe, sympathize, approval, solace.
(ANT.) depress, sadden, discourage, derision, dishearten, discouragement, antagonize.

cheerful *(SYN.)* glad, jolly, joyful, gay, happy, cherry, merry, joyous, lighthearted.
(ANT.) mournful, sad, glum, depressed, gloomy, sullen.

cherish *(SYN.)* prize, treasure, appreciate, nurse, value, comfort, hold dear, foster, nurture, sustain.
(ANT.) disregard, neglect, deprecate, scorn, reject, undervalue, abandon.

chest *(SYN.)* bosom, breast, coffer, box, case, trunk, casket, dresser, commode, cabinet, chifforobe.

chew *(SYN.)* gnaw, munch, bite, nibble.

chic *(SYN.)* fashionable, modish, smart, stylish, trendy.

chide *(SYN.)* admonish, rebuke, scold, reprimand, criticize, reprove.
(ANT.) extol, praise, commend.

chief *(SYN.)* chieftain, head, commander, captain, leader, principal, master, boss, leading, ruler.
(ANT.) servant, subordinate, secondary, follower, incidental, accidental, auxiliary, attendant.

chiefly *(SYN.)* mainly, especially, mostly.

childish *(SYN.)* immature, childlike, infantile, babyish.
(ANT.) mature, adult, seasoned, grownup.

chill *(SYN.)* coolness, cold, cool, coldness, brisk, frosty.
(ANT.) hot, warm, heat, heated, warmth.

chilly *(SYN.)* cold, frigid, freezing, arctic, cool, icy, passionless, wintry, unfeeling.
(ANT.) fiery, heated, passionate, ardent.

chirp *(SYN.)* peep, cheep, twitter, tweet, chirrup.

chivalrous *(SYN.)* noble, brave, polite, valorous, gallant, gentlemanly, courteous.
(ANT.) crude, rude, impolite, uncivil.

chivalry *(SYN.)* courtesy, nobility, gallantry, knighthood.

choice *(SYN.)* delicate, elegant, fine, dainty, exquisite, pure, refined, subtle, splendid, handsome, option, selection, beautiful, minute, pretty, pick, select, uncommon, rare, precious, valuable, thin, small.
(ANT.) coarse, rough, thick, blunt, large.

choke *(SYN.)* throttle, gag, strange.

choose *(SYN.)* elect, decide between, pick, select, cull, opt.
(ANT.) reject, refuse.

chop *(SYN.)* hew, cut, fell, mince.

chore *(SYN.)* routine, task, job, duty, work.

chronic *(SYN.)* persistent, constant, lingering, continuing, perennial, unending, sustained, permanent.
(ANT.) fleeting, acute, temporary.

chronicle *(SYN.)* detail, history, narrative, account, description, narration, recital.
(ANT.) misrepresentation, confusion, distortion.

chuckle *(SYN.)* titter, laugh, giggle.

chum *(SYN.)* friend, pal, buddy, companion.
cinema *(SYN.)* effigy, film, etching, appearance, drawing, engraving, illustration, likeness, image, panorama, painting, picture, photograph.
circle *(SYN.)* disk, ring, set, group. class, club, surround, encircle, enclose, round.
circuit *(SYN.)* circle, course, journey, orbit, revolution, tour.
circuitous *(SYN.)* distorted, devious, indirect, roundabout swerving, crooked, tortuous.
(ANT.) straightforward, straight, direct, honest.
circular *(SYN.)* chubby, complete, curved, bulbous, cylindrical, round, ringlike, globular, entire, rotund.
(ANT.) straight.
circumference *(SYN.)* border, perimeter, periphery, edge.
circumspection *(SYN.)* care, worry, solicitude, anxiety, concern, caution, attention, vigilance.
(ANT.) neglect, negligence, indifference.
circumstance *(SYN.)* fact, event, incident, condition, happening, position, occurrence, situation.
circumstances *(SYN.)* facts, conditions, factors, situation, background, grounds, means, capital, assets, rank, class.
cite *(SYN.)* affirm, assign, allege, advance, quote, mention, declare, claim, maintain.
(ANT.) refute, gainsay, deny, contradict.
citizen *(SYN.)* native, inhabitant, national, denizen, subject, dweller, resident.
city *(SYN.)* metropolis, municipality, town.
civil *(SYN.)* courteous, cultivated, accomplished, public, municipal, respectful, genteel, polite, considerate, gracious, urban.
(ANT.) uncouth, uncivil, impertinent, impolite, boorish.
civilization *(SYN.)* cultivation, culture, education, breeding, enlightenment, society, refinement.
(ANT.) ignorance, vulgarity.
civilize *(SYN.)* refine, tame, polish, cultivate, instruct, teach.
claim *(SYN.)* aver, declare, allege, assert, affirm, express, state, demand, maintain, defend, uphold.
(ANT.) refute, deny, contradict.
clamor *(SYN.)* cry, din, babel, noise, racket, outcry, row, sound tumult, shouting, shout, uproar.
(ANT.) hush, serenity, silence, tranquility, stillness, quiet.
clan *(SYN.)* fellowship, kindness, solidarity, family, brotherliness, association, fraternity.
(ANT.) discord, strife, opposition, acrimony.
clandestine *(SYN.)* covert, hidden, latent, private, concealed, secret, unknown.
(ANT.) exposed, known, conspicuous, obvious.
clarify *(SYN.)* educate, explain, expound, decipher, illustrate, clear, resolve, define, interpret, unfold.
(ANT.) darken, obscure, baffle, confuse.
clash *(SYN.)* clank, crash, clang, conflict, disagreement, opposition, collision, struggle, mismatch, contrast, disagree, collide, interfere.
(ANT.) accord, agreement, harmony, blend, harmonize, match, agree.
clasp *(SYN.)* grip, hold, grasp, adhere, clutch, keep, have, maintain, possess, occupy, retain, support, confine, embrace, fastening, check, detain, curb, receive.
(ANT.) relinquish, vacate, surrender, abandon.
class *(SYN.)* category, denomination, caste, kind, genre, grade, rank, order, elegance, classification, division, sort, family, species, set, excellence.
classic *(SYN.)* masterpiece.
classification *(SYN.)* order, category, class, arrangement, ordering, grouping, organization.
classify *(SYN.)* arrange, class, order, sort, grade, group, index.
clause *(SYN.)* condition, paragraph, limitation, article.
claw *(SYN.)* hook, talon, nail, scratch.
clean *(SYN.)* mop, tidy, neat, dustless, clear, unsoiled, immaculate, unstained, untainted, pure, dust, vacuum, scour, decontaminate, wipe, sterilize, cleanse, scrub, purify, wash, sweep.
(ANT.) stain, soil, pollute, soiled, impure, dirty, stain.
cleanse *(SYN.)* mop, purify, wash, sweep.
(ANT.) stain, soil, dirty, pollute.
clear *(SYN.)* fair, sunny, cloudless, transparent, apparent, limpid, distinct, intelligible, evident, unmistakable, understandable, unclouded, uncloudy, light, bright, certain, manifest, lucid, plain, obvious, unobstructed.
(ANT.) obscure, unclear, muddled, confused, dark, cloudy, blocked, obstructed, questionable, dubious, blockaded, foul, overcast.
clearly *(SYN.)* plainly, obviously, evidently, definitely, surely, certainly.
(ANT.) questionably, dubiously.
clemency *(SYN.)* forgiveness, charity, compassion, grace, mercy, leniency, pity, mildness.
(ANT.) punishment, vengeance, retribution.
clerical *(SYN.)* ministerial, pastoral, priestly, celestial, holy, sacred, secretarial.
clerk *(SYN.)* typist, office worker, office girl, saleslady, salesperson, salesclerk.
clever *(SYN.)* apt, dexterous, quick, adroit, quick-witted, talented, bright, skillful, witty, ingenious, smart, intelligent, shrewd, gifted, expert, sharp.
(ANT.) unskilled, slow, stupid, backward, maladroit, bungling, dull, clumsy.
cleverness *(SYN.)* intellect, intelligence, comprehension, mind, perspicacity, sagacity, fun.
(ANT.) sobriety, stupidity, solemnity,

commonplace, platitude.
client *(SYN.)* patron, customer.
cliff *(SYN.)* scar, bluff, crag, precipice, escarpment.
climate *(SYN.)* aura, atmosphere, air, ambience.
climax *(SYN.)* apex, culmination, peak, summit, consummation, height, acme, zenith.
(ANT.) depth, base, anticlimax, floor.
climb *(SYN.)* mount, scale, ascend.
(ANT.) descend.
clip *(SYN.)* snip, crop, cut, mow, clasp.
cloak *(SYN.)* conceal, cover, disguise, clothe, cape, guard, envelop, hide, mask, protect, shield.
(ANT.) divulge, expose, reveal, bare, unveil.
clod *(SYN.)* wad, hunk, gobbet, lump, chunk, clot, gob, dunce, dolt, oaf, fool.
clog *(SYN.)* crowd, congest, cram, overfill, stuff.
cloister *(SYN.)* monastery, priory, hermitage, abbey, convent.
close *(SYN.)* adjacent, adjoining, immediate, unventilated, stuffy, abutting, neighboring, dear, oppressive, mean, impending, nearby, near, devoted.
(ANT.) afar, faraway, removed, distant.
close *(SYN.)* seal, shut, clog, stop, obstruct, cease, conclude, complete, end, terminate, occlude, finish.
(ANT.) unlock, begin, open, unbar, inaugurate, commence, start.
closet *(SYN.)* cabinet, locker, wardrobe, cupboard.
cloth *(SYN.)* fabric, goods, material, textile.
clothe *(SYN.)* garb, dress, apparel.
(ANT.) strip, undress.
clothes *(SYN.)* array, attire, apparel, clothing, dress, garb, dress, garments, raiment, drapery, vestments.
(ANT.) nudity, nakedness.
clothing *(SYN.)* attire, clothes, apparel, array, dress, drapery, garments, garb, vestments.
(ANT.) nudity, nakedness.
cloud *(SYN.)* fog, mist, haze, mass, collection, obscure, dim, shadow.
cloudy *(SYN.)* dim, dark, indistinct, murky, mysterious, indefinite, vague, sunless, clouded, obscure, overcast, shadowy.
(ANT.) sunny, clear, distinct, limpid, lucid, clarified, cloudless, clearheaded, brilliant, bright.
club *(SYN.)* society, association, set, circle, organization, bat, cudgel, stick, blackjack.
clue *(SYN.)* sign, trace, hint, suggestion.
clumsy *(SYN.)* bungling, inept, rough, unpolished, bumbling, awkward, ungraceful, gauche, ungainly, unskillful, untoward.
(ANT.) polished, skillful, neat, graceful, dexterous, adroit.
cluster *(SYN.)* batch, clutch, group, bunch, gather, pack, assemble, crowd.
clutch *(SYN.)* grip, grab, seize, hold.
coalition *(SYN.)* combination, association, alliance, confederacy, entente, league, treaty.
(ANT.) schism, separation, divorce.
coarse *(SYN.)* unpolished, vulgar, refined, rough, smooth, impure, rude, crude, gruff, gross, cultivated, delicate, cultured.
(ANT.) delicate, smooth, refined, polished, genteel, cultivated, suave, fine, cultured.
coast *(SYN.)* seaboard, seashore, beach, shore, drift, glide, ride.
coax *(SYN.)* urge, persuade, wheedle, cajole.
(ANT.) force, bully, coerce.
coddle *(SYN.)* pamper, baby, spoil, indulge.
code *(SYN.)* crypt, cryptogram, cipher.
coerce *(SYN.)* constrain, compel, enforce, force, drive, oblige, impel.
(ANT.) prevent, persuade, convince, induce.
coercion *(SYN.)* emphasis, intensity, energy, dint, might potency, power, vigor, strength, compulsion, force, constraint, violence.
(ANT.) impotence, frailty, feebleness, weakness, persuasion.
cognizance *(SYN.)* apprehension, erudition, acquaintance, information, learning, knowledge, lore, science, scholarship, understanding.
(ANT.) illiteracy, misunderstanding, ignorance.
cognizant *(SYN.)* conscious, aware, apprised informed, mindful, observant, perceptive.
(ANT.) unaware, ignorant, oblivious, insensible.
coherent *(SYN.)* logical, intelligible, sensible, rational, commonsensical, reasonable.
coiffeur *(SYN.)* hairdresser.
coiffure *(SYN.)* haircut, hairdo.
coincide *(SYN.)* acquiesce, agree, accede, assent, consent, comply, correspond, concur, match, tally, harmonize, conform.
(ANT.) differ, disagree, protest, contradict.
coincidence *(SYN.)* accident, chance.
(ANT.) plot, plan, prearrangement, scheme.
coincident *(SYN.)* identical, equal, equivalent, distinguishable, same, like.
(ANT.) distinct, contrary, disparate, opposed.
coincidental *(SYN.)* unpredicted, unexpected, chance, unforeseen, accidental, fortuitous.
cold *(SYN.)* cool, freezing, chilly, frigid, icy, frozen, wintry, arctic, unfriendly, indifferent, phlegmatic, stoical, passionless, chill, unemotional, heartless, unfeeling.
(ANT.) hot, torrid, fiery, burning, ardent, friendly, temperate, warm, passionate.
collapse *(SYN.)* descend, decrease, diminish, fail, downfall, failure, decline, fall, drop, sink, subside, topple.
(ANT.) soar, steady, limb, mount, arise.
colleague *(SYN.)* companion, attendant, comrade, associate, crony, coworker,

mate, friend, partner.
(ANT.) enemy, stranger, adversary.
collect *(SYN.)* assemble, amass, concentrate, pile, accumulate, congregate, obtain, heap, gather, solicit, secure, procure, raise, get, mass, hoard, consolidate.
(ANT.) divide, dole, assort, dispel, distribute, disperse.
collected *(SYN.)* cool, calm, composed, peaceful, imperturbable, placid, sedate, quiet.
(ANT.) excited, violent, aroused, agitated.
collection *(SYN.)* amount, conglomeration, sum, entirety, aggregation, hoard, accumulation, pile, store, aggregate, total, whole.
(ANT.) part, unit, particular, element, ingredient.
collide *(SYN.)* hit, smash, crash, strike.
collision *(SYN.)* conflict, combat, duel, battle, encounter, crash, smash, fight, contention, struggle, discord.
(ANT.) concord, amity, harmony, consonance.
collusion *(SYN.)* combination, cabal, intrigue, conspiracy, plot, treason, treachery.
color *(SYN.)* hue, paint, pigment, complexion, dye, shade, tone, tincture, stain, tint, tinge.
(ANT.) paleness, transparency, achromatism.
colorful *(SYN.)* impressive, vivid, striking, full-color, multicolored, offbeat, weird, unusual.
(ANT.) flat, dull, uninteresting.
colossal *(SYN.)* enormous, elephantine, gargantuan, huge, immense, gigantic, prodigious.
(ANT.) little, minute, small, miniature, diminutive, microscopic, tiny.
combat *(SYN.)* conflict, duel, battle, collision, encounter, fight, contest, oppose, war, contention, struggle, discord.
(ANT.) consonance, harmony, concord, yield, surrender, succumb, amity.
combination *(SYN.)* association, confederacy, alliance, entente, league, compounding, mixture, blend, composite, federation, mixing, compound, blending, union.
(ANT.) separation, division, schism, divorce.
combine *(SYN.)* adjoin, associate, accompany, conjoin, connect, link, mix, blend, couple, unite, join.
(ANT.) detach, disjoin, divide, separate, disconnect.
come *(SYN.)* near, approach, reach, arrive, advance.
(ANT.) depart, leave, go.
comedian *(SYN.)* comic, wit, humorist, gagman, wag.
comely *(SYN.)* charming, elegant, beauteous, beautiful, fine, lovely, pretty, handsome lovely.
(ANT.) hideous, repulsive, foul, unsightly.
come-on *(SYN.)* lure, inducement, enticement, temptation, premium.
comfort *(SYN.)* contentment, ease, enjoyment, relieve, consolation, relief, cheer, console, calm, satisfaction, soothe, encourage, succor, luxury, solace.
(ANT.) depress, torture, discomfort, upset, misery, disturb, agitate, affliction, discompose, uncertainty, suffering.
comfortable *(SYN.)* pleasing, agreeable, convenient, cozy, welcome, acceptable, relaxed, restful, cozy, gratifying, easy, contented, rested, satisfying, pleasurable.
(ANT.) miserable, distressing, tense, strained, troubling, edgy, uncomfortable.
comical *(SYN.)* droll, funny, humorous, amusing, ludicrous, witty, ridiculous, odd, queer.
(ANT.) sober, solemn, sad, serious, melancholy.
command *(SYN.)* class, method, plan regularity, rank, arrangement, series, sequence, point, aim, conduct, manage, guide, bid, system, succession, bidding, direct, order, demand, direction, rule, dictate, decree.
(ANT.) consent, obey, misdirect, distract, deceive, misguide, license, confusion.
commandeer *(SYN.)* take, possession, seize, confiscate, appropriate.
commanding *(SYN.)* imposing, masterful, assertive, authoritative, positive.
commence *(SYN.)* open, start.
(ANT.) stop, end, terminate, finish.
commend *(SYN.)* laud, praise, applaud, recommend.
(ANT.) censure, blame, criticize.
commendable *(SYN.)* deserving, praiseworthy.
(ANT.) bad, deplorable, lamentable.
commendation *(SYN.)* approval, applause, praise, recommendation, honor, medal.
(ANT.) criticism, condemnation, censure.
commensurate *(SYN.)* keep, celebrate, observe, honor, commend, extol, glorify, laud, praise, honor.
(ANT.) decry, disgrace, disregard, overlook, profane, dishonor.
comment *(SYN.)* assertion, declaration, annotation, explanation, review, commentary, report, remark, observation, utterance, criticism, statement.
commerce *(SYN.)* business, engagement, employment, art, trade, marketing, enterprise, occupation.
(ANT.) hobby, pastime, avocation.
commission *(SYN.)* board, committee, command, permit, order, permission, delegate, authorize, deputize, entrust.
commit *(SYN.)* perpetrate, perform, obligate, do, commend, consign, relegate, bind, delegate, empower, pledge, entrust, authorize, trust.
(ANT.) neglect, mistrust, release, free, miscarry, fail, loose.
commitment *(SYN.)* duty, promise, responsibility, pledge.
committee *(SYN.)* commission, bureau, board, delegate, council.

commodious *(SYN.)* appropriate, accessible, adapted, favorable, handy, fitting, timely.
(ANT.) inconvenient, troublesome, awkward.
commodity *(SYN.)* article, merchandise, wares, goods.
common *(SYN.)* ordinary, popular, familiar, mean, low, general, vulgar, communal, mutual, shared, natural, frequent, prevalent, joint, conventional, plain, usual, universal.
(ANT.) odd, exceptional, scarce, noble, extraordinary, different, separate, outstanding, rare, unusual, distinctive, refined.
commonplace *(SYN.)* common, usual, frequent, ordinary, everyday.
(ANT.) distinctive, unusual, original.
commonsense *(SYN.)* perceptible, alive, apprehensible, aware, awake, cognizant, conscious, comprehending, perceptible.
(ANT.) unaware, impalpable, imperceptible.
commotion *(SYN.)* confusion, chaos, disarray, ferment, disorder, stir, tumult, agitation.
(ANT.) tranquillity, peace, certainty, order.
communicable *(SYN.)* infectious, virulent, catching, transferable, contagious.
(ANT.) hygienic, noncommunicable, healthful.
communicate *(SYN.)* convey, impart, inform, confer, disclose, reveal, relate, tell, advertise, publish, transmit, publicize, divulge.
(ANT.) withhold, hide, conceal.
communication *(SYN.)* disclosure, transmission, declaration, announcement, notification, publication, message, report, news, information.
communicative *(SYN.)* unreserved, open, frank, free, straightforward, unrestrained.
(ANT.) close-mouthed, secretive.
communion *(SYN.)* intercourse, fellowship, participation, association, sacrament, union.
(ANT.) nonparticipation, alienation.
community *(SYN.)* public, society, city, town, village, township.
compact *(SYN.)* contracted, firm, narrow, snug, close, constricted, packed, vanity, treaty, agreement, tense, taught, tight, niggardly, close-fisted, parsimonious, compressed, stingy.
(ANT.) slack, open, loose, relaxed, unconfined, unfretted, sprawling, lax.
companion *(SYN.)* attendant, comrade, consort, friend, colleague, partner, crony, mate, associate.
(ANT.) stranger, enemy, adversary.
companionship *(SYN.)* familiarity, cognizance, acquaintance, fellowship, knowledge, intimacy.
(ANT.) unfamiliarity, inexperience, ignorance.
company *(SYN.)* crew, group, band, party, throng, house, assemblage, troop, fellowship, association, business, concern, partnership, corporation, companionship, firm.
(ANT.) seclusion, individual, solitude, dispersion.
comparable *(SYN.)* allied, analogous, alike, akin, like, correspondent, correlative, parallel.
(ANT.) opposed, incongruous, dissimilar, unlike, different, divergent.
compare *(SYN.)* discriminate, match, differentiate, contrast, oppose.
comparison *(SYN.)* likening, contrasting, judgment.
compartment *(SYN.)* division, section.
compassion *(SYN.)* mercy, sympathy, pity, commiseration, condolence.
(ANT.) ruthlessness, hardness, brutality, inhumanity, cruelty.
compassionate *(SYN.)* sympathizing, benign, forbearing, good, tender, affable, humane, indulgent, kind, sympathetic, kindly.
(ANT.) inhuman, merciless, unkind, cold-hearted, unsympathetic, cruel.
compatible *(SYN.)* consistent, agreeing, conforming, accordant, congruous, harmonious, cooperative, agreeable, constant, consonant, correspondent.
(ANT.) discrepant, paradoxical, disagreeable, contradictory.
compel *(SYN.)* drive, enforce, coerce, constrain, force, oblige, impel.
(ANT.) induce, coax, prevent, wheedle, persuade, cajole, convince.
compensate *(SYN.)* remunerate, repay, reimburse, recompense, balance.
compensation *(SYN.)* fee, earnings, pay, payment, recompense, allowance, remuneration, remittance, settlement, stipend, repayment, salary, wages.
(ANT.) present, gratuity, gift.
compete *(SYN.)* rival, contest, oppose, vie.
(ANT.) reconcile, accord.
competence *(SYN.)* skill, ability, capability.
competent *(SYN.)* efficient, clever, capable, able, apt, proficient, skillful, fitted, qualified.
(ANT.) inept, incapable, unfitted, awkward, incompetent, inadequate.
competition *(SYN.)* contest, match, rivalry, tournament.
competitor *(SYN.)* rival, contestant, opponent.
(ANT.) ally, friend, colleague.
complain *(SYN.)* lament, murmur, protest, grouch, grumble, regret, moan, remonstrate, whine, repine.
(ANT.) rejoice, praise, applaud, approve.
complaint *(SYN.)* protest, objection, grievance.
complement *(SYN.)* supplement, complete.
(ANT.) clash, conflict.
complete *(SYN.)* consummate, entire, ended, full, thorough, finished, full, whole, concluded, over, done, terminate, unbroken, total, undivided.
(ANT.) unfinished, imperfect, incomplete, start, partial, begin, commence, lacking.

completion *(SYN.)* achievement, attainment, end, conclusion, close, finish, wind-up, accomplishment, realization.
(ANT.) omission, neglect, failure, defeat.
complex *(SYN.)* sophisticated, compound, intricate, involved, perplexing, elaborate, complicated.
(ANT.) basic, simple, rudimentary, uncompounded, uncomplicated, plain.
complexion *(SYN.)* paint, pigment hue, color, dye, stain, tincture, tinge, tint, shade.
(ANT.) paleness, transparency, achromatism.
compliant *(SYN.)* meek, modest, lowly, plain, submissive, simple, unostentatious, unassuming, unpretentious.
(ANT.) proud, vain, arrogant, haughty, boastful.
complicated *(SYN.)* intricate, involved, complex, compound, perplexing.
(ANT.) simple, plain, uncompounded.
compliment *(SYN.)* eulogy, flattery, praise, admiration, honor, adulation, flatter, commendation, tribute.
(ANT.) taunt, affront, aspersion, insult, disparage, criticism.
complimentary *(SYN.)* gratis, free.
comply *(SYN.)* assent, consent, accede, acquiesce, coincide, conform, concur, tally.
(ANT.) differ, dissent, protest, disagree.
component *(SYN.)* division, fragment, allotment, moiety, apportionment, scrap, portion, section, share, segment, ingredient, organ.
(ANT.) whole, entirety.
comport *(SYN.)* carry, conduct, behave, act, deport, interact, operate, manage.
compose *(SYN.)* forge, fashion, mold, make, construct, create, produce, shape, form, constitute, arrange, organize, make up, write, invent, devise, frame.
(ANT.) misshape, dismantle, disfigure, destroy.
composed *(SYN.)* calm, cool, imperturbable, placid, quiet, unmoved, sedate, peaceful, collected, tranquil.
(ANT.) aroused, violent, nervous, agitated, perturbed, excited.
composer *(SYN.)* author, inventor, creator, maker, originator.
composition *(SYN.)* paper, theme, work, essay, compound, mixture, mix.
composure *(SYN.)* calmness, poise, control, self-control, self-possession.
(ANT.) anger, rage, turbulence, agitation.
compound *(SYN.)* blend, confound, jumble, consort, aggregate, complicated, combination, combined, mixture, complex, join.
(ANT.) segregate, separate, divide, simple, sort.
comprehend *(SYN.)* apprehend, discern, learn, perceive, see, grasp, understand.
(ANT.) mistake, misunderstand, ignore.
comprehension *(SYN.)* insight, perception, understanding, awareness, discernment.
(ANT.) misconception, insensibility.
comprehensive *(SYN.)* wide, inclusive, complete, broad, full.
(ANT.) fragmentary, partial, limited, incomplete.
compress *(SYN.)* press, compact, squeeze, pack, crowd.
(ANT.) spread, stretch, expand.
comprise *(SYN.)* contain, hold, embrace.
(ANT.) emit, encourage, yield, discharge.
compulsion *(SYN.)* might, energy, potency, strength, vigor.
(ANT.) persuasion, impotence, frailty.
compulsory *(SYN.)* required, obligatory, necessary, unavoidable.
(ANT.) elective, optional, free, unrestricted.
computation *(SYN.)* reckoning, record.
(ANT.) misrepresentation.
compute *(SYN.)* count, calculate, determine, figure, reckon.
(ANT.) conjecture, guess, miscalculate.
comrade *(SYN.)* attendant, companion, colleague, associate, friend.
(ANT.) stranger, enemy, adversary.
con *(SYN.)* cheat, bamboozle, trick, swindle.
conceal *(SYN.)* disguise, cover, hide, mask, screen, secrete, veil, withhold.
(ANT.) reveal, show, disclose, expose.
concede *(SYN.)* permit, suffer, tolerate, grant, give, admit, acknowledge, allow, yield.
(ANT.) forbid, contradict, protest, refuse, deny, negate, resist.
conceit *(SYN.)* pride, vanity, complacency, conception, idea, egotism, self-esteem, caprice, fancy, whim.
(ANT.) humility, meekness, humbleness, modesty.
conceited *(SYN.)* proud, arrogant, vain, smug, egotistical.
(ANT.) humble, modest, self-effacing.
conceive *(SYN.)* design, create, imagine, understand, devise, concoct, perceive, frame, grasp, invent.
(ANT.) imitate, reproduce, copy.
concentrate *(SYN.)* localize, focus, condense, ponder, meditate, center, scrutinize.
(ANT.) scatter, diffuse, dissipate, disperse.
concentrated *(SYN.)* compressed, thick, dense.
(ANT.) sparse, quick, dispersed.
concept *(SYN.)* fancy, conception, image, notion, idea, sentiment, thought.
(ANT.) thing, matter, substance, entity.
conception *(SYN.)* consideration, deliberation, fancy, idea, notion, regard, thought, view.
concern *(SYN.)* matter, anxiety, affair, disturb, care, business, solicitude, interest, affect, involve, touch, trouble, interest, worry.
(ANT.) unconcern, negligence, disinterest, tire, bore, calm, soothe, indifference.
concerning *(SYN.)* regarding, about, respecting.
concerted *(SYN.)* united, joint, com-

bined.
(ANT.) individual, unorganized, separate.
concession *(SYN.)* admission, yielding, granting.
(ANT.) insistence, demand.
concise *(SYN.)* pity, neat, brief, compact, succinct, terse.
(ANT.) wordy, lengthy, verbose, prolix.
conclude *(SYN.)* decide, achieve, close, complete, end, finish, terminate, arrange, determine, settle, perfect, perform.
(ANT.) start, begin, commence.
concluding *(SYN.)* extreme, final, last, terminal, utmost.
(ANT.) first, foremost, opening, initial.
conclusion *(SYN.)* end, finale, termination, deduction, close, settlement, decision, finish, resolution, determination, completion, issue, judgment.
(ANT.) commencement, inception, opening, start, beginning.
conclusive *(SYN.)* decisive, eventual, final, terminal, ultimate.
(ANT.) original, first, inaugural.
concord *(SYN.)* agreement, unison, understanding, accordance, stipulation.
(ANT.) disagreement, discord, dissension.
concrete *(SYN.)* solid, firm, precise, definite, specific.
(ANT.) undetermined, vague, general.
concur *(SYN.)* agree, assent, consent, accede.
(ANT.) dissent, protest, differ.
condemn *(SYN.)* denounce, reproach, blame, upbraid, convict, rebuke, doom, judge, censure, reprehend, punish, reprobate, sentence.
(ANT.) condone, forgive, absolve, praise, applaud, extol, approve, pardon, laud, excuse, commend.
condense *(SYN.)* shorten, reduce, abridge, abbreviate, concentrate, digest, compress, diminish.
(ANT.) enlarge, increase, swell, expand.
condition *(SYN.)* circumstance, state, situation, case, plight, requirement, position, necessity, stipulation, predicament, provision, term.
conditional *(SYN.)* dependent, relying.
(ANT.) casual, original, absolute.
condolence *(SYN.)* commiseration, concord, harmony, pity, sympathy, warmth.
(ANT.) harshness, indifference, unconcern.
conduct *(SYN.)* control, deportment, supervise, manage, behavior, deed, actions, act, behave, manners, deportment.
confederate *(SYN.)* ally, abettor, assistant.
(ANT.) enemy, rival, opponent, adversary.
confederation *(SYN.)* combination, league, union, marriage, treaty.
(ANT.) separation, divorce.
confer *(SYN.)* gossip, grant, speak, tattle, blab, chat, deliberate, consult, award, give, bestow, talk, mutter.
(ANT.) retrieve, withdraw.
confess *(SYN.)* avow, acknowledge, admit, concede, grant, divulge, reveal.
(ANT.) disown, renounce, deny, conceal.
confession *(SYN.)* defense, justification, excuse, apology.
(ANT.) dissimulation, denial, complaint.
confidence *(SYN.)* firmness, self-reliance, assurance, faith, trust, pledge, declaration, self-confidence, reliance, self-assurance, courage, statement.
(ANT.) distrust, shyness, mistrust, bashfulness, diffidence, doubt, modesty, suspicion.
confident *(SYN.)* certain, sure, dauntless, self-assured.
(ANT.) uncertain, timid, shy.
confine *(SYN.)* enclose, restrict, hinder, fence, limit, bound.
(ANT.) release, expose, free, expand, open.
confirm acknowledge, establish, settle, substantiate, approve, fix, verify, assure, validate, ratify, corroborate, strengthen.
(ANT.) disclaim, deny, disavow.
confirmation *(SYN.)* demonstration, experiment, test, trail, verification.
(ANT.) fallacy, invalidity.
confirmed *(SYN.)* regular, established, habitual, chronic.
(ANT.) occasional, infrequent.
conflict *(SYN.)* duel, combat, fight, collision, discord, encounter, interference, inconsistency, contention, struggle, opposition, clash, oppose, battle, controversy, contend, engagement, contest, variance.
(ANT.) consonance, harmony, amity.
confiscate *(SYN.)* capture, catch, gain, purloin, steal, take, clutch, grip, seize, get, obtain, bear.
conflagration *(SYN.)* flame, glow, heat, warmth, fervor, passion, vigor.
(ANT.) apathy, cold, quiescence.
conform *(SYN.)* adapt, comply, yield, submit, obey, adjust, agree, fit, suit.
(ANT.) misapply, misfit, rebel, vary, disagree, disturb.
conformity *(SYN.)* congruence, accord, agreement, correspondence.
confound *(SYN.)* confuse, baffle, perplex, puzzle, bewilder.
confront *(SYN.)* confront, defy, hinder, resist, thwart, withstand, bar.
(ANT.) submit, agree, support, succumb.
confuse *(SYN.)* confound, perplex, mystify, dumbfound, baffle, puzzle, jumble, mislead, mix up, mistake, bewilder.
(ANT.) explain, instruct, edify, illumine, enlighten, illuminate, solve.
confused *(SYN.)* deranged, indistinct, disordered, muddled, bewildered, disconcerted, disorganized, perplexed.
(ANT.) organized, plain, clear, obvious.
confusion *(SYN.)* commotion, disarray, agitation, disorder, chaos, ferment, stir, perplexity, tumult, bewilderment, disarrangement, uncertainty, muss, mess, turmoil.

(ANT.) order, tranquillity, enlightenment, comprehension, understanding, tidiness, organization, peace.

congregate *(SYN.)* gather, forgather, meet, convene.
(ANT.) scatter, dispel, disperse, dissipate.

congress *(SYN.)* parliament, legislature, assembly.

congruous *(SYN.)* agreeing, conforming, constant, correspondent.
(ANT.) incongruous, inconsistent, discrepant.

conjecture *(SYN.)* law, supposition, theory.
(ANT.) proof, fact, certainty.

conjunction *(SYN.)* combination, junction, connection, link.
(ANT.) separation, disconnection, separation, diversion.

connect *(SYN.)* adjoin, link, combine, relate, join, attach, unite, associate, attribute, affix.
(ANT.) detach, separate, disjoin, untie, dissociation, disconnect, disassociation, unfasten.

connection *(SYN.)* conjunction, alliance, link, affinity, bond, tie, association, relationship, union.
(ANT.) isolation, dissociation, separation, disassociation, disunion.

conquer *(SYN.)* master, beat, humble, defeat, overcome, rout, win, succeed, achieve, gain, overpower, quell, subdue, crush, vanquish.
(ANT.) cede, yield, retreat, surrender.

conquest *(SYN.)* triumph, victory, achievement.
(ANT.) surrender, failure, defeat.

conscientious *(SYN.)* upright, straight, honest, incorruptible, scrupulous.
(ANT.) careless, irresponsible, slovenly.

conscious *(SYN.)* cognizant, informed, perceptive, aware, intentional, sensible, awake, purposeful, deliberate, sensible.
(ANT.) unaware, insensible, asleep, comatose, ignorant.

consecrate *(SYN.)* exalt, extol, hallow, honor.
(ANT.) mock, degrade, debase, abuse.

consecrated *(SYN.)* holy, divine, devout, spiritual.
(ANT.) evil, worldly, secular.

consent *(SYN.)* permission, leave, agree, let, assent, agreement, license, permit.
(ANT.) refusal, opposition, denial, dissent, prohibition.

consequence *(SYN.)* outcome, issue, result, effect, significance, importance.
(ANT.) impetus, cause.

consequential *(SYN.)* significant, important, weighty.
(ANT.) trivial, unimportant, minor, insignificant.

consequently *(SYN.)* hence, thence, therefore.

conservative *(SYN.)* conventional, reactionary, cautious, moderate, careful.
(ANT.) radical, liberal, rash, foolhardy, reckless.

conserve *(SYN.)* save, retain, reserve, guard, keep, support, sustain.
(ANT.) dismiss, neglect, waste, reject, discard.

consider *(SYN.)* heed, ponder, contemplate, examine, study, weigh, reflect, think about, regard, deliberate, respect.
(ANT.) ignore, overlook, disdain, disregard, neglect.

considerable *(SYN.)* much, noteworthy, worthwhile, significant, important.

considerate *(SYN.)* careful, considerate, heedful, prudent, kind, thoughtful, polite, introspective, reflective.
(ANT.) thoughtless, heedless, inconsiderate, selfish, rash.

consideration *(SYN.)* kindness, care, heed, politeness, empathy, notice, watchfulness, kindliness, thoughtfulness, courtesy, concern, sympathy, thought, attention, reflection, fee, pay, study.
(ANT.) omission, oversight, negligence.

consistent *(SYN.)* conforming, accordant, compatible, agreeing, faithful, constant, harmonious, expected, regular, congruous, correspondent.
(ANT.) paradoxical, discrepant, contrary, antagonistic, opposed, eccentric, inconsistent, incongruous.

consolation *(SYN.)* enjoyment, sympathy, relief, ease, contentment, comfort, solace.
(ANT.) discomfort, suffering, discouragement, torture, burden, misery.

console *(SYN.)* solace, comfort, sympathize with, assuage, soothe.
(ANT.) worry, annoy, upset, disturb, distress.

consolidate *(SYN.)* blend, combine, conjoin, fuse, mix, merge, unite.
(ANT.) decompose, separate, analyze, disintegrate.

consort *(SYN.)* companion, comrade, friend.
(ANT.) stranger, enemy, adversary.

conspicuous *(SYN.)* distinguished, clear, manifest, salient, noticeable, striking, obvious, prominent, visible.
(ANT.) hidden, obscure, neutral, common, inconspicuous.

conspiracy *(SYN.)* machination, combination, treason, intrigue, cabal, treachery, plot, collusion.

conspire *(SYN.)* plan, intrigue, plot, scheme.

constancy *(SYN.)* devotion, faithfulness, accuracy, precision, exactness.
(ANT.) faithlessness, treachery, perfidy.

constant *(SYN.)* continual, invariable, abiding, permanent, faithful, invariant, true, ceaseless, enduring, unchanging, steadfast, unchangeable, loyal, stable, immutable, staunch, steady, fixed.
(ANT.) fickle, irregular, wavering, off-and-on, infrequent, occasional, mutable.

constantly *(SYN.)* eternally, ever, evermore, forever, unceasingly.
(ANT.) rarely, sometimes, never, occasionally.

consternation *(SYN.)* apprehension, dismay, alarm, fear, fright, dread, horror, terror.

(ANT.) bravery, courage, boldness, assurance.

constitute *(SYN.)* compose, found, form, establish, organize, create, appoint, delegate, authorize, commission.

constitution *(SYN.)* law, code, physique, health, vitality.

constrain *(SYN.)* necessity, indigence, need, want, poverty.
(ANT.) luxury, freedom, uncertainty.

construct *(SYN.)* build, form, erect, make, fabricate, raise, frame.
(ANT.) raze, demolish, destroy.

construction *(SYN.)* raising, building, fabricating.

constructive *(SYN.)* useful, helpful, valuable.
(ANT.) ruinous, destructive.

construe *(SYN.)* explain, interpret, solve, render, translate.
(ANT.) distort, confuse, misconstrue.

consult *(SYN.)* discuss, chatter, discourse, gossip, confer, report, rumor, deliberate, speech, talk.
(ANT.) writing, correspondence, silence.

consume *(SYN.)* engulf, absorb, use up, use, expend, exhaust, devour, devastate, destroy, engross.
(ANT.) emit, expel, exude, discharge.

consumer *(SYN.)* user, buyer, purchaser.

consummate *(SYN.)* close, conclude, do finish, perfect, terminate.

consummation *(SYN.)* climax, apex, culmination, peak.
(ANT.) depth, base, floor.

contact *(SYN.)* meeting, touching.

contagious *(SYN.)* infectious, virulent, communicable, catching.
(ANT.) noncommunicable, healthful, hygienic.

contain *(SYN.)* embody, hold, embrace, include, accommodate, repress, restrain.
(ANT.) emit, encourage, yield, discharge.

contaminate *(SYN.)* corrupt, sully, taint, defile, soil, pollute, dirty, infect, poison.
(ANT.) purify.

contemplate *(SYN.)* imagine, recollect, consider, study, reflect upon, observe, deliberate, muse, ponder, plan, intend, view, regard, think about, reflect, think, mean.
(ANT.) forget, guess, conjecture.

contemplative *(SYN.)* simultaneous, meditative, thoughtful, contemporaneous, pensive, studious.
(ANT.) inattentive, indifferent, thoughtless.

contemporary *(SYN.)* modern, present, simultaneous, fashionable, coexisting, contemporaneous, up-to-date.
(ANT.) old, antecedent, past, ancient, succeeding, bygone.

contempt *(SYN.)* detestation, malice, contumely, disdain, derision, scorn.
(ANT.) respect, reverence, admiration, esteem, awe.

contemptible *(SYN.)* base, mean, vile, vulgar, nasty, low, detestable, selfish, miserable, offensive.
(ANT.) generous, honorable, noble, exalted, admirable.

contemptuous *(SYN.)* disdainful, sneering, scornful, insolent.
(ANT.) modest, humble.

contend *(SYN.)* dispute, combat, contest, assert, claim, argue, maintain.

content *(SYN.)* pleased, happy, contented, satisfied.
(ANT.) restless, dissatisfied, discontented.

contented *(SYN.)* delighted, fortunate, gay, happy, joyous, lucky, merry.
(ANT.) gloomy, blue, depressed.

contention *(SYN.)* combat, duel, struggle, discord, battle, variance.
(ANT.) concord, harmony, amity, consonance.

contentment *(SYN.)* delight, happiness, gladness, pleasure, satisfaction.
(ANT.) misery, sorrow, grief, sadness, despair.

contest *(SYN.)* dispute, debate, competition, tournament, oppose, discuss, quarrel, squabble.
(ANT.) allow, concede, agree, assent.

continence *(SYN.)* forbearance, temperance.
(ANT.) self-indulgence, excess, intoxication.

contingency *(SYN.)* likelihood, possibility, occasion, circumstance.

contingent *(SYN.)* depending, subject.
(ANT.) independent, original, casual.

continual *(SYN.)* constant, unceasing, everlasting, unremitting, endless, continuous, uninterrupted, regular, connected, consecutive, ceaseless.
(ANT.) periodic, rare, irregular, occasional, interrupted.

continue *(SYN.)* proceed, extend, endure, persist, resume, renew, recommence, last, remain, last, prolong, pursue.
(ANT.) check, cease, discontinue, stop, suspend.

continuous *(SYN.)* continuing, uninterrupted, ceaseless, unceasing, incessant, constant.
(ANT.) intermittent, irregular, sporadic.

contract *(SYN.)* condense, diminish, reduce, bargain, restrict, agreement, compact, pact, shrink, gel, treaty, shorten.
(ANT.) lengthen, extend, swell, expand, elongate.

contraction *(SYN.)* reduction, shortening.
(ANT.) enlargement, expansion, extension.

contradict *(SYN.)* gainsay, counter, oppose, confute, dispute.
(ANT.) verify, confirm, agree, support.

contradictory *(SYN.)* inconsistent, conflicting, incompatible, paradoxical, unsteady.
(ANT.) congruous, consistent, correspondent.

contrary *(SYN.)* disagreeable, perverse, hostile, stubborn, opposite, opposing, opposed, disagreeing, disastrous, conflicting, headstrong, unlucky.

(ANT.) lucky, agreeable, propitious, favorable, like, obliging, similar, complementary, tractable, fortunate.

contrast *(SYN.)* differentiate, compare, distinction, disagreement, distinguish, differ, discriminate, difference, oppose.
(ANT.) agreement, similarity, likeness.

contribute *(SYN.)* grant, give, donate, bestow, provide, offer.
(ANT.) deny, withhold.

contribution *(SYN.)* grant, gift, offering, donation.

contrition *(SYN.)* grief, regret, self-reproach.
(ANT.) self-satisfaction, complacency.

contrive *(SYN.)* devise, intend, plan, make, invent, plot, hatch, form, project, arrange, manage, maneuver, scheme, sketch.

control *(SYN.)* govern, regulate, rule, command, dominate, direct, manage, check, repress, curb, management, mastery, direction, restraint, superintend, restrain.
(ANT.) ignore, forsake, follow, submit, abandon.

controversy *(SYN.)* disagreement, dispute, debate.
(ANT.) agreement, harmony, accord, concord, decision.

convenience *(SYN.)* accessibility, aid, benefit, help, service, availability.
(ANT.) inconvenience.

convenient *(SYN.)* adapted, appropriate, fitting, favorable, handy, suitable, accessible, nearby, ready, available, advantageous, timely.
(ANT.) inconvenient, troublesome, awkward.

convention *(SYN.)* meeting, conference, assembly, practice, custom, rule.

conventional *(SYN.)* common, regular, usual, everyday, habitual, routine, accustomed.
(ANT.) exotic, unusual, bizarre, extraordinary.

conversant *(SYN.)* aware, intimate, familiar, versed, close, friendly, sociable.
(ANT.) affected, distant, cold, reserved.

conversation *(SYN.)* colloquy, dialogue, chat, parley, discussion, talk.

converse *(SYN.)* jabber, talk, argue, comment, harangue, plead, rant, spout, discuss, chat, talk, speak, reason.

conversion *(SYN.)* alteration, change, mutation, modification, metamorphosis.

convert *(SYN.)* change, alter, alter, turn, transform, shift, modify, exchange, win over, vary, veer.
(ANT.) establish, stabilize, settle, retain.

convey *(SYN.)* carry, bear, communicate, transport, transmit, support, sustain.
(ANT.) drop, abandon.

conveyance *(SYN.)* van, car, train, truck, plane.

convict *(SYN.)* felon, offender, criminal.

conviction *(SYN.)* opinion, position, view, faith, belief, confidence, feeling, reliance, trust.
(ANT.) doubt, heresy, incredulity, denial.

convince *(SYN.)* persuade, assure, exhort, induce, influence.
(ANT.) deter, compel, restrain, dissuade.

convivial *(SYN.)* jolly, social, jovial, gregarious.
(ANT.) solemn, stern, unsociable.

convoy *(SYN.)* with, attend, chaperon.
(ANT.) avoid, desert, quit, leave.

cool *(SYN.)* frosty, chilly, icy, cold, wintry, quiet, composed, collected, distant, unfriendly, quiet, moderate.
(ANT.) hot, warm, heated, overwrought, excited, hysterical, friendly, outgoing.

cooperate *(SYN.)* unite, combine, help, contribute, support.

coordinate *(SYN.)* attune, harmonize, adapt, match, balance.

copious *(SYN.)* ample, abundant, bountiful, overflowing, plentiful, profuse, rich.
(ANT.) scant, scarce, insufficient, meager, deficient.

copy *(SYN.)* facsimile, exemplar, imitation, duplicate, reproduction, likeness, print, carbon, transcript.
(ANT.) prototype, original.

cordial *(SYN.)* polite, friendly, affable, genial, earnest, gracious, warm, ardent, warmhearted, hearty, sincere.
(ANT.) unfriendly, cool, aloof, hostile, ill-tempered, reserved.

core *(SYN.)* midpoint, heart, kernel, center, middle.
(ANT.) outskirts, border, surface, outside, boundary, rim.

corporation *(SYN.)* business, organization, crew, group, troop, society, company, conglomerate, firm.
(ANT.) individual, dispersion, seclusion.

corpse *(SYN.)* cadaver, carcass, remains, body, form.
(ANT.) spirit, soul, mind, intellect.

corpulent *(SYN.)* obese, portly, chubby, stout.
(ANT.) slim, thin, slender, lean, gaunt.

correct *(SYN.)* true, set right, faultless, impeccable, proper, accurate, precise, mend, right, rebuke, punish, amend, rectify, better, emend, caution, discipline, exact, strict.
(ANT.) condone, aggravate, false, inaccurate, wrong, untrue, faulty.

correction *(SYN.)* order, improvement, regulation, instruction, amendment, emendation, remedy, rectification, repair, training, punishment.
(ANT.) confusion, turbulence, chaos.

correlative *(SYN.)* allied, correspondent, like, similar, parallel.
(ANT.) different, opposed, divergent.

correspond *(SYN.)* compare, coincide, match, agree, suit, fit, write.
(ANT.) differ, diverge, vary.

correspondent *(SYN.)* allied, alike, comparable, like, parallel, similar.
(ANT.) different, opposed, divergent, dissimilar.

corridor *(SYN.)* hallway, hall, foyer,

passage, lobby, passageway.
corrode *(SYN.)* erode.
corrupt *(SYN.)* crooked, untrustworthy, treacherous, debased, unscrupulous, wicked, evil, low, contaminated, perverted, bribe, depraved, corrupted, demoralize, degrade, venal, putrid, tainted, dishonest, impure.
(ANT.) upright, honest, pure, sanctify, edify, purify, sanctified, scrupulous.
corrupted *(SYN.)* crooked, dishonest, impure, spoiled, unsound.
cost *(SYN.)* price, value, damage, charge, loss, sacrifice, penalty, worth.
costly *(SYN.)* dear, expensive.
(ANT.) cheap, inexpensive.
costume *(SYN.)* dress, clothes, apparel, clothing, garb.
couch *(SYN.)* davenport, sofa, loveseat.
council *(SYN.)* caution, instruction, committee, cabinet, board, suggestion.
counsel *(SYN.)* guidance, attorney, lawyer, counselor, hint, imply, opinion, advice, offer, advise.
(ANT.) declare, dictate, insist.
count *(SYN.)* consider, number, enumerate, total, figure, compute, tally, estimate.
(ANT.) conjecture, guess, miscalculate.
countenance *(SYN.)* visage, face, aspect, support, appearance, approval, encouragement, favor.
(ANT.) forbid, prohibit.
counteract *(SYN.)* thwart, neutralize, offset, counterbalance, defeat.
counterfeit *(SYN.)* false, fraudulent, pretended, pretend, sham, imitate, forgery, artificial, bogus, fake, spurious, imitation, unreal.
(ANT.) authentic, natural, real, genuine, true.
country *(SYN.)* state, nation, forest, farmland.
(ANT.) city.
couple *(SYN.)* team, pair, accompany, associate, attach, combine, connect, brace, join, link, unite.
(ANT.) detach, separate, disjoin, disconnect.
courage *(SYN.)* fearlessness, boldness, chivalry, fortitude, mettle, spirit, daring, bravery, prowess, intrepidity, valor, resolution.
(ANT.) fear, timidity, cowardice.
courageous *(SYN.)* bold, dauntless, brave, daring, intrepid, valorous, plucky, fearless, heroic, valiant.
(ANT.) fearful, weak, timid, cowardly.
course *(SYN.)* passage, advance, path, road, progress, way, direction, bearing, route, street, track, trail, way.
courteous *(SYN.)* civil, respectful, polite, genteel, well-mannered, gracious, refined.
(ANT.) discourteous, rude, uncivil, impolite, boorish.
courtesy *(SYN.)* graciousness, politeness, respect.
(ANT.) discourtesy, rudeness.
covenant *(SYN.)* agreement, concord, harmony, unison, compact, stipulation.
(ANT.) variance, discord, dissension, difference.
cover *(SYN.)* clothe, conceal, disguise, curtain, guard, envelop, mask, cloak, shield, hide, screen, protect, embrace, top, lid, covering, stopper, protection, refuge, spread, overlay, include, veil.
(ANT.) bare, expose, reveal.
covert *(SYN.)* potential, undeveloped, concealed, dormant.
(ANT.) explicit, visible, manifest.
covetous *(SYN.)* grasping, greedy, acquisitive, avaricious.
(ANT.) generous.
coward *(SYN.)* milquetoast, cad.
(ANT.) hero.
cowardice *(SYN.)* dread, dismay, fright, dismay, panic, terror, timidity.
(ANT.) fearlessness, courage, bravery.
cowardly *(SYN.)* fearful, timorous, afraid, faint-hearted, yellow, pusillanimous, spineless.
cower *(SYN.)* wince, flinch, cringe, quail, tremble.
coy *(SYN.)* embarrassed, sheepish, shy, timid.
(ANT.) fearless, outgoing, bold, adventurous, daring.
crack *(SYN.)* snap, break, split.
cracker *(SYN.)* wafer, biscuit, saltine.
craft *(SYN.)* talent, skill, expertness, ability, cunning, guile, deceit, trade, profession, occupation.
crafty *(SYN.)* covert, clever, cunning, skillful, foxy, tricky, sly, underhand, shrewd.
(ANT.) frank, sincere, gullible, open, guileless, ingenuous.
craggy *(SYN.)* rough, rugged, irregular, uneven.
(ANT.) level, sleek, smooth, fine, polished.
crank *(SYN.)* cross, irritable, bad-tempered, testy.
(ANT.) cheerful, happy.
crash *(SYN.)* smash, shatter, dash.
crave *(SYN.)* want, desire, hunger for.
(ANT.) relinquish, renounce.
craving *(SYN.)* relish appetite, desire, liking, longing, passion.
(ANT.) renunciation, distaste, disgust.
crazy *(SYN.)* delirious, deranged, idiotic, mad, insane, demented, foolish, maniacal.
(ANT.) sane, sensible, sound, rational, reasonable.
creak *(SYN.)* squeak.
create *(SYN.)* fashion, form, generate, engender, formulate, make, originate, produce, cause, ordain, invent, beget, design, construct, constitute.
(ANT.) disband, abolish, terminate, destroy, demolish.
creative *(SYN.)* imaginative, ingenious, original, resourceful, clever, inventive, innovative, mystical.
(ANT.) unromantic, dull, literal.
credence *(SYN.)* confidence, faith, feeling, opinion, trust.
(ANT.) doubt, incredulity, denial.
credible *(SYN.)* conceivable, believable.
(ANT.) inconceivable, unbelievable.
credit *(SYN.)* believe, accept, belief,

trust, faith, merit, honor, apprehend, fancy, hold, support.
(ANT.) doubt, reject, question, distrust.
creditable *(SYN.)* worthy, praiseworthy.
(ANT.) dishonorable, discreditable, shameful.
credulous *(SYN.)* trusting, naive, believing, gullible, unsuspicious.
(ANT.) suspicious.
creed *(SYN.)* belief, precept, credo, faith, teaching.
(ANT.) practice, deed, conduct, performance.
creek *(SYN.)* brook, spring, stream, rivulet.
crime *(SYN.)* offense, insult, aggression, wrongdoing, wrong, misdeed.
(ANT.) right, genuineness, innocence, morality.
criminal *(SYN.)* unlawful, crook, gangster, outlaw, illegal, convict, delinquent, offender, malefactor, culprit, felonious, felon, transgressor.
cripple *(SYN.)* hurt, maim, damage, injure.
crippled *(SYN.)* deformed, disabled, maimed, hobbling, limping, unconvincing, unsatisfactory.
(ANT.) robust, sound, vigorous, athletic.
crisis *(SYN.)* conjuncture, emergency, pass, pinch, acme, climax, contingency, juncture, exigency, strait.
(ANT.) calm, normality, stability, equilibrium.
crisp *(SYN.)* crumbling, delicate, frail, brittle.
(ANT.) calm, normality, stability.
criterion *(SYN.)* measure, law, rule, principle, gauge, proof.
(ANT.) fancy guess, chance, supposition.
critic *(SYN.)* reviewer, judge, commentator, censor, defamer, slanderer, faultfinder.
critical *(SYN.)* exact, fastidious, caviling, faultfinding, accurate, risky.
(ANT.) shallow, uncritical, approving, insignificant, trivial, unimportant.
criticize *(SYN.)* examine, analyze, inspect, blame, censure, appraise.
(ANT.) neglect, overlook, approve.
crooked *(SYN.)* twisted, corrupt, hooked, curved, criminal, dishonest.
(ANT.) improved, raised, straight.
crop *(SYN.)* fruit, produce, harvest, cut, mow, reaping, result, yield.
cross *(SYN.)* mix, mingle, traverse, interbreed, annoyed, irritable, cranky.
(ANT.) cheerful.
crouch *(SYN.)* duck, stoop.
crow *(SYN.)* boast, brag.
crowd *(SYN.)* masses, flock, host, squeeze, mob, multitude, press.
crown *(SYN.)* coronet, apex, crest, circlet, pinnacle, tiara, skull, head.
(ANT.) base, bottom, foundation, foot.
crude *(SYN.)* rude, graceless, unpolished, green, harsh, rough, coarse.
(ANT.) finished, refined, polished.
cruel *(SYN.)* ferocious, mean, heartless, unmerciful, malignant, savage, brutal.
(ANT.) humane, forbearing, kind, compassionate, merciful, benevolent.
cruelty *(SYN.)* harshness, meanness, savagery, brutality.
(ANT.) compassion, kindness.
crumb *(SYN.)* jot, grain, mite, particle, shred.
(ANT.) mass, bulk, quantity.
crunch *(SYN.)* champ, gnaw, nibble.
crush *(SYN.)* smash, break, crash.
cry *(SYN.)* yowl, yell, roar, shout, bellow, scream, wail, weep, bawl, sob.
culprit *(SYN.)* delinquent, felon, offender.
cultivate *(SYN.)* plant, seed, farm, till, refine, educate, teach.
cultivation *(SYN.)* farming, horticulture, tillage, agriculture.
cultural *(SYN.)* civilizing, educational, elevating, instructive.
culture *(SYN.)* humanism, upbringing, cultivation, breeding, education.
(ANT.) illiteracy, vulgarity, ignorance.
cultured *(SYN.)* sophisticated, worldly.
(ANT.) crude, simple, uncouth.
cumbersome *(SYN.)* clumsy, awkward.
(ANT.) handy.
cunning *(SYN.)* clever, wily, crafty, foxy, skillful, tricky, ingenious, foxiness, ability, skill, wiliness, devious, shrewdness, slyness, cleverness, crooked.
(ANT.) gullible, honest, naive, openness, straightforward, simple, direct.
curb *(SYN.)* check, restraint, hinder.
(ANT.) aid, loosen, incite, encourage.
cure *(SYN.)* help, treatment, heal.
curiosity *(SYN.)* wonder, marvel, rarity.
(ANT.) apathy, indifference.
curious *(SYN.)* interrogative, interested.
(ANT.) unconcerned, incurious.
current *(SYN.)* up-to-date, modern.
(ANT.) antiquated, old, ancient, past.
curse *(SYN.)* ban, oath, denounce.
(ANT.) boon, blessing, advantage.
cursory *(SYN.)* frivolous, shallow, slight.
(ANT.) complete, deep, profound.
curt *(SYN.)* hasty, short, abrupt, blunt, rude, harsh.
(ANT.) friendly, smooth, gradual, polite.
curtail *(SYN.)* condense, reduce, limit, abbreviate.
(ANT.) lengthen, extend.
curtain *(SYN.)* blind, drapery, drape.
curve *(SYN.)* crook, deflect, bend, twist.
(ANT.) resist, stiffen, straighten.
cushion *(SYN.)* pillow, pad, check.
custodian *(SYN.)* guard, keeper, guardian, watchman.
custody *(SYN.)* guardianship, care.
(ANT.) neglect, disregard, indifference.
custom *(SYN.)* fashion, rule, routine, practice, usage.
customary *(SYN.)* common, usual.
(ANT.) exceptional, irregular, rare.
customer *(SYN.)* patron, client, buyer.
cut *(SYN.)* slash, gash, prick, slit, sever.
cut back *(SYN.)* decrease, reduce.
cut in *(SYN.)* butt in, interfere.
cut off *(SYN.)* cease, end, stop, terminate.
cut short *(SYN.)* stop, finish, end, quit.
cutting *(SYN.)* bitter, stern, caustic, scathing, harsh, acerbic.
cylindrical *(SYN.)* circular, curved, plump, rotund, spherical, round.

dab *(SYN.)* coat, pat, smear.
dabble *(SYN.)* splatter, toy, splash, fiddle, putter.
daft *(SYN.)* crazy, foolish, insane.
dagger *(SYN.)* knife, dirk, blade.
daily *(SYN.)* every day, diurnal, regularly.
dainty *(SYN.)* slender, pleasing, delicate, frail, pleasant, pretty, petite.
(ANT.) uncouth, vulgar, coarse, tough.
dam *(SYN.)* dike, levee, barrier, slow, stop, check, obstruct, block.
(ANT.) free, release, loose, unleash.
damage *(SYN.)* spoil, deface, impair, mar, hurt, injury, impairment, destruction, harm, injure.
(ANT.) repair, benefit, mend, rebuild, improve, ameliorate.
dame *(SYN.)* woman, lady.
damp *(SYN.)* humid, dank, moisture, wetness, dampness, humidity.
(ANT.) arid, dry.
dampen *(SYN.)* wet, depressed, moisten, dull, suppress, sprinkle, discouraged, retard, slow, muffle, inhibit.
(ANT.) dehumidify, increase, encourage.
dance *(SYN.)* bounce, flit, skip, sway, prance, bob, glide, caper, cavort, frisk.
dandle *(SYN.)* jounce, joggle, bounce, jiggle, nestle, cuddle, caress.
danger *(SYN.)* jeopardy, risk, threat, hazard, uncertainty, peril.
(ANT.) safety, immunity, security.
dangerous *(SYN.)* risky, insecure, threatening, critical, perilous, unsafe.
(ANT.) trustworthy, protected, safe.
dangle *(SYN.)* droop, swing, flap, hang.
dare *(SYN.)* brave, call, question, defy, risk, challenge, summon.
daring *(SYN.)* foolhardy, chivalrous, rash, fearless, courageous, intrepid.
(ANT.) timid, cowardice, timidity.
dark *(SYN.)* somber, obscure, gloomy, black, dim, evil, hidden, secret.
(ANT.) lucid, light, happy, cheerful.
darling *(SYN.)* dear, adored, sweetheart, favorite, cherished.
(ANT.) unlovable, rejected, forlorn.
darn *(SYN.)* repair, mend.
dart *(SYN.)* scurry, arrow, barb, hurry, dash, throw, missile, run, hasten.
dash *(SYN.)* pound, thump, beat, smite, buffet, thrash, smash, break, scurry.
(ANT.) stroke, encourage, defend.
data *(SYN.)* information, statistics.
date *(SYN.)* interview, appointment.
dated *(SYN.)* out-of-date, old-fashioned.
(ANT.) latest, current, fashionable, hot.
dawn *(SYN.)* sunrise, start, outset.
(ANT.) dusk, sunset, nightfall, end.
daze *(SYN.)* perplex, stun, puzzle, bewilder, upset, confuse, confusion.
dazzle *(SYN.)* surprise, stun, astonish, impress, bewilder, stupefy.
dead *(SYN.)* lifeless, deceased, dull.
(ANT.) animate, functioning, active.
deadly *(SYN.)* lethal, mortal, fatal.
deaf *(SYN.)* unhearing, unaware.
(ANT.) aware, conscious.
deal *(SYN.)* act, treat, attend, cope, barter, trade, bargain, apportion, give.
dear *(SYN.)* valued, esteemed, expensive, beloved, costly, darling.
(ANT.) hateful, reasonable, unwanted.
death *(SYN.)* decease, extinction, demise, passing.
(ANT.) life.
debase *(SYN.)* lower, degrade, alloy, adulterate, defile, humiliate, depress.
(ANT.) restore, improve, vitalize.
debris *(SYN.)* rubbish, litter, junk.
debt *(SYN.)* amount due, liability, obligation.
decay *(SYN.)* spoil, waste, disintegrate, perish, rot, collapse, decompose.
(ANT.) progress, increase, grow, flourish.
deceased *(SYN.)* lifeless, departed, dead.
(ANT.) living, alive.
deceit *(SYN.)* duplicity, cheat, fraud, chicanery, trick, cunning, deception.
(ANT.) truthfulness, openness.
deceitful *(SYN.)* false, fraudulent, insincere, dishonest, deceptive.
(ANT.) sincere, honest.
deceive *(SYN.)* cheat, defraud, hoodwink, mislead, swindle.
decency *(SYN.)* decorum, dignity, propriety, respectability.
decent *(SYN.)* befitting, fit, suitable, becoming, respectable, adequate, seemly.
(ANT.) vulgar, gross, improper, unsuitable, indecorous, indecent, coarse.
deception *(SYN.)* trick, cheat, sham, deceit, trickery, craftiness, treachery.
(ANT.) openness, frankness, candor, probity, truthfulness, honesty.
deceptive *(SYN.)* specious, fallacious, deceitful, false, delusive, unreliable.
(ANT.) honest, real, genuine, true, truthful, authentic.
decide *(SYN.)* resolve, determine, terminate, conclude, close, settle.
(ANT.) waver, hesitate, vacillate, doubt, suspend.
decipher *(SYN.)* render, unravel, construe, solve, decode, translate.
(ANT.) misconstrue, distort, misinterpret, confuse.
decision *(SYN.)* resolution, determination, settlement.
decisive *(SYN.)* determined, firm, decided, unhesitating, resolute.
declaration *(SYN.)* pronouncement, notice, affirmation, statement.
declare *(SYN.)* assert, promulate, affirm, tell, broadcast, express, proclaim,
(ANT.) deny, withhold, conceal.
decline *(SYN.)* descend, decay, dwindle, refuse, incline, wane, sink, depreciate.
(ANT.) accept, ascend, ameliorate, increase.
decompose *(SYN.)* rot, disintegrate, molder, decay, crumble.
decorate *(SYN.)* trim, paint, deck, enrich, color, beautify, enhance, furbish.
(ANT.) uncover, mar, deface, defame.
decoration *(SYN.)* ornamentation, embellishment, adornment, furnishing.
decoy *(SYN.)* lure, bait.
decrease *(SYN.)* lessen, wane, deduct, diminish, curtail, deduct, remove.
(ANT.) expansion, increase, enlarge, expand, grow.
decree *(SYN.)* order, edict, statute, declaration, announce, act.
decrepit *(SYN.)* feeble, weakened, rick-

ety, weak, run-down, tumble-down.
(ANT.) strong, forceful, vigorous, energetic, lusty.
decry *(SYN.)* lower, belittle, derogate, minimize, undervalue.
(ANT.) praise, commend, magnify.
dedicate *(SYN.)* sanctify, consecrate, hallow, devote, assign.
dedicated *(SYN.)* disposed, true, affectionate, fond, wedded.
(ANT.) indisposed, detached, untrammeled, disinclined.
deduct *(SYN.)* lessen, shorten, abate, remove, eliminate, curtail, subtract.
(ANT.) grow, enlarge, add, increase, amplify, expand.
deed *(SYN.)* feat, action, performance, act, operation, achievement, document, certificate, title.
(ANT.) intention, cessation, inactivity, deliberation.
deem *(SYN.)* hold, determine, believe, regard, reckon, judge, consider.
deep *(SYN.)* bottomless, low, unplumbed, acute, obscure, involved.
(ANT.) shallow.
deface *(SYN.)* spoil, impair, damage, mar, hurt, scratch, mutilate, disfigure.
(ANT.) mend, benefit, repair, enhance.
defamation *(SYN.)* invective. reproach, upbraiding, abuse, insult, outrage.
(ANT.) respect, approval, laudation, commendation.
default *(SYN.)* loss, omission, lack, failure, want, dereliction.
(ANT.) victory, achievement, sufficiency, success.
defeat *(SYN.)* quell, vanquish, beat, overcome, overthrow, subdue.
(ANT.) submit, retreat, cede, yield, surrender, capitulate, lose.
defect *(SYN.)* shortcoming, fault, omission, blemish, imperfection, forsake.
(ANT.) perfection, flawlessness, support, join, completeness.
defective *(SYN.)* faulty, imperfect, inoperative, flawed, inoperable.
(ANT.) flawless, perfect, faultless.
defend *(SYN.)* screen, espouse, justify, protect, vindicate, fortify, assert.
(ANT.) oppose, assault, submit, attack, deny.
defense *(SYN.)* resistance, protection, bulwark, fort, barricade, trench.
defer *(SYN.)* postpone, delay.
(ANT.) speed, hurry, expedite.
deference *(SYN.)* fame, worship, adoration, reverence, admiration, respect.
(ANT.) dishonor, derision, reproach, contempt.
defiant *(SYN.)* rebellious, antagonistic, obstinate.
(ANT.) yielding, submissive.
deficient *(SYN.)* lacking, short, incomplete, defective, scanty, insufficient.
(ANT.) enough, ample, sufficient, adequate.
defile *(SYN.)* pollute, march, corrupt, dirty, file, debase, contaminate.
(ANT.) purify.
define *(SYN.)* describe, fix, establish, label, designate, set, name, explain.
definite *(SYN.)* fixed, prescribed, certain, specific, exact, determined.
(ANT.) indefinite, confused, undetermined, equivocal.
definitely *(SYN.)* certainly, assuredly, absolutely, positively, surely.
definition *(SYN.)* sense, interpretation, meaning, explanation.
deft *(SYN.)* handy, adroit, clever, adept, dexterous, skillful, skilled.
(ANT.) inept, clumsy, maladroit, awkward.
defunct *(SYN.)* lifeless, dead, departed, expired, extinct, spiritless, inanimate.
(ANT.) living, alive, stirring.
defy *(SYN.)* hinder, oppose, withstand, attack, resist, confront, challenge.
(ANT.) yield, allow, relent, surrender, submit, accede.
degenerate *(SYN.)* dwindle, decline, weaken, deteriorate, decrease.
(ANT.) ascend, ameliorate, increase, appreciate.
degrade *(SYN.)* crush, reduce, subdue, abash, humble, lower, shame, demote.
(ANT.) praise, elevate, honor.
degree *(SYN.)* grade, amount, step, measure, rank, honor, extent.
deign *(SYN.)* condescend, stoop.
dejected *(SYN.)* depressed, downcast, sad, disheartened, blue, discouraged.
(ANT.) cheerful, happy, optimistic.
delectable *(SYN.)* tasty, delicious, savory, delightful, sweet, luscious.
(ANT.) unsavory, distasteful, unpalatable, acrid.
delegate *(SYN.)* emissary, envoy, ambassador, representative, commission.
delete *(SYN.)* erase, cancel, remove.
(ANT.) add.
deliberate *(SYN.)* studied, willful, intended, contemplated, premeditated.
(ANT.) fortuitous, hasty, accidental.
delicate *(SYN.)* frail, critical, slender, dainty, pleasing, fastidious, exquisite.
(ANT.) tough, strong, coarse, clumsy, hearty, hale, vulgar, rude.
delicious *(SYN.)* tasty, luscious, delectable, sweet, savory.
(ANT.) unsavory, distasteful, unpalatable, unpleasant, acrid.
delight *(SYN.)* joy, bliss, gladness, pleasure, ecstasy, happiness, rapture.
(ANT.) revolt, sorrow, annoyance, displeasure, disgust, displease, revulsion.
delightful *(SYN.)* pleasing, pleasant, charming, refreshing, pleasurable.
(ANT.) nasty, disagreeable, unpleasant.
delirious *(SYN.)* raving, mad, giddy, frantic, hysterical, violent.
deliver *(SYN.)* impart, publish, rescue, commit, communicate, free, address.
(ANT.) restrict, confine, capture, enslave, withhold, imprison.
deluge *(SYN.)* overflow, flood.
delusion *(SYN.)* mirage, fantasy, phantasm, vision, dream, illusion, phantom.
(ANT.) substance, actuality.
delve *(SYN.)* dig, look, search, scoop, explore, hunt.
demand *(SYN.)* claim, inquire, ask, need, require, obligation, requirement.
(ANT.) tender, give, present, waive, relinquish, offer.

demean *(SYN.)* comport, bear, operate, carry, act, manage, deport.
demeanor *(SYN.)* manner, way, conduct, actions, behavior.
demented *(SYN.)* insane, crazy, mad, mental, psychotic, lunatic.
demolish *(SYN.)* ruin, devastate, ravage, annihilate, wreck, destroy, raze.
(ANT.) erect, make, save, construct, preserve, build, establish.
demolition *(SYN.)* wrecking, destruction.
(ANT.) erection, construction.
demon *(SYN.)* fiend, monster, devil, ogre, spirit.
demonstrate *(SYN.)* evince, show, prove, display, illustrate, describe.
(ANT.) hide, conceal.
demonstration *(SYN.)* exhibit, show, presentation, exhibition, display, rally.
demur *(SYN.)* waver, falter, delay, stutter, doubt, vacillate, hesitate, scruple.
(ANT.) proceed, decide, resolve.
demure *(SYN.)* meek, shy, modest, diffident, retiring, bashful, coy.
den *(SYN.)* cave, lair, cavern.
denial *(SYN.)* disallowance, proscription, refusal, prohibition.
denounce *(SYN.)* condemn, blame, reprove, reprehend, censure, reproach.
(ANT.) condone, approve, forgive, commend, praise.
dense *(SYN.)* crowded, slow, close, obtuse, compact, dull, stupid.
(ANT.) sparse, quick, dispersed, clever, dissipated, empty, smart, bright.
dent *(SYN.)* notch, impress, pit, nick.
deny *(SYN.)* refuse, withhold, dispute, disavow, forbid, refute, contradict.
(ANT.) confirm, affirm, admit, confess, permit, allow, concede, assert.
depart *(SYN.)* quit, forsake, withdraw, renounce, desert, relinquish, die, perish, decease.
(ANT.) tarry, remain, come, abide, stay, arrive.
departure *(SYN.)* valediction, farewell.
depend *(SYN.)* trust, rely, confide.
dependable *(SYN.)* secure, trustworthy, certain, safe, trusty, reliable, tried.
(ANT.) unreliable, fallible, dubious, uncertain.
dependent *(SYN.)* relying, contingent, subordinate, conditional.
(ANT.) original, casual, absolute, independent.
depict *(SYN.)* explain, recount, describe, portray, characterize, relate, narrate.
deplore *(SYN.)* repine, lament, bemoan, wail, bewail, weep, grieve, regret.
deport *(SYN.)* exile, eject, oust, banish, expel, dismiss, ostracize, dispel, exclude.
(ANT.) receive, admit, shelter, accept, harbor.
deportment *(SYN.)* deed, behavior, manner, action, carriage, disposition, bearing, demeanor.
deposit *(SYN.)* place, put, bank, save, store, sediment, dregs, addition, entry.
(ANT.) withdraw, withdrawal.
depreciate *(SYN.)* dwindle, decrease, decay, belittle, disparage, weaken, minimize, descend, deteriorate.
(ANT.) ascend, ameliorate, praise, increase, applaud, appreciate.
depress *(SYN.)* deject, dishearten, sadden, dampen, devaluate, devalue, lessen, lower, cheapen, reduce, dispirit, discourage, sink.
(ANT.) exalt, cheer, exhilarate.
depression *(SYN.)* hopelessness, despondency, pessimism, dip, cavity, pothole, hole, despair, gloom, melancholy, sadness, sorrow, recession, decline, desperation, discouragement.
(ANT.) eminence, elation, optimism, happiness, confidence, elevation, hope.
deprive *(SYN.)* bereave, deny, strip.
(ANT.) provision, supply, provide.
derelict *(SYN.)* decrepit, shabby, dilapidated, neglected, forsaken, deserted, remiss, abandoned, lax.
dereliction *(SYN.)* want, lack, failure, miscarriage, loss, default, deficiency, omission, fiasco.
(ANT.) sufficiency, success, achievement, victory.
derision *(SYN.)* irony, satire, banter, raillery, sneering, gibe, ridicule.
derivation *(SYN.)* source, birth, inception, start, beginning, spring, commencement, foundation, origin.
(ANT.) issue, end, outcome, harvest, product.
derive *(SYN.)* obtain, acquire, get, receive.
descend *(SYN.)* wane, lower, move, slope, incline, decline, slant, sink.
(ANT.) increase, appreciate, ameliorate, ascend.
descendant *(SYN.)* child, issue, progeny, offspring.
describe *(SYN.)* portray, picture, recount, depict, relate, characterize, represent, narrate.
description *(SYN.)* history, record, recital, account, computation, chronicle, reckoning, narration, detail, narrative.
(ANT.) misrepresentation, confusion, caricature.
desecration *(SYN.)* profanation, insult, defamation, reviling, abuse, maltreatment, aspersion, perversion, dishonor.
(ANT.) respect, commendation, approval, laudation.
desert *(SYN.)* forsake, wilderness, resign, abjure, abandon, wasteland, waste, leave, surrender, abdicate, quit, barren, uninhabited.
(ANT.) uphold, defend, stay, maintain, accompany, join, support.
deserter *(SYN.)* runaway, renegade, fugitive, defector.
deserts *(SYN.)* right, compensation, due, reward, requital, condign.
deserve *(SYN.)* earn, warrant, merit.
design *(SYN.)* drawing, purpose, outline, devise, intend, draw, contrive, draft, cunning, plan, artfulness, delineation, scheming, sketch, intent, invent, objective, mean, contrivance, plotting, intention, create.
(ANT.) candor, accident, result, chance.
designate *(SYN.)* manifest, indicate,

show, specify, denote, reveal, name, appoint, select, assign, disclose, signify, imply, nominate, intimate.
(ANT.) divert, mislead, conceal, falsify, distract.

desirable *(SYN.)* coveted, wanted.

desire *(SYN.)* longing, craving, yearning, appetite, lust, long for, crave, covet, want, request, ask, need, wish, aspiration, urge.
(ANT.) hate, aversion, loathing, abomination, detest, loathe, abhor, distaste.

desist *(SYN.)* cork, stop, cease, hinder, terminate, abstain, halt, interrupt, seal, arrest, plug, bar.
(ANT.) promote, begin, speed, proceed, start.

desolate *(SYN.)* forlorn, waste, bare, lonely, abandoned, wild, deserted, uninhabited, empty, sad, miserable, wretched, unhappy, bleak, forsaken.
(ANT.) crowded, teeming, populous, happy, cheerful, fertile, attended.

despair *(SYN.)* discouragement, pessimism, depression, hopelessness, despondency, gloom, desperation.
(ANT.) elation, optimism, hope, joy, confidence.

desperado *(SYN.)* criminal, crook, thug, gangster, hoodlum.

desperate *(SYN.)* reckless, determined, despairing, wild, daring, hopeless, despondent, audacious.
(ANT.) optimistic, composed, hopeful, collected, calm, assured.

despicable *(SYN.)* vulgar, offensive, base, vile, contemptible, selfish, low, mean, worthless, nasty.
(ANT.) noble, exalted, admirable, generous, worthy, dignified.

despise *(SYN.)* hate, scorn, detest, loathe, disdain, abhor, condemn, dislike, abominate.
(ANT.) honor, love, approve, like, admire.

despite *(SYN.)* notwithstanding.

despoil *(SYN.)* plunder, rob, loot.

despondent *(SYN.)* sad, dismal, depressed, somber, ejected, melancholy, doleful, sorrowful.
(ANT.) joyous, cheerful, merry, happy.

despot *(SYN.)* tyrant, ruler, oppressor, dictator.

despotic *(SYN.)* authoritative, unconditional, absolute, tyrannous, entire, unrestricted.
(ANT.) dependent, conditional, qualified, accountable.

destiny *(SYN.)* fate, portion, outcome, consequence, result, fortune, doom, lot.

destitute *(SYN.)* poor, penurious, needy, impecunious, poverty-stricken, impoverished, indigent.
(ANT.) opulent, wealthy, affluent, rich.

destroy *(SYN.)* raze, devastate, ruin, end, demolish, wreck, extinguish, annihilate, exterminate, obliterate, waste, slay, kill, eradicate.
(ANT.) make, construct, start, create, save, establish.

destroyed *(SYN.)* rent, smashed, interrupted, flattened, wrecked, broken, ruptured, crushed.
(ANT.) whole, repaired, integral, united.

destruction *(SYN.)* ruin, devastation, extinction, demolition.
(ANT.) beginning, creation.

destructive *(SYN.)* deadly, baneful, noxious, deleterious, injurious, pernicious, fatal, detrimental.
(ANT.) salutary, beneficial, creative.

detach *(SYN.)* deduct, remove, subtract, curtail, divide, shorten, decrease, disengage, reduce, separate, diminish.
(ANT.) hitch, grow, enlarge, increase, connect, amplify, attack, expand.

detail *(SYN.)* elaborate, commission, part, itemize, portion, division, fragment, assign, circumstance, segment.

detain *(SYN.)* impede, delay, hold back, retard, arrest, restrain, stay.
(ANT.) quicken, hasten, expedite, forward, precipitate.

detect *(SYN.)* discover, reveal, find, ascertain, determine, learn, originate, devise.
(ANT.) hide, screen, lose, cover, mask.

determinant *(SYN.)* reason, incentive, source, agent, principle, inducement.
(ANT.) result, effect, consequence, end.

determine *(SYN.)* decide, settle, end, conclude, ascertain, induce, fix, verify, resolve, establish, necessitate.

detest *(SYN.)* loathe, hate, despise.
(ANT.) savor, appreciate, like, love.

detriment *(SYN.)* injury, harm, disadvantage, damage.
(ANT.) benefit.

detrimental *(SYN.)* hurtful, mischievous, damaging, harmful.
(ANT.) salutary, advantageous, profitable, beneficial.

develop *(SYN.)* evolve, unfold, enlarge, amplify, expand, create, grow, advance, reveal, unfold, mature, elaborate.
(ANT.) wither, contract, degenerate, stunt, deteriorate, compress.

development *(SYN.)* growth, expansion, progress, unraveling, elaboration, evolution, maturing, unfolding.
(ANT.) compression, abbreviation, curtailment.

deviate *(SYN.)* deflect, stray, divert, diverge, wander, sidetrack, digress.
(ANT.) preserve, follow, remain, continue, persist.

device *(SYN.)* tool, utensil, means, channel, machine, agent, vehicle, gadget, apparatus, tools, instrument, contrivance.
(ANT.) preventive, impediment, hindrance, obstruction.

devilish *(SYN.)* diabolical, fiendish, diabolic, satanic, demonic.

devious *(SYN.)* tortuous, winding, distorted, circuitous, tricky, crooked, roundabout, cunning, erratic, indirect.
(ANT.) straight, direct, straightforward, honest.

devise *(SYN.)* create, concoct, invent, originate.

devote *(SYN.)* assign, dedicate, give, apply.

(ANT.) withhold, relinquish, ignore, withdraw.

devoted *(SYN.)* attached, dedicated, prone, wedded, addicted, ardent, earnest, loyal, disposed, inclined, fond, affectionate, faithful.
(ANT.) untrammeled, disinclined, detached, indisposed.

devotion *(SYN.)* piety, zeal, ardor, loyalty, dedication, religiousness, consecration, affection, love, devoutness, fidelity, attachment.
(ANT.) unfaithfulness, aversion, alienation, indifference.

devour *(SYN.)* consume, gulp, gorge, waste, eat, ruin, swallow, destroy.

devout *(SYN.)* sacred, religious, spiritual, holy, theological, pietistic, pious, sanctimonious, reverent.
(ANT.) profane, skeptical, atheistic, secular, impious.

dexterity *(SYN.)* talent, capability, qualification, aptness, skill, ability.
(ANT.) unreadiness, incapacity, disability, incompetency.

dexterous *(SYN.)* clever, adroit, handy, deft, facile, skillful, skilled, proficient.
(ANT.) awkward, clumsy.

dialect *(SYN.)* slang, jargon, cant, speech, idiom, tongue, diction, vernacular.
(ANT.) nonsense, drivel, babble, gibberish.

dialogue *(SYN.)* interview, chat, discussion, conference, exchange, talk, conversation.

diary *(SYN.)* memo, account, journal, words.

dicker *(SYN.)* haggle, bargain, negotiate.

dictate *(SYN.)* deliver, speak, record, command, order, direct.

dictator *(SYN.)* oppressor, tyrant, despot, persecutor, overlord, autocrat.

die *(SYN.)* fade, wane, cease, depart, wither, decay, decline, sink, expire, perish, decease, go, diminish, fail, languish, decrease.
(ANT.) live, begin, grow, survive, flourish.

difference *(SYN.)* inequality, variety, disparity, discord, distinction, dissension, dissimilarity, disagreement, contrast, separation.
(ANT.) harmony, similarity, identity, agreement, likeness, compatibility, kinship, resemblance.

different *(SYN.)* unlike, various, distinct, miscellaneous, divergent, sundry, contrary, differing, diverse, variant, incongruous, divers, unlike, changed, dissimilar, opposite.
(ANT.) similar, congruous, same, alike, identical.

differentiate *(SYN.)* separate, discriminate, distinguish, perceive, detect, recognize, discern.
(ANT.) confuse, omit, mingle, confound, overlook.

difficult *(SYN.)* involved, demanding, arduous, trying, complicated, hard, laborious, perplexing, hard, intricate.
(ANT.) simple, easy, facile, effortless.

difficulty *(SYN.)* trouble, hardship, fix, predicament, trouble.
(ANT.) ease.

diffuse *(SYN.)* spread, sparse, scattered, scanty, dispersed, thin, rare.
(ANT.) concentrated.

dig *(SYN.)* burrow, excavate, appreciate, understand.

digest *(SYN.)* consume, eat, reflect on, study, shorten, consider, summarize, abridge, abstract, abridgment, synopsis.

dignified *(SYN.)* serious, solemn, noble, stately, elegant.

dignify *(SYN.)* honor, elevate.
(ANT.) shame, degrade, humiliate.

dignity *(SYN.)* stateliness, distinction, bearing.

digress *(SYN.)* divert, wander, bend, stray, deflect, sidetrack, crook.
(ANT.) preserve, continue, remain, follow, persist.

dilate *(SYN.)* increase, widen, amplify, enlarge, augment, expand.
(ANT.) shrink, contract, restrict, abridge.

dilemma *(SYN.)* fix, strait, condition, scrape, difficulty, plight.
(ANT.) ease, calmness, satisfaction, comfort.

diligent *(SYN.)* patient, busy, hard-working, active, perseverant, assiduous, industrious, careful.
(ANT.) unconcerned, indifferent, apathetic, lethargic, careless.

dim *(SYN.)* pale, shadowy, faint, faded, unclear, vague, darken, dull, indistinct.
(ANT.) brighten, brilliant, bright, illuminate, glaring.

dimension *(SYN.)* size, importance, measure, extent.

diminish *(SYN.)* suppress, lower, decrease, shrink, wane, abate, reduce, lessen, assuage.
(ANT.) enlarge, revive, amplify, increase.

diminutive *(SYN.)* small, wee, tiny, little, minute.
(ANT.) large, big, great, gigantic, huge.

din *(SYN.)* tumult, clamor, sound, babble, outcry, row, noise, racket.
(ANT.) quiet, stillness, hush.

dine *(SYN.)* lunch, eat, sup, feed.

dingy *(SYN.)* dull, dark, dismal, dirty, drab, murky, gray.
(ANT.) cheerful, bright.

dip *(SYN.)* immerse, plunge, submerge, wet, swim.

diplomacy *(SYN.)* knack, dexterity, skill, address, poise, tact, finesse.
(ANT.) vulgarity, blunder, awkwardness, incompetence.

diplomatic *(SYN.)* politic, adroit, tactful, discreet, judicious, gracious, polite, discriminating.
(ANT.) rude, churlish, gruff, boorish, impolite, coarse.

dire *(SYN.)* horrible, terrible, appalling, fearful, harrowing, grievous, ghastly, awful, horrid, terrifying, dreadful, frightful, horrifying, monstrous, horrendous, repulsive.
(ANT.) lovely, enchanting, fascinating,

beautiful, enjoyable.

direct *(SYN.)* rule, manage, bid, order, level, command, conduct, regulate, point, indicate, show, aim, control, sight, guide, instruct, train, govern.
(ANT.) swerving, untruthful, misguide, distract, indirect, crooked, deceive.

direction *(SYN.)* way, order, course, instruction, tendency, management, route, trend, guidance, administration, supervision, inclination.

directly *(SYN.)* immediately, straight.

dirt *(SYN.)* pollution, soil, filthiness, filth.
(ANT.) cleanliness, cleanness.

dirty *(SYN.)* muddy, base, pitiful, filthy, shabby, foul, soiled, nasty, mean, grimy, low, obscene, untidy, indecent, unclean, messy, squalid, contemptible, sloppy.
(ANT.) pure, neat, wholesome, clean, presentable.

disability *(SYN.)* inability, weakness, handicap, incapacity, injury, unfitness, incompetence, impotence.
(ANT.) power, ability, strength, capability.

disable *(SYN.)* weaken, incapacitate, cripple.
(ANT.) strengthen.

disabled *(SYN.)* deformed, limping, weak, crippled, maimed, defective, unsatisfactory, halt, unconvincing, feeble.
(ANT.) vigorous, athletic, sound, agile, robust.

disadvantage *(SYN.)* drawback, hindrance, handicap, inconvenience, obstacle.
(ANT.) advantage, benefit, convenience.

disagree *(SYN.)* quarrel, dispute, differ, conflict.
(ANT.) agree.

disagreement *(SYN.)* nonconformity, variance, difference, objection, challenge, remonstrance, dissent.
(ANT.) assent, acceptance, compliance, agreement.

disappear *(SYN.)* end, fade out, vanish.
(ANT.) emerge, appear.

disappoint *(SYN.)* fail, displease, mislead, dissatisfy.
(ANT.) please, satisfy, gratify.

disappointment *(SYN.)* dissatisfaction, defeat, discouragement, failure.
(ANT.) pleasure, satisfaction, gratification.

disapprove *(SYN.)* object to, disfavor, oppose.
(ANT.) approve.

disarm *(SYN.)* paralyze, demilitarize.

disaster *(SYN.)* casualty, mishap, misfortune, catastrophe, accident, adversity, ruin, calamity.
(ANT.) fortune, advantage, welfare.

disavow *(SYN.)* reject, revoke, disclaim, retract, disown.
(ANT.) recognize, acknowledge.

disband *(SYN.)* scatter, split, dismiss, separate.

disbelief *(SYN.)* doubt, incredulity, skepticism.
(ANT.) certainty, credulity.

discard *(SYN.)* scrap, reject.

discern *(SYN.)* distinguish, see, descry, separate, differentiate, perceive, discriminate, detect, observe, recognize.
(ANT.) omit, confuse, overlook, mingle, confound.

discernment *(SYN.)* perception, sharpness, intelligence, perspicacity, acuity, keenness.
(ANT.) dullness, stupidity.

discharge *(SYN.)* remove, relieve, dismiss, banish, unburden, shoot, fire, explosion, eject, detonation, liberation, release, unload, discard, send.
(ANT.) retain, employ, enlist, hire, accept, recall, detain.

disciple *(SYN.)* learner, follower, student, adherent, supporter, scholar, pupil, votary, devotee.
(ANT.) guide, leader.

discipline *(SYN.)* training, order, instruction, drill, restraint, regulation, practice, correction, control, self-control, train, teach, exercise.
(ANT.) carelessness, sloppiness, confusion, negligence, messiness, chaos, turbulence.

disclaim *(SYN.)* retract, reject, deny, renounce, disavow, revoke.
(ANT.) recognize, acknowledge.

disclose *(SYN.)* show, divulge, betray, uncover, discover, reveal, expose.
(ANT.) hide, cloak, mask, cover, obscure, conceal.

discomfit *(SYN.)* malaise, concern, confuse, baffle, perplex, disconcert.

discomfort *(SYN.)* malaise, concern, anxiety, uneasiness.

disconcerted *(SYN.)* disturbed, agitated, upset.

disconnect *(SYN.)* divide, separate, unhook, disengage, detach.
(ANT.) connect, bind, attach, unify, engage.

disconsolate *(SYN.)* depressed, downcast, sorrowful, dejected, dismal, sad, unhappy, wretched, somber, cheerless, morose, lugubrious, miserable, mournful.
(ANT.) delightful, merry, glad, cheerful, happy.

discontent *(SYN.)* displeased, disgruntled, unhappy, dissatisfied, vexed.

discontinue *(SYN.)* postpone, delay, adjourn, stay, stop, defer, suspend, end, cease, interrupt.
(ANT.) prolong, persist, continue, start, begin, proceed, maintain.

discord *(SYN.)* disagreement, conflict.
(ANT.) concord, accord, agreement.

discourage *(SYN.)* hamper, obstruct, restrain, block, dishearten, retard, check, dispirit, thwart, depress, hinder, stop.
(ANT.) expedite, inspire, encourage, promote, inspirit, assisi, further.

discourteous *(SYN.)* gruff, rude, vulgar, blunt, impolite, saucy, uncivil, boorish, rough.
(ANT.) stately, courtly, civil, dignified, genteel.

discover *(SYN.)* find out, invent, expose, ascertain, devise, reveal, learn, determine, detect.

(ANT.) hide, screen, cover, conceal, lose.

discredit *(SYN.)* disbelieve, dishonor, doubt, disgrace, shame.

discreet *(SYN.)* politic, discriminating, judicious, adroit, prudent, cautious, wise, tactful, careful, diplomatic.
(ANT.) incautious, rude, coarse, boorish, tactless, imprudent, indiscreet, careless, gruff.

discrepant *(SYN.)* incompatible, wavering, contrary, irreconcilable, unsteady, illogical, contradictory.
(ANT.) correspondent, compatible, consistent.

discriminating *(SYN.)* exact, particular, critical, accurate, discerning.
(ANT.) unimportant, shallow, insignificant, superficial.

discrimination *(SYN.)* perspicacity, discernment, racism, wisdom, bias, sagacity, intolerance, prejudice, intelligence, understanding.
(ANT.) thoughtlessness, senselessness, arbitrariness.

discuss *(SYN.)* gossip, plead, discourse, blab, lecture, talk, chat, spout, mutter, deliberate, consider, reason, comment.

discussion *(SYN.)* speech, chatter, lecture, conference, talk, dialogue, conversation, rumor.
(ANT.) silence, correspondence, writing.

disdain *(SYN.)* derision, hatred, contempt, scorn, contumely, reject, haughtiness, detestation.
(ANT.) respect, esteem, reverence, admire, prize, honor, admiration, awe, regard.

disdainful *(SYN.)* haughty, scornful, arrogant, contemptuous.
(ANT.) awed, admiring, regardful.

disease *(SYN.)* malady, disorder, ailment, illness, affliction, infirmity, complaint, sickness.
(ANT.) soundness, health, vigor.

disentangle *(SYN.)* unwind, untie, clear, unravel, unknot, unsnarl, untangle.

disfigured *(SYN.)* deformed, marred, defaced, scarred.

disgrace *(SYN.)* odium, chagrin, shame, mortification, embarrassment, humiliate, scandal, dishonor, mortification.
(ANT.) renown, glory, respect, praise, dignity, honor.

disgraceful *(SYN.)* ignominious, shameful, discreditable, disreputable, scandalous, dishonorable.
(ANT.) renowned, esteemed, respectable, honorable.

disguise *(SYN.)* excuse, simulation, pretension, hide, camouflage, make-up, cover-up, mask, conceal, screen, affectation, pretext.
(ANT.) show, reality, actuality, display, reveal, sincerity, fact.

disgust *(SYN.)* offend, repulse, nauseate, revolt, sicken.
(ANT.) admiration, liking.

disgusting *(SYN.)* repulsive, nauseating, revolting, nauseous, repugnant

dish *(SYN.)* serve, container, give, receptacle.

dishearten *(SYN.)* depress, sadden, discourage.

disheveled *(SYN.)* mussed, sloppy, rumpled, untidy.

dishonest *(SYN.)* crooked, impure, unsound, false, contaminated, venal, corrupt, putrid, thievish, vitiated, tainted.
(ANT.) upright, honest, straightforward.

dishonor *(SYN.)* disrepute, scandal, indignity, chagrin, mortification, shame, obloquy, defamation, humiliation, disgrace, scandal.
(ANT.) renown, glory, praise, honor, dignity.

disinclined *(SYN.)* unwilling, reluctant, loath.

disingenuous *(SYN.)* tricky, deceitful, scheming, dishonest, underhanded, cunning, artful, crafty, insidious.

disintegrate *(SYN.)* decompose, dwindle, spoil, decay, wane, ebb, decline, rot.
(ANT.) increase, flourish, rise, grow.

disinterested *(SYN.)* unbiased, open-minded, neutral, impartial, unprejudiced.

dislike *(SYN.)* aversion, dread, reluctance, abhorrence, disinclination, hatred, repugnance.
(ANT.) devotion, affection, enthusiasm, attachment.

disloyal *(SYN.)* false, treasonable, apostate, unfaithful, recreant, treacherous, untrue, perfidious, traitorous, faithless.
(ANT.) true, devoted, constant, loyal.

dismal *(SYN.)* dark, lonesome, somber, bleak, dull, sad, doleful, sorrowful, cheerless, depressing, dreary, funeral, gloomy, melancholy.
(ANT.) lively, gay, happy, lighthearted, charming, cheerful.

dismantle *(SYN.)* take apart, wreck, disassemble.

dismay *(SYN.)* disturb, bother, dishearten, horror, alarm, bewilder, frighten, scare, discourage, confuse.
(ANT.) encourage, hearten.

dismiss *(SYN.)* remove, discharge, discard, release, liberate, exile, banish, eject, oust.
(ANT.) retain, detain, engage, hire, accept, recall.

disobedient *(SYN.)* refractory, forward, unruly, insubordinate, defiant, rebellious, undutiful.
(ANT.) submissive, compliant, obedient.

disobey *(SYN.)* invade, break, violate, infringe, defile.

disorder *(SYN.)* tumult, chaos, jumble, confusion, muddle, turmoil, anarchy.
(ANT.) organization, neatness, system, order.

disorganization *(SYN.)* jumble, confusion, muddle, anarchy.
(ANT.) system, order.

disorganized *(SYN.)* muddled, confused, indistinct, bewildered, mixed.
(ANT.) organized, lucid, clear, plain.

disown *(SYN.)* deny, renounce, reject, repudiate, forsake, disinherit.

disparaging *(SYN.)* belittling, deprecatory, discrediting, deprecating.

disparage *(SYN.)* undervalue, depreciate, lower, belittle, derogate,

minimize, decry, discredit.
(ANT.) exalting, praise, aggrandize, magnify, commend.
disparagement *(SYN.)* lowering, decrying, undervaluing, belittling, minimizing.
(ANT.) praise, exalting, aggrandizement, magnification.
dispassionate *(SYN.)* calm, cool, composed, controlled, unemotional, imperturbable.
dispatch *(SYN.)* throw, impel, transmit, emit, cast, finish, report, message, send, speed, achieve, conclude, communication, promptness, discharge.
(ANT.) reluctance, get, retain, bring, slowness, hold.
dispel *(SYN.)* disseminate, scatter, disperse, separate, diffuse.
(ANT.) collect, accumulate, gather.
dispense *(SYN.)* deal, give, allot, assign, apportion, mete, distribute, grant, allocate, measure.
(ANT.) refuse, withhold, confiscate, retain, keep.
disperse *(SYN.)* dissipate, scatter, disseminate, diffuse, separate, dispel.
(ANT.) collect, amass, gather, assemble, accumulate.
dispirited *(SYN.)* downhearted, unhappy, dejected, disheartened, sad, depressed, melancholy.
(ANT.) cheerful, happy, optimistic.
displace *(SYN.)* remove, transport, lodge, shift, move.
(ANT.) retain, leave, stay, remain.
display *(SYN.)* parade, exhibit, show, expose, reveal, demonstrate, showing, uncover, flaunt.
(ANT.) hide, cover, conceal.
displeasure *(SYN.)* dislike, disapproval, dissatisfaction, distaste, discontentment.
disposal *(SYN.)* elimination, adjustment, removal, release, arrangement, administration, settlement.
dispose *(SYN.)* settle, adjust, arrange.
disposition *(SYN.)* behavior, character, deed, deportment, action, manner, bearing, temperament, nature, demeanor, personality, carriage.
dispossess *(SYN.)* eject, expel, evict, oust, dislodge.
disprove *(SYN.)* refute, deny, invalidate, controvert.
dispute *(SYN.)* squabble, debate, argument, controversy, contention, disagreement, bicker, contest, argue, contend, quarrel, contradict, discuss, deny, oppose, altercate.
(ANT.) harmony, concord, agreement, allow, concur, agree, concede, decision.
disregard *(SYN.)* slight, omit, ignore, inattention, oversight, skip, neglect, overlook.
(ANT.) regard, include.
disrepair *(SYN.)* ruin, decay, dilapidation, destruction.
disreputable *(SYN.)* dishonored, notorious, dishonorable, disgraced.
disrespectful *(SYN.)* fresh, impertinent, rude, impolite, impudent.
(ANT.) polite, respectful, courteous.
dissect *(SYN.)* examine, cut, analyze.
disseminate *(SYN.)* publish, circulate, spread, publish, broadcast.
dissent *(SYN.)* objection, challenge, disagreement, protest, remonstrance, difference, nonconformity, variance, noncompliance.
(ANT.) assent, acceptance, compliance, agreement.
dissertation *(SYN.)* thesis, treatise, disquisition.
dissimilar *(SYN.)* diverse, unlike, various, distinct, contrary, sundry, different, miscellaneous.
(ANT.) same, alike, similar, congruous.
dissimulation *(SYN.)* pretense, deceit, sanctimony, hypocrisy, cant.
(ANT.) honesty, candor, openness, frankness, truth.
dissipate *(SYN.)* misuse, squander, dwindle, consume, waste, lavish, diminish.
(ANT.) save, conserve, preserve, accumulate, economize.
dissolve *(SYN.)* liquefy, end, cease, melt, fade, disappear.
distant *(SYN.)* stiff, cold, removed, far, afar, unfriendly, remote, faraway, separated, aloof, reserved.
(ANT.) nigh, friendly, close, cordial, near.
distasteful *(SYN.)* disagreeable, unpleasant, objectionable.
distend *(SYN.)* swell, widen, magnify, expand, enlarge.
distinct *(SYN.)* plain, evident, lucid, visible, apparent, different, separate, individual, obvious, manifest, clear.
(ANT.) vague, indistinct, uncertain, obscure, ambiguous.
distinction *(SYN.)* importance, peculiarity, trait, honor, fame, characteristic, repute, quality, renown, prominence, attribute, property.
(ANT.) nature, substance, essence, being.
distinctive *(SYN.)* odd, exceptional, rare, individual, eccentric, special, strange.
(ANT.) ordinary, general, common, normal.
distinguish *(SYN.)* recognize, differentiate, divide, classify, descry, discern, separate, perceive, detect.
(ANT.) mingle, conjoin, blend, found, omit, confuse, overlook.
distinguished *(SYN.)* eminent, illustrious, renowned, celebrated, elevated, noted, important, famous, prominent.
(ANT.) ordinary, common, unknown, undistinguished, obscure, unimportant.
distort *(SYN.)* contort, falsify, twist, misrepresent.
distract *(SYN.)* occupy, bewilder, disturb, divert, confuse.
(ANT.) focus, concentrate.
distracted *(SYN.)* abstracted, preoccupied, absent.
(ANT.) attentive, attending, watchful, present.
distraction *(SYN.)* entertainment, confusion, amusement, diversion.

distress *(SYN.)* torment, misery, trouble, worry, pain, agony, torture, anguish, anxiety, disaster, wretchedness, peril, danger, suffering.
(ANT.) joy, solace, comfort, relief.
distribute *(SYN.)* deal, sort, allot, mete, classify, share, issue, dole, apportion, allocate, dispense, group.
district *(SYN.)* domain, place, territory, country, region, division, neighborhood, section, area, land.
distrust *(SYN.)* scruple, unbelief, suspect, mistrust, hesitation, suspense, uncertainty, doubt, suspicion, ambiguity.
(ANT.) faith, conviction, trust, belief, determination.
disturb *(SYN.)* perturb, vex, confuse, worry, agitate, derange, unsettle, perplex, rouse, bother, trouble, annoy, interrupt, discompose.
(ANT.) quiet, order, calm, settle, pacify, soothe.
disturbance *(SYN.)* disorder, commotion, confusion, riot, fight, brawl.
(ANT.) calm, tranquillify, serenity.
disturbed *(SYN.)* neurotic, psychopathic, psychoneurotic, psychotic.
(ANT.) normal.
diverge *(SYN.)* fork, separate.
(ANT.) converge, join, merge.
diverse *(SYN.)* unlike, various, different, several.
diversify *(SYN.)* change, modify, alter.
diversion *(SYN.)* entertainment, sport, distraction, amusement, recreation.
divert *(SYN.)* detract, amuse, confuse, distract, deflect, entertain, tickle.
(ANT.) tire, bore, weary.
divide *(SYN.)* share, split, detach, cleave, apportion, sunder, part, distribute, allocate, disunite, estrange, separate, allot, sever.
(ANT.) merge, unite, convene, join, gather, combine.
divine *(SYN.)* holy, supernatural, godlike, transcendent, celestial, heavenly.
(ANT.) mundane, wicked, blasphemous, profane, diabolical.
division *(SYN.)* partition, separation, sharing, section, segment, part, portion.
(ANT.) union, agreement.
divorce *(SYN.)* disjoin, disconnect, separate, divide.
divulge *(SYN.)* discover, release, expose, show, betray, reveal, admit, disclose, uncover.
(ANT.) hide, conceal, cloak, cover.
dizzy *(SYN.)* staggering, unsteady, giddy, light-headed, confused.
(ANT.) rational, clearheaded, unconfused.
do *(SYN.)* conduct, perform, work, suffice, accomplish, finish, transact, serve, discharge, execute, complete, carry on, make, settle, conclude, fulfill, consummate, produce, terminate, observe, practice.
docile *(SYN.)* pliant, tame, complaint, teachable, obedient, submissive, yielding.
(ANT.) unruly, obstinate, ungovernable, mulish.
dock *(SYN.)* moor, clip, anchor, tie.
doctor *(SYN.)* heal, treat, medic, remedy, cure.
doctrine *(SYN.)* tenet, precept, belief, dogma, teaching, principle, creed.
(ANT.) deed, practice, conduct, perform.
doctrinaire *(SYN.)* formal, dogmatic, overbearing, authoritarian, formal, arrogant, magisterial.
(ANT.) skeptical, indecisive, fluctuating.
document *(SYN.)* report, minute, memorial, vestige, account, note, trace.
dodge *(SYN.)* equivocate, recoil, elude, evade, avoid, duck.
dogma *(SYN.)* tenet, doctrine, belief, teaching, creed.
(ANT.) deed, practice, conduct, performance.
dogmatic *(SYN.)* formal, domineering, authoritarian, doctrinaire, opinionated, dictatorial, positive, arrogant, authoritative, overbearing, doctrinal, magisterial.
(ANT.) skeptical, indecisive, fluctuating.
doing *(SYN.)* feat, performance, act, deed, action, accomplishment, transaction.
(ANT.) intention, inactivity, cessation, inhibition.
dole *(SYN.)* deal, spread, allot, relief, divide, apportion, alms, welfare, distribute, dispense.
doleful *(SYN.)* dark, depressed, sad, dismal, dejected, bleak, dull, blue, sorrowful, unhappy, morose, lonesome, mournful, somber.
(ANT.) gay, lively, cheerful, joyous.
dolt *(SYN.)* blockhead, dunce.
domain *(SYN.)* place, division, region, territory, empire, country, charge, kingdom, realm, quarter, dominion, bailiwick, jurisdiction, land.
domestic *(SYN.)* family, tame, native, servant, homemade, household, internal.
(ANT.) alien, foreign, outside.
domesticate *(SYN.)* train, tame, housebreak, teach.
domicile *(SYN.)* dwelling, residence, home, abode.
dominate *(SYN.)* control, manage, rule, influence, subjugate, command, govern, tyrannize, direct, regulate.
(ANT.) follow, ignore, abandon, submit, forsake.
domination *(SYN.)* mastery, sway, ascendancy, transcendence.
don *(SYN.)* wear, slip on.
donation *(SYN.)* gift, bequest, present, benefaction, grant, contribution, offering, largess, boon.
(ANT.) earnings, purchase, deprivation, loss.
done *(SYN.)* complete, concluded, finished, over, terminated.
doom *(SYN.)* fortune, issue, result, destruction, destiny, consequence, fate, outcome, destine, ruin, death, lot.
doomed *(SYN.)* fated, predestined, destined, foreordained.

dormant *(SYN.)* unemployed, inert, lazy, unoccupied, idle, indolent.
(ANT.) working, employed, occupied, active, industrious.
dose *(SYN.)* quantity, amount, portion.
dote *(SYN.)* indulge, treasure, coddle, pamper, spoil.
(ANT.) ignore.
double *(SYN.)* copy, fold, duplicate.
doubt *(SYN.)* distrust, incredulity, suspicion, hesitation, uncertainty, question, scruple, ambiguity, skepticism, suspect, mistrust, unbelief, suspense.
(ANT.) conviction, belief, determination, trust, certainty.
doubtful *(SYN.)* uncertain, unsettled, dubious, questionable, unsure, undetermined.
doubtless *(SYN.)* certainly, undoubtedly, assuredly, positively, unquestionably.
dour *(SYN.)* gloomy, sulky, crabbed, morose, fretful.
(ANT.) joyous, pleasant, amiable, merry.
douse *(SYN.)* immerse, quench, dip, dunk, extinguish.
dowdy *(SYN.)* messy, unkempt, untidy, sloppy, shabby, frowzy.
downcast *(SYN.)* sad, disheartened, unhappy, downhearted, dejected, dispirited, discourage, depressed, glum.
downfall *(SYN.)* destruction, comedown.
downgrade *(SYN.)* reduce, lower, diminish, decrease, depreciate.
(ANT.) improve, upgrade, appreciate.
downhearted *(SYN.)* glum, discouraged, depressed, gloomy, downcast, sad, dejected.
(ANT.) enthusiastic, cheerful, happy.
downpour *(SYN.)* cloudburst, deluge, flood.
downright *(SYN.)* totally, positively, completely, definitely.
dowry *(SYN.)* endowment, gift, settlement, talent, ability.
drab *(SYN.)* flat, dull, lifeless, unattractive.
draft *(SYN.)* air, induction, wind, enrollment, drawing, outline.
drag *(SYN.)* heave, pull, tug, crawl, draw, tarry, tow, haul, delay.
drain *(SYN.)* empty, deprive, dry, filter, spend, tap, exhaust, waste, sap, use.
(ANT.) fulfill, fill.
drama *(SYN.)* show, play, production, piece.
dramatist *(SYN.)* playwright.
drape *(SYN.)* flow, cover, hang.
drastic *(SYN.)* severe, rough, extreme, violent, tough, intense.
draw *(SYN.)* tug, obtain, trace, lure, drag, attract, persuade, induce, haul, write, remove, extend, stretch, take out, allure, pull, prolong, extract, tow, draft, delineate, unsheathe, lure, depict, entice, sketch, infer.
(ANT.) shorten, contract, propel, alienate, drive.
drawback *(SYN.)* snag, hitch, disadvantage, handicap, deficiency, difficulty, check, obstacle, hindrance, impediment.
(ANT.) gain, benefit, windfall, advantage.
drawing *(SYN.)* likeness, print, view, engraving, portrait, sketch, illustration, picture, resemblance, scene.
drawn *(SYN.)* tired, haggard, taut, strained, harrowed, weary, tense, sapped, spent.
(ANT.) rested, relaxed, energetic, fresh.
draw out *(SYN.)* protract, extend, persist, prolong, lengthen, sustain, continue.
(ANT.) reduce, curtail, shorten, abridge.
draw up *(SYN.)* draft, write out, prepare, compose, indite, formulate, wail, stay.
dread *(SYN.)* awe, horror, fear, terror, alarm, reverence, apprehension, foreboding.
(ANT.) courage, boldness, assurance, confidence.
dreadful *(SYN.)* dire, inspiring, ghastly, appalling, horrid, impressive, terrible, awful, frightful, horrible, bad, hideous, awesome, outrageous, repulsive.
(ANT.) fascinating, beautiful, enjoyable, enchanting, lovely.
dream *(SYN.)* fantasy, wish, hope, vision, daydream, reverie, imagine, fantasize, fancy, invent, muse.
dream up *(SYN.)* cook up, create, think up, concost, contrive, originate, imagine, devise.
dreary *(SYN.)* dull, sad, bleak, lonesome, gloomy, chilling, somber, depressing, dismal, cheerless, dark.
(ANT.) lively, hopeful, gay, cheerful, bright, joyous.
dregs *(SYN.)* riffraff, scum, outcasts, dross, leftovers, flotsam.
drench *(SYN.)* wet, bathe, flood, soak, saturate.
dress *(SYN.)* clothing, costume, apparel, attire, wardrobe, garments, clothes, frock, garb.
(ANT.) undress, strip, divest, disrobe.
dresser *(SYN.)* dude, clotherhorse, fop, dandy.
dressing *(SYN.)* bandage, seasoning, medicine, sauce.
dressy *(SYN.)* flashy, swank, showy, dapper.
(ANT.) dowdy, drab, frumpy, shabby, tacky.
dribble *(SYN.)* fall, drip, leak, slaver, slobber.
drift *(SYN.)* roam, tendency, meander, sail, float, wander, intention, stray.
drifter *(SYN.)* hobo, tramp, vagabond.
drill *(SYN.)* employment, lesson, task, use, activity, operation, training.
(ANT.) relaxation, indolence, rest, idleness, repose.
drink *(SYN.)* gulp, swallow, imbibe, beverage, refreshment, potion.
drip *(SYN.)* dribble, drop, trickle.
drive *(SYN.)* impel, coerce, oblige, force, push, direct, constrain, journey, urge, enforce, trip, handle, ride, propel, control, run, compel.
driver *(SYN.)* motorist, operator,

teamster, trucker, motorman, pilot, coachman.
drone *(SYN.)* buzz, hum, loafer, idler, nonworker.
drool *(SYN.)* drivel, slaver, dribble, spit, gibber, jabber, twaddle, trickle, salivate.
droop *(SYN.)* dangle, weaken, hang, sink, fail, settle, sag, weary, languish, despond.
(ANT.) stand, tower, extend, rise, straighten.
drop *(SYN.)* droop, dribble, topple, collapse, downward, drip, trickle, tumble.
(ANT.) ascend, mount, steady, arise, soar.
drove *(SYN.)* flock, herd.
drown *(SYN.)* sink, inundate, submerge, immerse.
drowse *(SYN.)* nap, doze, catnap, snooze, sleep, slumber, rest.
drowsy *(SYN.)* dozing, torpid, soothing, dreamy, sleepy, comatose, lethargic.
(ANT.) alert, awake, sharp, keen, acute.
drub *(SYN.)* wallop, thrash, beat, thump, cane, flog, rout, outclass, overcome, defeat, outplay.
drubbing *(SYN.)* walloping, flogging, beating, pounding,thrashing, licking.
drudge *(SYN.)* work, labor, hack, slave, toil, grub.
drudgery *(SYN.)* toil, travail, effort, task, work, endeavor, labor.
(ANT.) recreation, indolence, leisure.
drug *(SYN.)* remedy, medicine, stupefy, anesthetize, numb, benumb.
drugged *(SYN.)* numb, doped, numbed, stupefied, dazed, groggy, denumbed.
druggist *(SYN.)* pharmacologist, chemist.
drunk *(SYN.)* tight, intoxicated, soused, drunken, inebriated, alcoholic.
drunkard *(SYN.)* sot, drunk, alcoholic, lush.
dry *(SYN.)* thirsty, dehydrated, vapid, plain, arid, uninteresting, drained.
(ANT.) fresh, wet, soaked, fascinating, attractive, lively, moist, interesting.
dub *(SYN.)* nickname, christen, came, call, bestow, entitle, label.
dubious *(SYN.)* unsure, uncertain, undecided, hesitant, spurious, unreliable.
(ANT.) decided, fixed, irrefutable, definite, genuine, unquestionable.
duck *(SYN.)* douse, dip, submerse, submerge, immerse, plunge, wet, souse.
(ANT.) raise, confront, face, elevate, cope with, undertake, assume.
duct *(SYN.)* pipe, tube, passage, vein, canal, funnel, gutter, main, trough, artery.
due *(SYN.)* payable, unpaid, owing, owed, imminent, expected.
duel *(SYN.)* competition, contest, engagement, rivalry, combat, strife.
dues *(SYN.)* assessment, fees, cost, levy, admission, fare, toll, demand, contribution.
duffer *(SYN.)* bungler, slouch, blunderer, novice, incompetent, fumbler.
(ANT.) master, expert, pro.
dull *(SYN.)* commonplace, slow, sad, dreary, boring, stupid, uninteresting, blunt, tedious, dulled, dumb, tiring.
(ANT.) clear, animated, interesting.
dullard *(SYN.)* dolt, dunce, moron, clod, blockhead, numskull.
dumb *(SYN.)* dull, witless, ignorant, mute, speechless, brainless, dense.
(ANT.) discerning, bright, alert, clever, intelligent.
dumbfound *(SYN.)* stagger, stun, nonplus, stupefy, overwhelm, amaze.
dumfounded *(SYN.)* shocked, astonished, flabbergasted, astounded.
dump *(SYN.)* heap, fling down, drop, empty, unload, clear out, dispose of.
(ANT.) store, fill, load, hoard, pack.
dunce *(SYN.)* deadhead, nitwit, booby, idiot, ignoramus, numskull, noddy.
dungeon *(SYN.)* jail, prison, keep, cell.
dunk *(SYN.)* plunge, douse, submerge.
(ANT.) uplift, elevate, recover.
dupe *(SYN.)* sucker, victim, gull, pushover, fool, cheat, deceive, defraud.
duplicate *(SYN.)* replica, replicate, facsimile, copy, reproduce, clone, double.
(ANT.) prototype.
duplicity *(SYN.)* dissimulation, deception, hypocrisy, deceitfulness.
(ANT.) openness, artlessness, candor, straightforwardness, genuineness.
durability *(SYN.)* might, strength, force, sturdiness, intensity, potency, vigor.
(ANT.) weakness, frailty, feebleness.
durable *(SYN.)* constant, firm, fixed, unchangeable, enduring, abiding.
(ANT.) unstable, temporary, perishable, transitory.
duration *(SYN.)* time, term, period, while, stage, era, epoch, interim.
duress *(SYN.)* force, demand, compulsion, emergency, pressure.
dusky *(SYN.)* sable, black, dark, darkish, swarthy, tawny, gloomy, overcast.
(ANT.) light, fair, white, pale, shining, clear, bright.
dusty *(SYN.)* sooty, unclean, dirty, musty, grubby, unswept, crumbly.
(ANT.) polished, immaculate, clean.
dutiful *(SYN.)* docile, faithful, obedient.
(ANT.) disobedient, willful, unruly.
duty *(SYN.)* bond, responsibility, accountability, faithfulness, function.
(ANT.) freedom, choice.
dwarf *(SYN.)* midget, runt, reduce, stunt, minimize, tiny.
(ANT.) mammoth, colossus, monster.
dwell *(SYN.)* inhabit, roost, settle, abide, live, reside.
dwelling *(SYN.)* seat, quarters, abode, home, hearth, residence, house.
dwell on *(SYN.)* insist, linger over, harp on, emphasize.
(ANT.) skip, neglect, skim over.
dwindle *(SYN.)* wane, decrease, diminish, fade, subside, ebb, shrivel.
(ANT.) enlarge, wax, increase, grow.
dying *(SYN.)* failing, expiring, waning, passing, final, declining, receding.
(ANT.) thriving, booming, flourishing.
dynamic *(SYN.)* active, forceful, kinetic, energetic, motive, mighty, vigorous.
(ANT.) sleepy, stable, inert, fixed, dead, still, uninspiring, ineffectual, listless.

eager *(SYN.)* avid, hot, anxious, fervent, enthusiastic, impatient, ardent, impassioned, yearning.
(ANT.) unconcerned, apathetic, impassioned, dull, uninterested, indifferent.
early *(SYN.)* betimes, opportune, first, beforehand, advanced, soon, shortly.
(ANT.) retarded, late, tardy, overdue.
earmark *(SYN.)* peculiarity, characteristic, brand, sign, stamp, trademark.
earn *(SYN.)* attain, win, get, achieve, obtain, gain, deserve, realize, collect, net, acquire, merit.
(ANT.) lose, waste, consume, forfeit.
earnest *(SYN.)* sincere, decided, determined, intent, serious, eager, resolute.
(ANT.) indifferent, frivolous, insincere.
earnings *(SYN.)* wages, pay, income.
earth *(SYN.)* globe, dirt, land, world, turf, soil, sod, ground.
earthly *(SYN.)* everyday, worldly.
(ANT.) heavenly.
earthy *(SYN.)* earthlike, coarse, earthen, crude, unrefined, vulgar.
(ANT.) tasteful, elegant, polished, refined.
ease *(SYN.)* lighten, alleviate, pacify, soothe, allay, comfort, contentedness, assuage, reduce, rest, facilitate, relaxation, calm, repose, mitigate, contentment, relax.
(ANT.) worry, disturb, confound, aggravate, difficulty, effort, trouble, intensify, distress.
easily *(SYN.)* readily, effortlessly, smoothly, naturally, facilely.
(ANT.) hardly, painfully, laboriously.
easiness *(SYN.)* repose, comfort, satisfaction, contentment, liberty, leisure, facility, simplicity.
(ANT.) unrest, torment, arduousness, difficulty, discomfort.
easy *(SYN.)* light, simple, facile, gentle, effortless, unhurried, comfortable, pleasant, cozy, relaxed, plain, uncomplicated, restful.
(ANT.) hard, demanding, awkward, strict, difficult, formal.
easygoing *(SYN.)* calm, mild, complacent, relaxed, unconcerned, serene, uncritical, carefree, unhurried.
(ANT.) severe, demanding, strict, harsh.
eat *(SYN.)* consume, swallow, dine, corrode, chew, lunch, devour, feast, breakfast, erode.
eavesdrop *(SYN.)* spy, snoop, overhear.
eavesdropper *(SYN.)* monitor, listener, snoop, spy.
ebb *(SYN.)* diminish, recede, decline, decrease, retreat, lessen.
(ANT.) wax, grow, thrive, increase, swell.
ebullient *(SYN.)* buoyant, exuberant.
(ANT.) lethargic, sad, depressed.
eccentric *(SYN.)* odd, irregular, unusual, abnormal, peculiar.
(ANT.) ordinary, conventional, normal.
eccentricity *(SYN.)* kink, whim, freak, caprice, foible, quirk, oddness, strangeness, aberration.
(ANT.) normality, conventionality.
ecclesiastical *(SYN.)* religious, clerical.
echelon *(SYN.)* rank, grade, place, status.
echo *(SYN.)* response, imitation, suggestion, trace, imitate, repeat.
eclectic *(SYN.)* selective, diverse, broad, liberal, comprehensive.
(ANT.) limited, narrow, rigid, confined.
eclipse *(SYN.)* conceal, screen, hide, cover, obscure, overcast, veil.
economical *(SYN.)* saving, thrifty, careful, frugal, provident, sparing.
(ANT.) wasteful, extravagant, lavish, improvident, prodigal.
economize *(SYN.)* pinch, scrimp, save.
economy *(SYN.)* saving, thrift.
ecstasy *(SYN.)* frenzy, gladness, de-light, madness, joy, glee, exaltation, pleasure, trance, rapture.
(ANT.) misery, melancholy, sadness.
ecstatic *(SYN.)* overjoyed, thrilled, delighted, happy, elated.
edge *(SYN.)* margin, brim, verge, brink, border, keenness, extremity, boundary, trim, periphery, rim, sting.
(ANT.) dullness, center, bluntness.
edgy *(SYN.)* tense, nervous, irritable.
edict *(SYN.)* declaration, order, ruling, decree, command, law, proclamation.
edifice *(SYN.)* construction, building, establishment.
edit *(SYN.)* check, revise, correct.
educate *(SYN.)* instruct, teach, train.
education *(SYN.)* training, development, knowledge, learning, cultivation, schooling, instruction, study.
eerie *(SYN.)* weird, fearful, ghastly, spooky, strange.
efface *(SYN.)* obliterate, erase.
effect *(SYN.)* produce, consequence, evoke, cause, make, complete, outcome, result, determine.
effective *(SYN.)* efficient, practical.
(ANT.) useless, wasteful, ineffective.
efficiency *(SYN.)* efficacy, capability, effectiveness, competency, ability.
(ANT.) wastefulness, inability.
efficient *(SYN.)* efficacious, skillful, capable, adept, competent, useful, effectual, effective, apt, proficient.
(ANT.) inefficient, unskilled.
effort *(SYN.)* labor, endeavor, pains, essay, trial, exertion, struggle, strain, try, attempt, strife, toil.
effortless *(SYN.)* simple, easy.
egg *(SYN.)* stir, ovum, incite, urge, arouse, embryo, provoke.
egghead *(SYN.)* intellectual, pedant.
egoism *(SYN.)* self-interest, conceit, pride, selfishness, egotism.
(ANT.) modesty, generosity.
eject *(SYN.)* remove, oust, eliminate.
(ANT.) include.
elaborate *(SYN.)* detail, develop, decorated, decorative, complex.
(ANT.) simplify, simple, unadorned.
elapse *(SYN.)* expire.
elastic *(SYN.)* yielding, flexible, adaptable, pliable.
elated *(SYN.)* delighted, rejoicing, overjoyed, jubilant.
(ANT.) sad, unhappy.
elder *(SYN.)* senior.
(ANT.) younger.
elderly *(SYN.)* aged, old.
(ANT.) young, youthful.
elect *(SYN.)* pick, appoint, choose.

electrify *(SYN.)* shock, charge, stir, upset, generate, agitate.
elegant *(SYN.)* tasteful, refined, cultivated, choice, superior, fine.
(ANT.) coarse, unpolished, tasteless.
elementary *(SYN.)* simple, primary, basic, uncomplicated, initial, beginning, fundamental.
(ANT.) involved, complex, sophisticated, complicated.
elevate *(SYN.)* raise, lift.
(ANT.) lower, drop.
elf *(SYN.)* devil, fairy, imp.
elicit *(SYN.)* summon.
eligible *(SYN.)* fit, suitable, qualified.
eliminate *(SYN.)* expel, eject, remove, dislodge, extirpate, erase, oust.
(ANT.) admit, involve.
elite *(SYN.)* nobility, upper-class, aristocracy, gentry.
(ANT.) mob, proletariat.
elongate *(SYN.)* prolong, lengthen.
elope *(SYN.)* escape, flee.
eloquent *(SYN.)* expressive, fluent, articulate, glib, meaningful.
(ANT.) inarticulate.
else *(SYN.)* different, another, other.
elude *(SYN.)* escape, miss, avoid, dodge.
(ANT.) add, include.
emaciated *(SYN.)* wasted, thin, starved, withered, shriveled, gaunt, shrunken, drawn, undernourished.
emancipate *(SYN.)* free, deliver, save.
(ANT.) restrain.
embankment *(SYN.)* shore, dam, bank, fortification, buttress.
embargo *(SYN.)* restriction, restraint.
embark *(SYN.)* board, depart.
embarrass *(SYN.)* discomfit, rattle, distress, hamper, fluster, entangle, abash, mortify, confuse, shame, trouble.
(ANT.) relieve, encourage, help.
embassy *(SYN.)* ministry, legation, consulate.
embed *(SYN.)* root, inset, enclose, plant.
embellish *(SYN.)* adorn, decorate.
embezzle *(SYN.)* pilfer, misuse, rob, misappropriate, steal, take.
embitter *(SYN.)* provoke, arouse, alienate, anger, inflame.
emblem *(SYN.)* token, mark, symbol, badge.
embody *(SYN.)* comprise, cover, embrace, include.
embrace *(SYN.)* espouse, accept, receive, comprehend, contain, welcome, comprise, cover, clasp, include, adopt, hug.
(ANT.) spurn, reject, bar, exclude, repudiate.
embroider *(SYN.)* decorate, adorn, stitch, trim, overstate, embellish, ornament, exaggerate, magnify.
emerge *(SYN.)* surface, show, appear.
emergency *(SYN.)* strait, pass, crisis, urgency, predicament, pinch.
eminent *(SYN.)* renowned, glorious, distinguished, noted, celebrated, elevated, glorious, important, conspicuous, prominent, famous.
(ANT.) ordinary, commonplace, unknown, undistinguished, common.
emissary *(SYN.)* envoy, minister, delegate, agent, spy.
emit *(SYN.)* expel, breathe, shoot, hurl, ooze, vent, belch, discharge.
emotion *(SYN.)* passion, turmoil, perturbation, affection, sentiment, feeling, trepidation, agitation.
(ANT.) dispassion, indifference, tranquillity, calm, restraint.
emotional *(SYN.)* ardent, passionate, stirring, zealous, impetuous, overwrought, enthusiastic.
(ANT.) tranquil, calm, placid.
emphasis *(SYN.)* accent, stress, insistence.
emphatic *(SYN.)* positive, definite, forceful, energetic, strong.
(ANT.) lax, quiet, unforceful.
employ *(SYN.)* avail, use, devote, apply, utilize, engage, sign, hire, retain, service, contract.
(ANT.) reject, discard.
employee *(SYN.)* laborer, worker, servant.
(ANT.) boss, employer.
employer *(SYN.)* owner, boss, management, proprietor, manager, superintendent, supervisor.
(ANT.) employee, worker.
employment *(SYN.)* occupation, work, business, position, job, service, engagement.
(ANT.) leisure, idleness, slothfulness.
empower *(SYN.)* enable, sanction, permit, warrant.
empty *(SYN.)* void, devoid, unfilled, barren, senseless, unoccupied, unfurnished, vacant, blank, evacuate, unload, hollow.
(ANT.) supplied, full, occupied.
emulate *(SYN.)* follow, imitate, copy.
enable *(SYN.)* authorize, empower, sanction, qualify.
enact *(SYN.)* legislate, portray, pass, stage, represent.
enchant *(SYN.)* charm, titillate, fascinate, bewitch, delight, thrill, captivate.
(ANT.) tire, bore.
encircle *(SYN.)* comprise, include, bound, encompass.
enclose *(SYN.)* envelop, confine, bound, surround, encompass, encircle, circumscribe.
(ANT.) open, exclude, distend, expose, develop.
encompass *(SYN.)* include, surround, encircle.
encore *(SYN.)* repetition, repeat, again.
encounter *(SYN.)* battle, meet, oppose, run into, face, collide.
encourage *(SYN.)* incite, favor, cheer, impel, countenance, inspirit, exhilarate, animate, hearten, embolden, support.
(ANT.) deter, dispirit, deject, dissuade.
encroach *(SYN.)* interfere, trespass, intrude, infringe.
encumber *(SYN.)* hamper, load, burden.
end *(SYN.)* completion, object, close, aim, result, conclusion, finish, extremity, intent, halt, stop, limit, purpose, cessation, expiration, termination.

(ANT.) opening, start, introduction, beginning, launch, inception.
endanger *(SYN.)* imperil, hazard, risk.
(ANT.) secure.
endear *(SYN.)* allure, charm.
endeavor *(SYN.)* strive, struggle, exertion, attempt, try, labor.
endless *(SYN.)* constant, nonstop, continuous, incessant, everlasting.
endorse *(SYN.)* approve, accept, sign, confirm, pass.
endow *(SYN.)* provide, furnish, bestow, give, contribute.
(ANT.) divest.
endure *(SYN.)* experience, undergo, sustain, last, bear, continue, remain, undergo, persist, brook, tolerate, suffer.
(ANT.) wane, die, perish, succumb, fail.
enemy *(SYN.)* foe, antagonist, rival, opponent, competitor, adversary, opposition.
(ANT.) colleague, ally, friend, accomplice.
energy *(SYN.)* strength, vim, force, power, stamina, vigor, might.
(ANT.) feebleness, lethargy.
enervate *(SYN.)* enfeeble, weaken, debilitate, exhaust, devitalize.
(ANT.) invigorate.
enfold *(SYN.)* clasp, surround, wrap, embrace, hug.
enforce *(SYN.)* make, drive, compel, execute, force.
engage *(SYN.)* absorb, occupy, employ, hold, involve, hire, agree, engross, retain, promise, commit, entangle.
(ANT.) fire, disengage, discharge, dismiss.
engaged *(SYN.)* affianced, betrothed, busy, occupied.
engaging *(SYN.)* fascinating, appealing, enticing, interesting, tempting, lovely, beguiling, charming, enchanting, engrossing, delightful, exquisite.
(ANT.) ordinary, boring.
engender *(SYN.)* develop, breed, cause, generate, produce.
engineer *(SYN.)* direct, conduct, guide, lead, manage.
engrave *(SYN.)* print, cut, impress, inscribe, carve, sketch.
engross *(SYN.)* engage, enthrall, occupy, fascinate, absorb.
engulf *(SYN.)* flood, swallow.
enhance *(SYN.)* better, uplift, improve.
enigma *(SYN.)* mystery, stumper, riddle.
enigmatic *(SYN.)* perplexing, confusing, puzzling, baffling, mystifying.
enjoy *(SYN.)* savor, like, relish.
enjoyment *(SYN.)* pleasure, delight, gratification.
(ANT.) abhorrence, displeasure.
enlarge *(SYN.)* widen, distend, amplify, broaden, extend, increase, augment, expand, dilate.
(ANT.) diminish, shrink, contract, decrease, wane, restrict.
enlighten *(SYN.)* inform, illuminate, clarify, teach, instruct.
(ANT.) confuse.
enlist *(SYN.)* enroll, prompt, join, induce, enter, register, persuade.
(ANT.) quit, leave, abandon.
enliven *(SYN.)* inspire, brighten, stimulate.
enmity *(SYN.)* antagonism, hatred, animosity, malignity, ill-will, antipathy, hostility, unfriendliness.
(ANT.) love, like, friendliness.
enormity *(SYN.)* heinousness, wickedness, barbarity, atrociousness.
enormous *(SYN.)* vast, huge, colossal, immense, gargantuan, elephantine, gigantic, stupendous, large.
(ANT.) small, slight, tiny, minute, infinitesimal, diminutive, little.
enough *(SYN.)* ample, adequate, sufficient, plenty.
(ANT.) inadequate, insufficient.
enrage *(SYN.)* anger, provoke, madden, inflame.
(ANT.) appease, soothe, calm.
enrich *(SYN.)* better, improve.
enroll *(SYN.)* record, list, recruit, register, enlist, write, induct.
(ANT.) quit, leave, abandon.
enshrine *(SYN.)* bury, entomb.
ensign *(SYN.)* banner, colors, flag, officer.
enslave *(SYN.)* keep, hold, capture.
ensue *(SYN.)* arise, succeed, follow, result.
ensure *(SYN.)* guarantee, assure, protect, defend, cover.
entangle *(SYN.)* confuse, snare, involve, ravel, snarl, tangle, trap.
enter *(SYN.)* join, go inside.
enterprise *(SYN.)* fete, deed, venture, project, adventure, undertaking, ambition, business, exploit.
enterprising *(SYN.)* energetic, resourceful.
(ANT.) lazy, indolent, sluggish, unresourceful.
entertain *(SYN.)* cheer, gladden, hold, consider, please, contemplate, divert, amuse, harbor, fascinate, interest.
(ANT.) repulse, tire, bore, disgust, annoy.
enthrall *(SYN.)* captivate, fascinate, enchant, charm, thrill.
enthusiasm *(SYN.)* fervor, fanaticism, zeal, ardor, intensity, devotion, excitement, eagerness, fervency, earnestness.
(ANT.) indifference, ennui, apathy, unconcern, detachment.
enthusiastic *(SYN.)* earnest, zealous, eager.
(ANT.) aloof, indifferent, unconcerned.
entice *(SYN.)* lure, attract, seduce.
entire *(SYN.)* complete, intact, whole, undivided.
(ANT.) divided, separated, incomplete, partial.
entirely *(SYN.)* altogether, thoroughly, wholly, solely.
entitle *(SYN.)* call, label, name, empower, allow, authorize, license, title.
entourage *(SYN.)* train, company, retinue, escort.
entrance *(SYN.)* inlet, portal, doorway, fascinate, entry, intrigue, door, thrill.
(ANT.) exit.

entreat *(SYN.)* implore, beg, plead.
entreaty *(SYN.)* plea, appeal.
entrust *(SYN.)* commit, charge, assign, delegate, consign, commission.
enumerate *(SYN.)* count, tally, list, number.
enunciate *(SYN.)* announce, express, speak, state.
envelop *(SYN.)* embrace, cover, conceal, surround, wrap.
environment *(SYN.)* neighborhood, habitat, surroundings, setting.
envision *(SYN.)* picture, imagine, visualize.
envoy *(SYN.)* delegate, emissary, representative, agent, messenger.
envy *(SYN.)* covetousness, jealousy, spitefulness, covet.
(ANT.) indifference, generosity.
epicure *(SYN.)* gourmand, gourmet, connoisseur, gastronome, epicurean, aesthete.
epidemic *(SYN.)* prevalent, scourge, plague, catching, widespread, pestilence, infectious.
episode *(SYN.)* happening, affair, occurrence, event, experience.
epoch *(SYN.)* age.
equal *(SYN.)* even, uniform, like, alike, equitable, same, identical, commensurate, equivalent, regular, parallel.
(ANT.) different, unequal, irregular, uneven.
equilibrium *(SYN.)* stability, steadiness, balance, firmness.
equip *(SYN.)* fit, rig, provide, outfit, prepare, furnish.
equipment *(SYN.)* utensils, material, apparatus.
equitable *(SYN.)* square, rightful, fair, due, just, fit.
(ANT.) partial, biased, unjust, uneven.
equity *(SYN.)* impartiality, fairness, justness, justice, fair-mindedness, even-handedness.
equivalent *(SYN.)* match, rival, equal, like, replacement.
equivocal *(SYN.)* oblique, ambiguous, vague, indeterminate, uncertain, obscure.
(ANT.) clear, precise, explicit, certain, clear-cut, definite.
equivocate *(SYN.)* temporize, evade, hedge, quibble, fudge, waffle, straddle.
era *(SYN.)* epoch, cycle, age, time, period.
eradicate *(SYN.)* remove, demolish, eliminate.
erase *(SYN.)* obliterate, remove, cancel.
(ANT.) add, include.
erect *(SYN.)* upright, build, straight, raise, construct, vertical.
(ANT.) flat, horizontal, raze, flatten, demolish.
erection *(SYN.)* building, construction, raising, fabrication.
erode *(SYN.)* rust, consume, disintegrate.
erotic *(SYN.)* carnal, fleshy, amatory, prurient, lewd, wanton, passionate, lecherous.
err *(SYN.)* slip, misjudge.
errand *(SYN.)* chore, duty, task, exercise.
errant *(SYN.)* roving, rambling, wandering, vagrant.
erratic *(SYN.)* irregular, abnormal, uneven, occasional, sporadic, changeable, unsteady, odd, eccentric, strange, extraordinary, unconventional, bizarre, peculiar, uncertain, unusual, unstable.
(ANT.) regular, steady, normal, ordinary.
erroneous *(SYN.)* wrong, mistaken, incorrect, inaccurate, false, untrue.
(ANT.) true, right, correct, accurate.
error *(SYN.)* inaccuracy, fault, slip, oversight, fallacy, mistake, blunder.
erudite *(SYN.)* sage, wise, learned, deep, profound.
erupt *(SYN.)* vomit.
escapade *(SYN.)* caper, antic, stunt, trick, prank.
escape *(SYN.)* shun, avoid, flee, decamp, elude, flight, avert, departure, abscond, fly, evade.
(ANT.) meet, confront, invite, catch.
escort *(SYN.)* conduct, lead, attend, accompany, protection, guard, guide, convoy, usher, squire.
especially *(SYN.)* unusually, principally, mainly, particularly, primarily.
essay *(SYN.)* test, thesis, undertake, paper, try.
essence *(SYN.)* substance, character, nature, principle, odor, meaning, basis, smell, perfume.
essential *(SYN.)* vital, intrinsic, basic, requisite, fundamental, indispensable, critical, requirement, necessity, necessary, important.
(ANT.) dispensable, unimportant, inessential.
establish *(SYN.)* prove, fix, found, settle, institute, raise, verify, conform, form, sanction, ordain, begin, organize.
(ANT.) upset, discontinue, scatter, disperse, refute, abolish, unsettle.
esteem *(SYN.)* revere, deem, appreciate, honor, value, think, admire, respect, hold, prize, reverence, regard.
(ANT.) scorn, disdain, depreciate, disregard, contempt, abhor.
estimate *(SYN.)* calculate, gauge, judge, rate, evaluate, compute, value, figure.
estimation *(SYN.)* judgment, viewpoint, opinion.
etch *(SYN.)* stamp, engrave, impress.
eternal *(SYN.)* undying, immortal, ceaseless, infinite, everlasting, deathless, perpetual, endless, timeless.
(ANT.) mortal, transient, finite, brief, temporary, passing.
etiquette *(SYN.)* decorum, formality.
evacuate *(SYN.)* withdraw, depart, leave, vacate.
evade *(SYN.)* miss, avoid, bypass.
(ANT.) confront, meet, face.
evaluate *(SYN.)* value, appraise, assay.
evaporate *(SYN.)* disappear, vanish.
(ANT.) condense, appear.
even *(SYN.)* smooth, level, still, square, same, flat, balanced, equal, parallel, identical.

(ANT.) irregular, bumpy, unbalanced, unequal, divergent.
evening *(SYN.)* twilight, dusk, sunset.
(ANT.) sunrise, dawn.
event *(SYN.)* issue, end, result, circumstance, occurrence, incident, consequence, happening, episode, outcome.
even-tempered *(SYN.)* composed, calm, cool.
(ANT.) hotheaded.
eventual *(SYN.)* consequent, ultimate.
(ANT.) present, current.
eventually *(SYN.)* ultimately.
ever *(SYN.)* continuously, always, constantly.
(ANT.) never.
everlasting *(SYN.)* permanent, ceaseless, endless, continual.
evermore *(SYN.)* always.
everyday *(SYN.)* commonplace, common, usual, ordinary, customary.
(ANT.) rare.
evict *(SYN.)* oust, put out, expel.
evidence *(SYN.)* grounds, clue, facts, testimony, data, sign, proof.
evident *(SYN.)* apparent, clear, obvious, indubitable, plain, conspicuous, patent, manifest, open, unmistakable.
(ANT.) hidden, unclear, uncertain, obscure, concealed.
evil *(SYN.)* immoral, harmful, badness, sinful, injurious, woe, bad, wicked.
(ANT.) goodness, moral, useful, upright, virtuous, beneficial, virtue, advantageous.
evoke *(SYN.)* summon, prompt.
evolve *(SYN.)* grow, advance, develop, result, emerge, unfold.
exact *(SYN.)* correct, faultless, errorless, detailed, accurate.
(ANT.) inaccurate, inexact, faulty.
exaggerate *(SYN.)* stretch, expand, amplify, embroider, heighten, overstate, caricature, magnify, enlarge.
(ANT.) understate, minimize, diminish, depreciate.
exalt *(SYN.)* erect, consecrate, raise, elevate, extol, dignify.
(ANT.) humble, degrade, humiliate.
examination *(SYN.)* investigation, inspection, test, scrutiny.
examine *(SYN.)* assess, contemplate, question, review, audit, notice, inquire, analyze, check, investigate, dissect, inspect, survey.
(ANT.) omit, disregard, overlook.
example *(SYN.)* pattern, archetype, specimen, illustration, model, instance, prototype, sample.
(ANT.) rule, concept, principle.
exasperate *(SYN.)* aggravate, anger, madden, irritate.
excavate *(SYN.)* unearth, dig, burrow.
exceed *(SYN.)* excel, beat, surpass, top.
exceedingly *(SYN.)* extremely, very, especially, unusually, surprisingly.
excel *(SYN.)* better, beat, surpass.
excellence *(SYN.)* distinction, superiority.
(ANT.) poorness, inferiority, badness.
excellent *(SYN.)* wonderful, fine, marvelous, superior.
(ANT.) poor, terrible, bad, inferior.
except *(SYN.)* omitting, barring, but, reject, excluding, save, exclude.
exception *(SYN.)* affront, offense, exclusion, deviation, omission, anomaly.
exceptional *(SYN.)* different, irregular, strange, unusual, abnormal.
excerpt *(SYN.)* abstract, extract.
excess *(SYN.)* surplus, intemperance, extravagance, immoderation, profusion, abundant, profuse, superfluity.
(ANT.) want, sparse, lack, dearth.
exchange *(SYN.)* barter, interchange, substitute, trade, change, swap.
excite *(SYN.)* arouse, incite, agitate, stimulate, awaken, disquiet.
(ANT.) lull, quiet, bore, pacify.
exclaim *(SYN.)* vociferate, cry, call out, cry out, ejaculate, shout.
exclamation *(SYN.)* shout, outcry, clamor.
exclude *(SYN.)* omit, restrain, hinder, bar, except, prevent.
(ANT.) welcome, involve, embrace, admit, accept, include.
exclusion *(SYN.)* exception, bar, rejection.
(ANT.) inclusion.
exclusive *(SYN.)* restricted, limited, restrictive, choice, selective, fashionable.
(ANT.) common, general, ordinary, unrestricted, unfashionable.
excursion *(SYN.)* voyage, tour, trip.
excuse *(SYN.)* exculpate, forgive, remit, acquit, free, pardon, condone, explanation, overlook, exempt, reason, justify, absolve.
(ANT.) revenge, punish, convict.
execute *(SYN.)* complete, accomplish, do, achieve, kill, perform.
exemplify *(SYN.)* show, illustrate.
exempt *(SYN.)* excuse, free, except, release.
exercise *(SYN.)* drill, task, use, activity, lesson, training, exertion, application, gymnastics, operation, practice.
(ANT.) rest, indolence, repose.
exertion *(SYN.)* attempt, effort, strain, endeavor.
exhale *(SYN.)* blow, breathe out.
exhaust *(SYN.)* drain, tire, empty, wear out, use, finish, fatigue.
(ANT.) renew, refresh, replace.
exhaustive *(SYN.)* comprehensive, thorough, extensive, complete.
(ANT.) incomplete.
exhibit *(SYN.)* demonstrate, display, reveal, betray, present, show, flaunt.
(ANT.) hide conceal, disguise.
exhilarate *(SYN.)* gladden, refresh, cheer, excite, stimulate.
exhort *(SYN.)* advise, urge, prompt.
exile *(SYN.)* expulsion, proscription, deportation, ostracism, expatriation, deport, extradition, expel, banishment.
(ANT.) retrieval, welcome, recall, admittance, reinstatement.
exist *(SYN.)* stand, live, occur, be.
exit *(SYN.)* leave, depart.
exodus *(SYN.)* leaving, exit, departure.
exonerate *(SYN.)* acquit, clear.
exorbitant *(SYN.)* unreasonable, outrageous, overpriced, preposterous, ex-

cessive.
(ANT.) normal, reasonable.
exotic *(SYN.)* strange, vivid, foreign.
(ANT.) dull, native.
expand *(SYN.)* unfold, enlarge, broaden, spread, inflate, swell, grow.
(ANT.) contract, shrivel, shrink.
expect *(SYN.)* await, think, hope.
expedient *(SYN.)* helpful, desirable, rush, hasten, useful, fitting, sensible.
(ANT.) delay.
expedition *(SYN.)* trek, speed, trip, haste, voyage, journey, hurry.
expel *(SYN.)* exile, dislodge, discharge, excommunicate, oust, eject, dismiss, banish, disown.
(ANT.) favor, recall, invite, admit.
expend *(SYN.)* consume, waste, spend.
(ANT.) ration, reserve, conserve.
expense *(SYN.)* charge, payment, price.
expensive *(SYN.)* costly, dear.
(ANT.) modest, inexpensive, cheap.
experience *(SYN.)* occurrence, episode, sensation, happening, existence, background, feeling, living, knowledge.
experienced *(SYN.)* expert, qualified, accomplished, skilled, practiced.
(ANT.) untutored, inexperienced, naive.
experiment *(SYN.)* trial, test, prove, research, examine, try, verify.
expert *(SYN.)* adept, handy, skillful, clever, specialist, authority, skilled, knowledgeable, ingenious.
(ANT.) unskilled, inexperienced.
expire *(SYN.)* terminate, die, cease, perish, pass, end, disappear.
(ANT.) commence, continue.
explain *(SYN.)* illustrate, decipher, expound, clarify, resolve, define, unravel, elucidate, unfold, justify, interpret.
(ANT.) darken, baffle, obscure.
explanation *(SYN.)* definition, description, interpretation, account, reason, justification, excuse.
explicit *(SYN.)* lucid, definitive, specific, express, clear, manifest.
(ANT.) vague, implicit, ambiguous.
exploit *(SYN.)* feat, deed, accomplishment, adventure.
explore *(SYN.)* research, hunt, probe, search, investigate, look, examine.
explosion *(SYN.)* bang, boom, blowup, flare-up, blast, detonation, outbreak, convulsion, furor, tantrum, paroxysm.
explosive *(SYN.)* fiery, rabid, eruptive, volcanic, fulminatory, inflammatory.
(ANT.) stable, inert, peaceful, calm.
exponent *(SYN.)* explicator, spokesman, supporter, expounder, interpreter.
expose *(SYN.)* uncover, display, bare, open, unmask, reveal.
(ANT.) hide, conceal, mask, covered.
exposition *(SYN.)* fair, bazaar, show, expo, exhibition.
expound *(SYN.)* clarify, present, explain, lecture, demonstrate.
express *(SYN.)* voice, tell, send, say, ship, declare, precise, specific, swift.
expression *(SYN.)* declaration, statement, look.
expressive *(SYN.)* suggestive, meaningful, telling, significant, thoughtful.
(ANT.) meaningless, nondescript.
expressly *(SYN.)* precisely, exactly, definitely, clearly.
(ANT.) tentatively, ambiguously.
expulsion *(SYN.)* ejection, discharge, removal, elimination.
expunge *(SYN.)* blot out, erase, cancel, obliterate, delete, efface, remove.
expurgate *(SYN.)* cleanse, purge, censor, edit, emasculate, abridge, blip.
exquisite *(SYN.)* delicate, delightful, attractive, dainty, beautiful, elegant, fine, superb, lovely, excellent, perfect.
(ANT.) vulgar, dull, ugly, unattractive.
extant *(SYN.)* subsisting, remaining, surviving, present, existing.
(ANT.) lost, defunct, extinct, vanished.
extemporaneous *(SYN.)* casual, impromptu, offhand.
extemporize *(SYN.)* improvise, devise.
extend *(SYN.)* lengthen, stretch, increase, offer, give, grant, expand.
(ANT.) abbreviate, shorten, curtail.
extension *(SYN.)* expansion, increase, stretching, enlargement.
extensive *(SYN.)* vast, wide, spacious, broad.
(ANT.) narrow, cramped, confined, restricted.
extent *(SYN.)* length, degree, range, amount, measure, size, compass, reach, magnitude, expanse, area.
extenuating *(SYN.)* exculpating, excusable, qualifying, justifying.
exterior *(SYN.)* surface, face, outside, covering, outer, external.
(ANT.) inside, lining, interior, inner.
exterminate *(SYN.)* slay, kill, destroy.
external *(SYN.)* outer, exterior, outside.
(ANT.) inner, internal, inside, interior.
externals *(SYN.)* images, effects, look, appearance, veneer, aspect.
extinct *(SYN.)* lost, dead, gone, vanished.
(ANT.) present, flourishing, alive, extant.
extinction *(SYN.)* eclipse, annihilation, obliteration, death, extirpation.
extinguish *(SYN.)* suppress, smother, quench.
extol *(SYN.)* laud, exalt, praise.
(ANT.) denounce, discredit, disparage.
extra *(SYN.)* surplus, spare, additional.
extract *(SYN.)* remove, essence.
(ANT.) penetrate, introduce.
extraordinary *(SYN.)* unusual, wonderful, marvelous, peculiar, noteworthy, remarkable, uncommon, exceptional.
(ANT.) commonplace, ordinary, usual.
extravagant *(SYN.)* excessive, exaggerated, lavish, wasteful, extreme.
(ANT.) prudent, frugal, thrifty, economical, provident.
extreme *(SYN.)* excessive, overdone, outermost, limit, greatest, utmost, furthest, extravagant.
(ANT.) reasonable, modest, moderate.
extricate *(SYN.)* rescue, free, clear, release, liberate.
exuberant *(SYN.)* ebullient, vivacious.
(ANT.) sad, depressed.
exult *(SYN.)* rejoice, delight.
eye *(SYN.)* watch, view, stare, look, inspect, glance.

fable *(SYN.)* legend, parable, myth, fib, falsehood, fiction, tale, story.
fabled *(SYN.)* legendary, famous, famed, historic.
fabric *(SYN.)* goods, textile, material, cloth, yard goods.
fabricate *(SYN.)* assemble, make, construct, create, manufacture, form.
(ANT.) raze, destroy, demolish.
fabrication *(SYN.)* deceit, lie, falsehood, untruth, forgery, deception.
(ANT.) reality, actuality, truth, fact.
fabulous *(SYN.)* amazing, marvelous, unbelievable, fantastic, astounding.
(ANT.) ordinary, commonplace, credible, proven, factual.
facade *(SYN.)* deception, mask, front, show, pose, veneer, guise, affectation.
face *(SYN.)* cover, mug, front, assurance, countenance, audacity, visage, expression, look, features, facade, encounter, meet, surface.
(ANT.) rear, shun, avoid, evade, back.
facet *(SYN.)* perspective, view, side.
facetious *(SYN.)* jocular, pungent, humorous, funny, clever, droll, witty, playful, jesting.
(ANT.) sober, serious, grave, weighty.
face to face *(SYN.)* opposing, confronting.
facile *(SYN.)* simple, easy, quick, uncomplicated, clever, fluent, skillful.
(ANT.) complex, difficult, complicated, laborious, hard, ponderous, painstaking, arduous.
facilitate *(SYN.)* help, speed, ease, promote, accelerate, expedite.
facilities *(SYN.)* aid, means, resources, conveniences.
facility *(SYN.)* ability, skill, ease, skillfulness, material.
(ANT.) effort, difficulty, labor.
facsimile *(SYN.)* reproduction, replica.
fact *(SYN.)* reality, deed, certainty, act, incident, circumstance, occurrence, event, truth, actuality.
(ANT.) falsehood, fiction, delusion.
faction *(SYN.)* clique, party, sect.
factitious *(SYN.)* false, sham, artificial, spurious, unnatural, affected.
(ANT.) natural, real, genuine, artless.
factor *(SYN.)* part, certain, element, basis, cause.
factory *(SYN.)* installation, plant, works.
factual *(SYN.)* true, correct, accurate. sure, genuine, authentic.
(ANT.) incorrect, erroneous, invented.
faculty *(SYN.)* power, capacity, talent, staff, gift, ability, qualification, ability, skill.
fad *(SYN.)* fashion, vogue, mania, rage.
faddish *(SYN.)* ephemeral, modish, temporary, passing, fleeting.
(ANT.) lasting, permanent, enduring.
fade *(SYN.)* pale, bleach, weaken, dim, decline, sink, discolor, fail, diminish.
fagged *(SYN.)* exhausted, tired, weary, jaded, pooped, worn.
fail *(SYN.)* neglect, weaken, flunk, miss, decline, disappoint, fade.
(ANT.) succeed, achieve, accomplish.
failing *(SYN.)* fault, foible, imperfection, frailty, defect, shortcoming.
(ANT.) steadiness, strength, integrity.
failure *(SYN.)* miscarriage, omission, decline, deficiency, fiasco, lack, dereliction, failing, unsuccessfulness, loss, default, want, insufficiency.
(ANT.) conquest, accomplishment, success, triumph, victory, hit, luck.
faint *(SYN.)* timid, faded, languid, half-hearted, dim, pale, wearied, feeble, indistinct, weak.
(ANT.) strong, sharp, forceful, glaring, clear, distinct, conspicuous, brave.
faint-hearted *(SYN.)* shy, cowardly, timid, bashful.
(ANT.) fearless, brave, stouthearted, courageous.
fair *(SYN.)* pale, average, light, sunny, mediocre, bright, just, clear, lovely, market, blond, honest, equitable, impartial, reasonable, comely.
(ANT.) ugly, fraudulent, foul, outstanding, dishonorable, unfair.
fairly *(SYN.)* equally, evenly, rather, impartially, passably, justly, somewhat.
fair-minded *(SYN.)* reasonable, fair, just, open-minded, honest, unprejudiced, impartial, evenhanded.
(ANT.) bigoted, narrow-minded, unjust, close-minded, partisan.
fairness *(SYN.)* equity, justice, evenhandedness, honesty.
(ANT.) favoritism, partiality, bias, one-sidedness.
fairy *(SYN.)* gnome, elf, pixie, sprite.
faith *(SYN.)* dependence, trust, reliance, creed, loyalty, doctrine, confidence, dogma, tenet, persuasion, constancy, credence, fidelity, religion, belief.
(ANT.) disbelief, doubt, infidelity.
faithful *(SYN.)* staunch, true, devoted, trusty, loyal, constant, credible, steadfast, strict, trust-worthy, accurate.
(ANT.) untrustworthy, faithless, inaccurate, wrong, false, disloyal, erroneous.
faithless *(SYN.)* treacherous, unfaithful, disloyal, perfidious, untrue.
(ANT.) loyal, true, unwavering, constant, faithful.
fake *(SYN.)* falsify, distort, pretend, feign, fraud, counterfeit, cheat, false, artificial, phony, imitation, forgery.
(ANT.) honest, pure, real, genuine, authentic.
falderal *(SYN.)* foolery, jargon, nonsense, gibberish, blather, balderdash.
fall *(SYN.)* drop, decline, diminish, droop, topple, decrease, sink, hang, descend, subside, plunge, collapse.
(ANT.) soar, climb, steady, rise, ascend.
fallacious *(SYN.)* untrue, false, wrong, erroneous, deceptive, illusory.
(ANT.) accurate, true, exact, real.
fallacy *(SYN.)* mistake, error, illusion, sophism, misconception, deception.
fall back *(SYN.)* retreat, recede, retire, withdraw, concede.
(ANT.) progress, advance, gain, prosper, proceed.
fallow *(SYN.)* idle, unprepared, unproductive. inactive.
(ANT.) prepared, productive, cultivated.
false *(SYN.)* incorrect, wrong, deceitful, fake, imitation, counterfeit.

(ANT.) genuine, loyal, true, honest.

falsehood *(SYN.)* untruth, lie, fib, story.
(ANT.) truth.

falsify *(SYN.)* misquote, distort, misstate, mislead, adulterate.

falter *(SYN.)* stumble, tremble, waver, hesitate, flounder.

fame *(SYN.)* distinction, glory, mane, eminence, credit, reputation, renown, acclaim, notoriety.
(ANT.) infamy, obscurity, anonymity, disrepute.

famed *(SYN.)* known, renowned, famous.
(ANT.) obscure, unknown, anonymous.

familiar *(SYN.)* informal, intimate, close, acquainted, amicable, knowing, cognizant, well-acquainted, versed, unreserved, friendly, sociable, affable, aware, known, courteous, intimate.
(ANT.) unfamiliar, distant, affected, reserved.

familiarity *(SYN.)* sociability, acquaintance, awareness, frankness, intimacy, understanding, knowledge, fellowship.
(ANT.) distance, ignorance, reserve, presumption, constraint, haughtiness.

family *(SYN.)* kin, tribe, folks, group, relatives.

famine *(SYN.)* want, deficiency, starvation, need.
(ANT.) excess, plenty.

famous *(SYN.)* distinguished, noted, glorious, illustrious, famed, celebrated, well-known, eminent, renowned, prominent, esteemed.
(ANT.) obscure, hidden, unknown.

fan *(SYN.)* arouse, spread, admirer, enthusiast, devotee, stir, aficionado, whip, follower.

fanatic *(SYN.)* bigot, enthusiast, zealot.

fancy *(SYN.)* love, dream, ornate, imagine, suppose, imagination, taste, fantasy, ornamented, elaborate, think.
(ANT.) plain, undecorated, simple, unadorned.

fantastic *(SYN.)* strange, unusual, odd, wild, unimaginable, incredible, unbelievable, unreal, bizarre, capricious.
(ANT.) mundane, ordinary, staid, humdrum.

fantasy *(SYN.)* illusion, dream, whim, hallucination, delusion, caprice, mirage, daydream, fancy.
(ANT.) bore.

far *(SYN.)* removed, much, distant, remote, estranged, alienated.
(ANT.) close, near.

fare *(SYN.)* prosper, eat, passenger, thrive, toil, progress, succeed.

farewell *(SYN.)* good-by, valediction, departure, leaving.
(ANT.) welcome, greeting.

farm *(SYN.)* grow, harvest, cultivate, ranch, hire, charter, plantation.

fascinate *(SYN.)* charm, enchant, bewitch, attract, enthrall.

fashion *(SYN.)* create, shape, style, mode, make, custom, form, manner, method, way, vogue.

fashionable *(SYN.)* chic, smart, stylish, modish, elegant, voguish.
(ANT.) dowdy, unfashionable.

fast *(SYN.)* fleet, firm, quick, swift, inflexible, stable, secure, expeditious, rapid, steady, solid, constant, speedy.
(ANT.) insecure, sluggish, unstable, loose, slow, unsteady.

fasten *(SYN.)* secure, bind, tie, join, fix, connect, attach, unite.
(ANT.) open, loose, free, loosen, release, separate.

fastidious *(SYN.)* choosy, selective, discriminating, picky, meticulous.

fat *(SYN.)* stout, plump, chubby, pudgy, obese, oily, fleshy, greasy, fatty, portly, corpulent, paunchy, wide, thick, rotund.
(ANT.) slim, gaunt, emaciated, thin, slender.

fatal *(SYN.)* killing, lethal, doomed, disastrous, deadly, fateful, mortal.
(ANT.) nonfatal.

fate *(SYN.)* end, fortune, doom, issue, destiny, necessity, portion, result, lot, chance, luck, outcome, consequence, kismet.

father *(SYN.)* cause, sire, breed, originate, founder, inventor.

fatherly *(SYN.)* protective, paternal, kind, paternalistic.

fathom *(SYN.)* penetrate, understand, interpret, comprehend.

fatigue *(SYN.)* weariness, lassitude, exhaustion, enervation, languor, tiredness.
(ANT.) vivacity, rejuvenation, energy, vigor.

fault *(SYN.)* defect, flaw, mistake, imperfection, shortcoming, error, weakness, responsibility, omission, blemish, blame, failure.
(ANT.) perfection, completeness.

faultfinding *(SYN.)* carping, censorious, critical, caviling, nit-picking.

faulty *(SYN.)* imperfect, broken, defective, damaged, impaired.
(ANT.) flawless, perfect, whole.

favor *(SYN.)* rather, resemble, liking, service, prefer, approval, like, support, patronize, benefit.
(ANT.) deplore, disapprove.

favorite *(SYN.)* prized, pet, choice, darling, treasured, preferred.

favoritism *(SYN.)* prejudice, bias, partiality.
(ANT.) fairness, impartiality.

fear *(SYN.)* horror, terror, fright, trepidation, alarm, consternation, dismay, cowardice, panic, anxiety, dread, scare, apprehension.
(ANT.) fearlessness, boldness, courage, assurance.

fearless *(SYN.)* bold, brave, courageous, gallant, dauntless, confident.
(ANT.) timid, fearful, cowardly.

feast *(SYN.)* dinner, banquet, barbecue.

feat *(SYN.)* performance, act, operation, accomplishment, achievement, doing, transaction, deed.
(ANT.) intention, deliberation, cessation.

feature *(SYN.)* trait, quality, characteristic, highlight, attribute.

fee *(SYN.)* payment, pay, remuneration, charge, recompense.

feeble *(SYN.)* faint, puny, exhausted, impair, delicate, weak, enervated, frail, powerless, forceless, sickly, decrepit, ailing.
(ANT.) strong, forceful, powerful, vigorous, stout.
feed *(SYN.)* satisfy, nourish, food, fodder, forage.
feel *(SYN.)* sense, experience, perceive.
feeling *(SYN.)* opinion, sensibility, tenderness, affection, impression, belief, sensation, sympathy, thought, passion, sentiment, attitude, emotion.
(ANT.) fact, imperturbability, anesthesia, insensibility.
fellowship *(SYN.)* clan, society, brotherhood, fraternity, camaraderie, companionship, comradeship, association.
(ANT.) dislike, discord, distrust, enmity, strife, acrimony.
felonious *(SYN.)* murderous, criminal, larcenous.
feminine *(SYN.)* womanly, girlish, ladylike, female, maidenly, womanish.
(ANT.) masculine, male, virile.
ferocious *(SYN.)* savage, fierce, wild, blood-thirsty, brutal.
(ANT.) playful, gentle, harmless, calm.
fertile *(SYN.)* rich, fruitful, teeming, plenteous, bountiful, prolific, luxuriant, productive, fecund.
(ANT.) unproductive, barren, sterile.
festival *(SYN.)* feast, banquet, regalement, celebration.
festive *(SYN.)* joyful, gay, joyous, merry, gala, jovial, jubilant.
(ANT.) sad, gloomy, mournful, morose.
fetching *(SYN.)* charming, attractive, pleasing, captivating, winsome.
feud *(SYN.)* dispute, quarrel, strife, argument, conflict, controversy.
(ANT.) amity, understanding, harmony, peace.
fiber *(SYN.)* line, strand, thread, string.
fickle *(SYN.)* unstable, capricious, restless, changeable, inconstant, variable.
(ANT.) stable, constant, trustworthy, steady, reliable, dependable.
fiction *(SYN.)* fabrication, romance, falsehood, tale, allegory, narrative, fable, novel, story, invention.
(ANT.) verity, reality, fact, truth.
fictitious *(SYN.)* invented, make-believe, imaginary, fabricated, unreal, counterfeit, feigned.
(ANT.) real, true, genuine, actual, proven.
fidelity *(SYN.)* fealty, devotion, precision, allegiance, exactness, constancy, accuracy, faithfulness, loyalty.
(ANT.) treachery, disloyalty.
fidget *(SYN.)* squirm, twitch, wriggle.
fiendish *(SYN.)* devilish, demonic, diabolical, savage, satanic.
fierce *(SYN.)* furious, wild, savage, violent, ferocious, vehement.
(ANT.) calm, meek, mild, gentle, placid.
fight *(SYN.)* contend, scuffle, struggle, battle, wrangle, combat, brawl, quarrel, dispute, war, skirmish, conflict.
figure *(SYN.)* design, pattern, mold, shape, form, frame, reckon, calculate, compute, determine.
fill *(SYN.)* glut, furnish, store, stuff, occupy, gorge, pervade, content, stock, fill up, supply, sate, replenish, satisfy.
(ANT.) void, drain, exhaust, deplete, empty.
filter *(SYN.)* screen, strainer, sieve.
filth *(SYN.)* pollution, dirt, sewage, foulness.
(ANT.) cleanliness, innocence, purity.
filthy *(SYN.)* foul, polluted, dirty, stained, unwashed, squalid.
(ANT.) pure, clean, unspoiled.
final *(SYN.)* ultimate, decisive, concluding, ending, terminal, last, conclusive, eventual, latest.
(ANT.) inaugural, rudimentary, beginning, initial, incipient, first, original.
finally *(SYN.)* at last, eventually, ultimately.
find *(SYN.)* observe, detect, discover, locate.
fine *(SYN.)* thin, pure, choice, small, elegant, dainty, splendid, handsome, delicate, nice, powdered, beautiful, minute, exquisite, subtle, pretty, refined.
(ANT.) thick, coarse, rough, blunt, large.
finicky *(SYN.)* fussy, meticulous, finical, fastidious, prim.
finish *(SYN.)* consummate, close, get done, terminate, accomplish, conclude, execute, perform, complete, end, achieve, fulfill, do, perfect.
(ANT.) open, begin, start, beginning.
fire *(SYN.)* vigor, glow, combustion, passion, burning, conflagration, ardor, flame, blaze, intensity, fervor.
(ANT.) apathy, cold.
firm *(SYN.)* solid, rigid, inflexible, stiff, unchanging, steadfast, dense, hard, unshakable, compact, business, company, corporation, partnership.
(ANT.) weak, limp, soft, drooping.
first *(SYN.)* chief, primary, initial, pristine, beginning, foremost, primeval, earliest, prime, primitive, original.
(ANT.) subordinate, last, least, hindmost, latest.
fishy *(SYN.)* suspicious, questionable, doubtful.
(ANT.) believable, credible.
fit *(SYN.)* adjust, suit, suitable, accommodate, conform, robust, harmonize, belong, seizure, spasm, attack, suited, appropriate, healthy, agree, adapt.
(ANT.) misfit, disturb, improper.
fitful *(SYN.)* variable, restless, fickle, capricious, unstable, changeable.
(ANT.) trustworthy, stable, constant, steady.
fitting *(SYN.)* apt, due, suitable, proper.
(ANT.) improper, unsuitable, inappropriate.
fix *(SYN.)* mend, regulate, affix, set, tie, repair, attach, settle, link, bind, determine, establish, define, place, rectify, stick, limit, adjust, fasten.
(ANT.) damage, change, mistreat, displace, alter, disturb, mutilate.
fixation *(SYN.)* fetish, obsession, infatuation, compulsion.

flair *(SYN.)* style, dash, flamboyance, drama, gift, knack, aptitude.
flamboyant *(SYN.)* showy, flashy, ostentatious, gaudy, ostentatious.
flame *(SYN.)* blaze, fire.
flash *(SYN.)* flare, flame, wink, twinkling, instant, gleam.
flashy *(SYN.)* tawdry, tasteless, pretentious, garish, flamboyant.
flat *(SYN.)* vapid, stale, even, smooth, tasteless, horizontal, dull, level, insipid, uninteresting, lifeless, boring.
(ANT.) tasty, racy, hilly, savory, stimulating, interesting, broken, sloping.
flattery *(SYN.)* compliment, praise, applause, blarney, acclaim.
flaunt *(SYN.)* exhibit, show off, display, parade.
(ANT.) conceal, hide, disguise.
flavor *(SYN.)* tang, taste, savor, essence, quality, character, season, spice.
flaw *(SYN.)* spot, imperfection, blemish, fault, deformity, blotch.
flee *(SYN.)* fly, abscond, hasten, escape, run away, decamp, evade.
(ANT.) remain, appear, stay, arrive.
fleece *(SYN.)* filch, rob, purloin, swindle, defraud, pilfer, cheat.
fleet *(SYN.)* rapid, swift, quick, fast.
(ANT.) unhurried, sluggish, slow.
fleeting *(SYN.)* brief, swift, passing, temporary.
(ANT.) stable, fixed, lasting, permanent.
fleshy *(SYN.)* overweight, chubby, stocky, plump, obese, stout.
(ANT.) spare, underweight, skinny.
flexible *(SYN.)* lithe, resilient, pliable, tractable, complaint, elastic, yielding, adaptable, agreeable, supple, pliant, easy, ductile.
(ANT.) hard, unbending, firm, brittle, inflexible, rigid, fixed.
flighty *(SYN.)* giddy, light-headed, frivolous, irresponsible.
(ANT.) solid, responsible, steady.
flimsy *(SYN.)* wobbly, weak, frail, fragile, unsteady, delicate, thin.
(ANT.) durable, stable, firm, strong.
fling *(SYN.)* pitch, throw, toss, fun, celebration, party.
flippant *(SYN.)* disrespectful, sassy, insolent, brazen, rude, impertinent.
(ANT.) courteous, polite, mannerly.
flit *(SYN.)* flutter, scurry, hasten, dart, skim.
flock *(SYN.)* gathering, group, flight, swarm, herd, school.
flog *(SYN.)* thrash, lash, switch, strike, paddle.
flood *(SYN.)* overflow, deluge, inundate, cascade.
florid *(SYN.)* gaudy, fancy, ornate, embellished.
(ANT.) spare, simple, plain, unadorned.
flourish *(SYN.)* succeed, grow, prosper, wave, thrive, bloom.
(ANT.) wither, wane, die, decline.
flout *(SYN.)* disdain, scorn, spurn, ignore, taunt, ridicule, mock.
flow *(SYN.)* proceed, abound, spout, come, stream, run, originate, emanate, result, pour, squirt, issue, gush, spurt.
fluctuate *(SYN.)* vary, oscillate, change, waver, hesitate, vacillate.
(ANT.) persist, stick, adhere, resolve.
fluent *(SYN.)* graceful, glib, flowing.
fluid *(SYN.)* liquid, running, liquefied.
flush *(SYN.)* abundant, flat, even, level.
fluster *(SYN.)* rattle, flurry, agitate, upset, perturb, quiver, vibrate.
fly *(SYN.)* flee, mount, shoot, decamp, hover, soar, flit, flutter, sail, escape, rush, spring, glide, abscond, dart, float.
(ANT.) sink, descend, plummet.
foam *(SYN.)* suds, froth, lather.
foe *(SYN.)* opponent, enemy, antagonist, adversary.
(ANT.) associate, ally, friend, comrade.
fog *(SYN.)* haze, mist, cloud, daze, confusion, stupor, vapor, smog.
foible *(SYN.)* frailty, weakness, failing, shortcoming, kink.
foist *(SYN.)* misrepresent, insinuate, falsify.
fold *(SYN.)* lap, double, overlap, clasp, pleat, tuck.
follow *(SYN.)* trail, observe, succeed, ensue, obey, chase, comply, accompany, copy, result, imitate, heed, adopt.
(ANT.) elude, cause, precede, avoid, flee.
follower *(SYN.)* supporter, devotee, henchman, adherent, partisan, votary, attendant, disciple, successor.
(ANT.) master, head, chief, dissenter.
following *(SYN.)* public, disciples, supporters, clientele, customers.
folly *(SYN.)* imprudence, silliness, foolishness, indiscretion, absurdity, imprudence, imbecility, stupidity, extravagance.
(ANT.) reasonableness, judgment, sense, prudence, wisdom.
fond *(SYN.)* affectionate, loving, attached, tender, devoted.
(ANT.) hostile, cool, distant, unfriendly.
fondness *(SYN.)* partiality, liking, affection.
(ANT.) hostility, unfriendliness.
food *(SYN.)* viands, edibles, feed, repast, nutriment, sustenance, diet, bread, provisions, meal, rations, victuals, fare.
(ANT.) want, hunger, drink, starvation.
fool *(SYN.)* oak, dunce, jester, idiot, simpleton, buffoon, harlequin, dolt, blockhead, numskull, clown, dope, trick, deceive, nincompoop.
(ANT.) scholar, genius, sage.
foolish *(SYN.)* senseless, irrational, crazy, silly, brainless, idiotic, simple, nonsensical, stupid, preposterous, asinine.
(ANT.) sane, sound, sensible, rational, judicious, wise, reasonable, prudent.
footing *(SYN.)* base, basis, foundation.
footloose *(SYN.)* uncommitted, free, detached, independent.
(ANT.) engaged, rooted, involved.
forbearance *(SYN.)* moderation, abstinence, abstention, continence.
(ANT.) greed, excess, intoxication.
forbid *(SYN.)* disallow, prevent, ban, prohibit, taboo, outlaw.
(ANT.) approve, let, allow, permit.
forbidding *(SYN.)* evil, hostile, un-

friendly, sinister, scary, repulsive.
(ANT.) pleasant, beneficent, friendly.
force *(SYN.)* energy, might, violence, vigor, intensity, dint, power, constraint, coercion, vigor, compel, compulsion, oblige, make, coerce, strength.
(ANT.) weakness, frailty, persuasion, feebleness, impotence, ineffectiveness.
forceful *(SYN.)* dynamic, vigorous, energetic, potent, drastic, intense.
(ANT.) lackadaisical, insipid, weak.
foreboding *(SYN.)* misgiving, suspicion, apprehension, presage, intuition.
forecast *(SYN.)* prophesy, predict, predetermine.
foregoing *(SYN.)* above, former, preceding, previous, prior.
(ANT.) later,coming, below, follow.
foreign *(SYN.)* alien, strange, exotic, different, unfamiliar.
(ANT.) commonplace, ordinary, familiar.
foreigner *(SYN.)* outsider, alien, newcomer, stranger.
(ANT.) native.
foreman *(SYN.)* super, boss, overseer, supervisor.
forerunner *(SYN.)* harbinger, proclaimer, informant.
foresee *(SYN.)* forecast, expect, anticipate, surmise, envisage.
forest *(SYN.)* grove, woodland, wood, copse, woods.
forestall *(SYN.)* hinder, thwart, prevent, obstruct, repel.
foretell *(SYN.)* soothsay, divine, predict.
forever *(SYN.)* evermore, always, everlasting, hereafter, endlessly.
(ANT.) fleeting, temporarily.
forfeit *(SYN.)* yield, resign, lose, sacrifice.
forgive *(SYN.)* exonerate, clear, excuse, pardon.
(ANT.) impeach, accuse, blame, censure.
forgo *(SYN.)* relinquish, release, surrender, waive, abandon.
(ANT.) keep, retain, safeguard.
forlorn *(SYN.)* pitiable, desolate, dejected, woeful, wretched.
(ANT.) optimistic, cherished, cheerful.
form *(SYN.)* frame, compose, fashion, arrange, construct, make up, devise, create, invent, mold, shape, forge, organize, produce, constitute, make.
(ANT.) wreck, dismantle, destroy, misshape.
formal *(SYN.)* exact, stiff, correct, outward, conformist, conventional, affected, regular, proper, ceremonious, decorous, methodical, precise, solemn, external, perfunctory.
(ANT.) heartfelt, unconstrained, easy, unconventional.
former *(SYN.)* earlier, one-time, previous, erstwhile, prior.
formidable *(SYN.)* alarming, frightful, imposing, terrible, terrifying, dire, fearful, forbidding.
(ANT.) weak, unimpressive, ordinary.
forsake *(SYN.)* abandon, desert, forgo, quit, discard, neglect.

forte *(SYN.)* gift, capability, talent, specialty, aptitude, bulwark.
forth *(SYN.)* out, onward, forward.
forthright *(SYN.)* honest, direct, candid, outspoken, blunt sincere, plain, explicit.
forthwith *(SYN.)* instantly, promptly, immediately.
(ANT.) afterward, later, ultimately, slowly.
fortify *(SYN.)* bolster strengthen, buttress, barricade, defend.
fortuitous *(SYN.)* successful, benign, lucky, advantageous, propitious, happy, favored, chance.
(ANT.) unlucky, condemned, persecuted.
fortunate *(SYN.)* happy, auspicious, fortuitous, successful, favored, advantageous, benign, charmed, lucky, felicitous, blessed, propitious, blissful.
(ANT.) ill-fated, cheerless, unlucky, unfortunate, cursed, condemned.
fortune *(SYN.)* chance, fate, lot, luck, riches, wealth, kismet, destiny.
fortuneteller *(SYN.)* soothsayer, clairvoyant, forecaster, oracle, medium.
forward *(SYN.)* leading, front, promote, elevate, advance, first, ahead, onward, further, foremost, aggrandize.
(ANT.) withhold, retard, hinder, retreat, oppose.
foul *(SYN.)* base, soiled, dirty, mean, unclean, polluted, impure, vile, evil, muddy, wicked, rainy, stormy, despicable, filthy.
(ANT.) pure, neat, wholesome, clean.
found *(SYN.)* organize, establish.
foundation *(SYN.)* support, root, base, underpinning, groundwork, bottom, establishment, substructure, basis.
(ANT.) top, cover, building.
foxy *(SYN.)* cunning, sly, artful, crafty, wily, sharp, shrewd, slick.
fraction *(SYN.)* fragment, part, section, morsel, share, piece.
fracture *(SYN.)* crack, break, rupture.
fragile *(SYN.)* delicate, frail, weak, breakable, infirm, brittle, feeble.
(ANT.) tough, hardy, sturdy, strong, stout, durable.
fragment *(SYN.)* scrap, piece, bit, remnant, part, splinter, segment.
fragrance *(SYN.)* odor, smell, scent, perfume, aroma.
fragrant *(SYN.)* aromatic, scented, perfumed.
frail *(SYN.)* feeble, weak, delicate, breakable, fragile.
(ANT.) sturdy, strong, powerful.
frame *(SYN.)* support, framework, skeleton, molding, border, mount.
frank *(SYN.)* honest, candid, open, unreserved, direct, sincere, straightforward.
(ANT.) tricky, dishonest.
frantic *(SYN.)* frenzied, crazed, raving, panicky.
(ANT.) composed, stoic.
fraud *(SYN.)* deception, guile, swindle, deceit, artifice, imposture, trick, cheat, imposition, duplicity, chicanery.
(ANT.) sincerity, fairness, integrity.

fraudulent *(SYN.)* tricky, fake, dishonest, deceitful.
fray *(SYN.)* strife, fight, battle, struggle, tussle, combat, brawl, melee, skirmish.
(ANT.) truce, agreement, peace, concord.
freak *(SYN.)* curiosity, abnormality, monster, oddity.
free *(SYN.)* munificent, clear, autonomous, immune, open, freed, bountiful, liberated, unfastened, immune, emancipated, unconfined, unobstructed, easy, artless, loose, familiar, bounteous, unrestricted, liberal, independent, careless, frank exempt.
(ANT.) stingy, clogged, illiberal, confined, parsimonious.
freedom *(SYN.)* independence, privilege, familiarity, unrestraint, liberty, exemption, liberation, immunity, license.
(ANT.) servitude, constraint, bondage, slavery, necessity.
freely *(SYN.)* liberally, generously, unstintingly.
freight *(SYN.)* chipping, cargo, load, shipment.
frenzy *(SYN.)* craze, agitation, excitement.
frequent *(SYN.)* usual, habitual, common, often, customary, general.
(ANT.) unique, rare, solitary, uncommon, exceptional, infrequent, scanty.
fresh *(SYN.)* recent, new, additional, further, refreshing, natural, brisk, novel, inexperienced, late, current, sweet, pure, cool.
(ANT.) stagnant, decayed, musty, faded.
fret *(SYN.)* torment, worry, grieve, anguish.
fretful *(SYN.)* testy, irritable, touchy, peevish, short-tempered.
(ANT.) calm.
friend *(SYN.)* crony, supporter, ally, companion, intimate, associate, advocate, comrade, mate, patron, acquaintance, chum, defender.
(ANT.) stranger, adversary.
friendly *(SYN.)* sociable, kindly, affable, genial, companionable, social, neighborly, amicable.
(ANT.) hostile, antagonistic, reserved.
friendship *(SYN.)* knowledge, familiarity, fraternity, acquaintance, intimacy, fellowship, comradeship, cognizance.
(ANT.) unfamiliarity, ignorance.
fright *(SYN.)* alarm, fear, panic, terror.
frighten *(SYN.)* scare, horrify, daunt, affright, appall, terrify, alarm, terrorize, astound, dismay, startle, panic.
(ANT.) soothe, embolden, compose, reassure.
frigid *(SYN.)* cold, wintry, icy, glacial, arctic, freezing.
fringe *(SYN.)* hem, edge, border, trimming, edging.
frisky *(SYN.)* animated, lively, peppy, vivacious.
frolic *(SYN.)* play, cavort, romp, frisk.
front *(SYN.)* facade, face, start, beginning, border, head.
(ANT.) rear, back.
frontier *(SYN.)* border, boundary.
frugal *(SYN.)* parsimonious, saving, stingy, provident, temperate, economical, sparing.
(ANT.) extravagant, wasteful, self-indulgent, intemperate.
fruitful *(SYN.)* fertile, rich, bountiful, teeming, fecund, productive, luxuriant.
(ANT.) lean, unproductive, barren, sterile.
fruitless *(SYN.)* barren, futile, vain, sterile, unproductive.
(ANT.) fertile, productive.
frustrate *(SYN.)* hinder, defeat, thwart, circumvent, outwit, foil, baffle, disappoint, balk, discourage, prevent.
(ANT.) promote, fulfill, accomplish.
fugitive *(SYN.)* deserter, runaway.
fulfill *(SYN.)* do, effect, complete, accomplish, realize.
full *(SYN.)* baggy, crammed, entire, satiated, flowing, perfect, gorged, soaked, complete, filled, packed, extensive, plentiful, replete, voluminous.
(ANT.) lacking, devoid, partial, empty.
full-grown *(SYN.)* ripe, adult, mature, developed, grown-up, complete.
(ANT.) green, young, unripe, adolescent.
fullness *(SYN.)* glut, repletion, enough, satiety, satiation, sufficiency, all, totality, satisfaction, overload, wholeness, aggregate, everything, sum.
(ANT.) need, want, hunger, lack, insufficiency, privation, emptiness, incompleteness.
full-scale *(SYN.)* major, all-out, lavish, comprehensive, unlimited, maximum.
(ANT.) indifferent, partial, minor.
fun *(SYN.)* merriment, pleasure, enjoyment, gaiety, sport, amusement.
function *(SYN.)* operation, activity, affair, ceremony, gathering, party.
fundamental *(SYN.)* basic, essential, primary, elementary.
funny *(SYN.)* odd, droll, ridiculous, queer, farcical, laughable, comic, curious, amusing, humorous, witty.
(ANT.) solemn, sad, sober, melancholy.
furious *(SYN.)* angry, enraged.
(ANT.) serene, calm.
furnish *(SYN.)* yield, give, endow, fit, produce, equip, afford, decorate, supply, appoint.
(ANT.) divest, denude, strip.
furthermore *(SYN.)* moreover, also.
furtive *(SYN.)* surreptitious, secret, hidden, clandestine.
(ANT.) honest, open.
fury *(SYN.)* wrath, anger, frenzy, rage, violence, fierceness.
(ANT.) calmness, serenity.
fuss *(SYN.)* commotion, bother, pester, annoy, irritate.
futile *(SYN.)* pointless, idle, vain, useless, worthless, minor.
(ANT.) weighty, important, worthwhile, serious, valuable.
future *(SYN.)* approaching, imminent, coming, impending.
(ANT.) former, past.
fuzzy *(SYN.)* indistinct, blurred.
(ANT.) lucid, clear.

gab *(SYN.)* jabber, babble, chatter, prattle, gossip.
gabble *(SYN.)* chatter, babble, jabber, blab, prate, gaggle, prattle, blather, gibberish.
gabby *(SYN.)* chatty, talkative, wordy, verbose.
gad *(SYN.)* wander, roam, rove, ramble, meander, cruise.
gadabout *(SYN.)* gypsy, wanderer, rambler.
gadget *(SYN.)* contrivance, device, doodad, jigger, thing, contraption.
gaffe *(SYN.)* blunder, boner, mistake, gaucherie, error, howler.
gag *(SYN.)* witticism, crack jest, joke.
gaiety *(SYN.)* joyousness, cheerfulness, high-spiritedness, joyfulness, light-heartedness.
(ANT.) melancholy, sadness, depression.
gain *(SYN.)* acquire, avail, account, good, interest, attain, favor, achieve, get, secure, advantage, earn, profit, procure, service, obtain, improvement, increase, behalf, net, reach, win, benefit.
(ANT.) trouble, lose, calamity, forfeit, handicap, lose, distress.
gainful *(SYN.)* lucrative, rewarding, profitable, beneficial, payable, productive.
(ANT.) unproductive, unprofitable, unrewarding.
gainsay *(SYN.)* refute, contradict, controvert, deny, refuse, inpugn, contravene, disavow, differ.
(ANT.) maintain, aver, affirm, asseverate.
gait *(SYN.)* stride, walk, tread, step.
gala *(SYN.)* ball, party, carnival, fete, festival.
gale *(SYN.)* burst, surge, outburst.
gall *(SYN.)* nerve, audacity, impudence, annoy, vex, anger, provoke, irritate.
gallant *(SYN.)* bold, brave, courageous, valorous, valiant, noble, polite, fearless, heroic, chivalrous.
gallantry *(SYN.)* valor, daring, courage, prowess, heroism, manliness, dauntlessness, graciousness, attentiveness, coquetry, gentleness, fearlessness, chivalrousness.
(ANT.) poltroonery, timidity, cowardice, cravenness, cloddishness.
gallery *(SYN.)* passageway, hall, aisle, hallway, passage, corridor.
galling *(SYN.)* vexing, irritating, annoying, distressful, irksome.
galore *(SYN.)* abounding, plentiful, profuse, rich, overflowing.
gamble *(SYN.)* game, wager, bet, hazard, risk, venture, chance.
gambol *(SYN.)* romp, dance, cavort, frolic.
game *(SYN.)* fun, contest, merriment, pastime, match, play, amusement, recreation, diversion, entertainment, competition, sport.
(ANT.) labor, hardship, work, business.
gamut *(SYN.)* extent, scope, sweep, horizon, range.
gang *(SYN.)* group, troop, band, company, horde, crew.
gangling *(SYN.)* rangy, lean, skinny, tall, lanky.
gangster *(SYN.)* crook, hoodlum, gunman, criminal.
gap *(SYN.)* cavity, chasm, pore, gulf, aperture, abyss, interval, space, hole, void, pore, break, opening.
gape *(SYN.)* ogle, stare, gawk.
garb *(SYN.)* clothing, dress, vesture, array, attire, clothes, drapery, apparel, garments, costume, raiment.
(ANT.) nudity, nakedness.
garbage *(SYN.)* refuse, waste, trash, rubbish.
garbled *(SYN.)* twisted, confused, distorted.
gargantuan *(SYN.)* colossal, monumental, giant, huge, large, enormous.
garments *(SYN.)* drapery, dress, garb, apparel, array, attire, clothes, vesture, raiment, clothing.
(ANT.) nakedness, nudity.
garnish *(SYN.)* decorate, embellish, trim, adorn, enrich, beautify, deck, ornament.
(ANT.) expose, strip, debase, uncover, defame.
garrulous *(SYN.)* chatty, glib, verbose, talkative, communicative, voluble.
(ANT.) silent, uncommunicative, laconic, reticent, taciturn.
gash *(SYN.)* lacerate, slash, pierce, cut, hew, slice.
gasp *(SYN.)* pant, puff, wheeze.
gather *(ANT.)* assemble, collect, garner, harvest, reap, deduce, judge, amass, congregate, muster, cull, glean, accumulate, convene.
(ANT.) scatter, disperse, distribute, disband, separate.
gathering *(SYN.)* meeting, crowd, throng, company, assembly.
gaudy *(SYN.)* showy, flashy, loud, bold, ostentatious.
gaunt *(ANT.)* lank, diaphanous, flimsy, gauzy, narrow, rare, scanty, meager, gossamer, emaciated, scrawny, tenuous, thin, fine, lean, skinny, spare, slim, slight, slender, diluted.
(ANT.) wide, fat, thick, broad, bulky.
gay *(SYN.)* merry, lighthearted, joyful, cheerful, sprightly, jolly, happy, joyous, gleeful, jovial, colorful, bright, glad.
(ANT.) glum, mournful, sad, depressed, sorrowful, somber, sullen.
gaze *(SYN.)* look, stare, view, watch, examine, observe, glance, behold, discern, seem, see, survey, witness, inspect, goggle, appear.
(ANT.) hide, overlook, avert, miss.
geld *(SYN.)* neuter, alter, spay, castrate.
gem *(SYN.)* jewel, semiprecious stone.
general *(SYN.)* ordinary, universal, usual, common, customary, regular, vague, miscellaneous, indefinite, inexact.
(ANT.) definite, particular, exceptional, singular, rare, particular, precise, exact, specific.
generally *(SYN.)* ordinarily, usually, customarily, normally, mainly.

(ANT.) seldom, infrequently, rare.

generate *(SYN.)* produce, bestow, impart, concede, permit, acquiesce, cede, relent, succumb, surrender, pay, supply, grant, relent, bear, afford, submit, waive, allow, breed, accord, accede, abdicate, resign, relinquish, surrender, quit.
(ANT.) assert, refuse, struggle, resist, dissent, oppose, deny, strive.

generation *(SYN.)* age, date, era, period, seniority, senescence, senility, time, epoch, dotage.
(ANT.) infancy, youth, childhood.

generosity *(SYN.)* magnanimity, benevolence, humanity, kindness, philanthropy, tenderness, altruism, liberality, charity, beneficence.
(ANT.) selfishness, malevolence, cruelty, inhumanity, unkindness.

generous *(SYN.)* giving, liberal, unselfish, magnanimous, bountiful, munificent, charitable, big, noble, beneficent.
(ANT.) greedy, stingy, selfish, covetous, mean, miserly.

genesis *(SYN.)* birth, root, creation, source, origin, beginning.

genius *(SYN.)* intellect, adept, intellectual, sagacity, proficient, creativity, ability, inspiration, faculty, originality, aptitude, brain, gift, prodigy, talent.
(ANT.) dullard, stupidity, doll, shallowness, moron, ineptitude, obtuseness.

genre *(SYN.)* chaste, order, set, elegance, class, excellence, kind, caste, denomination, grade.

genteel *(SYN.)* cultured, polished, polite, refined, elegant.
(ANT.) discourteous, churlish, common.

gentle *(SYN.)* peaceful, placid, tame, serene, relaxed, docile, benign, soothing, calm, soft, mild, amiable, friendly, kindly, cultivated.
(ANT.) nasty, harsh, rough, fierce, mean, violent, savage.

genuine *(SYN.)* real, true, unaffected, authentic, sincere, bona fide, unadulterated, legitimate, actual, veritable, definite, proven.
(ANT.) false, sham, artificial, fake, counterfeit, bogus, pretended, insincere, sham.

genus *(SYN.)* kind, race, species, type, variety, character, family, breed, sort.

germ *(SYN.)* pest, virus, contamination, disease, pollution, taint, infection, contagion, poison, ailment.

germinate *(SYN.)* vegetate, pullulate, sprout, develop, grow.

gesture *(SYN.)* omen, signal, symbol, emblem, indication, note, token, symptom, movement, sign, motion, indication.

get *(SYN.)* obtain, receive, attain, gain, achieve, acquire, procure, earn, fetch, carry, remove, prepare, take, ready, urge, induce, secure.
(ANT.) lose, surrender, forfeit, leave, renounce.

ghastly *(SYN.)* frightful, horrible, horrifying, frightening, grisly, hideous, dreadful.

ghost *(SYN.)* phantom, spook, apparition, specter, trace, hint, vestige, spirit.

ghoulish *(SYN.)* weird, eerie, horrifying, gruesome, sinister, scary.

giant *(SYN.)* monster, colossus, mammoth, superman, gigantic.
(ANT.) small, tiny, dwarf, runt, midget, infinitesimal.

gibe *(SYN.)* sneer, jeer, mock, scoff, boo, hoot, hiss.
(ANT.) approve.

giddy *(SYN.)* reeling, dizzy, flighty, silly, scatterbrained.
(ANT.) serious.

gift *(SYN.)* endowment, favor, gratuity, bequest, talent, charity, present, largess, donation, grant, aptitude, boon, offering, faculty, genius, benefaction.
(ANT.) purchase, loss, ineptitude, deprivation, earnings, incapacity.

gigantic *(SYN.)* huge, colossal, immense, large, vast, elephantine, gargantuan, prodigious, mammoth, monumental, enormous.
(ANT.) small, tiny, minute, diminutive, little.

giggle *(SYN.)* chuckle, jeer, laugh, roar, snicker, titter, cackle, guffaw, mock.

gild *(SYN.)* cover, coat, paint, embellish, sweeten, retouch, camouflage.

gingerly *(SYN.)* gentle, cautiously, carefully, gently.
(ANT.) roughly.

gird *(SYN.)* wrap, tie, bind, belt, encircle, surround, get set, prepare.
(ANT.) untie.

girl *(SYN.)* female, lass, miss, maiden, damsel.

girth *(SYN.)* measure, size, width, dimensions, expanse, proportions.

gist *(SYN.)* connotation, explanation, purpose, significance, acceptation, implication, interpretation, meaning.
(ANT.) redundancy.

give *(SYN.)* bestow, contribute, grant, impart, provide, donate, confer, deliver, present, furnish, yield, develop, offer, produce, hand over, award, allot, deal out, mete out, bend, sacrifice, supply.
(ANT.) withdraw, take, retain, keep, seize.

given *(SYN.)* handed over, presented, supposed, stated, disposed, assumed, inclined, bent.

glacier *(SYN.)* frigid, icy, iceberg.

glad *(SYN.)* happy, cheerful, gratified, delighted, joyous, merry, pleased, exulting, charmed, thrilled, satisfied, tickled, gay, bright.
(ANT.) sad, depressed, dejected, melancholy, unhappy, morose, somber, despondent.

gladness *(SYN.)* bliss, contentment, happiness, pleasure, well-being, beatitude, delight, satisfaction, blessedness.
(ANT.) sadness, sorrow, despair, misery, grief.

glade *(SYN.)* clearing.

gladiator *(SYN.)* battler, fighter, competitor, combatant, contender, contestant.

glamorous *(SYN.)* spellbinding, fascinating, alluring, charming, bewitching, entrancing, captivating, enchanting, attractive, appealing, enticing, enthralling.

glamour *(SYN.)* charm, allure, attraction, magnetism, fascination.

glance *(SYN.)* eye, gaze, survey, view, examine, inspect, discern, look, see, witness, peek, regard, skim, reflect, glimpse, behold, observe.
(ANT.) hide, miss, avert, overlook.

glare *(SYN.)* flash, dazzle, stare, glower, glow, shine, glaze, burn, brilliance, flare, blind, scowl.

glaring *(SYN.)* flagrant, obvious, blatant, prominent, dazzling.

glass *(SYN.)* cup, tumbler, goblet, pane, crystal.

glassy *(SYN.)* blank, empty, emotionless, vacant, fixed, expressionless.

glaze *(SYN.)* buff, luster, cover, wax, gloss, coat, polish, shellac.

gleam *(SYN.)* flash, glimmer, glisten, shimmer, sparkle, twinkle, glare, beam, glow, radiate, glimmering, shine, burn, reflection, blaze.

glean *(SYN.)* reap, gather, select, harvest, pick, separate, cull.

glee *(SYN.)* mirth, joy, gladness, enchantment, delight, cheer, bliss, elation, merriment.
(ANT.) depression, misery, dejection.

glen *(SYN.)* ravine, valley.

glib *(SYN.)* smooth, suave, flat, plain, polished, sleek, urbane.
(ANT.) rough, rugged, blunt, harsh, bluff.

glide *(SYN.)* sweep, sail, fly, flow, slip, coast, cruise, move easily, skim, slide.

glimmer *(SYN.)* blink, shimmer, flicker, indication, hint, clue, suggestion.

glimpse *(SYN.)* notice, glance, peek, see, impression, look, flash.

glint *(SYN.)* flash, gleam, peek, glance, glimpse, sparkle, glitter.

glisten *(SYN.)* shimmer, shine, glimmer, twinkle, glitter, glister, sparkle.

glitch *(SYN.)* mishap, snag, hitch, malfunction.

glitter *(SYN.)* glisten, glimmer, sparkle, shine, twinkle.

gloat *(SYN.)* triumph, exult, glory, rejoice, revel.

global *(SYN.)* universal, international, worldwise.

globe *(SYN.)* orb, ball, world, earth, map, universe, sphere.

gloom *(SYN.)* bleakness, despondency, misery, sadness, woe, darkness, dejection, obscurity, blackness, shadow, shade, dimness, shadows, melancholy.
(ANT.) joy, mirth, exultation, cheerfulness, light, happiness, brightness, frivolity.

gloomy *(SYN.)* despondent, dismal, glum, somber, sorrowful, sad, dejected, disconsolate, dim, dark, morose, dispirited, moody, grave, pensive.
(ANT.) happy, merry, cheerful, high-spirited, bright, sunny, joyous.

glorify *(SYN.)* enthrone, exalt, honor, revere, adore, dignify, enshrine, consecrate, praise, worship, laud, venerate.
(ANT.) mock, dishonor, debase, abuse, degrade.

glorious *(SYN.)* exalted, high, noble, splendid, supreme, elevated, lofty, raised, majestic, famous, noted, stately, distinguished, celebrated, renowned, famed, magnificent, grand, proud, impressive, elegant, sublime.
(ANT.) ridiculous, low, base, ignoble, terrible, ordinary.

glory *(SYN.)* esteem, praise, respect, reverence, admiration, honor, dignity, worship, eminence, homage, deference.
(ANT.) dishonor, disgrace, contempt, reproach, derision.

gloss *(SYN.)* luster, shine, glow, sheen.

glossary *(SYN.)* dictionary, thesaurus, wordbook, lexicon.

glossy *(SYN.)* smooth, glistening, shiny, sleek, polished.
(ANT.) matte, dull.

glow *(SYN.)* beam, glisten, radiate, shimmer, sparkle, glare, blaze, scintillate, shine, light, gleam, burn, flare, flame, radiate, dazzle, blush, redden, heat, warmth, flicker.

glower *(SYN.)* scowl, stare, frown, glare.
(ANT.) beam, grin, smile.

glowing *(SYN.)* fiery, intense, passionate, zealous, enthusiastic, ardent, eager, fervent, favorable, impassioned, keen, complimentary, vehement.
(ANT.) cool, indifferent, apathetic, nonchalant.

glue *(SYN.)* bind, fasten, cement, paste.

glum *(SYN.)* morose, sulky, fretful, crabbed, sullen, dismal, dour, moody.
(ANT.) joyous, merry, amiable, gay, pleasant.

glut *(SYN.)* gorge, sate, content, furnish, fill, pervade, satiate, stuff, replenish, fill up, satisfy, stock.
(ANT.) empty, exhaust, deplete, void, drain.

glutton *(SYN.)* pig, hog, greedy eater.

gluttony *(SYN.)* ravenousness, piggishness, devouring, insatiability.
(ANT.) satisfaction, fullness.

gnarled *(SYN.)* twisted, knotted, rugged, knobby, nodular.

gnash *(SYN.)* gnaw, crunch, grind.

gnaw *(SYN.)* chew, eat, gnash, grind, erode.

go *(SYN.)* proceed, depart, flee, move, vanish, exit, walk, quit, fade, progress, travel, become, fit, agree, leave, suit, harmonize, pass, travel, function, operate, withdraw.
(ANT.) stay, arrive, enter, stand, come.

goad *(SYN.)* incite, prod, drive, urge, push, shove, jab, provoke, stimulate.

goal *(SYN.)* craving, destination, desire, longing, objective, finish, end, passion, aim, object, aspiration.

gobble *(SYN.)* devour, eat fast, gorge, gulp, stuff.

goblet *(SYN.)* cup, glass.

goblin *(SYN.)* troll, elf, dwarf, spirit.

godlike *(SYN.)* holy, supernatural, heavenly, celestial, divine, transcendent.
(ANT.) profane, wicked, blasphemous,

diabolical, mundane.
godly *(SYN.)* pious, religious, holy, pure, divine, spiritual, righteous, saintly.
golden *(SYN.)* shining, metallic, bright, fine, superior, nice, excellent, valuable.
(ANT.) dull, inferior.
gong *(SYN.)* chimes, bells.
good *(SYN.)* honest, sound, valid, cheerful, honorable, worthy, conscientious, moral, genuine, humane, kind, fair, useful, skillful, adequate, friendly.
(ANT.) bad, imperfect, vicious, undesirable, unfriendly, unkind, evil.
good-by *(SYN.)* so long, farewell.
good-bye *(SYN.)* farewell.
good-hearted *(SYN.)* good, kind, thoughtful, kindhearted, considerate.
(ANT.) evil-hearted.
good-humored *(SYN.)* pleasant, good-natured, cheerful, sunny, amiable.
(ANT.) petulant, cranky.
goodness *(SYN.)* good, honesty, integrity, virtue, righteousness.
(ANT.) sin, evil, dishonesty, corruption.
goods *(SYN.)* property, belongings, holdings, possessions, merchandise.
good will *(SYN.)* agreeability, harmony, willingness, readiness.
gore *(SYN.)* impale, penetrate, puncture, gouge.
gorge *(SYN.)* ravine, devour, stuff, gobble, valley, defile, pass, cram, fill.
gorgeous *(SYN.)* grand, ravishing, glorious, stunning, brilliant, divine.
(ANT.) homely, ugly, squalid.
gory *(SYN.)* bloody.
gossamer *(SYN.)* dainty, fine, filmy, delicate, sheer, transparent.
gossip *(SYN.)* prate, rumor, prattle, bearsay, meddler, tattler, chatter.
gouge *(SYN.)* scoop, dig, carve, burrow, excavate, chisel, notch.
gourmet *(SYN.)* gourmand, gastronome, connoisseur.
govern *(SYN.)* manage, oversee, reign, preside over, supervise, direct, command, sway, administer, control.
(ANT.) assent, submit, acquiesce.
government *(SYN.)* control, direction, rule, command, authority.
governor *(SYN.)* controller, administrator, director, leader, manager.
gown *(SYN.)* garment, robe, frock, dress, costume, attire.
grab *(SYN.)* snatch, grip, clutch, seize, grasp, capture, pluck.
grace *(SYN.)* charm, beauty, handsomeness, loveliness, dignify, fairness, honor, distinguish, sympathy.
(ANT.) eyesore, homeliness, deformity, ugliness, disfigurement.
graceful *(SYN.)* elegant, fluid, natural, supple, beautiful, comely, flowing.
(ANT.) clumsy, awkward, gawky, ungainly, deformed.
gracious *(SYN.)* warm-hearted, pleasing, friendly, engaging, agreeable, kind, amiable, kindly, nice, good, courteous, polite, generous.
(ANT.) surly, hateful, churlish, rude, disagreeable, impolite, thoughtless, discourteous, ill-natured.
grade *(SYN.)* kind, rank, elegance, denomination, sort, arrange, category, classify, rate, group, place, mark.
gradual *(SYN.)* deliberate, sluggish, dawdling, laggard, slow, leisurely, moderate, easy, delaying.
(ANT.) quick, swift, fast, speedy, rapid.
graduate *(SYN.)* pass, finish, advance.
graft *(SYN.)* fraud, theft, cheating, bribery, dishonesty, transplant.
grain *(SYN.)* speck, particle, plant, bit, seed, temper, fiber, character, texture, markings, nature, tendency.
grand *(SYN.)* great, elaborate, splendid, royal, stately, noble, considerable.
(ANT.) unassuming, modest, insignificant, unimportant, humble.
grandeur *(SYN.)* resplendence, majesty, distinction, glory.
grandiose *(SYN.)* grand, lofty, magnificent, stately, noble, pompous, dignified, imposing, sublime, majestic.
(ANT.) lowly, ordinary, common.
grandstand *(SYN.)* bleachers, gallery.
granite *(SYN.)* stone, rock.
grant *(SYN.)* confer, allocate, deal, divide, mete, appropriation, assign, benefaction, distribute, allowance, donate, award, mete out, deal out.
(ANT.) refuse, withhold, confiscate, keep, retain.
granular *(SYN.)* grainy, sandy, crumbly, rough, gritty.
graph *(SYN.)* design, plan, stratagem, draw up, chart, sketch, cabal, machination, outline, plot.
graphic *(SYN.)* vivid, lifelike, significant, meaningful, pictorial, descriptive.
grapple *(SYN.)* grip, seize, clutch, clasp, grasp, fight, struggle.
grasp *(SYN.)* clutch, grip, seize, apprehend, capture, snare, hold, clasp.
(ANT.) release, lose, throw, liberate.
grasping *(SYN.)* possessive, greedy, selfish, acquisitive, mercenary.
(ANT.) liberal, unselfish, generous.
grate *(SYN.)* file, pulverize, grind, scrape, scratch, scrape, annoy, irritate.
grateful *(SYN.)* beholden, obliged, appreciative, thankful, indebted.
(ANT.) ungrateful, unappreciative, grudging, thankless.
gratify *(SYN.)* charm, please, satisfy.
(ANT.) frustrate.
gratifying *(SYN.)* contentment, solace, relief, comfort, ease, succor, consolation, enjoyment.
(ANT.) suffering, torment, affliction, discomfort, torture, misery.
grating *(SYN.)* harsh, rugged, severe, stringent, coarse, gruff, jarring, rigorous, strict.
(ANT.) smooth, melodious, gentle, soft.
gratis *(SYN.)* complimentary, free.
gratitude *(SYN.)* gratefulness, thankfulness, appreciation.
(ANT.) ungratefulness.
gratuity *(SYN.)* tip, bonus, gift.
grave *(SYN.)* sober, grim, earnest, serious, important, momentous, sedate, solemn, somber, imposing, vital, essential, staid, consequential, thoughtful.

(ANT.) light, flighty, trivial, insignificant, unimportant, trifling, merry, gay, cheery, frivolous.
gravel *(SYN.)* stones, pebbles, grain.
gravitate *(SYN.)* incline, tend, lean, approach, toward.
gravity *(SYN.)* concern, importance, seriousness, pull, movement.
(ANT.) triviality.
graze *(SYN.)* scrape, feed, rub, brush, contact, skim.
grease *(SYN.)* fat, oil, lubrication.
greasy *(SYN.)* messy, buttery.
great *(SYN.)* large, numerous, eminent, illustrious, big, gigantic enormous, immense, vast, weighty, fine.
(ANT.) minute, common, menial, ordinary, paltry, unknown.
greed *(SYN.)* piggishness, lust, desire, greediness, avarice, covetousness.
(ANT.) selflessness, generosity.
greedy *(SYN.)* selfish, devouring, ravenous, avaricious, covetous, rapacious, gluttonous, insatiable, voracious.
(ANT.) full, generous, munificent, giving, satisfied.
green *(SYN.)* inexperienced, modern, novel, recent, further, naive, fresh, natural, raw, unsophisticated, undeveloped, immature, unripe, additional, brisk, artless.
(ANT.) hackneyed, musty, decayed, faded, stagnant.
greenhorn *(SYN.)* tenderfoot, beginner, apprentice, amateur, novice.
greenhouse *(SYN.)* hothouse.
greet *(SYN.)* hail, accost, meet, address, talk to, speak to, welcome, approach.
(ANT.) pass by, avoid.
gregarious *(SYN.)* outgoing, civil, affable, hospitable, sociable.
(ANT.) inhospitable, antisocial, disagreeable, hermitic.
grief *(SYN.)* misery, sadness, tribulation, affliction, heartache, woe, trial, anguish, mourning, distress, lamentation.
(ANT.) happiness, solace, consolation, comfort, joy.
grief-stricken *(SYN.)* heartsick, ravaged, devastated, wretched, forlorn, desolate, wretched.
(ANT.) joyous, blissful, content.
grievance *(SYN.)* injury, wrong, injustice, detriment, complaint, damage, prejudice, evil, objection, protest, accusation, harm.
(ANT.) improvement, benefit, repair.
grieve *(SYN.)* lament, brood over, mourn, weep, wail, sorrow, distress, bemoan, hurt, deplore.
(ANT.) revel, carouse, celebrate, rejoice, gladden, soothe.
grieved *(SYN.)* contrite, remorseful, beggarly, mean, pitiful, shabby, vile, sorrowful, pained, hurt, sorry, contemptible, worthless.
(ANT.) splendid, delighted, cheerful, impenitent, unrepentant.
grievous *(SYN.)* gross, awful, outrageous, shameful, lamentable, regrettable.
(ANT.) agreeable, comforting, pleasurable.
grill *(SYN.)* cook, broil, question, interrogate, barbecue, grating, gridiron, cross-examine.
grim *(SYN.)* severe, harsh, strict, merciless, fierce, horrible, inflexible, adamant, ghastly, frightful, unyielding, rigid, stern.
(ANT.) pleasant, lenient, relaxed, amiable, congenial, smiling.
grimace *(SYN.)* expression, mope.
grimy *(SYN.)* unclean, grubby, soiled.
grin *(SYN.)* beam, smile, smirk.
grind *(SYN.)* mill, mash, powder, crush, crumble, pulverize, smooth, grate, sharpen, even.
grip *(SYN.)* catch, clutch, apprehend, trap, arrest, grasp, hold, bag, suitcase, lay hold of, clench, command, control, possession, domination, comprehension, understanding, seize.
(ANT.) release, liberate, lose, throw.
gripe *(SYN.)* protest, grumbling.
grit *(SYN.)* rub, grind, grate, sand, gravel, pluck, courage, stamina.
groan *(SYN.)* sob, wail, howl, moan, whimper, wail, complain.
groggy *(SYN.)* dazed, dopy, stupefied, stunned, drugged, unsteady.
(ANT.) alert.
groom *(SYN.)* tend, tidy, preen, curry, spouse, consort.
groove *(SYN.)* furrow, channel, track, routine, slot, scratch.
groovy *(SYN.)* marvelous, delightful, wonderful.
grope *(SYN.)* fumble, feel around.
gross *(SYN.)* glaring, coarse, indelicate, obscene, bulky, great, total, whole, brutal, grievous, aggregate, earthy, rude, vulgar, entire, enormous, plain, crass, rough, large.
(ANT.) appealing, delicate, refined, proper, polite, cultivated, slight, comely, trivial, decent.
grotesque *(SYN.)* strange, weird, odd, incredible, fantastic, monstrous, absurd, freakish, bizarre, peculiar, deformed, disfigured, queer.
grotto *(SYN.)* tunnel, cave, hole, cavern.
grouch *(SYN.)* protest, remonstrate, whine, complain, grumble, murmur, mope, mutter, repine.
(ANT.) praise, applaud, rejoice.
grouchy *(SYN.)* cantankerous, grumpy, surly.
(ANT.) cheerful, contented, pleasant.
ground *(SYN.)* foundation, presumption, surface, principle, underpinning, premise, base, bottom, fix, basis, soil, land, earth, set, root, support, establish, dirt, presupposition.
(ANT.) implication, superstructure, trimming, derivative.
groundless *(SYN.)* baseless, unfounded, unwarranted, needless.
grounds *(SYN.)* garden, lawns, dregs, foundation, leftovers, reason, sediment, cause, basis, premise, motive.
groundwork *(SYN.)* support, bottom, base, underpinning, premise, presupposition, principle, basis.
(ANT.) trimming, implication, deriva-

tive, superstructure.

group *(SYN.)* crowd, clock, party, troupe, swarm, bunch, brook, assembly, herd, band, mob, brood, class, throng, cluster, flock, lot, collection, pack, horde, gathering, aggregation.
(ANT.) disassemble.

grouse *(SYN.)* mutter, grumble, gripe, scold, growl, complain.

grovel *(SYN.)* creep, crawl, cower, cringe, slouch, stoop, scramble.

groveling *(SYN.)* dishonorable, lowly, sordid, vile, mean, abject, despicable, ignoble, menial, servile, vulgar, ignominious.
(ANT.) lofty, noble, esteemed, exalted, righteous.

grow *(SYN.)* extend, swell, advance, develop, enlarge, enlarge, germinate, mature, expand, flower, raise, become, cultivate, increase, distend.
(ANT.) wane, shrink, atrophy, decay, diminish, contract.

growl *(SYN.)* complain, snarl, grumble, gnarl, roar, clamor, bellow.

grown-up *(SYN.)* full-grown, adult, of age, mature, big, senior.
(ANT.) little, childish, junior, juvenile.

growth *(SYN.)* expansion, development, unfolding, maturing, progress, elaboration, evolution.
(ANT.) degeneration, deterioration, curtailment, abbreviation, compression.

grub *(SYN.)* gouge, dig, scoop out, burrow, tunnel, excavate, plod, toil, drudge.

grubby *(SYN.)* unkempt, grimy, slovenly, dirty.
(ANT.) tidy, spruce, neat, clean, well-groomed.

grudge *(SYN.)* malevolence, malice, resentment, bitterness, spite, animosity, enmity, rancor, ill will.
(ANT.) kindness, love, benevolence, affection, good will, friendliness.

grudgingly *(SYN.)* reluctantly, unwillingly, under protest, involuntarily.

grueling *(SYN.)* taxing, exhausting, excruciating, trying, arduous, grinding, crushing.
(ANT.) effortless, easy, light, simple.

gruesome *(SYN.)* hideous, frightful, horrible, loathsome, ghastly, grisly.
(ANT.) agreeable, soothing, delightful, charming.

gruff *(SYN.)* scratchy, crude, incomplete, unpolished, stormy, brusque, rude, rough, uncivil, churlish, violent, harsh, imperfect, craggy, irregular, deep, husky, approximate, tempestuous, blunt.
(ANT.) civil, courteous, polished, calm, even, sleek, smooth, finished, gentle, placid, pleasant, tranquil.

grumble *(SYN.)* protest, complain.

grumpy *(SYN.)* ill-tempered, cranky, grouchy, surly, cross-grained, crabbed, fractious, pettish, disgruntled, moody.
(ANT.) winsome, amiable, pleasant, cheery.

guarantee *(SYN.)* bond, pledge, token, warrant, earnest, surety, bail, commitment, promise, secure, swear, assure, sponsor, certify, warranty, insure, endorse, security.

guarantor *(SYN.)* voucher, sponsor, warrantor, signatory, surety.

guaranty *(SYN.)* warranty, token, deposit, earnest, pledge, stake.

guard *(SYN.)* protect, shield, veil, cloak, conceal, disguise, envelop, preserve, hide, defend, cover, sentry, protector, shroud, curtain.
(ANT.) unveil, expose, ignore, neglect, bare, reveal, disregard, divulge.

guarded *(SYN.)* discreet, cautious.
(ANT.) audacious, reckless, careless.

guardian *(SYN.)* curator, keeper, protector, custodian, patron, watchdog, champion.

guess *(SYN.)* estimate, suppose, think, assume, reason, believe, reckon, speculate, notion, surmise, hypothesis, imagine, consider, opinion.
(ANT.) know.

guest *(SYN.)* caller, client, customer, patient, visitor, company.
(ANT.) host.

guide *(SYN.)* manage, supervise, conduct, direct, lead, steer, escort, pilot, show, squire, usher, control, affect, influence, regulate.
(ANT.) follower, follow.

guild *(SYN.)* association, union, society.

guile *(SYN.)* deceitfulness, fraud, wiliness, trick, deceit, chicanery, cunning, deception, craftiness, sneakiness.
(ANT.) sincerity, openness, honesty, truthfulness, candor, frankness.

guileless *(SYN.)* open, innocent, naive, sincere, simple, candid.
(ANT.) treacherous, plotting.

guilt *(SYN.)* sin, blame, fault, offense.

guilty *(SYN.)* culpable, to blame, responsible, criminal, blameworthy.
(ANT.) blameless, innocent, guiltless.

guise *(SYN.)* aspect, pretense, mien, look, air, advent, apparition, appearance, dress, garb, coat, cover, clothes, show, manner, form, demeanor, arrival.

gulch *(SYN.)* gorge, ravine, canyon.

gulf *(SYN.)* ravine, cut, break, crack, chasm, canyon, abyss, cleft, separation, bay, sound, inlet.

gullible *(SYN.)* trustful, naive, innocent, unsuspecting, deceivable, believing.
(ANT.) skeptical, sophisticated.

gully *(SYN.)* ditch, gorge, ravine, valley, gulch, gulf.

gulp *(SYN.)* devour, swallow, gasp.

gun *(SYN.)* fire, shoot, weapon, discharge, pistol, firearm, revolver.

gush *(SYN.)* pour, spurt, stream, rush out, spout, flood, flush, chatter.

gust *(SYN.)* blast, wind, outbreak.

gutter *(SYN.)* ditch, groove, drain, channel, trench, sewer, trough.

gymnasium *(SYN.)* playground, arena, court, athletic field.

gymnastics *(SYN.)* drill, exercise, acrobatics, calisthenics.

gyp *(SYN.)* swindle, cheat, defraud.

gypsy *(SYN.)* nomad.

habit *(SYN.)* usage, routine, compulsion, use, wont, custom, disposition, practice, addiction, fashion.
habitation *(SYN.)* abode, domicile, lodgings, dwelling, home.
habitual *(SYN.)* general, usual, common, frequent, persistent, customary, routine, regular, often.
(ANT.) solitary, unique, exceptional, occasional, unusual, scanty, rare.
habituated *(SYN.)* used, accustomed, adapted, acclimated, comfortable, familiarized, addicted, settled.
hack *(SYN.)* cleave, chop, slash, hew, slice, pick, sever, mangle.
hackneyed *(SYN.)* stale, stereotyped, trite, commonplace, ordinary, banal, common, unique.
(ANT.) novel, stimulating, modern, fresh, creative, momentous.
hag *(SYN.)* beldam, crone, vixen, granny, ogress, harridan, virage.
haggard *(SYN.)* drawn, careworn, debilitated, spent, gaunt, worn.
(ANT.) bright, fresh, clear-eyed, animated.
haggle *(SYN.)* dicker, bargain.
hail *(SYN.)* welcome, approach, accost, speak to, address, greet.
(ANT.) pass by, avoid.
hairdo *(SYN.)* hairstyle, coiffure, haircut.
hairdresser *(SYN.)* beautician, barber.
hairless *(SYN.)* shorn, bald, baldpated, depilitated.
(ANT.) hirsute, hairy, unshaven.
hair-raising *(SYN.)* horrifying, exciting, alarming, thrilling, startling, frightful, scary, breathtaking.
hairy *(SYN.)* bearded, shaggy, hirsute, bewhiskered.
hale *(SYN.)* robust, well, wholesome, hearty, healthy, sound, strong, vigorous, salubrious.
(ANT.) noxious, frail, diseased, delicate, infirm, injurious.
half-baked *(SYN.)* crude, premature, makeshift, illogical, shallow.
half-hearted *(SYN.)* uncaring, indifferent, unenthusiastic, cool.
(ANT.) eager, enthusiastic, earnest.
half-wit *(SYN.)* dope, simpleton, nitwit, dunce, idiot, fool.
hall *(SYN.)* corridor, lobby, passage, hallway, vestibule, foyer.
hallow *(SYN.)* glorify, exalt, dignify, aggrandize, consecrate, elevate, ennoble, raise, erect.
(ANT.) dishonor, humiliate, debase, degrade.
hallowed *(SYN.)* holy, sacred, beatified, sacrosanct, blessed, divine.
hallucination *(SYN.)* fantasy, mirage, dream, vision, phantasm, appearance, aberration, illusion.
halt *(SYN.)* impede, obstruct, terminate, stop, hinder, desist, check, arrest, abstain, discontinue, hold, end, cork, interrupt, bar, cease.
(ANT.) start, begin, proceed, speed, beginning, promote.
halting *(SYN.)* imperfect, awkward, stuttering, faltering, hobbling, doubtful, limping, wavering.
(ANT.) decisive, confident, smooth, graceful, facile.
hammer *(SYN.)* beat, bang, whack, pound, batter, drive, tap, cudgel.
hamper *(SYN.)* prevent, impede, thwart, restrain, hinder, obstruct.
(ANT.) help, assist, expedite, encourage, facilitate.
hamstrung *(SYN.)* disabled, helpless, paralyzed.
hand *(SYN.)* assistant, helper, support, aid, farmhand, laborer.
handicap *(SYN.)* retribution, penalty, disadvantage, forfeiture, hindrance, chastisement.
(ANT.) reward, pardon, compensation, remuneration.
handily *(SYN.)* readily, skillfully, easily, dexterously, smoothly, adroitly, deftly.
handkerchief *(SYN.)* bandanna, kerchief, scarf.
handle *(SYN.)* hold, touch, finger, clutch, grip, manipulate, feel, grasp, control, oversee, direct, treat, steer, supervise, run, regulate.
hand out *(SYN.)* disburse, distribute, deal, mete, circulate.
hand over *(SYN.)* release, surrender, deliver, yield, present, fork over.
handsome *(SYN.)* lovely, pretty, fair, comely, beautiful, charming, elegant, good-looking, large, generous, liberal, beauteous, fine.
(ANT.) repulsive, ugly, unattractive, stingy, small, mean, petty, unsightly, meager, homely, foul, hideous.
handy *(SYN.)* suitable, adapted, appropriate, favorable, fitting, near, ready, close, nearby, clever, helpful, useful, timely, accessible.
(ANT.) inopportune, troublesome, awkward, inconvenient.
hang *(SYN.)* drape, hover, dangle, suspend, kill, sag, execute, lynch.
hang in *(SYN.)* continue, endure, remain, persevere, resist, persist.
hang-up *(SYN.)* inhibition, difficulty, snag, hindrance, block.
hanker *(SYN.)* wish, yearn, long, desire, pine, thirst, covet.
haphazard *(SYN.)* aimless, random, purposeless, casual, indiscriminate, accidental.
(ANT.) determined, planned, designed, deliberate.
hapless *(SYN.)* ill-fated, unfortunate, jinxed, luckless, wretched.
happen *(SYN.)* occur, take place, befchance, betide, transpire, come to pass, chance, befall.
happening *(SYN.)* episode, event, scene, incident, affair, experience, phenomenon, transaction.
happiness *(SYN.)* pleasure, gladness, delight, beatitude, bliss, contentment, satisfaction, joy, joyousness, blessedness, joyfulness, felicity, elation, well-being.
(ANT.) sadness, sorrow, despair, misery, grief.
happy *(SYN.)* gay, joyous, cheerful, fortunate, glad, merry, contented,

satisfied, lucky, blessed, pleased, opportune, delighted.
(ANT.) gloomy, morose, sad, sorrowful, miserable, inconvenient, unlucky, depressed, blue.

happy-go-lucky *(SYN.)* easygoing, carefree, unconcerned.
(ANT.) prudent, responsible, concerned.

harangue *(SYN.)* oration, diatribe, lecture, tirade, exhortation.

harass *(SYN.)* badger, irritate, molest, pester, taunt, torment, provoke, tantalize, worry, aggravate, annoy, nag, plague, vex.
(ANT.) please, soothe, comfort, delight, gratify.

harbinger *(SYN.)* sign, messenger, proclaim, forerunner, herald.

harbor *(SYN.)* haven, port, anchorage, cherish, entertain, protect, shelter.

hard *(SYN.)* difficult, burdensome, arduous, rigid, puzzling, cruel, strict, unfeeling, severe, stern, impenetrable, compact, tough, solid, onerous, rigorous, firm, intricate, harsh, perplexing.
(ANT.) fluid, brittle, effortless, gentle, tender, easy, simple, plastic, soft, lenient, flabby, elastic.

hard-boiled *(SYN.)* unsympathetic, tough, harsh, unsentimental.

harden *(SYN.)* petrify, solidify.
(ANT.) loose, soften.

hardheaded *(SYN.)* stubborn, obstinate, unyielding, headstrong.

hardhearted *(SYN.)* merciless, hard, unmerciful, callous, pitiless, ruthless.

hardly *(SYN.)* barely, scarcely.

hard-nosed *(SYN.)* shrewd, tough, practical.

hardship *(SYN.)* ordeal, test, effort, affliction, misfortune, trouble, experiment, proof, essay, misery, examination, difficulty, tribulation.
(ANT.) consolation, alleviation.

hardy *(SYN.)* sturdy, strong, tough, vigorous.
(ANT.) frail, decrepit, feeble, weak, fragile.

harm *(SYN.)* hurt, mischief, misfortune, mishap, damage, wickedness, cripple, injury, evil, detriment, ill, infliction, wrong.
(ANT.) favor, kindness, benefit, boon.

harmful *(SYN.)* damaging, injurious, mischievous, detrimental, hurtful, deleterious.
(ANT.) helpful, salutary, profitable,, advantageous, beneficial.

harmless *(SYN.)* protected, secure, snag, dependable, certain, painless, innocent, trustworthy.
(ANT.) perilous, hazardous, insecure, dangerous, unsafe.

harmonious *(SYN.)* tuneful, melodious, congenial, amicable.
(ANT.) dissonant, discordant, disagreeable.

harmony *(SYN.)* unison, bargain, contract, stipulation, pact, agreement, accordance, concord, accord, understanding, unity, coincidence.
(ANT.) discord, dissension, difference, variance, disagreement.

harness *(SYN.)* control, yoke.

harry *(SYN.)* vex, pester, harass, bother, plague.

harsh *(SYN.)* jarring, gruff, rugged, severe, stringent, blunt, grating, unpleasant, tough, stern, strict, unkind, rigorous, cruel, coarse.
(ANT.) smooth, soft, gentle, melodious, soothing, easy, mild.

harvest *(SYN.)* reap, gather, produce, yield, crop, gain, acquire, fruit, result, reaping, product, proceeds, glean, garner.
(ANT.) plant, squander, lose, sow.

haste *(SYN.)* speed, hurry, rush, rapidity, flurry, scramble.
(ANT.) sloth, sluggishness.

hasten *(SYN.)* hurry, sprint, quicken, rush, precipitate, accelerate, scurry, run, scamper, dispatch, press, urge, dash, expedite, speed.
(ANT.) retard, tarry, detain, linger, dawdle, delay, hinder.

hasty *(SYN.)* quick, swift, irascible, lively, nimble, brisk, active, speedy, impatient, testy, sharp, fast, rapid.
(ANT.) slow, dull, sluggish.

hat *(SYN.)* helmet, bonnet.

hatch *(SYN.)* breed, incubate, brood.

hate *(SYN.)* loathe, detest, despise, disfavor, hatred, abhorrence, abominate, abhor, dislike.
(ANT.) love, cherish, approve, admire, like.

hateful *(SYN.)* loathsome, detestable, offensive.
(ANT.) likable, loving, admirable.

hatred *(SYN.)* detestation, dislike, malevolence, enmity, rancor, ill will, loathing, hate, hostility, abhorrence, aversion, animosity.
(ANT.) friendship, love, affection, attraction.

haughty *(SYN.)* proud, stately, vainglorious, arrogant, disdainful, overbearing, supercilious, vain.
(ANT.) meek, ashamed, lowly, humble.

haul *(SYN.)* draw, pull, drag, tow.

have *(SYN.)* own, possess, seize, hold, control, occupy, acquire, undergo, maintain, experience, receive, gain, affect, include, contain, get, take, obtain.
(ANT.) surrender, abandon, renounce, lose.

havoc *(SYN.)* devastation, ruin, destruction.

hazard *(SYN.)* peril, chance, dare, risk, offer, conjecture, jeopardy, danger.
(ANT.) safety, defense, protection, immunity.

hazardous *(SYN.)* perilous, precarious, threatening, unsafe, dangerous, critical, menacing, risky.
(ANT.) protected, secure, safe.

hazy *(SYN.)* uncertain, unclear, ambiguous, dim, obscure, undetermined, vague, unsettled, indefinite.
(ANT.) specific, clear, lucid, precise, explicit.

head *(SYN.)* leader, summit, top, culmination, director, chief, master, commander, supervisor, start, source,

crest, beginning, crisis.
(ANT.) foot, base, bottom, follower, subordinate, underling.
headstrong *(SYN.)* obstinate, stubborn, willful.
(ANT.) easygoing, amenable.
headway *(SYN.)* movement, progress.
heady *(SYN.)* thrilling, intoxicating, exciting, electrifying.
heal *(SYN.)* restore, cure.
healthy *(SYN.)* wholesome, hale, robust, sound, well, vigorous, strong, hearty, healthful, hygienic, salubrious, salutary.
(ANT.) noxious, diseased, unhealthy, delicate, frail, infirm, injurious.
heap *(SYN.)* collection, mound, increase, store, stack, pile, gather, accumulate, amass, accrue, accumulation, collect.
(ANT.) dissipate, scatter, waste, diminish, disperse.
hear *(SYN.)* heed, listen, detect, harken, perceive, regard.
heart *(SYN.)* middle, center, sympathy, nucleus, midpoint, sentiment, core, feeling, midst.
(ANT.) outskirts, periphery, border, rim, boundary.
heartache *(SYN.)* anguish, mourning, sadness, sorrow, affliction, distress, grief, lamentation, tribulation.
(ANT.) happiness, joy, solace, comfort, consolation.
heartbroken *(SYN.)* distressed, forlorn, mean, paltry, worthless, contemptible, wretched, crestfallen, disconsolate, downhearted, comfortless, brokenhearted, low.
(ANT.) noble, fortunate, contented, significant.
hearten *(SYN.)* encourage, favor, impel, urge, promote, sanction, animate, cheer, exhilarate, cheer.
(ANT.) deter, dissuade, deject, discourage, dispirit.
heartless *(SYN.)* mean, cruel, ruthless, hardhearted, pitiless.
(ANT.) sympathetic, kind.
heart-rending *(SYN.)* heartbreaking, depressing, agonizing.
hearty *(SYN.)* warm, earnest, ardent, cordial, sincere, gracious, sociable.
(ANT.) taciturn, aloof, cool, reserved.
heat *(SYN.)* hotness, warmth, temperature, passion, ardor, zeal, inflame, cook, excitement, warm.
(ANT.) cool, chill, coolness, freeze, coldness, chilliness, iciness, cold.
heated *(SYN.)* vehement, fiery, intense, passionate.
heave *(SYN.)* boost, hoist, raise.
heaven *(SYN.)* empyrean, paradise.
heavenly *(SYN.)* superhuman, godlike, blissful, saintly, holy, divine, celestial, angelic, blessed.
(ANT.) wicked, mundane, profane, blasphemous, diabolical.
heavy *(SYN.)* weighty, massive, gloomy, serious, ponderous, cumbersome, trying, burdensome, harsh, grave, intense, dull, grievous, concentrated, severe, oppressive, sluggish.
(ANT.) brisk, light, animated.
heckle *(SYN.)* torment, harass, tease, hector, harry.
heed *(SYN.)* care, alertness, circumspection, mindfulness, consider, watchfulness, reflection, study, attention, notice, regard, obey, ponder, respect, meditate, mind, observe, deliberate, examine, contemplate, weigh, esteem, application.
(ANT.) negligence, oversight, over look, neglect, ignore, disregard, indifference, omission.
heedless *(SYN.)* sightless, headlong, rash, unmindful, deaf, unseeing, oblivious, ignorant, inattentive, disregardful, blind.
(ANT.) perceiving, sensible, aware, calculated, discerning.
height *(SYN.)* zenith, peak, summit, tallness, mountain, acme, apex, elevation, altitude, prominence, maximum, pinnacle, culmination.
(ANT.) base, depth, anticlimax.
heighten *(SYN.)* increase, magnify, annoy, chafe, intensify, amplify, aggravate, provoke, irritate, concentrate, nettle.
(ANT.) soothe, mitigate, palliate, soften, appease.
heinous *(SYN.)* abominable, grievous, atrocious.
hello *(SYN.)* greeting, good evening, good afternoon, good morning.
(ANT.) farewell, good-bye, so long.
help *(SYN.)* assist, support, promote, relieve, abet, succor, back, uphold, further, remedy, encourage, aid, facilitate, mitigate.
(ANT.) afflict, thwart, resist, hinder, impede.
helper *(SYN.)* aide, assistant, supporter.
helpful *(SYN.)* beneficial, serviceable, wholesome, useful, profitable, advantageous, good, salutary.
(ANT.) harmful, injurious, useless, worthless, destructive, deleterious, detrimental.
helpfulness *(SYN.)* assistance, cooperation, usefulness, serviceability, kindness, neighborliness, willingness, collaboration, supportiveness, readiness.
(ANT.) antagonism, hostility, opposition.
helpless *(SYN.)* weak, feeble, dependent, disabled, inept, unresourceful, incapable, incompetent.
(ANT.) resourceful, competent, enterprising.
helplessness *(SYN.)* impotence, feebleness, weakness, incapacity, ineptitude, invalidism, shiftless, awkwardness.
(ANT.) power, strength, might, potency.
helter-skelter *(SYN.)* haphazardly, chaotically, irregularly.
hem *(SYN.)* bottom, border, edge, rim, margin, pale, verge, flounce, boundary, fringe, brim, fence, hedge, frame.
hem in *(SYN.)* enclose, shut in, confine, restrict, limit.
hence *(SYN.)* consequently, thence, therefore, so, accordingly.
herald *(SYN.)* harbinger, crier, envoy,

forerunner, precursor, augury, forecast.
herculean *(SYN.)* demanding, heroic, titanic, mighty, prodigious, laborious, arduous, overwhelming, backbreaking.
herd *(SYN.)* group, pack, drove, crowd, flock, gather.
heretic *(SYN.)* nonconformist, sectarian, unbeliever, sectary, schismatic, apostate, dissenter.
heritage *(SYN.)* birthright, legacy, patrimony, inheritance.
hermit *(SYN.)* recluse, anchorite, eremite.
hero *(SYN.)* paladin, champion, idol.
heroic *(SYN.)* bold, courageous, fearless, gallant, valiant, valorous, brave, chivalrous, adventurous, dauntless, intrepid, magnanimous.
(ANT.) fearful, weak, cringing, timid, cowardly.
heroism *(SYN.)* valor, bravery, gallant, dauntless, bold, courageous, fearless.
hesitant *(SYN.)* reluctant, unwilling, disinclined, loath, slow, averse.
(ANT.) willing, inclined, eager, ready, disposed.
hesitate *(SYN.)* falter, waver, pause, doubt, demur, delay, vacillate, wait, stammer, stutter, scruple.
(ANT.) proceed, resolve, continue, decide, persevere.
hesitation *(SYN.)* distrust, scruple, suspense, uncertainty, unbelief, ambiguity, doubt, incredulity, skepticism.
(ANT.) determination, belief, certainty, faith, conviction.
hidden *(SYN.)* undeveloped, unseen dormant, concealed, quiescent, latent, potential, inactive.
(ANT.) visible, explicit, conspicuous, evident.
hide *(SYN.)* disguise, mask, suppress, withhold, veil, cloak, conceal, screen, camouflage, shroud, pelt, skin, leather, cover.
(ANT.) reveal, show, expose, disclose, uncover, divulge.
hideous *(SYN.)* frightful, ugly, shocking, frightening, horrible, terrible, horrifying, terrifying, grisly, gross.
(ANT.) lovely, beautiful, beauteous.
high *(SYN.)* tall, eminent, exalted, elevated, high-pitched, sharp, lofty, proud, shrill, raised, strident, prominent, important, powerful, expensive, dear, high-priced, costly, grave, serious, extreme, towering.
(ANT.) low, mean, tiny, stunted, short, base, lowly, deep, insignificant, unimportant, inexpensive, reasonable, trivial, petty, small.
highly *(SYN.)* extremely, very, extraordinarily, exceedingly.
high-minded *(SYN.)* lofty, noble, honorable.
(ANT.) dishonorable, base.
high-priced *(SYN.)* dear, expensive, costly.
(ANT.) economical, cheap.
high-strung *(SYN.)* nervous, tense, wrought-up, intense.
(ANT.) calm.
highway *(SYN.)* parkway, speedway, turnpike, superhighway, freeway.
hilarious *(SYN.)* funny, side-splitting, hysterical.
(ANT.) depressing, sad.
hinder *(SYN.)* hamper, impede, block, retard, stop, resist, thwart, obstruct, check, prevent, interrupt, delay, slow, restrain.
(ANT.) promote, further, assist, expedite, advance, facilitate.
hindrance *(SYN.)* interruption, delay, interference, obstruction, obstacle, barrier.
hinge *(SYN.)* rely, depend, pivot.
hint *(SYN.)* reminder, allusion, suggestion, clue, tip, taste, whisper, implication, intimate, suspicion, mention, insinuation.
(ANT.) declaration, affirmation, statement.
hire *(SYN.)* employ, occupy, devote, apply, enlist, lease, rent, charter, rental, busy, engage, utilize, retain, let, avail.
(ANT.) reject, banish, discard, fire, dismiss, discharge.
history *(SYN.)* narration, relation, computation, record, account, chronicle, detail, description, narrative, tale, recital.
(ANT.) confusion, misrepresentation, distortion, caricature.
hit *(SYN.)* knock, pound, strike, hurt, pummel, beat, come upon, find, discover, blow, smite.
hitch *(SYN.)* tether, fasten, harness, interruption, hindrance, interference.
hoard *(SYN.)* amass, increase, accumulate, gather, save, secret, store, cache, store, accrue, heap.
(ANT.) dissipate, scatter, waste, diminish, squander, spend, disperse.
hoarse *(SYN.)* deep, rough, husky, raucous, grating, harsh.
(ANT.) clear.
hoax *(SYN.)* ploy, ruse, wile, device, cheat, deception, antic, imposture, stratagem, stunt, guile, fraud.
(ANT.) openness, sincerity, candor, exposure, honesty.
hobbling *(SYN.)* deformed, crippled, halt, lame, unconvincing, unsatisfactory, defective, feeble, disabled maimed, weak.
(ANT.) robust, vigorous, agile, sound, athletic.
hobby *(SYN.)* diversion, pastime, avocation.
(ANT.) vocation, profession.
hobo *(SYN.)* derelict, vagrant, vagabond, tramp.
hoist *(SYN.)* heave, lift, elevate, raise, crane, elevator, derrick.
hold *(SYN.)* grasp, occupy, possess, curb, contain, slow, carry, adhere, have, clutch, keep, maintain, clasp, grip, retain, detain, accommodate, restrain, observe, conduct, check, support.
(ANT.) vacate, relinquish, surrender, abandon.
holdup *(SYN.)* heist, robbery, stickup,

delay, interruption, slowdown.
hole *(SYN.)* cavity, void, pore, opening, abyss, chasm, gulf, aperture, tear, pit, burrow, lair, den, gap.
hollow *(SYN.)* unfilled, vacant, vain, meaningless, flimsy, false, hole, cavity, depression, hypocritical, depressed, empty, pit, insincere.
(ANT.) sound, solid, genuine, sincere, full.
holocaust *(SYN.)* fire, burning, extermination, butchery, disaster, massacre.
holy *(SYN.)* devout, divine, blessed, consecrated, sacred, spiritual, pious, sainted, religious, saintly, hallowed.
(ANT.) worldly, sacrilegious, unconsecrated, evil, profane, secular.
homage *(SYN.)* reverence, honor, respect.
home *(SYN.)* dwelling, abode, residence, seat, quarters, hearth, domicile, family, house, habitat.
homely *(SYN.)* uncommonly, disagreeable, ill-natured, ugly, vicious, plain, hideous, unattractive, deformed, surly, repellent, spiteful.
(ANT.) fair, handsome, pretty, attractive, comely, beautiful.
homesick *(SYN.)* lonely, nostalgic.
honest *(SYN.)* sincere, trustworthy, truthful, fair, ingenuous, candid, conscientious, moral, upright, open, frank, forthright, honorable, just.
(ANT.) fraudulent, tricky, deceitful, dishonest, lying.
honesty *(SYN.)* frankness, openness, fairness, sincerity, trustworthiness, justice, candor, honor, integrity, responsibility, uprightness.
(ANT.) deceit, dishonesty, trickery, fraud, cheating.
honor *(SYN.)* esteem, praise, worship, admiration, homage, glory, respect, admire, heed, dignity, revere, value, deference, venerate, reverence, consider, distinction, character, principle, uprightness, honesty, adoration.
(ANT.) scorn, dishonor, despise, neglect, abuse, shame, reproach, disdain, contempt, derision, disgrace.
honorable *(SYN.)* fair, noble, creditable, proper, reputable, honest, admirable, true, trusty, eminent, respectable, esteemed, just, famed, illustrious, noble, virtuous, upright.
(ANT.) infamous, disgraceful, shameful, dishonorable, ignominious.
honorary *(SYN.)* gratuitous, complimentary.
hoodlum *(SYN.)* crook, gangster, criminal, hooligan, mobster.
hop *(SYN.)* jump, leap.
hope *(SYN.)* expectation, faith, optimism, anticipation, expectancy, confidence, desire, trust.
(ANT.) pessimism, despair, despondency.
hopeful *(SYN.)* optimistic, confident.
(ANT.) despairing, hopeless.
hopeless *(SYN.)* desperate, despairing, forlorn, fatal, incurable, disastrous.
(ANT.) promising, hopeful.
hopelessness *(SYN.)* gloom, discouragement, depression, pessimism, despondency.
(ANT.) hope, optimism, confidence, elation.
horde *(SYN.)* host, masses, press, rabble, swarm, throng, bevy, crush, mob, multitude, crowd, populace.
horizontal *(SYN.)* even, level, plane, flat, straight, sideways.
(ANT.) upright, vertical.
horrendous *(SYN.)* awful, horrifying, terrible, dreadful, horrid, ghastly.
(ANT.) splendid, wonderful.
horrible *(SYN.)* awful, dire, ghastly, horrid, terrible, repulsive, frightful, appalling, horrifying, dreadful, ghastly, fearful.
(ANT.) enjoyable, enchanting, beautiful, lovely, fascinating.
horrid *(SYN.)* repulsive, terrible, appalling, dire, awful, frightful, fearful, shocking, horrible, horrifying, horrid, ghastly, dreadful, revolting, hideous.
(ANT.) fascinating, enchanting, enjoyable, lovely, beautiful.
horror *(SYN.)* dread, awe, hatred, loathing, foreboding, alarm, apprehension, aversion, terror.
(ANT.) courage, boldness, assurance, confidence.
horseplay *(SYN.)* tomfoolery, clowning, shenanigans.
hospital *(SYN.)* infirmary, clinic, sanatorium, rest home, sanitarium.
hospitality *(SYN.)* warmth, liberality, generosity, graciousness, welcome.
hostile *(SYN.)* unfriendly, opposed, antagonistic, inimical, adverse, warlike.
(ANT.) friendly, favorable, amicable, cordial.
hostility *(SYN.)* grudge, hatred, rancor, spite, bitterness, enmity, malevolence.
(ANT.) love, friendliness, good will.
hot *(SYN.)* searching, fervent, hot-blooded, passionate, peppery, ardent, burning, fiery, impetuous, scalding, heated, sizzling, blazing, frying, roasting, warm, intense, torrid, pungent.
(ANT.) indifferent, apathetic, impassive, passionless, bland, frigid, cold, freezing, cool, phlegmatic.
hot air *(SYN.)* bombast, blather, jabber, gabble.
hotbed *(SYN.)* sink, nest, well, den, nursery, cradle, source, incubator, seedbed.
hot-blooded *(SYN.)* passionate, ardent, excitable, wild, fervent, fiery, impetuous, rash, brash, intense, impulsive.
(ANT.) stolid, impassive, cold, staid.
hotel *(SYN.)* hostel, motel, inn, hostelry.
hotheaded *(SYN.)* rash, touchy, short-tempered, reckless, unruly.
(ANT.) levelheaded, cool-headed, calm.
hound *(SYN.)* harry, pursue, pester, harass.
hourly *(SYN.)* frequently, steadily, constantly, unfailingly, periodically, perpetually, ceaselessly, continually, incessantly.
(ANT.) occasionally, seldom.
house *(SYN.)* building, residence,

abode, dwelling.
housebreaker *(SYN.)* robber, thief, prowler, cracksman, burglar.
household *(SYN.)* manage, family, home.
householder *(SYN.)* homeowner, occupant.
housing *(SYN.)* lodgings, shelter, dwelling, lodgment, case, easing, quarters, domicile, enclosure, console, bracket.
hovel *(SYN.)* cabin, hut, sty, shack, hole, shed.
hover *(SYN.)* hang, drift, poise, stand by, linger, impend, waver, hand around.
however *(SYN.)* notwithstanding, still, nevertheless, but, yet.
howl *(SYN.)* bellow, yowl, wail, yell, cry.
hub *(SYN.)* pivot, center, core, heart, axis, basis, focus, nucleus.
hubbub *(SYN.)* uproar, tumult, commotion, clamor, bustle, turmoil, racket, confusion.
(ANT.) peacefulness, stillness, silence, quiet, quiescence.
huckster *(SYN.)* peddler, adman, hawker, salesman, pitchman.
huddle *(SYN.)* mass, herd, bunch, crowd, cram, gather, shove, pack, flock, ball, conglomeration, knot, clump, medley, scrum.
hue *(SYN.)* pigment, tint, shade, dye, complexion, paint, stain, color, tone, tincture.
(ANT.) transparency, achromatism, paleness.
huffy *(SYN.)* sensitive, vulnerable, testy, offended, thin-skinned, touchy, irascible, cross, offended.
(ANT.) tough, placid, stolid, impassive.
hug *(SYN.)* embrace, coddle, caress, kiss, pet, press, clasp, fondle, cuddle.
(ANT.) tease, vex, spurn, buffet, annoy.
huge *(SYN.)* great, immense, vast, ample, big, capacious, extensive, gigantic, enormous, vast, tremendous, large, wide, colossal.
(ANT.) short, small, mean, little, tiny.
hulking *(SYN.)* massive, awkward, bulky, ponderous, unwieldy, overgrown, lumpish, oafish.
hullabaloo *(SYN.)* clamor, uproar, din, racket, tumult, hubbub, commotion, noise, blare.
(ANT.) calm, peace, silence.
hum *(SYN.)* whir, buzz, whiz, purr, croon, murmur, intone, vibrate.
human *(SYN.)* hominid, mortal, fleshly, individual, person.
humane *(SYN.)* lenient, tender, tolerant, compassionate, clement, forgiving, kind, forbearing, thoughtful, kindhearted, kindly, gentle, merciful.
(ANT.) remorseless, cruel, heartless, pitiless, unfeeling, brutal.
humanist *(SYN.)* scholar, sage, classicist, savant.
humanitarian *(SYN.)* benefactor, philanthropist.
humanitarianism *(SYN.)* good will, beneficence, philanthropy, welfarism, humanism.
humanity *(SYN.)* generosity, magnanimity, tenderness, altruism, beneficence, kindness, charity, philanthropy.
(ANT.) selfishness, unkindness, cruelty, inhumanity.
humble *(SYN.)* modest, crush, mortify, simple, shame, subdue, meek, abase, break, plain, submissive, compliant, unpretentious, unassuming, abash, unostentatious, lowly, polite, courteous, unpretending, degrade.
(ANT.) praise, arrogant, exalt, illustrious, boastful, honor, elevate.
humbly *(SYN.)* deferentially, meekly, respectfully, unassumingly, diffidently, modestly, subserviently, submissively.
(ANT.) insolently, proudly, grandly, arrogantly.
humbug *(SYN.)* drivel, gammon, bosh, nonsense, rubbish, inanity.
humdrum *(SYN.)* commonplace, prosy, mundane, insipid, tedious, routine, dull, boring.
(ANT.) interesting, stimulating, arresting, striking, exciting.
humid *(SYN.)* moist, damp, misty, muggy, wet, watery, vaporous.
(ANT.) parched, dry, desiccated.
humiliate *(SYN.)* corrupt, defile, depress, pervert, abase, degrade, disgrace, adulterate, humble, shame, lower, impair, deprave, depress.
(ANT.) restore, raise, enhance, improve, vitalize.
humiliation *(SYN.)* chagrin, dishonor, ignominy, scandal, abasement, mortification, disrepute, odium, disgrace, shame.
(ANT.) honor, praise, glory, dignity, renown.
humor *(SYN.)* jocularity, wit, temperament, sarcasm, irony, joking, amusement, joke, disposition, waggery, fun, clowning, satire, mood.
(ANT.) sorrow, gravity, seriousness.
humorous *(SYN.)* funny, ludicrous, witty, curious, queer, amusing, comical, farcical, laughable, droll.
(ANT.) sober, unfunny, melancholy, serious, sad, solemn.
hunger *(SYN.)* desire, longing, inclination, relish, stomach, zest, craving, liking, passion.
(ANT.) satiety, repugnance, disgust, distaste, renunciation.
hungry *(SYN.)* famished, thirsting, craving, avid, longing, starved, ravenous.
(ANT.) gorged, satisfied, full, sated.
hunt *(SYN.)* pursuit, investigation, examination, inquiry, pursue, track, chase, search, quest, seek, probe, scour, exploration.
(ANT.) cession, resignation, abandonment.
hurl *(SYN.)* throw, cast, propel, fling, toss, pitch, thrust.
(ANT.) retain, pull, draw, haul, hold.
hurried *(SYN.)* rushed, hasty, swift, headlong, slipshod, careless, impulsive, superficial.
(ANT.) deliberate, slow, dilatory, thorough, prolonged.
hurry *(SYN.)* quicken, speed, ado, rush,

accelerate, run, hasten, race, urge, bustle, expedite, precipitate.
(ANT.) retard, tarry, hinder, linger, dawdle, delay, hinder.

hurt *(SYN.)* damage, harm, grievance, detriment, pain, injustice, injure, abuse, distress, disfigured, mar, afflict, spoil, affront, insult, wound, dishonor, wrong, mischief.
(ANT.) improvement, repair, compliment, help, praise, benefit.

hurtful *(SYN.)* harmful, damaging, maleficent, injurious, baleful, noxious.
(ANT.) remedial, beneficial, good, salutary.

hurtle *(SYN.)* charge, collide, rush, crash, lunge, bump, fling.

husband *(SYN.)* spouse, mate.

hush *(SYN.)* quiet, silence, still.

husk *(SYN.)* shell, hull, pod, skin, covering, crust, bark.

husky *(SYN.)* strong, brawny, strapping, muscular.
(ANT.) feeble, weak.

hustle *(SYN.)* hasten, run, race, hurry, speed.

hut *(SYN.)* cottage, shanty, cabin, shed.

hutch *(SYN.)* box, chest, locker, trunk, coffer, bin.

hybrid *(SYN.)* mule, mixture, crossbreed, cross, mongrel, mutt, composite.

hygiene *(SYN.)* cleanliness, sanitation, health, hygienics, prophylaxis.

hygienic *(SYN.)* robust, strong, well, wholesome, hale, healthy, sound, salubrious.
(ANT.) frail, noxious, infirm, delicate, diseased, injurious.

hyperbole *(SYN.)* puffery, exaggeration, embellishment, overstatement, ballyhoo, amplification, magnification.

hypercritical *(SYN.)* faultfinding, captious, censorious, finicky, exacting, carping, querulous, nagging, finical, hairsplitting.
(ANT.) lax, easygoing, indulgent, lenient, tolerant.

hypnotic *(SYN.)* soothing, opiate, sedative, soporific, entrancing, spellbinding, arresting, charming, engaging, gripping.

hypnotize *(SYN.)* entrance, dazzle, mesmerize, fascinate, spellbind.

hypocrisy *(SYN.)* pretense, deceit, dissembling, fakery, feigning, pharisaism, sanctimony, cant, dissimulation.
(ANT.) openness, candor, truth, directness, forthrightness, honesty, frankness.

hypocrite *(SYN.)* cheat, deceiver, pretender, dissembler, fake, fraud, charlatan.

hypocritical *(SYN.)* dissembling, two-faced, insincere, dishonest, duplicitous, deceitful, phony.
(ANT.) heartfelt, true, genuine, honest.

hypothesis *(SYN.)* law, theory, supposition, conjecture.
(ANT.) proof, fact, certainty.

hypothetical *(SYN.)* conjectural, speculative, theoretical.

idea *(SYN.)* conception, image, opinion, sentiment, concept, fancy, notion, thought, impression.
(ANT.) thing, matter, entity, object, substance.

ideal *(SYN.)* imaginary, supreme, unreal, visionary, perfect, faultless, fancied, exemplary, utopian.
(ANT.) imperfect, actual, material, real, faulty.

idealistic *(SYN.)* extravagant, dreamy, fantastic, fanciful, ideal, maudlin, imaginative, mawkish, sentimental, poetic, picturesque.
(ANT.) practical, literal, factual, prosaic.

identify *(ANT.)* recollect, apprehend, perceive, remember, confess, acknowledge, name, describe, classify.
(ANT.) ignore, forget, overlook, renounce, disown, repudiate.

identity *(SYN.)* uniqueness, personality, character, individuality.

ideology *(SYN.)* credo, principles, belief.

idiom *(SYN.)* language, speech, vernacular, lingo, dialect, jargon, slang, tongue.
(ANT.) babble, gibberish, drivel, nonsense.

idiot *(SYN.)* buffoon, harlequin, dolt, jester, dunce, blockhead, imbecile, numb-skull, simpleton, oaf, nincompoop, fool, moron.
(ANT.) philosopher, genius, scholar, sage.

idiotic *(SYN.)* asinine, absurd, brainless, irrational, crazy, nonsensical, senseless, preposterous, silly, ridiculous, simple, stupid, foolish, inane, moronic, half-witted, simpleminded, dimwitted.
(ANT.) prudent, wise, sagacious, judicious, sane, intelligent, bright, brilliant, smart.

idle *(SYN.)* unemployed, dormant, lazy, inactive, unoccupied, indolent, slothful, inert, unused.
(ANT.) occupied, working, employed, active, industrious, busy, engaged.

idol *(SYN.)* unoccupied, unused, inactive, unemployed.

idolize *(SYN.)* revere, worship, adore.
(ANT.) despise.

ignoble *(SYN.)* dishonorable, ignominious, lowly, menial vile, sordid, vulgar, abject, base, despicable, groveling, mean, vile.
(ANT.) righteous, lofty, honored, esteemed, noble, exalted.

ignominious *(SYN.)* contemptible, abject, despicable, groveling, dishonorable, ignoble, lowly, low, menial, mean, sordid, servile, vulgar, vile.
(ANT.) lofty, noble, esteemed, righteous, exalted.

ignorant *(SYN.)* uneducated, untaught, uncultured, illiterate, uninformed, unlearned, unlettered, untrained, unaware, unmindful.
(ANT.) cultured, literate, educated, erudite, informed, cultivated, schooled, learned, lettered.

ignore *(SYN.)* omit, slight, disregard,

overlook, neglect, skip.
(ANT.) notice, regard, include.
ill *(SYN.)* diseased, ailing, indisposed, morbid, infirm, unwell, unhealthy, sick, unhealthy.
(ANT.) robust, strong, healthy, well, sound, fit.
ill-use *(SYN.)* defame, revile, vilify, misemploy, disparage, abuse, traduce, asperse, misapply, misuse.
(ANT.) protect, cherish, respect, honor, praise.
ill-advised *(SYN.)* injudicious, ill-considered, imprudent.
ill-at-ease *(SYN.)* nervous, uncomfortable, uneasy.
(ANT.) comfortable.
illegal *(SYN.)* prohibited, unlawful, criminal, illicit, outlawed, illegitimate.
(ANT.) permitted, lawful, honest, legal, legitimate.
illiberal *(SYN.)* fanatical, bigoted, intolerant, narrow-minded, dogmatic, prejudiced.
(ANT.) progressive, liberal radical.
illicit *(SYN.)* illegitimate, criminal, outlawed, unlawful, prohibited, illegal, unauthorized.
(ANT.) legal, honest, permitted, lawful, licit.
ill-natured *(SYN.)* crabby, cranky, grouchy, cross, irascible.
illness *(SYN.)* complaint, infirmity, ailment, disorder, malady, sickness.
(ANT.) healthiness, health, soundness, vigor.
illogical *(SYN.)* absurd, irrational, preposterous.
ill-tempered *(SYN.)* crabby, cranky, cross, grouchy.
ill-treated *(SYN.)* harmed, mistreated, abused, maltreated.
illuminate *(SYN.)* enlighten, clarify, irradiate, illustrate, light, lighten, explain, interpret, clarify, elucidate, brighten, illumine.
(ANT.) obscure, confuse, darken, obfuscate, shadow, complicate.
illusion *(SYN.)* hallucination, vision, phantom, delusion, fantasy, dream, mirage.
(ANT.) substance, actuality, reality.
illusive *(SYN.)* fallacious, delusive, false, specious, misleading, deceptive, deceitful, delusory.
(ANT.) real, truthful, authentic, genuine, honest.
illustrate *(SYN.)* decorate, illuminate, adorn, show, picture, embellish, demonstrate.
illustration *(SYN.)* likeness, painting, picture, print, scene, sketch, view, engraving, drawing, panorama, photograph, cinema, etching, effigy, film, appearance, portrayal, resemblance, image, portrait.
illustrator *(SYN.)* painter, artist.
illustrious *(SYN.)* prominent, eminent, renowned, famed, great, vital, elevated, majestic, noble, excellent, dignified, big, gigantic, enormous, immense, huge, vast, large, countless, numerous, celebrated, critical, momentous, august, weighty, grand, fine, magnificent, serious, important.
(ANT.) menial, common, minute, diminutive, small, obscure, ordinary, little.
image *(SYN.)* reflection, likeness, idea, representation, notion, picture, conception.
imaginary *(SYN.)* fanciful, fantastic, unreal, whimsical.
(ANT.) actual, real.
imagination *(SYN.)* creation, invention, fancy, notion, conception, fantasy, idea.
imaginative *(SYN.)* inventive, poetical, fanciful, clever, creative, mystical, visionary.
(ANT.) prosaic, dull, unromantic, literal.
imagine *(SYN.)* assume, surmise, suppose, conceive, dream, pretend, conjecture, fancy, opine, envisage, think, envision, guess, picture.
imbecile *(SYN.)* idiot, numbskull, simpleton, blockhead, dolt, dunce, jester, buffoon, harlequin, nincompoop, clown, fool, oaf.
(ANT.) scholar, genius, philosopher, sage.
imbibe *(SYN.)* absorb, consume, assimilate, engulf, engage, occupy, engross.
(ANT.) dispense, exude, discharge, emit.
imitate *(SYN.)* duplicate, mimic, follow, reproduce, mock, ape, counterfeit, copy, simulate, impersonate.
(ANT.) invent, distort, alter, diverge.
imitation *(SYN.)* replica, reproduction copy, duplicate, facsimile, transcript, exemplar.
(ANT.) prototype, original.
immaculate *(SYN.)* clean, spotless, unblemished.
(ANT.) dirty.
immature *(SYN.)* young, boyish, childish, youthful, childlike, puerile, girlish, juvenile, callow.
(ANT.) old, senile, aged, elderly, mature.
immeasurable *(SYN.)* unlimited, endless, eternal, immense, interminable, unbounded, immeasurable, boundless, illimitable,infinite.
(ANT.) limited, confined, bounded, finite, circumscribed.
immediate *(SYN.)* present, instant, instantaneous, near, close, next, prompt, direct.
(ANT.) distant, future.
immediately *(SYN.)* now, presently, instantly, promptly, straightway, directly, instantaneously, forthwith.
(ANT.) sometime, hereafter, later, shortly, distantly.
immense *(SYN.)* enormous, large, gigantic, huge, colossal, elephantine, great, gargantuan, vast.
(ANT.) small, diminutive, little, minuscule, minute, petit, tiny.
immensity *(SYN.)* hugeness, enormousness, vastness.
immerse *(SYN.)* plunge, dip, dunk, sink, submerge, engage, absorb, engross, douse.

(ANT.) uplift, elevate, recover.

immigration *(SYN.)* settlement, colonization.
(ANT.) exodus, emigration.

imminent *(SYN.)* nigh, impending, overhanging, approaching, menacing, threatening.
(ANT.) retreating, afar, distant, improbable, remote.

immoderation *(SYN.)* profusion, surplus, extravagance, excess, intemperance, superabundance.
(ANT.) lack, want, deficiency, dearth, paucity.

immoral *(SYN.)* sinful, wicked, corrupt, bad, indecent, profligate, unprincipled, antisocial, dissolute.
(ANT.) pure, high-minded, chaste, virtuous, noble.

immortal *(SYN.)* infinite, eternal, timeless, undying, perpetual, ceaseless, endless, deathless, everlasting.
(ANT.) mortal, transient, finite, ephemeral, temporal.

immune *(SYN.)* easy, open, autonomous, unobstructed, free, emancipated, clear, independent, unrestricted, exempt, liberated, familiar, loose, unconfined, frank, unfastened, careless, freed.
(ANT.) confined, impeded, restricted, subject.

immutable *(SYN.)* constant, faithful, invariant, persistent, unchanging, unalterable, continual, ceaseless, enduring, fixed, permanent, abiding, perpetual, unwavering.
(ANT.) mutable, vacillating, wavering, fickle.

impact *(SYN.)* striking, contact, collision.

impair *(SYN.)* harm, injure, spoil, deface, destroy, hurt, damage, mar.
(ANT.) repair, mend, ameliorate, enhance, benefit.

impart *(SYN.)* convey, disclose, inform, tell, reveal, transmit, notify, confer, divulge, communicate, relate.
(ANT.) hide, withhold, conceal.

impartial *(SYN.)* unbiased, just, honest, fair, reasonable, equitable.
(ANT.) fraudulent, dishonorable, partial.

impartiality *(SYN.)* indifference, unconcern, impartiality, neutrality, disinterestedness, apathy, insensibility.
(ANT.) passion, ardor, fervor, affection.

impasse *(SYN.)* standstill, deadlock, stalemate.

impede *(SYN.)* hamper, hinder, retard, thwart, check, encumber, interrupt, bar, clog, delay, obstruct, block, frustrate, restrain, stop.
(ANT.) assist, promote, help, advance, further.

impediment *(SYN.)* barrier, bar, block, difficulty, check, hindrance, snag, obstruction.
(ANT.) assistance, help, aid, encouragement.

impel *(SYN.)* oblige, enforce, drive, coerce, force, constrain.
(ANT.) induce, prevent, convince, persuade.

impending *(SYN.)* imminent, nigh, threatening, overhanging, approaching, menacing.
(ANT.) remote, improbable, afar, distant, retreating.

impenetrable *(SYN)* rigid, tough, harsh, strict, unfeeling, rigorous, intricate, arduous, penetrable, cruel, difficult, severe, stern, firm, hard, compact.
(ANT.) soft, simple, gentle, tender, brittle, fluid, flabby, elastic, lenient, easy, effortless.

imperative *(SYN.)* critical, instant, important, necessary, serious, urgent, cogent, compelling, crucial, pressing, impelling, importunate, exigent, insistent.
(ANT.) trivial, insignificant, unimportant, petty.

imperceptible *(SYN.)* invisible, indiscernible, unseen, indistinguishable.
(ANT.) seen, evident, visible, perceptible.

imperfection *(SYN.)* flaw, shortcoming, vice, defect, blemish, failure, mistake, omission, fault, error.
(ANT.) correctness, perfection, completeness.

imperil *(SYN.)* jeopardize, risk, endanger, hazard, risk.
(ANT.) guard, insure.

impersonal *(SYN.)* objective, detached, disinterested.
(ANT.) personal.

impersonate *(SYN.)* mock, simulate, imitate, ape, counterfeit, mimic, copy, duplicate.
(ANT.) alter, invent, diverge, distort.

impertinence *(SYN)* impudence, presumption, sauciness, effrontery, audacity, rudeness, assurance, boldness, insolence.
(ANT.) truckling, politeness, diffidence, subserviency.

impertinent *(SYN.)* rude, offensive, insolent, disrespectful, arrogant, brazen, impudent, insulting, contemptuous, abusive.
(ANT.) polite, respectful, considerate, courteous.

impetuous *(SYN.)* rash, heedless, quick, hasty, careless, passionate, impulsive.
(ANT.) cautious, reasoning, careful, prudent, thoughtful, calculating.

implicate *(SYN.)* reproach, accuse, blame, involve, upbraid, condemn, incriminate, rebuke, censure.
(ANT.) exonerate, absolve, acquit.

implore *(SYN.)* beg, pray, request, solicit, crave, entreat, beseech, ask, importune, supplicate, adjure, appeal, petition.
(ANT.) give, cede, bestow, favor, grant.

imply *(SYN.)* mean, involve, suggest, connote, hint, mention, indicate, insinuate, signify.
(ANT.) state, assert, declare, express.

impolite *(SYN.)* rude, unpolished, impudent, boorish, blunt, discourteous, rough, saucy, surly, savage, insolent, gruff, uncivil, coarse, ignorant, crude, illiterate, raw, primitive, vulgar, un-

taught.
(ANT.) genteel, courteous, courtly, dignified, polite, stately, noble, civil.
import *(SYN.)* influence, significance, stress, emphasis, importance, value, weight.
(ANT.) triviality, insignificance.
important *(SYN.)* critical, grave, influential, momentous, well-known, pressing, relevant, prominent, primary, essential, weighty, material, considerable, famous, principle, famed, sequential, notable, significant, illustrious, decisive.
(ANT.) unimportant, trifling, petty, trivial, insignificant, secondary, anonymous, irrelevant.
impose *(SYN.)* levy, require, demand.
imposing *(SYN.)* lofty, noble, majestic, magnificent, august, dignified, grandiose, high, grand, impressive, pompous, stately.
(ANT.) ordinary, undignified, humble, common, lowly.
imposition *(SYN.)* load, onus, burden.
impossible *(SYN.)* preposterous.
impregnable *(SYN.)* safe, invulnerable, secure, unassailable.
(ANT.) vulnerable.
impress *(SYN.)* awe, emboss, affect, mark, imprint, indent, influence.
impression *(SYN.)* influence, indentation, feeling, opinion, mark, effect, depression, guess, thought, belief, dent, sensibility.
(ANT.) fact, insensibility.
impressive *(SYN.)* arresting, moving, remarkable, splendid, thrilling, striking, majestic, grandiose, imposing, commanding, affecting, exciting, touching, stirring.
(ANT.) regular, unimpressive, commonplace.
impromptu *(SYN.)* casual, unprepared, offhand, extemporaneous.
improper *(SYN.)* unfit, unsuitable, inappropriate, naughty, indecent, unbecoming.
(ANT.) fitting, proper, appropriate.
improve *(SYN.)* better, reform, refine, ameliorate, amend, help, upgrade, rectify.
(ANT.) debase, vitiate, impair, corrupt, damage.
improvement *(SYN)* growth, advance, progress, betterment, development, advancement, progression.
(ANT.) relapse, regression, decline, retrogression, delay.
imprudent *(SYN.)* indiscreet, thoughtless, desultory, lax, neglectful, remiss, careless, inattentive, heedless, inconsiderate, reckless, ill-advised, irresponsible, unconcerned.
(ANT.) careful, meticulous, accurate.
impudence *(SYN.)* boldness, insolence, rudeness, sauciness, assurance, effrontery, impertinence, presumption, audacity.
(ANT.) politeness, truckling, subserviency, diffidence.
impudent *(SYN.)* forward, rude, abrupt, prominent, striking, bold, fresh, impertinent, insolent, pushy, insulting, brazen.
(ANT.) bashful, flinching, polite, courteous, cowardly, retiring, timid.
impulse *(SYN.)* hunch, whim, fancy, urge, caprice, surge, pulse.
impulsive *(SYN.)* passionate, rash, spontaneous, heedless, careless, hasty, quick, impetuous.
(ANT.) reasoning, calculating, careful, prudent, cautious.
impure *(SYN.)* dishonest, spoiled, tainted, contaminated, debased, corrupt, profligate, unsound, putrid, corrupted, crooked, depraved, vitiated, venal.
imputation *(SYN.)* diary, incrimination, arraignment, indictment.
(ANT.) exoneration, pardon, exculpation.
inability *(SYN.)* incompetence, incapacity, handicap, disability, impotence, weakness.
(ANT.) power, strength, ability, capability.
inaccurate *(SYN.)* false, incorrect, mistaken, untrue, askew, wrong, awry, erroneous, fallacious, imprecise, faulty, amiss.
(ANT.) right, accurate, true, correct.
inactive *(SYN.)* lazy, unemployed, indolent, motionless, still, inert, dormant, idle, unoccupied.
(ANT.) employed, working, active, industrious, occupied.
inadequate *(SYN.)* insufficient, lacking, short, incomplete, defective, scanty.
(ANT.) satisfactory, enough, adequate, ample, sufficient.
inadvertent *(SYN.)* careless, negligent, unthinking, thoughtless.
inane *(SYN.)* trite, insipid, banal, absurd, silly, commonplace, vapid, foolish, stupid, hackneyed.
(ANT.) stimulating, novel, fresh, original, striking.
inanimate *(SYN.)* deceased, spiritless, lifeless, gone, dull, mineral, departed, dead, insensible, vegetable, unconscious.
(ANT.) living, stirring, alive, animate.
inattentive *(SYN.)* absent-minded, distracted, abstracted, preoccupied.
(ANT.) watchful, attending, attentive.
inaugurate *(SYN.)* commence, begin, open, originate, start, arise, launch, enter, initiate.
(ANT.) end, terminate, close, complete, finish.
incense *(SYN.)* anger, enrage, infuriate.
incentive *(SYN.)* impulse, stimulus, inducement, encouragement.
(ANT.) discouragement.
inception *(SYN.)* origin, start, source, opening, beginning, outset, commencement.
(ANT.) end, termination, close, completion, consummation.
incessant *(SYN.)* perennial, uninterrupted, continual, ceaseless, continuous, unremitting, eternal, constant, unceasing, unending, perpetual, everlasting.

(ANT.) rare, occasional, periodic, interrupted.

incident *(SYN.)* happening, situation, occurrence, circumstance, condition, event, fact.

incidental *(SYN.)* casual, contingent, trivial, undersigned, chance, fortuitous, accidental, secondary, unimportant, unintended.
(ANT.) intended, fundamental, planned, calculated, willed, decreed.

incidentally *(SYN.)* by the way.

incinerate *(SYN.)* sear, char, blaze, scald, singe, consume, scorch, burn.
(ANT.) quench, put out, extinguish.

incisive *(SYN.)* neat, succinct, terse, brief, compact, condensed, neat, summary, concise.
(ANT.) wordy, prolix, verbose, lengthy.

incite *(SYN.)* goad, provoke, urge, arouse, encourage, cause, stimulate, induce, instigate, foment.
(ANT.) quiet, bore, pacify, soothe.

inclination *(SYN.)* bent, preference, desire, slope, affection, bent, bias, disposition, bending, penchant, incline, attachment, predisposition, predication, tendency, prejudice, slant, lean, leaning.
(ANT.) nonchalance, apathy, distaste, aversion, reluctance, disinclination, uprightness, repugnance.

incline *(SYN.)* slope, nod, lean.
(ANT.) straighten.

include *(SYN.)* contain, hold, accommodate, embody, encompass, involve, comprise, embrace.
(ANT.) omit, exclude, discharge.

income *(SYN.)* earnings, salary, wages, revenue, pay, return, receipts.

incomparable *(SYN.)* peerless, matchless, unequaled.

incompetency *(SYN.)* inability, weakness, handicap, impotence, disability, incapacity.
(ANT.) strength, ability, power, capability.

incomprehensible *(SYN.)* unintelligible, indecipherable.

inconceivable *(SYN.)* unbelievable, unimaginable, impossible.
(ANT.) possible, believable.

incongruous *(SYN.)* inconsistent, contrary, incompatible, irreconcilable, contradictory, unsteady, incongruous, wavering, paradoxical, vacillating, discrepant, illogical.
(ANT.) consistent, compatible, correspondent.

inconsiderate *(SYN.)* unthinking, careless, unthoughtful, unmindful.
(ANT.) logical, consistent.

inconsistency *(SYN)* discord, variance, contention, conflict, controversy, interference.
(ANT.) harmony, concord, amity, consonance.

inconsistent *(SYN.)* fickle, wavering, variable, changeable, contrary, unstable, illogical, contradictory, irreconcilable, discrepant, paradoxical, incompatible, self-contradictory, incongruous, unsteady, fitful, shifting.
(ANT.) unchanging, steady, logical, stable, uniform, constant.

inconspicuous *(SYN.)* retiring, unnoticed, unostentatious.
(ANT.) obvious, conspicuous.

inconstant *(SYN.)* fickle, shifting, changeable, fitful, vacillating, unstable, wavering.
(ANT.) stable, constant, steady, uniform, unchanging.

inconvenient *(SYN.)* awkward, inappropriate, untimely, troublesome.
(ANT.) handy, convenient.

incorrect *(SYN.)* mistaken, wrong, erroneous, inaccurate.
(ANT.) proper, accurate, suitable.

increase *(SYN.)* amplify, enlarge, grow, magnify, multiply, augment, enhance, expand, intensify, swell, raise, greater, prolong, broaden, lengthen, expansion, accrue, extend, heighten.
(ANT.) diminish, reduce, atrophy, shrink, shrinkage, decrease, lessening, lessen, contract.

incredible *(SYN.)* improbable, unbelievable.
(ANT.) plausible, credible, believable.

incriminate *(SYN.)* charge, accuse, indict, arraign, censure.
(ANT.) release, exonerate, acquit, absolve, vindicate.

incrimination *(SYN.)* imputation, indictment, accusation, charge, arraignment.
(ANT.) exoneration, pardon, exculpation.

indebted *(SYN.)* obliged, grateful, beholden, thankful, appreciative.
(ANT.) unappreciative, thankless.

indecent *(SYN.)* impure, obscene, pornographic, coarse, dirty, filthy, smutty, gross, disgusting.
(ANT.) modest, refined, decent, pure.

indeed *(SYN.)* truthfully, really, honestly, surely.

indefinite *(SYN.)* unsure, uncertain, vague, confused, unsettled, confusing.
(ANT.) decided, definite, equivocal.

independence *(SYN.)* liberation, privilege, freedom, immunity, familiarity, liberty, exemption, license.
(ANT.) necessity, constraint, compulsion, reliance, dependence, bondage, servitude.

independent *(SYN.)* free, unrestrained, voluntary, autonomous, self-reliant, uncontrolled, unrestricted.
(ANT.) enslaved, contingent, dependent, restricted.

indestructible *(SYN.)* enduring, lasting, permanent, unchangeable, abiding, constant, fixed, stable, changeless.
(ANT.) unstable, temporary, transitory, ephemeral.

indicate *(SYN.)* imply, denote, signify, specify, intimate, designate, symbolize, show, manifest, disclose, mean, reveal.
(ANT.) mislead, falsify, distract, conceal, falsify.

indication *(SYN.)* proof, emblem, omen, sign, symbol, token, mark, portent, gesture, signal.

indict *(SYN.)* charge, accuse, in-

criminate, censure, arraign.
(ANT.) acquit, vindicate, absolve, exonerate.
indictment *(SYN.)* incrimination, arraignment, imputation, charge.
(ANT.) pardon, exoneration, exculpation.
indifference *(SYN.)* unconcern, apathy, impartiality, disinterestedness, insensibility, neutrality.
(ANT.) ardor, passion, affection, fervor.
indifferent *(SYN.)* uncaring, insensitive, cool, unconcerned.
(ANT.) caring, concerned, earnest.
indigence *(SYN.)* necessity, destitution, poverty, want, need, privation, penury.
(ANT.) wealth, abundance, plenty, riches, affluence.
indigenous *(SYN.)* inborn, native, inherent, domestic, aboriginal, plenty, endemic, innate, natural.
indigent *(SYN.)* wishing, covetous, demanding, lacking, requiring, wanting, claiming, craving.
indignant *(SYN.)* irritated, irate, angry, aroused, exasperated.
(ANT.) calm, serene, content.
indignation *(SYN.)* ire, petulance, passion, choler, anger, wrath, temper, irritation, exasperation, animosity, resentment, rage.
(ANT.) self-control, peace, forbearance, patience.
indignity *(SYN.)* insolence, insult, abuse, affront, offense.
(ANT.) homage, apology, salutation.
indirect *(SYN.)* winding, crooked, devious, roundabout, cunning, tricky, tortuous, circuitous, distorted, erratic, swerving.
(ANT.) straightforward, direct, straight, honest.
indiscretion *(SYN.)* imprudence, folly, absurdity, extravagance.
(ANT.) prudence, sense, wisdom, reasonableness, judgment.
indispensable *(SYN.)* necessary, fundamental, basic, essential, important, intrinsic, vital.
(ANT.) optional, expendable, peripheral, extrinsic.
indistinct *(SYN.)* cloudy, dark, mysterious, vague, blurry, ambiguous, cryptic, dim, obscure, enigmatic, abstruse, hazy, blurred, unintelligible.
(ANT.) clear, lucid, bright, distinct.
indistinguishable *(SYN.)* identical, like, coincident, equal, same, equivalent.
(ANT.) dissimilar, opposed, contrary, disparate, distinct.
individual *(SYN.)* singular, specific, unique, distinctive, single, particular, undivided, human, apart, marked, person, different, special, separate.
(ANT.) universal, common, general, ordinary.
individuality *(SYN.)* symbol, description, mark, kind, character, repute, class, standing, sort, nature, disposition, reputation, sign.
indolent *(SYN.)* slothful, lazy, idle, inactive, slow, sluggish, torpid, supine, inert.
(ANT.) diligent, active, assiduous, vigorous, zestful, alert.
indomitable *(SYN.)* insurmountable, unconquerable, invulnerable, impregnable, unassailable.
(ANT.) weak, puny, powerless, vulnerable.
induce *(SYN.)* evoke, cause, influence, persuade, effect, make, originate, prompt, incite, create.
inducement *(SYN.)* incentive, motive, purpose, stimulus, reason, impulse, cause, principle, spur, incitement.
(ANT.) result, attempt, action, effort, deed.
induct *(SYN.)* instate, establish, install.
(ANT.) eject, oust.
indulge *(SYN.)* humor, satisfy, gratify.
indulgent *(SYN.)* obliging, pampering, tolerant, easy.
indurate *(SYN.)* impenitent, hard, insensible, tough, obdurate, callous, unfeeling.
(ANT.) soft, compassionate, tender, sensitive.
industrious *(SYN.)* hard-working, perseverant, busy, active, diligent, assiduous, careful, patient.
(ANT.) unconcerned, indifferent, lethargic, careless, apathetic, lazy, indolent, shiftless.
inebriated *(SYN.)* drunk, tight, drunken, intoxicated, tipsy.
(ANT.) sober, clearheaded, temperate.
ineffective *(SYN.)* pliant, tender, vague, wavering, defenseless, weak, inadequate, poor, irresolute, frail, decrepit, delicate, vacillating, assailable, exposed, vulnerable.
(ANT.) sturdy, robust, strong, potent, powerful.
inept *(SYN.)* clumsy, awkward, improper, inappropriate.
(ANT.) adroit, dexterous, adept, appropriate, proper, apt, fitting.
inequity *(SYN.)* wrong, injustice, unfairness, grievance, injury.
(ANT.) righteousness, lawfulness, equity, justice.
inert *(SYN.)* lazy, dormant, slothful, inactive, idle, indolent, motionless, unmoving, fixed, static.
(ANT.) working, active, industrious, occupied.
inertia *(SYN.)* indolence, torpidity, idleness, slothfulness, indolence, sluggishness, supineness.
(ANT.) assiduousness, activity, alertness, diligence.
inevitable *(SYN.)* definite, fixed, positive, sure, undeniable, indubitable, certain, assured, unquestionable, secure.
(ANT.) uncertain, probable, doubtful, questionable.
inexpensive *(SYN.)* low-priced, cheap, inferior, mean, beggarly, common, poor, shabby, modest, economical.
(ANT.) expensive, costly, dear.
inexperienced *(SYN.)* naive, untrained, uninformed, green.
(ANT.) experienced, skilled, sophisticated, trained, seasoned.

inexplicable *(SYN.)* hidden, mysterious, obscure, secret, dark, cryptic, enigmatical, incomprehensible, occult, recondite, inscrutable, dim.
(ANT.) plain, simple, clear, obvious, explained.
infamous *(SYN.)* shocking, shameful, scandalous.
infantile *(SYN.)* babyish, naive, immature, childish.
(ANT.) mature, grownup, adult.
infect *(SYN.)* pollute, poison, contaminate, defile, sully, taint.
(ANT.) purify, disinfect.
infection *(SYN.)* virus, poison, ailment, disease, pollution, pest, germ, taint, contamination, contagion.
infectious *(SYN.)* contagious, virulent, catching, communicable, pestilential, transferable.
(ANT.) noncommunicable, hygienic, healthful.
infer *(SYN.)* understand, deduce, extract.
inference *(SYN.)* consequence, result, conclusion, corollary, judgment, deduction.
(ANT.) preconception, foreknowledge, assumption, presupposition.
inferior *(SYN.)* secondary, lower, poorer, minor, subordinate, mediocre.
(ANT.) greater, superior, better, higher.
infinite *(SYN.)* immeasurable, interminable, unlimited, unbounded, eternal, boundless, illimitable, immense, endless, vast, innumerable, numberless, limitless.
(ANT.) confined, limited, bounded, circumscribed, finite.
infinitesimal *(SYN.)* minute, microscopic, tiny, submicroscopic.
(ANT.) gigantic, huge, enormous.
infirm *(SYN.)* feeble, impaired, decrepit, forceless, languid, puny, powerless, enervated, weak, exhausted.
(ANT.) stout, vigorous, forceful, lusty, strong.
infirmity *(SYN.)* disease, illness, malady, ailment, sickness, disorder, complaint.
(ANT.) soundness, health, vigor, healthiness.
inflame *(SYN.)* fire, incite, excite, arouse.
(ANT.) soothe, calm.
inflammation *(SYN.)* infection, soreness, irritation.
inflammatory *(SYN.)* instigating, inciting, provocative.
inflate *(SYN.)* expand, swell, distend.
(ANT.) collapse, deflate.
inflexible *(SYN.)* firm, stubborn, headstrong, immovable, unyielding, uncompromising, dogged, contumacious, determined, obstinate, rigid, unbending, unyielding, steadfast.
(ANT.) submissive, compliant, docile, amenable, yielding, flexible, giving, elastic.
inflict *(SYN.)* deliver, deal, give, impose, apply.
influence *(SYN.)* weight, control, effect, sway.
influenced *(SYN.)* sway, affect, bias, control, actuate, impel, stir, incite.
influential *(SYN.)* important, weighty, prominent, significant, critical, decisive, momentous, relevant, material, pressing, consequential, grave.
(ANT.) petty, irrelevant, mean, trivial, insignificant.
inform *(SYN.)* apprise, instruct, tell, notify, advise, acquaint, enlighten, impart, warn, teach, advise, relate.
(ANT.) delude, mislead, distract, conceal.
informal *(SYN.)* simple, easy, natural, unofficial, familiar.
(ANT.) formal, distant, reserved, proper.
informality *(SYN.)* friendship, frankness, liberty, acquaintance, sociability, intimacy, unreserved.
(ANT.) presumption, constraint, reserve, distance, haughtiness.
information *(SYN.)* knowledge, data, intelligence, facts.
informative *(SYN.)* educational, enlightening, instructive.
informer *(SYN.)* tattler, traitor, betrayer.
infrequent *(SYN.)* unusual, rare, occasional, strange.
(ANT.) commonplace, abundant, usual, ordinary, customary, frequent, numerous.
ingenious *(SYN.)* clever, skillful, talented, adroit, dexterous, quick-witted, bright, smart, witty, sharp, apt, resourceful, imaginative, inventive, creative.
(ANT.) dull, slow, awkward, bungling, unskilled, stupid.
ingenuity *(SYN.)* cunning, inventiveness, resourcefulness, aptitude, faculty, cleverness, ingenuousness.
(ANT.) ineptitude, clumsiness, dullness, stupidity.
ingenuous *(SYN.)* open, sincere, honest, candid, straightforward, plain, frank, truthful, free, naive, simple, innocent, unsophisticated.
(ANT.) scheming, sly, contrived, wily.
ingredient *(SYN.)* component, element, constituent.
inhabit *(SYN.)* fill, possess, absorb, dwell, occupy, live.
(ANT.) relinquish, abandon, release.
inherent *(SYN.)* innate, native, congenital, inherent, intrinsic, inborn, inbred, natural, real.
(ANT.) extraneous, acquired, external, extrinsic.
inhibit *(SYN.)* curb, constrain, hold back, restrain, bridle, hinder, repress, suppress, stop, limit.
(ANT.) loosen, aid, incite, encourage.
inhuman *(SYN.)* merciless, cruel, brutal, ferocious, savage, ruthless, malignant, barbarous, barbaric, bestial.
(ANT.) kind, benevolent, forbearing, gentle, compassionate, merciful, humane, humane.
inimical *(SYN.)* hostile, warlike, adverse, antagonistic, opposed, unfriendly.
(ANT.) favorable, amicable, cordial.
iniquitous *(SYN.)* baleful, immoral, per-

nicious, sinful, wicked, base, bad, evil, noxious, unsound, villainous, unwholesome.
(ANT.) moral, good, excellent, honorable, reputable.

iniquity *(SYN.)* injustice, wrong, grievance, unfairness, injury.
(ANT.) lawful, equity, righteousness, justice.

initial *(SYN.)* original, first, prime, beginning, earliest, pristine, chief, primeval, primary, foremost, basic, elementary.
(ANT.) latest, subordinate, last, least, hindmost, final, terminal.

initiate *(SYN.)* institute, enter, arise, inaugurate, commence, originate, start, open, begin.
(ANT.) terminate, complete, end, finish, close, stop.

initiative *(SYN.)* enthusiasm, energy, vigor, enterprise.

injure *(SYN.)* harm, wound, abuse, dishonor, damage, hurt, impair, spoil, disfigure, affront, insult, mar.
(ANT.) praise, ameliorate, help, preserve, compliment, benefit.

injurious *(SYN.)* detrimental, harmful, mischievous, damaging, hurtful, deleterious, harmful, destructive.
(ANT.) profitable, helpful, advantageous, salutary, beneficial, useful.

injury *(SYN.)* harm, detriment, damage, injustice, wrong, prejudice, grievance, mischief.
(ANT.) repair, benefit, improvement.

injustice *(SYN.)* unfairness, grievance, iniquity, wrong, injury.
(ANT.) righteousness, justice, equity, lawfulness.

inmate *(SYN.)* patient, prisoner.

inn *(SYN.)* motel, lodge, hotel.

innate *(SYN.)* native, inherent, congenital, innate, real, inborn, natural, intrinsic, inbred.
(ANT.) extraneous, acquired, external, extrinsic.

innocent *(SYN.)* pure, sinless, blameless, innocuous, lawful, naive, faultless, virtuous, not guilty.
(ANT.) guilty, corrupt, sinful, culpable, sophisticated, wise, worldly.

innocuous *(SYN.)* naive, pure, innocent, blameless, virtuous, lawful, faultless, innocuous, sinless.
(ANT.) sinful, corrupt, unrighteous, culpable, guilty.

inquire *(SYN.)* ask, solicit, invite, demand, claim, entreat, interrogate, query, beg, request, question, investigate, examine.
(ANT.) dictate, insist, reply, command, order.

inquiring *(SYN.)* prying, searching, curious, inquisitive, peering, snoopy, peeping, meddling, interrogative.
(ANT.) unconcerned, indifferent, uninterested, incurious.

inquiry *(SYN.)* investigation, quest, research, examination, interrogation, exploration, query, question, scrutiny, study.
(ANT.) inattention, inactivity, disregard, negligence.

inquisitive *(SYN.)* meddling, peeping, nosy, interrogative, peering, searching, prying, snoopy, inquiring, curious.
(ANT.) unconcerned, indifferent, incurious, uninterested.

insane *(SYN.)* deranged, mad, foolish, idiotic, demented, crazy, delirious, maniacal, lunatic.
(ANT.) sane, rational, reasonable, sound, sensible, coherent.

insanity *(SYN.)* delirium, aberration, dementia, psychosis, lunacy, madness, frenzy, mania, craziness, derangement.
(ANT.) stability, rationality, sanity.

insecure *(SYN.)* uneasy, nervous, uncertain, shaky.
(ANT.) secure.

insensitive *(SYN.)* unfeeling, impenitent, callous, hard, indurate, obdurate, tough.
(ANT.) soft, compassionate, tender, sensitive.

insight *(SYN.)* intuition, acumen, penetration, discernment, perspicuity.
(ANT.) obtuseness.

insignificant *(SYN.)* trivial, paltry, petty, small, frivolous, unimportant, insignificant, trifling.
(ANT.) momentous, serious, important, weighty.

insincere *(SYN.)* false, dishonest, deceitful.
(ANT.) honest, sincere.

insinuate *(SYN.)* imply, mean, suggest, connote, signify, involve.
(ANT.) express, state, assert.

insipid *(SYN.)* tasteless, dull, stale, flat, vapid.
(ANT.) racy, tasty, savory, exciting.

insist *(SYN.)* command, demand, require.

insolence *(SYN.)* boldness, presumption, sauciness, effrontery, audacity, assurance, impertinence, rudeness.
(ANT.) politeness, truckling, diffidence, subserviency.

insolent *(SYN.)* arrogant, impertinent, insulting, rude, brazen, contemptuous, abusive, offensive, disrespectful.
(ANT.) respectful, courteous, polite, considerate.

inspect *(SYN.)* observe, discern, eye, behold, glance, scan, stare, survey, view, regard, see, watch, witness, examine, investigate.
(ANT.) overlook, miss, avert, hide.

inspection *(SYN.)* examination, retrospect, survey, revision, reconsideration, critique, criticism, review.

inspiration *(SYN.)* creativity, aptitude, genius, originality, ability, faculty, sagacity, talent, proficient, master, gift, adept, intellectual, thought, impulse, idea, notion, hunch.
(ANT.) dullard, moron, shallowness, ineptitude, stupidity, obtuseness, dolt.

install *(SYN.)* establish.

instance *(SYN.)* occasion, illustration, occurrence, example, case.

instant *(SYN.)* flash, moment.

instantaneous *(SYN.)* hasty, sudden unexpected, rapid, abrupt, immediate.

(ANT.) slowly, anticipated, gradual.
instantly *(SYN.)* now, presently, directly, forthwith, immediately, rapidly straight-away, at once, instantaneously.
(ANT.) sometime, distantly, hereafter, later, shortly.
instinct *(SYN.)* intuition, feeling.
instinctive *(SYN.)* offhand, voluntary, willing, spontaneous, automatic, impulsive, extemporaneous.
(ANT.) rehearsed, planned, compulsory, prepared, forced.
institute *(SYN.)* ordain, establish, raise, form, organize, sanction, fix, found, launch, begin, initiate.
(ANT.) overthrow, upset, demolish, abolish, unsettle.
instruct *(SYN.)* teach, tutor, educate, inform, school, instill, train, inculcate, drill.
(ANT.) misinform, misguide.
instruction *(SYN.)* advise, warning, information, exhortation, notification, admonition, caution, recommendation, counsel, suggestion, teaching, training, education, command, order.
instrument *(SYN.)* channel, device, utensil, tool, agent, apparatus, means, vehicle, medium, agent, implement.
(ANT.) obstruction, hindrance, preventive, impediment.
insubordinate *(SYN.)* rebellious, unruly, defiant, disorderly, disobedient, undutiful, refractory, intractable, mutinous.
(ANT.) obedient, compliant, submissive, dutiful.
insufficient *(SYN.)* limited, lacking, deficient, short, inadequate.
(ANT.) ample, protracted, abundant, big, extended.
insulation *(SYN.)* quarantine, segregation, seclusion, withdrawal, isolation, loneliness, alienation, solitude.
(ANT.) union, communion, association, fellowship, connection.
insult *(SYN.)* insolence, offense, abuse, dishonor, affront, insult, indignity, offend, humiliate, outrage.
(ANT.) compliment, homage, apology, salutation, flatter, praise.
integrated *(SYN.)* mingled, mixed, combined, interspersed, desegregated, nonsectarian, interracial.
(ANT.) separated, divided, segregated.
integrity *(SYN.)* honesty, openness, trustworthiness, fairness, candor, justice, rectitude, sincerity, uprightness, soundness, wholeness, honor, principle, virtue.
(ANT.) fraud, deceit, cheating, trickery, dishonesty.
intellect *(SYN.)* understanding, judgment.
intellectual *(SYN.)* intelligent.
intelligence *(SYN.)* reason, sense, intellect, understanding, mind, ability, skill, aptitude.
(ANT.) feeling, passion, emotion.
intelligent *(SYN.)* clever, smart, knowledgeable, well-informed, alert, discerning, astute, quick, enlightened, smart, bright, wise.
(ANT.) insipid, obtuse, dull, stupid, slow, foolish, unintelligent, dumb.
intend *(SYN.)* plan, prepare, scheme, contrive, outline, design, sketch, plot, project, delineate.
intense *(SYN.)* brilliant, animated, graphic, lucid, bright, expressive, vivid, deep, profound, concentrated, serious, earnest.
(ANT.) dull, vague, dusky, dim, dreary.
intensify *(SYN.)* accrue, augment, amplify, enlarge, enhance, extend, expand, heighten, grow, magnify, raise, multiply.
(ANT.) reduce, decrease, contract, diminish.
intent *(SYN.)* purpose, design, objective, intention, aim.
(ANT.) accidental, result, chance.
intensity *(SYN.)* force, potency, power, toughness, activity, durability, fortitude, vigor, stamina.
(ANT.) weakness, feebleness, infirmity, frailty.
intention *(SYN.)* intent, purpose, objective, plan, expectation, aim, object.
(ANT.) chance, accident.
intentional *(SYN.)* deliberate, intended, studied, willful, contemplated, premeditated, designed, voluntary, purposeful, planned.
(ANT.) fortuitous, accidental, chance.
intentionally *(SYN.)* purposefully, deliberately, maliciously.
(ANT.) accidentally.
interest *(SYN.)* attention, concern, care, advantage, benefit, profit, ownership, credit, attract, engage, amuse, entertain.
(ANT.) apathy, weary, disinterest.
interested *(SYN.)* affected, concerned.
(ANT.) unconcerned, indifferent, uninterested.
interesting *(SYN.)* engaging, inviting, fascinating, attractive.
(ANT.) boring, tedious, uninteresting, wearisome.
interfere *(SYN.)* meddle, monkey, interpose, interrupt, tamper, butt in, intervene.
interference *(SYN.)* prying, intrusion, meddling, obstacle, obstruction.
interior *(SYN.)* internal, inmost, inner, inward, inside, center.
(ANT.) outer, adjacent, exterior, external, outside.
interject *(SYN.)* intrude, introduce, insert, inject, interpose.
(ANT.) overlook, avoid, disregard.
interminable *(SYN)* immense, endless, immeasurable, unlimited, vast, unbounded, boundless, eternal, infinite.
(ANT.) limited, bounded, circumscribed, confined.
internal *(SYN.)* inner, interior, inside, intimate, private.
(ANT.) outer, external, surface.
interpose *(SYN.)* arbitrate, inject, intervene, meddle, insert, interject, introduce, intercede, intrude, interfere.
(ANT.) overlook, avoid, disregard.
interpret *(SYN.)* explain, solve, trans-

late, construe, elucidate, decode, explicate, render, unravel, define, understand.
(ANT.) misinterpret, falsify, confuse, distort, misconstrue.
interrogate *(SYN.)* quiz, analyze, inquire, audit, question, contemplate, assess, dissect, notice, scan, review, view, check, survey, scrutinize, examine.
(ANT.) overlook, omit, neglect, disregard.
interrupt *(SYN.)* suspend, delay, postpone, defer, adjourn, stay, discontinue, intrude, interfere.
(ANT.) prolong, persist, continue, maintain, proceed.
interval *(SYN.)* pause, gap.
intervene *(SYN.)* insert, intercede, meddle, inject, introduce, interpose, mediate, interfere, interrupt, intrude.
(ANT.) overlook, avoid, disregard.
intimacy *(SYN.)* fellowship, friendship, acquaintance, frankness, familiarity, unreserved, liberty.
(ANT.) presumption, distance, haughtiness, constraint, reserve.
intimate *(SYN.)* chummy, confidential, friendly, loving, affectionate, close, familiar, near, personal, private, secret.
(ANT.) conventional, formal, ceremonious, distant.
intimation *(SYN.)* reminder, implication, allusion, hint, insinuation.
(ANT.) declaration, statement, affirmation.
intolerant *(SYN.)* fanatical, narrow-minded, prejudiced, bigoted, illiberal, dogmatic, biased.
(ANT.) tolerant, radical, liberal, progressive, broad-minded, fair.
intoxicated *(SYN.)* inebriated, tipsy, drunk, tight, drunken, high.
(ANT.) sober, temperate, clearheaded.
intrepid *(SYN.)* brave, fearless, insolent, abrupt, rude, pushy, adventurous, daring, courageous, prominent, striking, forward, imprudent.
(ANT.) timid, bashful, flinching, cowardly, retiring.
intricate *(SYN.)* compound, perplexing, complex, involved, complicated.
(ANT.) simple, plain, uncompounded.
intrigue *(SYN.)* design, plot, cabal, machination, stratagem, scheme, attract, charm, interest, captivate.
intrinsic *(SYN.)* natural, inherent, inbred, congenital, inborn, native.
(ANT.) extraneous, acquired, external, extrinsic.
introduce *(SYN.)* acquaint, present, submit, present, offer, propose.
introduction *(SYN.)* preamble, prelude, beginning, prologue, start, preface.
(ANT.) finale, conclusion, end, epilogue, completion.
intrude *(SYN.)* invade, attack, encroach, trespass, penetrate, infringe, interrupt.
(ANT.) vacate, evacuate, abandon, relinquish.
intruder *(SYN.)* trespasser, thief, prowler, robber.
intuition *(SYN.)* insight, acumen, perspicuity, penetration, discernment, instinct, clairvoyance.
invade *(SYN.)* intrude, violate, infringe, attack, penetrate, encroach, trespass.
(ANT.) vacate, abandon, evacuate, relinquish.
invalidate *(SYN.)* annul, cancel, abolish, revoke, abrogate.
(ANT.) promote, restore, sustain, establish, continue.
invaluable *(SYN.)* priceless, precious, valuable.
(ANT.) worthless.
invasion *(SYN.)* assault, onslaught, aggression, attack, intrusion.
(ANT.) surrender, opposition, resistance, defense.
invective *(SYN.)* insult, abuse, disparagement, upbraiding, reproach, defamation, aspersion.
(ANT.) laudation, plaudit, commendation.
invent *(SYN.)* devise, fabricate, design, concoct, frame, conceive, contrive, create, originate, devise.
(SYN.) reproduce, copy, imitate.
inventive *(SYN.)* fanciful, imaginative, visionary, poetical, clever, creative.
(ANT.) unromantic, literal, dull, prosaic.
inventiveness *(SYN)* cunning, cleverness, ingeniousness, aptitude.
(ANT.) ineptitude, clumsiness, dullness, stupidity.
invert *(SYN.)* upset, turn about, transpose, countermand, revoke, reverse, overturn, repeal.
(ANT.) maintain, stabilize, endorse.
investigate *(SYN.)* look, probe, ransack, scrutinize, ferret, examine, seek, explore, search, scour, inspect, study.
investigation *(SYN.)* exploration, interrogation, quest, question, scrutiny, inquiry, query, examination, study, research.
(ANT.) inattention, disregard, inactivity, negligence.
invigorating *(SYN.)* bracing, fortifying, vitalizing, stimulating.
invincible *(SYN.)* insurmountable, unconquerable, impregnable, indomitable, invulnerable, unassailable.
(ANT.) powerless, weak, vulnerable.
invisible *(SYN.)* indistinguishable, unseen, imperceptible, indiscernible.
(ANT.) evident, visible, seen, perceptible.
invite *(SYN.)* bid, ask, encourage, request, urge.
inviting *(SYN.)* appealing, attractive, tempting, luring, alluring.
(ANT.) unattractive, uninviting.
involuntary *(SYN.)* reflex, uncontrolled, automatic, unintentional.
(SYN.) voluntary, willful.
involve *(SYN.)* include, embrace, entangle, envelop, incriminate, embroil, implicate, contain, complicate, confuse.
(ANT.) separate, disconnect, extricate, disengage.
involved *(SYN.)* compound, intricate,

complicated, complex, perplexing.
(ANT.) plain, uncompounded, simple.
invulnerable *(SYN.)* indomitable, unassailable, invincible, unconquerable, insurmountable, impregnable.
(ANT.) weak, puny, powerless, vulnerable.
irate *(SYN.)* incensed, enraged, angry.
ire *(SYN.)* indignation, irritation, wrath, anger, animosity, fury, passion, temper, exasperation, petulance, rage.
(ANT.) peace, patience, conciliation, self-control, forbearance.
irk *(SYN.)* irritate, bother, disturb, pester, trouble, vex, tease, chafe, annoy, inconvenience, provoke.
(ANT.) console, soothe, accommodate, gratify.
irrational *(SYN.)* inconsistent, preposterous, self-contradictory, unreasonable, absurd, foolish, nonsensical, ridiculous.
(ANT.) sensible, sound, rational consistent, reasonable.
irregular *(SYN.)* eccentric, unusual, aberrant, devious, abnormal, unnatural, capricious, variable, unequal, disorderly, unsettled, random, disorganized.
(ANT.) regular, methodical, fixed, usual, ordinary, even.
irrelevant *(SYN.)* foreign, unconnected, remote, alien, strange.
(ANT.) germane, relevant, akin, kindred.
irresolute *(SYN.)* frail, pliant, vacillating, ineffective, wavering, weak, yielding, fragile, pliable.
(ANT.) robust, potent, sturdy, strong, powerful.
irresponsible *(SYN.)* unreliable.
irritable *(SYN.)* hasty, hot, peevish, testy, irascible, fiery, snappish, petulant, choleric, excitable, touchy.
(ANT.) composed, agreeable, tranquil, calm.
irritate *(SYN.)* irk, molest, bother, annoy, tease, disturb, inconvenience, vex, trouble, pester, inflame, chafe.
(ANT.) console, gratify, accommodate, soothe, pacify, calm.
irritable *(SYN.)* peevish, testy, sensitive, touchy.
(ANT.) happy, cheerful.
irritation *(SYN.)* chagrin, mortification, vexation, annoyance, exasperation.
(ANT.) pleasure, comfort, gratification, appeasement.
isolate *(SYN.)* detach, segregate, separate, disconnect.
(ANT.) happy, cheerful.
isolated *(SYN.)* lone, single, alone, desolate, secluded, solitary, deserted.
(ANT.) surrounded, accompanied.
isolation *(SYN.)* quarantine, seclusion, separation, solitude, alienation, retirement, loneliness, withdrawal, segregation, detachment.
(ANT.) fellowship, union, association, communion, connection.
issue *(SYN.)* flow, proceed, result, come, emanate, originate, abound.
itemize *(SYN.)* register, detail, record.

jab *(SYN.)* thrust, poke, nudge, prod, shove, jolt, boost, tap, slap, rap.
jack *(SYN.)* fellow, guy, boy, toiler, guy, man, worker.
jacket *(SYN.)* wrapper, envelope, coat, sheath, cover, folder, enclosure, skin.
jade *(SYN.)* hussy, wanton, trollop.
jag *(SYN.)* notch, snag, protuberance, barb, dent, cut, nick, indentation.
jagged *(SYN.)* crooked, bent, ragged, pointy, notched, aquiline, furcated.
(ANT.) smooth.
jail *(SYN.)* stockade, prison, reformatory, penitentiary, keep, dungeon, brig, confine, lock up, detain.
jam *(SYN.)* force, pack, ram, crowd, push, wedge, squeeze, stuff, load.
jamboree *(SYN.)* celebration, fete, spree, festival, festivity, carousal.
janitor *(SYN.)* custodian, doorkeeper, caretaker, superintendent, gatekeeper.
jar *(SYN.)* rattle, shake, bounce, jolt.
jargon *(SYN.)* speech, idiom, dialect, vernacular, diction, argot.
(ANT.) gibberish, babble, nonsense.
jaunt *(SYN.)* journey, trip, tour, excursion, outing, voyage, expedition.
jazzy *(SYN.)* garish, vivacious, loud, splashy, exaggerated, flashy.
jealous *(SYN.)* covetous, envious.
jealousy *(SYN.)* suspicion, envy, resentfulness, greed, covetousness.
(ANT.) tolerance, liberality.
jeer *(SYN.)* taunt, mock, scoff, deride, make fun of, gibe, sneer.
(ANT.) flatter, praise, compliment, laud.
jeering *(SYN.)* mockery, sneering, derision, sarcasm, irony, ridicule.
jell *(SYN.)* finalize, congeal, set, solidify, shape up, take form.
jeopardize *(SYN.)* risk, dare, expose, imperil, chance, venture, hazard.
(ANT.) know, guard, determine.
jerk *(SYN.)* quiver, twitch, shake, spasm, jolt, yank, fool.
jet *(SYN.)* squirt, spurt, gush, inky, nozzle.
jetty *(SYN.)* pier, breakwater, buttress.
jewel *(SYN.)* ornament, gemstone, gem, bauble, stone.
jig *(SYN.)* caper, prance, jiggle, leap.
jiggle *(SYN.)* shimmy, agitate, jerk, twitch, wiggle.
jilt *(SYN.)* abandon, get rid of, reject, desert, forsake, leave.
jingle *(SYN.)* chime, ring, tinkle.
jinx *(SYN.)* hex, whammy, curse.
jittery *(SYN.)* jumpy, nervous, quivering, shaky, skittery.
job *(SYN.)* toil, business, occupation, post, chore, stint, career, duty.
jobless *(SYN.)* idle, unoccupied, inactive, unemployed.
jocularity *(SYN.)* humor, wit, joke, facetiousness, waggery.
(ANT.) sorrow, gravity.
jog *(SYN.)* gait, trot, sprint, run, lope.
join *(SYN.)* conjoin, unite, attach, accompany, associate, assemble, fit.
(ANT.) separate, disconnect, split, sunder, part, divide, detach.
joint *(SYN.)* link, union, connection, junction, coupling, common.

(ANT.) divided, separate.
joke *(SYN.)* game, jest, caper, prank, anecdote, quip, tease, banter, laugh.
joker *(SYN.)* wisecracker, humorist, comedian, trickster, comic, jester, wit.
jolly *(SYN.)* merry, joyful, gay, happy, sprightly, pleasant, jovial, gleeful.
(ANT.) mournful, depressed, glum.
jolt *(SYN.)* sway, waver, startle, rock, jar, jerk, bounce, quake, bump, shake.
jot *(SYN.)* note, write, record.
jounce *(SYN.)* bounce, jolt, bump, jostle, jar, shake.
journal *(SYN.)* account, diary, log, chronicle, magazine, newspaper.
journey *(SYN.)* tour, passage, cruise, voyage, pilgrimage, jaunt, trip, outing.
joy *(SYN.)* pleasure, glee, bliss, elation, mirth, felicity, rapture, delight.
(ANT.) grief, depression, unhappiness, sorrow, misery, gloom, affliction.
joyful *(SYN.)* gay, lucky, opportune, cheerful, happy, blissful, jovial, merry.
(ANT.) gloomy, sad, blue, solemn, serious, grim, morose, glum, depressed.
joyous *(SYN.)* jolly, gay, blithe, merry, gleeful, cheerful, jovial.
(ANT.) sad, gloomy, sorrowful.
jubilant *(SYN.)* exulting, rejoicing, overjoyed, triumphant, elated, delighted.
(ANT.) dejected.
jubilee *(SYN.)* gala, holiday, celebration.
judge *(SYN.)* umpire, think, estimate, decide, arbitrator, condemn, decree.
judgment *(SYN.)* wisdom, perspicacity, discernment, decision, common sense.
(ANT.) thoughtlessness, senselessness.
judicious *(SYN.)* sensible, wise, well-advised, thoughtful.
(ANT.) ignorant.
jug *(SYN.)* bottle, jar, flask, flagon.
jumble *(SYN.)* disarrangement, tumult, agitation, ferment, turmoil.
(ANT.) peace, arrange, compose.
jump *(SYN.)* leap, caper, skip, bound, jerk, vault, hop, spring.
junction *(SYN.)* coupling, joining, union, crossroads, intersection, weld.
(ANT.) separation.
jungle *(SYN.)* woods, thicket, undergrowth, forest, bush.
junior *(SYN.)* secondary, inferior, minor, lower, younger.
junk *(SYN.)* rubbish, scraps, trash, waste, dump, discard, castoffs, debris.
junky *(SYN.)* tawdry, ramshackle, tattered, tacky, shoddy.
jurisdiction *(SYN.)* power, commission, warrant, authority, authorization.
just *(SYN.)* fair, trustworthy, precise, exact, candid, upright, honest.
(ANT.) tricky, dishonest, unjust, corrupt.
justice *(SYN.)* justness, rectitude, equity, law, fairness, impartiality, right.
(ANT.) unfairness, inequity, wrong.
justify *(SYN.)* uphold, excuse, defend, acquit, exonerate, absolve, clear, vindicate.
(ANT.) convict.
jut *(SYN.)* project, protrude, stick out.
(ANT.) indent, recess.
juvenile *(SYN.)* youthful, childish.
(ANT.) old, aged, adult, mature.

kaiser *(SYN.)* czar, caesar, caliph, mogul, tycoon, khan, cazique.
kavass *(SYN.)* badel, macebearer, constable.
keck *(SYN.)* vomit, belch, retch.
keen *(SYN.)* clever, cunning, acute, penetrating, exact, severe, shrewd, wily, astute, sharp, bright, intelligent.
(ANT.) stupid, shallow, dull, blunted, slow, bland, gentle, obtuse, blunt.
keep *(SYN.)* maintain, retain, observe, protect, confine, sustain, continue, preserve, save, guard, restrain, reserve.
(ANT.) abandon, disobey, dismiss, discard, ignore, neglect, lose, reject, relinquish.
keeper *(SYN.)* warden, jailer, ranger, gaoler, guard, turnkey, watchman, escort, custodian.
keeping *(SYN.)* congeniality, uniformity.
keepsake *(SYN.)* reminder, memorial, relic, souvenir, memento, hint.
keg *(SYN.)* container, drum, tub, barrel, receptacle, reservatory, capsule, cask.
kelpie *(SYN.)* sprite, naiad, pixy.
kelson *(SYN.)* bottom, sole, toe, foot, root, keel.
kempt *(SYN.)* neat, trim, tidy, spruce.
ken *(SYN.)* field, view, vision, range, scope.
kennel *(SYN.)* swarm, flock, covy, drove, herd, pound, doghouse.
kerchief *(SYN.)* neckcloth, hankerchief, scarf, headpiece, babushka.
kern *(SYN.)* peasant, carle, serf, tike, tyke, countryman.
kernel *(SYN.)* marrow, pith, backbone, soul, heart, core, nucleus.
ketch *(SYN.)* lugger, cutter, clipper, ship, barge, sloop.
kettle *(SYN.)* pan, caldron, vat, pot, teapot, vessel, receptacle, receiver.
key *(SYN.)* opener, explanation, tone, lead, cause, source, note, pitch.
keynote *(SYN.)* core, model, theme, pattern, standard, gist.
keystone *(SYN.)* backbone, support.
khan *(SYN.)* master, czar, kaiser, padishah, caesar.
kick *(SYN.)* punt, remonstrate, boot.
kickback *(SYN.)* repercussion, backfire, rebound.
kickoff *(SYN.)* beginning, opening, commencement, outset, start.
kid *(SYN.)* joke, tease, fool, jest, tot, child.
kidnap *(SYN.)* abduct, snatch, shanghai.
kill *(SYN.)* execute, put to death, slay, butcher, assassinate, murder, cancel, destroy, slaughter, finish, end.
(ANT.) save, protect, animate, resuscitate, vivify.
killing *(SYN.)* massacre, genocide, slaughter, carnage, butchery, bloodshed.
killjoy *(SYN.)* wet blanket, sourpuss, party-pooper.
kin *(SYN.)* relatives, family, folks, relations.
kind *(SYN.)* humane, affable, compassionate, benevolent, merciful, tender, sympathetic, breed, indulgent.
(ANT.) unkind, cruel, merciless, severe,

mean, inhuman.

kindle *(SYN.)* fire, ignite, light, arouse, excite, set afire, stir up, trigger, move, provoke, inflame.
(ANT.) pacify, extinguish, calm.

kindly *(SYN.)* warm, kindhearted, kind, warmhearted.
(ANT.) mean, cruel.

kindred *(SYN.)* family, relations, relatives, consanguinity, kinsfolk, affinity.
(ANT.) strangers, disconnection.

kinetic *(SYN.)* vigorous, active, dynamic, energetic, mobile, forceful.

king *(SYN.)* sovereign, ruler, chief, monarch, potentate.

kingdom *(SYN.)* realm, empire, monarchy, domain.

kingly *(SYN.)* kinglike, imperial, regal, royal, majestic.

kink *(SYN.)* twist, curl, quirk.

kinship *(SYN.)* lineage, blood, family, stock, relationship.

kismet *(SYN.)* fate, end, fortune.

kiss *(SYN.)* pet, caress, fondle, cuddle, osculate, embrace.
(ANT.) vex, spurn, annoy, tease, buffet.

kit *(SYN.)* outfit, collection, furnishings, equipment, rig, gear, set.

knack *(SYN.)* cleverness, readiness, deftness, ability, ingenuity, skill, talent, aptitude, talent, know-how, art, adroitness, skillfulness.
(ANT.) inability, clumsiness, awkwardness, ineptitude.

knave *(SYN.)* rogue, rascal, villain, scoundrel.

knead *(SYN.)* combine, massage, blend.

knickknack *(SYN.)* trinket, bric-a-brac, trifle.

knife *(SYN.)* sword, blade.

knightly *(SYN.)* valiant, courageous, gallant, chivalrous, noble.

knit *(SYN.)* unite, join, mend, fasten, connect, combine, heal.

knob *(SYN.)* doorknob, handle, protuberance, bump.

knock *(SYN.)* thump, tap, rap, strike, hit, jab, punch, beat, pound, bang, hammer, thwack.

knockout *(SYN.)* stunning, overpowering, stupefying, overwhelming.

knoll *(SYN.)* hill, elevation, hump, mound, butte.

knot *(SYN.)* cluster, gathering, collection, group, crowd, twist, snarl, tangle.

know *(SYN.)* perceive, comprehend, apprehend, recognize, understand, discern, discriminate, ascertain, identify.
(ANT.) doubt, suspect, dispute, ignore.

knowing *(SYN.)* sage, smart, wise, clever, sagacious, shrewd.

knowledge *(SYN.)* information, wisdom, erudition, learning, apprehension.
(ANT.) misunderstanding, ignorance, stupidity, illiteracy.

knurl *(SYN.)* gnarl, knot, projection, burl, node, lump.

kosher *(SYN.)* permitted, okay, fit, proper, acceptable.

kowtow *(SYN.)* stoop, bend, kneel, genuflect, bow.

kudos *(SYN.)* acclaim, praise, approbation, approval.

label *(SYN.)* mark, tag, title, name, marker, stamp, sticker, ticket, docket, identity.

labor *(SYN.)* toil, travail, effort, task, childbirth, work, parturition, striving, workers, effort, industry, workingmen.
(ANT.) recreation, indolence, idleness, leisure.

laboratory *(SYN.)* lab, workroom, workshop.

laborer *(SYN.)* wage earner, helper, worker, toiler, blue-collar worker.

laborious *(SYN.)* tiring, difficult, hard, burdensome, industrious, painstaking.
(ANT.) simple, easy, relaxing, restful.

labyrinth *(SYN.)* complex, maze, tangle.

lace *(SYN.)* openwork, fancywork, embroidery, edging.

lacerate *(SYN.)* mangle, tear roughly.

laceration *(SYN.)* cut, wound, puncture, gash, lesion, injury.

lack *(SYN.)* want, need, shortage, dearth, scarcity, require.
(ANT.) profusion, quantity.

lackey *(SYN.)* stooge, flatterer, flunky.

lacking *(SYN.)* insufficient, short, deficient, incomplete, defective, scanty.
(ANT.) satisfactory, enough, ample, sufficient, adequate.

lackluster *(SYN.)* dull, pallid, flat, lifeless, drab, dim.

laconic *(SYN.)* short, terse, compact, brief, curt, succinct, concise.

lacquer *(SYN.)* polish, varnish, gild.

lad *(SYN.)* youth, boy, fellow, stripling.

laden *(SYN.)* burdened, weighted.

ladle *(SYN.)* scoop, dipper.

lady *(SYN.)* matron, woman, dame, gentlewoman.

ladylike *(SYN.)* feminine, womanly, maidenly, womanish, female.
(ANT.) masculine, male, virile, mannish, manly.

lag *(SYN.)* dawdle, loiter, linger, poke, dilly-dally, delay, tarry, slowdown.

laggard *(SYN.)* dallier, idler, lingerer, slowpoke, dawdler.

lair *(SYN.)* retreat, burrow, den, nest, mew, hole.

lambaste *(SYN.)* berate, scold, censure.

lame *(SYN.)* feeble, maimed, disabled, crippled, deformed, hobbling, unconvincing, weak, poor, inadequate, halt.
(ANT.) vigorous, convincing, plausible, athletic, robust, agile, sound.

lament *(SYN.)* deplore, wail, bemoan, bewail, regret, grieve, mourning, lamentation, moaning, wailing, mourn.
(ANT.) celebrate, rejoice.

lamentable *(SYN.)* unfortunate.

lamp *(SYN.)* light, beam, illumination, shine, insight, knowledge, radiance.
(ANT.) shadow, darkness, obscurity, gloom.

lampoon *(SYN.)* skit, tirade, burlesque, parody, satire.

lance *(SYN.)* cut, pierce, perforate, stab, puncture, impale, knife.

land *(SYN.)* earth, continent, ground, soil, domain, estate, field, realm, plain, surface, arrive, descend, country, island, region, alight, shore, sod, tract.

landlord *(SYN.)* owner, landholder,

landowner, proprietor.
landmark *(SYN.)* keystone, monument, milestone, point, cornerstone.
landscape *(SYN.)* panorama, environs, countryside, scenery, scene.
landslide *(SYN.)* rockfall, avalanche.
lane *(SYN.)* alley, way, road, path, aisle, pass, channel, avenue, artery, passage.
language *(SYN.)* dialect, tongue, speech, lingo, jargon, cant, diction, idiom, patter, phraseology, vernacular, words.
(ANT.) gibberish, nonsense, babble, drivel.
languid *(SYN.)* feeble, drooping, irresolute, dull, lethargic, weak, faint.
(ANT.) forceful, strong, vigorous.
languish *(SYN.)* decline, sink, droop, wither, waste, fail, wilt, weaken.
(ANT.) revive, rejuvenate, refresh.
languor *(SYN.)* weariness, depression, torpor, inertia, apathy.
lanky *(SYN.)* skinny, gaunt, lean, scrawny, slender, thin.
(ANT.) chunky, stocky, obese, fat.
lantern *(SYN.)* torch, light, lamp.
lap *(SYN.)* drink, lick, fold over.
lapse *(SYN.)* decline, sink, slump.
larceny *(SYN.)* pillage, robbery, stealing, theft, burglary, plunder.
lard *(SYN.)* grease, fat.
large *(SYN.)* great, vast, colossal, ample, extensive, capacious, sizable, broad, massive, grand, immense, big, enormous, huge, giant, mammoth, wide.
(ANT.) tiny, little, short, small.
largely *(SYN.)* chiefly, mainly, principally, mostly.
lariat *(SYN.)* lasso, rope.
lark *(SYN.)* fling, frolic, play, fun, spree, joke, revel, celebration.
lascivious *(SYN.)* lecherous, raunchy, lustful, wanton, lewd.
lash *(SYN.)* thong, whip, rod, cane, blow, strike, hit, beat, knout.
lass *(SYN.)* maiden, girl, damsel.
(ANT.) woman.
lasso *(SYN.)* lariat, rope, noose, snare.
last *(SYN.)* terminal, final, ultimate, remain, endure, concluding, latest, utmost, end, conclusive, hindmost, continue, extreme.
(ANT.) first, initial, beginning, opening, starting, foremost.
latch *(SYN.)* clasp, hook, fastener, lock, closing, seal, catch.
late *(SYN.)* overdue, tardy, behind, advanced, delayed, new, slow, recent.
(ANT.) timely, early.
lately *(SYN.)* recently, yesterday.
latent *(SYN.)* potential, undeveloped, unseen, dormant, secret, concealed, inactive, hidden, obscured, covered, quiescent.
(ANT.) visible, evident, conspicuous, explicit, manifest.
lather *(SYN.)* suds, foam, froth.
lateral *(SYN.)* sideways, glancing, tangential, marginal, skirting, side.
latitude *(SYN.)* range, scope, freedom, extent.
latter *(SYN.)* more recent, later.
(ANT.) former.
lattice *(SYN.)* grating, screen, frame, trellis, openwork, framework, grid.
laud *(SYN.)* commend, praise, extol, glorify, compliment.
(ANT.) criticize, belittle.
laudable *(SYN.)* creditable, praiseworthy, commendable, admirable.
laudation *(SYN.)* applause, compliment, flattery, praise, commendation, acclaim, extolling, glorification.
(ANT.) criticizing, condemnation, reproach, disparagement, censure.
laugh *(SYN.)* chuckle, giggle, snicker, cackle, titter, grin, smile, roar, guffaw, jeer, mock.
laughable *(SYN.)* funny, amusing, comical, humorous, ridiculous.
launch *(SYN.)* drive, fire, propel, start, begin, originate, set afloat, initiate.
(ANT.) finish, stop, terminate.
launder *(SYN.)* bathe, wash, scrub, scour.
laurels *(SYN.)* glory, distinction, recognition, award, commendation, reward, honor.
lavatory *(SYN.)* toilet, washroom, bathroom, latrine.
lavish *(SYN.)* squander, waste, dissipate, scatter, abundant, free, plentiful, liberal, extravagant, ample, wear out, prodigal, generous, spend.
(ANT.) economize, save, conserve, accumulate, sparing, stingy, preserve.
law *(SYN.)* decree, formula, statute, act, rule, ruling, standard, principle, ordinance, proclamation, regulation, order, edict.
lawful *(SYN.)* legal, permissible, allowable, legitimate, authorized, constitutional, rightful.
(ANT.) prohibited, criminal, illicit, illegal, illegitimate.
lawless *(SYN.)* uncivilized, uncontrolled, wild, savage, untamed, violent.
(ANT.) obedient, law-abiding, tame.
lawlessness *(SYN.)* chaos, anarchy.
lawn *(SYN.)* grass, meadow, turf.
lawyer *(SYN.)* counsel, attorney, counselor.
lax *(SYN.)* slack, loose, careless, vague, lenient, lazy.
(ANT.) firm, rigid.
lay *(SYN.)* mundane, worldly, temporal, place, dispose, bet, wager, hazard, risk, stake, site, earthly, profane, laic, arrange, location, put, set, ballad, deposit, position, song, secular.
(ANT.) spiritual, unworldly, remove, misplace, disturb, mislay, disarrange, ecclesiastical, religious.
lay off *(SYN.)* discharge, bounce, fire, dismiss.
layout *(SYN.)* plan, arrangement, design.
lazy *(SYN.)* slothful, supine, idle, inactive, sluggish, inert, indolent, torpid.
(ANT.) alert, ambitious, forceful, diligent, active, assiduous.
lea *(SYN.)* pasture, meadow.
leach *(SYN.)* remove, extract, seep, dilute, wash out.
lead *(SYN.)* regulate, conduct, guide, escort, direct, supervise, command, come first, steer, control.

(ANT.) follow.

leader *(SYN.)* master, ruler, captain, chief, commander, principal, director, head, chieftain.
(ANT.) follower, servant, disciple, subordinate, attendant.

leading *(SYN.)* dominant, foremost, principal, first, main, primary.

league *(SYN.)* entente, partnership, association, confederacy, coalition, society, alliance, federation, union.
(ANT.) separation, schism.

leak *(SYN.)* dribble, flow, drip, opening, perforation.

lean *(SYN.)* rely, tilt, slim, slender, slope, incline, tend, trust, bend, tendency, slant, depend, spare, scant, lanky, thin, meager, inclination, narrow, sag.
(ANT.) rise, heavy, fat, erect, straighten, portly, raise.

leaning *(SYN.)* trend, proclivity, bias, tendency, bent, predisposition, proneness.
(ANT.) disinclination, aversion.

leap *(SYN.)* vault, skip, caper, dive, hurdle, jump, bound, start, hop, plunge, spring.

learn *(SYN.)* gain, find out, memorize, acquire, determine.

learned *(SYN.)* erudite, knowing, enlightened, deep, wise, discerning, scholarly, intelligent, educated, sagacious.
(ANT.) simple, uneducated, ignorant, illiterate, unlettered, foolish.

learning *(SYN.)* science, education, lore, apprehension, wisdom, knowledge, scholarship, erudition.
(ANT.) misunderstanding, ignorance, stupidity.

lease *(SYN.)* charter, let, rent, engage.

leash *(SYN.)* chain, strap, shackle, collar.

least *(SYN.)* minutest, smallest, tiniest, trivial, minimum, fewest, slightest.
(ANT.) most.

leave *(SYN.)* give up, retire, desert, abandon, withdraw, relinquish, will, depart, quit, liberty, renounce, go, bequeath, consent, allowance, permission, freedom, forsake.
(ANT.) come, stay, arrive, tarry, remain, abide.

lecherous *(SYN.)* lustful, sensual, carnal, lascivious.

lecture *(SYN.)* talk, discussion, lesson, instruct, speech, conference, sermon, report, recitation, address, oration, discourse.
(ANT.) writing, meditation, correspondence.

ledge *(SYN.)* eaves, ridge, shelf, rim, edge.

lee *(SYN.)* shelter, asylum, sanctuary, haven.

leech *(SYN.)* barnacle, bloodsucker, parasite.

leer *(SYN.)* eye, grimace, ogle, wink, squint.

leeway *(SYN.)* reserve, allowance, elbowroom, slack, clearance.

leftovers *(SYN.)* scraps, remains, residue, remainder.

legacy *(SYN.)* bequest, inheritance, heirloom.

legal *(SYN.)* legitimate, rightful, honest, allowable, allowed, permissible, lawful, permitted, authorized.
(ANT.) illicit, illegal, prohibited, illegitimate.

legalize *(SYN.)* authorize, ordain, approve, sanction.

legate *(SYN.)* envoy, agent, representative, emissary.

legend *(SYN.)* saga, fable, allegory, myth, parable, tale, story, folklore, fiction, chronicle.
(ANT.) history, facts.

legendary *(SYN.)* fictitious, traditional, mythical, imaginary, fanciful.

legible *(SYN.)* plain, readable, clear, distinct.
(ANT.) illegible.

legion *(SYN.)* outfit, unit, troop, regiment, company, battalion, force, army, team, division.

legislation *(SYN.)* resolution, ruling, lawmaking, regulation, enactment, statute, decree.

legislator *(SYN.)* statesman, congressman, senator, politician, lawmaker.

legitimate *(SYN.)* true, real, bona fide, lawful, proper, right, valid, correct, unadulterated, authentic, rightful, legal, sincere.
(ANT.) sham, counterfeit, artificial, false.

leisure *(SYN.)* respite, intermission, ease, relaxation, rest, calm, tranquillity, recreation, peace, pause.
(ANT.) motion, commotion, tumult, agitation, disturbance.

leisurely *(SYN.)* sluggish, laggard, unhurried, relaxed, casual, dawdling, slow, deliberate.
(ANT.) hurried, swift, pressed, rushed, forced, fast, speedy, quick.

lend *(SYN.)* entrust, advance, confer.

length *(SYN.)* reach, measure, extent, distance, span, longness, stretch.

lengthen *(SYN.)* stretch, prolong, draw, reach, increase, grow, protract, extend.
(ANT.) shrink, contract, shorten.

leniency *(SYN.)* grace, pity, compassion, mildness, charity, mercy, clemency.
(ANT.) vengeance, punishment, cruelty.

lenient *(SYN.)* tender, humane, clement, tolerant, compassionate, merciful, relaxed, forgiving, gentle, mild, lax, kind.
(ANT.) unfeeling, pitiless, brutal, remorseless.

leprechaun *(SYN.)* gnome, imp, goblin, fairy, elf, sprite, banshee.

lesion *(SYN.)* wound, blemish, sore, trauma, injury.

less *(SYN.)* fewer, smaller, reduced, negative, stinted.
(ANT.) more.

lessen *(SYN.)* shorten, reduce, deduct, subtract, curtail, diminish, shrink, dwindle, decline, instruction, teaching, remove, decrease.
(ANT.) swell, grow, enlarge, increase,

expand, multiply, amplify.
lesson *(SYN.)* exercise, session, class, assignment, section, recitation.
let *(SYN.)* admit, hire out, contract, allow, permit, consent, leave, grant, rent.
(ANT.) deny.
letdown *(SYN.)* disillusionment, disappointment.
lethal *(SYN.)* mortal, dangerous, deadly, fatal, devastating.
lethargic *(SYN.)* sluggish, logy, slow, listless, phlegmatic, lazy.
(ANT.) vivacious, energetic.
lethargy *(SYN.)* numbness, stupor, daze, insensibility, torpor.
(ANT.) wakefulness, liveliness, activity, readiness.
letter *(SYN.)* note, letter, mark, message, character, symbol, sign, memorandum.
letup *(SYN.)* slowdown, slackening, lessening, abatement, reduction.
levee *(SYN.)* dike, breakwater, dam, embankment.
level *(SYN.)* smooth, even, plane, equivalent, uniform, horizontal, equal, flatten, equalize, raze, demolish, flat.
(ANT.) uneven, sloping, hilly, broken.
level-headed *(SYN.)* reasonable, sensible, calm, collected, cool.
leverage *(SYN.)* clout, power, influence, weight, rank.
levity *(SYN.)* humor, triviality, giddiness, hilarity, fun, frivolity.
levy *(SYN.)* tax, duty, tribute, rate, assessment, exaction, charge, custom.
(ANT.) wages, remuneration, gift.
lewd *(SYN.)* indecent, smutty, course, gross, disgusting, impure.
(ANT.) pure, decent, refined.
liability *(SYN.)* indebtedness, answerability, obligation, vulnerability.
liable *(SYN.)* answerable, responsible, likely, exposed to, subject, amenable, probable, accountable.
(ANT.) immune, exempt, independent.
liaison *(SYN.)* union, coupling, link, connection, alliance.
liar *(SYN.)* fibber, falsifier, storyteller, fabricator, prevaricator.
libel *(SYN.)* slander, calumny, vilification, aspersion, defamation.
(ANT.) defense, praise, applause, flattery.
liberal *(SYN.)* large, generous, unselfish, openhanded, broad, tolerant, kind, unprejudiced, open-minded, lavish, plentiful, ample, abundant, extravagant, extensive.
(ANT.) restricted, conservative, stingy, confined.
liberality *(SYN.)* kindness, philanthropy, beneficence, humanity, altruism, benevolence, generosity, charity.
(ANT.) selfishness, cruelty, malevolence.
liberate *(SYN.)* emancipate, loose, release, let go, deliver, free, discharge.
(ANT.) subjugate, oppress, jail, confine, restrict, imprison.
liberated *(SYN.)* loose, frank, emancipated, careless, liberal, freed, autonomous, exempt, familiar.
(ANT.) subject, clogged, restricted, impeded.
liberty *(SYN.)* permission, independence, autonomy, license, privilege, emancipation, freedom.
(ANT.) constraint, imprisonment, bondage, captivity.
license *(SYN.)* liberty, freedom, liberation, permission, exemption, authorization, warrant, allow, consent, permit, sanction, approval, unrestraint.
(ANT.) servitude, constraint, bondage, necessity.
lick *(SYN.)* taste, lap, lave.
lid *(SYN.)* top, cover, cap, plug, cork, stopper.
lie *(SYN.)* untruth, fib, illusion, delusion, falsehood, fiction, equivocation, prevarication, repose, location, perjury, misinform, site, recline, similitude.
(ANT.) variance, truth, difference.
life *(SYN.)* sparkle, being, spirit, vivacity, animation, buoyancy, vitality, existence, biography, energy, liveliness, vigor.
(ANT.) demise, lethargy, death, languor.
lift *(SYN.)* hoist, pick up, elevate, raise, heft.
light *(SYN.)* brightness, illumination, beam, gleam, lamp, knowledge, brilliance, fixture, bulb, candle, fire, ignite, burn, dawn, incandescence, flame, airy, unsubstantial, dainty, luminosity, shine, radiance, giddy, enlightenment, weightless, understanding.
(ANT.) darken, gloom, shadow, extinguish, darkness.
lighten *(SYN.)* diminish, unburden, reduce, brighten.
light-headed *(SYN.)* giddy, silly, dizzy, frivolous.
(ANT.) sober, clear-headed, rational.
lighthearted *(SYN.)* carefree, merry, gay, cheerful, happy, glad.
(ANT.) somber, sad, serious, melancholy.
like *(SYN.)* fancy, esteem, adore, love, admire, care for, prefer, cherish.
(ANT.) disapprove, loathe, hate, dislike.
likely *(SYN.)* liable, reasonable, probable, possible.
likeness *(SYN.)* similarity, resemblance, representation, image, portrait.
(ANT.) difference.
likewise *(SYN.)* besides, as well, also, too, similarly.
liking *(SYN.)* fondness, affection, partiality.
(ANT.) antipathy, dislike.
limb *(SYN.)* arm, leg, member, appendage, part, bough.
limber *(SYN.)* bending, flexible, elastic, pliable.
(ANT.) inflexible, stiff.
limbo *(SYN.)* exile, banishment, purgatory.
limelight *(SYN.)* spotlight, notice, notoriety, fame, prominence.
limerick *(SYN.)* jingle, rhyme.
limit *(SYN.)* terminus, bound, extent, confine, border, restriction, boundary,

restraint, edge, frontier, check, end, limitation.
(ANT.) endlessness, vastness, boundlessness.

limn *(SYN.)* depict, portray, sketch, paint, illustrate.

limp *(SYN.)* soft, flabby, drooping, walk, limber, supple, flexible, hobble, stagger.
(ANT.) stiff.

limpid *(SYN.)* clear, open, transparent, unobstructed.
(ANT.) cloudy.

line *(SYN.)* row, file, series, array, sequence, wire, seam, wrinkle, crease, boundary, arrangement, kind, type, division.

lineage *(SYN.)* race, family, tribe, nation, strain, folk, people, ancestry, clan.

linger *(SYN.)* wait, rest, bide, delay, dwadle, stay, loiter, remain, dilly-dally, tarry.
(ANT.) leave, expedite.

lingo *(SYN.)* vernacular, dialect, language, jargon, speech.

link *(SYN.)* unite, connector, loop, couple, attach, connective, connection, coupling, juncture, bond.
(ANT.) separate, disconnect, split.

lip *(SYN.)* edge, brim, rim.

liquid *(SYN.)* watery, fluent, fluid, flowing.
(ANT.) solid, congealed.

liquidate *(SYN.)* pay off, settle, defray.

liquor *(SYN.)* spirits, alcohol, drink, booze.

lissome *(SYN.)* nimble, quick, lively, flexible, agile.

list *(SYN.)* roll, register, slate, enumeration, series.

listen *(SYN.)* overhear, attend to, heed, hear, list, hearken.
(ANT.) ignore, scorn, disregard, reject.

listless *(SYN.)* uninterested, tired, lethargic, unconcerned, apathetic.
(ANT.) active.

literal *(SYN.)* exact, verbatim, precise, strict, faithful.

literally *(SYN.)* actually, exactly, really.

literate *(SYN.)* informed, educated, learned, intelligent, versed, knowledgeable.
(ANT.) unread, illiterate, ignorant, unlettered.

literature *(SYN.)* books, writings, publications.

lithe *(SYN.)* supple, flexible, bending, limber, pliable.
(ANT.) stiff.

litigious *(SYN.)* quarrelsome, disputatious, argumentative.

litter *(SYN.)* rubbish, trash, scatter, clutter, strew, debris, rubble, disorder.

little *(SYN.)* tiny, petty, miniature, diminutive, puny, wee, significant, small, short, brief, bit, trivial.
(ANT.) huge, large, big, long, immense.

liturgy *(SYN.)* ritual, sacrament, worship, service.

live *(SYN.)* dwell, reside, abide, survive, exist, alive, occupy, stay, active.
(ANT.) die.

livelihood *(SYN.)* keep, sustenance, support, subsistence, job, trade, profession, vocation.

lively *(SYN.)* blithe, vivaciousness, clear, vivid, active, frolicsome, brisk, fresh, animated, energetic, live, spry, vigorous, quick, nimble, bright, exciting, supple.
(ANT.) stale, dull, listless, slow, vapid.

livestock *(SYN.)* animals, cattle.

livid *(SYN.)* grayish, furious, pale, enraged.

living *(SYN.)* support, livelihood, existent, alive.

load *(SYN.)* oppress, trouble, burden, weight, freight, afflict, encumber, pack, shipment, cargo, lade, tax.
(ANT.) lighten, console, unload, mitigate, empty, ease.

loafer *(SYN.)* loiterer, bum, idler, sponger, deadbeat.

loan *(SYN.)* credit, advance, lend.

loath *(SYN.)* reluctant, unwilling, opposed.

loathe *(SYN.)* dislike, despise, hate, abhor, detest, abominate.
(ANT.) love, approve, like, admire.

loathsome *(SYN.)* foul, vile, detestable, revolting, abominable, atrocious, offensive, odious.
(ANT.) pleasant, commendable, alluring, agreeable, delightful.

lob *(SYN.)* toss, hurl, pitch, throw, heave.

lobby *(SYN.)* foyer, entry, entrance, vestibule, passageway, entryway.

local *(SYN.)* limited, regional, restricted, particular.

locality *(SYN.)* nearness, neighborhood, district, vicinity.
(ANT.) remoteness.

locate *(SYN.)* discover, find, unearth, site, situate, place.

located *(SYN.)* found, residing, positioned, situated, placed.

location *(SYN.)* spot, locale, station, locality, situation, place, area, site, vicinity, position, zone, region.

lock *(SYN.)* curl, hook, bolt, braid, ringlet, plait, close, latch, tuft, fastening, bar, hasp, fasten, tress.
(ANT.) open.

locker *(SYN.)* wardrobe, closet, cabinet, chest.

locket *(SYN.)* case, lavaliere, pendant.

locomotion *(SYN.)* movement, travel, transit, motion.

locution *(SYN.)* discourse, cadence, manner, accent.

lodge *(SYN.)* cabin, cottage, hut, club, chalet, society, room, reside, dwell, live, occupy, inhabit, abide, board, fix, settle.

lodger *(SYN.)* guest, tenant, boarder, occupant.

lofty *(SYN.)* high, stately, grandiose, towering, elevated, exalted, sublime, majestic, scornful, proud, grand, tall, pompous.
(ANT.) undignified, lowly, common, ordinary.

log *(SYN.)* lumber, wood, board, register, record, album, account.

logical *(SYN.)* strong, effective, telling, convincing, reasonable, sensible, rational, sane, sound, cogent.
(ANT.) crazy, illogical, irrational, unreasonable, weak.
logy *(SYN.)* tired, inactive, lethargic, sleepy, weary.
loiter *(SYN.)* idle, linger, wait, stay, tarry, dilly-dally, dawdle.
loll *(SYN.)* hang, droop, recline, relax.
lone *(SYN.)* lonely, sole, unaided, single, deserted, isolated, secluded, apart, alone, solitary.
(ANT.) surrounded, accompanied.
loner *(SYN.)* recluse, maverick, outsider, hermit.
loneliness *(SYN.)* solitude, isolation, seclusion, alienation.
lonely *(SYN.)* unaided, isolated, single, solitary, lonesome, unaccompanied, deserted, alone, desolate.
(ANT.) surrounded, attended.
lonesome *(SYN.)* secluded, remote, unpopulated, barren, empty, desolate.
long *(SYN.)* lengthy, prolonged, wordy, elongated, extended, lingering, drawn out, lasting, protracted, extensive, length, prolix, far-reaching, extended.
(ANT.) terse, concise, abridged, short.
long-standing *(SYN.)* established.
long-winded *(SYN.)* boring, dull, wordy.
(ANT.) curt, terse.
look *(SYN.)* gaze, witness, seem, eye, behold, see, watch, scan, view, appear, stare, discern, glance, examine, examination, peep, expression, appearance, regard, study, survey.
(ANT.) overlook, hide, avert, miss.
loom *(SYN.)* emerge, appear, show up.
loop *(SYN.)* ringlet, noose, spiral, fastener.
loose *(SYN.)* untied, unbound, lax, vague, unrestrained, dissolute, limp, undone, baggy, disengaged, indefinite, slack, careless, heedless, unfastened, free, wanton.
(ANT.) restrained, steady, fastened, secure, tied, firm, fast, definite, inhibited.
loosen *(SYN.)* untie, undo, loose, unchain.
(ANT.) tie, tighten, secure.
loot *(SYN.)* booty, plunder, take, steal, rob, sack, rifle, pillage, ravage, devastate.
lope *(SYN.)* run, race, bound, gallop.
lopsided *(SYN.)* unequal, twisted, uneven, askew, distorted.
loquacious *(SYN.)* garrulous, wordy, profuse, chatty, verbose.
lord *(SYN.)* peer, ruler, proprietor, nobleman, master, owner, governor.
lore *(SYN.)* learning, knowledge, wisdom, stories, legends beliefs, teachings.
lose *(SYN.)* misplace, flop, fail, sacrifice, forfeit, mislay, vanish, surrender.
(ANT.) succeed, locate, place, win, discover, find.
loss *(SYN.)* injury, damage, want, hurt, need, bereavement, trouble, death, failure, deficiency.
lost *(SYN.)* dazed, wasted, astray, forfeited, preoccupied, used, adrift, bewildered, missing, distracted, consumed, misspent, absorbed, confused, mislaid, gone, destroyed.
(ANT.) found, anchored.
lot *(SYN.)* result, destiny, bunch, many, amount, fate, cluster, group, sum, portion, outcome, number, doom, issue.
lotion *(SYN.)* cosmetic, balm, cream.
lottery *(SYN.)* wager, chance, drawing, raffle.
loud *(SYN.)* vociferous, noisy, resounding, stentorian, clamorous, sonorous, thunderous, shrill, blaring, roaring, deafening.
(ANT.) soft, inaudible, murmuring, subdued, quiet, dulcet.
lounge *(SYN.)* idle, loaf, laze, sofa, couch, davenport, relax, rest, lobby, salon, divan.
louse *(SYN.)* scoundrel, knave, cad, rat.
lousy *(SYN.)* revolting, grimy, rotten, dirty, disgusting.
lovable *(SYN.)* charming, attractive, delightful, amiable, sweet, cuddly.
love *(SYN.)* attachment, endearment, affection, adoration, liking, devotion, warmth, tenderness, friendliness, adore, worship, like, cherish, fondness.
(ANT.) loathing, detest, indifference, dislike, hate, hatred.
loveliness *(SYN.)* grace, pulchritude, charm, attractiveness, comeliness, fairness, beauty.
(ANT.) ugliness, eyesore, disfigurement.
lovely *(SYN.)* handsome, fair, charming, pretty, attractive, delightful, beautiful, beauteous, exquisite, comely.
(ANT.) ugly, unsightly, homely, foul, hideous, repulsive.
lover *(SYN.)* fiance, suitor, courter, sweetheart, beau.
loving *(SYN.)* close, intimate, confidential, affectionate, friendly.
(ANT.) formal, conventional, ceremonious, distant.
low *(SYN.)* mean, vile, despicable, vulgar, abject, groveling, contemptible, lesser, menial.
(ANT.) righteous, lofty, esteemed, noble.
lower *(SYN.)* subordinate, minor, secondary, quiet, soften, disgrace, degrade, decrease, reduce, diminish, lessen, inferior.
(ANT.) greater, superior, increase.
low-key *(SYN.)* subdued, muted, calm, controlled, restrained, understated.
lowly *(SYN.)* lowborn, humble, base, low, mean, common, average, simple.
(ANT.) royal, noble.
loyal *(SYN.)* earnest, ardent, addicted, inclined, faithful, devoted, affectionate, prone, fond, patriotic, dependable, true.
(ANT.) indisposed, detached, disloyal, traitorous, untrammeled.
loyalty *(SYN.)* devotion, steadfastness, constancy, faithfulness, fidelity, patriotism, allegiance.
(ANT.) treachery, falseness, disloyalty.
lubricate *(SYN.)* oil, grease, anoint.
lucent *(SYN.)* radiant, beaming, vivid, illuminated, lustrous.

lucid *(SYN.)* plain, visible, clear, intelligible, unmistakable, transparent, limpid, translucent, open, shining, light, explicit, understandable, clear-cut, distinct.
(ANT.) unclear, vague, obscure.
luck *(SYN.)* chance, fortunate, fortune, lot, fate, fluke, destiny, karma.
(ANT.) misfortune.
lucky *(SYN.)* favored, favorable, auspicious, fortunate, successful, felicitous.
(ANT.) unlucky, condemned, unfortunate, persecuted.
lucrative *(SYN.)* well-paying, profitable, high-paying, productive, beneficial.
ludicrous *(SYN.)* absurd, ridiculous.
lug *(SYN.)* pull, haul, drag, tug.
luggage *(SYN.)* bags, valises, baggage, suitcases, trunks.
lugubrious *(SYN.)* mournful, sad, gloomy, somber, melancholy.
lukewarm *(SYN.)* unenthusiastic, tepid, spiritless, detached, apathetic, mild.
lull *(SYN.)* quiet, calm, soothe, rest, hush, stillness, pause, break, intermission, recess, respite, silence.
lumber *(SYN.)* logs, timber, wood.
luminous *(SYN.)* beaming, lustrous, shining, glowing, gleaming, bright, light, alight, clear, radiant.
(ANT.) murky, dull, dark.
lummox *(SYN.)* yokel, oaf, bumpkin, clown, klutz.
lump *(SYN.)* swelling, protuberance, mass, chunk, hunk, bump.
lunacy *(SYN.)* derangement, madness, aberration, psychosis, craziness.
(ANT.) stability, rationality.
lunge *(SYN.)* charge, stab, attack, push.
lurch *(SYN.)* topple, sway, toss, roll, rock, tip, pitch.
lure *(SYN.)* draw, tug, drag, entice, attraction, haul, attract, temptation, persuade, pull, draw on, allure.
(ANT.) drive, alienate, propel.
lurid *(SYN.)* sensational, terrible, melodramatic, startling.
lurk *(SYN.)* sneak, hide, prowl, creep.
luscious *(SYN.)* savory, delightful, juicy, sweet, pleasing, delicious, tasty.
(ANT.) unsavory, nauseous, acrid.
lush *(SYN.)* tender, succulent, ripe.
lust *(SYN.)* longing, desire, passion, appetite, craving, aspiration, urge.
(ANT.) hate, aversion, loathing.
luster *(SYN.)* radiance, brightness, glister, honor, fame, effulgence, gloss.
(ANT.) dullness, obscurity, darkness.
lustful *(SYN.)* amorous, sexy, desirous, passionate, wanton.
lusty *(SYN.)* healthy, strong, mighty, powerful, sturdy, strapping, hale.
(ANT.) weak.
luxuriant *(SYN.)* abundant, flourishing, dense, lush, rich.
luxurious *(SYN.)* rich, lavish, deluxe.
(ANT.) simple, crude, sparse.
luxury *(SYN.)* frills, comfort, extravagance, elegance, splendor, prosperity, swankiness, well-being.
(ANT.) poverty.
lyric *(SYN.)* musical, text, words.
lyrical *(SYN.)* poetic, musical.

macabre *(SYN.)* ghastly, grim, horrible, gruesome.
machine *(SYN.)* motor, mechanism, device, contrivance.
machinist *(SYN.)* engineer.
mad *(SYN.)* incensed, crazy, insane, angry, furious, delirious, provoked.
(ANT.) sane, calm, healthy, rational, lucid, cheerful, happy.
madam *(SYN.)* dame, woman, lady, matron, mistress.
madder *(SYN.)* ruddle.
madness *(SYN.)* derangement, delirium, aberration, mania, insanity, craziness.
(ANT.) stability, rationality.
magazine *(SYN.)* journal, periodical, arsenal, armory.
magic *(SYN.)* sorcery, wizardry, charm, legerdemain, enchantment, black art.
magical *(SYN.)* mystical, marvelous, magic, miraculous, bewitching.
magician *(SYN.)* conjuror, sorcerer, wizard, witch, artist, trickster.
magistrate *(SYN.)* judge, adjudicator.
magnet *(SYN.)* lure, temptation.
magnetic *(SYN.)* pulling, attractive, alluring, drawing, enthralling, seductive.
magnetism *(SYN.)* allure, irresistibility, attraction, appeal.
magnificence *(SYN.)* luxury, grandeur, splendor, majesty, dynamic.
magnificent *(SYN.)* rich, luxurious, splendid, wonderful, impressive.
(ANT.) simple, plain.
magnify *(SYN.)* heighten, exaggerate, amplify, expand, stretch, caricature.
(ANT.) compress understate, depreciate, belittle.
magnitude *(SYN.)* mass, bigness, size, area, volume, dimensions, greatness.
maid *(SYN.)* chambermaid, servant.
maiden *(SYN.)* original, foremost, first, damsel, lass, miss.
(ANT.) accessory, secondary.
mail *(SYN.)* dispatch, send, letters, post, correspondence.
main *(SYN.)* essential, chief, highest, principal, first, leading, cardinal.
(ANT.) supplemental, subordinate, auxiliary.
mainstay *(SYN.)* buttress, pillar, refuge, reinforcement, support, backbone.
maintain *(SYN.)* claim, support, uphold, defend, vindicate, sustain, continue.
(ANT.) neglect, oppose, discontinue.
maintenance *(SYN.)* subsistence, livelihood, living, support, preservation.
majestic *(SYN.)* magnificent, stately, noble, august, grand, imposing, sublime, lofty, high, grandiose, dignified.
(ANT.) humble, lowly, undignified.
majesty *(SYN.)* grandeur, dignity, nobility, splendor, distinction.
major *(SYN.)* important, superior, larger, chief, greater, uppermost.
(ANT.) inconsequential, minor.
make *(SYN.)* execute, cause, produce, establish, assemble, create, shape.
(ANT.) unmake, break, undo, demolish.
make-believe *(SYN.)* pretend, imagined, simulated, false, fake, unreal.
maker *(SYN.)* inventor, creator, producer, builder, manufacturer.

makeshift *(SYN.)* proxy, deputy, understudy, expedient, agent, alternate.
(ANT.) sovereign, head, principal.
make-up *(SYN.)* composition, formation, structure cosmetics.
male *(SYN.)* masculine, virile.
(ANT.) female, womanly, feminine.
malfunction *(SYN.)* flaw, breakdown, snag, glitch, failure.
malice *(SYN.)* spite, grudge, enmity, ill will, malignity, animosity, rancor.
(ANT.) love, affection, toleration.
malicious *(SYN.)* hostile, malignant, virulent, bitter, rancorous, evil-minded, malevolent, spiteful, wicked.
(ANT.) kind, benevolent, affectionate.
malign *(SYN.)* misuse, defame, revile, abuse, traduce, asperse, misapply.
(ANT.) praise, cherish, protect, honor.
malignant *(SYN.)* harmful, deadly, killing, lethal, mortal, destructive, hurtful.
(ANT.) benign, harmless.
malodorous *(SYN.)* reeking, fetid, smelly, noxious, vile, rancid, offensive,
malpractice *(SYN.)* wrongdoing, misdeed, abuse, malfeasance, error, mismanagement, dereliction, fault, sin.
maltreat *(SYN.)* mistreat, ill-treatment, abuse.
maltreatment *(SYN.)* disparagement, perversion, aspersion, invective, defamation, profanation.
(ANT.) respect, approval, laudation, commendation.
mammoth *(SYN.)* enormous, immense, huge, colossal, gigantic, gargantuan.
(ANT.) minuscule, tiny, small.
man *(SYN.)* person, human being, society, folk, soul, individual, mortal.
(ANT.) woman.
manage *(SYN.)* curb, govern, direct, bridle, command, regulate, repress, check, restrain, dominate, guide.
(ANT.) forsake, submit, abandon, mismanage, bungle.
manageable *(SYN.)* willing, obedient, docile, controllable, tractable, submissive, governable, wieldy.
(ANT.) recalcitrant, unmanageable, wild.
management *(SYN.)* regulation, administration, supervision, direction.
manager *(SYN.)* overseer, superintendent, supervisor, director, boss, executive.
mandate *(SYN.)* order, injunction, command, referendum, dictate, writ.
mandatory *(SYN.)* compulsory, required, obligatory, imperative, necessary.
(ANT.) optional.
maneuver *(SYN.)* execution, effort, proceeding, enterprise, working, action, operation, agency, instrumentality.
(ANT.) rest, inaction, cessation.
mangle *(SYN.)* tear apart, cut, maim, wound, mutilate, injure, break.
manhandle *(SYN.)* maltreat, maul, abuse, ill-treat.
manhood *(SYN.)* maturity, manliness.
(ANT.) youth.
manic *(SYN.)* excited, hyped up, agitated.
manifest *(SYN.)* open, evident, lucid, clear, distinct, unobstructed, cloudless, apparent, intelligible, apparent.
(ANT.) vague, overcast, unclear, cloudy, hidden, concealed.
manifesto *(SYN.)* pronouncement, edict, proclamation, statement, declaration.
manifold *(SYN.)* various, many, multiple, numerous, abundant, copious, profuse.
(ANT.) few.
manipulate *(SYN.)* manage, feel, work, operate, handle, touch, maneuver.
manly *(SYN.)* strong, brave, masculine, manful, courageous, stalwart.
man-made *(SYN.)* artificial.
(ANT.) natural.
manner *(SYN.)* air, demeanor, custom, style, method, deportment, mode, habit, practice, way, behavior, fashion.
mannerism *(SYN.)* eccentricity, quirk, habit, peculiarity, idiosyncrasy, trait.
mannerly *(SYN.)* well-bred, gentlemanly, courteous, suave, polite, genteel.
manor *(SYN.)* land, mansion, estate, domain, villa, castle, property, palace.
manslaughter *(SYN.)* murder, killing, assassination, homicide, elimination.
mantle *(SYN.)* serape, garment, overgarment, cover, cloak, wrap.
manual *(SYN.)* directory, guidebook, handbook, physical, laborious, menial.
manufacture *(SYN.)* construct, make, assemble, fabricate, produce, fashion, build.
manure *(SYN.)* fertilizer, droppings, waste, compost.
manuscript *(SYN.)* copy, writing, work, paper, composition, document.
many *(SYN.)* numerous, various, divers, multitudinous, sundry, multifarious, several, manifold, abundant, plentiful.
(ANT.) infrequent, meager, few, scanty.
map *(SYN.)* sketch, plan, chart, graph, itinerary.
mar *(SYN.)* spoil, hurt, damage, impair, harm, deface, injure.
(ANT.) repair, benefit, mend.
marathon *(SYN.)* relay, race, contest.
march *(SYN.)* promenade, parade, pace, hike, walk, tramp.
margin *(SYN.)* boundary, border, rim, edge.
marine *(SYN.)* naval, oceanic, nautical, ocean, maritime.
mariner *(SYN.)* seafarer, gob, seaman, sailor.
marionette *(SYN.)* doll, puppet.
maritime *(SYN.)* shore, coastal, nautical.
mark *(SYN.)* stain, badge, stigma, vestige, sign, feature, label, characteristic, trace, brand, trait, scar, indication.
marked *(SYN.)* plain, apparent, noticeable, evident, decided, noted, special, noteworthy.
market *(SYN.)* supermarket, store, bazaar, mart, stall, marketplace, plaza, emporium.
maroon *(SYN.)* desert, leave behind, forsake, abandon, jettison.

marriage *(SYN.)* wedding, matrimony, nuptials, espousal, union, alliance, association.
(ANT.) divorce, celibacy, separation.
marrow *(SYN.)* center, core, gist, essential, soul.
marry *(SYN.)* wed, espouse, betroth.
marsh *(SYN.)* bog, swamp, mire, everglade, estuary.
marshal *(SYN.)* adjutant, officer, order, arrange, rank.
mart *(SYN.)* shop, market, store.
martial *(SYN.)* warlike, combative, militant, belligerent.
(ANT.) peaceful.
martyr *(SYN.)* victim, sufferer, tortured, torment, plague, harass, persecute.
marvel *(SYN.)* phenomenon, wonder, miracle, astonishment, sensation.
marvelous *(SYN.)* rare, wonderful, extraordinary, unusual, exceptional, miraculous, wondrous, amazing.
(ANT.) usual, common, ordinary.
mascot *(SYN.)* pet, amulet, charm.
masculine *(SYN.)* robust, manly, virile, strong, bold, male, lusty, vigorous, hardy, mannish.
(ANT.) weak, emasculated, feminine, effeminate, womanish, female.
mash *(SYN.)* mix, pulverize, crush, grind, crumble, granulate.
mask *(SYN.)* veil, disguise, cloak, secrete, withhold, hide, cover.
(ANT.) uncover, reveal, disclose.
masquerade *(SYN.)* pretend, disguise, pose, impersonate, costume party.
mass *(SYN.)* society, torso, body, remains, association, carcass, bulk.
(ANT.) spirit, mind, intellect.
massacre *(SYN.)* butcher, murder, carnage, slaughter, execute, slay, genocide, killing, butchery, extermination.
(ANT.) save, protect, vivify, animate.
massage *(SYN.)* knead, rub, stroke.
massive *(SYN.)* grave, cumbersome, heavy, sluggish, ponderous, serious.
(ANT.) light, animated, small, tiny.
mast *(SYN.)* pole, post.
master *(SYN.)* owner, employer, leader, ruler, chief, head, lord, teacher.
(ANT.) slave, servant.
masterful *(SYN.)* commanding, bossy, domineering, dictatorial, cunning.
masterly *(SYN.)* adroit, superb, skillful, expert.
(ANT.) awkward, clumsy.
mastermind *(SYN.)* prodigy, sage, guru, mentor.
masterpiece *(SYN.)* prizewinner, classic, perfection, model.
mastery *(SYN.)* sway, sovereignty, domination, transcendence, ascendancy, influence, jurisdiction, prestige.
mat *(SYN.)* cover, rug, pallet, bedding, pad.
match *(SYN.)* equivalent, equal, contest, balance, resemble, peer, mate.
matchless *(SYN.)* peerless, incomparable, unequaled, unrivaled, excellent.
(ANT.) ordinary, unimpressive.
mate *(SYN.)* friend, colleague, associate, partner, companion, comrade.
(ANT.) stranger, adversary.
material *(SYN.)* sensible, momentous, germane, bodily, palpable, important, physical, essential, corporeal, tangible, substance, matter, fabric.
(ANT.) metaphysical, spiritual, insignificant, mental, immaterial, irrelevant, intangible.
materialize *(SYN.)* take shape, finalize, embody, incarnate, emerge, appear.
maternal *(SYN.)* motherly.
(ANT.) fatherly.
mathematics *(SYN.)* measurements, computations, numbers, calculation, figures.
matrimony *(SYN.)* marriage, wedding, espousal, union.
(ANT.) virginity, divorce.
matrix *(SYN.)* template, stamp, negative, stencil, mold, form, die, cutout.
matron *(SYN.)* lady.
matted *(SYN.)* tangled, clustered, rumpled, shaggy, knotted, gnarled, tousled.
matter *(SYN.)* cause, thing, substance, occasion, material, moment, topic, stuff, concern, theme, subject, consequence, affair, business, interest.
(ANT.) spirit, immateriality.
mature *(SYN.)* ready, matured, complete, ripe, consummate, mellow, aged, seasoned, full-grown.
(ANT.) raw, crude, undeveloped, young, immature, innocent.
maudlin *(SYN.)* emotional, mushy, sentimental, mawkish.
maul *(SYN.)* pummel, mistreat, manhandle, beat, batter, bruise, abuse.
mausoleum *(SYN.)* shrine, tomb, vault.
maverick *(SYN.)* nonconformist, oddball, outsider, dissenter, loner.
mawkish *(SYN.)* sentimental, emotional, nostalgic.
maxim *(SYN.)* rule, code, law, proverb, principle, saying, adage, motto.
maximum *(SYN.)* highest, largest, head, greatest, supremacy, climax.
(ANT.) minimum.
may *(SYN.)* can, be able.
maybe *(SYN.)* feasibly, perchance, perhaps, possibly.
(ANT.) definitely.
mayhem *(SYN.)* brutality, viciousness, ruthlessness.
maze *(SYN.)* complex, labyrinth, network, muddle, confusion, snarl, tangle.
meadow *(SYN.)* field, pasture, lea, range, grassland.
meager *(SYN.)* sparse, scanty, mean, frugal, deficient, slight, paltry, inadequate.
(ANT.) ample, plentiful, abundant, bountiful.
meal *(SYN.)* refreshment, dinner, lunch, repast, breakfast.
mean *(SYN.)* sordid, base, intend, plan, propose, expect, indicate, denote, say, signify, suggest, express, average, nasty, middle, contemptible, offensive, vulgar, unkind, cruel, despicable, vile, low, medium.
(ANT.) dignified, noble, exalted,

thoughtful, gentle, openhanded, kind, generous, admirable.

meander *(SYN.)* wind, stray, wander, twist

meaning *(SYN.)* gist, connotation, intent, purport, drift, acceptation, implication, sense, import, interpretation, denotation, signification, explanation, purpose, significance.

meaningful *(SYN.)* profound, deep, expressive, important, crucial.

meaningless *(SYN.)* nonsensical, senseless, unreasonable, preposterous.

means *(SYN.)* utensil, channel, agent, money, riches, vehicle, apparatus, device, wealth, support, medium, instrument.

(ANT.) preventive, impediment, hindrance.

measly *(SYN.)* scanty, puny, skimpy, meager, petty.

measure *(SYN.)* law, bulk, rule, criterion, size, volume, weight, standard, dimension, breadth, depth, test, touchstone, trial, length, extent, gauge.

(ANT.) guess, chance, supposition.

measureless *(SYN.)* immeasurable, immense, boundless, limitless, infinite, vast.

(ANT.) figurable, ascertainable, measurable.

meat *(SYN.)* lean, flesh, food.

mecca *(SYN.)* target, shrine, goal, sanctuary, destination.

mechanic *(SYN.)* repairman, machinist.

mechanism *(SYN.)* device, contrivance, tool, machine, machinery.

medal *(SYN.)* decoration, award, badge, medallion, reward, ribbon, prize, honor.

meddle *(SYN.)* tamper, interpose, pry, snoop, intrude, interrupt, interfere, monkey.

meddlesome *(SYN.)* forward, bothersome, intrusive, obtrusive.

media *(SYN.)* tools, instruments, implements.

mediate *(SYN.)* settle, intercede, umpire, intervene, negotiate, arbitrate, referee.

medicinal *(SYN.)* helping, healing, remedial, therapeutic, corrective.

medicine *(SYN.)* drug, medication, remedy, cure, prescription, potion.

mediocre *(SYN.)* medium, mean, average, moderate, fair, ordinary.

(ANT.) outstanding, exceptional.

meditate *(SYN.)* remember, muse, think, judge, mean, conceive, contemplate, deem, suppose, purpose, consider, picture, reflect, believe, plan, reckon.

medium *(SYN.)* modicum, average, middling, median.

(ANT.) extreme.

medley *(SYN.)* hodgepodge, mixture, assortment, conglomeration, mishmash, miscellany.

meek *(SYN.)* subdued, dull, tedious, flat, docile, domesticated, tame, insipid, domestic.

(ANT.) spirited, exciting, savage, wild.

meet *(SYN.)* fulfill, suffer, find, collide, gratify, engage, connect, converge, encounter, unite, join, satisfy, settle, greet, answer, undergo, answer, meeting, contest, match, assemble, discharge, gather, convene, congregate, confront, intersect.

(ANT.) scatter, disperse, separate, cleave.

melancholy *(SYN.)* disconsolate, dejected, despondent, glum, somber, pensive, moody, dispirited, depressed, gloomy, dismal, doleful, depression, downcast, gloom, sadness, sad, grave, downhearted, sorrowful.

(ANT.) happy, cheerful, merry.

meld *(SYN.)* unite, mix, combine, fuse, merge, blend, commingle, amalgamate.

melee *(SYN.)* battle royal, fight, brawl, free-for-all, fracas.

mellow *(SYN.)* mature, ripe, aged, cured, full-flavored, sweet, smooth, melodious, develop, soften.

(ANT.) unripened, immature.

melodious *(SYN.)* lilting, musical, lyric, dulcet, mellifluous, tuneful, melodic.

melodramatic *(SYN.)* dramatic, ceremonious, affected, stagy, histrionic, overwrought, sensational, stagy.

(ANT.) unemotional, subdued, modest.

melody *(SYN.)* strain, concord, music, air, song, tune, harmony.

melt *(SYN.)* dissolve, liquefy, blend, fade out, vanish, dwindle, disappear, thaw.

(ANT.) freeze, harden, solidify.

member *(SYN.)* share, part, allotment, moiety, element, concern, interest, lines, faction, role, apportionment.

(ANT.) whole.

membrane *(SYN.)* layer, sheath, tissue, covering.

memento *(SYN.)* keepsake, token, reminder, trophy, sign, souvenir, remembrance.

memoirs *(SYN.)* diary, reflections, experiences, autobiography, journal, confessions.

memorable *(SYN.)* important, historic, significant, unforgettable, noteworthy, momentous, crucial, impressive.

(ANT.) passing, forgettable, transitory, commonplace.

memorandum *(SYN.)* letter, mark, token, note, indication, remark, message.

memorial *(SYN.)* monument, souvenir, memento, remembrance, commemoration, reminiscent, ritual, testimonial.

memorize *(SYN.)* study, remember.

memory *(SYN.)* renown, remembrance, reminiscence, fame, retrospection, recollection, reputation.

(ANT.) oblivion.

menace *(SYN.)* warning, threat, intimidation, warn, threaten, imperil, forebode.

menagerie *(SYN.)* collection, zoo, kennel.

mend *(SYN.)* restore, better, refit, sew, remedy, patch, correct, repair, rectify, ameliorate, improve, reform, recover,

fix.
(ANT.) hurt, deface, rend, destroy.
mendacious *(SYN.)* dishonest, false, lying, deceitful, deceptive, tricky.
(ANT.) honest, truthful, sincere, creditable.
mendicant *(SYN.)* ragamuffin, vagabond, beggar.
mental *(SYN.)* unskilled, lowly, degrading, tedious, humble, routine.
mental *(SYN.)* reasoning, intellectual, rational, thinking, conscious, reflective, thoughtful.
(ANT.) physical.
mentality *(SYN.)* intellect, reason, understanding, liking, disposition, judgment, brain, inclination, faculties, outlook.
(ANT.) materiality, corporeality.
mention *(SYN.)* introduce, refer to, reference, allude, enumerate, speak of.
mentor *(SYN.)* advisor, tutor, sponsor, guru, teacher, counselor, master, coach.
mercenary *(SYN.)* sordid, corrupt, venal, covetous, grasping, avaricious, greedy.
(ANT.) liberal, generous.
merchandise *(SYN.)* stock, wares, goods, sell, commodities, promote, staples, products.
merchant *(SYN.)* retailer, dealer, trader, storekeeper, salesman, businessman.
merciful *(SYN.)* humane, kindhearted, tender, clement, sympathetic, forgiving, tolerant, forbearing, lenient, compassionate, tenderhearted, kind.
(ANT.) remorseless, cruel, unjust, mean, harsh, unforgiving, vengeful, brutal, unfeeling, pitiless.
merciless *(SYN.)* carnal, ferocious, brute, barbarous, gross, ruthless, cruel, remorseless, bestial, savage, rough, pitiless, inhuman.
(ANT.) humane, courteous, merciful, openhearted, kind, civilized.
mercurial *(SYN.)* fickle, unstable, volatile, changeable, inconstant, capricious, flighty.
mercy *(SYN.)* grace, consideration, kindness, clemency, mildness, forgiveness, pity, charity, sympathy, leniency, compassion.
(ANT.) punishment, retribution, ruthlessness, cruelty, vengeance.
mere *(SYN.)* only, simple, scant, bare.
(ANT.) substantial, considerable.
merely *(SYN.)* only, barely, simply, hardly.
meretricious *(SYN.)* gaudy, sham, bogus, tawdry, flashy, garish.
merge *(SYN.)* unify, fuse, combine, amalgamate, unite, blend, commingle.
(ANT.) separate, decompose, analyze.
merger *(SYN.)* cartel, union, conglomerate, trust, incorporation, combine, pool.
meridian *(SYN.)* climax, summit, pinnacle, zenith, peak, acme, apex, culmination.
merit *(SYN.)* worthiness, earn, goodness, effectiveness, power, value, virtue, goodness, quality, deserve, excellence, worth.
(ANT.) sin, fault, lose, consume.
merited *(SYN.)* proper, deserved, suitable, adequate, earned.
(ANT.) unmerited, improper.
meritorious *(SYN.)* laudable, excellent, commendable, good, praise-worthy, deserving.
merry *(SYN.)* hilarious, lively, festive, joyous, sprightly, mirthful, blithe, gay, cheery, joyful, jolly, happy, gleeful, jovial, cheerful.
(ANT.) sorrowful, doleful, morose, gloomy, sad, melancholy.
mesh *(SYN.)* grid, screen, net, complex.
mesmerize *(SYN.)* enthrall, transfix, spellbind, bewitch, charm, fascinate, hypnotize.
mess *(SYN.)* dirtiness, untidiness, disorder, confusion, muddle, trouble, jumble, difficulty, predicament, confuse, dirty.
message *(SYN.)* letter, annotation, memo, symbol, indication, sign, note, communication, memorandum, observation, token.
messenger *(SYN.)* bearer, agent, runner, courier, liaison, delegate, page.
messy *(SYN.)* disorderly, dirty, confusing, confused, disordered, sloppy, untidy, slovenly.
(ANT.) orderly, neat, tidy.
metallic *(SYN.)* grating, harsh, clanging, brassy, brazen.
metamorphosis *(SYN.)* transfiguration, change, alteration, rebirth, mutation.
mete *(SYN.)* deal, assign, apportion, divide, give, allocate, allot, measure.
(ANT.) withhold, keep, retain.
meteoric *(SYN.)* flashing, blazing, swift, brilliant, spectacular, remarkable.
meter *(SYN.)* record, measure, gauge.
method *(SYN.)* order, manner, plan, way, mode, technique, fashion, approach, design, procedure.
(ANT.) disorder.
methodical *(SYN.)* exact, definite, ceremonious, stiff, accurate, distinct, unequivocal.
(ANT.) easy, loose, informal, rough.
meticulous *(SYN.)* precise, careful, exacting, fastidious, fussy, perfectionist.
metropolitan *(SYN.)* civic, city, municipal.
mettle *(SYN.)* intrepidity, resolution, boldness, prowess, bravery, fearlessness.
(ANT.) fear, timidity, cowardice.
microscopic *(SYN.)* tiny, precise, fine, detailed, minute, infinitesimal, minimal.
(ANT.) general, huge, enormous.
middle *(SYN.)* midpoint, nucleus, center, midst, median, central, intermediate, core.
(ANT.) end, rim, outskirts, beginning, border, periphery.
middleman *(SYN.)* dealer, agent, distributor, broker, representative, intermediary.
midget *(SYN.)* gnome, shrimp, pygmy, runt, dwarf.
(ANT.) giant.

midst *(SYN.)* center, heart, middle, thick.
midway *(SYN.)* halfway, midmost, inside, central, middle.
mien *(SYN.)* way, semblance, manner, behavior, demeanor, expression, deportment.
miff *(SYN.)* provoke, rile, chagrin, irk, irritate, affront, offend, annoy, exasperate.
might *(SYN.)* force, power, vigor, potency, ability, strength.
(ANT.) frailty, vulnerability, weakness.
mighty *(SYN.)* firm, fortified, powerful, athletic, potent, muscular, robust, strong, cogent.
(ANT.) feeble, weak, brittle, insipid, frail, delicate.
migrant *(SYN.)* traveling, roaming, straying, roving, rambling, transient, meandering.
(ANT.) stationary.
migrate *(SYN.)* resettle, move, emigrate, immigrate, relocate, journey.
(ANT.) stay, remain, settle.
migratory *(SYN.)* itinerant, roving, mobile, vagabond, unsettled, nomadic, wandering.
mild *(SYN.)* soothing, moderate, gentle, tender, bland, pleasant, kind, meek, calm, amiable, compassionate, temperate, peaceful, soft.
(ANT.) severe, turbulent, stormy, excitable, violent, harsh, bitter.
milieu *(SYN.)* environment, background, locale, setting, scene, circumstances.
militant *(SYN.)* warlike, belligerent, hostile, fighting, pugnacious, aggressive, combative.
(ANT.) peaceful.
military *(SYN.)* troops, army, service, soldiers.
milksop *(SYN.)* namby-pamby, weakling, sissy, coward.
mill *(SYN.)* foundry, shop, plant, factory, manufactory.
millstone *(SYN.)* load, impediment, burden, encumbrance, hindrance.
mimic *(SYN.)* simulate, duplicate, copy, imitate, mock, counterfeit, simulate.
(ANT.) invent, distort, alter.
mince *(SYN.)* shatter, fragment, chop, smash.
mind *(SYN.)* intelligence, psyche, disposition, intention, understanding, intellect, spirit, brain, inclination, mentality, soul, wit, liking, brain, sense, watch, faculties, judgment, reason.
(ANT.) matter, corporeality.
mindful *(SYN.)* alert, aware, watchful, cognizant, watchful, sensible, heedful.
mine *(SYN.)* shaft, lode, pit, excavation, drill, dig, quarry, source.
mingle *(SYN.)* unite, coalesce, fuse, merge, combine, amalgamate, unify, conjoin, mix, blend, commingle.
(ANT.) separate, analyze, sort, disintegrate.
miniature *(SYN.)* small, little, tiny, midget, minute, minuscule, wee, petite, diminutive.
(ANT.) outsize.
minimize *(SYN.)* shorten, deduct, belittle, decrease, reduce, curtail, lessen, diminish, subtract.
(ANT.) enlarge, increase, amplify.
minimum *(SYN.)* lowest, least, smallest, slightest.
(ANT.) maximum.
minister *(SYN.)* pastor, clergyman, vicar, parson, curate, preacher, prelate, chaplain, cleric, deacon, reverend.
minor *(SYN.)* poorer, lesser, petty, youth, inferior, secondary, smaller, unimportant, lower.
(ANT.) higher, superior, major, greater.
minority *(SYN.)* youth, childhood, immaturity.
minstrel *(SYN.)* bard, musician.
mint *(SYN.)* stamp, coin, strike, punch.
minus *(SYN.)* lacking, missing, less, absent, without.
minute *(SYN.)* tiny, particular, fine, precise, jiffy, instant, moment, wee, exact, detailed, microscopic.
(ANT.) large, general, huge, enormous.
miraculous *(SYN.)* spiritual, supernatural, wonderful, marvelous, incredible, preternatural.
(ANT.) commonplace, natural, common, plain, everyday, human.
mirage *(SYN.)* vision, illusion, fantasy, dream, phantom.
(ANT.) reality, actuality.
mire *(SYN.)* marsh, slush, slime, mud.
mirror *(SYN.)* glass, reflector, reflect.
mirth *(SYN.)* joy, glee, jollity, joyousness, gaiety, joyfulness, laughter, merriment.
(ANT.) sadness, gloom, seriousness.
misadventure *(SYN.)* accident, adversity, reverse, calamity, catastrophe, hardship, mischance, setback.
misappropriate *(SYN.)* embezzle, steal, purloin, plunder, cheat, filch, defraud.
misbehave *(SYN.)* trespass, act badly.
(ANT.) behave.
miscalculate *(SYN.)* miscount, blunder, confuse, err, mistake, misconstrue.
miscarriage *(SYN.)* omission, want, decay, fiasco, default, deficiency, loss, abortion, prematurity.
(ANT.) success, sufficiency, achievement.
miscarry *(SYN.)* flounder, fall short, falter, go wrong, fail.
(ANT.) succeed.
miscellaneous *(SYN.)* diverse, motley, indiscriminate, assorted, sundry, heterogeneous, mixed, varied.
(ANT.) classified, selected, homogeneous, alike, ordered.
miscellany *(SYN.)* medley, gallimaufry, jumble, potpourri, mixture, collection.
mischief *(SYN.)* injury, harm, damage, evil, ill, prankishness, rascality, roguishness, playfulness, wrong, detriment, hurt.
(ANT.) kindness, boon, benefit.
mischievous *(SYN.)* roguish, prankish, naughty, playful.
(ANT.) well-behaved, good.
misconduct *(SYN.)* transgression, delinquency, wrongdoing, negligence.

miscreant *(SYN.)* rascal, wretch, rogue, sinner, criminal, villain, scoundrel.
miscue *(SYN.)* blunder, fluff, mistake, error, lapse.
misdemeanor *(SYN.)* infringement, transgression, violation, offense, wrong.
miser *(SYN.)* cheapskate, tightwad.
(ANT.) philanthropist.
miserable *(SYN.)* abject, forlorn, comfortless, low, worthless, pitiable, distressed, heartbroken, disconsolate, despicable, wretched, uncomfortable, unhappy, poor, unlucky, paltry, contemptible, mean.
(ANT.) fortunate, happy, contented, joyful, content, wealthy, honorable, lucky, noble, significant.
miserly *(SYN.)* stingy, greedy, acquisitive, tight, tightfisted, cheap, mean, parsimonious, avaricious.
(ANT.) bountiful, generous, spendthrift, munificent, extravagant, openhanded, altruistic.
misery *(SYN.)* suffering, woe, evil, agony, torment, trouble, distress, anguish, grief, unhappiness, anguish, tribulation, calamity, sorrow.
(ANT.) fun, pleasure, delight, joy.
misfit *(SYN.)* crank, loner, deviate, fifth wheel, individualist.
misfortune *(SYN.)* adversity, distress, mishap, calamity, accident, catastrophe, hardship, ruin, disaster, affliction.
(ANT.) success, blessing, prosperity.
misgiving *(SYN.)* suspicion, doubt, mistrust, hesitation, uncertainty.
misguided *(SYN.)* misdirected, misled, misinformed, wrong, unwise, foolish, erroneous, unwarranted, ill-advised.
mishap *(SYN.)* misfortune, casualty, accident, disaster, adversity, reverse.
(ANT.) intention, calculation, purpose.
mishmash *(SYN.)* medley, muddle, gallimaufry, hodge-podge, hash.
misjudge *(SYN.)* err, mistake, miscalculate.
mislay *(SYN.)* misplace, lose.
(ANT.) discover, find.
mislead *(SYN.)* misdirect, deceive, misinform, deceive, delude.
misleading *(SYN.)* fallacious, delusive, deceitful, false, deceptive, illusive.
(ANT.) real, genuine, truthful, honest.
mismatched *(SYN.)* unfit, unsuitable, incompatible, unsuited.
misplace *(SYN.)* lose, mislay, miss.
(ANT.) find.
misrepresent *(SYN.)* misstate, distort, falsify, twist, belie, garble, disguise.
miss *(SYN.)* lose, want, crave, yearn for, fumble, drop, error, slip, default, omit, lack, need, desire, fail.
(ANT.) suffice, have, achieve, succeed.
misshapen *(SYN.)* disfigured, deformed, grotesque, malformed, ungainly, gnarled, contorted.
missile *(SYN.)* grenade, shot, projectile.
missing *(SYN.)* wanting, lacking, absent, lost, gone, vanished.
mission *(SYN.)* business, task, job, stint, work, errand, assignment, delegation.
missionary *(SYN.)* publicist, evangelist, propagandist.
mist *(SYN.)* cloud, fog, haze, steam, haze.
mistake *(SYN.)* slip, misjudge, fault, blunder, misunderstand, confuse, inaccuracy, misinterpret, error.
(ANT.) truth, accuracy.
mistaken *(SYN.)* false, amiss, incorrect, awry, wrong, misinformed, confused, inaccurate, askew.
(ANT.) true, correct, suitable, right.
mister *(SYN.)* young man, gentleman, esquire, fellow, buddy.
mistreat *(SYN.)* wrong, pervert, oppress, harm, maltreat, abuse.
mistrust *(SYN.)* suspect, doubt, distrust, dispute, question, skepticism, apprehension.
(ANT.) trust.
misunderstand *(SYN.)* misjudge, misinterpret, jumble, confuse, mistake.
(ANT.) perceive, comprehend.
misunderstanding *(SYN)* clash, disagreement, dispute, conflict, misinterpretation.
misuse *(SYN.)* defame, malign, abuse, misapply, traduce, asperse, revile, vilify.
(ANT.) protect, honor, respect, cherish.
mite *(SYN.)* particle, mote, smidgen, trifle, iota, corpuscle.
mitigate *(SYN.)* soften, soothe, abate, assuage, relieve, allay, diminish.
(ANT.) irritate, agitate, increase.
mix *(SYN.)* mingle, blend, consort, fuse, alloy, combine, jumble, fraternize, associate, concoct, commingle, amalgamate, confound, compound, join.
(ANT.) divide, sort, segregate, dissociate, separate.
mixture *(SYN.)* diversity, variety, strain, sort, change, kind, confusion, heterogeneity, jumble, mess, assortment, breed, mix, hodge-podge, subspecies.
(ANT.) likeness, sameness, homogeneity, monotony.
moan *(SYN.)* wail, groan, cry, lament.
moat *(SYN.)* fortification, ditch, trench, entrenchment.
mob *(SYN.)* crowd, host, populace, swarm, riot, bevy, horde, rabble, throng, multitude.
mobile *(SYN.)* free, movable, portable.
(ANT.) stationary, immobile, fixed.
mock *(SYN.)* taunt, jeer, deride, scoff, scorn, fleer, ridicule, tease, fake, imitation, sham, gibe, sneer, fraudulent, flout.
(ANT.) praise, applaud, real, genuine, honor, authentic, compliment.
mockery *(SYN.)* gibe, ridicule, satire, derision, sham, banter, irony, sneering, scorn, travesty, jeering.
(ANT.) admiration, praise.
mode *(SYN.)* method, fashion, procedure, design, manner, technique, way, style, practice, plan.
(ANT.) disorder, confusion.
model *(SYN.)* copy, prototype, type, example, ideal, imitation, version, facsimile, design, style, archetype, pattern, standard, mold.

(ANT.) reproduction, imitation.
moderate *(SYN.)* lower, decrease, average, fair, reasonable, abate, medium, conservative, referee, umpire, suppress, judge, lessen, assuage.
(ANT.) intensify, enlarge, amplify.
moderation *(SYN.)* sobriety, forbearance, self-control, restraint, continence, temperance.
(ANT.) greed, excess, intoxication.
moderator *(SYN.)* referee, leader, arbitrator, chairman, chairperson, master of cermonies, emcee.
modern *(SYN.)* modish, current, recent, novel, fresh, contemporary, new.
(ANT.) old, antiquated, past, bygone, ancient.
modernize *(SYN.)* refurnish, refurbish, improve, rebuild, renew, renovate.
modest *(SYN.)* unassuming, virtuous, bashful, meek, shy, humble, decent, demure, unpretentious, prudish, moderate, reserved.
(ANT.) forward, bold, ostentatious, conceited, immodest, arrogant.
modesty *(SYN.)* decency, humility, propriety, simplicity, shyness.
(ANT.) conceit, vanity, pride.
modicum *(SYN.)* particle, fragment, grain, trifle, smidgen, bit.
modification *(SYN.)* alternation, substitution, variety, change, alteration.
(ANT.) uniformity, monotony.
modify *(SYN.)* shift, vary, alter, change, convert, adjust, temper, moderate, curb, exchange, transform, veer.
(ANT.) settle, establish, retain, stabilize.
modish *(SYN.)* current, fashionable, chick, stylish, voguish.
modulate *(SYN.)* temper, align, balance, correct, regulate, adjust, modify.
module *(SYN.)* unit, measure, norm, dimension, component, gauge.
modus operandi *(SYN.)* method, technique, system, means, process, workings, procedure.
mogul *(SYN.)* bigwig, personage, figure, tycoon, magnate, potentate.
molety *(SYN.)* part, scrap, share, allotment, piece, division, portion.
moist *(SYN.)* damp, humid, dank, muggy, clammy.
moisten *(SYN.)* wet, dampen, sponge.
(ANT.) dry.
moisture *(SYN.)* wetness, mist, dampness, condensation, evaporation, vapor, humidity.
(ANT.) aridity, dryness.
mold *(SYN.)* make, fashion, organize, produce, forge, constitute, create, combine, construct, form, pattern, format.
(ANT.) wreck, dismantle, destroy, misshape.
moldy *(SYN.)* dusty, crumbling, dank, old, deteriorating.
molest *(SYN.)* irk, disturb, trouble, annoy, pester, bother, vex, inconvenience.
(ANT.) console, accommodate.
mollify *(SYN.)* soothe, compose, quiet, humor, appease, tranquilize, pacify.
molt *(SYN.)* slough off, shed, cast off.
molten *(SYN.)* fusible, melted, smelted, redhot.
moment *(SYN.)* flash, jiffy, instant, twinkling, gravity, importance, consequence, seriousness.
momentary *(SYN.)* concise, pithy, brief, curt, terse, laconic, compendious.
(ANT.) long, extended, prolonged.
momentous *(SYN.)* critical, serious, essential, grave, material, weighty, consequential, decisive, important.
(ANT.) unimportant, trifling, mean, trivial, tribial, insignificant.
momentum *(SYN.)* impetus, push, thrust, force, impulse, drive, vigor, propulsion, energy.
monarch *(SYN.)* ruler, king, queen, empress, emperor, sovereign.
monastic *(SYN.)* withdrawn, dedicated, austere, unworldly, celibate, abstinent, ascetic.
monastery *(SYN.)* convent, priory, abbey, hermitage, cloister.
money *(SYN.)* cash, bills, coin, notes, currency, funds, specie, capital.
monger *(SYN.)* seller, hawker, huckster, trader, merchant, shopkeeper, retailer, vendor.
mongrel *(SYN.)* mixed-breed, hybrid, mutt.
monitor *(SYN.)* director, supervisor, advisor, observe, watch, control.
monkey *(SYN.)* tamper, interfere, interrupt, interpose.
monogram *(SYN.)* mark, stamp, signature
monograph *(SYN.)* publication, report, thesis, biography, treatise, paper, dissertation.
monologue *(SYN.)* discourse, lecture, sermon, talk, speech, address, soliloquy, oration.
monomania *(SYN.)* obsessiveness, passion, single-mindedness, extremism.
monopoly *(SYN.)* corner, control, possession.
monotonous *(SYN.)* dull, slow, tiresome, boring, humdrum, dilatory, tiring, irksome, tedious, burdensome, wearisome.
(ANT.) interesting, riveting, quick, fascinating, exciting, amusing.
monsoon *(SYN.)* storm, rains.
monster *(SYN.)* brute, beast, villain, demon, fiend, wretch.
monstrous *(SYN.)* tremendous, huge, gigantic, immense, enormous, revolting, repulsive, shocking, horrible, hideous, terrible.
(ANT.) diminutive, tiny, miniature, small.
monument *(SYN.)* remembrance, memento, commemoration, souvenir, statue, shrine.
monumental *(SYN.)* enormous, huge, colossal, immense, gigantic, important, significant.
(ANT.) trivial, insignificant, tiny, miniature.
mood *(SYN.)* joke, irony, waggery, temper, disposition, temperament, sar-

casm.
(ANT.) sorrow, gravity.
moody *(SYN.)* morose, fretful, crabbed, changeable, sulky, dour, short-tempered, testy, temperamental, irritable, peevish, glum.
(ANT.) good-natured, even-tempered, merry, gay, pleasant, joyous.
moor *(SYN.)* tether, fasten, tie, dock, anchor, bind.
moorings *(SYN.)* marina, slip, harbor, basin, landing, dock, wharf, pier, anchorage.
moot *(SYN.)* unsettled, questionable, problematical, controversial, contestable.
mop *(SYN.)* wash, wipe, swab, scrub.
mope *(SYN.)* gloom, pout, whine, grumble, grieve, sulk, fret.
(ANT.) rejoice.
moral *(SYN.)* just, right, chaste, good, virtuous, pure, decent, honest, upright, ethical, righteous, honorable, scrupulous.
(ANT.) libertine, immoral, unethical, licentious, amoral, sinful.
morale *(SYN.)* confidence, spirit, assurance.
morality *(SYN.)* virtue, strength, worth, chastity, probity, force, merit.
(ANT.) fault, sin, corruption, vice.
morals *(SYN.)* conduct, scruples, guidelines, behavior, life style, standards.
morass *(SYN.)* fen, march, swamp, mire.
morbid *(SYN.)* sickly, unwholesome, unhealthy, ghastly, awful, horrible, shocking.
(ANT.) pleasant, healthy.
more *(SYN.)* further, greater, farther, extra, another.
(ANT.) less.
moreover *(SYN.)* further, in addition, also, furthermore, besides.
mores *(SYN.)* standards, rituals, rules, customs, conventions, traditions.
moron *(SYN.)* subnormal, dunce, blockhead, imbecile, retardate, simpleton.
morose *(SYN.)* gloomy, moody, fretful, crabbed, sulky, glum, dour, surly, downcast, sad, unhappy.
(ANT.) merry, gay, amiable, joyous, pleasant.
morsel *(SYN.)* portion, fragment, bite, bit, scrap, amount, piece, taste, tidbit.
(ANT.) whole, all, sum.
mortal *(SYN.)* fatal, destructive, human, perishable, deadly, temporary, momentary, final.
(ANT.) superficial, divine, immortal.
mortgage *(SYN.)* stake, post, promise, pledge.
mortician *(SYN.)* funeral director, embalmer.
mortified *(SYN.)* embarrassed, humiliated, abashed, ashamed.
mortify *(SYN.)* humiliate, crush, subdue, abase, degrade, shame.
(ANT.) praise, exalt, elevate.
mortuary *(SYN.)* morgue, crematory, funeral parlor.
most *(SYN.)* extreme, highest, supreme, greatest, majority.
(ANT.) least.
mostly *(SYN.)* chiefly, generally, largely, mainly, principally, especially.
mother *(SYN.)* bring about, produce, breed, mom, mama, watch, foster, mind, nurse, originate, nurture.
(ANT.) father.
motion *(SYN.)* change, activity, movement, proposition, action, signal, gesture, move, proposal.
(ANT.) stability, immobility, stillness.
motionless *(SYN.)* still, undisturbed, rigid, fixed, stationary, unresponsive.
motivate *(SYN.)* move, prompt, stimulate, induce, activate, propel, arouse.
motive *(SYN.)* inducement, purpose, cause, incentive, reason, incitement.
(ANT.) deed, result, attempt, effort.
motor *(SYN.)* engine, generator, machine.
motto *(SYN.)* proverb, saying, adage, byword, saw, slogan, catchword, aphorism.
mound *(SYN.)* hillock, hill, heap, pile, stack, knoll, accumulation, dune.
mount *(SYN.)* scale, climb, increase, rise, prepare, ready, steed, horse, tower.
(ANT.) sink, descend.
mountain *(SYN.)* alp, mount, pike, peak, ridge, height, range.
mounting *(SYN.)* backing, pedestal, easel, support, framework.
mourn *(SYN.)* suffer, grieve, bemoan, sorrow, lament, weep, bewail.
(ANT.) revel, celebrate, carouse.
mournful *(SYN.)* sorrowful, sad, melancholy, gloomy, woeful, rueful, disconsolate.
(ANT.) joyful, cheerful, happy.
mourning *(SYN.)* misery, trial, distress, affliction, tribulation, sorrow, woe.
(ANT.) happiness, solace, comfort, joy.
move *(SYN.)* impel, agitate, persuade, induce, push, instigate, advance, stir.
(ANT.) halt, stop, deter, rest.
movement *(SYN.)* activity, effort, gesture, move, proposition, crusade.
(ANT.) stillness, immobility.
moving *(SYN.)* poignant, stirring, touching.
mow *(SYN.)* prune, cut, shave, crop, clip.
much *(SYN.)* abundance, quantity, mass, ample, plenty, sufficient, substantial.
muck *(SYN.)* filth, mire, dirt, rot, sludge, sewage.
muddle *(SYN.)* disorder, chaos, mess.
muddled *(SYN.)* disconcerted, confused, mixed, bewildered, perplexed.
(ANT.) plain, lucid, organized.
muff *(SYN.)* blunder, bungle, spoil, mess, fumble.
muffle *(SYN.)* soften, deaden, mute, quiet, drape, shroud, veil, cover.
(ANT.) louden, amplify.
multiply *(SYN.)* double, treble, increase, triple, propagate, spread, expand.
(ANT.) lessen, decrease.
multitude *(SYN.)* crowd, throng, mass, swarm, host, mob, army, legion.
(ANT.) scarcity, handful.

mum *(SYN.)* mute, silent, quiet, still, close-mouthed, secretive.
mumble *(SYN.)* stammer, whisper, hesitate, mutter.
(ANT.) shout, yell.
municipal *(SYN.)* urban, metropolitan.
munificent *(SYN.)* bountiful, full, generous, forthcoming, satisfied.
(ANT.) voracious, insatiable, grasping, ravenous, devouring.
murder *(SYN.)* homicide, kill, slay, slaughter, butcher, killing, massacre, assassinate, execute.
(ANT.) save, protect, vivify, animate.
murderer *(SYN.)* slayer, killer, assassin.
murky *(SYN.)* gloomy, dark, obscure, unclear, impenetrable.
(ANT.) cheerful, light.
murmur *(SYN.)* mumble, whine, grumble, whimper, lament, mutter, complaint, remonstrate, complain, repine.
(ANT.) praise, applaud, rejoice.
muscle *(SYN.)* brawn, strength, power, fitness, vigor, vim, stamina, robustness.
museum *(SYN.)* exhibit hall, treasure house, gallery, repository.
mushroom *(SYN.)* multiply, proliferate, flourish, spread, grow, pullulate.
music *(SYN.)* symphony, harmony, consonance.
musical *(SYN.)* tuneful, melodious, dulcet, lyrical, harmonious.
must *(SYN.)* ought to, should, duty, obligation, ultimatum.
musty *(SYN.)* mildewed, rancid, airless, dank, stale, decayed, rotten, funky.
mute *(SYN.)* quiet, noiseless, dumb, taciturn, hushed, peaceful, speechless, uncommunicative, silent.
(ANT.) raucous, clamorous, noisy.
mutilate *(SYN.)* tear, cut, clip, amputate, lacerate, dismember, deform, castrate.
mutinous *(SYN.)* revolutionary, rebellious, unruly, insurgent, turbulent, riotous.
(ANT.) dutiful, obedient, complaint.
mutiny *(SYN.)* revolt, overthrow, rebellion, rebel, coup, uprising.
mutter *(SYN.)* complain, mumble, whisper, grumble, murmur.
mutual *(SYN.)* correlative, interchangeable, shared, alternate, joint, common.
(ANT.) unshared, unrequited, separate.
muzzle *(SYN.)* restrain, silence, bridle, bind, curb, suppress, gag, stifle.
myriad *(SYN.)* considerable, many.
mysterious *(SYN.)* hidden, mystical, secret, cryptic, incomprehensible.
(ANT.) simple, obvious, clear, plain.
mystery *(SYN.)* riddle, difficulty, enigma, puzzle, strangeness, conundrum.
(ANT.) solution, key, answer, resolution.
mystical *(SYN.)* secret, cryptic, hidden, dim, obscure, dark, cabalistic.
(ANT.) simple, explained, plain, clear.
mystify *(SYN.)* puzzle, confound, bewilder, stick, get, floor, bamboozle.
myth *(SYN.)* fable, parable, allegory, fiction, tradition, lie, saga, legend.
(ANT.) history.

nag *(SYN.)* badger, harry, provoke, tease, bother, annoy, molest, taunt, vex, torment, worry, annoy, pester, irritate, pick on, horse, torment.
(ANT.) please, comfort, soothe.
nail *(SYN.)* hold, fasten, secure, fix, seize, catch, snare, hook, capture.
(ANT.) release.
naive *(SYN.)* frank, unsophisticated, natural, artless, ingenuous, simple, candid, open, innocent.
(ANT.) worldly, cunning, crafty.
naked *(SYN.)* uncovered, unfurnished, nude, bare, open, unclad, stripped, exposed, plain, mere, simple, barren, unprotected, bald, defenseless, unclothed, undressed.
(ANT.) covered, protected, dressed, clothed, concealed, suppressed.
name *(SYN.)* title, reputation, appellation, style, fame, repute, renown, denomination, appoint, character, designation, surname, distinction, christen, denominate, mention, specify, epithet, entitle, call, label.
(ANT.) anonymity, misnomer, hint, misname.
nap *(SYN.)* nod, doze, sleep, snooze, catnap, siesta, slumber, drowse, forty winks.
narcissistic *(SYN.)* egotistical, egocentric, self-centered, egotistic.
narcotics *(SYN.)* opiates, drugs, sedatives, tranquilizers, barbiturates.
narrate *(SYN.)* recite, relate, declaim, detail, rehearse, deliver, review, tell, describe, recount.
narrative *(SYN.)* history, relation, account, record, chronicle, detail, recital, description, story, tale.
(ANT.) distortion, caricature, misrepresentation.
narrow *(SYN.)* narrow-minded, illiberal, bigoted, fanatical, prejudiced, close, restricted, slender, cramped, confined, meager, thin, tapering, tight.
(ANT.) progressive, liberal, wide,
narrow-minded *(SYN.)* close-minded, intolerant, partisan, arbitrary, bigoted.
(ANT.) tolerant, liberal, broad-minded.
nascent *(SYN.)* prime, introductory, emerging, elementary.
nasty *(SYN.)* offensive, malicious, selfish, mean, disagreeable, unpleasant, foul, dirty, filthy, loathsome, disgusting, polluted, obscene, indecent, sickening, nauseating, obnoxious, revolting, odious.
(ANT.) generous, dignified, noble, admirable, pleasant.
nation *(SYN.)* state, community, realm, nationality, commonwealth, kingdom, country, republic, land, society, tribe.
native *(SYN.)* domestic, inborn, inherent, natural, aboriginal, endemic, innate, inbred, indigenous, hereditary, original, local.
(ANT.) alien, stranger, foreigner, outsider, foreign.
natty *(SYN.)* chic, well-dressed, sharp, dapper.
natural *(SYN.)* innate, genuine, real,

unaffected, characteristic, native, normal, regular, inherent, original, simple, inbred, inborn, hereditary, typical, authentic, honest, legitimate, pure, customary.
(ANT.) irregular, false, unnatural, formal, abnormal.

naturally *(SYN.)* typically, ordinarily, usually, indeed, normally, plainly, of course, surely, certainly.
(ANT.) artificially.

nature *(SYN.)* kind, disposition, reputation, character, repute, world, quality, universe, essence, variety, features, traits.

naught *(SYN.)* nought, zero, nothing.

naughty *(SYN.)* unmanageable, insubordinate, disobedient, mischievous, unruly, bad, misbehaving, disorderly, wrong, evil, rude, improper, indecent.
(ANT.) obedient, good, well-behaved.

nausea *(SYN.)* sickness, vomiting, upset, queasiness, seasickness.

nauseated *(SYN.)* unwell, sick, queasy, squeamish.

nautical *(SYN.)* naval, oceanic, marine, ocean.

naval *(SYN.)* oceanic, marine, nautical, maritime.

navigate *(SYN.)* sail, cruise, pilot, guide, steer.

near *(SYN.)* close, nigh, dear, adjacent, familiar, at hand, neighboring, approaching, impending, proximate, imminent, bordering.
(ANT.) removed, distant, far, remote.

nearly *(SYN.)* practically, close to, approximately, almost.

neat *(SYN.)* trim, orderly, precise, clear, spruce, nice, tidy, clean, well-kept, clever, skillful, adept, apt, tidy, dapper, smart, proficient, expert, handy, well-done, shipshape, elegant, well-organized.
(ANT.) unkempt, sloppy, dirty, slovenly, messy, sloppy, disorganized.

nebulous *(SYN.)* fuzzy, indistinct, indefinite, clouded, hazy.
(ANT.) definite, distinct, clear.

necessary *(SYN.)* needed, expedient, unavoidable, required, essential, indispensable, urgent, imperative, inevitable, compelling, compulsory, obligatory, needed, exigent.
(ANT.) optional, nonessential, contingent, casual, accidental, unnecessary, dispensable, unneeded.

necessity *(SYN.)* requirement, fate, destiny, constraint, requisite, poverty, exigency, compulsion, want, essential, prerequisite.
(ANT.) option, luxury, freedom, choice, uncertainty.

necromancy *(SYN.)* witchcraft, charm, sorcery, conjuring, wizardry.

need *(SYN.)* crave, want, demand, claim, desire, covet, wish, lack, necessity, requirement, poverty, require, pennilessness.

needed *(SYN.)* necessary, indispensable, essential, requisite.
(ANT.) optional, contingent.

needle *(SYN.)* goad, badger, tease, nag, prod, provoke.

needless *(SYN.)* nonessential, unnecessary, superfluous, useless, purposeless.

needy *(SYN.)* poor, indigent, impoverished penniless, destitute.
(ANT.) affluent, well-off, wealthy, well-to-do.

nefarious *(SYN.)* detestable, vicious, wicked, atrocious, horrible, vile.

negate *(SYN.)* revoke, void, cancel, nullify.

neglect *(SYN.)* omission, default, heedlessness, carelessness, thoughtlessness, disregard, negligence, oversight, omission, ignore, slight, failure, overlook, omit, skip, pass over, be inattentive, miss.
(ANT.) diligence, do, protect, watchfulness, care, attention, careful, attend, regard, concern.

negligent *(SYN.)* imprudent, thoughtless, lax, careless, inattentive, indifferent, remiss, neglectful.
(ANT.) careful, nice, accurate, meticulous.

negligible *(SYN.)* trifling, insignificant, trivial, inconsiderable.
(ANT.) major, vital, important.

negotiate *(SYN.)* intervene, talk over, mediate, transact, umpire, referee, arbitrate, arrange, settle, bargain.

neighborhood *(SYN.)* environs, nearness, locality, district, vicinity, area, section, locality.
(ANT.) remoteness.

neighboring *(SYN.)* bordering, near, adjacent, next to, surrounding, adjoining.

neighborly *(SYN.)* friendly, sociable, amiable, affable, companionable, congenial, kind, cordial, amicable.
(ANT.) distant, reserved, cool, unfriendly, hostile.

neophyte *(SYN.)* greenhorn, rookie, amateur, beginner, apprentice, tyro, student.

nepotism *(SYN.)* bias, prejudice, partronage, favoritism.

nerve *(SYN.)* bravery, spirit, courage, boldness, rudeness, strength, stamina, bravado, daring, impudence, mettle, impertinence.
(ANT.) frailty, cowardice, weakness.

nervous *(SYN.)* agitated, restless, excited, shy, timid, upset, disturbed, shaken, rattle, high-strung, flustered, tense, jittery, strained, edgy, perturbed, fearful.
(ANT.) placid, courageous, confident, calm, tranquil, composed, bold.

nest *(SYN.)* den, refuge, hideaway.

nestle *(SYN.)* cuddle, snuggle.

net *(SYN.)* snare, trap, mesh, earn, gain, web, get, acquire, secure, obtain.

nettle *(SYN.)* irritate, vex, provoke, annoy, disturb, irk, needle, pester.

neurotic *(SYN.)* disturbed, psychoneurotic.

neutral *(SYN.)* nonpartisan, uninvolved, detached, impartial, cool, unprejudiced, indifferent, inactive.
(ANT.) involved, biased, partisan.

neutralize *(SYN.)* offset, counteract, nullify, negate.

nevertheless *(SYN.)* notwithstanding, however, although, anyway, but, regardless.
new *(SYN.)* modern, original, newfangled, late, recent, novel, young, firsthand, fresh, unique, unusual.
(ANT.) antiquated, old, ancient, obsolete, outmoded.
newborn *(SYN.)* baby, infant, cub, suckling.
news *(SYN.)* report, intelligence, information, copy, message, advice, tidings, knowledge, word, story, data.
next *(SYN.)* nearest, following, closest, successive, succeeding, subsequent.
nibble *(SYN.)* munch, chew, bit.
nice *(SYN.)* pleasing, pleasant, agreeable, thoughtful, satisfactory, friendly, enjoyable, gratifying, desirable, fine, good, cordial.
(ANT.) nasty, unpleasant, disagreeable, unkind, inexact, careless, thoughtless.
niche *(SYN.)* corner, nook, alcove, cranny, recess.
nick *(SYN.)* cut, notch, indentation, dash, score, mark.
nickname *(SYN.)* byname, sobriquet.
nigh *(SYN.)* close, imminent, near, adjacent, approaching, bordering, neighboring, impending.
(ANT.) removed, distant.
nightmare *(SYN.)* calamity, horror, torment, bad dream.
nil *(SYN.)* zero, none, nought, nothing.
nimble *(SYN.)* brisk, quick, active, supple, alert, lively, spry, light, fast, speedy, swift, agile.
(ANT.) slow, heavy, sluggish, clumsy.
nincompoop *(SYN.)* nitwit, idiot, fool, moron, blockhead, ninny, idiot, simpleton.
nip *(SYN.)* bite, pinch, chill, cold, squeeze, crispness, sip, small.
nippy *(SYN.)* chilly, sharp, bitter, cold, penetrating.
nit-picker *(SYN.)* fussbudget, precise, purist, perfectionist.
nitty-gritty *(SYN.)* essentials, substance, essence.
noble *(SYN.)* illustrious, exalted, dignified, stately, eminent, lofty, grand, elevated, honorable, honest, virtuous, great, distinguished, majestic, important, prominent, magnificent, grandiose, aristocratic, upright, well-born.
(ANT.) vile, low, base, mean, dishonest, common, ignoble.
nocturnal *(SYN.)* nightly.
nod *(SYN.)* bob, bow, bend, tip, signal.
node *(SYN.)* protuberance, growth, nodule, cyst, lump, wen.
noise *(SYN.)* cry, sound, din, babel, racket, uproar, clamor, outcry, tumult, outcry, sounds, hubbub, bedlam, commotion, rumpus, clatter.
(ANT.) quiet, stillness, hush, silence, peace.
noisome *(SYN.)* repulsive, disgusting, revolting, obnoxious, malodorous, rotten, rancid.
noisy *(SYN.)* resounding, loud, clamorous, vociferous, stentorian, tumultuous.
(ANT.) soft, dulcet, subdued, quiet, silent, peaceful.
nomad *(SYN.)* gypsy, rover, traveler, roamer, migrant, vagrant, wanderer.
nominate *(SYN.)* propose, choose, select.
nomination *(SYN.)* appointment, naming, choice, selection, designation.
nominee *(SYN.)* sapirant, contestant, candidate, competitor.
nonbeliever *(SYN.)* skeptic, infidel, atheist, heathen.
nonchalant *(SYN.)* unconcerned, indifferent, cool, casual, easygoing.
noncommittal *(SYN.)* neutral, tepid, undecided, cautious, guarded, uncommunicative.
nonconformist *(SYN.)* protester, rebel, radical, dissenter, renegade, dissident, eccentric.
nondescript *(SYN.)* unclassifiable, indescribable, indefinite.
nonentity *(SYN.)* nothing, menial, nullity.
nonessential *(SYN.)* needless, unnecessary.
nonpareil *(SYN.)* unsurpassed, exceptional, paramount, unrivaled.
nonplus *(SYN.)* confuse, perplex, dumfound, mystify, confound, puzzle, baffle, bewilder.
(ANT.) illumine, clarify, solve, explain.
nonsense *(SYN.)* balderdash, rubbish, foolishness, folly, ridiculousness, stupidity, absurdity, poppycock, trash.
nonsensical *(SYN.)* silly, preposterous, absurd, unreasonable, foolish, irrational, ridiculous, stupid, senseless.
(ANT.) sound, consistent, reasonable.
nonstop *(SYN.)* constant, continuous, unceasing, endless.
nook *(SYN.)* niche, corner, recess, cranny, alcove.
noose *(SYN.)* snare, rope, lasso, loop.
normal *(SYN.)* ordinary, uniform, natural, unvaried, customary, regular, healthy, sound, whole, usual, typical, characteristic, routine, standard.
(ANT.) rare, erratic, unusual, abnormal.
normally *(SYN.)* regularly, frequently, usually, customarily.
nosy *(SYN.)* inquisitive, meddling, peering, searching, prying, snooping.
(ANT.) unconcerned, incurious, uninterested.
notable *(SYN.)* noted, unusual, uncommon, noteworthy, remarkable, conspicuous, distinguished, distinctive, celebrity, starts, important, striking, special, memorable, extraordinary, rare, exceptional, personality.
(ANT.) commonplace, ordinary, usual.
notch *(SYN.)* cut, nick, indentation, gash.
note *(SYN.)* sign, annotation, letter, indication, observation, mark, symbol, comment, remark, token, message, memorandum, record, memo, write, list, inscribe, notice.
noted *(SYN.)* renowned, glorious, celebrated, famous, illustrious, well-known, distinguished, famed, notable.

(ANT.) unknown, hidden, infamous, ignominious.

noteworthy *(SYN.)* consequential, celebrated, exceptional, prominent.

notice *(SYN.)* heed, perceive, hold, mark, behold, descry, recognize, observe, attend to, remark, note, regard.
(ANT.) overlook, disregard, skip.

notify *(SYN.)* apprise, acquaint, instruct, tell, advise, warn, teach, inform.
(ANT.) mislead, delude, conceal.

notion *(SYN.)* image, conception, sentiment, abstraction, thought, idea.
(ANT.) thing, matter, substance, entity.

notorious *(SYN.)* celebrated, renowned, famous, well-known, popular.

nourish *(SYN.)* strengthen, nurse, feed, supply, nurture, sustain, support.

nourishment *(SYN.)* nutriment, food, sustenance, support.
(ANT.) starvation, deprivation.

novel *(SYN.)* fiction, narrative, allegory, tale, fable, story, romance, invention, different, unusual, strange, original, new, unique, fresh, firsthand, odd.
(ANT.) verity, history, truth, fact.

novice *(SYN.)* beginner, amateur, newcomer, greenhorn, learner, apprentice.
(ANT.) expert, professional, adept.

now *(SYN.)* today, at once, right away, immediately, at this time, present.
(ANT.) later.

noxious *(SYN.)* poisonous, harmful, damaging, toxic, detrimental.
(ANT.) harmless.

nucleus *(SYN.)* core, middle, heart, focus, hub, kernel.

nude *(SYN.)* naked, unclad, plain, open, defenseless, mere, bare, exposed.
(ANT.) dressed, concealed, protected, clothed, covered.

nudge *(SYN.)* prod, push, jab, shove, poke, prompt.

nugget *(SYN.)* clump, mass, lump, wad, chunk, hunk.

nuisance *(SYN.)* annoyance, bother, irritation, pest.

nullify *(SYN.)* abolish, cross out, delete, invalidate, obliterate, cancel, expunge.
(ANT.) perpetuate, confirm, enforce.

numb *(SYN.)* unfeeling, dull, insensitive, deadened, anesthetized, stupefied.

number *(SYN.)* quantity, sum, amount, volume, aggregate, total, collection.
(ANT.) zero, nothing, nothingness.

numeral *(SYN.)* figure, symbol, digit.

numerous *(SYN.)* many, several, manifold, various, multitudinous, diverse.
(ANT.) scanty, meager, few, scarce.

nuptials *(SYN.)* marriage, wedding, espousal, wedlock, matrimony.
(ANT.) virginity, divorce, celibacy.

nurse *(SYN.)* tend, care for, nourish, nurture, feed, foster, train, mind, attend.

nurture *(SYN.)* hold dear, foster, sustain, appreciate, prize, bring up, rear.
(ANT.) dislike, disregard, abandon.

nutriment *(SYN.)* food, diet, sustenance, repast, meal, fare, edibles.
(ANT.) hunger, want, starvation.

nutrition *(SYN.)* nourishment, sustenance, food, nutriment.

oaf *(SYN.)* boor, clod, clown, lummox, fool, lout, dunce, bogtrotter.

oasis *(SYN.)* shelter, haven, retreat, refuge.

oath *(SYN.)* promise, pledge, vow, profanity, curse, agreement, commitment.

obdurate *(SYN.)* insensible, callous, hard, tough, unfeeling, insensitive.
(ANT.) soft, compassionate, tender.

obedience *(SYN.)* docility, submission, subservience, compliance.
(ANT.) rebelliousness, disobedience.

obedient *(SYN.)* dutiful, yielding, tractable, compliant, submissive.
(ANT.) rebellious, intractable, insubordinate, obstinate.

obese *(SYN.)* portly, fat, pudgy, chubby, plump, rotund, stout, thickset.
(ANT.) slim, gaunt, lean, thin, slender.

obey *(SYN.)* submit, yield, mind, comply, listen to, serve, conform.
(ANT.) resist, disobey.

object *(SYN.)* thing, aim, intention, design, end, objective, particular, mark.
(ANT.) assent, agree, concur, approve.

objection *(SYN.)* disagreement, protest, rejection, dissent, challenge.
(ANT.) acceptance, compliance.

objectionable *(SYN.)* improper, offensive, unbecoming, deplorable.

objective *(SYN.)* aspiration, goal, passion, desire, aim, hope, purpose, drift.
(ANT.) biased, subjective.

objectivity *(SYN.)* disinterest, neutrality, impartiality.

obligate *(SYN.)* oblige, require, pledge, bind, force, compel.

obligation *(SYN.)* duty, bond, engagement, compulsion, account, contract.
(ANT.) freedom, choice, exemption.

oblige *(SYN.)* constrain, force, impel, enforce, coerce, drive, gratify.
(ANT.) persuade, convince, allure, free, induce, disoblige, prevent.

obliging *(SYN.)* considerate, helpful, thoughtful, well-meaning, accommodating.
(ANT.) discourteous.

obliterate *(SYN.)* terminate, destroy, eradicate, raze, extinguish.
(ANT.) make, save, construct, establish.

oblivious *(SYN.)* sightless, unmindful, headlong, rash, blind, senseless.
(ANT.) sensible, aware, calculated.

oblong *SYN.)* rectangular, elliptical, elongated.

obnoxious *(SYN.)* hateful, offensive, nasty, disagreeable, repulsive.

obscene *(SYN.)* indecent, filthy, impure, dirty, gross, lewd, pornographic, coarse, disgusting, bawdy, offensive, smutty.
(ANT.) modest, pure, decent, refined.

obscure *(SYN.)* cloudy, enigmatic, mysterious, abstruse, cryptic, dim, indistinct, dusky, ambiguous, dark, indistinct, unintelligible, unclear, shadowy, fuzzy, blurred, vague.
(ANT.) clear, famous, distinguished, noted, illumined, lucid, bright, distinct.

obsequious *(SYN.)* fawning, flattering, ingratiating.

observance *(SYN.)* protocol, ritual,

ceremony, rite, parade, pomp, solemnity, formality.
(ANT.) omission.

observant *(SYN.)* aware, alert, careful, mindful, watchful, heedful, considerate, attentive, anxious, circumspect, cautious, wary.
(ANT.) unaware, indifferent, oblivious.

observation *(SYN.)* attention, watching, comment, opinion, remark, notice, examination.

observe *(SYN.)* note, behold, discover, notice, perceive, eye, detect, inspect, keep, commemorate, mention, utter, watch, examine, mark, view, express, see, celebrate.
(ANT.) neglect, overlook, disregard, ignore.

observer *(SYN.)* examiner, overseer, lookout, spectator, bystander, witness, watcher.

obsession *(SYN.)* preoccupation, mania, compulsion, passion, fetish, infatuation.

obsolete *(SYN.)* old, out-of-date, ancient, archaic, extinct, old-fashioned, discontinued, obsolescent, venerable, dated, antiquated.
(ANT.) modern, stylish, current, recent, fashionable, extant.

obstacle *(SYN.)* block, hindrance, barrier, impediment, snag, check, deterrent, stoppage, hitch, bar, difficulty, obstruction.
(ANT.) help, aid, assistance, encouragement.

obstinate *(SYN.)* firm, headstrong, immovable, stubborn, determined, dogged, intractable, uncompromising, inflexible, willful, bullheaded, contumacious, obdurate, unbending, unyielding, pertinacious.
(ANT.) yielding, docile, amenable, submissive, pliable, flexible, compliant.

obstruct *(SYN.)* clog, barricade, impede, block, delay, hinder, stop, close, bar.
(ANT.) promote, clear, aid, help, open, further.

obstruction *(SYN.)* block, obstacle, barrier, blockage, interference.

obtain *(SYN.)* get, acquire, secure, win, procure, attain, earn, gain, receive, assimilate.
(ANT.) surrender, forfeit, lose, forego, miss.

obtrusive *(SYN.)* blatant, garish, conspicuous.

obtuse *(SYN.)* blunt, dull, slow-witted, unsharpened, stupid, dense, slow.
(ANT.) clear, interesting, lively, bright, animated, sharp.

obviate *(SYN.)* prevent, obstruct, forestall, preclude, intercept, avert, evade.

obvious *(SYN.)* plain, clear, evident, palpable, patent, self-evident, apparent, distinct, understandable, manifest, unmistakable.
(ANT.) concealed, hidden, abstruse, obscure.

obviously *(SYN.)* plainly, clearly, surely, evidently, certainly.

occasion *(SYN.)* occurrence, time, happening, excuse, opportunity, chance.

occasional *(SYN.)* random, irregular, sporadic, infrequent, periodically, spasmodic.
(ANT.) chronic, regular, constant.

occasionally *(SYN.)* seldom, now and then, infrequently, sometimes, irregularly.
(ANT.) regularly, often.

occlude *(SYN.)* clog, obstruct, choke, throttle.

occupant *(SYN.)* tenant, lodger, boarder, dweller, resident, inhabitant.

occupation *(SYN.)* employment, business, enterprise, job, trade, vocation, work, profession, matter, interest, concern, affair, activity, commerce, trading, engagement.
(ANT.) hobby, pastime, avocation.

occupy *(SYN.)* dwell, have, inhabit, absorb, hold, possess, fill, busy, keep.
(ANT.) relinquish, abandon, release.

occur *(SYN.)* take place, bechance, come about, befall, chance, transpire, betide, happen.

occurrence *(SYN.)* episode, event, issue, end, result, consequence, happening, circumstance, outcome.

ocean *(SYN.)* deep, sea, main, briny.

odd *(SYN.)* strange, bizarre, eccentric, unusual, single, uneven, unique, queer, quaint, peculiar, curious, unmatched, remaining, singular.
(ANT.) matched, common, typical, normal, familiar, even, usual, regular.

odious *(SYN.)* obscene, depraved, vulgar, despicable, mean, wicked, sordid, foul, base, loathsome, depraved, vicious, displeasing, hateful, revolting, offensive, repulsive, horrible, obnoxious, vile.
(ANT.) decent, upright, laudable, attractive, honorable.

odor *(SYN.)* fume, aroma, fragrance, redolence, smell, stink, scent, essence, stench.

odorous *(SYN.)* scented, aromatic, fragrant.

odyssey *(SYN.)* crusade, quest, journey, voyage.

offbeat *(SYN.)* uncommon, eccentric, strange, unconventional, peculiar.

off-color *(SYN.)* rude, improper, earthy, suggestive, salty.

offend *(SYN.)* annoy, anger, vex, irritate, displease, provoke, hurt, grieve, pain, disgust, wound, horrify, stricken, insult, outrage.
(ANT.) flatter, please, delight.

offender *(SYN.)* criminal, culprit, lawbreaker, miscreant.

offense *(SYN.)* indignity, injustice, transgression, affront, outrage, misdeed, sin, insult, atrocity, aggression, crime.
(ANT.) morality, gentleness, innocence, right.

offensive *(SYN.)* attacking, aggressive, unpleasant, revolting, disagreeable, nauseous, disgusting.
(ANT.) pleasing, defending, defensive, pleasant, attractive, agreeable.

offer *(SYN.)* suggestion, overture, proposal, present, suggest, propose, try, submit, attempt, tender.

(ANT.) withdrawal, denial, rejection.
offhand *(SYN.)* informal, unprepared, casual, impromptu, spontaneous.
(ANT.) considered, planned, calculated.
office *(SYN.)* position, job, situation, studio, berth, incumbency, capacity, headquarters, duty, task, function, work, post.
officiate *(SYN.)* regulate, administer, superintend, oversee, emcee.
offset *(SYN.)* compensate, counterbalance, cushion, counteract, neutralize, soften, balance.
offshoot *(SYN.)* outgrowth, addition, by-product, supplement, appendage, accessory, branch.
offspring *(SYN.)* issue, children, progeny, descendants.
often *(SYN.)* frequently, repeatedly, commonly, generally, many times, recurrently.
(ANT.) seldom, infrequently, rarely, occasionally, sporadically.
ogle *(SYN.)* gaze, stare, eye, leer.
ogre *(SYN.)* fiend, monster, devil, demon.
ointment *(SYN.)* lotion, pomade, balm, emollient.
old *(SYN.)* antique, senile, ancient, archaic, old-fashioned, superannuated, obsolete, venerable, antiquated, elderly, discontinued, abandoned, aged.
(ANT.) new, youthful, recent, modern, young.
old-fashioned *(SYN.)* outmoded, old, dated, ancient.
(ANT.) modern, fashionable, current, new.
olio *(SYN.)* potpourri, variety, mixture, jumble.
omen *(SYN.)* sign, gesture, indication, proof, portent, symbol, token, emblem, signal.
ominous *(SYN.)* unfavorable, threatening, sinister, menacing.
omission *(SYN.)* failure, neglect, oversight, default.
(ANT.) inclusion, notice, attention, insertion.
omit *(SYN.)* exclude, delete, cancel, eliminate, ignore, neglect, skip, leave out, drop, miss, bar, overlook, disregard.
(ANT.) insert, notice, enter, include, introduce.
omnipotent *(SYN.)* all-powerful, almighty, divine.
oncoming *(SYN.)* imminent, approaching, arriving, nearing.
onerous *(SYN.)* intricate, arduous, hard, perplexing, difficult, burdensome, puzzling.
(ANT.) simple, easy, facile, effortless.
one-sided *(SYN.)* unfair, partial, biased, prejudiced.
(ANT.) impartial, neutral.
ongoing *(SYN.)* advancing, developing, continuing, progressive.
onlooker *(SYN.)* witness, spectator, observer, bystander.
only *(SYN.)* lone, sole, solitary, single, merely, but, just.
onset *(SYN.)* commencement, beginning, opening, start, assault, attack, charge, offense, onslaught.
(ANT.) end.
onslaught *(SYN.)* invasion, aggression, attack, assault, offense, drive, criticism, onset, charge, denunciation.
(ANT.) vindication, defense, surrender, opposition, resistance.
onus *(SYN.)* load, weight, burden, duty.
onward *(SYN.)* ahead, forward, frontward.
(ANT.) backward.
ooze *(SYN.)* seep, leak, drip, flow, filter.
opacity *(SYN.)* obscurity, thickness, imperviousness.
opaque *(SYN.)* murky, dull, cloudy, filmy, unilluminated, dim, obtuse, indistinct, shadowy, dark, obscure.
(ANT.) light, clear, bright.
open *(SYN.)* uncovered, overt, agape, unlocked, passable, accessible, unrestricted, candid, plain, clear, exposed, unclosed, unobstructed, free, disengaged, frank, unoccupied, public, honest, ajar, available.
open *(SYN.)* unbar, unfold, exhibit, spread, unseal, expand, unfasten.
(ANT.) close, shut, conceal, hide.
open-handed *(SYN.)* kind, generous, charitable, lavish, extravagant, bountiful.
(ANT.) mean, stingy.
openhearted *(SYN.)* frank, honest, candid, sincere, ingenuous, straightforward.
(ANT.) insincere, devious.
opening *(SYN.)* cavity, hole, void, abyss, aperture, chasm, pore, gap, loophole.
openly *(SYN.)* sincerely, frankly, freely.
(ANT.) secretly.
open-minded *(SYN.)* tolerant, fair, just, liberal, impartial, reasonable, unprejudiced.
(ANT.) prejudiced, bigoted.
operate *(SYN.)* comport, avail, behave, interact, apply, manage, utilize, demean, run, manipulate, employ, act, exploit, exert, exercise, practice, conduct.
(ANT.) neglect, waste.
operation *(SYN.)* effort, enterprise, mentality, maneuver, action, instrumentality, performance, working, proceeding, agency.
(ANT.) inaction, cessation, rest, inactivity.
operative *(SYN.)* busy, active, industrious, working, effective, functional.
(ANT.) inactive, dormant.
opiate *(SYN.)* hypnotic, tranquilizer, narcotic.
opinion *(SYN.)* decision, feeling, notion, view, idea, conviction, belief, judgment, sentiment, persuasion, impression.
(ANT.) knowledge, fact, misgiving, skepticism.
opinionated *(SYN.)* domineering, overbearing, arrogant, dogmatic, positive, magisterial, obstinate, pertinacious.
(ANT.) questioning, fluctuating, indecisive, skeptical, open-minded, indecisive.

opponent *(SYN.)* competitor, foe, adversary, contestant, enemy, rival, contender, combatant, antagonist.
(ANT.) comrade, team, ally, confederate.
opportune *(SYN.)* fitting, suitable, appropriate, proper, favorable, felicitous.
opportunity *(SYN.)* possibility, chance, occasion, time, contingency, opening.
(ANT.) obstacle, disadvantage, hindrance.
oppose *(SYN.)* defy, resist, withstand, combat, bar, counteract, confront, thwart, struggle, fight, contradict, hinder, obstruct.
(ANT.) submit, support, agree, cooperate, succumb.
opposed *(SYN.)* opposite, contrary, hostile, adverse, counteractive, unlucky, antagonistic, unfavorable, disastrous.
(ANT.) lucky, benign, propitious, fortunate, favorable.
opposite *(SYN.)* reverse, contrary, different, unlike, opposed.
(ANT.) like, same, similar.
opposition *(SYN.)* combat, struggle, discord, collision, conflict, battle, fight, encounter, discord, controversy, inconsistency, variance.
(ANT.) harmony, amity, concord, consonance.
oppress *(SYN.)* harass, torment, vex, afflict, annoy, harry, pester, hound, worry, persecute.
(ANT.) encourage, support, comfort, assist, aid.
oppression *(SYN.)* cruelty, tyranny, persecution, injustice, despotism, brutality, abuse.
(ANT.) liberty, freedom.
oppressive *(SYN.)* difficult, stifling, burdensome, severe, domineering, harsh, unjust, overbearing, overwhelming.
oppressor *(SYN.)* bully, scourge, slave-driver.
opprobrium *(SYN.)* disgrace, contempt, reproach, shame, discredit.
opt *(SYN.)* choose, prefer, pick, select.
optical *(SYN.)* seeing, visual.
optimism *(SYN.)* faith, expectation, optimism, anticipation, trust, expectancy, confidence, hope.
(ANT.) despair, pessimism, despondency.
optimistic *(SYN.)* happy, cheerful, bright, glad, pleasant, radiant, lighthearted.
(ANT.) pessimistic.
option *(SYN.)* preference, choice, selection, alternative, election, self-determination.
optional *(SYN.)* selective, elective, voluntary.
(ANT.) required.
opulence *(SYN.)* luxury, abundance, fortune, riches, wealth, plenty, affluence.
(ANT.) need, indigence, want, poverty.
opulent *(SYN.)* wealthy, rich, prosperous, well-off, affluent, well-heeled.
oracle *(SYN.)* authority, forecaster, wizard, seer, mastermind, clairvoyant.
oral *(SYN.)* voiced, sounded, vocalized, said, uttered, verbal, vocal, spoken.
(ANT.) recorded, written, documentary.
orate *(SYN.)* preach, lecture, sermonize.
oration *(SYN.)* address, lecture, speech, sermon, discourse, recital, declamation.
orb *(SYN.)* globe, sphere, ball, moon.
orbit *(SYN.)* path, lap, course, circuit, revolution, revolve, circle.
orchestra *(SYN.)* ensemble, band.
orchestrate *(SYN.)* coordinate, direct, synchronize, organize.
ordain *(SYN.)* constitute, create, order, decree, decide, dictate, command, rule, bid, sanction, appoint.
(ANT.) terminate, disband.
ordeal *(SYN.)* hardship, suffering, test, affliction, trouble, fortune, proof, examination, trial, experiment, tribulation, misery.
(ANT.) consolation, alleviation.
order *(SYN.)* plan, series, decree, instruction, command, system, method, aim, arrangement, class, injuction, mandate, instruct, requirement, dictate, bidding.
(ANT.) consent, license, confusion, disarray, irregularity, permission.
order *(SYN.)* guide, command, rule, direct, govern, manage, regulate, bid, conduct.
(ANT.) misguide, deceive, misdirect, distract.
orderly *(SYN.)* regulated, neat, well-organized, disciplined, methodical, shipshape.
(ANT.) sloppy, messy, haphazard, disorganized.
ordinarily *(SYN.)* commonly, usually, generally, mostly, customarily, normally.
ordinary *(SYN.)* common, habitual, normal, typical, usual, conventional, familiar, accustomed, customary, average, standard, everyday, inferior, mediocre, regular, vulgar, plain.
(ANT.) uncommon, marvelous, extraordinary, remarkable, strange.
ordance *(SYN.)* munitions, artillery.
organ *(SYN.)* instrument, journal, voice.
organic *(SYN.)* living, biological, animate.
organism *(SYN.)* creature, plant, micro-organism.
organization *(SYN.)* order, rule, system, arrangement, method, plan, regularity, scheme, mode, process.
(ANT.) irregularity, chaos, disarrangement, chance, disorder, confusion.
organize *(SYN.)* assort, arrange, plan, regulate, systematize, devise, categorize, classify, prepare.
(ANT.) jumble, disorder, disturb, confuse, scatter.
organized *(SYN.)* planned, neat, orderly, arranged.
orient *(SYN.)* align, fit, accustom, adjust.
orifice *SYN.)* vent, slot, opening, hole.
origin *(SYN.)* birth, foundation, source, start, commencement, inception, beginning, derivation, infancy, parentage, spring, cradle.

(ANT.) product, issue, outcome, end.
original *(SYN.)* primary, fresh, new, initial, pristine, creative, first, primordial, inventive, primeval, novel, introductory.
(ANT.) banal, trite, subsequent, derivative, later, modern, terminal.
originality *(SYN.)* unconventionality, genius, novelty, creativity, imagination.
originate *(SYN.)* fashion, invent, cause, create, make, initiate, inaugurate, organize, institute, produce, engender, commence, found, establish, form, begin, arise, generate, formulate.
(ANT.) demolish, terminate, annihilate, disband, destroy.
originator *(SYN.)* creator, inventor, discoverer.
(ANT.) follower, imitator.
ornament *(SYN.)* decoration, ornamentation, adornment, embellishment, trimming, garnish.
ornamental *(SYN.)* ornate, decorative.
ornate *SYN.)* florid, overdone, elaborate, showy, flowery, pretentious.
ornery *(SYN.)* disobedient, firm, unruly, stiff, rebellious, stubborn, headstrong, willful, contrary, rigid, mean, difficult, malicious, cross, disagreeable.
(ANT.) pleasant.
orthodox *(SYN.)* customary, usual, conventional, correct, proper, accepted.
(ANT.) different, unorthodox.
oscillate *(SYN.)* vary, change, hesitate, waver, undulate, fluctuate, vacillate.
(ANT.) persist, resolve, adhere, stick, decide.
ostentation *(SYN.)* parade, show, boasting, pageantry, vaunting, pomp, display, flourish.
(ANT.) reserve, humility, unobtrusiveness, modesty.
ostentatious *(SYN.)* flashy, showy, overdone, fancy, pretentious, garish.
ostracize *(SYN.)* hinder, omit, bar, exclude, blackball, expel, prohibit.
other *(SYN.)* distinct, different, extra, further, new, additional, supplementary.
ought *(SYN.)* must, should, be obliged.
oust *(SYN.)* eject, banish, exclude, expatriate, ostracize, dismiss, exile, expel.
(ANT.) shelter, accept, receive, admit, harbor.
outbreak *(SYN.)* riot, revolt, uprising, disturbance, torrent, eruption, outburst.
outburst *(SYN.)* outbreak, eruption, torrent, ejection, discharge.
outcast *(SYN.)* friendless, homeless, deserted, abandoned, forsaken, disowned, derelict, forlorn, rejected.
outcome *(SYN.)* fate, destiny, necessity, doom, portion, consequence, result, end, fortune, effect, issue, aftermath.
outcry *(SYN.)* scream, protest, clamor, noise, uproar.
outdated *(SYN.)* old-fashioned, unfashionable, old, outmoded.
(ANT.) stylish.
outdo *(SYN.)* outshine, defeat, excel, beat, surpass.
outer *(SYN.)* remote, exterior, external.
outfit *(SYN.)* garb, kit, gear, furnish, equip, rig, clothing, provisions.
outgoing *(SYN.)* leaving, departing, friendly, congenial, amicable.
(ANT.) unfriendly, incoming.
outing *(SYN.)* journey, trip, excursion, jaunt, expedition, junket.
outlandish *(SYN.)* peculiar, odd, weird, curious, strange, queer, exotic, bazaar.
(ANT.) ordinary, common.
outlast *(SYN.)* survive, endure, outlive.
outlaw *(SYN.)* exile, bandit, outcast, badman, convict, criminal, fugitive, desperado.
outlay *(SYN.)* expense, costs, spending, disbursement, expenditure, charge.
outlet *(SYN.)* spout, opening, passage.
outline *(SYN.)* form, sketch, brief, draft, figure, profile, contour, chart.
outlook *(SYN.)* viewpoint, view, prospect, opportunity, position, attitude, future.
outlying *(SYN.)* external, remote, outer, out-of-the-way, surburban, rural.
outnumber *(SYN.)* exceed.
output *(SYN.)* yield, crop, harvest, proceeds, productivity, production.
outrage *(SYN.)* aggression, transgression, vice, affront, offense, insult.
(ANT.) morality, right, gentleness.
outrageous *(SYN.)* shameful, shocking, disgraceful, insulting, nonsensical.
(ANT.) prudent, reasonable, sensible.
outright *(SYN.)* entirely, altogether, completely, quite, fully, thoroughly.
outside *(SYN.)* covering, exterior, surface, facade, externals, appearance.
(ANT.) intimate, insider.
outsider *(SYN.)* immigrant, stranger, foreigner, alien, newcomer, bystander.
(ANT.) countryman, friend, acquaintance, neighbor, associate.
outspoken *(SYN.)* rude, impolite, unceremonious, brusque, unrestrained, vocal, open, straight-forward, blunt.
(ANT.) suave, tactful, shy, polished, polite, subtle.
outstanding *(SYN.)* well-known, important, prominent, leading, eminent.
(ANT.) insignificant, unimportant.
outward *(SYN.)* apparent, outside, exterior, visible.
outweigh *(SYN.)* predominate, supersede, counteract, dwarf.
outwit *(SYN.)* baffle, trick, outsmart, bewilder, outdo, outmaneuver, confuse.
oval *(SYN.)* egg-shaped, elliptical, ovular.
ovation *(SYN.)* fanfare, homage, applause, tribute, cheers, acclamation.
overall *(SYN.)* comprehensive, complete, general, extensive, wide-spread, entire.
overbearing *(SYN.)* domineering, masterful, autocratic, dictatorial.
(ANT.) humble.
overcast *(SYN.)* dim, shadowy, cloudy, murky, dark, mysterious, gloomy, somber, dismal, hazy, indistinct.
(ANT.) sunny, bright, distinct, limpid, clear.

overcome *(SYN.)* quell, beat, crush, surmount, humble, conquer, defeat.
(ANT.) retreat, surrender, capitulate, cede, lose.
overdue *(SYN.)* tardy, advanced, slow, delayed, new.
(ANT.) timely, early, beforehand.
overflow *(SYN.)* run over, flood, spill, cascade, inundate.
overflowing *(SYN.)* ample, plentiful, teeming, abundant, copious, profuse.
(ANT.) insufficient, scant, deficient, scarce.
overhang *(SYN.)* protrude, extend, projection.
overhaul *(SYN.)* recondition, rebuild, service, repair, condition, revamp.
overhead *(SYN.)* high, above, aloft, expenses, costs.
overlap *(SYN.)* overhang, extend, superimpose.
overload *(SYN.)* burden, weight, oppress, afflict, weigh, trouble, encumber, tax.
(ANT.) ease, lighten, console, alleviate, mitigate.
overlook *(SYN.)* miss, disregard, exclude, cancel, omit, skip, ignore.
(ANT.) notice, enter, include, introduce.
overpass *(SYN.)* span, bridge, viaduct.
overpower *(SYN.)* overcome, conquer, defeat, surmount, overwhelm.
(ANT.) surrender.
overrated *(SYN.)* exaggerated, misrepresented.
overrule *(SYN.)* disallow, nullify, cancel, override, repeal, revoke.
overrun *(SYN.)* spread, exceed, beset, infest, flood, abound.
oversee *(SYN.)* direct, run, operate, administer, superintend, boss, manage, supervise.
overshadow *(SYN.)* dominate, control, outclass, surpass, domineer.
oversight *(SYN.)* omission, charge, superintendence, surveillance, inattention, error, inadvertence, neglect.
(ANT.) scrutiny, care, attention.
overstep *(SYN.)* surpass, exceed, trespass, transcend, impinge, violate.
overt *(SYN.)* honest, candid, frank, plain, open, apparent, straightforward.
overtake *(SYN.)* outdistance, reach, catch, pass.
overthrow *(SYN.)* defeat, demolish, overcome, destroy, ruin, rout.
(ANT.) revive, restore, construct.
overture *(SYN.)* offer, bid, proposal, prelude, introduction, presentation.
(ANT.) finale.
overturn *(SYN.)* demolish, overcome, vanquish, upset, supplant, destroy.
(ANT.) uphold, construct, build, preserve, conserve.
overweight *(SYN.)* pudgy, stout, heavy, obese, fat.
overwhelm *(SYN.)* crush, surmount, vanquish, conquer, astonish, surprise.
owe *(SYN.)* be liable, be indebted.
own *(SYN.)* monopolize, hold, possess, maintain, have.
owner *(SYN.)* landholder, partner, proprietor, possessor.
pace *(SYN.)* rate, gait, step.
pacific *(SYN.)* peaceful, calm, serene, undisturbed, composed.
(ANT.) turbulent, wild, excited, frantic.
pacify *(SYN.)* appease, lull, relieve, quell, soothe, allay, assuage, calm, satisfy, compose, placate, alleviate.
(ANT.) incense, inflame, arouse, excite.
pack *(SYN.)* prepare, stow, crowd, stuff, bundle, parcel, load, crowd, gang, mob.
package *(SYN.)* parcel, packet, load, bundle, box, bottle, crate.
packed *(SYN.)* filled, complete, plentiful, crammed, fall, replete, gorged, satiated, copious, entire, extensive.
(ANT.) lacking, depleted, devoid, vacant, insufficient, partial, empty.
pageant *(SYN.)* show, display, spectacle.
pain *(SYN.)* twinge, ache, pang, agony, distress, grief, anguish, throe, paroxysm, suffering, misery.
(ANT.) happiness, pleasure, comfort, relief, solace, ease, delight, joy.
painful *(SYN.)* hurting, galling, poignant, bitter, grievous, agonizing, aching.
(ANT.) sweet, pleasant, soothing.
painting *(SYN.)* image, picture, portrayal, scene, view, sketch, illustration, panorama, likeness, representation.
pair *(SYN.)* team, couple, mate, match.
pale *(SYN.)* colorless, white, pallid, dim, faint, whiten, blanch.
(ANT.) flushed, ruddy, bright, dark.
pamphlet *(SYN.)* leaflet, brochure.
pang *(SYN.)* throb, pain, hurt.
panic *(SYN.)* fear, terror, fright, alarm, apprehension, trembling, horror, dread.
(ANT.) tranquillity, composure, calmness, serenity, calm, soothe.
pant *(SYN.)* wheeze, puff, gasp.
pantry *(SYN.)* cupboard, storeroom.
paper *(SYN.)* journal, newspaper, document, article, essay.
parable *(SYN.)* fable, saga, legend, myth, allegory, chronicle, fiction.
(ANT.) history, fact.
parade *(SYN.)* procession, cavalcade, succession, train, file, cortege, retinue, sequence, march, review, pageant, strut.
paradise *(SYN.)* utopia, heaven.
parallel *(SYN.)* allied, analogous, comparable, corresponding, akin, similar.
(ANT.) opposed, different, incongruous.
paralyze *(SYN.)* numb, deaden.
parcel *(SYN.)* packet, package, bundle.
parched *(SYN.)* dry, arid, thirsty, drained, dehydrated, desiccated.
(ANT.) moist, damp.
pardon *(SYN.)* condone, overlook, remit, absolve, acquit, forgive, excuse.
(ANT.) punish, accuse, condemn.
parley *(SYN.)* interview, talk, conference, chat, dialogue, colloquy.
part *(SYN.)* piece, section, allotment, portion, segment, element, member.
(ANT.) whole, entirety.
partake *(SYN.)* dispense, parcel, allot, assign, distribute, partition, ap-

propriate, divide, portion, share.
(ANT.) condense, aggregate, combine.
partial *(SYN.)* unfinished, undone, incomplete, prejudiced, unfair.
(SYN.) comprehensive, complete.
participate *(SYN.)* join, share, partake.
participation *(SYN.)* communion, sacrament, union, intercourse, association, fellowship.
(ANT.) nonparticipation, alienation.
particle *(SYN.)* mite, crumb, scrap, atom, corpuscle, grain, iota, shred, smidgen, grain, speck, bit, spot.
(ANT.) quantity, bulk, mass.
particular *(SYN.)* peculiar, unusual, detailed, specific, fastidious.
(ANT.) general, rough, universal, comprehensive, undiscriminating.
partition *(SYN.)* distribution, division, separation, screen, barrier, separator, divider, wall.
(ANT.) unification, joining.
partner *(SYN.)* colleague, comrade, friend, crony, consort, associate, companion, mate, participant.
(ANT.) stranger, enemy, adversary.
pass *(SYN.)* proceed, continue, move, go, disregard, ignore, exceed, gap.
(ANT.) note, consider, notice.
passage *(SYN.)* section, passageway, corridor, section, voyage, tour.
passenger *(SYN.)* traveler, tourist, rider, voyager, commuter.
passion *(SYN.)* feeling, affection, turmoil, sentiment, perturbation.
(ANT.) tranquillity, indifference, calm, restraint, dispassion, apathy, coolness.
passionate *(SYN.)* fiery, ardent, burning, glowing, irascible, fervid.
(ANT.) quiet, calm, cool, apathetic.
passive *(SYN.)* relaxed, idle, stoical, enduring, inert, inactive, patient.
(ANT.) dynamic, active, aggressive.
past *(SYN.)* done, finished, gone, over, former.
(ANT.) future, present, ahead.
patch *(SYN.)* restore, fix, repair, ameliorate, correct, remedy, sew.
(ANT.) rend, destroy, hurt, injure.
path *(SYN.)* avenue, street, trail, walk, course, road, route, thoroughfare.
pathetic *(SYN.)* piteous, sad, affecting, moving, poignant, pitiable, touching.
(ANT.) funny, comical, ludicrous.
patience *(SYN.)* perseverance, composure, endurance, fortitude, long-suffering, forbearance, calmness, passiveness, serenity, courage, persistence.
(ANT.) restlessness, nervousness, impatience, unquite, impetuosity.
patient *(SYN.)* indulgent, forbearing, composed, passive, quiet, unexcited.
(ANT.) high-strung, hysterical.
patrol *(SYN.)* inspect, watch, guard.
patron *(SYN.)* purchaser, buyer, client, customer.
patronize *(SYN.)* support.
pattern *(SYN.)* guide, example, original, model, design, figure, decoration.
pause *(SYN.)* falter, hesitate, waver, demur, doubt, scruple, delay, rest.
(ANT.) proceed, continue, decide, resolve, persevere, continuity.
pawn *(SYN.)* tool, puppet, stooge.
pay *(SYN.)* earnings, salary, allowance, stipend, wages, payment, compensation, recompense.
(ANT.) gratuity, present, gift.
payable *(SYN.)* unpaid, due, owed, owing.
peace *(SYN.)* hush, repose, serenity, tranquillity, silence, stillness, calmness.
(ANT.) noise, tumult, disturbance.
peaceable *(SYN.)* mild, calm, friendly, peaceful, amiable, gentle, pacific.
(ANT.) aggressive, hostile, warlike.
peaceful *(SYN.)* pacific, calm, undisturbed, quiet, serene, mild, placid.
(ANT.) noisy, violent, agitated.
peak *(SYN.)* climax, culmination, summit, zenith, height, acme, consummation, apex, top, point, crest.
(ANT.) depth, floor, base, anticlimax, base, bottom.
peculiar *(SYN.)* odd, eccentric, extraordinary, unusual, individual, particular.
(ANT.) ordinary, common, normal.
peculiarity *(SYN.)* characteristic, feature, mark, trait, quality, attribute, property, distinctiveness.
pedantic *(SYN.)* formal, scholastic, erudite, academic, learned, bookish, theoretical, scholarly.
(ANT.) simple, common-sense, ignorant, practical, unlearned.
peddle *(SYN.)* sell, vend, hawk.
pedestrian *(SYN.)* stroller, walker.
pedigree *(SYN.)* descent, line, parentage, lineage, ancestry, family.
peek *(SYN.)* glimpse, look, peer, peep.
peel *(SYN.)* rind, skin, peeling.
peep *(SYN.)* squeak, cheep, chirp.
peer *(SYN.)* match, rival, equal, parallel, peep, glimpse, examine, peek, scrutinize.
peeve *(SYN.)* nettle, irk, irritate, annoy, vex.
peevish *(SYN.)* ill-natured, irritable, waspish, touchy, petulant, snappish, fractious, ill-tempered, fretful.
(ANT.) pleasant, affable, good-tempered, , genial, good-natured.
pen *(SYN.)* coop, enclosure, cage.
penalize *(SYN.)* dock, punish.
penalty *(SYN.)* fine, retribution, handicap, punishment, chastisement, disadvantage, forfeiture, forfeit.
(ANT.) remuneration, compensation, reward, pardon.
penchant *(SYN.)* disposition, propensity, tendency, partiality, inclination, bent, tendency, slant, bias.
(ANT.) justice, fairness, equity, impartiality.
penetrate *(SYN.)* bore, hole, pierce, enter.
penetrating *(SYN.)* profound, recondite, abstruse, deep, solemn, piercing, puncturing, boring, sharp, acute.
(ANT.) superficial, trivial, shallow, slight.
peninsula *(SYN.)* spit, headland, neck, point.
penitent *(SYN.)* remorseful, sorrowful, regretful, contrite, sorry, repentant.

(ANT.) remorseless, objurgate.

penniless *(SYN.)* poor, destitute, impecunious, needy, poverty-stricken, needy.
(ANT.) rich, wealthy, affluent, opulent, prosperous, well-off.

pensive *(SYN.)* dreamy, meditative, thoughtful, introspective, reflective, contemplative.
(ANT.) thoughtless, heedless, inconsiderate, precipitous, rash.

penurious *(SYN.)* avaricious, greedy, parsimonious, miserly, stingy, acquisitive, tight.
(ANT.) munificent, extravagant, bountiful, generous, altruistic.

penury *(SYN.)* poverty, want, destitution, necessity, indigence, need, privation.
(ANT.) riches, affluence, abundance, plenty, wealth.

people *(SYN.)* humans, person.

perceive *(SYN.)* note, conceive, see, comprehend, understand, discern, recognize, apprehend, notice, observe, distinguish, understand, grasp.
(ANT.) overlook, ignore, miss.

perceptible *(SYN.)* sensible, appreciable, apprehensible.
(ANT.) imperceptible, absurd, impalpable.

perception *(SYN.)* understanding, apprehension, conception, insight, comprehension, discernment.
(ANT.) misconception, ignorance, misapprehension, insensibility.

perceptive *(SYN.)* informed, observant, apprised, cognizant, aware, conscious, sensible, mindful, discerning, sharp, acute, observant.
(ANT.) unaware, ignorant, oblivious, insensible.

perfect *(SYN.)* ideal, whole, faultless, immaculate, complete, superlative, absolute, unqualified, utter, sinless, holy, finished, blameless, entire, excellent, pure, flawless, ideal.
(ANT.) incomplete, defective, imperfect, deficient, blemished, lacking, faulty, flawed.

perfectionist *(SYN.)* purist, pedant.

perform *(SYN.)* impersonate, pretend, act, play, do, accomplish, achieve, complete.

performance *(SYN.)* parade, entertainment, demonstration, movie, show, production, ostentation, spectacle, presentation, offering.

performer *(SYN.)* entertainer, actress, actor.

perfume *(SYN.)* cologne, scent, essence.

perfunctory *(SYN.)* decorous, exact, formal, external, correct, affected, methodical, precise, stiff, outward, proper, solemn.
(ANT.) unconventional, easy, unconstrained, natural, heartfelt.

perhaps *(SYN.)* conceivable, possible, maybe.
(ANT.) absolutely, definitely.

peril *(SYN.)* jeopardy, risk, danger, hazard.
(ANT.) safety, immunity, protection, defense, security.

perilous *(SYN.)* menacing, risky, hazardous, critical, dangerous, precarious, unsafe, insecure, threatening.
(ANT.) safe, firm, protected, secure.

period *(SYN.)* era, age, interval, span, tempo, time, epoch, duration, spell, date.

periodical *(SYN.)* uniform, customary, orderly, systematic, regular, steady.
(ANT.) exceptional, unusual, abnormal, rare, erratic.

perish *(SYN.)* die, sink cease, decline, decay, depart, wane, wither, languish, expire, cease, pass away.
(ANT.) grow, survive, flourish, begin, live.

perishable *(SYN.)* decomposable, decayable.

permanent *(SYN.)* constant, durable, enduring, abiding, fixed, changeless, unchangeable, lasting, indestructible, stable, continuing, long-lived, persistent, persisting, everlasting, unchanging, unaltered.
(ANT.) unstable, transient, ephemeral, temporary, transitory, passing, inconstant, fluctuating.

permeate *(SYN.)* penetrate, pervade, run through, diffuse, fill, saturate, infiltrate.

permissible *(SYN.)* allowable, fair, tolerable, admissible, justifiable, probable, warranted.
(ANT.) unsuitable, inadmissible, irrelevant.

permission *(SYN.)* authorization, liberty, permit, authority, consent, leave, license, freedom.
(ANT.) refusal, prohibition, denial, opposition.

permissive *(SYN.)* easy, tolerant, open-minded, unrestrictive.
(ANT.) restrictive.

permit *(SYN.)* let, tolerate, authorize, sanction, allow, grant, give.
(ANT.) refuse, resist, forbid, protest, object, prohibit, disallow.

perpendicular *(SYN.)* standing, upright, vertical.
(ANT.) horizontal.

perpetrate *(SYN.)* commit, perform, do.
(ANT.) neglect, fail, miscarry.

perpetual *(SYN.)* everlasting, immortal, ceaseless, endless, timeless, undying, infinite, eternal, unceasing, continuing, continual, continuous, permanent, constant, eternal.
(ANT.) transient, mortal, finite, temporal ephemeral, inconstant, intermittent, fluctuating.

perpetually *(SYN.)* continually, ever, incessantly, eternally, forever, always, constantly.
(ANT.) rarely, sometimes, never, occasionally, fitfully.

perplex *(SYN.)* confuse, dumbfound, mystify, puzzle, bewilder, confound, nonplus.
(ANT.) solve, explain, illumine, instruct, clarify.

perplexed *(SYN.)* confused, disorganized, mixed, bewildered, deranged,

disordered, muddled, disconcerted.
(ANT.) plain, obvious, clear, lucid, organized.

perplexing *(SYN.)* intricate, complex, involved, compound, complicated.
(ANT.) uncompounded, plain, simple.

persecute *(SYN.)* harass, hound, torment, worry, vex, torture, harry, afflict, annoy, oppress, pester, ill-treat, victimize, maltreat.
(ANT.) support, comfort, assist, encourage, aid.

persevere *(SYN.)* remain, abide, endure, last, persist, continue.
(ANT.) vacillate, desist, discontinue, cease, waver, lapse.

perseverance *(SYN.)* persistency, constancy, pertinacity, steadfastness, tenacity, industry.
(ANT.) sloth, cessation, laziness, idleness, rest.

persist *(SYN.)* endure, remain, abide, persevere, continue, last.
(ANT.) vacillate, waver, desist, cease, discontinue, stop.

persistence *(SYN.)* persistency, constancy, perseverance, steadfastness, tenacity.
(ANT.) cessation, rest, sloth, idleness.

persistent *(SYN.)* lasting, steady, obstinate, stubborn, fixed, enduring, immovable, constant, indefatigable, dogged.
(ANT.) wavering, unsure, hesitant, vacillating.

person *(SYN.)* human, individual, somebody, someone.

personal *(SYN.)* secret, private.
(ANT.) general, public.

personality *(SYN.)* make-up, nature, disposition, character.

perspicacity *(SYN.)* intelligence, understanding, discernment, judgment, wisdom, sagacity.
(ANT.) thoughtlessness, stupidity, arbitrariness, senselessness.

persuade *(SYN.)* entice, coax, exhort, prevail upon, urge, allure, induce, influence, win over, convince.
(ANT.) restrain, deter, compel, dissuade, coerce, discourage.

persuasion *(SYN.)* decision, feeling, notion, view, sentiment, conviction, belief, opinion.
(ANT.) knowledge, skepticism, fact, misgiving.

persuasive *(SYN.)* winning, alluring, compelling, convincing, stimulating, influential.
(ANT.) dubious, unconvincing.

pertain *(SYN.)* refer, relate, apply.

pertinacious *(SYN.)* firm, obstinate, contumacious, head-strong, dogged, inflexible, obdurate, uncompromising, determined, immovable, unyielding.
(ANT.) yielding, docile, amenable, submissive, compliant.

pertinent *(SYN.)* apt, material, relevant, relating, applicable, to the point, germane, apropos, apposite, appropriate.
(ANT.) unrelated, foreign, alien, extraneous.

perturbed *(SYN.)* agitated, disturbed, upset, flustered.

pervade *(SYN.)* penetrate, saturate, fill, diffuse, infiltrate, run through, permeate.

perverse *(SYN.)* obstinate, ungovernable, sinful, contrary, fractious, peevish, forward, disobedient, wicked, intractable, petulant.
(ANT.) docile, agreeable, tractable, obliging.

perversion *(SYN.)* maltreatment, outrage, desecration, abuse, profanation, misuse, reviling.
(ANT.) respect.

pervert *(SYN.)* deprave, humiliate, impair, debase, corrupt, degrade, abase, defile.
(ANT.) improve, raise, enhance.

perverted *(SYN.)* wicked, perverse, sinful.

pest *(SYN.)* annoyance, bother, nuisance, bother, irritant, irritation.

pester *(SYN.)* disturb, annoy, irritate, tease, bother, chafe, inconvenience, molest, trouble, vex, harass, torment, worry.
(ANT.) console, soothe, accommodate, gratify.

pet *(SYN.)* darling, favorite, caress.

petition *(SYN.)* invocation, prayer, request, appeal, entreaty, supplication, suit, plea, application, solicitation, entreaty.

petty *(SYN.)* paltry, trivial, frivolous, small, unimportant, trifling, insignificant.
(ANT.) important, serious, weighty, momentous, grand, vital, significant, generous.

petulant *(SYN.)* irritable, ill-natured, fretful, snappish, peevish, ill-tempered, waspish, touchy.
(ANT.) pleasant, affable, good-tempered, genial, good-natured.

phantom *(SYN.)* apparition, ghost, specter.

phase *(SYN.)* period, stage, view, condition.

phenomenon *(SYN.)* occurrence, fact, happening, incident.

philanthropy *(SYN.)* kindness, benevolence, charity, generosity, tenderness, liberality, humanity, magnanimity, altruism.
(ANT.) unkindness, inhumanity, cruelty, malevolence, selfishness.

phlegmatic *(SYN.)* unfeeling, passionless, listless, cold, lethargic, sluggish, slow, lazy.
(ANT.) passionate, ardent, energetic.

phony *(SYN.)* counterfeit, artificial, ersatz, fake, synthetic, unreal, spurious, feigned, assumed, bogus, sham, false, forged.
(ANT.) real, genuine, natural, true.

phrase *(SYN.)* expression, term, word, name.

physical *(SYN.)* material, bodily, carnal, corporeal, natural, somatic, corporal.
(ANT.) spiritual, mental.

pick *(SYN.)* cull, opt, select, elect, choose.

(ANT.) reject, refuse.

picture *(SYN.)* etching, image, painting, portrait, print, representation, sketch, appearance, cinema, effigy, engraving, scene, view, illustration, panorama, resemblance, likeness, drawing, photo-graph.

piece *(SYN.)* portion, bit, fraction, morsel, scrap, fragment, amount, part, quantity, unit, section, portion.
(ANT.) sum, whole, entirety, all, total.

piecemeal *(SYN.)* gradually, partially.
(ANT.) whole, complete, entire.

pierce *(SYN.)* puncture, perforate.

pigheaded *(SYN.)* inflexible, stubborn, obstinate.

pigment *(SYN.)* shade, tint, color, dye, hue, complexion, tincture, stain, tinge.
(ANT.) transparency, paleness.

pile *(SYN.)* accumulation, heap, collection, amass.

pilgrim *(SYN.)* wanderer, traveler.

pilgrimage *(SYN.)* trip, journey, tour, expedition.

pillar *(SYN.)* support, prop, column, shaft.

pillow *(SYN.)* bolster, cushion, pad.

pilot *(SYN.)* helmsman, aviator, steersman.

pin *(SYN.)* clip, fastening, peg, fastener.

pinch *(SYN.)* squeeze, nip.

pinnacle *(SYN.)* crown, zenith, head, summit, chief, apex, crest, top.
(ANT.) bottom, foundation, base, foot.

pioneer *(SYN.)* guide, pilgrim, pathfinder, explorer.

pious *(SYN.)* devout, religious, spiritual, consecrated, divine, hallowed, holy, saintly, sacred, reverent.
(ANT.) worldly, sacrilegious, evil, secular, profane, irreligious, impious.

pirate *(SYN.)* plunderer, buccaneer, privateer.

pistol *(SYN.)* gun, revolver, weapon, handgun.

pit *(SYN.)* well, cavity, hole, excavation.

pitch *(SYN.)* throw, cast, toss, propel, hurl, fling, thrust, establish.
(ANT.) retain, draw, hold, pull, haul.

pitcher *(SYN.)* jug.

piteous *(SYN.)* poignant, touching, affecting, moving, pitiable, sad, pathetic.
(ANT.) funny, ludicrous, comical.

pitfall *(SYN.)* lure, snare, wile, ambush, bait, intrigue, trick, trap, artifice, net, snare.

pitiable *(SYN.)* poignant, touching, moving, affecting, sad.
(ANT.) ludicrous, funny, comical.

pitiful *(SYN.)* distressing, pathetic, pitiable.

pitiless *(SYN.)* unmerciful, mean, unpitying, merciless, cruel.
(ANT.) gentle, kind.

pity *(SYN.)* sympathy, commiseration, condolence, mercy, compassion, charity, mercy.
(ANT.) ruthlessness, hardness, cruelty, inhumanity, brutality, vindictiveness.

pivotal *(SYN.)* crucial, critical, essential, central.
(ANT.) peripheral, unimportant.

place *(SYN.)* lay, arrange, dispose, put, deposit, space, region, location, plot, area, spot.
(ANT.) mislay, remove, disarrange, disturb, misplace.

placid *(SYN.)* pacific, serene, tranquil, calm, imperturbable, composed, peaceful, quiet, still, undisturbed, unruffled.
(ANT.) wild, frantic, turbulent, stormy, excited.

plagiarize *(SYN.)* recite, adduce, cite, quote, paraphrase, repeat, extract.
(ANT.) retort, contradict, misquote, refute.

plague *(SYN.)* hound, pester, worry, harass, annoy, persecute, torment, vex, afflict, badger, torture, epidemic, trouble.
(ANT.) encourage, aid, comfort, assist, support.

plain *(SYN.)* candid, simple, flat, smooth, clear, evident, sincere, unpretentious, level, distinct, absolute, visible, open, frank, palpable, undecorated, ordinary, unembellished, unadorned.
(ANT.) embellished, abstruse, abrupt, rough, broken, insincere, adorned, fancy, elaborate, beautiful, ornamented.

plan *(SYN.)* design, purpose, sketch, devise, invent, contrive, intend, draw, create, scheme, plot, method, procedure.

plane *(SYN.)* level, airplane.

plastic *(SYN.)* pliable, moldable, supple, flexible, synthetic.

platform *(SYN.)* stage, pulpit.

plausible *(SYN.)* likely, practical, credible, feasible, possible, probable.
(ANT.) impracticable, impossible, visionary.

play *(SYN.)* entertainment, amusement, pastime, sport, game, fun, diversion, recreation, show, performance, drama, theatrical.
(ANT.) work, labor, boredom, toil.

playful *(SYN.)* sportive, frolicsome, frisky.

plaything *(SYN.)* game, trinket, toy, gadget.

playwright *(SYN.)* scriptwriter, dramatist.

plea *(SYN.)* invocation, request, appeal, entreaty, supplication, petition, suit.

plead *(SYN.)* beseech, defend, rejoin, supplicate, discuss, beg, appeal, ask, implore, argue, entreat.
(ANT.) deprecate, deny, refuse.

pleasant *(SYN.)* agreeable, welcome, suitable, charming, pleasing, amiable, gratifying, acceptable, pleasurable, enjoyable, nice, satisfying, satisfactory, acceptable, affable, mild, friendly.
(ANT.) offensive, disagreeable, obnoxious, unpleasant, horrid, sour, difficult, nasty.

please *(SYN.)* satisfy, suffice, fulfill, content, appease, gratify, satiate, compensate, remunerate.
(ANT.) dissatisfy, annoy, tantalize, frustrate, displease, vex.

pleasing *(SYN.)* luscious, melodious, sugary, delightful, agreeable, honeyed,

mellifluous, engaging, pleasant, charming, engaging.
(ANT.) repulsive, sour, acrid, bitter, offensive, irritating, annoying.
pleasure *(SYN.)* felicity, delight, amusement, enjoyment gratification, happiness, joy, satisfaction, gladness, well-being.
(ANT.) suffering, pain, vexation, trouble, affliction, discomfort, torment.
pledge *(SYN.)* promise, statement, assertion, declaration, assurance, agreement, oath, commitment, agree, vow, swear.
pledge *(SYN.)* bind, obligate, commit.
(ANT.) renounce, release, neglect, mistrust.
plentiful *(SYN.)* ample, profuse, replete, bountiful, abundant, plenteous, luxurious, fullness, fruitful, copious.
(ANT.) rare, scanty, deficient, scarce, insufficient.
plenty *(SYN.)* fruitfulness, bounty, fullness, abundance.
(ANT.) want, scarcity, need.
pliable *(SYN.)* elastic, supple, flexible, compliant, pliant, resilient, ductile.
(ANT.) rigid, unbending, hard, brittle, stiff.
plight *(SYN.)* dilemma, situation, difficulty, condition, predicament, fix, scrape, state.
(ANT.) satisfaction, ease, comfort, calmness.
plot *(SYN.)* design, plan, scheme, cabal, conspiracy, diagram, sketch, graph, chart, machination, intrigue.
plotting *(SYN.)* cunning, scheming, objective, artfulness, contrivance, purpose, intent, design.
(ANT.) accident, chance, result, candor, sincerity.
ploy *(SYN.)* ruse, guile, antic, deception, hoax, subterfuge, wile, cheat, artifice, fraud, trick.
(ANT.) honesty, sincerity, openness, exposure, candor.
pluck *(SYN.)* yank, snatch, jerk, pull.
plug *(SYN.)* cork, stopper.
plump *(SYN.)* obese, portly, stout, thickset, rotund, chubby, fat, paunchy, stocky, corpulent, pudgy, stout, fleshy.
(ANT.) slim, thin, gaunt, lean, slender, skinny.
plunder *(SYN.)* ravage, strip, sack, rob, pillage, raid, loot.
plunge *(SYN.)* immerse, dip, submerge.
pocketbook *(SYN.)* purse, handbag.
poem *(SYN.)* lyric, verse, poetry.
poetry *(SYN.)* rhyme, verse.
pogrom *(SYN.)* massacre, carnage, slaughter, butchery.
poignant *(SYN.)* pitiable, touching, affecting, impressive, sad, tender, moving, heart-rending.
point *(SYN.)* direct, level, train, aim, locality, position, spot, location.
(ANT.) distract, misguide, deceive, misdirect.
pointed *(SYN.)* keen, sharp, penetrating, shrewd, witty, quick, acute, penetrating, cutting, piercing, astute, severe.
(ANT.) shallow, stupid, bland, blunt, gentle.
pointless *(SYN.)* vain, purposeless.
poise *(SYN.)* composure, self-possession, equanimity, equilibrium, carriage, calmness, balance, self-control, assurance, control, dignity.
(ANT.) rage, turbulence, agitation, anger, excitement.
poison *(SYN.)* corrupt, sully, taint, infect, befoul, defile, contaminate, venom, toxin, virus.
(ANT.) purify, disinfect.
poke *(SYN.)* punch, stab, thrust, jab.
policy *(SYN.)* procedure, system, rule, approach, tactic.
polish *(SYN.)* brighten, shine, finish, brightness, gloss.
(ANT.) tarnish, dull.
polished *(SYN.)* glib, diplomatic, urbane, refined, sleek, suave, slick.
(ANT.) rough, blunt, bluff, harsh, rugged.
polite *(SYN.)* civil, refined, well-mannered, accomplished, courteous, genteel, urbane, well-bred, cultivated, considerate, thoughtful, mannerly, respectful.
(ANT.) uncouth, impertinent, rude, boorish, uncivil, discourteous.
pollute *(SYN.)* contaminate, poison, taint, sully, infect, befoul, defile, dirty.
(ANT.) purify, disinfect, clean, clarify.
pomp *(SYN.)* flourish, pageantry, vaunting, show, boasting, ostentation, parade, display.
(ANT.) reserve, humility, modesty.
pompous *(SYN.)* high, magnificent, stately, august, dignified, grandiose, noble, majestic, lofty, imposing, arrogant, vain, pretentious.
(ANT.) lowly, undignified, humble, common, ordinary.
ponder *(SYN.)* examined, study, contemplate, investigate, meditate, muse, scrutinize, cogitate, reflect, weigh, deliberate, consider.
ponderous *(SYN.)* burdensome, trying, gloomy, serious, sluggish, massive, heavy, cumbersome, grievous, grave, dull, weighty.
(ANT.) light, animated, brisk.
poor *(SYN.)* penniless, bad, deficient, destitute, inferior, shabby, wrong, scanty, pecunious, indigent, needy, poverty-stricken, unfavorable, impoverished, penniless.
(ANT.) wealthy, prosperous, rich, fortunate, good, excellent.
poppycock *(SYN.)* rubbish, babble, twaddle, nonsense.
popular *(SYN.)* favorite, general, common, familiar, prevalent, liked, prevailing, well-liked, approved, accepted, celebrated, admired, ordinary.
(ANT.) unpopular, esoteric, restricted, exclusive.
populous *(SYN.)* dense, thronged, crowded.
porch *(SYN.)* patio, veranda.
pornographic *(SYN.)* impure, indecent, obscene, coarse, dirty, filthy, lewd, smutty, offensive, disgusting.
(ANT.) refined, modest, pure, decent.

port *(SYN.)* harbor, refuge, anchorage.
portable *(SYN.)* transportable, movable.
portal *(SYN.)* entry, doorway, opening, inlet, entrance.
(ANT.) exit, departure.
portend *(SYN.)* foreshadow, presage, foretoken.
portentous *(SYN.)* significant, critical, momentous.
(ANT.) trivial.
portion *(SYN.)* share, bit, parcel, part, piece, section, fragment, division, quota, segment, allotment.
(ANT.) whole, bulk.
portly *(SYN.)* majestic, grand, impressive, dignified, stout, fat, heavy, obese.
(ANT.) slender, thin, slim.
portrait *(SYN.)* painting, representation, picture, likeness.
portray *(SYN.)* depict, picture, represent, sketch, describe, delineate, paint.
(ANT.) misrepresent, caricature, suggest.
pose *(SYN.)* model.
position *(SYN.)* caste, site, locality, situation, condition, standing, incumbency, office, bearing, posture, berth, place, job, pose, rank, attitude, location, place, spot, station, job, situation, occupation.
positive *(SYN.)* sure, definite, fixed, inevitable, undeniable, indubitable, assured, certain, unquestionable, unmistakable.
(ANT.) uncertain, doubtful, questionable, probably, unsure, dubious, confused, negative, adverse.
positively *(SYN.)* unquestionably, surely, certainly, absolutely.
possess *(SYN.)* own, obtain, control, have, seize, hold, occupy, affect, hold, control.
(ANT.) surrender, abandon, lose, renounce.
possessed *(SYN.)* entranced, obsessed, consumer, haunted, enchanted.
possession *(SYN.)* custody, ownership, occupancy.
possessions *(SYN.)* commodities, effects, goods, property, merchandise, wares, wealth, belongings, stock.
possible *(SYN.)* likely, practical, probable, feasible, plausible, credible, practicable.
(ANT.) visionary, impossible, improbable.
possibility *(SYN.)* opportunity, chance, contingency, occasion.
(ANT.) obstacle, disadvantage, hindrance.
possible *(SYN.)* feasible, practical, practicable, doable.
possibly *(SYN.)* perchance, perhaps, maybe.
post *(SYN.)* position, job, berth, incumbency, situation, shaft, pole, fort, base, station.
postpone *(SYN.)* delay, stay, suspend, discontinue, defer, adjourn, interrupt, put off.
(ANT.) persist, prolong, maintain, continue, proceed.
postulate *(SYN.)* principle, adage, saying, proverb, truism, byword, aphorism, axiom, fundamental, maxim.
potency *(SYN.)* effectiveness, capability, skillfulness, efficiency, competency, ability.
(ANT.) wastefulness, inability, ineptitude.
potent *(SYN.)* mighty, influential, convincing, effective.
(ANT.) feeble, weak, powerless, impotent.
potential *(SYN.)* likely, possible, dormant, hidden, latent.
pouch *(SYN.)* container, bag, sack.
pound *(SYN.)* buffet, beat, punch, strike, thrash, defeat, subdue, pulse, smite, belabor, knock, thump, overpower, palpitate, rout, vanquish.
(ANT.) fail, surrender, stroke, defend, shield.
pour *(SYN.)* flow.
pout *(SYN.)* brood, sulk, mope.
poverty *(SYN.)* necessity, need, want, destitution, privation, indigence, distress.
(ANT.) plenty, abundance, wealth, riches, affluence, richness, comfort.
power *(SYN.)* potency, might, authority, control, predominance, capability, faculty, validity, force, vigor, command, influence, talent, ability, dominion, competency.
(ANT.) incapacity, fatigue, weakness, disablement, impotence, ineptitude.
powerful *(SYN.)* firm, strong, concentrated, enduring, forcible, robust, sturdy, tough, athletic, forceful, hale, impregnable, hardy, mighty, potent.
(ANT.) feeble, insipid, brittle, delicate, fragile, weak, ineffectual, powerless.
practical *(SYN.)* sensible, wise, prudent, reasonable, sagacious, sober, sound, workable, attainable.
(ANT.) stupid, unaware, impalpable, imperceptible, absurd, impractical.
practically *(SYN.)* almost, nearly.
practice *(SYN.)* exercise, habit, custom, manner, wont, usage, drill, tradition, performance, action, repetition.
(ANT.) inexperience, theory, disuse, idleness, speculation.
practiced *(SYN.)* able, expert, skilled, adept.
(ANT.) inept.
prairie *(SYN.)* plain, grassland.
praise *(SYN.)* applaud, compliment, extol, laud, glorify, commend, acclaim, eulogize, flatter, admire, celebrate, commendation, approval.
(ANT.) criticize, censure, reprove, condemn, disparage, disapprove, criticism, negation.
pray *(SYN.)* supplicate, importune, beseech, beg.
prayer *(SYN.)* plea, suit, appeal, invocation, supplication, petition, entreaty, request.
preach *(SYN.)* teach, urge, moralize, lecture.
preamble *(SYN.)* overture, prologue, beginning, introduction, prelude, start,

foreword, preface.
(ANT.) end, finale, completion, conclusion, epilogue.
precarious *(SYN.)* dangerous, perilous, threatening, menacing, critical, risky, unsafe, hazardous.
(ANT.) secure, firm, protected, safe.
precaution *(SYN.)* foresight, forethought, care.
precedence *(SYN.)* preference, priority.
precedent *(SYN.)* model, example.
precept *(SYN.)* doctrine, tenet, belief, creed, teaching, dogma.
(ANT.) practice, conduct, performance, deed.
precious *(SYN.)* dear, useful, valuable, costly, esteemed, profitable, expensive, priceless, dear.
(ANT.) poor, worthless, cheap, mean, trashy.
precipice *(SYN.)* bluff, cliff.
precipitate *(SYN.)* speedy, swift, hasty, sudden.
precipitous *(SYN.)* unannounced, sudden, harsh, rough, unexpected, sharp, abrupt, hasty, craggy, steep, precipitate.
(ANT.) expected, smooth, anticipated, gradual.
precise *(SYN.)* strict, exact, formal, rigid, definite, unequivocal, prim, ceremonious, distinct, accurate, correct.
ANT.) loose, easy, vague, informal, careless, erroneous.
precisely *(SYN.)* specifically, exactly.
precision *(SYN.)* correction, accuracy, exactness.
preclude *(SYN.)* hinder, prevent, obstruct, forestall, obviate, thwart, impede.
(ANT.) permit, aid, expedite, encourage, promote.
preclusion *(SYN.)* omission, exception, exclusion.
(ANT.) standard, rule, inclusion.
predicament *(SYN.)* dilemma, plight, situation, condition, fix, difficulty, strait, scrape.
(ANT.) satisfaction, comfort, east, calmness.
predict *(SYN.)* forecast, foretell.
prediction *(SYN.)* forecast, prophecy.
predilection *(SYN.)* attachment, inclination, affection, bent, desire, penchant, disposition, preference.
ANT.) repugnance, aversion, apathy, distaste, nonchalance.
predominant *(SYN.)* highest, paramount, cardinal, foremost, main, first, leading, supreme, principal, essential, prevalent, dominant, prevailing.
(ANT.) subsidiary, auxiliary, supplemental, minor, subordinate.
predominate *(SYN.)* prevail, outweigh, rule.
preface *(SYN.)* foreword, introduction, preliminary, prelude, prologue, preamble.
prefer *(SYN.)* select, favor, elect, fancy.
preference *(SYN.)* election, choice, selection, alternative, option.
prejudice *(SYN.)* bias, favoritism, unfairness, partiality.
prejudiced *(SYN.)* fanatical, narrow-minded, dogmatic, bigoted, illiberal, intolerant.
(ANT.) radical, liberal, tolerant, progressive.
preliminary *(SYN.)* introductory, preparatory, prelude, preface.
premature *(SYN.)* early, untimely, unexpected.
(ANT.) timely.
premeditated *(SYN.)* intended, voluntary, contemplated, designed, intentional, willful, deliberate, studied.
(ANT.) fortuitous, accidental.
premeditation *(SYN.)* intention, deliberation, forethought, forecast.
(ANT.) hazard, accident, impromptu, extemporization.
premise *(SYN.)* basis, presupposition, assumption, postulate, principle, presumption.
(ANT.) superstructure, derivative, trimming, implication.
preoccupied *(SYN.)* abstracted, distracted, absorbed, meditative, inattentive, absent, absent-minded.
(ANT.) attentive, alert, conscious, present, attending, watchful.
prepare *(SYN.)* contrive, furnish, ready, predispose, condition, fit, arrange, plan, qualify, make ready, get ready.
preposterous *(SYN.)* foolish, nonsensical, silly, contradictory, unreasonable, absurd, inconsistent, irrational, self-contradictory.
(ANT.) sensible, rational, consistent, sound, reasonable.
prerequisite *(SYN.)* essential, requirement, necessity, condition, demand.
prerogative *(SYN.)* grant, right, license, authority, privilege.
(ANT.) violation, encroachment, wrong, injustice.
prescribe *(SYN.)* order, direct, designate.
presence *(SYN.)* nearness, attendance, closeness, vicinity, appearance, bearing, personality.
present *(SYN.)* donation, gift, today, now, existing, current, largess, donate, acquaint, introduce, being, give, gratuity, boon, grant.
(ANT.) reject, spurn, accept, retain, receive.
presentable *(SYN.)* polite, well-bred, respectable, well-mannered.
presently *(SYN.)* shortly, soon, directly, immediately.
preserve *(SYN.)* protect, save, conserve, maintain, secure, rescue, uphold, spare, keep, can, safeguard, defend, rescue.
(ANT.) impair, abolish, destroy, abandon, squander, injure.
preside *(SYN.)* officiate, direct, administrate.
press *SYN.)* impel, shove, urge, hasten, push, compress, squeeze, hug, crowd, propel, force, drive, embrace, smooth, iron, insist on, pressure, promote, urgency, jostle.

(ANT.) oppose, pull, falter, drag, retreat, ignore.

pressing *(SYN.)* impelling, insistent, necessary, urgent, compelling imperative, instant, serious, important, cogent, exigent, importunate.
(ANT.) unimportant, trifling, insignificant, petty, trivial.

pressure *(SYN.)* force, influence, stress, press, compulsion, urgency, constraint, compression.
(ANT.) relaxation, leniency, ease, recreation.

prestige *(SYN.)* importance, reputation, weight, influence, renown, fame, distinction.

presume *(SYN.)* guess, speculate, surmise, imagine, conjecture, apprehend, believe, think, assume, suppose, deduce.
(ANT.) prove, ascertain, demonstrate, know, conclude.

presumption *(SYN.)* boldness, impertinence, insolence, rudeness, assurance, effrontery, impudence, assumption, audacity, supposition, sauciness.
(ANT.) politeness, truckling, diffidence.

presumptuous *(SYN.)* bold, impertinent, fresh, imprudent, rude, forward, arrogant.

pretend *(SYN.)* feign, stimulate, act, profess, make believe, imagine, fake, sham, affect.
(ANT.) expose, reveal, display, exhibit.

pretense *(SYN.)* mask, pretext, show, affection, disguise, garb, semblance, simulation, fabrication, lie, excuse, falsification, deceit, subterfuge.
(ANT.) sincerity, actuality, truth, fact, reality.

pretentious *(SYN.)* gaudy, ostentatious.
(ANT.) simple, humble.

pretty *(SYN.)* charming, handsome, lovely, beauteous, fair, comely, attractive, beautiful, elegant.
(ANT.) repulsive, foul, unsightly, homely, plain, hideous.

prevail *(SYN.)* win, succeed, predominate, triumph.
(ANT.) yield, lose.

prevailing *(SYN.)* common, current, general, habitual, steady, regular, universal.

prevalent *(SYN.)* ordinary, usual, common, general, familiar, popular, prevailing, widespread, universal, frequent.
(ANT.) odd, scarce, exceptional, extraordinary.

prevent *(SYN.)* impede, preclude, forestall, stop, block, check, halt, interrupt, deter, slow, obviate, hinder, obstruct, thwart.
(ANT.) expedite, help, allow, abet, aid, permit, encourage, promote.

previous *(SYN.)* former, anterior, preceding, prior, antecedent, earlier, aforesaid, foregoing.
(ANT.) subsequent, following, consequent, succeeding, later.

prey *(SYN.)* raid, seize, victimize.

price *(SYN.)* worth, cost, expense, charge, value.

pride *(SYN.)* self-respect, vanity, glory, superciliousness, haughtiness, conceit, arrogance, self-importance, pretension, egotism, satisfaction, fulfillment, enjoyment, self-esteem.
(ANT.) modesty, shame, humbleness, lowliness, meekness, humility.

prim *(SYN.)* formal, puritanical, priggish, prudish.

primarily *(SYN.)* mainly, chiefly, firstly, essentially, originally.
(ANT.) secondarily.

primary *(SYN.)* first, principal, primeval, pristine, beginning, original, initial, fundamental, elementary, chief, foremost, earliest, main, prime.
(ANT.) subordinate, last, secondary, least, hindmost, latest.

prime *(SYN.)* first, primary, chief, excellent, best, superior, ready.

primeval *(SYN.)* fresh, primary, novel, inventive, creative, primordial, original, first, new, initial.
(ANT.) trite, modern, subsequent, banal, later, terminal, derivative.

primitive *(SYN.)* antiquated, early, primeval, prehistoric, uncivilized, uncultured, simple, pristine, old, aboriginal, unsophisticated, rude, rough, primary.
(ANT.) sophisticated, modish, civilized, cultured, cultivated, late.

principal *(SYN.)* first, leading, main, supreme, predominant, chief, foremost, highest, prime, primary, leader, headmaster, paramount, essential, cardinal.
(ANT.) supplemental, secondary, auxiliary, subsidiary, accessory, minor, subordinate.

principle *(SYN.)* law, method, axiom, rule, propriety, regulation, maxim, formula, order, statute.
(ANT.) exception, hazard, chance, deviation.

print *(SYN.)* issue, reprint, publish, letter, sign, fingerprint, mark, picture, lithograph, engraving, etching.

prior *(SYN.)* previous, aforesaid, antecedent, sooner, earlier, preceding, former, foregoing.
(ANT.) succeeding, following, later, consequent, subsequent.

prison *(SYN.)* brig, jail, stockade, penitentiary.

pristine *(SYN.)* primordial, creative, first, original, fresh, inventive, novel, primary, initial.
(ANT.) trite, terminal, derivative, modern, banal, subsequent, plagiarized, later.

private *(SYN.)* concealed, hidden, secret, clandestine, unknown, personal, surreptitious, covert, individual, particular, special, latent.
(ANT.) exposed, known, closed, general, public, conspicuous, disclosed, obvious.

privilege *(SYN.)* liberty, right, advantage, immunity, freedom, license, favor, sanction.
(ANT.) restriction, inhibition, prohibition, disallowance.

prize *(SYN.)* compensation, bonus, award, premium, remuneration, reward, bounty, esteem, value, rate, recompense, requital.
(ANT.) charge, punishment, wages, earnings, assessment.
probable *(SYN.)* presumable, likely.
probe *(SYN.)* stretch, reach, investigate, examine, examination, scrutiny, scrutinize, inquire, explore, inquiry, investigation, extend.
(ANT.) miss, short.
problem *(SYN.)* dilemma, question, predicament, riddle, difficulty, puzzle.
procedure *(SYN.)* process, way, fashion, form, mode, conduct, practice, manner, habit, system, operation, management, plan.
proceed *(SYN.)* progress, continue, issue, result, spring, thrive, improve, advance, emanate, rise.
(ANT.) retard, withhold, withdraw, hinder, retreat, oppose.
proceeding *(SYN.)* occurrence, business, affair, deal, negotiation, transaction, deed.
proceedings *(SYN.)* account, record, document.
proceeds *(SYN.)* result, produce, income, reward, intake, fruit, profit, store, yield, product, return, harvest, crop.
process *(SYN.)* method, course, system, procedure, operation, prepare, treat.
procession *(SYN.)* cortege, parade, sequence, train, cavalcade, file, retinue, succession.
proclaim *(SYN.)* declare, assert, make known, promulgate, state, assert, broadcast, express, announce, aver, advertise, tell, publish, profess.
proclamation *(SYN.)* declaration, announcement, promulgation.
procrastinate *(SYN.)* waver, vacillate, defer, hesitate, delay, postpone.
procreate *(SYN.)* generate, produce, beget, engender, originate, propagate, sire, create, father.
(ANT.) murder, destroy, abort, kill, extinguish.
procure *(SYN.)* secure, gain, win, attain, obtain, get, acquire, earn.
(ANT.) lose.
prod *(SYN.)* goad, nudge, jab, push.
produce *(SYN.)* harvest, reaping, bear, result, originate, bring about, store, supply, make, create, crop, proceeds.
(ANT.) conceal, reduce, destroy, consume, waste, hide.
product *(SYN.)* outcome, result, output, produce, goods, commodity, stock, merchandise.
productive *(SYN.)* fertile, luxuriant, rich, bountiful, fruitful, creative, fecund, teeming, plenteous, prolific.
(ANT.) wasteful, unproductive, barren, impotent, useless, sterile.
profanation *(SYN.)* dishonor, insult, outrage, defamation, abuse.
(ANT.) plaudit, commendation, laudation, respect, approval.
profane *(SYN.)* deflower, violate, desecrate, pollute, dishonor, ravish, debauch.
profess *(SYN.)* declare, assert, make known, state, protest, announce, aver, express, broadcast, avow, tell.
(ANT.) suppress, conceal, repress, withhold.
profession *(SYN.)* calling, occupation, vocation, employment.
(ANT.) hobby, avocation, pastime.
proffer *(SYN.)* extend, tender, volunteer, propose, advance.
(ANT.) reject, spurn, accept, receive, retain.
proficient *(SYN.)* competent, adept, clever, able, cunning, practiced, skilled, versed, ingenious, accomplished, skillful, expert.
(ANT.) untrained, inexpert, bungling, awkward, clumsy.
profit *(SYN.)* gain, service, advantage, return, earnings, emolument, improvement, benefit, better, improve, use, avail.
(ANT.) waste, loss, detriment, debit, lose, damage, ruin.
profitable *(SYN.)* beneficial, advantageous, helpful, wholesome, useful, gainful, favorable, beneficial, serviceable, salutary, productive, good.
(ANT.) harmful, destructive, injurious, deleterious, detrimental.
profound *(SYN.)* deep, serious, knowing, wise, intelligent, knowledgeable, recondite, solemn, abstruse, penetrating.
(ANT.) trivial, slight, shallow, superficial.
profuse *(SYN.)* lavish, excessive, extravagant, improvident, luxuriant, prodigal, wasteful, exuberant, immoderate, plentiful.
(ANT.) meager, poor, economical, sparse, skimpy.
profusion *(SYN.)* immoderation, superabundance, surplus, extravagance, intemperance, superfluity.
(ANT.) lack, paucity, death, want, deficiency.
program *(SYN.)* record, schedule, plan, agenda, calendar.
progress *(SYN.)* advancement, improvement, development, betterment, advance, movement, improve, progression.
(ANT.) delay, regression, relapse, retrogression, decline.
progression *(SYN.)* gradation, string, train, chain, arrangement, following, arrangement, order.
prohibit *(SYN.)* hinder, forbid, disallow, obstruct, prevent, stop, ban, interdict, debar.
(ANT.) help, tolerate, allow, sanction, encourage, permit.
prohibition *(SYN.)* prevention, ban, embargo, restriction.
(ANT.) allowance, permission.
prohibitive *(SYN.)* forbidding, restrictive.
project *(SYN.)* design, proposal, scheme, contrivance, outline, homework, activity, purpose, bulge, protrude, throw, cast, device, plan.

(ANT.) production, accomplishment, performance.
prolific *(SYN.)* fertile, rich, fruitful, teeming, fecund, bountiful, luxuriant, productive, plenteous.
(ANT.) unproductive, barren, sterile, impotent.
prolong *(SYN.)* extend, increase, protract, draw, stretch, lengthen.
(ANT.) shorten.
prominent *(SYN.)* distinguished, illustrious, outstanding, renowned, influential, famous, well-known, noted, notable, important, conspicuous, eminent, leading, celebrated.
(ANT.) low, vulgar, ordinary, common.
promise *(SYN.)* assurance, guarantee, pledge, undertaking, agreement, bestowal, word, contract, oath, vow.
promote *(SYN.)* advance, foster, encourage, assist, support, further, aid, help, elevate, raise, facilitate, forward.
(ANT.) obstruct, demote, hinder.
prompt *(SYN.)* punctual, timely, exact, arouse, evoke, occasion, induce, urge, ineffect, cite, suggest, hint, cause, mention, propose, make, precise, originate. *(ANT.) laggardly, slow, tardy, dilatory.*
promptly *(SYN.)* immediately, instantly, straightway, forthwith, directly, instantaneously, presently.
(ANT.) later, sometime, hereafter, distantly, shortly.
prone *(SYN.)* apt, inclined, disposed, likely, predisposed.
pronounce *(SYN.)* proclaim, utter, announce, articulate, enunciate.
pronounced *(SYN.)* clear, definite.
(ANT.) minor, unnoticeable.
proof *(SYN.)* evidence, verification, confirmation, experiment, demonstration, testimony, trial, protected, impenetrable, corroboration, test.
(ANT.) fallacy, invalidity, failure.
propel *(SYN.)* drive, push, transfer, actuate, induce, shift, persuade, move.
(ANT.) stay, deter, halt, rest, stop.
proper *(SYN.)* correct, suitable, decent, peculiar, legitimate, right, conventional, decent, just, well-mannered, seemly, fit, appropriate, fitting, respectable, special.
property *(SYN.)* real estate, effects, possessions, quality, characteristic.
(ANT.) poverty, destitution, want, deprivation.
prophecy *(SYN.)* augury, prediction.
prophet *(SYN.)* fortuneteller, oracle, seer, soothsayer, clairvoyant.
proportion *(SYN.)* steadiness, poise, composure, relation, balance, equilibrium, comparison, section, part, arrange, adjust, symmetry.
(ANT.) unsteadiness, imbalance, fall.
proposal *(SYN.)* plan, proposition, tender, scheme, program, offer, suggestion, overture.
(ANT.) rejection, acceptance, denial.
propose *(SYN.)* offer, proffer, recommend, plan, mean, expect, move, design, propound, present, tender.
(ANT.) fulfill, perform, effect.
proposition *(SYN.)* proposal, motion.
propound *(SYN.)* bring forward, offer, advance, allege, propose, assign.
(ANT.) retreat, hinder, withhold, retard.
proprietor *(SYN.)* master, owner.
(ANT.) slave, servant.
(ANT.) exciting, different, extraordinary.
proscribe *(SYN.)* forbid, ban, prohibit.
(ANT.) permit, allow.
prospect *(SYN.)* anticipation, expectation, candidate, buyer, explore, search.
prospective *(SYN.)* planned, proposed.
prosper *(SYN.)* succeed, win, achieve, gain, rise, prevail, flourish, thrive.
(ANT.) miscarry, wane, miss, fail.
prosperous *(SYN.)* rich, wealthy, affluent, well-to-do, sumptuous, well-off, flourishing, thriving, opulent.
(ANT.) impoverished, indigent, beggarly, needy, destitute, poor.
prostrate *(SYN.)* prone, supine, overcome, recumbent, crushed.
protect *(SYN.)* defend, preserve, save, keep, conserve, safeguard, maintain, guard, shield, secure.
(ANT.) impair, abandon, destroy, abolish, injure.
protection *(SYN.)* safeguard, shelter, security, bulwark, fence, guard, safety, assurance, defense, refuge, shield.
protest *(SYN.)* dissent, noncompliance, disagree, objection, disagreement.
(ANT.) acquiesce, assent, compliance, concur, comply, acceptance, approval.
prototype *(SYN.)* model, archetype, specimen, instance, illustration, example, pattern, sample.
(ANT.) rule, concept, precept, principle.
protract *(SYN.)* extend, strain, distend, expand, spread, stretch, elongate.
(ANT.) tighten, contract, loosen, shrink.
protuberance *(SYN.)* prominence, projection, bulge, protrusion, swelling.
proud *(SYN.)* overbearing, vain, arrogant, haughty, stately, vain, glorious.
(ANT.) humble, meek, ashamed, lowly.
prove *(SYN.)* manifest, verify, confirm, demonstrate, establish, show, affirm, examine, corroborate, try, test.
(ANT.) contradict, refute, disprove.
proverb *(SYN.)* maxim, byword, saying, adage, byword, saw, motto, apothegm.
provide *(SYN.)* supply, endow, afford, produce, yield, give, fit, equip, furnish, bestow, fit out.
(ANT.) strip, denude, divest, despoil.
provident *(SYN.)* saving, thrifty, economical, frugal, sparing.
(ANT.) wasteful, lavish, extravagant.
provision *(SYN.)* supply, fund, condition, arrangement, accumulation, reserve, store, hoard.
provisions *(SYN.)* stock, supplies, store.
provoke *(SYN.)* excite, stimulate, agitate, arouse, incite, stir up, vex, bother, disquiet, excite, irritate, annoy.
(ANT.) quell, allay, pacify, calm, quiet.
prowl *(SYN.)* sneak, slink, lurk.
proximate *(SYN.)* nigh, imminent, adjacent, neighboring, bordering, close, impending, approaching.
(ANT.) removed, distant, far.
proxy *(SYN.)* representative, equivalent,

makeshift, alternate, deputy, substitute, expedient, lieutenant.
(ANT.) sovereign, head, principal.
prudence *(SYN.)* watchfulness, care, heed, vigilance, wariness, carefulness, tact, judgment, wisdom, common, foresight, caution.
(ANT.) rashness, recklessness, abandon, foolishness, carelessness.
prudent *(SYN.)* reasonable, sensible, sound, discreet, practical, judicious, sagacious, sensible, provident, sage, intelligent, sober, careful, wise.
(ANT.) stupid, unaware, absurd.
pry *(SYN.)* peer, peep, meddle, peek.
prying *(SYN.)* inquisitive, meddling, curious, inquiring, nosy, peering, searching, interrogative, snoopy.
(ANT.) unconcerned, incurious, indifferent, uninterested.
psyche *(SYN.)* judgment, reason, understanding, brain, intellect, mentality, soul, mind, faculties, spirit.
(ANT.) materiality, body, matter.
public *(SYN.)* common, civil, governmental, federal, unrestricted, people, society, open.
publish *(SYN.)* distribute, issue, declare, announce, reveal, proclaim, publicize.
pull *(SYN.)* attract, induce, prolong, draw, tow, drag, remove, take out, persuade, allure, entice, extract.
(ANT.) shorten, alienate, drive, propel.
pulsate *(SYN.)* beat, throb, palpitate.
pump *(SYN.)* interrogate, question, ask, inquire, quiz, examine, query.
(ANT.) state, answer, respond, reply.
punish *(SYN.)* correct, pummel, chasten, reprove, strike, castigate, chastise.
(ANT.) release, exonerate, reward, pardon, acquit, free.
punishment *(SYN.)* correction, discipline.
(ANT.) turbulence, chaos, confusion.
pupil *(SYN.)* student, undergraduate.
purchase *(SYN.)* get, procure, buy, shopping, acquire, obtain.
(ANT.) sell, dispose of, vend.
pure *(SYN.)* chaste, absolute, clean, immaculate, untainted, spotless.
(ANT.) corrupt, mixed, defiled, foul, tainted, adulterated, polluted.
purify *(SYN.)* cleanse, wash, clean, mop.
(ANT.) soil, dirty, sully, stain, pollute.
purpose *(SYN.)* intention, end, goal, aim, objective, application, use, drift.
(ANT.) hazard, accident, fate.
pursue *(SYN.)* persist, track follow, hunt, hound, chase, trail.
(ANT.) evade, abandon, flee, elude.
pursuit *(SYN.)* hunt, chase.
push *(SYN.)* jostle, shove, urge, press, thrust, force, drive, crowd, hasten.
(ANT.) ignore, falter, halt, drag, oppose.
pushy *(SYN.)* impudent, abrupt, prominent, insolent, forward, brazen.
(ANT.) retiring, timid, cowardly.
put *(SYN.)* set, place, state, express, say, assign, attach, establish.
puzzle *(SYN.)* mystery, mystify, confound, perplex, riddle, conundrum.
(ANT.) key, solution, solve, explain, answer, resolution, illumine, clue.

quack *(SYN.)* faker, fake, fraud, gaggle, clack, gabble, bluffer, cackle, dissembler, charlatan, impostor.
quackery *(SYN.)* charlatanism, deceit, make-believe, fakery, duplicity, dissimulation, pretense, fraudulence, sham, counterfeiting, show.
(ANT.) integrity, probity, veracity, sincerity, honesty.
quaff *(SYN.)* swig, swill, swallow, lap up, sip, drink, ingurgitate, guzzle, imbibe.
quagmire *(SYN.)* swamp, bog, fen, ooze, morass, slough, marsh, plight, predicament, dilemma, impasse, fix, entanglement, quicksand, hole, quandary.
quail *(SYN.)* recoil, cower, flinch, blench, wince, falter, shrink, shake, hesitate, faint, droop.
(ANT.) brave, resist, defy, withstand.
quaint *(SYN.)* odd, uncommon, old-fashioned, antique, antiquated, queer, unusual, curious, eccentric, peculiar, picturesque, singular, whimsical, droll, charming, fanciful, droll, strange.
(ANT.) usual, normal, common, novel, ordinary, modern, current, commonplace, familiar.
quake *(SYN.)* shake, tremble, shudder, quiver, pulsate, stagger, shiver, temblor, vibrate, quaver, throb, earthquake.
qualification *(SYN.)* efficiency, adaptation, restriction, aptness, skill, ability, faculty, talent, power, aptitude, competence, suitability, capability, fitness, condition, dexterity.
(ANT.) unreadiness, incapacity, disability.
qualified *(SYN.)* clever, skillful, efficient, suitable, able, capable, fit, fitted, suited, bounded, limited, contingent, eligible, delimited, adept, circumscribed, equipped, modified, competent.
(ANT.) deficient, inept, impotent, categorical, unlimited, unfitted, unfit, incapable, unsuitable, inadequate.
qualify *(SYN.)* fit, suit, befit, ready, prepare, empower, lessen, moderate, soften, capacitate, condition, adapt, label, designate, name, call, equip, train, restrict, restrict, limit, change.
(ANT.) unfit, incapacitate, disable, disqualify, enlarge, reinforce, aggravate.
quality *(SYN.)* trait, feature, attribute, value, peculiarity, grade, caliber, character, distinction, rank, condition, status, characteristic, kind, nature, constitution, mark, type, property.
(ANT.) nature, inferiority, mediocrity, triviality, indifference, inferior, shoddy, second-rate, being, substance, essence.
qualm *(SYN.)* doubt, uneasiness, anxiety, suspicion, skepticism, question, pang, compunction, twinge, regret, uncertainty, demur, fear, remorse, misgiving.
(ANT.) security, comfort, confidence, easiness, invulnerability, firmness.
quandary *(SYN.)* predicament, perplexity, confusion, uncertainty, puzzle, plight, bewilderment, fix, difficulty, entanglement, impasse, doubt, dilemma.

(ANT.) ease, relief, certainty, assurance.

quantity *(SYN.)* sum, measure, volume, content, aggregate, bulk, mass, portion, amount, number, multitude, extent.
(ANT.) zero, nothing.

quarantine *(SYN.)* segregate, separate, confine, isolate, seclude.

quarrel *(SYN.)* contention, argument, affray, dispute, altercation, squabble, feud, difference, disagree, bicker, differ, spar, fight, bickering, tiff, argue, disagreement, spat.
(ANT.) peace, friendliness, reconciliation, amity, agreement, sympathy, accord, concur, support, agree, unity, harmony.

quarrelsome *(SYN.)* testy, contentious, edgy, peevish, irritable, snappish, argumentative, disputatious, cranky, belligerent, combative, disagreeable.
(ANT.) genial, friendly, peaceful, easygoing, peaceable, tempered.

quarry *(SYN.)* prey, quest, game, victim, goal, aim, prize, objective.

quarter *(SYN.)* place, source, fount, well, origin, mainspring, ruth, mercy, pity, compassion, clemency, spring, benevolence, forbearance.
(ANT.) ruthlessness, brutality, cruelty, barbarity, harshness, ferocity.

quarters *(SYN.)* residence, rooms, lodgings, dwelling, flat, billets, chambers, accommodations.

quash *(SYN.)* void, annul, overthrow, nullify, suppress, cancel, quench, quell, repress, invalidate.
(ANT.) reinforce, sustain, authorize, sanction, validate, incite.

quasi *(SYN.)* would-be, partial, synthetic, nominal, imitation, bogus, sham, counterfeit, mock.
(ANT.) certified, real, legitimate.

quaver *(SYN.)* tremble, shake, hesitate, trill, oscillate, waver, vibrate, shiver, quiver, falter, quake.

quay *(SYN.)* dock, wharf, pier, jetty, bank.

queasy *(SYN.)* sick, squeamish, nauseated, uneasy, queer, restless, nauseous, uncomfortable.
(ANT.) untroubled, comfortable, easy, relaxed.

queen *(SYN.)* empress, diva, doyenne, goddess, star.

queer *(SYN.)* odd, quaint, curious, unusual, droll, strange, peculiar, extraordinary, singular, uncommon, eccentric, weird, funny, nutty, screwy, wacky, deviant, whimsical.
(ANT.) familiar, usual, normal, common, commonplace, plain, patent, conventional, ordinary.

queerness *(SYN.)* oddity, oddness, freakishness, strangeness, singularity, outlandishness, anomaly, weirdness.
(ANT.) normality, familiarity, commonness, standardization.

quell *(SYN.)* subdue, calm, pacify, quiet, cool, hush, appease, lull, mollify, reduce, crush, smother, suppress, stifle, extinguish.
(ANT.) encourage, foment, arouse, foster, incite.

quench *(SYN.)* extinguish, stop, suppress, sate, allay, abate, stifle, slacken, put out, slake, satisfy.
(ANT.) set, light, begin, start, kindle.

querulous *(SYN.)* faultfinding, fretful, carping, critical, complaining, censorious, captious, petulant.
(ANT.) pleased, easygoing, contented, carefree.

query *(SYN.)* inquire, interrogate, demand, investigate, probe, examine, question, inquiry, ask.
(ANT.) answer.

quest *(SYN.)* investigation, interrogation, research, examination, search, question, exploration, seek, pursue, journey, hunt, pursuit, explore, query.
(ANT.) negligence, inactivity, disregard.

question *(SYN.)* interrogate, quiz, doubt, ask, pump, challenge, inquiry, uncertainty, interview, suspect, inquire, dispute, demand, examine, query.
(ANT.) accept, solution, reply, assurance, rejoinder, state, answer, result, response, attest, avow, confidence, respond.

questionable *(SYN.)* uncertain, doubtful, dubious, implausible, debatable, hypothetical, unlikely.
(ANT.) obvious, assured, indubitable, proper, unimpeachable, seemly, conventional, sure, certain.

queue *(SYN.)* file, row, line, series, chain, tier, sequence, string.

quibble *(SYN.)* cavil, shift, evasion, equivocation, dodge, sophism, prevaricate, quiddity, palter.

quick *(SYN.)* rapid, touchy, shrewd, active, hasty, testy, nimble, irascible, discerning, fast, swift, precipitate, excitable, speedy, sharp, impatient, acute, abrupt, curt, brisk, clever, keen, sensitive, lively.
(ANT.) inattentive, dull, gradual, patient, slow, unaware, unhurried, backward, deliberate, sluggish.

quicken *(SYN.)* expedite, forward, rush, hurry, accelerate, push, hasten, dispatch, facilitate, speed.
(ANT.) slow, impede, hinder, hamper, delay, kill, deaden, retard, block.

quickly *(SYN.)* soon, rapidly, fast, at once, promptly, presently, swiftly, hastily, fleety, headlong.
(ANT.) deliberately, slowly, later, gradually.

quickness *(SYN.)* energy, vigor, intensity, action, movement, briskness, exercise, motion, rapidity, agility, enterprise.
(ANT.) sloth, idleness, inertia, dullness.

quick-witted *(SYN.)* astute, shrewd, alert, keen, penetrating, quick, knowing, intelligent, clever.
(ANT.) slow, dull, unintelligent, plodding.

quiescent *(SYN.)* latent, resting, silent, tranquil, undeveloped, still, quiet, dormant, secret, unseen, inactive.
(ANT.) visible, aroused, evident, active, patent, astir, manifest.

quiet *(SYN.)* meek, passive, hushed, peaceful, calm, patient, quiescent, motionless, tranquil, gentle, undisturbed, mild, peace, silent, quiescence, hush, modest, quietude, rest, tranquillity, calmness, repose, silence, placid, serenity, soundless, immobile, still.
(ANT.) disturbed, agitation, excitement, loud, disturbance, restless, noisy, boisterous, anxious, perturbed, noise, agitated.
quietness *(SYN.)* tranquillity, repose, calm, silence, quietude, calmness, stillness, quietism, muteness, noiselessness, placidity, seclusion, soundlessness.
(ANT.) flurry, disturbance, fuss, turbulence, agitation, uproar, tumult.
quintessence *(SYN.)* heart, soul, extract, essence, distillation, core.
(ANT.) contingency, adjunct, excrescence, nonessential.
quip *(SYN.)* jest, sally, wisecrack, witticism, joke, jibe, pleasantry.
quirk *(SYN.)* mannerism, idiosyncrasy, foible, peculiarity, oddity, quiddity, vagary, habit, trait, eccentricity.
quirky *(SYN.)* odd, weird, whimsical, pe-cuiar, pixilated, erratic, kinky.
(ANT.) normal, conventional, steady.
quisling *(SYN.)* collaborationist, traitor, subversive, betrayer.
(ANT.) partisan, loyalist.
quit *(SYN.)* leave, stop, desist, depart, abandon, resign, withdraw, refrain, retreat, cease, vacate, end, relinquish, discontinue, halt, lay off, surrender.
(ANT.) persevere, remain, stay, endure, persist, abide, continue.
quite *(SYN.)* somewhat, rather, completely, truly, absolutely, really, entirely.
(ANT.) hardly, merely, barely, somewhat.
quitter *(SYN.)* shirker, dropout, defeatist, piker, loser, malingerer.
quiver *(SYN.)* quake, shake, shudder, tremble, vibrate, shiver.
quixotic *(SYN.)* unrealistic, romantic, visionary, impractical, idealistic, chimerical, lofty, fantastic, fey.
(ANT.) pragmatic, realistic, prosaic, practical.
quiz *(SYN.)* challenge, interrogate, inquire, pump, doubt, question, ask, dispute, test, query, examine.
(ANT.) reply, say, inform, respond, accept, answer, state.
quizzical *(SYN.)* teasing, coy, mocking, derisive, insolent, arch, bantering, puzzled, questioning, baffled.
(ANT.) respectful, obsequious, uninterested, normal, everyday, usual, serious, attentive.
quota *(SYN.)* share, portion, apportionment, ratio, proportion, allotment.
quotation *(SYN.)* quote, selection, excerpt, repetition, cutting, reference.
quote *(SYN.)* refer to, recite, paraphrase, adduce, repeat, illustrate, cite, echo, plagiarize.
(ANT.) retort, contradict, refute.

rabble *(SYN.)* throng, mob, horde, crowd.
rabid *(SYN.)* frantic, frenzied, violent, raging, raving, zealous, fanatical.
(ANT.) normal, sound, sober, moderate.
race *(SYN.)* meet, run, clan, stock, lineage, strain, match, course, stream, hasten, compete, folk, competition, dash, contest, contend, hurry, speed, tribe.
(ANT.) linger, dawdle, dwell.
rack *(SYN.)* frame, framework, bracket, scaffold, skeleton.
racket *(SYN.)* sound, cry, babel, noise, uproar, hubbub, clamor, fuss, disturbance, din, tumult, fracas, clatter.
(ANT.) stillness, hush, silence, quiet, tranquillity, peace.
racy *(SYN.)* interesting, vigorous, lively, spirited, animated, entertaining.
radiance *(SYN.)* luster, brilliancy, brightness, splendor, effulgence, glowing.
(ANT.) gloom, darkness, obscurity.
radiant *(SYN.)* showy, superb, brilliant, illustrious, dazzling, grand, shining, bright, effulgent, beaming, sumptuous.
(ANT.) dark, unimpressive, dull, dim, lusterless, ordinary.
radiate *(SYN.)* spread, emit, diffuse, shed, irradiate, shine, gleam, illuminate.
radical *(SYN.)* ultra, innate, essential, organic, complete, revolutionary, insurgent, natural, total, fundamental, extreme, basic, original, thorough.
(ANT.) extraneous, moderate, conservative, superficial, shallow, established.
radius *(SYN.)* orbit, reach, extent, scope, sphere, range, sweep.
raft *(SYN.)* pontoon, platform, float.
rag *(SYN.)* dishcloth, dishrag, cloth.
ragamuffin *(SYN.)* tatterdemalion, wretch, beggar, vagabond, mendicant.
rage *(SYN.)* passion, ire, exasperation, fashion, fad, vogue, craze, anger, temper, fury, irritation, mania, rave, rant, storm, fume, overflow, wrath.
(ANT.) peace, forbearance, conciliation, patience.
raging *(SYN.)* raving, severe, passionate, boisterous, violent, fierce, wild, passionate, acute, intense, powerful.
(ANT.) feeble, soft, calm, quiet.
ragged *(SYN.)* tattered, torn, worn, shredded, seedy, threadbare, shabby.
raid *(SYN.)* assault, attack, invasion, arrest, invade, seizure, maraud, foray.
rail *(SYN.)* railing, fence, bar.
railing *(SYN.)* balustrade, banister, barrier, fence.
rain *(SYN.)* shower, drizzle, rainstorm, sprinkle, deluge, down-pour.
raise *(SYN.)* grow, muster, elevate, heave, cultivate, awake, rouse, excite, enlarge, increase, rise, breed, hoist, bring up, rear, gather, exalt, lift.
(ANT.) destroy, decrease, lessen, cut, depreciate, lower, abase, debase, drop, demolish, level.
rakish *(SYN.)* dapper, dashing, smart, debonair, natty, swanky, showy.
rally *(SYN.)* muster, convoke, summon,

convene, convention, assemblage.
ramble *(SYN.)* err, amble, saunter, wander, roam, saunter, walk, deviate, stroll, digress, stray.
(ANT.) stop, linger, stay, halt, settle.
rambling *(SYN.)* incoherent, erratic.
(ANT.) straightfoward, coherent.
rambunctious *(SYN.)* stubborn, defiant, unruly, aggressive, contrary.
ramification *(SYN.)* aftermath, extension, branch, offshoot, result, consequence.
rampage *(SYN.)* tumult, outbreak, uproar, rage, frenzy, ebullition, storm.
rampant *(SYN.)* excessive, flagrant, boisterous, menacing.
(ANT.) bland, calm, mild.
ramshackle *(SYN.)* rickety, decrepit, flimsy, dilapidated, shaky.
rancid *(SYN.)* spoiled, rank, tainted, sour, musty, putrid, rotten, purtrescent.
(ANT.) pure, fresh, wholesome, fragrant.
rancor *(SYN.)* spite, grudge, malice, animosity, malevolence, hostility.
(ANT.) kindness, toleration, affection.
random *(SYN.)* haphazard, chance, unscheduled, unplanned, casual.
(ANT.) intentional, specific, particular.
range *(SYN.)* expanse, extent, limit, area, grassland, pasture, plain, change, wander, roam, travel, rove.
rank *(SYN.)* estate, blood, range, grade, standing, hue, eminence, level, class, order, classify, dense, wild, rotten, degree, standing, arrange, sort, row.
(ANT.) shame, disrepute, stigma, humiliation.
ransack *(SYN.)* pillage, loot, rummage, plunder, despoil, ravish, search.
ransom *(SYN.)* release, deliverance, compensation, redeem.
rant *(SYN.)* declaim, rave, harangue.
rap *(SYN.)* thump, knock, blow, whack.
rapacious *(SYN.)* greedy, wolfish, avaricious, ravenous, grasping, predatory.
rapid *(SYN.)* speedy, quick, swift, fast.
(ANT.) deliberate, halting, sluggish, slow.
rapidity *(SYN.)* motion, enterprise, action, vigor, liveliness, activity, quickness, exercise, energy.
(ANT.) sloth, dullness, inertia, idleness.
rapine *(SYN.)* destruction, pillage, robbery, marauding, spoiling.
rapport *(SYN.)* harmony, fellowship, agreement, mutuality, accord, empathy.
rapture *(SYN.)* joy, gladness, ecstasy, bliss, transport, exultation, delight, happiness, enchantment, ravishment.
(ANT.) woe, misery, wretch, depression.
rare *(SYN.)* unique, strange, precious, uncommon, infrequent, choice, singular, occasional, unusual, fine, matchless, undone, incomparable, scarce.
(ANT.) worthless, common, commonplace, usual, everyday, customary.
rarely *(SYN.)* scarcely, hardly infrequently, occasionally, sparingly, barely.
(ANT.) usually, continually, often.
rascal *(SYN.)* scoundrel, villain, trickster, rogue, scamp, swindler, imp, prankster.
rash *(SYN.)* quick, careless, passionate, thoughtless, hotheaded, reckless, foolhardy, eruption, dermatitis, heedless.
(ANT.) thoughtful, considered, prudent, reasoning, calculating, careful.
raspy *(SYN.)* gruff, harsh, dissonant, grinding, hoarse, grating, strident.
rate *(SYN.)* try, adjudicate, consider, decide, condemn, decree, estimate, speed, pace, measure, judge, arbitrate, velocity, ratio, evaluate, evaluate.
ratify *(SYN.)* validate, certify, confirm, establish, support, endorse, uphold.
rating *SYN.)* assessment, position, assignment, status, classification.
ration *(SYN.)* portion, allowance, distribute, measure, allotment, share, percentage.
rational *(SYN.)* sound, wise, sane, intelligent, sober, sensible, judicious, sober.
(ANT.) irrational, absurd, insane.
rationality *(SYN.)* cause, aim, intelligence, reason, basis, understanding, ground, argument, mind, sense.
raucous *(SYN.)* raspy, harsh, grating, hoarse, discordant, rowdy.
(ANT.) dulcet, pleasant, sweet.
ravage *(SYN.)* ruin, despoil, strip, waste, destroy, pillage, plunder, sack, havoc.
(ANT.) conserve, save, accumulate.
rave *(SYN.)* rage, storm, laud, praise.
ravenous *(SYN.)* hungry, voracious, craving, starved, gluttonous, famished.
(ANT.) replete, gorged, satiated, full.
ravine *(SYN.)* chasm, gorge, crevasse, canyon, abyss.
ravish *(SYN.)* violate, debauch.
ravishing *(SYN.)* enchanting, captivating, bewitching, fascinating, alluring.
(ANT.) loathsome, disgusting, repulsive.
raw *(SYN.)* harsh, rough, coarse, unrefined, undone, uncooked, unprocessed, crude, unpolished, natural.
(ANT.) finished, refined, processed.
ray *(SYN.)* beam.
raze *(SYN.)* ravage, wreck, destroy, flatten, annihilate, obliterate, demolish.
(ANT.) make, erect, construct, preserve, establish, save.
reach *(SYN.)* overtake, arrive at, extent, distance, scope, range, extend, attain, stretch.
(ANT.) fail, miss.
react *(SYN.)* result, reply, respond.
(ANT.) overlook, disregard.
reaction *(SYN.)* result, response, reception, repercussion.
readable *(SYN.)* understandable, distinct, legible, plain, clear, comprehensible.
(ANT.) obliterated, illegible, defaced.
readily *(SYN.)* quickly, promptly, easily.
ready *(SYN.)* mature, ripe, complete, seasonable, done, arrange, prompt, prepared, completed, quick, mellow.
(ANT.) undeveloped, immature, green.
real *(SYN.)* true, actual, positive, authentic, genuine, veritable.

(ANT.) counterfeit, unreal, fictitious, false, sham, supposed.
realization *(SYN.)* completion, achievement, performance, accomplishment, comprehension, insight.
(ANT.) failure.
realize *(SYN.)* discern, learn, comprehend, appreciate, perfect, actualize, understand, apprehend, know, see.
(ANT.) misunderstand, misapprehend.
really *(SYN.)* truly, actually, honestly, undoubtedly, positively, genuinely.
ANT.) questionably, possibly, doubtfully.
realm *(SYN.)* land, domain, farm, kingdom, sphere, department, estate, world.
reap *(SYN.)* gather, harvest, gain, glean, produce, cul, pick, acquire, garner.
(ANT.) plant, seed, sow, lose, squander.
reaping *(SYN.)* proceeds, result, crop, yield, fruit, produce.
rear *(SYN.)* posterior, raise, lift, train, nurture, rump, back, elevate, construct, build, foster.
reason *(SYN.)* intelligence, objective, understanding, mind, aim, argument, cause, aim, judgment, common sense, sanity, gather, assume, sake, motive.
reasonable *(SYN.)* prudent, rational, logical, sage, sound, moderate, intelligent, sensible, discreet.
(ANT.) unaware, imperceptible, insane, absurd, stupid, illogical, irrational.
rebel *(SYN.)* revolutionary, traitor, mutineer, mutiny, revolt, disobey.
rebellion *(SYN.)* revolt, uprising, coup, overthrow, insurrection, revolution.
(ANT.) submission, obedience, repression, peace.
rebellious *(SYN.)* unruly, forward, defiant, undutiful, disobedient.
(ANT.) obedient, compliant, submissive.
rebirth *(SYN.)* renascence, renaissance, revival.
rebuff *(SYN.)* snub, oppose, resist, reject, refuse, slight, opposition.
(ANT.) welcome, encourage, support.
rebuild *(SYN.)* restore, renew, refresh, reconstruct, renovate.
rebuke *(SYN.)* chide, scold, reproach, censure, upbraid, scolding, condemn.
(ANT.) praise, exonerate, absolve.
rebuttal *(SYN.)* contradiction, defense, answer.
(ANT.) argument, validation, corroboration.
recall *(SYN.)* recollect, remembrance, withdraw, retract, remember, recollection, reminisce, mind, memory, remind.
(ANT.) forget, overlook, ignore.
recede *(SYN.)* withdraw, ebb, retire, retreat.
receive *(SYN.)* entertain, acquire, admit, accept, shelter, greet, obtain, welcome.
(ANT.) reject, offer, give, bestow, discharge, impart.
recent *(SYN.)* novel, original, late, new, newfangled, fresh, modern, current.
(ANT.) old, antiquated, ancient.
reception *(SYN.)* gathering, party.
recess *(SYN.)* hollow, opening, nook, cranny, dent, respite, rest, break, pause.
(ANT.) gather, convene.
recession *(SYN.)* slump, depression.
recipe *(SYN.)* instructions, formula, prescriptions, procedure, method.
recital *(SYN.)* history, account, relation, chronicle, narrative, detail, narration.
(ANT.) distortion, confusion, misrepresentation.
recite *(SYN.)* describe, narrate, declaim, rehearse, tell, mention, repeat, detail, recapitulate, report, list, relate, deliver.
reckless *(SYN.)* thoughtless, inconsiderate, careless, imprudent, rash, indiscreet, unconcerned.
(ANT.) careful, nice, accurate.
reclaim *(SYN.)* reform, rescue, reinstate, regenerate, recycle.
recline *(SYN.)* stretch, sprawl, repose, rest, lounge, loll, incline.
recluse *(SYN.)* hermit, eremite, loner, anchorite.
recognize *(SYN.)* remember, avow, own, know, admit, apprehend, recollect, recall, concede, acknowledge, confess.
(ANT.) disown, ignore, renounce.
recollect *(SYN.)* recall, remember,, memory, reflect, call to mind, reminisce.
(ANT.) forget.
recollection *(SYN.)* remembrance, retrospection, impression, recall.
(ANT.) forgetfulness, oblivion.
recommend *(SYN.)* hind, refer, advise, commend, suggest, counsel, allude, praise, approve, intimate, advocate.
(ANT.) disapprove, declare, insist.
recommendation *(SYN.)* instruction, justice, trustworthiness, counsel, admonition, caution, integrity, uprightness.
(ANT.) fraud, deceit, trickery, cheating.
reconcile *(SYN.)* meditate, unite, adapt, adjust, settle, reunite, appease.
recondition *(SYN.)* rebuild, overhaul, restore, service.
reconsider *(SYN.)* ponder, reevaluate, mull over, reflect, reassess.
record *(SYN.)* enter, write, register, chronicle, history, account, document.
recount *(SYN.)* report, convey, narrate, tell, detail, recite, describe, repeat.
recoup *(SYN.)* regain, recover, repay, retrieve.
recover *(SYN.)* regain, redeem, recapture, retrieve, salvage, better, improve, mend, heal.
(ANT.) debilitate, succumb, worsen.
recreation *(SYN.)* entertainment, amusement, enjoyment, diversion, fun.
recrimination *(SYN.)* vindication, reproach, dissension, accusation, countercharge.
recruit *(SYN.)* trainee, beginner, volunteer, draftee, select, enlist, novice.
recuperate *(SYN.)* regain, retrieve, cure, recapture, redeem, rally, convalesce, revive, recover, repossess, restore.
(ANT.) sicken, weaken, lose, regress, forfeit.
redeem *(SYN.)* claim, recover, repossess, regain, reclaim, cash in, retrieve.

reduce *(SYN.)* lessen, decrease, lower, downgrade, degrade, suppress, lower, abate, diminish.
(ANT.) enlarge, swell, raise, elevate, revive, increase, amplify.
reduction *(SYN.)* shortening, abridgment, abbreviation.
(ANT.) amplification, extension, enlargement.
reek *(SYN.)* odor, stench, stink, smell.
refer *(SYN.)* recommend, direct, commend, regard, concern, relate, suggest, mention.
referee *(SYN.)* judge, arbitrator, umpire, arbiter, moderator, mediator, intermediary.
reference *(SYN.)* allusion, direction, mention, concern, respect, referral.
refine *(SYN.)* purify, clarify, improve, clean.
(ANT.) pollute, debase, muddy, downgrade.
refined *(SYN.)* purified, cultured, cultivated, courteous, courtly.
(ANT.) rude, coarse, crude, vulgar.
refinement *(SYN.)* culture, enlightenment, education, civilization.
(ANT.) vulgarity, ignorance, boorishness.
reflect *(SYN.)* muse, mirror, deliberate, cogitate, think, reproduce, ponder, consider, reason, meditate, contemplate.
reflection *(SYN.)* warning, conception, intelligence, appearance, likeness, image, cogitation, notification.
reform *(SYN.)* right, improve, correction, change, amend, improvement, better, betterment, correct, rectify.
(ANT.) spoil, damage, aggravate, vitiate.
refresh *(SYN.)* exhilarate, renew, invigorate.
(ANT.) exhaust, tire.
refreshing *(SYN.)* bracing, cool, brisk, fresh.
refreshment *(SYN.)* food, snack, drink, nourishment, exhilaraton, stimulation.
refuge *(SYN.)* safety, retreat, shelter, asylum, sanctuary, harbor.
(ANT.) peril, exposure, jeopardy, danger.
refuse *(SYN.)* spurn, rebuff, decline, reject, trash, rubbish, withhold, disallow, waste, garbage, deny, demur.
(ANT.) allow, accept, welcome, grant.
refute *(SYN.)* rebut, disprove, confute, falsify, controvert, contradict.
(ANT.) prove, confirm, accept, establish.
regain *(SYN.)* redeem, retrieve, recover, repossess, recapture.
(ANT.) lose.
regalement *(SYN.)* feast, dinner, celebration, entertainment.
regard *(SYN.)* estimate, value, honor, affection, notice, care, consideration, consider, relation, respect, attend, thought, reference, care, attention, esteem, concern, liking.
(ANT.) neglect, disgust, antipathy.
regards *(SYN.)* salutations, greetings, good wishes, respects, remembrances.
regenerate *(SYN.)* improve, reconstruct, remedy, reestablish, rebuild.
regime *(SYN.)* direction, government, administration, management, dynasty, command, leadership.
regimented *(SYN.)* ordered, directed controlled, orderly, rigid, disciplined.
(ANT.) loose, free, unstructured.
region *(SYN.)* belt, place, spot, territory, climate, area, zone, locality, station, locale.
register *(SYN.)* catalog, record, book, list, roll, enter, roster, chronicle.
regressive *(SYN.)* revisionary, retrograde.
(ANT.) progressive, civilized, advanced.
regret *(SYN.)* sorrow, qualm, lament, grief, compunction, bemoan, concern, scruple, misgiving, remorse, contrition.
(ANT.) obduracy, complacency.
regular *(SYN.)* steady, orderly, natural, normal, customary, usual, habitual, even, uniform, systematic, unvaried, methodical, symmetrical.
(ANT.) odd, exceptional, unusual, irregular, abnormal, rare.
regulate *(SYN.)* control, manage, govern, direct, legislate, set, adjust, systematize.
regulation *(SYN.)* method, rule, axiom, guide, control, standard, canon, precept, restraint, requirement.
(ANT.) chaos, deviation, hazard, turbulence, confusion.
rehabilitate *(SYN.)* renew, restore, rebuild, reestablish, repair, reconstruct.
rehearse *(SYN.)* repeat, practice, train, learn, coach, prepare, perfect, direct.
reign *(SYN.)* dominion, power, rule, sovereignty, govern, domination.
reimburse *(SYN.)* recompense, remunerate, compensate, remit.
rein *(SYN.)* restriction, bridle, check, deterrent, curb, restraint, barrier, control.
reinforce *(SYN.)* brace, strengthen, fortify, intensify, support.
reiterate *(SYN.)* reproduce, recapitulate, duplicate, repeat, rephrase.
reject *(SYN.)* spurn, rebuff, decline, renounce, expel, discard, withhold, deny, refuse.
(ANT.) endorse, grant, welcome, accept.
rejection *(SYN.)* dissent, nonconformity, variance, challenge, remonstrance, difference, noncompliance.
(ANT.) assent, acceptance, compliance.
rejoice *(SYN.)* celebrate, delight, enjoy, revel, exhilarate, elate.
rejuvenate *(SYN.)* refresh, rekindle, overhaul, revitalize, animate, invigorate.
(ANT.) deplete, weaken, exhaust, eneverate.
relapse *(SYN.)* worsen, deteriorate, regress, weaken, fade, worsen, sink fail.
(ANT.) strengthen, progress, advance, get well, rehabilitate.
relate *(SYN.)* refer, beat, report, describe, tell, correlate, narrate,

recount, compare, connect.
relation *(SYN.)* entente, compact, coalition, alliance, connection, relationship, association, partnership, similarity, kinsman, treaty, marriage.
(ANT.) separation, divorce.
relationship *(SYN.)* link, tie, alliance, connection, union, bond, affinity, conjunction.
(ANT.) separation, disunion.
relative *(SYN.)* dependent, proportional, about, pertinent, regarding.
relax *(SYN.)* slacken, loosen, repose, rest, recline, unwind.
(ANT.) increase, tighten, intensify.
relaxation *(SYN.)* comfort, ease, rest, enjoyment, lull, recess, breather, loafing.
relaxed *(SYN.)* welcome, pleasing, casual, acceptable, informal, restful, agreeable.
(ANT.) formal, planned, wretched, distressing, troubling.
release *(SYN.)* liberate, emancipate, relinquish, proclaim, publish, liberation, announce, deliver, free, discharge.
(ANT.) restrict, imprison, subjugate.
relegate *(SYN.)* entrust, authorize, remand, refer, assign.
relent *(SYN.)* cede, yield, surrender, give, relax, abdicate, relinquish, waive.
(ANT.) strive, assert, struggle.
relentless *(SYN.)* eternal, stubborn, tenacious, dogged, ceaseless, incessant, ceaseless, persistent, determined.
relevant *(SYN.)* related, material, apt, applicable, fit, relating, germane.
(ANT.) foreign, alien, unrelated.
reliable *(SYN.)* trusty, tried, certain, secure, trustworthy, dependable.
(ANT.) unreliable, eccentric, questionable, erratic, dubious.
reliance *(SYN.)* faith, confidence, trust.
(ANT.) mistrust, doubt, skepticism.
relic *(SYN.)* remains, fossil, throwback, heirloom, souvenir, keepsake, heirloom.
relief *(SYN.)* help, aid, comfort, ease, backing, patronage, alms, support.
(ANT.) hostility, defiance, antagonism, resistance.
relieve *(SYN.)* diminish, soothe, calm, abate, pacify, ease, lessen, replace, spell, lighten, comfort, alleviate.
(ANT.) disturb, irritate, agitate, trouble, aggravate, worry.
religion *(SYN.)* tenet, belief, dogma, faith, creed, persuasion.
religious *(SYN.)* godly, reverent, faithful, devout, zeal, pious, divine, holy, devoted, sacred, theological.
(ANT.) profane, irreligious, skeptical, impious, lax, atheistic.
religiousness *(SYN.)* love, zeal, affection, devoutness, fidelity, ardor.
(ANT.) indifference, apathy, unfaithfulness.
relinquish *(SYN.)* capitulate, submit, yield, abandon, cede, sacrifice, disclaim.
(ANT.) overcome, conquer, rout, resist.
relish *(SYN.)* enjoyment, satisfaction, delight, gusto, appreciation, condiment, like, enjoy, enthusiasm.
(ANT.) distaste, antipathy, disfavor, dislike.
reluctance *(SYN.)* disgust, hatred, repulsion, abhorrence, distaste, repugnance, aversion.
(ANT.) enthusiasm, affection, devotion.
reluctant *(SYN.)* slow, averse, hesitant, unwilling, loath, disinclined, balky.
(ANT.) ready, eager, willing, disposed.
rely *(SYN.)* confide, trust, lean, depend.
(ANT.) mistrust, disbelieve, question, distrust.
remain *(SYN.)* survive, rest, stay, abide, halt, endure, dwell, tarry, continue, linger.
(ANT.) finish, leave, terminate, dissipate.
remainder *(SYN.)* leftover, residue, rest, surplus, balance, excess.
remains *(SYN.)* residue, balance, rest, remnants, relics, discards, waste, junk.
remark *(SYN.)* comment, state, utterance, mention, note, observe, observation, annotation, declaration, statement.
remarkable *(SYN.)* exciting, impressive, overpowering, unusual, affecting, thrilling, splendid, special, noteworthy, extraordinary, touching, august.
(ANT.) ordinary, unimpressive, commonplace, average, regular.
remedy *(SYN.)* redress, help, cure, relief, medicine, restorative, rectify, alleviate, medication, correct, reparation.
remember *(SYN.)* recollect, reminisce, recall, memorize, mind, retain, remind.
(ANT.) forget, overlook, disregard.
remembrance *(SYN.)* monument, memory, recollection, memento, recall, keepsake, souvenir, retrospection.
remiss *(SYN.)* delinquent, lax, careless, negligent, oblivious, forgetful, absentminded, sloppy, irresponsible.
remit *(SYN.)* send, pay, forward, forgive, pardon, overlook, excuse, reimburse.
remittance *(SYN.)* payment.
remnant *(SYN.)* remains, remainder, rest, residue, trace, relic.
remodel *(SYN.)* remake, reshape, rebuild, redecorate, renovate, modify, change, alter, convert, refurbish, update.
remonstrate *(SYN.)* grouch, protest, complain, grumble, murmur, repine, dispute.
(ANT.) rejoice, applaud, praise.
remorse *(SYN.)* sorrow, qualm, contrition, regret, compunction, repentance.
(ANT.) obduracy, complacency.
remorseless *(SYN.)* savage, unrelenting, crude, barbaric, merciless, cruel, fiendish, brutal, callous.
(ANT.) kind, refined, polite, civilized.
remote *(SYN.)* inconsiderable, removed, slight, far, unlikely, distant, inaccessible, unreachable, isolated, sequestered.

(ANT.) visible, nearby, current, near, close.

remove *(SYN.)* transport, eject, move, vacate, withdraw, dislodge, transfer, doff, displace, eliminate, murder, kill, oust, extract.
(ANT.) insert, retain, leave, stay, keep.

removed *(SYN.)* aloof, distant, cool, remote.

remuneration *(SYN.)* wages, payment, pay, salary, compensation, reimbursement, reward.

render *(SYN.)* become, make, perform, do, offer, present, give, submit.

rendition *(SYN.)* interpretation, version, depiction, expression, characterization.

renegade *(SYN.)* defector, insurgent, dissenter, rebel, maverick, mutineer, betrayer.

renege *(SYN.)* let down, doublecross, deceive.

renew *(SYN.)* restore, renovate, overhaul, revise, modernize, reshape, redo.

renounce *(SYN.)* resign, disown, revoke, abandon, quit, retract, forgo, leave, forsake, abdicate, reject, relinquish, deny.
(ANT.) assert, uphold, recognize, maintain.

renovate *(SYN.)* restore, rehabilitate, rebuild, refresh, renew, overhaul, redesign.

renown *(SYN.)* honor, reputation, eminence, acclaim, glory, repute, luster, fame, notability.
(ANT.) obscurity, anonymity, disgrace.

renowned *(SYN.)* noted, famous, distinguished, well-known, glorious, celebrated.
(ANT.) unknown, infamous, hidden, obscure.

rent *(SYN.)* payment, rental, let, lease, hire.

repair *(SYN.)* rebuilding, mend, renew, tinker, correct, patch, restore, adjust, reconstruction, remedy, amend, rehabilitation, retrieve.
(ANT.) harm, break.

repartee *(SYN.)* badinage, banter.

repast *(SYN.)* feast, banquet, meal, refreshment, snack.

repeal *(SYN.)* end, cancel, nullify, annul, quash, abolish, cancellation, rescind, abolition, abrogate.

repeat *(SYN.)* reiterate, restate, redo, rehearse, quote, remake, relate, iterate, reproduce.

repeated *(SYN.)* continuous, frequent, recurrent, continual.

repel *(SYN.)* check, repulse, rebuff, reject, decline, discourage.
(ANT.) lure, attract.

repellent *(SYN.)* sickening, offensive, disgusting, nauseating, repugnant, obnoxious.

repent *(SYN.)* deplore, regret, rue, lament.

repentance *(SYN.)* penitence, remorse, sorrow, compunction, qualm, grief.
(ANT.) obduracy, complacency.

repentant *(SYN.)* regretful, sorrowful, contrite, sorry, penitent.
(ANT.) remorseless, obdurate.

repetitious *(SYN.)* repeated, monotonous, boring, tiresome, humdrum.

repine *(SYN.)* protest, lament, complain, whine, regret, grouch, murmur, grumble.
(ANT.) rejoice, applaud, praise.

replace *(SYN.)* alternate, return, reinstate.

replacement *(SYN.)* understudy, proxy, second, alternate, substitute, replica, surrogate.

replenish *(SYN.)* store, pervade, fill, stock, occupy, supply.
(ANT.) empty, void, deplete, exhaust, drain.

replica *(SYN.)* reproduction, copy, exemplar, imitation, duplicate, facsimile.
(ANT.) prototype.

reply *(SYN.)* retort, rejoinder, answer, retaliate, respond, confirmation.
(ANT.) summoning, inquiry.

report *(SYN.)* declare, herald, publish, announce, summary, publish, advertise.
(ANT.) suppress, conceal, withhold, bury.

reporter *(SYN.)* journalist.

repose *(SYN.)* hush, quiet, tranquillity, rest, peace, slumber, calm, stillness, sleep, calmness, dormancy.
(ANT.) tumult, excitement, agitation.

reprehensible *(SYN.)* criminal, immoral, damnable, culpable, wrong, wicked.

represent *(SYN.)* picture, draw, delineate, portray, depict, denote, symbolize.
(ANT.) misrepresent, caricature.

representation *(SYN.)* effigy, film, likeness, portrait, print, scene, appearance, drawing, scene, view, cinema.

representative *(SYN.)* delegate, agent, substitute, surrogate.

repress *(SYN.)* limit, stop, check, bridle, curb, restrain, constrain, suppress.
(ANT.) loosen, aid, incite, liberate, encourage.

reprimand *(SYN.)* rate, scold, vituperate, berate, lecture, blame, admonish, upbraid.
(ANT.) praise, approve.

reproach *(SYN.)* defamation, dishonor, insult, profanation, abuse, disparagement, misuse, reviling.
(ANT.) respect, laudation, approval, plaudit.

reproduction *(SYN.)* replica, copy, exemplar, transcript, duplicate, photocopy.

reproof *(SYN.)* rebuke, punishment, blame, censure, disapproval, scorn, disdain, admonition.

repugnance *(SYN.)* disgust, hatred, reluctance, abhorrence, aversion, loathing, antipathy, distaste, repulsion.
(ANT.) devotion, affection, enthusiasm, attachment.

repulsive *(SYN.)* repellent, ugly, homely, deformed, horrid, offensive, plain, uncomely.
(ANT.) fair, pretty, attractive, hand-

some.

reputable *(SYN.)* honest, upstanding, trustworthy, straightforward, upright, reliable.
(ANT.) notorious, corrupt, disreputable.

reputation *(SYN.)* class, nature, standing, name, fame, kind, renown, prominence, character, distinction, disposition, repute.

repute *(SYN.)* class, nature, standing, kind, character, reputation, disposition, sort.

request *(SYN.)* sue, implore, petition, desire, appeal, question, entreaty, beseech, ask, pray, supplicate.
(ANT.) require.

require *(SYN.)* exact, need, order, command, order, lack, claim, demand, want.

requirement *(SYN.)* demand, need, necessity, condition, provision, prerequisite.

requisite *(SYN.)* vital, necessary, basic, fundamental, indispensable, essential, needed.
(ANT.) casual, nonessential, peripheral, accidental.

rescind *(SYN.)* annul, quash, revoke, abolish, invalidate, abrogate, withdraw.

rescue *(SYN.)* liberate, ransom, release, deliver, deliverance, liberation.

research *(SYN.)* exploration, quest, scrutiny, exploration, interrogation, query, examination, study, investigation.
(ANT.) inattention, disregard, negligence.

resemblance *(SYN.)* parity, similitude, analogy, likeness, correspondence.
(ANT.) distinction, difference.

resemble *(SYN.)* duplicate, mirror, look like.

resentfulness *(SYN.)* envy, jealousy, covetousness, suspicion.
(ANT.) liberality, geniality, tolerance, difference.

resentment *(SYN.)* displeasure, bitterness, indignation, rancor, outrage, hostility.
(ANT.) complacency, understanding, good will.

reservation *(SYN.)* skepticism, restriction, objection, limitation, doubt.

reserve *(SYN.)* fund, hold, keep, store, accumulation, save, stock, maintain, supply.
(ANT.) waste, squander.

reserved *(SYN.)* cautious, fearful, timorous, wary, aloof, chary, sheepish, restrained, proper, unfriendly, bashful, diffident.
(ANT.) forward, bold, wild, immodest, brazen, abandoned, friendly.

reside *(SYN.)* inhabit, dwell, abide, live, lie.

residence *(SYN.)* home, dwelling, stay, seat, abode, quarters, domicile, living quarters.

residue *(SYN.)* balance, remainder, rest, ashes, remnants, dregs, leftovers, ends.

resign *(SYN.)* vacate, withdraw, leave, surrender, quit.

resignation *(SYN.)* perseverance, endurance, fortitude, composure, forbearance.
(ANT.) unquiet, nervousness, impatience.

resigned *(SYN.)* forbearing, stoical, assiduous, passive, accepting, composed, uncomplaining.
(ANT.) turbulent, chafing.

resilience *(SYN.)* rubbery, springy, buoyant, elasticity.
(ANT.) unresponsive, fixed, rigid, stolid.

resist *(SYN.)* defy, attack, withstand, hinder, confront, oppose.
(ANT.) relent, allow, yield, accede.

resolute *(SYN.)* firm, resolved, set, determined, decided.
(ANT.) irresolute, wavering, vacillating.

resolution *(SYN.)* resolve, courage, determination, persistence, statement, verdict, recommendation, decision, steadfastness, dedication, perseverance.
(ANT.) indecision, inconstancy.

resolve *(SYN.)* determination, resolution, courage, settle, decide, persistence, determine, confirm, decision, steadfastness.
(ANT.) integrate, indecision, inconstancy.

resort *(SYN.)* motel, lodge, hotel, solve.

resound *(SYN.)* echoe, ring, reverberate.

resource *(SYN.)* store, source, supply, reserve.

resourceful *(SYN.)* inventive, ingenious, creative, clever, imaginative, skillful.

respect *(SYN.)* honor, approval, revere, heed, value, admire, esteem, point, detail, admiration, reverence, regard, feature, particular, venerate, consider.
(ANT.) disrespect, neglect, abuse, scorn, disregard, despise.

respectable *(SYN.)* becoming, respected, proper, seemly, tolerable, decent, acceptable, fair, adequate, passable, suitable, honorable, valuable.
(ANT.) unsavory, vulgar, gross, disreputable, reprehensible.

respectful *(SYN.)* courteous, polite, well-behaved, well-bred, compliant, submssive.
(ANT.) disobedient, impertinent, rude, flippant.

respite *(SYN.)* deferment, adjounment, suspension.

respond *(SYN.)* rejoin, answer, reply, acknowledge, retort.
(ANT.) overlook, disregard.

response *(SYN.)* reply, acknowledgment, answer, retort, rejoinder.
(ANT.) summoning, inquiry.

responsibility *(SYN.)* duty, obligation, accountability, trust-worthiness, trust, liability, commitment.

responsible *(SYN.)* answerable, chargeable, trustworthy, liable, accountable, able, capable, upstanding, reliable, solid, indebted, creditable.
(ANT.) careless, free, negligent.

rest *(SYN.)* ease, intermission, calm, quiet, balance, surplus, repose, lounge, inactivity, motionlessness, immobility,

standstill, relax, remainder, excess, surplus, relaxation, slumber, peace, tranquillity, leisure.
(ANT.) tumult, commotion, motion, agitation.
restful *(SYN.)* peaceful, quiet, tranquil, calm.
(ANT.) tumultuous, upsetting, agitated, disturbed.
restitution *(SYN.)* recompense, satisfaction, refund, amends, retrieval.
restive *(SYN.)* balky, disobedient, fractious, impatient, unruly, fidgety, uneasy.
restless *(SYN.)* sleepless, unquiet, transient, active, agitated, disturbed, jumpy, nervous, uneasy, disquieted, irresolute.
(ANT.) quiet, tranquil, calm, peaceable.
restore *(SYN.)* repair, recover, rebuild, reestablish, renovate, return, renew, mend, reinstall, revive, rehabilitate, replace.
restrain *(SYN.)* limit, curb, constraint, stop, bridle, control, reserve, constrain, repress, check, suppress, hinder.
(ANT.) incite, aid, loosen.
restraint *(SYN.)* order, self-control, reserve, control, regulation, limitation, confinement.
(ANT.) freedom, liberty, confusion.
restrict *(SYN.)* fetter, restrain, confine, limit, engage, attach, connect, link, tie, bind.
(ANT.) broaden, enlarge, untie, loose, free.
restriction *(SYN.)* curb, handicap, check, boundary, ban, limitation, control, deterrent.
result *(SYN.)* effect, issue, outcome, resolve, end, consequence, happen, determination, conclusion, reward, aftermath.
(ANT.) cause, beginning, origin.
resume *(SYN.)* restart, continue, recommence, reassume.
resurgence *(SYN.)* rebirth, comeback, recovery, revival, resuscitation, rejuvenation, renewal.
resuscitate *(SYN.)* restore, revive, resurrect.
retain *(SYN.)* keep, hold, recall, remember, employ, hire, engage.
retainer *(SYN.)* aide, assistant, lackey, attendant, servant.
retaliate *(SYN.)* repay, revenge, return, avenge.
(ANT.) condone, forgive, overlook, excuse, forget.
retard *(SYN.)* detain, slacken, defer, impede, hold back, delay, postpone.
(ANT.) accelerate, speed, hasten, rush.
retention *(SYN.)* reservation, acquisition, holding, tenacity, possession.
reticent *(SYN.)* reserved, subdued, quiet, shy, withdrawn, restrained, bashful, silent.
(ANT.) outspoken, forward, opinionated.
retire *(SYN.)* resign, quit, abdicate, depart, vacate.
retiring *(SYN.)* timid, bashful, withdrawn, modest, reticent, quiet, reserved.
(ANT.) gregarious, assertive, bold.
retort *(SYN.)* reply, answer, response, respond, rejoin, rejoinder, retaliate.
(ANT.) summoning, inquiry.
retreat *(SYN.)* leave, depart, retire, withdraw, retirement, withdrawal, departure, shelter, refuge.
(ANT.) advanced.
retrench *(SYN.)* reduce, scrape, curtail.
retribution *(SYN.)* justice, vengeance, reprisal, punishment, comeuppance, vindictiveness, revenge, retaliation.
retrieve *(SYN.)* regain, recover, recapture, repossess, reclaim, salvage, recoup.
retrograde *(SYN.)* regressive, backward, declining, deteriorating, worsening.
(ANT.) onward, progression, advanced.
return *(SYN.)* restoration, replace, revert, recur, restore, retreat.
(ANT.) keep, take, retain.
reveal *(SYN.)* discover, publish, communicate, impart, uncover, tell, betray, divulge, disclose.
(ANT.) conceal, cover, obscure, cloak, hide.
revel *(SYN.)* rejoice, wallow, bask, enjoy, delight, savor, gloat, luxuriate, relish.
revenge *(SYN.)* vindictiveness, reprisal, requital, vengeance, repayment, repay, retribution, reparation.
(ANT.) reconcile, forgive, pity.
revenue *(SYN.)* take, proceeds, income, profit, return.
revere *(SYN.)* admire, honor, worship, respect, venerate, adore.
(ANT.) ignore, despise.
reverence *(SYN.)* glory, worship, homage, admiration, dignity, renown, respect, esteem, veneration, adoration.
(ANT.) dishonor, derision, reproach.
reverse *(SYN.)* overthrow, unmake rescind, opposite, invert, contrary, rear, back, misfortune, defeat, catastrophe, upset, countermand, revoke.
(ANT.) vouch, stabilize, endorse, affirm.
revert *(SYN.)* revive, relapse, backslide, rebound, retreat, recur, go back.
(ANT.) keep, take, appropriate.
review *(SYN.)* reconsideration, examination, commentary, retrospection.
revile *(SYN.)* defame, malign, vilify, abuse, traduce, asperse, scandalize.
(ANT.) honor, respect, cherish, protect.
revise *(SYN.)* change, alter, improve, correct, amend, update, rewrite, polish.
revision *(SYN.)* inspection, survey, retrospection, commentary, critique.
revival *(SYN.)* renaissance, exhumation, resurgence, renewal, revitalization.
revive *(SYN.)* refresh, lessen, decrease, renew, reduce, lower, abate, reanimate, diminish, reawaken, rejuvenate, suppress.
(ANT.) increase, amplify, intensify.
revoke *(SYN.)* nullify, cancel, abolish, quash, rescind, abrogate.
revolt *(SYN.)* mutiny, rebel, disgust, revolution, uprising, rebellion,

upheaval, takeover, insurgence, abolish.
revolting *(SYN.)* hateful, odious, abominable, foul, vile, detestable.
(ANT.) delightful, agreeable, pleasant.
revolution *(SYN.)* rebellion, mutiny, turn, coup, revolt, overthrow, cycle.
revolutionary *(SYN.)* insurgent, extremist, radical, subversive, mutinous.
revolve *(SYN.)* spin, wheel, rotate, circle, circle, turn, whirl, gyrate.
(ANT.) travel, proceed, wander.
revolver *(SYN.)* gun, pistol.
revulsion *(SYN.)* reversal, rebound, backlash, withdrawal, recoil.
reward *(SYN.)* bounty, premium, meed, award, compensation, prize, recompense, bonus, remuneration, accolade, wages.
(ANT.) charge, wages, punishment.
rewarding *(SYN.)* pleasing, productive, fruitful, profitable, favorable, satisfying, gratifying, fulfilling.
rhetoric *(SYN.)* style, verbosity, expressiveness, eloquence, fluency, flamboyance.
rhyme *(SYN.)* poem, verse, poetry, ballad, ditty, rhapsody, sonnet.
ribald *(SYN.)* suggestive, off-color, indecent, spicy, rude, vulgar.
rich *(SYN.)* ample, costly, wealthy, fruitful, prolific, abundant, well-off, affluent, plentiful, fertile, bountiful, luxuriant.
(ANT.) poor, unfruitful, beggarly, barren, impoverished, scarce, scanty, unproductive, destitute.
rickety *(SYN.)* unsound, unsteady, flimsy, unstable, shaky, decrepit, wobbly.
(ANT.) steady, solid, sturdy.
ricochet *(SYN.)* recoil, backfire, rebound, bounce, deviate, boomerang.
rid *(SYN.)* free, clear, shed, delivered, eliminate, disperse, unload, purge.
riddle *(SYN.)* puzzle, mystery, conundrum, problem, question, enigma.
(ANT.) key, solution, answer, resolution.
ride *(SYN.)* tour, journey, motor, manage, drive, control, guide.
ridge *(SYN.)* hillock, backbone, spine, crest, mound, hump.
ridicule *(SYN.)* gibe, banter, mock, jeering, deride, tease, taunt, satire, mockery, derision.
(ANT.) praise, respect.
ridiculous *(SYN.)* silly, nonsensical, absurd, accurate, inconsistent, farcical, proper, laughable, apt, preposterous, foolish.
(ANT.) sound, reasonable, consistent.
rife *(SYN.)* widespread, abundant, innumerable, rampant, teeming.
rifle *(SYN.)* plunder, pillage, rummage, ransack, rob, steal.
rift *(SYN.)* crevice, fault, opening, crack, flaw, fissure, split, breach, opening.
right *(SYN.)* correct, appropriate, suitable, ethical, fit, real, legitimate, justice, factual, just, directly, virtue, true, definite, straight, honorably, seemly.
(ANT.) immoral, unfair, wrong, bad, improper.
righteous *(SYN.)* ethical, chaste, honorable, good, virtuous, good, noble.
(ANT.) sinful, libertine, amoral, licentious.
rigid *(SYN.)* strict, unyielding, stiff, stern, austere, rigorous, inflexible, stringent, unbendable, severe, harsh, unbending.
(ANT.) supple, flexible, mild, compassionate, pliable, limp, relaxed.
rigorous *(SYN.)* unfeeling, rough, strict, blunt, cruel, hard, severe, grating, coarse, jarring, stern, stringent.
(ANT.) soft, mild, tender, gentle, smooth.
rile *(SYN.)* irritate, nettle, hector, exasperate, provoke, gripe.
rim *(SYN.)* verge, frontier, border, outskirts, edge, brink, lip, limit, termination, boundary, fringe, brim, margin.
(ANT.) core, mainland, center.
rind *(SYN.)* layer, cover, skin, hide, peel, crust, bark.
ring *(SYN.)* fillet, band, loop, circlet, circle, surround, encircle, peal, sound, resound, jingle, tinkle.
ringleader *(SYN.)* provoker, troublemaker, leader, instigator, chief, inciter, agitator.
rinse *(SYN.)* launder, cleanse, wash, soak, immerse, laundering, rinsing, immerse, bathe, clean.
riot *(SYN.)* disturbance, disorder, outburst, commotion, insurgence, uproar, panic, boisterousness, lark, hoot, wow, sensation, caper, roister, frolic, eruption, confusion, tumult, revolt.
riotous *(SYN.)* boisterous, wild, rambunctious, roisterous, tumultuous, turbulent, noisy, loud, rowdy, rollicking.
rip *(SYN.)* tear, rend, wound, rive, cleave, cut, slit, slash, lacerate, shred, scramble, dart, dash, split, disunite.
(ANT.) unite, join, repair.
ripe *(SYN.)* ready, finished, mature, complete, full-grown, develop, mellow, seasonable, full-fledged, primed, disposed, keen, avid, consummate.
(ANT.) raw, crude, undeveloped, premature, unprepared, unripe, immature.
ripen *(SYN.)* grow, season, age, mature, mellow, develop, progress, maturate.
rip into *(SYN.)* assail, lash out at, attack, charge.
rip-off *(SYN.)* fraud, dishonesty, gyp, racket, swindle, exploitation, heist, theft, extortion, thievery, larceny, shakedown.
riposte *(SYN.)* rejoinder, comeback, quip, retort, response, reply, wisecrack.
ripple *(SYN.)* wave, ruffle, wavelet, gurgle, undulate, gurgle, corrugation, rumple, crumple, spurtle, dribble, bubble.
rise *(SYN.)* thrive, awaken, ascend, climb, mount, tower, arise, wake, scale, flourish, prosper, advance, proceed, soar.
(ANT.) fall, drop, plunge, fade, slump,

decline, sinking, depression, waning, comedown, setback, retrogression, descend.

risk *(SYN.)* hazard, peril, danger, endanger, chance, jeopardy, threat, vulnerability, contingency, precariousness, shakiness.
(ANT.) protection, safety, immunity, defense.

risky *(SYN.)* menacing, chancy, threatening, critical, perilous, insecure, unsafe, dicey, unsound, dangerous.
(ANT.) guarded, safe, certain, firm, secure.

rite *(SYN.)* pomp, solemnity, ceremony, observance, ceremonial, formality.

ritual *(SYN.)* pomp, solemnity, ceremony, parade, rite, ritualism, prescription, routine, custom, tradition.

rival *(SYN.)* enemy, opponent, contestant, compete, foe, adversary, oppose.
(ANT.) colleague, confederate, allay.

rivalry *(SYN.)* contest, struggle, duel, race, vying, opposition, contention, competition.
(ANT.) alliance, collaboration, partnership, cooperation, teamwork, coalition.

river *(SYN.)* brook, stream, headstream, watercourse, tributary, creek.

rivet *(SYN.)* weld, bolt, fasten, attach, secure, bind, join, staple, nail, couple.

road *(SYN.)* street, way, highway, pike, drive, highway, expressway, boulevard.

roam *(SYN.)* err, saunter, deviate, rove, range, wander, digress, ramble, stroll.
(ANT.) stop, linger, stay, halt, settle.

roar *(SYN.)* cry, bellow, yell, shout, yowl, howl, bawl, hoot, bang, boom, blast, blare, scream, whoop, holler, yelp.

roast *(SYN.)* deride, ridicule, kid, ride, mock, tease, twit, parody, burlesque.

rob *(SYN.)* fleece, steal, despoil, pilfer, pillage, sack, loot, plunder, burglarize, ransack, hold up, rip off, thieve.

robbery *(SYN.)* larceny, plundering, thievery, stealing, theft, pillage, swiping, caper, snatching, burglary, plunder.

robe *(SYN.)* housecoat, bathrobe, dressing gown, caftan, muumuu, smock, cape.

robot *(SYN.)* computer, android, automaton, pawn, workhorse, drudge, laborer.

robust *(SYN.)* well, hearty, hale, sound, healthy, strong, able-bodied, stalwart.
(ANT.) fragile, feeble, debilitated, reserved, refined, puny, frail, delicate, infirm.

rock *(SYN.)* pebble, boulder, stone, gravel, granite, roll, sway, swagger, limestone.

rocky *(SYN.)* unstable, faint, rocklike, stony, pebbly, gravelly, trembly, rough.
(ANT.) effortless, easy, slight, simple, sound, rugged, stout, hardy, strong.

rod *(SYN.)* bar, pole, wand, stick, pike, staff, billy, baton.

rogue *(SYN.)* criminal, rascal, outlaw, scoundrel, scamp, good-for-nothing, villain.

roil *(SYN.)* churn, muddy, rile, mire, disturb.

roister *(SYN.)* bluster, swagger, swashbuckle, vaunt, bluff, flourish, rollick.

role *(SYN.)* task, part, function, characterization, portrayal, face, character.

roll *(SYN.)* revolve, rotate, whirl, swing, rock, waver, reel, lumber, swagger, stagger, progress, proceed, turn, spin.

roll up *(SYN.)* amass, collect, accumulate, gather.

romance *(SYN.)* affair, enchantment, novel, tale, adventure, enterprise, daring, story.

romantic *(SYN.)* poetic, mental, dreamy, fanciful, imaginative.
(ANT.) homely, faint-hearted, familiar, unromantic, pessimistic, unemotional.

romp *(SYN.)* caper, gambol, frolic, play, conquer, triumph, horseplay, frisk.
(ANT.) defeat, rout.

room *(SYN.)* enclosure, cell, chamber, space, stay, lodge, cubicle, reside.

roomy *(SYN.)* broad, large, wide, sizable, generous, capacious, ample, spacious, extensive, commodious, vast.
(ANT.) tight, limited, crowded, confined, narrow.

roost *(SYN.)* coop, henhouse, perch, hutch, residence, abode, hearth, lodgings.

root *(SYN.)* reason, bottom, groundwork, cause, support, base, underpinning, beginning, mainspring, source, basis.
(ANT.) cover, top, building.

rooted *(SYN.)* fixed, fast, firm, steadfast, immovable, stationary.

root out *(SYN.)* dispose of, uproot, cut out, pluck out.

rope *(SYN.)* string, wire, cord, cable, line, strand, rigging, ropework, cordage.

roster *(SYN.)* list, census, muster, enrollment, listing, register.

rosy *(SYN.)* reddish, pink, healthy, fresh, cheerful, bright, happy, glowing, flushed, promising, favorable.
(ANT.) pale, pallid, gray, wan, disheartening, ashen, unfavorable, gloomy.

rot *(SYN.)* putrefy, waste, decay, mold, decompose, dwindle, spoil, decline, decomposition, wane, rotting, ebb.
(ANT.) increase, rise, grow, luxuriate.

rotary *(SYN.)* axial, rotating, turning, gyral, revolving, rolling, whirling, rotational.

rotate *(SYN.)* spin, twirl, wheel, circle, twist, orbit, invert, swivel, gyrate, wind, alternate, recur, intermit, pivot.
(ANT.) stop, arrest, stand.

rotation *(SYN.)* turning, rolling, succession, gyration, revolution, return, rhythm, swirling, spinning, whirling.

rotten *(SYN.)* decayed, decomposed, spoiled, putrid, contaminated, tainted.
(ANT.) unspoiled, pure, sweet, fresh.

rough *(SYN.)* jagged, scratchy, crude, incomplete, severe, craggy, stormy.
(ANT.) calm, polished, civil, mild.

roughly *(SYN.)* nearly, about, approximately.

round *(SYN.)* rotund, chubby, curved, bulbous, entire, complete, spherical,

circular, bowed.
(ANT.) slender, trim, slim, thin, lean.
rouse *(SYN.)* waken, awaken, stimulate, excite, summon, arise, stir.
(ANT.) rest, calm, sleep, restrain, sedate.
rousing *(SYN.)* exciting, galvanic, stimulating, electric, moving, exhilarating, stirring, breathtaking, inciting.
(ANT.) flat, uninteresting, drab, monotonous, boring, tiresome, slow.
route *(SYN.)* street, course, trail, way, avenue, passage, thoroughfare, track, road, path.
routine *(SYN.)* way, habit, use, custom, practice, fashion, method, system, channel, circuit.
(ANT.) unusual, rare, uncommon.
rover *(SYN.)* traveler, adventurer, wanderer, voyager.
row *(SYN.)* file, order, series, rank, progression, sequence, arrangement.
rowdy *(SYN.)* disorderly, unruly, brawling, roughneck, scrapper.
royal *(SYN.)* lordly, regal, noble, courtly, ruling, stately, dignified.
(ANT.) servile, common, low, humble.
rub *(SYN.)* shine, polish, scour, scrape.
rubbish *(SYN.)* debris, garbage, trash, waste, junk, clutter.
rude *(SYN.)* gruff, impudent, blunt, impolite, boorish, insolent, saucy, rough.
(ANT.) courtly, civil, stately, genteel, calm, dignified, polished, courteous.
rudimentary *(SYN.* essential, primary, fundamental, original, imperfect.
ruffle *(SYN.)* rumple, disarrange, disorder, disturb, trimming, frill.
rug *(SYN.)* floor-covering, carpet.
rugged *(SYN.)* jagged, craggy, scratchy, irregular, uneven, harsh, severe, tough.
(ANT.) smooth, level, even.
ruin *(SYN.)* wreck, exterminate, devastate, annihilate, raze, demolish, spoil.
(ANT.) save, establish, preserve.
ruination *(SYN:)* obliteration, annihilation, havoc, catastrophe.
rule *(SYN.)* law, guide, order, regulation, dominion, sovereignty, control.
ruler *(SYN.)* commander, chief, leader, governor, yardstick.
ruling *(SYN.)* judgment, decision, decree.
rummage *(SYN.)* root, scour, ransack.
rumor *(SYN.)* innuendo, hearsay, gossip.
rumple *(SYN.)* tousle, furrow, crease, wrinkle, dishevel.
run *(SYN.)* race, hurry, speed, hasten, sprint, dart, scamper, dash.
runaway *(SYN.)* refugee, deserter, fugitive.
run-down *(SYN.)* ramshackle, dilapidated, tumble-down, weakened, unhealthy, summary, outline, draft.
rupture *(SYN.)* fracture, fissure, cleft, severance.
rural *(SYN.)* country, farm, rustic, backwoods.
(ANT.) citified, urban.
rush *(SYN.)* dash, speed, hurry, run.
(ANT.) tarry, linger.

sabotage *(SYN.)* subversion, treason, treachery, damage, disable, subvert.
sack *(SYN.)* pouch, bag.
sacrament *(SYN.)* communion, fellowship, association, intercourse.
(ANT.) nonparticipation, alienation.
sacred *(SYN.)* consecrated, blessed, devout, divine, holy, religious.
(ANT.) profane, evil, sacrilegious, worldly, secular, blasphemous.
sad *(SYN.)* dejected, cheerless, despondent, depressed, disconsolate, doleful.
(ANT.) happy, cheerful, glad, merry.
safe *(SYN.)* dependable, certain, harmless, secure, snug, trustworthy.
(ANT.) hazardous, dangerous, unsafe, insecure, perilous.
safeguard *(SYN.)* fence, bulwark, protection, shelter, refuge, shield, guard, defense, security.
sag *(SYN.)* incline, bend, lean, slant, tend, depend, rely, trust, fail.
(ANT.) rise, raise, erect, straighten.
saintly *(SYN.)* virtuous, moral, holy, devout, righteous, good.
sake *(SYN.)* motive, reason, purpose, benefit, advantage, welfare.
salary *(SYN.)* compensation, allowance, earnings, pay, fee, payment.
(ANT.) gratuity, present, gift.
saloon *(SYN.)* pub, bar.
salute *(SYN.)* receive, greet.
salvage *(SYN.)* retrieve, rescue, recover.
salvation *(SYN.)* release, rescue, deliverance.
same *(SYN.)* equal, coincident, equivalent, like, indistinguishable.
(ANT.) disparate, contrary, dissimilar, opposed, distinct.
sample *(SYN.)* example, case, illustration, model, instance, pattern.
sanction *(SYN.)* approval, approbation, authorization, authority, let, permit.
(ANT.) reproach, reprimand, stricture, censure, object, forbid, refuse, resist.
sanctuary *(SYN.)* harbor, haven, asylum, refuge, retreat, shelter.
(ANT.) danger, hazard, exposure, jeopardy, peril.
sane *(SYN.)* balanced, rational, normal, sound, reasonable.
(ANT.) crazy, insane, irrational.
sanitary *(SYN.)* purified, clean, hygienic, disinfected.
(ANT.) soiled, fouled, unclean, dirty.
sap *(SYN.)* undermine, exhausted, drain, weaken.
sarcastic *(SYN.)* biting, acrimonious, cutting, caustic, derisive, sardonic.
(ANT.) agreeable, affable, pleasant.
satire *(SYN.)* cleverness, fun, banter, humor, irony, raillery, pleasantry.
(ANT.) platitude, sobriety, commonplace, solemnity, stupidity.
satisfaction *(SYN.)* beatitude, bliss, delight, contentment, pleasure.
(ANT.) grief, misery, sadness, despair.
satisfactory *(SYN.)* ample, capable, adequate, commensurate, enough.
(ANT.) scant, lacking, deficient, unsatisfactory, poor.
satisfy *(SYN.)* compensate, appease, content, gratify, fulfill, suitable.

(ANT.) displease, dissatisfy, annoy, frustrate, tantalize.
saturate *(SYN.)* fill, diffuse, infiltrate, penetrate, permeate, run through.
saucy *(SYN.)* insolent, bold, impudent, impertinent.
(ANT.) shy, demure.
savage *(SYN.)* brutal, cruel, barbarous, ferocious, inhuman, merciless.
(ANT.) compassionate, forbearing, benevolent, gentle, humane, kind.
save *(SYN.)* defend, conserve, keep, maintain, guard, preserve, protect.
(ANT.) abolish, destroy, abandon, impair, injure.
savory *(SYN.)* delectable, delightful, delicious, palatable, luscious, tasty.
(ANT.) distasteful, nauseous, acrid, unpalatable, unsavory.
say *(SYN.)* converse, articulate, declare, express, discourse, harangue, talk.
(ANT.) hush, refrain, be silent.
saying *(SYN.)* aphorism, adage, byword, maxim, proverb, motto.
scalding *(SYN.)* hot, scorching, burning, torrid, warm, fervent, ardent.
(ANT.) cool, cold, freezing, passionless, frigid, bland.
scale *(SYN.)* balance, proportion, ration, range, climb, mount.
scamp *(SYN.)* troublemaker, rascal.
scan *(SYN.)* examine, study.
scandal *(SYN.)* chagrin, humiliation, abashment, mortification, dishonor.
(ANT.) glory, honor, dignity, praise.
scandalize *(SYN.)* aspersé, defame, abuse, disparage, revile, vilify, traduce.
(ANT.) honor, respect, cherish.
scant *(SYN.)* succinct, summary, concise, terse, inadequate, deficient, insufficient, limited, lacking.
(ANT.) ample, big, extended, abundant, protracted.
scarce *(SYN.)* occasional, choice, infrequent, exceptional, rare, uncommon.
(ANT.) frequent, ordinary, usual, customary, abundant, numerous, worthless.
scare *(SYN.)* alarm, papal, affright, astound, dismay, daunt, frighten.
(ANT.) compose, reassure, soothe.
scared *(SYN.)* apprehensive, afraid, faint-hearted, frightened, fearful.
(ANT.) bold, assured, courageous, composed, sanguine.
scarf *(SYN.)* kerchief.
scatter *(SYN.)* dispel, disperse, diffuse, disseminate, separate, dissipate, spread.
(ANT.) assemble, accumulate, amass, gather, collect.
scene *(SYN.)* exhibition, view, display.
scent *(SYN.)* fragrance, fume, aroma, incense, perfume, odor, redolence.
schedule *(SYN.)* program, timetable.
scheme *(SYN.)* conspiracy, cabal, design, machination, intrigue, plot, plan, chart, stratage, diagram, graph.
scheming *(SYN.)* create, design, intend, mean, draw, sketch, purpose.
scholar *(SYN.)* intellectual, pupil, learner, disciple, sage, student, savant.
(ANT.) dunce, idiot, fool, ignoramus.
scholarly *(SYN.)* bookish, erudite, formal, academic, learned, pedantic, theoretical, scholastic.
(ANT.) practical, simple, ignorant.
scholarship *(SYN.)* cognizance, erudition, apprehension, information, learning, knowledge, science, wisdom.
(ANT.) illiteracy, stupidity, ignorance.
science *(SYN.)* enlightenment, discipline, knowledge, scholarship.
(ANT.) superstition, ignorance.
scoff *(SYN.)* ridicule, belittle, mock.
scold *(SYN.)* berate, blame, lecture, rate, rebuke, censure, admonish, reprehend, upbraid, reprimand, criticize.
(ANT.) commend, praise, approve.
scorch *(SYN.)* burn, char, consume, blaze, incinerate, sear, singe, scald.
(ANT.) put out, quench, extinguish.
score *(SYN.)* reckoning, tally, record, mark, rating.
scorn *(SYN.)* contumely, derision, contempt, detestation, hatred, disdain.
(ANT.) esteem, respect, awe.
scoundrel *(SYN.)* rogue, villain, cad.
scour *(SYN.)* wash, clean, scrub.
scowl *(SYN.)* glower, frown, glare.
scrap *(SYN.)* fragment, rag, apportionment, part, portion, piece, section, share, segment, crumb, junk.
(ANT.) whole, entirety.
scrape *(SYN.)* difficulty, dilemma, condition, fix, predicament, plight, situation, strait, scour, rub, scratch.
(ANT.) comfort, ease, calmness.
scratch *(SYN.)* scrape, scar.
scrawny *(SYN.)* gaunt, skinny, spindly.
(ANT.) husky, burly.
scream *(SYN.)* screech, shriek, yell.
screech *(SYN.)* yell, cry, scream, shriek.
screen *(SYN.)* partition, cover, separation, protection.
script *(SYN.)* penmanship, hand, handwriting, text, lines.
scrub *(SYN.)* cleanse, mop, purify, clean, sweep, wash, scour.
(ANT.) polluie, dirty, stain, sully.
scrupulous *(SYN.)* conscientious, candid, honest, honorable, fair.
(ANT.) dishonest, fraudulent, lying deceitful, tricky, careless.
seal *(SYN.)* emblem, stamp, symbol, crest, signet.
search *(SYN.)* exploration, examination, investigation, inquiry, pursuit, hunt.
(ANT.) resignation, abandonment.
searching *(SYN.)* inquiring, inquisitive, interrogative, nosy, curious, peeping, peering, snoopy, prying.
(ANT.) indifferent, unconcerned, incurious, uninterested.
season *(SYN.)* mature, perfect, ripen, develop, age.
seasoned *(SYN.)* veteran, skilled.
secluded *(SYN.)* deserted, desolate, isolated, alone, lonely, lone, unaided.
(ANT.) attended, surrounded.
seclusion *(SYN.)* insulation, isolation, loneliness, alienation, quarantine, segregation, separation, retirement.
(ANT.) fellowship, union, connection, association, communion.
secondary *(SYN.)* minor, poorer, inferior, lower, subordinate.

(ANT.) greater, higher, superior.
secret *(SYN.)* concealed, hidden, latent, covert, private, surreptitious, unknown.
(ANT.) disclosed, exposed, known, obvious, conspicuous, open, public.
secrete *(SYN.)* clothe, conceal, cover, cloak, curtain, envelop, disguise, hide.
(ANT.) divulge, reveal, expose, unveil.
section *(SYN.)* district, country, domain, dominion, division, land, place.
secular *(SYN.)* lay earthly, laic, mundane, temporal, profane, worldly.
(ANT.) religious, spiritual, unworldly.
security *(SYN.)* bond, earnest, pawn, bail, guaranty, pledge, token, surety.
sedate *(SYN.)* controlled, serene, calm, composed, unruffled.
sediment *(SYN.)* residue, grounds.
see *(SYN.)* contemplate, descry, behold, discern, espy, distinguish, glimpse.
seek *(SYN.)* explore, hunt, examine, look, investigate, probe, ransack.
seem *(SYN.)* look, appeal.
(ANT.) exist, be, disappear, withdraw, vanish.
segment *(SYN.)* apportionment, division, fragment, moiety, allotment.
(ANT.) whole, entirety.
segregate *(SYN.)* exclude, separate.
(ANT.) include, combine.
seize *(SYN.)* check, detain, hinder, apprehend, arrest, obstruct, stop.
(ANT.) free, liberate, release, activate, discharge, loosen.
seldom *(SYN.)* infrequently, scarcely.
select *(SYN.)* cull, opt, pick, choose, elect, prefer.
(ANT.) reject, refuse.
selection *(SYN.)* election, choice, alternative, option, preference.
self-denial *(SYN.)* abstinence, continence, abstention, forbearance.
(ANT.) gluttony, excess, greed, intoxication, self-indulgence.
self-important *(SYN.)* egotistical, proud, conceited, egocentric.
self-indulgence *(SYN.)* egotism, narrowness, self-centeredness, self-seeking, stinginess, ungenerousness.
(ANT.) charity, magnanimity, altruism, liberality.
selfish *(SYN.)* illiberal, narrow, self-centered, self-seeking, mercenary, stingy, ungenerous, greedy, mean, miserly.
(ANT.) charitable.
self-satisfied *(SYN.)* smug, complacent.
sell *(SYN.)* market, retail, merchandise, vend, trade, barter.
send *(SYN.)* discharge, emit, dispatch, cast, propel, impel, throw, transmit, forward, ship, convey, mail.
(ANT.) get, hold, retain, receive, bring.
senile *(SYN.)* antiquated, antique, aged, ancient, archaic, obsolete, old, elderly, old-fashioned, venerable.
(ANT.) new, youthful, young, modern.
senior *(SYN.)* superior, older, elder.
(ANT.) minor, junior.
sensation *(SYN.)* feeling, image, impression, apprehension, sense, sensibility, perception, sensitiveness.
(ANT.) insensibility, torpor, stupor, apathy.
sensational *(SYN.)* exciting, marvelous, superb, thrilling, startling, spectacular.
sense *(SYN.)* perception, sensation, feeling, awareness, insight, consciousness, appreciate, discern, perceive.
senseless *(SYN.)* dense, dull, crass, brainless, dumb, foolish, stupid.
(ANT.) discerning, intelligent, alert, clever, bright.
sensibility *(SYN.)* sensation, emotion, feeling, passion, tenderness, sentiment.
(ANT.) coldness, imperturbability, anesthesia, insensibility, fact.
sensible *(SYN.)* apprehensible, perceptible, appreciable, alive, aware, awake, cognizant, comprehending, perceiving, conscious, sentient, intelligent, discreet, practical, judicious, prudent, sagacious, reasonable, sage, sober, wise, sound.
(ANT.) impalpable, imperceptible, absurd, stupid, unaware, foolish.
sensitive *(SYN.)* perceptive, prone, impressionable, responsive, tender, sore.
(ANT.) dull, hard, callous, insensitive.
sentence *(SYN.)* convict, condemn.
(ANT.) acquit, pardon, absolve acquit.
sentiment *(SYN.)* affection, emotion, sensation, feeling, sensibility, passion.
(ANT.) coldness, imperturbability, anesthesia, insensibility, fact.
sentimental *(SYN.)* extravagant, fanciful, fantastic, dreamy, fictitious, idealistic, ideal, maudlin, imaginative, mawkish, poetic, romantic, picturesque.
(ANT.) literal, practical, prosaic.
separate *(SYN.)* part sever, sunder, divide, allot, dispense, share.
(ANT.) convene, join, gather, combine.
separation *(SYN.)* insulation, isolation, loneliness, alienation, quarantine.
(ANT.) communion, fellowship, union, association, connection.
sequence *(SYN.)* chain, graduation, order, progression, arrangement, following, series, succession, train, string.
serene *(SYN.)* composed, imperturbable, calm, dispassionate, pacific, placid, peaceful, quiet. tranquil, still, undisturbed, unruffled.
(ANT.) frantic, turbulent, wild, excited, stormy, agitated, turbulent.
serenity *(SYN.)* calmness, hush, calm, quiet, peace, quiescence, rest, silence.
(ANT.) tumult, excitement, noise, agitation, disturbance.
series *(ANT.)* following, chain, arrangement, graduation, progression, order, sequence, train, string.
serious *(SYN.)* important, momentous, great, earnest, grave, sedate, sober.
(ANT.) trivial, informal, relaxed, small.
servant *(SYN.)* attendant, butler, domestic, valet, manservant, maid.
serve *(SYN.)* assist, attend, help, succor, advance, benefit, forward, answer.
(ANT.) command, direct, dictate, rule.
service *(SYN.)* advantage, account, avail, benefit, behalf, favor, good, gain.
(ANT.) distress, calamity, trouble.

set *(SYN.)* deposit, dispose, lay, arrange, place, put, position, pose, station, appoint, fix, assign, settle, establish.
(ANT.) mislay, misplace, disturb, remove, disarrange.
settle *(SYN.)* close, conclude, adjudicate, decide, end, resolve, agree upon, establish, satisfy, pay, lodge, locate, reside, determine, abide, terminate.
(ANT.) suspend, hesitate, doubt, vacillate, waver.
settlement *(SYN.)* completion, close, end, finale, issue, conclusion, termination, deduction, decision, inference.
(ANT.) commencement, prelude, start, inception, beginning.
sever *(SYN.)* part, divide, sunder, split, cut, separate.
(ANT.) convene, connect, gather, join, unite, combine.
several *(SYN.)* some, few, a handful.
severe *(SYN.)* arduous, distressing, acute, exacting, hard, harsh, intense.
(ANT.) genial, indulgent, lenient, yielding, merciful, considerate.
sew *(SYN.)* mend, patch, fix, stitch, refit, restore, repair.
(ANT.) destroy, hurt, deface, injure.
shabby *(SYN.)* indigent, impecunious, needy, penniless, worn, ragged, destitute, poor, threadbare, deficient, inferior, scanty.
(ANT.) rich, wealthy, ample, affluent, opulent, right, sufficient, good.
shack *(SYN.)* hovel, hut, shanty, shed.
shackle *(SYN.)* chain, fetter, handcuff.
shade *(SYN.)* complexion, dye, hue, paint, color, stain, pigment, darkness, shadow, tincture, dusk, gloom, blacken, darken, conceal, screen, tint, tinge.
(ANT.) transparency, paleness.
shady *(SYN.)* shifty, shaded, questionable, doubtful, devious.
shaggy *(SYN.)* hairy, unkempt, uncombed, woolly.
shake *(SYN.)* flutter, jar, jolt, quake, agitate, quiver, shiver, shudder, rock, totter, sway, tremble, vibrate, waver.
shaky *(SYN.)* questionable, uncertain, iffy, faltering, unsteady.
(ANT.) sure, definite, positive, certain.
shallow *(SYN.)* exterior, cursory, flimsy, frivolous, slight, imperfect, superficial.
(ANT.) complete, deep, abstruse, profound, thorough.
sham *(SYN.)* affect, act, feign, assume, pretend, simulate, profess.
(ANT.) exhibit, display, reveal, expose.
shame *(SYN.)* chagrin, humiliation, abashment, disgrace, mortification.
(ANT.) pride, glory, praise, honor.
shameful *(SYN.)* disgraceful, dishonorable, disreputable.
(ANT.) honorable, renowned, respectable, esteemed.
shameless *(SYN.)* unembarrassed, unashamed, brazen, bold, impudent.
(ANT.) demure, modest.
shape *(SYN.)* create, construct, forge, fashion, form, make, mold, figure.
(ANT.) disfigure, misshape, dismantle.
shapeless *(SYN.)* rough, amorphous, vague.
shapely *(SYN.)* attractive, well-formed, curvy, alluring.
(ANT.) shapeless.
share *(SYN.)* parcel, bit, part, division, portion, ration, piece, fragment, allotment, partake, apportion, participate, divide, section.
(ANT.) whole.
shared *(SYN.)* joint, common, reciprocal, correlative, mutual.
(ANT.) unrequited, dissociated.
sharp *(SYN.)* biting, pointed, cunning, acute, keen, rough, fine, cutting, shrill.
(ANT.) gentle, bland, shallow, smooth, blunt.
sharpen *(SYN.)* whet, hone, strop.
shatter *(SYN.)* crack, rend, break, pound, smash, burst, demolish, shiver, infringe.
(ANT.) renovate, join, repair, mend.
shattered *(SYN.)* fractured, destroyed, reduced, separated, broken, smashed, flattened, rent, wrecked.
(ANT.) united, integral, whole.
shawl *(SYN.)* stole, scarf.
sheepish *(SYN.)* coy, embarrassed, shy, humble, abashed, diffident, timid.
(ANT.) daring, outgoing, adventurous.
sheer *(SYN.)* thin, transparent, clear, simple, utter, absolute, abrupt, steep, see through.
sheet *(SYN.)* leaf, layer, coating, film.
shelter *(SYN.)* retreat, safety, cover, asylum, protection, sanctuary, harbor, guard, haven, security.
(ANT.) unveil, expose, bare, reveal.
shield *(SYN.)* envelop, cover, clothe, curtain, protest, protection, cloak, guard, conceal, defense, shelter, hide, screen, veil, shroud.
(ANT.) unveil, divulge, reveal, bare.
shift *(SYN.)* move, modify, transfer, substitute, vary, change, alter, spell, turn, transfigure.
(ANT.) settle, establish, stabilize.
shifting *(SYN.)* wavering, inconstant, changeable, fitful, variable, fickle.
(ANT.) uniform, stable, unchanging.
shiftless *(SYN.)* idle, lazy, slothful.
(ANT.) energetic.
shifty *(SYN.)* shrewd, crafty, tricky.
shimmer *(SYN.)* glimmer, shine, gleam.
(ANT.) dull.
shine *(SYN.)* flicker, glisten, glow, blaze, glare, flash, beam, shimmer, glimmer, radiate, brush, polish, twinkle, buff, luster, gloss, scintillate, radiance, gleam.
shining *(SYN.)* dazzling, illustrious, showy, superb, brilliant, effulgent, magnificent, splendid, bright.
(ANT.) ordinary, dull, unimpressive.
shiny *(SYN.)* bright, glossy, polished, glistening.
(ANT.) lusterless, dull.
shipshape *(SYN.)* clean, neat.
(ANT.) sloppy, messy.
shiver *(SYN.)* quiver, quake, quaver, tremble, shudder, shake, break, shatter.
shock *(SYN.)* disconcert, astonish, surprise, astound, amaze, clash, distur-

bance, bewilder, outrage, horrify, revolt, agitation, stagger, blow, impact, collision, surprise, startle, upset, stun.
(ANT.) prepare, caution, admonish.
shocking *(SYN.)* hideous, frightful, severe, appalling, horrible, awful.
(ANT.) safe, happy, secure, joyous.
shore *(SYN.)* seaside, beach, coast.
(ANT.) inland.
short *(SYN.)* abrupt, squat, concise, brief, low, curtailed, dumpy, small.
(ANT.) extended, ample, protracted.
shortage *(SYN.)* deficiency, deficit, shortfall.
(ANT.) surplus, enough.
shorten *(SYN.)* curtail, limit, cut, abbreviate, reduce, abridge, lessen, restrict.
(ANT.) lengthen, elongate.
shortening *(SYN.)* reduction, abridgment, abbreviation.
(ANT.) enlargement, amplification.
short-handed *(SYN.)* understaffed.
shortly *(SYN.)* soon, directly, presently.
shortsighted *(SYN.)* myopic, nearsighted, unimaginative, unthinking, thoughtless.
shout *(SYN.)* ejaculate, cry, yell, roar, vociferate, bellow, exclaim.
(ANT.) whisper, intimate.
shove *(SYN.)* propel, drive, urge, crowd, jostle, force, push, promote.
(ANT.) retreat, falter, oppose, drag, halt.
shovel *(SYN.)* spade.
show *(SYN.)* flourish, parade, point, reveal, explain, array, movie, production, display, exhibit, note, spectacle, demonstrate, entertainment, tell, usher, guide, prove, indicate, present, lead, demonstration.
showy *(SYN.)* ceremonious, stagy, affected, theatrical, artificial.
(ANT.) unaffected, modest, unemotional, subdued.
shred *(SYN.)* particle, speck, iota, mite, bit, smidgen, tear, slit, cleave, rip, disunite, wound, rend, mince, tatter, lacerate.
(ANT.) bulk, unite, quantity, mend, aggregate, repair.
shrewd *(SYN.)* cunning, covert, artful, stealthy, foxy, astute, ingenious, guileful, crafty, sly, surreptitious, wily, tricky, clever, intelligent, clandestine.
(ANT.) frank, sincere, candid, open.
shriek *(SYN.)* screech, scream, howl, yell.
shrill *(SYN.)* keen, penetrating, sharp, acute, piercing, severe.
(ANT.) gentle, bland, shallow.
shrink *(SYN.)* diminish, shrivel, dwindle.
shrivel *(SYN.)* wizen, waste, droop, decline, sink, dry, languish, wither.
(ANT.) renew, refresh, revive, rejuvenate.
shun *(SYN.)* escape, avert, forestall, avoid, forbear, evade, ward, elude, dodge, free.
(ANT.) encounter, confront, meet.
shut *(SYN.)* seal, finish, stop, close, terminate, conclude, clog, end, obstruct.
(ANT.) begin, open, start, unbar, inaugurate, unlock, commence.
shy *(SYN.)* reserved, fearful, bashful, retiring, cautious, demure, timid, shrinking, wary, chary.
(ANT.) brazen, bold, immodest, self-confident, audacious.
sick *(SYN.)* ill, morbid, ailing, unhealthy, diseased, unwell, infirm.
(ANT.) sound, well, robust, strong.
sickness *(SYN.)* illness, ailment, disease, complaint, disorder.
(ANT.) soundness, healthiness, vigor.
side *(SYN.)* surface, face, foe, opponent, rival, indirect, secondary, unimportant.
siege *(SYN.)* blockade.
sieve *(SYN.)* screen, strainer, riddle, colander.
sight *(SYN.)* eyesight, vision, scene, view, display, spectacle, eyesore.
sightless *(SYN.)* unmindful, oblivious, blind, unseeing, heedless, ignorant.
(ANT.) sensible, discerning, aware, perceiving.
sign *(SYN.)* omen, mark, emblem, token, suggestion, indication, clue, hint, approve, authorize, signal, gesture, symbol, portent.
signal *(SYN.)* beacon, sign, alarm.
significance *(SYN.)* connotation, drift, acceptation, explanation, implication, gist, importance, interpretation, intent, weight, meaning, purpose, purport, sense, signification.
significant *(SYN.)* grave, important, critical, material, indicative, meaningful, crucial, momentous, telling, vital, weighty.
(ANT.) irrelevant, insignificant, meaningless, unimportant, negligible.
signify *(SYN.)* designate, imply, denote, intimate, reveal, indicate, manifest, mean, communicate, show, specify.
(ANT.) distract, divert, mislead, conceal, conceal.
silence *(SYN.)* motionless, peaceful, placid, hushed, stillness, quiescent, still, soundlessness, quiet, tranquil, noiselessness, hush, muteness, undisturbed.
(ANT.) strident, loud, racket, disturbed, clamor, agitated, perturbed.
silent *(SYN.)* dumb, hushed, mute, calm, noiseless, quiet, peaceful, still, soundless, speechless, tranquil, uncommunicative, taciturn.
(ANT.) communicative, loud, noisy, raucous, talkative, clamorous.
silhouette *(SYN.)* contour, delineation, brief, draft, form, figure, outline, profile, plan, sketch.
silly *(SYN.)* asinine, brainless, crazy, absurd, foolish, irrational, witless, nonsensical, simple, ridiculous, stupid.
(ANT.) sane, wise, judicious, prudent.
similar *(SYN.)* alike, akin, allied, comparable, analogous, correlative, corresponding, correspondent, parallel, resembling, like.
(ANT.) dissimilar, divergent, opposed, different, incongruous.
similarity *(SYN.)* likeness, parity, analogy, correspondence, resemblance,

similitude.
(ANT.) distinction, variance, difference.
simple *(SYN.)* effortless, elementary, pure, easy, facile, mere, single, uncompounded, homely, humble, unmixed, plain, artless, naive, frank, natural, unsophisticated, open, asinine, foolish, credulous, silly.
(ANT.) artful, complex, intricate, adorned, wise.
simpleton *(SYN.)* idiot, fool, ignoramus.
simulate *(SYN.)* copy, counterfeit, duplicate, ape, imitate, impersonate, mock, mimic.
(ANT.) distort, diverge, alter, invent.
sin *(SYN.)* evil, crime, iniquity, transgress, guilt, offense, ungodliness, trespass, vice, transgression, wickedness, wrong.
(ANT.) purity, goodness, purity, virtue, righteousness.
sincere *(SYN.)* earnest, frank, heartfelt, genuine, candid, honest, open, true, straightforward, faithful, truthful, upright, trustworthy, unfeigned.
(ANT.) hypocritical, insincere, affected, dishonest, untruthful.
sincerity *(SYN.)* fairness, frankness, honesty, justice, candor, integrity, openness, responsibility, rectitude, uprightness.
(ANT.) deceit, dishonesty, cheating.
sinful *(SYN.)* bad, corrupt, dissolute, antisocial, immoral, licentious, profligate, evil, indecent, unprincipled, vicious.
(ANT.) pure, noble, virtuous.
sing *(SYN.)* chant, croon, hum, carol, intone, lilt, warble.
singe *(SYN.)* burn, char, consume, blaze, incinerate, scorch, sear, scald.
(ANT.) put out, quench, extinguish.
single *(SYN.)* individual, marked, particular, distinctive, separate, special, specific, lone, one, solitary, sole, unwed, unmarried, singular, unique.
(ANT.) ordinary, universal, general.
singular *(SYN.)* exceptional, eccentric, odd, peculiar, rate, extraordinary, strange, unusual, striking, characteristic, remarkable, rare, individual, distinctive, uncommon, special.
(ANT.) general, normal, ordinary.
sink *(SYN.)* diminish, droop, subside, hang, decline, fall, extend, downward, drop, descend.
(ANT.) mount, climb, soar, steady, arise.
sinless *(SYN.)* faultless, holy, immaculate, perfect, blameless, holy, consummate, ideal, excellent, superlative, supreme.
(ANT.) defective, faulty, blemished, imperfect.
sip *(SYN.)* drink, taste, swallow.
sire *(SYN.)* breed, create, father, engender, beget, generate, procreate, originate, produce, propagate.
(ANT.) destroy, ill, extinguish, murder, abort.
site *(SYN.)* place, position, location, situation, station, locality.
situation *(SYN.)* circumstance, plight, state, site, location, placement, locale, predicament, position, state, condition.
size *(SYN.)* bigness, bulk, dimensions, expanse, amplitude, measurement, area, extent, largeness, magnitude, mass, greatness, volume.
skeptic *(SYN.)* doubter, infidel, agnostic, deist, questioner, unbeliever.
(ANT.) believer, worshiper, adorer.
skepticism *(SYN.)* hesitation, questioning, wavering, doubting, distrust, mistrust, suspicion.
(ANT.) confidence, reliance, trust.
sketch *(SYN.)* draft, figure, form, outline, contour, delineation, drawing, picture, represent, silhouette, draw, profile.
sketchy *(SYN.)* indefinite, vague, incomplete, indistinct.
(ANT.) definite, detailed, complete.
skill *(SYN.)* cunning, deftness, dexterity, ability, adroitness, cleverness, talent, readiness, skillfulness.
(ANT.) ineptitude, inability.
skillful *(SYN.)* adept, clever, able, accomplished, competent, expert, ingenious, cunning, proficient, practiced, versed, skilled.
(ANT.) untrained, inept, clumsy, inexpert, bungling, awkward.
skimpy *(SYN.)* cheap, scanty, meager.
(ANT.) abundant, generous.
skin *(SYN.)* outside, covering, peel, rind, shell, pare.
skinny *(SYN.)* gaunt, thin, raw-boned.
(ANT.) fat, hefty, heavy.
skip *(SYN.)* drop, eliminate, ignore, exclude, cancel, delete, disregard, omit, overlook neglect, miss.
(ANT.) notice, introduce, include, insert.
skirmish *(SYN.)* brawl, battle, conflict, combat, dispute, encounter, contend, quarrel, squabble, scuffle, wrangle, struggle.
slack *(SYN.)* lax, limp, indefinite, free, disengaged, unbound, untied, unfastened, vague, dissolute, heedless, careless, unrestrained, limp, lazy, loose, inactive, sluggish, wanton.
(ANT.) restrained, tied, right, stiff, taunt, rigid, fast, inhibited.
slander *(SYN.)* libel, calumny, backbiting, aspersion, scandal, vilification.
(ANT.) praise, flattery, commendation, defense.
slang *(SYN.)* jargon, dialect.
slant *(SYN.)* disposition, inclination, bias, bent, partiality, slope, tilt, pitch, penchant, prejudice, proneness, proclivity, turn, incline, lean, tendency.
(ANT.) justice, fairness, impartiality, equity.
slash *(SYN.)* gash, cut, slit, lower, reduce.
slaughter *(SYN.)* butcher, kill, massacre, slay, butchering, killing.
slave *(SYN.)* bondservant, serf.
slavery *(SYN.)* captivity, imprisonment, serfdom, confinement, bondage, thralldom, servitude, enslavement.
(ANT.) freedom, liberation.

slay *(SYN.)* assassinate, kill, murder.
sleek *(SYN.)* smooth, polished, slick.
(ANT.) blunt, harsh, rough, rugged.
sleep *(SYN.)* drowse, nap, nod, catnap, repose, doze, rest, slumber, snooze.
sleepy *(SYN.)* tired, drowsy, nodding.
slender *(SYN.)* lank, lean, meager, emaciated, gaunt, scanty, rare, skinny, scrawny, slight, spare, trim, slim, tenuous, thin.
(ANT.) fat, broad, overweight, thick, wide, bulky.
slide *(SYN.)* glide, slip, skim, skid.
slight *(SYN.)* lank, lean, meager, emaciated, gaunt, fine, narrow, scanty, scrawny, skinny, sparse, small, rare, slender, spare, insignificant, tenuous, unimportant, slim, thin.
(ANT.) regard, notice, enormous, large, major, huge, include.
slim *(SYN.)* thin, slender, lank, slight, weak, insignificant, unimportant.
slip *(SYN.)* error, fault, inaccuracy, shift, err, slide, mistake, glide, blunder.
(ANT.) precision, truth, accuracy.
slipshod *(SYN.)* sloppy, careless.
(ANT.) careful.
slit *(SYN.)* slash, cut, tear, slot.
slogan *(SYN.)* catchword, motto.
slope *(SYN.)* incline, leaning, inclination, bending, slant.
sloth *(SYN.)* indolence, idleness, inactivity, inertia, supineness, sluggishness, torpidity.
(ANT.) alertness, assiduousness, diligence, activity.
slothful *(SYN.)* indolent, idle, inactive, lazy, inert, supine, sluggish, torpid.
(ANT.) alert, diligent, active, assiduous.
slovenly *(SYN.)* sloppy, bedraggled, unkempt, messy.
(ANT.) meticulous, neat.
slow *(SYN.)* deliberate, dull, delaying, dawdling, gradual, leisurely, tired, sluggish, unhurried, late, behindhand, delayed.
(ANT.) rapid, quick, swift, speedy, fast.
sluggish *(SYN.)* dull, deliberate, dawdling, delaying, laggard, gradual, leisurely, tired, slow, lethargic.
(ANT.) quick, rapid, fast, speedy, swift, energetic, vivacious.
slumber *(SYN.)* drowse, catnap, nod, doze, repose, sleep, rest, snooze.
slump *(SYN.)* drop, decline, descent.
sly *(SYN.)* covert, artful, astute, crafty, clandestine, foxy, furtive, cunning, insidious, guileful, stealthy, subtle, shrewd, tricky, surreptitious, underhand, wily, secretive.
(ANT.) sincere, ingenuous, open, candid.
small *(SYN.)* little, minute, petty, diminutive, puny, wee, tiny, trivial, slight, miniature.
(ANT.) immense, enormous, large, huge.
smart *(SYN.)* dexterous, quick, skillful, adroit, apt, clever, bright, witty, ingenious, sharp, intelligent.
(ANT.) foolish, stupid, unskilled, awkward, clumsy, bungling, slow, dumb.
smash *(SYN.)* burst, crush, demolish, destroy, break, crack, fracture, pound, fringe, rack, rupture, shatter, rend.
(ANT.) mend, renovate, restore, repair.
smear *(SYN.)* wipe, rub, spread.
smell *(SYN.)* fragrance, fume, odor, perfume, incense, aroma, fetidness, stench, stink, scent, sniff, detect, bouquet.
smidgen *(SYN.)* crumb, mite, small, bit, particle, shred, speck, scrap.
(ANT.) bulk, mass, quantity, aggregate.
smile grin.
(ANT.) frown.
smite *(SYN.)* knock, hit, dash, beat, belabor, buffet, pound, punch, pummel, thrash, thump, defeat, overthrow, overpower, subdue, vanquish, rout.
(ANT.) surrender, fail, defend, shield, stroke.
smooth *(SYN.)* polished, sleek, slick, glib, diplomatic, flat, level, plain, suave, urbane, even, unwrinkled.
(ANT.) rugged, harsh, rough, blunt, bluff, uneven.
smother *(SYN.)* suffocate, asphyxiate, stifle.
smutty *(SYN.)* disgusting, filthy, impure, coarse, dirty, lewd, offensive, obscene, pornographic.
(ANT.) modest, refined, decent, pure.
snag *(SYN.)* difficulty, bar, barrier, check, hindrance, obstruction.
(ANT.) assistance, help, encouragement.
snappish *(SYN.)* ill-natured, ill-tempered, fractious, irritable, fretful, peevish, testy, touchy, petulant.
(ANT.) good-tempered, pleasant, good-natured, affable, genial.
snappy *(SYN.)* quick, stylish, chic.
snare *(SYN.)* capture, catch, arrest, clutch, grasp, grip, lay, apprehend, seize, trap, net.
(ANT.) throw, release, lose, liberate.
snarl *(SYN.)* growl.
snatch *(SYN.)* grasp, seize, grab.
sneak *(SYN.)* steal, skulk, slink.
sneer *(SYN.)* fleer, flout, jeer, mock, gibe, deride, taunt, scoff, scorn.
(ANT.) laud, flatter, praise, compliment.
sneering *(SYN.)* derision, gibe, banter, jeering, mockery, raillery, sarcasm, ridicule, satire.
sniveling *(SYN.)* whimpering, sniffling, weepy, whining, blubbering.
snobbish *(SYN.)* uppity, conceited, snooty, snobby, snotty.
snoopy *(SYN.)* inquisitive, interrogative, curious, inquiring, meddling, peeping, prying, peering.
(ANT.) uninterested, incurious, unconcerned, indifferent.
snub *(SYN.)* rebuke, insult, slight.
snug *(SYN.)* constricted, close, contracted, compact, firm, narrow, taut, tense, stretched, tight, cozy, comfortable, sheltered.
(ANT.) loose, lax, slack, relaxed, open.
soak *(SYN.)* saturate, drench, steep, wet.
soar *(SYN.)* flutter, fly, flit, float, glide, sail, hover, mount.
(ANT.) plummet, sink, fall, descend.

sob *(SYN.)* weep, cry, lament.
sober *(SYN.)* sedate, serious, staid, earnest, grave, solemn, moderate.
(ANT.) ordinary, joyful, informal, boisterous, drunk, fuddled, inebriated.
sobriety *(SYN.)* forbearance, abstinence, abstention, self-denial, moderation, temperance.
(ANT.) self-indulgence, excess, intoxication.
social *(SYN.)* friendly, civil, gregarious, affable, communicative, hospitable, sociable, group, common, genial, polite.
(ANT.) inhospitable, hermitic, antisocial, disagreeable.
society *(SYN.)* nation, community, civilization, organization, club, association, fraternity, circle, association, company, companionship.
soft *(SYN.)* gentle, lenient, flexible, compassionate, malleable, meek, mellow, subdued, mild, tender, supple, yielding, pliable, elastic, pliant.
(ANT.) unyielding, rough, hard, tough, rigid.
soften *(SYN.)* assuage, diminish, abate, allay, alleviate, mitigate, relieve, soothe, solace.
(ANT.) irritate, increase, aggravate, agitate.
soil *(SYN.)* defile, discolor, spot, befoul, blemish, blight, stain, sully, earth, dirt, loam, dirty.
(ANT.) purify, honor, cleanse, bleach, decorate.
solace *(SYN.)* contentment, ease, enjoyment, comfort, consolation, relief, succor.
(ANT.) torture, torment, misery, affliction, discomfort.
sole *(SYN.)* isolated, desolate, deserted, secluded, unaided, lone, alone, only, single, solitary.
(ANT.) surrounded, accompanied, attended.
solemn *(SYN.)* ceremonious, imposing, formal, impressive, reverential, ritualistic, grave, sedate, earnest, sober, staid, serious, dignified.
(ANT.) ordinary, joyful, informal, boisterous, cheerful, gay, happy.
solicit *(SYN.)* beg, beseech, request, seek, pray.
solicitous *(SYN.)* anxious, concerned.
solicitude *(SYN.)* concern, worry, anxiety, care, attention, regard, vigilance, caution, wariness.
(ANT.) indifference, disregard, neglect, negligence.
solid *(SYN.)* hard, dense, compact, firm.
(ANT.) loose.
solitary *(SYN.)* isolated, alone, lonely, deserted, unaided, secluded, only, single, lone, sole.
(ANT.) surrounded, attended, accompanied.
solitude *(SYN.)* loneliness, privacy, refuge, retirement, seclusion, retreat, alienation, asylum, concealment.
(ANT.) publicity, exposure, notoriety.
solution *(SYN.)* explanation, answer.
solve *(SYN.)* explain, answer, unravel.
somatic *(SYN.)* corporeal, corporal, natural, material, bodily, physical.
(ANT.) spiritual, mental.
somber *(SYN.)* dismal, dark, bleak, doleful, cheerless, natural, physical, serious, sober, gloomy, grave.
(ANT.) lively, joyous, cheerful, happy.
sometimes *(SYN.)* occasionally.
(ANT.) invariably, always.
soon *(SYN.)* shortly, early, betimes, beforehand.
(ANT.) tardy, late, overdue, belated.
soothe *(SYN.)* encourage, console, solace, comfort, cheer, gladden, sympathize, calm, pacify.
(ANT.) dishearten, depress, antagonize, aggravate, disquiet, upset, unnerve.
soothing *(SYN.)* gentle, benign, docile, calm, mild, placid, peaceful, serene, soft, relaxed, tractable, tame.
(ANT.) violent, savage, fierce, harsh.
sophisticated *(SYN.)* cultured, worldly, blase, cultivated, urbane, cosmopolitan, suave, intricate, complex, advanced.
(ANT.) uncouth, ingenuous, simple, naive, crude.
sorcery *(SYN.)* enchantment, conjuring, art, charm, black, magic, voodoo, witchcraft, wizardry.
sordid *(SYN.)* vicious, odious, revolting, obscene, foul, loathsome, base, depraved, debased, vile, vulgar, abject, wicked, ignoble, despicable, mean, low, worthless, wretched, dirty, unclean.
(ANT.) upright, decent, honorable.
sore *(SYN.)* tender, sensitive, aching, hurting, painful.
sorrow *(SYN.)* grief, distress, heartache, anguish, misery, sadness, mourning, trial, tribulation, gloom, depression.
(ANT.) consolation, solace, joy, happiness, comfort.
sorrowful *(SYN.)* dismal, doleful, dejected, despondent, depressed, disconsolate, gloomy, melancholy, glum, moody, somber, sad, grave, aggrieved.
(ANT.) merry, happy, cheerful, joyous.
sorry *(SYN.)* hurt, pained, sorrowful, afflicted, grieved, contrite, repentant, paltry, poor, wretched, remorseful, mean, shabby, contemptible, worthless, vile, regretful, apologetic.
(ANT.) delighted, impenitent, cheerful, unrepentant, splendid.
sort *(SYN.)* class, stamp, category, description, nature, character, kind, type, variety.
(ANT.) peculiarity, deviation.
sound *(SYN.)* effective, logical, telling, binding, powerful, weighty, legal, strong, conclusive, valid.
(ANT.) weak, null, counterfeit.
sour *(SYN.)* glum, sullen, bitter, peevish, acid, rancid, tart, acrimonious, sharp, bad-tempered, unpleasant, cranky.
(ANT.) wholesome, kindly, genial, benevolent, sweet.
source *(SYN.)* birth, foundation, agent, determinant, reason, origin, cause, start, incentive, motive, spring, induce-

ment, principle, beginning.
(ANT.) product, harvest, outcome, issue, consequence, end.
souvenir *(SYN.)* memento, monument, commemoration, remembrance.
sovereign *(SYN.)* monarch, king, emperor, queen, empress.
sovereignty *(SYN.)* command, influence, authority, predominance, control, sway.
(ANT.) debility, incapacity, disablement, ineptitude, impotence.
space *(SYN.)* room, area, location.
spacious *(SYN.)* capacious, large, vast, ample, extensive, wide, roomy, large.
(ANT.) limited, confined, narrow, small, cramped.
span *(SYN.)* spread, extent.
spare *(SYN.)* preserve, safeguard, uphold, conserve, protect, defend, rescue, reserve, additional, unoccupied.
(ANT.) impair, abolish, injure, abandon.
sparing *(SYN.)* economical, thrifty, frugal.
(ANT.) lavish.
sparkle *(SYN.)* gleam, glitter, twinkle, beam, glisten, radiate, shine, blaze.
spat *(SYN.)* quarrel, dispute, affray, wrangle, altercation.
(ANT.) peace, friendliness, agreement, reconciliation.
spawn *(SYN.)* yield, bear.
speak *(SYN.)* declare, express, say, articulate, harangue, converse, talk, utter.
(ANT.) refrain, hush, quiet.
special *(SYN.)* individual, uncommon, distinctive, peculiar, exceptional, unusual, extraordinary, different, particular.
(ANT.) general, widespread, broad, prevailing, average, ordinary.
specialist *(SYN.)* authority, expert.
species *(SYN.)* variety, type, kind, class, sort.
specific *(SYN.)* limited, characteristic, definite, peculiar, explicit, categorical, particular, distinct, precise.
(ANT.) generic, general, nonspecific.
specify *(SYN.)* name, call, mention, appoint, denominate, designate, define.
(ANT.) miscall, hint.
specimen *(SYN.)* prototype, example, sample, model, pattern, type.
speck *(SYN.)* scrap, jot, bit, mite, smidgen, crumb, iota, particle, spot.
(ANT.) quantity, bulk, aggregate.
spectacle *(SYN.)* demonstration, ostentation, movie, array, exhibition, show, display, performance, parade, splurge.
spectator *(SYN.)* viewer, observer.
speculate *(SYN.)* assume, deduce, surmise, apprehend, imagine, consider, view, think, guess, suppose, conjecture.
(ANT.) prove, demonstrate, conclude.
speech *(SYN.)* gossip, discourse, talk, chatter, lecture, conference, discussion, address, dialogue, articulation, accent.
(ANT.) silence, correspondence, writing, meditation.
speed *(SYN.)* forward, push, accelerate, hasten, rapidity, dispatch, swiftness.
(ANT.) impede, slow, block, retard.
spellbound *(SYN.)* fascinated, entranced, hypnotized, mesmerized, rapt.
spend *(SYN.)* pay, disburse, consume.
(ANT.) hoard, save.
spendthrift *(SYN.)* squanderer, profligate.
sphere *(SYN.)* globe, orb, ball, environment, area, domain.
spherical *(SYN.)* round, curved, globular.
spicy *(SYN.)* indecent, off-color, suggestive, indelicate.
spin *(SYN.)* revolve, turn, rotate, whirl, twirl, tell, narrate, relate.
spine *(SYN.)* vertebrae, backbone.
spineless *(SYN.)* weak, limp, cowardly.
(ANT.) brave, strong, courageous.
spirit *(SYN.)* courage, phantom, verve, fortitude, apparition, mood, soul, ghost.
(ANT.) listlessness, substance, languor.
spirited *(SYN.)* excited, animated, lively, active, vigorous, energetic.
(ANT.) indolent, lazy, sleepy.
spiritless *(SYN.)* gone, lifeless, departed, dead, insensible, deceased, unconscious.
(ANT.) stirring, alive, living.
spiritual *(SYN.)* sacred, unearthly, holy, divine, immaterial, supernatural.
(ANT.) material, physical, corporeal.
spite *(SYN.)* grudge, rancor, malice, animosity, malevolence, malignity.
(ANT.) kindness, toleration, affection.
spiteful *(SYN.)* vicious, disagreeable, surly, ill-natured.
(ANT.) pretty, beautiful, attractive, fair.
splendid *(SYN.)* glorious, illustrious, radiant, brilliant, showy, superb, bright.
(ANT.) ordinary, mediocre, dull.
splendor *(SYN.)* effulgence, radiance, brightness, luster, magnificence, display.
(ANT.) darkness, obscurity, dullness.
splinter *(SYN.)* fragment, piece, sliver, chip, shiver.
split *(SYN.)* rend, shred, cleave, disunite, sever, break, divide, opening, lacerate.
(ANT.) repair, unite, join, sew.
spoil *(SYN.)* rot, disintegrate, waste, decay, ruin, damage, mold, destroy.
(ANT.) luxuriate, grow, flourish.
spoken *(SYN.)* verbal, pronounced, articulated, vocal, uttered, oral.
(ANT.) written, documentary.
spokesman *(SYN.)* agent, representative.
spontaneous *(SYN.)* impulsive, voluntary, automatic, instinctive, willing, extemporaneous, natural, unconscious.
(ANT.) planned, rehearsed, forced, studied, prepared.
sport *(SYN.)* match, play, amusement, fun, pastime, entertainment, athletics.
sporting *(SYN.)* considerate, fair, sportsmanlike.
spot *(SYN.)* blemish, mark, stain, flaw,

blot, location. place, site, splatter.
spotty *(SYN.)* erratic, uneven, irregular, inconsistent.
(ANT.) regular, even.
spout *(SYN.)* spurt, squirt, tube, nozzle.
spray *(SYN.)* splash, spatter, sprinkle.
spread *(SYN.)* unfold, distribute, open, disperse, unroll, unfurl, scatter, jelly.
(ANT.) shut, close, hide, conceal.
sprightly *(SYN.)* blithe, hopeful, vivacious, buoyant, lively, light, nimble.
(ANT.) hopeless, depressed, sullen, dejected, despondent.
spring *(SYN.)* commencement, foundation, start, beginning, inception, jump, cradle, begin, birth, bound, originate.
(ANT.) issue, product, end.
sprinkle *(SYN.)* strew, spread, scatter, rain.
spruce *(SYN.)* orderly, neat, trim, clear, nice.
(ANT.) unkempt, sloppy, dirty.
spry *(SYN.)* brisk, quick, agile, nimble, energetic, supple, alert, active, lively.
(ANT.) heavy, sluggish, inert, clumsy.
spur *(SYN.)* inducement, purpose, cause, motive, impulse, reason, incitement.
(ANT.) effort, action, result, attempt.
squabble *(SYN.)* bicker, debate, altercate, contend, discuss, argue, quarrel.
(ANT.) concede, agree, assent.
squalid *(SYN.)* base, indecent, grimy, dirty, pitiful, filthy, muddy, nasty.
(ANT.) wholesome, clean, pure.
squander *(SYN.)* scatter, lavish, consume, dissipate, misuse.
(ANT.) preserve, conserve, save, accumulate.
squeamish *(SYN.)* particular, careful.
stab *(SYN.)* stick, gore, pierce, knife, spear, bayonet.
stability *(SYN.)* steadiness, balance, proportion, composure, symmetry.
(ANT.) imbalance, fall, unsteadiness.
stable *(SYN.)* firm, enduring, constant, fixed, unwavering, steadfast, steady.
(ANT.) irresolute, variable, changeable.
stack *(SYN.)* mass, pile, mound, heap, accumulate.
staff *(SYN.)* pole, stick, club, personnel, crew, employees.
stage *(SYN.)* frame, platform, boards, theater, scaffold, period, phase, step, direct, produce, present.
stagger *(SYN.)* totter, sway, reel, vary, falter, alternate.
staid *(SYN.)* solemn, sedate, earnest, sober, grave.
(ANT.) joyful, informal, ordinary.
stain *(SYN.)* blight, dye, tint, befoul, spot, defile, mark, dishonor, disgrace, smirch, blot, tint, blemish, discolor, color, tinge.
(ANT.) honor, bleach, decorate, purify.
stair *(SYN.)* staircase, stairway, steps.
stake *(SYN.)* rod, pole, picket, post, pale, bet, wager, concern, interest.
stale *(SYN.)* tasteless, spoiled, old, inedible, dry, uninteresting, trite, flat, dull, vapid, insipid.
(ANT.) new, fresh, tasty.
stalk *(SYN.)* dog, follow, track, shadow, hunt.
stall *(SYN.)* hesitate, stop, delay, postpone.
stammer *(SYN.)* falter, stutter.
stamp *(SYN.)* crush, trample, imprint, mark, brand, block, seal, die.
stand *(SYN.)* tolerate, suffer, stay, stand up, endure, bear, abide, halt, arise, rise, remain, sustain, rest.
(ANT.) run, yield, advance.
standard *(SYN.)* law, proof, pennant, emblem, touchstone, measure, example, gauge, model, banner, symbol, test.
(ANT.) guess, chance, irregular, unusual, supposition.
standing *(SYN.)* rank, position, station, status.
standpoint *(SYN.)* position, viewpoint, attitude.
staple *(SYN.)* main, principal, chief, essential, necessary.
stare *(SYN.)* gaze.
stark *(SYN.)* utter, absolute, sheer, complete, rough, severe, harsh, grim.
start *(SYN.)* opening, source, commence, onset, surprise, shock, beginning, origin, begin, initiate, jerk, jump, advantage, lead, commencement, outset.
(ANT.) end, completion, termination, close.
startle *(SYN.)* astonish, disconcert, aback, alarm, shock, agitate, surprise, astound, amaze, stun.
(ANT.) caution, prepare, admonish, forewarn.
starved *(SYN.)* longing, voracious, hungry, craving, avid, famished.
(ANT.) satisfied, sated, gorged, full.
state *(SYN.)* circumstance, predicament, case, situation, condition, affirm, declare, express, nation, country, status, assert, recite, tell, recount.
(ANT.) imply, conceal, retract.
stately *(SYN.)* lordly, elegant, regal, sovereign, impressive, magnificent, courtly, grand, imposing, majestic, noble, supreme, dignified.
(ANT.) low, common, mean, servile, humble, vulgar.
statement *(SYN.)* announcement, mention, allegation, declaration, thesis, assertion, report.
station *(SYN.)* post, depot, terminal, position, place.
status *(SYN.)* place, caste, standing, condition, state, rank, position.
statute *(SYN.)* law, ruling, decree, rule.
(ANT.) intention, deliberation.
stay *(SYN.)* delay, continue, hinder, check, hold, hindrance, support, brace, line, rope, linger, sojourn, abide, halt, stand, rest, remain, tarry, arrest, wait.
(ANT.) hasten, progress, go, depart, advance, leave.
stead *(SYN.)* place.
steadfast *(SYN.)* solid, inflexible, constant, stable, unyielding, secure.
(ANT.) unstable, insecure, unsteady.
steadfastness *(SYN.)* persistence, industry, tenacity, constancy, persis-

tency.
(ANT.) laziness, sloth, cessation.
steady *(SYN.)* regular, even, unremitting, stable, steadfast, firm, reliable, solid.
steal *(SYN.)* loot, rob, swipe, burglarize, pilfer, shoplift, embezzle, snitch.
(ANT.) restore, buy, return, refund.
stealthy *(SYN.)* sly, secret, furtive.
(ANT.) direct, open, obvious.
steep *(SYN.)* sharp, hilly, sheer, abrupt, perpendicular, precipitous.
(ANT.) gradual, level, flat.
steer *(SYN.)* manage, guide, conduct, lead, supervise, escort, navigate, drive, control, direct.
stem *(SYN.)* stalk, trunk, arise, check, stop, orginate, hinder.
stench *(SYN.)* odor, fetor, fetidness, stink, aroma, smell, fume, scent.
step *(SYN.)* stride, pace, stage, move, action, measure, come, go, walk.
stern *(SYN.)* harsh, rigid, exacting, rigorous, sharp, severe, strict, hard, unyielding, unmitigated, stringent.
(ANT.) indulgent, forgiving, yielding, lenient, considerate.
stew *(SYN.)* ragout, goulash, boil, simmer.
stick *(SYN.)* stalk, twig, rod, staff, pole, pierce, spear, stab, puncture, gore, cling, adhere, hold, catch, abide, remain, persist.
stickler *(SYN.)* nitpicker, perfectionist, disciplinarian.
sticky *(SYN.)* tricky, delicate, awkward.
stiff *(SYN.)* severe, unbendable, unyielding, harsh, inflexible, unbending, rigid, firm, hard, solid, rigorous.
(ANT.) supple, yielding, compassionate, mild, lenient, resilient.
stifle *(SYN.)* choke, strangle, suffocate.
stigma *(SYN.)* trace, scar, blot, stain, mark, vestige.
still *(SYN.)* peaceful, undisturbed, but, mild, hushed, calm, patient, modest, nevertheless, motionless, meek, quiescent, stationary, besides, however, quiet, hush, tranquil, serene, placid.
(ANT.) agitated, perturbed, loud.
stimulate *(SYN.)* irritate, excite, arouse, disquiet, rouse, activate, urge, invigorate, animate, provoke.
(ANT.) quell, calm, quiet, allay.
stimulus *(SYN.)* motive, goad, arousal, provocation, encouragement.
(ANT.) discouragement, depressant.
stingy *(SYN.)* greedy, penurious, avaricious, mean, penny-pinching, cheap, selfish, miserly, tight, tightfisted.
(ANT.) munificent, generous, giving, extravagant, openhanded, bountiful.
stipulate *(SYN.)* require, demand.
stir *(SYN.)* instigate, impel, push, agitate, induce, mix, rouse, move, propel.
(ANT.) halt, stop, deter.
stock *(SYN.)* hoard, store, strain, accumulation, supply, carry, keep, provision, fund, breed, sort.
(ANT.) sameness, likeness, homogeneity, uniformity.
stolid *(SYN.)* obtuse, unsharpened, dull, blunt, edgeless.
(ANT.) suave, tactful, polished, subtle.
stone *(SYN.)* pebble, gravel, rock.
stony *(SYN.)* insensitive, unsentimental, cold.
stoop *(SYN.)* bow, bend, lean, crouch.
stop *(SYN.)* terminate, check, abstain, hinder, arrest, close, bar, cork, halt, end, conclude, obstruct, finish, quit, pause, discontinue, stay, impede, cease.
(ANT.) start, proceed, speed, begin.
store *(SYN.)* amass, hoard, collect, market, shop, reserve, supply, deposit, bank, save, accrue, increase, stock.
(ANT.) dissipate, waste, disperse.
storm *(SYN.)* gale, tempest, tornado, thunderstorm, hurricane, rage, rant, assault, besiege.
stormy *(SYN.)* rough, inclement, windy, blustery, roaring, tempestuous.
(ANT.) quiet, calm, tranquil, peaceful.
story *(SYN.)* yarn, novel, history, tale, falsehood, account, fable, anecdote, narrative, fabrication, lie, level, floor, fiction, report.
stout *(SYN.)* plump, obese, chubby, fat, paunchy, overweight, portly, heavy, sturdy, strong, pudgy, thickset.
(ANT.) thin, slender, flimsy, gaunt, slim.
straight *(SYN.)* erect, honorable, square, just, direct, undeviating, unbent, right, upright, honest, uncurving, directly, moral, correct, orderly, vertical.
(ANT.) dishonest, bent, circuitous, twisted, crooked.
straightforward *(SYN.)* forthright, direct, open, candid, aboveboard.
(ANT.) devious.
strain *(SYN.)* stock, kind, variety, stretch, breed, tighten, harm, injure, screen, filter, sprain, sort.
strainer *(SYN.)* colander, sieve, filter.
strait *(SYN.)* fix, situation, passage, condition, dilemma, channel, trouble, predicament, difficulty, distress, crisis.
(ANT.) ease, calmness, satisfaction, comfort.
strange *(SYN.)* bizarre, peculiar, odd, abnormal, irregular, unusual, curious, uncommon, singular, extraordinary, foreign, eccentric, unfamiliar, queer.
(ANT.) regular, common, familiar, conventional.
stranger *(SYN.)* foreigner, outsider, newcomer, alien, outlander, immigrant.
(ANT.) friend, associate, acquaintance.
strap *(SYN.)* strip, belt, thong, band.
strategy *(SYN.)* technique, management, tactics, approach.
stray *(SYN.)* ramble, rove, deviate, lost, strayed, wander, digress, roam, stroll.
(ANT.) linger, stop, halt, settle.
stream *(SYN.)* issue, proceed, flow, come, abound, spout, run, brook.
street *(SYN.)* way, road, boulevard, avenue.
strength *(SYN.)* power, might, toughness, durability, lustiness, soundness, vigor, potency.

(ANT.) weakness, frailty, feebleness.
strengthen *(SYN.)* verify, assure, confirm, fix, sanction, ratify, substantiate.
strenuous *(SYN.)* forceful, energetic, active, vigorous, determined.
stress *(SYN.)* urgency, press, emphasize, accentuate, accent, weight, strain, importance, compulsion, pressure.
(ANT.) relaxation, lenience, ease.
stretch *(SYN.)* strain, expand, elongate, extend, lengthen, spread, distend, protract, distort.
(ANT.) tighten, loosen, slacken, contract.
strict *(SYN.)* rough, stiff, stringent, harsh, unbending, severe, rigorous.
(ANT.) easygoing, lenient, mild.
strife *(SYN.)* disagreement, conflict, discord, quarrel, difference, unrest.
(ANT.) tranquillity, peace, concord.
strike *(SYN.)* pound, hit, smite, beat, assault, attack, affect, impress, overwhelm, sitdown, walkout, slowdown.
striking *(SYN.)* arresting, imposing, splendid, august, impressive, thrilling, stirring, awesome, aweinspiring.
(ANT.) ordinary, unimpressive, commonplace, regular.
strip *(SYN.)* disrobe, undress, remove, uncover, peel, ribbon, band, piece.
stripped *(SYN.)* open, simple, bare, nude, uncovered, exposed, bald, plain, naked, barren, defenseless.
(ANT.) protected, dressed, concealed.
strive *(SYN.)* aim, struggle, attempt, undertake, design, endeavor, try.
(ANT.) omit, abandon, neglect, decline.
stroke *(SYN.)* rap, blow, tap, knock, feat, achievement, accomplishment, caress.
stroll *(SYN.)* amble, walk, ramble.
strong *(SYN.)* potent, hale, athletic, mighty, sturdy, impregnable, resistant.
(ANT.) feeble, insipid, brittle, weak, bland, fragile.
structure *(SYN.)* construction, framework, arrangement.
struggle *(SYN.)* fray, strive, fight, contest, battle, skirmish, oppose, clash.
(ANT.) peace, agreement, truce.
stubborn *(SYN.)* obstinate, firm, determined, inflexible, obdurate.
(ANT.) docile, yielding, amenable.
student *(SYN.)* pupil, observer, disciple, scholar, learner.
studio *(SYN.)* workroom, workshop.
study *(SYN.)* weigh, muse, master, contemplate, reflect, examination, examine.
stuff *(SYN.)* thing, subject, material, theme, matter, substance, fill, ram, cram, pack, textile, cloth, topic.
(ANT.) spirit, immateriality.
stumble *(SYN.)* sink, collapse, tumble, drop, topple, lurch, trip, fall.
(ANT.) steady, climb, soar, arise.
stun *(SYN.)* shock, knock out, dumbfound, take, amaze, alarm.
(ANT.) forewarn, caution, prepare.
stunning *(SYN.)* brilliant, dazzling, exquisite, ravishing.
(ANT.) drab, ugly.
stunt *(SYN.)* check, restrict, hinder.
stupid *(SYN.)* dull, obtuse, half-witted, brainless, foolish, dumb, witless, idiotic.
(ANT.) smart, intelligent, clever, quick, bright, alert, discerning.
stupor *(SYN.)* lethargy, torpor, daze, languor, drowsiness, numbness.
(ANT.) wakefulness, liveliness, activity.
sturdy *(SYN.)* hale, strong, rugged, stout, mighty, enduring, hardy, well-built.
(ANT.) fragile, brittle, insipid, delicate.
style *(SYN.)* sort, type, kind, chic, smartness, elegance.
subdue *(SYN.)* crush, overcome, rout, beat, reduce, lower, defeat, vanquish.
(ANT.) retreat, cede, surrender.
subject *(SYN.)* subordinate, theme, case, topic, dependent, citizen, matter.
sublime *(SYN.)* lofty, raised, elevated, supreme, exalted, splendid, grand.
(ANT.) ordinary, vase, low, ridiculous.
submerge *(SYN.)* submerse, dunk, sink, dip, immerse, engage, douse, engross.
(ANT.) surface, rise, uplift, elevate.
submissive *(SYN.)* deferential, yielding, dutiful, compliant.
(ANT.) rebellious, intractable, insubordinate.
submit *(SYN.)* quit, resign, waive, yield, tender, offer, abdicate, cede, surrender.
(ANT.) fight, oppose, resist, struggle, deny, refuse.
subordinate *(SYN.)* demean, reduce, inferior, assistant, citizen, liegeman.
(ANT.) superior.
subsequent *(SYN.)* later, following.
(ANT.) preceding, previous.
subside *(SYN.)* decrease, lower, sink, droop, hang, collapse, downward.
(ANT.) mount, steady, arise, climb.
subsidy *(SYN.)* support, aid, grant.
substance *(SYN.)* stuff, essence, importance, material, moment, matter.
(ANT.) spirit, immaterial.
substantial *(SYN.)* large, considerable, sizable, actual, real, tangible, influential.
(ANT.) unimportant, trivial.
substitute *(SYN.)* proxy, expedient, deputy, makeshift, replacement, alternate, lieutenant, representative, surrogate, displace, exchange, equivalent.
(ANT.) sovereign, master, head.
substitution *(SYN.)* change, mutation, vicissitude, alteration, modification.
(ANT.) uniformity, monotony.
subterfuge *(SYN.)* pretext, excuse, cloak, simulation, disguise, garb, pretension.
(ANT.) reality, truth, actuality, sincerity.
subtle *(SYN.)* suggestive, indirect.
(ANT.) overt, obvious.
subtract *(SYN.)* decrease, reduce, curtail, deduct, diminish, remove, lessen.
(ANT.) expand, increase, add, enlarge, grow.
succeed *(SYN.)* thrive, follow, replace, achieve, win, flourish, prevail, inherit.
(ANT.) flop, miscarry, anticipate, fail.
success *(SYN.)* prosperity, luck.
(ANT.) failure.
successful *(SYN.)* fortunate, favorable,

lucky, triumphant.
succession *(SYN.)* chain, course, series, order, string, arrangement, progression, train, following.
successive *(SYN.)* serial, sequential.
succinct *(SYN.)* pithy, curt, brief, short, compendious, terse.
(ANT.) prolonged, extended, long, protracted.
sudden *(SYN.)* rapid, swift, immediate, abrupt, unexpected, unforeseen, hasty.
(ANT.) slowly, anticipated.
suffer *(SYN.)* stand, experience, endure, bear, feel, allow, let, permit, sustain.
(ANT.) exclude, banish, overcome.
suffering *(SYN.)* distress, ache, anguish, pain, woe, misery, torment.
(ANT.) ease, relief, comfort.
sufficient *(SYN.)* fitting, enough, adequate, commensurate, satisfactory.
(ANT.) scant, deficient.
suffix *(SYN.)* ending.
(ANT.) prefix.
suggest *(SYN.)* propose, offer, refer, advise, hint, insinuate, recommend.
(ANT.) dictate, declare, insist.
suggestion *(SYN.)* exhortation, recommendation, intelligence, caution, admonition, warning, advice.
suit *(SYN.)* conform, accommodate, fit.
(ANT.) misapply, disturb.
suitable *(SYN.)* welcome, agreeable, acceptable, gratifying.
(ANT.) offensive, disagreeable.
sullen *(SYN.)* moody, fretful, surly, crabbed, morose, dour.
(ANT.) merry, gay, pleasant, amiable.
sullen *(SYN.)* fretful, morose, crabbed, dismal, silent, sulky, bitter, sad, somber, glum, gloomy, dour, moody.
(ANT.) pleasant, joyous, merry.
sultry *(SYN.)* close, hot, stifling.
sum *(SYN.)* amount, total, aggregate, whole, increase, append, add.
(ANT.) sample, fraction, reduce.
summarize *(SYN.)* abstract, abridge.
(ANT.) restore, add, unite, return.
summary *(SYN.)* digest, outline, abstract, synopsis, concise, brief, short.
summit *(SYN.)* peak, top, head, crest, zenith, apex, crown, pinnacle.
(ANT.) bottom, foundation, base, foot.
summon *(SYN.)* invoke, call, invite.
(ANT.) dismiss.
sundry *(SYN.)* miscellaneous, several, different, various, divers.
(ANT.) similar, identical, alike, same.
sunny *(SYN.)* cheery, cheerful, fair, joyful, happy, cloudless.
(ANT.) overcast, cloudy.
superb *(SYN.)* splendid, wonderful, extraordinary, marvelous.
superficial *(SYN.)* flimsy, shallow, cursory, slight, exterior.
(ANT.) thorough, deep, abstruse.
superintendent *(SYN.)* manager, supervisor, overseer, director, administrator.
superior *(SYN.)* greater, finer, better, employer, boss.
(ANT.) inferior.
superiority *(SYN.)* profit, mastery, advantage, good, service, edge, utility.
(ANT.) obstruction, harm, impediment.
supervise *(SYN.)* rule, oversee, govern, command, direct, superintend.
(ANT.) submit, forsake, abandon.
supervision *(SYN.)* oversight, inspection, surveillance, management.
supervisor *(SYN.)* manager, boss, foreman, director.
supplant *(SYN.)* overturn, overcome.
(ANT.) uphold, conserve.
supple *(SYN.)* lithe, pliant, flexible, limber, elastic, pliable.
(ANT.) stiff, brittle, rigid, unbending.
supplement *(SYN.)* extension, complement, addition, extend, add.
supplicate *(SYN.)* beg, petition, solicit, adjure, beseech, entreat, ask, pray.
(ANT.) cede, give, bestow, grant.
supplication *(SYN.)* invocation, plea, appeal, request, entreaty.
supply *(SYN.)* provide, inventory, hoard, reserve, store, accumulation.
support *(SYN.)* groundwork, aid, favor, base, prop, assistance, comfort, basis.
(ANT.) discourage, abandon, oppose.
supporter *(SYN.)* follower, devotee, adherent, henchman, attendant, disciple, votary.
(ANT.) master, head, chief.
suppose *(SYN.)* believe, presume, deduce, apprehend, think, assume, imagine, speculate, guess, conjecture.
(ANT.) prove, demonstrate, ascertain.
supposition *(SYN.)* theory, conjecture.
(ANT.) proof, fact.
suppress *(SYN.)* diminish, reduce, overpower, abate, lessen, decrease, subdue, lower.
(ANT.) revive, amplify, intensify.
supreme *(SYN.)* greatest, best, highest, main, principal, cardinal, first, chief, foremost, paramount.
(ANT.) supplemental, minor, subsidiary.
sure *(SYN.)* confident, fixed, inevitable, certain, positive, trustworthy.
(ANT.) probable, uncertain, doubtful.
surface *(SYN.)* outside, exterior, cover.
surge *(SYN.)* heave, swell, grow.
(ANT.) wane, ebb, diminish.
surname *(SYN.)* denomination, epithet, title, name, appellation, designation.
surpass *(SYN.)* pass, exceed, excel, outstrip, outdo.
surplus *(SYN.)* extravagance, intemperance, superabundance, excess, immoderation, remainder, extra, profusion, superfluity.
(ANT.) want, lack, dearth, paucity.
surprise *(SYN.)* miracle, prodigy, wonder, awe, phenomenon, marvel, bewilderment, wonderment, rarity.
(ANT.) expectation, triviality, indifference, familiarity.
surrender *(SYN.)* relinquish, resign, yield, abandon, sacrifice, submit, cede.
(ANT.) overcome, rout, conquer.
surround *(SYN.)* confine, encompass, circle, encircle, girdle, fence, circumscribe, limit, envelop.
(ANT.) open, distend, expose, enlarge.
surveillance *(SYN.)* inspection, oversight, supervision, management.
survey *(SYN.)* scan, inspect, view, examine, inspection, examination.

survive *(SYN.)* live, remain, continue.
(ANT.) die, fail, succumb.
suspect *(SYN.)* waver, disbelieve, presume, suppose, mistrust, distrust, question, suspected, assume, defendant, questionable, suspicious, doubt.
(ANT.) decide, believe, trust.
suspend *(SYN.)* delay hang, withhold, interrupt, postpone, dangle, adjurn, poise, defer, swing.
(ANT.) persist, proceed, maintain.
suspicious *(SYN.)* suspecting, distrustful, doubtful, doubting, questioning, suspect, skeptical, unusual.
suspicion *(SYN.)* unbelief, distrust, suspense, uncertainty, doubt.
(ANT.) determination, conviction.
sustain *(SYN.)* bear, carry, undergo, foster, keep, prop, help, advocate, back, encourage, maintain, assist, suffer, approve, uphold, support.
(ANT.) betray, oppose, destroy.
swallow *(SYN.)* gorge, gulp, eat.
swamp *(SYN.)* fen, bog, marsh, quagmire, morass, flood, overcome, deluge.
swarm *(SYN.)* throng, horde, crowd.
sway *(SYN.)* control, affect, stir, actuate, impel, impress, bend, wave, swing, persuade, influence.
swear *(SYN.)* declare, state, affirm, vouchsafe, curse, maintain.
(ANT.) demur, oppose, deny.
sweat *(SYN.)* perspiration, perspire.
sweeping *(SYN.)* extensive, wide, general, broad, tolerant, comprehensive, vast.
(ANT.) restricted, confined.
sweet *(SYN.)* engaging, luscious, pure, clean, fresh, melodious, winning.
(ANT.) bitter, harsh, nasty, irascible.
swell *(SYN.)* increase, grow, expand.
(ANT.) diminish, shrink.
swift *(SYN.)* quick, fast, fleet, speedy, rapid, expeditious.
swindle *(SYN.)* bilk, defraud, con, deceive, cheat, guile, imposture, deception, artifice, deceit, trick.
(ANT.) sincerity, honesty, fairness.
swing *(SYN.)* rock, sway, wave.
switch *(SYN.)* shift, change, turn.
swoon *(SYN.)* faint.
symbol *(SYN.)* sign, character.
sympathetic *(SYN.)* considerate, compassionate, gentle, benevolent, good.
(ANT.) unkind, merciless, unsympathetic, indifferent, intolerant, cruel.
sympathize *(SYN.)* gladden, sheer, solace, comfort, encourage, soothe.
(ANT.) depress, antagonize.
sympathy *(SYN.)* compassion, agreement, tenderness, commiseration, pity.
(ANT.) indifference, unconcern, antipathy, malevolence.
symptom *(SYN.)* indication, sign.
synopsis *(SYN.)* outline, digest.
synthetic *(SYN.)* counterfeit, artificial, phony, unreal, bogus, sham.
(ANT.) natural, true, genuine.
system *(SYN.)* organization, procedure, regularity, arrangement, mode, order.
(ANT.) confusion, chance, disorder.
systematic *(SYN.)* orderly, organized.
(ANT.) irregular, random.

table *(SYN.)* catalog, list, schedule, postpone, chart, index, delay, put off.
tablet *(SYN.)* pad, notebook, capsule, sketchpad, pill, lozenge.
taboo *(SYN.)* banned, prohibited, forbidden, restriction.
(ANT.) accepted, allowed, sanctioned.
tack *(SYN.)* add, join, attach, clasp.
tackle *(SYN.)* rigging, gear, apparatus, equipment, grab, seize, catch, down.
tacky *(SYN.)* gummy, sticky, gooey.
tact *(SYN.)* dexterity, poise, diplomacy, judgment, savoir faire, skill, finesse.
(ANT.) incompetence, vulgarity, blunder, rudeness, awkwardness.
tactful *(SYN.)* discreet, considerate, judicious, adroit, sensitive, diplomatic.
(ANT.) coarse, gruff, tactless, boorish, unfeeling, churlish, rude.
tag *(SYN.)* sticker, label, mark, identification, marker, name.
tail *(SYN.)* rear, back, follow, end, shadow, pursue, trail, heel.
tailor *(SYN.)* modiste, couturier, modify, redo, shape, fashion.
taint *(SYN.)* spot, stain, tarnish, soil, mark, discolor.
(ANT.) cleanse, disinfect, clean.
tainted *(SYN.)* crooked, impure, vitiated, profligate, debased, spoiled.
take *(SYN.)* accept, grasp, catch, confiscate, clutch, adopt, assume.
taking *(SYN.)* charming, captivating, winning, attractive.
takeover *(SYN.)* revolution, merger, usurpation, confiscation.
tale *(SYN.)* falsehood, history, yarn, chronicle, account, fable, fiction.
talent *(SYN.)* capability, knack, skill, endowment, gift, cleverness, aptitude.
(ANT.) ineptitude, incompetence.
talented *(SYN.)* skillful, smart, adroit, dexterous, clever, apt, quick-witted.
(ANT.) dull, clumsy, awkward, unskilled.
talk *(SYN.)* conversation, gossip, report, speech, communicate, discuss, confer.
(ANT.) silence, correspondence, meditation, writing.
tall *(SYN.)* elevated, high, towering, big, lofty, imposing, gigantic.
(ANT.) tiny, low, short, small, stunted.
tally *(SYN.)* score, count, compute, reckon, calculate, estimate, list, figure.
tamper *(SYN.)* mix in, interrupt, interfere, meddle, interpose.
tang *(SYN.)* zest, sharpness, tartness.
tangible *(SYN.)* material, sensible, palpable, corporeal, bodily.
(ANT.) metaphysical, mental, spiritual.
tangle *(SYN.)* confuse, knot, snarl, twist, ensnare, embroil, implicate.
tangy *(SYN.)* pungent, seasoned, sharp.
tantalize *(SYN.)* tease, tempt, entice, titillate, stimulate, frustrate.
tantrum *(SYN.)* outburst, fit, fury, conniption, rampage.
tap *(SYN.)* pat, rap, hit, strike, blow, faucet, spout, spigot, bunghole.
tape *(SYN.)* ribbon, strip, fasten, bandage, bind, record, tie.
taper *(SYN.)* narrow, candle, decrease, lessen.
tardy *(SYN.)* slow, delayed, overdue,

late, belated.
(ANT.) prompt, timely, punctual, early.
target *(SYN.)* aim, goal, object, objective.
tariff *(SYN.)* duty, tax, levy, rate.
tarnish *(SYN.)* discolor, blight, defile, sully, spot, befoul, disgrace, stain.
(ANT.) honor, purify, cleanse, bleach.
tarry *(SYN.)* dawdle, loiter, linger, dally, remain, delay, procrastinate.
tart *(SYN.)* sour, acrid, pungent, acid, sharp, distasteful, bitter.
(ANT.) sweet, delicious, pleasant.
task *(SYN.)* work, job, undertaking, labor, chore, duty, stint.
taste *(SYN.)* tang, inclination, liking, sensibility, flavor, savor, try, sip.
(ANT.) indelicacy, disinclination, antipathy, insipidity.
tasteful *(SYN.)* elegant, choice, refined, suitable, artistic.
(ANT.) offensive, unbecoming.
tasteless *(SYN.)* flavorless, insipid, unpalatable, rude, unrefined.
tasty *(SYN.)* delectable, delicious, luscious, palatable, tempting.
tattered *(SYN.)* ragged, torn, shoddy, shabby, frazzled, frayed, tacky, seedy.
taunt *(SYN.)* tease, deride, flout, scoff, sneer, annoy, bother, ridicule, jeer.
(ANT.) praise, compliment, laud, flatter.
taunting *(SYN.)* ironic, caustic, cutting, sardonic, derisive, biting, acrimonious.
(ANT.) pleasant, agreeable, affable.
taut *(SYN.)* tight, constricted, firm, stretched, snug, tense, extended.
(ANT.) slack, loose, relaxed, open, lax.
tavern *(SYN.)* pub, bar, cocktail lounge.
tax *(SYN.)* duty, assessment, excise, levy, toll, burden, strain, tribute, tariff.
(ANT.) reward, gift, remuneration
taxi *(SYN.)* cab, taxicab.
teach *(SYN.)* inform, school, educate, train, inculcate, instruct, instill, tutor.
(ANT.) misinform, misguide.
teacher *(SYN.)* tutor, instructor.
team *(SYN.)* company, band, party, crew, gang, group.
tear *(SYN.)* rend, shred, sunder, cleave, rip, lacerate, teardrop, disunite, rend, divide, drop, wound, split, slit, sever.
(ANT.) mend, repair, join, unite, sew.
tease *(SYN.)* badger, harry, bother, irritate, nag, pester, taunt, vex, annoy.
(ANT.) please, delight, soothe, comfort.
technical *(SYN.)* industrial, technological, specialized, mechanical.
technique *(SYN.)* system, method, routine, approach, procedure.
teem *(SYN.)* abound, swarm.
teeter *(SYN.)* sway, hesitate, hem and haw, waver.
telecast *(SYN.)* broadcast.
televise *(SYN.)* telecast.
tell *(SYN.)* report, mention, state, betray, announce, recount, relate, narrate, rehearse, mention, utter, confess.
telling *(SYN.)* persuasive, convincing, forceful, effective.
temper *(SYN.)* fury, choler, exasperation, anger, passion, petulance, disposition, nature, rage, soothe, soften, wrath, indignation, irritation, pacify, animosity, mood, resentment.
(ANT.) peace, self-control, forbearance, conciliation.
temperament *(SYN.)* humor, mood, temper, nature, disposition.
temperamental *(SYN.)* testy, moody, touchy, sensitive, irritable.
(ANT.) calm, unruffled, serene.
temperance *(SYN.)* abstinence, sobriety, self-denial, forbearance, abstention.
(ANT.) intoxication, excess, self-indulgence, gluttony, wantonness.
temperate *(SYN.)* controlled, moderate, cool, calm, restrained.
(ANT.) excessive, extreme, prodigal.
tempest *(SYN.)* draft, squall, wind, blast, gust, storm, hurricane, commotion, tumult, zephyr.
(ANT.) calm, tranquillity, peace.
tempo *(SYN.)* measure, beat, cadence, rhythm.
temporal *(SYN.)* mundane, earthly, lay, profane, worldly, terrestrial, laic.
(ANT.) spiritual, ecclesiastical, unworldly, religious, heavenly.
temporary *(SYN.)* brief, momentary, shortlived, fleeting, ephemeral, passing, short, transient.
(ANT.) lasting, permanent, immortal, everlasting, timeless, abiding.
tempt *(SYN.)* entice, allure, lure, attract, seduce, invite, magnetize.
tenacious *(SYN.)* persistent, determined, unchanging, unyielding.
tenable *(SYN.)* correct, practical, rational, reasonable, sensible, defensible.
tenacity *(SYN.)* perseverance, steadfastness, industry, constancy, persistence, pertinacity.
(ANT.) laziness, rest, cessation, idleness, sloth.
tenant *(SYN.)* renter, lessee, lodger, leaseholder, dweller, resident.
tend *(SYN.)* escort, follow, care for, lackey, watch, protect, take care of, attend, guard, serve.
tendency *(SYN.)* drift, inclination, proneness, leaning, bias, aim, leaning, disposition, predisposition, propensity, trend, impulse.
(ANT.) disinclination, aversion, deviation.
tender *(SYN.)* sympathetic, sore, sensitive, painful, gentle, meek, delicate, fragile, proffer, bland, mild, loving, offer, affectionate, soothing, propose, moderate, soft.
(ANT.) rough, severe, fierce, chewy, tough, cruel, unfeeling, harsh.
tenderfoot *(SYN.)* novice, apprentice, beginner, amateur.
tenderhearted *(SYN.)* kind, sympathetic, merciful, softhearted, understanding, sentimental, affectionate, gentle, sensitive.
tenderness *(SYN.)* attachment, kindness, love, affection, endearment.
(ANT.) repugnance, indifference, aversion, hatred, repulsive.
tenet *(SYN.)* dogma, belief, precept, doctrine, creed, opinion.
(ANT.) deed, conduct, practice, perfor-

mance.

tense *(SYN.)* strained, stretched, excited, tight, nervous.
(ANT.) loose, placid, lax, relaxed.

tension *(SYN.)* stress, strain, pressure, anxiety, apprehension, distress.

tentative *(SYN.)* hypothetical, indefinite, probationary, conditional.

tenure *(SYN.)* administration, time, regime, term.

tepid *(SYN.)* temperate, mild, lukewarm.
(ANT.) boiling, scalding, passionate, hot.

term *(SYN.)* period, limit, time, boundary, duration, name, phrase, interval, session, semester, expression, word.

terminal *(SYN.)* eventual, final, concluding, decisive, ending, fatal, latest, last, ultimate, conclusive.
(ANT.) original, first, rudimentary, incipient, inaugural.

terminate *(SYN.)* close, end, finish, abolish, complete, cease, stop, conclude, expire, culminate.
(ANT.) establish, begin, initiate, start, commence.

terminology *(SYN.)* vocabulary, nomenclature, terms, phraseology.

terms *(SYN.)* stipulations, agreement, conditions, provisions.

terrible *(SYN.)* frightful, dire, awful, gruesome, horrible shocking, horrifying, terrifying, horrid, hideous, appalling, shocking.
(ANT.) secure, happy, joyous, pleasing, safe.

terrific *(SYN.)* superb, wonderful, glorious, great, magnificent, divine, colossal, sensational, marvelous.

terrify *(SYN.)* dismay, intimidate, startle, terrorize, appall, frighten, petrify, astound, alarm, affright, horrify, scare.
(ANT.) soothe, allay, reassure, compose, embolden.

territory *(SYN.)* dominion, province, quarter, section, country, division, region, domain, area, place, district.

terror *(SYN.)* fear, alarm, dismay, horror, dread, consternation, fright, panic.
(ANT.) calm, security, assurance, peace.

terse *(SYN.)* concise, incisive, succinct, summary, condensed, compact, neat, pithy, summary.
(ANT.) verbose, wordy, lengthy, prolix.

test *(SYN.)* exam, examination, trial, quiz, analyze, verify, validate.

testify *(SYN.)* depose, warrant, witness, state, attest, swear.

testimony *(SYN.)* evidence, attestation, declaration, proof, witness, confirmation.
(ANT.) refutation, argument, disproof, contradiction.

testy *(SYN.)* ill-natured, irritable, snappish, waspish, fractious, fretful, touchy, ill-tempered, peevish, petulant.
(ANT.) pleasant, affable, good-tempered, genial, good-natured.

tether *(SYN.)* tie, hamper, restraint, bridle.

text *(SYN.)* textbook, book, manual.

textile *(SYN.)* material, cloth, goods, fabric.

texture *(SYN.)* construction, structure, makeup, composition, grain, finish.

thankful *(SYN.)* obliged, grateful, appreciative.
(ANT.) thankless, ungrateful, resenting.

thaw *(SYN.)* liquefy, melt, dissolve.
(ANT.) solidify, freeze.

theater *(SYN.)* arena, playhouse, battlefield, stadium, hall.

theatrical *(SYN.)* ceremonious, melodramatic, stagy, artificial, affected, dramatic, showy, dramatic, compelling.
(ANT.) unemotional, subdued, modest, unaffected.

theft *(SYN.)* larceny, robbery, stealing, plunder, burglary, pillage, thievery, depredation.

theme *(SYN.)* motive, topic, argument, subject, thesis, text, point, paper, essay, composition.

theoretical *(SYN.)* bookish, learned, scholarly, pedantic, academic, formal, erudite, scholastic.
(ANT.) practical, ignorant, commonsense, simple.

theory *(SYN.)* doctrine, guess, presupposition, postulate, assumption, hypothesis, speculation.
(ANT.) practice, verity, fact, proof.

therefore *(SYN.)* consequently, thence so, accordingly, hence, then.

thick *(SYN.)* compressed, heavy, compact, viscous, close, concentrated, crowded, syrupy, dense.
(ANT.) watery, slim, thin, sparse, dispersed, dissipated.

thief *(SYN.)* burglar, robber, criminal.

thin *(SYN.)* diluted, flimsy, lean, narrow, slender, spare, emaciated, diaphanous, gauzy, meager, slender, tenuous, slim, rare, sparse, scanty, lank, gossamer, scanty, slight.
(ANT.) fat, wide, broad, thick, bulky.

think *(SYN.)* picture, contemplate, ponder, esteem, intend, mean, imagine, deliberate, contemplate, recall, speculate, recollect, deem, apprehend, consider, devise, plan, judge, purpose, reflect, suppose, assume, meditate, muse.
(ANT.) forget, conjecture, guess.

thirst *(SYN.)* appetite, desire, craving, longing.

thirsty *(SYN.)* arid, dry, dehydrated, parched, craving, desirous.
(ANT.) satisfied.

thorn *(SYN.)* spine, barb, prickle, nettle, bramble.

thorough *(SYN.)* entire, complete, perfect, total, finished, unbroken, perfect, careful, thoroughgoing, consummate, undivided.
(ANT.) unfinished, careless, slapdash, imperfect, haphazard, lacking.

thoroughfare *(SYN.)* avenue, street, parkway, highway, boulevard.
(ANT.) byway.

though *(SYN.)* in any case, notwithstanding, however, nevertheless.

thought *(SYN.)* consideration, pensive,

attentive, heedful, prudent, dreamy, reflective, introspective, meditation, notion, view, deliberation, sentiment, fancy, idea, impression, reasoning, contemplation, judgment, regard.
(ANT.) thoughtlessness.

thoughtful *(SYN.)* considerate, attentive, dreamy, pensive, provident, introspective, meditative, cautious, heedful, kind, courteous, friendly, pensive.
(ANT.) thoughtless, heedless, inconsiderate, rash, precipitous, selfish.

thoughtless *(SYN.)* inattentive, unconcerned, negligent, lax, desultory, inconsiderate, careless, imprudent, inaccurate, neglectful, indiscreet, remiss.
(ANT.) meticulous, accurate, nice, careful.

thrash *(SYN.)* whip, beat, defeat, flog, punish, flog, strap, thresh.

thread *(SYN.)* yarn, strand, filament, fiber, string, cord.

threadbare *(SYN.)* shabby, tacky, worn, ragged, frayed.

threat *(SYN.)* menace, warning, danger, hazard, jeopardy, omen.

threaten *(SYN.)* caution, warning, forewarn, menace, intimidate, loom.

threatening *(SYN.)* imminent, nigh, approaching, impending, overhanging, sinister, foreboding.
(ANT.) improbable, retreating, afar, distant, remote.

threshold *(SYN.)* edge, verge, start, beginning, doorsill, commencement.

thrift *(SYN.)* prudence, conservation, saving, economy.

thrifty *(SYN.)* saving, economical, sparing, frugal, provident, stingy, saving, parsimonious.
(ANT.) wasteful, spendthrift, intemperate, self-indulgent, extravagant.

thrill *(SYN.)* arouse, rouse, excite, stimulation, excitement, tingle.
(ANT.) bore.

thrive *(SYN.)* succeed, flourish, grow, prosper.
(ANT.) expire, fade, shrivel, die, fail, languish.

throb *(SYN.)* pound, pulsate, palpitate, beat, pulse.

throe *(SYN.)* pang, twinge, distress, suffering, pain, ache, grief, agony.
(ANT.) pleasure, relief, ease, solace, comfort.

throng *(SYN.)* masses, press, crowd, bevy, populace, swarm, rabble, horde, host, mass, teem, mob, multitude.

throttle *(SYN.)* smother, choke, strangle.

through *(SYN.)* completed, done, finished, over.

throughout *(SYN.)* all over, everywhere, during.

throw *(SYN.)* propel, cast, pitch, toss, hurl, send, thrust, fling.
(ANT.) retain, pull, draw, haul, hold

thrust *(SYN.)* jostle, push, promote, crowd, force, drive, hasten, push, press, shove, urge.
(ANT.) ignore, falter, retreat, drag, oppose, halt.

thug *(SYN.)* mobster, hoodlum, mugger, gangster, assassin, gunman.

thump *(SYN.)* blow, strike, knock, jab, poke, pound, beat, clout, bat, rap, bang.

thunderstruck *(SYN.)* amazed, astounded, astonished, awed, flabbergasted, surprised, dumbfounded, bewildered, spellbound.

thus *(SYN.)* hence, therefore, accordingly, so, consequently.

thwart *(SYN.)* defeat, frustrate, prevent, foil, stop, baffle, circumvent hinder, obstruct, disappoint, balk, outwit.
(ANT.) promote, accomplish, fulfill, help, further.

ticket *(SYN.)* stamp, label, tag, seal, token, pass, summons, certificate, ballot, sticker, slate, citation.

tickle *(SYN.)* delight, entertain, thrill, amuse, titillate, excite.

ticklish *(SYN.)* fragile, delicate, tough, difficult.

tidings *(SYN.)* message, report, information, word, intelligence, news.

tidy *(SYN.)* trim, clear, neat, precise, spruce, orderly, shipshape.
(ANT.) disheveled, unkempt, sloppy, dirty, slovenly.

tie *(SYN.)* bond, join, relationship, bind, restrict, fetter, connect, conjunction, association, alliance, union, fasten, engage, attach, restrain, oblige, link, affinity.
(ANT.) separation, disunion, unfasten, open, loose, untie, free, isolation.

tier *(SYN.)* line, row, level, deck, layer.

tiff *(SYN.)* bicker, squabble, argue, row, clash, dispute, altercation.

tight *(SYN.)* firm, taut, penny-pinching, constricted, snug, taut, parsimonious, secure, fast, strong, sealed, fastened, watertight, locked, close, compact, stingy.
(ANT.) slack, lax, open, relaxed, loose.

till *(SYN.)* plow, work, moneybox, depository, cultivate, vault.

tilt *(SYN.)* slant, slope, incline, tip, lean.

timber *(SYN.)* lumber, wood, logs.

time *(SYN.)* epoch, span, term, age, duration, interim, period, tempo, interval, space, spell, season.

timeless *(SYN.)* unending, lasting, perpetual, endless, immemorial.
(ANT.) temporary, mortal, temporal.

timely *(SYN.)* prompt, exact, punctual, ready, precise.
(ANT.) slow, dilatory, tardy, late.

timepiece *(SYN.)* clock, watch.

timetable *(SYN.)* list, schedule.

timid *(SYN.)* coy, humble, sheepish, abashed, embarrassed, modest, bashful, diffident, shamefaced, retiring, fearful, faint-hearted, shy, timorous.
(ANT.) gregarious, bold, daring, adventurous, fearless, outgoing.

tinge *(SYN.)* color, tint, dye, stain, flavor, imbue, season, impregnate.

tingle *(SYN.)* shiver, chime, prickle.

tinker *(SYN.)* potter, putter, fiddle with, dawdle, dally, dabble.

tinkle *(SYN.)* sound, peal, ring, jingle, chime, toll.

tint *(SYN.)* color, tinge, dye, stain, hue,

tone, shade.
tiny *(SYN.)* minute, little, petty, wee, slight, diminutive, miniature, small, insignificant, trivial, puny.
(ANT.) huge, large, immense, big, enormous.
tip *(SYN.)* point, end, top, peak, upset, tilt, reward, gift, gratuity, clue, hint, suggestion, inkling.
tirade *(SYN.)* outburst, harangue, scolding.
tire *(SYN.)* jade, tucker, bore, weary, exhaust, weaken, wear out, fatigue.
(ANT.) restore, revive, exhilarate, amuse, invigorate, refresh.
tired *(SYN.)* weary, exhausted, fatigued, run-down, sleepy, faint, spent, wearied, worn, jaded.
(ANT.) rested, fresh, hearty, invigorated, energetic, tireless, eager.
tireless *(SYN.)* active, enthusiastic, energetic, strenuous.
(ANT.) exhausted, wearied, fatigued.
tiresome *(SYN.)* dull, boring, monotonous, tedious.
(ANT.) interesting.
titan *(SYN.)* colossus, powerhouse, mammoth.
title *(SYN.)* epithet, privilege, name, appellation, claim, denomination, due, heading, ownership, right, deed, designation.
toast *(SYN.)* salutation, pledge, celebration.
toddle *(SYN.)* stumble, wobble, shuffle.
toil *(SYN.)* labor, drudgery, work, travail, performance, business, achievement, employment, occupation, slave, sweat, effort.
(ANT.) recreation, ease, vacation, relax, loll, play, leisure, repose.
token *(SYN.)* mark, sign, sample, indication, evidence, symbol.
tolerant *(SYN.)* extensive, vast, considerate, broad, patient, large, sweeping, liberal, wide.
(ANT.) intolerant, bigoted, biased, restricted, narrow, confined.
tolerate *(SYN.)* endure, allow, bear, authorize, permit, brook, stand, abide.
(ANT.) forbid, protest, prohibit, discriminating, unreasonable.
toll *(SYN.)* impost, burden, rate, assessment, duty, custom, excise, tribute, levy, burden, strain.
(ANT.) reward, wages, gift, remuneration.
tomb *(SYN.)* vault, monument, catacomb, grave, mausoleum.
tone *(SYN.)* noise, sound, mood, manner, expression, cadence.
tongs *(SYN.)* tweezers, hook, grapnel, forceps.
tongue *(SYN.)* diction, lingo, cant, jargon, vernacular, dialect, idiom, speech, phraseology.
(ANT.) nonsense, drivel, babble, gibberish.
too *(SYN.)* furthermore, moreover, similarly, also, in addition, besides, likewise.
tool *(SYN.)* devise, medium, apparatus, agent, implement, utensil, agent, vehicle, instrument.
(ANT.) preventive, hindrance, impediment, obstruction.
top *(SYN.)* crown, pinnacle, peak, tip, cover, cap, zenith, apex, crest, chief, head, summit.
(ANT.) bottom, foundation, base, foot.
topic *(SYN.)* subject, thesis, issue, argument, matter, theme, point.
topple *(SYN.)* collapse, sink, fall, tumble.
torment *(SYN.)* pain, woe, pester, ache, distress, misery, harass, throe, annoy, vex, torture, anguish, suffering, misery.
(ANT.) relief, comfort, ease, gratify, delight.
torpid *(SYN.)* sluggish, idle, lazy, inert, inactive, supine, slothful, indolent, motionless, lethargic.
(ANT.) alert, assiduous, diligent, active.
torpor *(SYN.)* lethargy, daze, numbness, stupor, drowsiness, insensibility, languor.
(ANT.) wakefulness, liveliness, activity, alertness, readiness.
torrent *(SYN.)* flood, downpour, deluge.
torrid *(SYN.)* scorching, ardent, impetuous, passionate, scalding, warm, fiery, sultry, tropical, intense, sweltering, burning, hot.
(ANT.) passionless, impassive, cold, frigid, apathetic, freezing, phlegmatic, indifferent, temperate.
torso *(SYN.)* form, frame, body.
(ANT.) soul, mind, spirit, intellect.
torture *(SYN.)* anguish, badger, plague, distress, ache, forment, pester, pain, hound, agony, woe, worry, vex, persecute, suffering, throe, afflict, misery.
(ANT.) aid, relief, comfort, ease, support, encourage, mitigation.
toss *(SYN.)* throw, cast, hurl, pitch, tumble, thrust, pitch, fling, propel.
(ANT.) retain, pull, draw, haul, hold.
total *(SYN.)* entire, complete, concluded, finished, thorough, whole, entirely, collection, aggregate, conglomeration, unbroken, perfect, undivided, consummate, full.
(ANT.) part, element, imperfect, unfinished, ingredient, particular, lacking.
tote *(SYN.)* move, transfer, convey, drag, carry.
totter *(SYN.)* falter, stagger, reel, sway, waver, stumble, wobble.
touch *(SYN.)* finger, feel, handle, move, affect, concern, mention, hint, trace, suggestion, knack, skill, ability, talent.
touch-and-go *(SYN.)* dangerous, risky, perilous, hazardous.
touching *(SYN.)* pitiable, affecting, moving, sad, adjunct, bordering, tangent, poignant, tender, effective, impressive, adjacent.
(ANT.) removed, enlivening, animated, exhilarating.
touchy *(SYN.)* snappish, irritable, fiery, choleric, testy, hot, irascible, nervous, excitable, petulant, sensitive, short-tempered, jumpy, peevish.
(ANT.) composed, agreeable, tranquil, calm, serene, stolid, cool.
tough *(SYN.)* sturdy, difficult, trying, vi-

cious, incorrigible, troublesome, hard, stout, leathery, strong, laborious, inedible, sinewy, cohesive, firm, callous, obdurate, vicious.
(ANT.) vulnerable, submissive, easy, brittle, facile, weak, fragile, compliant, tender, frail.
toughness *(SYN.)* stamina, sturdiness, fortitude, durability, intensity, force, might, stoutness, power, sturdiness, vigor.
(ANT.) weakness, feebleness, infirmity, frailty.
tour *(SYN.)* rove, travel, go, visit, excursion, ramble, journey, roam.
(ANT.) stop, stay.
tourist *(SYN.)* traveler, sightseer, vagabond, voyager.
tournament *(SYN.)* tourney, match, contest, competition.
tout *(SYN.)* vend, importune, peddle, solicit, sell, hawk.
tow *(SYN.)* tug, take out, unsheathe, haul, draw, remove, extract, pull, drag.
(ANT.) propel, drive.
towering *(SYN.)* elevated, exalted, high, lofty, tall, proud, eminent.
(ANT.) base, mean, stunted, small, tiny, low.
town *(SYN.)* hamlet, village, community, municipality.
toxic *(SYN.)* deadly, poisonous, fatal, lethal, harmful.
(ANT.) beneficial.
toy *(SYN.)* play, romp, frolic, gamble, stake, caper, plaything, wager, revel.
trace *(SYN.)* stigma, feature, indication, trait, mark, stain, scar, sign, trial, trace, suggestion, characteristic, vestige, symptoms.
track *(SYN.)* persist, pursue, follow, sign, mark, spoor, trace, path, route, road, carry, hunt, chase.
(ANT.) escape, evade, abandon, flee, elude.
tract *(SYN.)* area, region, territory, district, expanse, domain.
tractable *(SYN.)* yielding, deferential, submissive, dutiful, compliant, obedient.
(ANT.) rebellious, intractable, insubordinate, obstinate.
trade *(SYN.)* business, traffic, commerce, dealing, craft, occupation, profession, livelihood, swap, barter, exchange.
trademark *(SYN.)* logo, brand name, identification, emblem, insignia, monogram.
tradition *(SYN.)* custom, legend, folklore, belief, rite, practice.
traduce *(SYN.)* defame, malign, vilify, revile, abuse, asperse, scandalize, disparage.
(ANT.) protect, honor, cherish, praise, respect, support, extol.
tragedy *(SYN.)* unhappiness, misfortune, misery, adversity, catastrophe.
tragic *(SYN.)* miserable, unfortunate, depressing, melancholy, mournful.
(ANT.) happy, cheerful, comic.
trail *(SYN.)* persist, pursue, chase, follow, drag, draw, hunt, track.
(ANT.) evade, flee, abandon, elude, escape.
train *(SYN.)* direct, prepare, aim, point, level, teach, drill, tutor, bid, instruct, order, command.
(ANT.) distract, deceive, misguide, misdirect.
traipse *(SYN.)* roam, wander, saunter, meander.
trait *(SYN.)* characteristic, feature, attribute, peculiarity, mark, quality, property.
traitor *(SYN.)* turncoat, betrayer, spy, double-dealer, conspirator.
traitorous *(SYN.)* disloyal, faithless, apostate, false, recreant, perfidious, treasonable, treacherous.
(ANT.) devoted, true, loyal, constant.
tramp *(SYN.)* bum, beggar, rover, hobo, march, stamp, stomp, vagabond, wanderer, vagrant.
(ANT.) laborer, worker, gentleman.
trample *(SYN.)* crush, stomp, squash.
tranquil *(SYN.)* composed, calm, dispassionate, imperturbable, peaceful, pacific, placid, quiet, still, serene, undisturbed, unruffled.
(ANT.) frantic, stormy, excited, disturbed, upset, turbulent, wild.
tranquillity *(SYN.)* calmness, calm, hush, peace, quiet, quiescence, quietude, repose, serenity, rest, stillness, silence, placid.
(ANT.) disturbance, agitation, excitement, tumult, noise.
transact *(SYN.)* conduct, manage, execute, treat, perform.
transaction *(SYN.)* business, deal, affair, deed, settlement, occurrence, negotiation, proceeding.
transcend *(SYN.)* overstep, overshadow, exceed.
transcribe *(SYN.)* write, copy, rewrite, record.
transfer *(SYN.)* dispatch, send, transmit, remove, transport, transplant, consign, move, shift, reasign, assign, relegate.
transform *(SYN.)* change, convert, alter, modify, transfigure, shift, vary, veer.
(ANT.) establish, continue, settle, preserve, stabilize.
transgression *(SYN.)* atrocity, indignity, offense, insult, outrage, aggression, injustice, crime, misdeed, trespass, sin, wrong, vice.
(ANT.) innocence, morality, gentleness, right.
transient *(SYN.)* ephemeral, evanescent, brief, fleeting, momentary, temporary, short-lived.
(ANT.) immortal, abiding, permanent, lasting, timeless, established.
transition *(SYN.)* change, variation, modification.
translate *(SYN.)* decipher, construe, decode, elucidate, explicate, explain, interpret, solve, render, unravel.
(ANT.) distort, falsify, misinterpret, confuse, misconstrue.
transmit *(SYN.)* confer, convey, communicate, divulge, disclose, impart, send, inform, relate, notify, reveal, dispatch, tell.

(ANT.) withhold, hide, conceal.

transparent *(SYN.)* crystalline, clear, limpid, lucid, translucent, thin, evident, manifest, plain, evident, explicit, obvious, open.
(ANT.) opaque, muddy, turbid, thick, questionable, ambiguous.

transpire *(SYN.)* befall, bechance, betide, happen, chance, occur.

transport *(SYN.)* carry, bear, convey, remove, move, shift, enrapture, transfer, lift, entrance, ravish, stimulate.

transpose *(SYN.)* change, switch, reverse.

trap *(SYN.)* artifice, bait, ambush, intrigue, net, lure, pitfall, ensnare, deadfall, snare, ruse, entrap, bag, trick, stratagem, wile.

trash *(SYN.)* refuse, garbage, rubbish, waste.

trashy *(SYN.)* insignificant, worthless, slight.

trauma *(SYN.)* ordeal, upheaval, jolt, shock, disturbance.

travail *(SYN.)* suffering, torment, anxiety, distress, anguish, misery, ordeal.

travel *(SYN.)* journey, go, touring, ramble, rove, voyage, cruise, tour, roam.
(ANT.) stop, stay, remain, hibernate.

travesty *(SYN.)* farce, joke, misrepresentation, counterfeit, mimicry.

treachery *(SYN.)* collusion, cabal, combination, intrigue, conspiracy, machination, disloyalty, betrayal, treason, plot.
(ANT.) allegiance, steadfastness, loyalty.

treason *(SYN.)* cabal, combination, betrayal, sedition, collusion, intrigue, conspiracy, machination, disloyalty, treachery, plot.

treasure *(SYN.)* cherish, hold dear, abundance, guard, prize, appreciate, value, riches, wealth, foster, sustain, nurture.
(ANT.) disregard, neglect, dislike, abandon, reject.

treat *(SYN.)* employ, avail, manipulate, exploit, operate, utilize, exert, act, exercise, practice, handle, manage, deal, entertain, indulge, host, negotiate, tend, attend, heal, use.
(ANT.) neglect, overlook, ignore, waste.

treaty *(SYN.)* compact, agreement, pact, bargain, covenant, alliance, marriage.
(ANT.) schism, separation, divorce.

trek *(SYN.)* tramp, hike, plod, trudge.

tremble *(SYN.)* flutter, jolt, jar, agitate, quake, quiver, quaver, rock, shake shudder, shiver, totter, sway, vibrate, waver.

trembling *(SYN.)* apprehension, alarm, dread, fright, fear, horror, terror, panic.
(ANT.) composure, calmness, tranquillity, serenity.

tremendous *(SYN.)* enormous, huge, colossal, gigantic, great, large.

tremor *(SYN.)* flutter, vibration, palpitation.

trench *(SYN.)* gully, gorge, ditch, gulch, moat, dugout, trough.

trenchant *(SYN.)* clear, emphatic, forceful, impressive, meaningful.

trend *(SYN.)* inclination, tendency, drift, course, tendency, direction.

trendy *(SYN.)* modish, faddish, stylish, voguish, popular, current.

trepidation *(SYN.)* apprehension, alarm, dread, fright, fear, horror, panic, terror.
(ANT.) boldness, bravery, fearlessness, courage, assurance.

trespass *(SYN.)* atrocity, indignity, affront, insult, outrage, offense, aggression, crime, misdeed, injustice, vice, wrong, sin.
(ANT.) evacuate, vacate, relinquish, abandon.

trespasser *(SYN.)* invader, intruder, encroacher.

trial *(SYN.)* experiment, ordeal, proof, test, examination, attempt, effort, endeavor, essay, affliction, misery, hardship, suffering, difficulty, misfortune, tribulation, trouble.
(ANT.) consolation, alleviation.

tribe *(SYN.)* group, race, clan, bunch.

tribulation *(SYN.)* anguish, distress, agony, grief, misery, sorrow, torment, suffering, woe, disaster, calamity, evil, trouble, misfortune.
(ANT.) elation, delight, joy, fun, pleasure.

tribunal *(SYN.)* arbitrators, judges, decision-makers, judiciary.

trick *(SYN.)* artifice, antic, deception, device, cheat, fraud, hoax, guile, imposture, ruse, ploy, stratagem, trickery, deceit, jest, joke, prank, defraud, subterfuge, wile, stunt.
(ANT.) exposure, candor, openness, honesty, sincerity.

trickle *(SYN.)* drip, drop, dribble, leak, seep.

tricky *(SYN.)* artifice, antic, covert, cunning, foxy, crafty, furtive, guileful, insidious, sly, shrews, stealthy, surreptitious, subtle, underhand, wily.
(ANT.) frank, candid, ingenuous, sincere, open.

trifling *(SYN.)* insignificant, frivolous, paltry, petty, trivial, small, unimportant.
(ANT.) momentous, serious, important, weighty.

trigger *(SYN.)* generate, provoke, prompt, motivate, activate.

trim *(SYN.)* nice, clear, orderly, precise, tidy, spruce, adorn, bedeck, clip, shave, prune, cut, shear, compact, neat, decorate, embellish, garnish.
(ANT.) deface, deform, spoil, mar, important, serious, momentous, weighty.

trimmings *(SYN.)* accessories, adornments, decorations, garnish, ornaments.

trinket *(SYN.)* bead, token, memento, bauble, charm, knickknack.

trio *(SYN.)* threesome, triad, triple.

trip *(SYN.)* expedition, cruise, stumble, err, journey, jaunt, passage, blunder, bungle, slip, excursion, tour, pilgrimage, voyage, travel.

trite *(SYN.)* common, banal, hackneyed, ordinary, stereotyped, stale.
(ANT.) modern, fresh, momentous, stimulating, novel, new.
triumph *(SYN.)* conquest, achievement, success, prevail, win, jubilation, victory, ovation.
(ANT.) succumb, failure, defeat.
triumphant *(SYN.)* celebrating, exultant, joyful, exhilarated, smug.
trivial *(SYN.)* insignificant, frivolous, paltry, petty, trifling, small, unimportant.
(ANT.) momentous, important weighty, serious.
troops *(SYN.)* militia, troopers, recruits, soldiers, enlisted men.
trophy *(SYN.)* award, memento, honor, testimonial, prize.
tropical *(SYN.)* sultry, sweltering, humid, torrid.
trouble *(SYN.)* anxiety, affliction, calamity, distress, hardship, grief, pain, misery, sorrow, woe, annoyance.
(ANT.) console, accommodate, gratify, soothe, joy, peace.
troublemaker *(SYN.)* rebel, scamp, agitator, demon, devil, ruffian.
troublesome *(SYN.)* bothersome, annoying, distressing, irksome, disturbing, trying, arduous, vexatious, arduous.
(ANT.) amusing, accommodating, gratifying, easy, pleasant.
truant *(SYN.)* delinquent, absentee, vagrant, malingerer.
truce *(SYN.)* armistice, cease-fire, interval, break, intermission, respite.
true *(SYN.)* actual, authentic, accurate, correct, exact, genuine, real, veracious, veritable, constant, honest, faithful.
(ANT.) erroneous, counterfeit, false, spurious, fictitious, faithless, inconstant.
truly *(SYN.)* indeed, actually, precisely, literally, really, factually.
truncate *(SYN.)* prune, clip, pare.
truss *(SYN.)* girder, brace, framework, shoring.
trust *(SYN.)* credence, confidence, dependence, reliance, faith.
(ANT.) incredulity, doubt, skepticism, mistrust.
trusted *(SYN.)* trustworthy, reliable, true, loyal, staunch, devoted.
trustworthy *(SYN.)* dependable, certain, reliable, secure, safe, sure, tried.
(ANT.) fallible, dubious, questionable, unreliable, uncertain.
truth *(SYN.)* actuality, authenticity, accuracy, correctness, exactness.
(ANT.) falsity, falsehood, fiction, lie, untruth.
truthful *(SYN.)* frank, candid, honest, sincere, open, veracious, accurate, correct, exact, reliable.
(ANT.) misleading, sly, deceitful.
try *(SYN.)* endeavor, attempt, strive, struggle, undertake, afflict, test, prove, torment, trouble, essay, examine.
(ANT.) decline, ignore, abandon, omit, neglect, comfort, console.
trying *(SYN.)* bothersome, annoying, distressing, irksome, disturbing.
(ANT.) amusing, easy, accommodating, pleasant, gratifying.
tryout *(SYN.)* audition, trial, chance, test.
tryst *(SYN.)* rendezvous, meeting, appointment.
tub *(SYN.)* basin, vessel, sink, bowl.
tube *(SYN.)* hose, pipe, reed.
tubular *(SYN.)* hollow, cylindrical.
tuck *(SYN.)* crease, fold, gather, bend.
tuft *(SYN.)* bunch, group, cluster.
tug *(SYN.)* pull, wrench, tow, haul, draw, yank, jerk.
tuition *(SYN.)* instruction, schooling, teaching, education.
tumble *(SYN.)* toss, trip, fall, sprawl, wallow, lurch, flounder, plunge.
tumble-down *(SYN.)* ramshackle, decrepit, broken-down, dilapidated.
tumult *(SYN.)* chaos, agitation, commotion, confusion, disarrangement.
(ANT.) peacefulness, order, peace, certainty, tranquillity.
tune *(SYN.)* song, concord, harmony, air, melody, strain.
(ANT.) aversion, discord, antipathy.
tunnel *(SYN.)* passage, grotto, cave.
turbulent *(SYN.)* gusty, blustery, inclement, rough, roaring, stormy.
(ANT.) clear, calm, quiet, peaceful.
turf *(SYN.)* lawn, grassland, sod, grass.
turmoil *(SYN.)* chaos, agitation, commotion, confusion, disarray.
(ANT.) order, peace, certainty, quiet, tranquillity.
turn *(SYN.)* circulate, circle, invert, rotate, revolve, spin, twist, twirl, whirl.
(ANT.) fix, stand, arrest, stop, continue, endure, proceed, perpetuate.
turret *(SYN.)* watchtower, belfry, steeple, tower, cupola, lookout.
tussle *(SYN.)* wrestle, struggle, contend, battle, fight, scuffle.
tutor *(SYN.)* instruct, prime, school, teach, train, prepare, drill.
twig *(SYN.)* sprig, branch, shoot, stem.
twilight *(SYN.)* sunset, sundown, nightfall, eventide, dusk.
twin *(SYN.)* lookalike, imitation, copy, double, replica.
twine *(SYN.)* string, cordage, rope, cord.
twinge *(SYN.)* smart, pang, pain.
twinkle *(SYN.)* shine, gleam, glisten, sparkle, glitter, shimmer, scintillate.
twirl *(SYN.)* rotate, spin, wind, turn, pivot, wheel, swivel, whirl.
twist *(SYN.)* bow, bend, crook, intertwine, curve, incline, deflect, braid.
(ANT.) resist, break, straighten, stiffen.
twitch *(SYN.)* fidget, shudder, jerk.
tycoon *(SYN.)* millionaire, industrialist, businessman.
tyke *(SYN.)* rascal, urchin, brat, ragamuffin, imp.
type *(SYN.)* mark, emblem, sign, category, symbol, kind, class.
(ANT.) deviation, monstrosity, eccentricity, peculiarity.
typhoon *(SYN.)* hurricane, cyclone, storm, tornado, whirlwind, twister.
typical *(SYN.)* common, accustomed, conventional, familiar, customary.
(ANT.) marvelous, extraordinary.
tyrant *(SYN.)* dictator, autocrat, despot.

ugly *(SYN.)* hideous, homely, plain, deformed, repellent, uncomely, repulsive, unsightly, nasty, unpleasant.
(ANT.) beautiful, fair, pretty, attractive, handsome, comely, good.
ultimate *(SYN.)* extreme, latest, final, concluding, decisive, hindmost, last.
(ANT.) foremost, opening, first, beginning, initial.
umbrage *(SYN.)* anger, displeasure.
umpire *(SYN.)* judge, referee, arbitrator.
unadulterated *(SYN.)* genuine, clear, clean, immaculate, spotless, pure.
(ANT.) foul, sullied, corrupt, tainted, polluted, tarnished, defiled.
unalterable *(SYN.)* fixed, unchangeable, steadfast, inflexible.
unanimity *(SYN.)* accord, agreement.
unannounced *(SYN.)* hasty, precipitate, abrupt, unexpected.
(ANT.) courteous, expected, anticipated.
unassuming *(SYN.)* humble, lowly, compliant, modest, plain, meek, simple, unostentatious, retiring, submissive.
(ANT.) haughty, showy, pompous, proud, vain, arrogant, boastful.
unattached *(SYN.)* apart, separate, unmarried, single, free, independent.
(ANT.) committed, involved, entangled.
unavoidable *(SYN.)* inescapable, certain, inevitable, unpreventable.
unawares *(SYN.)* abruptly, suddenly, unexpectedly, off guard.
unbalanced *(SYN.)* crazy, mad, insane.
unbearable *(SYN.)* insufferable, intolerable.
(ANT.) tolerable, acceptable.
unbeliever *(SYN.)* dissenter, apostate, heretic, schismatic, nonconformist.
unbending *(SYN.)* firm, inflexible, decided, determined, obstinate.
(ANT.) flexible.
unbiased *(SYN.)* honest, equitable, fair, impartial, reasonable, unprejudiced.
(ANT.) partial, fraudulent, dishonorable.
unbroken *(SYN.)* complete, uninterrupted, continuous, whole.
unburden *(SYN.)* clear, disentangle, divest, free.
uncanny *(SYN.)* amazing, remarkable, extraordinary, strange.
uncertain *(SYN.)* dim, hazy, indefinite, obscure, indistinct, unclear, undetermined, unsettled, ambiguous, unsure, doubtful, questionable, dubious.
(ANT.) explicit, lucid, specific, certain, unmistakable, precise, clear.
uncertainty *(SYN.)* distrust, doubt, hesitation, incredulity, scruple, ambiguity, skepticism, uncertainty, suspense, suspicion, unbelief.
(ANT.) faith, belief, certainty, conviction, determination.
uncivil *(SYN.)* impolite, rude, discourteous.
(ANT.) polite.
uncivilized *(SYN.)* barbaric, barbarous, barbarian, brutal, crude, inhuman, cruel, merciless, rude, remorseless, uncultured, savage, unrelenting.
(ANT.) humane, kind, polite, refined.
unclad *(SYN.)* exposed, nude, naked, bare, stripped, defenseless, uncovered.
(ANT.) concealed, protected, clothed, covered, dressed.
uncommon *(SYN.)* unusual, rare, odd, scarce, strange, peculiar, queer, exceptional, remarkable.
(ANT.) ordinary, usual.
uncompromising *(SYN.)* determined, dogged, firm, immovable, contumacious, headstrong, inflexible, obdurate, intractable, obstinate, pertinacious.
(ANT.) docile, compliant, amenable, yielding, submissive, pliable.
unconcern *(SYN.)* disinterestedness, impartiality, indifference, apathy, insensibility, neutrality.
(ANT.) affection, fervor, passion, ardor.
unconditional *(SYN.)* unqualified, unrestricted, arbitrary, absolute, pure, complete, actual, authoritative, perfect, entire, ultimate, tyrannous.
(ANT.) conditional, contingent, accountable, dependent, qualified.
unconscious *(SYN.)* lethargic, numb, comatose.
uncouth *(SYN.)* green, harsh, crude, coarse, ill-prepared, rough, raw, unfinished, unrefined, vulgar, rude, impolite, discourteous, unpolished, ill-mannered, crass.
(ANT.) well-prepared, cultivated, refined, civilized, finished.
uncover *(SYN.)* disclose, discover, betray, divulge, expose, reveal, impart, show.
(ANT.) conceal, hide, cover, obscure, cloak.
undependable *(SYN.)* changeable, unstable, uncertain, shifty, irresponsible.
(ANT.) stable, dependable, trustworthy.
under *(SYN.)* beneath, underneath, following, below, lower, downward.
(ANT.) over, above, up, higher.
undercover *(SYN.)* hidden, secret.
undergo *(SYN.)* endure, feel, stand, bear, indulge, suffer, sustain, experience, let, allow, permit, feel, tolerate.
(ANT.) overcome, discard, exclude, banish.
underhand *(SYN.)* sly, secret, sneaky, secretive, stealthy, crafty.
(ANT.) honest, open, direct, frank.
undermine *(SYN.)* demoralize, thwart, erode, weaken, subvert, sabotage.
underscore *(SYN.)* emphasize, stress.
understand *(SYN.)* apprehend, comprehend, appreciate, conceive, discern, know, grasp, hear, learn, realize, see, perceive.
(ANT.) misunderstand, mistake, misapprehend, ignore.
understanding *(SYN.)* agreement, coincidence, concord, accordance, concurrence, harmony, unison, compact, contract, arrangement, bargain, covenant, stipulation.
(ANT.) variance, difference, discord, dissension, disagreement.
understudy *(SYN.)* deputy, agent, proxy, representative, agent, alternate, lieutenant, substitute.
(ANT.) head, principal, sovereign, master.

undertake *(SYN.)* venture, attempt.
undertaking *(SYN.)* effort, endeavor, attempt, experiment, trial, essay.
(ANT.) laziness, neglect, inaction.
undersigned *(SYN.)* casual, chance, contingent, accidental, fortuitous, incidental, unintended.
(ANT.) decreed, planned, willed, calculated.
undesirable *(SYN.)* obnoxious, distasteful, objectionable, repugnant.
(ANT.) appealing, inviting, attractive.
undivided *(SYN.)* complete, intact, entire, integral, total, perfect, unimpaired, whole.
(ANT.) partial, incomplete.
undoing *(SYN.)* ruin, downfall, destruction, failure, disgrace.
undying *(SYN.)* endless, deathless, eternal, everlasting, ceaseless, immortal, infinite, perpetual, timeless.
(ANT.) transient, mortal, temporal, ephemeral, finite, impermanent.
unearthly *(SYN.)* metaphysical, ghostly, miraculous, marvelous, preternatural, superhuman, spiritual, foreign, strange, weird, supernatural.
(ANT.) physical, plain, human, natural, common, mundane.
uneducated *(SYN.)* uncultured, ignorant, illiterate, uninformed, unlearned, untaught, unlettered.
(ANT.) erudite, cultured, educated, literate, formed.
unemployed *(SYN.)* inert, inactive, idle, jobless, unoccupied.
(ANT.) working, occupied, active, industrious, employed.
uneven *(SYN.)* remaining, single, odd, unmatched, rugged, gnarled, irregular.
(ANT.) matched, even, flat, smooth.
unexceptional *(SYN.)* commonplace, trivial, customary.
unexpected *(SYN.)* immediate, hasty, surprising, instantaneous, unforeseen, abrupt, rapid, startling, sudden.
(ANT.) slowly, expected, gradual, predicted, anticipated, planned.
unfaithful *(SYN.)* treacherous, disloyal, deceitful, capricious.
(ANT.) true, loyal, steadfast, faithful.
unfasten *(SYN.)* open, expand, spread, exhibit, unbar, unlock, unfold, unseal.
(ANT.) shut, hide, conceal, close.
unfavorable *(SYN.)* antagonistic, contrary, adverse, opposed, opposite, disastrous, counteractive, unlucky.
(ANT.) benign, fortunate, lucky, propitious.
unfeeling *(SYN.)* hard, rigorous, cruel, stern, callous, numb, hard, strict, unsympathetic, severe.
(ANT.) tender, gentle, lenient. humane.
unfold *(SYN.)* develop, create, elaborate, amplify, evolve, mature, expand.
(ANT.) wither, restrict, contract, stunt, compress.
unfurnished *(SYN.)* naked, mere, bare, exposed, stripped, plain, open, simple.
(ANT.) concealed, protected, covered.
ungainly *(SYN.)* clumsy, awkward, bungling, clownish, gawky.
(ANT.) dexterous, graceful, elegant.
unhappy *(SYN.)* sad, miserable, wretched, melancholy, distressed, depressed, wretched.
(ANT.) joyful, happy, joyous, cheerful.
unhealthy *(SYN.)* infirm, sick, diseased, sickly.
(ANT.) vigorous, well, healthy, hale.
uniform *(SYN.)* methodical, natural, customary, orderly, normal, consistent, ordinary, regular, unvarying, unchanging, systematic, steady, unvaried.
(ANT.) rare, unusual, erratic, abnormal, exceptional, changeable.
unimportant *(SYN.)* petty, trivial, paltry, trifling, insignificant, indifferent, minor, petty.
uninformed *(SYN.)* illiterate, uncultured, uneducated, ignorant, unlearned, untaught, unlettered.
(ANT.) informed, literate, erudite, cultured, educated.
uninhibited *(SYN.)* loose, open, liberated, free.
(ANT.) constrained, tense, suppressed.
unintelligible *(SYN.)* ambiguous, cryptic, dark, cloudy, abstruse, dusky, mysterious, indistinct, obscure, vague.
(ANT.) lucid, distinct, bright, clear.
uninteresting *(SYN.)* burdensome, dilatory, dreary, dull, boring, slow humdrum, monotonous, sluggish, tedious, tardy, wearisome, tiresome.
(ANT.) entertaining, exciting, quick, amusing.
union *(SYN.)* fusion, incorporation, combination, joining, concurrence, solidarity, agreement, unification, concord, harmony, alliance, unanimity, coalition, confederacy, amalgamation, league, concert, marriage.
(ANT.) schism, disagreement, separation, discord.
unique *(SYN.)* exceptional, matchless, distinctive, choice, peculiar, singular, rare, sole, single, incomparable, uncommon, solitary, unequaled.
(ANT.) typical, ordinary, commonplace, frequent, common.
unison *(SYN.)* harmony, concurrence, understanding, accordance, concord, agreeable, coincidence.
(ANT.) disagreement, difference, discord, variance.
unite *(SYN.)* attach, blend, amalgamate, combine, conjoin, associate, connect, embody, consolidate, join, link, fuse, unify, merge.
(ANT.) sever, divide, separate, sever, disrupt, disconnect.
universal *(SYN.)* frequent, general, popular, common, familiar, prevailing, prevalent, usual.
(ANT.) scarce, odd, regional, local, extraordinary, exceptional.
unkempt *(SYN.)* sloppy, rumpled, untidy, messy, bedraggled.
(ANT.) presentable, well-groomed, tidy, neat.
unkind *(SYN.)* unfeeling, unsympathetic, unpleasant, cruel, harsh.
(ANT.) considerate, sympathetic, amiable, kind.

unlawful *(SYN.)* illegitimate, illicit, illegal, outlawed, criminal, prohibited.
(ANT.) permitted, law, honest, legal, legitimate, authorized.
unlike *(SYN.)* dissimilar, different, distinct, contrary, diverse, divergent, opposite, incongruous, variant, miscellaneous, divers.
(ANT.) conditional, accountable, contingent, qualified, dependent.
unlucky *(SYN.)* cursed, inauspicious, unfortunate.
(ANT.) prosperous, fortunate, blessed.
unmerciful *(SYN.)* cruel, merciless, heartless, brutal.
unmistakable *(SYN.)* clear, patent, plain, visible, obvious.
unnecessary *(SYN.)* pointless, needless, superfluous, purposeless.
unoccupied *(SYN.)* empty, vacant, uninhabited.
unparalleled *(SYN.)* peerless, unequaled, rare, unique, unmatched.
unpleasant *(SYN.)* offensive, disagreeable, repulsive, obnoxious, unpleasing.
unqualified *(SYN.)* inept, unfit, incapable, incompetent, unquestioned, absolute, utter.
unreasonable *(SYN.)* foolish, absurd, irrational, inconsistent, nonsensical, ridiculous, silly.
(ANT.) reasonable, sensible, sound, consistent, rational.
unruffled *(SYN.)* calm, smooth, serene, unperturbed.
unruly *(SYN.)* unmanageable, disorganized, disorderly, disobedient.
(ANT.) orderly.
unsafe *(SYN.)* hazardous, insecure, critical, dangerous, perilous, menacing, risky, precarious, threatening.
(ANT.) protected, secure, firm, safe.
unselfish *(SYN.)* bountiful, generous, liberal, giving, beneficent, magnanimous, openhanded, munificent.
(ANT.) miserly, stingy, greedy, selfish, covetous.
unsightly *(SYN.)* ugly, unattractive, hideous.
unsophisticated *(SYN.)* frank, candid, artless, ingenuous, naive, open, simple.
(ANT.) sophisticated, cunning, crafty.
unsound *(SYN.)* feeble, flimsy, weak, fragile, sick, unhealthy, diseased, invalid, faulty, false.
unstable *(SYN.)* fickle, fitful, inconstant, capricious, changeable, restless.
(ANT.) steady, stable, constant.
unswerving *(SYN.)* fast, firm, inflexible, constant, secure, stable, solid, steady.
(ANT.) sluggish, insecure, unsteady, unstable, loose, slow.
untainted *(SYN.)* genuine, pure, spotless, clean, clear, unadulterated.
(ANT.) polluted, tainted, sullied, tarnished, defiled, corrupt, foul.
untamed *(SYN.)* fierce, savage, uncivilized, barbarous, outlandish, rude, undomesticated, desert, wild, frenzied.
(ANT.) quiet, calm, civilized, placid.
untidy *(SYN.)* messy, sloppy, disorderly.
unusual *(SYN.)* capricious, abnormal, devious, eccentric, aberrant, irregular.
(ANT.) methodical, regular, usual, fixed, ordinary.
unyielding *(SYN.)* fast, firm, inflexible, constant, solid, secure, stable, steadfast, unswerving, steady.
(ANT.) sluggish, slow, insecure, loose, unsteady, unstable.
upbraid *(SYN.)* blame, censure, berate, admonish, rate, lecture, rebuke.
(ANT.) praise, commend, approve.
uphold *(SYN.)* justify, espouse, assert, defend, maintain, vindicate.
(ANT.) oppose, submit, deny, attack.
upright *(SYN.)* undeviating, right, unswerving, direct, erect, unbent.
(ANT.) bent, dishonest, crooked, circuitous, winding.
uprising *(SYN.)* revolution, mutiny, revolt, rebellion.
uproar *(SYN.)* noise, disorder, commotion, tumult, disturbance.
upset *(SYN.)* disturb, harass, bother, annoy, haunt, molest, inconvenience, perplex, pester, tease, plague, trouble.
(ANT.) soothe, relieve, please, gratify.
upshot *(SYN.)* conclusion, result.
urbane *(SYN.)* civil, considerate, cultivated, courteous, genteel, polite, accomplished, refined, well-mannered.
(ANT.) rude, uncouth, boorish, uncivil.
urge *(SYN.)* craving, desire, longing, lust, appetite, aspiration, yearning.
(ANT.) loathing, hate, distaste, aversion, compel, dissuade, discourage.
urgency *(SYN.)* emergency, exigency, pass, pinch, strait, crisis.
urgent *(SYN.)* critical, crucial, exigent, imperative, impelling, insistent.
(ANT.) trivial, petty, insignificant.
usage *(SYN.)* use, treatment, custom, practice, tradition.
use *(SYN.)* custom, practice, habit, training, usage, manner, apply, avail employ, operate, utilize, exert, exhaust, handle, manage, accustom.
(ANT.) disuse, neglect, waste, ignore, overlook, idleness.
useful *(SYN.)* beneficial, helpful, good, serviceable, wholesome, advantageous.
(ANT.) harmful, injurious, deleterious, destructive, detrimental.
useless *(SYN.)* bootless, empty, idle, pointless, vain, valueless, worthless.
(ANT.) profitable, potent, effective.
usher *(SYN.)* guide, lead.
usual *(SYN.)* customary, common, familiar, general, normal, habitual, accustomed, everyday, ordinary, regular.
(ANT.) irregular, exceptional, rare, extraordinary, abnormal.
utensil *(SYN.)* instrument, tool, vehicle, apparatus, device, implement.
(ANT.) hindrance, obstruction.
utilize *(SYN.)* use, apply, devote, busy, employ, occupy, avail.
(ANT.) reject, banish, discard.
utopian *(SYN.)* perfect, ideal, faultless, exemplary, supreme, visionary, unreal.
(ANT.) real, imperfect, actual, faulty.
utter *(SYN.)* full, perfect, whole, finished, entire, speak, say, complete.
(ANT.) imperfect, deficient, lacking, faulty, incomplete.

vacancy *(SYN.)* void, emptiness, vacuum, hollowness, blankness, vacuity, depletion, nothingness.
(ANT.) *plenitude, fullness, profusion, completeness.*
vacant *(SYN.)* barren, empty, blank, bare, unoccupied, void, vacuous.
(ANT.) *filled, packed, employed, full, replete, busy, engaged.*
vacate *(SYN.)* abjure, relinquish, abdicate, renounce, abandon, resign, surrender, desert, waive, quit, leave.
(ANT.) *stay, support, uphold, maintain.*
vacation rest, holiday, recess, break.
(ANT.) *labor, work, routine.*
vacillate *(SYN.)* hesitate, oscillate, undulate, change, fluctuate, vary, waver.
(ANT.) *adhere, persist, stick, decide.*
vacillating *(SYN.)* contrary, illogical, contradictory, contrary, inconsistent, incongruous, incompatible, paradoxical, irreconcilable, unsteady, wavering.
(ANT.) *correspondent, congruous, consistent, compatible.*
vacuity *(SYN.)* space, emptiness, vacuum, void, blank, nothingness, ignorance, unawareness, senselessness, mindlessness, chatter, nonsense, froth, absurdity.
(ANT.) *matter, fullness, content, substance, knowledge, intelligence.*
vacuous *(SYN.)* dull, blank, uncomprehending, imbecillic, foolish, thoughtless, distracted, absent-minded.
(ANT.) *responsive, alert, attentive, bright, intelligent, aware.*
vacuum *(SYN.)* void, gap, emptiness, hole, chasm, nothingness, abyss.
vagabond *(SYN.)* pauper, ragamuffin, scrub, beggar, mendicant, starveling, wretch, tatterdemalion, hobo, tramp.
(ANT.) *responsible, established, rooted, installed, reliable.*
vagary *(SYN.)* notion, whim, fantasy, fancy, daydream, caprice, conceit, quirk, whimsy, impulse.
vagrant *(SYN.)* hobo, rover, tramp, beggar, bum, wanderer, vagabond.
(ANT.) *settled, worker, laborer, rooted, ambitious, gentleman.*
vague *(SYN.)* indefinite, hazy, dim, indistinct, ambiguous, obscure, undetermined, unclear, unsure, unsettled.
(ANT.) *certain, spelled out, specific, lucid, clear, definite, distinct, explicit, precise, unequivocal.*
vain *(SYN.)* fruitless, empty, bootless, futile, idle, abortive, ineffectual, unavailing, vapid, pointless, valueless, useless, trivial, unfruitful, worthless, unsuccessful, proud, conceited.
(ANT.) *meek, modest, potent, rewarding, self-effacing, diffident, profitable, effective, humble.*
vainglory *(SYN.)* conceit, pride, self-esteem, arrogance, self-respect, superciliousness, haughtiness, vanity.
(ANT.) *shame, modesty, meekness, humility, lowliness.*
valet *(SYN.)* groom, dresser, attendant, manservant.
valiant *(SYN.)* bold, brave, courageous, adventurous, audacious, chivalrous, daring, fearless, dauntless, heroic, brave, gallant, magnanimous, intrepid, unafraid, valorous, dauntless.
(ANT.) *weak, fearful, cowardly, timid.*
valid *(SYN.)* cogent, conclusive, effective, convincing, binding, efficacious, logical, powerful, legal, sound, weighty, well-founded, real, genuine, actual, true, trustworthy, authentic, strong, telling, logical, authentic.
(ANT.) *weak, unconvincing, void, unproved, null, spurious, counterfeit.*
validate *(SYN.)* corroborate, substantiate, support, confirm, prove, uphold, sustain, authenticate.
(ANT.) *disprove, contradict, cancel.*
valise *(SYN.)* satchel, bag, baggage.
valley *(SYN.)* dale, dell, lowland, basin, gully, vale, ravine.
(ANT.) *highland, hill, upland, headland.*
valor *(SYN.)* courage, heroism, bravery, boldness, intrepidity, fearlessness.
valuable *(SYN.)* profitable, useful, costly, precious, dear, expensive, worthy, important, high-priced, esteemed.
(ANT.) *trashy, poor, cheap, worthless.*
value *(SYN.)* price, merit, usefulness, value, virtue, utility, appreciate, prize, hold dear, treasure, excellence, benefit, cost, rate, evaluate, appraise, esteem, importance, worth, worthiness.
(ANT.) *valuelessness, uselessness, cheapness.*
vanish *(SYN.)* evaporate, disappear.
(ANT.) *appear.*
vanity *(SYN.)* complacency, egotism, pride, self-esteem, conceit, caprice, fancy, idea, conception, notion, haughtiness, self-respect, whim, smugness, vainglory, arrogance, imagination.
(ANT.) *meekness, humility, diffidence.*
vanquish *(SYN.)* defeat, crush, humble, surmount, master, beat, conquer, overcome, rout, quell, subjugate, subdue.
(ANT.) *surrender, cede, lose, retreat, capitulate.*
vapid *(SYN.)* hackneyed, inane, insipid, trite, banal, commonplace.
(ANT.) *striking, novel, fresh, original, stimulating.*
vapor *(SYN.)* steam, fog, mist, smog, haze, steam.
variable *(SYN.)* fickle, fitful, inconstant, unstable, shifting, changeable, unsteady, wavering, vacillating.
(ANT.) *unchanging, uniform, stable, un-wavering, steady, constant.*
variant *(SYN.)* dissimilar, different, distinct, contrary, diverse, divergent, opposite, unlike, incongruous, divers, sundry, various, miscellaneous.
(ANT.) *similar, same, congruous, identical, alike.*
variation *(SYN.)* change, alternation, alteration, substitution, variety, substitute, mutation, exchange, vicissitude.

(ANT.) uniformity, stability, monotony.
variety *(SYN.)* dissimilarity, diversity, heterogeneity, assortment, change, difference, medley, mixture, miscellany, variousness, form, type, class, breed, sort, kind, strain, stock.
(ANT.) likeness, monotony, uniformity, sameness, homogeneity.
various *(SYN.)* miscellaneous, sundry, divers, several, contrary, distinct, dissimilar, divergent, unlike, incongruous, opposite, different.
(ANT.) identical, similar, same, alike, congruous.
vary *(SYN.)* exchange, substitute, alter, change, modify, shift, convert, transform, transfigure, diversify, veer.
(ANT.) settle, stabilize, continue, establish, preserve.
vassalage *(SYN.)* confinement, captivity, imprisonment, slavery, thralldom.
(ANT.) liberation, freedom.
vast *(SYN.)* big, capacious, extensive, huge, great, ample, immense, wide, unlimited, enormous, measureless, large.
(ANT.) tiny, small, short, little.
vault *(SYN.)* caper, jerk, jump, leap, bound, crypt, sepulcher, hop, spring, safe, start, tomb, grave, catacomb, skip.
vaunt *(SYN.)* crow, flaunt, glory, boast.
(ANT.) minimize, humble, deprecate, apologize.
vaunting *(SYN.)* flourish, display, ostentation, parade, show, pomp.
(ANT.) modesty, reserve, humility.
vehement *(SYN.)* excitable, fervent, ardent, burning, fiery, glowing, impetuous, hot, trascible, passionate.
(ANT.) calm, quiet, cool, apathetic, deliberate.
veil *(SYN.)* clothe, conceal, cover, cloak, web, hide, curtain, disguise, gauze, film, envelop, screen, mask, shield, film.
(ANT.) reveal, unveil, bare, divulge.
velocity *(SYN.)* quickness, rapidity, speed, swiftness.
venal *(SYN.)* greedy, mercenary, sordid, corrupt.
(ANT.) liberal, honorable, generous.
venerable *(SYN.)* antiquated, aged, antique, ancient, elderly, old, superannuated, old-fashion.
(ANT.) young, new, youthful, modern.
venerate *(SYN.)* approve, esteem, admire, appreciate, wonder, respect.
(ANT.) dislike, despise.
vengeance *(SYN.)* requital, reprisal, reparation, retribution, revenge.
(ANT.) forgiveness, remission, pardon, mercy.
venom *(SYN.)* toxin, poison, bitterness, spite, hate.
vent *(SYN.)* eject, emit, expel, shoot, spurt, emanate, hurl, shed, belch, discharge, breathe.
venture *(ANT.)* speculate, attempt, test, dare, hazard, gamble, chance, risk.
(ANT.) insure, secure, protect.
verbal *(SYN.)* oral, spoken, literal, unwritten, vocal.
(ANT.) printed, written, recorded.
verbose *(SYN.)* communicative, glib, chattering, chatty, garrulous, loquacious, talkative.
(ANT.) uncommunicative, silent.
verbosity *(SYN.)* long-windedness, verboseness, redundancy, wordiness.
(ANT.) terseness, laconic, conciseness.
verdict *(SYN.)* judgment, finding, opinion, decision.
verge *(SYN.)* lip, rim, edge, margin, brink, brim.
verification *(SYN.)* confirmation, demonstration, evidence, proof, test, experiment, testimony, trial.
(ANT.) terseness, laconic, conciseness.
verify *(SYN.)* confirm, substantiate, acknowledge, determine, assure, establish, approve, fix, settle, ratify, strengthen, corroborate, affirm, sanction.
veritable *(SYN.)* authentic, correct, genuine, real, true, accurate, actual.
(ANT.) false, fictitious, spurious, erroneous, counterfeit.
versed *(SYN.)* conversant, familiar, intimate, knowing, acquainted, aware.
(ANT.) inclined, level, prone, oblique.
version *(SYN.)* interpretation, rendition.
vertical *(SYN.)* erect, perpendicular, upright.
(ANT.) horizontal.
very *(SYN.)* exceedingly, extremely, greatly, considerably.
vessel *(SYN.)* craft, boat, ship.
vestige *(SYN.)* stain, scar, mark, brand, stigma, characteristic, trace, feature, trait, symptoms, hint, token, suggestion, indication.
veto *(SYN.)* refusal, denial, refuse, deny, negate, forbid, prohibit.
(ANT.) approve, approval.
vex *(SYN.)* embitter, exasperate, aggravate, annoy, chafe, bother, provoke, pester, plague, anger, nettle, anger.
(ANT.) soften soothe, palliate, mitigate.
vexation *(SYN.)* chagrin, irritation, annoyance, mortification, irritation, pique.
(ANT.) comfort, pleasure, appeasement, gratification.
vibrate *(SYN.)* flutter, jar, quake, jolt, quaver, agitate, transgression, wickedness, ungodliness, tremble, wrong.
vice *(SYN.)* iniquity, crime, offense, evil, guilt, sin, ungodliness, wickedness, depravity, corruption, wrong.
(ANT.) righteousness, virtue, goodness, innocence, purity.
vicinity *(SYN.)* district, area, locality, neighborhood, environs, proximity, nearness, adjacency.
(ANT.) remoteness, distance.
vicious *(SYN.)* bad, evil, wicked, sinful, corrupt, cruel, savage, dangerous.
victimize *(SYN.)* cheat, dupe, swindle, deceive, take advantage of.
victor *(SYN.)* champion, winner.
(ANT.) loser.
victory *(SYN.)* conquest, jubilation, triumph, success, achievement, ovation.
(ANT.) defeat, failure.
view *(SYN.)* discern, gaze, glance, be-

hold, eye, discern, stare, watch, examine, witness, prospect, vision, vista, sight, look, panorama, opinion, judgment, belief, impression, perspective, range, regard, thought, observation, survey, scene, conception, outlook, inspect, observe.
(ANT.) miss, overlook, avert, hide.

viewpoint *(SYN.)* attitude, standpoint, aspect, pose, disposition, position, stand, posture.

vigilant *(SYN.)* anxious, attentive, careful, alert, circumspect, cautious, observant, wary, watchful, wakeful.
(ANT.) inattentive, neglectful, careless.

vigor *(SYN.)* spirit, verve, energy, zeal, fortitude, vitality, strength, liveliness.
(ANT.) listlessness.

vigorous *(SYN.)* brisk, energetic, active, blithe, animated, frolicsome, strong, spirited, lively, forceful, sprightly, vivacious, powerful, supple.
(ANT.) vapid, dull, listless, insipid.

vile *(SYN.)* foul, loathsome, base, depraved, debased, sordid, vulgar, wicked, abject, ignoble, mean, worthless, sinful, bad, low, wretched, evil, offensive, objectionable, disgusting.
(ANT.) honorable, upright, decent, laudable, attractive.

vilify *(SYN.)* asperse, defame, disparage, abuse, malign, revile, scandalize.
(ANT.) protect, honor, praise, cherish.

village *(SYN.)* hamlet, town.
(ANT.) metropolis, city.

villain *(SYN.)* rascal, rogue, cad, brute, scoundrel, devil, scamp.

villainous *(SYN.)* deleterious, evil, bad, base, iniquitous, unsound, sinful, unwholesome, wicked.
(ANT.) honorable, reputable, moral, good, excellent.

violate *(SYN.)* infringe, break.

violent *(SYN.)* strong, forcible, forceful.
(ANT.) gentle.

vindicate clear, assert, defend, absolve, excuse, acquit, uphold, support.
(ANT.) accuse, convict, abandon.

violate *(SYN.)* disobey, invade, defile, break, desecrate, pollute, dishonor, debauch, profane, deflower, ravish.

violence *(SYN.)* constraint, force, compulsion, coercion.
(ANT.) weakness, persuasion, feebleness, impotence, frailty.

violent *(SYN.)* strong, forceful, powerful, forcible, angry, fierce, savage, passionate, furious.
(ANT.) gentle.

virgin *(SYN.)* immaculate, genuine, spotless, clean, chaste, untainted, innocent, guiltless, pure, untouched, modest, unused, undefiled, pure.
(ANT.) foul, tainted, defiled, sullied, polluted, corrupt.

virtue *(SYN.)* integrity, probity, purity, chastity, goodness, rectitude, effectiveness, force, honor, power, efficacy, quality, strength, merit, righteousness, advantage, excellence, advantage.
(ANT.) fault, vice, lewdness, corruption.

virulent *(SYN.)* hostile, malevolent, malignant, bitter, spiteful, wicked.
(ANT.) kind, affectionate, benevolent.

vision *(SYN.)* dream, hallucination, mirage, eyesight, sight, fantasy, illusion, specter, revelation, phantom, spook, ghost, imagination, farsightedness, keenness, foresight, apparition.
(ANT.) verity, reality.

visit *(SYN.)* attend, see, call on, appointment.

visitor *(SYN.)* caller, guest.

vista *(SYN.)* view, scene, aspect.

vital *(SYN.)* cardinal, living, paramount, alive, essential, critical, basic, indispensable, urgent, life-and-death.
(ANT.) lifeless, unimportant, inanimate, nonessential.

vitality *(SYN.)* buoyancy, being, life, liveliness, existence, spirit, vigor.
(ANT.) death, lethargy, dullness, demise.

vivacious *(SYN.)* lively, spirited.

vivid *(SYN.)* brilliant, striking, clear, bright, intense, lively, strong, graphic.
(ANT.) dim, dusky, vague, dull, dreary.

vocal *(SYN.)* said, uttered, oral, spoken, definite, outspoken, specific.

vocation *(SYN.)* commerce, employment, business, art, job, profession, trade, occupation, career, calling, work, trading.
(ANT.) pastime, hobby, avocation.

void *(SYN.)* barren, emptiness, space, annul, cancel, empty, bare, unoccupied, meaningless, invalid, useless.
(ANT.) employed, full, replete, engaged.

volatile *(SYN.)* effervescent, resilient, buoyant, animated, cheerful, hopeful.
(ANT.) depressed, sullen, hopeless, dejected, despondent.

volition *(SYN.)* desire, intention, pleasure, preference, choice, decision, resolution, testament, wish, will.
(ANT.) disinterest, compulsion, indifference.

voluble *(SYN.)* glib, communicative, verbose, loquacious, chatty, chattering.
(ANT.) uncommunicative, laconic, taciturn, silent.

volume *(SYN.)* capacity, skill, power, talent, faculty, magnitude, mass, book.
(ANT.) stupidity, inability, impotence, incapacity.

voluntary *(SYN.)* extemporaneous, free, automatic, spontaneous, offhand.
(ANT.) forced, planned, required, rehearsed, compulsory, prepared.

volunteer *(SYN.)* extend, offer, present, advance, propose, tender, sacrifice.
(ANT.) receive, spurn, reject, accept, retain.

voodoo *(SYN.)* art, conjuring, legerdemain, magic, witchcraft, wizardry.

voracious *(SYN.)* insatiable, ravenous.

vow *(SYN.)* oath, pledge, swear, promise.

voyage *(SYN.)* tour, journey, excursion.

vulgar *(SYN.)* ordinary, popular, common, general, crude, coarse, low.
(ANT.) polite, refined, select, aristocratic.

vulnerable *(SYN.)* unguarded, defenseless, unprotected.

wacky *(SYN.)* strange, crazy, peculiar.
wad *(SYN.)* hunk, clump, chunk.
wafer *(SYN.)* cracker, lozenge.
waft *(SYN.)* convey, glide, sail, float.
wage *(SYN.)* conduct, pursue, make.
wager *(SYN.)* stake, bet, play, gamble, speculate, risk, chance.
wages *(SYN.)* payment, compensation, fee, allowance, pay, salary, earnings.
wagon *(SYN.)* carriage, buggy, cart, surrey, stagecoach.
waif *(SYN.)* guttersnipe, ragamuffin, tramp, vagrant, urchin.
wail *(SYN.)* mourn, moan, cry, bewail, lament, bemoan, sorrow.
wait *(SYN.)* linger, tarry, attend, bide, watch, delay, await, abide, stay, serve, pause, remain, rest, minister, expect.
(ANT.) hasten, act leave, expedite.
waive *(SYN.)* renounce, abandon, surrender, relinquish, forgo.
(ANT.) uphold, maintain.
wake *(SYN.)* awaken, rouse, waken, arouse, stimulate, activate.
(ANT.) doze, sleep.
waken *(SYN.)* wake, arouse, rouse, awaken, stimulate, activate.
(ANT.) doze, sleep.
walk *(SYN.)* step, stroll, march, amble, saunter, hike, lane, path, passage.
wall *(SYN.)* barricade, divider, partition, panel, stockade.
wallow *(SYN.)* plunge, roll, flounder.
wan *(SYN.)* colorless, haggard, gaunt, pale, pallid, pasty, pale.
wander *(SYN.)* rove, stroll, deviate, ramble, digress, roam, range, err.
(ANT.) linger, stop, settle.
wane *(SYN.)* abate, weaken, fade, ebb, decrease, wither, subside.
want *(SYN.)* penury, destitution, crave, desire, requirement, poverty, wish, require, need, privation.
(ANT.) wealth, plenty, abundance.
wanton *(SYN.)* lecherous, immoral, loose, lewd, salacious, lustful.
war *(SYN.)* battle, hostilities, combat, fight, strife, contention.
warble *(SYN.)* sing, trill, chirp.
ward *(SYN.)* annex, wing, section.
warden *(SYN.)* custodian, guard, guardian, keeper, turnkey, jailer, curator.
ward off *(SYN.)* repel, thwart, deflect, foil, deter, forestall, repulse.
wardrobe *(SYN.)* chiffonier, bureau, closet, armoire.
warehouse *(SYN.)* arsenal, store-house, depository.
wares *(SYN.)* merchandise, staples, inventory, commodities, goods.
wariness *(SYN.)* heed, care, watchfulness, caution, vigilance.
(ANT.) carelessness, abandon.
warlike *(SYN.)* hostile, unfriendly, combative, belligerent, antagonistic, pugnacious, opposed, aggressive.
(ANT.) cordial, peaceful, amicable.
warm *(SYN.)* sincere, cordial, hearty, earnest, sympathetic, ardent, heated, gracious, temperate, enthusiastic.
(ANT.) cool, aloof, brisk, indifferent.
warmhearted *(SYN.)* loving, kind, kindhearted, friendly, generous.
warmth *(SYN.)* friendliness, cordiality, geniality, understanding, compassion.
warn *(SYN.)* apprise, notify, admonish, caution, advise, inform.
warning *(SYN.)* advice, information, caution, portent, admonition, indication, notice, sign.
warp *(SYN.)* turn, bend, twist, distort.
warrant *(SYN.)* pledge, assurance, warranty, guarantee, authorize, approve, mandate, sanction.
warrior *(SYN.)* combatant, fighter, soldier, mercenary, guerrilla.
wary *(SYN.)* careful, awake, watchful, heedful, attentive, alive, mindful.
(ANT.) unaware, indifferent, apathetic.
wash *(SYN.)* launder, cleanse, rub, touch, reach, border, wet, clean, scrub.
(ANT.) soil, dirty, stain.
waspish *(SYN.)* irritable, petulant, fractious, testy, snappish, touchy.
(ANT.) pleasant, genial.
waste *(SYN.)* forlorn, bleak, wild, solitary, dissipate, abandoned, spend, deserted, bare, consume, dwindle, decay, misspend, decrease, wither.
(ANT.) cultivated, attended.
wasteful *(SYN.)* wanton, costly, lavish, extravagant.
watch *(SYN.)* inspect, descry, behold, distinguish, guard, attend, observe, contemplate, espy, perceive, look at, protect, chronometer, timepiece.
watchful *(SYN.)* alert, careful, attentive, vigilant, wary, cautious.
waterfall *(SYN.)* cascade, cataract.
wave *(SYN.)* ripple, whitecap, undulation, breaker, surf, swell, sea, surge.
waver *(SYN.)* question, suspect, flicker, deliberate, doubt, distrust, hesitate.
(ANT.) confide, trust, believe, decide.
wavering *(SYN.)* fickle, shifting, variable, changeable, vacillating, fitful.
(ANT.) unchanging, constant, uniform.
wavy *(SYN.)* rippling, serpentine, curly.
wax *(SYN.)* raise, heighten, expand, accrue, enhance, extend, multiply, enlarge, augment, amplify.
(ANT.) contract, reduce, atrophy, diminish.
way *(SYN.)* habit, road, course, avenue, route, mode, system, channel, track, fashion, method, walk, approach.
waylay *(SYN.)* surprise, accost, ambush, attack, pounce, intercept.
wayward *(SYN.)* stubborn, headstrong, contrary, obstinate, naughty, disobedient, rebellious, refractory.
weak *(SYN.)* frail, debilitated, delicate, poor, wavering, infirm, bending, lame, defenseless, vulnerable, fragile, pliant.
(ANT.) strong, potent, sturdy, powerful.
weaken *(SYN.)* exhaust, sap, disable, devitalize.
weakness *(SYN.)* incompetence, inability, impotence, handicap, fondness, liking, affection, disability, incapacity.
(ANT.) strength, ability, dislike, power.
wealth *(SYN.)* fortune, money, riches, possessions, abundance, opulence, affluence, property, quantity, luxury.
(ANT.) want, need.
wealthy *(SYN.)* rich, exorbitant,

prosperous, affluent, successful.
(ANT.) poverty-stricken, poor, indigent, impoverished, beggarly, destitute, needy.
wear *(SYN.)* erode, fray, grind, apparel, clothes, garb, attire.
wearied *(SYN.)* weak, languid, faint, irresolute, feeble, timid.
(ANT.) brave, vigorous.
weary *(SYN.)* faint, spent, worn, tired, fatigued, exhausted, tiresome, bored.
(ANT.) rested, hearty, fresh.
weasel *(SYN.)* cheat, traitor, be-trayer.
weave *(SYN.)* lace, interlace, plait, intertwine, braid, knit.
web *(SYN.)* netting, network, net, cobweb, trap, entanglement.
wed *(SYN.)* espouse, marry.
wedlock *(SYN.)* marriage, union, espousal, wedding, matrimony.
wedge *(SYN.)* chock, jam, lodge.
wee *(SYN.)* small, tiny, miniature, petite, microscopic, minute.
weep *(SYN.)* mourn, sob, bemoan, cry, lament, whimper, wail.
weigh *(SYN.)* heed, deliberate, consider, study, ponder, contemplate.
(ANT.) neglect, ignore.
weight *(SYN.)* importance, emphasis, load, burden, import, stress, influence, heaviness, pressure, value.
(ANT.) triviality, levity, insignificance, lightness, buoyancy.
weird *(SYN.)* odd, eerie, strange, unnatural, peculiar, spooky.
welcome *(SYN.)* take, entertain, greet, accept, receive, reception, gain, greeting, shelter.
(ANT.) reject, impart, discharge.
weld *(SYN.)* solder, connect, fuse, bond.
welfare *(SYN.)* good, prosperity.
well *(SYN.)* hearty, happy, sound, hale, beneficial, good, convenient, expedient, healthy, favorably, fully, thoroughly, surely, adequately, satisfactorily, competently, certainly.
(ANT.) infirm, depressed, weak.
well-being *(SYN.)* delight, happiness, satisfaction, contentment, gladness.
(ANT.) sorrow, grief, sadness, despair.
well-bred *(SYN.)* cultured, polite, genteel, courtly, refined, cultivated.
(ANT.) crude, vulgar, boorish, rude.
well-known *(SYN.)* famous, illustrious, celebrated, noted, eminent, renowned.
(ANT.) unknown, ignominious, obscure, hidden.
wet *(SYN.)* moist, dank, soaked, damp, drenched, dampen, moisten.
(ANT.) arid, dry, parched.
wharf *(SYN.)* pier, dock.
wheedle *(SYN.)* coax, cajole, persuade.
whim *(SYN.)* fancy, notion, humor, quirk, caprice, whimsy, inclination.
whimsical *(SYN.)* quaint, strange, curious, odd, unusual, droll, eccentric.
(ANT.) normal, usual, familiar.
whine *(SYN.)* whimper, moan, complain.
whip *(SYN.)* scourge, thrash, beat, lash.
whirl *(SYN.)* rotate, twirl, spin, revolve, reel.
whole *(SYN.)* total, sound, all, intact, complete, well, hale, integral, unimpaired, healed, entire, uncut, undivided, unbroken, undamaged, intact.
(ANT.) partial, defective, imperfect, deficient.
wholesome *(SYN.)* robust, well, hale, healthy, sound, salubrious, good, hygienic, salutary, nourishing, healthful, strong, nutritious, hearty.
(ANT.) frail, noxious, infirm, delicate, injurious, diseased.
wicked *(SYN.)* deleterious, iniquitous, immoral, bad, evil, base, ungodly, unsound, sinful, bitter, blasphemous, malicious, evil-minded, profane.
(ANT.) moral, good, reputable, honorable.
wide *(SYN.)* large, broad, sweeping, extensive, vast, expanded.
(ANT.) restricted, narrow.
width *(SYN.)* wideness, extensiveness, breadth.
wield *(SYN.)* handle, brandish.
wild *(SYN.)* outlandish, uncivilized, untamed, irregular, wanton, foolish, mad, barbarous, rough, waste, desert, uncultivated, boisterous, unruly, savage, primitive, giddy, unrestrained, silly, wayward, uncontrolled, impetuous, crazy, ferocious, undomesticated, desolate.
(ANT.) quiet, gentle, placid, tame, restrained, civilized.
willful *(SYN.)* intentional, designed, contemplated, studied, premedi-tated.
(ANT.) fortuitous.
will *(SYN.)* intention, desire, volition, decision, resolution, wish, resoluteness, choice, determination, pleasure.
(ANT.) disinterest, coercion, indifference.
willing *(SYN.)* agreeing, energetic, enthusiastic, consenting, agreeable, eager.
wilt *(SYN.)* sag, droop, weaken.
wily *(SYN.)* cunning, foxy, sly, crafty.
win *(SYN.)* gain, succeed, prevail, achieve, thrive, obtain, get, acquire, earn, flourish.
(ANT.) lose, miss, forfeit, fail.
wind *(SYN.)* gale, breeze, storm, gust, blast, air, breath, flurry, puff, blow, hurricane, typhoon, cyclone, tornado, suggestion, hint, clue, zephyr, squall, coil, crank, screw, meander, wander, twist, weave, draft.
winsome *(SYN.)* winning, charming, agreeable.
wisdom *(SYN.)* insight, judgment, learning, sense, discretion, reason, prudence, erudition, foresight, intelligence, sageness, knowledge, information, sagacity.
(ANT.) nonsense, foolishness, stupidity, ignorance.
wise *(SYN.)* informed, sagacious, learned, penetrating, enlightened, advisable, prudent, profound, deep, erudite, scholarly, knowing, sound, intelligent, expedient, discerning.
(ANT.) simple, shallow, foolish.
wish *(SYN.)* crave, hanker, long, hunger, yearning, lust, craving, yearn, want, appetite, covet, longing, desire, urge.
(ANT.) hate, aversion, loathing, dis-

taste.

wit *(SYN.)* sense, humor, pleasantry, satire, intelligence, comprehension, understanding, banter, mind, wisdom, intellect, wittiness, fun, drollery, humorist, wag, comedian, raillery, irony, witticism.
(ANT.) solemnity, commonplace, sobriety.

witch *(SYN.)* magician, sorcerer, enchanter, sorceress, enchantress, warlock.

witchcraft *(SYN.)* enchantment, magic, wizardry, conjuring, voodoo.

withdraw *(SYN.)* renounce, leave, abandon, recall, retreat, go, secede, desert, quit, retire, depart, retract, remove, forsake.
(ANT.) enter, tarry, abide, place, stay.

wither *(SYN.)* wilt, languish, dry, shrivel, decline, fade, decay, sear, waste, wizen, weaken, droop, sink, fail, shrink.
(ANT.) renew, refresh, revive.

withhold *(SYN.)* forbear, abstain, repress, check, refrain.
(ANT.) persist, continue.

withstand *(SYN.)* defy, contradict, bar, thwart, oppose, hinder, combat, resist, counteract.
(ANT.) succumb, cooperate, support.

witness *(SYN.)* perceive, proof, spectator, confirmation, see, attestation, watch, observe, eyewitness, declaration, notice, testimony.
(ANT.) refutation, contradiction, argument.

witty *(SYN.)* funny, talented, apt, bright, adroit, sharp, clever.
(ANT.) foolish, slow, dull, clumsy, awkward.

wizard *(SYN.)* magician, conjuror, sorcerer.

wizardry *(SYN.)* voodoo, legerdemain, conjuring, witchcraft, charm.

woe *(SYN.)* sorrow, disaster, trouble, evil, agony, suffering, anguish, sadness, grief, distress, misery, torment, misfortune.
(ANT.) pleasure, delight, fun.

womanly *(SYN.)* girlish, womanish, female, ladylike.
(ANT.) mannish, virile, male, masculine.

wonder *(SYN.)* awe, curiosity, miracle, admiration, surprise, wonderment, marvel, conjecture, amazement, question, astonishment.
(ANT.) expectation, familiarity, indifference, apathy, triviality.

wonderful *(SYN.)* extraordinary, marvelous, astonishing, amazing, remarkable, astounding.

wont *(SYN.)* practice, use, custom, training, habit, usage, manner.
(ANT.) inexperience, disuse.

word *(SYN.)* phrase, term, utterance, expression, articulate.

wordy *(SYN.)* talkative, verbose, garrulous.

work *(SYN.)* opus, employment, achievement, performance, toil, business, exertion, occupation, labor, job, product, accomplishment, travail, effort.
(ANT.) recreation, leisure, vacation, ease.

working *(SYN.)* busy, active, industrious.
(ANT.) lazy, dormant, passive, inactive.

world *(SYN.)* globe, earth, universe.

worldly *(SYN.)* bodily, fleshy, animal, carnal, corporeal, gross, voluptuous, base.
(ANT.) refined, temperate, exalted, spiritual.

worn *(SYN.)* tired, jaded, exhausted, wearied, faint, weary.
(ANT.) invigorated, fresh, rested.

worry *(SYN.)* concern, trouble, disquiet, anxiety, fear, pain, harry, gall, grieve, persecute, annoy, disturb, fidget, chafe, agonize, bother, haze, pester, uneasiness, fret.
(ANT.) console, comfort, contentment, satisfaction, peace.

worship *(SYN.)* honor, revere, adore, idolize, reverence, glorify, respect, deify, venerate.
(ANT.) curse, scorn, blaspheme, despise.

worth *(SYN.)* value, price, deserving, excellence, utility, worthiness, merit.
(ANT.) uselessness, cheapness.

worthless *(SYN.)* empty, idle, abortive, ineffectual, bootless, vain, unavailing.
(ANT.) meek, effective, modest, potent.

wound *(SYN.)* mar, harm, damage, hurt, dishonor, injure, injury, spoil, wrong.
(ANT.) compliment, benefit, help.

wrangle *(SYN.)* spat, bickering, affray, argument, dispute, quarrel, altercation, contention, squabble.
(ANT.) peace, friendliness, reconciliation, harmony.

wrap *(SYN.)* cover, protect, shield, cloak, mask, clothe, curtain, guard.
(ANT.) reveal, bare, unveil, expose.

wrath *(SYN.)* fury, anger, irritation, rage, animosity, passion, temper, petulance, choler, resentment.
(ANT.) patience, conciliation, peace.

wreck *(SYN.)* ravage, devastation, extinguish, destroy, annihilate, damage, raze, demolish, destruction, ruin.
(ANT.) construct, preserve, establish.

wrench *(SYN.)* tug, jerk, twist.

wrestle *(SYN.)* fight, tussle, grapple.

wretch *(SYN.)* cad, knave, scoundrel.

wretched *(SYN.)* forlorn, miserable, comfortless, despicable, paltry, low, worthless, disconsolate, sorry, mean.
(ANT.) noble, contented, happy, significant.

wring *(SYN.)* twist, extract.

writer *(SYN.)* creator, maker, author, father, composer.

writhe *(SYN.)* twist, squirm.

wrong *(SYN.)* awry, incorrect, improper, amiss, naughty, inappropriate, criminal, faulty, erroneous, bad, evil, imprecise, inaccurate, askew, sin, incorrectness, false, unsuitable, impropriety, wickedness, immoral.
(ANT.) proper, true, correct, suitable.

wry *(SYN.)* amusing, witty, dry, droll.

yacht *(SYN.)* sailboat, boat, cruiser.
yak *(SYN.)* chatter, babble, jabber, talk.
yank *(SYN.)* pull, wrest, draw, haul, tug, jerk, wrench, heave, extract, grab, wrest, snatch, nab, twitch, wring, extract.
yap *(SYN.)* howl, bark.
yard *(SYN.)* pen, confine, court, enclosure, compound, garden, courtyard.
yardstick *(SYN.)* measure, criterion, gauge.
yarn *(SYN.)* wool, tale, narrative, thread, story, fiber, anecdote, spiel.
yaw *(SYN.)* tack, change course, pitch, toss, roll.
yawn *(SYN.)* open, gape.
yearly *(SYN.)* annually.
yearn *(SYN.)* pine, long for, want, desire, crave, wish for, hope for.
yearning *(SYN.)* hungering, craving, desire, longing, appetite, lust, urge, aspiration, wish.
(ANT.) distaste, loathing, abomination, hate.
yell *(SYN.)* call, scream, shout, whoop, howl, roar, holler, wail, bawl.
yellow *(SYN.)* fearful, cowardly, chicken.
(ANT.) bold, brave.
yelp *(SYN.)* screech, squeal, howl, bark, yap.
yen *(SYN.)* longing, craving, fancy, appetite, desire, lust, hunger.
yet *(SYN.)* moreover, also, additionally, besides.
yield *(SYN.)* produce, afford, breed, grant, accord, cede, relent, succumb, bestow, allow, permit, give way, submit, bear, surrender, supply, fruits, give up, abdicate, return, impart, harvest, permit, accede, acquiesce, crop, capitulate, pay, concede, generate, relinquish.
(ANT.) assert, deny, refuse, resist, struggle, oppose, strive.
yielding *(SYN.)* dutiful, submissive, compliant, obedient, tractable.
(ANT.) rebellious, intractable, insubordinate.
yoke *(SYN.)* tether, leash, bridle, harness.
yokel *(SYN.)* hick, peasant, hayseed, innocent.
young *(SYN.)* immature, undeveloped, youthful, underdeveloped, juvenile, junior, underage.
(ANT.) old, mature, elderly.
youngster *(SYN.)* kid, lad, stripling, minor, youth, child, fledgling.
(ANT.) adult, elder.
youthful *(SYN.)* childish, immature, young, boyish, childlike, callow, girlish, puerile, juvenile, adolescent, growing, robust, active, peppy.
(ANT.) old, elderly, senile, aged, mature.
yowl *(SYN.)* yell, shriek, cry, wail, whoop, howl, scream.

zany *(SYN.)* clownish, comical, foolish, silly, scatterbrained.
zap *(SYN.)* drive, vim, pep, determination.
zeal *(SYN.)* fervor, eagerness, passion, feverency, vehemence, devotion, intensity, excitement, earnestness, inspiration, warmth, ardor, fanaticism, enthusiasm.
(ANT.) unconcern, ennui, apathy, indifference.
zealot *(SYN.)* champion, crank, fanatic, bigot.
zealous *(SYN.)* enthusiastic, fiery, keen, eager, fervid, ardent, intense, vehement, fervent, glowing, hot, impassioned, passionate.
(ANT.) cool, nonchalant, apathetic.
zenith *(SYN.)* culmination, apex, height, acme, consummation, top, summit, pinnacle, climax, peak.
(ANT.) floor, nadir, depth, base, anticlimax.
zero *(SYN.)* nonexistent, nil, nothing, none.
zest *(SYN.)* enjoyment, savor, eagerness, relish, satisfaction, gusto, spice, tang, pleasure, exhilaration.
zestful *(SYN.)* delightful, thrilling, exciting, stimulating, enjoyable.
zip *(SYN.)* vigor, vim, energy, vitality, spirited, animation, provocative.
zone *(SYN.)* region, climate, tract, belt, sector, section, district, locality, precinct, territory.
zoo *(SYN.)* menagerie.
zoom *(SYN.)* zip, fly, speed, whiz, roar, race.